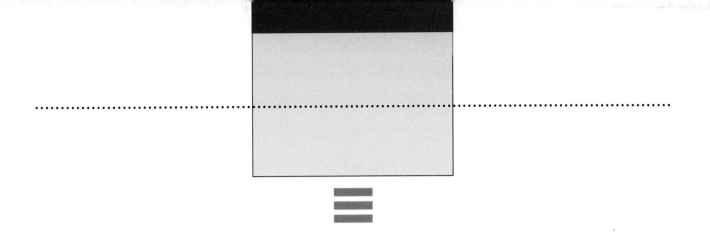

MARKETING

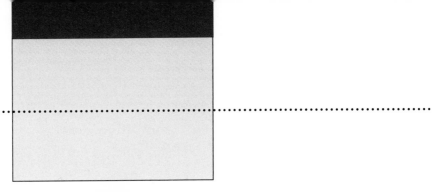

FIFTH EDITION

MARKETING

CONTEMPORARY CONCEPTS AND PRACTICES

William F. Schoell
University of Southern Mississippi

Joseph P. Guiltinan
University of Notre Dame

Allyn and Bacon   Boston   London   Toronto   Sydney   Tokyo   Singapore

Executive Editor: Richard Wohl
Series Editor: Susan Nelle Barcomb
Development Editor: Judith S. Fifer
Series Editorial Assistants: Carol Alper, Sarah Carter
Production Supervisor: Elaine Ober
Production Coordinator: Leslie K. Olney
Copy Editor: Jo-Anne Naples
Text Designer: Stuart Paterson, Image House Inc.
Composition Buyer: Linda Cox
Manufacturing Buyer: Megan Cochran
Cover Administrator: Linda Dickinson
Cover Designer: Susan Slovinsky

Copyright © 1992, 1990, 1988, 1985, 1982 by Allyn and Bacon
A Division of Simon & Schuster, Inc.
160 Gould Street
Needham Heights, MA 02194

Library of Congress Cataloging-in-Publication Data

Schoell, William F.
   Marketing: contemporary concepts and practices / William F.
Schoell, Joseph P. Guiltinan. — 5th ed.
      p.   cm.
   Includes bibliographical references and index.
   ISBN 0-205-13150-6
   1. Marketing.   I. Guiltinan, Joseph P.   II. Title.
HF5415.S357   1991
658.8—dc20   91-29546
                                    CIP

Printed in the United States of America
10 9 8 7 6 5 4 3 2 1   95 94 93 92 91

For Rosie, Shannon, Bryan, and William Jr.
For Sharon, Joanna, Jennifer, and Shannon

ABOUT THE
AUTHORS

● **William F. Schoell** ● is currently Professor of Marketing at the University of Southern Mississippi. He received his Ph.D. from the University of Arkansas, Fayetteville. Bill Schoell has also taught marketing at the University of New Orleans and University College of Tulane University. Bill is a co-author of *Introduction to Business: A Contemporary View,* currently in its sixth edition, and *Introduction to Canadian Business,* currently in its fourth edition. For many years, Bill served on the editorial staff of the Marketing Abstracts Section of the *Journal of Marketing.* He currently teaches in the International Project Seminar Series in International Business.

● **Joseph P. Guiltinan** ● is Professor of Marketing and Associate Dean of the College of Business Administration at the University of Notre Dame. Previously, he has held faculty positions at the University of Massachusetts and the University of Kentucky. He received his D.B.A. degree from Indiana University. Joe Guiltinan has authored numerous articles and papers on the topics of marketing strategy, pricing, channels of distribution, and services marketing. His work has appeared in the *Journal of Marketing, Journal of Consumer Research, Journal of Retailing, Journal of Health Care Marketing,* and *Social Forces.* Additionally, he is co-author of *Marketing Management: Strategies and Programs,* currently in its fourth edition, and several monographs on pricing financial services.

As co-authors, Bill Schoell and Joe Guiltinan bring together a blend of skills, experiences, and interests that contribute to their development of a truly teachable/learnable basic marketing text. Each member of this writing partnership has taught Principles of Marketing courses for many years to both large and small group classes, and is especially attuned to the need for a basic marketing text and supplements that will both introduce students to and excite them about the world of contemporary marketing.

BRIEF

CONTENTS

CONTENTS

Target

3

Marketing Management and the Planning Process 74

Comprehensive Case 1: Greenmarketing: A Fad or a Viable Strategy? 99

SECTION II

UNDERSTANDING AND SELECTING TARGET MARKETS 105

· ·

Z 8's

*doer user +procedure
Motivation
research*

4

Marketing Research 106

3 ≡SS
5 ID

5

The Consumer Market and Buying Behavior 140

17

Personal Selling 554

**Comprehensive Case 5:
Hill & Knowlton:
Coping with Crises 584**

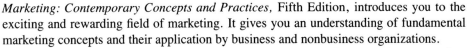

TO THE

STUDENT

Marketing: Contemporary Concepts and Practices, Fifth Edition, introduces you to the exciting and rewarding field of marketing. It gives you an understanding of fundamental marketing concepts and their application by business and nonbusiness organizations.

We organized the subject matter into seven sections. Section One provides an overview of the nature of marketing, its environment, and its management. Section Two focuses on understanding and selecting target markets. It discusses marketing research, consumer and organizational buying behavior, market segmentation, and targeted marketing. Sections Three through Six look at the elements of the marketing mix—product, distribution, promotion, and price. Section Seven covers the implementation and control of marketing strategies and takes a close look at services marketing, nonprofit marketing, and international marketing.

To Help You Learn

We kept you, the user of this text, in mind throughout the revision process. One of our major goals was to stimulate you to *want* to learn about marketing. Thus we designed the following features into the text to help you to learn.

- **Learning Objectives** • The list of learning objectives at the beginning of each chapter tells you what to expect and what you should be able to accomplish after reading each chapter. The objectives also provide a convenient way for you to review how well the material in each chapter has been learned.

- **Chapter Opening Vignette** • Each chapter opens with a real-world example that focuses on one or more topics that are discussed in the chapter. These vignettes help to convey the excitement and relevance of marketing today and to provide a framework for each chapter. Following the vignette is a brief discussion that ties together the vignette and what is to be covered in each chapter.

- **Advertisements** • Actual advertisements are included throughout the text to illustrate and dramatize major marketing concepts and practices. The ads reinforce learning and demonstrate the relevance of topics discussed to real-world marketing organizations, both business and nonprofit. The chapter discussion includes specific reference to the ad.

- **Photographs** • The photographs in the text were selected to reinforce and illustrate specific points made in the chapter discussion and to highlight the cultural diversity of today's marketing environment. Each photo serves a special purpose which is elaborated upon in the accompanying caption.

- **Tables and Figures** • Whenever appropriate, tables and figures are included to supplement text discussion of related material. The chapter discussion makes a specific reference to each table or figure. You will not find complex material that is not covered in the chapter.

- **Examples** • Hundreds of examples of marketing concepts, strategies, and practices are included throughout the text. These examples were drawn from a variety of real-world business and nonbusiness organizations. They show how individuals, *Fortune 500* companies, small businesses, and nonprofit organizations apply the concepts and strategies you are learning about in marketing their goods, services, ideas, or other offerings to consumers such as yourself and to organizational buyers such as hospitals, wholesalers, manufacturers, or governments. Most of the examples feature organizations that are familiar to you in order to help you relate the new material to your existing knowledge.

- **Global Marketing Box** • Chapter 22 focuses specifically on international marketing. However, each chapter contains a boxed feature that focuses specifically on global marketing. We want to enhance your awareness of marketing's increasingly global dimension and its implications. In marketing today, you must ''think global.''

- **Ethics in Marketing Box** • Each chapter also contains a boxed feature that focuses on marketing ethics. You will have many opportunities to reflect upon some of the most pressing ethical issues in contemporary marketing. Think carefully about the issues and questions we raise in these boxes because in the not too distant future you may confront ethical dilemmas that are very much like the ones we look at in these boxes.

- **Summary of Learning Objectives** • The Summary of Learning Objectives at the end of each chapter is designed to help you review and prepare for exams.

- **Review Questions** • Each chapter has a group of review questions. Because they relate directly to material covered in the chapter, you can answer these questions completely from material presented in the chapter. They provide another opportunity for you to test your understanding of chapter content.

- **Discussion Questions** • Each chapter also has a set of discussion questions that call upon you to reflect upon the material you learned in the chapter. These questions will stimulate creativity, in-depth critical thinking, and discussion.

- **Application Exercise** • Each chapter has an application exercise that asks questions that pertain to the chapter opening vignette. This gives you an opportunity to apply the knowledge you acquired in the chapter to a situation you were introduced to before reading the chapter.

- **Key Concepts** • At the end of each chapter is a list of key concepts. These terms are printed in boldface type and are called out in the margin. To help you in building your marketing vocabulary, they are defined in one-sentence definitions.

- **Short Cases** • Two short cases appear at the end of each chapter. Each case includes questions that pertain to chapter content. They include questions that will require you to apply the material you learned in the chapter. The cases will also help you to sharpen your analytical and creative skills. Many of the cases are built around business or nonprofit organizations that are familiar to you. Some of the cases focus on small businesses that are unfamiliar to you. In either case, however, the cases depict the real world of marketing.

• **Comprehensive Cases** • A comprehensive case appears at the end of each section of the text. These real-world cases are longer, more in-depth, and more complex than the end-of-chapter cases. They also include questions for analysis and discussion and give you another opportunity to put yourself in the shoes of the marketing decision maker.

• **Glossary** • Because vocabulary building is important in any introductory course, a glossary is provided at the end of the text. It lists and defines the key concepts that appear in each chapter. It also indicates the page number on which the term first appears in the text.

• **Indexes** • The Name and Subject Indexes can help you prepare for exams. For example, if you remember reading in the text about a particular company's marketing strategy and you want to refer to it, look up the company's name in the Name Index. Or if you want to review the material you read about a particular topic, look the topic up in the Subject Index.

• **Study Guide** *Plus* • A comprehensive study guide is available to help you study and understand the material covered in the text. It can be a major help—especially in preparing for exams. If the study guide is not available in your bookstore your instructor can tell you how to order a copy from Allyn and Bacon.

We hope that you will both enjoy and profit from your first course in marketing. As in previous editions, we sincerely solicit your comments about the text and its supplements. We believe what we say in this book about customer satisfaction! While we relish receiving favorable feedback, please let us know from the student perspective what we can do to improve.

ACKNOWLEDGMENTS

We would like to thank the following professors who provided many of the cases that appear at the end of chapters:

Lyn S. Amine, St. Louis University
Donald G. Anderson, Ouachita Baptist University
Dennis J. Elbert, University of North Dakota
John W. Gillett, University of North Dakota
W. Fred Lawrence, University of North Dakota
James D. Porterfield, Pennsylvania State University
Thomas K. Pritchett, Kennesaw State College

We would also like to thank Leslie Brunetta for writing the comprehensive cases, and Julie A. Tober and James Peavler for their contributions to the end-of-chapter cases.

The authors of the supplements have also contributed greatly to the overall teaching/learning package. Thanks to

Caroline Fisher, Loyola University, New Orleans
Douglas L. Fugate, Western Kentucky University
Anthony J. Lucas, Community College of Allegheny County
Gayle J. Marco, Robert Morris College
Dennis Pitta, University of Baltimore
Betty McLemore Pritchett, Kennesaw State College
Thomas K. Pritchett, Kennesaw State College
Thomas D. Smith, Texas Wesleyan College

Thanks also to reviewers, chapter consultants, and users who have provided their comments, which are greatly appreciated:

David M. Andrus, Kansas State University
Deanna Barnwell, Memphis State University
James L. Brock, Montana State University
John Brunnell, Broome Community College
Valeriano Cantu, Angelo State University
Stephen B. Castleberry, Northern Illinois University
William A. Cunningham, Memphis State University
Lee D. Dahringer, Emory University
Rose Dikis, Ohio University
Alan J. Dubinsky, University of Kentucky
Robert Dwyer, University of Cincinnati

Jerry Elder, Southeast Missouri State University
Linda Felicetti, Clarion State College
S. J. Garner, East Kentucky University
Marc H. Goldberg, Portland State University
Jon M. Hawes, University of Akron
Jack Heinsius, Modesta Junior College
Ross R. Higa, University of Hawaii
Nancy B. Higgins, Montgomery College
Herbert Katzenstein, St. John's University
Maryon King, Southern Illinois University at Carbondale
Victor LaFrenz, Mohawk Valley Community College
Edward Laurie, San Jose State University
George H. Lucas, Jr., Memphis State University
Suzanne McCall, East Texas State University
Margaret McCloud, Eastern Michigan University
Barbara A. McCuen, University of Nebraska at Omaha
William C. Moser, Ball State University
James A. Muncy, Clemson University
Patrick E. Murphy, University of Notre Dame
Bruce I. Newman, DePaul University
Nick Nicholas, Salisbury State College
Thomas Ponzurick, West Virginia University
Thomas K. Pritchett, Kennesaw State College
Michael Reilly, Montana State University
Winston Ring, University of Wisconsin—Milwaukee
Maurice Sampson, Philadelphia Community College
Philip B. Schary, Oregon State University
Joan Sepic-Mizis, St. Louis Community College
Robert Smiley, Indiana State University
Michael F. Smith, Temple University
Nancy Stephens, Arizona State University
Joseph Stern, Trenton State College
Vincent P. Taiani, Indiana University
Ron Taylor, Mississippi State University
Bill Thompson, University of Texas-Pan American
Leon E. Totten, III, Western New England College
Jane Wayland, Virginia Commonwealth University
Ron Weir, East Tennessee State University
Van R. Wood, Texas Tech University
Gene Wunder, Ball State University

Thanks also to those students and instructors who sent us their comments about the previous edition and its supplements. Your feedback is invaluable in ensuring that future editions will provide the types of innovative and exciting topics and features that set this text apart.

Special thanks are also due to the professionals at Allyn and Bacon who have provided expertise, encouragement, and support throughout the revision process: Elaine Ober, production administrator; Richard Wohl, executive editor; Susan Nelle Barcomb, senior series editor; Judith Fifer, development editor; Carolyn Harris, marketing manager; JoAnne

Naples, copyeditor and permissions editor; Judy Fiske, production director; Sandi Kirshner, marketing director; Carol Alper, senior editorial assistant; Sarah Carter, editorial assistant; and Leslie Olney, production coordinator.

We also want to thank all the organizations that granted permission for us to use their advertisements and provided information for this edition. Thanks to The Body Shop for providing the video to accompany the case on The Body Shop. And a special thank-you to CNN for use of their video material in this edition of Schoell and Guiltinan's *Marketing: Contemporary Concepts and Practices*.

Ancillary Materials for the Instructor

The following supplements are available for instructors:

> Annotated Instructor's Edition
> Instructor's Resource Manual
> Test Bank
> Allyn and Bacon Test Manager
> Call-In and FAX Testing Service
> Acetate Transparencies
> Videos
> Video User's Manual
> Business Line Fax Service
> Software Exercises
> Student Study Guide *Plus*

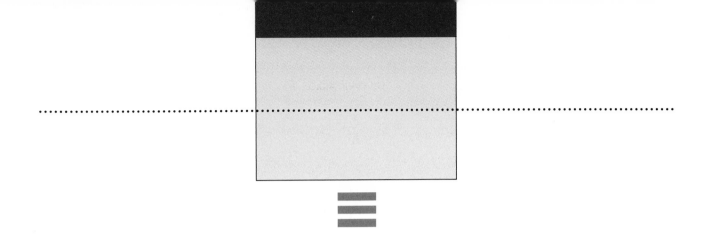

MARKETING

MARKETING: ITS ENVIRONMENT AND MANAGEMENT

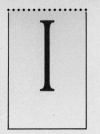

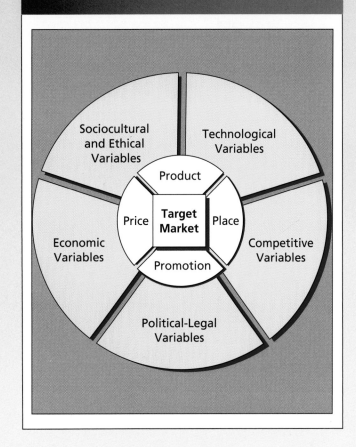

The three chapters in Section One provide an overview of contemporary marketing and an introduction to what the field of marketing is all about.

Chapter 1 traces the origins of marketing and defines what it is. It examines different types of marketers, what they do, what they market, and to whom they market. It explains the marketing concept and how it is implemented. It also explains the major elements involved in formulating a marketing strategy and introduces the concepts of a target market and a marketing mix.

Chapter 2 looks at the complex and rapidly changing environmental setting within which marketing managers formulate their marketing strategies and the marketing process takes place. It analyzes the uncontrollable variables in this environment: economic, competitive, technological, sociocultural and ethical, and political-legal. It explains the increasing importance of the global dimension of the marketing environment and the importance to marketers of environmental monitoring.

Chapter 3 examines the nature of marketing management. It takes an in-depth look at strategic planning at two different levels in the organization—strategic planning for the organization as a whole and marketing planning. The discussion focuses on strategic planning as a long-run on-going process through which top management seeks to relate the organization to its environment. It also explains the marketing planning process in terms of its three major elements—establishing marketing objectives, developing marketing strategies, and developing marketing plans.

The Comprehensive Case at the end of this Section, Greenmarketing, focuses on contemporary environmentalism and its impact on marketers. It illustrates the concepts of social responsibility, societal marketing, the elements in the marketing environment, marketing ethics, and strategic planning.

1

WHAT IS
MARKETING?

After reading this chapter you will be able to

1. explain how production and marketing create utility.

2. explain the significance of the marketing functions and identify those functions.

3. identify the three major types of marketers and the two major types of markets.

4. trace the evolution of marketing in the United States through three major eras.

5. explain the emergence and meaning of the traditional marketing concept and how the concept is being broadened.

6. explain what is involved in formulating a marketing strategy.

An old sales tool, the satisfaction guarantee, is fast becoming one of the hot marketing gimmicks of the 1990s. If the customer doesn't like what he or she bought, the company must make good—by fixing what's wrong, replacing the product, or returning the customer's money.

In September 1990 Xerox launched its Total Satisfaction Guarantee, an offer, good for at least three years, to give a disgruntled buyer of any Xerox product an identical or comparable machine. During that same month Mannington Resilient Floors, the number 2 vinyl-flooring marketer, came out with a no-questions-asked one-year warranty for its new, top-of-the-line Mannington Gold brand. If you don't like the way the puce floor looks with your hot pink drapes, Mannington will rip out the floor free of charge and replace it.

It's a strategy for tough times. Many goods and services are considered virtual commodities these days, that is, products for which all brands are alike. A guarantee is often the only way to distinguish a product—or a company—from its rivals. It's also a good tactic for cementing brand loyalty. That's particularly true now, when sluggish markets often make keeping current customers far less costly than prospecting for new ones.

"We're seeing a huge upsurge in satisfaction guarantees," says Sheree Marr of Walker Customer Satisfaction Measurements, one of a number of consulting firms that have sprung up to help companies learn exactly what their customers mean by *satisfaction*. According to one estimate, the U.S. "satisfaction measurement business" could now be a $100 million industry.

There are traps to watch out for, however. What does *satisfaction* mean? There's no easy answer. Quality is one thing: A company can set and meet an internal standard for zero defects on its line of widgets. But satisfaction is based more on customers' somewhat fuzzy expectations than on outright needs.

The trick is to pose pointed questions to different groups of customers who have specific criteria for satisfaction. Xerox sends out 40,000 detailed surveys a month to monitor satisfaction. Xerox asks specific questions. It asks administrators how they like the billing process, asks machine operators how well their machines work, and surveys purchasing agents on their relationship with the local Xerox office.

Xerox also discovered that its customers preferred a replacement model to a money-back guarantee. Why? A refund, Xerox found, would have sent the embarrassing signal that the purchasing agent had made the wrong decision in the first place. Moreover, a money-back guarantee ends the relationship and sends the customer to another vendor.

Mannington Resilient Floors didn't have a clue to what satisfied its customers until it started gearing up for its guarantee program last year. "We were stunned by what we heard," says Thomas McAndrews, Mannington's president. "It turns out people were broadly dissatisfied with the industry, and with us."

Part of the problem was the level of consumer expectation. Vinyl-flooring industry parlance uses the terms *no wax* and *never wax*. Not surprisingly, vinyl buyers assumed those terms meant exactly what they said—no more waxing their floors. Big mistake. The industry uses those terms to mean that people need not wax every time they mop. But some polishing is required. Once Mannington learned that customers took the terms literally, it elected to drop these terms from its advertising.[1]

Ultimately, customer satisfaction is what marketing is all about. Marketers are in the business of providing satisfaction. They study their target customers to learn what they want, design offerings intended to satisfy those wants, and monitor customer satisfaction.

In this chapter we look at the origins of marketing and define what *marketing* is. We then trace its evolution in the United States and examine the marketing concept. The chapter ends with a brief discussion of the processes involved in developing a marketing strategy. To begin, let's go back in time to the days of the cave-dweller. That is where we will find marketing's roots.

MARKETING'S ORIGINS

Marketing is a want-satisfying social process. To understand the origins of this process, we will look briefly at the evolution of exchange.

The Exchange Process

Early cave-dwellers produced everything they consumed, were entirely self-sufficient, and were totally independent of one another. Gradually, however, they left their caves and formed villages with the others. This created an opportunity for trade, or exchange, which could occur if there were a division of labor. That is, if each villager specialized—concentrating on producing what he or she could produce best—surpluses and economic growth might result through exchange. In the process, however, the individual would become dependent on the productive efforts of other specialists.

Notice that the division of labor resulted when the villagers *perceived the opportunity* to exchange. A villager with grain but no cattle, for example, might perceive the opportunity to exchange grain with another villager who had cattle but no grain. Exchange, therefore, does not result from, but rather contributes to, surpluses and economic growth.

If a good or a service satisfies a particular want of a particular person, then it is useful and valuable to that person. If it can command something else in return, it also has value in exchange. Thus two people who engage in exchange do so for the same basic reason. Person A has something of value that person B wants, and person B has something of value that person A wants.

What are human needs and human wants? *Needs* are physiological or psychological states that are common to all humans regardless of their culture. For example, all people need food and clothing, but their culture influences what they will *want* to eat or wear in order to satisfy those needs. In this text, however, we will use the terms *needs* and *wants* interchangeably.

Whether a person needs or wants something, it is something of value to that person. The something of value that is exchanged is created through production. In our highly interdependent economy, millions of production specialists exchange their something of value with millions of others. The process of exchange itself, however, is marketing. Although the exchange process is much more complicated now than it was thousands of years ago, production and marketing are still the two basic functions that underlie the exchange process.

The Creation of Utility

Production and marketing create utility. *Utility* is the satisfaction, value, or usefulness a user receives from a good or service in relation to the user's wants. There are four basic types of utility: form, place, time, and possession (or ownership).

utility

Moving products to places where they are needed creates place utility. In some cases, the modes of transportation are primitive in comparison to the modes that are available in more economically developed countries.

[© Marc & Evelyne Berheim from Rapho Guillumette]

Production activities create *form utility* by putting the good or service into a usable form in relation to a specific person's wants. Rock musicians combine their musical talents with musical instruments and other production facilities to create a performance. Michael Foods washes, inspects, and mechanically cracks eggs at the rate of three hundred a minute. The liquid is pasteurized at high heat and then poured into aseptic packages. Compared with natural eggs, the company's Easy Eggs are easier to transport, store, and use. Shell eggs can cause salmonella poisoning. Pasteurizing makes Easy Eggs disease-free.[2]

Marketing people typically provide guidance to production people regarding targeted customers' wants. For example, several years ago General Electric Company was about to discontinue making microwave ovens when its marketing people discovered that many potential buyers did not buy the ovens because they take up too much counter space. Thus GE began producing a microwave oven that was positioned above the stove, and sales increased tremendously.[3] Nevertheless, although marketing inputs may guide the creation of form utility, it is production activities that actually create form utility.

Marketing functions create place, time, and possession utility. *Place utility* is the value added to goods or services as a result of having them available where customers want to buy them. Auto Critic franchises dispatch mobile inspection units to check out used cars, vans, or trucks for potential buyers. At the used-car lot an Auto Critic certified mechanic examines the car and test drives it.[4] Airport chaplaincies, such as Tri-Faith chapel at JFK International Airport, help fulfill the spiritual needs of travelers and airport employees by offering services in airports.[5] A company in Michigan rents and delivers to party sites an 8-by-25-foot redwood-and-cedar house that contains a hot tub.[6] Fast-food restaurants, including Pizza Hut, are opening outlets in school cafeterias and dorms.[7] The "couch potato" is served by an increasing variety of restaurants that provide home delivery.

Time utility is the value added to goods or services by having them available when customers want to buy them. Drive-through-only hamburger chains, such as Rally's, offer no inside seating, but customers get in and out in about forty-five seconds.[8] Video rental machines add time utility to video rental services. Automated teller machines add time utility to banking services. Urgent-care clinics add time utility to medical services.

Possession utility is the value added to goods or services that comes about as a result of the passage of legal title to the buyer through a sales transaction. It gives buyers the right to consume what they have purchased for cash or credit or by swapping one good or service

FIGURE 1–1

The Nature of Exchange

*Or something else of value—ideas, images, concepts, places, and people.

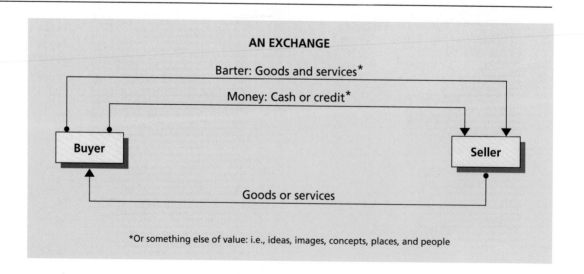

AN EXCHANGE

Barter: Goods and services*

Money: Cash or credit*

Buyer   **Seller**

Goods or services

*Or something else of value: i.e., ideas, images, concepts, places, and people

for another. Credit, for example, enables people to enjoy the possession of homes, cars, and many other goods even if they cannot pay the full purchase price in cash at the time of purchase.

Thus place, time, and possession utility are created when goods or services are available where and when customers want to buy them and when a sale is made. Some people admit the importance of form utility but underestimate the importance of place, time, and possession utility. In other words, they appreciate production activities but do not fully appreciate the marketing function. Actually, marketing is a catalyst that makes the total utility of a product a reality for consumers.

WHAT IS MARKETING?

Marketing is the process of planning and executing the conception, pricing, promotion, and distribution of ideas, goods, and services to create exchanges that satisfy individual and organizational objectives.[9] The discussions that follow elaborate on this definition.

marketing

What Is Exchange?

Exchange is the process by which two or more individuals or organizations give and receive something of value. Exchange involves an actual trading of something of value. *Barter* means the buyer and seller exchange goods or services directly; for example, one person may swap a used car for another person's boat and outboard motor, or a lawyer may swap legal services for dental services. Instead of engaging in barter, the buyer could pay cash or buy on credit.

As shown in Figure 1–1, the something of value that is exchanged between buyer and seller can be a good, a service, money, or something else of value, such as ideas, images, concepts, places, and people. Figure 1–2 provides several examples of exchanges.

exchange

FIGURE 1–2

Examples of Exchanges

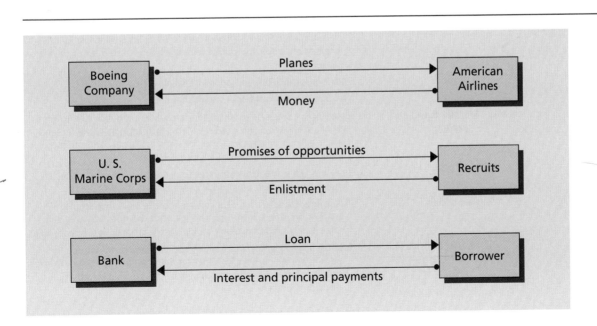

What Are Marketing Functions?

Marketing functions are the activities that create utility and facilitate the exchange process by bridging the distance, time, and possession gaps that usually separate the participants in an exchange. By bridging the gaps, marketing creates utility and facilitates the exchange process.

Table 1–1 identifies and describes the basic marketing functions: buying or leasing, selling or leasing, transporting, storing, standardizing and grading, financing, risk taking, and market information gathering. For example, transportation bridges the distance gap by moving goods from one geographical location to another—from where they are produced to where they are consumed. Thus videocassette recorders (VCRs) are made in Japan but used throughout the United States. Storage bridges the time gap by holding products until buyers want them. Thousands of retailers in the United States have VCRs in inventory waiting to be purchased by consumers.

Who Performs Marketing Functions?

Marketing functions are performed by the participants in an exchange. These functions can be shifted and shared among the participants, but they *cannot* be eliminated. Someone must perform them. As we will see in chapter 11, the participants may include producers, wholesalers, retailers, facilitating intermediaries (middlemen), and final consumers.

Campbell Soup Company, a producer, ships truckloads of soup to large retailers, such as Kroger Company. Kroger stores the soup in its warehouses and then transports it in case lots to Kroger supermarkets in the area. Campbell Soup does not sell directly to small,

TABLE 1–1   The Marketing Functions

Function	Nature
Buying or leasing	Identifying, selecting, and evaluating sources of supply; negotiating terms of purchase or lease.
Selling or leasing	Identifying, locating, and communicating with targeted customers; stimulating demand through personal selling, advertising, sales promotion, publicity, public relations; negotiating terms of sale or lease.
Transporting	Moving goods from one geographical location to another.
Storing	Holding goods until buyers want them.
Standardizing and grading	Establishing size and quality standards, sorting goods according to those standards, and grading them; facilitating the buying and selling functions by reducing the need to inspect and sample goods.
Financing	Providing the financial resources to produce, transport, store, promote, sell, and buy goods or services.
Risk taking	Assuming, transferring, and controlling the risk inherent in the marketing effort, including the risk that the good may not sell, that it may be damaged or stolen, or that it may become obsolete.
Market information gathering	Identifying and analyzing market opportunity, developing and administering surveys, conducting market experiments, gathering information about competitors, providing usable information to decision makers.

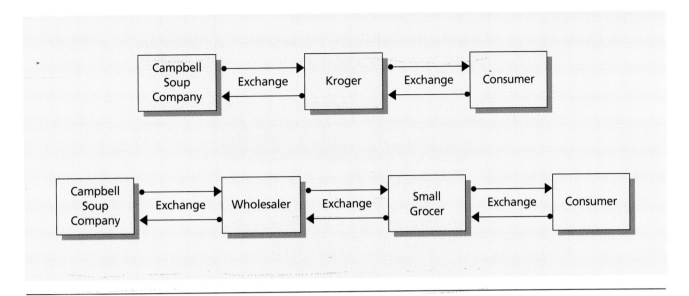

independently owned grocery stores that buy only three or four cases at a time. Instead, it sells in large quantities to wholesalers, and the wholesalers resell in smaller quantities to grocery stores. Unlike small retail stores, Kroger does not need an independent wholesaler to store and transport Campbell's soup because it performs these functions itself. The owners of small grocery stores, however, shift the storage and transportation functions to wholesalers.

In most cases the exchange process is more complicated than that shown in Figure 1–1, where the buyer and seller deal directly with each other, using no intermediaries. Figure 1–3 shows that more than one exchange is involved in getting soup from the producer to consumers. Kroger, the wholesaler, and the small grocery store are all intermediaries.

In addition to intermediaries such as wholesalers and retailers, facilitating intermediaries are often involved in exchanges when the other participants cannot or choose not to perform certain functions. Thus many companies turn to advertising agencies, marketing research firms, and transportation companies. They may lack sufficient resources to set up their own in-house advertising and research departments and trucking operations, or they may believe outsiders can perform these specialized tasks more efficiently or more effectively than they can. The Dun & Bradstreet ad explains how this facilitating intermediary helps its clients perform the risk-taking function.

Even final consumers perform marketing functions. In the past, when you ordered a take-out pizza over the phone, you usually picked it up yourself. Now many pizza places deliver. Domino's Pizza was the first to focus on home delivery. Domino's assumes the transportation function from the consumer. Some supermarkets now take phone or fax orders and deliver. On the other hand, many department stores, which once had their own fleets of trucks and provided free delivery, now charge for the service. In this case the consumer shares the cost of transportation with the stores. Some supermarkets have passed on to their customers certain other functions, such as marking prices on merchandise and bagging groceries, in return for lower prices.

The ways in which marketing functions are shifted and shared are continually changing. For example, Xerox once had its salespeople call on customers. Later, when it began to make small copiers and other office products targeted to smaller customers, such as doctors and lawyers, it opened its own retail stores. Xerox subsequently sold these stores,

Dun & Bradstreet is a facilitating intermediary that helps marketers perform the risk-taking function.

(Dun & Bradstreet Information Services.)

marketer

however, because the company found it was cheaper to sell through independent retailers who assumed the costs of running the stores.[10]

Who Are Marketers?

A *marketer* is an individual or organization that performs marketing functions to facilitate exchanges for the purpose of satisfying human wants. Both business organizations and nonprofit organizations are marketers, seeking to receive something of value as a result of an exchange.

• **Individuals** • As individuals, we are all marketers. For example, you market yourself to your professor when you pay attention in class, do well on exams, and ask questions that reflect your genuine interest in course content. The something of value you hope to receive in exchange is a good grade. If you have not already done so, you will soon be marketing yourself to potential employers. Other examples of individual marketers might include your professor trying to make her course relevant to you, a politician seeking public office, a person seeking a spouse, an employee seeking a promotion, or a would-be actor doing his own marketing because he cannot afford to hire an agent.

• **Business Organizations** • Organizations seeking to earn a financial return for their owners are business organizations. The owners are sole proprietors, partners, or stockholders.

Business marketers are involved in many types of business activities. General Electric and Procter & Gamble, for example, are manufacturers, Sears and Wal-Mart are retailers, and Super Valu and McKesson are wholesalers. Retailers and wholesalers are intermediaries who stand between producers and those producers' final customers. Business marketers such as Kelly Services (temporary help) and Federal Express are service providers, as opposed to goods providers. Other examples of service providers are law firms, airlines, advertising agencies, and financial services companies.

Of course, many business organizations are involved in more than one type of business activity. Sears, for example, is involved in retailing goods and providing financial services. Super Valu engages in both wholesaling and retailing. General Electric manufactures goods ranging from home appliances to jet engines and offers financial services through its GE Capital subsidiary.

• **Nonprofit Organizations** • Nonprofit organizations are also marketers. As a spokesperson for the Sierra Club said recently, "We recruit more and more from the profit-making world." Although the Sierra Club is a nonprofit organization, its yearly budget is $52 million.[11]

Many major traditional churches and synagogues have difficulty appealing to baby boomers. This is not the case at the customer-oriented Willow Creek Community Church in South Barrington, Illinois. The pastor's answer for attracting thirty and forty year olds—marketing. He went from door-to-door to ask nonchurchgoers why they didn't go to church and then designed a church to satisfy their expressed needs. An average of 14,500 people show up every Sunday.[12]

The Girl Scouts organization consists of more than 3 million girls and 700,000 adult volunteer leaders, consultants, board members, and staff specialists. The organization has two missions: to address the needs of girls growing up in a changing society and to obtain the funds to reach that goal. An executive of the Girl Scouts recently said: "From now until the year 2000, we need to become more expert in reading demographics, responding to trends, and appreciating the differences as this country grows exceedingly diverse. Attracting support so we can meet the needs of this rapidly growing society is becoming more of a priority for us."[13] Clearly, the Girl Scouts organization is involved in marketing.

What Do Marketers Market?

Marketers, whether they are individuals, business organizations, or nonprofit organizations, seek to market their offerings. A *market offering* is anything of value that is presented by a marketer to potential customers. It may be a product, such as a tangible good or an intangible service or an idea, a cause, an image, a concept, a place, or a person. To simplify our discussion throughout this text, we will often use the term *product* to refer to a market offering, whether it is a tangible good, an intangible service, or anything else of value.

market offering

Procter & Gamble markets tangible goods such as Charmin, Crisco, and Tide. Federal Express markets an intangible service, overnight delivery of packages. IBM markets a good (computers) and a service (their installation).

The Democratic and Republican parties market their ideas on political issues, and numerous charitable organizations market the idea of contributing money to help them accomplish their objectives, such as saving children and curing cancer. Other organizations market ideas such as conserving natural resources, maintaining equality, and reducing pollution.

The marketing of social ideas and causes is called social marketing. More specifically, *social marketing* is the design, implementation, and control of programs seeking to increase the acceptability of a social idea, cause, or practice in target groups.[14] Examples

social marketing

of social ideas and causes are safe driving, family planning, blood donation, church attendance, and support of higher education. During recent years the American Medical Association and several drug and food companies have been involved in cholesterol-education programs.

Images are also marketed. Colleges market themselves as "academically distinguished" and as "the place to go to prepare for a rewarding career." Companies market themselves as good community citizens or as pioneers in developing new technology. Entertainers and politicians who "have an image to protect" do so by marketing that image.

The Selective Service System markets the *concept* of registration for the draft. Other examples of concept marketing include the marketing activities of organizations that advocate the neutering of pets, organ donation, and safe sex.

Places are marketed also. In addition to being marketed for vacations, they may be marketed as ideal for rearing children or for retirement. Many efforts are undertaken to market places as sites for political conventions, Super Bowl games, trade shows, or industry.

People, too, are marketed. Political parties market their candidates, model agencies market models, and booking agents market entertainers.

To Whom Do Marketers Market?

Mothers Against Drunk Driving (MADD) markets its cause to several targets, including voters, drivers, police officers, judges, jurors, and legislators. Although these are not necessarily mutually exclusive groups, each may require a slightly different marketing approach. For example, MADD representatives have appeared before legislative bodies in support of tougher drunk-driving laws. To keep the pressure on judges to give stiff sentences to those convicted of drunk driving, MADD members are often present in the courtroom when sentences are handed down.

To whom does your college market itself? In addition to its customer-students, who else is targeted? If it is a four-year college, there are probably several departments in which marketing activities take place. The admissions office may engage in marketing activities to recruit graduating high school and junior college students in the college's market area. The college may hire a professional to produce a videotape for the recruiters to use. A department of continuing education may place ads in local newspapers describing courses for older part-time students. A department of conferences and workshops may target potential users of campus facilities to hold meetings, conferences, and workshops on campus. An alumni association may solicit financial and other types of support from the college's alumni. A department of research and sponsored programs may solicit grants for research. The dean of the business school may seek financial and other support by setting up an advisory board consisting of outstanding businesspeople in the region. This may also help in marketing graduates to potential employers, which the college's placement office also does.

A public relations department may market the college to people living in the community. One focus might be on the college's financial impact—how much money it brings into the community—and the human resources available at the college for consulting purposes. If the college is state-supported, the market will also include members of the legislature and persons appointed by state government officials to oversee the allocation of funds to state-supported colleges and universities. Other possible markets might include National Merit finalists and prospective faculty members. Clearly colleges seek to market to numerous people in addition to their current students.

What about markets for businesses? Consider the markets that Raytheon Company targets. It sells Amana, Speed Queen, Caloric, and Modern Maid appliances to consumers through wholesalers and retailers. These products may also be sold to businesses such as laundromats and nonprofit organizations such as churches. Raytheon also does business with the federal government. It modernizes battleships, builds Patriot missile systems, and manufactures airplanes. Some of its planes are sold to businesses too. Raytheon also does a considerable amount of business in international markets.

All markets can be divided into two basic types, consumer and organizational. *Ultimate consumers* are people who acquire products for their personal or household use. All individuals are ultimate consumers, and they make up the consumer market.

Organizational buyers are entities such as businesses, governments, and nonprofit organizations that purchase products (1) for use in making other products, (2) to resell, or (3) to carry on the organization's operations. They do not buy for personal or household use. Wholesalers, retailers, manufacturers, governments, and all other buyers except ultimate consumers are organizational buyers. The Iowa Department of Economic Development's ad seeks to attract organizational buyers to locate in Iowa.

In addition to marketing products to ultimate consumers and organizational buyers, organizations also market themselves to their noncustomer publics. Examples of these publics are employees, labor unions, suppliers, legislators, stockholders, regulatory agencies, zoning boards, tax assessors, consumer groups, environmental groups, and people in the vicinity of a proposed new plant. These publics also are called *stakeholders*.

In the next section we will trace the evolution of marketing in the United States. We will see why it has become increasingly important for marketers to put their targeted customers' wants first—not their own wants.

ultimate consumers

organizational buyers

The Iowa Department of Economic Development is targeting organizational buyers with this ad.

(Iowa Department of Economic Development.)

MARKETING'S EVOLUTION IN THE UNITED STATES

As Figure 1–4 shows, marketing in the United States has evolved through three eras: (1) the production era, (2) the sales era, and (3) the marketing era. Marketers too can be categorized as production, sales, or market oriented.

The Production Era

Figure 1–4 also shows the four phases of the production era, which began with the arrival of the earliest settlers in America and lasted until the early twentieth century. Like some people in the most underdeveloped nations in the world today, the earliest families in the United States could consume only what they produced for themselves. During this *subsistence phase,* each family's major concern was to produce enough for its own survival.

As small towns began to form, people with different skills came together and engaged in exchange beyond the immediate family. During this *made-to-order phase,* production and consumption became separate activities. Customers told producers what they wanted, and producers offered them custom-tailored products. Under this job order system, products were sold before they were produced. It was only natural, therefore, to consider production more important than selling.

However, producers lost valuable production time while waiting for orders, so gradually there began a shift to speculative production—making products in advance of customer orders. Although speculative production required producers to anticipate their customers' needs, this was not a major problem during the *early production for market phase.* Producers and consumers were located near one another, they knew one another personally, and production was still more important than selling.

In the second half of the nineteenth century the full effects of the Industrial Revolution were beginning to be felt in the United States. The concepts of interchangeable machine parts and mass production were being implemented vigorously. The basic idea of mass

FIGURE 1–4

The Evolution of the Marketing Era

Production Era •••••••••••••••••••••••••••••••••••► Sales Era ••••••► Marketing Era					
Subsistence Phase	Made-to-Order Phase	Early Production for Market Phase	Mass Production for Market Phase		
1600s	**1700s**	**1800 -1849**	**1850 -1899**	**1900 -1949**	**1950 -**
Producer and consumer are one and the same.	Initial separation of production and consumption activities. Custom-tailored market offerings. Production to order.	Beginning of speculative production.	Emergence of selling specialists to improve distribution efficiency.	General shift from a seller's market to a buyer's market. Recognition of the need for mass selling. Emergence of consumerism.	Focus on potential buyer wants. Emergence of the marketing concept.

production is that unit costs of production will decline as the volume of output increases. This, however, is of little practical value unless the output can be sold. Thus, in order to engage in mass production, producers had to sell to a greater number of customers than were available in their local markets. Producers (production specialists) therefore began turning to intermediaries such as wholesalers and retailers (selling specialists) to find customers for them. This *mass production for market phase* lasted until the early twentieth century.

During the entire production era producers were production oriented. It was a *seller's market*—an environment in which demand is greater than supply. Much more attention was given to production than to selling.

The Sales Era

As producers sought to intensify their use of mass production, they came to realize that production economies hinged on the ability to sell what had been produced. It became clear that mass selling was necessary to support mass production. This was the sales era.

During the early part of the sales era there was a shift in many industries to a *buyer's market*—an environment in which supply is greater than demand. Naturally, selling became more important than production. To maximize their sales, producers with excess inventories turned increasingly to hard-sell techniques such as high-pressure tactics and deceptive and fraudulent advertising. The production orientation gave way to a sales orientation, and selling became the name of the game.

The use of hard-sell techniques became so commonplace that consumers revolted, which led to the birth of consumerism. *Consumerism* is a movement to strengthen the power of consumers in relation to the power of producers and sellers. Our first consumer movement occurred in the early 1900s. Upton Sinclair's book *The Jungle* (1906) exposed the filthy conditions in meat-packing plants and stimulated consumer protest that led to the passage in 1906 of the Pure Food and Drug Act and the Meat Inspection Act. The consumer movement showed that the marketing system required some government regulation to protect consumers.

A second consumerist era began in the 1930s. A book by Stuart Chase and F. J. Schlink, *Your Money's Worth* (1934) criticized such hard-sell tactics as deceptive, misleading, and fraudulent advertising and helped secure passage of the Wheeler-Lea Act (1938). This act gives the Federal Trade Commission (FTC), a government agency, power to prosecute firms that use deceptive ads and other deceptive sales practices.

Consumerism declined as the United States entered World War II. Consumer products were scarce during the war because production lines were converted to military production. This meant the return of a seller's market (demand greater than supply). After the war, as the United States shifted from a wartime to a peacetime economy, people were anxious to spend money on the consumer products that began to appear. Thus the seller's market continued, at least for a while.

The production orientation and the sales orientation are nonmarket orientations that can take several forms. For example, some companies are engineering oriented; that is, they produce what their engineers think are good products. Chrysler Corporation manufactured its Airflow automobile models during the 1930s because its engineers said the tear-shaped design minimized wind resistance. Unfortunately for Chrysler, however, relatively few buyers cared about wind resistance. They preferred the boxlike car design and did not buy Airflow models because they thought they did not look right. Later, in the early 1980s, Ford Motor Company turned away from boxlike cars in favor of sleeker, more aerodynamically styled cars. The new cars sold because, by the 1980s, consumers wanted such styling.

seller's market

buyer's market

Selling now important

consumerism

Another variation of the production orientation focuses on manufacturing efficiency. For example, in 1977 General Motors Corporation (GM) equipped some Oldsmobiles with Chevrolet engines but failed to inform buyers. Although this eased some of GM's production problems initially, it later cost GM millions of dollars to settle lawsuits brought against it by unhappy buyers who didn't want Chevrolet engines in their Oldsmobiles.

One version of the sales orientation focuses on maximizing sales volume. The assumption here is that by maximizing sales, companies eventually maximize profits. This, however, can be a dangerous assumption. Selling at profitless prices bankrupts a firm in the long run. The firm sells itself out of business. Square D Company's electrical division sales increased 14 percent in a recent year. But the division's operating income dropped 10 percent, largely because the sales force was pushing for volume and sometimes made unprofitable deals. Thus management now bases commissions in part on divisional profits, not just on sales volume.[15] One expert on competitiveness says firms should pursue "good" customers—those who value service more than price and who pay bills on time. "Bad" customers, on the other hand, are always asking for price breaks and pay their bills late. Although the firm may lose some accounts, it will make more profit by concentrating on getting more "good" customers.[16]

Another form of the sales orientation is the product orientation. The company persists in trying to sell its existing products despite evidence that they are not what most potential customers want. For example, NCR Corporation lost its dominance in the cash register business in the early 1970s by failing to switch fast enough from its electromechanical cash registers to electronic point-of-sale terminals.

Some products are still made to order.

(Marvin Windows.)

For convenience we refer to any nonmarket orientation, either sales or production, as a production orientation. Production-oriented companies do not recognize that they are first and foremost in the business of satisfying their present and potential customers. Market-oriented companies, on the other hand, do.

The Marketing Era

By the middle of the twentieth century, producers began to recognize the advantage of the close customer contact that had existed during the made-to-order phase of the production era. That type of direct seller-customer relationship, however, became less practical as firms grew larger; and it became clear to producers that they would have to research the market to learn about potential customers' wants. This is not to say, however, that products are no longer made to order. Examples of made-to-order goods are custom-made men's suits, custom-built houses, and, as indicated in its ad, Marvin windows. Stewart and Stevenson Services Inc. is the leading supplier of custom-built diesel and gas-turbine generators in the United States. The firm buys products from many engine manufacturers and customizes them for its customers.[17]

During the marketing era producers turned from a sales orientation to a market orientation and began to focus on potential customers' wants. Instead of focusing on the seller's need to move inventory (a sales orientation), they focused on the potential customers' wants by producing the products these buyers wanted (a market orientation). Thus the marketing concept was born.

THE MARKETING CONCEPT

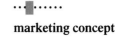

marketing concept

The *marketing concept,* which emerged in the 1950s, is a philosophy of management that advocates that a business organization (1) exists to satisfy targeted customers' wants, (2) approaches decision making from a systems view of management, and (3) seeks to earn a satisfactory return on the owners' investment in the firm.

Customer Orientation

As shown in Figure 1–5, production comes first in production-oriented firms, and to them *marketing* means simply selling whatever products are produced. The focus is on the producer's need to move inventory, not on the needs of targeted customers.

Figure 1–5 also shows that, in market-oriented (or customer-oriented) firms, the wants of present and potential customers come first. Customers are the focal point for all decision making in the organization, and all functional areas (design, engineering, research and development, production, marketing, finance, and so on) are geared to satisfy targeted customers' wants. As suggested in the Canon ad, customer-oriented firms research the market, first to learn what their targeted customers want and then to design and develop a market offering that satisfies these wants. The belief is that it is easier to market a product that potential customers really want than it is to make a product and then convince potential buyers that it is what they want.

Although research does not guarantee success, the odds favor firms that try to learn what potential customers want *before* they produce products. For example, soft-drink manufacturers discovered through research that sizable groups of consumers do not want sugar, caffeine, and sodium. This led to the development of sugar-free, decaffeinated, and sodium-free soft drinks.

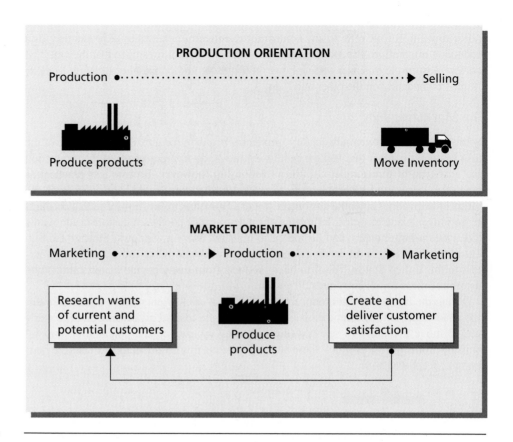

PRODUCTION ORIENTATION

Production ●···➤ Selling

Produce products   Move Inventory

MARKET ORIENTATION

Marketing ●················➤ Production ●················➤ Marketing

Research wants
of current and
potential customers

Produce
products

Create and
deliver customer
satisfaction

FIGURE 1–5

Comparison of Production and
Market Orientation

Note in Figure 1–5 that customer-oriented firms do not consider the marketing task complete once a sale has been made. Such firms provide after-sale services and, through research, check up on how satisfied their customers are and on what they can do to enhance that satisfaction. Fidelity Investments, the largest marketer of mutual funds in the United States, recently named a vice president of corporate quality management. Soliciting customer criticism is a big part of that person's job. In a recent client survey, for example, Fidelity found, quite unexpectedly, that customers value polite treatment even ahead of investment performance and the accuracy of statements.[18]

Companies such as General Electric, Coca-Cola, and British Airways are investing millions of dollars to improve complaint handling. Programs include toll-free telephone systems, intensive staff training, and liberal refund policies. The purpose is to turn company critics into loyal supporters.

Clearly, customer-oriented organizations focus on providing product quality, creating customer satisfaction and service, and getting close to the customer. As explained in the Global Marketing box, the type of marketing system within which a firm operates plays a big part in determining how customer oriented that company is likely to be.

● **Product Quality** ● The chairman and chief executive officer of Westinghouse Electric Corporation says that quality is the key to American business success in world markets. He asserts that the essence of quality is satisfying customers by ''doing the right thing right the first time.'' His references to *customers* go beyond traditional customers. He regards

Our copiers are designed from a different point of view.

At Canon, we approach copying from a different perspective. Yours.

You wanted copiers that combine quality and performance. We gave you that, along with superior technology and a design that makes them remarkably easy to use.

Because different work environments have different needs, we designed a copier line that's more than just the industry's largest, it's the most varied. Our models range from com-

pact desk-top units to high-speed copying systems to the most advanced digital full color copying available.

And to keep your business productive, we developed a wide variety of feeding and finishing options as well as faster copy speeds.

In short, before any Canon copier is designed by us, it's designed by you. It's no wonder we're America's most popular copier. For information, call toll-free **1-800-OK-CANON**.

Canon
The choice is Canon.

An ad that reflects a customer orientation.

(© 1990. Photograph by Tim Bieber, Inc.)

the units in an organization that use the outputs of another unit as customers of the first unit.[19]

Whirlpool now assembles the guts of a washing machine, fills the tub with water, and runs through a wash cycle, right on the assembly line. Then and only then is the machine's steel jacket slipped on and its control panel attached. The company's head of manufacturing says, "Building from the inside out has allowed us to shift from an inspection mentality to a build-it-right-the-first-time policy."[20]

The recent heavy focus on product quality in the United States is due in large part to the dedication of Japanese firms to total quality, which has enabled them to take big market shares of such U.S. industries as the auto, machine tool, and consumer electronics industries. Consider that in response to a recall of 3,500 Mazdas sold in Japan and the Middle East, Mazda Motor Corporation cut the salaries of its chairman and seventeen other top executives by up to 10 percent for three months.[21]

• **Customer Satisfaction and Service** • The NYNEX ad focuses on the importance of customer satisfaction. So does Xerox Corporation's "Total Satisfaction Guarantee," which covers all Xerox equipment delivered after September 5, 1990. As we saw at the beginning of this chapter, Xerox promises customer satisfaction with each product or it will replace the product free of charge for up to three years from the purchase date. According to a Xerox spokesperson: "We're putting the customer in charge. The customer is the sole arbiter and decision maker."[22]

An ad that discusses the importance to NYNEX of customer satisfaction.

(© 1990 NYNEX Corporation.)

The American Management Association says that 65 percent of the average company's business comes from its present satisfied customers. The Customer Service Institute estimates that it costs five times as much to acquire a new customer as it does to service an existing one. Ways to provide high-quality service include determining target customers' wants, training and motivating employees to satisfy them, and following up to gauge customers' appraisals of service quality.[23]

Studies also show that customers tell twice as many people about bad experiences as good ones. Technical Assistance Research Programs—a Washington, D.C., consulting firm that has been studying corporate complainers for over ten years—has developed a model that calculates the return on company dollars invested in units that handle complaints and inquiries. The average return for makers of consumer durables such as washing machines and refrigerators is 100 percent. In other words, if manufacturers spend $1 million, they get $2 million in benefits. For banks the return is as much as 170 percent. The payoff can be even higher in retailing.[24]

During the 1980s firms focused mainly on improving product quality as the key to becoming more competitive. In the 1990s the focus is shifting to improving the caliber of customer care. As one consultant said, "If manufacturers concentrate only on product quality, they may miss much of what satisfies their customers and influences them to repurchase their products."[25]

But it is harder for manufacturers and service providers to improve customer service than to implement zero-defect quality campaigns. *Good service* is often hard to define; customers asked to describe the perfect service provider tend to give such vague answers as "nice," "helpful," "courteous." To find out what customers really want, one research firm asks a sampling of its clients' customers to act out situations, such as checking into a hotel room. The researcher then attempts to gauge customers' reactions to service. Otherwise, he says, ''if I interview [people] at home when they're not traveling, they don't remember what they liked and didn't like.''[26]

As mentioned earlier, marketers also are paying more attention to employee satisfaction. According to one expert, ''Employees are quick to recognize a superficial effort, and

GLOBAL MARKETING

It helps to distinguish between macro-marketing and micromarketing when looking at marketing's global dimension. *Macromarketing* is the study of overall marketing systems, of how those systems affect society and how society affects them. *Micromarketing* is the study of marketing activities of a specific organization.

An individual organization's marketing activities are affected by the type of macromarketing system within which the organization operates. For example, there is no incentive for a state-owned enterprise in a totally planned, centrally directed economy to implement the marketing concept. There is no incentive to be customer oriented because government planners, not consumers, determine which goods and services will be produced and made available to consumers.

The situation is quite different in a market economy. Consumers, not government planners, determine which goods and services will be produced. Marketers in Eastern Europe are still adjusting to the change from centrally planned economies to market economies. They are learning the importance of serving and satisfying their target customers.

One of the main reasons Japanese companies have been so successful in exporting their products to other countries is that they take the time to study their target markets overseas. But many Japanese consumers believe their standard of living does not reflect Japan's

national wealth because the political system favors producers. For example, the country's complex distribution system and protections for small farmers were designed to feed a hungry country and guarantee full employment after World War II. Many consumers today want politicians to push consumer issues harder. A recent poll of 10,000 Japanese voters found that 47 percent agreed with U.S. demands that Japan should review its economic structure and open its markets.

The unification of Germany has created market opportunities for firms in many countries. Caterpillar, for example, stepped up exports of earthmovers in anticipation of heavy reconstruction. The U.S.-Canadian Free Trade Agreement has stimulated greater exchange between the two countries. Meanwhile, the United States and Mexico are moving closer to free trade, which will give many U.S.-based firms greater access to a growing export market. These are all examples of how developments in the macromarketing environment create market opportunities for micromarketers.

Macromarketing also relates to the societal marketing concept. Examples of macromarketing issues here include the effects on the marketing system of wasting natural resources and polluting the environment.

Source: Information about Japan is from ''Japan's Silent Majority Starts to Mumble,'' *Business Week,* April 23, 1990, pp. 52–54.

employee support is absolutely essential for the [customer satisfaction] program to be successful."[27]

● **Closeness to the Customer** ● Most colleges and universities spend a lot of time and effort on student recruitment. Many are now recognizing that it's just as important, perhaps even more important, to devote time and effort to student retention.

Businesses, too, are recognizing that customer retention strategies are desirable. Customer-oriented marketers are interested in building and maintaining good relationships with their customers. Some marketers call this "getting close to the customer."

At Procter & Gamble's Duncan Hines angel food cake factory in Jackson, Tennessee, the line workers are given letters from customers who have problems with the product. One worker called up a customer whose angel food cake did not rise and helped figure out why by asking such questions as "How long did you beat the mix?" and "At what temperature did you bake it?" According to P&G's chief executive officer, "What we've said to the worker is, this is the only place we make angel food cake, and you're responsible for it, and if you want to talk to the consumer, we'd like you to talk to the consumer."[28]

Consider another example of getting close to the customer. Local phone companies have handled AT&T's billing since the breakup of the Bell System of telephone companies. In effect, a layer of insulation has come between AT&T and its customers. In 1990 AT&T introduced the Universal credit card, in part to help the company strengthen its relationship with nonbusiness long-distance callers. The Universal card enables AT&T to get closer to its customers and to become more involved in their everyday lives. AT&T expects that customers will prefer to rely on a single company for both long-distance service and bank card credit. For either use the customer receives a bill from AT&T; the envelope containing the bill may also include promotional and informational brochures.[29]

Systems View of Management

Over three decades ago management expert Peter Drucker said that the only valid definition of *business purpose* is "to create a customer." The key to profitable growth of a company—individual customer satisfaction and service—requires participation from every person in the organization.

In the systems view of management the focus is on the interdependence of an organization's employees, divisions, and departments and on the need to coordinate their activities to satisfy targeted customers' wants and to achieve a satisfactory rate of return on investment. The systems view recognizes that an organization is made up of subsystems (divisions and departments) and that the organization itself is a subsystem of its industry.

The systems view also recognizes that the organization is a subsystem of the socioeconomic system in which it exists. Just as a person is a citizen of a community, so is a business organization a corporate citizen. The notion of social responsibility as part of corporate citizenship is becoming increasingly important. *Social responsibility* is the concept that businesses are part of the larger society in which they exist and are accountable to society for their performance. Businesses must therefore act responsibly in their dealings with their various publics, or stakeholders.

social responsibility

WiteOut Corporation, for example, developed a new formula for its correction fluid after it learned that as many as twenty young people die annually as a result of sniffing correction fluid for a cheap high. WiteOut replaced the solvent trichloroethane with another that is nonintoxicating.[30]

U.S. West Communications has replaced push-button pay phones with rotary-dial models in some drug-infested neighborhoods. Drug dealers, who typically wear pagers, can send and receive messages with their pagers and touch-tone phones. But most pagers will not work with dial phones. Thus the company's effort helped reduce the drug traffic in these neighborhoods.[31]

In the effort to function in a socially responsible manner, marketers often encounter ethical dilemmas. ***Marketing ethics*** is judgments about what is morally right and wrong for marketing organizations and their employees in their role as marketers. The Ethics in Marketing box focuses on the growing importance of marketing's ethical dimension.

marketing ethics

Goal Orientation

The marketing concept views customer orientation as the means to the end of achieving the organization's goals. By providing market offerings that satisfy its targeted customers' wants, the organization will achieve its own goals too. These goals can be expressed in many ways—for example, achieving a specified percentage increase in profitable volume of sales or in market share. For the sake of simplicity, we say that the firm seeks to earn a satisfactory rate of return on the owners' investment in the firm.

THE SOCIETAL MARKETING CONCEPT

Although the marketing concept is a philosophy of *business* management, many individual and nonbusiness marketers have adopted and implemented it in recent years. Thus the applicability of the concept is being broadened.

Some people argue in favor of broadening both the marketing concept itself and its applicability. They believe that the traditional concept focuses on selected customers' wants at the expense of societal well-being. These people advocate making the marketing

The societal marketing concept requires marketers to accept their social responsibility. How can a marketer strike a balance among targeted customer's wants, customer's long-run best interests, society's long-run best interests, and the firm's long-run financial goals?

[© Dan Budnik]

concept more compatible with the concept of the social responsibility of business. For example, they question whether it is socially responsible to market gas-guzzling cars and overpackaged products that use up scarce resources.

societal marketing concept

Related to the concept of social responsibility is the *societal marketing concept*—a philosophy that requires marketers to accept their social responsibility. That is, marketers should strike a balance among targeted customers' wants, customers' long-run best interests, society's long-run best interests, and the firm's long-run financial goals. This concept is even tougher than the traditional marketing concept to implement.

ETHICS IN MARKETING

According to a former chairman of the board of the U.S. Chamber of Commerce: "The vast majority of business people are honest. The few who are not create problems for all of business. It is up to each business leader to set a conspicuous example of integrity and to make certain that . . . subordinates know that exemplary behavior will be demanded and required at every level of the enterprise. . . . The key is the CEO, with strong backing from the board of directors, determined to establish and enforce strict ethical behavior throughout the organization.''

The Business Roundtable, which is made up of the chief executive officers of two hundred major corporations, completed a landmark study several years ago of how big business deals with ethical questions. The recommendations: greater commitment of top management to ethics programs, written codes that clearly communicate management expectations, programs to implement the guidelines, and surveys to monitor compliance.

And according to a national survey of small-business executives, 39 percent of respondents believed their companies had been hurt by "questionable business practices," especially bribes, kickbacks, price collusion, and conflicts of interest. Some analysts say that small firms are

more subject to ethical transgressions than large firms—for several reasons. One is that small firms do not have the legal responsibility of full disclosure that large, publicly owned corporations have. Another is that small firms often lack a system of internal controls that would tend to make potential chiselers think twice.

Another recent study compared the ethics of big- and small-firm managers. Managers of small businesses found it more acceptable to discriminate against women, trade on inside information, and pad expense accounts than did big-business managers. The small-business managers also found it more acceptable to evade taxes, copy computer software, and engage in collusion on contract bids. On the other hand, the small-business managers had stricter ethical standards on six other issues: making misleading advertising claims, reporting misleading financial results, giving faulty investment advice, showing favoritism in promotions, acquiescing in a dangerous design flaw, and promoting cigarette smoking as healthful.

A recent survey of corporate executives found that two-thirds of upper-level executives thought people are "occasionally" unethical in their business dealings, another 15 percent believed people are

Notice that the societal marketing concept requires marketers to consider not only their customers' wants but also the wants of other people whose welfare is affected by their operations. It requires marketers to recognize that they exist within a larger social system that includes noncustomer stakeholders.

One example of societal marketing is green marketing. *Green marketing* is the development and implementation of marketing programs that are designed to enhance an organization's environmental image. For example, many marketers are using such environmental terms as *environmentally friendly, biodegradable,* and *recyclable* in their

green marketing

"often" unethical and 16 percent considered people "seldom" without ethics. Additionally, nearly one in four executives believed ethical standards can impede successful careers. Still, 54 percent thought business executives and managers have higher ethical standards and behavior than the general population.

In the midst of a multitude of recent scandals in business, corporations are rushing to formulate codes of ethics, business schools are rushing to add courses on business ethics, and consultants are being hired to put "integrity" into corporate cultures. And, as we will explain in greater detail in chapter 2, the American Marketing Association completed a major revision of its code of ethics several years ago.

Of course, ethical issues also arise in the marketing activities of nonprofit organizations. One example is the methods some organizations use to accomplish their goals. For example, some people might question the ethics of using TV commercials in an effort to find adoptive parents for children in foster care. In New York City the Human Resources Administration used ten-second ads featuring children, with a one-sentence description of each child and his or her interests. In New Orleans two J.C. Penney stores invited the Louisiana

department of social services to select children who were willing to be brought to the stores. There they were dressed in the latest fashions, given tips on modeling, and sent onstage. An invited group of prospective parents got a chance to size up the kids and obtain information on adoption applications and processing.

Why is ethics important to marketing? As we explain in this chapter, marketing is a pervasive activity in business and nonprofit organizations. It directly links the organization and its target customers, and there are countless opportunities for unethical practices to influence this linkage, ranging from the padding of expense accounts to the bribing of potential customers.

Sources: "Businesses Are Signing Up for Ethics 101," *Business Week*, February 15, 1988, pp. 56–57; Timothy D. Schellhardt, "Managing: What Bosses Think about Corporate Ethics," *Wall Street Journal*, April 6, 1988, p. 21; Michael Allen, "Small Business Jungle," *Wall Street Journal* (Special Supplement), June 10, 1988, p. 19R; Robert T. Gray, "Making Ethics Come Alive," *Nation's Business*, June 1988, pp. 65–66; Buck Brown, "Enterprise: Ethics in Small Firms vs. Ethics in Big Firms," *Wall Street Journal*, March 23, 1989, p. B1; "American Notes: Putting Kids on Display," *Time*, April 30, 1990, p. 43; "New York City Airs Ads to Adopt Foster Children," *Wall Street Journal*, October 8, 1990, p. B4.

DRUNK DRIVING IS ONE PROBLEM THE BREWERS
ARE FACING HEAD ON.

One sure way to get drunk drivers off the road is to hire a cab for them. So we do. Alert Cab is a program that offers a free or reduced

taxi ride to anyone who is unable to drive safely home from a bar or restaurant. The bartender has a confidential telephone number to

call when summoning a cab. Alert Cab, though, is just one way to keep drunk drivers off the road. We also support "Designated Driver"

programs such as I'm Driving. And we've developed Think When You Drink, a television campaign that urges people to not drive drunk.

The Beer Institute is also active at the community level. A.D.D.Y.—Alcohol, Drugs, Driving and You—educates teenagers on how drugs

and alcohol affect judgment and driving performance. And our Community Assistance Fund provides money directly for education and

prevention programs. □ None of these programs, however, is designed to take the place of responsible drinking. To learn more about everything

we're doing to address the problem of alcohol abuse write James C. Sanders, President of the Beer Institute, 1225 Eye Street, NW, Suite 825,

Washington, D.C. 20005. □ We're doing something about the problem of alcohol abuse. With your help we can find a solution together.

BEER INSTITUTE

The Beer Institute is the trade association for American brewers and their suppliers. It is dedicated to responsible consumption of their fine quality beers.

An example of demarketing by a trade association.

(Beer Institute.)

advertising. Procter & Gamble is one of many firms that seeks to make its products environmentally friendly. Examples include redesigning Crisco oil bottles to use 28 percent less plastic, compressing Pampers into smaller plastic packs, and offering superconcentrated detergents that require 15 percent less packaging.[32]

Developing and implementing a green marketing program is a complex process. Many states have passed laws that regulate environmental claims in an effort to end consumer confusion and cynicism about green marketing—what some people are calling "green-collar fraud." Rhode Island totally bans most green marketing as misleading.[33]

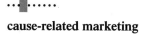

cause-related marketing

Green marketers sometimes engage in cause-related marketing. *"Cause-related marketing* is the process of formulating and implementing marketing activities that are characterized by an offer from the firm to contribute a specified amount to a designated cause when customers engage in revenue-providing exchanges that satisfy organizational and individual objectives."[34] An example is Procter & Gamble's recent newspaper coupon for Tide and Bold detergents. P&G offered to donate 10 cents per coupon redeemed (up to $100,000) to Keep America Beautiful. The ad also provided information about P&G's efforts to reduce the environmental impact of its packaging and proposed that consumers help the cause of a cleaner environment by supporting recycling programs.[35]

demarketing

A marketer may even need to engage in demarketing to implement the societal marketing concept. *Demarketing* is a strategy a marketer undertakes in an attempt to reduce demand for its goods or services. Conservation used to be a dirty word in the electric utility industry because it meant less demand. More recently, however, a huge demand for electricity in the face of growing public opposition to new power plants ("not in my backyard") and the desire to avoid being blamed for the greenhouse effect are making conservation a must for electric utilities.[36] The Beer Institute ad is an example of demarketing by a trade association.

IMPLEMENTING THE MARKETING CONCEPT

Because it is a philosophy, the marketing concept will accomplish nothing until it is put into practice. Among the incentives to do this are intensive competition for customers, the growing selectivity of buyers in making purchasing decisions, the potential for more government regulation of marketing activities and practices that do not provide customer satisfaction, and the need to develop customer loyalty and to realize the firm's return on investment goal.

Nevertheless, the marketing concept has not been universally implemented. Some organizations are still basically production oriented. Their owners are willing to accept a lower rate of return on investment, and their top management is unwilling to assume the risk of changing the firm's orientation. And some firms that claim to have adopted the marketing concept are really still production oriented. There is a big difference between adopting a concept and implementing it.

Nonprofit organizations have good reason to implement the marketing concept. Rising social problems in the 1990s, ranging from drugs to AIDS, have intensified the competition for charitable donations, especially in light of reduced corporate giving and of cutbacks in government support because of budget pressures.[37]

We discussed the social responsibility of marketers earlier in this chapter. In the case of charitable organizations, donors are asking more and more questions about how their donations are being used. Thus some people are advocating that charities issue routine statements in which they explain how they spend their money. These organizations also probably should educate the public about the nature of fund-raising.[38]

Top Management's Role

Because implementation of the marketing concept affects all departments and personnel, the chief executive officer must market the concept to other members of upper-level management and enlist their support in marketing it to lower-level managers. Although the concept ultimately must be embraced by all personnel from top to bottom, the stimulus for change must come from the top. The heads of production, finance, engineering, and other departments must often be convinced that implementing the marketing concept is not the equivalent of making the marketing manager the boss. In fact, getting a sales-oriented marketing manager to adopt the concept can be a challenge in itself.

The changes a firm must make to improve quality and adopt a customer orientation are so fundamental that they must take root in the company's *culture*—the values, attitudes, heroes, myths, and symbols that have been in the organization forever. The firm's chief executive officer should guide the change, and it will likely take five to ten years for a significant improvement.[39]

Organizational Restructuring

Many companies have had to restructure their organizations in order to implement the marketing concept. This usually includes creating an information system for gathering data about targeted customers and their wants. As the focus shifts from a production to a market orientation, the importance of researching the wants of targeted customers becomes critical.

IBM recently went through a restructuring effort. More than 65,000 staffers were retrained as salespeople or pushed into product and software development, where they are in direct contact with customers. IBM now has nearly 25 percent of its work force in sales and marketing. As a company executive said recently: "IBM needs to bring products out in six months instead of a year or longer. Every IBM operation should use 'closed-loop development.' This means staying in constant touch with leading-edge customers during product development and modifying the product to their needs."[40]

Implementation Problems

Organizations rarely find it easy to implement the marketing concept. This is perhaps the major reason some firms are reluctant to adopt it.

Research of targeted customer wants, for example, does not guarantee that the firm will be able to specify exactly what customers want. Or the research may suggest the existence of a want for a product, but the firm may lack the resources and capabilities to produce it. Perhaps not enough people want it to make its production sufficiently profitable.

Personnel problems are also likely to arise. Some people feel threatened by the marketing concept, especially those who do not understand or accept it. Perhaps a production manager, for example, would be more willing to accept it if it were called the customer satisfaction concept rather than the marketing concept. It's not easy to overcome functional or departmental politics in a business organization.

Another potential problem is impatience. The education and reorganization processes may require several years. Unless results are immediately forthcoming, some people want to revert to the old ways of doing things.

As we have seen, the marketing concept views customer orientation as the means to the end of achieving the organization's goals. By providing market offerings that satisfy targeted customer wants, the organization will achieve its goals too. Clearly, there is a need for marketing strategy to guide the organization's marketing effort.

DEVELOPING A MARKETING STRATEGY

marketing strategy

A *marketing strategy* is a broad plan of action for using an organization's resources to meet its marketing objectives. It defines a specific target market as the focus for the marketing effort and specifies a marketing mix to satisfy that market. Thus, as we will see in greater detail in chapter 3, the formulation of a marketing strategy involves selecting and analyzing one or more target markets and creating and maintaining a marketing mix to satisfy them.

In formulating their marketing strategies, marketing managers must deal with *uncontrollable variables* in the marketing environment. The sociocultural, ethical, technological, competitive, political-legal, and economic variables in this environment are essentially givens in marketing strategy development.

For example, Hartmarx, the maker of several brands of men's suits, including Hickey-Freeman, Johnny Carson, and Sansabelt, says changes in the workplace and shifting lifestyles have contributed to slippage in sales of U.S.-made men's suits. The wave of leveraged buyout of the late 1980s emptied many offices of potential suit shoppers. Also, many firms are moving to suburban office parks, where casual dress is more acceptable. Meanwhile, the personal computer makes it possible for some employees to work at home, reducing the suit to an occasional requirement.[41]

....

The promotion variable in the marketing mix is developed with the target market in mind.

[© Bob Daemmrich]

Marketing strategies must be developed within the limits dictated by the uncontrollable variables in the marketing environment. Thus we will examine the marketing environment in chapter 2 before we look at the marketing strategy planning process in chapter 3.

Selecting and Analyzing a Target Market

········

target market

A *target market* is a well-defined set of present and potential customers that an organization attempts to satisfy. Many hotels target business travelers, who account for more than 70 percent of all hotel stays. For example, hotel chains may try to attract corporate clients by providing them with executive services such as stenography, photocopying, and the Dow Jones news wire.[42] General Motors' goal is to sell 80 percent of the cars made by its Saturn division to import buyers. A Saturn spokesperson says, "We're really out to get the guy who's driving the Civic or the Corolla."[43]

In section 2 of this text, "Understanding and Selecting Target Markets," we explain how firms use marketing research to study markets and choose customer targets. Much of this research focuses on understanding buyer behavior in the two basic types of markets identified in this chapter: consumer and organizational markets. We also explain how marketers can divide markets into segments in order to do a more effective job of satisfying the people in the chosen segments.

Creating and Maintaining a Marketing Mix

········

marketing mix

Unlike the largely uncontrollable variables in the marketing environment, marketing mix variables are *controllable* by marketing managers. A *marketing mix* is the combination of the four controllable variables—product, place, promotion, and price (the four *P*s)—that an organization creates to satisfy its target market. The organization's market offering is the result of combining the four controllable variables in the marketing mix. Marketing

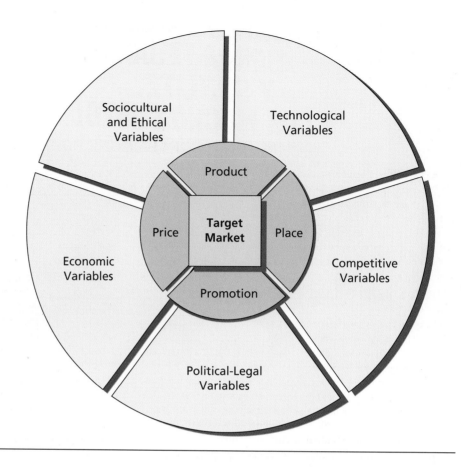

Sociocultural and Ethical Variables

Technological Variables

Product

Price

Target Market

Place

Economic Variables

Competitive Variables

Promotion

Political-Legal Variables

FIGURE 1–6

· ·

The Target Market and the Uncontrollable and Controllable Variables

managers blend these variables to create a mix that satisfies the target market. (See Figure 1–6.)

In sections 3 through 6 of this book we provide a detailed look at the marketing mix. We devote a separate section to each of the marketing mix variables and examine the concepts, techniques, and activities that are involved in blending these variables to create customer-satisfying marketing mixes for targeted customers.

The *product variable* is the bundle of perceived attributes that has the potential to satisfy targeted customer wants. The product can be a tangible good, an intangible service, or a combination of the two. As we saw earlier in the chapter, the product can also be an idea, a cause, an image, a concept, a place, or a person.

The *place variable* seeks to create time, place, and possession utility by having the product available where and when targeted customers will want to buy it. The objective is to distribute the right product to the right place at the right time and in the right quantity.

The primary focus of the *promotion variable* is communication between the organization and its targeted customers. Promotion activities such as advertising and personal selling seek to inform, remind, and persuade the target market about the organization and its offerings.

The *price variable* establishes the amount of money or other consideration that the seller seeks from the buyer in exchange for the product. Pricing activities also include the establishment of policies concerning trade-in allowances, discounts, and other adjustments to the basic asking price (list price) to arrive at an actual selling price for the target market.

In section 7, "Implementing, Controlling, and Extending Marketing," we take an in-depth look at how management implements and controls its marketing strategies. We also look at the special opportunities and challenges in services and in nonprofit and international marketing.

SUMMARY OF LEARNING OBJECTIVES

1. Explain how production and marketing create utility.
Production activities create form utility by putting the good or service into a usable form in relation to a specific person's wants. Marketing functions create place, time, and possession utility. Place utility is the value added to goods or services as a result of having them available where customers want to buy them. Time utility is the value added to goods or services by having them available when customers want to buy them. Possession utility is the value added to goods or services that comes about as a result of the passage of legal title to the buyer through a sales transaction.

2. Explain the significance of the marketing functions and identify those functions.
Marketing functions create utility and facilitate the exchange process by bridging the distance, time, and possession gaps that usually separate the participants in an exchange. By bridging the gaps, marketing creates utility and facilitates the exchange process. The marketing functions are buying or leasing, selling or leasing, transporting, storing, standardizing and grading, financing, risk taking, and market information gathering.

3. Identify the three major types of marketers and the two major types of markets.
The three major types of marketers are individuals, business organizations, and nonprofit organizations. All markets can be divided into two basic types, consumer and organizational.

4. Trace the evolution of marketing in the United States through three major eras.
The *production era* had four phases: the subsistence phase, the made-to-order phase, the early production for market phase, and the mass production for market phase. During the entire production era producers were production oriented. It was a seller's market. In the *sales era* it became clear that mass selling was necessary to support mass production. During the early part of this era there was a shift in many industries to a buyer's market. The use of hard-sell techniques in the sales era led to the birth of consumerism. During the *marketing era* producers turned from a sales orientation to a market orientation and began to focus on potential customers' wants.

5. Explain the emergence and meaning of the traditional marketing concept and how the concept is being broadened.
The marketing concept emerged during the marketing era. It is a philosophy of management that advocates that a business organization exists to satisfy targeted customers' wants, approaches decision making from a systems view of management, and seeks to earn a satisfactory return on the owners' investment in the firm. Although the marketing concept is a philosophy of *business* management, many individual and nonbusiness marketers have adopted and implemented it in recent years. Thus the applicability of the concept is being broadened. Some people advocate making the marketing concept itself more compatible with the concept of the social responsibility of business. The result is the societal marketing concept.

6. Explain what is involved in formulating a marketing strategy.
A marketing strategy is a broad plan of action for using an organization's resources to meet its marketing objectives. The formulation of a marketing strategy involves selecting and analyzing one or more target markets and creating and maintaining a marketing mix to satisfy them. In formulating their marketing strategies, marketing managers must deal with uncontrollable variables in the marketing environment.

Review Questions

1. How do production and marketing activities create utility?

2. What are marketing functions? Can they be eliminated? Explain.

3. What is a market offering?

4. How do the production, sales, and marketing eras differ.

5. What is a seller's market? Is a marketer more likely to be production oriented or market oriented in a seller's market? Explain.

6. What is meant by *customer orientation*?

7. How does the societal marketing concept broaden the traditional marketing concept?

8. What are some of the problems an organization might encounter in implementing the marketing concept?

9. What is a marketing strategy?

10. What are the uncontrollable variables in the marketing environment and the controllable variables in the marketing mix?

Discussion Questions

1. Comment on the following statement: In order to increase manufacturing efficiency, improve product quality, and do a better job of satisfying its customers, companies that manufacture products should be headed by people whose background is in manufacturing.

2. Why should a charitable organization consider itself a marketer? Are there any possible risks to the organization in doing so? Explain.

3. Americans import a large volume of products from abroad, but many of the same types of products are made in the United States. Does this mean that the foreign producers are more market oriented than U.S. producers? Explain.

4. As part of their effort to get closer to the customer, some marketers actively solicit customer complaints. What are the relative merits of doing so?

5. Is green marketing a fad? Explain.

6. Is cause-related marketing ethical? Explain.

Application Exercise

Reread the material about customer satisfaction at the beginning of this chapter and answer the following questions:

1. What do Xerox and Mannington receive in exchange for their customer satisfaction guarantees?

2. Why is customer satisfaction so important in the 1990s?

3. Why are marketers spending a large amount of money on customer satisfaction measurement?

4. Is satisfaction a subjective concept? Explain.

Key Concepts

The following key terms were introduced in this chapter:

utility
marketing
exchange
marketing functions
marketer
market offering
social marketing
ultimate consumers

organizational buyers
seller's market
buyer's market
consumerism
marketing concept
social responsibility
marketing ethics

societal marketing concept
green marketing
cause-related marketing
demarketing
marketing strategy
target market
marketing mix

CASES

Glen Ellen Wine—Success Through Marketing

Winemaking is probably the second most ancient profession. Through the ages, most winemakers have gone about their business in the same way: grow the grapes, crush the grapes, age the juice, sell the wine. But these days, it's not a business anyone enters into lightly. You have to buy hundreds of acres in areas where the soil and the climate are just right—and usually also where land prices have been driven sky-high by other vintners. You have to buy hundreds of thousands if not millions of dollars worth of barrels and temperature-control and chemical analysis equipment. In fact, many winemakers who are considered successful invest $2 in their winemaking operations for every $1 in wine sales. Common wisdom has it that the only way to make lots of money owning a winery is to make sure that you're born to parents whose parents already own one.

So how did the Benziger family of California's Glen Ellen winery manage to earn $12 million on sales of $80 million in 1989 when they'd only been in business since 1980? Marketing. Instead of focusing on the capital-intensive production end of the winemaking business, they concentrated on finding out what wine-drinkers wanted and getting it to them.

The Benzigers' original idea had been to go about winemaking in the traditional way—by running a boutique winery that would make a small amount of fine wine. They made their first sauvignon blanc and chardonnay from other vineyards' grapes because their own vines wouldn't mature for years. The wines won widely publicized contests and quickly sold out. The family decided to take a new tack and to make their prime business buying and blending other vintners' surplus wines.

Based on their previous retail experience, Bruno and Mike Benziger thought there would be a huge market for wine that was better quality than $3-a-bottle jug wine but less expensive than $8-a-bottle-and-up premium wine, a market ignored by other wineries. *Proprietor's Reserve* labels were usually kept for limited-edition premium wines, but Bruno decided to break with tradition and affix it to his new $4-to-$7 chardonnays. Other winemakers weren't happy, but customers were: Glen Ellen sold 42,000 cases of its first vintage. The Benzigers discovered California gold: by buying surplus wine at $2 and $3 per gallon, their margins were tremendous. Today, in addition to buying surplus wines, Glen Ellen buys grapes. But the Benzigers subcontract most of their winemaking to other vineyards (where they carefully supervise the process), thereby avoiding traditional capital costs.

What Glen Ellen does invest in is marketing, to the tune of about $2.5 million every year. One liquor retailer says more than just its high quality and low price sells Glen Ellen wine: ''There is more marketing expertise and support from the winery and that's critical for us. Promotional programs are backed up with more research and the proper point of purchase material.''

Questions

1. What types of utility does Glenn Ellen create?

2. What marketing functions does Glenn Ellen perform?

3. What target market do you think Glen Ellen is trying to reach?

4. Which of its actions show that Glen Ellen has a customer orientation?

The Greening of Lucky Charms

JAMES D. PORTERFIELD, *Pennsylvania State University*

There they were, tumbling out of a box of Lucky Charms. Among the pink hearts, yellow moons, blue diamonds, green clovers, and orange stars, were lots of innocent-looking green marshmallow bits shaped like trees.

Most corporate environmental efforts aren't quite so ''green.'' By including the small green tree charm in the company's popular frosted oat cereal, General Mills, the giant food products manufacturer, had served notice it was joining the ranks of firms trying to demonstrate social responsibility with a ''green'' program.

New television advertising portrays the brand's spokesperson, Lucky Leprechaun, setting off into the woods to hide some of his marshmallow bits—but the trees have all been cut down to stumps. To counteract these damaging environmental practices, the company is offering a free tree seedling and instructions for planting it to anyone who purchases two boxes of Lucky Charms. Another element of General Mills' Lucky Charms campaign includes hiring an ''arborist,'' who visits with elementary school children and teaches them the value of planting trees.

Critics, including those employed in the logging industry, are seeing red instead of green over the campaign. Especially infuriating to them is the implication that people who cut down trees are bad because they leave stumps. Noting that responsible logging companies replant trees, critics charge General Mills with ''cheap shot ambush commercialism.'' Some have gone so far as to assert that processed cereal does worse damage to people than processed timber, and dozens of loggers and their families have

let such feelings be known at General Mills' Minneapolis headquarters. Michael Crouse, the publisher of *Loggers World* magazine, accuses General mills of ''jumping on the environmental bandwagon.'' As for General Mills' claim that they are giving something back to the environment, Mr. Crouse calls that only fair. After all, he points out, all those Lucky Charms boxes are made out of paper taken from trees.

The company acknowledged the ruckus it had stirred up when it released a statement saying that its ''ads weren't intended to denigrate the U.S. timber industry.'' A spokesperson elaborated by saying: ''We didn't mean to perpetuate the myth that they cut down trees and don't replace them.''

Welcome, General Mills, to the not-so-friendly world of environmentally friendly marketing.

Questions

1. Is General Mills creating utility by adding tree-shaped green marshmallow bits to its Lucky Charms cereal? Explain.

2. Would you describe the campaign built around Lucky Charms as *green marketing* or *cause-related marketing*? Explain.

3. What ends, beyond those offered by the spokesperson, might General Mills' Lucky Charms social marketing campaign satisfy for the company?

4. Are there other marketing techniques that General Mills might have implemented to ''give something back to the environment'' without offending any particular group? Identify and explain the techniques.

2

THE MARKETING
ENVIRONMENT

After reading this chapter you will be able to

1. identify the major variables in the marketing environment.

2. identify the major issues that confront marketers in the economic environment.

3. explain the nature of competition.

4. explain how technology affects marketing.

5. identify the major elements of the sociocultural and ethical environment.

6. identify the major elements of the political-legal environment.

7. explain the meaning and nature of environmental monitoring.

As it appeared that a possible recession was looming in 1990, a growing number of companies started studying just how products performed in the 1981–1982 recession. "The past is the best indicator of the future," according to a marketing consultant. But the fact that many changes had occurred during the 1980s made it clear that reading the tea leaves from eight years ago was a dicey business.

Consumers certainly had changed—demanding more quality, variety, and convenience. More women were working. Microwave ovens, in only a quarter of U.S. homes at the beginning of the 1981–1982 recession, were zapping meals in about 80 percent of homes in 1990. In addition, inflation was higher going into the earlier recession. After all those factors, and more, will sales of Velveeta, for instance, soar 34 percent as they did in that recession?

"Everything is dynamic, and there are constantly things going on that could change buying habits," says a market researcher. To illustrate: In the 1981–1982 recession, sales of place mats declined 64 percent. But that was probably caused as much by changing lifestyles—fewer families sitting down together for meals—as by penny-pinching by consumers, marketing specialists say.

Still, the earlier recession offers some obvious lessons. People do opt for less expensive products. Sales of hot dogs jumped 11 percent and sausage soared 23 percent in 1982 alone. Private-label products, such as canned tuna, boomed largely because of their lower prices.

Moreover, people tended to shy away from restaurants and eat more meals at home. In 1982 sales of baking ingredients rose 21 percent. Most anything that helped stretch homemade meals was also in demand: salad dressing, gravy, sauces, stuffing mixes, and dehydrated soups.

An analysis of data on grocery product sales during the 1981–1982 recession also dispels some myths. Sales of sweets, for one, turned sour. Despite their image as "affordable luxuries," chewing gum and desserts ranging from pudding to gelatin and ice cream topping—and even bags of sugar—all showed sales declines. Confection sales, with candy-bar volume declining, were sluggish. Makers of candy and gum suggest that price increases, made to cover cost increases in the late 1970s, were a major factor.

But some marketers and others believe an economic slowdown gives consumers reasons, besides health, to cut back on sugar. A sociologist who has studied food and society says: "A lot of people look at sugar as a reward or luxury. During a recession more people are saying 'I can't afford luxury anymore.'"

Other unpredictable findings: The recession sparked light bulb and battery sales. In the early 1980s, when retailers were "clawing for every dollar," they promoted light bulbs to help lure shoppers. Batteries gained because people typically didn't abandon such pleasure-oriented items as cameras, radios, and boom boxes, which are big battery users.

Even when people tried to trim food spending, marketers say, they generally wouldn't part with variety. Sales of Mexican food rose 21 percent, while frozen Chinese foods jumped 61 percent. Even raisin sales jumped 15 percent as more people tossed the fruit into salads and oatmeal to pep up taste. "During the recession, when people couldn't go out to eat, they began to rebel against the monotony of taste by seeking out ethnic and exotic foods," says a new-products consultant.

Moreover, the overwhelming preference for foods that taste fresh turned into a boon for plain frozen vegetables (sales surged 89 percent) at the expense of their cheaper, canned counterparts (sales rose just 5 percent).

The clear lesson, according to marketing experts, is that even in a recession some downscale products can be risky, especially if they collide with lifestyle trends. Says a New York market researcher, "It is unarguable that consumers are more demanding today."[1]

All organizations affect and are affected by the overall environment in which they operate. A major element in that environment is the economic environment. Most marketers have to adjust their strategies as the economy slips into a recession, as it did in 1981 and 1990.

The focus in this chapter is on the marketing environment in the United States. We analyze it in terms of economic, competitive, technological, sociocultural and ethical, and political-legal variables. (See Figure 2–1.) Although we discuss the uncontrollable variables one at a time, keep in mind that they are in dynamic interaction in the real world. Furthermore, even though these variables are basically uncontrollable, marketing managers can control how they deal with them. Management's effectiveness in dealing with these variables affects how the organization will be influenced by them. More than ever marketers must identify and monitor environmental forces that are relevant to their organizations and must forecast changes in them if they are to develop effective marketing plans and strategies. For a growing number of organizations, this monitoring effort must include the international environment.

THE ECONOMIC ENVIRONMENT

The economic environment has a major impact on marketers and their present and potential customers. In the discussions that follow we look at the business cycle; consumer spending

FIGURE 2–1

The Marketing Environment

behavior; the postindustrial service economy; inflation, disinflation, and deflation; debt; shortages; and unemployment.

The Business Cycle

As we were reminded once again during the 1990–1991 recession, our economy is subject to ups and downs in the level of business and economic activity. The *business cycle* is the sequence of changes (swings) that occur in an economy's overall level of business and economic activity. It consists of prosperity (boom), recession (slowdown), depression (bust), and recovery (upswing). (See Figure 2–2.) These swings in business and economic activity occur because of such factors as variations in the overall supply of and demand for products, the ability and willingness of consumers to buy products and of businesses to invest in new plant and equipment, the volume of consumer spending, employment levels, interest rates, and government spending and tax policies. Personal consumption and housing expenditures together account for 70 percent of the U.S. gross national product (GNP).[2] Thus the economy usually slows when consumer spending falls off.

Swings in the business cycle usually require marketers to adjust their marketing efforts. During an upswing, for example, consumers are generally in a buying mood because they are optimistic about the economic outlook. During a downswing consumers begin doubting their ability to maintain their accustomed levels of consumption. They try to save more and spend less. Many fast-food chains developed new low-price menus during the last recession to help consumers pinch pennies.

Not all marketers are affected equally by the business cycle. Some are essentially unaffected by a recession. Utilities and drug companies are examples. Cyclical businesses are hurt by recessions. For example, shipments in the home appliance industry fell 7.9 percent

business cycle

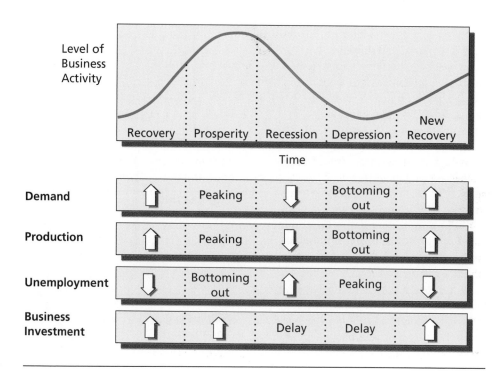

FIGURE 2–2
....

The Business Cycle

in 1990, hurt by the weak economy, low consumer confidence, and the conflict in the Middle East.[3] But business picked up for home appliance repair firms as consumers tried to extend the life of their appliances. This is an example of a *countercyclical business*. Other examples include firms in the debt collection, home improvement, security, and pawnshop businesses. For example, pawnshops cater primarily to cash-poor blue-collar workers during relatively good economic periods. But during recessions newly laid-off executives can be found pawning their Rolexes.[4]

The 1990–1991 recession came on the heels of the heavy consumer spending of the 1980s. Marketers responded in different ways. Some cut their promotion budgets to save money. Others increased their promotion budgets, believing they could take sales away from rivals who had cut theirs. Some reallocated their promotion funds, perhaps spending more on sales promotions such as coupons and less on network TV advertising. Others started new ad campaigns focusing on such consumer concerns as value and savings. An example is a Quaker Oats ad saying that a bowl "costs you one nickel and four pennies." Ads for many hotels and motels featured discounts. Days Inns' "Beat the Bad Times" campaign is an example. Many supermarkets started pushing their private labels (store brands) of products such as cereals and canned vegetables.[5]

Consumer Spending Behavior

Swings in the business cycle cause many consumers to change their spending behavior. Our spending behavior is determined by factors such as our buying power and our willingness to spend. It is also determined by many other factors, such as personal and sociocultural influences (which we will examine in chapter 5).

Consumer buying power depends on current income, credit, accumulated wealth, and the overall state of the economy. Current income, the major source of buying power in the

United States, is the amount of money received from such sources as salary, rent, investments, pensions, and subsidies. _Disposable income_ is after-tax income that is available for either spending or saving. _Discretionary income_ is what remains of disposable income after necessities are purchased. Consumer credit includes installment credit (which requires monthly payments on the outstanding balance) and noninstallment credit (which requires paying off charge purchases in full by a specific date every month). Accumulated wealth includes liquid wealth (assets easily converted to cash) and nonliquid wealth (assets not easily converted to cash).

Swings in the business cycle affect the overall state of the economy because they affect price levels and interest rates. Thus if current income, accumulated wealth, and credit are held constant, an increase in price levels causes a decline in buying power. As we will see shortly, this is called _inflation_.

Our overall willingness to spend is influenced by our ability to buy the general state of the economy, job security, and so on. Our willingness to spend in order to buy specific products depends mainly on their relative prices and their perceived usefulness to us in satisfying our wants.

As the world's economies become increasingly interdependent, it is more and more difficult for a country to be unaffected by economic developments abroad. For example, even if the U.S. economy is not in a recession, recessions in the economies of our trading partners to have a negative economic impact in the United States. Those foreign customers are likely to reduce their spending on American-made goods as a result of the recession.

The Postindustrial Service Economy

During the 1950s and 1960s our economy began changing from an industrial economy based on the manufacture of tangible goods to a postindustrial economy based on the creation of intangible services. This change is often referred to as the decline of smokestack America. Manufacturing industries are the chief source of jobs in an industrial economy. Service industries are the chief source of jobs in a postindustrial economy. The service industries include everything from computer software development to business consulting, from haircuts to telecommunications. Examples of service providers are banks, consulting firms, hotel chains, restaurants, and airlines. In our economy more and more old-line manufacturing firms are moving into services. Notice in the Chrysler ad that the auto maker offers commercial leasing and lending services through Chrysler Capital.

The conventional wisdom is that the service industries mitigate recessions because they rarely lay off people and help spark recoveries by bolstering personal income and steadily creating jobs. But many service industries were hurt in the 1990–1991 recession. Although the service industries remain less cyclical than manufacturing, they have become more volatile.[6]

Inflation, Disinflation, and Deflation

inflation

Inflation is a decline in buying power caused by price levels rising more rapidly than incomes. This decline was a major problem for marketers in the late 1970s and early 1980s, when U.S. inflation was double-digit. Inflation pushes up production and marketing costs while reducing consumer buying power. Consumers who expect inflation to get worse develop an _inflationary psychology_. They spend their money faster because today's prices look like bargains compared to tomorrow's expected prices. They have little incentive to save. In a typical recent year Americans saved less than 6 percent of their annual household income. Families in Japan save about 17 percent.[7]

Chrysler has found growth opportunities in the service industries.

(Chrysler Capital.)

disinflation

deflation

Beginning in 1982 the economy entered a period of disinflation. _**Disinflation**_ is a sustained reduction in the inflation rate, caused by prices rising at a declining rate. In such an environment buy-now, pay-later consumer spending patterns are less likely than during inflationary periods. Marketers therefore must cope with consumers who are more price-sensitive—who shop for the best prices.

By the mid-1980s deflation was a reality in some parts of the United States. _**Deflation**_ is falling prices. For marketers whose prices are falling, deflation means decreased revenues and lower profits, unless the marketers can offset deflation's effects with greater sales volume. In recent years inflation has averaged about 4 to 5 percent a year.

Debt

There has been a major increase in federal, corporate, and consumer debt. Huge annual federal budget deficits have added to the national debt, mergers and acquisitions have added to corporate debt, and heavy consumer borrowing has added to consumer debt.

The enormity of the debt, especially of the federal budget deficits, contributes to uncertainty about the future direction of interest rates. Whether consumers expect interest rates to rise or to fall is a big factor in their decision to buy products on credit, especially durable

goods such as houses, furniture, major appliances, and cars. Their perceived ability to pay down their debt also affects their spending decisions.

Shortages

A crew on a spaceship must conserve and recycle the resources on board. We must do likewise with the natural resources here on earth. As we saw in chapter 1, *demarketing* is a strategy marketers use to reduce demand.

Marketers may also have to direct demand away from products that are in short supply and toward products that are made from more plentiful materials. Price increases caused by shortages may lead consumers to stop buying products that are in short supply, to hoard them, or to switch to substitute products.

During the 1990 Christmas season many catalog retailers understocked their inventory and back-ordered merchandise for their customers. They did not want to risk being saddled with unsalable inventory during a recession.[8] Shortages are a common occurrence in many of the formerly communist economies in Eastern Europe and in the Soviet Union. For example, a major shortage of cigarettes occurred in the Soviet Union in summer 1990. It was caused by antiquated manufacturing equipment, ethnic unrest in domestic cigarette-producing areas, and a lack of foreign currency with which to buy foreign-made cigarettes. As a result, a pack of foreign cigarettes sold for between $17 and $25 on the black market.[9]

Unemployment

People are unemployed when, although they are able and willing to work and are actively looking for work, they do not have jobs. During the 1991–1992 recession, thousands of college graduates were looking for jobs but could not find them. *Underemployment,* another problem, occurs when people who are qualified by education, training, or experience to take higher-level jobs must take lower-level jobs or face the prospect of being unemployed. Many college graduates took jobs waiting tables to ride out the recession.

Unemployment reduces the buying power of the unemployed and leads to higher taxes for the employed, to pay for welfare, social services, unemployment compensation, food stamps, and so on. This reduces the effective buying power of the employed. The fear of being laid off may lead employed people to save more and spend less.

THE COMPETITIVE ENVIRONMENT

competition

Competition is rivalry among marketers that seek to satisfy markets. Increasingly, this rivalry is taking on global proportions, as firms based in different countries compete for the same customers.

The broadest view of competition is that it is generic—all marketers compete for general customer buying power. American Airlines, Daimler-Benz, Toshiba, and the Salvation Army are in generic competition with one another. A narrower perspective is that competition is rivalry among marketers that market *substitutable offerings*. Amtrak competes with the airlines and Greyhound. A still narrower perspective is that competition is rivalry among marketers that market *directly similar offerings*. From this viewpoint American Airlines competes with other airlines, both domestic and international.

Practically speaking, a marketer tends to consider its competitors to be the marketers that are in the same market area and whose offerings are either directly similar to or substitutable for its offerings. Thus the owner of a McDonald's restaurant in downtown Atlanta probably considers all fast-food restaurants in downtown Atlanta to be competitors—but not all downtown restaurants or all fast-food restaurants in the suburbs.

Types of Market Structures

The strength of the competition and the number and type of competitors an organization faces are affected by the type of market structure in which it operates. The four basic types of market structure are (1) pure competition, (2) monopolistic competition, (3) oligopoly, and (4) monopoly.

pure competition

• **Pure Competition** • In the market structure of *pure competition* there are many small buyers and sellers, a homogeneous product, easy entry into and exit from the industry, perfect information in the hands of buyers and sellers, and identical conditions under which all buyers buy and all sellers sell. Pure competition, of course, does not exist in the real world. Buyers and sellers do not have perfect information, different brands within a product category are not homogeneous, buyers and sellers do not operate under the same conditions, and so on.

monopolistic competition

• **Monopolistic Competition** • In the market structure of *monopolistic competition* there are many sellers and many buyers, but the offerings of each seller are somewhat different. The more consumers perceive a seller's offering to differ in desirable ways from rival offerings, the more control that seller has over its price. Buyers perceive no close substitutes for the offering. If they want it, they have to buy it from that seller.

Auto service shops, computer software manufacturers, day care providers, and garment manufacturers typically operate under conditions of monopolistic competition. Numerous firms are already in these industries, and it is relatively easy for new competitors to enter the market. For long-run success a firm operating in a monopolistically competitive market must continually strive to differentiate itself and its market offerings from those of its competitors. This is a never-ending process, because rivals tend to copy product features, advertising campaigns, or anything else that enables them to enjoy an advantage.

- **Oligopoly** • In the market structure of *oligopoly* a few large firms account for the bulk of the industry's sales. Each oligopolist has a large number of the industry's customers, the actions of one firm tend to directly affect the other firms in the industry, and each firm tries to anticipate what the others will do. Examples of oligopolistic industries are ready-to-eat breakfast cereals, major home appliances, automobiles, steel, aluminum, elevators, oil refining, cola drinks, automobile tires, cigarettes, and disposable diapers. For example, Procter & Gamble and Kimberly-Clark have a combined 85 percent share of the disposable diaper market.[10]

oligopoly

In *differentiated oligopoly* buyers perceive differences among competitors' offerings. Examples are automobiles, household appliances, and cigarettes. Marketers achieve and protect this differentiation through product design, product features, and advertising. In *undifferentiated oligopoly* buyers perceive competitors' offerings to be pretty much the same. Examples are steel, aluminum, and cement. To help achieve some differentiation a cement producer might emphasize quick delivery.

It is difficult to enter an oligopolistic industry and to compete with oligopolists. Imagine the financial resources a firm would need to enter the tire manufacturing industry. Oligopolists typically enjoy huge economies of scale not available to a newcomer. The newcomer would also lack certain specialized production and marketing skills. Furthermore, well-entrenched brand names would be enough to discourage a potential entrant.

- **Monopoly** • In the market structure of *monopoly* one firm produces a product that has no close substitute. For example, a firm with a patent on a process or a product for which there are no substitutes is a monopolist. Some people might argue that Nintendo is close to being a monopolist. The company, which supplies all the hardware and software needed to transform a family TV into an interactive electronic playground, accounts for more than 80 percent of worldwide sales of video games.[11]

monopoly

Public utilities are another example. One firm selling natural gas and electricity may serve all of the people in a city. Those who buy its offerings must pay the monopolist's price. Its rates, however, are regulated by government. It is a *natural monopoly*. Such a firm is allowed to operate as a monopoly because the government believes that one company can serve the people more effectively than can several competing companies.

Table 2–1 summarizes the important characteristics of the major types of market structures.

The Changing Nature of Competition

Researchers studying economic data from both 1939 and 1958 found that about half the nation's output was produced under truly competitive conditions.[12] The U.S. economy during the 1960s was also divided roughly into two equal parts. One half fit the model of *managed competition,* which included the auto manufacturing industry, dominated by the Big Three—GM, Ford, and Chrysler; the steel manufacturing industry, dominated by U.S. Steel; and the detergent industry, dominated by Procter & Gamble and Colgate-Palmolive. The other half was considerably more freewheeling.

TABLE 2–1 Important Characteristics of the Major Types of Market Structures

Market Structure	Number of Sellers	Size of Sellers	Control over Price	Product	Entry into Industry
Pure competition	Many	Small	None	Homogeneous	Easy
Monopolistic competition	Many	Varies	Depends on extent of differentiation	Differentiated	Relatively easy
Differentiated oligopoly	Few	Large	Considerable (prices tend to be stable)	Differentiated	Difficult
Undifferentiated oligopoly	Few	Large	Considerable (prices tend to be stable)	Fairly homogeneous	Difficult
Monopoly	One	Varies	Maximum	No close substitutes	Difficult

The 1970s saw major changes affecting the nature of competition. Chief among them were rapidly changing technology, the import invasion, and the beginning of the deregulation movement. In 1980 William G. Shepherd, a professor of economics, said that three-quarters of the nation's output was produced under truly competitive conditions. He cited several examples of industries in which competition was less managed than in the past. The office copier industry, once dominated by Xerox, was transformed by the arrival of imports in the 1970s. The automotive rentals industry, once dominated by three companies, was opened to new entrants as a result of an antitrust action. In railroad transportation, deregulation in 1976 and 1980 brought route and rate competition.

The 1980s witnessed an entrepreneurial boom that grew out of the profound market changes in the 1970s. For example, every stage in the growth of the microelectronics industry—from the development of the transistor to the development of the latest applications software—was pioneered by upstart firms. In the auto industry the import invasion forced the Big Three auto makers to cut costs through layoffs and heavy reliance on outsourcing (buying parts from outside vendors rather than making the parts themselves). That set the stage for hundreds of firms to supply the auto industry. Entrepreneurship was a cause as well as an effect of increased competition.

What happened in the 1970s was that markets were destabilized—some by new technologies, others by deregulation or imports. That opened niches for growth-oriented entrepreneurs. Today, as we will see later in the chapter, technology continues to change the marketplace and create new opportunities. But many U.S. industries have already reacted to the import threat or the opportunities of deregulation and are in the process of restabilizing. One example is air transportation. Although many new airlines were created after the late 1970s deregulation, by the end of the 1980s most of them had been bought up or shaken out and the industry was increasingly being dominated by three or four players. Many people wonder if the entrepreneurial boom of the 1980s will continue throughout the rest of the 1990s or if we will see more of the managed markets of the 1960s.

In the United States more and more universities are teaching entrepreneurship, more and more incubators (where start-up companies can get low-cost space and services) are springing up, more and more entrepreneurs are helping each other through self-help clubs, and franchising is still a very popular way of going into business. On a global scale the decline of Marxism and socialism has been accompanied by a zest for enterprise in many countries where enterprise was previously dormant or suppressed.[13]

How Do Marketers Compete?

As we will explain in the next chapter, organizations must select where (in which markets) they will compete and how they will compete. A marketer has two basic options in dealing with competitors. One is to do as they are doing—imitation. This is a me-too marketing philosophy: "If it works for them, it will work for me too."

Malt-O-Meal company competes in an oligopolistic industry dominated by Kellogg, General Mills, and Quaker Oats. Its strategy: "Don't fight 'em; copy 'em." It still makes hot cereal, as it has for over seventy years. But its main products are low-cost, high-margin clones of the biggest-selling cold cereals. Malt-O-Meal's Toasty O's look and taste like General Mills' Cheerios. Tootie Fruities imitate Kellogg's Fruit Loops. Malt-O-Meal uses few coupons and has no TV ads. Its bags, not boxes, of cereal, however, typically are priced at about half of what the major brands cost.[14]

The other approach is to seek a differential advantage. A *differential advantage* is the benefit enjoyed when a marketer offers a unique product that customers will buy from it rather than from its rivals. The firm has a competitive advantage over its rivals because it and its market offering are different from its rivals and their offerings in ways that are important to its customers. The Andersen Consulting ad discusses the importance of rapid responses to changing customer demands. Blockbuster Video created a differential advantage by taking a business typified by small, seedy, mom-and-pop neighborhood rental shops and going national with stores that resemble supermarkets. It set the terms of the trade, with a huge tape selection (no porno section), three-night rental, and attractive, freshly painted, and brightly lighted family-oriented stores.[15] The challenge for Blockbuster is to hold onto its differential advantage in light of rapidly changing technology and inroads by imitative competitors.

The process of developing and maintaining a differential advantage is what much of marketing is all about. In the process a firm may engage in price competition or nonprice competition.

• **Price Competition** • During the recent recession, prices of many products declined. They included Caribbean vacations, dining out, and housing. When consumers cut spending, marketers often must respond by cutting prices. But many marketers routinely rely mainly on price to differentiate themselves from their rivals. Examples of price-based competitors include discount brokerage firms, discount car rental firms, and discount stores. Rexhall Industries has become a competitor in the recreational vehicle business along with much bigger rivals, such as Winnebago and Fleetwood, mainly by offering lower prices than the rivals. The company also believes in the imitation strategy. As the founder says, "In this industry, we call it R&C: research and copy."[16]

The main problem with price competition is that other firms can often meet a competitor's lower price or can lower their prices even more, thereby possibly setting off a price war. Using price as the major competitive tool may not provide a lasting advantage.

• **Nonprice Competition** • Given the difficulties of price competition, some marketers prefer *nonprice competition*—a market situation in which rivals minimize the importance of price as a competitive tool. Instead of focusing on price, a marketer might create a unique market offering for a segment (niche) of the larger market that rivals are targeting.

A *market niche* is an area of unfulfilled need in a market. Church & Dwight Company

differential advantage

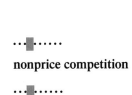

nonprice competition

market niche

Firms that make a slow response to changing customer demands will lose out to competitors.

(Used by permission of Andersen Consulting.)

pursued a niche strategy when it introduced its Arm & Hammer Dental Care toothpaste and tooth powder with baking soda. The niche the company targeted is people who are more concerned about oral hygiene than about the taste of the product.[17]

In addition to targeting market niches, marketers can engage in nonprice competition by focusing on a nonprice element in the marketing mix—the product, its distribution, or its promotion. A. Schulman Inc. is a relatively small firm in the specialty plastics industry that competes with overseas giants such as BASF and Hoechst and domestic giants such as Dow and Monsanto. The company's chairman and president states his business philosophy: "We don't talk price, we talk quality." While other companies struggle to make the lowest-cost commodity plastics, Schulman focuses on high-priced specialty items. Practically every product it makes has features that cannot be easily matched by the competition.[18]

Oligopolists, especially, tend to avoid price competition for two reasons. First, an oligopolist may avoid raising its price if it fears rivals will not follow. It might lose customers who think the rivals' market offerings are just as good, especially in the case of an undifferentiated oligopoly. Second, if one firm cuts its price and the others follow, a price war could result. Thus prices can remain fairly stable without illegal price fixing because the rivals recognize their interdependence. In some cases there is a price leader whom all firms follow on price changes.

Mergers and Acquisitions

An unprecedented number of mergers and acquisitions occurred during the 1980s, including Philip Morris Company's buyout of Kraft Inc. and Grand Metropolitan PLC's purchase of Pillsbury Company. Critics argued that the intensity of merger activity created too much uncertainty among firms. Thus, instead of devoting time to such strategic activities as analyzing market opportunities and developing new products, too many executives were said to be spending their time thinking about what companies they wanted to take over or trying to figure out what companies would like to take over their companies.[19]

Among early 1990s acquisitions were Matsushita Electric Industrial Company's acquisition of MCA and AT&T's acquisition of NCR Corporation. The 1980s takeovers typically involved junk bonds and leveraged buyouts. In the 1990s it's more a case of large, well-financed domestic and foreign-based corporations making strategic acquisitions to build their own businesses. Many find it less costly to expand into businesses related to their core businesses through acquisition than to start from scratch by building plants and developing brands.[20]

Another type of strategic activity involves competitors entering into a *marketing alliance*. One of the earliest involved two pharmaceutical companies, London-based Glaxo Holdings and Switzerland-based Hoffman-LaRoche. In 1981 Glaxo knew its antiulcer drug Zantac had tremendous potential, but the company's marketing capability was no match for that of SmithKline Beckman, which dominated the market with its antiulcer drug Tagamet. Thus Glaxo formed an alliance with competitor Hoffman-LaRoche to market Zantac. More recently Glaxo has made similar marketing deals with firms in Argentina, Ecuador, and South Africa. It has even agreed to market its rivals' drugs. In addition to making numerous marketing alliances, the pharmaceutical industry is becoming increasingly dominated by global giants as a result of mergers and acquisitions.[21]

There are other types of alliances too. For example, General Motors, Ford, and Chrysler formed an alliance to develop battery technology for electric cars. This is seen by some observers as opening a new era of cooperation by the Big Three against foreign rivals. It reflects a major shift in their competitive strategies. Meanwhile a Japanese alliance of auto makers and the Japanese government is working to develop an electric-powered vehicle.[22]

THE TECHNOLOGICAL ENVIRONMENT

Technology is the knowledge to do new or old tasks in a better way. The result of technological development—a new product, process, or idea—is an *invention*. Introducing inventions in the marketplace is called *innovation*. The 3M ad focuses on the importance of innovation.

technology

A major source of new technology is scientific research. Research and development (R&D) is an important function of many businesses. Nonbusiness sources of new technology include governments, universities, research hospitals, and research foundations.

Basic research seeks new concepts. *Applied research* seeks to transfer technology from the lab to the marketplace. The Council on Competitiveness, a private think tank, was established to help U.S. firms compete globally. In a recent report it said: ''Pioneering research and Nobel prizes are not enough. Unless ideas can be pushed, pulled or cajoled

An ad that discusses the importance of innovation.

(Courtesy of 3M.)

from the laboratory to the marketplace, America's jobs, standard of living and, ultimately, national security will be at risk.'' In other words, the council recognizes that the United States has good universities and top researchers but that it stumbles when it comes to translating scientific know-how into marketable products.[23]

In 1990 the federal government spent about $70 billion on science and technology, up from $30 billion in 1980. Some people favor allocating a huge portion of the R&D money to space projects and defense. They believe military R&D will ultimately lead to commercial applications, or spin-offs, of that technology. Other people want the federal government to shift R&D money to the development of industrial technologies that lead quickly to industrial applications—marketable products. Of course, the success of such a shift would depend on the ability of U.S. firms to bring technology to market rapidly, something Japanese firms have been doing much more successfully in recent years.[24]

Controversy regarding how federal R&D funds should be allocated is part of the larger issue of the federal government's proper role in advancing the nation's industrial power. Advocates of *industrial policy* want the government to play a much larger role in identifying and providing financial support to key industries and key technologies, just as Japan and some European countries do. Advocates say this is necessary for U.S. firms to become more competitive in world markets and for our standard of living to rise. Opponents of industrial policy say such decisions should be left to market forces.

The United States funds about twice as much R&D as Japan and Germany combined. But we have lagged behind both countries in industry-funded R&D as a percent of gross national product for two decades. Furthermore, industry spending in both countries has been growing at a faster rate than it has in the United States.[25]

Technology and Society

Many applications of technology have raised our standard of living, given us a tremendous variety of new products, increased productivity, contributed to longer and healthier lives, given us more leisure time, and reduced the need for humans to perform dangerous and unhealthy jobs.

Some applications of technology, nevertheless, have had negative side effects, contributing to social problems such as pollution, crime, and job stress. But further applications of technology may reduce or overcome some of the negative effects of previous applications. Thus, although some applications of technology create pollution, others clean up pollution.

Many ethical and legal issues arise in connection with technology. Recently a woman who was eight months pregnant with an implanted embryo produced with the sperm and eggs supplied by a husband and wife sued the spouses. She sought custody of the baby she was carrying for them, even though she had no genetic connection to it. Who is the baby's mother?[26] What about controlling the spread of technology for manufacturing nuclear, chemical, and biological weapons? What about the ethics of genetic engineering?

One thing is certain. The pace of technological change is accelerating rapidly and many people feel unprepared to cope with it. Some job skills, for example, can quickly become technologically obsolete, and some workers must either learn new skills or face the dismal prospect of unemployment.

Technology and Marketing

Marketing helps deliver the benefits of new technology to society. Turning technological know-how into marketable products, however, requires a good marketing organization. One reason many inventors sell their ideas to larger and more effective marketing organizations is that the inventors do not know how to market their ideas.

• **Impact on the Nature of Competition** • Technological development can create a new competitor. For example, hospitals are facing increasingly stiff competition from new home health care devices. Many of the devices use "telemonitoring" technology—phone-linked computer systems that allow health care professionals to make, in effect, an electronic house call. An example is MDphone, a briefcase-sized device used to revive heart attack patients. One man bought MDphone a couple weeks before his wife was scheduled to have a heart transplant. Prior to the transplant she suffered a heart attack. By opening MDphone, her husband automatically connected himself to a nurse, who told him to hook up the device's electrodes to his wife's chest. "Stand back," she yelled to the husband, just before a 2,500-volt electrical current shocked his wife's heart to life.[27]

• **Impact on Costs and Productivity** • The application of new technology may enable an organization to lower its production and marketing costs, increase its productivity, and gain a competitive advantage. The traditional approach to drug development involves screening thousands of chemicals in hit-or-miss search. This helps explain why it can now cost more than $200 million to bring one drug to market. A recent study showed that R&D spending by major international drug makers as a share of revenues doubled in the 1980s. But the number of new drugs introduced has declined steadily since 1960.

A new wave of R&D called "rational drug design" brings together biotechnology and chemistry in an effort to streamline and enhance drug development and reshape the biotech and pharmaceutical industries. Many in the business believe rational drug design will restore the drug industry's R&D productivity.[28]

• **Impact on the Marketing Mix** • As we saw in chapter 1, the elements in a marketing mix are product, place (distribution), promotion, and price—the four *P*s. Technology can also affect each of these elements.

Technology affects the types of *products* marketers can offer. Pitney Bowes is replacing its old postage meters and scales with new models that replenish postage electronically by telephone. No longer does the user have to take the meter to a post office.[29] Technology made the old machines obsolete.

Technology also affects the way products are *distributed*. More and more retailers are using scanners to track sales and inventory. Many also automatically reorder through computers that "talk" to suppliers' computers.

Promotion is also affected by technology. MerchanTec International's InstAward uses electronic countertop terminals in restaurants and satellite technology to identify, track, and reward frequent customers. To enroll in an InstAward program, consumers fill out an application at the restaurant. The application is processed at MerchanTec, an electronic file is created to store data about the customer—name, address, and so on—and the customer is issued a plastic card to use when making purchases. Data collected over time can be used to target promotions at specific customers. For example, a customer who has not eaten at a restaurant during the past several weeks can be sent a coupon through the mail.[30]

Pricing too is affected by technology. Imagine the problems travel agents would encounter without computers to inform them of the discount fares offered by airlines.

....

THE SOCIOCULTURAL AND ETHICAL ENVIRONMENT

The marketer's relationship to society and to its culture makes up the sociocultural environment. Because this environment affects how people live, including how they behave as consumers, it is important for marketers to understand it.

People, of course, are the most important element in the sociocultural environment, and changes involving them are of major importance to marketers. The "graying" of America—the aging of the population—is one reason the "oldies but goodies" is one of the fastest-growing radio formats.[31] An aging population and fear of contracting AIDS or other sexually transmitted diseases help explain the decline in the divorce rate in recent years.[32] Much of the explanation for the transformation of small cities such as Naples, Fort Myers, and Fort Pierce, Florida, into rapidly growing metropolitan areas lies in their attractiveness to retirees.[33] As the Nexxus ad suggests, marketers can find market opportunities in the "graying" of America.

Consider also the recent changes in a basic sociocultural influence on consumer behavior—the family. Approximately 65 percent of the 45.1 million married couples drawing paychecks in the United States today are dual-income pairs.[34] Dual-career couples are bringing changes in American lifestyles. Men are feeling increased pressure to spend more time with their children and to perform household chores. Having a demanding career and

Bring out your finest silver.

Nexxus Simply Silver Shampoo is formulated to make silver, gray and white hair absolutely glisten.

Just one use and you'll see the difference.

The gentle botanicals in Simply Silver cleanse and moisturize your hair adding shine and lustre, enhancing your natural color.

Your silver hair will sparkle every day with Simply Silver Shampoo.

Available only at hair-styling salons.

Nexxus

Where you go for beautiful hair.

The "graying" of America offers market opportunities for many firms.

(Courtesy of R.A.O. Communications. Art direction: Broūn. Photography: Broūn. Copywriters: Applegate/Slay.)

being a good parent is becoming as stressful for men as it has been for women.[35] Many marketers are focusing attention on men in their role as fathers. The number of households headed by women is also growing. Like dual-career couples, these people have little free time. Thus they demand convenience and more and more services.

Cultural Diversity

As we will see in chapters 7 and 8, marketers often develop separate marketing mixes for specific market segments. Race and nationality are among the many variables that can be used in breaking a market down into smaller segments.

The United States is more racially and ethnically diverse than ever before. Consider that nearly 50 percent more people became naturalized citizens in the 1980s than during the previous decade.[36] The top five countries of origin were the Philippines, Vietnam, Mexico, China, and Korea.[37] The 1990 U.S. Census showed that minority groups increased at a rate at least twice that of the white majority. In 1990 the white majority fell to 80.3 percent, the lowest in the twentieth century. The Hispanic population has grown nine times faster than

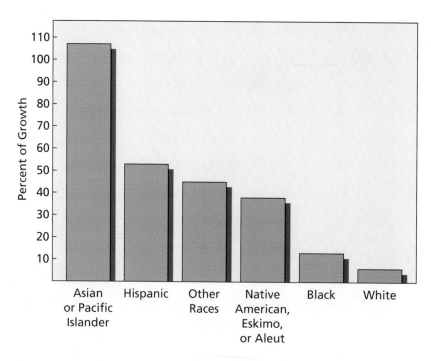

FIGURE 2–3
....

Growth of Racial and Ethnic Groups in the United States

[1]Hispanics can be of any race.

Source: U.S. Census Bureau

the white population since 1980; Asian-Amerian growth has been eighteen times faster, and African-American two times.[38] (See Figure 2–3.) There also has been a dramatic dispersion of minority groups into all areas of the nation. Americans everywhere, in major metropolitan areas as well as rural areas, are being exposed as never before to different cultures.[39]

By the year 2000, 30 percent of Americans will be Hispanic or of a racial minority, up from 20 percent now; and 80 percent of new workers will be minorities or women. By 2015 Hispanics are projected to be the biggest minority in the United States.[40] By 2056 the ''average'' U.S. resident, as defined by Census statistics, will trace his or her descent to Africa, Asia, the Hispanic world, the Pacific Islands, Arabia—almost anywhere but white Europe. According to Molefi Asante, chairman of the department of African-American studies at Temple University: ''Once America was a microcosm of European nationalities. Today America is a microcosm of the world.''[41]

Between the 1980 and 1990 Census the number of Asian-Americans more than doubled. Thus more and more firms are targeting them. For example, AT&T offers price promotions during Asian holidays such as Parents' Day in Korea and Moon Festival in Hong Kong and Taiwan. Equitable, MetLife, and New York Life Insurance advertise in Asian-language media and have hired bilingual Asian sales agents. MetLife angered potential customers, however, when it ran an ad in a Korean magazine showing a family in traditional dress—Chinese dress! Anheuser-Busch sells eight varieties of California-grown rice to Asian-Americans. Each as a different Asian label to cover a range of nationalities and tastes.[42]

Cultural Values

As we will see in chapter 5, all cultures have certain values that are resistant to change. But marketers must remain alert to detect signs of shifting beliefs and values in order to spot

More and more marketers in the United States are targeting a culturally diverse market.

[© Bob Daemmrich]

developing threats or opportunities and to help ensure that their marketing strategies reflect the values of the relevant culture. Interfaith marriages created an opportunity for MixedBlessing to market interfaith cards—for example, one showing a Christmas tree transforming into a Star of David. Although interfaith marriages are increasing, there is considerable opposition to the cards from some Jewish and Christian leaders who reject the merging of symbols.[43]

Shifts in our cultural values affect marketers. Heightened concern about sexually trans-mitted diseases presented condom manufacturers with an opportunity to advertise their products to women. The same concern was perceived as a threat to many of the bars that cater to the swinging singles lifestyle. Operation Desert Shield and Operation Desert Storm brought forth a newfound patriotism that was reflected in many ad campaigns.

Social trends such as the concern with nutrition, smoking, and drunk-driving are making people wary of fatty foods, secondhand smoke, and drinking too heavily. McDonald's introduced its McLean Deluxe hamburger to appeal to people concerned about fat in their foods. Hotels, motels, restaurants, retail stores, and many other businesses are affected by the antismoking trend. Wrigley's spotted opportunity and started an ad campaign targeted to people who smoke but can't always light up when they want to. The campaign urged them to chew Spearmint gum. More and more brewers have added nonalcoholic drinks to their lineups. The Distilled Spirits Council sponsored a campaign titled ''Know the Mean-ing of the Word'' to help differentiate between alcohol use and alcohol abuse.[44]

Of course, the sociocultural environment in the United States is not homogeneous. The rap group 2 Live Crew stood trial for obscenity in Hollywood, Florida, and jurors in Cin-cinnati participated in an obscenity trial against an art museum for displaying some works of Robert Mapplethorpe. Rising cultural conservatism and growing attacks on violent and obscene lyrics played a role in the decision of most major record companies to voluntarily apply an ''Explicit Lyrics'' sticker to albums with crude language or explicit references to sex or violence.[45]

Our cultural values also have spillover effects on the other elements in the marketing environment. Honesty, integrity, and fairness are basic cultural values in the United States. They are reflected in the political-legal environment in the form of laws prohibiting such practices as fraudulent advertising and deceptive packaging. Those values also have their impact in the competitive environment in terms of what is considered fair competition.

How does the growing cultural diversity in the United States affect our cultural values? Some people argue that a society needs a universally accepted set of cultural values. Otherwise, they argue, social cohesion will be impossible to achieve. In general, these people believe we should focus more on our unity than on our diversity. They point to the frictions among the various ethnic groups in the culturally diverse Soviet Union and believe immigrants to the United States should be pressured to conform to Western values.[46]

Firms that do business in the United States often market to diverse subcultures. Some might target Mexican-American subculture. But to do so successfully requires an in-depth knowledge of the market. There are differences among Mexicans, Puerto Ricans, Cubans, and the other nationalities that make up the U.S. Hispanic population. For example, Cuban-Americans are concentrated in southern Florida, Puerto Ricans are concentrated in New York, and Mexican-Americans are concentrated in the southwestern states. Growing recognition of such facts has led to a big increase in the use of regionalization by national

GLOBAL MARKETING

Global economic interdependence is probably inevitable in the long run. In varying degrees the U.S. economy affects and is affected by the economic environment in other countries. Consider the actual and potential impact of the fall of communism in Eastern Europe, the economic integration of Western Europe, the growing economic power of many Asian countries, and free trade among the United States, Canada, and Mexico.

U.S.-based companies are competing ever more intensely with foreign-based companies both at home and abroad. Whereas General Motors, Ford, and Chrysler have cut back some of their automobile operations in the United States, Japanese-owned or jointly owned companies have expanded their auto

operations here. Disney, Paramount, and Time Warner are the only U.S.-owned movie firms. Universal, MCA, Columbia Pictures, MGM-UA, and 20th Century-Fox are foreign-owned rivals.

The growth of research and development (R&D) in other nations has eroded the dominant leadership role the United States has enjoyed for the past several decades. More and more technology is being transferred from the United States to other countries as a result of licenses granted by U.S. firms to foreign firms, many of which make products for U.S.-based firms to market in the United States. On the other hand, there is a growing flow of new technology from other countries to the United States.

International marketers must recognize

firms. *Regionalization* is a marketing strategy that seeks to cater to regional preferences within a larger market. Domino's Pizza offers different toppings in different regions. Campbell Soup Company divides the United States into twenty-two regions in line with its commitment to regionalization.[47]

····■······

regionalization

As indicated in the Global Marketing box, the marketing environment is becoming increasingly global in scope. As we will see in chapter 22, international marketers must be especially familiar with and sensitive to intercultural differences.

In the discussions that follow we focus on a topic —marketing ethics. The sociocultural environment plays the major role in determining what constitutes ethical and unethical marketing practices and what constitutes marketing's social responsibility.

Marketing Ethics

Ethical concerns and questions arise in all areas of marketing. As we said in chapter 1, marketing ethics is judgments about what is morally right and wrong for organizations and their employees in their role as marketers. Individual employees formulate codes of ethics (guides to ethical behavior) on the basis of their personal value systems. Their ethics are the standards against which they judge a particular action to be right or wrong. Organizations also have ethical codes by which they expect their members to abide.

Professionals who experience a conflict between employer and personal ethics can resolve the issue by adhering to the ethical code established by their professional association. The code for the American Marketing Association (AMA) is presented in the Ethics in Marketing box. Companies too are sometimes guided by third parties. Thus some trade

sociocultural and ethnic diversity, which includes language, aesthetics, cultural values and attitudes, and customs and taboos. Recently legislators in Prague voted to rename their country the Czech and Slovak Federative Republic to provide equal ethnic billing.

Ideas about marketing's social responsibility and marketing ethics often differ. Our notions about social responsibility may have little relevance in less developed countries. More and more colleges of business administration in the United States are adding courses in ethics. In Japan, however, little distinction is made between ethics and social norms. The Japanese philosophy of education emphasizes rote learning and socialization. Ethical theories are studied mainly for their intellectual and historical value. They need not be applied in real life ethical situations because society tells one what is right and what is wrong.

Politics to a large extent affects trade and other business possibilities. Can you imagine Pizza Hut doing business in China and the Soviet Union when the Cold War was in full swing? On the other hand, terrorism—hijackings, bombings, and kidnappings—by extremist political factions has become a major risk and cost of conducting international business.

Source: The information about ethics and social norms in Japan is from Richard E. Wokutch, "Corporate Social Responsibility Japanese Style," *Executive*, May 1990, pp.56–74.

ETHICS IN MARKETING

The following is the American Marketing Association's revised Code of Ethics. It was developed in 1985 by a panel of AMA members including both business-people and academics. The previous code was much less detailed; it was ten points listed on the back of the AMA membership card.

Members of the American Marketing Association (AMA) are committed to ethical professional conduct. They have joined together in subscribing to this Code of Ethics embracing the following topics.

Responsibilities of the Marketer

Marketers must accept responsibility for the consequences of their activities and make every effort to ensure that their decisions, recommendations, and actions function to identify, serve and satisfy all relevant publics: customers, organizations and society. Marketers' professional conduct must be guided by:

1. The basic rule of professional ethics: not knowingly to do harm;

2. The adherence of all applicable laws and regulations;

3. The accurate representation of their education, training and experience; and

4. The active support, practice and promotion of this Code of Ethics.

Honesty and Fairness

Marketers shall uphold and advance the integrity, honor and dignity of the marketing profession by:

1. Being honest in serving consumers, clients, employees, suppliers, distributors and the public;

2. Not knowingly participating in conflict of interest without prior notice to all parties involved; and

3. Establishing equitable fee schedules including the payment or receipt of usual, customary and/or legal compensation for marketing exchanges.

Rights and Duties of Parties in the Marketing Exchange Process

Participants in the marketing exchange process should be able to expect that:

1. Products and services offered are safe and fit for their intended uses;

2. Communications about offered products and services are not deceptive;

3. All parties intend to discharge their obligations, financial and otherwise, in good faith; and

4. Appropriate internal methods exist for equitable adjustment and/or redress of grievances concerning purchases.

It is understood that the above would include, *but is not limited to*, the following responsibilities of the marketer:

In the area of product development and management,

- disclosure of all substantial risks associated with product or service usage;
- identification of any product component substitution that might materially change the product or impact on the buyer's purchase decision;

- identification of extra-cost added features.

In the area of promotions,

- avoidance of false and misleading advertising;
- rejection of high pressure manipulations, or misleading sales tactics;
- avoidance of sales promotions that use deception or manipulation.

In the area of distribution,

- not manipulating the availability of a product for purpose of exploitation;
- not using coercion in the marketing channel;
- not exerting undue influence over the reseller's choice to handle a product.

In the area of pricing,

- not engaging in price fixing;
- not practicing predatory pricing;
- disclosing the full price associated with any purchase.

In the area of marketing research,

- prohibiting selling or fund raising under the guise of conducting research;
- maintaining research integrity by avoiding misrepresentation and omission of pertinent research data;
- treating outside clients and suppliers fairly.

Organizational Relationships

Marketers should be aware of how their behavior may influence or impact on the behavior of others in organizational rela-

tionships. They should not demand, encourage or apply coercion to obtain unethical behavior in their relationships with others, such as employees, suppliers or customers. Marketers should:

1. Apply confidentiality and anonymity in professional relationships with regard to privileged information;
2. Meet their obligations and responsibilities in contracts and mutual agreements in a timely manner;
3. Avoid taking the work of others, in whole, or in part, and represent this work as their own or directly benefit from it without compensation or consent of the originator or owner;
4. Avoid manipulation to take advantage of situations to maximize personal welfare in a way that unfairly deprives or damages their organization or others.

Any AMA member found to be in violation of any provision of this Code of Ethics may have his or her Association membership suspended or revoked.

What are the strengths of this code? What about weaknesses? Do you have any recommendations for improving the code?

Source: American Marketing Association, *Code of Ethics*, rev. ed. (Chicago: American Marketing Association, 1985). Reprinted by permission.

associations and Better Business Bureaus have ethical codes to which their member firms subscribe. In some cases regulatory agencies such as the Federal Trade Commission may issue guidelines that help firms formulate their ethical codes. Nevertheless, ethical problems do arise.

Suppose an employee in a company's new-product development department discovers that a new oven cleaner, scheduled to be introduced on the market the following week, is potentially dangerous to users if they fail to follow precisely the instructions printed on the package. The employee feels a strong personal obligation to do something and believes the company's ethical code also requires that corrective action be taken. Thus the employee discusses the problem with the head of the product development department, who tells the employee not to be concerned. What should the employee do?

To do nothing might violate both personal and company ethical codes. To blow the whistle on the boss by bringing the matter to the attention of higher-ups in the company would undoubtedly alienate the boss. Would upper management support the employee's action? If the employee is unsure of upper management support, should the person call the Consumer Product Safety Commission about the situation?

The answers to these questions require serious deliberation. The person's job will be in jeopardy if the company's ethical code is more puff than substance. Yet the employee can-

An ad that reflects Texaco's commitment to its various stakeholders.

(This advertisement reprinted courtesy of Texaco Inc.)

"DO IT RIGHT."

"We have a corporate responsibility to do business with a conscience. This includes ensuring that the issues we are all passionate about—the environment and the quality of life—are not overlooked."

Victor Simon is a Texaco Senior Petroleum Engineer. He is committed to making certain that Texaco's oil and gas operations in the Eastern U.S. are conducted in a manner consistent with environmental safeguards.

"This responsibility includes more than just being attentive to government regulations. In every step of our operations, from obtaining emission permits to ensuring on-site safety, simply meeting legislated standards isn't enough. We can and *do* exceed such standards when we believe it is the right thing to do. We have an obligation to our employees, our contractors, our customers and the people in the communities around us to act with their interest in mind, not just react."

Victor and his group have a commitment to corporate quality that goes beyond standard business practice. They have a driving desire to succeed without wasting time or energy; to make sure that when a job is done, it's done right the first time and every time.

"Basically, good business isn't just bottom-line efficiency. It's also safety on the job—whether you're drilling, producing or supplying. It's respect for the environment and for each other."

It's also people like Victor.

Victor Simon
Senior Petroleum Engineer
Texaco

Star of the
American Road

TEXACO – WE'VE GOT THE ENERGY.

not push the issue aside. Perhaps one way for companies to deal with such a situation is to set up in-house procedures for reviewing employee allegations about wrongdoing, without the need for employees to make formal accusations.

Marketing's Social Responsibility

As we saw in chapter 1, the societal marketing concept stresses marketing's social responsibility—a long-run view of company, customer, and societal welfare. As the Texaco ad suggests, the concept recognizes that marketers are obligated not only to provide stockholders with a satisfactory rate of return on their investment, to provide attractive pay and working conditions for employees, and to provide want-satisfying offerings for customers but also to fulfill obligations to other publics. In Figure 2–4, the community at large includes various subgroups to which the organization has obligations. Other examples are minorities, women, older people, and people with disabilities. In other words, the societal marketing concept requires marketers to consider the wants of all people whose welfare is affected by their operations.

• **Socially Responsible Behavior** • What constitutes socially responsible behavior, however, is not always simple to determine. Suppose a polluting metals smelting plant is located in an economically depressed area. Although the plant is only marginally profit-

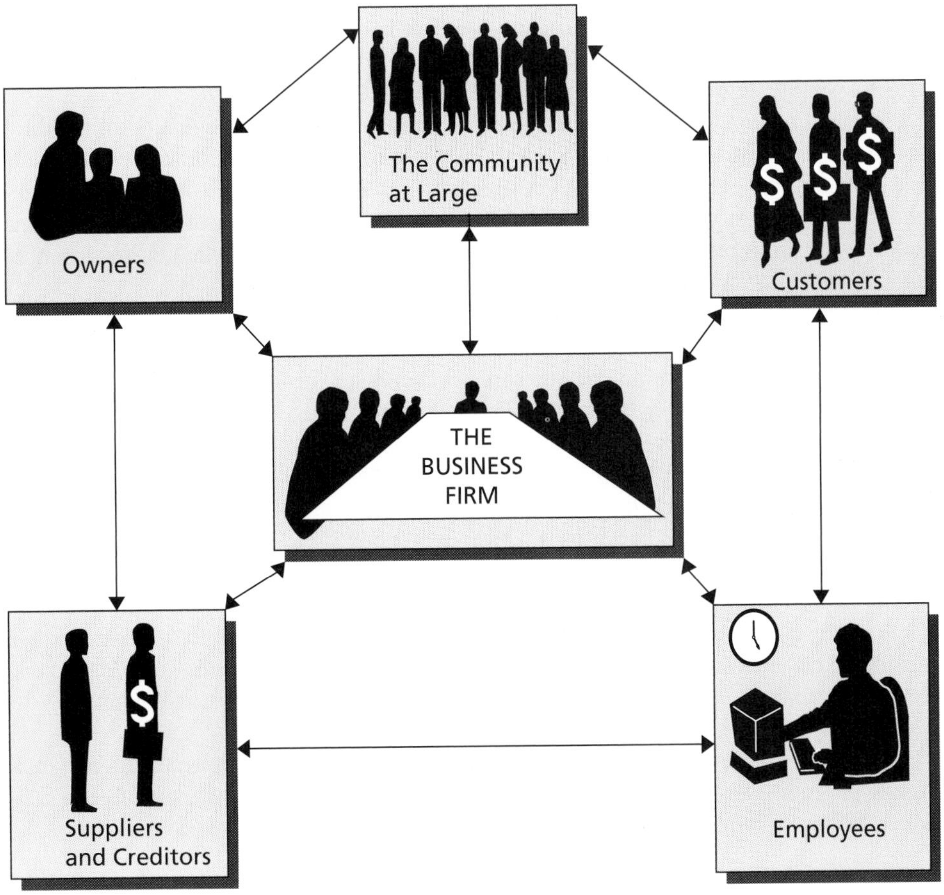

FIGURE 2–4

Examples of a Firm's Publics, or Stakeholders

able, management decides to continue operations because it has long-term commitments to supply customers from that plant; it feels an obligation to the workers, who would have difficulty finding work elsewhere; and it would need to make a tremendous investment to replace the plant with a modern, less polluting facility.

From the traditional perspective of social responsibility, management is acting responsibly. It has considered customer, employee, and stockholder interests. But is the decision to keep a polluting plant operating really in the best interests of the people whose well-being is negatively affected by the pollution? Would closing the plant be more socially responsible?

• **Consumerism** • As we saw in chapter 1, the United States experienced its first consumerist era in the early 1900s and a second one in the 1930s. Both were started largely in response to the failure of businesses to accept their social responsibility to their customers. A third consumerist era began in 1962, when President John F. Kennedy set forth four consumer rights: (1) the right to choose from an adequate number of products; (2) the right to be informed of all the important facts about products, such as price, durability, and safety hazards; (3) the right to be heard by producers and government when treatment is unfair or when a question or complaint arises; and (4) the right to safety in the use of all products.

Rachel Carson's *Silent Spring* (1962) attacked the irresponsible use of pesticides, and Ralph Nader's *Unsafe at Any Speed* (1965) attacked the defects in the Corvair auto. Nader has helped pass laws relating to packaging, product safety, warranties, and information on consumer financing plans.

Marketers now realize more than ever that it costs much less to keep present customers than to develop new ones. Thus it makes good business sense to maintain good customer relations. The ad describing General Motors' Third Party Arbitration Program is an example of a positive response to consumerism.

The field of customer relations has been growing ever since the beginning of the third consumerist era. More and more organizations are setting up consumer affairs departments and installing toll-free numbers for consumers to call for information or to register complaints. It is estimated that only 5 to 10 percent of dissatisfied consumers will take the time to write or call to register their complaints. Thus the typical dissatisfied customer either endures the dissatisfaction quietly or shifts to another brand.[48]

Modern consumerism has grown to encompass equal opportunity, product safety, product warranties, honest advertising, child protection, full disclosure by lenders, fair packaging and labeling, nutrition, health care, occupational health and safety, ecological concerns, and other consumer interests. These are broad categories of concern. For example, ecological concerns encompass conservation of resources, recycling of used resources, and control over pollution in all its forms. Perhaps consumerism has become a permanent part of the marketing environment. One of the more recent forms of marketing to emerge from ecological concerns is "green marketing."

• **Green Marketing** • Especially since the twentieth anniversary of Earth Day, in 1990, many organizations have become involved in green marketing. Recently more than a hundred business leaders gathered in New York at the Power of Green conference to discuss two subjects: increasing brand loyalty via environmental tie-ins and enhancing the corporate image by communicating a solid "Green" personality.[49]

As we saw in chapter 1, green marketing is the development and implementation of marketing programs designed to enhance an organization's environmental image. Green marketers believe environmental concerns are influencing the buying decisions of more and

General Motors' Third Party Arbitration Program is a positive response to consumerism.

(Courtesy of General Motors Corporation.)

more consumers. A recent Gallup poll revealed that 76 percent of Americans think of themselves as "environmentalists."[50] The environmental awakening that culminated in the first Earth Day, in 1970, was essentially defined by young idealists. The twentieth Earth Day was characterized by an explosion of environmental populism. Millions of "ordinary" Americans became involved.[51]

As environmental concerns enter into more buying decisions and as more and more marketers turn to green marketing, environmental claims proliferate. In some cases the claims amount to little more than "green gimmickry." In others the claims are confusing, misleading, or even deceptive. Thus efforts are being made to develop uniform national guidelines for environmental marketing claims in order to prevent "green-collar" fraud. Various types of seals of approval have been developed to cope with this problem.

Most of the high-grade "recycled" paper being sold contains factory scrap that never left the mill plus trimmings from "converters," which make such products as envelopes. Conservatree Paper Company, however, markets paper products containing postconsumer fiber—used paper that would otherwise end up in landfills.[52]

Conservatree has developed a ranking system for its products to help end the confusion surrounding "recycled" paper. The rankings are intended to inform consumers about which papers use the most deinked fibers. Conservatree hopes the labeling system will catch on and help increase demand for genuine recycled paper. That would encourage paper mills to buy deinking equipment and wastepaper that is now ending up in landfills or being burned.[53]

Environmentalism is a corporate philosophy at some companies. Lost Arrow Corporation makes Patagonia outdoor clothing. The company's travel manager says: "Our line is outdoor clothing. What good is it if there's no outdoors to go to?" The company reimburses an employee who pays hotel maids $3 a day not to change her sheets when she's staying in a hotel for more than one night. The company also keeps a master calendar showing who's traveling where and when and encourages employees to coordinate their trips to avoid unnecessary travel.[54]

One of the most innovative packages of all times was the L'eggs plastic egg—the package for L'eggs pantyhose. But in the summer of 1991 the company announced it would

Mexico's changing political environment affects the way marketers do business in that country.

(Albert Frank-Guenther Law, Inc., NY, NY, ad agency; Art direction: Dominic Algieri; Creative director/copy: Jon Saunders; photography: Susumu Sato.)

BANCA SERFIN

It's bright.
It's clear.
And it's evident in all the major avenues of Mexico's economy.

Areas once restricted by regulatory bottlenecks are now wide open. And the message behind Mexico's reforms is full speed ahead.

The ways you can go are many. Such as foreign investment and trade. A thriving maquiladora industry with low production costs. The privatization of key industries. Or the redevelopment of our country's infrastructure, to name a few.

Mapping the right course for your company is easy. Just talk to the people at Banca Serfin.

As Mexico's first full-service bank, we're at the forefront of our country's revitalization. Which means we have everything it takes to help you succeed. From general investment advice and merchant banking, to leasing, trade finance, swaps, factoring and foreign exchange.

Opportunity in Mexico is now in the fast lane. With Banca Serfin, it won't pass you by.

Mexico Is Sending Business A New Signal.

| Mexico City | New York | Tokyo | London | Toronto | Los Angeles | Nassau | Belize | Seoul |
| (525) 512-7768 | (212) 635-2300 | (813) 273-5911 | (4471) 408-2151 | (416) 360-8900 | (213) 624-6610 | (212) 635-2300 | (5012) 78970 | (813) 273-5911 |

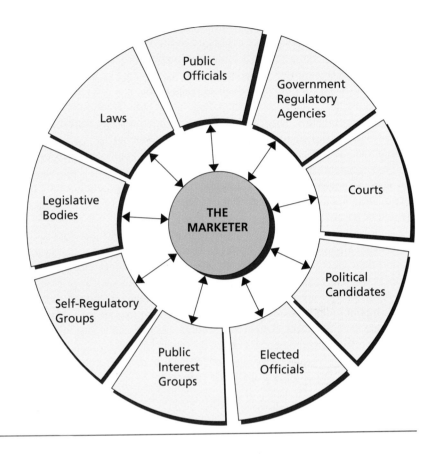

FIGURE 2–5

Elements in the Political-Legal
Environment

drop the plastic egg in favor of a new recycled-cardboard box.[55] Even the nuclear power industry is turning to green marketing. Nuclear power is being offered as a solution to such environmental problems as acid rain, global warming, and the hole in the earth's ozone shield.

Of course, the green movement is not restricted to the United States. In fact, it started in Western Europe and today is involved in national politics throughout Western Europe. Environmentalism is a global concern. Thus many marketers throughout the world have become green marketers.

THE POLITICAL-LEGAL ENVIRONMENT

In today's increasingly global economy marketers must remain alert to developments in the global political environment. The Banca Serfin ad discusses Mexico's changing political environment. Knowledge of those changes might make Mexico a more attractive place for foreign firms to do business. Likewise the lifting of sanctions by the United States against South Africa in the summer of 1991 created opportunity for many U.S. firms to do business in South Africa. Political changes in the Soviet Union, Eastern Europe, China, and the Middle East also affect their relative attractiveness as potential markets.

Figure 2–5 identifies the elements in the political-legal environment in the United States that affect the marketer. Of course, the same elements would be present in the political-legal environment of most other countries, although the relative influence of the different elements might vary. Also notice in Figure 2–5 that marketers try to influence the political-legal environment. An example is lobbying Congress or state legislatures.

A great deal of controversy has erupted in recent years about former U.S. government officials who lobby for foreign interests in Washington, D.C. For example, since 1973 one-third of all former top officials in the Office of the U.S. Trade Representative have registered as foreign agents, mostly for Japanese companies. The controversy also raises the issue of what patriotism means in today's global economy.[56]

Regardless of the particular country, government is the major element in the political-legal environment. In the United States, government regulatory agencies such as the Federal Trade Commission and the Consumer Product Safety Commission play a major role in regulating marketing practices. For example, they work to prevent false advertising and the sale of unsafe products.

Candidates for public office, nongovernment self-regulatory groups, and public interest groups also affect the political-legal environment. Candidates seek to persuade voters to support their views on such matters as government spending, taxation, the obligations of business to society, and regulation of marketing activities such as pricing and advertising. Self-regulatory groups such as Better Business Bureaus encourage businesses to police themselves in order to lessen the perceived need for government to do so. Public interest groups are also important. Action for Children's Television wants tighter government regulation of television commercials targeted to children. Protests and boycotts also are common. Feminist groups called for a boycott of *Esquire* magazine after an issue appeared with the cover story "Your Wife: An Owner's Manual."[57]

Government and Marketers

In addition to regulating the economy, government also seeks to stabilize it to prevent serious recessions, high unemployment, and so on. Furthermore, government provides highways to facilitate the transportation function, a postal service to facilitate the communication function, and statistical data to facilitate the marketing information function.

The share of gross national product (GNP) spent by federal, state, and local governments is close to 40 percent.[58] The U.S. government is the biggest single customer in the world.

Finally, in addition to its roles as regulator, stabilizer, facilitator, and customer, government can be a competitor. United Parcel Service and Federal Express compete with the U.S. Postal Service, and private colleges compete with state colleges.

Marketing and the Law

The relationship between government and business during most of the history of the United States has been based on the philosophy of *laissez faire,* or "let businesses compete." Government once allowed rivals to compete without regulation. This approach worked rather well when firms were small and their products simple.

Until 1890 the U.S. government relied mainly on common law to protect competition. However, common law, which is built on previous court decisions, proved inadequate. Previous court decisions dealt with small businesses and local markets. Courts in the late 1800s, however, were dealing with cases involving large businesses and national markets. This was the period during which big business trusts were trying to monopolize industries.

Therefore, in 1890 Congress passed the Sherman Act. Instead of having to rely on common law, the courts now had a statutory (written) law for dealing with antitrust cases. The Sherman Act outlaws "every contract, combination, or conspiracy in restraint of trade" as well as monopolies and attempts to monopolize trade or commerce. The objective was to preserve and protect competition.

In 1990 Procter & Gamble dropped its plan to market Maalox antacid and other products made by Rhone-Poulenc Rorer. The Justice Department had filed an antitrust lawsuit against the firms because it would give P&G, the maker of Pepto-Bismol, too big a share of the over-the-counter stomach remedies market.[59]

The Great Depression of the 1930s forced government to focus again on the need to protect competition. Many small retailers, especially grocery stores, were being forced out of business because they could not compete with big grocery chains. The big chains bought products from manufacturers in large volume and demanded and got quantity discounts much larger than could be justified on the basis of high-volume cost savings. Such discounts enabled the big chains to drastically underprice their smaller independent rivals, thereby running many of them out of business.

The large number of small-business failures aggravated an already huge unemployment problem, and the resulting public outcry led Congress to pass the Robinson-Patman Act in 1936. This act made it illegal for sellers to discriminate against small buyers by granting unjustifiably large discounts to big chains on large-volume purchases. Table 2–2 identifies the major federal antitrust laws.

We indicated earlier in the chapter that the United States experienced a second consumerist era during the 1930s. Note in Table 2–2 that the Wheeler-Lea Act of 1938 was the first federal law to make unfair or deceptive acts or practices in commerce unlawful if they injure *consumers*. This law put the Federal Trade Commission in the business of protecting consumers. Table 2–3 gives several examples of agencies that are involved in consumer protection at the federal level. Every state also provides some protection against consumer fraud through the state attorney general's office. Many states have some form of consumer representation in the governor's office as well.

TABLE 2–2   Major Antitrust Laws

Date	Act	Provisions
1890	Sherman Act	Outlaws every contract, combination, or conspiracy in restraint of trade; monopolies; and attempts to monopolize trade or commerce.
1914	Clayton Act	Sherman Act amendment that spells out actions that are illegal if they substantially lessen competition or tend to create a monopoly.
1914	Federal Trade Commission (FTC) Act	Makes unlawful unfair methods of competition in commerce if they injure a competitor.
1936	Robinson-Patman Act	Clayton Act amendment dealing with price discrimination, brokerage allowances, and promotional allowances.
1938	Wheeler-Lea Act	FTC Act amendment that makes unlawful unfair or deceptive acts or practices in commerce if they injure consumers.
1950	Celler-Kefauver Act	Clayton Act amendment that allows the FTC to prevent asset acquisition mergers if the effect may be to substantially lessen competition or to tend to create a monopoly.
1975	FTC Improvement Act	Strengthens the FTC's ability to protect consumers.

TABLE 2–3   Examples of Federal Consumer Protection Agencies

Agency	Consumer Protection
Department of Agriculture	Sets and enforces inspection and labeling standards for dairy products, eggs, meat, and other food products.
Postal Service	Seeks to prevent the use of the mail for promoting fraudulent selling schemes.
Federal Trade Commission	Promotes and protects free and fair competition, investigates false and deceptive advertising, and enforces truthful labeling laws.
Food and Drug Administration	Enforces laws relating to the purity and truthful labeling of food, drugs, and cosmetics.
Securities and Exchange Commission	Oversees the operation of the securities exchanges and the issuance and sales of corporate securities to help prevent fraud.
National Highway Traffic Safety Administration	Sets motor vehicle safety standards.
Environmental Protection Agency	Sets and enforces standards of quality for air, water, and other environmental elements.
Consumer Product Safety Commission	Helps prevent unsafe consumer products from reaching the market.

State attorneys general used to focus on prosecuting misdeeds by small, local firms. Now they are fighting questionable advertising, mergers, pricing practices, and the like. For example, a group of twenty-two states recently sued Sandoz Pharmaceuticals, charging the company with violating antitrust laws in marketing one of its drugs.[60]

In addition to engaging in lobbying to influence the political-legal environment, marketers use other approaches to accomplish the same objective. One is advertising their positions on public issues. Ads for the U.S. Council for Energy Awareness discuss what the council perceives as a need for the United States to rely more on nuclear energy.

Another approach is cooperating with regulatory agencies in drafting proposed regulations. For example, businesses covered by the 1990 Americans with Disabilities Act must be ready to serve disabled people as they do all other customers. The law guarantees disabled people the chance to partake ''fully and equally,'' like anybody else, in a business's services and goods. For example, retail stores are not required to write all of their price tags in Braille for visually impaired customers. But salesclerks must be available to read prices to such customers. After the law was passed, the Equal Employment Opportunity Commission (EEOC) sought input from businesspeople and others to use in writing fair regulations.[61]

The majority of marketers seek to abide by the law. Ethical marketers adhere not only to the letter of the law but also to its spirit. Some marketers, however, intentionally violate it if they believe the chance of getting caught is slim or the penalty is minor. Such behavior is not only illegal but socially irresponsible and unethical as well.

Unintentional violations of the law are more common. They occur either because the marketer is unaware of the law or because provisions in the law are vague. Sometimes there are conflicting mandates to cope with. Marketers should keep abreast of legislative developments and current court interpretations of existing laws.

Although a particular law may remain unchanged, its interpretation and the degree of its enforcement can change over the years. Compliance can be improved by awareness of and adherence to guidelines published by the agencies that enforce the law.

Firms that may be affected by proposed changes in regulatory agencies' rules must be given an opportunity to express their viewpoint. Notices of possible changes are published in the *Federal Register*. Their purpose is to solicit comment so serious problems that might arise after the rules are implemented can instead be solved in advance.

Regulatory agencies seek to encourage firms to comply voluntarily with regulations. *Voluntary compliance* is a practice by which a firm agrees to do what a regulatory agency advises without the need for a hearing. For example, if a firm is considering a change in its pricing policies, it might ask the FTC to provide an advisory opinion to clarify whether the new policy is lawful. If the opinion is unfavorable, the firm may comply voluntarily and rescind the new policy. In this way the firm avoids costly legal proceedings.

voluntary compliance

Regulatory agencies also issue trade practice rules and trade regulation rules. *Trade practice rules* are purely advisory rules that are developed by regulatory agencies in conjunction with industry representatives to guide firms in avoiding future violations of the law. *Trade regulation rules* are binding rules that are published by regulatory agencies and are used to bring cases against alleged violators.

trade practice rules

trade regulation rules

Federal agencies such as the FTC often settle cases informally. Thus, if a firm agrees to discontinue a practice that the agency believes is in violation of the rules, the firm simply signs a consent order. A *consent order* is an agreement by a firm to "cease and desist" a practice that is presumed to be in violation of regulatory rules. If the firm refuses to stop the practice, the agency issues a formal complaint, and one of its examiners holds a hearing and makes a decision. That decision may then be reviewed by the full agency if necessary. Beyond this stage, the firm may appeal through the courts.

consent order

Regulation, Deregulation, and Reregulation

Federal regulation of business began with the Interstate Commerce Act of 1889 and the Sherman Act of 1890. Since then the pendulum of regulation has swung back and forth.

The first two decades of this century witnessed a big increase in federal regulation in an attempt to control the excesses of huge monopolies, such as Standard Oil and U.S. Steel. Even more laws were passed during the Great Depression to protect the basic rights of workers, retirees, consumers, and investors. Public confidence in business recovered during the Eisenhower years after World War II, and government regulation eased up.

During the 1960s and 1970s many laws were passed in the areas of consumer protection, minority and women's rights, occupational safety and health, and environmental protection. During the Nixon administration (1969–1974) the Occupational Safety and Health Administration, the Environmental Protection Agency, and the Consumer Product Safety Commission were created. These regulatory agencies initially pursued vigorous programs, and their rules generally were strictly enforced.

It was during the late 1960s that initial steps were taken toward deregulation of business by government. The deregulation movement gained strength in the late 1970s, beginning in 1978 when Congress gave the airlines more freedom to add routes and to change fares without government approval. It was after the election of Ronald Reagan to the presidency, in 1980, however, that the movement gained major momentum. Three industries—telecommunications, finance, and transportation—were deregulated. The Regulatory Flexibility Act of 1981 also reduced the regulation of small businesses.

The enforcement of some of the consumer, environmental, and antimerger laws weakened during the early 1980s, in response partly to the 1981–1982 recession and partly to the hands-off philosophy of the Reagan administration. In 1984 the antitrust division of the Department of Justice revised its guidelines for mergers in industries facing foreign competition, in declining industries, and in industries in which mergers would improve efficiency. A flood of mergers followed.

In 1988, the last full year of the Reagan administration, the administration toughened up its antitrust enforcement. President Bush has carried this forward and has demonstrated a more assertive regulatory posture.[62]

Recently there have been calls for reregulation. In some cases it is firms in the deregulated industries that want to slow the process of deregulation. In other cases it is consumers concerned about oil spills, faulty airplanes, insider trading scandals, high rates charged by cable TV systems, the savings and loan bailout, failing banks and insurance companies, skyrocketing medical costs, and other problems who are calling for more regulation.

ENVIRONMENTAL MONITORING

Not only is an organization's very existence derived from its environment, that environment is also the source of the market opportunities and threats. Therefore, it is important for marketers to systematically monitor, or scan, the environment to detect changes that may present a new opportunity (or threat) and to adapt their plans and strategies to the changes. *Environmental monitoring* is the process by which a marketing organization identifies, analyzes, and forecasts the impact of relevant environmental forces on it.

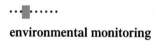

environmental monitoring

The Monitoring Process

A marketer that scans business periodicals regularly will be exposed to some general environmental developments relevant to the organization. At the other extreme, some organizations—General Electric, for example—have specialized environmental scanning groups. These groups regularly monitor a variety of environmental forces and report to other planners in the company.

Once an event, or trend, has been forecasted, its significance must be interpreted. Eastman Kodak Company probably underestimated the potential impact of developments in instant photography made by Polaroid Corporation. Kodak initially assumed that the market for instant photography was small and that instant photography did not compete with regular photography. It was wrong. More recently Polaroid probably underestimated the impact that low-cost 35 mm cameras would have on instant photography.

U.S. officials say several foreign governments have been using their spy networks to obtain business secrets from U.S. firms and give them to firms in their countries. According to a Federal Bureau of Investigation official, "A number of nations friendly to the U.S. have engaged in industrial espionage, collecting information with their intelligence services to support private industry." Their governments have a tradition of working more closely with businesses than we have in the United States. The global competitiveness of U.S. firms is a major concern in this country. Many people fear that U.S. firms are operating at a disadvantage when it comes to intelligence gathering and sharing.[63]

What to Monitor?

It would be too costly to monitor every facet of an environment. But, selecting environmental forces to monitor is risky, because other developments—in forces that lie outside the defined scope of the organization's monitoring effort—can affect the organization. For example, some typewriter manufacturers that did not monitor technological developments in computer software were ill-prepared to forecast the impact of word processing would have on their business.

An organization's size, resources, and geographic scope influence its approach to monitoring. A small, independent bank whose customers are mostly local farmers will think of the economic environment in terms of its customers' good or bad harvests. Such a perspective is vastly different from that of Chase Manhattan Bank, whose concept of the economic environment is global.

For many firms, however, monitoring the economic environment includes keeping tabs on the federal government's fiscal policy (taxation and spending) and on the Federal Reserve System's monetary policy (manipulation of the money supply and credit). Increased government spending on defense, for example, is a favorable development for firms in the defense industries; and a tight money policy, pushing interest rates up, is an unfavorable development for firms in the construction and housing industries. Government and private sources such as banks provide an abundance of information about economic trends and forecasts.

Monitoring the marketing activities of *competitors* is essential to revealing new-product offerings, product deletions, price reductions, new distribution outlets, and new promotional campaigns. Touring competitors' plants, disassembling competitors' products, and questioning competitors' customers, suppliers, and even former employees are among information-gathering activities. Other sources of information about competitors' activities include trade and business publications, newspapers, corporate annual reports, business conferences, and trade shows.

The *technological environment* can be monitored by scanning scientific journals, observing new products at trade shows, and attending technological conferences. A growing number of firms in high-technology industries are engaging in technology forecasting. This involves gathering and interpreting evidence of scientific advances in a field and forecasting the direction of technological change and its impact on the firm.

It is also desirable to monitor the *sociocultural environment*. Two important sources to monitor are ad agency reports that track sociocultural and consumer trends and books written by experts on consumers' changing lifestyles and values. Toward the end of the 1980s these sources were advising that the conspicuous consumption and ''shop till you drop'' lifestyles that dominated the 1980s would soon be fading away and saving, caution, and moderation would be coming into vogue.[64]

Careful monitoring of *political campaigns* sheds light on major political issues and the various candidates' approaches to coping with them. Other developments should be evaluated in terms of their implications for the political environment. For example, the 1990 Census showed that more than half of all Americans live in suburbs, up from 23 percent in 1950 and 43.8 percent in 1980. Because of reapportionment, cities will lose power in Congress and in state legislatures.[65] Traditionally this would favor Republicans, because suburbanites tend to vote more for Republican candidates. But as the suburbs become more culturally diverse, the traditional voting pattern may become obsolete.

Firms that engage in international marketing should monitor the political-legal environment in the countries in which they are engaged in business or plan to engage in business operations. Monitoring is especially important but more complex in countries whose political systems lack stability.

The attempted coup in the Soviet Union in August, 1991 underscores the difficulty of forecasting developments in the political environment. President Gorbachev had selected

August 20 for the signing of a new union treaty with the Russian and Kazakh republics. But on August 18, while Gorbachev was at his Crimean vacation retreat, coup plotters demanded that he sign a decree proclaiming a state of emergency and transfer his powers to Vice President Yanayev. Gorbachev refused. Meanwhile, Boris Yeltsin, president of the Russian republic, emerged as the leader against the coup. After several days of citizen uprising, Gorbachev returned to Moscow on August 22. The failed coup seems to have helped speed the processes of democratization and decentralization. The Soviet Union began crumbling as, one after another most of the republics declared their independence. For international marketers, those several days changed the nature of market opportunity in that vast region of the world.

SUMMARY OF LEARNING OBJECTIVES

1. Identify the major variables in the marketing environment.
The major variables are economic, competitive, technological, sociocultural and ethical, and political-legal variables.

2. Identify the major issues that confront marketers in the economic environment.
The major issues are the business cycle; consumer spending behavior; the postindustrial service economy; inflation, disinflation, and deflation; debt; shortages; and unemployment.

3. Explain the nature of competition.
Competition is rivalry among marketers that seek to satisfy markets. The broadest view of competition is that it is generic—all marketers compete for general customer buying power. A narrower perspective is that competition is rivalry among marketers who market substitutable offerings. A still narrower perspective is that competition is rivalry among marketers who market directly similar offerings. The four basic types of market structure are pure competition, monopolistic competition, oligopoly, and monopoly.

4. Explain how technology affects marketing.
Technology is the knowledge to do new or old tasks in a better way. Technological progress can affect the nature of competition, costs and productivity, and the elements in the marketing mix.

5. Identify the major elements of the sociocultural and ethical environment.
The marketer's relationship to society and to its culture makes up the sociocultural environment. The major elements are cultural diversity, cultural values, marketing ethics, social responsibility, and green marketing.

6. Identify the major elements of the political-legal environment.
The major elements are government regulatory agencies, courts, political candidates, elected officials, public interest groups, self-regulatory groups, legislative bodies, laws, and public officials.

7. Explain the meaning and nature of environmental monitoring.
Environmental monitoring is the process by which a marketing organization identifies, analyzes, and forecasts the impact of relevant environmental forces on it. Because it would be too costly to monitor every facet of an environment, monitoring typically focuses on tracking developments in the forces that are identified as being important to the organization.

Review Questions

1. What is the significance of the business cycle to marketers?
2. What is a postindustrial economy?
3. What are the basic types of market structures? Explain each.
4. What is nonprice competition?
5. How does basic research differ from applied research?
6. What is meant by *cultural diversity*?
7. What is the significance of cultural values to marketers?
8. What is the significance to marketers that the marketing environment is becoming increasingly global in scope?
9. Why is the field of customer relations growing?
10. What is green marketing?
11. What elements in the political-legal environment affect marketers?
12. Why do marketers engage in environmental monitoring?

Discussion Questions

1. What can the U.S. government do to help U.S. firms compete more effectively in international markets?

2. How does cultural diversity in the United States affect the development of marketing strategies?

3. Is green marketing a fad? Explain.

4. In the spring of 1991 Louis Sullivan, Secretary of Health and Human Services, asked fans to stop attending sporting events sponsored by tobacco companies. He said he was appealing to individuals because his plea to the tobacco industry to stop sponsoring sporting events "fell on indifferent ears." How should tobacco companies respond?

Application Exercise

Reread the material about the 1981–1982 recession at the beginning of this chapter and answer the following questions:

1. Do you agree with the marketing consultant's statement, "the past is the best indicator of the future"? Explain.

2. In addition to swings in the business cycle, what types of events can cause changes in consumer buying habits?

3. Do recessions affect all marketers equally? Explain.

Key Concepts

The following key terms were introduced in this chapter:

business cycle	oligopoly	regionalization
inflation	monopoly	voluntary compliance
disinflation	differential advantage	trade practice rules
deflation	nonprice competition	trade regulation rules
competition	market niche	consent order
pure competition	technology	environmental monitoring
monopolistic competition		

CASES

Environmental Clean-Up Makes (Dollars and) Sense

She went from cleaning up hazardous waste sites to advising corporate clients in six years. Meet Gail Brice, a successful entrepreneur and owner of Brice Enviro Ventures, a Newport Beach, California, firm that helps small environmental companies find capital.

She's only one of many entrepreneurs who have entered a hot industry: environmental services. Says one venture capitalist, "A good environmental idea makes money because it just makes good sense." This industry attributes its growth to a combination of increasing environmental regulation, rising consumer expectations, and a widening recognition by businesses that pro-environment action is as much good business as it is humanitarian.

By looking at the history of environmental regulation imposed on U.S. business in the 1970s and 1980s, it's easy to see why firms specializing in hazardous waste handling, air- and water-pollution control, recycling, and environmental consulting are in high demand and will continue to be through the 1990s. Revenues for the industry could double, from $120 billion in 1989 to $240 billion in 2000.

The growing environmental services industry has set the stage for some classic examples of entrepreneurs identifying market niches. Sandra Clark, for example, owns a $10 million hazardous waste hauling company that used to be a home-based scrap hauling service. She recommends sticking with "narrow market niches, specific service regions, or with certain types of clients."

Brice is another example. When she opened her company, she narrowed her focus to targeting investors and larger companies interested in financing or acquiring environmental firms. This knowledge of the competitive environment was a factor in her start-up's success. In exchange for matching the targeted investors with small environmental firms, she is paid a finder's fee and equity in her client firms.

Combined with her targeting wisdom was her perception of an emerging socioeconomic trend. Brice understood that many marketers were beginning to see and act on the value of social responsibility. They realized that consumers were voting in favor of the environment with their wallets at the grocery store checkout; they'd have to clean up their act. She saw this trend developing and grabbed hold.

Furthermore, in founding a service company, her timing couldn't have been better in the present postindustrial service economy. Service companies are the sources of growth for the 1990s and beyond. And, according to one expert, the environmental services industry is recession-resistant. Since regulation makes demand go up, much business spending is not discretionary. In fact, a 1990 study done by Stanford University and Deloitte & Touche, an accounting firm, found that a large industrial company might spend as much as $450 million a year on routine compliance costs. Environmental factors are certainly the most significant factors shaping the economy today.

Questions

1. Why are investors interested in financing environmental firms?

2. How would you describe the market structure in which environmental service firms compete?

3. What issues or trends did Brice possibly perceive in the sociocultural environment?

4. Is the environmental services industry recession-resistant? Explain.

Ionics, Inc.—The Wave of the Future

When in early 1991 the Iraqi army opened Kuwaiti oil reservoirs and sent oil gushing into the Persian Gulf, the world was shocked. But people weren't concerned about the waste of valuable oil—they were concerned about the wanton destruction of invaluable water.

Experts predict that in the 1990s clean water will replace oil as the natural resource of chief concern to the nations of the world. Population growth, increasing industrialization, and many other factors threaten the earth's limited fresh water supply. Each of these factors requires the use of massive amounts of clean water—and each can produce polluted water.

Worldwide water problems open opportunities to companies able to understand the variables operating in this complex international marketplace. Ionics, Inc., of Watertown, Massachusetts, seems to be such a company.

Ionics markets products applicable to all phases of the water problem. For example, the first step in cleaning up water is to discover what is polluting it. Ionics is a leading manufacturer of analytic instruments and chemicals to test for water pollution and of equipment to purify it.

Ionics is also involved in the highly competitive consumer water business. A survey by the International Bottled Water Association showed that by late 1990 over six hundred brands of bottled water were available in the United States alone. Even Ionics's small share of this market provides about 20 percent of its total revenue.

But the bulk of the business of Ionics, Inc., is not in testing water or in providing pure water but in removing unwanted chemicals and other contaminants from unusable water. About 60 percent of total revenue comes from building and selling desalination plants to countries, cities, and private industry. Ionics has built more than two thousand such plants all over the world, including several in the Middle East. And demand is growing rapidly as pure water becomes scarcer. Even in the United States, particularly in drought-stricken California, cities are seriously considering desalination to provide domestic water.

According to Arthur L. Goldstein, president and chief executive of Ionics, Inc., "You build a desalination plant when three things come together: Bad water, money, and some kind of change," such as a sudden population shift or higher government standards for domestic water purity.

Bad water, money, and change also affect the recycling of industrial water supplies. One of the most important changes expected in this market is more stringent government regulation of wastewater discharges. Under stricter standards, water-dependent industries may find it cost-effective to recycle their own water, creating an increased demand for the kinds of chemicals, equipment, and technical expertise that Ionics has already proven it has.

Ionics appears to have read the external variables well and stands poised to take advantage of the coming together of bad water, money, and the changing environment in the 1990s.

Questions

1. How important to Ionics is the international environment?

2. What type of market structure do you think governs Ionics's building and sale of desalination plants? Its bottled water sales?

3. If water does become "the oil of the 1990s," what are some potential ethical dilemmas that Ionics could face?

4. Which elements of the marketing environment should Ionics monitor? Why?

3

MARKETING MANAGEMENT AND THE PLANNING PROCESS

After reading this chapter you will be able to

1. explain the steps in strategic planning.

2. identify the types of organizational growth and consolidation strategies.

3. understand the uses and types of portfolio analysis.

4. describe the steps in marketing planning.

5. explain the basic elements of a marketing strategy.

6. understand the marketing mix concept and its components.

At the 1990 annual meeting of Quaker Oats Company, William Smithburg, the chairman and president, announced that the company would increase marketing spending by 10 to 15 percent in the coming year, while focusing on core products such as cereals and Gatorade. After the meeting Smithburg said: "We see this year as a turnaround year, a refocusing year in which we expect to balance growth and returns. Our interest in growth is clear through our investment in new products."

Quaker Oats Company had developed a broad line of consumer goods sold in the United States and abroad over a period of many years. By 1990 its North American business included

- *Hot cereals*. The company held a 61 percent share of a $775 million market with its Quaker line.
- *Ready-to-eat cereals*. The company held a 7.6 percent share of a $7.5 billion market with its Quaker, Life, and Cap'n Crunch lines.
- *Aunt Jemima products*. These products include breakfast syrups, pancake mixes, and frozen breakfast products. With a 23 percent share, Aunt Jemima is the leader in the $580 million syrup market.

- *Wholesome snacks*. This category includes granola bars and rice and grain cakes. Quaker is the leader in both categories, which together are a $545 million market.
- *Celeste pizza and corn products*. Celeste's share of frozen pizza is a modest 6 percent, but the line is strong in selected regions, and Quaker is the leader in the cornmeal and grits categories.
- *Pet foods*. This industry has three segments: dry, semimoist, and moist. Overall it is a $6.1 billion industry, and Quaker's brands dominate the small semimoist category (with Ken-L-Ration and Gainesburgers) and the very large premium category (with Kibbles n'Bits).
- *Golden Grain*. This business includes the Rice-A-Roni and Noodle Roni lines, Ghirardelli chocolates, and some regional pasta business.
- *Grocery specialties*. Gatorade, Van Camp canned beans, and Wolf Brand chili are included here. The Gatorade and Van Camp lines are both category leaders, and Wolf Brand has a 13 percent national share even though it competes in only four states.

Nearly 80 percent of Quaker's brands were first or second in their categories. The company's annual report assessed the best opportunities among these brands: "Brands that meet the needs of good nutrition and convenience have the potential for future growth and are usually value-added in nature. Therefore, they have higher profit contribution potential.'' The company viewed its cereal and Gatorade products as clearly meeting those criteria; it saw many other products as having some valuable characteristics. However, during 1989 and 1990, Quaker received far more attention in two other product categories: pet food and toys.

Quaker had acquired the Gaines line of pet foods in 1986 to expand its semimoist dog food business. Although demand was not growing, the purchase gave Quaker a 75 percent share of the semimoist market and 15 percent of the total dog food market. Subsequently, however, competitors Mars (owner of the Kal Kan brand) and Ralston-Purina initiated a strong new product effort backed by extensive advertising and price cutting. Quaker was put on the defensive, responded slowly, and suffered a 14.5 per-cent loss in sales between 1988 and 1989, with profitability declining sharply.

More dramatic was the demise of Quaker's Fisher-Price toy business. Long dominant in the preschool toy market, the division sought new avenues of sales growth by expanding into electronic toys just as competitors were targeting the preschool market. (Mattel, for instance, had licensed the Walt Disney name for a line of sixty-five preschool toys.) The shift to electronics taxed Fisher-Price's technical and production capabilities. Additionally, the company learned that its quality image for preschool toys mattered little to school-aged children. Sales dropped 17 percent in 1989, and the division suffered a $100 million negative change in profits between 1988 and 1989. In 1990 Quaker decided to sell the Fisher-Price division.[1]

Certainly the Quaker Oats Company of the 1990s has grown far from its roots. Although it remains primarily a food company, Quaker's wide mix of products makes it far more than an ''oats'' company. Quaker is like many other organizations in that, over time, management modifies the firm's product lines and changes the relative level of resources committed to each line. Such actions usually are influenced by changes in the environment. New technology, changing attitudes toward health and nutrition, and shifting competition can change the growth rate and profit opportunities in various markets.

Because the environment can change dramatically, organizations must be prepared to review and occasionally to redefine the scope of the markets they serve and to revise the priorities they attach to different businesses or products. Top management is usually responsible for these types of marketing decisions, which are made through the process of strategic planning.

WHAT IS MARKETING MANAGEMENT?

marketing management

Marketing management is the process of planning, implementing, and controlling marketing activities and decisions in order to facilitate exchanges. The steps in this process are

After reading this chapter you will be able to

1. explain the need for information management.

2. describe what a marketing information system is and what it does.

3. describe the relationship between a marketing information system and marketing research.

4. give examples of marketing research activities.

5. identify and describe the steps in the marketing research process.

D o you buy Cheerios? Don't be surprised if a competing cereal maker starts writing you personal letters touting its new, better-than-oats, "all-natural" cereal.

Maybe you regularly buy the same brand of dog food for the family pooch. Before long you may get a letter from the ASPCA (American Society for the Prevention of Cruelty to Animals) asking for a donation to support its animal shelter in New York City.

Welcome to the brave new world of supermarket scanners, where the laser devices that tally what's in your grocery cart will soon do a lot more than help control the store's inventory and generate detailed receipts for you. By drawing on computerized data from the scanners and the credit cards you use at the check-out counter, marketers, manufacturers, and even nonprofit groups that want to get a message to you will soon be able to know your family's buying habits and brand preferences.

Citicorp has put special ID cards into 2.3 million households in such cities as Chicago, Dallas, Denver, and Los Angeles. Consumers agree to use them at certain supermarkets—for example, Jewel, Vons, and Pathmark—where Citicorp's computers take their purchase information from the store scanners.

Citicorp then sells this information to marketers, who will be able to tailor messages to specific individuals and be fairly sure their messages reach them. Databases linked to cable TV and magazine subscriber lists will be able to tell advertisers whether you're responding to their pitches.

Citicorp, which expects to lure supermarket customers into its financial services network through its ID cards, projects that by 1995 it will be gathering and selling data on the purchases of 40 million American households. That will mean processing information on 30 billion transactions a year at 14,000 nationwide retail outlets, through computers with memories holding trillions of bits of data. The information, sifted and sorted to whatever specifications the client wants, will be distributed daily to scores of manufacturers and retailers, including Pillsbury, Ralston Purina, and PepsiCo.

In 1990 Citicorp bought a small interest in Information Resources, Inc. (IRI), a pioneer in gathering and massaging scanner data. IRI already collects data from scanners in 2,700 stores around the country.

Other firms, too, are gearing up for the coming of the scanner age. Several years ago Dun & Bradstreet, an information services company, acquired the marketing research house of A. C. Nielsen Company. Although Nielsen is better known for its television ratings, its biggest business has always been reporting buying trends through an index that measures sales in a national sample of stores. Nielsen now has scanner links to nearly 5,000 stores and a pilot program in 16,000 homes, where consumers use scanner wands to record purchases when they get back from the store. At the end of every week someone in the house places the wand against a telephone mouthpiece, dials an 800 number, and communicates about fifteen seconds' worth of squeaks back to the Nielsen computer. Nielsen then analyzes and sells the data to such companies as General Foods, Coca-Cola, Miles, and Clairol.[1]

Citicorp and Dun & Bradstreet are just two of the many firms involved in collecting and selling data. Marketing research organizations such as these are in the business of providing their clients with information to be used in decision making. Of course, many of the clients, such as General Foods and Coca-Cola, also do a great deal of marketing research internally. In other words, they have their own marketing research departments that engage in the marketing research process.

We begin this chapter with an explanation of the differences between data and information and the importance of information management to organizations today. Next we show what a marketing information system is and discuss the benefits it can bring to organizations. Then we move on to an in-depth look at marketing research.

INFORMATION MANAGEMENT

Consider the problems three marketing managers face in deciding whether to go ahead with development of a new product. The desk of the first manager is cluttered with pages of opinions, forecasts, and recommendations from the sales force, finance and production personnel, and potential customers, as well as detailed statistics on market test results. The desk of the second manager contains only a pen and several pieces of paper. The desk of the third manager holds several reports summarizing the same type of data the first manager has in raw form. The first manager has too much data (data overload), the second has too little, and the third has relevant information. The third manager is benefiting from a systematic approach to data gathering, which pulls together the information needed for decision making.

Data and information are not the same. *Information* is data that have been converted to a useful form for decision making—for solving a problem. It is relevant, timely, accurate, and cost-effective; and it reduces risk in decision making.

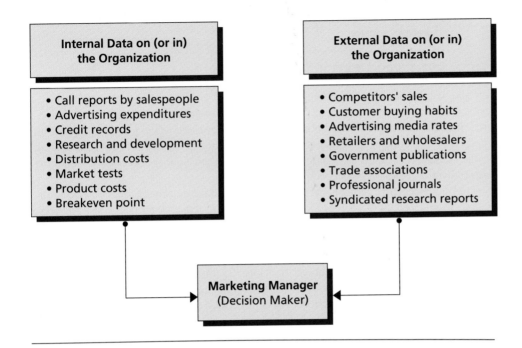

Internal Data on (or in) the Organization	External Data on (or in) the Organization
• Call reports by salespeople • Advertising expenditures • Credit records • Research and development • Distribution costs • Market tests • Product costs • Breakeven point	• Competitors' sales • Customer buying habits • Advertising media rates • Retailers and wholesalers • Government publications • Trade associations • Professional journals • Syndicated research reports

Marketing Manager
(Decision Maker)

FIGURE 4–1

Examples of Data That Affect
Marketing Managers

Marketing managers face an immense volume of raw *data*. In Figure 4–1, the data flowing from the left to the marketing manager are generated internally. The data flowing from the right are generated externally. If these data are to be useful, the data flow must be managed.

Marketing managers must consider the cost of collecting and converting data into information when specifying their informational needs. Seldom will they have all the information they want. Thus the cost of additional information must be weighed against its value for planning, implementing, and controlling marketing operations.

Some managers want "all the information" before making decisions. At the other extreme are managers who want to make decisions without taking time to get any information. They rely primarily on their accumulated personal experience. In the middle are managers who weigh the value of additional information against its cost to increase the probability of making better decisions.

Note in Figure 4–1 that syndicated research reports are generated externally. Donnelley Marketing is an example of a commercial supplier; it sells demographic data sorted by zip code. An information supplier might also be hired to collect information for a marketer's specific purposes. Many marketing research firms conduct specific research investigations for clients.

As suggested earlier, the investment in marketing intelligence activities should never exceed the value of the information to the marketer. If an information specialist can provide information more efficiently than the user, the specialist should be consulted. Outsiders often bring fresh insight into problems and may approach the task more objectively than company marketing or information managers.

The firm's sales force should also be trained in intelligence gathering. Its close contact with the market can make it a useful data source for manufacturers, retailers, and wholesalers. Too often, however, salespeople are trained only in selling techniques. The Global Marketing box discusses the nature of intelligence gathering by Japanese firms.

THE MARKETING INFORMATION SYSTEM

**marketing information
system (MIS)**

In recent years many firms have begun to view their overall marketing information management from a systems perspective. A ***marketing information system (MIS)*** is ''a structured, interacting complex of persons, machines, and procedures designed to generate an orderly flow of pertinent information collected from intra- and extra-firm sources, for use as the bases for decision making in specific responsibility areas of marketing management.''[2]

An MIS gives marketing managers a steady flow of accurate, timely, and relevant information, from a variety of sources, which can be used to make better decisions. An MIS, however, cannot reduce decision making to an exact science. The experience, intuition, and judgment of marketing managers also play a part. But it is the relevant, timely, and accurate information that is the key to good decision making. This includes monitoring the key environmental variables discussed in chapter 2. Information managers (information suppliers) must understand the decisions marketing managers (information users) face and the information they need to make better decisions. Good communication between the two types of managers reduces risk in decision making and helps the marketing manager develop and implement good plans.

GLOBAL

MARKETING

Michael Pincus, chairman of Thunderstone Software and chief scientist at Mnemotrix Systems, spends a lot of time convincing U.S. firms they must mount corporate intelligence networks to keep an eye on their rivals around the world. Several years ago Pincus visited the Tokyo headquarters of Marubeni Corporation, Japan's fourth-largest trading company. In an unassuming room, row upon row of clerical workers were filing away slips of paper, photographs, charts, and reports sent from far-flung employees on competing businesses and businesspeople. Until a few years ago most U.S. firms thought they had better things to do with their employees' time. Now many are picking up on the Japanese practice.

Japan's corporate intelligence networks date to the days immediately following World War II. Many Japanese military intelligence officers who helped rebuild the country's economy later went to work for Japan's enormous trading companies. Today these companies form the basis of the country's market intelligence system.

Almost unnoticed, Japan's market research goals have changed over the past few years. In the 1960s and 1970s, with Japanese firms relying largely on copycat technology, Japan's appetite for U.S. patents and other technology was enormous. Japanese intelligence gatherers flocked with their cameras to U.S. factories and to U.S. patent offices to see the plans for cars, stereos, and computer

MIS Design and Organization

The objectives that information suppliers and information users set for a firm's MIS influence its design and how its functions will be performed. Although there is no one best model, the following functions are always performed by an MIS:

1. Gathering data.
2. Processing data.
3. Analyzing data.
4. Storing and retrieving data.
5. Evaluating information.
6. Disseminating information to marketing managers.

These functions are identified by the same numbers in Figure 4–2, which gives an overview of how an MIS works. Once the marketing manager, perhaps with the information supplier's assistance, has defined a problem, the information supplier can check the availability of information in the information bank. If additional information is needed, it must be decided if it is worth the cost. If it is not worth the cost, the marketing decision is made without acquiring additional information. If it is decided to acquire additional information, however, external and internal data are gathered, stored in the data bank, and retrieved

chips. But now, with Japan in the forefront of high technology in many areas, much Japanese intelligence work has come to look more like marketing research.

Japanese firms collect data on virtually everything. If a Japanese executive has lunch with an American, he will probably take note of the American's hobbies and family. Does the U.S. executive have a golf trophy in his office? Does he mention his children? What kind of food does he like? The answers to such questions are often sent to the home office to be kept on file. To an American such information may seem either trivial or too personal. But for a Japanese executive it is all part of understanding the competitor. Acquiring information is only half the battle. It doesn't really become intelligence until you acquire it in a focused fashion and know how to use it. One way to use such information is to concentrate your intelligence efforts on a specific rival.

Fast emerging as a battleground for Japanese information gathering are the research labs at American universities, where tomorrow's commercial technology is being explored. At Stanford alone, Japanese corporations have endowed six permanent chairs and one visiting professorship, all in either engineering or business.

Source: Adapted from Patrice Duggan and Gale Eisenstodt, ''The New Face of Japanese Espionage,'' by permission of *Forbes* magazine from the November 12, 1990, issue, p. 96.

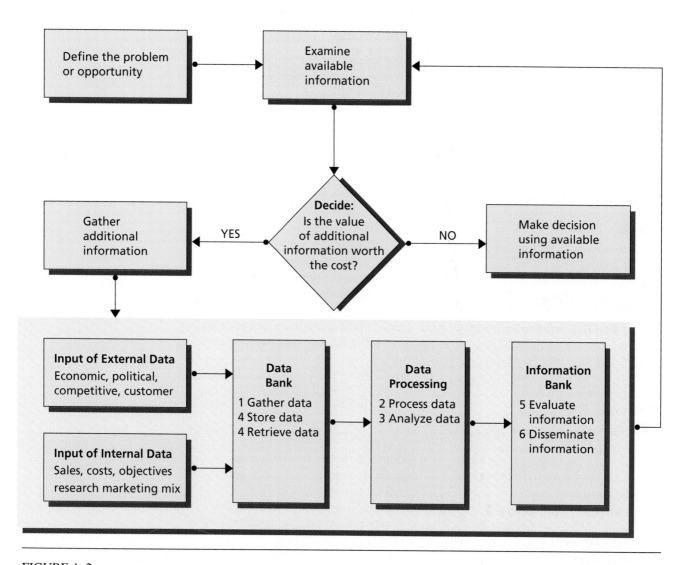

FIGURE 4–2
. . . .

A Marketing Information
System

from the data bank. These data are then processed, analyzed, and placed in the information bank for evaluation and dissemination to the marketing manager.

As Figure 4–2 shows, the input is raw data (that is, raw external and internal data are put into the MIS). The output is relevant information from the information bank. This information is what the marketing manager needs to make a decision. Thus an MIS is an organization's master plan for developing and maintaining a continuous flow of relevant marketing information to decision makers. It is a valuable tool for planning, implementing, and controlling the marketing effort.

An MIS is made up of two basic types of data subsystems. One deals with routinely collected internal and external data. Examples of routinely collected *internal data* are data on sales, inventories, product costs, accounts payable, and accounts receivable that are supplied by the accounting department. Examples of routinely collected *external data* are population projections, surveys of buying power, and trade association statistics.

The other data subsystem deals with data that are collected for a special purpose. The subsystem of the MIS that deals with the collection of special-purpose data is called marketing research. The information bank depicted in Figure 4–2 contains both routine and special-purpose data that have been converted into information available for decision-making purposes.

In recent years many organizations have decentralized the MIS. Because of advances in personal computers, software, and communications, information users increasingly have direct access to information stored in the MIS. They can therefore bypass the information suppliers and interact directly with the MIS through their desktop or laptop computers.

Thus the emphasis in marketing information management is shifting to the concept of a *marketing decision support system (MDSS)*. Because information is of little value to managers who do not use it in decision making, the emphasis is on making the MDSS user friendly. Today's marketing managers are using the MDSS to identify market opportunities; to build models that enable them to better understand causal relationships, such as that between advertising expenditures and sales; and to engage in what-if planning.

In the discussions that follow, we take a closer look at marketing research.

MARKETING RESEARCH

Although informal marketing research has been practiced ever since firms began to market their products, formal marketing research has developed only during the past six or seven decades. The key distinction is that the formal approach is *systematic*. It follows an orderly sequence in which each step is subordinated to a larger systematic whole to provide reliable information for decision making. The American Marketing Association defines *marketing research* as follows:

> Marketing research is the function which links the consumer, customer, and public to the marketer through information—information used to identify and define marketing opportunities and problems; generate, refine, and evaluate marketing actions; monitor marketing performance; and improve understanding of marketing as a process.
>
> Marketing research specifies the information required to address these issues; designs the method for collecting information; manages and implements the data collection process; analyzes the results; and communicates the findings and their implications.[3]

We will simplify the definition as follows: *Marketing research* is the process of identifying and defining a marketing problem or opportunity, specifying and collecting the data required to address these issues, analyzing the results, and communicating information to decision makers.

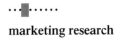

marketing research

Marketing research helps an organization identify and solve problems. It can also help an organization identify and evaluate a market opportunity and develop the effort needed to exploit it.

Of course, what constitutes a problem from one point of view can represent an opportunity from another. For example, Pitney Bowes is best known for its mail-metering machines. When the firm's profit growth started to slow down several years ago, it tripled its marketing research budget to help find a way to push past the postage machine business. A major conclusion of the research is that the paperless society is a pipe dream; paper will continue to clog offices and mailboxes. Thus Pitney Bowes focused on automating the handling of paper and introduced a string of new products to change the way firms mail and ship products.[4]

Waterford Wedgwood PLC, the Ireland-based maker of fine crystal and china, has for many years promoted its products as the ultimate in Irish handmade luxury. It recently con-

TABLE 4–1 Examples of Marketing Research Activities

· ·

Forecasting sales	Designing products and packages
Measuring market share	Locating warehouses and stores
Identifying market trends	Processing orders
Measuring the organization's image	Managing inventory
Measuring brand images	Analyzing audience characteristics
Developing target customer profiles	Scheduling advertisements

· ·

sidered shifting production out of Ireland and using machines to make some lines. But before doing so, Waterford undertook marketing research. It tested reaction in the United States (its major market) by marketing four machine-made gift items produced to Waterford specifications by a German company. Waterford's consumer research in the United States had indicated that customers cared more about the Waterford label than about where the crystal is made. Nevertheless, Waterford executives decided to await the results of the market test prior to making a final decision.[5] Table 4–1 provides additional examples of marketing research activities.

In most organizations, MIS activities and research activities are concentrated in a marketing research department. Although an organization's size and need for research influence the manner in which the department is organized, the head of the research department typically reports to the marketing manager, who coordinates marketing research with technical research and development. Good communication and coordination are essential if research objectives are to be stated clearly, if the project is to be carried out efficiently, and if the findings are to be used effectively in decision making.

If help from outside specialists is needed, their efforts must be coordinated with those of internal personnel throughout the research process. Even organizations that have their own internal marketing research departments often use outside marketing research firms for some projects. For example, J. D. Power & Associates is an automotive marketing research firm that conducts customer satisfaction surveys. Most car manufacturers also buy some of the two hundred reports the company puts out each year. Most of the studies are based on questionnaires that are mailed to car owners.[6]

· ·

THE MARKETING RESEARCH PROCESS

A firm's marketing manager must communicate informational needs to the firm's director of marketing research, who conducts the research project. The marketing manager does not have to be an expert on research techniques but must be able to state informational needs and assess the research findings. The researcher, on the other hand, has to be an expert on research techniques and must be able to understand and satisfy the marketing manager's informational needs.

Figure 4–3 presents a logical five-step approach to the marketing research process. It also includes a rough approximation of the extent of participation by the marketing manager and the researcher in each step of the process. The manager's main role is to state, and eventually solve, problems for which research is needed. The researcher's main role is to design and implement a research project that will help the manager solve the problems.

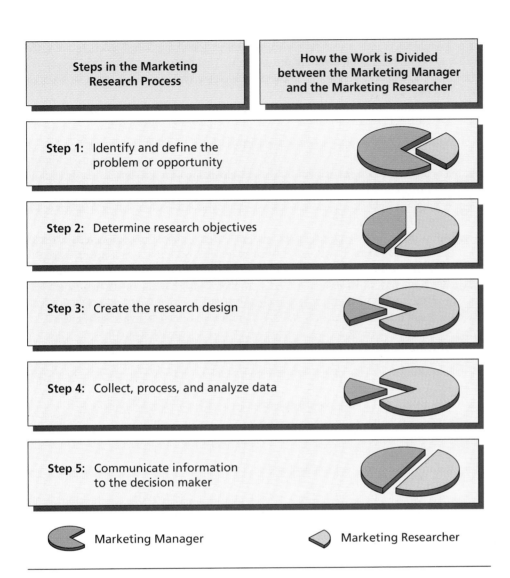

Steps in the Marketing Research Process	How the Work is Divided between the Marketing Manager and the Marketing Researcher
Step 1: Identify and define the problem or opportunity	
Step 2: Determine research objectives	
Step 3: Create the research design	
Step 4: Collect, process, and analyze data	
Step 5: Communicate information to the decision maker	

Marketing Manager   Marketing Researcher

FIGURE 4–3
....

The Relative Participation of the Marketing Manager and the Marketing Researcher in the Marketing Research Process

If the findings are to be accurate and objective, marketing researchers must apply the scientific method: They should be orderly and rational in their approach, be objective and avoid interjecting personal bias into their work, be thorough and precise, and interpret their findings honestly.

Identifying and Defining the Problem or Opportunity

No research project should begin until the marketing manager has clearly communicated the nature of the problem or opportunity to the researcher.

Identifying and defining the problem is the first step in the process of finding a solution. Failure to meet sales objectives, an excessive increase in uncollectible accounts, and abnormal turnover of salespeople are signals, or symptoms, of deeper problems. Marketers and researchers want to identify and define the problems behind these symptoms. A poor diagnosis will lead to an ineffective solution.

For example, a marketer who states the problem as "declining sales" is only tipping the researcher off to the general nature of the problem. This is a symptom, and the researcher must probe more deeply first to identify and then to clearly define the problem as one that is researchable.

After the decision maker states what he or she believes is the problem, the researcher begins a preliminary exploration of the problem situation. Confirming or rejecting the problem *as stated by the decision maker* is a crucial phase of the research project.

Talking to knowledgeable persons in the firm helps the researcher develop familiarity with the problem. It also sheds light on the reasons behind the manager's interpretation. This is very important when the researcher is an outside consultant.

For example, a sales manager who notices that sales are declining might interpret the problem as ineffective advertising. The researcher therefore is asked to investigate the effectiveness of the firm's advertising. In talking with salespeople, wholesalers, and retailers of the firm's products, however, the researcher discovers that their support began to decline when a rival firm introduced a new product that gave them a bigger margin on sales. They make more profit by selling the rival's product. This gives the researcher a new perspective on the problem. It also makes it clear that an investigation of advertising effectiveness will not help solve the problem. A different type of research project is needed.

Determining Research Objectives

Once the researcher and the manager have a better feel for the problem, they can determine the objectives of the research project. In general, a research investigation will have one of four basic objectives—to explore, to describe, to test hypotheses, or to predict.

Researchers conduct *exploratory research* (such as the preliminary exploration just described) when they need more information about the problem, when tentative hypotheses need to be formulated more specifically, or when new hypotheses are needed. One purpose of the preliminary exploration is to gather data that suggest meaningful research questions.

Researchers conduct *descriptive research* when they need to describe such things as a market or a part (segment) of a market by developing summary statistics of it. Soft-drink marketers use this type of research to describe the characteristics and wants of different groups of consumers.

If the objective is to test hypotheses about the relationship between an independent and a dependent variable, the researcher engages in *causal research*. For example, descriptive research may suggest that a price reduction is associated with increased sales of a product, but it does not say definitely that the price cut was the actual *cause* of the sales increase. Sales may have increased because of other factors, such as an increase in customer buying power or a decline in competitors' marketing efforts. Causal research, on the other hand, tries to show either that the price cut (independent variable) is the cause of increased sales (dependent variable) or that the price cut is *not* the cause of increased sales. This requires the researcher to keep all factors other than price and sales constant—at best, a difficult task.

If the objective is to forecast future values, such as the number of votes or sales revenues, *predictive research* is used. Political pollsters use predictive research to forecast how many people will vote for a particular candidate in an upcoming election. Businesses engage in sales forecasting to predict sales of their products during a specific time period.

Creating the Research Design

The creation of the research design is probably the single most important step in the research process. The **research design** is the grand plan for conducting a marketing research investigation; it specifies the data that are needed and the procedures for collect-

---

**Step 3
Create the
Research
Design**

↓

Determine data
needs

↓

Determine data
sources

↓

Determine primary
data collection
method

↓

Determine how to
contact survey
participants

↓

Design data
collection
instrument

↓

Design sampling
plan

FIGURE 4–4
· ·

Steps in Creating the Research
Design

· · ▪ · · · · · ·

research design

ing, processing, and analyzing the data. The task requires a great deal of creativity on the researcher's part. It does not lend itself to simply selecting a design from among available alternatives; instead, the design must be developed in light of the investigation's specific research objectives.

There are, however, several types of commonly conducted research projects, with several widely used designs for conducting them. For example, a number of common research designs are used for appraising the effectiveness of an organization's advertising. Figure 4–4 outlines the steps involved in creating the research design.

• **Determine Data Needs** • Research objectives must be translated into specific information needs if the researcher is to satisfy the manager's information needs. For example, the U.S. Army engages in marketing research for many purposes. Suppose it decides to undertake a research project with the objective of finding out what steps it can take to improve the quality of recruits. The information necessary to satisfy the research objective might include

■ A detailed description of recruiting incentives currently being offered by the U.S. Army and by the other branches of the military.
■ Young people's attitudes toward existing recruiting incentives offered by the U.S. Army and by the other branches of the military.
■ The demographic and lifestyle characteristics of current Army enlistees who are high achievers.

The availability, currency, and reliability of secondary data cannot always be taken for granted. In some cases, even census data are lacking.

[© Robert Frerck]

- Forecasts for each of the next ten years of the number of new enlistees who will have graduated in the top fourth of their high school class.
- A detailed description of recruiting activities currently in use at recruiting centers.
- Comparative data on pay earned by young people in various branches of the military and in civilian types of employment, by age and education.
- A forecast of unemployment rates for the next decade, by state.
- Mental aptitude scores of last year's recruits, by age.

····■······

primary data

····■······

secondary data

In determining their data needs, researchers distinguish between primary data and secondary data. *Primary data* are data that are collected through original research for a specific purpose. The data must not have been collected previously. The big advantage of primary data is that they relate specifically to the problem at hand. In gathering them, the researcher may sharpen the research project's focus and uncover new problems. The main disadvantages of primary data are the cost and time required to collect them.

Secondary data are data that were previously collected by people either inside or outside the organization to meet their needs. If those needs are similar to the researcher's needs, there may be no reason to collect primary data. Secondary data are usually cheaper and

TABLE 4–2 ■ Illustrative External Sources of Secondary Marketing Data

General Sources

Bureaus of business research in colleges and universities
Chambers of commerce
Government agencies
Public libraries
Trade associations

Specialized Sources for Client Subscribers

Donnelley Marketing	A. C. Nielsen Company
Information Resources Inc.	Opinion Research Corporation
Market Facts, Inc.	Pulse, Inc.
Market Research Corporation of America	

Specific Publications

Census of Business
Census of Housing
Census of Manufactures
Census of Population, Current Population Reports
County and City Data Book
Economic Indicators
Facts for Marketers
Index of Publications of Bureaus of Business and Economic Research
Marketing Information Guide
Measuring Markets: A Guide to the Use of Federal and State Statistical Data
Monthly Catalog of U.S. Government Publications
Sales Management Magazine: Annual Survey of Buying Power
Statistical Abstract of the United States
Survey of Current Business
Wall Street Journal Index

faster to collect, but researchers must always consider their relevance, accuracy, credibility, and timeliness.

• **Determine Data Sources** • Secondary data can come from internal or external sources. The major internal source is company records. Public libraries, trade associations, and government publications are important external sources. (See Table 4–2.) All secondary sources should be exhausted before primary data collection is considered.

Secondary data can be collected from an originating source or a nonoriginating source. Population data for Chicago, for example, can be secured from detailed census publications (the originating source). They can also be secured from the *Statistical Abstract of the United States* (a nonoriginating source), which takes its data from the detailed census publications. Using the originating source usually is better because the data are more complete and often more accurate. It also provides more explanation of definitions and the research methodology used in collecting the data. This helps researchers evaluate the usefulness of the data for their needs.

Primary data can also come from internal or external sources. The major internal source is company personnel. Retailers, wholesalers, customers, and competitors are important

Customer satisfaction measurement involves collecting primary data.

(Copy: Chilton Research Services. Artwork: Chilton Company Art Department. Naughton Studios.)

external sources. Knowing what primary data are needed gives the researcher a hint about who might have them. Data on customer expectations about the firm's product and price are primary data if they have not been collected previously by the firm. To gather these data, the researcher may have to question customers by mail, telephone, or in person. The Chilton Research Services ad discusses the importance of customer satisfaction measurement. Chilton collects primary data from its client's customers.

Secondary data can be very helpful in defining the problem and determining research objectives, and they may be sufficient to meet the researcher's needs. But if these data cannot provide all the needed information, primary data must be collected. The discussions that follow focus on primary data.

• **Determine Primary-Data Collection Method** • The researcher can gather primary data through (1) observation, (2) experimentation, and (3) surveys. (See Figure 4–5.)

observational research

• *Observational Research* • The gathering of primary data through direct or indirect monitoring and recording of behavior is *observational research*. In direct-observation techniques, humans or mechanical and electronic devices can be used to record the behavior being observed. For example, a manufacturer of breakfast cereals who wants to study the attention-producing value of a new package might station observers with cameras and tape recorders behind the supermarket aisles where the cereal is shelved. The observers would monitor the actions of shoppers directly. If the research is highly *structured*, the observers are told what to watch and record. If it is highly *unstructured*, those determinations are left up to the observers.

Indirect observation involves making inferences about past behavior. For example, the

FIGURE 4–5

Types and Sources of Data and Collection Methods

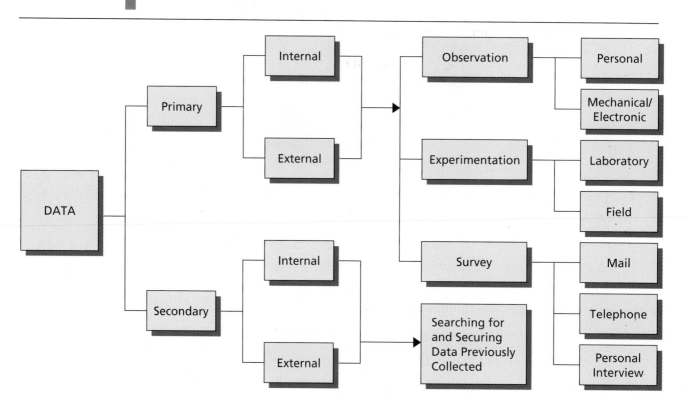

owner of a car repair shop could make inferences about the radio listening habits of customers by noting the stations customers had their radios tuned to when they brought their cars in for servicing.

Observation may be more objective than surveys because no questions are asked. The observation method focuses on what people do (direct observation) or did (indirect observation), not on what they say they do or did. Observers, however, can interpret only the behavior they witness directly. This interpretation may be inaccurate or biased. A shopper may pick up a package of cereal, examine it, and walk away without buying it. The shopper might have wanted it but might not have had enough money to buy it. An observer, however, might interpret this behavior as lack of interest in the product. In other words, we do not know why the shopper left the package. Some things, such as motives, simply cannot be observed.

As we saw at the beginning of this chapter, the use of mechanical, and especially electronic, observational devices is growing rapidly. A. C. Nielsen Company uses a people-meter in developing rating points for TV shows. The meter continuously monitors individual viewer choices and stores the data so they can be retrieved nightly by computer through telephone lines. The top of the meter box has touch-sensitive panels that bear the names of the family members as well as "visitors" to the TV viewing room. Touch-sensitive panels are also used to record the sex and age of visitors.

Observation can be used to get information that people are unable or unwilling to provide to interviewers. For example, most consumers who took the time to read a new product's label probably would be unable to tell a researcher how long they spent reading it. Some people might be unwilling to admit to a researcher that they regularly buy generic products. Table 4–3 gives several examples of observational research.

• *Experimental Research* • The gathering of primary data by manipulating an independent variable (such as advertising or price) to observe the effect of the change on a dependent variable (such as sales) is ***experimental research.*** By attempting to hold all other factors constant while manipulating price, it might be possible to estimate how many units of a product would be demanded at various prices. Experimental research can be conducted in a laboratory or a field setting.

experimental research

A soft-drink manufacturer, for example, might decide to taste-test proposed reformulations of its product in taste labs prior to introducing the reformulated product on the market. The influence on sales of the type of sweetener used in the soft drink could be tested

TABLE 4–3   Examples of Observational Research

1. A hotel uses researchers to observe how front desk personnel handle check-ins and check-outs.
2. A soft-drink bottler uses researchers to observe shelf-space allocation among rival brands of soft drinks in local supermarkets.
3. A shopping mall uses researchers to record license plate numbers on shoppers' cars in the parking lot as part of the research effort to determine the mall's ability to attract out-of-state customers.
4. A clothing store uses researchers to visit competitive stores to check on their prices.
5. A public library installs an electronic device at the entrance to record the number of times the door opens.

in the taste labs by participants who give their reactions to various formulations. The only independent variable operating is the type of sweetener. Thus the lab setting is unlike the real world, where other variables might influence consumer reaction. For example, a lower-priced rival brand is not in the lab but might be on the supermarket shelf and might reduce the sales of the researcher's soft drink.

Researchers conduct experimentation in the real world when they use a field setting. The field setting is more realistic than the lab setting but is harder to control. For example, an advertising manager who wants to test the effectiveness of a proposed newspaper ad selects two cities similar in population characteristics, income distribution, and so on. One is the control city and the other the test city. The ad appears in the test city's newspaper but not in the control city's newspaper. After the ad appears, sales of the product are recorded. Any difference in sales in the two cities is attributed to the ad.

Three assumptions are made: (1) two or more similar cities can be found, (2) the control city's environment can be controlled, and (3) test conditions are the same as those that will exist when the ad is run in the real market. But locating two almost identical cities for testing is not always easy. Also, if a rival withdraws its product in the control city, sales of the researcher's product might increase. If test city sales are lower than those in the control city, the researcher might incorrectly conclude that the ad is ineffective. Thus it is practi-

An ad that suggests the importance of cultural differences on survey research responses.

(Custom Research Inc., Minneapolis–New York–Chicago–San Francisco.)

An ad that describes a marketing research firm's Hispanic Panel.

(NFO Research Inc., Toledo, Ohio.)

cally impossible to ensure that test conditions will be the same as conditions in the real market.

● *Survey Research* ● The most commonly used and most flexible method for gathering primary data is survey research. **Survey research** is the gathering of primary data from respondents by mail, by telephone, or in person. As the CRI ad suggests, country-to-country cultural differences can affect survey research responses.

survey research

It took U S West Inc., the telecommunications company, four years and 15,000 interviews to find out the demographics of its customers. As a result of those interviews the firm recently was reorganized into groups reflecting different constituents. Examples include families with and without children, Hispanic consumers, and younger consumers.[7] Firms that target the Hispanic population in the United States can use the services offered by NFO Research. Its ad discusses the firm's Hispanic panel, which help NFO's clients obtain custom survey research from the Hispanic population.

Like observational research, survey research can be highly structured or highly unstructured. In a structured survey, all respondents are asked the same list of questions in the same way. In an unstructured survey, interviewers are free to ask their own questions to encourage respondents to open up. Three types of data are usually sought in survey research: facts, opinions, and motives.

In a *factual survey* respondents are asked questions such as "What brand of toothpaste do you use?" The purpose is to gather facts unavailable from secondary sources. In an *opinion survey* respondents are asked to give opinions, although they believe they are reporting facts. An example of an opinion survey question is "Which brand of toothpaste offers the best protection against cavities?" In a *motivational survey* respondents are asked to interpret and report their motives. These surveys ask "why" questions—for example, "Why do you buy Colgate toothpaste?" Many marketing research investigations are based entirely on survey research. It is a highly flexible method for gathering data.

- **Determine How to Contact Survey Participants** • Survey research data can be obtained from mail, telephone, or personal interview surveys. Table 4–4 discusses the relative advantages and disadvantages of each.

- *Mail Survey* • When the geographical area to be covered is large, the questions are simple, time is not a major factor, and the questionnaire is relatively short, the mail survey is favored. Respondents can answer at their convenience, and there are no interviewers to bias the results.

- *Telephone Survey* • When the questionnaire is short, time is limited, and research funds are scarce, the telephone survey is favored. The response rate usually is higher than for mail surveys. Well-trained interviewers can establish rapport quickly and ask respondents probing questions. Coincidental measurement also is possible. For example, interviewers can ask people questions about which TV programs or ads they are watching while the programs or ads are on the air.

Techniques have been developed to draw telephone samples without having to rely on phone directories that do not list all phone subscribers. One type of nondirectory telephone sample is generated by random-digit dialing. With this procedure, at least some digits of each sample telephone number are generated randomly. Thus the sample will include both listed and unlisted numbers. One potential disadvantage, however, is that some unassigned (nonworking) phone numbers will be drawn and must be called.

Technological advances are leading to greater use of telephone surveys. Wide-Area Telecommunications Service (WATS) lines and new technology are making telephone surveys less costly and less time-consuming. Telephone interviewers at some marketing research firms are working with data entry terminals. The interviewers read the questions off the video screen and enter the respondents' answers into the computer.

The Ethics in Marketing box discusses what the marketing research industry is doing to battle unethical practices such as "sugging."

- *Personal Interview Survey* • The most direct type of survey is the personal interview survey, because respondent and interviewer are in face-to-face contact. Audiovisual aids can be used and rapport can be built, which may make it possible to conduct longer interviews. Whenever a survey requires respondents to do something they cannot do by mail or phone—taste a new flavor of soft drink, for example, or smell a new brand of air freshener—a personal interview survey is necessary. This type of survey can be based on individual or group interviewing.

Individual interviewing is conducted on a one-on-one basis—in the respondent's home, on the street, or in a shopping mall. The trend in recent years has been to conduct these interviews in central location testing facilities in shopping malls in order to reduce costs.

Group interviewing—usually called the *focus group interview*—is a form of survey

focus group interview

research in which a moderator (a highly trained interviewer) meets with eight to twelve participants and leads them through a discussion on a given topic to develop hypotheses about an existing or potential product or marketing problem that might lead to more specific marketing research projects. Starting off with broad questions, the moderator gradually moves the group to a more focused discussion of specific issues.

Forum Corporation, a service-quality consulting firm in Boston, recently helped a bank

TABLE 4–4   Comparison of Mail, Telephone, and Personal Interview Surveys

Criteria	Mail Survey	Telephone Survey	Personal Interview Survey
Cost (assuming a good response rate)	Often lowest	Usually in-between	Usually highest
Ability to probe	No personal contact or observation	Some chance for gathering additional data through elaboration on questions, but no personal observation	Greatest opportunity for observation, building rapport, and additional probing
Respondent ability to complete at own convenience	Yes	No	Perhaps, if interview time is prearranged with respondent
Interviewer bias	No chance	Some, perhaps because of voice inflection, etc.	Greatest chance
Ability to decide who actually responds to the questionnaire within a household	Least	Some	Greatest
Sampling problems	Lack of up-to-date, accurate mailing list; low response rates	Lack of up-to-date, accurate phone subscriber list; unlisted numbers; no phone; refusals	Not-at-homes; refusals
Impersonality	Greatest	Some, because of lack of face-to-face contact	Least
Complex questions	Least suitable	Somewhat suitable	Most suitable
Visual aids in survey	Little opportunity	No opportunity	Greatest opportunity
Opportunity for building rapport	Least	Some	Greatest
Potential negative respondent reaction	"Junk mail"	"Junk calls"	Invasion of privacy
Interviewer control over interview environment	Least	Some, in selection of time to call	Greatest
Time lag between soliciting and receiving response	Greatest	Least	May be considerable if a large area is involved
Suitable types of questions	Simple, mostly dichotomous (yes-no) and multiple-choice questions	Some opportunity for open-ended questions, especially if interview is recorded	Greatest opportunity for open-ended questions
Requirement for technical skills in conducting interview	Least	Medium	Greatest

Walker Research does a biennial study of public cooperation with and attitudes toward survey research. Among other things, the study documents the extent to which the U.S. public is contacted by telemarketers who pose as survey researchers to get screening information about sales prospects. According to a recent Walker study, 48 percent of adult Americans are aware of being involved in such a disguised sales pitch, and 21 percent had the experience within the prior year.

The Research Industry Coalition (RIC) recently added a weapon in its arsenal to battle "sugging" (selling under the guise of marketing research) and "frugging" (fund-raising under the guise of marketing research). "A Statement about Certain Unacceptable Practices when Performed under the Guise of Research" has been sent to the press and other parties as well as to violators, such as errant telemarketers and fund-raisers.

According to RIC chairwoman Diane Bowers of the Council of American Survey Research Organizations (CASRO), the coalition was formed as an outgrowth of an industry summit meeting. Sugging and frugging are major concerns in the marketing research industry. The statement says the following practices are *not* legitimate or acceptable as elements of professionally conducted research:

- Requiring a monetary payment or soliciting monetary contributions as part of a research process.
- Offering goods or services for sale or using participant contacts to generate sales leads.
- Revealing the identity of respondents to a survey or of participants in a research process without their permission.

Telemarketers and fund-raisers who engage in these practices will receive the statement along with a letter asking them to stop. Bowers admits the watchdog has no teeth, since the only way to force compliance is to sue, and "we're not in the business of conducting lawsuits."

That's why the coalition also sends violators a copy of the revised postal regulations that resulted from a related lawsuit won by the U.S. Postal Service. Bowers is confident many companies will comply once they realize their practices are under scrutiny.

The statement also will be sent to various interested government groups to help them document the proper use of research. According to Bowers, it "shows we're very concerned about regulating ourselves."

Other leading professional and trade associations supporting the statement include the American Marketing Association, the American Association for Public Opinion Research, the American Psychological Association (Division 23), the Marketing Research Association, the National Association of Broadcasters, the National Council on Public Polls, the Newspaper Advertising Bureau, the Qualitative Research Consultants Association, and the Travel and Tourism Research Association.

Sources: The information about Walker Research is from Jack Honomichl, " 'We're Legitimate' Is an Idea Whose Time Is Right," *Marketing News,* January 7, 1991, p. 37. The rest of the box is adapted by permission from "Research Group to Warn Violators," *Marketing News,* November 12, 1990, p. 5, published by the American Marketing Association.

whose customers said they simply wanted friendly service. Through focus groups, it learned that it was most important to customers that, in especially busy periods, every available bank official was helping at service windows. According to a Forum spokesperson, "If you have people doing other things than serving customers, they have to be out of sight."[8]

• **Design the Data Collection Instrument** • Marketing researchers use two main types of instruments for collecting primary data: mechanical and electronic devices and questionnaires. Various types of data collection forms are then used to record the results of experiments.

• *Mechanical and Electronic Devices* • Among the mechanical and electronic devices available for collecting primary data are such devices as the turnstile counters that monitor visitor traffic flow at Walt Disney World and the mechanical device that counts the cars that pass through a major highway intersection. As we saw at the beginning of this chapter, services such as Information Resources Inc. use a combination of cable television, supermarket scanner devices, and computers to track every commercial that plays in their consumer panelists' homes and every purchase the panelists make at the supermarket. The panelists are given coded identification cards to use when they shop at supermarkets covered by these firms' scanner networks.[9]

• *Questionnaires* • Just as survey research is the most common method for gathering primary data, the questionnaire is the most common instrument for collecting these data.

In designing a questionnaire, researchers must exercise great care in deciding (1) which questions to ask, (2) the form in which to ask the questions, (3) how to word the questions, and (4) how to sequence the questions.

The research objectives should guide decisions about *which* questions to ask. Questions that are irrelevant to the research objectives do not belong on the questionnaire. Nor do questions that are likely to create suspicion and antagonism. Care is needed to avoid asking questions that require information not readily available to respondents, such as asking a father what brand of aerobic shoes his teenage daughter buys. It is also a mistake to ask questions that respondents are unwilling or unable to answer.

The *form* in which the questions are presented is very important. Open-ended questions, such as those in Figure 4–6(a) do not provide respondents with a choice of answers. Instead, respondents formulate their own answers in their own words. Close-ended questions, such as those in Figure 4–6(b), give respondents all the possible answers to each question; respondents then simply choose one.

The *choice of words* can make the difference between a good and a poor questionnaire. Words should be simple and unambiguous so they will mean the same thing to all respondents. They should not be biased, create misunderstandings, or lead respondents into giving the answer that the researcher wants.

The *sequencing* of questions should be planned carefully. Starting off with difficult and highly personal questions, for example, can antagonize respondents and lead to refusals to participate. Pretesting a questionnaire on a sample of respondents before using it in the full survey is always advisable. Figure 4–6(c) shows a hypothetical questionnaire along with commentary about the quality of the questions.

Validity and reliability are major issues in marketing research. They should always be considered in questionnaire development. *Validity* is a measurement instrument's ability to measure what it is supposed to measure. *Reliability* is a measurement instrument's ability to produce essentially identical results after repeated use. It indicates the extent to which a measure is free from random error and yields consistent results.

The validity and reliability of data can easily be compromised if respondents cannot answer the questions accurately. An example is asking a respondent questions about a product he or she has never consumed or even heard of and failing to include a "don't know" category on the questionnaire.

• *Interviewing Techniques* • Among the major interviewing techniques researchers use are direct, depth, and projective interviewing. The choice of technique influences the form in which questions are asked—open-ended or close-ended.

Direct interviewing is a marketing research technique that uses direct questions designed to elicit specific responses. An example is "How many miles per gallon of gasoline do you get with your car?" The interviewer records the specific answer by checking the correct response:

☐ 1–16 miles   ☐ 26–34 miles
☐ 17–25 miles   ☐ more than 34 miles

Direct questions elicit direct responses and are used when survey results are to be analyzed quantitatively. For example, the researcher can determine the percentage of respondents who selected each of the four possible responses.

A researcher who wants a fuller response might use depth interviewing. *Depth interviewing* is a marketing research technique that uses open-ended questions to permit respondents to talk to and interact with the interviewer. The open-ended question "What do you think about your car's fuel economy?" permits respondents to interact with the interviewer, who might interject responses such as "Why?" and "Tell me more."

validity

reliability

direct interviewing

depth interviewing

QUESTION FORM A	QUESTION FORM B	QUESTION FORM C

QUESTION FORM A

1. Totally Open
"What do you think of Subaru of America"

_____

_____

2. Sentence Completion
"In buying a new car, the most important thing to keep in mind is _____ "

3. Word Association
"Domestic cars" _____
"Foreign cars" _____
"Auto dealerships" _____
"Subaru" _____

4. Picture Completion

Enjoying your new car?

QUESTION FORM B

1. Dichotomous
"Do you think air bags should be required equipment on all new cars?
Yes ☐
No ☐

2. Multiple Choice
"What age group are you in?"
Under 20 ___   40–49 ___
21–29 ___   50–60 ___
30–39 ___   Over 60 ___

3. Semantic Differential
"Subaru of America"
Large _ _ _ _ _ Small
Modern _ _ _ _ _ Old-fashioned

4. Rating Scale
"Customer service at Subaru dealers is"
1. ___ excellent
2. ___ very good
3. ___ good
4. ___ fair
5. ___ poor

QUESTION FORM C

1. What is your age?
Too personal a question to begin a questionnaire. Should be at the end and provide age ranges.

2. What kind of car(s) do you presently own?
Ambiguous question. What does "kind" mean? Brand name, size, model, country of origin, convertible or hard top? What if the respondent leases instead of owns?

3. How much did you pay for safety equipment the last time you bought a new car?
The respondent probably will be unable to provide this information because he or she does not have it.

4. Don't you think passive restraint systems make for safer and more economical cars than other types of systems?
Yes ☐   No ☐
What does *passive restraint* mean? Two subjects are being asked about– *safety* and *economy*. It is also a leading question.

5. Have you ever felt guilty for driving your car after you had too much to drink, thereby inviting a serious accident?
Yes ☐   No ☐
Most people would probably not be willing to answer this question.

FIGURE 4–6
....

Examples of Open-Ended Questions, Close-Ended Questions, and Faulty Questions ▪

...▪......

projective interviewing

Skilled interviewers can use open-ended questions to elicit more qualitative information. Respondents who say they get seventeen to twenty-five miles per gallon do not provide much information about whether they consider that satisfactory or whether better mileage might be an effective feature to emphasize in advertising a new car. When open-ended questions are used, the number of people interviewed usually is smaller than in the direct-question surveys. Also, responses to open-ended questions are harder to tabulate because they are not as clear-cut.

Projective interviewing is a marketing research technique that seeks to get respondents to reveal subconscious feelings and opinions. It is used when researchers think respondents will refuse or be unable to provide the needed information. If the technique is successful, the respondents project their own feelings and opinions into the situation.

Look back at Figure 4–6(a). In a word association test, respondents are asked to say the first word that comes to mind when they are given a stimulus word by the interviewer. This can be useful in studying ad appeals and brand and company images. In a picture completion test, respondents are asked to project themselves into a situation by filling in words in the empty balloon.

motivational research

Depth and projective interviewing are techniques of motivational research. *Motivational research* is a type of marketing research that attempts to develop deeper insight into the whys of consumer behavior by analyzing the motives behind it. Traditional marketing research focuses on overt aspects of consumer behavior—who buys, where, when, and so on. Motivational research studies fewer respondents in greater depth. Trained psychologists are often employed to do the research.

Motivational research began in the 1950s, and it seemed quite sinister at the time. In his book *The Hidden Persuaders,* Vance Packard cautioned, ''With all this interest in manipulating the customer's subconscious, the old slogan 'let the buyer beware' began taking on a new and more profound meaning.''

Today motivational research is more sophisticated but less suspected of being sinister. McCann-Erickson ad agency uses a battery of psychological techniques to understand the emotional bond between consumers and brands. For example, it asks consumers to write newspaper obituaries for brands. The agency says it learns a lot about a product's image when people describe the brand either as young and virile and the victim of a tragic accident, or as a worn-out product succumbing to old age.[10] Chesebrough-Pond's succeeded with Elizabeth Taylor's Passion perfume after marketing researchers found that Taylor's struggles with weight control, substance abuse, and men ''made Liz more approachable. Women figured, if Liz can get control of her life, why can't I? That forged a very strong bond.''[11]

• **Design the Sampling Plan** • Suppose that Subaru wants to survey people in the United States who bought Subarus during the last three years to assess their opinions about the car. The marketing manager could get a list of the names of these people rather easily. Then each buyer could be surveyed—most likely by mail. Since this particular survey would include all persons in the population, it would be a complete enumeration, or a census, of the population.

If Procter & Gamble wanted to survey users of Crest toothpaste, it would have a much tougher job because the firm does not have a list of their names. The population is not as well defined as in the Subaru example. Sampling, therefore, is necessary.

A *population,* or universe, is the frame from which sample items are selected. The entire population is selected in a complete enumeration. Otherwise, only part of the population is selected. Items (persons, stores, cars, and so on) selected from their relevant populations are called *sampling units*. A *sample* is a set of units, or items, selected from a population. Most marketing research is based on sampling.

sample

Both complete censuses and samples can contain errors. Two types of errors are nonsampling errors and sampling error. Examples of *nonsampling errors* are incorrect recording of respondents' answers and incorrect transferring of data from questionnaires by data entry terminal operators. *Sampling error* is the error that the sample is not representative of the population from which it was selected.

• *Sampling Decisions* • Three basic issues must be decided in order to draw a sample: (1) the sampling unit, (2) the type of sample, and (3) the sample size.

What should the sampling unit be for Subaru? Whose opinions are wanted in a household buying unit that contains two spouses and two teenage drivers? This decision will influence the design of the questionnaire.

Next, a decision is needed about the type of sample. A good sampling plan will produce a sample that is representative of the characteristics of the population from which it is drawn. Two basic types of samples are probability (random) samples and nonprobability (nonrandom) samples.

A *probability (or random) sample* is a selection in which each item in a population has a known chance of being included through strict statistical procedures. The selection process cannot be arbitrary or based on judgment. A random sample's probability of representativeness can be mathematically appraised. In other words, sampling error can be measured. Table 4–5 discusses two types of probability sampling techniques.

probability (or random) sample

A *nonprobability (or nonrandom) sample* is a selection in which not every item in a population has a known chance of being included because researcher judgment enters into the selection. A nonprobability sample's probability of representativeness cannot be mathematically appraised. Sampling error cannot be measured. The sample's representativeness depends on how good the researcher's judgment is. Table 4–6 discusses two types of nonprobability sampling techniques.

nonprobability (or nonrandom) sample

Finally, a decision is needed about sample size. In general, industrial product marketers tend to use smaller samples than consumer product marketers. One reason is that the number of industrial buyers is far smaller than the number of ultimate consumers. Nevertheless, samples typically used in consumer research projects are far less than 1 percent of the population.

At any rate, the adequacy of sample size can be measured statistically only for probability samples. Increasing the sample size can reduce only sampling error; nonsampling errors can still affect the results. The determination of sample size requires statistical procedures beyond our scope.

• *Sampling and Marketing Research* • Both probability and nonprobability samples have a place in marketing research. The major advantages of a probability sample are that

TABLE 4–5   Two Types of Probability (Random) Sampling Techniques

Simple Random Sampling

This requires the researcher to have a list of all items in the population. Sampling units are selected in a random fashion. For example, assume each student in your class is assigned a sequential number written on a card and all students' cards are put in a container and mixed up. A blindfolded person could choose sampling units from the population by picking out cards. Each card has an equal chance of being chosen for the sample.

Stratified Sampling

This requires the researcher to divide the population into mutually exclusive subgroups (strata) based on a common characteristic. The basis for stratification (age, income, occupation, sex, etc.) should be characteristics that are relevant to the research project. In studying leisure activities of people in the population the researcher may believe that age is relevant. Thus the population is stratified by age. People in a particular stratum are of similar age, but each stratum differs from others with respect to age. Simple random sampling could be used to select sampling units from each stratum. A researcher needs more information on the population to select a stratified sample than to select a simple random sample, and he or she must be able to place each item in the population in the proper stratum.

TABLE 4–6   Two Types of Nonprobability (Nonrandom) Sampling Techniques

···

Convenience Sampling

Sampling units are chosen by the researcher simply on the basis of convenience. Examples
include on-the-street interviews by television reporters, asking people in a supermarket their
opinions about a new brand of detergent, and conducting taste tests with supermarket
customers. People not at the same place on the street on the same date and time that the TV
reporter is there clearly do not have a chance of being included in the sample. Nor do people
who are not in that particular supermarket at the date and time opinions or taste reactions
are being sought.

Judgment Sampling

Sampling units are chosen by the researcher on the basis of the person's opinion as to their
representativeness. Examples include selecting a sample of salespeople for their opinions as
input in preparing a sales forecast, selecting cities in which to test market new products, and
a TV reporter's selection of people to interview to get an informed view of the likely outcome
of an upcoming election. The representativeness of these samples depends on the judgment
of the person doing the selecting.

···

sampling error can be measured and that the sample size needed can be determined in
advance. Its major practical drawbacks are that probability techniques must be used to
select sample items and that much time and cost and knowledge of statistics are needed to
develop a probability sample.

Sampling error cannot be statistically measured for a nonprobability sample. Its presence and extent must be judged subjectively. The sample size also is based on judgment.
Since the cost, time, and statistical expertise required are much less, however, most marketing research projects are based on nonprobability samples.

Collecting, Processing, and Analyzing the Data

Once the researcher has determined data needs, data sources, and the framework and procedures with which to collect, process, and analyze the data, the problem becomes one of
searching for and securing the data. In collecting data, the researcher implements the
research design. Even large firms with their own marketing research departments sometimes use outside specialists to help in this step.

• **Data Collection** • The data *collection* step in the marketing research process is often
the most costly. The potential for error is also very high. To help ensure that the research
design is being implemented correctly, the researcher must monitor every phase of its
implementation. In a personal interview survey, for example, it is especially important to
monitor the fieldwork. The researcher might take a sample of completed questionnaires and
call the respondents to verify that they were, in fact, interviewed.

The researcher is also concerned about nonresponse error. Respondents who are not at
home when the interviewer calls and respondents who refuse to participate in the survey
can cause problems. There is always the concern that those persons might have systematically responded to questions differently from those who did participate in the survey. Thus

the researcher wants to ensure that follow-up calls are made in the case of not-at-homes and that interviewers make a genuine effort to encourage all those they call on to participate.

• **Data Processing** • After the data are collected, they must be *processed*. Collected data must be edited and coded to facilitate their analysis. Editors go through completed questionnaires to eliminate those completed by the wrong respondent and to check for readability of the responses. Editing also involves setting up categories for the data in accordance with the research design. For example, in a survey of cigarette smokers to determine brand usage, the categories might consist of brands, types of cigarettes (filtered, unfiltered, menthol), city size, household income, and sex of respondent.

Coding assigns the data to proper categories. For example, Carlton 120's might be coded brand number 1 and Century Lights 100's brand number 2. Cities of 20,000 population or less might be coded city size number 1, those with 1 million or more people number 5, and so on. Sometimes questionnaires are precoded (the codes are printed on the questionnaires) to permit data entry terminal personnel to enter responses directly from the questionnaire. Data processing activities, of course, lend themselves to the use of computers. Thus the data often are put into a computer-readable form and then read into a computer file and stored.

• **Data Analysis** • Next the data are *analyzed*. Actually, data analysis techniques should be planned in advance of data collection as part of the research design. For example, more data might be collected if computers are used than if the analysis is to be done by hand. Evaluating data as they become available during the investigation also helps the researcher gain insight into areas that should be examined in greater depth during analysis and interpretation and may help in identifying other techniques for data analysis. These techniques range from the simple to the complex, and in some cases outside specialists are used. Nevertheless, the researcher's job is to study the data to determine their meaning, in order to convert the data to relevant information for decision makers.

Data analysis involves descriptive analysis—describing responses, calculating averages, and so on—in order to transform raw data into an understandable form for the subsequent interpretation of the data. *Tabulation* involves arranging the data in a table, graph, or other summary format to facilitate interpretation. One-way tabulations provide answers to questions such as ''What percentage of the survey respondents were male?''

More sophisticated data analysis techniques may also be used as the researcher moves beyond the description of the data to complex statistical analysis of them. *Cross-tabulation* is often used to show how one variable relates to another. For example, two-way tabulations provide answers to such questions as ''What is the relationship between gender and brand loyalty in the automobile market?'' It is in the data analysis stage that meaningful information emerges—information that pertains to the problem that was defined in the first step of the research process.

Communicating Information to the Decision Maker

The final step in the research process involves interpreting the findings and communicating this information to the marketing manager. As the Equifax ad points out, ''Pertinent, timely information, properly analyzed and interpreted, is the strongest foundation for making intelligent decisions.''

Communication problems often exist between researchers and managers. Directors of marketing research are staff specialists who are familiar with the technical jargon of marketing research. Marketing managers are line executives who are often unfamiliar with

Elrick and Lavidge is an Equifax company. Equifax is The Information Source for business, industry and government in North America. Equifax responds to the information needs of its 60,000 customers—through more than 1,100 locations—an estimated one and a half million times each workday. Equifax's customers include banks, retailers, manufacturers, insurance companies, public utilities, government agencies and financial services organizations. Elrick and Lavidge capabilities include:
Professional project/program methodology design
Specialized targeted sampling systems
Computer-assisted telephone interviewing from seven telephone centers with more than 250 positions
Mall interviewing from more than 40 permanent locations
Qualitative interviewing from more than 45 focus group facilities
Face-to-face interviewing in homes, offices, stores and factories on a nationwide basis
Auditing and observation capabilities in over 200 cities
Data refinement analysis and reporting
Database creation and management
Good Research Helps You Make Better Business Decisions
How? By providing you with the information you need. Pertinent, timely information, properly analyzed and interpreted, is the strongest foundation for making intelligent decisions. Our customers know this and keep coming back to us for their research needs. They realize that the information we provide helps them make better business decisions.
We're Elrick and Lavidge. We provide our customers with information in every critical area of the marketing and research process, from data collection to processing and analysis. We've been serving business and industry of all kinds since 1951. Today we are linking traditional research projects with databases, models and segmentation systems. And we intend to stay in the forefront of providing good research and to assist our customers in making better business decisions.
Our nationwide organization offers dedicated, experienced personnel and full-service facilities to work on your project locally or throughout the nation.
We would like to meet with you to discuss your marketing research goals. Contact any of our offices. We would be happy to answer your questions and provide additional information describing our specialized services. Call us today.
EQUIFAX The Information Source
ELRICK & LAVIDGE MARKETING RESEARCH
ATLANTA (404) 938-3233
CHICAGO (708) 449-5300
CINCINNATI (513) 772-1990
LOS ANGELES (213) 316-2253
NEW YORK AREA (201) 599-0755
SAN FRANCISCO (415) 434-0536

Marketing researchers help marketing managers make better decisions.

(Reproduced with the permission of Elrick & Lavidge.)

technical jargon. Thus, as Figure 4–7 suggests, effective marketing researchers, whether on the organization's payroll or working for a marketing research company hired by the organization, possess both information skills and working relationship skills.

In communicating their research findings to decision makers, some researchers prepare several versions of their reports, each tailored to meet the needs of specific individuals. Others prepare one report and target specific sections to specific users. Among the criteria for judging the quality of a research report are completeness, organization, understandability, interest level, currency, accuracy, clarity, and conciseness.

The researcher usually makes an oral presentation to the decision makers. This too should be tailored to a particular audience's level of sophistication and needs. It helps sell the decision makers on the value of the research and its results—one of the researcher's key tasks—and gives the decision makers the opportunity to ask questions.

MARKETING RESEARCH IN SMALL BUSINESSES AND NONPROFIT ORGANIZATIONS

Small businesses and nonprofit organizations also engage in marketing research. Small retail store operators, for example, can use the video cameras that are installed in their

Information Skills	Working Relationship Skills
Ability to	**Ability to**
• Find out why information is being sought • Determine if the information already exists • Determine if the question really can be answered • Determine the best way(s) to obtain the information • Make the information absorbable	• Understand the culture in which the client or manager is embedded (the values held by the organization) • Empathize with the individuals who will take action • Avoid the self-induced alienation of the superior specialist caused by overuse of technical jargon • Avoid the fear of becoming emotionally involved (instead of simply gathering data dispassionately, researchers should use imagination and creative intuition to make their work exciting and productive)

FIGURE 4–7

The Marketing Researcher's Information and Working Relationship Skills

stores for security purposes to observe the effects of point-of-purchase displays on customers. Many small businesses use drawings for prizes to generate a customer list. Customers who participate supply information that can be used to develop a mailing list.

Careful listening during face-to-face conversations with customers can yield insight into what they want. Careful questioning of customers might produce information about what the firm's competitors are doing.

Secondary sources of information include local Better Business Bureaus, business and economic research bureaus at nearby colleges, and local Chambers of Commerce. Small firms can also turn to the growing number of information brokers who supply firms with hard-to-find information quickly. As awareness of electronic information access systems increases among small businesses, so will their use of these brokers.[12]

Small firms can engage in simple versions of experimental research. Large supermarket chains can use scanner data to evaluate the effectiveness of in-store merchandising tactics. Such data could be used to test alternate placements of products within a store. For example, should foil-packaged sauce mixes be displayed together or spread around the store according to their contents (spaghetti sauce mix near bottled spaghetti sauce, gravy mix near canned gravy, and so on)?[13] A small grocery can achieve the same results by observing sales given the alternate placements.

Museums, labor unions, clinics, hospitals, civic groups, political parties, churches, and numerous other nonbusiness organizations also use marketing research to gather information on target contributors, members, patients, and so on. For example, an art museum director was planning a program to expose low-income children to the art world. She wanted to invite government supporters, private sponsors, and influential citizens to observe the first night's "encounter with culture"; but she decided to preface this with several telephone calls to museums in other cities to see if they had tried similar events. As a result of the calls, she decided to change her plans. Another museum that tried the same approach had disastrous results. The museum's big contributors were horrified to observe children hollering in the museum corridors and actually touching the works of art. Donations dropped sharply.[14]

SUMMARY OF LEARNING OBJECTIVES

1. Explain the need for information management.

Marketing managers face an immense volume of raw data. These data are generated internally and externally. If the data are to be useful to the manager, the data flow must be managed. Data must be converted to information for decision making.

2. Describe what a marketing information system is and what it does.

A marketing information system (MIS) is a structured, interacting complex of persons, machines, and procedures designed to generate an orderly flow of pertinent information collected from intra- and extra-firm sources, for use as the bases for decision making in specific responsibility areas of marketing management. It gives marketing managers a steady flow of accurate, timely, and relevant information, from a variety of sources, which can be used to make better decisions. An MIS performs these functions: gathering data, processing data, analyzing data, storing and retrieving data, evaluating information, and disseminating information to marketing managers.

3. Describe the relationship between a marketing information system and marketing research.

An MIS is made up of two basic types of data subsystems. One deals with routinely collected internal and external data. The other deals with data that are collected for a special purpose. The sub-system of the MIS that deals with the collection of special-purpose data is called marketing research. Marketing research is the process of identifying and defining a marketing problem or opportunity, specifying and collecting the data required to address these issues, analyzing the results, and communicating information to decision makers.

4. Give examples of marketing research activities.

Examples include forecasting sales, measuring market share, identifying market trends, measuring the organization's image, measuring brand images, developing target customer profiles, designing products and packages, locating warehouses and stores, processing orders, managing inventory, analyzing audience characteristics, and scheduling advertisements.

5. Identify and describe the steps in the marketing research process.

Step 1 is identifying and defining the problem or opportunity. After the decision maker states what he or she believes is the problem, the researcher begins a preliminary exploration of the problem situation. Step 2 is determining research objectives. In general, a research investigation will have one of four basic objectives—to explore (exploratory research), to describe (descriptive research), to test hypotheses (causal research), or to predict (predictive research). Step 3 is creating the research design. This involves determining data needs, determining data sources, determining the primary data collection method, determining how to contact survey participants, designing the data collection instrument, and designing the sampling plan. Step 4 is collecting, processing, and analyzing the data. In collecting data, the researcher implements the research design. Processing involves editing and coding collected data to facilitate their analysis. Data analysis involves descriptive analysis in order to transform raw data into an understandable form for the subsequent interpretation of the data. Step 5 is communicating information to the decision maker. This involves interpreting the findings and communicating this information to the marketing manager.

Review Questions

1. Are data and information the same thing? Explain.

2. How does a marketing information system help marketers make better decisions?

3. How do routinely collected data in a marketing information system differ from data that are collected for a special purpose?

4. What is the key distinction between informal and formal marketing research?

5. Why is communication between information suppliers and information users important?

6. What are the five steps in the marketing research process?

7. What are (a) exploratory research, (b) descriptive research, (c) causal research, and (d) predictive research?

8. What is a research design? Explain what is involved in creating a research design.

9. How do primary data and secondary data differ?

10. What are (a) observational research, (b) experimental research, and (c) survey research?

11. What are the relative advantages and disadvantages of (a) mail surveys, (b) telephone surveys, and (c) personal interview surveys?

12. What are four major decisions that must be made in designing a questionnaire?

13. How do direct interviewing and depth interviewing differ?

14. How do probability samples differ from nonprobability samples?

Discussion Questions

1. Marketing researchers in the United States often must deal with the issue of cultural diversity. How might such diversity affect the collection of data by the survey method?

2. Unilever and Procter & Gamble entered the cosmetics business several years ago. Unilever, the Anglo-Dutch packaged-goods producer, markets Faberge and Elizabeth Arden cosmetics. P&G markets Cover Girl and Clarion makeup lines. Both firms devote a lot of time and money to conducting marketing research. Traditionally, however, firms in the cosmetics industry spend relatively little on marketing research. They tend to focus more on creative intuition. Would you expect this tradition to change? Explain.

3. Marketers today often have ''mountains of data'' to support their decision making. Can they have too much data? Explain.

4. What steps can marketing research firms take to regulate themselves to prevent harassment and safeguard privacy during the conducting of surveys? Are those steps sufficient, or should government regulate survey researchers? Explain.

5. What role should experience play when a marketing manager is making decisions?

6. How important are listening skills to marketing researchers? Explain.

Application Exercise

Reread the material about supermarket scanning at the beginning of this chapter and answer the following questions:

1. How does the concept of the marketing information system (MIS) fit into the scanner age?

2. Are the data that Pillsbury and PepsiCo buy from Citicorp primary data or secondary data as far as Pillsbury and PepsiCo are concerned? Explain.

3. Which data collection method is Citicorp using: observation, experimentation, or survey? Explain.

4. Do supermarket scanning and the building of huge databases of shopper behavior raise ethical issues? Explain.

Key Concepts

The following key terms were introduced in this chapter:

marketing information system (MIS)
marketing research
research design
primary data
secondary data
observational research

experimental research
survey research
focus group interview
validity
reliability
direct interviewing
depth interviewing

projective interviewing
motivational research
sample
probability (or random) sample
nonprobability (or nonrandom) sample

Caller ID

In 1990, Bell Atlantic telephone company unveiled the first major breakthrough in domestic telephone technology since the home answering machine—Caller ID. Caller ID allows telephone users to screen incoming calls by displaying the caller's telephone number. Who would want such a service? People who have tiresome relatives they'd rather hear from at their own convenience. People who have been bothered in the past by obscene phone calls. And people who don't like having their dinners interrupted by fund raisers, survey takers, and replacement window sellers. It's this last group of people who have direct marketing and marketing research specialists worried.

They're worried because Caller ID ". . . will drastically limit the number of homes we go into," according to the vice president of one marketing research firm. Because Caller ID allows you to display the originating number of an incoming call anytime the phone rings, you can wait until the caller starts to leave a message on your answering machine before answering the phone if you don't recognize the number. (Market research done prior to the Caller ID launch indicated that the people most likely to buy Caller ID service already have answering machines.) If you don't recognize the caller's voice or name, chances are you won't pick up the phone. And that means that the telemarketer or market researcher has paid for the call, for the caller's time, and for the time and effort of selecting your number to be included in the database for nothing.

Moreover, the presence of Caller ID may skew market research survey results: a random no-answer has different statistical significance than a conscious, "I don't want to hear from you" no-answer, but the researcher probably won't be able to tell what kind of no-answer has occurred.

What worries telemarketers and market researchers even more is that if you have Caller ID, you're probably just the type of person they're most eager to reach out and touch. Caller ID costs $60 to $80 to install plus $6.50 per month in extra service charges. If you're willing to spend that much for a new luxury item, you're probably willing to buy other luxuries. Many market researchers' best clients want to know what your tastes and attitudes are.

As of late 1990, Bell Atlantic was selling Caller ID in five mid-Atlantic states and in the District of Columbia. But, as the result of a legal suit, Pennsylvania's Commonwealth Court had blocked Bell Atlantic from selling the service in that state, ruling that Caller ID violated the privacy of the caller. Those supporting the Court's ban claimed that the presence of Caller ID could cause people to fear losing their anonymity if they phoned suicide or other hotlines. They also said that automatically providing one's phone number—which could later be used in direct marketing efforts—shouldn't be the price of calling a business to ask questions about its services. Bell Atlantic appealed the ban. Whether it won its appeal or not, though, it expected Caller ID to achieve 18 to 20 percent market penetration within five years. And the nation's other regional telephone companies were in the process of applying for permission to market the service.

Questions

1. Which of the six functions always performed by an MIS would Caller ID likely affect?

2. Do you think Caller ID could make telephone surveying obsolete?

3. How may Caller ID affect the relative merits of mail and telephone surveys?

4. One legislator has proposed making the availability of a blocking service—a service that allows a caller to block the ability of the receiver to display the caller's number—mandatory in Caller ID markets. How might this affect the impact of Caller ID on telephone market research?

What Is Welch's?

JAMES D. PORTERFIELD, *Pennsylvania State University*

"What is Welch's?" That's a strange question, especially when asked by the company's Chief Executive Officer. After noticing that Welch's sales volume was declining despite 2-percent-per-year industry growth, that is the question asked by Everett Baldwin, CEO of the fruit-products manufacturer.

In an effort to find an answer, Baldwin turned to Jordan Case McGrath, Welch's advertising agency. The agency then asked Booz Allen consultants to study the consumers' points of view, and market research produced encouraging results. First, people associated Welch's with quality. Second, while grape juice and grape jelly came to mind first, consumers easily associated Welch's with other fruit products. The findings launched a host of new marketing efforts as Baldwin set out to reposition Welch's as a marketer of fruit, not just grape, products.

From letterhead to packaging, Baldwin wanted a new look for Welch's that would underscore the firm's century-old heritage yet enable him to introduce new products. Working from the belief that consumers' reactions to packaging are especially important at the point of product selection, the company's designers called on Perception Research Services to measure consumers' reactions to new package designs before they were introduced on grocery store shelves.

Perception Research Services used focus groups, consumer attitude surveys, eye tracking, and recognition measures to determine consumers' reactions. By gauging these reactions early, the designers could focus on distinguishing Welch's products at the all-important product display area in stores.

The role of market research in guiding the designers' work was remarkable in this process. Fueled by fears that their creativity and designs will be destroyed by statisticians who speak in unrecognizable jargon, designers usually view research results with doubt and generally mistrust researchers. In this case, however, by improving research methods and using language that laypeople understand, researchers helped Welch's designers increase the chances for success in a new package design.

A look at an assortment of Welch's products shows the outcome. A uniform type style unites all product categories. The company's name is emblazoned on every label in the same location. An elaborate bunch of grapes adorns the top and right edge of grape products' labels and is dropped from labels of other fruit products. Finally, a light wallpaper-like background design used on grape products is replaced with a bold solid color on other products.

Welch's now has a brand and corporate identity to help it achieve its business objectives: capturing a proud history and announcing a broader range of fruit products (not to mention giving sales a real boost).

Questions

1. If you were a marketing manager and Everett Baldwin asked you the question, ''What is Welch's?'' what type of research would you do first? Explain.

2. What was the purpose of using three market research organizations to collect and analyze data for Welch's? Why not use just one?

3. Which technique would be the most effective for gathering data on consumer reaction to the new Welch's packages?

4. What would be your follow-up plan for achieving the company's business objectives?

5

THE CONSUMER
MARKET AND
BUYING BEHAVIOR

OBJECTIVES

After reading this chapter you will be able to

1. understand and use a simplified model of the consumer decision-making framework.

2. contrast complex and programmed decisions.

3. explain the meaning of cognitive dissonance and how consumers and marketers attempt to reduce it.

4. identify and analyze the personal influences on consumer behavior.

5. identify and analyze the sociocultural influences on consumer behavior.

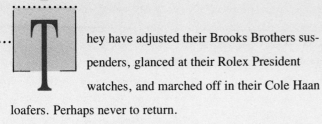

They have adjusted their Brooks Brothers suspenders, glanced at their Rolex President watches, and marched off in their Cole Haan loafers. Perhaps never to return.

The demise of yuppies, those young exhibitionists of consumerism, brings a smile to many working stiffs, but others aren't so happy to see them go. These days, marketers of brands such as Häagen-Dazs and BMW—icons of an era of self-indulgence and conspicuous consumption—are scrambling to cope with the new values of the 1990s.

Marketing experts are still debating the new psychology of consumers, but a wholesome profile is being crafted. As baby boomers have aged and had children of their own, family values have replaced the quest for individual gratification. In an uncertain economic climate, overt materialism has become less fashionable. Nowadays, young professionals are apt to choose the Gap over Gucci, even if money is no object. And some boomers now fret over problems more global than personal, including the deteriorating environment.

"In the 1980s, Ralph Lauren's print advertising worked because it looked like photos of George Bush's extended family," says John Lister, executive vice president of a New York consulting firm. The ads showed Lauren's clothes and household furnishings as part of a sporty, affluent lifestyle plenty of consumers coveted. "But now we're entering an age of more reasonable aspirations," Lister says.

That leaves many marketers of yesterday's status symbols desperately trying to distance themselves from the dated yuppie image. Those companies now stress real product attributes in their advertising, rather than trying to conjure up a fantasy-laden lifestyle. Marketers from Club Med to Häagen-Dazs are pitching to families and older individuals. Some other elite brands—such as BMW and Filofax—are rolling out budget models. According to a New York image consultant, "The products that have a value separate from their brand image are the ones that will continue to flourish."

Absolut, the yuppie status symbol of the 1980s, is an example of a product that may be losing its luster. Although sales of the vodka grew an astonishing 42 percent annually from 1985 to 1988 and rose 24 percent in 1989, the rate of sales growth has slowed in recent years.

Vodka had traditionally been a generic category until Absolut turned the market on its head in 1979. Conventional wisdom was that all vodka was tasteless, odorless, colorless—and created equal. The one exception, Stolichnaya, played up its Russian roots rather than taking aim at the young and self-consciously stylish.

Then came Absolut, with a break-the-mold ad campaign featuring witty wordplay and art from the likes of Keith Haring and Andy Warhol. The ads gave Absolut ''designer'' cachet and reappeared in endless variations throughout the 1980s. But the persistent imagery now breeds fatigue in certain circles.

Absolut faces one of marketing's toughest tricks: continuing to be fashionable among the trend-setting types who first embraced it even as it increasingly goes mass market. Some believe Absolut is destined for a backlash from its original fans. ''The avant-garde is growing restless,'' says a spokesperson from a consulting firm that specializes in youth marketing. ''Vodka drinkers will begin to seek alternatives because Absolut has become too much of a yuppie status symbol.'' One occasional Absolut drinker puts it this way: ''It's kind of embarrassing to order something so obvious. It's almost becoming a cliché.''[1]

No other generation has received more attention from marketers than the baby boom generation. One segment of baby boomers who commanded a lot of attention during the mid-1980s was the young urban professionals—the yuppies. But by the start of the 1990s the yuppie image was dated. Like Absolut, many of the other status symbols of the 1980s were losing their luster. Their marketers need new strategies for coping with changing patterns of consumer values and behavior.

In order to influence consumer behavior, marketers must understand what affects consumers' decisions. In this chapter we look at the types of decisions consumers make and the personal and sociocultural influences on their decisions. The personal influences include learning, motivation, perception, attitudes, and personality and lifestyles. The sociocultural influences include the family, reference groups, social classes, and culture. Let's begin with a brief look at the framework within which consumers make decisions.

THE FRAMEWORK FOR CONSUMER DECISIONS

Many fast-food drive-through customers appear to buy lunch much the way they buy gasoline—location and price are the criteria. According to a spokesperson for a marketing research firm that tracks the quick-service scene, ''They look at it more as a fuel stop than a dining experience.'' The heavy users of drive-through service, who tend to be young, single males, consider price and speed important. On the other hand, older people often regard eating out as a social occasion and are unlikely to meet at a fast-food restaurant.[2] The consumer behavior of younger and older consumers differs in significant ways.

Consumer behavior is the subset of human behavior that is concerned with the decisions and acts of individuals in purchasing and using products. In attempting to explain and predict consumer buying decisions, marketers make extensive use of the social sciences, including psychology, sociology, social psychology, economics, and cultural anthropology.

Figure 5–1, a simplified model of the consumer decision-making framework, shows the major influences on consumer buying decisions. In this chapter we examine the types of decisions consumers make and how the personal influences (learning, motivation, perception, attitudes, and personality and lifestyles) and sociocultural influences (family, reference group, social class, and culture) affect these decisions. The personal influences are highly interrelated both with each other and with sociocultural influences. Thus, although we will discuss each one individually, we need to remember that they are interrelated in complex ways. It is the interaction of these influences that affects consumers' buying decisions.

Ordinarily, there are many differences in the ways consumers make buying decisions. Even when two people appear to make a decision in the same way, the importance of certain factors in their choices might be different. For example, two consumers who need new tires might consult friends, read *Consumer Reports,* comparison shop at five stores, and finally buy the same brand. But they might have had very different reasons for their choices. One might have been looking for safety features and a product warranty, and the other might have been more interested in mileage, price, and appearance.

The buying decisions consumers make can be divided into two major types, based on

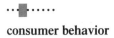

consumer behavior

FIGURE 5–1

A Model of the Consumer Decision-Making Framework

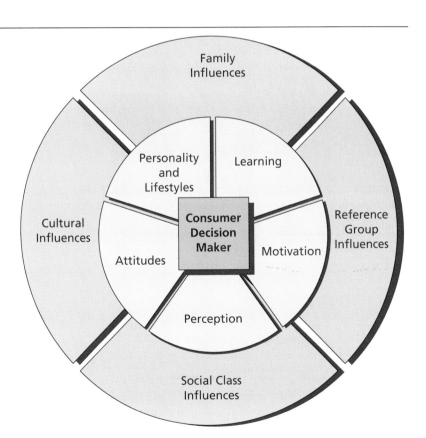

the nature of the decision process—complex decisions and programmed decisions. Complex decision making and programmed decision making are at opposite ends of a continuum. As we move to the right on the continuum, the decision-making process changes from extensive problem solving to limited problem solving to routine decision making. Thus the decision process becomes simpler as we move in the direction of a programmed decision.

COMPLEX DECISIONS

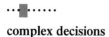

complex decisions

Consumers making complex decisions are in an active learning situation and are receptive to information about products and brands—where they are available, what they cost, and so on. *Complex decisions* are decisions that consumers make through extensive problem solving rather than through routine behavior. Consumers often seek information from such sources as advertising, brochures, friends and relatives, store personnel, Better Business Bureaus, and *Consumer Reports* in the decision process. As suggested by the Seldane ad, providing information to help consumers make complex decisions is part of the marketing effort.

Consumers making complex decisions are receptive to product information.

(Courtesy of Marion Merrell Dow Inc.)

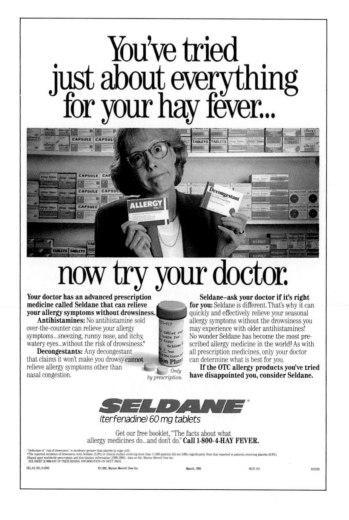

Consumers use complex decision making for *high-involvement purchases*—those that include a high amount of economic, psychological, or performance risk. The product's *economic importance* depends on its cost relative to the consumer's disposable income. Even inexpensive products may be considered economically important (involving economic risk) to low-income consumers.

Psychological importance is related to the social consequences of using the product (its social value) or its personal significance to the consumer. Purchases of high-fashion clothing generally involve psychological risk and are high-involvement.

The *performance risk* for a product is related to the consequences of buying a product that performs poorly. Products that last a long time, such as houses, cars, and major appliances, also involve performance risk because the consumer ordinarily will own them for a long time. Thus some home builders and car and appliance manufacturers offer money-back guarantees to their customers.

Decisions that the consumer has never made before are usually high-involvement decisions as well. For example, newlyweds who are buying furniture and appliances for the first time are making high-involvement decisions. Buying decisions for products that involve high risk can be high-involvement even though they might not be first-time purchases, however.

Some entrepreneurs are finding market opportunity in helping their customers make complex decisions. For example, clients tell New York–based Auto Consumers Inc. what new car they want and the firm does the haggling. The firm also advises clients against certain models and extras.[3]

Stages in Complex Decision Making

The process for making complex decisions is shown in Figure 5–2. Let's look briefly at each stage.

- **Awareness of Needs** • Your buying behavior results from your awareness of deficits in your assortment of products. This awareness may range from a vague feeling of dissatisfaction to a clear, unambiguous desire. You constantly scan your situation to identify imbalances in your assortment and assign priority rankings to missing items.

Certain factors can lead to changes in a person's deficits and their priority ranking. One such factor is exposure to new products or information. Consider, for example, the information released in recent years about skin cancer and its impact on the demand for products such as Sea & Ski's Block Out. Other factors include depleting the supply of a regularly used product, having more money to spend, changing social activities, changing goals, and experiencing mood changes. Deficits are continually changing, and marketers cannot always predict buyer behavior from them.

- **Information Processing** • Information processing involves the search for information and its perception, organization, and retention. Consumers start searching for information when they recognize a need for which they have no predetermined buying solution. They may turn to information they already have. For example, they may recall prior experiences or the experiences of friends in making a similar decision. The more similar the previous decision, the more likely the present decision will be based on it. But if the decision is not similar, they search for more information from external sources such as family members, ads, and salespeople.

In general, consumers will seek more information when they believe a decision is important in terms of economic, psychological, and time considerations. The more money

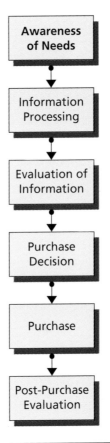

FIGURE 5–2

Stages in Complex Decision Making

involved relative to one's disposable income, the greater the perceived psychological risk in making the decision, and the longer the period during which the product will be used, the more information the consumer will seek. Also, more information is sought when a person's prior experiences do not fit the decision at hand.

The June 1988 issue of *Consumer Reports* stated that the Suzuki Samurai ''is so likely to roll over . . . that it is unfit for its intended use.'' In September 1988 the National Highway Traffic Safety Administration (NHTSA), a federal safety agency, refused to order a recall, on the ground that the Samurai is no more unsafe than any Jeeplike vehicle. *Consumer Reports* and the NHTSA based their judgments on different statistics and road tests. The end result for many consumers, however, was confusion.[4]

• **Evaluation of Information** • Consumers typically get information about products in bits and pieces and from different sources. They must sort this information into categories such as price, durability, and safety. The categories they use depend on their prior experiences and on what they learn in gathering information. Suppose you want to buy a riding lawn mower. You may bring to the decision situation some habitually used categories to sort information, such as price, service, and warranty. Additional categories, such as motor horsepower and number of gears, may be added by talking with other people and comparing models.

Information from different sources may be treated differently. For example, friends may be a more or less important source of information than ads, depending on how reliable and credible the friends have been in the past. A consumer may rely on ads to learn about new products but rely on a friend's advice about product durability. Information in ads may also be discounted if it is inconsistent with that provided by friends whose opinions are highly valued.

• **Purchase Decision** • At some point, the consumer must stop searching for and evaluating information and must choose a *buying alternative*. A buying alternative for a consumer product includes the product itself, the package, the store, and the method of purchase. The consumer makes a ''satisfying compromise'' regarding product features and other factors—for example, a person may be willing to pay a higher price to get a washing machine with a gentle cycle.

• **Purchase** • A purchase decision is not the same as the actual purchase. The time delay between the decision to purchase and the actual purchase may depend on a variety of circumstances, such as a shortage of cash. When the purchase is made, the original purchase decision may not be followed because of any number of variables, such as the unavailability of the chosen brand or a price increase.

• **Post-Purchase Evaluation** • The final stage in making a complex decision involves an evaluation of the decision. In other words, the decision-making process does not end when the purchase is made; the consumer evaluates the decision and uses this evaluation for future decision making.

Cognitive Dissonance

cognitive dissonance

In evaluating a decision, consumers often experience post-purchase doubt. *Cognitive dissonance* is the state of psychological tension or post-purchase doubt that a consumer experiences after making a difficult purchasing choice. It is a feeling of uneasiness that arises when the buyer chooses one purchase alternative and rejects others although each has some desirable unique features. Thus the rejected alternatives will have desirable features that the selected alternative (the product that the consumer purchased) does not have. The consumer, in effect, asks, "Did I make the right decision?" Buyers of the Suzuki Samurai who subsequently saw the June 1988 issue of *Consumer Reports* likely experienced cognitive dissonance.

The greater the economic and psychological importance of the decision and the greater the similarity between the product purchased and one or more of the rejected alternatives, the greater the amount of dissonance the buyer is likely to experience. Furthermore, the less the opportunity for the buyer to reverse the decision (return the product), the greater the amount of dissonance experienced.

• **How Consumers Reduce Dissonance** • Many decisions produce dissonance. Consumers try to reduce dissonance by reevaluating the information they obtained prior to the decision and by searching for more information. They may (1) deny or distort information, (2) seek confirming opinions from others, (3) discredit the information source, (4) minimize the issue's importance, or (5) change the overall evaluation of the chosen alternative.

Suppose you believe Toyotas, Hondas, and Nissans are equally attractive, but you buy a Toyota. You may lower the overall appeal that the Honda and Nissan had for you by changing their positive characteristics to negative ones and rejecting some of the positive

An ad that helps reduce dissonance.

(Courtesy of Ford Motor Company.)

information because of its source. You may turn to other Toyota owners to reinforce your decision, or you may simply conclude that there are no real differences among the three makes.

If you cannot distort, reevaluate, or discredit the information you obtained before making the decision, you may seek new information. But your search for and use of new information will be biased. Favorable information will be readily used, but positive information about Hondas and Nissans and negative information about Toyotas will be ignored or discounted. You will notice more Toyotas on the highway and pay more attention to Toyota ads.

• **How Marketers Reduce Dissonance** • Marketers can help consumers reduce dissonance by providing information consumers can use to reduce it and by ensuring that poor product performance is corrected as soon as possible. They can also use post-purchase communications such as letters and brochures to help buyers reduce dissonance. Many car dealers send reassuring letters to new-car buyers. The money-back guarantees for homes, cars, and appliances that we mentioned earlier are another example. Extended service contracts can also help reduce dissonance. About one-third of all car buyers sign up for such contracts, which cover repairs for one or more years after the manufacturer's warranty expires.[5] The Ford ad explains the company's Lifetime Service Guarantee, a car repair guarantee that lasts a lifetime.

Dissonance that is not reduced or eliminated leads to future complex decisions about products in that category. On the other hand, the more times a consumer makes a buying decision that produces satisfaction, the greater the chance that the decision will become programmed.

PROGRAMMED DECISIONS

···■·····
programmed decisions

Consumers, of course, make many purchases routinely, without engaging in the complex decision making we have described. *Programmed decisions* are routine decisions that result from the learning process consumers engage in when making complex decisions.

Programmed decisions differ from complex decisions in that they usually (1) are not difficult to make; (2) do not involve high economic, performance, or psychological risk; and (3) are made frequently. Deciding among brands of toothpaste, bath soap, cigarettes, and breakfast cereals are programmed decisions for most consumers. These items are simple-decision products because of the low risks involved in using them and the high frequency of their purchase. In other words, they are *low-involvement products.*

Consumer Behavior in Programmed Decisions

Decisions to buy frequently purchased products are usually handled in a programmed way to save time and effort. The programmed decision sequence is much shorter and simpler than that for complex decisions. Consumers making programmed decisions tend to exhibit three characteristics: (1) their behavior is under external stimulus control, (2) they are not receptive to new information, and (3) their behavior is relatively consistent in making these decisions.

• **External Stimulus Control** • If you are aware of a need, you buy the product that satisfies it. But in making a programmed decision, you may be aware of the need before going shopping, or you may not realize the need until you see the product while shopping. The same brand may be bought on either basis at different times. The programmed decision sequence in Figure 5–3 assumes that need awareness results from seeing the normally purchased brand. Thus the consumer's behavior is under external stimulus control.

• **Not Receptive to New Information** • A programmed decision does not involve much thinking by the consumer. The consumer is not actively receptive to new information but buys out of force of habit.

Product and store loyalty are well-developed programmed decisions to buy a particular brand or to buy from a particular store. Switching brand-loyal customers is hard because they either do not look at ads or point-of-purchase displays of competing brands or they consider them irrelevant.

The information seeking and processing that do occur in programmed decision making usually are limited to cursory checks of different sizes and styles of the product or of nearby competing brands. This minimal effort is not a real consideration of alternate products. It is a casual check to make sure that price and other product features are within a reasonable range.

• **Relatively Consistent Behavior** • In making programmed decisions, a person's behavior is relatively consistent, no matter what the product category. Buying several types of toilet articles at discount stores instead of at supermarkets or drugstores may be characteristic of your buying habits. It may reflect your strategy of finding the lowest price for normally purchased products or your desire to find a convenient place to buy a number of items at one time.

Shifts in Types of Buying Decisions

The division between programmed and complex buying decisions is not permanent. Programmed decisions can become complex if (1) new products become available, (2) the consumer has used one brand for a long time and wants variety, (3) people whose opinions the consumer respects suggest new ways of doing something, (4) the consumer's living situation changes a great deal, or (5) outstanding advertising attracts the consumer's attention.

Successful complex decisions also can become programmed. The process through which buying decisions are changed from complex to programmed is called learning. Learning is one of the personal influences on consumer behavior.

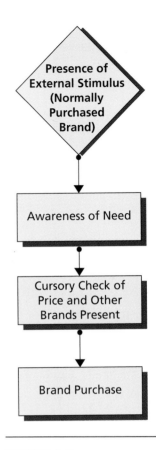

FIGURE 5–3

Decision Sequence in Programmed Decisions

PERSONAL INFLUENCES ON CONSUMER BEHAVIOR

Now that we have a basic understanding of the two types of buying decisions, let's turn to the personal influences that are specific to a given consumer's psychological makeup and that affect the person's buying decisions. These influences are learning, motivation, perception, attitudes, and personality and lifestyles.

Learning

Marketers want their targeted customers to know about their products. Prospective customers can learn about a product in two basic ways—through direct experience and through indirect experience. First, they can actually use the product. Marketers often give away

···■······

learning

free samples of new products or make them available in trial size packages so consumers will try them; this is *direct experience*. Second, consumers can learn about products through *indirect experience*—information obtained from friends, relatives, ads, and salespeople or from observing the behavior of others.

Learning is the process through which a relatively permanent change in behavior results from the consequences of past behavior. If a consumer's buying behavior leads to satisfying consequences, it has been positively reinforced and the purchase will tend to be repeated. By this process, consumer decisions become more and more like the programmed decisions described previously.

Some marketers seek to build brand loyalty among children by creating clubs. Children can join Burger King's Kids Club for free and receive a newsletter five times a year as well as posters, stickers, and literature on subjects such as nutrition and technology.[6] According to the publisher of the *Marketing to Kids Report* newsletter, "A club is an ongoing involvement that builds a solid relationship with youngsters."[7] Delta Air Lines, Toys "R" Us, and Fox Broadcasting also have kids clubs. According to experts, kids clubs can cost several million dollars a year to operate. Some marketers have ended their clubs. Kraft General Foods, for example, ended its Honeycomb Hideout Club in 1990. According to a

ETHICS IN
MARKETING

Along with daily doses of reading, writing, and arithmetic, children in many public schools around the United States are getting lessons on brand loyalty. Like never before, some of the nation's best-known marketers, including Coca-Cola, IBM, and Reebok, are devising ways to slip advertising messages into the nation's schools. The pace has escalated as officials in financially strapped school districts look to the business community for support. Many consumer product companies are happy to oblige—with a few strings attached.

The best-known classroom pitchman remains Christopher Whittle, chairman of Whittle Communications. His launch in March 1990 of a closed-circuit TV network that includes two minutes of ads on a daily news program for students touched off a barrage of criticism. Yet the controversy has hardly dissuaded other companies from launching their own educational marketing programs. One example is Scholastic Inc., one of the largest U.S. publishers of books and magazines for children. It cranks out single-sponsor magazines and other teaching tools for some forty firms, including AT&T and Mars Inc.'s M&M/ Mars division.

Marketers are so interested in the classroom because the kids' market is so big. Teenagers alone buy an estimated $78 billion in goods each year—and they cajole their parents into spending up to twice that amount. Moreover, although TV viewers at home often zap to another channel at commercial breaks, kids in the classroom are a captive audience to whom ads may seem a welcome break from studies. And because school marketing is relatively untried, there's little clutter to cut through. "The kids we're reaching are consumers in training," said a marketing researcher.

Others are far less enthusiastic about the trend. Consumers Union, publisher of *Consumer Reports* magazine, recently released a study that decries the "non-company spokesperson, ''It didn't draw enough of a response'' to give Honeycomb cereal a big sales boost. Some firms have backed away from the clubs because of criticism from consumer activists.[8] As the Ethics in Marketing box points out, some marketers also try to teach brand loyalty to students while they are in school.

Brand loyalty develops through positive reinforcement and repetition of the buying behavior. Brands can be arranged in a hierarchy based on the number of satisfactory purchases. The brands that are most rewarding are most likely to be bought. PepsiCo renamed its caffeine-free colas to make them more rewarding. The old names, Pepsi Free and Diet Pepsi Free, were replaced with Caffeine-Free Pepsi and Caffeine-Free Diet Pepsi. According to the publisher of *Beverage Digest,* ''The problem with Pepsi Free was that consumers didn't know if that meant sugar free, caffeine free or just what.''[9]

When a well-established buying habit is weakened by unsatisfactory experiences, the weakening is called *extinction.* Although you may not switch to some other brand or store after one bad experience, the more of them you have the less likely you will buy that brand or shop at that store again. The Tetley's ad is an example of advertising that seeks to switch consumers who are loyal to rival brands.

New habits are broken faster than old ones because new habits have not been repeated

stop advertising barrage on America's children.'' Some school administrators are doing heavy soul-searching. On the one hand, harried teachers have been receptive to packaged teaching aids, such as the AT&T Adventure Club, a program developed for AT&T by Scholastic. The program, which includes student newsletters, classroom posters, and teaching guides, is designed to foster understanding of communications and to build AT&T brand awareness among first-graders.

But many educators complain that companies are more interested in expanding markets than minds. School officials say marketers and their hired guns can't be trusted to develop unbiased educational materials. ''Parents are entrusting their kids to the schools,'' says a state superintendent of public instruction. ''We have no right to sell access to that captive market.'' Another educator says opening school doors to marketers now will result in an intolerable situation

down the road. ''Will we eventually be selling one-minute spots in fifth-grade geography? The classroom should be a marketplace of ideas, not products.''

The issue of commercialism in schools has become a top concern for the national Parent-Teacher Association. According to a spokesperson for the group: ''Parents are getting fed up with marketers. We can't just sell off our curricula to the highest bidder.''

Is it ethical for advertisers to target a captive audience? Is it ethical for school officials to permit commercial messages to be presented in taxpayer-supported public schools? What other ethical issues are involved here?

Source: Adapted from Kathleen Deveny, ''Consumer-Products Firms Hit the Books, Trying to Teach Brand Loyalty in School,'' *Wall Street Journal,* July 17, 1990, pp. B1, B6. Reprinted by permission of the *Wall Street Journal,* © Dow Jones & Company, Inc., 1990. All rights reserved.

as often. Customers may switch to a new brand for a while and then switch back to the old brand as the big advertising push for the new one slacks off. Older brands therefore require less advertising than newer brands to keep their market share.

We also learn indirectly through observing others. If you observe that another person's behavior leads to reinforcement, you may imitate that behavior when you are in the same situation. *Imitation* is a key factor in consumer adoption of new products. This is one reason marketers use celebrities in their advertising.

The observation does not have to be direct. We are influenced by the experiences of others that are communicated to us as well. Thus we learn about products through what our friends and relatives, and even advertisers, tell us. This ability to learn *indirectly* through the communication of the experience of others accounts for the popularity of testimonials in advertising. But regardless of our learning experiences, we will not purchase a product unless we are motivated.

Motivation

motivation

Even when a buying decision is programmed, consumers will not make a purchase unless the product is needed. Consumer behavior is directed toward meeting needs. ***Motivation*** is the driving force that causes a person to take action to satisfy specific needs. Marketers use motivational research to try to discover the whys of consumer behavior by analyzing the major motives that influence it. If marketers can identify these motives and develop marketing mixes that appeal to them, they can generate consumer motivation to buy.

One step in understanding motivation is to classify needs into categories. Psychologist Abraham Maslow categorized needs into five categories. His *hierarchy of needs* is a ranking of human needs starting with the most basic physiological needs and ranging in decreasing dominance through safety, love and belonging, esteem, and self-actualization needs. (See Figure 5–4.) Each category represents a cluster of specific needs. The most basic needs provide the foundation for higher-level needs. The physiological needs, which relate to a person's survival, must be satisfied before any needs from higher categories can emerge. Thus a hungry person would be concerned with getting something to eat before thinking about what surroundings would make a meal more agreeable.

hierarchy of needs

FIGURE 5–4

Maslow's Hierarchy of Needs

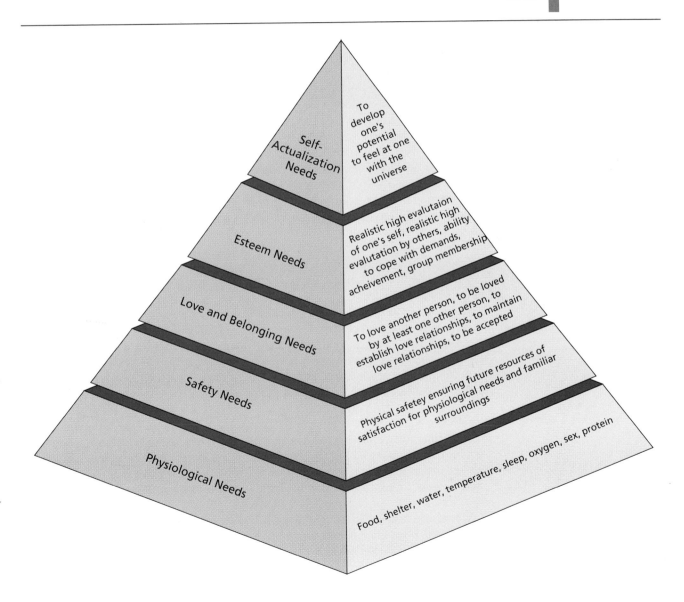

The marketer can use this concept of basic and higher-level needs in deciding how to approach the consumer. The consumer's motivation to satisfy the most basic needs may be directed toward a general category of goods or services. These generalized needs are called *primary buying motives*. The hungry consumer, for example, may buy at the nearest fast-food restaurant.

But to get consumers interested in a particular brand, the marketer needs to elicit *selective buying motives* aimed at arousing interest in a particular product within the general category. Thus arousing a consumer's hunger by showing a hamburger on TV does not guarantee that the consumer will go to Burger King. The Eveready Battery Company focuses on consumers' safety needs and arouses the selective buying motive with the slogan "Peace of mind from a name you can trust."

Marketers advertise their products and train their salespeople in selling techniques in the hope of motivating prospective customers to buy. But whether a given prospect buys or not will depend to some extent on how the person perceives the advertising and the salesperson. If the prospect does not pay attention to the advertising and perceives the salesperson as being too aggressive, the prospect probably will not buy. In the discussion that follows we take a closer look at the perception process.

Perception

We are constantly bombarded by an ever-changing flow of marketing stimuli—TV and radio commercials, newspaper and magazine ads, billboard messages, merchandise displays, stores, products, salespeople, and so on. Many of these stimuli, however, are irrelevant to what we are trying to accomplish and therefore are not admitted to our awareness. Thus you may be sitting in front of a TV set while a commercial is being broadcast and be unaware of it because you do not perceive it.

perception

Perception is the process through which an individual selects relevant stimuli (information) from the environment, organizes them, and assigns meaning to them. In other words, we choose what information to pay attention to, we organize it, and then we interpret what we see, hear, touch, taste, and smell in a way that is meaningful to us. We change and reorganize the information so that it is consistent with our knowledge, goals, and experiences. Our behavior, therefore, is determined by how we perceive our environment, not by what is really there.

According to the president of Perception Research Services, an eye-tracking facility: "The average supermarket shopper is exposed to 17,000 products in a shopping visit that lasts less than 30 minutes—and 60 percent of the purchases are unplanned. Eye tracking shows which products have stopping power."[10] As supermarket shelves become more and more cluttered, eye tracking will probably become more important to marketers who want to maximize the chances that consumers will pay attention to their products on the shelves.

• **Selective Nature of Perception** • The perception process is highly selective. Of all the marketing stimuli in our environment, each of us is exposed to only a small portion. If an advertiser places an ad in *Time* magazine, but you do not read *Time,* you will not be exposed to that ad. Even if you do read the magazine, you may not notice the ad. We pay attention only to information that interests us at the moment. This is called *selective exposure*.

We are also selective in terms of how we deal with the information we pay attention to. For example, if we admit information from an ad to our awareness, but that information is inconsistent with our feelings or beliefs, we may distort the information to make it consistent. This is called *selective distortion*.

Finally, we are selective in what we retain of the information we perceive. In other words, we tend to remember only what we want to remember. This is called *selective retention*.

Obviously, marketers need to be aware of the selective processes if they want to get their messages across to their targeted audiences. Some pop-in-the-microwave dinners can be stored for months at room temperature. These "shelf-stable meals" have been in existence for years, but they remain a high-tech product in search of a market. Although most U.S. consumers have at least one microwave oven, fewer than 25 percent have tried shelf-stable dinners. The big reason is fear. According to a marketing consultant: "When you say 'shelf-stable,' you run into the perception that it has lots of stuff in it—chemicals—to keep it fresh. Today, people are talking fresh, no preservatives." Actually, however, shelf-stable foods have few or no preservatives. Like canned foods, they are cooked at high temperatures that kill bacteria and allow the products to be stored for months without refrigeration.[11]

Marketers also must recognize the way consumers attach meaning to objects and events in their environment.

• Consumer Meaning • As we have seen, consumers assign meaning to objects or events in their environment through the perception process. Thus, in order to create satisfaction for their target markets, marketers should understand how targeted customers perceive their marketing activities. Consider, for example, the meanings target customers assign to products—functional meanings and subjective meanings.

• *Functional Meanings* • A product's functional meanings reflect how well the product will do something for you. They are an objective assessment of its quality, price, and utility. Most consumers agree on the functional meanings of products because the meanings are shared readily. Even new uses can be adopted without much trouble. Vans, originally designed for commercial use, became popular as recreational vehicles during the 1970s but declined in popularity as the price of gasoline soared. Minivans were introduced in the 1980s, and many buyers perceived them as essential rather than recreational vehicles. To those people, the minivan is a family workhorse, not a weekend plaything.[12]

• *Subjective Meanings* • The meanings consumers give to products that are unrelated to the products' intended functions are subjective meanings. Two types of subjective meanings are social and symbolic meanings.

Marketers are often faced with consumer behavior that appears illogical. After looking at several scarves in a discount store, a woman selects one and seems to consider it appropriate. Its price is $19.95. But after thinking about it for fifteen minutes, she returns it to the counter and leaves the store. A few days later she sees the same scarf in an exclusive department store, looks at it for a moment, and buys it for $40.

From an external frame of reference she made an irrational decision. If the marketer could enter her frame of reference and discover the meanings she is attaching to this experience, her behavior might make sense. The woman may have wanted to give the scarf as a gift and thus did not want to buy it from a discount store. This is an example of the *social meaning* of products.

Symbolic meaning is important too. Many consumer products made and marketed in Japan are created to appear as if they were made in the United States. Thus advertising and package design often feature pastures, plantations, and log cabins. Japan's Mister Donut stores started looking more "American" after a Japanese firm bought the chain from an American firm. Confident that a 1950s image would increase sales, the new owner put pink neon flamingos by the windows of new outlets and installed revolving merry-go-rounds. A specially made tape of 1950s music, interspersed with comments—in English—by a disc jockey also plays in the outlets. According to the new owner, ''There's a nostalgic feeling among the Japanese people'' for that era. ''We were miserable after the war. And America was our dream.''[13]

Colors have a strong influence on symbolic meaning. For example, beverage industry executives say that gold has become the ''accepted consumer visual cue'' for products without caffeine.[14]

• *Measurement of Consumer Meaning* • Marketers would like to know what meanings consumers attach to their products or organizations in order to develop better marketing mixes. To determine how consumers interpret their experience with a product or organization, marketers use projective techniques and semantic differential scales.

Projective techniques, which were discussed in chapter 4, can help in measuring a product's symbolic meanings. For example, the meanings attached to instant coffee were measured by giving two groups of people shopping lists that were identical except for the type of coffee listed (instant versus drip grind). The groups were then asked to describe the person who bought these groceries. Differences in their descriptions were attributed to the type of coffee on the lists. Shoppers with the instant coffee on the list were perceived to be lazy and poor homemakers. This study was published in 1950. In a repeat of the experiment, published in 1970, homemakers who used drip grind coffee were seen as old-fashioned.[15]

Another projective technique is the use of illustrations to determine the symbolic meaning of a brand name. Two groups might be given cartoons or pictures of a situation. The product would be identified by brand name in one picture but not in the other. Any differences in the descriptions of the person who would buy each product would thus be due to the meanings the subjects attach to the brand name.

Meanings can also be measured by semantic differential scales. *Semantic differential scales* are methods for measuring the meanings consumers attach to products, brand names, or organizations, whereby the consumers rate the subject on a seven-point scale between pairs of antonyms (opposites). Specific aspects of the brand or firm can be measured, and comparisons can be made with other brands or firms. Consumer reactions to store layout, store personnel, product assortment, and pricing policies also can be measured individually by retailers. Figure 5–5 shows some of the scales that could be used to measure consumer reactions to store personnel.

Perception is closely related to attitudes. The meanings consumers attach to products influence their attitudes toward them. In turn, attitudes determine what will be selectively perceived.

semantic differential scales

Attitudes

attitudes

Marketers are concerned with consumer attitudes toward their products because attitudes influence consumer buying decisions. *Attitudes* are enduring feelings, evaluations, and response tendencies directed toward an object or idea. Attitudes toward a brand involve overall positive and negative feelings and evaluations—likes and dislikes.

As mentioned earlier, attitudes affect the perception process through selectivity. Typically, we selectively *screen out* information that conflicts with our attitudes, selectively *distort* information to make it consistent with our attitudes, and selectively *retain* information that reinforces our attitudes. Thus attitudes can affect the learning process too.

We saw how consumers can learn about products through direct and indirect experience. Attitudes themselves are learned (formed) through information acquired directly through

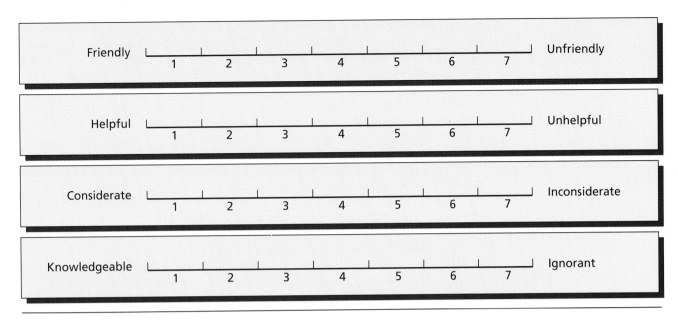

previous experiences with an object and indirectly through interactions with other people. Attitudes can also be reinforced. Thus the greater the number of repeat purchases of a certain brand, the more information we acquire about that brand and the more difficulty marketers of competitive brands will have in changing our attitudes toward that brand. Because attitudes are also acquired through interactions with others, word-of-mouth can benefit marketers when attitudes toward their offerings are positive and can damage marketers when attitudes are negative.

• **Attitude Measurement** • Because attitudes can affect consumer buying decisions, marketers attempt to measure them. Measurement includes some of the same methods used to measure consumer meaning—projective techniques and semantic differential scales, which are also called attitude scales. Among the dimensions that might be measured are attitudes toward a product and its package, store location, price, quality of salespeople, store hours, and advertisements.

In measuring attitudes, however, we are not measuring buying intentions. People can have favorable attitudes about a product and still not intend to buy it. Many millions of people have a positive attitude about Mercedes-Benz automobiles even though they have never bought one and probably never will. Measuring attitudes and forecasting sales are two very different activities. Although a survey of consumer attitudes toward a proposed new product might indicate a strong attitude for or against it, and therefore influence the decision of whether to proceed with its development, such a survey is not a sales forecast. We discuss sales forecasting in chapter 8.

• **Attitude Change** • Because they are predispositions to behave in a consistent way, attitudes, especially strongly held attitudes, are resistant to change. This does not mean, however, that attitudes do not change or cannot be changed. Consider the history of changes in attitudes about big cars, infant formulas, tonsillectomies, synthetic fibers, condoms, calcium, jogging, eggs, meat, poultry, pasta, and salads. Cruise lines have been combating their pricey image for many years. Even in the best of times, the main reason most consumers have never taken a cruise is the price. According to an industry spokesperson, "People see the price and say, I don't want to spend that much on a vacation." The industry has been trying to educate people about cruising's value.[16]

A marketer whose offering is met with strongly negative attitudes on the part of a significant number of targeted customers may try to change these attitudes to make them more positive. This is extremely difficult, perhaps impossible, to do and involves a lengthy and costly marketing effort. It is much easier to adapt a marketing mix to existing attitudes than it is to try to change existing attitudes toward the marketing mix. Marketers must also consider existing attitudes when planning new market offerings.

There have, however, been some successful attempts to change consumer attitudes. Honda Motor Company many years ago launched an ad campaign built around the theme "You meet the nicest people on a Honda" to help dispel the attitude held by many potential Honda buyers that motorcycle riders were unsavory characters.

In studying attitudes and attitude change, marketers have found that both are influenced by the consumer's personality and lifestyles.

Personality and Lifestyles

Personality and lifestyles are related concepts, both identifying long-term behavior patterns.

personality

• **Personality** • The behavior pattern termed *personality* is the collection of relatively permanent tendencies to behave in consistent ways in certain situations. Because of this consistency, we can categorize people on the basis of such personality traits as self-confidence, aggressiveness, extroversion, introversion, gregariousness, friendliness, compulsiveness, sociability, and adaptability. Such traits affect the way people behave. Thus self-confident people and insecure people probably behave differently in choosing products and brands to buy and stores to shop in.

Marketers therefore have attempted to use personality inventories, in the belief that personality traits affect buying behavior. In general, however, such attempts have not met with much success. One problem is measurement. Most personality inventories have been developed for clinical use and are not suitable for the general population. In other words, it is hard to classify the personality traits of specific consumers and to demonstrate strong correlations between certain personality types and their choices of specific products and brands to buy or specific stores to shop in.

Perhaps the major use of personality factors in contemporary marketing is the attempt to develop a brand or store image that fits with what are often assumed to be some of the personality traits of targeted customers. For example, ads for More and Virginia Slims cigarettes seek to appeal to different types of personalities.

self-concept

Self-concept is closely related to personality. *Self-concept,* or self-image, is the image or perception of oneself. Your self-concept is the result of the interaction of both personal and sociocultural influences on your behavior. In general, consumers buy products and brands and shop in stores whose images are consistent and compatible with their self-concept. Marketers therefore seek to tailor their market offerings and store images to match and enhance their targeted customers' self-images.

lifestyles

• **Lifestyles** • Among the many recent U.S. trends in lifestyles are a shift toward personal independence and individualism and a preference for a healthy, natural lifestyle. *Lifestyles* are the consistent patterns that people follow in their lives, including how they spend their time and money, and are identified through people's activities, interests, and opinions of themselves and the world around them. Some marketers include attitudes in their measurements of lifestyles.

Trends in lifestyles are important to marketers, and they respond to them in a number of ways. Campbell Soup Company introduced its Souper Combo, a microwavable bowl of soup and a sandwich, in Chicago. Sales skyrocketed. But by the time the product was on supermarket shelves nationwide, in 1989, most new food products were emphasizing health—low sodium, few calories, and so on. Souper Combos were regular food, with fat. Campbell therefore canceled the product in late 1990.[17] Concern about cholesterol levels is one reason that annual per capita consumption of chicken rose from forty pounds in 1970 to more than seventy pounds in 1990.[18]

Lifestyles have received a great deal of attention and research from marketers and will be discussed further in chapter 7. Lifestyles evolve from the individual's personality and attitudes, combined with the sociocultural influences discussed in the following section.

SOCIOCULTURAL INFLUENCES ON CONSUMER BEHAVIOR

A consumer's wants, learning experiences, motives, perceptions, attitudes, and personality and lifestyle are influenced by the person's family, reference groups, social class, and culture. The discussions that follow focus on these sociocultural influences on consumer behavior.

The Family

The most basic of all groups to which a person belongs is the family. To make good marketing decisions, marketers must understand that

1. Many buying decisions are made in the family unit.

2. Consumer behavior starts in the family unit. Children learn patterns of marketplace behavior from their parents.

3. The family roles and product preferences children observe are the models they imitate, alter, or reject in establishing their own families. Transmitting brand preferences from one generation to the next to maintain brand loyalty is an important part of the marketer's effort.

4. Family buying decisions are a mixture of family interaction and individual decision making. Products bought on the basis of family interaction must be marketed differently from those bought on the basis of individual decisions.

5. The family acts as an interpreter of cultural and social forces for the individual.

We now look at the family life cycle, the family structure, and the changing roles of family members.

family life cycle

• **The Family Life Cycle** • The series of life stages people pass through is the *family life cycle;* it includes childhood, marriage, childbirth, childrearing, and eventual dissolution of marriage through the death of a spouse or by divorce. It describes the process of family formation and dissolution.

Table 5–1 shows a modernized view of the family life cycle, reflecting both the high divorce rate and the decision of many couples not to have children. One divorce occurs for

TABLE 5–1 ▮ A Modernized View of the Family Life Cycle

....

1. Young single
2. Young married without children
3. Other young
   a. Young divorced without children
   b. Young married with children
   c. Young divorced with children
4. Middle-aged
   a. Middle-aged married without children
   b. Middle-aged divorced without children
   c. Middle-aged married with young and adolescent children
   d. Middle-aged divorced with young and adolescent children
   e. Middle-aged married without dependent children
   f. Middle-aged divorced without dependent children
5. Older
   a. Older married
   b. Older unmarried (divorced, widowed)
6. All other
   All adults and children not accounted for by the family life cycle stages

....

Source: Adapted by permission of the University of Chicago Press. From Patrick E. Murphy and William A. Staples, "A Modernized Family Life Cycle," *Journal of Consumer Research,* June 1979, p. 16.

every two marriages in the United States.[19] Today an estimated 40 percent of people in their twenties are children of divorce.[20]

The singles market is made up of single, separated, widowed, and divorced people. Although people in this group have some wants in common, there are also many differences. For example, a young single's wants will differ in many ways from those of an elderly surviving spouse.

As we will see in chapter 7, the baby boom generation is especially important to many marketers. These 72 million Americans were born between 1946 and 1964. The group is so large that marketers cannot afford to ignore its requirements. Small subgroups within the boomer group are also targeted. An example is the 4 million or so young urban professionals (yuppies) of the mid-1980s. When today's twentysomething generation was born, the baby boom was fading into the so-called baby-bust. This relatively small group is much less understood by marketers than the baby boom group. For the most part, however, baby-busters reject the habits and values of the baby boomers. They tend to view the boomers as self-centered, fickle, and impractical.[21]

Today, 12 percent of the U.S. population (29 million people) is over age sixty-five.[22] The graying of America is also having a major impact on many marketers. The casino town of Laughlin, Nevada, is 90 miles south of Las Vegas. The casino companies here target older gamblers and other cost-conscious players who yearn for the low-key atmosphere of yesterday's Las Vegas.[23]

Longer life expectancy is having an impact too. For example, 5 million Americans will be over the age of eighty-five by the year 2000. In a report issued by the Older Women's League, the president of the league stated, "The empty nest is nothing more than a myth, because if women's nests empty at all they fill again very quickly with elderly parents or other relatives who need care and support.'' The report noted that although care of children and elderly parents is a family issue, three out of every four care givers to the elderly are women.[24]

- **Family Structure** • Your family of orientation—the family into which you were born—influences your views about religion, politics, education, and numerous other elements of your life, including your buying behavior. The family you create through marriage is your family of procreation, a separate economic unit that buys products such as housing, furniture, and home appliances. Its influence on buying behavior is even more direct than that of the family of orientation.

A *nuclear family unit* is composed of a mother, father, and their children. An *extended family unit* consists of the nuclear family unit and grandparents, unmarried aunts and uncles, cousins, married children, and divorced children and their offspring who live with the nuclear family. Four- and five-generation families living under the same roof are rapidly becoming commonplace. At the low end of the age spectrum, teenage pregnancies and out-of-wedlock births are adding new generations to households. At the high end, people are living longer, though they often have chronic illnesses that require constant care. In the middle, couples in their twenties, thirties, and forties are divorcing more often, sending daughters and sons and their children back to the parental nest.[25]

Today only 7 percent of American households fit the 1950s image of breadwinner husband, homemaker wife, and two children. In the current family most children live with parents who both work. One out of two children lives at some point in a one-parent household. During a routine week, most parents juggle up to four different kinds of child care.[26]

- **Changing Roles and Task Sharing** • For many years marketers operated under the assumption that women, mostly ''housewives,'' made about 80 percent of all consumer purchases because they enjoyed the social pleasures of shopping. The typical employed woman in past years was (1) a young and single woman, (2) a married woman who had to work to supplement her husband's income, or (3) a married woman whose husband had died or left home. Women who held jobs outside the home were in the minority.[27]

Today 65 percent of all mothers with children at home are employed.[28] Between now and the end of the century, women will make up 65 percent of the new entrants into the work force.[29] These women have less time for shopping, and their consumer behavior differs significantly from that of the traditional stereotyped housewife.

Children not yet in their teens are shopping and cooking for the family. Sociologists use the term *self-nurturing* to describe children's after-school independence. General Foods is revising its view of mother as the all-powerful gatekeeper of the kitchen. Because of kids' growing influence over food purchases, General Foods is increasingly marketing to children. Kraft is tailoring more of its food advertising to girls twelve to nineteen.[30] Meanwhile, kids as young as six are microwaving their own child-oriented product lines, such as Kid's Kitchen, Kid Cuisine, and My Own Meals.[31]

A recent study by Teenage Research Unlimited of people twelve through nineteen years of age shows that 29 percent of driving-age teens have their own car and 44 percent of teens have their own VCR. About 69 percent help sway family vacation plans. Parents consider their teens to be the experts on such purchases as CD players and TVs. Clearly, teens are buying more big-ticket items for themselves and their families. According to the president of the research firm, ''Unlike their parents, teens have never been intimidated by high technology.[32]

As the Quorum ad suggests, fathers are taking a more active role in raising children, and

An ad that reflects the fact that fathers are taking a more active role in raising children.

(The MacDougall Company.)

this is being increasingly recognized by marketers. United Airlines, for example, installed changing tables in the men's rooms at Los Angeles airports and at Chicago's O'Hare Airport for fathers traveling with babies.[33]

Many marketers are targeting the large number of households with children in which both spouses are employed. Some marketers focus on working parents who feel guilty that they don't have more time to spend with their kids. Parents of "latchkey kids" spend heavily on flashy toys and new clothes to make up for the lack of "quality time" with their kids.[34] Sales of children's personal-care products are growing at an annual rate of more than 10 percent. William & Clarissa sells trendy toiletries under the Kids brand in 20,000 stores nationwide.[35] Some experts say that yuppie parents who purchased products to make up for the lack of time spent with their children paved the way for today's rejection of the yuppie brand of materialism among the twentysomething generation.[36]

Reference Groups

reference group

A family is an example of a reference group. A ***reference group*** is any group that positively or negatively influences a person's attitudes or behavior. It serves as a guide or model for that person. Reference groups vary in size, composition, and structure. They may be membership groups, aspirational groups, or dissociative groups.

A *membership reference group* is a group to which a person formally or actually belongs. The person is perceived and accepted by others as belonging to that group. Families, fraternities, churches, synagogues, and work groups are membership reference groups. *Aspirational reference groups* are groups to which a person wishes (aspires) to belong. Sometimes a person does not wish to be associated with a particular group because the person rejects its values or behaviors; these groups are called *dissociative reference groups*. The person behaves in such a way as to not be associated with the group.

range of acceptable behavior

• **Acceptable Behavior** • The survival of any group depends on its ability to define and enforce group norms. A *range of acceptable behavior,* or a range of group norms, is the limits of a group's values, beliefs, and behaviors, to which members must conform more or less according to their status.

As Figure 5–6 shows, your range of acceptable behavior varies according to your status position in the group. Notice that high-status members (A) have a much wider range of acceptable behavior than people who aspire to group membership or who are new members (C). People in status position C have the narrowest range of acceptable behavior and must conform closely to group norms. Behavior that falls outside the limits set by the group is punished. Buying an inappropriate product, for example, may lead to loss of membership in the group.

• **Psychosocial Risk** • The most important determinant of whether a consumer will be influenced by reference groups in buying a product is the product's conspicuousness—whether it can be seen and identified by others and whether it stands out and attracts attention—in short, its social value. Examples of products with a high social value are cars, houses, clothes, jewelry, beer, colleges, and luggage. Products such as antifreeze, sugar, and light bulbs have little or no social value, and their purchase is not influenced much by reference groups.

Buying decisions for products with high social value are risky for consumers when reference groups lack well-defined norms. The degree of psychosocial risk is determined by the possibility of negative consequences of the purchase decision, the probability of their occurrence, and their severity. Buying a dress for a Christmas party may involve great risk.

FIGURE 5–6

The Relationship between Range of Acceptable Behavior and Status Position in the Group

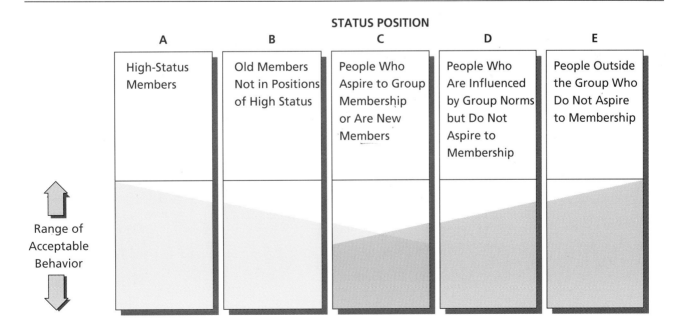

STATUS POSITION

A	B	C	D	E
High-Status Members	Old Members Not in Positions of High Status	People Who Aspire to Group Membership or Are New Members	People Who Are Influenced by Group Norms but Do Not Aspire to Membership	People Outside the Group Who Do Not Aspire to Membership

Range of Acceptable Behavior

Buying peanut butter may involve little or none. Marketers try to reduce the consumer's perceived risk. Women who wanted to wear their leotards with a skirt but were skeptical probably were helped by the ad slogan "Danskins are not just for dancing."

• **Opinion Leadership** •   The values of social groups change. Change usually is introduced by persons who have freedom to behave differently because of their high status, specialized skills, or knowledge. In many cases other members look to these innovators, or opinion leaders, to define what is acceptable behavior. Often this includes advice and information about new products.

Marketers of products such as cosmetics, liquor, tobacco, and high-fashion clothing often target trendy urbanites who are thought to be trend setters. According to the president of Paddington Corporation, which markets J&B scotch: "In the fashion business you want the right people wearing your clothes. We want the right people drinking our scotch." Publications such as *Details* and *L.A. Style* report on the most fashionable nightspots and cater to the irreverent tastes of their readers. For example, *Details* runs a column on cosmetic surgery called "Knifestyles of the Rich and Famous."[37]

Opinion leadership is a shared task. A person with multiple reference groups may turn to several opinion leaders in different groups for advice and information about new products. That person's buying behavior, therefore, cannot be predicted simply on the basis of one opinion leader or one reference group. The person may look to a work associate for advice about life insurance, to a friend for advice about clothes, and to a neighbor for advice about lawn care products.

Reference group influence, however, is not dictatorial. A suburban couple whose friends have all bought camcorders may be under pressure to buy one. The brand, features, when and where they will buy it, and how much they will spend are individual decisions.

The next section looks at a larger grouping of reference groups—social classes. There are several such groupings in the United States. Individuals or families in a given social class are perceived by others in the society to be roughly equal in terms of their social position. A person's or a family's social position is a major influence on consumer behavior.

Social Classes

social classes

Contrary to popular belief, the United States is not a classless society. There is a social class structure, although it is not as rigid as that in many other countries. *Social classes* are the relatively stable and homogeneous divisions in society into which individuals, families, or groups that share similar values, lifestyles, interests, and behaviors can be placed. The social class structure is a larger grouping of reference groups. Its characteristics are as follows: (1) people are conscious of it, (2) social interactions generally occur between people on the same class level, and (3) people within a social class are very much alike in terms of values, interests, and behavior.

Your social class limits the reference groups to which you can belong and influences your future opportunities by the values it places on education and vocational goals. It is the background against which your family unit and reference groups function.

A combination of the following factors, in order of their importance, can be used to measure a family's social class in the United States: (1) occupation, (2) source of income, (3) type of house, (4) dwelling area, (5) education, (6) interaction patterns, (7) kinship, and (8) family ancestry.

• **Social Class Characteristics** •   Table 5–2 summarizes the characteristics of the six social classes in the United States. Although there can be a wide range of behaviors, lifestyles, and incomes within any particular class, the range is wider among classes. The per-

TABLE 5–2 ■ Social Class Structure in the United States

....

Upper Class
_____

Capitalist class (1%): Their investment decisions shape the national economy; income mostly from assets, earned and/or inherited; prestigious university connections.

Upper-middle class (14%): Upper managers, professionals, owners of medium-size businesses; college educated; family income ideally runs nearly twice national average.

Middle Class
_____

Middle class (33%): Middle level white-collar, top level blue-collar; education past high school typical; income somewhat above national average.

Working class (32%): Middle level blue-collar, lower level white-collar; income runs slightly below national average; education is also slightly below.

Marginal and Lower Class
_____

Working poor (11–12%): Below mainstream U.S. living standard, but above the poverty line; low-paid service workers, operatives; some high school.

Underclass (8–9%): Depend primarily on welfare system for sustenance; living standard below poverty line; not regularly employed; lack schooling.

....

Source: Excerpted by permission from Richard P. Coleman, "The Continuing Significance of Social Class to Marketing," *Journal of Consumer Research,* December 1983, p. 267. This class structure was abstracted by Coleman from Dennis Gilbert and Joseph A. Kahl, *The American Class Structure: A New Synthesis* (Homewood, Ill.: Dorsey Press, 1982), chap. 11, "The American Class Structure: A Synthesis." Copyright © 1982 Dorsey Press. Reprinted by permission.

centage figures for each class are not rigid; nor are they reflective of the buying power of the various classes. For example, there is a disproportionately large amount of discretionary income (income remaining after paying taxes and buying necessities) in the upper class.

Keep in mind, however, that no value judgments are associated with the terms *lower, middle,* and *upper.* In other words, it is improper to rationalize that people in higher social classes are happier, more fulfilled, or better than people in lower classes.

One of the most meaningful conclusions to be drawn from the study of social classes is that income alone does not determine consumers' lifestyles or buying behavior. Although there is some general relationship between a person's or a family's income level and social class, the income levels of different people in the same social class can differ greatly. Furthermore, individuals and families can belong to different social classes even if they have similar income levels, and they will tend to spend their money in different ways.

■ **Social Class and Marketing Decision Making** ■ Understanding of social class helps marketers select advertising media (radio, television, newspapers, magazines, and so on) and choose specific stations, newspapers, or magazines that will reach targeted customers. For example, the *New Yorker* is more likely to reach targeted customers in the middle and upper classes than is the *National Enquirer.*

A person's social class is also a good indicator of shopping behavior. Lower-class people tend to shop closer to home, do not use interest rate information as much, do not engage in as much prepurchase information gathering, and have less knowledge of shopping alternatives than higher-class people.

Stores project definite class images. Personnel in higher-status stores, such as Neiman-Marcus, behave differently and look different from those in middle- or lower-class stores. Higher-class stores smell different and have less merchandise in the display windows. Width of aisles, lighting, and choice of materials and fixtures affect consumers' perceptions of store status.

As we will see in chapter 7, an understanding of social class helps marketers select their target markets. The similarities in selecting and using products and the goals of each class suggest that social class measures can be used to divide a large market into smaller segments, each of which is made up of people who are similar in terms of the characteristics that were used to divide the overall market.

The family, reference groups, and social classes are social influences on consumer behavior. They all operate within a larger culture. In the next section we take a closer look at culture and how it influences consumer behavior.

Culture

culture

Consumer behavior is the individual's attempt to obtain satisfactions for needs. Culture determines the products available for satisfying those needs and the behaviors used to obtain these satisfactions. *Culture* is the sum total of knowledge, beliefs, values, customs, and artifacts that we use to adapt to our environment and that we hand down to succeeding generations. As is clear from the Global Marketing box, culture also determines what is acceptable in advertising products.

As we will see in greater detail in chapter 22, international marketers must be especially sensitive to cultural differences in the countries in which they do business. These differences sometimes can be very great. For example, in Saudi Arabia women cannot drive,

By now everybody is used to Super Bowl promotions for such products as beer, soft drinks, and cars. The 1990 Super Bowl was different. It marked the first Super Bowl tie-in by a laxative. The "Phillips Milk of Magnesia Super Bowl Flush" was a contest. Radio disc jockeys in nine cities asked listeners to call in to name the most frequently performed activity during the Super Bowl. (The answer is toilet flushing.) In mid-January 1990 Phillips held a drawing of all those who gave correct answers. Nine lucky winners got tickets to the Super Bowl.

Advertisers in the United States used to tiptoe around such words as *laxative, toilet paper,* and *diarrhea.* Suddenly, makers of toilet paper and laxatives and other digestive cures are positively reveling in bathroom talk. The spate of new ads caused some people to ask just how far the limits of good taste could be stretched. Others insisted that this was just the beginning of what was to come in the 1990s.

Procter & Gamble tested a TV commercial for its Charmin bathroom tissue showing a clown using the toilet in a men's room. The spot depicted the clown entering the men's room and closing the door of the stall. His head soon pops up over the door, though, with a red face and steam pouring out of his ears— apparently because the toilet paper he's using isn't Charmin. The ad's tagline: "Life without Charmin can really be a pain."

Upjohn's Kaopectate began running its first-ever commercial in which an actor announces he has diarrhea. A man going through customs at an airport is asked by the customs agent if he has anything to declare. His succinct answer: "Diarrhea." And Milk of Magnesia introduced a commercial focusing on an immobile roll of toilet paper that starts moving after its constipated owner takes a dose of the stuff.

Advertising is becoming more and more global in nature. The new frankness in ads for bathroom products in the United States reflects the influence of European advertising. In Europe, bodily functions are described with sometimes alarming candor.

Source: Adapted from JoAnne Lipman, "Bathroom Is No Longer Taboo as Subject for Ads," *Wall Street Journal,* January 19, 1990, p. B4. Reprinted by permission of the *Wall Street Journal,* © Dow Jones & Company, Inc., 1990. All rights reserved.

drink alcohol, vote, sit in a theater or on a beach with a man, or even show their face and hair. Saudi men cannot drink alcohol and must adhere to a rigid dress code. During the Persian Gulf war, there were many instances where the American and Saudi cultures clashed because of different perspectives on the role of women—especially female U.S. soldiers.[38]

• **Cultural Values** • Among important cultural values in the United States are good health, education, freedom, and, as suggested in the Ryder ad, individualism. Quality in the goods and services we buy is also a cultural value. *Cultural values* are values that result from assigning worth to objects or behaviors on the basis of need satisfaction; objects and behaviors that are highly valued are transmitted to succeeding generations.

Valued objects in primitive cultures are related directly to the physiological and safety

cultural values

First, I accepted the promotion. Then, it hit me. A new job in a new city meant moving to a new apartment. And I have so much stuff, I didn't know where to begin. But you know what they say: "If you want something done right, do it yourself." So I did.

When you move, rely on Ryder to help. Our handbook will guide you through a smooth and successful move. For a free copy, call 1-800-327-3399.

RYDER.
We're there at every turn™

An ad that reflects the cultural value of individualism.

(Ogilvy & Mather for Ryder Truck Rental, Inc.)

needs in Maslow's hierarchy. Camels, goats, and yaks are the units of wealth, status, and exchange. By contributing meat, milk, hides, and hair, they are crucial to the continued existence of people. Valued objects in more industrialized cultures often satisfy higher-order needs; they may include continuing education programs, travel, and vacation homes.

Behaviors that satisfy needs are highly valued and are transmitted to succeeding generations. Those that are inappropriate for foreseeable future circumstances are not transmitted. Some behaviors, however, become so highly valued that they are transmitted to succeeding generations even when they are no longer functional. Hunting was a necessary skill for survival during the frontier period. It no longer serves a survival function but is a major sport supporting several industries, including camping equipment, firearms, and outdoor clothing.

Often the young are taught to believe in and strive for the attainment of certain behaviors passed down but no longer functional. These often become cultural myths that can be used to market many products. By developing products that incorporate the myths into their design, marketers can decrease the expense and time necessary to build product acceptance. Tying products to cultural myths through ad campaigns can create customer loyalty or develop new markets for existing products. The "Marlboro man" in cigarette ads is a variation of the rugged individualist ideal of masculinity.

Cultural values are resistant to change, but they can and often do change over time. Our cultural values with respect to such things as marriage, children, work and leisure, and civil rights have changed over time.

West Germany emerged several years ago as one of the world's richest nations. It enjoyed the largest trade surplus, the greatest per capita concentration of high-performance cars, the best wages for the shortest workweek, and the most rewarding all-round standard of living among major industrialized nations. In the early 1960s the average German family spent half its income on food and household goods; today the figure is slightly over 20 percent. Nearly as much—15 percent—is devoted to leisure activities and holidays. According to a recent survey, modern Germany "has changed from a working society to a leisure society." The average person devotes 4 hours a day to leisure activities, in contrast to about 1.5 hours forty years ago. This new leisure can be seen in lingering lunch breaks, overflowing cafes, and empty offices and on packed golf courses or deserted city streets on weekends. Although the people work less, they manage to produce more and still maintain quality.[39]

subculture

• **Subcultures** • There are many subcultures in the United States, in addition to the dominant culture. A *subculture* is a group that shares values and behavior patterns that differ in important ways from those of the dominant culture.

We must use a combination of such factors as age, social class, religion, geographic location, family size, and national origin to identify a subculture. Among the many U.S. subcultures are the Hispanic, teenage, elderly, and Native American subcultures. Although members of a subculture share many of the values held by people in the dominant culture, they also have many of their own.

The people within a particular subculture tend to be very similar with respect to certain characteristics, such as attitudes and values. By studying the subcultures that exist within

Marketers who target native Americans must have an indepth understanding of their traditions and values.

[© J. B. Diederich]

the dominant culture, marketers can develop marketing mixes that are tailored to a subculture's wants.

Cultural diversity is a source of opportunities and challenges for marketers. A hospital in a large urban market wanted to design promotion strategies for a rapidly growing number of young African-American, Hispanic, and Asian patients. Management assumed it could use the same message it had targeted to whites, merely substituting pictures of African-Americans, Hispanics, and Asians. The hospital's promotion was based on the concept of caring and responsive service delivery. But research showed the use of African-American models and testimonials would not be sufficient. A combination of focus groups and personal interviews indicated that minorities wanted to know that the hospital was first-rate in services, that its equipment was up-to-date, and that its medical procedures were state-of-the-art. The hospital would come across as a caring hospital only if it demonstrated a commitment to being a leading care resource. That image, however, could not be sold simply by saying so in ads.[40]

Los Angeles County's major ethnic groups have grown tremendously in recent years. Many of the new arrivals cling to their ethnic identity, preserving their language and customs. As one second-generation Chinese American in the county remarked: "We do not think in American terms of a melting pot. We prefer the metaphor of a rainbow or a salad."[41] Marketers who seek customers in ethnic subcultures must recognize that the melting-pot concept is a myth and that multilingual or multicultural marketing mixes are often required.

SUMMARY OF LEARNING OBJECTIVES

1. Understand and use a simplified model of the consumer decision-making framework.

The model shows the major influences on consumer buying decisions. At its center is the consumer decision maker. The personal influences on consumer buying decisions are motivation, perception, learning, personality and lifestyles, and attitudes. The sociocultural influences are family, reference group, social class, and culture. The interaction of personal and sociocultural influences affects consumers' buying decisions.

2. Contrast complex and programmed decisions.

Complex decisions are decisions that consumers make through extensive problem solving rather than through routine behavior. Programmed decisions are routine decisions that result from the learning process consumers engage in when making complex decisions. Programmed decisions differ from complex decisions in that they usually are not difficult to make; do not involve high economic, performance, or psychological risk; and are made frequently.

3. Explain the meaning of cognitive dissonance and how consumers and marketers attempt to reduce it.

Cognitive dissonance is the state of psychological tension or post-purchase doubt that a consumer experiences after making a difficult purchasing choice. Consumers try to reduce dissonance by reevaluating the information they obtained prior to the decision and by searching for more information. Marketers can help consumers

reduce dissonance by providing information consumers can use to reduce it and by ensuring that poor product performance is corrected as soon as possible. They can also use post-purchase communications such as letters and brochures to help buyers reduce dissonance.

4. Identify and analyze the personal influences on consumer behavior.

The personal influences are learning, motivation, perception, attitudes, and personality and lifestyles. *Learning* is the process through which a relatively permanent change in behavior results from the consequences of past behavior. *Motivation* is the driving force that causes a person to take action to satisfy specific needs. *Perception* is the process through which an individual selects relevant stimuli (information) from the environment, organizes them, and assigns meaning to them. *Attitudes* are enduring feelings, evaluations, and response tendencies directed toward an object or idea. *Personality* is the collection of relatively permanent tendencies to behave in consistent ways in certain situations. *Lifestyles* are the consistent patterns that people follow in their lives, including how they spend their time and money, and are identified through people's activities, interests, and opinions of themselves and the world around them.

5. Identify and analyze the sociocultural influences on consumer behavior.

The sociocultural influences are family, reference groups, social class, and culture. The most basic of all groups to which a person belongs is the *family*. A *reference group* is any group that positively or negatively influences a person's attitudes or behavior. *Social classes* are the relatively stable and homogeneous divisions in society into which individuals, families, or groups that share similar values, lifestyles, interests, and behaviors can be placed. *Culture* is the sum total of knowledge, beliefs, values, customs, and artifacts that we use to adapt to our environment and that we hand down to succeeding generations.

Review Questions

1. How do complex decisions differ from programmed decisions?

2. What are the stages in the decision-making process for complex decisions? Explain each stage.

3. What is cognitive dissonance? How can consumers and marketers reduce it?

4. "The only way for consumers to learn is through direct experience." Do you agree? Why or why not?

5. How do primary buying motives and selective buying motives differ?

6. Is perception a selective process? Explain.

7. "It is easy for marketers to change consumers' attitudes through advertising." Do you agree? Why or why not?

8. What is the family life cycle?

9. What is the meaning of *range of acceptable behavior* in the context of reference groups?

10. How does an understanding of the social class structure in the United States helps marketers in their decision making? Give an example.

11. What are cultural values?

12. What is a subculture?

Discussion Questions

1. Give an example from your own experience of a programmed decision shifting to a complex decision. Also give an example of a complex decision becoming programmed.

2. In 1968 Abbie Hoffman was arrested for wearing an American flag shirt. The Vietnam-era censorship gave the shirt instant cachet among political activists. During recent years, however, flag fashion in apparel has been popular. How would you explain this in terms of symbolic meaning?

3. More and more consumers and businesses are changing their attitudes toward the environment and are expressing concerns about environmental issues. What are the implications for consumer buying behavior? What about business behavior?

4. Visit a local supermarket to observe the great variety of cat food available for purchase. Many more brands and varieties of food are available today than were available twenty years ago. How does this greater variety affect buyer behavior?

Application Exercise

Reread the material about yuppies at the beginning of this chapter and answer the following questions:

1. What are the implications for marketers of family values replacing the quest for individual gratification among aging baby boomers?

2. Are the functional meanings of products becoming more important than the subjective meanings? Explain.

3. Are brands that start out as status symbols inevitably going to end up being targeted to the mass market? Explain.

Key Concepts

The following key terms were introduced in this chapter:

consumer behavior
complex decisions
cognitive dissonance
programmed decisions
learning
motivation
hierarchy of needs

perception
semantic differential scales
attitudes
personality
self-concept
lifestyles
family life cycle

reference group
range of acceptable behavior
social classes
culture
cultural values
subculture

CASES

Environmentally Mean or Truly "Green"?

Today, landfills in the East are overflowing and garbage dumps in the Midwest are expected to be tapped out by 1994 or 1995. Does it take this situation to get the couch-potato segment of the population to change their buying habits? Or, have consumers sincerely embraced the "green" movement by changing their buying behavior? It's debatable.

Despite all the environmental hoopla bombarding consumers in the early 1990s, as corporations scramble to develop earth-safe brands and packaging, curbside recycling services grow, and the media overflows with environmental advertising and information, "actual support for the environmental movement in this country is about one inch deep," says Alan Caruba, executive director of the National Anxiety Center. In other words, pretty shallow. "People's commitments to this are just not there, as indicated by the enormous numbers of inefficient cars they drive, tobaccos they consume, and disposable products they still buy."

A different viewpoint is expressed by Jonathan Asher, vice president for marketing services at Gerstman-Meyers, a New York package-design consulting firm that monitors consumer and corporate attitudes and behavior on environmental trends. His firm's annual study showed that about 84 percent of consumers are changing some buying patterns due to their concern about environmental issues. He illustrates the consumer decision-making framework with the statement, "Attitudes come first, behavior follows."

He admits, however, that the factor that may finally force the masses to consciously buy environmentally safe products will be the increased cost of garbage removal. Furthermore, Asher concedes that some consumers, as well as manufacturers and retailers, "are waiting for the government to come in and set up ground rules." One reason some consumers aren't fully committed is that they're misinformed. Many consumers don't realize, for example, that plastics can be as or more recyclable than paper and paperboard. All in all, Asher believes that Americans are making great strides and that more and better information will increase awareness and change buying habits. What do you think?

Questions

1. How do the concepts of perception and selective exposure affect a consumer's decision to purchase or ignore environmentally safe products?

2. How do consumers' reference groups influence them to change/not change their buying behavior concerning "green" products?

3. How is the environmental movement consistent with the 1990s lifestyle trend?

4. How do marketers use symbolic meaning on packaging to emphasize their products' environmentally safe qualities? Give two or three examples of methods used.

Marketing to Hispanics

About 25 million Spanish-speaking people live in the United States, and according to the Bureau of Labor Statistics, Hispanics will compose 10 percent of the workforce by the end of the nineties. The Hispanic subculture is the fastest-growing minority in the United States.

With so large a potential target market, we might expect that companies would be clamoring for a share, but that is not happening. On a national level, only a few very large companies direct advertising to Spanish speakers, and they tend to be sellers of staples rather than of specifically Hispanic-oriented products. Procter & Gamble, Kraft, AT&T, Kinney Shoes, Coca Cola, Anheuser-Busch, and Burger King are some prominent contributors to national advertising campaigns directed at Hispanics.

Why aren't there more advertisers? There are several reasons. Hispanics are generally considered to have much in common. They share a language, most have similar cultural backgrounds, and they are more likely to be Catholic than the rest of the popu-

lation. They tend to value strong nuclear families, and their divorce rate is lower than average. These similarities should help companies develop marketing campaigns with wide appeal.

Marketing to Hispanics should also be aided by the growth in Spanish-language media in recent years. Two national television networks, Telemundo and Univision, have become accessible to most TV markets thanks to the widespread availability of cable TV. At the same time, national Hispanic magazines, such as the family-oriented *La Familia de Hoy* and *Mi Bebe,* have provided vehicles for national marketing campaigns.

But Hispanics, along with having much in common, are also diverse. Although they share a common language, Mexicans, Puerto Ricans, Cubans, and El Salvadorans, for example, speak quite different dialects and have somewhat different concerns. In fact, in Los Angeles, Mexican-Americans are protesting that both Telemundo and Univision are too heavily dominated by Cubans and Cuban interests.

Furthermore, most Hispanics are bilingual, and many advertisers believe that bilingual Hispanics, especially younger ones who are products of U.S. education, can be reached by general English-language marketing efforts. This is especially true since younger Hispanics—who are more likely than older Hispanics to spend their money—tend not to use the Spanish-language media as much as their elders.

In spite of difficulties in determining just how to reach the Hispanic market, some experts hold that marketers should use Spanish in their efforts. According to Teresa Ménendez, president of Ménendez International, Miami, a Spanish message tells the potential consumer that ''the manufacturer thinks the Hispanic market is important enough to recognize with a piece of advertising.''

Questions

1. What are some arguments in favor of marketing campaigns directed at Hispanics?

2. To what Hispanic cultural values might a marketer direct a marketing campaign?

3. What information would you, as a marketer, want to acquire before creating a marketing campaign directed at a Hispanic audience?

4. What kinds of products could be marketed just as well in English as in Spanish to a Hispanic audience?

6

ORGANIZATIONAL MARKETS AND BUYING BEHAVIOR

OBJECTIVES

After reading this chapter you will be able to

1. distinguish between the consumer market and organizational markets.

2. describe the major characteristics of the industrial market.

3. explain the industrial procurement process in terms of the types of industrial buying situations.

4. identify and explain the steps in the industrial procurement process.

5. identify and explain the participants in industrial buying decisions.

6. identify important purchasing decision criteria.

7. explain why consumer and industrial marketing mixes are typically different.

"We're interested in marriages," says James Blue, "not weekend romances." Blue is general manager of the Boeing Commercial Airplane Group's Materiel Division. He does business with at least 3,500 suppliers to Boeing.

Most important, Blue is at the forefront of forging Japanese-style relationships between Boeing and its suppliers. He does this by working with the suppliers early in the design stages and by awarding them long-term contracts that they can take to their bankers. His twofold goal: locking in favorable prices and getting a better handle on quality control.

Prior to 1984 Boeing's purchasing was done by each individual airliner program. The people in charge of building 747s, for example, would take care of their procurement needs. Likewise with the 757 team, the 737 team, and so on. But as the Commercial Airplane Group began growing rapidly, it became obvious that procurement needed to be brought under centralized control. The 400-passenger 747-400, for example, contains some 6 million parts, which come from more than 1,500 suppliers. The Materiel Division was created to source and keep track of all these components intelligently.

The change made sense and was long overdue. After all, some 40 percent of an airplane's cost is controlled by this division. Recalls Blue, "We realized that this [procurement control] is where the leverage is." So for the first time, for example, Boeing's buyers could combine similar parts orders for various jet models and get more competitive prices than if they had bought the items separately.

Blue took over the Materiel Division in early 1987 and began pushing the ideas of longer-term contracts and of involving the suppliers as early as possible in the actual design and engineering of parts changes—and, most important, in the specifications for its new planes.

In the past, building planes was like building houses: There were commonly six hundred or more requests from customers for changes from the basic specifications. From now on, however, Boeing customers will have less of a free hand in designing their planes. The general manager of Boeing's New Airplane Division came up with the idea of a catalog that the customer can use to pick options. That way both the customer and Boeing can keep track of their cost. With the catalog the number of change requests on the 747-400 (such as the types of lavatories and the location of galleys) has been reduced to fifty or less.

Boeing has also found that more secure contracts increase its own efficiency by smoothing out shipping and supply glitches. Several years ago, when Boeing foresaw the development of a critical shortage of galleys, seats, and lavatories, for example, it dispatched teams to overseas suppliers to get them to increase capacity. In a year the suppliers of these key components boosted production and capacity by nearly 50 percent. Boeing has about 125 experts around the world whose job is to keep their eyes on suppliers and offer help when needed. Early in 1989 Boeing was battling a thousand parts shortages on the 747-400. The company had shaved that to about thirty late in 1990.[1]

Boeing, an industrial marketer, sells planes to airlines, which are industrial buyers. Clearly, much of Boeing's success hinges on how effectively it works with its suppliers in performing the procurement function. Boeing and its suppliers have a mutually beneficial type of partnership arrangement. Boeing benefits from the close supplier–buyer relationship in that the company achieves favorable prices from suppliers and better quality control. Boeing's suppliers benefit from getting a better handle on Boeing's purchase requirements (getting close to their customer) and from long-term contracts the suppliers can use to help secure financing from banks. Ultimate consumers, of course, do not buy planes from Boeing.

Up to this point we have focused on the consumer market. In this chapter, however, we deal with the major types and characteristics of organizational markets. We also examine the procurement function in considerable detail. We conclude with a brief comparison of consumer and organizational marketing mixes.

ORGANIZATIONAL MARKETS

Buyers in the consumer market buy products for personal or household consumption. Buyers in organizational markets buy products to satisfy the needs of the organizations to which they belong. These needs can be classified into three product types:

1. Products needed to make other consumer or industrial products, such as the jet engines Pratt & Whitney sells to Boeing.

2. Products needed to carry on the organization's operations, such as the computers American Airlines buys to operate its reservations system.

3. Products bought for resale, such as the hardware items that K mart buys for resale to its customers.

Many marketers sell in both consumer and organizational markets. Goodyear, for example, sells auto tires through its Goodyear stores to ultimate consumers. It also sells tires to

TABLE 6–1 ■ Standard Industrial Classification (SIC) Divisions and Code Numbers

Divisions	Code Numbers
Agriculture, forestry, and fishing	01–09
Mining	10–14
Construction	15–17
Manufacturing	20–39
Transportation, communications, electric, gas, and sanitary services	40–49
Wholesale trade	50–51
Retail trade	52–59
Finance, insurance, and real estate	60–67
Services	70–89
Public administration	91–97
Nonclassifiable establishments	99

Source: Executive Office of the President, Office of Management and Budget, Standard Industrial Classification Manual, 1987.

automobile manufacturers, which are organizational buyers. ServiceMaster has separate divisions for consumer services and industrial services.[2]

Sometimes marketers switch their focus. Cellular phone companies are targeting the consumer market in order to expand beyond the organizational market.[3] Business travelers fled Continental Airlines in the mid-1980s because the airline targeted leisure travelers with low fares and low service. Early in 1991 Continental announced that it was phasing in a host of improvements to attract business travelers.[4]

All buyers other than ultimate consumers are organizational buyers. *Organizational marketing* is the branch of marketing that is concerned with providing products to all buyers except ultimate consumers. Sometimes it is referred to as *business-to-business marketing*.

organizational marketing

Because of the wide diversity of customers in organizational markets, the markets can be divided in many ways. The *Standard Industrial Classification (SIC) system* is a system developed by the U.S. Bureau of the Census that breaks down organizational markets into eleven major industries, with further divisions into subindustries and products.

Standard Industrial Classification (SIC) system

The SIC classifies industries according to the product produced or the operation performed at each "establishment" in the United States. A code is assigned to each establishment, which can be a factory, mine, farm, bank, mill, store, college, and so on. Thus a manufacturing company that has several plants will be assigned several codes. The code assigned to each of its establishments depends on the principal product produced there.

Notice in Table 6–1 that manufacturing is assigned codes 20–39. Major group 28 of the manufacturing code is chemicals and allied products, industry group number 281 is industrial inorganic chemicals, and industry number 2812 is alkalines and chlorine.

We now focus on three major types of organizational markets: (1) the industrial market, (2) the reseller market, and (3) the government market. (See Figure 6–1.)

The Industrial Market

As Figure 6–1 indicates, the *industrial market* is made up of buyers from all the industries represented in Table 6–1, except for wholesale and retail trade, government, and nonclassifiable establishments. The agriculture, forestry, fishing, mining, construction, and

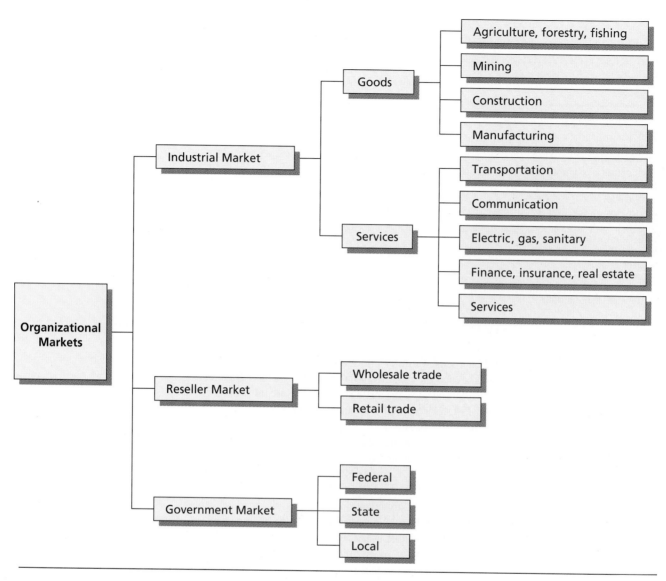

FIGURE 6–1

Types of Organizational
Markets

**value added by
manufacturing**

manufacturing industries turn out goods and account for just under half of all the industrial firms. The rest is accounted for by industries that deal primarily in services. The industrial market is both the largest and the most diverse of the three major types of organizational markets.

The largest dollar volume of purchases in the industrial market is accounted for by manufacturers. Two-thirds of the manufacturing plants in the United States have fewer than 20 employees. Only 5 percent of them have more than 250 employees. But this small percentage of larger manufacturing plants accounts for about 65 percent of total value added by manufacturing.

Value added by manufacturing is the worth added to a product as a result of processing or manufacturing operations that caused a change in the product's form utility. Clearly a very small percentage of manufacturers accounts for a very large percentage of the value added by manufacturing. In other words, there is a great deal of concentration in terms of value added by manufacturing. Because these large manufacturers represent such huge sales potential, industrial marketers often create tailor-made marketing mixes for each potential customer.

An important distinction to marketers who sell to manufacturers is that between original equipment manufacturers and user accounts. An *original equipment manufacturer (OEM)* is a firm that buys industrial products from a supplier and incorporates them into the product it produces and markets. Automobile components manufacturers view car manufacturers as OEMs because the components the car manufacturers buy become part of the vehicles they offer for sale.

Those same car manufacturers, however, can be viewed by some suppliers as user accounts. A *user account* is a manufacturer that buys industrial products that facilitate the manufacturer's production process but are not incorporated into the product the manufacturer markets. Thus car manufacturers are user accounts to marketers of robots and machine tools.

Industrial marketers often sell to both OEMs and user accounts. A manufacturer of temperature controls may sell the controls to manufacturers of large commercial air-conditioning units, which incorporate the controls into their products. These customers are OEMs. But when the temperature controls manufacturer sells the controls to a cold storage warehouse operator who uses them to regulate temperature in a warehouse, the customer is a user account. Different marketing mixes are needed to serve these different target markets.

Manufacturers often distinguish between an original equipment market and a replacement market. As we mentioned earlier, Goodyear sells tires as component parts (an industrial product) to auto manufacturers in the original equipment market. Goodyear, however, also sells tires to consumers (a consumer product) in the replacement market, or aftermarket. Again, different marketing mixes are needed. Also, developments in one market can affect the other market. For example, tire producers in 1990 found that excess capacity coupled with weak car sales led producers to dump tires intended for the original equipment market into the replacement market. This action drove prices down in the replacement market.[5]

As we saw earlier, the industrial market is the largest and most diverse of the three major types of organizational markets. The sections that follow take a look at some of the major characteristics of the industrial market that distinguish it from the consumer market. Figure 6–2 summarizes these characteristics.

Some of the characteristics are descriptive of all three major types of organizational markets. For example, buyers in industrial, reseller, and government markets are professionals who engage in more specification buying, handle more complex negotiations, and make greater use of leasing than do ultimate consumers.

• **Derived Demand** • The demand for industrial products is a derived demand; it results from the demand for consumer products. *Derived demand* is a situation in which the demand for one product results from the existing demand for another product. If there were no demand for cars, there would be no demand for the component parts, such as tires and headlights, made by automotive suppliers.

Aluminum is used as a component material in manufacturing cars, appliances, and beverage containers. Thus changes in the demand for automobiles and appliances, as well as changes in consumer preferences for packaging materials, cause changes in the demand for aluminum.

original equipment manufacturer (OEM)

user account

derived demand

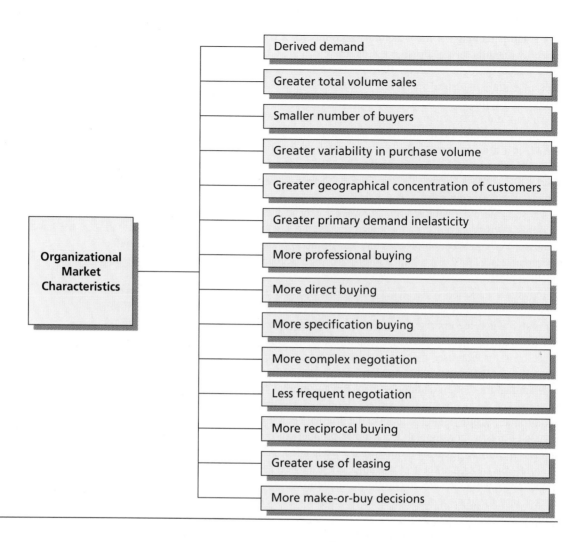

FIGURE 6–2
· ·

Characteristics of the
Industrial Market ▪

Given the nature of derived demand, industrial marketers should gain an in-depth understanding of their own customers—and their customers' customers, and so on—until they reach the ultimate consumer. Most industrial buyers would prefer to deal with a supplier that understands the requirements of both the industrial buyer and the buyer's customers.[6]

Briggs & Stratton Corporation advertises its lawn mower engines to encourage consumers to buy lawn mowers with Briggs & Stratton engines. The firm also promotes its engines to original equipment manufacturers, such as Toro Company, that use engines as component parts in their lawn mowers.

Figure 6–3 shows that a mild increase in consumer demand is magnified into a steep increase in demand in the industrial market. Notice also that a mild decrease in consumer demand leads to a much steeper decrease in demand in the industrial market. When it appears that a boom is just beginning in sales of home appliances, appliance manufacturers revise their sales forecasts upward. The tendency is to be optimistic, and the purchasing department is instructed to increase inventories of component parts. Thus the anticipated increase in sales in the consumer market leads to a big boom in the components market.

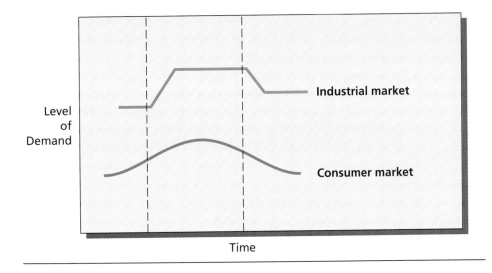

FIGURE 6–3

Derived Demand

The situation also works in reverse. When sales start to taper off in the consumer mar-ket, appliance manufacturers drastically cut back on inventories of component parts to avoid being caught with excess inventories. They are as pessimistic in reducing their inven-tories as they had been optimistic in increasing them.

Derived demand is a factor in the business cycle. A sharp drop in ultimate consumer demand for new cars leads automakers to cut back on employment and output. They will buy less steel, and steel producers will buy less coal to fire their blast furnaces. Coal mining firms will lay off workers, and this leads to reduced buying of all types of consumer prod-ucts. Manufacturers of auto components, such as batteries and tires, will also cut production.

These examples illustrate the interdependence of U.S. industry. The cutback in coal production in our example was caused by an event far removed from the coal industry—a decline in the demand for cars. Fluctuations in consumer demand send out shock waves in the industrial market that tend to magnify the further back we get from the ultimate con-sumer. Consumer confidence in the economy can produce extreme optimism among businesspeople, and the lack of it can lead to extreme pessimism. Thus we often refer to the industrial market as a boom-or-bust industry.

• **Greater Total Sales Volume** • Total dollar sales in the industrial market are greater than total dollar sales in the consumer market, even though there are far fewer industrial buyers than ultimate consumers. A car bought by an ultimate consumer counts as one sale in the consumer market. But many sales transactions occurred in the process of manufac-turing that car. Iron ore was mined and sold to a steel producer, which in turn sold steel to the automaker. Hundreds of other industrial transactions also occurred before the car rolled off the assembly-line.

• **Smaller Number of Buyers** • A typical industrial marketer sells to a much smaller number of buyers than a typical consumer products marketer would. In some cases an industrial marketer may have only one major customer. Firms that sell to industrial buyers usually have less trouble identifying potential customers than do firms that sell to ultimate consumers. Millions of consumers buy General Electric home appliances, but there are far fewer potential buyers for GE's aircraft engines.

• **Greater Variability in Purchase Volume** • There is greater variability among industrial buyers in their purchase volume than there is in the consumer market. An automobile components manufacturer might sell thousands of units of a particular component part to an auto manufacturer in the original equipment market under a multiyear contract. It might also sell a much smaller number to an automobile parts wholesaler in a one-time sale in the after-market. A do-it-yourself mechanic might buy that part at a retail auto parts dealer only once during the life of a car.

Because of this variability in purchase volume, industrial marketers often develop different marketing mixes for different customers, based on the customers' purchase volume. Many industries offer a high degree of concentration—a few firms may account for the bulk of the industry's sales and purchases.

• **Greater Geographical Concentration of Customers** • Industrial buyers are geographically concentrated. Manufacturers are concentrated in the metropolitan areas of big industrial East–North Central states, Middle Atlantic states, and California. Over half are located in seven states: New York, California, Pennsylvania, Illinois, Ohio, New Jersey, and Michigan.

There is also considerable geographical concentration in some industries. For example, the aircraft and microelectronics industries are concentrated on the West Coast. New York and Chicago are important financial centers; Tulsa, Dallas, and Houston are important petroleum centers. A large proportion of the agricultural output of the United States is accounted for by relatively few states. Of the beer manufactured in the United States in 1990, 53 percent was produced in five states—Colorado, Texas, California, New York, and Wisconsin.[7]

• **Greater Primary Demand Inelasticity** • As we will explain more fully in chapter 18, the demand for a product is *price elastic* when (1) a price cut causes total revenue (price per unit times the number of units sold) to increase or (2) a price hike causes total revenue to decrease. The demand is *price inelastic* when (1) a price cut causes total revenue to decrease or (2) a price hike causes total revenue to increase.

Because of the derived demand for industrial products, industrial marketers have less opportunity to stimulate *primary demand* (demand for a product category) through price cuts than do consumer product marketers. Thus the primary demand for industrial products is more price inelastic than the primary demand for consumer products.

For example, auto manufacturers buy headlights as component parts for automobiles. If the price of headlights goes down, the manufacturers are unlikely to increase their purchases of headlights greatly. If they expect the price cut to be temporary, they may stockpile some—but this merely amounts to a change in the *timing* of orders, not an overall increase in the long-run *volume* of purchases. The cost of headlights accounts for a small part of the total cost of producing a car, and a reduction of a few cents in the selling price of cars is unlikely to stimulate car sales. Furthermore, the price of headlights could go up considerably before it would have much effect on sales of headlights.

But when substitutes are available for a particular industrial product, price increases often will lead to reduced sales as buyers switch to the substitutes. Also, price can play a crucial role in selecting suppliers. Although the overall demand for headlights (primary demand) is highly inelastic, the demand for each producer's brand of headlights (selective demand) is price elastic. Thus a headlight supplier whose price is less than that of rival producers offering comparable quality and service is likely to make more sales.

• **More Professional Buying** • Industrial buyers generally take a more formalized approach to buying than ultimate consumers do. For more costly and complex purchases, buying committees, made up of people with various types of expertise, often participate in the buying decision. Industrial buyers are professional buyers, and selling to them requires professional salespeople.

The professionals who handle the buying for their organizations are called purchasing agents, or purchasing managers. The National Association of Purchasing Management (NAPM), a professional organization, awards purchasing managers who meet its certification requirements the Certified Purchasing Manager (CPM) designation. The Ethics in Marketing box presents the NAPM's Principles and Standards of Purchasing Practice.

• **More Direct Buying** • Most ultimate consumers buy products from retailers instead of directly from producers. But many industrial buyers buy products directly from producers. Consumers who are do-it-yourself auto mechanics buy their repair and replacement parts from retail stores. Automobile manufacturers buy component parts directly from manufacturers. The larger the purchase volume, the more complex and costly the industrial product, and the more after-sale service it requires, the more likely it will be bought directly from the producer.

• **More Specification Buying** • Industrial marketers also engage in more production to order than consumer product marketers. A firm that manufactures products for Sears will follow Sears's specifications in producing the product. This type of purchasing is often called *contract buying,* or *specification buying.* Cargill is the largest grain seller in the world and the largest egg producer in the United States. The eggs it sells under the Sunny Fresh label are produced by contract growers who raise the chickens according to Cargill's specifications.[8]

Hershey sold a lot of Desert Bars to the U.S. Army during operations Desert Shield and Desert Storm. Designed to meet the Army's specifications for "heat-resistant" milk chocolate that tastes good, the Desert Bar could stand up to temperatures of well over 100 degrees without melting.[9]

• **More Complex Negotiation** • Considerable buyer-seller negotiation exists in the purchase and sale of many industrial products, especially expensive and complicated products. Product specifications, delivery dates, payment terms, and price may be subject to negotiation. In many cases buyer representatives will meet with seller representatives to negotiate sales contracts. This negotiation may continue over several months. Thus a considerable amount of time can pass between the industrial salesperson's first sales call and the prospective customer's decision to buy or not buy.[10]

General Electric and Pratt & Whitney are the world's two leading aircraft engine makers. Both firms competed to design the engine for Japan's FSX fighter plane. The Japan Defense Agency awarded the contract to General Electric after a three-year battle between the two firms for the business.[11]

• **Less Frequent Negotiation** • Computer-assisted buying is becoming more prevalent in the industrial market, mainly in purchasing frequently used maintenance, repair, and operating supplies (MRO items). In order to match these buyers' requirements more effectively and efficiently, many suppliers have entered into long-term contractual relationships with buyers. One approach is called blanket ordering. ***Blanket ordering*** is a procurement method in which the buyer and supplier enter into a long-term contract under which the supplier offers speedy and reliable delivery or a reduced price for repeat purchases of supplies and the buyer must use that supplier for the duration of the agreement.

In many cases buyers enter into annual vendor contracts. Blanket ordering simplifies the buyer's inventory management and reduces purchasing costs while it helps the seller develop customer loyalty and reduce selling costs through less frequent negotiation.

- **More Reciprocal Buying** • As we will see later in the chapter, there is a good deal of reciprocal buying in industrial marketing. A marketer may buy from its supplier primarily because that supplier also buys from the marketer.

- **Greater Use of Leasing** • An alternative to purchasing is ***leasing***—a renting arrangement in which a lessor grants use of a product to a lessee for a period of time in return for stated regular payments. The lessee rents the product instead of owning it. Businesses and other organizations lease computers, trucks, photocopying equipment, cars, and airplanes. Approximately 40 percent of all passenger jets flying are leased by the airlines.[12] The Ryder ad invites prospective customers to call or write for information about Ryder Full Service Leasing.

Leasing is much more common in the industrial market than in the consumer market. But in recent years there has been a big increase in consumer leasing of such goods as cars,

ETHICS IN MARKETING

The National Association of Purchasing Management's principles and standards of purchasing practice are presented here. Carefully evaluate each of the eleven standards.

Principles and Standards of Purchasing Practice

- Loyalty to your company
- Justice to those with whom you deal
- Faith in your profession

From these principles are derived the NAPM standards of purchasing practice.

1. Avoid the intent and appearance of unethical or compromising practice in relationships, actions, and communications.

2. Demonstrate loyalty to the employer by diligently following the lawful instructions of the employer, using reasonable care and only authority granted.

3. Refrain from any private business or professional activity that would create a conflict between personal interests and the interest of the employer.

4. Refrain from soliciting or accepting money, loans, credits, or prejudicial discounts, and the acceptance of gifts, entertainment, favors, or services from present or potential suppliers which might influence, or appear to influence, purchasing decisions.

5. Handle information of a confidential

musical instruments, furniture, appliances, TVs, and household maintenance and repair goods. The carmakers like leasing to consumers because it makes higher-priced cars more affordable and stimulates more frequent trade-ins. The main appeal to consumers is no down payment and monthly payments that can run 20 to 30 percent less than for buying the same car.

A lessor of industrial products might choose to lease its products rather than sell them outright for a variety of reasons. Heavy research, development, and production costs associated with a product may require such a high price that few customers could afford to buy it. This is why the earliest computers were leased rather than sold. Another reason is that the lessor may find it easier to make sales of complementary products needed to operate the leased product. For example, IBM sells paper to its lessees. Lessors of sophisticated products generally require considerable financial resources because the costs are not recovered as quickly as they are from an outright sale.

A lessee also can enjoy several benefits from leasing:

1. Leasing may eliminate the need to borrow funds to buy the product, which can be important when interest rates are high, borrowing power is limited, or better uses exist for the funds that would have been committed in an outright purchase.

2. A lessee can replace leased equipment with more modern equipment without the losses involved in selling obsolete equipment.

3. Lease payments may offer a tax advantage because they are a deductible business expense.

or proprietary nature to employers and/or suppliers with due care and proper consideration of ethical and legal ramifications and governmental regulations.

6. Promote positive supplier relationships through courtesy and impartiality in all phases of the purchasing cycle.

7. Refrain from reciprocal agreements which restrain competition.

8. Know and obey the letter and spirit of laws governing the purchasing function and remain alert to the legal ramifications of purchasing decisions.

9. Encourage that all segments of society have the opportunity to partici-pate by demonstrating support for small, disadvantaged and minority-owned businesses.

10. Discourage purchasing's involvement in employer sponsored programs of personal purchases which are not business related.

11. Enhance the proficiency and stature of the purchasing profession by acquiring and maintaining current technical knowledge and the highest standards of ethical behavior.

Source: Adopted May 1990. Reprinted with permission from the publisher, the National Association of Purchasing Management, ''Principles and Standards of Purchasing Practice,'' *NAPM Insights,* vol. 1, no. 9, September 1990, p. 27.

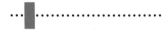

An ad that discusses some of the advantages of leasing.

(Courtesy of Ryder Transportation Resources.)

4. Maintenance and repair service usually is provided as part of the lease agreement.

5. Equipment can be leased only when needed, unlike purchased equipment, which may lie idle for extended periods of time.

However, the cash payments on a lease often are considerably higher than financed purchase payments, and use restrictions may be imposed on the equipment by the lessor.

make-or-buy decision

• **More Make-or-Buy Decisions** • Another area of importance in the industrial market is the *make-or-buy decision*—the choice an industrial buyer makes between manufacturing its own goods (or performing services) and buying the goods (or hiring the services) from vendors. Instead of buying component parts from vendors, a manufacturer might consider making the part for itself. If the results of a cost-benefit analysis indicate that this would be the more profitable alternative, the manufacturer very likely would fill some of its own product requirements. Temple-Inland is the third-largest maker of corrugated boxes in the United States. Almost all of the output of the firm's six containerboard plants is used by its thirty-two box plants around the country.[13]

Can makers have been hurt by a trend among some of their largest beverage-making customers, especially the major beer companies, of making their own cans to cut costs. Anheuser-Busch has enough capacity to make most of its own cans. But in recent years it has been supplying 40 percent of its own needs and using the rest of its capacity to make soft-drink cans. The extra capacity helps the firm win good prices from its can suppliers.[14]

The make-or-buy decision is complex, especially when a "make" decision requires expanding the firm's production system or buying another firm. General Electric bought Intersil, a semiconductor maker, in 1981 to expand in electronics, expecting to put its own semiconductors into its products. But GE's failure in such markets as mobile phones and its subsequent decision to stop making televisions cut its need to make its own semiconductors. GE sold its semiconductor business in 1988.[15] Table 6–2 lists several factors that might favor making rather than buying and also lists some of the potential drawbacks.

Modern firms recognize the important role the purchasing department can play in make-or-buy planning. The discussion of the procurement function later in the chapter assumes the firm "buys" rather than "makes."

TABLE 6–2  The Make-or-Buy Decision

A Firm Might Favor Making Rather than Buying Some of Its Requirements When:

1. No suitable vendors exist.
2. The firm requires such small quantities that no vendor is interested in supplying the firm.
3. The product is so specialized that vendors cannot, or do not want to, meet the potential buyer's specifications.
4. The product was designed by the using firm and it wants to protect its design and manufacturing process from other firms.
5. The user can produce the product more cheaply than vendors.
6. The user wants to demonstrate its ability to produce part of its requirements to gain bargaining leverage in negotiating with vendors who fill its other requirements.
7. Producing some of its requirements may utilize excess manufacturing capacity.
8. The amount used is sufficient for the firm to realize economies of scale in producing the product.

Some of the Potential Drawbacks to Making Rather than Buying Are:

1. New equipment and skills may be needed and the firm may be entering a new line of business.
2. Demand for the end product (the product the part is used to make) is questionable or marginal.
3. Existing producers may control patents or sources of materials.
4. Production scheduling may be upset.
5. The firm has to keep up with the latest technology in producing the part or the end product will deteriorate relative to its competitors'.
6. There is a reduced chance for reciprocal buying arrangements.
7. Alienated vendors can be a source of adverse word-of-mouth advertising and the firm loses goodwill.
8. The firm locks itself into one supplier—itself.

The Reseller Market

As Figure 6–1 indicates, the *reseller market* is made up of firms that engage in wholesale and retail trade. These resellers (wholesaling intermediaries and retailers) buy products from their suppliers and resell them to their customers. Except for products that producers sell directly to final buyers, all products are sold through resellers.

When a reseller sells a product, the product is in essentially the same form it was in when the reseller bought it from the supplier. Thus resellers are not concerned with creating form utility. Instead, they focus on creating time, place, and possession utility. In doing so, they create *value added by marketing*—the worth added to a product by resellers that equals the resellers' sales revenues minus their cost of goods sold and their cost of purchased services.

Because their main business is reselling to customers the products they buy from suppliers, resellers must be careful in deciding what products to buy. They must think of themselves as buyers for their customers, instead of resellers for their suppliers. These wholesaling intermediaries and retailers are in business to satisfy their customers' wants.

Resellers also buy products necessary to conduct their own business operations. These products include light bulbs, floor cleaners, data processing equipment, and buildings. They are used, not resold, and the buying procedures are essentially the same as those followed by manufacturers in buying products they need to conduct their operations. We will take an in-depth look at retailing and wholesaling in chapters 12 and 13.

The Government Market

The government market in the United States consists of one federal government (the largest customer in the world), 50 state governments, and over 80,000 local governments. The actual number of potential customers in the government market is even greater than these figures suggest, because the figures do not include semiautonomous agencies that states, cities, and counties use to provide certain services and that are under the administrative or fiscal control of these government units—for example, state institutions of higher education.

There is a lot of red tape in selling to the government because taxpayers want assurance that government gets what it pays for and that there is no favoritism in selecting suppliers. In general, government purchases are affected by social, political, and economic goals. Some purchases, for example, are reserved for minority-owned small businesses. Roughly one-third of all federal government buying is from small firms.

THE PROCUREMENT FUNCTION

In the discussions that follow, the focus is on procurement in the industrial market. We look at the procurement function in terms of (1) the types of industrial buying, (2) the industrial buying process, (3) participants in industrial buying decisions, (4) the role of purchasing departments, and (5) purchasing decision criteria. Following those discussions is a brief look at procurement in reseller and government markets.

Types of Industrial Buying

As Figure 6–4 shows, industrial buying can be divided into buyclasses. *Buyclasses* are the three types of industrial buying situations: (1) new task, (2) modified rebuy, and (3) straight rebuy.[16]

value added by marketing

buyclasses

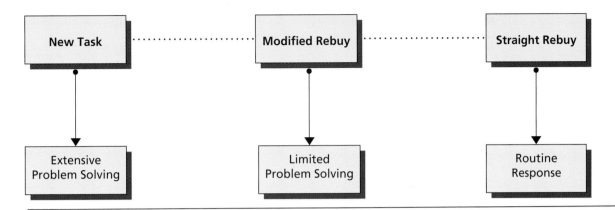

```
┌─────────────┐      ┌─────────────────┐      ┌─────────────────┐
│  New Task   │······│  Modified Rebuy │······│  Straight Rebuy │
└─────────────┘      └─────────────────┘      └─────────────────┘
       │                      │                        │
       ▼                      ▼                        ▼
┌─────────────┐      ┌─────────────────┐      ┌─────────────────┐
│  Extensive  │      │     Limited     │      │     Routine     │
│   Problem   │      │     Problem     │      │    Response     │
│   Solving   │      │     Solving     │      │                 │
└─────────────┘      └─────────────────┘      └─────────────────┘
```

FIGURE 6–4

Three Types of Industrial
Buying (Buyclasses)

• **New Task Buying** • In new task buying the organization faces a new need or problem and the buyer gathers information from vendors who can offer products to satisfy the need or solve the problem. This type of buying decision is complex and involves extensive problem solving. For example, the federal government's requirements for greater fuel efficiency led automakers to search for vendors and products that could help them meet the more-miles-per-gallon requirement. This created an opportunity for firms such as PPG Industries Inc. to sell automakers on the benefits of fiberglass-reinforced plastic in reducing car weight by replacing component parts made of steel. In 1989 General Motors launched the Chevrolet Lumina APV (all-purpose vehicle), the Pontiac Trans Sport, and the Oldsmobile Silhouette, the largest mass-market vehicles ever produced with plastic bodies.[17]

Alcan Aluminum's strategy in recent years has been to make advanced, high-quality aluminum for use primarily in planes and cars. Alcan promotes the lightweight, corrosion-resistant metal as a means of improving fuel efficiency and extending the life of a car. Recently Ferrari and Jaguar introduced auto chassis made of the company's product.[18] Meanwhile, Ford and Reynolds Metals are building a prototype aluminum car.[19]

New task buying is common when a firm begins production of a new product. In such cases the reputations of potential suppliers are the major factor in choosing suppliers. Those with problem-solving sales personnel have the upper hand. New task buying involves more time than the other two buying processes, and more people usually participate in the buying decision.

• **Modified Rebuy Buying** • The buyer in modified rebuy buying seeks to modify product specifications, delivery schedules, prices, or suppliers. For example, when energy costs started going up, firms in the construction industry started shifting from ordinary flat glass to insulating glass. Although modified rebuy buying is less complex than new task buying, several people may still participate in the decisions. Rival suppliers that can offer products and customer support services that better match the buyer's needs can take business from the present supplier. These buying situations cause the present vendor to be concerned about losing the customer. Potential vendors consider it an opportunity to win new business.

• **Straight Rebuy Buying** • Straight rebuy buying means buying a product that has been purchased before with satisfactory results from an established vendor. Rival suppliers have a tough time taking business from such an entrenched supplier. Straight rebuy decisions are programmed buying decisions. Such order-reorder buying requires less time than new task or modified rebuy buying and often is automated because of its repetitive and routine nature.

Industrial marketers must tailor their marketing efforts to the type of buying situation they face. An ''in'' supplier (a vendor that is currently supplying the buyer) in a new task situation has an established relationship with the buyer and is in a better position than ''out'' suppliers to anticipate the buyer's problems and requirements. An ''in'' supplier in a modified rebuy situation should try to change the buying situation to a straight rebuy by providing superior service. An ''out'' supplier would want to prevent this by presenting the buyer with innovative solutions to problems. An ''in'' supplier in a straight rebuy situation may retain that status by continued good service and responsiveness to changing requirements. An ''out'' supplier has the difficult task of demonstrating to decision makers that it has the capabilities that merit its consideration as a potential supplier.

The Industrial Buying Process

buyphases

We will now describe the industrial buying process that applies primarily to new task buying. Our discussion will be similar to the discussion of complex decisions in chapter 5. Modified and straight rebuys generally do not involve all these steps because they require less extensive problem solving. The steps are called buyphases. *Buyphases* are the problem-solving steps used by industrial buyers primarily in new task buying: (1) recognizing a need; (2) specifying the need; (3) searching for potential suppliers; (4) inviting, acquiring, and analyzing vendor proposals; (5) selecting the vendor and placing the order; and (6) following up.[20] (See Figure 6–5.) The buyer's commitment to a particular vendor increases in successive buyphase stages, and there is less opportunity for other vendors to make proposals.

FIGURE 6–5

Steps in the Industrial Buying Process (Buyphases)

• **Recognizing a Need** • Need recognition is the starting place in the procurement process. It can result from internal or external developments. Internal developments include (1) the user of a piece of machinery demonstrates its inefficiency to a supervisor, (2) the purchasing agent believes the firm is receiving poor after-sale service from its

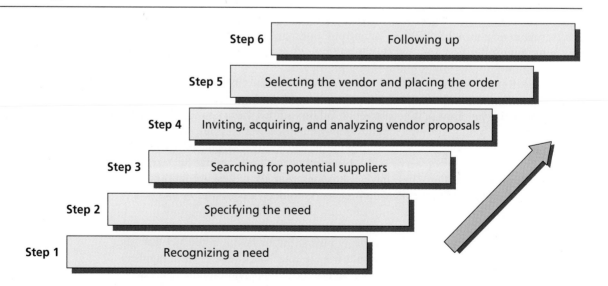

Step 6   Following up

Step 5   Selecting the vendor and placing the order

Step 4   Inviting, acquiring, and analyzing vendor proposals

Step 3   Searching for potential suppliers

Step 2   Specifying the need

Step 1   Recognizing a need

present supplier and wants to seek a new one, (3) a major piece of equipment becomes obsolete and must be replaced, (4) inventory reaches the reorder point, and (5) the firm wants to market a new product and needs new equipment to produce it.

External developments include (1) a vendor's salesperson calls on the purchasing agent to demonstrate a product that will save the firm money, (2) a vendor sends a brochure to the production manager explaining how its equipment can reduce maintenance costs, (3) attendance at a trade association meeting or a trade show convinces top managers that the firm's equipment is obsolete, (4) an article in a trade journal discusses a new data processing system that will cut costs and make information available to decision makers faster, and (5) a vendor uses advertising, such as the Philips Lighting ad.

Before plastic, many apparel makers made their buttons from tagua, an ivorylike nut found in the rain forests of Ecuador and Colombia. Concern about saving rain forests and elephants played a large role in the efforts of an environmental group (Conservation International) to link two clothing makers (Patagonia and Smith & Hawken) together with tagua nut suppliers in northwestern Ecuador. Together they are reviving the tagua-nut industry.[21] Industrial marketers must capitalize on every opportunity to convert internal and external developments to sales. They do this by developing effective ad campaigns and professional

An ad that seeks to stimulate need recognition.

You'll save enough with Philips SL* to buy an SL from a different manufacturer.

Philips SL* Lamps can save you a carload of money. Let's say you have a 500 room hotel. If you put SL* Lamps in your corridors alone, you'll save $66,000 over the life of the lamps.

That's because an SL* can reduce energy costs by an amazing 76% compared to incandescents. Also, they last up to 13 times longer than incandescents, so you'll save even more on maintenance costs.

There are SL* Lamps for general lighting, high-hat downlighting, decorative lighting and a brand new one for low lumen areas. Each fits right into an ordinary incandescent socket and produces the same warm light.

To find out more about Philips incredibly efficient SL*, call 1-800-631-1259 and talk to our Lighting Team. Then you can start picking out the color of your other SL.

It's time to change your bulb.™

Philips Lighting

PHILIPS

sales forces to reach people and help them recognize their needs and help solve their problems.

- **Specifying the Need** • In specifying its need the buyer identifies and describes in detail the quantity and quality of the needed product. It develops the specifications of what it needs to buy. USAA, which does all its insurance business over the phone and through the mail, recently decided that it needed a document retrieval system to cope with a huge amount of paper. Company trucks leave headquarters for the post office several times daily to pick up mail addressed to USAA. In requesting bids from several vendors, USAA supplied them with a thick rules document that specified precisely how the system would have to work. Part of the detailed specifications stated that the system would have to ''turn the page''—store one page and bring up another on the screen—in one second. It had to bring the image to the screen from the hard disk connected to the mainframe computer in five seconds. It had to bring the image from the optical disks, where everything is finally stored, to the screen in fifteen seconds or less.[22]

Customers are increasingly asking manufacturers of machine tools (machines used to shape metal parts in manufacturing) to work more closely with them to meet their requirements. Often toolmakers participate in the early stages of the design of their customers' products. In effect, suppliers and customers work together like partners. As we saw at the beginning of this chapter, such cooperative relationships are replacing the traditional, often adversarial, relationships between suppliers and their customers.

- **Searching for Potential Suppliers** • The buyer who is searching for potential suppliers will identify vendors that are likely to be able to supply the needed product. Industrial marketers place great value on a good reputation to help create word-of-mouth advertising so their names will get around. They also make sure they are listed in appropriate trade directories. If they are unknown, they cannot be included on a list of qualified potential suppliers. Offshore procurement of industrial products is growing. Thus the search for potential suppliers is more and more an international search.

- **Inviting, Acquiring, and Analyzing Vendor Proposals** • Buyers invite qualified vendors to submit proposals for evaluation. Perhaps the vendor will respond by mailing a catalog or sending a sales representative to make a call. In seeking proposals for complex equipment the buyer may request vendors to submit detailed specifications and make a personal presentation. Industrial marketers must be skilled in preparing written and oral presentations and should receive assistance from technical people, such as engineers, in preparing them.

- **Selecting the Vendor and Placing the Order** • Choosing the vendor that best satisfies the firm's needs and placing the order require the buyer to prepare a list of desired vendor attributes. Examples of these attributes are (1) technical support services, (2) dependable delivery, (3) reasonable credit terms, and (4) adequate product warranties. Each vendor is rated in terms of these criteria, and one or more vendors are selected. But prior to actual placement of the order, there may be some further negotiation on the product's specifications, price, delivery date, and so on. In the end, however, the final order is written.

- **Following Up** • The follow-up involves an evaluation of product and vendor performance. Again, value and vendor analysis can help in this stage. They are discussed later in the chapter.

Participants in Industrial Buying Decisions

Of course, organizations do not buy products; people do the buying. A *buying center* is the set of people who determine both what will be purchased to fill an organization's needs and from whom the products will be purchased. Five types of actors can play a role in industrial buying decisions: (1) users, (2) influencers, (3) gatekeepers, (4) deciders, and (5) buyers.[23]

buying center

• **Users** • The people who will use the product are users. Secretaries use personal computers, factory workers use machine tools, and warehouse personnel use forklift trucks. Users' input is often sought in buying decisions. Salespeople must recognize this, perhaps by talking with them to learn about their needs and problems.

• **Influencers** • The people inside and outside the organization who help shape buying decision criteria are influencers. They have some voice in setting product specifications and evaluating vendor offerings. Finance personnel may set maximum price limits on buying alternatives, engineering personnel may set tolerance limits for precision equipment, and an outside consulting engineer may be called on to evaluate the merits of several vendors' product designs. These people cannot be ignored by salespeople.

• **Gatekeepers** • The people who control the flow of information into, within, and out of the buying organization are gatekeepers. Secretaries can turn away vendor salespeople, and a production manager can establish policies preventing vendor salespeople from talk-

Gatekeepers often are confronted with delicate ethical issues as they seek to control the flow of information into, within, and out of the buying organization.

[© John Curtis]

ing to assembly-line workers. Selling to gatekeepers often requires considerable human relations skill.

- **Deciders** • The persons authorized to make the final choice of what will be bought are deciders. When very costly products are involved, the deciders may be members of top management. For less expensive, routinely purchased products the decider is also the buyer.

- **Buyers** • The persons authorized to handle the details of contracting with suppliers are buyers—often called purchasing agents. But if the contract is a long-term one involving considerable purchase commitments, members of top management may participate as buyers.

The industrial salesperson who is selling to a buying center must determine which persons in the organization are playing which roles in each buying situation and how much power each has in the purchase decision. This helps the salesperson tailor buying appeals to the different actors. He or she is selling to an organization *and* to the individuals who participate in buying decisions. Therefore, personal and sociocultural influences on consumer behavior are relevant in selling to people in buying centers.

················
multiple buying influence

Multiple buying influence exists within a buying center. ***Multiple buying influence*** is a situation in which several persons participate in an industrial buyer's buying decision. As Table 6–3 shows, multiple buying influence is especially likely to exist in new task buying. In such situations, salespeople often must choose between concentrating their efforts on the people they think are key buying influences or on trying to reach all participants in the buying center. Two challenging tasks are identifying the people with the most power in a given buying situation and scheduling appointments with them. A participant's power may vary according to buyphase and from one purchase to the next. In many cases those who are the most powerful and influential are often the most inaccessible to salespeople.

Only users and buyers may be involved in purchases of routinely bought supplies such as paper clips and light bulbs. At the other extreme, all five actors may participate in buying long-lived, costly products such as heavy equipment and buildings. In either case a person may play more than one role.

The Role of Purchasing Departments

Purchasing departments of small industrial buyers may consist of one or two people who handle all the buying. Industrial salespeople who call on them serve essentially as consultants—as extensions of the purchasing department.

TABLE 6–3   Characteristics of Industrial Buyclasses

Buyclasses	Problem Solving	Decision Type	Extent of Multiple Buying Influence	Time Required for Decision
New task buying	Extensive	Very complex	Maximally present	Maximum
Modified rebuy buying	Limited	Somewhat complex	Somewhat present	Somewhat lengthy
Straight rebuy buying	Routine response (often automated)	Programmed	None	Least

Purchasing departments of large industrial buyers, on the other hand, may be staffed by numerous purchasing specialists, each buying only one or a few categories of products. Industrial salespeople calling on these purchasing specialists must be able to provide highly detailed product information regarding cost, quality, performance, durability, and so on. Large industrial buyers increasingly practice centralized buying, rather than allowing individual departments or divisions to make their own purchases. These centralized purchasing departments handle the procurement function.

As we saw at the beginning of this chapter, in today's industrial market there is a growing spirit of cooperation between buyers and their suppliers. As we will see in chapter 13, the just-in-time system enables manufacturers to keep their inventories to a bare minimum because they rely on their suppliers to deliver exactly on time the supplies they need to keep their plants operating without interruption. The details involved in making such a system work require a great deal of cooperation between producers and their suppliers. Blanket ordering, which we discussed earlier, is another example of cooperation. The long-term relationship between the buyer and the supplier facilitates the development of a cooperative relationship.

Yet another type of cooperation involves corporate purchasing agreements. *Corporate purchasing agreements* are statements of intention by the buyer to buy and the seller to sell a given quantity of a product at a specified price during the next year. Although these agreements are not legally binding, they give the supplier insight into the buyer's product requirements. The manufacturer-supplier can thereby do a better job of scheduling production and the distributor-supplier a better job of buying and managing inventory. The buyer benefits because the risk of the supplier being out of stock is reduced.

corporate purchasing agreements

Increasingly, organizations are making deals with airlines to get discounts on air travel. Businesses and their travel agents are gathering more information on employee travel patterns. This enables them to tell an airline how many people will be flying on a certain route during a certain period. Airlines can use this information to fill empty planes. The special rates almost never apply to all travel by one company. Instead, the airlines will limit an agreement to a specific route and insist that the company promise to fly a certain number of people on that route in a given period.[24]

More and more organizations now recognize the strategic importance of purchasing. Increasingly, purchasing jobs are at the vice-presidential level. Many firms have developed incentive systems to reward exceptional performance in handling the procurement function, very much like the bonuses salespeople receive for exceeding their sales quotas.

Depending on the product, the purchasing department may provide different types of advice and perform different types of services in the buying process. It usually makes the price and quality decision on its own when buying routinely purchased items. But it works much more closely with executives in other departments in buying expensive, long-lived products or services. Value analysis and vendor analysis are two important tasks of the purchasing department.

Value analysis is also an important part of step 2 of the industrial buying process—specifying the need. *Value analysis* is the review of existing product specifications to eliminate inessential cost factors and to develop greater capability for the present cost for products purchased or manufactured in-house. In small firms one person often is accountable for all the organization's buying. This person may work closely with the sales representatives of one or more vendors in conducting a value analysis study.

value analysis

The salesperson serves as a consultant to the purchasing agent, who may lack detailed and specialized knowledge of product characteristics and functions. In larger organizations, as mentioned earlier, purchasing department personnel often specialize by product categories. A major part of the salesperson's job here is to provide the detailed technical information people in the purchasing department request and to answer specific technical questions. Frequently, a committee of engineers, cost accountants, and production and finance personnel is formed to work with purchasing department personnel to review the specifications set by the user department.

Vendor analysis is an important part of step 5 of the industrial buying process—selecting the vendor. *Vendor analysis* is the evaluation of the performance capability of potential suppliers through the rating of their past performance in technical, financial, managerial, and other areas. It is a way to substitute facts for feelings in selecting suppliers. Value and vendor analysis are also integral parts of the follow-up step in the industrial buying process.

Purchasing Decision Criteria

Industrial buyers consider many factors in their purchasing decisions. Most are economic, or rational, factors, but emotional factors are also present. An industrial marketer must analyze the prospective buyer's situation and develop a total product for solving the problem or capitalizing on an opportunity.

GLOBAL
MARKETING

In 1983 Westinghouse Electric acquired Unimation Inc., the inventor of industrial robots. Soon after General Electric, United Technologies, IBM, and Cincinnati Milacron jumped into the robot business. Today all these companies have quit the robot business, whipped by the Japanese, who had licensed the technology from America. Westinghouse bailed out fully in 1987. Cincinnati Milacron, the final major holdout, left the business in September 1990.

There were signs from the start that the robot industry was doomed in the United States. In 1967 inventor Joseph Engelberger appeared on "The Tonight Show Starring Johnny Carson" with a robot that opened a can of Budweiser and led the band. The audience laughed, and talent agents called to book the act. The Japanese government, however, flew Engelberger first class to Tokyo to address seven hundred industrialists and to field questions for six hours. Americans saw the robot as a novelty. The Japanese saw it as a solution.

When U.S. manufacturers belatedly took notice, they too were receptive. Saddled with high labor costs, the auto industry, particularly, saw robotics as a way to match Japan's lower car production costs.

It was strategically important, in order to beat Japanese competition, that Unimation excel in electrically driven gears and control systems. But Unimation stayed instead with its hydraulic robots, the Unimates. These robots were prone to leaks because of a design flaw that would have been prohibitively expensive to fix. So the devices were equipped with drip pans, which overflowed unpredictably, sometimes halting assembly lines where they were in use.

A Ford Motor Company executive said the company would place an order for robots and drip pans if Unimation would spend the proceeds from the sale of drip pans to rid its robots of their need for drip pans. But according to an operations manager at Unimation at the time, "Our guys said why fix it when we were mak-

In recent years a great deal of attention has been given to systems selling. *Systems selling* is the marketing of a total product offering that will provide a total solution to a customer's problem. The concept began in the military as systems buying. Military procurement offices used to buy different components for a total weapons system from different vendors. The military would then put the system together itself. During the 1960s the emphasis shifted to dealing with a prime contractor who delivered the total system. The contractor handled all the details of subcontracting with suppliers of system components.

Loral Corporation's radars, sensors, and electronics provide the eyes and brains for a broad range of U.S. aircraft, submarines, tanks, and satellites. Its core strength is in building electronic warfare systems, which are based on radar, cameras, and sensors. For example, Loral supplied electronic warfare systems for McDonnell Douglas's F-15 fighter, which was used in operation Desert Storm. Loral is a component and subsystem supplier to McDonnell Douglas. Of course, Loral also subcontracts work out to other vendors.[25]

As another example, manufacturers who want to automate manufacturing operations need more than robots; they also need solid-state and process controls. Solid-state controls

········■······

systems selling

ing money on the drip pan, not to mention the extra hydraulic fluid.''

In 1983, the year that Westinghouse bought Unimation, General Motors, a major Unimation customer, was growing so impatient with the pace of U.S. robot development that it entered the business itself, in a joint venture with Fanuc Ltd. of Japan. GM had explored a partnership with eight U.S. robot makers, including Unimation, but most didn't ''want to be swallowed up'' by GM. Such relationships are common in Japan.

The executive vice president for advance product technology at Westinghouse, who studied the Unimation operation, says: ''The first thing I learned was that the robots made a difference where they had been fully integrated in the manufacturing process. Systems integration was the key. Joe Engelberger had never thought of that. All Unimation was doing was shipping robots out as a commodity.''

Indeed, by the mid-1980s robot fever had cooled because buyers had learned

that they had to make significant changes in their processes in order to integrate the robots. And it had dawned on U.S. industry that a robot's control systems had to be custom-designed to fit in with whatever process a robot was intended to help. Japanese robot makers, meanwhile, were helping customers redesign products and processes to make them more ''robot-friendly.''

No wonder that in the United States, though not in Japan, many manufacturers today are robot-shy. ''We used to spend a lot of money just to keep the robots working reliably,'' says the director of engineering at Whirlpool Corporation. In some operations, the appliance maker has done away with robots.

Source: Adapted from Amal Kumar Naj. ''Product Failure: How U.S. Robots Lost the Market to Japan in Factory Automation,'' *Wall Street Journal*, November 6, 1990, pp. A1, A10. Reprinted by permission of the *Wall Street Journal,* © Dow Jones & Company, Inc., 1990. All rights reserved.

allow translation of low-voltage commands from computers into high-energy commands that drive robots and machine tools. Process controls monitor manufacturing processes and send information about them to a computer.[26] The Global Marketing box explains how U.S. manufacturers of robots underestimated the importance of systems integration to their customers and how this contributed to their losing out to Japanese manufacturers.

As the NYNEX ad suggests, systems selling enables a buyer to deal with one vendor and assures the buyer that the various components of the total system will be compatible. Among the important purchasing decision criteria are dependability, product quality, cost, vendor production capacity, after-sale service, vendor reliability and integrity, reciprocity, and emotional factors.

• **Dependability** •   Effective marketers provide the level of service that their target customers want with respect to such criteria as devising delivery schedules, stocking repair parts, and handling customer complaints. A major concern in selecting suppliers is their dependability in providing services, such as meeting promised delivery dates. Late deliveries can cause production scheduling problems and downtime in production operations. Early deliveries can cause storage and inventory problems.

• **Product Quality** •   Another crucial factor is product quality. In many U.S. industries the price quoted by the supplier was once the major factor in selecting suppliers. More and more, however, especially in the industries that have lost market share to the Japanese,

An ad that focuses on systems selling.

(Courtesy of NYNEX Corporation.)

We'd like to propose to you.

Wouldn't it be more efficient to consider one comprehensive proposal instead of seven? A proposal that is prepared by a full-service integrated systems provider, NYNEX. The immediate result would be a cleaner desk.

Instead of looking at many unrelated proposals, let us show you one that's well thought out. We'll help you put together a cost-effective information system. A system that will fully integrate your computers, software and networks. We can even develop entirely new systems that meet your unique needs. What's more, we can offer your staff a wide range of training programs that teach your people how to use them.

So call us at 1 800 535-1535. This could be the beginning of a beautiful relationship.

Need to communicate? Need to compute? The answer is

manufacturers have refocused their attention on quality. As we said in chapter 1, the customer orientation is focusing more and more on the areas of product quality and customer satisfaction and service. Industrial marketers tend to insist on strict quality control procedures.

• **Cost** • Industrial buyers set quality standards for the parts they buy, and they try to buy parts that meet their standards at the least cost. Value analysis helps buyers avoid setting quality standards that are too high or too low. Because the cost of component parts must be included in the finished product's price, industrial buyers want to avoid buying overdesigned parts. They also want to avoid underdesigned parts that will lower the finished product's quality.

• **Vendor Production Capacity** • A vendor's production capacity is another important consideration. Buyers want assurances that suppliers can meet their present and forecasted volume requirements. Otherwise, orders will back up. When Benetton started out as a family business in Italy, the company entered into contracts with many mom-and-pop subcontractors to manufacture clothing. This approach worked reasonably well at first, but Benetton has had many problems with it in more recent years. A major problem is that competitors can shift from one low-cost manufacturer to another while Benetton is stuck with about 85 percent of its production inside high-cost Italy. One result is delays of up to ten months in filling orders for outlets in Canada and the United States.[27]

Many buyers practice multiple sourcing. *Multiple sourcing* is the establishment of a buying relationship with two or more vendors rather than with only one. Although buying from more than one source ensures that a strike, major accident, or natural catastrophe at supplier A's plants will not completely shut off supplies, buying a relatively large share of total requirements from A may help the buyer negotiate favorable purchase terms with that supplier. Multiple sourcing is especially important in industries subject to supply shortages.

multiple sourcing

On the other hand, a growing number of organizations are buying from fewer suppliers. They are cutting out purchases from vendors who do not live up to their expectations in such areas as product quality, price, and dependability. Single sourcing is becoming more popular as suppliers and buyers work to build a partnership relationship.

• **After-Sale Service** • The ability of industrial marketers to provide service on the products they lease or sell to their customers is a very important consideration. Breakdowns in equipment can cause expensive downtime in production operations if the equipment is not repaired promptly. Concern about after-sale service can extend to the capabilities of independent dealers who resell the manufacturer's product.

• **Vendor Reliability and Integrity** • Industrial buyers also want assurance that vendors can meet the buyers' product specifications. This concern extends to the vendors' production, service, engineering, and sales personnel. Vendors' integrity in living up to service and warranty commitments also is important.

reciprocity

• **Reciprocity** • A common element in industrial marketing is reciprocity. *Reciprocity* is an arrangement under which a customer buys from a vendor if the vendor buys from the customer. Reciprocal buying arrangements can take many forms and involve several firms. Company A might try to influence B to buy from C, which is A's customer. Reciprocity's importance as a buying strategy depends a great deal on environmental variables. For example, it can help offset declining sales during a recession without costly advertising.

Multiple sourcing for a growing number of U.S.-based firms involves buying from suppliers in other countries.

[© D. Eisermann/Argus/Focus]

Reciprocity among small firms often is based on friendship. But it goes way beyond friendship in some larger firms. Some have trade relations departments that use computers to analyze their purchases and sales by supplier and customer. This helps identify opportunities for reciprocal dealings with suppliers and customers.

Reciprocity, of course, can be used to restrain trade. Thus the Federal Trade Commission and the antitrust division of the Justice Department sometimes take a close look at reciprocal dealings. Another risk is that reciprocal buying and selling deals negotiated by upper-level managers will demoralize purchasing and sales personnel.

Reciprocity is taking on a new twist in the United States. United States suppliers and customers are starting to do for each other what foreign rivals have been doing for many years—exchange a financial stake for guaranteed business. To secure a broader market for its cars in the auto rental industry, Chrysler has acquired Thrifty Rent-a-Car System, Snappy Rental Inc., and Dollar Rent A Car Systems. Chrysler is not alone in buying high-volume customers. Ford has put money into Hertz and Budget Rent A Car. General Motors has done the same with Avis and National Car Rental System. Mitsubishi Motors recently acquired Value Rent A Car.[28]

• **Emotional Factors** • Industrial buyers are professionals, but they are also influenced by emotional factors in their buying behavior. Within a buying center there may be several participants, each of whom wants recognition and status. Ads for business jets explain how the planes can save executives time but also feature attractive interiors to reinforce their status needs.

Emotional factors are most likely to enter into buying decisions when rival vendors offer essentially the same total product. Friendship with the vendor or the vendor's salespeople takes on more importance when rival offerings are practically identical.

RESELLER PROCUREMENT

Resellers, both retailers and wholesalers, are in business to offer the product assortment that their customers want to buy. They are in business to function as purchasing agents for their customers. Unlike many industrial buyers that have only recently come to recognize the importance of purchasing, resellers have always recognized that effective buying is the key to success in retailing and wholesaling.

Like buyers in the industrial market, resellers have buying centers in which participants engage in a buying decision process to determine what and how much to buy, from whom, and under what terms. But there are some differences between buying in the industrial and reseller markets.

For example, many producers expend effort trying to induce wholesalers and retailers to stock new products. Wholesalers also often try to persuade retailers to add new items. The buying decision comes down to a choice of whether to add the new item. This buying situation differs from the new task situation faced by buyers in the industrial market in at least one major way. A new task situation *requires* a purchase to solve an existing problem. The buyer in the industrial market may not even know which suppliers have the capabilities to meet the buyer's requirements.

In chapters 12 and 13 we will look at some of the major factors that influence the buying decisions of retailers and wholesalers. We will also see that they are working hard to improve their buying skills. This, of course, means that vendors who call on resellers must improve their own marketing skills.

GOVERNMENT PROCUREMENT

The U.S. government engages in two major types of buying: civilian and military. Civilian procurement is handled by the individual government departments, branches, bureaus, and agencies when the products being purchased are not commonly used by all of them. For example, the National Aeronautics and Space Administration buys some products that are not used by other government units. The General Services Administration (GSA), however, centralizes the procurement of branded products and highly standardized products that are commonly used by government units. Office furniture is an example.

Military procurement is handled in much the same fashion. The GSA's largest customer is the Department of Defense (DOD). Each branch of the military buys for itself products for which it is the only user. Additionally, coordinated department procurement programs make it possible for an individual branch to buy for the combined needs of the DOD. Otherwise, the Defense Logistics Agency (DLA) buys products that the army, navy, and air force use in common. The assistant secretary of defense for acquisitions and logistics is responsible for acquiring weapon systems, for procurement policy, and for production planning. The office also coordinates all procurement activities of the major DOD components.[29]

The top twenty-five Pentagon contractors account for about half of total defense spending. Examples include McDonnell Douglas, General Dynamics, General Electric, and Raytheon. Some defense contractors derive the vast majority of their sales revenues from defense sales. For example, Lockheed derives 91 percent of its sales revenues from the Pentagon and Martin Marietta 75 percent. Other major defense contractors are much less dependent on defense spending. For example, IBM derives less than 5 percent of its sales from government purchases—and defense contracts are only a fraction of that amount.[30]

Pentagon spending tops $200 billion annually, and roughly half a million people work in the DOD's acquisition bureaucracy. The secretary of defense recently proposed major changes to the defense acquisition and management system. Among the changes is a reduction in the acquisition and management work force.[31]

State and local governments have units, such as school districts and highway departments, that buy products on their own. Many also have an agency similar to the GSA. The purpose is to centralize procurement in order to receive favorable prices and services from vendors through volume purchasing.

Procurement Procedures

Government units buy on either an advertised bid basis or a negotiated contract basis. The objective of both types of buying is competitive procurement.

When procurement is by advertised bid, suppliers who want to sell to a government agency must request placement on the agency's list of qualified bidders. This is the usual procedure for off-the-shelf items such as office furniture and personal computers. The agency will issue an "invitation for bid," much of which eventually becomes the contract. The invitation for bid sets out the specifications (specs), delivery requirements, and contract terms. The agency mails invitations to firms on the list of qualified bidders. The accepted bid is usually the one that meets the specs at the lowest price. For purchases of equipment the agency may request bids that also include maintenance on the equipment over its useful life. If the product turns out to cost the winning bidder more than expected, the government may or may not adjust the price.

Bidding firms must pay close attention to the buying agency's very exact specifications. This is not a major problem in the case of standardized products. But in the case of non-standardized products the bidder must decide if it has the resources and capability to meet the agency's specs.

A government agency that wants to buy a product it cannot describe in precise detail will negotiate a contract directly with a prospective supplier. The agency issues a "request for proposals." Bidders prepare their own proposals, and terms are open for negotiation.[32] This is the usual procedure in buying complex military hardware such as high-technology fighter aircraft. The firm that can provide it at the best price will be awarded the contract.

Negotiated contracts can take many forms. Price can be based on cost plus an agreed-upon percentage for profit, or a fixed price can be set. Critics of cost-plus pricing argue that suppliers have no incentive to hold costs down. A fixed-price-and-incentive contract enables the firm to earn more profit by decreasing costs. There also may be provisions for renegotiating the contract if it appears that the supplier will make more than a reasonable profit.

Customer-Oriented Government Marketers

Government marketers often tend to be production oriented, especially when the government buys on a bid basis. A firm simply requests listing on a bidder's list, and the government buying unit tells the firm what it wants, down to the most minute specification. Little opportunity exists for competing on any basis other than price. Negotiated contracts offer more opportunity to stress product design and personal selling. A growing number of government marketers are setting up marketing departments. Some also are taking the initiative in developing offerings that match specific agency needs rather than waiting for the agency to send out an invitation for bid.

In the case of requests for proposals, it is also advisable for prospective suppliers to be customer oriented. We mentioned the Loral corporation earlier in this chapter. Follow-on contracts are important to all defense firms. In a recent year 75 percent of Loral's sales stemmed from existing business. To win upgrade business, Loral commits resources to improving its products well before its customers are ready to buy or fund such improvements. For example, Loral independently added innovative infrared technology to some radar warning receivers previously sold to the Air Force. According to a rear admiral, Loral computers governing the firing of Tomahawk missiles substantially exceeded navy requirements for reliability. These missiles played an important role in operation Desert Storm.[33]

COMPARING CONSUMER AND INDUSTRIAL MARKETING MIXES

Because industrial buyers and ultimate consumers buy for different reasons, marketing mixes developed to serve them are typically different. Let's look at some of the major differences.

Product

Most consumer products in the United States are produced in anticipation of purchase by consumers (speculative production) instead of being produced to individual customer specification. There are, of course, exceptions, such as custom-built homes, commissioned artwork, and custom-made clothing. As the International trucks ad suggests, custom manufacturing (job order production), however, is much more common in industrial marketing.

Boeing has modified its 747 airplane on several occasions to meet the requirements of specific airlines. A buyer, for example, may want to change the upper deck's configuration so more passengers can be transported. Boeing's 777 airplane will begin flying commercially in 1995. The plane's wings are so long that airlines will have the option of ordering wingtips that fold up as the plane approaches the gate. This feature was initially requested by American Airlines, a potential customer. Although military airplanes have used folding wings safely for decades, they have never appeared on a commercial jet.[34]

A long period can pass between the time the marketer starts to learn about the potential customer's needs and delivery of the product to satisfy those needs. In the interim the marketer has to draw up specifications for the product, submit design and cost proposals, and secure a purchase contract. Service before the sale is an important part of the product component of the marketing mix.

The seller's ability to provide after-sale service is important to many consumers in buying home appliances and cars. But to industrial buyers the ability to provide after-sale service is critical. For example, in a continuous process operation such as cola bottling, the industrial buyer may have to shut down a plant because of a breakdown in a conveyor belt system.

Industrial marketers engage in more custom manufacturing than consumer products marketers.

(Navistar International Transportation Corp. Agency: Young & Rubicam, Chicago.)

Industrial buyers typically are concerned about a product's functional features, whereas consumers tend to be more interested in styling. A firm contemplating the purchase or leasing of a fleet of cars for its salespeople is much more interested in maintenance contracts, mileage, and repair history than is a person buying a car for personal use. Similarly, the role of packaging in the consumer market is essentially one of promotion. In the industrial market it is essentially one of protection.

Place

Consumers typically buy products in retail stores—the buyer goes to the seller. In industrial marketing the seller, who is often the manufacturer, usually goes directly to the buyer. For example, large-volume buyers are called on by IBM's sales representatives. Small-volume buyers, however, can be served through independent retail dealers. Without these dealers IBM would likely miss sales to small accounts for which the firm could not justify the expense of a personal call by an IBM sales representative. But in general the larger the order size and the more complex the equipment, the more likely the buyer will buy directly from the manufacturer.

Tandy Corporation, long a leading personal computer maker, had never made much headway with corporate PC buyers. Several years ago Tandy adopted a new strategy. Its Radio Shack stores would no longer sell PCs to firms with at least $100 million in sales. Instead Tandy's Grid Systems subsidiary would sell to them. About half of Grid's sales were to corporations, and it became the number 3 laptop computer maker in the United States. The strategy was to place the Grid name on Tandy-built high-end PCs. Grid also inherited 61 of Tandy's 354 computer stores plus a hundred of its salespeople.[35]

Promotion

Consumer product marketers such as Procter & Gamble and Gillette rely heavily on advertising in mass media—TV, radio, and mass-circulation magazines. Industrial marketers rely more on personal selling by their own sales forces, industrial trade shows, and advertising in specialized media such as *Hardware Age* to promote their products. This promotion is targeted to users, influencers, gatekeepers, deciders, and buyers.

Many types of industrial products are bought infrequently. A bank, for example, does not buy a heating and air-conditioning system very often. Even many small items that are used daily are bought under supply contracts negotiated between the buyer and the seller. But the marketer cannot ignore these customers. Sales calls are still needed. They keep customers informed of product developments and keep salespeople up-to-date on potential buyers and their needs.

As we said earlier, many firms are centralizing the purchasing function. This has led some industrial marketers to reorganize their sales organizations. Instead of regional or district salespeople calling on a firm's various plants, the central buying unit is serviced by a national account salesperson. Because the volume involved in such an account is much larger than that of a regional account, the national account salesperson must be a dedicated professional.

Price

In many countries consumers haggle over the selling prices of the products they buy. This is much less common in consumer product marketing in the United States. But seller-buyer negotiation of prices in industrial marketing is very common. Just as the product often is tailored to the individual industrial buyer, so is the price. This may help the salesperson create a differential advantage for the firm's total offering to the buyer. Leasing is also more common in industrial marketing.

SUMMARY OF LEARNING OBJECTIVES

1. Distinguish between the consumer market and organizational markets.

Buyers in the consumer market buy products for personal or household consumption. Buyers in organizational markets buy products to satisfy the needs of the organizations to which they belong. The three major types of organizational markets are the industrial market, the reseller market, and the government market.

2. Describe the major characteristics of the industrial market.

The major characteristics are as follows: derived demand, a situation in which the demand for one product results from the existing demand for another product; greater total sales volume; smaller number of buyers; greater variability in purchase volume; greater geographical concentration of customers; greater primary demand inelasticity; more professional buying; more direct buying; more specification buying; more complex negotiation; less frequent negotiation; more reciprocal buying; greater use of leasing; and more make-or-buy decisions.

3. Explain the industrial procurement process in terms of the types of industrial buying situations.

Industrial buying can be divided into three types of industrial buying situations (buyclasses): new task, modified rebuy, and straight rebuy. In new task buying the organization faces a new need or problem and the buyer gathers information from vendors who can offer products to satisfy the need or solve the problem. The buyer in modified rebuy buying seeks to modify product specifications, delivery schedules, prices, or suppliers. Straight rebuy buying means buying a product that has been purchased before with satisfactory results from an established vendor.

4. Identify and explain the steps in the industrial procurement process.

The steps in the industrial procurement process are called buyphases. They are (1) recognizing a need, which can result from internal or external developments; (2) specifying the need, which involves the buyer identifying and describing in detail the quantity and quality of the needed product; (3) searching for potential suppliers, which focuses on identifying vendors that are likely to be able to supply the needed product; (4) inviting, acquiring, and analyzing vendor proposals, which involves buyers inviting qualified vendors to submit proposals for evaluation; (5) selecting the vendor

and placing the order, which means choosing the vendor that best satisfies the firm's needs and placing the order with that vendor; and (6) following up, which involves an evaluation of product and vendor performance.

5. Identify and explain the participants in industrial buying decisions.

A buying center is the set of people who determine both what will be purchased to fill an organization's needs and from whom the products will be purchased. Five types of participants are involved in industrial buying decisions: (1) users—the people who will use the product; (2) influencers—the people inside and outside the organization who help shape buying decision criteria; (3) gate-keepers—the people who control the flow of information into, within, and out of the buying organization; (4) deciders—the persons authorized to make the final choice of what will be bought; and (5) buyers—the persons authorized to handle the details of contracting with suppliers.

6. Identify important purchasing decision criteria.

The criteria include dependability, product quality, cost, vendor production capacity, after-sale service, vendor reliability and integrity, reciprocity, and emotional factors.

7. Explain why consumer and industrial marketing mixes are typically different.

Consumer and industrial marketing mixes are typically different because industrial buyers and ultimate consumers buy for different reasons.

·················· ▌ ··················

Review Questions

1. What is the main difference between buyers in the consumer market and buyers in organizational markets?

2. Which of the organizational markets is the largest and the most diverse? What broad industry groupings are included in this market?

3. What are the major characteristics of the industrial market?

4. What is the significance of the fact that the demand for industrial products is a derived demand?

5. What are the advantages and disadvantages of an industrial marketer's decision to produce some of its own goods rather than buying them from vendors (the make-or-buy decision?)

6. How does new task buying differ from straight rebuy buying?

7. What are the six buyphases in the procurement function? Explain each one.

8. What is a buying center? Identify the actors who can play a role in industrial buying decisions.

9. What is the significance of value analysis and vendor analysis?

10. What are the major industrial purchasing decision criteria?

11. How does the advertised bid basis for buying differ from the negotiated contract basis in government procurement?

Discussion Questions

1. Early in 1991 the U.S. economy was in a recession, the United States was involved in Operation Desert Storm, and air travelers were concerned about war-related terrorism. How did these developments affect airlines? What about airplane manufacturers?

2. Some of AT&T's big financial services customers switched to competitors such as MCI Communications after AT&T entered into the credit card business. Why do you think those firms switched vendors?

3. In recent years the U.S. government has undertaken many privatization efforts. In other words, it has been turning over some jobs that it formerly performed for itself to government contractors—privately owned businesses. Privatization is also occurring at the state and local government levels. Why? Is the decision to privatize similar to the make-or-buy decision? Explain.

4. Lockheed is an example of a government contractor that is highly dependent on government procurement. In recent years Lockheed has sought to reduce its dependence on government contracts. Why?

Application Exercise

Reread the material about Boeing at the beginning of this chapter and answer the following questions:

1. What does James Blue mean when he says "We're interested in marriages, not weekend romances"?

2. Are there any disadvantages to buyers from forging closer relationships with their suppliers? Explain.

3. What are the advantages and disadvantages of multiple sourcing and single (or sole) sourcing?

Key Concepts

The following key terms were introduced in this chapter:

organizational marketing
Standard Industrial
    Classification (SIC)
    system
value added by
    manufacturing
original equipment
    manufacturer (OEM)
user account

derived demand
blanket ordering
leasing
make-or-buy decision
value added by marketing
buyclasses
buyphases
buying center

multiple buying influence
corporate purchasing
    agreements
value analysis
vendor analysis
systems selling
multiple sourcing
reciprocity

CASES

Ball Corp. "Can" Do

In each of seven Ball Corp. factories scattered around the United States, 1500 beer and soda cans fly off the assembly line every minute. The factories churn out the cans 24 hours a day, seven days a week. Ball's Findley, Ohio, plant alone made about 400 million steel cans, 1.1 billion aluminum cans, and 7 billion can ends in 1990.

That year, Ball took in about $1.2 billion selling its cans and can ends to beer giant Anheuser-Busch, to PepsiCo and Coca-Cola, and to many makers of private-label beers and soft drinks. But Ball still controls only about 12 percent of the market, running a distant fourth in the ultra-competitive U.S. can business. During the last decade, Ball, like most can makers, saw its profit margins and stock prices soar and then sink. In the mid-1980s, Ball and other can makers were operating near full capacity. They raised their prices to boost their margins up to about 12 percent.

Smelling even larger profits, they independently started adding manufacturing capacity. Collectively, however, they added enough capacity that they began to make a lot more cans than customers wanted. Soft-drink makers started demanding steep discounts, and Ball's and other can makers' profit margins suddenly started to plummet. Now, in the 1990s, Ball executives realize that the only way to increase profits is to increase the number of cans Ball sells.

Ball started investing in this project long ago, spending at least $55 million annually over the last decade in plant improvements designed to lower costs and raise product quality. For drink cans, quality means not just making cans that don't have holes, but also making cans that are uniformly precise in terms of shape, size, and texture. "A can that runs like butter through a customer's filling line is worth a premium," says Delmont Davis, Ball's president. Although each can costs Ball's customers a cent or less, if it jams the filling line or otherwise causes the soda or beer to end up anywhere else but inside it, it may cost the drink maker many dollars in lost time and lost product.

Improving quality was a relatively easy task: it mostly depended upon actions within Ball itself. Other steps on the road to increased sales volume will be more difficult. Industry analysts say that Ball's biggest competitors, American National Can and Crown Cork & Seal, control so much of the market that—in addition to having lower costs as a result of economies of scale and their clout with raw material suppliers—they can often call the tune to their customers. In contrast, Ball depends on Anheuser-Busch alone for 22 percent of its sales and 14 percent of its operating profits so that it often has to dance to this giant's music. What makes matters worse is that Anheuser-Busch has the manufacturing capacity to make most of its own cans anytime it wants to—it already makes about 40 percent of its own cans and sells others to soft-drink makers. If Ball wants more for its cans than Anheuser-Busch wants to pay, Ball will be the loser. Thus, analysts say, although Ball makes 8 to 9.5 percent operating profit

margins from most of its customers, it can only demand 6 percent from Anheuser-Busch.

Some analysts say that Ball's only real hope for expansion in the can market is either to move into faster-growing foreign markets or to acquire another can maker. One interesting possibility: Anheuser-Busch has reportedly thought about selling its can plants. Should Ball think about buying them?

Questions

1. Are Ball's customers original equipment manufacturers (OEMs) or user accounts?

2. How could the ultimate consumers of Ball's customers' products affect the derived demand for Ball's cans?

3. How have customers' make-or-buy decisions affected Ball's business?

4. Into what buyclass do most of Ball's sales probably fall? What implications does this fact have for Ball's future?

Raytheon: From Vacuum Tubes to SCUD-Busting

The fact that a company succeeds in marketing to the government doesn't guarantee that it can successfully compete in other organizational markets. Many a successful government contractor has flopped in the industrial marketplace. For example, General Dynamics, one of the largest and most successful defense contractors, could not compete in the telecommunications market. Grumman became notorious when it tried to make buses, and McDonnell Douglas has struggled in the commercial airliner business. So when a major government contractor makes good, it makes news. One such contractor is Raytheon Corp., now famous as the manufacturer of the SCUD-busting Patriot missile.

To be sure, the road to success in nongovernment markets was not easy for Raytheon. Before the second world war the company made vacuum tubes for radios. During the war it thrived as a manufacturer of microwave tubes for radar systems. When the company began to make vacuum tubes again after the war, however, it discovered they had become obsolete.

Raytheon continued its government contracting by becoming a major maker of cold-war missile systems. Today, Raytheon has built upon its knowledge of sophisticated electronics to become a major supplier of missiles, radar, electronic jammers, and communications systems. Before the Gulf War even began Raytheon had increased its funded backlog of government contracts by 6 percent, to $6.7 billion, in the first half of 1990. The success of the Patriot missile during the Gulf War has assured additional contracts to expand and develop Patriot technology.

But Raytheon doesn't want to be purely a defense contractor.

To find a way into other markets, Raytheon initially used its electronics expertise to try to diversify into consumer goods. The company built an excellent television set, but found that it had no network to distribute them. That experience taught Raytheon an important lesson: knowing the product does not guarantee knowing how to market it.

In 1965, to gain entry into the appliance market, Raytheon bought Amana, then a small and well-respected refrigerator manufacturer. In two years Amana introduced the first consumer microwave oven, based on a Raytheon engineer's discovery of microwave cooking. This time the company not only offered state-of-the-art technology but offered it under a familiar company name. Amana microwaves were tremendously successful. Raytheon built on this base by buying Caloric (ovens and ranges) and Speed Queen (washers and dryers).

Raytheon has used similar buying strategies to enter industrial markets, focusing on light aircraft and energy services. The company now owns United Engineers & Constructors, which engineers power plants; the Badger Corp., which sets up refineries and chemical plants; Cedar Rapids Corp., which markets rock crushing, asphalt, and paving machines; Seismograph Services Corp., which does geophysical mapping; and, biggest of all, Beech Aircraft, which has already become a successful innovator in the commercial and business aircraft industry. Raytheon hopes that its energy services businesses will profit by getting into the business of environmental cleanups.

Today, while maintaining a successful government contracting business, Raytheon earns 40 percent of its total revenues in nongovernment markets, and profits from the nongovernment businesses are growing: in 1989 more than 70 percent of Raytheon's $52 million increase in pretax earnings came from its commercial businesses. Raytheon has come a long way from vacuum tubes.

Questions

1. Why do you think Raytheon does not want to be purely a defense contractor?

2. The United States government wants to buy more sophisticated missiles based on Patriot technology. What buyclass is involved in such procurement? Explain.

3. Does Raytheon engage in systems selling? Explain.

4. Is multiple buying influence present in government procurement? Explain.

MARKET
SEGMENTATION

After reading this chapter you will be able to

1. explain the mass-market strategy.

2. contrast the concentration strategy and the multi-segment strategy.

3. identify the major issues involved in the decision to pursue a segmentation strategy.

4. identify categories of segmentation variables and give examples of specific variables in each category for segmenting the consumer market.

5. give examples of segmentation variables for organizational markets.

I t's long past the peak dinner hour, but the Kentucky Fried Chicken outlet on 125th Street in Harlem is still so packed that some customers ease the tedium of a forty-five-minute wait by rapping the jingle for the product many came for: "Hot Wings, get into a new thing!" Georgi Olivero, the store's supervisor, boasts that this relatively new outlet is already one of the top performers in yearly sales. It is a particular feat considering the many competitive fast-food outlets in the neighborhood.

After blanketing the suburbs in the 1960s and '70s, the fast-food chains in the '80s turned to their last frontier: the inner city. Now the hamburger and fried chicken forces play a central role in ghetto life. In many poor neighborhoods the fast-food restaurant has emerged as a safe, clean, air-conditioned refuge from what lies just outside the door. It can also offer status. Being able to afford a steady diet of fast food shows a customer has some financial muscle.

But with their emphasis on high-fat, high-sodium, and high-sugar products, fast-food restaurants are also significant factors in the cycle of poor nutrition affecting the health of many low-income, undereducated Americans.

Fully 25 percent of the hamburger industry's sales now come from inner-city consumers. Poor areas hold an unusually high proportion of what the industry calls "heavy users," people who consume fast food at least eight times a month. One Burger King manager says his company's statistics show African-Americans 30 percent more likely than whites to be heavy users of fast food and Hispanics at least 20 percent more likely. He also says that young African-American males are the heaviest consumers, particularly men aged eighteen to twenty-four who haven't graduated from high school.

An African-American McDonald's franchisee who owns three outlets in Harlem estimates that 85 to 90 percent of his inner-city customers eat at his stores about four times a week. They also order 20 percent more large fries and large sandwiches than customers at his stores in more affluent Englewood, New Jersey, and downtown Manhattan. But they order only half as many salads.

Over the past decade fast-food companies have steadily stepped up their pitch to African-Americans and Hispanics. Although African-Americans make up about 12 percent of the population, executives estimate the Big Three burger flippers devote 15 percent to 20 percent of their ad budgets to wooing them. Thomas J. Burrell, chairman of Burrell Advertising Inc., which handles McDonald's advertising directed at African-Americans, estimates that ads appealing to this group increased at least sixfold during the '80s. "It wasn't growing before because people weren't aware of the vast potential of this market segment," he explains. "The market is big and sufficiently unique to require a targeted effort."

African-Americans, a disproportionate number of whom have low incomes and lack many entertainment options, watch a hefty 74.1 hours a week of television, 44 percent more than whites in general. That means plenty of exposure to the fast-food industry's thousands of messages. Critics decry the targeting, comparing it to targeting by some tobacco and alcohol producers.[1]

It appears that more and more marketers are practicing market segmentation. Some are focusing their marketing effort on smaller and smaller market niches. Does market segmentation make sense in the fast-food business? If inner-city consumers do have special wants in regard to fast food, then it makes sense to target that segment. But if inner-city consumers are really no different from other consumers of fast food in terms of what they want, then it does not make sense to segment the market.

In this chapter we contrast the mass-market strategy with market segmentation strategies. We look at the reasons marketers engage in market segmentation and how they might go about segmenting both consumer and organizational markets.

MARKET MATCHING STRATEGIES

market

Any organization that seeks to match its capabilities and resources with market requirements must have an in-depth understanding of its own capabilities and resources and of the markets it seeks to serve. A *market* is a set of individuals or organizations that desire a product and are willing and able to buy it.

The number of individuals or organizations in a market is a major determinant of sales for products such as bread, home appliances, medical care, and office cleaners. Most marketers, however, are interested mainly in the people in the population who are potential customers or users. Unless people desire the marketer's product, they are nonprospects. Dentists know that many people do not desire dental checkups. But as marketers, dentists try to influence consumer desires. Thus the American Dental Association promotes the benefits of preventive dental care.

Willingness and ability to buy mean that prospective buyers have buying power, are willing to spend, and are eligible to buy. People who desire a new car but cannot afford one are not in the market for the product. Even people who have the buying power are not in the market if they are unwilling to spend—to give up some of their buying power to buy the product. If they have the buying power and are willing to spend, they are not in the market if they are not eligible to buy. Thus people below the legal age to make a contract are ineligible to buy a new car on credit.

In matching their capabilities and resources with market requirements, marketers must identify and select their target markets. In identifying their target markets, they can pursue either a mass-market strategy or a market segmentation strategy.

The Mass-Market Strategy

In marketing the Model-T, Henry Ford offered one marketing mix for all car buyers: one product (not even a choice of colors—all Model-Ts were black), one distribution system, one promotion program, and one price. Ford used the mass-market strategy. The *mass-market strategy* is a strategy that defines the market as all potential buyers of brands in a product category and offers them one marketing mix. (See Figure 7–1.) Such a strategy enabled Ford to schedule long production runs and to hold to a minimum inventory costs, distribution costs, promotion costs, and marketing research costs. Ford was the lowest-cost mass producer of cars.

mass-market strategy

Organizations that use the mass-market strategy assume either (1) that people in the market for a product category have very similar characteristics and wants and that one marketing mix will satisfy them all; or (2) that people in that market have different characteristics and wants but that it is not worth the cost of identifying the differences and developing two or more marketing mixes.

The mass-market strategy is sometimes accompanied by a strategy of product differentiation. *Product differentiation* is a marketing strategy that seeks to create a difference in people's minds between a marketer's brand and rival brands that are serving the same mass market. Advertising, packaging, and minor physical changes can help differentiate the marketer's brand from its rivals. If the features chosen to differentiate the brand are important and believable to the people in the mass market, this product differentiation will help increase sales. Kimberly-Clark says its Kleenex toilet tissue is differentiated by its

product differentiation

FIGURE 7–1

Market Matching Strategies

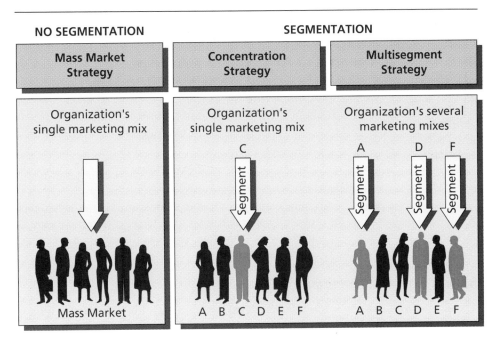

NO SEGMENTATION	SEGMENTATION	
Mass Market Strategy	Concentration Strategy	Multisegment Strategy

"through-dried" process of blow-drying the tissue, which produces a softer finish than the roll driers typically used to remove the water used in paper making.[2]

Marketers sometimes search for consumer characteristics and wants that are common to people of different ages, races, sexes, and incomes. Since, for example, a good-tasting, nutritious cereal is probably a common want of people of all ages, the use of several ad appeals may enable a cereal marketer to combine different age groups into one mass market that can be served with one basic product. This is called *market aggregation*. The Quaker Oats Company used to target its Life cereal to nutrition-conscious adults but has now succeeded in broadening Life's appeal to include children. Thus Life has become an all-family cereal. The Nexxus ad is another example of a market aggregation strategy.

In some cases product differentiation may not lead to a larger market for the product. Although it may increase the probability of purchase by some target customers, it may, in fact, reduce the number of potential buyers. Therefore, product differentiation sometimes is used along with a strategy of market segmentation.

Market Segmentation Strategies

The mass-market strategy works if the market is homogeneous. But if the market is made up of people with very different characteristics and wants, the market is *heterogeneous* and one marketing mix will not satisfy everyone in it. As the Global Marketing box explains, the Japanese market has become increasingly heterogeneous. Marketers who wish to do an effective job of marketing to people in a heterogeneous market must identify the characteristics and wants of different groups of people within the overall market, because one marketing mix will not satisfy all of them. Nor will product differentiation by itself be sufficient to cater to all of their wants.

···■······

market segmentation

Market segmentation is the process of identifying smaller markets (groups of people or organizations) that exist within a larger market. These groups are called *market segments*. The people in a given segment are supposed to be similar in terms of the criteria by which they were segmented. At the same time, people in different segments are supposed to differ in terms of these criteria.

Market segmentation enables a marketer to divide a heterogeneous market into smaller submarkets, or market segments. In each of these smaller segments, the people's wants and characteristics are essentially homogeneous. Therefore the marketer can develop a specific

GLOBAL

MARKETING

There is less ethnic, religious, and cultural diversity in Japan than in a nation of immigrants such as the United States. And most Japanese, according to regular polls, consider themselves middle class. As recently as 1978 books for foreign companies eyeing the Japanese market included such chapters as "Concentration and Uniformity—the Formation of a Mammoth Homogeneous Market."

But for the most part the Japanese market is now uniform only in comparison with the U.S. market. Market researchers see large differences in income levels and lifestyles in Japan. The Japanese rich—the top 10 percent of the population, making more than 10 million yen (approximately $70 thousand) a year—can be divided into five distinct groups. These range from the "overts," who spend heavily, particularly on foreign goods, art, and travel; to the "conservatives," who tend to save their money or spend it on such things as their children's education. Studies of women, the elderly, and the young have turned up similar findings.

Largely as a result of this knowledge,

niche marketing is in full bloom in Japan. Cigarettes are a good example. There are now U.S. brands aimed at young men, such as Lucky Strike, and those aimed at older men, such as Kent. There are Capri and Virginia Slims for women. Japan Tobacco also sells many products aimed at various niches, including Dean for young men and Alex for young women.

Goldstar Company, the giant South Korean manufacturer of home electronics and other products, says that market segmentation in Japan—where it does about $90 million of business a year—is enabling it to invade the country with its lower-priced products. "The market wasn't there before," says Kim Young Jun, managing director of Goldstar's overseas business operations. "There was no demand for the low end, only high-end products. Now there is a market we can get into."

Source: Adapted from Damon Darlin, "Myth and Marketing in Japan," *Wall Street Journal,* April 6, 1989, p. B1. Reprinted by permission of the *Wall Street Journal,* © Dow Jones & Company, Inc., 1989. All rights reserved.

marketing mix for the particular segment that is chosen as the target market. If more than one segment is chosen, a separate marketing mix can be developed for each segment.

Market segmentation also enables marketers to see clearly the diversity that may exist within a given market. It may lead them to uncover market opportunities—to identify a market segment whose wants are not being filled by offerings currently on the market. It also helps marketers develop marketing mixes that are tailored to the characteristics and wants of the people in the segments that are identified and selected as target markets.

For many years Kodak and Fuji have divided the film market into two segments—the consumer segment and the professional segment. More recently the companies recognized a new segment—advanced amateur photographers, people who consider themselves artier than occasional snapshooters. Kodak targets its Ektar film and Fuji targets its Reala film to this segment.[3]

Instead of trying to please everybody with one marketing mix, and probably ending up satisfying nobody very well, marketers who practice targeted marketing focus on pleasing one or more segments of a market. They seek the best possible match between the characteristics and wants of particular market segments and their marketing mixes. There are two types of market segmentation strategies: the concentration strategy and the multisegment strategy. (See Figure 7–1.)

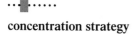

concentration strategy

• **The Concentration Strategy** • Casinos put forth a lot of effort targeting penny-pinching slot machine players and high rollers. On the other hand, Players International's Players Club targets middle-market gamblers. Players says these gamblers are often overlooked by casino marketing programs. The casinos say the middle market is so diverse that such gamblers are harder to target.[4]

The *concentration strategy* is the marketing strategy of focusing marketing effort on one segment of a larger market and developing one marketing mix for that segment. This strategy is used more often in marketing industrial products than in marketing consumer products. The single segment selected to be the firm's target market can be of any size but typically is relatively small.

• *Advantages of Concentration* • Because all its effort is focused on a single segment of the total market, the firm can research target customers' characteristics and wants in great detail and can devote itself to satisfying that segment. The firm is less likely to fall into the trap of trying to satisfy everybody and ending up satisfying nobody. Long production runs may be possible; and distribution, promotion, and price can be keyed to satisfying one target segment. As mentioned earlier, a firm trying to enter a market dominated by a few large firms may gain easier entry by concentrating on a small segment that the existing competitors are overlooking.

A&W Brands is a tiny company compared to PepsiCo and Coca-Cola. It is the market leader in niche soft drinks such as root beer, cream soda, grapefruit soda, and spicy ginger. One of A&W's competitors recently commented about A&W's niche strategy: "It's no different than a halfback in football. You can't run at the pile, so you have to hit the holes."[5]

If a firm concentrates on a segment so small that only one firm can make a satisfactory profit, potential rivals may continue to ignore that segment. Carmike Cinema has two hundred movie theaters in a dozen southern states. Its strategy is to avoid built-up urban and suburban areas that are attractive to its larger rivals, such as General Cinema and United Artists Communications. In some small towns Carmike is a monopolist—there are no other theaters.[6]

Many organizations, however, want to concentrate on the segment of the mass market that has the most people. This sometimes is referred to as the *majority fallacy*. Stiff competition among rivals for the big segment occurs while smaller segments are neglected. The neglect provides opportunity for smaller firms to position themselves in these smaller segments.

• *Disadvantages of Concentration* • The major disadvantage of the concentration strategy is that the organization cannot spread its marketing risk. Thus a decline in the selected segment's buying power, a change in tastes, or the entry of rivals can have a negative impact on profitability.

Sometimes a firm that focuses exclusively on one market segment develops a specialist image in that segment. As a result it may encounter difficulties in directing its effort to other segments. Thus Gerber, best known for its line of baby food, failed in the 1970s in its effort to market ''Singles''—single-serving meals for adults. It was not until 1989 that Gerber reentered the adult food market with a line of flavored applesauces called Fruit Classics.

• **The Multisegment Strategy** • Some firms start out with a concentration strategy and, once they are successful, begin to expand into other segments. In other words, they pursue the multisegment strategy. The *multisegment strategy* is a marketing strategy of developing two or more marketing mixes for two or more market segments. Sara Lee Corporation's L'eggs appeals to the budget-minded hosiery buyer, Hanes and Sheer Energy offer mid-priced hosiery, and the Donna Karan line is targeted to upscale customers.[7]

multisegment strategy

• *Advantages of the Multisegment Strategy* • By using a multisegment strategy rather than a concentration strategy an organization can usually serve a greater number of potential customers. Japanese car manufacturers, for example, once concentrated on U.S. buyers of subcompacts. Several years ago they switched to a multisegment strategy. Today they also are targeting buyers of compact, mid-sized, and upscale cars.

An organization may be able to use excess capacity by appealing to additional market segments. Elderhostels offer people sixty and over short-term noncredit courses that are designed especially to appeal to them. Elderhostels help many colleges cope with declining undergraduate enrollments and use dormitories and cafeterias that otherwise might be idle.

• *Disadvantages of the Multisegment Strategy* • The major disadvantage of the multisegment strategy is that the organization may spread itself too thinly. It may focus on too many segments with too many marketing mixes. For example, some loyalists believe Porsche cheapened its image when it introduced the ''low-priced'' ($19,900) 924-S in 1987. Many potential buyers of the 924-S turned instead to higher-performance models from Honda and Mazda.[8]

For the firm, focusing on too many segments may drive up production costs because shorter production runs are necessary to produce a greater variety of products. Marketing costs also tend to go up when new marketing channels and promotion programs are needed.

Some consumerists argue that marketers sometimes segment markets too much. They say that dividing up the detergent, soft-drink, and car markets, for example, into so many segments causes higher prices for consumers in all the segments and wastes natural resources. Consider that several years ago J. D. Power & Associates (a marketing research firm) divided the luxury car market into two segments—big and expensive cars and European and expensive cars. Today the firm identifies six separate segments: near-luxury cars, traditional luxury cars, high-style luxury cars, low-price international luxury cars, high-price international luxury cars, and luxury sports cars. All are aimed at the U.S. ''affluent market,'' estimated at 4 million households. Perhaps too many cars are chasing too few consumers.[9]

The goal of market segmentation is to satisfy as precisely as possible the wants of consumers in target segments. The societal marketing concept, which we looked at in chapter 1, suggests that perhaps there should be limits to market segmentation in order to conserve productive resources and reduce marketing costs.

Should the Organization Pursue a Segmentation Strategy?

Research on both current and potential customers is the best place to start in deciding whether to pursue a strategy of market segmentation. Progressive Corporation writes many insurance policies on risky customers that most other insurers turn down. The company does a lot of marketing research. After analyzing reams of accident and arrest statistics, it found that drunk drivers with children are least likely to get in trouble again by mixing alcohol and gasoline. Similarly, most insurers that insure motorcyclists charge them by the weight of their motorcycles. Because Progressive's researchers found that middle-aged bikers are a pretty safe bet, the company uses age as its key underwriting criterion.[10]

Five important questions should enter into the decision of whether to pursue a strategy of market segmentation:

1. Are potential customers' characteristics and wants heterogeneous?
2. Can segments be identified and compared in terms of relative attractiveness?
3. Is at least one segment large enough to serve profitably?
4. Can the segments be reached by developing a marketing mix that is designed to match the market opportunity the segments represent?
5. Will the segments be responsive to the marketing mix developed for them?

If the mass market is homogeneous, one marketing mix will be sufficient and a segmentation strategy is not necessary. If the market's characteristics and wants are only slightly different, the mass-market strategy can be accompanied by a strategy of product differentiation. The more heterogeneous its wants are, however, the more attractive a segmentation strategy becomes.

In order to segment a market, it is necessary to identify (define) segments so they can be compared in terms of their relative attractiveness to the organization. The marketer must identify one or more characteristics of people in the mass market that can be used to divide them into segments based on those characteristics. In order to compare the segments' relative attractiveness, the marketer must develop estimates of the revenue potential and the cost of the marketing effort that will be needed to make the desired impact on each segment.

The identification and comparison of market segments enables the marketer to determine if there is at least one segment that is large enough to be served profitably. Unless there is at least one such segment, there is no reason to pursue a segmentation strategy any further.

Assuming that one or more potentially profitable segments have been identified and selected, the marketer still faces the task of reaching them. A separate marketing mix must be tailored to the requirements of each segment selected for targeting. The organization must possess the resources and capabilities to do so at an acceptable rate of return on the investment in the segmentation effort. If it does not possess them, segmentation should not be attempted.

Finally, the decision to pursue a segmentation strategy should always be supported with research showing that the selected segments will be responsive to the marketing mix

One of the most important questions a marketer can ask when deciding whether to pursue a strategy of market segmentation is ''Will the segments be responsive to the marketing mix developed for them''?
[Courtesy of Mattel, Inc.]

planned for them. Unless the targeted segments respond, the segmentation effort will be a misallocation of the organization's resources. In other words, the marketing mix planned for the targeted segment will not generate sales sufficient to make the effort profitable.

Kmart, J. C. Penney, Wal-Mart, and Sears are mass merchandisers, or mass marketers. But they do not practice mass marketing. They recognize that one marketing mix will not satisfy a heterogeneous market; consequently, they target specific market segments with separate marketing mixes.

In other words, *mass marketing* and *mass marketer* are not synonymous. Mass marketers do aim at clearly defined target markets. Thus Kroger's cheese shops and delis are targeted to gourmet shoppers, and Kmart's upgraded apparel lines are targeted to higher-income shoppers. Perhaps the reason mass marketers are so often confused with mass marketing is the fact that they typically take aim at large market segments.

Let's take a closer look at some possible ways to segment the consumer market. We will look at segmentation in organizational markets later in the chapter.

SEGMENTING THE CONSUMER MARKET

segmentation variable

A *segmentation variable* is some characteristic of people in the overall (mass) market that aids in dividing it. Figure 7–2 shows four categories of segmentation variables that are often used in segmenting the consumer market: (1) geographic variables, (2) demographic

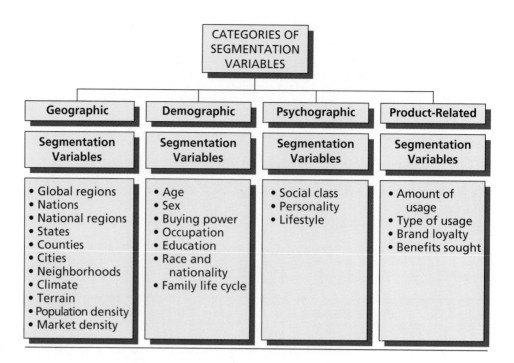

CATEGORIES OF
SEGMENTATION
VARIABLES

Geographic	Demographic	Psychographic	Product-Related
Segmentation Variables	**Segmentation Variables**	**Segmentation Variables**	**Segmentation Variables**
• Global regions • Nations • National regions • States • Counties • Cities • Neighborhoods • Climate • Terrain • Population density • Market density	• Age • Sex • Buying power • Occupation • Education • Race and nationality • Family life cycle	• Social class • Personality • Lifestyle	• Amount of usage • Type of usage • Brand loyalty • Benefits sought

FIGURE 7–2
· ·

Examples of Segmentation Variables for the Consumer Market

variables, (3) psychographic variables, and (4) product-related variables. Figure 7–2 also gives examples of specific segmentation variables for each of these categories. For example, age and sex are demographic segmentation variables.

One-variable segmentation means that only one characteristic is used to divide the mass market. *Multivariate segmentation* means that more than one characteristic is used to divide the mass market. The major advantage of one-variable segmentation is that it is easier to do. The major limitation is that, because the segment is defined less precisely than it is in multivariate segmentation, it is not much help in developing a uniquely satisfying marketing mix. Thus a magazine targeted to women in general would have less appeal to women aged eighteen to thirty-four than does *Redbook,* a magazine targeted to women eighteen to thirty-four years of age.

Marketing research plays a major role in market segmentation. For example, a recent study by the alcoholic beverage research publication *Impact* was based on diaries kept by twelve thousand people. It covered beverage consumption by location, time of day, sex, age, geographic region, and household income. Among the findings: People in the South drank the most alcoholic beverages, households with incomes of $35,000 and above drank the most of every type of alcoholic beverage, and men consumed 75.2 percent of all alcohol.[11]

The more categories of segmentation variables and the more specific the variables used in each category to segment a market, the greater is the number of segments created and the more detailed is the description of people in each segment. In Figure 7–3 four variables were used to segment the market—the demographic variables of sex, race, and age and the geographic variable of population density (small towns and rural areas versus metropolitan areas).

Multivariate segmentation provides marketers with more information about the people in a particular segment than does one-variable segmentation. This should help in developing more satisfying marketing mixes for them. But because there are fewer people in

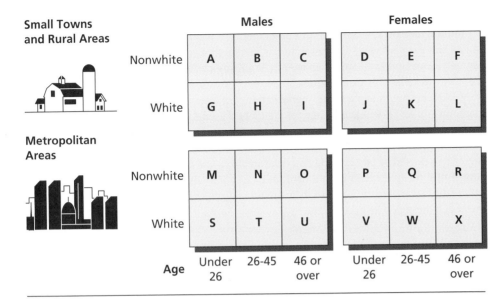

Small Towns and Rural Areas

Metropolitan Areas

		Males			Females		
Nonwhite		A	B	C	D	E	F
White		G	H	I	J	K	L
Nonwhite		M	N	O	P	Q	R
White		S	T	U	V	W	X
Age		Under 26	26-45	46 or over	Under 26	26-45	46 or over

FIGURE 7–3

Four-Variable Segmentation

each segment with multivariate segmentation, the potential for sales in each segment is diminished.

In deciding between one-variable and multivariate segmentation, the marketer must determine if the use of additional variables will help in developing better marketing mixes—ones that are more precisely attuned to satisfying the marketer's intended segments. If the use of additional variables does not help in developing more satisfying mixes, then there is no need to use them. The segmentation variables that an organization uses should help it (1) identify segments that are large enough to serve profitably, (2) develop marketing mixes for the selected segments, and (3) identify segments that can be reached.

Marketing effort should not be misdirected to segments that are too small to be served profitably. In organizational marketing an individual buyer often constitutes a market segment. The individual buyer is in a segment with no other buyers. For example, many of Sears's suppliers consider Sears to be a market segment by itself. Traditionally, one person would rarely constitute a market segment in the consumer market. Among the few exceptions are individuals for whom a contractor builds custom-built homes. Each home is made to order for an individual customer.

More recently, however, some consumer product marketers have gone beyond segmenting markets on the basis of regions, states, and cities. Increasingly they are targeting specific neighborhoods, and even a single supermarket. The supermarket scanners that we discussed in chapter 4 are helping to make this possible. For example, Frito-Lay used store-specific marketing when it introduced its lower-oil, light line of snack chips nationally. The company first found those stores whose customers fit the products' demographic profile: white-collar workers 35 to 54 years old, earning more than $35 thousand a year. By increasing promotional spending, running in-store taste programs, and lobbying retailers to give more space to the pricier chips in the selected stores, Frito-Lay got the line off to a running start. In other words, store-specific marketing helped Frito-Lay to reduce the risk of new product failure.[12]

As we will see in the discussion of direct marketing in chapter 16, direct marketers of many consumer products seek to target specific individuals—*segments of one*. Some call this *individualized marketing*. For example, Waldenbooks, a unit of Kmart, has enrolled 3.7 million members, at $5 each, in a program that rewards frequent book buyers with discounts and extra service. The program has increased store visits by club members by 43 percent. The membership program enables Waldenbooks to target specific individuals who are heavy readers with specific titles.[13]

Marketers should avoid using segmentation variables that are irrelevant in developing marketing mixes. For example, age would not be a useful variable for segmenting the market for typewriter correction fluid.

Finally, certain segmentation variables should not be used if they do not help in reaching segments selected as target markets. For example, some consumers are compulsive shoppers. But a retailer would have a hard time targeting advertisements to people with this personality characteristic because there are no magazines, radio programs, or other media that reach these people exclusively.

Geographic Segmentation

geographic segmentation

Geographic differences in consumer behavior often lead to the development of separate marketing mixes for targeted geographic segments. For example, according to a recent survey on consumer spending, urban households spent an average of $1,800 a year on food at home and rural households spent only $1,400. Urban households also spent an average of $300 on alcohol, compared with $200 for rural households.[14]

Geographic segmentation is the division of a mass market into units such as nations, regions, states, cities, and neighborhoods. Figure 7–2 identified examples of geographic segmentation variables. Table 7–1 gives typical examples of breakdowns for each of those variables.

• **Global Regions to Neighborhoods** • As we will see in chapter 22, international marketers often divide the global market along regional or national lines. Two or more nations whose people are sufficiently homogeneous in characteristics and wants that are important to the marketer can be treated as one market segment. The European Community (EC) was formed in 1957 with the eventual purpose of creating a single European market. The twelve

TABLE 7–1 Examples of Typical Breakdowns for Geographic Segmentation Variables

Variable	Examples of Typical Breakdowns
Global region	Latin America, Western Europe, North America
Nation	Brazil, France, United States
National region	Pacific, East South Central, New England
State size	Large, medium, small
County size	Large, medium, small
City size	Nonmetropolitan, metropolitan area type
Neighborhood	Inner-city, suburban
Climate	Northern, southern
Terrain	Plains, mountains, hills, desert
Population density	Urban, suburban, rural
Market density	High potential, medium potential, low potential

TABLE 7–2 ▪ Major Types of Metropolitan Areas

....

Metropolitan Statistical Area (MSA)

A free-standing urban area. It has either a city of 50,000 population or an urbanized area of 50,000 population, and a total metropolitan area population of at least 100,000. Examples are the New Haven–Meriden, Connecticut, area; Syracuse, New York; Sheboygan, Wisconsin; Fargo, North Dakota; and Peoria, Illinois.

Primary Metropolitan Statistical Area (PMSA)

A large urbanized county, or a cluster of socially and economically integrated counties, either of which has close ties to neighboring areas. The area contains more than 1 million people. Examples include the area of Aurora–Elgin, Joliet, and Waukegan, Illinois, and the area of Gary-Hammond, Indiana.

Consolidated Metropolitan Statistical Area (CMSA)

A large area that includes several PMSAs. The Los Angeles CMSA consists of the following PMSAs: Anaheim–Santa Ana, Los Angeles–Long Beach, Oxnard–Ventura, and Riverside–San Bernardino.

....

member countries are considered by some marketers to be a single market segment—the "United States of Europe."

Japanese cars have long been more popular on the coasts than in the Midwest, where the Big Three U.S. automakers employ thousands of people and hometown loyalties run deep. Thus Nissan has increased its regional advertising budget and plans advertising that will "include Midwestern sensitivities."[15]

Automobile manufacturers consider California to be a separate market segment because its emissions laws are more stringent than federal laws. Regions within a state may be targeted also. Marketers of retirement villages in Arkansas know that the influx of retirees is concentrated in the Ozark and Ouachita mountain highlands.[16] *Atlanta* magazine is targeted to people in Atlanta. Local historic preservation groups typically confine their efforts to specific neighborhoods. The U.S. Bureau of the Census divides metropolitan areas into census tracts; it reports income, age, and other market data for each tract.

Climate and terrain can also be used to divide a market. Some hair spray manufacturers target people in high-humidity areas, and some moisturizing lotion manufacturers target people in dry climates. Subaru entered the U.S. market by targeting the snowy New England and Rocky Mountain states with its four-wheel-drive car.

• **Population Density and Market Density** • An area's population density is the number of people per square mile. Nations, states, cities, and neighborhoods vary in population density. Table 7–2 identifies the three major types of metropolitan areas—MSAs, PMSAs, and CMSAs—where roughly three out of every four Americans live. Because of the high concentration of people in these areas, some marketers focus most, or even all, of their effort on these areas.

market density

Market density interests marketers more than population density. *Market density* is the number of people per square mile in an area who are potential customers for a given marketer's offering. The market density for products targeted to Hispanics is higher in San Antonio than in many other cities with roughly equal land area and population size.

Dividing a market solely on the basis of geographic variables tends to result in the creation of a large segment that is still too heterogeneous for effective marketing. Thus marketers often segment a market by combining two or more categories of segmentation variables, as we will see in the discussions that follow.

Demographic Segmentation

demographic segmentation

As chapter 2 suggested, marketers must pay close attention to demographic trends. *Demography* is the study of population statistics, such as the number of births, deaths, marriages, and age groupings. ***Demographic segmentation*** is the division of a mass market on the basis of statistical data such as age, sex, and buying power. (See Figure 7–2.) This approach to segmentation is the most often used approach, because demographic variables are easy to measure through observation and surveys. Population data collected and reported by the U.S. Bureau of the Census can also be used to segment markets.

In the discussions that follow, we focus on the demographic variables of age, sex, buying power, occupation, education, race and nationality, and family life cycle. The Ethics in Marketing box raises several issues about the use of demographic variables to segment markets.

ETHICS IN MARKETING

Late in 1989 R. J. Reynolds Tobacco Company announced its intention to test market a menthol cigarette the following February in Philadelphia. A spokesperson for the company said research showed that some African-American smokers ''prefer a lighter menthol'' cigarette; and the new brand, Uptown, was designed to give smokers a lighter menthol taste than the company's Salem brand.

Uptown was the first cigarette that was to be explicitly targeted to African-Americans. Because of strong opposition from groups ranging from the American Cancer Society to the Junior League, however, Reynolds in late January 1990 announced its cancellation of plans to test market Uptown. Louis Sullivan, secretary of health and human services, said in a speech: ''Uptown's message is more disease, more suffering and more death for a group already bearing more than its share of smoking-related illness and mortality.'' This was the first time that a sec-

retary of health and human services had ever singled out a specific brand of cigarette for criticism.

Tobacco companies, of course, had marketed to African-Americans prior to the Uptown episode. But the approach was more subtle. For example, tobacco companies say that menthol brands are aimed at the general public. But the companies have pitched the products in African-American publications, on billboards in African-American neighborhoods, and by sponsoring African-American events. Marketers and antismoking activists agree that Reynolds's big mistake was in its blatant declaration that Uptown was aimed at African-Americans.

R. J. Reynolds said it had simply decided to be upfront about its intentions. A company spokesperson said, ''We're an honest company; what do you say when the audience is going to be predominantly black?'' In a statement, the company said that pressure from antismoking ''zealots'' succeeded in limiting

• **Age** • Figure 7–4 shows the actual percentages of the U.S. population by age group for 1990 and the projected percentages for 2000 and 2010. Age is an important segmentation variable for many products because consumer wants change as people grow older. Gerber Products Company recently developed a line of toddler (ages one to three) foods in an effort to retain many of the ten thousand baby "customers" it loses every day as these babies grow older.[17] Some Florida McDonald's restaurants offer Senior Citizen Bingo during slow morning hours.[18] As explained in the Johnson & Johnson ad, Johnson's Baby Sunblock SPF 15 lotion is made for babies.

The number of age segments used depends on the particular market and product. Some manufacturers of children's clothing divide the market into infant, toddler, junior, preschool, and so on. Procter & Gamble's Pampers Phases are disposable diapers with different absorbency and design features for the four stages of a child's early years. For example, the diaper for "crawlers" has wider tape fasteners because babies old enough to crawl put more stress on the tapes. The infant size has a longer back sheet, because infants spend much of their time lying down.[19]

Demographers refer to the baby boom generation (the 76 million Americans born between 1946 and 1964) as "the pig in the python"—"a moving bulge that distorts and distends everything around it as it rumbles through the stages of life."[20] Marketers have

choices for African-American smokers, resulting in "a further erosion of the free enterprise system."

In announcing its decision to cancel test marketing of Uptown, R. J. Reynolds said it could not get accurate results from the test market under such adverse conditions. Some marketing experts predicted that the Uptown fiasco would make it increasingly difficult in the future for tobacco and liquor companies to target their brands to minorities, women, and youths.

After the Uptown fiasco, an antismoking group released copies of a marketing plan for another new brand of cigarettes, Dakota, which R. J. Reynolds was supposed to test market in April 1990 in Houston. According to the plan, Dakota was to target young, poorly educated white women. The ad campaign was to focus on a certain group of women whose favorite pastimes, according to the marketing plan, include "cruising," "partying," and attending "hot rod

shows" and "tractor pulls" with their boyfriends. When asked about the marketing plan, Louis Sullivan said, "It is especially reprehensible to lure young people into smoking and potential lifelong nicotine addiction."

As more and more better-educated Americans have quit smoking, tobacco companies have focused more and more marketing effort on the poor, minorities, young women, and consumers in foreign markets, especially in developing countries in the Third World.

Sources: The Uptown material is adapted from James R. Schiffman, "Uptown's Fall Bodes Ill for Niche Brands," *Wall Street Journal,* January 22, 1990, pp. B1, B6. Reprinted by permission of the *Wall Street Journal,* © Dow Jones & Company, Inc., 1990. All rights reserved. The Dakota material is adapted from Michael Specter, "New Cigarette Targets Young, White Women," *New Orleans Times-Picayune,* February 18, 1990, p. A6. © 1990 the *Washington Post.* Reprinted with permission.

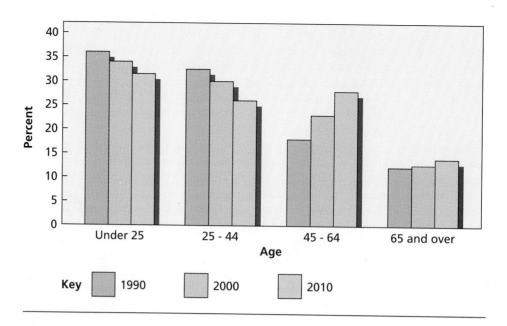

FIGURE 7–4

• •

Percent of the U.S. Population
by Age Group, Actual and Projected for Selected Years

*Projections.
Source: U.S. Census Bureau.

studied and catered to baby boomers more than to any other age segment. In the year 2000 the youngest baby boomers will be thirty-six years old and the oldest will be fifty-four. This is a major plus for marketers because that age group in the past has spent the most money of all age groups.[21]

Unlike the baby boomers, who share many characteristics and wants in common, the over-sixty-five segment includes people whose characteristics and wants are increasingly heterogeneous. Because more and more people are living into their eighties and nineties, the over-sixty-five segment spans thirty or more years. There are, for example, significant differences in health and income between people sixty-five to seventy-five and those over eighty-five.

The graying of America has tremendous implications for marketers. Americans over fifty are the most affluent group of all. Although they account for 35 percent of the adult population, they have nearly half the nation's discretionary income (current income minus taxes and spending for necessities) and control 77 percent of all assets. They also have more free time to spend it. For example, between 1970 and 1990 the labor force participation rate of men aged fifty-five to sixty-four fell from 83 percent to 67 percent.[22]

Nevertheless, in a national survey 80 percent of respondents fifty-five or older were dissatisfied with the way marketers market to them. For example, 70 percent said they found packages and bottles difficult to open, and nearly 60 percent said the lettering on labels is too small to read. Nearly one-third had boycotted goods and services because of inappropriate age stereotyping in ads.[23]

Kellogg put a name on its Bran Flakes—40+ Bran Flakes. *Lear's* magazine was launched "for the woman who wasn't born yesterday." Centrum Silver is promoted as "the first complete multivitamin for adults 50+." But the aging of America is also having an impact on the types of goods and services offered to all consumers, not just older consumers. Whirlpool has redesigned all its major appliances to conform to the needs of an older market. For example, it has replaced the hard-to-read operating instructions on washing machine lids with high-contrast oversize graphics.[24]

The use of age as a segmentation variable should be preceded by marketing research that

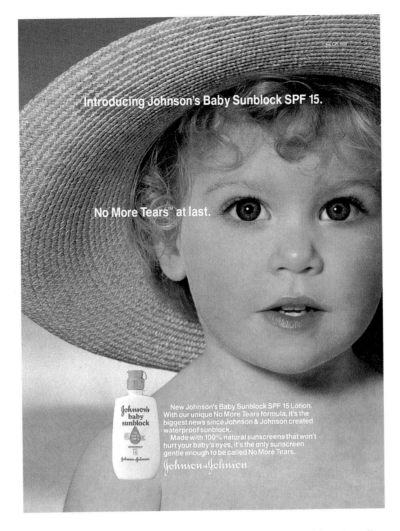

Introducing Johnson's Baby Sunblock SPF 15.

No More Tears™ at last.

New Johnson's Baby Sunblock SPF 15 Lotion. With our unique No More Tears formula, it's the biggest news since Johnson & Johnson created waterproof sunblock.
Made with 100% natural sunscreens that won't hurt your baby's eyes, it's the only sunscreen gentle enough to be called No More Tears.

An ad that reflects market segmentation based on age.

(Courtesy of Johnson & Johnson.)

demonstrates that age is a meaningful variable for the product under consideration. For example, in recent years brokerage firms and money management firms have focused more attention on people over fifty years of age and less attention on the 1980s-type yuppies. But experts advise these firms that they should not suddenly start running ads depicting groups of gray-haired investors. One expert says: "You are not advertising to people who think they are older. You are advertising to people who think they are younger and will live longer." Adds another: "People portray themselves as being 10 to 20 years younger than they are. We've found that in some cases, portraying older people in print ads tends to be extremely ineffective and in some cases turns them off."[25] Johnson & Johnson introduced its Affinity shampoo as the shampoo for women over forty. Because of poor sales, Affinity was repositioned for a more general audience.

One study suggests that marketers may be missing out when they segment older consumers by age. In the study, age did not make much difference in buying habits. The study found instead that people age along biophysical and psychosocial lines in different ways. Two other studies agree that older people should be grouped by attitude more than age.[26]

• **Sex** • Sex is also used as a basis for segmenting markets for such products as shampoo, cigarettes, razors, toys, and hair sprays. A growing number of clinics and hospitals are expanding their women's health care programs because women are the major health care consumers. After age fourteen, women visit physicians 25 percent more often—and are hospitalized 15 percent more often—than men.[27]

Men account for nearly half of the 65 million Americans who want to lose weight. But women are much more likely to diet. Slim-Fast's TV ads featuring sports heroes such as Tommy Lasorda, manager of the Los Angeles Dodgers, were designed to broaden the product's appeal to men. Before Lasorda's endorsement men accounted for only about 10 percent of Slim-Fast's customers. After the endorsement the figure shot up to between 30 and 35 percent.[28]

The use of sex as a segmentation variable must take into account changes in traditional sex roles and be based on careful marketing research. For example, more fathers are becoming involved in child-rearing. Research indicates that there are larger numbers of men at childbirth classes and in the delivery room itself. There have been modest increases in male involvement in feeding, diapering, babysitting, and similar child-caring chores. There has also been a tremendous increase in the number of father "self-help" books.[29]

Simmons College in Boston is an all-female school. Its MBA program emphasizes organizational behavior courses that examine how women compete differently from men.[30]

Sex may not always be an especially strong segmentation variable, however. For example, despite all the brands of cigarettes that have been targeted to women—including Virginia Slims, More, Dawn, Capri, Superslims, Chelsea, Spring Lemon Lights, and Eve Ultra Light 120s—the vast majority of women smokers still smoke mass-appeal brands such as Marlboro.[31] Many brands that were targeted to women failed.

First Women's Bank was founded in 1975 to cater to professional women. It nearly folded in 1986. In late 1988 the bank asked the state banking department for permission to change its name to First New York Bank for Business. According to the bank's chair and chief executive officer: "We found the name gave us no special competitive advantage. When we went to upscale professional women for business, they said 'I'm good enough to go to a regular bank.' "[32]

• **Buying Power** • Many markets can be segmented by buying power. American Express, MasterCard, and VISA target their gold cards to higher-income people who want more services and are willing and able to pay higher fees for them. Stuarts Department Stores is a retail chain that targets primarily lower-income shoppers. As the company's chief executive officer says: "I don't want the moderate- and upper-income shoppers. They have more places to shop than they know what to do with."[33]

Household buying power affects people's ability to buy, the types and quality of products they buy, and where they buy. *Sales & Marketing Management* magazine's annual *Survey of Buying Power* provides an index of buying power for regions, states, and metropolitan areas in the United States. The index indicates the relative buying power of each specific geographic area—the proportion of aggregate national buying power contained in the area. As we saw in chapter 2, the three main sources of buying power are current income, accumulated wealth (or assets), and credit.

Buying power, of course, is not distributed evenly among households. A disproportionate share of the total income in the United States goes to the richest one-fifth of families. In 1990 the top 1 percent of families accounted for 12.6 percent of the country's after-tax family income.[34] As mentioned earlier, Americans over fifty account for 35 percent of the adult population, but they have nearly half the nation's discretionary income and control 77 percent of all assets. The average African-American household's income is less than that of the average white household's income, and households in the Northeast have more buying power than those in the Southeast. Dual-earner families (both spouses employed) are becoming increasingly common.[35] When teenagers are present, they do much of the family shopping, often deciding which products and brands to buy. When these teenagers also work, the families are called multiple-earner families.

• **Occupation** • Because consumers' occupations may affect what they buy, occupation can be used as a segmentation variable. Typical occupational breakdowns include professional and technical workers; managers, officials, and proprietors; clerical and sales workers; craftsmen; supervisors; operatives; farmers; the retired; students; homemakers; and the unemployed. The proportion of white-collar workers in the U.S. labor force is increasing, and the proportion of blue-collar workers is decreasing.

Some physicians are targeting professional athletes (sports medicine), and others are targeting performers (arts medicine).[36] Some hotels offer suites that provide more space and comfort than ordinary rooms and are designed to appeal to the business traveler who stays three or four days instead of the usual two. Extended-stay hotels are targeted to corporate users that need temporary quarters for relocated employees and for training and educational programs, such as computer classes, that require workers to be away from home. Antique & Contemporary Leasing in Washington, D.C., targets diplomats, corporate executives, government officials, and developers building and showing expensive houses. Many of these people expect to be in the area only a brief time before their careers take them elsewhere.[37]

Occupation is one factor that is used to measure a person's or a family's social class. There are often significant differences between some of the spending patterns of people in different occupations who earn the same amount of money. Occupation can therefore be a more important determinant of consumer behavior than income. A junior executive and a plumber may have the same income, but they tend to spend it differently.

• **Education** • Consumers' education levels may also affect their buying behaviors. Breakdowns in education level are grade school or less, some high school, high school graduate, some college, and college graduate. Higher educational levels are generally associated with higher incomes. Better-educated people are more likely than less educated people to engage in comparison shopping, to shop outside the town in which they live, to read *Consumer Reports,* and to complain about faulty products and poor service. Elderly people who are college educated are much more active in sailing, golf, tennis, photography, home entertaining, and theater and concert attendance than are elderly people without a college background.[38]

The army, navy, air force, and marines use different recruiting programs and techniques for college students than for high school dropouts. Public broadcasting stations make a special effort to reach the more highly educated people in their communities for contributions. Both are examples of the use of education level to segment markets.

There are 13 million college students in the United States, but many marketers make the mistake of assuming they can reach students through their mainstream promotions. For example, Tambrands' ran an ad for its First Response home pregnancy test that featured a happy couple, with the man asking, ''So which is it, yes or no?'' and the woman responding, ''Now, why do you think I'm smiling?'' The ad was highly criticized in a focus group. Students in the group said the scenario implied that the test was positive—which to most students is a big negative.[39]

• **Race and Nationality** • As we saw in chapter 2, although many people like to think of the United States as a great melting pot, in which all people are basically alike, this is a myth. Many racial and ethnic groups exist within the overall market—for example, white,

African-American, Hispanic, and Asian. African-Americans currently are the largest minority group in the country, but Hispanics will become the largest minority group in the next century. Asians, however, are the fastest-growing minority group. During the decade of the 1980s the Asian population in the United States increased 80 percent.[40] Product preferences and buying behavior often differ among and within these groups.

Where there are large concentrations of particular ethnic groups, geographic and ethnic variables can be combined to segment the market. For example, Cuban Americans are heavily concentrated in southern Florida, Mexican-Americans are mostly concentrated in the southwestern states, and Puerto Ricans are concentrated in New York City. Of the U.S. Hispanic population, over half is in Texas and California. Nearly half of the Asian population is in six urban areas—Honolulu, Los Angeles, San Francisco, New York, Chicago, and San Jose.[41] California is the most ethnically diverse state. Roughly 40 percent of the population is African-American, Hispanic, or Asian. By 2000 this share may rise to half.[42]

Great care must be exercised in using race and nationality to divide markets. It would be a mistake, for example, to view any market as homogeneous. There are many segments within any given racial or ethnic market. For example, the Hispanic market is not homogeneous. The average Cuban-American has a higher income and is older than the average Mexican-American or Puerto Rican in this country.[43] Hispanics do not all speak the same type of Spanish. Asians' languages are also different, and Asian immigrants are no longer primarily from China and Japan. The last two decades have seen an influx of immigration from Southeast Asia. Furthermore, although the early immigrants from those countries tended to be well educated and middle class, the newest immigrants often were peasants.[44]

• **Family Life Cycle** • As we saw in chapter 5, the family life cycle describes the process of family formation and dissolution. Each stage in the cycle reflects changes in the family, and these changes affect the family's expenditure patterns. Thus such variables as marital status, presence or absence of children, and age of children can be used to divide markets.

For example, newly married couples are an important segment for home appliance manufacturers, and the young divorced with children segment is important to Parents Without Partners and to child-care firms such as Kinder-Care Learning Centers. Financial institutions pitch loan programs to young families and savings programs to older families.

A household is made up of all persons who live in a housing unit such as an apartment, a mobile home, or a house. Households are divided into four major groups: (1) married couples with dependent children (27 percent); (2) married couples without dependent children (30 percent); (3) people living alone (24 percent); and (4) other families and nonfamilies, such as unmarried couples, roommates, and single-parent families (19 percent).[45] Over half of African-American children under eighteen and nearly a third of Hispanic children live with only one parent; 19 percent of white children live with one parent.[46]

The singles market is a heterogeneous group, including people who have never been married, divorced people, widows and widowers, and those married but with the spouse absent. Marketers that focus on the singles market, or on any of its segments, include the owners of singles' apartment buildings and condominiums, singles' bars, gourmet shops, and churches and synagogues that offer special programs for singles.

Psychographic Segmentation

psychographic segmentation

Geographic and demographic variables traditionally have been the major variables for segmenting markets. Nevertheless, there may be considerable psychographic differences among the people within a given geographic or demographic group. *Psychographic segmentation* is the division of a mass market on the basis of social class, personality characteristics, or lifestyles.

• **Social Class** • As we saw in chapter 5, social class influences consumer behavior. The different characteristics and wants of people in the different classes make social class a useful basis for segmenting markets such as those for liquor, furniture, financial services, cars, clothing, hotels, and leisure activities. Retailers, especially, often use social class in segmenting their markets. Prestige department stores, for example, cater to the upper classes, and discount department stores and other retailers target the lower classes.

Marketers that use social class to segment a market build in product features, design advertisements, furnish stores, and develop the other elements of their marketing mixes to appeal to people in targeted social classes. For example, Villeroy & Boch, a 240-year-old German firm, targets its fine china to the upwardly mobile as they move upward. Old World product, Old World grace, and Old World service are offered at the company's first store in the United States on an elegant stretch of Madison Avenue in New York.[47]

• **Personality** • When marketers attempt to segment markets by personality variables, they try to offer brands whose images (or brand personalities) will appeal to the consumer personalities they identify. Typical breakdowns include compulsive, competitive, extroverted, gregarious, authoritarian, ambitious, and aggressive. Banks that promote themselves as friendly and whose customer service personnel are instructed to address customers by their first names are trying to appeal to gregarious people. Some cosmetics marketers and mutual funds target aggressive individuals.

Although some studies have suggested a link between several personality characteristics and buyer behavior, the results of many studies have not been conclusive. Nevertheless, some marketers, as just indicated, try to divide markets on the basis of personality, believing that personality does influence which products and brands individual consumers buy.

Marketers sometimes use personality inventories to gain insight into the psychological makeup of target customers. There are problems with this method, however. One is the difficulty of measuring personality characteristics. Existing personality inventories, such as the Minnesota Multiphasic Personality Inventory (MMPI), were developed for clinical use, not for the purpose of segmenting markets. A second problem relates to identifying target customers. A retail store manager may suspect that compulsiveness is an important characteristic of the store's best customers. But how can customers who have this personality trait be identified? A third problem, as suggested earlier, is the reachability of the segments. Suppose gregarious people are good prospects to bank at a first-name-basis bank. How would the bank direct ads at this segment? There are no magazines or TV programs that reach this segment exclusively.

Marketers who try to segment on the basis of personality therefore generally focus on a personality characteristic they believe is valued positively by most people in the culture. They assume that many people have or want to have this personality characteristic and advertise their brands as being suitable for people with the characteristic. For example, Lady Stetson ads say: ''Wear it. Live it. A Declaration of Independence.''

• **Lifestyle** • Segmentation by lifestyle is a more recent method of identifying aspects of people's lives that affect buying behavior. It involves asking respondents to indicate how strongly they agree or disagree with a series of statements (perhaps twenty to twenty-five pages of statements) pertaining to their activities, interests, and opinions (called AIO statements). By analyzing their responses, the marketer can determine if there are distinctive groupings of consumers.

If groupings do exist, the marketer has a lifestyle profile of the consumers in each group. The marketer gains a better understanding of consumers' lifestyles, of how the purchase of a product fits in with their lifestyles, of what other products they might buy, and of what types of advertising themes might appeal to them. Merchants that target low-income people, such as Stuarts Department Stores, know their customers' lifestyles inside out, including shopping habits. The merchants know, for example, that their customers do not buy seasonal merchandise until the weather breaks.[48]

The Mirage and the Excalibur are two recently built hotel/casinos in Las Vegas. The Mirage caters to the "high-roller" gambler's lifestyle. The Excalibur caters to the "low-roller" gambler's lifestyle and bills itself as a "one-of-a-kind, must-see entertainment megastore."[49]

Although psychographics is not an exact science, it can show that the people in a given segment tend to be similar in attitudes, values, aspirations, motives, and personality characteristics. Table 7–3 lists several variables under each of the AIO dimensions, along with the demographic variables that are often included in such inventories.

By studying responses to statements about the variables under the *activities* dimension, marketers can divide people into groups on the basis of how they spend their time. Analysis of the responses under the *interests* dimension helps in dividing people according to the importance they place on things in their lives. Finally, examination of the responses under the *opinions* dimension enables marketers to divide people according to their opinions about themselves and about broad issues. When this information is coupled with such demographic information as age, education, and income, a profile of people in each lifestyle segment can be put together. Lifestyle analysis provides insight into how people live their lives on a daily basis. It should therefore yield meaningful information about their product requirements and buyer behavior.

Many psychographic studies have been conducted in recent years in an attempt to define psychographic segments within the U.S. adult population. VALS (Values and Lifestyles) was developed by SRI International, a research firm. On the basis of a survey of almost three thousand people throughout the nation, VALS classified people into four comprehensive groups (need-driven, outer-directed, inner-directed, and combined outer- and

TABLE 7–3   Lifestyle Dimensions

Activities	Interests	Opinions	Demographics
Work	Family	Themselves	Age
Hobbies	Home	Social issues	Education
Social events	Job	Politics	Income
Vacation	Community	Business	Occupation
Entertainment	Recreation	Economics	Family size
Club membership	Fashion	Education	Dwelling
Community	Food	Products	Geography
Shopping	Media	Future	City size
Sports	Achievements	Culture	Stage in life cycle

Source: Reprinted by permission, from Joseph T. Plummer, "The Concept and Application of Life Style Segmentation," *Journal of Marketing*, January 1974, p. 34, published by the American Marketing Association.

inner-directed), which were subdivided into nine lifestyles. People in each lifestyle grouping had similar profiles of responses to the VALS lifestyle statements. A VALS 2 classification that was subsequently developed categorized consumers as belonging to one of five basic lifestyle groups (strugglers, action-oriented, status-oriented, principle-oriented, and actualizers). The VALS studies are the most widely used by marketers in segmenting markets on the basis of lifestyle.

There are, however, many other classifications of lifestyles. For example, shopping is one of the variables listed under the activities dimension in Table 7–3. In a study to develop profiles of holiday shopping lifestyles, respondents were given statements such as the following to agree or disagree with:

- ''Before I shop, I look at the newspaper ads or other shopping ads to compare prices.''
- ''It's fun to get dressed up a bit to go holiday shopping.''
- ''Something should be done to curb advertising during the holiday season.''

By analyzing responses to these and many other AIO statements, the marketer developed the four shopping profiles presented in Table 7–4.[50]

Notice also in Table 7–3 that vacation is one of the variables listed under the activities dimension. Research conducted by Gilmore Research Group identified the following travel profiles: (1) adventure seekers, (2) older stay-at-homes, (3) fun seekers, (4) family travel planners, (5) solitude seekers, (6) intense travelers, and (7) no-nonsense travelers.[51]

Advertising agencies, marketing consultants, and newspapers are among the sources of information on lifestyle segments. Thus an increasing amount of descriptive information is becoming available on an increasing variety of psychographic segments. In developing a marketing strategy for a brand, the marketer can look for relationships between the characteristics of the brand and the characteristics of various identified psychographic groups. Another approach is for the marketer to develop a custom-tailored set of psychographic segments that might be more appropriate for its own product or brand.

In recent years, as more and more marketers have been engaging in regional marketing, geodemographic segmentation has become increasingly popular. Utilities, financial services institutions, health care organizations, retailers, and packaged-goods companies are among the types of users. *Geodemographic segmentation* clusters potential customers into neighborhood lifestyle categories that enable the marketer to determine what ''type'' of people live in a particular area and to identify areas with the greatest demand for a particular good or service. Donnelley Marketing Information Services has developed a ClusterPlus geodemographic system that combines demographics and socioeconomic or lifestyle characteristics.

geodemographic segmentation

Sears is a good example of regional marketing using geodemographic analysis. Sears geocodes its credit card customer database to find its best customers and identify growth segments to target. The analysis also can be used to determine which merchandise is best suited to an area's needs.

For example, several years ago Sears opened two ''intercept'' stores in previously underrepresented locations in the Chicago area. Both stores were customized to match the lifestyles of people in the market areas they served.

Chicago's Old Town district has a heavy concentration of apartment dwellers and singles. Thus the Sears store there featured a Brand Central superstore; departments such as hardware, home improvements, and ready-to-assemble furniture; and concession services, such as a bakery and cafe, a floral shop, an optical department, and a shoe repair department.

TABLE 7–4 ■ Holiday Shopping Lifestyles

....

Extravagant Elves

Affluent, able, and willing to pay for special gifts and celebrations, they go all out to stimulate the magic of the season. They begin shopping early, but stretch it out, buying impractical, whimsical, or wildly extravagant gifts—always chic, always good quality, very often store-wrapped—on credit. Generally childless couples or single—young or older retirees—they're liberal rock-music lovers who, even as adults, hang stockings.

Hearth Huggers

Like Christmas but don't go hog-wild: are concerned about the commercialization, believing the celebrations were better when they were kids. They get caught up in the spirit of the holidays, with traditional, warm, family-oriented gatherings, often religious. They send Christmas cards, have all-purpose backup gifts on hand, shop carefully, and usually finish long before Christmas.

Soured Spirits

Have little to spend, so are bummed out by the commercialization of Christmas. Most would enjoy the holidays more if the gift-giving weren't part of it. They'll buy fewer gifts than any other group and especially dislike the idea of buying gifts for co-workers. They tend to choose practical gifts (often asking recipients what they'd like), sometimes give handmade items, will drive miles to hit sales but spend little time on gift selection. Shop late—very often not until two weeks before Christmas—and generally pay cash. Might be older, separated, or divorced and favor pickups and country music.

Sugarplums

Traditionalists—many are homemakers with children—who shift into high gear during the holidays. They bake cookies, donate to charities, cook big turkey dinners, and buy scads of gifts. They go all out, largely to ensure that their kids love Christmas as much as they did. They'll shop around for the best deals, but won't cut back on the number of gifts, even in rocky financial times. Prefer easy-listening music and do up Christmas in the most old-fashioned way.

....

Source: Elizabeth Snead, ''Unwrapping Your Christmas Presence,'' *USA Today,* December 3, 1990, p. 4D. Copyright 1990, *USA Today.* Reprinted with permission.

Chicago's South Side is an area that consists primarily of single-family households with children. The Sears store there offered more clothing than the Old Town store and had a Kids & More department.[52]

Product-Related Segmentation

........■......

product-related segmentation

Among other ways to segment a market are the consumer's amount of usage of the product, the type of usage of the product, brand loyalty, and benefits sought from the product. These are examples of product-related segmentation. *Product-related segmentation* is the division of a mass market on the basis of characteristics of the consumer's relationship to the product.

■ **Amount of Usage** ■ The consumer's amount of usage is either the quantity of a product that is consumed or the number of interactions with a retailer, such as store visits, during a specific period of time. For any given product or type of retailer, there are users and nonusers. For example, many consumers have never purchased a personal computer or ordered merchandise from a Land's End catalog or flown on a plane. All of these people are nonusers of those products or retailers.

Users can be divided into heavy users, moderate users, and light users. The Hertz ad is targeted to heavy users of car rental services. The 80/20 principle holds that a disproportionate share of total consumption of many products is accounted for by the heavy users. Thus, according to the principle, 80 percent of a bank's revenues are generated by 20 percent of its customers. Although the percentages are not exact, the general idea often holds.

Adolph Coors Company launched Keystone beer in 1990. This was the company's first entry in the popular-priced category. Because men aged twenty-five to fifty-four drink nearly all the popular-priced beer sold, Coors targeted Keystone to them. Coors also was one of the leaders in targeting women with its beer ads, especially with its Coors Light ad campaigns.[53]

An ad that reflects market segmentation based on amount of usage.

(Copyright Hertz System, Inc., 1990.)

Infrequent (light) users can be important to a firm's profitability too. Priority Overnight Service accounts for about 51 percent of Federal Express's revenues, and infrequent users account for about a third of the Priority Overnight Service. These users are important because they forfeit the price breaks given to larger-volume customers.[54]

Nonusers can be divided into at least two groups—prospects and nonprospects. Prospects might become users; nonprospects are unlikely to ever become users. Prospects may have neutral attitudes about the product, whereas nonprospects may have strong negative attitudes about it. Thus prospects are more important than nonprospects. Several years ago Sterling Drug introduced Bayer aspirin with a microthin coating to make it easier for people to swallow the product. This increased its appeal to some nonusers who were prospects.

- **Type of Usage** • Some markets can be segmented on the basis of how the product is used. For example, Chrysler owns three car rental firms. Its Snappy Rental specializes in providing replacement cars for people who need them after an accident with their own cars. Dollar Rent A Car has rental facilities in airport terminals, and 80 percent of its customers are business travelers. Thrifty Rent-a-Car operates out of off-airport locations. Less than half of Thrifty's customers rent cars for business purposes.[55]

Japanese camera makers are preparing for the era of the TPO (time, place, and occasion). They reason that families will own several cameras, each for a different purpose. For weddings and foreign travel, a sophisticated single lens reflex 35 mm camera. For parties, a simple point-and-shoot 35 mm camera. For the beach and camping, an underwater or weatherproof camera.[56] Coca-Cola was consumed as a breakfast drink in some parts of the United States long before it was promoted by the company as such.

- **Brand Loyalty** • Brand and store loyalty can be used to segment markets. *Brand loyalty* is the degree to which a buying unit, such as a household, concentrates its purchases over time on a particular brand within a product category.

Suppose the users of a particular brand of soap can be divided into loyal and nonloyal buyers. By studying the geographic, demographic, and psychographic characteristics of its most loyal users, the marketer might get a better understanding of the brand's target market. Likewise, by studying its less loyal buyers, the marketer might get a better understanding of its major rivals. Persuading nonloyal users to become loyal requires a different type of marketing effort from what is needed to keep presently loyal users. Perhaps cents-off coupons are needed to increase loyalty among nonloyal users. The concept of brand loyalty is not all that exact, and it can be misunderstood. Branding will be discussed further in chapter 9.

- **Benefits Sought** • As suggested in the Topol ad, some markets can be segmented on the basis of benefits. *Benefit segmentation* is the division of a mass market on the basis of the benefits that people seek from the product. Consumers are grouped directly into various benefit segments that are based on what they want the product to do for them.

Benefit segmentation requires the marketer to determine the benefits people are seeking in the product category. Then the marketer must determine the characteristics of the people who want each benefit, divide people seeking similar benefits into groups, and identify the brands currently on the market that provide each benefit. This should enable the marketer to more clearly identify the benefit segment to which the firm's brand appeals. It might also help in focusing on a new benefit that is not being provided by existing brands and facilitate the introduction of a brand that offers this benefit.

Rally's, In-N-Out Burger, and other small take-out-only eateries offer their customers

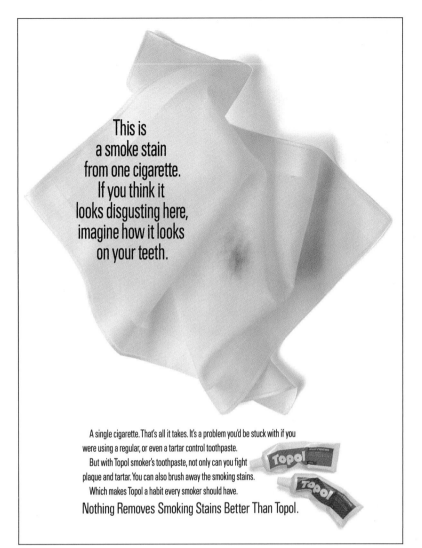

An ad that reflects benefit segmentation.

(Bob Kuperman, Creative; Michael Smith, Director; Dion Hughes, Copywriter. Chiat/Day/ Mojo, Los Angeles.)

low prices and very fast service. Warner-Lambert's Cristal gum is targeted at consumers thirty-five years old and over who have crowns, caps, or bridges. Cristal is a sugarless gum that won't stick to dentures.[57] Ultralight cigarettes are targeted to people who want a smoother, lighter taste than that available from light cigarettes.

SEGMENTING ORGANIZATIONAL MARKETS

The focus of market segmentation in the consumer market is ultimate consumers. The focus in organizational markets is industries, organizations, buying centers within organizations, and individuals within buying centers.

Secondary data may be sufficient in focusing on industries and organizations. Standard Industrial Classification (SIC) data, the *Census of Retail Trade*, the *Census of Wholesale*

Buying procedures in organizational markets in China are very different from those in the U.S. This influences a U.S. marketer's approach to segmenting organizational markets in China.

Trade, the *Census of Service Industries,* the *Census of Transportation,* the *Census of Manufactures,* the *Census of Mineral Industries,* and the *Census of Construction Industries* can be very helpful. But segmenting buying centers and the individuals within them usually involves gathering primary data. The marketer's sales force is often a major source of such data, as are noncompetitive suppliers who sell to these organizations.

Caterpillar Tractor Company can market its products in such diverse industries as agriculture, mining, and construction. It is important, therefore, for Cat to have an in-depth knowledge of how these industries differ and how they are similar. Although they all require some of the types of products Cat makes—products ranging from backhoes to excavators—not all may need Cat's D10 tractor, which stands 15 feet tall, weighs 73 tons, and sells for over half a million dollars.[58] Such a huge tractor might be used only in the construction industry. But there can be significant differences within a particular industry, just as there are differences among industries. As far as Cat is concerned, for example, the requirements of companies that build interstate highways are vastly different from those of small farmers.

Segmenting Organizations

Once the industry focus has been narrowed, the marketer can turn to segmenting the organizations within the industries. The objective is to identify segmentation variables that are good predictors of differences in buying behavior.

Using *size* of organization as a segmentation variable often reveals important differences among potential buyers. Size can be measured in various ways. Among them are number of establishments, volume of shipments, annual sales volume, and number of employees. Cat is less likely to sell farm tractors to small farmers than are Deere & Company and Kubota.

Segmenting on the basis of *geographic location* can also be useful. The same regional and metropolitan area breakdowns used in segmenting the consumer market can be used in segmenting organizational markets. As far as Cat is concerned, the mining industry is more concentrated geographically than the construction industry. Organizations in the areas of concentration can be considered to constitute one segment, and those outside may be treated as one or more other segments.

The *structure of the procurement function* is another method of dividing organizations. The buying behavior of organizations that centralize the procurement function is different from that of organizations that decentralize it. Cat has dealt with huge multinational construction project management companies for many years. More recently Cat has been targeting small-scale owner-operators who build houses, repair roads, and install sewers. These two types of customers would, of course, handle the procurement function differently.

Organizational markets can also be divided on the basis of the buyer's *use of the product*. Among the possible breakdowns are (1) where the product is used (office, factory, warehouse), (2) how the product is used (to make other products, to use in conducting operations, to resell), and (3) the rate of usage (nonuse, light use, moderate use, heavy use). Some of Cat's machinery can be used on the farm or on construction sites. Most of Cat's sales are to customers that use the products in conducting their operations, but the company also sells diesel engines to original equipment manufacturers. Of course, Cat can also segment on the basis of usage rate. Some of its competitors probably focus more on light users than does Cat. Light users probably do not require all the quality that Cat builds into its equipment.

As we saw in chapter 6, the three types of industrial buying are new task, modified rebuy, and straight rebuy—the buyclasses. The *type of buying situation* the prospective customer is facing, of course, affects marketing mix requirements. Organizations facing new task buying situations need vendor salespeople who have the skills and time necessary to help their prospects solve their problems. This will require a greater commitment of resources by the vendor than is the case in straight rebuy situations in which the vendor is the ''in'' supplier. But in a straight rebuy situation in which the vendor is an ''out'' supplier, the vendor must be prepared to invest the time and effort necessary to convince the prospect to reevaluate the current supplier and must be prepared to offer a superior product. Small emerging contractors traditionally purchased their equipment from Deere or JI Case.[59] Cat's distributors must work hard to change their ''out'' supplier status with these customers.

Organizations can often be segmented on the basis of their *inventory requirements*. We discussed the growing spirit of cooperation between organizational buyers and their suppliers in chapter 6. A vendor could consider those buyers who use the just-in-time system as a market segment. Another segment might be composed of organizations that have corporate purchasing agreements with the vendor.

Another basis for segmenting might be the prospective customers' *buying criteria*. An example is the relative importance attributed to a product's performance, price, and after-sale service. Cat has certified eight hundred of its four thousand major suppliers around the world. These certified suppliers probably consider Cat to be a segment unto itself. Certified companies receive preferential treatment in return for meticulous attention to quality.[60]

Segmenting Buying Centers within Organizations

Once the organizations have been segmented, it may be desirable to divide them further on the basis of similarities and differences among their buying centers. The *composition of buying centers* may provide one basis for segmenting buying centers. For example, buying centers that include members of top management might be expected to behave differently from buying centers that have no representation from top management. Engineering personnel may have more influence in some buying centers than in others.

Receptivity to being approached by prospective suppliers may also offer a basis for segmentation. Some buying centers are more approachable than others.

Segmenting Individuals within Buying Centers

In segmenting the individuals within buying centers, organizational marketers can use many of the same variables that are used to segment ultimate consumers. *Personality variables,* for example, may influence individuals' approaches to handling risk and making decisions. Individuals who value social relationships may not be receptive to being approached by an "out" supplier.

SUMMARY OF LEARNING OBJECTIVES

1. Explain the mass-market strategy.

The mass-market strategy is a strategy that defines the market as all potential buyers of brands in a product category and offers them one marketing mix. Organizations that use this strategy assume either (1) that people in the market for a product category have very similar characteristics and wants and that one marketing mix will satisfy them all; or (2) that people in that market have different characteristics and wants but that it is not worth the cost of identifying the differences and developing two or more marketing mixes.

2. Contrast the concentration strategy and the multisegment strategy.

The concentration strategy and the multisegment strategy are two types of market segmentation strategies. The concentration strategy is the marketing strategy of focusing marketing effort on one segment of a larger market and developing one marketing mix for that segment. The multisegment strategy is a marketing strategy of developing two or more marketing mixes for two or more market segments.

3. Identify the major issues involved in the decision to pursue a segmentation strategy.

There are five major issues: (1) Are potential customers' characteristics and wants heterogeneous? (2) Can segments be identified and compared in terms of relative attractiveness? (3) Is at least one segment large enough to serve profitably? (4) Can the segments be reached by developing a marketing mix that is designed to match the market opportunity the segments represent? (5) Will the segments be responsive to the marketing mix developed for them?

4. Identify categories of segmentation variables and give examples of specific variables in each category for segmenting the consumer market.

The categories are geographic, demographic, psychographic, and product-related. Geographic variables include global regions, nations, national regions, states, counties, cities, neighborhoods, climate, terrain, population density, and market density. Demographic variables include age, sex, buying power, occupation, education, race and nationality, and family life cycle. Psychographic variables include social class, personality, and lifestyle. Product-related variables include amount of usage, type of usage, brand loyalty, and benefits sought.

5. Give examples of segmentation variables for organizational markets.

Examples include size of organization, geographic location, structure of the procurement function, use of the product, type of buying situation, inventory requirements, buying criteria, composition of buying centers, receptivity to being approached by prospective suppliers, and personality variables.

Review Questions

1. What are the requirements for the existence of a market?

2. What is the mass-market strategy?

3. What is product differentiation?

4. Why would a marketer want to segment a market?

5. What are the advantages and disadvantages of the concentration strategy?

6. What are the advantages and disadvantages of the multisegment strategy?

7. What factors influence the choice between one-variable and multivariate segmentation?

8. Why are marketers more interested in market density than in population density?

9. How might a marketer go about segmenting a market on the basis of personality?

10. Why are AIO statements used in lifestyle segmentation?

11. Why is the heavy user so important to many marketers?

12. What are the similarities and differences between market segmentation in the consumer market and market segmentation in organizational markets?

Discussion Questions

1. Is the practice of market segmentation the result of differences in wants among consumers, or are those differences the result of market segmentation? Explain.

2. Why do some marketers insist on practicing market segmentation when it probably adds to the cost of marketing products?

3. What are the implications of the growing cultural diversity of the United States for the practice of market segmentation?

4. The gay market is an important market for many types of products. What are the advantages and disadvantages to an organization of making a direct appeal to this market?

5. Is market segmentation a more useful strategy to marketers in the consumer market or to marketers in organizational markets? Explain.

Application Exercise

Reread the material about fast-food chains at the beginning of this chapter and answer the following questions:

1. Why do fast-food chains practice market segmentation?

2. Which segmentation variables are useful to marketers of fast foods?

3. What ethical issues might arise in connection with the practice of market segmentation in the fast-food industry?

Key Concepts

The following key terms were introduced in this chapter:

market
mass-market strategy
product differentiation
market segmentation
concentration strategy

multisegment strategy
segmentation variable
geographic segmentation
market density
demographic segmentation

psychographic segmentation
geodemographic
   segmentation
product-related segmentation
brand loyalty
benefit segmentation

CASES

A&W Goes Beyond Root Beer

In 1919, Roy Allen and Frank Wright opened the first A&W roadside draft root beer stand in Lodi, California. Americans' romance with the automobile was just revving up, and a mug of ice cold A&W sure tasted good to lots of sun-baked California motorists. Cashing in on their early success, Allen and Wright sold A&W franchises, and more of their roadside root beer stands started to pop up all across the country.

For decades, A&W did a pretty fair business as a fast-food-and-drink company, competing against other small take-out chains such as McDonald's and Kentucky Fried Chicken. But when some of its rivals began to surge forward on the strength of aggressive franchising and advertising strategies during the 1960s and 1970s, A&W was left in the dust. On the soda front, A&W root beer lagged far, far behind soft-drink leaders Coca-Cola and Pepsi. These two giants had early recognized the marketing value of selling their products by the bottle at stores as well as by the glass at soda fountains, but A&W wasn't sold in bottles until 1971.

Yet despite this sluggishness—and although its sales figures were insignificant compared to Coke's or Pepsi's—A&W quickly became the largest-selling national-brand root beer once it appeared in bottles. This achievement seemed to satisfy United Brands, which had acquired A&W and made the bottling decision, and it let A&W drift through the 1970s. New owners kept an equally light hand on A&W's steering wheel through the early 1980s.

But in 1986 Lou Lowenkron, a frustrated A&W executive with twenty-five years experience marketing soft-drinks for Pepsi, Canada Dry, and Cadbury Schweppes, put together a highly leveraged buyout of A&W. In three years, Lowenkron tripled A&W's sales.

How? By finally cashing in on the strength of the A&W brand as he targeted markets the cola giants had ignored. A&W had always meant just root beer. Now Lowenkron brought out A&W Cream, the first national-brand cream soda. Within months, A&W Cream had captured about half of the $350 million cream soda market. He bought Squirt, a grapefruit soda that had lots of fans in the upper Midwest and along the West Coast, and started to take it national. He licensed the rights to bottle Country Time Lemonade, a General Foods product, and set out to boost its sales. And he acquired a ginger soda called Vernors, previously

sold only in Michigan and Ohio, which he also believed had a wider potential market.

By 1989 A&W had the top-selling root beer, cream soda, and lemonade in the United States. Squirt and Vernors were coming on strong. The company was still minuscule compared to Pepsi or Coca-Cola: A&W took in only $780 million, or 3 percent, of the $26 billion Americans spent on soda that year. But many industry analysts expected Lowenkron's focus on minority tastes to result in 5 percent annual A&W sales volume growth; meanwhile, the whole soda industry's growth rate hovered at 1 percent. And it seems Lowenkron has proven that, in the root beer race at least, he can beat the cola warriors in their own stadiums: many bottlers who hold PepsiCo and Coca-Cola Enterprises franchises won't buy Pepsi's Mug or Coke's Ramblin' Root Beer—they prefer to sell A&W.

Questions

1. What marketing strategy did A&W practice before Lou Lowenkron took over the company?

2. Has Lowenkron succeeded because his competitors practice a mass-market strategy? Explain your answer.

3. Is there any evidence of the majority fallacy in this case? Explain.

4. What possible dangers are there in A&W's expansion?

A New Generation of American Dolls

When Susan White of Marion, Massachusetts, decided to buy dolls for her adopted Korean children, she had one important criterion: "I wanted the dolls to look like them."

A few years ago, that might have been a problem. Until recently, about the only place a shopper could find a doll that wasn't white was in the special section of "dolls from around the world." And even when dolls of color were available, they varied from white dolls in color only. Mattel Toys, maker of the popular Barbie dolls, introduced a black fashion doll in 1968, but the doll did not have realistic African-American features.

Toymakers have now caught on to the fact that dolls with particular ethnic features could capture different segments of the market. Minority populations are growing at a faster rate than the majority, and by the year 2000 African-Americans will make up 18 percent of the population of the United States. Similarly, a specialized Hispanic-American market is just beginning to develop. Today, all of the major toy manufacturers have introduced ethnic dolls to the mass market, and they are found in every children's store and department, from exclusive shops to discount outlets. In 1990 dolls accounted for $1.28 billion in wholesale toy orders—about 14 percent of the total toy market.

Mattel's entry into this newly segmented market is Shani (which means "marvellous" in Swahili), with her friends Asha and Nichelle. The dolls have realistic African-American features and help fill what Mattel perceived as "an absence of positive play products for African-American children." The dolls were developed by African-American employees, with advice from African-American mothers both inside and outside of the company. Deborah Mitchell, Mattel's product manager for Shani and her friends, is herself an African-American who grew up playing with a white Barbie doll. She sees Shani as a doll African-American girls can "dream through." Similarly, Susan White, who wanted dolls that looked like her Korean children, has found an array of Asian dolls, from Barbie to collector's dolls.

Tyco Toys, one of the newer entrants into the doll market, makes all of its dolls in both black and white. The company claims that there is not yet enough demand to create Hispanic and Asian dolls, since the company would have to retool its doll-making apparatus. However, it seems likely that, as doll manufacturing companies become aware of the growing economic importance of ethnic minorities in the United States, they will begin to make more dolls that look more like today's Americans.

Questions

1. Can the mass-market strategy work in the doll industry? Explain.

2. How might a marketer use a concentration strategy to enter the doll market?

3. Do you agree with Tyco Toys's assessment of the situation in the doll industry? Explain.

4. Which segmentation variables would you advise doll marketers to consider if they wanted to segment the market? Explain.

TARGETED
MARKETING

After reading this chapter you will be able to

1. identify the steps in developing a targeted marketing strategy.

2. identify the three key characteristics of an ideal market segment.

3. distinguish between potentials and forecasts.

4. identify the major sales forecasting methods.

Small brewers account for a tiny fraction of the American beer market, which totals an annual 180 million barrels, or over 5 billion gallons. In the high-price market, which accounts for about 10 percent of all beer consumed, microbrewers had about 4 percent of the market in 1990, compared to less than 1 percent in 1986.

In 1990 there were some three hundred microbreweries, compared with about fifty in 1985. Production is growing at a rate of 30 to 50 percent annually. That growth has come at the expense of imported beers, which have lost market share since 1988. A few of the most successful microbrewers have grown enough to become big players in their areas.

Successful microbrewers gain an edge by knowing their local markets and giving a nod to local character. In Seattle, where microbrewers have 2 percent of the entire market and 40 percent of the high end, Red Hook Ale Brewery's Ballard Bitter has the motto ''Ya sure, ya betcha,'' targeting the city's Scandinavian community. The brewery also makes a Red Hook Extra Special Bitter, a lighter beer aimed at customers along the Pacific Coast.

''We view imported beers as highly vulnerable,'' says the brewery's founder.

Boston's Mass Bay Brewing Company, which has become the largest brewer in the state, targets the home crowd with invitations for brewery tours and a picture of a whaler on the label of its beer, Harpoon Ale. The brewery weans locals off the imports by touting freshness. ''These are perishable products,'' says the company's founder. ''It's not motor oil.''

Most importers, meanwhile, stick with national advertising, giving microbrewers a chance to distinguish themselves by tailoring marketing to local tastes. ''The closest we get to local advertising is calling it 'New Mexico's No. 1 Import,' '' says the president of the firm that imports Corona into the United States.

Tom Pastorius started the Pennsylvania Brewing company in Pittsburgh several years ago. Much of the brewery's support comes from the well-off white males in the twenty-five to forty-five age group. Pastorius says the beer appeals to ''serious'' beer drinkers of all stripes. He claims that his draft beer tastes better because, unlike the imports, it has no additives and hasn't been shipped.

There's a sobering side, however. The Institute for Brewing Studies reports that ten small brewers closed their doors last year and large numbers continue to lose money. So Pastorius is cautious about expanding, preferring to put in long hours rather than hire more workers. He also must rely on wholesalers to pick up the beer themselves at his brewery. And he is wary about expanding too far outside the Pittsburgh area, worrying that the beer could lose its local magic: Costs would rise, and quality might suffer.

There are other competitive disadvantages for the local brewer. Pastorius's products have a shorter shelf life than the bigger brands. And like other hometown brews, its Penn Pilsner is heavier and more filling than most imports, so drinkers drink less of it.

Nevertheless, in markets such as Seattle and San Francisco the small breweries are clearly eating into import sales. In Pittsburgh fifty area bars and restaurants have Penn Pilsner on tap, and hundreds of pubs and distributors carry the beer in bottles. Pastorius has asked the city's zoning committee for permission to expand capacity by ten times. He seeks 5 percent of the local market.

That level may be within reach if Pastorius can win over more customers like Pittsburgh taxi driver Steve Cable, who switched from Beck's. "If I can get a local beer that's as good as a German beer, I'll get the local beer," he says.[1]

Microbreweries in the United States seek to identify segments that the megabreweries such as Anheuser-Busch and Miller Brewing either did not recognize and therefore overlooked or recognized but rejected because possible sales in those segments were too small to justify targeting them. These microbreweries recognized an opportunity to target segments that were not previously targeted.

As we will see in this chapter, however, the demand for beer has flattened out, and the megabreweries are now targeting smaller market segments. We discussed the rationale of market segmentation in the previous chapter. In this chapter we take a look at the steps involved in developing a targeted marketing strategy. We show how a newly organized hypothetical microbrewery, Real Beer Company (RBC), developed a targeted marketing strategy—how it identified several segments in the market, selected one of those segments as the target of its marketing effort, and positioned its product in the target market. Marketers need estimates of the size (revenue potential) of the various segments they identify in order to decide which, if any, segments to target. Thus we also look at market forecasting and sales forecasting in this chapter.

DEVELOPING A TARGETED MARKETING STRATEGY

Figure 8–1 identifies the sequence of steps the Real Beer Company has taken in developing its targeted marketing strategy. The process begins with the definition of the relevant

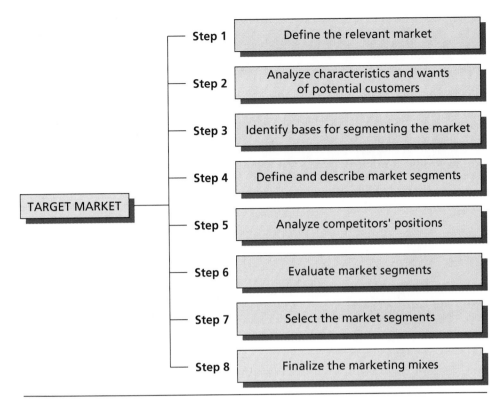

Step 1 — Define the relevant market

Step 2 — Analyze characteristics and wants of potential customers

Step 3 — Identify bases for segmenting the market

Step 4 — Define and describe market segments

TARGET MARKET

Step 5 — Analyze competitors' positions

Step 6 — Evaluate market segments

Step 7 — Select the market segments

Step 8 — Finalize the marketing mixes

FIGURE 8–1

The Eight Steps in Developing a Targeted Marketing Strategy

market and ends with the development of a marketing mix for the segment selected as the target market.

Defining the Relevant Market

Before attempting to define market segments or potential rivals, a company should define its relevant market. RBC could have defined its market in terms of the *product category* (beer), a particular *product form* (light versus regular beer), or *specific brands* (Miller Lite versus RBC's brand). The Sharp's ad focuses on another form of beer—a nonalcoholic brew.

A firm attempting to develop a market-matching strategy should begin with a broad definition of its relevant market in order to avoid a product orientation—defining an exact product to offer before researching potential customers' characteristics and wants. Thus RBC has defined its relevant market in terms of the product category—beer.

All Brand Importers imports rather than brews beer. This very successful company also defines its relevant market in terms of the product category. As the company's marketing vice president says, "Our competition is not just imported beers, it is all beers."[2]

Analyzing Characteristics and Wants of Potential Customers

After defining its relevant market, RBC collected data that describe the characteristics and wants of beer drinkers in its hometown, city A. This involved secondary research—gathering and using data already available in published form. In addition, RBC did some primary research—for example, surveying beer drinkers in city A. Some of the data RBC collected are shown in Figure 8–2.

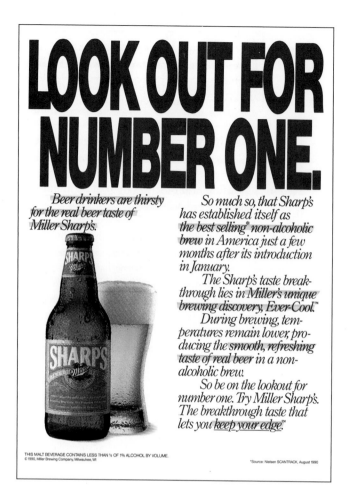

Identifying Bases for Segmenting the Market

Given the data in Figure 8–2, RBC can proceed to identify bases for segmenting the market. Geographic, demographic, psychographic, and product-related segmentation all appear to be possibilities. Specific segmentation variables, based on the data in Figure 8–2, might include *geographic* (suburban versus central-city dweller), *demographic* (age, sex, income, occupation), *psychographic* (personality), and *product-related* (amount of usage and benefits sought).

Because the objective of market segmentation is to create groups that are different in terms of their characteristics and wants, any characteristics or wants that are common to practically all beer drinkers are irrelevant as bases for segmentation. Figure 8–2 indicates that 99 percent of beer drinkers in city A prefer 12-ounce cans or bottles. RBC therefore must offer its beer in 12-ounce cans and bottles. The market cannot be segmented on the basis of container size because, practically speaking, there would be too few customers in that segment who want beer in containers larger or smaller than 12 ounces.

Defining and Describing Market Segments

market segment profile

After RBC has identified possible segmentation variables, it can proceed to define the various market segments by developing market segment profiles. A *market segment profile* is a description of the characteristics and wants of people or organizations in a market segment. The people in one segment will be highly similar to one another in terms of their characteristics and wants (intrasegment homogeneity) but different from the people in other segments in terms of their characteristics and wants (intersegment heterogeneity).

On the basis of the data in Figure 8–2 and more complete data available to RBC, the company defines eight market segments (see Table 8–1): (1) traditionalists, (2) machos,

FIGURE 8–2
....

Selected Characteristics and Wants of Beer Drinkers in City A

Geographic and Demographic Characteristics   **Number of Beer Drinkers: 100,000**

Residence	81% city dwellers		19% suburban
Sex	70% male		30% female
Age	65% 35 and under		35% over 35
Income	76% $20,000 per year and under		24% over $20,000
Type of worker	37% white collar	63% blue collar	
Education	24% college graduates	76% not college graduates	

Psychographic and Product-Related Characteristics

Personality	52% outgoing		48% not outgoing
Level of use	53% heavy	34% medium	13% light
Level of use with meals	53% at least occasionally	47% never	
Brand loyality	64% strong	26% some	10% no

Wants

Tastes	28% heavy	46% medium	26% light
Alcoholic content	70% care	30% do not care	
Preference for pastueurization	70% yes	15% indifferent	15% no
Foaminess	85% yes	15% no	
Carbonation	80% want high	20% do not	
Caloric content	25% care	75% do not care	
Container type: home consumption	55% bottles	45% cans	
Container type; away from home	30% tap	45% bottles	25% cans
Container size	99% 12-ounce	1%	
Multiple packs	70% 6-pack	15% 12-pack	15% 24-pack
Price	52% above average	33% medium	15% low

TABLE 8–1   Beer Market Segment Profiles

Segments	Traditionalists	Machos	Sociables
Number of people	25,000	20,000	13,000
Principal benefits sought	Medium taste in a medium-priced beer	Full-bodied taste in an above-average-priced beer	Fairly light but good taste regardless of price
Geographic and demographic characteristics	City, middle-aged, males, blue-collar, high school education, income under $20,000	City, young, males, blue-collar, high school education, income under $20,000	Nice neighborhood in city, young, males and females, white-collar, college graduates, income over $20,000
Psychographic characteristics	Conservative, family men, TV sports spectators	Outgoing, patronize taverns, participate in weekend sports with friends	Extroverted, joiners of organizations
Product-related characteristics	Heavy users, often drink with meals, very brand loyal	Heavy users, often drink with meals, brand loyal	Moderate users, seldom drink with meals, some brand loyalty
Favorite brands	A, B, C, D	E, F, G	H, I, J

(3) sociables, (4) status seekers, (5) bargain hunters, (6) true connoisseurs, (7) the fitness conscious, and (8) occasional sippers.

Analyzing Competitors' Positions

After defining and describing the eight market segments, RBC identifies the major competitors in each of the segments. One approach is to survey a sample of consumers in each segment to determine how they would rate the various brands on the market in terms of determinant attributes. *Determinant attributes* are the features of a product that decide the buyer's choice of a particular brand. These features are important to the consumer, who perceives that alternate brands differ in terms of possessing these features.

Suppose that RBC's research indicated that the two basic determinant attributes are light versus heavy taste and low versus high price. From Table 8–1 it would appear that machos want robust taste at a reasonable price, the fitness conscious want light taste and a medium price, status seekers want the prestige of a premium-priced import, and bargain hunters want medium taste at a bargain price. Price and taste, therefore, are determinant attributes.

A product's *position* refers to consumers' perceptions of the product's attributes relative to those of competitive offerings. Thus it is current and potential customers, not marketers, who position products in consumers' minds. But if a marketer can determine how its product is positioned, relative to competitive offerings, in consumers' minds, it can adopt various positioning strategies in an effort to *manage* the product's position. The goal is to set the brand apart by establishing a unique position in the market. This requires a careful analysis of competitive offerings and of the market segments the marketer wants to penetrate.

Product positioning is the effort aimed at creating and maintaining in the minds of tar-

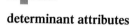

determinant attributes

product positioning

TABLE 8–1 ■ Continued

Status Seekers	Bargain Hunters	True Connoisseurs	The Fitness Conscious	Occasional Sippers
11,000	10,000	8,000	8,000	5,000
Prestige of a premium-priced imported medium-heavy beer	Medium-heavy taste at below-market price	Stout, heavy-tasting beer at a lower price than imported beer	Light taste in a medium-priced beer	Light taste in a low-priced beer that goes down easy
Suburbs, mostly young males, white-collar, college graduates, income over $20,000	City, middle-aged, mostly males, blue-collar, high school education, income under $20,000	City, practically all males, blue-collar, high school education, income under $20,000	Suburbs, young males and females, white-collar, some college, income near $20,000	City, mostly females, white-collar, high school education, income under $20,000
Extroverted, active in community affairs, cosmopolitan, assertive	Introverted, home centered, nonassertive, drink mostly at home	Very outgoing, beer drinking is an art, drink at home and "with the boys"	Avoid overindulgence, jog, play tennis, etc., "me" oriented	Introverted, feel guilty about drinking, compulsive
Moderate users, very seldom drink with meals, very brand loyal	Moderate users, sometimes drink with meals, no brand loyalty	Heavy users, often drink with meals, always searching for the right brand	Light to moderate users, almost never drink with meals, some brand loyalty	Light users, practically never drink with meals, some brand loyalty
K, L	M, N, O, P	Q, R	S, T	U, V

get customers the intended image for the product relative to the image of competitive offerings so target customers will perceive the product as possessing the attributes they want. Marketing researchers use several techniques to measure people's perceptions of competitive offerings in a product category. These measures are used to develop *product position maps*, which show the positions occupied by rival brands and suggest where new brands might be positioned. Such maps provide one way to select a desired position for a brand.

Figure 8–3 is a product position map. The dots indicate where RBC's respondents perceive the positions of the brands currently on the market. The circles indicate the various ideal-brand positions for each of the eight market segments RBC identified. The areas of the circles are proportional to the size of each market segment as determined by RBC's research. For example, circle F (true connoisseurs) is roughly one-third the size of circle A (traditionalists) because true connoisseurs accounted for 8 percent of the 100,000 beer drinkers in city A and traditionalists accounted for 25 percent.

True connoisseurs ideally want a heavy-tasting beer and are willing to pay a relatively high price for it. The two dots near circle F are the perceived positions of the two closest existing brands on the market. In actual practice, of course, these brands would be identified by brand name.

Consumers generally prefer existing brands that are near their ideal-brand positions. Thus customers in market segment A would probably buy the brands represented by the six dots near circle A. Because the three dots at the lower right of circle A are very close together, there is probably considerable and direct interbrand competition among them. Regardless of the segments RBC chooses, it will have to include many of the same features that brands positioned nearby possess.

RBC must also be careful in interpreting the product position map, because one of the

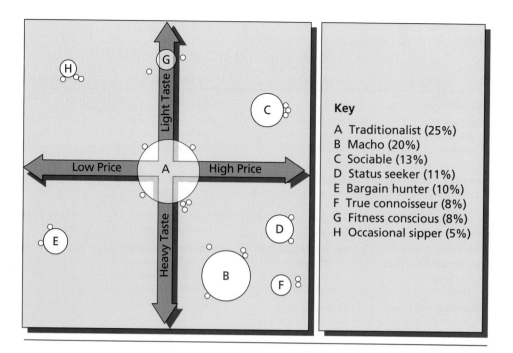

FIGURE 8–3

· ·

Product Position Map

Key

A Traditionalist (25%)
B Macho (20%)
C Sociable (13%)
D Status seeker (11%)
E Bargain hunter (10%)
F True connoisseur (8%)
G Fitness conscious (8%)
H Occasional sipper (5%)

underlying assumptions in the use of such maps is that potential consumers share the same perceptions of various brands. If certain brands of beer on the market are less familiar and are distributed less intensively than others, the chances are good that consumers will vary in their perceptions of a given brand of beer.

Evaluating Market Segments

In order to evaluate the relative attractiveness of the eight market segments, RBC must estimate the revenue potential and the cost of developing the effort needed to make the desired market impact in each segment. Serving a market segment profitably requires that the cost of the marketing effort be *less* than the sales revenues realized from serving it.

• **Estimating Revenue Potential** • Estimating revenue potential in one or more market segments involves preparing quantitative estimates of demand—demand measurement, or market measurement. Such estimates should be developed for the short run, the intermediate run, and the long run and should specify the product, the competition, and the geographic area covered by the estimate.

In RBC's case, for example, the short run probably encompasses six months and the long run may extend four or five years into the future. On the other hand, the long run for an electric utility may extend twenty-five or thirty years into the future. Such companies must estimate demand for electricity many years into the future because it takes many years to design and construct a generating plant. Several years may go by before the company even secures design approval from various regulatory agencies.

To estimate revenue potential in one or more market segments, RBC must engage in sales forecasting. This topic is covered in the last section of the chapter.

• **Estimating the Cost of the Marketing Effort** • In addition to estimating the revenue potential of the eight market segments, RBC must estimate the cost of the effort needed to make the desired impact on them. This helps in ranking the segments in terms of relative attractiveness.

RBC's assumptions about rivals' marketing efforts affect its estimates of the effort it will need to make in order to achieve the desired impact in each segment. For example, suppose RBC introduces a beer that gains rapid and widespread acceptance among consumers in a segment that other brewers have overlooked. How long will it be before rivals begin to introduce brands targeted to this same segment? If RBC estimates that rivals will retaliate quickly, it will want to gain a solid foothold as soon as possible. This will require a more costly marketing effort than would be needed if rivals were not expected to react so quickly.

Because estimating the competitive reaction is so uncertain, it is usually better for a marketer to overestimate than to underestimate the cost of the marketing effort necessary to make a desired market impact. Underestimation could prove disastrous. Suppose RBC, after having committed its resources to penetrating one or more segments, had to abandon the effort because it did not have access to the financial resources needed to increase its advertising and to widen the product's distribution. Also, the committed resources are usually not recoverable. On the other hand, it is wise to avoid an overcommitment to any one segment—putting all one's eggs in a single basket.

It is a good practice to involve personnel from different departments when developing cost estimates. This helps ensure better estimation and increases people's commitment to making the desired market impact.

Selecting Market Segments

Through the process of market segmentation, RBC has identified the major segments that exist in the beer market. It must now decide how to match its resources and capabilities to the market opportunities those segments present. Should RBC pursue a mass-market strategy and ignore differences in the characteristics and wants of the people in the segments it has identified? Or should it pursue a concentration strategy or a multisegment strategy? The answers to these questions will determine RBC's market coverage strategy.

In deciding on that strategy, RBC must consider such factors as its overall company objectives, its resources and capabilities, the level of competition, and the estimated competitive reaction to its entry into one or more segments. The estimated cost of the effort, and RBC's confidence in its estimates of revenue potential and costs, must also be considered.

On the basis of RBC's research, management concludes that the mass-market strategy will not be effective. One beer will not satisfy everybody because the market is heterogeneous. However, the greater the number of market segments RBC seeks to serve, the more costly the effort will be. RBC's management believes the company's resources are inadequate to support a multisegment strategy. Thus RBC decides to pursue a concentration strategy in entering the market.

Having made this decision, RBC must now select the specific market segment to target. This selection is guided by three key characteristics of an ideal market segment:

1. Its unique requirements can be satisfied with the firm's resources and capabilities at a satisfactory return on investment.

2. It represents an opportunity that potential rivals have not recognized.

3. It has the capacity to grow in size.

Although there may be few actual cases where all these characteristics are present, the characteristics can be useful in assessing opportunities. Thus, after a careful assessment of each market segment, RBC decides to rank the segments according to several criteria in order to facilitate the selection process.

TABLE 8–2   Real Beer Company's Target Market Selection

Potential Segment	Ranking of Revenue Potential	Ranking of Compatibility*	Estimated Speed of Competitive Reaction**	Confidence in Estimates***	Estimated Effort in Dollars
A Traditionalists	5	4	S	V	3,000,000
B Machos	2	2	S	M	2,500,000
C Sociables	4	5	I	C	2,000,000
D Status seekers	3	3	I	V	2,300,000
E Bargain hunters	6	6	S	C	1,200,000
F True connoisseurs	1	1	L	C	1,500,000
G Fitness conscious	7	7	L	V	1,100,000
H Occasional sippers	8	8	L	M	1,000,000

*Compatibility with company objectives, resources and capabilities, special strengths and weaknesses, and desired image.

**L = long-range
I = intermediate-range
S = short-range

***V = very little
C = considerable
M = much

Table 8–2 shows RBC's ranking of the eight segments in terms of (1) revenue potential; (2) compatibility with company objectives, resources and capabilities, special strengths and weaknesses, and desired image; (3) estimated speed of competitive reaction; (4) RBC's confidence in the estimates; and (5) the estimated cost of the effort needed to make the desired market impact on the target. The revenue-potential ranking is based on RBC's estimated ability to penetrate that particular segment. Thus, although segment A (traditionalists) accounts for the largest number of beer drinkers in city A, RBC knows that its resources are insufficient to penetrate this segment in any depth. Therefore, the revenue ranking is estimated on the basis of RBC's relative ability to penetrate that segment.

Suppose RBC (1) can invest $3 million in its marketing effort, (2) wants to avoid segments that rivals are expected to go after quickly, and (3) wants to pursue a conservative approach to entering the market. Given these constraints, several segments can be eliminated from further consideration.

Segment A is eliminated because the estimated cost of the effort will exhaust RBC's resources and the company has very little confidence in its estimates. Segment B is unattractive mainly because competitors are expected to react quickly to RBC's entry and RBC has much confidence in these estimates. Segments E, G, and H are unattractive in terms of revenue potential and compatibility.

Three segments remain—C, D, and F. RBC selects F (true connoisseurs) because that segment is ranked first in both revenue potential and compatibility. The estimated competitive reaction is long term—which will provide more time to phase the effort in gradually. Less time would be available for segments C and D. The lower estimated cost of the effort is also attractive because RBC wants to pursue a conservative approach to entering the market.

Finalizing the Marketing Mixes

Now that it has a target market, the true connoisseurs, RBC can finalize a specific marketing mix tailored to the target market's characteristics and wants. Although RBC did some preliminary thinking about marketing mixes when, for example, it was evaluating the various market segments, now that it has a specific target market it can develop the details of a specific marketing mix that will appeal to its target market. This requires decision making about product, distribution, promotion, and price—topics that are discussed in the next eleven chapters of this text.

Step 5 in developing a targeted marketing strategy, the analysis of competitors' positions, provides insight into how RBC should enter segment F. Let's return to Figure 8–3. RBC apparently is targeting a position in the market that has at least two rival brands positioned nearby. As suggested in step 5, if RBC wants to compete for customers in segment F, it must include many of the same features of nearby brands. Thus it will analyze the nearby brands carefully to identify those features. RBC will also attempt to find some basis for achieving a differential advantage relative to those brands.

Suppose the two dots nearest to segment F are, in reality, two brands of high-priced, imported, heavy-tasting, full-bodied beer. Apparently price could be a possible basis for differentiating RBC's brand from those brands. As Table 8–1 indicates, the beer drinkers in segment F want a heavy-tasting beer that is priced lower than imported beer.

RBC will therefore position its brand as a stout beer that is heavy, dark, and high in alcohol (like the imports positioned nearby) but that is lower-priced and, because it is made in the United States, fresher than the imports. It should have a strong appeal to blue-collar male workers who want a fresh and heavy-tasting stout beer that is priced lower than the imports.

The major product decisions can now be made. RBC's brand will be a stout, heavy, dark beer that is high in alcohol. The brand name, Stout & Proud, will help build the brand's image as a beer that is heavier and stronger than other domestically brewed beers and

Are these people representative of the market segment that Stout and Proud is targeting? If not, which segment do they represent?

[© Francesco Ruggeri]

fresher than imported beers. The label on the 12-ounce bottle will state that Stout & Proud is not pasteurized or carbonated and will feature the phrase "a beer that is brewed in the USA with real beer drinkers in mind."

Initial distribution will focus primarily on selected taverns in city A. As progress is made in securing initial sales, distribution will gradually be expanded, as output permits, to selected additional taverns, supermarkets, and restaurants. To help encourage tavern owners to stock Stout & Proud, RBC will focus on the higher profit margin the tavern owner can make from selling the brand.

Promotion will be carefully integrated with the other marketing mix elements. RBC will hire several "ambassadors of goodwill" to visit targeted taverns and "buy a round" for tavern patrons. Informal "Stout & Proud Challenges Brand X" tests in such a setting will also help generate word-of-mouth advertising. The major form of initial advertising will be outdoor ads—billboards in targeted areas of city A. The theme for these ads will be "At last—a fresh-tasting, real, and affordable stout beer brewed in the USA. Ask your tavern operator about Stout & Proud." (The Ethics in Marketing Box focuses on several issues that pertain to promotion in the beer industry.)

Stout & Proud will be priced between the highest-priced domestic heavy-tasting brands

ETHICS IN MARKETING

When the National Football League (NFL) announced plans in 1990 to scramble satellite signals carrying its games, some sports bars and restaurants nationwide decided to boycott. But they did not target the NFL or the networks. They boycotted their supplier, Anheuser-Busch.

The confrontation was over "out-of-market" games—Chicago–Los Angeles games, say, shown in a New York bar. These network telecasts, caught by satellite dishes, are shown in many of the nation's hundred thousand sports bars. The NFL says these "pirates" cut into league and team revenue by stealing copyrighted signals.

But bar owners see things differently. "For years, we've been showing the games, promoting the NFL. And now this," says one bar owner who is a defendant in a recent NFL lawsuit. "Now, because of greed, they want to start charging money." Some would say that the bars are the greedy ones. Still,

their battle with the NFL shows how a group of small-business owners can rally together against a common peril and how an industry giant (Anheuser-Busch) was pressured to come to their support.

Sports bars have scored big in the past decade by bringing a stadium atmosphere to the all-American pastime of watching-the-game-on-TV. And out-of-market games have given the bars a steady flow of displaced fans longing to see their home teams do battle. During the 1980s the NFL tried to stop these "pirates" with satellite dishes through warnings and occasional lawsuits. The league says the networks, which paid $3.6 billion for the rights to broadcast NFL games over four seasons, are being cheated whenever satellite-dish owners pick up "clean feeds" without commercials from the networks' sponsors.

At first the league was more concerned about bars showing local games blacked out because the home team did not sell out the stadium. The NFL argued that the

of beer and the lowest-priced comparable imports. The price should be especially appealing to heavy users, who might otherwise limit their consumption of truly satisfying beer to special occasions and drink lesser brands the majority of the time.

As we saw in chapter 7, one of the important questions that pertains to the decision to pursue a segmentation strategy is: Is at least one segment large enough to be served profitably? In this context, *large enough* refers to sufficient revenue potential in the segment. As we mentioned earlier in this chapter, marketers need estimates of the size (revenue potential) of the various segments they identify in order to decide which, if any, segments to target. In the discussions that follow we take a look at how the marketer can go about estimating revenue potential.

SALES FORECASTING

As we have seen, step 6 in developing a targeted marketing strategy involves estimating the revenue potential in each segment and the cost of the marketing effort needed to make

practice dissuaded fans from going to the game. When the league has gone to court over this issue, it has won. But soon more bars began showing out-of-market games, and the league went after them too.

Bar owners did not want the satellite signals scrambled, so they considered trying to make the NFL listen by boycotting Anheuser-Busch, which in 1990 had signed a four-year, $90 million deal to advertise on ABC's "Monday Night Football" and "SuperBowl XXV." The owners figured that Anheuser would rather have people sitting in bars drinking its beer than watching commercials about it. More than a thousand bars joined the boycott. After its distributors received cancellation calls, Anheuser executives called for an end to the boycott, saying that although they favored the position of the bars, they didn't control the broadcasting rights.

But Anheuser executives did tell the networks and the NFL, "We are very sympathetic with the plight of these people." After about a week, the NFL announced that the networks would not scramble the NFL broadcasts during the 1990 season, citing technical difficulties, among other things. The Anheuser boycott was halted.

Many sports bars say they would pay a reasonable price for access to the games. But some fear they may be forced to pay as much as $300 per game for pro games in the near future—the same amount that some bars already pay to receive certain unscrambled college football games.

What ethical issues are involved here?

Source: Adapted from Mark Robichaux, "How a Huddle of Sports Bars Beat an NFL Blitz," *Wall Street Journal,* November 9, 1990, pp. B1, B2. Reprinted by permission of the *Wall Street Journal,* © Dow Jones & Company, Inc., 1990. All rights reserved.

the desired impact on each segment. How much of this revenue potential the firm can realize—given its objectives, capabilities, and so on—must also be estimated. As Table 8–2 shows, Real Beer Company ranked the revenue potential in each of the eight segments it had identified.

Estimating revenue potential requires *demand measurement*. Demand can be measured by (1) product level, (2) competitive level, (3) geographic area, and (4) time frame. On the product level a firm can measure consumer demand for one brand or for all of its brands in a given product category. On the competitive level, a firm can measure the demand for its products or the demand for the products of all producers in its industry. The geographic area should always be specified. Is demand being measured for the entire world? For the entire nation? For one sales territory? (The Global Marketing box suggests the importance to Heineken of the global marketplace.) Finally, the marketer must also specify the estimate's time frame—short-term, intermediate-term, or long-term.

Two concepts are important in estimating revenue potential: potentials and forecasts.

Potentials are concerned with what is *possible*. Forecasts are concerned with what is *expected*.

Potentials and Forecasts

It is possible to estimate potentials and forecasts for the economy as a whole, for industries, and for firms and their specific brands of products. Economic potential is a country's total possible gross national product (GNP) during a future period of time, and an economic forecast is an estimate of the expected GNP during a future period of time.

Market potential is the maximum possible sales of a specific product in a specific market (or market segment) over a specific time period for all sellers in the industry, given that all sellers are putting forth their maximum marketing effort under an assumed set of environmental conditions. Market potential sets an upper limit for industry sales.

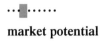

market potential

Market potential in the beer industry can refer to total sales of beer or to total sales of a particular form of beer (light, dark). It can be estimated for an entire market or for only a segment of that market. The segment can be defined in terms of any of the segmentation variables discussed in chapter 7. For example, RBC could estimate market potential in city A only. Or it could estimate market potential within a certain age or income segment of people in city A.

Market potential data help in evaluating which opportunities the marketer should pursue—for example, in determining which market segments to target. Such data also help in deciding the level of marketing effort that should be committed to the various segments and in providing benchmarks for evaluating performance in selected (targeted) segments.

A *market forecast* is an estimate of the expected sales of a specific product in a specific market (or market segment) over a specific time period for all sellers in the industry, given an expected level of industry effort and an expected set of environmental conditions. In other words, the market forecast is the portion of market potential that is expected to be realized.

market forecast

The market potential for imported beers has increased in recent years. Will it continue to grow?

[© Ted Cordingley]

sales potential

······

sales forecast

Sales potential is the upper limit of sales that a firm could possibly reach for a specific product in a specific market (or market segment) over a specific time period, given a maximum level of marketing effort and an assumed set of environmental conditions. A firm's sales potential, therefore, is the share of market potential that it might capture if it maximized its marketing effort.

A *sales forecast* is an estimate of the number of units or the dollar sales volume a firm expects to reach for a specific product in a specific market (or market segment) over a specific time period, given an intended level and type of marketing effort by the firm and an expected set of environmental conditions. Clearly, the marketing strategy must be specified before a sales forecast can be developed.

Figure 8–4 shows the steps in demand measurement. The process begins with environmental monitoring, a topic discussed in chapter 2. This monitoring provides input regarding the environmental conditions that will most likely exist during the time periods for which demand is being measured.

Consider the importance of environmental monitoring in the brewing industry. In recent years brewing companies have been targeting smaller and smaller market niches as the demand for beer has leveled off. In addition to light beers, a number of other types of beer are being targeted to the 129 million beer drinkers in the United States. Among them are dry beers, bottled draft beers, red beers, seasonal beers, pale ales, dry malt liquor, and no-alcohol beers.

Dry beer was introduced in Japan in 1987 by Asahi Breweries when it launched its Super Dry beer. Soon other Japanese brewing companies introduced their brands of dry beer and began selling them in the United States. Early in 1991 Asahi unveiled its Z (pronounced zed) beer, a brand that tastes crisper and lighter than Super Dry. Other brewers soon followed with their new brands of non-dry beer. Kirin Brewery, for example, launched its Ichiban Shibori.[3]

No-alcohol beer was very popular abroad before it caught on in the United States. No-alcohol imports include Clausthaler from Germany, Moussy from Switzerland, and Kaliber from Ireland. Moussy is even served on tap. Domestic no-alcohol beers include Anheuser-Busch's O'Doul's and Miller Brewing's Sharp's.

Microbreweries have been popular for some time in the United States. More recently the brew pub, a combination of restaurant and microbrewery that has existed in Europe for many years, has also become popular in the United States. Some say the brew pub appeals to the post-singles-bar generation that wants something like the old neighborhood bar, a safe place where the bartender and the patrons all have familiar faces.[4]

According to one expert, brewers are acting more like packaged-goods companies in their constant development of new products. Instead of being concerned that the new labels will cut into the sales of their existing labels (cannibalization), they are focusing more on their overall "family" of labels.[5]

If overall consumption of domestic and imported beer continues to decline, the larger

FIGURE 8–4

···························

Steps in Measuring Demand

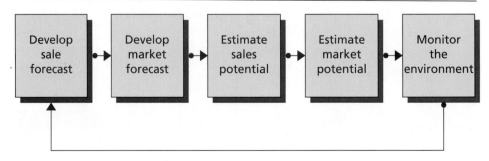

breweries can be expected to continue introducing new varieties—and they will be targeted at smaller and smaller market segments. In other words, more and more niche products will be targeted at smaller and smaller market niches. This probably is not an encouraging development as far as small brewers are concerned.

Let's return to our discussion of Figure 8–4. Given the likely environmental scenario, step 2 in Figure 8–4 requires that the marketer estimate market potential. Market potential is estimated on the basis of maximum marketing effort on the part of all marketers in the industry. Then sales potential is estimated on the basis of a maximum marketing effort by the firm. Next the market forecast is prepared, in light of the forecaster's expectations regarding the level of marketing effort that all firms in the industry will put forth. The sales forecast is then developed on the basis of the marketing effort that the firm's management intends to make, given the expected set of environmental conditions.

Market potential and sales potential are often affected by the activities of rivals. For example, Miller Brewing's successful introduction of Miller Lite helped expand this product form's market potential. It also helped create sales potential for other brewers, which subsequently introduced their brands of light beer. Similarly, Japan's Kirin brewing company's introduction of dry beer helped expand this product form's market potential. It also helped create sales potential for Michelob Dry, Old Style Special Dry, and Rainier Special Dry. The Coors ad is targeted to women, which may help expand market and sales potential.

Coors's ad campaign targeted to women may expand market and sales potential.

(Advertisement copy provided courtesy of Coors Brewing Company.)

A firm whose marketing effort is more effective than its rivals' may secure a greater share of market potential. Suppose a firm invests twice as much in its marketing effort as does its closest competitor. If each of those dollars has the same payoff in terms of generating sales, the firm's sales potential will be higher than its rivals' sales potential.

Seldom, however, does increased investment in marketing effort produce a *proportional* increase in sales. A firm may spend $1 million on advertising to increase its sales by switching some buyers of rival brands to its brand. But tripling its advertising expenditures would probably not triple its sales by producing three times as much brand switching.

The first $1 million may cause some *nonloyal buyers* of rival brands to switch. Eventually, however, the advertiser must face the much tougher task of switching *loyal buyers* of rival brands. Thus each additional dollar spent in a marketing effort to switch loyal buyers will be less productive than each initial dollar spent on switching nonloyal buyers of rival brands. ***Marketing effort response elasticity*** is the relationship between the percentage change in expenditures on marketing effort and the percentage change in sales.

Estimating Market and Sales Potential

Two basic approaches to estimating sales potential are the breakdown approach and the build-up approach. The ***breakdown approach*** is the approach to estimating sales potential that assumes that a product's sales potential varies with the country's general level of business activity. Thus the marketer begins with the economic forecast, estimating market potential and sales potential on the basis of it. This enables the marketer to break down a forecast of GNP into forecasts of industry sales, company sales, and brand sales.

Economic forecasts are readily available from many sources, including the federal government. Market forecasts are usually available from industry trade associations. Thus Real Beer Company might turn to the American Homebrewers' Association or to industry publications such as *Beverage Industry*. Armed with the economic and market forecasts, RBC can focus on forecasting its sales.

The ***build-up approach*** is the approach to estimating sales potential that begins with an estimate of the number of units of the product category a typical buyer in a typical sales territory will buy, then multiplies that number by the number of potential buyers in that territory, and does the same for all the other territories. Adding the figures provides an estimate of market potential. Estimating the share of that market potential the firm will capture at a given level of marketing effort provides an estimate of sales potential. Whereas the breakdown approach is a top-down approach, the build-up approach is a bottom-up, or grass-roots, approach.

Developing the Sales Forecast

In estimating sales potential, RBC is interested in assessing marketing effort response elasticity—the impact of various levels of marketing effort on sales potential. In developing a sales forecast, however, RBC is estimating the sales volume (number of units or dollar sales volume) that it will *actually achieve* during a specific time period given a specified level of marketing effort. As we saw earlier, sales cannot be forecasted until after the level of marketing effort has been specified.

RBC's sales forecast is an important planning and control tool. Numerous activities are planned on the basis of it. Among them are scheduling production; determining inventory levels; establishing financial, transportation, and personnel requirements; and procuring raw materials and equipment. The forecast also sets a sales performance standard against which actual sales results can be compared for control purposes.

Among the major sales forecasting methods are (1) the jury of executive opinion, (2) the

marketing effort response elasticity

breakdown approach

build-up approach

sales force composite, (3) surveys of buyer intentions, (4) expert surveys, (5) the Delphi method, (6) market tests, (7) simple trend analysis, (8) regression analysis, and (9) the substitute method. Figure 8–5 shows that forecasting methods are developed on the basis of what people say, what they do, or what they have done.

The choice of a sales forecasting method depends on such factors as the cost involved, the forecast's time period, the market's stability or volatility, and the availability of past sales data and of personnel with forecasting skills. Obviously, RBC has no past sales data with which to work. Thus some of the sales forecasting methods identified in Figure 8–5 would not be suitable for RBC.

Some sales forecasting methods are highly qualitative, and others are highly quantitative. Rather than relying exclusively on one method, marketers often use several. Some methods, for example, are better for short-range forecasts, and others are more suitable for long-range forecasts. In some cases forecasters use two or more methods for the same forecast in order to compare results.

• **Jury of Executive Opinion** • If the executives in an organization's various departments are knowledgeable about the factors that influence sales, and if they are current on marketing developments, the jury of executive opinion might be used to forecast sales. The *jury of executive opinion* is the sales forecasting method that involves combining and averaging the sales projections of executives in different departments to arrive at a sales forecast.

Even firms with established products often use this method to supplement forecasts based on other forecasting techniques. Perhaps the major drawback to the method is that recent experiences weigh more heavily than distant ones, which can result in too much optimism (or pessimism) regarding future sales.

• **Sales Force Composite** • Because salespeople are in direct contact with their customers, the sales force composite is widely used. The *sales force composite* is the sales forecasting method that involves asking salespeople to forecast attainable sales volume in

jury of executive opinion

sales force composite

FIGURE 8–5

Information Bases for Various Sales Forecasting Methods

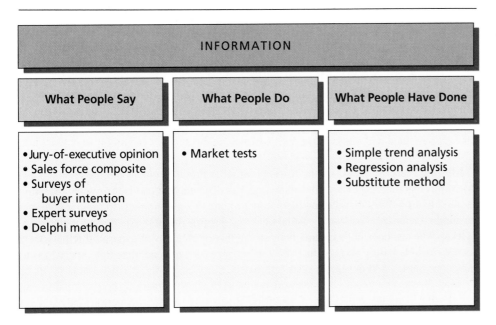

INFORMATION		
What People Say	**What People Do**	**What People Have Done**
• Jury-of-executive opinion • Sales force composite • Surveys of buyer intention • Expert surveys • Delphi method	• Market tests	• Simple trend analysis • Regression analysis • Substitute method

their territories for a given time period and combining those projections to produce a total sales forecast.

Like executives, though, salespeople can be overly optimistic or pessimistic. In addition, management must keep the sales force informed about company marketing plans that might affect the sales outlook in their territories—such as the planned launch of a new ad campaign during the period covered by the forecast.

survey of buyer intentions

• **Surveys of Buyer Intentions** • Many organizational marketers that sell to relatively few customers use a survey of buyer intentions. The *survey of buyer intentions* is the sales forecasting method that requires asking potential buyers if they intend to buy a certain product during a specific time period and, if so, how many units and from whom they will buy them.

RBC might find it useful to survey potential retailers and wholesalers. Many consumer products succeed or fail on the basis of how much selling effort retailers give to the product. Furthermore, the willingness of wholesalers and retailers to stock a new product often hinges on their feelings about its marketability.

expert survey

• **Expert Surveys** • RBC could use expert surveys to bring outside expertise into the sales forecasting process. The *expert survey* is the sales forecasting method that involves the participation of people outside the organization who have special knowledge and experience in the market under consideration—for example, economists, consultants, and retired executives.

Delphi method

• **Delphi Method** • A more complex version of the expert survey is the Delphi method. The *Delphi method* is the sales forecasting method that involves surveying (often by mail) a panel of experts from inside and outside the organization—sometimes from across the nation or throughout the world—to obtain their anonymous estimates and explanations, then having them repeat the process, after they are shown a summary of the results, for as many times as necessary until a consensus emerges.

Each panelist prepares an anonymous estimate of the sales revenue and explains in writing the rationale for submitting that figure. After all the estimates have been submitted, someone summarizes the results. The results are then given to the panelists, who are asked to submit a second anonymous estimate based on the material included in the summary. This process is repeated one or more times, and then a final summary is prepared.

The logic is that, through repeated submissions of estimates based on the summaries, extreme estimates should be eliminated. The goal is to receive a group of individually prepared estimates that fall within a fairly narrow range. Because the panelists remain anonymous, no one is put on the defensive for an estimate. Because of RBC's limited financial resources, small size, and limited market area, the Delphi method is less suitable than the less sophisticated and less costly expert survey would be.

market test

• **Market Tests** • RBC might distribute Stout & Proud in one or more markets to test potential customer response to the marketing mix. The *market test* is the sales forecasting method that involves distributing the product in one or more markets to predict potential customer response by measuring actual sales and generalizing test experiences to the entire market. The test does not measure intentions to buy or opinions of experts. If RBC selects its test markets wisely and conducts the test properly, it can generalize test experiences to the entire market and develop a sales forecast.

Market tests are also used to measure response elasticity to various levels of marketing effort—for example, the effect of increased advertising or price reductions on purchase volume. Such a test also gives RBC an opportunity to iron out bugs in the marketing mix while the product is being tested. Market tests, however, can be expensive and time-consuming, and there is no guarantee that buyer response in the test market will continue beyond the period of the test or that test results will be duplicated in other markets. We will discuss market testing in greater detail in chapter 10.

• **Simple Trend Analysis** • RBC has no use for simple trend analysis, because this type of analysis is based on historical sales data. *Simple trend analysis* is the sales forecasting technique that assumes future sales will be determined by the same variables that caused past sales and that the relationships among the variables will remain the same. For example, suppose a company had sales last year of $1,000,000 and that sales had been increasing by 10 percent in each of the last three years. The sales forecast for the current year would therefore be $1,000,000 + 10 percent of $1,000,000, or $1,100,000.

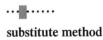

simple trend analysis

Simple trend analysis is suitable for products with a history of stable demand and is more accurate for short-term than for long-term forecasts. There are many complex statistical techniques for refining simple trend analysis. Time-series analysis, for example, enables the forecaster to take into consideration seasonal and longer-term sales fluctuations when developing the sales forecast.

• **Regression Analysis** • Like simple trend analysis, regression analysis is based on historical sales data and therefore cannot be used by RBC. *Regression analysis* is the statistical technique for developing a mathematical formula that defines a relationship between changes in past sales (the dependent variable) and one or more independent predictor variables (such as GNP, per capita income, or industry advertising expenditures). Simple regression uses only one independent variable. Multiple regression uses more than one independent variable.

regression analysis

Suppose that the forecaster at RBC had historical sales data available and observed a relationship between past sales and the average daily temperature in RBC's sales territories. RBC could use simple regression analysis to develop a mathematical formula to describe the relationship between sales and this independent predictor variable. By plugging the needed information (average daily temperatures) into the formula, RBC could forecast sales on the basis of this independent variable. The formula, however, does not prove a cause and effect relationship. In other words, there is no proof that changes in the temperature actually cause sales to go up or down.

• **The Substitute Method** • Companies such as Polaroid, Kodak, Bic, and Scripto-Tokai are always replacing older versions of cameras and mechanical pens with newer models. The new products replace older ones that show declining profit potential. The *substitute method* is the technique for forecasting sales of a new product that involves analyzing the sales of the older product it will replace and projecting sales of the new product on the basis of that analysis.

substitute method

SUMMARY OF LEARNING OBJECTIVES

1. **Identify the steps in developing a targeted marketing strategy.**
(1) Define the relevant market, (2) analyze characteristics and wants of potential customers, (3) identify bases for segmenting the market, (4) define and describe market segments, (5) analyze competitors' positions, (6) evaluate market segments, (7) select the market segments, and (8) finalize the marketing mixes.

2. Identify the three key characteristics of an ideal market segment.

(1) Its unique requirements can be satisfied with the firm's resources and capabilities at a satisfactory return on investment, (2) it represents an opportunity that potential rivals have not recognized, and (3) it has the capacity to grow in size.

3. Distinguish between potentials and forecasts.

These two concepts are important in estimating revenue potential in market segments. Potentials are concerned with what is possible. Forecasts are concerned with what is expected.

4. Identify the major sales forecasting methods.

(1) The jury of executive opinion, (2) the sales force composite, (3) surveys of buyer intentions, (4) expert surveys, (5) the Delphi method, (6) market tests, (7) simple trend analysis, (8) regression analysis, and (9) the substitute method.

Review Questions

1. What is involved in developing a targeted marketing strategy?

2. What role does a product position map play in targeted marketing?

3. Why is estimating revenue potential important in developing a targeted marketing strategy?

4. What is an ideal market segment?

5. How does market potential differ from sales potential?

6. What are the steps in measuring demand?

7. What is marketing effort response elasticity?

8. Why is a sales forecast an important planning and control tool?

9. What are the three information bases for the various sales forecasting methods?

10. What is the underlying logic of the Delphi method of sales forecasting?

Discussion Questions

1. We looked briefly at the 80/20 principle in chapter 7. What are its implications for the brewing industry?

2. "Increasingly, all brewing companies are becoming niche marketers." Do you agree? Explain.

3. In most states it is legal for consumers to brew their own beer for their own household consumption. Home brewing is becoming quite popular. Some people say this is a logical extension of the organic food movement, since home brew has no additives or preservatives. Others say home brewing is a response to the sameness of commercial beers. How would you explain the growth in popularity of home brewing?

4. There were hundreds of brewing companies in the United States in the early part of this century. Today a handful of brewing companies account for 90 percent or more of the U.S. beer market. Is brand proliferation more of a problem in the brewing industry today than it was earlier in this century? Explain.

5. Should brewing companies support changing the federal law that prohibits labeling beer bottles and cans with the alcohol content? Explain.

6. Simple trend analysis and regression analysis are based on historical sales data. Are those methods useful in the brewing industry, given the changes in that environment during recent years?

Application Exercise

Reread the material about microbreweries at the beginning of this chapter and answer the following questions:

1. What do you think is the major factor underlying the success of microbreweries?

2. How important is the concept of targeted marketing to microbreweries? Explain.

3. How can microbreweries survive in a market dominated by giants such as Anheuser-Busch and Miller Brewing?

4. How much growth should a microbrewery such as the Pennsylvania Brewing Company pursue?

Key Concepts

The following key terms were introduced in this chapter:

market segment profile
determinant attributes
product positioning
market potential
market forecast
sales potential
sales forecast

marketing effort response
   elasticity
breakdown approach
build-up approach
jury of executive opinion
sales force composite
survey of buyer intentions

expert survey
Delphi method
market test
simple trend analysis
regression analysis
substitute method

....

CASES

Enterprise Rent-A-Car

Avis Rent-A-Car's famous slogan was, "When you're Number 2, you try harder." When Enterprise Rent-A-Car was starting out, its slogan could have been, "When you're way behind Number 2, you try something else."

The biggest market for rental cars has always been business and vacation travellers who pick their cars up at airports. Long-time market leaders Hertz and Avis have made fortunes at this business and have so dominated the market that they've almost always been able to set the terms for price competition with their rivals. So when Jack Taylor, head of a car leasing business, decided to enter the car rental market in the early 1960s, he looked for opportunities away from the airports. What he discovered was that some auto insurance adjusters, who handled claims for stolen cars, wanted to provide cars to clients until their claims were settled. The major agencies charged higher rates than the insurance companies wanted to pay. By offering these adjusters the cars they wanted at the prices they wanted, Taylor gave Enterprise Rent-A-Car a strong start.

Fortune smiled on Taylor in the early 1970s: lawsuits brought by dissatisfied insurance policyholders resulted in court rulings that insurance companies had to compensate clients for their lack of a car between the time of a theft and a claim settlement. The number of insurance companies looking for reasonably priced rental cars boomed, and so did Enterprise's revenues.

Extrapolating from his experience with the adjusters, Taylor started going after drivers lacking wheels while their cars were in the body shop. These drivers preferred Enterprise over Hertz or Avis for the same reason the claims adjusters did: Enterprise could turn a profit by charging customers less than 60 percent what the big agencies charged. Why? Largely because vacation travellers (for whom car rental is essentially a luxury) and busi-

ness travellers (whose employers pay for their cars) usually want to rent new cars; Hertz and Avis rarely keep a car longer than six months. Theft and accident victims need a reasonable car that runs; Enterprise can therefore keep renting out a car for about three years so that their fixed costs are substantially lower.

Focusing on this "replacement car" segment of the car rental market and maintaining high customer service standards has paid off. The privately owned company was expected to pull in over $1 billion in revenues in 1991. Since 1984 the company has grown by a whopping 27 percent annually, and industry analysts expect that Taylor should be able to sustain this growth rate for some time. The four leaders in the replacement car segment of the market take home less than half of its sales dollars. Even though the segment as a whole grows by only 4 percent a year, there's plenty more room for Enterprise to stretch. Taylor has yet to open offices in twenty of the country's top one hundred markets. And meanwhile, Taylor has begun to pioneer a new segment ignored by the rent-a-car giants: visiting friends and relatives and college students home on break who could temporarily use a reliable but inexpensive car.

Questions

1. Describe the profile of the market segment Enterprise is trying to reach.

2. Does Enterprise's market segment possess the key characteristics of an ideal market segment? Explain.

3. What would the two axes on an Enterprise product position map probably be labeled? Explain.

4. Which approach to estimating market and sales potential do you think Enterprise probably took? Explain.

No Pink PCs, Please!

LYN S. AMINE, *St. Louis University*

Selling personal computers (PCs) used to be easy. All marketers had to do was announce the newest technological feature and then wait for corporate purchasing officers to place their orders. Now the market for PCs has exploded. There are multiple shapes and sizes, an intimidating range of choices for individual features such as memory size, processing speed, graphic capabilities, and built-in software, and perhaps now, even customization to the gender of the buyer. PC marketers are fully aware that women are well represented in the ranks of management and that they use computers on a daily basis both at work and at home. Yet the question remains—how should PCs be marketed to women?

In 1986, Qume Corporation of Milpitas, California, figured it could appeal directly to women with pastel colors for the control buttons of its laser printers and the function keys of its computer terminals. Qume engineers even deepened the handles and knobs of its printers to make them easier for women with long finger-nails to use. Sales did not show any improvement after these changes.

Following a similar approach to product development, con-sultant Marie Norwood tried to market a gender-oriented software program called Women's Ware. It included a checkbook balancer and budget planner, and the package was designed to look like a pair of slacks on a hanger. The name was later changed to Wom-en's Ware (For Modern Men Too), but the program did not sell and was quickly taken off the market.

Some companies, such as Zenith Data Systems Corporation and Apple Computer Inc., are trying a more subtle approach to the computer market using ad layouts that feature women along-side their male colleagues in realistic work settings. Toshiba Cor-poration went even further, using a layout for its print campaign that showed a woman directing an otherwise all-male meeting with a Toshiba laptop sitting on the conference table.

The problem seems to be for marketers to find a happy medium in their advertising approach that recognizes the presence and influence of women in the workplace, yet does not single them out for special or patronizing treatment. As Bruce Mowery, director of information and communication at Apple Computer Inc. has stated, "There's an opportunity there. But no one has come up with the secret code." Perhaps some wisdom can be gained by listening to those who have been marketing consumer products successfully for a long time. "When two audiences buy for the exact same reasons, you don't try and draw distinctions," is the advice from Scott Cook, former marketing executive for Procter & Gamble Corporation, who now sells software.

If gender-based product development and advertising were pursued in the PC industry, one might well expect to see whole offices decorated with pastel computers—pink for girls and blue for boys. The possibilities would be endless. Royal purple might be used for top management and fire engine red for newly recruited MBAs. Then, instead of using a "power tie" or silk bow to indicate one's ascent up the corporate hierarchy, one could rely on an annual change of PC color to transmit the right success messages.

Questions

1. Do you agree with Scott Cook's statement, "When two audi-ences buy for the exact same reasons, you don't try and draw distinctions"? Explain.

2. What types of market segmentation might have more potential than gender-based segmentation for PC marketers?

3. What kinds of market segment profiles could you think of for PC users?

4. How might the activities of rivals affect market potential in the PC industry?

Essence: Hitting the Target

• Introduction •

When Edward Lewis and three friends, Clarence O. Smith, Jonathan Blount, and Cecil Hollingsworth, launched *Essence* magazine in 1970, they confronted some rather massive obstacles. First, they had no experience in magazine publishing. Second, they were underfunded: they had initially sought $1.5 million for their venture but had come up with only $130,000. Third, they were entering an area of the marketplace that other publishers had declared a no-go zone. And fourth, major advertisers—the providers of the magazine publishing industry's lifeblood—weren't interested in giving them any business.

Except for the first of these obstacles, the others were all related to the fact that Lewis and his friends were African-American and that they proposed to launch a magazine for African-American women. As Lewis himself believes, his problems with potential backers and advertisers didn't in most cases stem from overt racism. Rather, what Lewis and his friends encountered among the white business community back in 1970 was more subtle: a lack of awareness both of the complexities of African-American culture and of blacks—

and particularly of black women—as an untapped and lucrative market for its products. "We had to sell the market," says Lewis, "sell advertisers that this was a viable market in terms of advertising support." Today, despite the fact that Lewis (who oversees editorial, circulation, and accounting operations) and remaining partner Clarence Smith (who oversees marketing advertising sales, and research operations) have turned their original $130,000 into the $38 million Essence Communications empire, they still have to sell that market every day.

• The Beginnings of Essence •

When Ed Lewis and his three friends started out, they had two primary goals, to be of service to the African-American community and to make money. A women's magazine, they believed, would make these goals compatible: although magazines such as *Ebony* and *Jet* and newspapers aimed at African-American readers had existed for years, there was no African-American equivalent of *Vogue, Cosmopolitan, Ladies' Home Journal,* or *McCall's.* By talking to friends and relatives and by putting together focus groups, they learned that a magazine targeted at black women would be warmly received. But just because African-American women didn't yet have a magazine to call their own

didn't mean that just anything would do. Lewis had originally planned to title the magazine "Sapphire," which he said "captured the Black woman as we viewed her—a rare gem of strength and beauty." The focus groups, however, gave "Sapphire" the thumbs down. Thumbs up went to "Essence," so *Essence* it was.

When the first issue of *Essence,* originally a fashion magazine, hit the newsstands in May 1970, eager readers snapped up 50,000 copies. But Smith could see that, despite such encouraging sales, he had a long road ahead of him—he had been able to sell only thirteen pages of advertising. Subscriptions and newsstand sales rarely cover magazines' production and operating costs, so revenue from selling advertising space is absolutely necessary. *Essence* was running at a heavy loss, and the only way it survived at first was with the help of a few financial backers who wanted to help Lewis prove that such a magazine could succeed.

The resistance Smith ran into from advertisers was usually two-fold: first, that African-American women did not make up a large enough market to warrant a separate advertising effort and, second, that these women were already exposed to their advertisements in the general market print media. They simply didn't believe that advertising in an

African-American women's magazine would result in a significant number of added product sales. Companies who made products expressly for African-American women, such as hair relaxers and make-up product lines in tones complimentary to darker skins, advertised in *Essence*—the match was obvious. But most of the major consumer goods marketers Smith targeted didn't see the point.

Smith responded that it was true that African-Americans watched the same television shows and read the same magazines as other Americans and therefore saw the same advertisements and commercials. But they remained a vast, untapped market for advertisers' products, he said. In the early 1970s, African-Americans made up about 12 percent of the American population and had a buying income that was over $100 billion and climbing. True, African-American median family income was about half that of white median family income. But the advances brought about by the Civil Rights movement in the 1960s—the removal of many educational and occupational barriers—meant that a

greater percentage of African-Americans than whites was upwardly mobile. Held back for so long, many were now able to go to college and to get jobs that entitled them to join the middle and upper income echelons and they were eager to acquire the appropriate belongings. In many cities, especially in the South, African-Americans were shopping more in major department stores and shopping centers: ignored in their own segregated neighborhoods by most major marketers, they were now being exposed to many of the consumer products and luxury items whites were already accustomed to examining in stores. For all of these reasons, a significant number of the more than 20 million African-Americans in the United States were eager to hear what marketers had to say, Smith told advertisers.

What African-Americans heard in the early 1970s, however, was that most major marketers didn't care about—and maybe didn't even really want—their business. Major marketers very, very rarely used African-American actors or models in their advertisements; to many African-

Americans, it seemed the marketers didn't want to show them using their products. And readers knew that *Ebony, Jet,* and *Essence* needed advertising revenues to survive. These publications were more than just read-'em-once-and-throw-'em-away magazines to most of their readers. They were institutions that provided not only news and information from an African-American perspective, but affirmation of the value of the African-American experience. Many readers took major marketers' unwillingness to advertise in these magazines as proof of their unwillingness to see the magazines—and, by extension, the aspirations of the magazines' readers—succeed.

Historically accustomed to being spurned by shopkeepers and other businesses, individual African-Americans protested in a way that reserved the most power and dignity for themselves—by refusing to give their money to those who didn't welcome them. Symbolically snubbed by advertisers, many reacted in the same way, Lewis said, by steering their consumer dollars to those marketers who actively sought their business. By advertising in *Ebony, Jet,* or *Essence,* he explained, advertisers would welcome African-American consumers in terms that were meaningful to them.

• The *Essence* Advantage •

And, Lewis added, *Essence* offered something other African-American magazines didn't. It was aimed exclusively at women. And—just as in white families—a very large amount of purchases were either solely at the discretion of or heavily influenced by women.

Essence had originally been primarily a fashion magazine. But through surveys, letters, and focus

Clarence O. Smith

Edward Lewis

groups, its editors had learned that what *Essence* readers really wanted was a magazine that focused on important issues in their lives such as jobs, housing, and education. The editors therefore transformed *Essence* into a women's service magazine, containing articles on career advancement, child-raising, civil rights issues, home decoration, cooking, upcoming elections, black celebrities and other personalities, fashion, and new products. Sales climbed steadily—throughout the 1970s, *Essence* was one of the fastest-growing women's magazines in the country. And Lewis knew from continuing surveys and focus groups and from the letters that poured through his mail-slot that *Essence* readers very much considered the magazine *theirs* and that they gave thoughtful attention to everything in it, including the ads.

Lewis also knew that his readership included the very people advertisers usually hoped to reach. They were homemakers and professionals, aged 18–49, and had an average household income in the lower-middle to middle-middle class range. And, in some respects, they were more attractive marketing targets than their white counterparts. Market research done by *Essence* and other organizations showed that, because shoddy, unbranded or unknown-brand name products had often been all that was available in the urban or rural ghettos in which many of them had grown up, they much preferred brand products. Once convinced of a brand's quality and value, they tended to be intensely loyal to it. Because entertaining at home was an important part of African-American culture and because they were used to being slapped with negative stereotypes about the way they lived, they were highly conscious of the

quality and image of their household furnishings. Thus, as a group, they tended to spend more for such items as china, silverware, furniture and other household goods than whites having similar incomes. And, again, because of civil rights advances, they tended to be more upwardly mobile than their white counterparts. Catching their attention could pay large dividends.

• **Changing Times** •

During the later 1970s, some marketers began to see the point of Lewis' and other African-American magazine publishers' arguments. As African-Americans continued to migrate northward and toward the cities, their percentage in the populations of many urban markets increased. As they were admitted into many of the manufacturing unions, African-American manual workers' spending power increased enormously. And as many more African-Americans graduated from college, the middle and upper class swelled.

Meanwhile, competition in all sectors of the economy was growing as more marketers—both domestic and foreign—entered the marketplace. Many marketers saw their best chance for success in more refined marketing efforts that included target marketing, niche marketing, and more sophisticated advertising appeals. Now, a few African-American models and actors began to show up in advertisements. Partly, this was simply an effort to avoid charges of racism from both African-Americans and whites who were committed to a more fully integrated society. But partly it resulted from a recognition on the part of many marketers that African-Americans did in fact number among their

current and potential customers and that it made sense to appeal to them.

Some mainstream marketers also began to see the logic of appealing directly to potential African-American customers through the media most likely to reach them. Avon Products, for instance, which markets a full range of personal grooming and cosmetics products, began to place a full schedule of advertisements in both *Essence* and *Ebony* to make sure that it was reaching African-American women and men. Other marketers, such as General Motors, Ford Motor, IBM, McDonald's, and Hertz, as well as most cigarette and liquor marketers, also began to make advertising in the African-American print media an integral piece of their total marketing effort. By the end of the 1970s, each issue of *Essence* had about 100 pages of ads.

• **The Success of Essence Communications** •

The 1980s were a boom period for *Essence*. Sales continued to climb until by 1990 monthly circulation topped 850,000 copies, which meant—according to standard rules used in the publishing industry—that *Essence* had about 4.1 million readers. *Essence* was still the only lifestyle magazine for African-American women, in part due still to the difficulty African-American entrepreneurs had drumming up capital and advertising revenue, but in part also due to *Essence*'s domination of the market.

During the 1980s, Lewis and Smith decided to capitalize on much of the information they had learned about African-American women and their concerns and desires. They began to move out into other areas of the marketplace. In the early 1980s, they invested $2 million in the production of "Essence: The Television Program," a weekly half-hour syndicated show that by 1985 was carried in fifty-five markets. In 1984, through their Essence Direct Mail Marketing subsidiary, they formed a joint venture with a subsidiary of Hanover House to produce *Essence By Mail*, a 5-times-a-year mail order catalog marketing fashion and home goods to a target audience of 20-to-50-year-old African-American women. They licensed the Essence name to a clothing manufacturer for a line of lingerie. And in 1985, in concert with Donald McHenry (ambassador to the UN during the Carter administration), and J. Bruce Llewellyn (former official in the Carter administration and a leading black entrepreneur), they paid about $70 million to buy Buffalo's WKBW-TV television station. By the late 1980s, Lewis and Smith had grown Essence Communications into the seventh largest black- or Hispanic-owned company in the country, worth $38 million.

- **But Fighting the Same Old Battles** -

It seemed as though Lewis and Smith had proved that there was money to be made by targeting the African-American market. And this market had not yet reached its peak. Lewis knew that African-American women especially should be an increasingly attractive target to marketers. While there were now about 11 million African-American women aged 18 and older, by 1998 there would be about 18 million. And they had more and more money to spend: in the two-year period of 1987 and 1988, for instance, the percentage of African-American women with household incomes between $30,000

and $35,000 grew by 85 percent and the percentage with household incomes between $35,000 and $40,000 grew by 83 percent.

But Smith still had trouble convincing most marketers either that this was true or that the black print media was an effective way to reach the market. In 1986, for instance,

They learned that a magazine targeted at African-American women would be warmly received.

Essence was only able to sell 974 pages of advertising when *Working Woman,* a mainstream women's magazine that had comparable circulation, book size, and advertising rates, was able to sell 1,246 pages. Such disparities remained throughout the 1980s despite Smith's hard sell to potential advertisers.

To some extent, Smith was still running into the same arguments from advertisers that he had first encountered. Many thought that by using African-American models and actors in their advertisements in mainstream magazines and television, they were already succeeding in reaching the African-American community. Few marketers doubted the Simmons Market Research Bureau's finding that *Essence* and *Ebony* each reached about 24 percent of the African-American market. But they also felt reassured by a report from BBDO International, one of the world's largest advertising and marketing research firms, that found that in terms of percentage of African-

American households reached, such general audience magazines as *Parade, TV Guide, People, National Enquirer, Reader's Digest,* and *Sports Illustrated* didn't rank far behind *Ebony* and *Essence.* As they were already reaching African-Americans *and* whites through these magazines, many marketers rea-

soned, why should they spend extra money trying to reach African-Americans again through additional print media? At the same time, the report also bolstered many marketers' belief that it wasn't cost effective to spend the extra time and money on aiming ads in general market magazines directly to African-Americans. While the magazines reached a large percentage of African-American households, these still made up a very small percentage of the magazines' total readership. Using African-American models should be enough to attract attention, they reasoned.

"The general media may be using a few more black models, but a cosmetic approach doesn't work," Edward Lewis contended. He seconded *Ebony* publisher Johnson's response to the BBDO report: "Just because blacks are reading these other publications doesn't mean they're believing them. Reaching is not selling."

The controversy engendered by

the BBDO report highlighted a long-standing problem in the argument between advertisers and African-American media owners about how best to reach African-American consumers. Advertisers criticized the African-American magazines for an absence of documented reader research to back up their claims that their magazines could cost-effectively sell advertisers' products. African-American magazine publishers criticized the advertisers and their advertising agencies and market research firms for historically and currently failing to conduct a proportional share of research on the lifestyles, attitudes, and buying habits of African-Americans

In 1990, Clarence Smith decided to do something about this problem. He set up a panel of 9,157 *Essence* readers who had agreed to participate in focus groups and to answer the survey questions of companies who signed up to become *Essence*'s custom research clients. Each panelist submitted detailed information about herself including education, income, number of children, lifestyle, and buying habits so that research clients could put together tightly controlled focus groups.

Smith predicted that this new market research division of Essence Communications would become the survey organization advertisers and others would turn to when they wanted information about the lifestyles of African-Americans. He also hoped that it would finally show for a fact that African-Americans were more strongly influenced by advertisements appearing in African-American publications than in general audience media. By late 1990, Chic hosiery had already signed on and Pillsbury, RJR Nabisco, and Sesame Street had expressed interest in this latest Lewis venture.

• Questions •

1. How would you assess Edward Lewis's and Clarence Smith's marketing research effort?

2. Lewis and Smith claim that many major marketers are ignorant of or place too little importance on differences between consumer behavior motivation in the African-American and white communities. Based on the evidence in the case, what motivations should advertisers consider when targeting African-American customers and how important do you think they are?

3. From a marketing standpoint, what is the basis of the argument between Smith and many major marketers? What are the main points of discussion in this argument?

4. What role does the majority fallacy play in the *Essence* story?

THE PRODUCT

. . . .

Sociocultural and Ethical Variables

Technological Variables

Product

Price | **Target Market** | Place

Economic Variables

Competitive Variables

Promotion

Political-Legal Variables

Section one explained the major elements involved in formulating a marketing strategy—selecting a target market and developing a marketing mix. Section Two examined the concept of the target market in considerable detail. This and the next three sections look more closely at the major elements of a marketing mix—product, distribution (place), promotion, and price—and at the decisions and activities involved in developing and maintaining effective marketing mixes. The two chapters in this section focus specifically on the product element of the marketing mix.

Chapter 9 examines what a product is and presents an approach to classifying both consumer and industrial goods and services. It distinguishes between a product mix and a product line in multiproduct organizations and explains packaging and labeling. It also focuses on the importance of branding and examines several branding strategies.

Chapter 10 takes an in-depth look at product development and management. It explains the importance of product objectives and positioning and emphasizes the stages of new-product development. It introduces the product life cycle concept and explains its relationship to fashion cycles and to the product adoption and diffusion processes. Finally, the chapter examines the major issues involved in managing products as they progress through their life cycles, what is meant by product liability, and what is involved in a product recall.

The Comprehensive Case at the end of this Section traces the birth of the Body Shop—Anita Roddick's company—in England through its emergence as an international manufacturing–retail chain of natural-ingredient cosmetics stores. It illustrates the full meaning of the ''product'' and the concepts of product mix and product line, branding, packaging, the new-product development process, product life cycle, and the diffusion process.

9

THE PRODUCT OFFERING

OBJECTIVES

After reading this chapter you will be able to

1. explain what consumer and industrial products are and how they are classified.

2. distinguish between a product mix and a product line.

3. discuss the meaning and importance of brand equity.

4. identify the key decisions involved in branding strategy.

5. explain the various objectives of packaging and labeling.

Lander Associates is a San Francisco–based consulting firm that likes to be known as "a world leader in identity management." One of the firm's specialties is to find out how people feel about a brand. Working for Castle & Cook, Lander researchers learned that the company's Dole brand evoked far more than pineapple in consumers' minds. It also evoked "freshness" and "sunshine."

Further research showed that this imaging could be traced to a major decision made by Dole management a decade earlier. For many years Dole pineapple was packed in a gooey, sweet syrup and a royal blue can. In 1974 the company began packaging products in their natural juices and simultaneously changed the label to a bright, sunny yellow. Subsequently, Lander Associates extended the packaging imagery by dropping the small pineapple crown logo above the Dole "o." In a new design the "o" became a yellow sunburst.

The Dole brand had been used on bananas, pineapple juice, and a line of fruit-based frozen desserts. The new information about the brand name has prompted the firm to attach it to fresh vegetables such as bell peppers, lettuce, cauliflower, and celery—product categories in which branding had never been successful. By 1990 Dole had captured 20 percent of the national market share in several of these categories. By 1991 industry observers believed the company had grown so much in value because of the brand name that Castle & Cook would be enticed into selling the Dole line to a major food manufacturer.[1]

Typically, product decisions are the most important decisions in developing a firm's marketing mix. The various product features and attributes are the source of the benefits and satisfactions that a firm can deliver to its customers. Additionally, as we will see in subsequent sections, decisions on the other marketing mix elements are significantly influenced by the product characteristics.

The discussion of the Dole brand demonstrates that consumers' perceptions of benefits may not be based solely on an inspection of the product's characteristics. Indeed, some benefits (such as freshness) are difficult to evaluate in advance of use. Brand names, packaging, and labeling are therefore as much a part of the product decision as is specification of the product's materials, special features or options, and other tangible characteristics.

This chapter examines what a product is, develops a system for classifying products, and introduces the concepts of product mix and product line. It also examines the types of and purposes for branding and discusses the major issues associated with packaging and labeling decisions.

WHAT IS A PRODUCT?

As we noted in chapter 1, throughout this book we use the term *product* to include both tangible goods and intangible services. Figure 9–1 shows, for example, that a person who buys psychiatric counseling receives nothing tangible; the product is a totally intangible service. At the other extreme, a person who buys a package of paper clips receives nothing intangible; the product is a totally tangible good. In between these extremes, a person who buys a restaurant meal receives a combination of an intangible service and a tangible, nondurable good. Practically all the products we buy are a combination of intangible service and tangible good.

product

A *product* is a bundle of perceived tangible and intangible attributes that has the potential to satisfy present and potential customer wants and is received in exchange for money or other consideration. Consider, for example, the product of the very successful Carnival Cruise Line. Carnival's core, or generic, product could be considered to be transportation. But Carnival has augmented that core product to such an extent that the cruise ships themselves have become the destination. The shipboard experience, not the ports of call, is Carnival's augmented product. That experience includes the benefits offered by the ships' casinos, movie theaters, and nightclubs.

FIGURE 9–1

A Continuum of Product
Tangibility

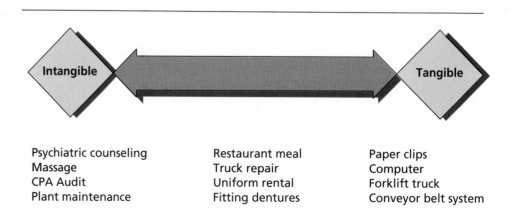

Psychiatric counseling	Restaurant meal	Paper clips
Massage	Truck repair	Computer
CPA Audit	Uniform rental	Forklift truck
Plant maintenance	Fitting dentures	Conveyor belt system

Tangible goods are often augmented by accompanying intangible services. Mainframe computer makers provide technical services to assist their customers in installing new equipment and revising software. Manufacturers of such consumer goods as automobiles and stereos offer warranties (although few warranties are as long term as the one discussed in the Peachtree ad).

Product Meanings

A product has meaning to the marketer, target customers, and society. Production-oriented organizations view a product as a manifestation of the resources used to produce it. Thus a production-oriented microcomputer manufacturer might view the product as a boxlike object that contains microchips, wires, plastic, and so on. Target customers such as college students will view it differently. To them the microcomputer is a bundle of benefits or satisfactions that will help them solve problems. For example, some of them may want to use the computer along with a word-processing program to solve the problem of how to produce typed papers on short notice.

A product warranty is often part of the product offering.

(Peachtree Windows and Doors, Inc.)

Market-oriented organizations view a product from the target customers' perspective. They realize that the product is their major vehicle for delivering customer satisfaction and that there is no need to distribute, promote, and price a product that offers no customer benefits, because the product will not sell.

The key to understanding the product meaning is to view it from the target customers' perspective—as a bundle of benefits or satisfactions that can help customers solve problems. Cosmetic companies combine chemicals to make lipstick, camera manufacturers produce mechanical devices that take pictures, and vitamin manufacturers produce pills. Marketers enhance these products for their target markets. Lipstick becomes beauty and hope, cameras become tools for capturing and preserving the present, and vitamins become hope for a healthier and fuller life. As the Bayer ad suggests, a brand name may provide additional meaning to a product. Bayer hopes people see trust as part of its product. In chapter 1 we discussed form, time, place, and possession utility. We could add image, or psychological utility to reflect a product's ability to provide satisfaction through the buyer's *perception* of its personal and social benefits.

Product Design

The major issue in product design is selecting the characteristics and attributes a product will have. This means specifying the attributes to be included and the levels of those attributes. Thus an automobile manufacturer must decide on such attributes as a car's total

From the target customer's perspective the product concept is a bundle of benefits and satisfactions.

(Courtesy Glenbrook Laboratories, Division of Sterling Drug Inc.)

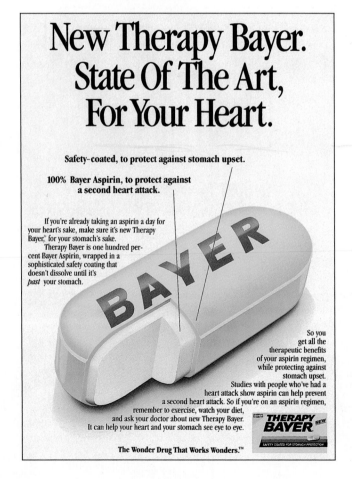

weight and the weight of its doors. Such decisions will determine the level of the benefits (such as fuel economy and ease of closing doors) that the customer will receive. To make intelligent decisions, product designers must know which benefits are most important to the buyer and how much of each attribute is desired. For example, at what point will consumers give up better gasoline mileage for the greater safety that heavier cars may offer?

Often the benefits are determined when the company knows what specific problem a customer is trying to solve. For example, the Therapy Bayer product in the advertisement is a response to a problem encountered by many users of aspirin. The safety coating solves the problem of stomach upset.

Perhaps the most talked about issue in the area of product design today is quality. ***Product quality*** is ''the totality of features and characteristics of a product [good] or service that bear on its ability to satisfy stated or implied needs.''[2]

product quality

The American Society for Quality Control distinguishes between grade and quality. *Grade* represents the addition or deletion of features or characteristics to satisfy additional needs, usually at a higher cost. Thus many service stations offer three grades of gasoline, shirt manufacturers offer different weights of cloth, and a Buick dealer offers Regals, LeSabres, and Park Avenues. The top-of-the-line item in each case is the highest-grade item.

Quality, on the other hand, refers to satisfying customer requirements. The Regal and the Park Avenue can be of equal quality (even though they differ in grade) as long as both provide high levels of customer satisfaction by conforming to customer requirements. The challenge of assuring quality, then, is not merely a question of using manufacturing techniques that assure reliable products. The products must also be designed to fulfill customer needs. An important recent development in product design that is intended to help firms meet this challenges is a process called ***quality function deployment***—the process of providing a formal way of linking information on customers' preferences for attributes to engineering specifications to ensure that marketing and research and development are collaborating effectively in achieving quality.[3]

quality function deployment

Styling (color, shape, size, and so on) is important for products ranging from tissue

Fashion or style obsolescence is psychological in nature. New models make old models obsolete. Is it ethical to promote fashion obsolescence?

[© Dan Budnik]

paper to office furniture. Styling should facilitate a product's function. Product designers are increasingly emphasizing the human side of their products' design—human-factors engineering, or *ergonomics*. Porter-Cable Corporation's engineers developed a prototype for an improved professional circular saw that, for example, was much lighter than competitive models. But the company had to bring in a design team to help overcome the prototype's biggest problem—it didn't look good. The company had to be cautious about departing from traditional appearance for the saw, keeping the emphasis on ruggedness and performance, or else risk a product failure.[4]

Customers also expect a certain level of product *performance*. Automakers in the 1950s and 1960s engaged in a "horsepower derby" when they realized people wanted high-performance cars. During the energy crunch of the 1970s, however, performance for cars and many other products came to be measured by what it cost to use them. In more recent years "muscle" cars have become popular again.

The *materials* that go into making a product can be very important. Material selection decisions can affect a product's sales appeal and should not be made solely by production managers. Materials shortages in some industries and questions regarding safety and health may lead firms to search for alternatives. Cost considerations can also be a factor.

Product design must include the benefits that intermediaries expect as well. Although final customers come first, intermediaries should not be overlooked. Grocers, for example, do not want packages that take up too much shelf space. L'eggs pantyhose are now being sold in cardboard packages rather than the familiar plastic eggs to reduce space requirements.

CLASSIFYING GOODS AND SERVICES

Scientists classify similar plants and animals into groups to study them. Marketers classify goods and services into groups to develop generalizations about desirable marketing mixes for the different groups. For example, we can divide products into three classes based on durability: (1) <u>nondurable goods</u>, (2) <u>durable goods</u>, and (3) <u>services</u>.[5]

    A *nondurable good,* such as a bar of bath soap, a soft drink, or a roll of paper towels, is consumed in one or a very limited number of uses. A *durable good,* such as an automobile, a washing machine, or a personal computer, lasts for many uses. Unlike nondurables and durables, which are both tangible, services, such as health care, haircuts, and psychiatric counseling, are intangible activities, benefits, or satisfactions that are offered for sale.

As we saw in chapter 2, our economy has evolved from an industrial economy based on manufacturing tangible goods to a postindustrial economy based on creating intangible services. A *service business* is a business that provides an intangible product for its customers. Nonprofit organizations, both private and government, also provide many services. Services differ from physical products in that they are intangible and production and consumption occur together. Hotels, laundries, beauty shops, movie theaters, car-repair shops, airlines, banks, and real estate companies are among the many types of service firms. Most are small in comparison to manufacturers of physical products and have greater difficulty reducing costs and increasing productivity through mechanization and automation. Because of the growing importance of services in our economy, chapter 21 takes an in-depth look at their marketing.

In the discussions that follow, we divide products (tangible goods and intangible services) into two broad types, consumer and industrial. **Consumer products** are goods and

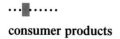

consumer products

services that are bought to satisfy personal and household wants. ***Industrial products*** are goods and services that are bought to use in producing other consumer or industrial products or in conducting an organization's operations. It is the purpose for which a product is bought that determines whether the product is a consumer product or an industrial product.

Some products, such as lipstick and haircuts, are destined exclusively for use by ultimate consumers. Others, such as railroad boxcars and business interruption insurance, are destined exclusively for use by industrial users. But many products can be used by both ultimate consumers and industrial users. For example, the car a family buys for family use is a consumer product. That same make and model is an industrial product if a firm buys it for a salesperson's use. In the late 1980s Canon introduced the RC-250 electronic still-video camera at a suggested list price of just under $800. Earlier still-video models from Canon, Hitachi, Kodak, and Sony were priced around $2,000, a price that restricted their potential as a consumer product.[6]

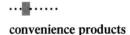

industrial products

Classifying Consumer Products

Several systems can be used to classify consumer products, but the one used most is buyer behavior. This classification system is based on differences in the buying behavior of the people who buy the products (how they perceive and shop for products), not on differences in the products themselves. Any product, therefore, could be classified differently depending on the buyer's behavior. The system works because many consumers behave alike in buying a given type of product. This helps marketers in making generalizations to guide development of their marketing mixes. The four classes of consumer products are (1) convenience products, (2) shopping products, (3) specialty products, and (4) unsought products.[7]

Convenience Products • Consumers do not think it is worth the effort to compare the price and quality of convenience products. ***Convenience products*** are low-priced items or services that consumers buy frequently with a minimum of shopping effort. Examples include chewing gum, hand soap, and automatic car washes. Because buyers are unwilling to shop actively for convenience products, the products are available in many outlets, including, for some, vending machines. Three subclasses are (1) staple products, (2) impulse products, and (3) emergency products.

convenience products

Examples of *staple products* for many consumers include bread, milk, and bus or subway transportation. These products are bought regularly and routinely. The only real thinking about such a product occurs when the buyer initially adds it to the list of regularly consumed products. Thereafter it is bought routinely because the decision is programmed. Supermarket shoppers who do not use a written shopping list rely on the store's display of products to remind them of what they need. The in-store cue reminds the shopper that the staple is almost depleted at home. This is why complementary products such as snacks and snack spreads are located close together.

Purchases of *impulse products* are completely unplanned. Exposure to the product triggers the want. Before going shopping you could prepare a list of the staple products you would buy, but not the impulse products. The desire to buy staple products may cause you to go shopping. The desire to buy impulse products is a result of your shopping. This is why impulse products are located where they will be noticed. *People* and *Us* magazines, Tic Tac mints, and blood pressure analyzers are impulse products for many consumers. These products are displayed and made available in heavy traffic areas, such as checkout aisles in supermarkets and store corridors in shopping malls.

Purchases of *emergency products* result from urgent and compelling needs. If your windshield wiper blades fail during a rainstorm, you will drive into the nearest service station to replace them. You will pay more than if you had anticipated this need and bought them at a discount store. Special one-hour service for cleaning and pressing clothing is an example of an emergency product offered by dry cleaners and hotels. Ambulance and wrecker services also offer emergency products.

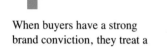

shopping products

• **Shopping Products** • Consumers think it is worth the time, cost, and effort to compare shopping products because they perceive more risk in buying these products. *Shopping products* are goods or services that consumers will purchase only after making price and quality comparisons. These products can be homogeneous or heterogeneous.

Consumers consider *homogeneous shopping products* to be alike. A person who thinks all top-of-the-line 17-cubic-foot refrigerators are very similar will limit the shopping effort to making price comparisons. Thus retailers tend to engage in price competition. Manufacturers also may stress differences in design and try to distinguish between the physical product and its product-related services. One manufacturer might set up service centers to differentiate its product from rivals'. A retailer might advertise that the refrigerator's price includes ninety days of interest-free financing. Consumers who want to stretch their

When buyers have a strong brand conviction, they treat a product as a specialty product.

(Etienne Aigner, Inc., 730 Fifth Avenue, New York City 10019.)

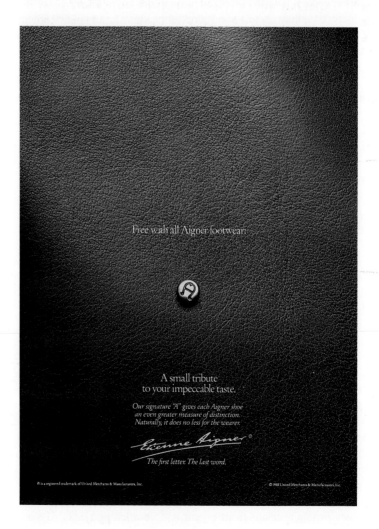

Free with all Aigner footwear.

A small tribute
to your impeccable taste.

Our signature "A" gives each Aigner shoe
an even greater measure of distinction.
Naturally, it does no less for the wearer.

Etienne Aigner®

The first letter. The last word.

® is a registered trademark of United Merchants & Manufacturers, Inc.   © 1988 United Merchants & Manufacturers, Inc.

disposable income are more likely to consider a product as a homogeneous shopping product than as a convenience product. Examples here might include oil change and lubrication, income-tax preparation, and long-distance telephone service.

Consumers consider *heterogeneous shopping products* to be different, or nonstandardized. They shop for the best price-quality combination. Price is often secondary to style and quality when price comparisons are hard to make. Using price to compare clothing, jewelry, cars, furniture, and apartments is difficult, because quality and style vary within each product class. A couple searching for an apartment may spend a lot of time comparing decor, floor plans, distance from bus lines, and so on. Once they find the ''right'' apartment, price becomes important. If the rent is reasonable compared to the alternatives, they probably will lease the apartment. Other examples of heterogeneous shopping products are child care and nursing care.

• **Specialty Products** • Consumers will make a special effort to buy specialty products. *Specialty products* are goods or services for which the buyer has a strong conviction as to brand, style, or type. Steinway pianos, Leica cameras, Steuben glassware, Rolls-Royce automobiles, and St. Jude's Children's Hospital are examples. Consumers will go out of their way to find these specialty products because of their perceived quality and other benefits. A person may willingly travel two hundred miles to the nearest dealer who sells the Rolls-Royce. There is no comparison shopping; the consumer searches to locate a specialty product.

specialty products

Physicians, attorneys, and tax consultants who enjoy a loyal following of patients and clients are selling specialty products. Most consumer services that involve a high degree of skill are considered specialty products. Marketers try to create specialty status for their products with advertising phrases such as ''accept no substitutes,'' ''insist on the real thing,'' and ''it's worth the trip from anywhere.'' They build customer loyalty when consumers consider their brands to be specialty products. A specialty product can be less intensively distributed than a convenience or shopping product because buyers will search to find it. The Etienne Aigner ad reflects the company's belief that its products have specialty status.

• **Unsought Products** • There are two types of unsought products—regularly unsought products and new unsought products. *Unsought products* are goods or services that potential buyers do not know exist or do not want to think about buying.

unsought products

Caskets, life insurance, a lawyer's services in preparing a will, and a physician's services in giving a cancer checkup are regularly unsought products. They are existing products that consumers do not want to think about buying, although they may eventually purchase them. Marketers face a tough challenge in persuading consumers to buy them. The American Cancer Society tries to motivate people to have checkups and to learn to recognize cancer's symptoms. Many people lack the motivation to visit a lawyer to prepare a will.

Products that are totally new and unfamiliar to consumers are new unsought products. The marketer's task here is to inform target customers of a product's existence and to lift it out of the new unsought category by stimulating demand for it. Oral polio vaccine at one time was a new unsought product. But heavy promotion and acceptance of the product practically eradicated polio. More recently, many parents apparently have forgotten about the dreaded disease. Thus we see ads urging parents to have their children take the vaccine.

Figure 9–2 gives an overview of the four classes of consumer products, along with their subclasses.

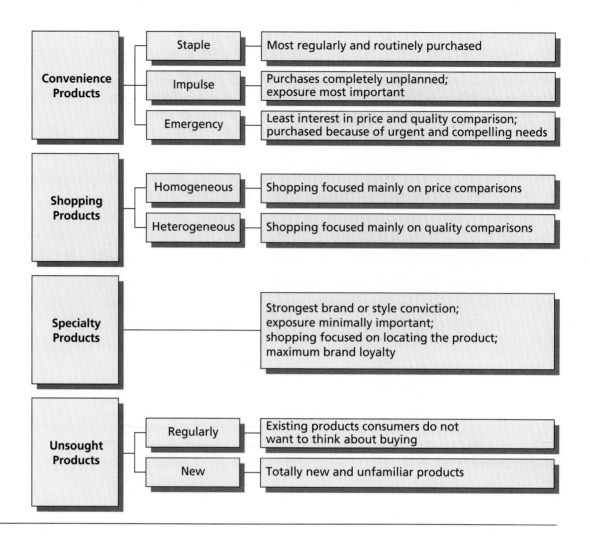

FIGURE 9–2

Classification of Consumer
Products

Using the Classification System

Because the system for classifying consumer products is based on buyer behavior, it is actually consumers who determine in which category a given product belongs in a given situation. Thus any given product may be classified differently by different consumers, or differently by the same consumer in different situations. For example, many consumers consider the services of dentists to be a specialty product. These consumers, therefore, are loyal patients who make a special effort to visit their regular dentist. On the other hand, consumers who shop for the best price and buy dental services from dental clinics that advertise low prices probably consider dental services to be a homogeneous shopping good. Then, too, for many people, dental services are a regularly unsought product.

In buying the same product in different situations, a given consumer might behave differently. To continue with the dental services example, a consumer who has just moved to a new town might shop around to gather information about price and quality before selecting a dentist. To that person, dental services are a heterogeneous shopping product. If the same person were to develop a toothache while vacationing in an unfamiliar town, he or she would likely consider dental services an emergency product.

These examples suggest that marketers should not be product oriented in thinking about their market offerings. They should view their products from their target customers' perspective. Marketers who understand that consumers differ in their perceptions of products and in their shopping behavior often can come up with new approaches to segmenting the mass market for a product category. Dental clinics that advertise low prices and ''no appointment necessary'' appeal to different market segments than do traditional dentists.

Classifying Industrial Products

Industrial products can be classified into two categories, based on how they will be used. The first category, *entering products,* includes products that will become part of the product they are used to produce: (1) raw materials, (2) component parts, and (3) component materials. The second category, *support products,* includes products that will be needed to conduct the organization's operations: (1) installations, (2) accessory equipment, (3) supplies, and (4) business services. (See Figure 9–3.)

• **Raw Materials** • Raw materials are expense items because their cost is charged off in the year they are bought. *Raw materials* are industrial products that have undergone only enough processing to permit convenient and economical handling, transportation, and storage. Two broad subclasses are farm products (such as tobacco, wheat, and soybeans) and natural products (such as the products of mines, forests, and the sea). The eggs a farmer sells to a household are a consumer product. Those sold to a bakery are a raw material. The same is true of natural products. Fish sold to a household are a consumer product; those sold to a canning factory are an industrial product.

Buying procedures depend on the current and anticipated market supply, price, and the percentage of the finished product's total production cost that is due to the raw material. If supplies are adequate, raw materials are bought routinely when inventory reaches the reorder point. If supplies are short, purchasing is less routine, and higher-level executives join in the buying decision. They might try to ensure adequate supplies by dealing directly with producers rather than distributors and by forward buying. *Forward buying* involves entering into contracts with suppliers to buy products that will be delivered in installments over a period of time. Supply problems also may lead users to search for new sources and substitute materials.

Raw materials often are bulky, low in value, and found at locations far removed from where they are needed. Thus transportation costs are very important. In an effort to hold these costs down, some firms, such as large grain marketers and oil companies, own their own transportation equipment.

raw materials

FIGURE 9–3

Classification of Industrial Products

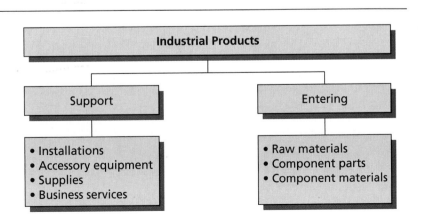

CHAPTER 9   THE PRODUCT OFFERING   **287**

component parts

component materials

installations

accessory equipment

supplies

•   **Component Parts and Materials**   •   Motors for lawn mowers and headlights for cars are examples of component parts. *Component parts* are industrial products that either are ready for direct assembly into the finished product or require only a minor amount of further processing. Standardized parts are available ready-made from many suppliers. Specialized parts are made to order.

Component materials are industrial products that include semimanufactured and semi-processed materials that require further processing before becoming part of the finished product. Examples are paper, textiles, cement, and leather.

Component parts and materials become part of the finished product and are expense items. The buyer is interested in quality, price, and the seller's delivery capability, since an out-of-stock situation might force the buyer to shut down operations. When the buyer needs a large, continuous supply, top-level executives in both the buying and selling firms may negotiate a long-term contract, especially when consistency of quality is important and quality varies among suppliers.

•   **Installations**   •   Installations do not become part of the finished product and they last for many years. *Installations* are industrial products that are capital items, including land and major equipment. Subcategories of land include such assets as plant sites, mineral rights, factories, warehouses, stores, and office buildings. Major equipment includes such assets as blast furnaces, printing presses, and elevators. Major equipment is either standard or custom-made. Lathes typically are standardized to suit many types of buyers. Custom-made major equipment, such as packaging machinery, is built to individual customer specifications.

Except for land, installations depreciate over time. Because of their high cost, high-level executives from different departments often participate in the buying decision (multiple-buying influence). The high cost of buying may lead to leasing, especially when the lessor includes service in the lease price. For example, a retailer who leases a store from a shopping center owner may receive maintenance services.

•   **Accessory Equipment**   •   Typewriters, photocopiers, cash registers, store fixtures, and forklift trucks are examples of accessory equipment. *Accessory equipment* is industrial products that are capital items that are less substantial than installations. Accessory equipment does not become part of the finished product, and compared to major equipment, it has a shorter useful life. With certain exceptions (such as the one noted in the Beechcraft ad), accessory equipment is less expensive than major equipment and is usually purchased with little influence from the firm's top executives.

•   **Supplies**   •   Supplies do not become part of the finished product. *Supplies* are industrial products that are expense items and include maintenance supplies, repair supplies, and operating supplies. These three subclasses of supplies often are referred to as *MRO* items.

Maintenance supplies are used to keep the plant and equipment in good working condition. Examples are brooms, sweeping compounds, and wiping cloths. Repair supplies are used to keep equipment in operating condition or to repair inoperable equipment. Truck mufflers, nuts and bolts, and power transmission belts are examples. Operating supplies include natural gas, pencils, and typewriter ribbons.

Supplies typically are bought routinely when needed. Janitorial supplies, for example, are bought routinely from the source that offers the best combination of price and service. Supplies are often standardized, so quality usually does not vary much among suppliers. Some operating supplies, such as coal for an electricity generating station, are bought under long-term contracts with several suppliers.

Although most accessory equipment is modest in cost, items such as business aircraft fall into this category because they help support general business operations.

(Beech Aircraft Corporation.)

• **Business Services** • Banks, insurance companies, advertising agencies, accounting and law firms, employment agencies, and management consulting firms all provide business services. *Business services* are intangible industrial products that are expense items and that do not become part of the finished product they are used to make. Some examples of business services are purchased maintenance services (such as landscaping and window washing), purchased repair services (such as those bought from plumbing and electrical contractors), and operating services (such as in-plant lunches and uniform rental). Buyers of business services have decided that buying the service from outside specialists is less costly than having company employees perform it. Multiple-buying influence may be present when the cost of the service exceeds a set amount.

business services

In looking at individual firms, we usually find that businesses tend to produce and market products in only one or a few of the classifications discussed here. However, as we noted in chapter 3, many large firms have engaged in extensive diversification. As firms increase the number of products they sell, they begin to encounter a variety of decisions relating to product mix and product line.

PRODUCT MIX AND PRODUCT LINE

··-■-·····

product mix

··-■-·····

product line

A *product mix* is an organization's entire offering of product items. Philip Morris has a product mix that includes cigarettes, coffee, cereal, and ice cream.

A *product line* is a group of products that are related because of customer, marketing, or production considerations. Sealtest, Breyer's, Frusen Glädje, and Light 'n Lively represent Philip Morris's ice cream line; Maxwell House, Sanka, Maxim, Yuban, and Brim constitute the company's coffee line.

As Table 9–1 suggests, there are many reasons to avoid dependence on a limited line of products. In the Philip Morris case the company's original dependence on the heavily regulated and nongrowing cigarette market in the United States was a major reason for diversification.

A product mix has two dimensions: breadth and depth. *Breadth* refers to the number of different product lines. *Depth* refers to the number of product items within each line. The product mix can be expanded along either dimension. Figure 9–4 illustrates breadth and depth for a portion of the Philip Morris product mix.[8]

··-■-·····

complementary products

A product line can be composed of two types of related products: complementary products or substitute products. **Complementary products** are products for which the purchase of one increases the likelihood that the second will be purchased. Typically, complementary relationships exist for two reasons. First, one product may enhance the value or the effective use of the other product. For example, flash attachments enhance the value of cameras and tennis balls enhance the value of tennis rackets. Second, buyers may encounter savings in time and effort by purchasing two or more products from the same source. Thus most people have savings accounts at the same institution that they use for checking.

··-■-·····

substitute products

Substitute products are products that satisfy the same basic needs but differ slightly in terms of specific characteristics. At a bank six-month and one-year certificates of deposit are substitutes in that both serve the same basic purpose but differ in terms of the interest rate and the length of time for which the consumer's money is committed.

Philip Morris could market its Lender's bagels and Philadelphia cream cheese as complements. The company's various beers and coffees are examples of lines composed of substitutes. These relationships are important to recognize for two reasons. First, it may be economical to conduct joint advertising or selling activities by tying closely related products together. Second, changes in sales of one product can significantly affect the sales of others in the product line.

FIGURE 9–4

Philip Morris's Product Mix and Product Line (Partial Listing) ■

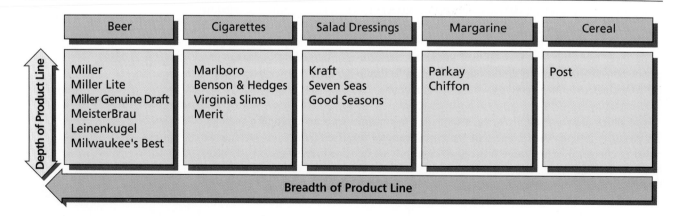

TABLE 9–1 ■ Reasons Many Firms Do Not Want to Limit Themselves
to One Product

. . . .

1. To counteract the effects of the product life cycle on a one-product firm.
2. To even out seasonal sales patterns.
3. To use company resources and capabilities more effectively.
4. To capitalize on intermediary and consumer acceptance of established products.
5. To spread production and marketing costs over a wider product mix.
6. To become better known and respected by intermediaries and consumers.

. . . .

For lines composed of substitutes, the issue of cannibalization must be kept in mind. *Cannibalization* is the situation that exists when an organization's new product achieves its sales mainly by taking away customers of its established products. Estimates are that as many as half the sales of a newly introduced low-tar version of an established brand of cigarettes come from that established brand's sales.[9]

 cannibalization

To avoid cannibalization, the company should not identify the new product too closely with established products. Instead it should target the new product to different market segments. Cannibalization can be desirable in some cases. If buyers switch from low-priced, low-profit products to higher-priced, higher-profit substitutes, overall profits will rise. Thus Philip Morris might like to encourage Sealtest buyers to shift to "premium" ice creams such as Frusen Glädje.

. . . .

BRANDS

In our discussion of Dole at the beginning of the chapter we noted that sometimes the most important attribute of the product is the *brand*—a name, term, design, symbol, or any other feature that identifies one seller's good or service as distinct from those of other sellers.[10] The *brand name* is that part of a brand that can be spoken—letters, numbers, or words. McDonald's is a brand name. The *brand mark,* or logo, is that part of a brand name that cannot be spoken and is most commonly a symbol, picture, design, distinctive lettering, color, or a combination of these. It is recognizable by sight but is not pronounceable. McDonald's Golden Arches are an example.

brand

brand name

brand mark

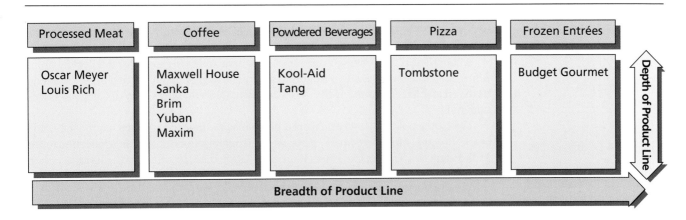

The McDonald's brand mark is recognizable throughout the world.

[© Jeremy Nicholl]

trademark

A *trademark* is a legal term meaning the same as brand. A trademark may be eligible for registration, as it is in the United States through the Patent and Trademark Office of the Department of Commerce. If registered, the trademark obtains additional protection, mainly exclusive use, but special efforts are necessary to keep the registration and the exclusive use.[11] On the package or label the circled *R* or *Reg. T.M.* following a brand mark or brand name indicates that it is a registered trademark. *Service marks* are trademarks for services. Examples include Sheraton Club International (a service mark of the Sheraton Corporation) and Discover (a service mark of Sears).

Protecting Brands

The terms *patent* and *copyright* are often used in marketing. Let's take a closer look at their meaning before we discuss brand protection.

patent

A *patent* is the protection of an invention (a product), a chemical formula, or a new way of doing something (a process) from imitation for a period of seventeen years. It cannot be renewed except by special act of Congress. After Hoffmann-LaRoche's patent on Valium expired in 1985, other pharmaceutical companies were able to market the drug under its generic name, diazepam.

copyright

A *copyright* is the granting to creators of dramatic, musical, and other intellectual properties or their heirs the exclusive rights to their published or unpublished works for as long as the creator lives, plus fifty years. The Copyright Office of the Library of Congress issues copyrights.

The Lanham Act of 1946 established provisions for registering brand names and brand marks. To apply for a trademark, a person or an organization submits an application to the U.S. Patent and Trademark Office. If the application is accepted, the office issues a permit that protects the applicant's right to use the trademark. Under the 1946 act, the right to use the permit was good for twenty years and was renewable every twenty years.

Registration of brand names and brand marks is not required in the United States, as it is in many other countries, because under common law original usage establishes ownership. But registration is wise because, although rebuttable, it is evidence of the registrant's exclusive ownership rights. In effect, it shifts the burden of proof to whoever wishes to challenge these rights. The federal government, however, is not in the business of policing the use of brands and trademarks. This is the owners' responsibility.

One of the biggest challenges some marketers face is preventing their brand names from becoming common descriptive terms for product categories. In other words, the owner of a brand name does not want it to become generic. *Aspirin, linoleum, nylon, cellophane, cola, raisin bran, elevator,* and *zipper,* once trademarks, became generic names because their owners did not effectively establish and defend their legal claims to the names. Some trademarks are considered generic by many people although their owners have exclusive rights to them. Examples are Jell-O, Coke, Xerox, Band-Aid, and Kleenex.

Marketers often use advertising to help protect their trademarks. Xerox ads explain that Xerox is a registered trademark, not a synonym for photocopying. Federal Express Corporation ads explain that Federal Express is a registered trademark, not just any overnight package service.

Branding Objectives

Brand marks and trademarks have existed for centuries. In medieval Europe trade guilds required tradesmen to "mark" each of their products to document its source. But long before that brick makers in ancient Egypt used symbols (brand marks) to identify their bricks. Brand names first appeared in the sixteenth century, when whiskey distillers burned their names in the top of each barrel to alert consumers to the source of the product and to prevent substitution with cheaper products.

In the eighteenth and nineteenth centuries branding took on broader purposes. Names or pictures of places, famous people, or animals were used as brand names to increase memorability and to differentiate products. Often the brand name was selected to enhance the perceived value of the product. The brand Old Smuggler Scotch whiskey was chosen because, at the time (1835), the special distilling processes used by bootleggers had resulted in a favorable reputation for smuggled whiskey.[12]

Today the primary objectives of branding remain much the same and a major purpose of advertising is to enhance the ***degree of brand familiarity***—the level of awareness of a product by any given person. A product may be unrecognized, recognized, rejected, accepted, preferred, or insisted upon. (See Figure 9–5.) Brand familiarity is a major cue in consumer choice behavior. It also affects marketing mix planning. Marketing research is often used to gain insight into the degree of brand familiarity a product has among target customers.

degree of brand familiarity

FIGURE 9–5

A Continuum of Brand Familiarity

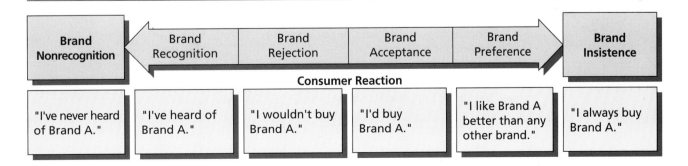

Brand Nonrecognition	Brand Recognition	Brand Rejection	Brand Acceptance	Brand Preference	Brand Insistence

Consumer Reaction

| "I've never heard of Brand A." | "I've heard of Brand A." | "I wouldn't buy Brand A." | "I'd buy Brand A." | "I like Brand A better than any other brand." | "I always buy Brand A." |

Brand nonrecognition means that potential buyers consider a branded product to be homogeneous with other brands in the product category because they do not recognize it. Typical examples for many consumers are mops and paper clips. *Brand recognition* means that potential buyers have heard or read about the brand and remember it. They can recognize it among other brands in the product category.

Brand rejection means that the brand is known but not acceptable. Potential buyers will not buy the product even though they recognize it because they have a poor image of the brand. Attempts by marketers to overcome poor brand images are costly, time-consuming, and difficult.

Brand acceptance means that potential buyers accept the brand as one purchase alternative when buying a brand within the product category. The brand meets at least their minimal product expectations. *Brand preference* means the brand is accepted and preferred

GLOBAL
MARKETING

As the Iron Curtain surrounding Eastern Europe came down at the end of the 1980s, many U.S. firms began to develop marketing strategies directed toward the nearly half billion consumers in that region. Indeed, many American marketing managers probably expected that East European consumers could hardly wait for their technology and well-known brands.

But a study by Signal International Ltd., a British research firm, suggests that U.S. firms have a challenging road ahead. Signal's brand recognition survey showed that Pepsi and Coca-Cola are uniformly well known, and that Levi's and McDonald's also enjoy a high level of recognition. In general, though, Japanese and Western European brands are far better known, and East Europeans have a much higher opinion of products made in those nations. Especially in categories such as furniture, sportswear, and appliances they look to Western Europe. For electronics and leisure products they look to Japan.

Researchers ascribe the secondary position of American products to two factors. First, Western European brands

are more familiar because of the proximity of the countries. Second, the United States is not a tremendously admired nation in Hungary and the eastern part of Germany, and this bias carries over to products.

However, it is possible to be successful in these markets. The Johnson Wax logo is highly regarded in Hungary because Johnson has been selling household care products there for a long time. This slow-but-steady philosophy of building brand equity can be contrasted with Sara Lee's strategy. Rather than pushing its L'eggs and Hanes hosiery brands into Europe, the company acquired Dim SA of Paris, Europe's leading hosiery maker, to gain a foothold. The big question confronting American managers now is whether it is too late for the slow-but-steady strategy, as firms from throughout Europe and Asia scramble to enter this market.

Source: Adapted from Michael Arndt, "U.S. Brands Fall Flat in Europe," *Chicago Tribune,* December 10, 1990, sec. 4, pp. 1–2. Copyrighted, 1990, Chicago Tribune. All rights reserved. Used with permission.

over others in the same product category. *Brand insistence* means the customer considers only one brand in the product category acceptable. It is unlikely that a marketer can achieve true brand insistence for most products and customers.

As the Global Marketing box suggests, firms wishing to do business overseas need to pay close attention to the development of brand familiarity.

Brand Equity and Branding Strategy

Branding helps build brand and company images and develop customer loyalty. When products are branded, advertising and in-store displays are meaningful, which facilitates self-service retailing. Brand promotion helps create a differential advantage for the owner and makes nonprice competition possible. Meat-packers, for example, are increasingly selling branded beef to supermarkets. Branded beef offers higher margins and the chance to win consumer loyalty.[13] Although most consumer products in the United States are branded, some are not, because the sellers are unwilling or unable to maintain consistent quality and to promote their brands.

Certain products, such as nails and safety pins, are hard to differentiate, although manufacturers can use packaging to create a difference. Lemons, bananas, and other fruits were once considered homogeneous, but branding has changed this. As we saw at the start of the chapter, Dole has been successful in branding fresh vegetables.

The most successful brands develop *brand equity*—the added value that a brand name brings to a product beyond the product's functional value. This equity can be developed by consistently delivering high quality, building strong associations between a brand name and a category or a set of benefits (such as Dole's association with freshness), and developing a consistent imagery through the use of logos, trademarks, characters, or spokespersons.[14]

brand equity

Brand equity helps a firm establish customer and distributor loyalty. Thus, when a brand with strong equity is used on a new product, the likelihood that people will try the new product is enhanced. Some firms (including Hershey, Crayola, Coca-Cola, and Harley-Davidson) allow other companies to license their brand for use on noncompeting products (for example, Coca-Cola shirts and Harley-Davidson beach towels).

A firm may also use a strong brand on its own new products. A *product line extension* is the use of an old brand on a new product within an existing product line. Maxwell House decaffeinated coffee is an example. A *brand franchise extension* is the application of an old brand to a new product line. The decision by Dole to begin branding fresh vegetables is a brand franchise extension because fresh vegetables were not substitutes for any existing Dole products.

product line extension

brand franchise extension

The various uses of brand equity mean that firms have three options in product mix branding: (1) family branding, (2) individual branding, and (3) combination branding.

- **Family Branding** • The option known as a *family brand* (or blanket brand) is a brand that is applied to an entire product mix or to all products in a particular line. Examples of family brands applied to an entire product mix are Heinz, Campbell, Levi's, and Kraft. Sears uses different family brands for different product lines—Allstate (insurance), Craftsman (tools), Die-Hard (batteries), Kenmore (appliances), and so on.

family brand

- **Individual Branding** • When products are unrelated or differ greatly in price, quality, use, and intended market segment, *individual brands* are used. Procter & Gamble's Pringles, Crisco, Tide, and Pampers are unrelated in nature. P&G's Crest and Gleem toothpastes are related in quality and nature and appeal to different market segments. Anheuser-

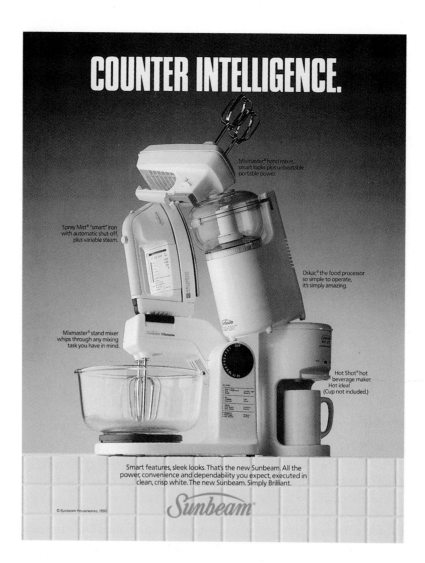

Combination branding allows a series of trademarked brands to be linked under a common, well-known umbrella.

(Courtesy of Sunbeam Housewares.)

Busch targets different brands of beer to different market segments. Busch and Natural Light are targeted to drinkers of popular-priced beer; Bud and Bud Light are targeted to drinkers of premium beer; and Michelob, Michelob Light, and Michelob Dark are targeted to drinkers of super premium beer.

Carrying multiple brands within a product category gives a firm greater pricing flexibility. It is not unusual for a rival to take direct aim at an established brand by introducing a cheaper version. The firm could counterattack by lowering its brand's quality and price, but this might hurt the brand and company image. It might therefore launch a *fighting brand* to compete directly with the newly introduced rival brand. For example, Coors launched its Keystone brand of beer to compete with lower-priced brands.

• **Combination Branding** •   Some firms combine individual brands with the trade, or company, name. Kellogg's Rice Krispies is an example. In the case of Betty Crocker Super Moist cake mix and Betty Crocker Creamy Deluxe frosting, General Mills has combined individual brands with its trade character, Betty Crocker. General Motors uses individual brands on its cars but associates them by promoting GM's "Mark of Excellence." The Sunbeam ad provides another example of combination branding.

Qualities of a Good Brand Name

The odds for successful branding are increased substantially if a good brand name is chosen. Although no exact formula exists for selecting a good brand name, some guidelines can help in evaluating names.

One guideline is that a good brand name should suggest the product's benefits or uses. Examples are Sundown (sunscreen), Slender (diet food), Windex and Glass Plus (window cleaners), Stir 'n Frost (cake mix), and Softsoap (soap in a pump dispenser).

Another guideline is that a good brand name should be easy to pronounce, recognize, and remember. Underalls (pantyhose and panties all in one) is an example. Firms that market their products in several countries may encounter problems with brand names because of language and other cultural differences. Hershey had to change the name of its crispy candy bar Whatchamacallit when it introduced the product to Canada. Special Crisp was easier for French-speaking Canadians to handle. Consider the problems facing the Xi´a Xi´ang brand in the ad, however. Though hard to pronounce, the brand may be easy to remember.

In general brand names should be short and simple and should suggest action. (Examples are Purex's Toss 'n Soft fabric softener, Close-Up toothpaste, and Surf detergent.) This helps in advertising and displaying the product. Distinctiveness and uniqueness also are important. Ideal Cement and Standard Coffee are not distinctive or unique.

Finally, brand names should be appropriate to the product and the target market. L'eggs and FemIron are appropriate for women. Cover Girl makeup may be appropriate for young women but perhaps not for older women.

It is hard to develop a brand name that satisfies all these requirements. But the rapid rate at which new brand names are appearing, as well as their potential psychological importance, justifies the effort to develop good ones. Roughly one-half million brand names are in use or registered for use.

Manufacturer and Dealer Brands

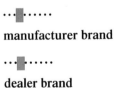

manufacturer brand

dealer brand

Brands can be classified according to ownership, as manufacturer brands or dealer brands. A *manufacturer brand* (or national brand) is a brand that is owned by a manufacturer. Delco is a manufacturer brand of batteries owned by General Motors. A *dealer brand* (or distributor, private, store, house, or middleman brand) is a brand that is owned by an intermediary such as a wholesaler or retailer. Die-Hard is a dealer brand of batteries owned by Sears.

• **Manufacturers and Branding** • Manufacturers can brand their products under (1) their own brands (manufacturer brands), (2) retailer or wholesaler brands (dealer brands), or (3) a combination of the two (a mixed-brand approach).

Manufacturers that apply their own brand to all their products generally are large, well-financed, multiproduct firms. Manufacturers that sell entirely under dealer brands are usually small and lack the financial and marketing resources to promote their own brands. Such firms typically produce a few products for one or more large retailers, such as Sears and J. C. Penney, under their brands. The manufacturer is totally dependent on the retailer for marketing effort at the retail level. A growing number of manufacturers follow a mixed-brand approach. That is, a portion of their output is sold under their own brand and another

portion under the dealer's brand. A mixed-brand approach enables the firm to use excess production capacity and may improve its working-capital position if intermediaries place large orders and pay promptly. There is no guarantee, however, that an intermediary will not shift to another supplier.

• **Intermediaries and Branding** • Most wholesalers and retailers (intermediaries) carry only manufacturer brands because of their advantages. Manufacturers promote the brands, the brands usually have a faster turnover rate than dealer brands, and intermediaries do not risk antagonizing a multiproduct manufacturer by offering products under their own dealer's brand in direct competition with products offered under the manufacturer's brand. In addition, intermediaries do not have to be concerned with sustaining the quality of a dealer brand, which can be a big problem when the product is produced by various manufacturers over a period of time.

Many intermediaries, however, find it advantageous to carry their own brands even though they have to promote them without help from manufacturers. Carrying their own brands enables intermediaries to appeal to price buyers. Manufacturers can sell a dealer-branded product to an intermediary at a lower price than the same product under their own brand because manufacturers do not have to promote dealer brands. Thus the intermediary's profit margin usually is greater on its own brand. Intermediaries can also have their brands manufactured to their specifications. Manufacturers have the power to cut dealers off and open their own sales outlets; this cannot happen if the dealer carries its own brand.

Sears built its business on its own brands. For decades the giant retailer carried its own brands exclusively. That policy changed in 1989. Along with its move to everyday low pricing, Sears started emphasizing manufacturer brands. It began with carpeting. The first burst of ads in early 1989 featured carpets at "our lowest price every single day." The ads showed the Sears name and guarantee alongside the carpet manufacturer's name. Later, Brand Central appliance and electronics departments were added. These departments offer products under such manufacturer brands as Amana, General Electric, Whirlpool, GoldStar, Hoover, Eureka, Sony, and Panasonic.

The Battle of the Brands

Manufacturer and dealer brands have been competing for market share for several decades. This *battle of the brands* heated up when giant retail chains began promoting their own brands. Some manufacturers refuse to produce dealer brands. Others sell more units under dealer brands than under their own brands.

Price used to be the only appeal of dealer brands, which were lower not only in price but in quality. Over the years, however, the quality gap has narrowed considerably. The price gap has not narrowed quite as much. Meanwhile, buyers have become more knowledgeable about these facts, and as a result serious inroads have been made by dealer brands in many industries.

Starting in the 1970s some consumers and marketers began taking greater interest in no-brand buying and selling. No-brand (generic) grocery products include canned products, paper products, plastic bags, mouthwash, shampoo, and detergents. Generic beer, liquor, cigarettes, and prescription drugs are also marketed.

Generic products are available in fewer package sizes, have plain packages and labels indicating the product name, are not advertised, and are of "standard" quality that meets applicable government standards. The major attraction of generics is that they are priced lower than manufacturer brands and dealer brands.

PACKAGING

An important part of many products is *packaging*—the design and production of the container or wrapper for a product. It may be the key factor in market success, as in the case of toothpaste in a pump dispenser.

In some countries, consumers buy products such as sugar, flour, and coffee in bulk from barrels and sacks. But most consumer products in the United States are sold in packaged form. Packaging requires that consumers have faith in the packager's integrity and that society have control over those who violate ethical packaging standards. Self-service retailing would be less efficient, perhaps impossible, without it.

packaging

Packaging Objectives

The most obvious objective of packaging is to *contain* the contents. Packaging also *protects* the contents as the product moves through its marketing channel and while it is in use.

A package also prolongs the shelf life of a product and protects against spoilage, deterioration, leakage, crushing, crumbling, evaporation, dehydration, unlawful tampering, and shoplifting. Effective packaging makes it possible to market products such as Ruffles potato chips and Sun-Maid raisins with no preservatives added. An important goal in designing packaging is to determine the protection needed and to minimize the cost of providing it.

Promoting the contents is another important packaging objective, especially in self-service retailing. L'eggs' attention-getting egg-shaped package played a major role in positioning the brand. By putting stockings into a grocery item package, L'eggs turned them into a commodity to be stocked up on, like eggs, butter, milk, and flour. A package also serves as a silent salesperson and can deliver promotional impact after the product is in use. Children, for example, are very responsive to illustrations of premiums that are included in the package.

The package can create a differential advantage for a brand by offering an additional consumer benefit. Pringle's crumble-proof can and Squeeze Parkay margarine are examples of products for which customer satisfaction was enhanced by packaging.

Packaging Decisions

Important packaging decisions include (1) organizational responsibility, (2) package design, (3) package changes, (4) reuse packaging, (5) multiple packaging, and (6) package safety.

Most consumer products companies have reassigned *organizational responsibility* for packaging from traffic managers, who arrange transportation of products through their marketing channels, to specialized packaging committees or vice presidents of packaging. The committees may include packaging engineers, intermediaries, materials procurement personnel, and designers.

Many consumer products marketers use both their own *package design personnel* and design consultants from ad agencies and container makers to keep pace with changing consumer tastes, new packaging materials, and environmental changes. Marketers also are taking a close look at cost considerations in package design. For example, more than half the cost of making a can of beer or soft drink is accounted for by the aluminum can. Many industries have shown greater interest in recent years in recycling packaging materials and avoiding overpackaging. The recognition of consumer interest in recycling is presumably the reason for the Del Monte ad.

Package changes may be desirable when sales or promotional effectiveness is declining, new and improved packaging materials are available, the present package is defective, intermediaries and final buyers want a package change, or currently used packaging materials are in short supply.

Aseptic packages such as Borden Sippin' packs for orange juice and the Brik Pak for milk keep the contents fresh for months without refrigeration. Another innovation in packaging is Hercules Inc.'s package that keeps supermarket fruits and vegetables fresh by lulling them into hibernation and preserving their just-picked quality for weeks. The package's main feature is a lunglike membrane on top that regulates its inner atmosphere.[15]

Unfortunately, the benefits of aseptic packaging are largely offset by the difficulties in recycling the containers, which are made of hard-to-separate paper, plastic, and foil. In 1990 Maine became the first state to ban these containers.

Reuse packaging means the package can serve other purposes after the contents have been consumed. Examples are coffee cans, plastic margarine containers, and attractive decanters for liquor. A major goal of reuse packaging is to stimulate repurchases.

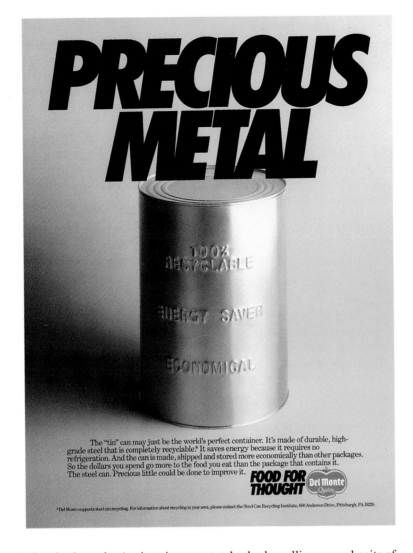

The "tin" can may just be the world's perfect container. It's made of durable, high-grade steel that is completely recyclable.* It saves energy because it requires no refrigeration. And the can is made, shipped and stored more economically than other packages. So the dollars you spend go more to the food you eat than the package that contains it. The steel can. Precious little could be done to improve it. **FOOD FOR THOUGHT** Del Monte Quality

*Del Monte supports steel can recycling. For information about recycling in your area, please contact the Steel Can Recycling Institute, 680 Anderson Drive, Pittsburgh, PA 15220.

Recyclable packaging has become an important factor in product decisions.

(Reprinted with permission of Del Monte Corporation.)

The main goal of *multiple packaging* is to increase total sales by selling several units of the product in one package. Multiple packaging is often used along with sales promotion activities such as two-for-one sales. It reduces the costs of unit handling and inventory control. Products that are used up slowly, such as silver polish, are not good candidates for multiple packaging.

Laws relating to packaging typically have resulted from misleading and deceptive packaging. Increasing attention is being focused on *package safety*, especially for products that are potentially dangerous to children. Child-proof medicine bottles and tamper-proof controls on insecticides are examples of safe packaging.

Among packaging advances that are designed to thwart tampering are packages that change colors when punctured, such as orange juice cartons that are pierced with syringes. Another method is designed to reveal tampering with lids. To do this, a hair-sized bundle of fiber optic strands is run from the top of the lid to the side and is attached along the way to the container itself. As long as that connection remains intact, a bright dot of light shows up where the strands meet the lid's side. The light disappears if the connection is broken by movement of the lid.[16]

label

LABELING

A *label* is the printed material that appears on a product package. Clothing labels often are on tags, and labels are sometimes imprinted into the product, such as the label on Mason jars.

The Fair Packaging and Labeling Act of 1966 requires the following information on a product's package or label: (1) type of product, (2) producer or processor's name and location, (3) net quantity, and, if applicable, (4) number and size of servings. Many similar laws cover foods, toys, drugs, cosmetics, furs, and textiles. For example, food labels must show sodium content if other nutritional data are disclosed.

ETHICS IN
MARKETING

In recent years consumer groups and government regulatory agencies have devoted increasing attention to product labeling and packaging decisions. In 1990 the U.S. Congress passed a sweeping new labeling bill. According to a U.S. senator, the new legislation will mean that "a bold health claim on the front of the package won't be contradicted by the fine print on the back." Basically, the legislation sets guidelines as to what is required to make claims. For example, products can be called "cholesterol free" only if they contain, per serving, less than 2 milligrams of cholesterol, less than 5 grams of total fat, and less than 2 grams of saturated fat.

One might ask why such legislation was deemed necessary. Should it be inferred that a large number of firms have misled the public about their "low fat, low-calorie, low-sodium, high fiber" products? Or have the benefits claimed for such products been exaggerated? To what extent is it ethical to link a nutritional advantage (such as high fiber) to a

health consequence (such as reduced risk of colon cancer)? How strong should this relationship be to support the claim?

A number of other ethical questions can arise in labeling and packaging. Should firms have to divulge in layman's terms that preservatives have been added to extend a product's shelf life? Should manufacturers or retailers be expected to use biodegradable packaging when it is not essential to protect the product? Rather than increasing prices as costs increase, some firms may reduce the amount of a product in a package, but consumers may not notice the change in net weight on the label. What is your view on the appropriateness of that practice? Can you think of some guidelines that an ethical food manufacturer could use in designing labels or making packaging decisions?

Sources: Information from Andrea Dorfman, "Less Baloney on the Shelves," *Time,* November 5, 1990, p. 79; Rodney Ferguson, "FDA Moves to Rewrite Food Labels," *Wall Street Journal,* July 13, 1990, p. B1.

When only the brand appears on the product item, it has a *brand label*. Chiquita stickers on bananas are an example of brand labeling.

A *grade label* identifies product quality by a letter, number, or word. *Choice* and *prime* stamped on beef are grade labels. Supporters of compulsory grade labeling contend that (1) brand labels do not give enough information about products, and this makes comparative shopping difficult; (2) grade labels are simple for sellers to use and easy for consumers to understand; and (3) price competition would replace a lot of nonprice competition based on alleged brand superiority if each brand in a product category carried a quality grade. Opponents say compulsory grade labeling seeks to force an objective standard rating on subjective factors such as taste and fashion. How, for example, could wine be graded? They also argue that it would be hard to grade complex products such as cars.

A middle position between brand and grade labeling is *informative labeling*. An informative label gives written or illustrative objective information about the product's ingredients, use, care, performance capability, life expectancy and limitations, precautions, nutrition, and number of servings. Major home appliance manufacturers must show on their labels the estimated cost of running each make and model for one year, based on average utility rates. As the Ethics in Marketing box suggests, however, a number of ethical issues in labeling (as well as in packaging) will challenge marketing managers regardless of the scope of new legislation.

An effectively designed label can enhance communication with target customers and build brand and company images. The labels on various flavors of Kellogg's Pop-Tarts, for example, feature common typography, although different colors are used for different flavors. This makes it easy for consumers to recognize the different flavors while also helping to achieve brand unity.

Attention-producing graphics are especially important for labels that cover a large part of the package. The bold graphics on cans of Coke call attention to the product on the shelf.

Label changes should be considered carefully. For example, during the summer of 1988, Adolph Coors Company changed the label on its beer to read "Original Draft" instead of "Banquet Beer." Sales increased everywhere except in southern California and west Texas. Many customers there believed the beer had been changed too. A company spokesperson said the reason could be that Coors is new in much of the country, and customer loyalties are not as well established in those markets as they are in southern California, where Coors has been sold since 1937, and in Texas, where the beer has been popular since 1948. At any rate, by the end of 1988 Coors had started using the old label in southern California and in El Paso, Texas.[17]

SUMMARY OF LEARNING OBJECTIVES

1. Explain what consumer and industrial products are and how they are classified.

Consumer products are goods and services that are bought to satisfy personal and household wants. *Industrial products* are goods and services that are bought to use in producing other consumer or industrial products or in conducting an organization's operations. One system for classifying consumer products is buyer behavior.

The four classes of consumer products are (1) convenience products, (2) shopping products, (3) specialty products, and (4) unsought products. Industrial products are classified according to the uses to which they are put. The first category is entering products—products that become part of the product they are used to produce: raw materials, component parts, and component materials. The second category is support products—products that will be needed to conduct the organization's operations: installations, accessory equipment, supplies, and business services.

2. Distinguish between a product mix and a product line.

A product mix is an organization's entire offering of product lines. A product line is a group of products that are related because of customer, marketing, or production considerations.

3. Discuss the meaning and importance of brand equity.

Brand equity is the added value that a brand name brings to a product beyond the product's functional value. It is important in that it helps build customer and distributor loyalty and often the brand can be applied to new products, thus improving the chances of their success.

4. Identify the key decisions involved in branding.

In developing a branding strategy managers should establish the brand name (the part of the brand that can be spoken) and the brand mark (or logo) and consider protecting them through registration and appropriate advertising. The strategy should also be designed to achieve brand familiarity, a high level of awareness of the brand among customers. In multiproduct firms managers must also decide whether to use family branding (applying the same brand to all products), individual branding of each product, or combination branding in which individual products have both a company and an individual brand.

5. Explain the various objectives of packaging and labeling.

Packaging is important when it protects or maintains product quality during shipping or storage; when it creates a differential advantage by offering an additional benefit; and when it can be used to help promote a brand. Environmental responsibility can also be an important packaging objective.

Labeling helps consumers understand the contents of a package. Additionally, some firms use labels to provide product usage information such as recommended serving sizes and to build brand and company images.

· · · · · · · · · · · · · · · · · · · ▌ · · · · · · · · · · · · · · · · · · ·

Review Questions

1. How do production-oriented and market-oriented views of the product differ.

2. How does classifying consumer products on the basis of buyer behavior help marketers?

3. What are the four major classes of consumer products. List the subclasses under each.

4. Which classes of industrial products become part of the product they are used to produce (entering products)? Which classes are needed to conduct the organization's operations (support products)?

5. Which types of industrial products are capital items? Which are expense items?

6. What is meant by *product mix* and *product line*?

7. What does cannibalization mean in the context of product management?

8. What are the degrees of brand familiarity? Explain each.

9. How can a firm build brand equity?

10. What are the advantages and disadvantages of family branding to a marketer?

11. What is the difference between a manufacturer brand and a dealer brand?

12. What are the objectives of packaging?

13. What is compulsory grade labeling?

Discussion Questions

1. Why are so many providers of services small businesses?

2. Why do consumers not think it is worth the effort to compare price and quality for convenience products?

3. How would you describe the product offering of a plastic surgeon?

4. An exclusive restaurant in a large city may have only one unit, whereas McDonald's and Burger King may have ten or more units. Explain this in terms of the classification system for consumer products.

5. Most new nondurable consumer goods introduced in the 1980s were product line extensions. What do you think the reasons are for this?

Application Exercise

Reread the material about Dole at the beginning of the chapter and answer the following questions:

1. Would Dole vegetables be considered a convenience, shopping, or specialty product? Explain.

2. So far Dole has been successful in using brand franchise extensions. Can you think of other product categories where the Dole brand equity could be successfully transferred? Explain.

3. What role could packaging play in Dole's product offering for vegetables? Is it irrelevant? Explain.

Key Concepts

The following key terms were introduced in this chapter:

product	installations	trademark
product quality	accessory equipment	patent
quality function deployment	supplies	copyright
consumer products	business services	degree of brand familiarity
industrial products	product mix	brand equity
convenience products	product line	product line extension
shopping products	complementary products	brand franchise extension
specialty products	substitute products	family brand
unsought products	cannibalization	manufacturer brand
raw materials	brand	dealer brand
component parts	brand name	packaging
component materials	brand mark	label

···   ···

CASES

Lasting Impressions: Montblanc

Dennis J. Elbert, *University of North Dakota*
John W. Gillett, *University of North Dakota*

Despite the predictions of many prognosticators, the writing instrument is not obsolete. Throughout the last hundred years many futurists predicted that with the development of the telephone, the typewriter, and the computer, writing instruments would be eliminated. However, each time technology makes another breakthrough, writing instruments seem to adapt and grow, not perish.

As our society moves towards the service sector (with 80 percent of all jobs service jobs), the result is more and more white collar employment. For many people in these jobs the pen has become a status symbol or a badge of success. Look, for example, at the fountain pen.

Once thought to have been totally replaced by the ballpoint pen, the fountain pen made a tremendous comeback in the late 1980s. Fountain pens, users say, have an executive, high-status quality. Some executives will sign important documents only with their favorite fountain pen; others will use only a particular brand of pen or color of ink. According to the Writing Instrument Manufacturer's Association, unit sales of fountain pens have grown steadily since 1985.

Fountain pens range in price from under $2 for disposables to several thousand dollars for special pens made of precious metals. The standard in recent years for up-and-coming executives has been the German-made Montblanc. Montblanc's Diplomat model has a black or burgundy finish, a 14-karat gold nib and, of course, Montblanc's snowflake trademark on the cap. Many consider this item, which retails typically for around $250, the power pen of choice. For the truly impressive signature, one should obtain the 18-karat gold Diplomat, with 18-karat gold nib, which sells for roughly seven thousand dollars. Montblanc also manufactures ballpoint pens and mechanical pencils that sell for approximately $90. All have the snowflake emblem on the cap so the pen is easily identifiable in the pocket as well as in the hand.

Fountain pens were invented in 1884 and served most of America's writing needs until 1939 when Lazlo Biro invented the ballpoint. Ballpoints were easy to use, disposable, and relatively inexpensive. Ballpoints dominated the writing market until the mid-1980s, when fountain pens started making a comeback. Perhaps the reason for the comeback is tied to a combination of nostalgia, prestige, and the fountain pen's one-hundredth birthday.

Americans have always responded well to accessories that exude prestige, and most feel that fountain pens exude a lot. For example, an expensive fountain pen requires several layers of lacquer and a gold nib and looks like a piece of art.

Compared to a disposable plastic ballpoint pen with Holiday Inn or U.S. Government stamped on it, the fountain pen looks and writes like a winner. Many payment contracts have been signed with a Bic or a Papermate, but the Japanese used a Parker Duofold fountain pen owned by General Douglas MacArthur when they signed the surrender papers in 1945. Compared to using a ballpoint, writing with a fountain pen is slower, maintaining the pen is part of the ritual, and using the right kind of paper is important. Purchasing a fountain pen takes time because writing nibs are available in a variety of styles. Each makes a distinctive mark on the paper. Serious fountain pen owners never lend their pen to others as a different handwriting may alter the shape of the nib.

Some fashion experts have predicted that a 25-year cycle exists with all clothing items. Perhaps fountain pens have a 100-year cycle. What people are wondering about now is how long the comeback will last. Is today's fountain pen going to be tossed with yesterday's red power suspenders? The true fountain pen lover says never.

Questions

1. Discuss the various product meanings consumers might attach to the pen category.

2. In terms of the classes of consumer products, where would pens fit?

3. Do you think Montblanc is a good brand name? Why or why not?

4. What factors would you consider in making a packaging decision about the Montblanc fountain pen?

Nissan's Fantasy Cars

Lyn S. Amine, *St. Louis University*

"The customer we had in mind," said the project manager of Silvia, a hot-selling 1989 sporty new Nissan model for sale in Japan, "is a 27-year-old who takes his girlfriend out to dinner. When he drives her home, her father, who meets them on the doorstep, is about to tell his daughter that her new man is too young. Then he sees the car, and changes his mind." This fantasy of the new Silvia owner is a long way from the traditional image of the workaholic Japanese salaryman, with his regulation white Toyota, that Westerners visualized during the 1980s. Car buyers in Japan are changing, and Japanese car producers are having to move quickly to keep one step ahead of the changing demands of consumers in their home market.

To satisfy customers who demand increasingly fashionable designs in their automobiles, Japanese automakers have turned to flexible manufacturing systems (FMS) and shorter model lives. Models are changed every four years instead of every seven to eight years, as in Europe and the United States. Using FMS, Japanese car producers can turn out several models on the same production line and adapt quickly to changes in market demand. This flexibility in marketing more than compensates for the increased costs of small batch production.

Examples of the types of cars that cater to fantasy niche markets in Japan are Nissan's Be-1 and Pao. Be-1 was styled by a fashion designer. The strange-looking minicar, Pao, sells for 40 percent more than similarly sized conventional cars. The aptly named S-cargo is a snail-shaped, light delivery van, scheduled to sell for only two years in order to underscore its exclusive image. Nissan's Cefiro is a midsized, Yuppie sports car that can be ordered with a choice of seats, wheels, windows, engine, and even suspension systems, designed to satisfy each new owner's desire for a unique vehicle. Nissan's upmarket Cima sells for about $33,000–$35,000 and has an optional in-car navigation system. This helps the driver find any of the 30 thousand preprogrammed, prestigious destinations, such as golf-clubs, hotels, and department stores in Tokyo, Osaka, and Nagoya.

The combined effects of FMS, computerized order entry, rapid model changes, just-in-time management techniques, and innovative styling are allowing Japanese car producers to pursue niche markets using customized marketing methods. The result is a range of fast-changing fantasy cars that are positioned to appeal to small segments of consumers. These methods also offer Japanese automakers important advantages in mainstream markets overseas. For example, Nissan's Infiniti is targeted to the larger market of upscale consumers in the United States who are looking for luxurious performance cars that offer the styling of European cars and the reliability of the ''Made in Japan'' label.

Questions

1. How do you think Nissan's management defines product quality?

2. How might styling considerations differ for a car that is intended to be sold in Japan, versus a car that will be sold in the United States?

3. Obviously Nissan has a deep product line. Do you think cannibalization is likely to be a problem for the company? Explain.

4. What type of product-mix branding option would you recommend for Nissan?

10

PRODUCT
DEVELOPMENT AND
MANAGEMENT

After reading this chapter you will be able to

1. explain the various meanings of *new product*.

2. identify organizational arrangements for new-product development.

3. identify and explain the stages in the new-product development process.

4. explain the elements of the product adoption and diffusion processes.

5. explain the concept of the product life cycle and discuss the use of the product life cycle concept in product management.

On Super Bowl Sunday in 1990 Gillette launched its new Sensor razor. Backed by $110 million in advertising and promotional support in North America alone, Sensor became perhaps Gillette's most successful new product in the company's ninety-year history. One year after introduction the company had produced 26 million razors and 424 million replacement cartridges—about 30 percent above the most ambitious forecasts.

The history behind Sensor is a long one. Gillette had been working on radically new shaving technologies since 1977 to improve on the dual-blade nondisposable razors. Initially, the company tried to make the blade cartridge more open for easier cleaning and to give the blades more room to operate. But its engineers became more ambitious and decided to find a way to allow each of the two blades to move independently, thus increasing the quality of the shave. Eventually, the engineers developed a technology for laser-welding the blades and their plastic springs onto steel sheets. In the process, twenty-two new patents were developed.

Because of the advanced laser technology and the instrumentation required to manufacture a product with many moving parts, Gillette's investment in the manufacturing equipment used to produce Sensor amounted to $200 million. The manufacturing processes were much different from what the company's experience had been, requiring many hours of collaboration between research and development personnel and production supervisors.

Product design considerations also were linked to findings from the company's marketing research. For example, as the impact of disposable razors on the shaving market increased (to a 42 percent share of all razors sold), Gillette's image began to decline. As one marketing manager put it, consumers viewed the Gillette razors as "cheap, plastic, and blue." Designers saw the new stainless steel shell of the razor as a way to project the sturdier image Gillette wanted.

Research also showed that permanent razors with replaceable cartridges (also known as razor systems) were rated as superior to disposables in consumer usage tests and that users of systems valued quality over price. Since disposables were far less profitable than systems, the idea of targeting the systems segment of the market with a technologically advanced product seemed reasonable. It was also anticipated that as the superior performance of Sensor became known, the product would draw sales from disposables users who previously had viewed the razor as a commodity.

After one year, data showed that 29 percent of Sensor buyers had been disposables users (half using Gillette disposables), 64 percent had been systems users (54 percent using Gillette products and 10 percent using competing products), and the remainder had been users of electric razors and other shaving methods. About nine months after the Sensor's introduction Gillette introduced a $15 silver-plated version, an $85 platinum-plated version, and a $225 sterling silver version. Sensor had captured 8.8 percent of the North American razor market dollars by the start of 1991.[1]

Not all new products are as successful as the Gillette Sensor appears to have been. Nor do most new products involve the level of financial commitment exemplified by that product. However, all new products do have certain common elements. First, a substantial risk is involved in introducing new products. Consumer acceptance is never guaranteed. Additionally, competitors often react to successful new-product introductions with competing offerings. (Schick had a competing razor ready to launch against Sensor before the end of 1990.) Second, substantial costs are often associated with new-product introductions. These costs can include manufacturing, research and development, and marketing costs, as the Sensor example demonstrated. Usually, the more innovative the product, the higher the costs. Finally, all successful new products eventually become old products. Today the challenges faced by the managers responsible for Gillette's Sensor are different from the challenges they faced in first bringing the product to market.

In this chapter we examine the new-product development process that firms use to manage the risks and costs associated with development. We also examine the processes of new-product adoption and diffusion that govern the market's acceptance of an innovation. Finally, using the concept of the product life cycle, we examine how the product management job changes over time.

NEW PRODUCTS

The primary source of growth for most organizations is new products. For high-technology firms the accelerating pace of technological development makes new-product development critical for survival. In 1990 the computer and instrument manufacturer Hewlett-Packard generated 50 percent of its sales from products that had been developed in the previous three years.[2]

What Is a New Product?

Product newness should be defined from two distinct points of view: newness to the firm and newness to the market.

The manufacturer of Baby Love products have gradually added new products that are entries into related categories. [Courtesy of Soft Sheen Products, Inc.]

• **Newness to the Firm** • From the firm's point of view, a new product could fall into any of the four categories shown in Figure 10–1. *Product modification* is the process by which the quality of an existing product is enhanced. If Gillette chose to improve the blades in its disposable razor, this degree of newness would apply. *Product line development* is the process of increasing the depth of an existing product line by adding a new product of a different grade, often to serve a new segment of the same market. The Sensor is an example of product line development. Often product line development is accomplished using an existing brand name. As discussed in chapter 9, this is called a product line extension of the brand. *Entry into related category* is the development of a new product that serves similar customer needs. This product may be complementary to existing products (for example, Gillette's foamy shaving cream). *Entry into entirely new category* is essentially a diversification strategy. Diversification strategies were discussed in chapter 3.

The importance to the company of recognizing the degree of newness is that the firm is more knowledgeable about producing and marketing less-new products, so it is probably better able to assess its costs and risks in such cases. Because the risk of entry into entirely new categories is high, firms often enter such categories by acquisition. Procter & Gamble

FIGURE 10–1

Degrees of Product Newness from the Firm's Viewpoint

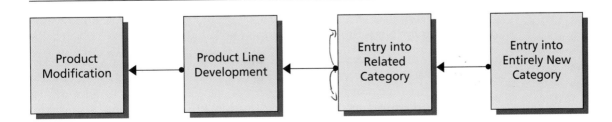

FIGURE 10–2
....

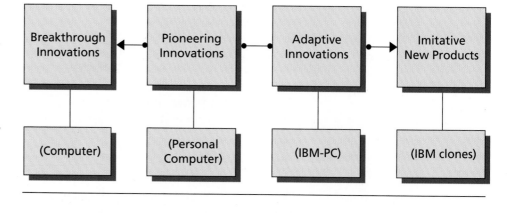

Degrees of Product Newness
from the Market's Viewpoint

Sources: The typology was adapted
from C. Merle Crawford, *New Products Management,* 3d ed. (Homewood,
Ill.: Richard D. Irwin, 1991), pp.
53–55; it also reflects the conceptual
work of Thomas Robertson, ''The
Process of Innovation and the Diffusion of Innovation,'' *Journal of Marketing,* January 1967, p. 15.

...▪......

breakthrough innovations

...▪......

pioneering innovations

...▪......

adaptive innovations

...▪......

imitative new products

has chosen this route to enter a variety of new markets. The company's acquisition of Rich-ardson-Vicks provided an effective way of entering the cold remedies market (through the Vicks line) and the hand lotion market (through the Oil of Olay line).

• **Newness to the Market** • New products will also differ in terms of the ease with which buyers will accept them. Usually acceptance is related to the degree of innovative-ness, as portrayed in Figure 10–2.

Breakthrough innovations are innovations that involve major changes in technology that lead to the creation of new product categories. Examples are the television, the tele-phone, the videocassette recorder, and the computer. *Pioneering innovations* are improve-ments in form or function that are so significant as to make existing products in the category obsolete or to create entirely new benefits and usage options for a product category. Color television, the cellular phone, the camcorder, and the personal computer are examples. *Adaptive innovations* are innovations that involve enhancements to established product forms that will compete with existing brands or suppliers but that may have some special distinctive feature. The IBM PC and subsequently the IBM PS/2 are examples, as are the Apple IIe and the Apple Macintosh. The least innovative approach is *imitative new prod-ucts*—products that copy an existing product and whose companies try to compete by underpricing the competition or perhaps by providing superior reliability and quality. Imi-tations do not involve significant form or function improvements. The computer firms that market IBM clones attempt to offer comparable features at lower prices.

As was the case with newness to the firm, the greater the newness to the market, the greater the risk. In particular, the ultimate degree of market acceptance becomes less cer-tain as the degree of market newness increases. The extent to which a firm pursues highly innovative new products will certainly affect the way it organizes itself for new-product development.

Organizing for New-Product Development

Top management's mission statement sets the tone for an organization's new-product development activity. This activity requires cooperation and coordination among different departments, and top management must provide the framework for it. Four popular approaches to organizing for new-product development are (1) the new-product committee;

(2) the new-product department; (3) the product, or brand, manager; and (4) the project team.

● **New-Product Committee** ● The approach to organizing for new-product development in which managers from different functional areas (production, marketing, finance, and R&D) review and act on new-product ideas generated elsewhere in the organization is the *new-product committee*. The committee brings together different types of expertise and helps build support among the managers for any ideas they accept. Disadvantages relate to the potential for buck passing, overconservatism, too much compromise, and time-consuming committee deliberations. Nevertheless, the committee structure is the most common approach to organizing for new-product development.

new-product committee

● **New-Product Department** ● The approach to organizing for new-product development in which a separate, formally structured unit handles all phases of the new-product development process is the *new-product department*. We will discuss this process later in the chapter. In some cases new-product ideas that are accepted by the committee are turned over to the new-product department for development and testing. New-product development is the full-time job of the person who heads the department. This person often reports directly to the firm's president.

new-product department

● **Product (or Brand) Manager** ● The person who is assigned one product, or product line, that has been approved for development and is responsible for determining its objectives and marketing strategies is the *product (or brand) manager*. But product managers almost never have direct authority over people whose cooperation is vital to their effectiveness. They select target markets and develop marketing mixes, but they do not, for example, have line authority over the sales force. Thus they must be skilled in winning the cooperation and support of others.

product (or brand) manager

Procter & Gamble gave birth to the product manager system in 1931. Sales of its new Camay soap were far behind sales of Ivory soap, the firm's oldest and most successful brand. So the company decided that each brand would have its own manager. The Camay manager would compete against the Ivory manager as if they worked for different companies.

Many multiproduct consumer products companies have copied the system that P&G created. Within each firm each brand gets individualized attention, and these brands and managers often compete for market share. These firms believe that intrafirm competition is good. Each brand manager, however, must be able to work effectively with the firm's research department, advertising department, and so on. In some cases product managers handle an entire line of related products. The product manager system also is common in department stores. Each merchandise manager manages the marketing effort for a given line of merchandise.

Critics argue that product managers sometimes neglect new-product development because they spend too much time managing existing products. Thus in some firms there are two types of product managers: *new*-product development managers handle initial development and test marketing of new products. Full-scale introduction of products that pass their test marketing is the task of product managers who manage assigned products through their life cycles.

Several years ago P&G and several other companies began to alter the brand manager system. One reason for the change was brand proliferation. The firms created the position of category manager, the person who oversees an entire product category. Category managers have the authority to coordinate marketing strategy among the product managers who rank below them.

P&G has eighty-plus brands and thirty-nine categories of U.S. business, from diapers to cake mixes. Each category is run by a category manager with direct profit responsibility. The basic thrust is to develop marketing strategies by focusing on categories and fitting brands together, as opposed to developing competing brand strategies and then dividing up company resources among them. Another focus is to allow for more coordinated marketing on a regular basis, as opposed to having managers from the different functional areas working together only on special projects.[3]

• **Project Team** • The approach to organizing for new-product development in which specialists from various functional areas who share an interest in a particular new product are given extensive authority in developing a new-product idea is the *project team* (also sometimes called a task force). The Texaco ad gives an example of a situation in which a project team is appropriate. Usually this approach is used when a major new technical

···■·····

project team

···■·····················

Special project teams are often used when new technology is involved in the product development process.

(This advertisement reprinted courtesy of Texaco Inc.)

"ROCK THE BOAT."

"At Texaco, we're free to rock the boat. To go with an unconventional idea when only a few can see the potential. One of those ideas resulted in a major development in gasoline technology."

Dan Daly is a research chemist at the Texaco Research Center in Beacon, N.Y. He's a member of the special team that developed Texaco's System³ gasoline.

The challenge: To clean up deposits in the intake systems of today's high-tech engines.

"We could have used a pre-existing additive package. That would have kept us at par with the current technology in the industry. But we chose to go beyond that. To be innovative, even if it did mean taking a risk."

The result: A remarkable system of gasolines that keep new cars running like new and can help restore performance to older cars. In fact, in the BMW test run on each of the six leading national gasolines, only System³ removed deposits on dirty intake valves.

This new generation of fuels has met with strong consumer acceptance.

"It's exhilarating to know you've developed something that can improve car performance."

Right, Dan. Because your team made waves, we made a better product for our customers.

Dan Daly
Chemist
Texaco Research Center

Star of the American Road

TEXACO – WE'VE GOT THE ENERGY.

development requiring the full and coordinated attention of a number of specialists is called for. Often the team will be physically separated from the rest of the firm and linked directly to top management. At the innovative 3M Company, many teams are formed by the initiative of someone who develops the idea and then recruits the other team members from functional areas such as marketing, manufacturing, finance, and any needed technical areas.[4]

Venture Capitalism

Venture capitalists are individuals or businesses that are willing to provide equity capital to entrepreneurs who have new products or ideas that are as yet unproven in the market but that have a good chance of becoming successful. Venture capitalists helped finance the growth of firms such as Apple Computer, Federal Express, and Genentech.

Many large corporations have internalized the concept of venture capitalism. IBM has units within the firm that investigate market opportunities beyond the company's core business. Through these units IBM has taken a low-risk approach to entering such emerging business areas as producing industrial robots, writing customized software, and selling directory-assistance equipment to telephone companies.

THE NEW-PRODUCT DEVELOPMENT PROCESS

new-product development process

The *new-product development process* is the sequence of stages a product must pass through prior to arriving at the introductory stage of the product life cycle: idea generation, idea screening, concept development and testing, business analysis, product development, market testing, and commercialization. Before proceeding to each successive stage, management has to decide whether to proceed, to seek more information, or to abandon the new-product development process.

Idea Generation

The goal in the first stage of the development process is to generate a steady flow of new-product ideas. Ideas must be received and channeled to persons or departments with the authority to act on them.

The obvious internal source of new ideas is the R&D department. Other internal sources are sales personnel; repair, service, and production personnel; and executives at all levels.

External sources include the new-products section in trade journals, which may stimulate other new-product ideas; observation of competitors and their customers; and research done on the firm's own customers. Companies that want to remain or become market driven in their new-product development effort, rather than being purely technology driven, are involving target customers earlier in the product development process. For example, as the Samsonite ad indicates, Samsonite uses consumer ideas extensively in new-product design.

Trade associations, private researchers, ad agencies, and universities are other external sources. In 1991 McDonald's introduced its McLean Deluxe sandwich, a product based on technology developed at Auburn University.[5] Government agencies, such as the Consumer Product Safety Commission, can also provide ideas.

Inventors who are skilled in engineering and production but lack marketing skill sometimes approach firms with new-product ideas. Some firms have a not-invented-here

Many new products are developed from analyzing customers' problems.

(Reprinted with permission. © Copyright 1988 Samsonite Corporation; all rights reserved.)

prejudice against outside inventors' ideas. Other firms welcome ideas from outside experts.

Firms also may set up teams that meet periodically to generate new ideas. To get maximum idea input in these brainstorming sessions, criticism and censorship are withheld. Table 10–1 discusses four techniques used by these teams.

As the Global Marketing box on page 318 illustrates, the range of sources of new-product ideas is complex for firms that market globally.

Idea Screening

Great care is needed in the idea generation stage to maximize creativity and minimize evaluation. Critical appraisal of ideas occurs in the idea screening stage, because a firm can afford to undertake development of only a limited number of product ideas. The less promising ones must be dropped. The major costs are those involved in rejecting good ideas (drop error) and accepting poor ideas (go error).

TABLE 10–1 ■ Examples of Techniques for Generating New-Product Ideas

....

1. Brainstorming:
   Each team member gives every new product idea he or she has.

2. Forced relationships:*
   Listing all the characteristics of an object that are markedly different from the product to be changed. For example, "How can you improve a chair by making it more like a car?"

3. Fantasy:
   Team members project themselves mentally into a situation. To generate new service ideas for airlines, team members could be asked to take an imaginary airplane trip.

4. Heuristic ideation technique:**
   This is a systematic method of considering all possible combinations of two variables to generate new ideas. A grid using packaging and food products could be constructed so that each type of packaging is paired with each type of food. New ideas might include grape jelly in tubes and margarine in squeezable containers.

....

*See Alex F. Osborn, *Applied Imagination*, 3d ed. (New York: Scribner, 1963), pp. 213–214.

**See Edward M. Tauber, "HIT: Heuristic Ideation Technique—A Systematic Procedure for New Product Search," *Journal of Marketing*, January 1972, pp. 58–61.

Rejecting good ideas leads to lost opportunities. Accepting poor ideas leads to increasing costs, because the costs associated with the later stages of the development process are much higher than those in the idea stages. The longer it takes to scrap a poor idea, the more costly it is to the firm.

New-product ideas may be evaluated according to criteria established by management. Often these criteria appear in checklists, such as the one in Figure 10–3. Although some checklists are designed to yield a quantitative score for each idea, the main purpose of this screening is to identify the major strengths and weaknesses of each idea. Different managers have different views about how an idea should be rated on a given criteria. Screening procedures can result in discussions that clarify those views as well as identifying any fatal flaws in an idea.

Many times a product idea will be rejected not because it is a bad idea but because it doesn't fit the objectives, strategy, or resources of the company. Once a new idea has been rated on each dimension, management will determine whether to proceed to the next stage. Most ideas do not survive the screening stage.

Concept Development and Testing

Product ideas that do survive the screening stage are refined into product concepts. A *product concept* is a statement of the benefits to be offered by a new product and of the product attributes that will provide those benefits.[6] The statement may also specify the target audience for the product.

One of the most famous new concepts in recent decades was the one formulated by Miller Lite. The dual benefits of "tastes great, less filling" were the cornerstone of the product concept. But integral to the concept were the attribute of fewer calories and advertising that showed that the product was for athletes and other "tough guys" who probably would not accept a wimpy beer just because it had fewer calories.

A *product concept test* is a procedure used to determine potential customers' reactions

...■......

product concept test

to a new product concept. Typically, customers are given a statement of the product concept (possibly with a picture of the product) and asked for a series of reactions. Among the questions that might be asked are Who would use this product? For what purposes would this product be used? and What is the likelihood you would try this product? (On a 5-point scale the likelihood would range from ''definitely would try'' to ''definitely would not try.'')

GLOBAL MARKETING

The question of where new products come from can have a slightly different answer when the situation is viewed in a global context. Indeed, the definition of *new product* may be different.

In some cases new-product ideas can come from products or ideas that are ignored in the country of origin. As we saw in chapter 6, Japan's current dominance in the robotics industry has been traced to 1967, when inventor Joseph Engelberger introduced a robot that opened a can of beer and led the band on ''The Tonight Show.'' Although American talent agents followed up by seeking to book the act, Japanese officials flew Engelberger to Tokyo to address industry leaders on the business significance of his invention.

Clearly, new technology lies at the root of many new products. But staying on top of every relevant technological development can be costly, especially in such fields as biotechnology. Accordingly, many firms follow the pattern developed by Britain's Glaxo Pharmaceutical. To broaden its product line while remaining focused in R&D, Glaxo has developed arrangements with Japanese pharmaceutical firms to cross-license new proprietary drugs. Thus drugs resulting from Glaxo technology become new products for the Japanese firms and vice versa.

Alternatively, a new product may be new not to the company but only to a particular nation or region. Product concepts that are successful in one country may not be effective elsewhere, however. When General Mills launched its first breakfast cereals in Europe in 1991 it decided to introduce Honey Nut Cheerios and Golden Grahams into France, Spain, and Portugal. Company officials chose those two brands rather than the company's strongest brands (Cheerios and Wheaties) or the fast-growing nutritional brands because the key product concepts and benefits of these alternatives did not seem appropriate for the intended markets. Specifically, Europeans were seen to be interested in sweetness (hence the selection of Honey Nut Cheerios over regular Cheerios) and to lack a strong awareness of health or nutritional issues. As far as Wheaties were concerned, General Mills officials believed the brand's image was linked too closely with the ''American athletic heritage'' because of the extensive degree to which Wheaties ads featured sports heroes.

Sources: Kenichi Ohmae, ''The Global Logic of Strategic Alliances,'' *Harvard Business Review,* March–April 1989, pp. 143–149; Amal Kumar Naj, ''How U.S. Robots Lost the Market to Japan in Factory Automation,'' *Wall Street Journal,* November 6, 1990, pp. A1, A10; Richard Gibson, ''Cereal Venture Is Planning Honey of a Venture in Europe,'' *Wall Street Journal,* November 14, 1990, pp. B1, B12.

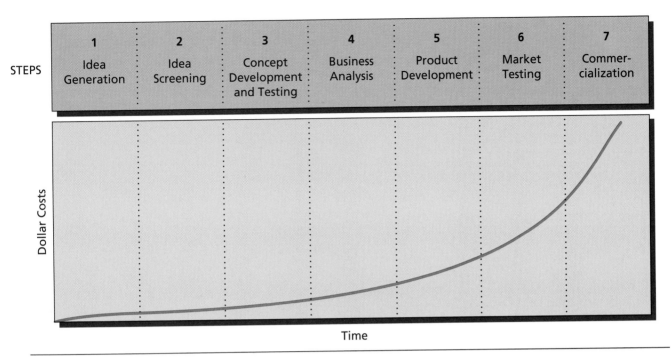

| STEPS | 1 Idea Generation | 2 Idea Screening | 3 Concept Development and Testing | 4 Business Analysis | 5 Product Development | 6 Market Testing | 7 Commer-cialization |

Time

Dollar Costs

FIGURE 10–3

A New-Product Screening Checklist

Business Analysis

After the product concept has been developed, management creates a preliminary marketing strategy for the proposed product's introduction. Issues that may be considered at this stage include the likely impact of the introduction on other products the firm markets and whether the proposed product and the technology for producing it can be protected with a patent. The main focus in this stage, however, is to evaluate the proposed product's business attractiveness.

Such an evaluation requires that management perform demand analysis, cost analysis, and profitability analysis. *Demand analysis* includes forecasting market and sales potential, and estimating the competitive reaction. *Cost analysis* includes estimating research and development, production, and marketing costs. Demand and cost factors are brought together in the *profitability analysis*. Each organization has its own requirements regarding a minimum acceptable return on investment of the proposed product or a minimum acceptable period of time for recovering the initial cash investment in the product. Environmental factors must be considered throughout the process of assessing the product's business attractiveness.

Product Development

If the product concept survives the business analysis stage, it is committed to technical and marketing development. The R&D and engineering departments develop one or more physical versions of the product concept—product prototypes. Each prototype must embody the key attributes that target customers want. It must also be subjected to manufacturing methods research to determine the most efficient method of volume production.

Once developed, the prototype is tested. *Functional tests* such as the one portrayed in the Ford ad, are used to ensure that product performance and safety standards are met. *Consumer tests* are used to measure the product's suitability to the target market.

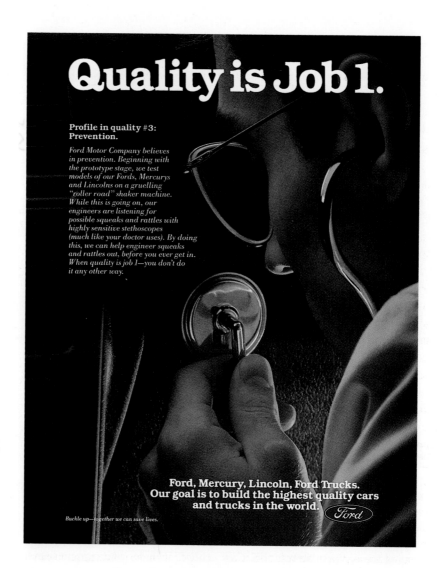

Quality is Job 1.

Profile in quality #3: Prevention.

Ford Motor Company believes in prevention. Beginning with the prototype stage, we test models of our Fords, Mercurys and Lincolns on a gruelling "roller road" shaker machine. While this is going on, our engineers are listening for possible squeaks and rattles with highly sensitive stethoscopes (much like your doctor uses). By doing this, we can help engineer squeaks and rattles out, before you ever get in. When quality is job 1—you don't do it any other way.

Ford, Mercury, Lincoln, Ford Trucks. Our goal is to build the highest quality cars and trucks in the world. *Ford*

Buckle up—together we can save lives.

Prototypes of the final product are often tested to be sure they fulfill the product concept.

(Courtesy of Ford Motor Company.)

Information gathered in this stage is the basis for deciding whether to continue, postpone, or drop further development. Although this go or no-go decision is made at each stage in the process, once technical and marketing development begins, costs increase sharply. (See Figure 10–4.) Up to this point, the only costs incurred are research costs. A go decision now leads to market entry costs. The manufacturing department plans for materials procurement, production facilities, and personnel. Meanwhile the marketing department develops a final plan for introducing the product and managing it into the future. Ideally all the development work in this stage will have ironed out any bugs in the product.

The drive for shorter product development cycles is especially evident in prototype development in the auto industry. In design and engineering shops engineers are building mathematical models of cars on computer-aided design systems. This reduces the need for clay mockups and the construction and testing of dozens of prototypes. The computer designs, which contain detailed specifications, also help the factory get a head start on tooling production equipment. There is no longer any need to wait for design engineers to take measurements from clay mockups and pass those specifications on to manufacturing.[7]

FIGURE 10–4

The Relative Costs Incurred in
Each Stage of the New-Product
Development Process

A New Product Screening Checklist

	Lowest ◄—— Rating ——► Highest				
	1	2	3	4	5
Technical difficulty	—	—	—	—	—
Fit with research skills	—	—	—	—	—
Patentability	—	—	—	—	—
Fit with manufacturing skills	—	—	—	—	—
Availability of manufacturing capacity	—	—	—	—	—
Access to raw materials or components	—	—	—	—	—
Ability to be cost competitive	—	—	—	—	—
Market size	—	—	—	—	—
Market growth rate	—	—	—	—	—
Degree of cannibalization	—	—	—	—	—
Intensity of competition	—	—	—	—	—
Newness to market	—	—	—	—	—
Fit with sales force	—	—	—	—	—
Fit with distribution system	—	—	—	—	—
Total investment required	—	—	—	—	—
Overall market risk	—	—	—	—	—
Ability to differentiate offering	—	—	—	—	—
Fit with corporate strategy/mission	—	—	—	—	—

Especially in the case of durable goods, the product development phase of the project may lead to a significant alteration of the product concept. The original concept may not prove feasible in a technical sense or market conditions may change, leading to a shift in strategy. For example, in 1983 General Motors conceived the Saturn as being a $6,000 car with 60 miles per gallon highway fuel efficiency and competing in the subcompact market. By launch time in 1990 the product's price had nearly doubled and its mileage ratings were cut nearly in half.[8]

Market Testing

If a go decision is made, market testing of the actual product begins, under realistic purchase conditions. The basic purposes of this final screening are (1) to determine if targeted customers will buy the product, (2) to test the other marketing mix elements, and (3) to prepare more reliable sales and profit forecasts. If test results are unfavorable, the product's introduction is postponed or the product is dropped. Ideally, individual product features that can be evaluated before the market test should be pretested.

The amount of time and money invested in market testing depends on such factors as the organization's financial resources, the degree of product newness, and the pressure to get the product to market before competitors introduce their versions of it. In general, the greater the innovativeness of a new product, the greater the commitment of time and money to market testing. At the other extreme, a new product that is little more than a minor modification of an existing product may not even be subjected to market testing.

Market testing can be approached in many ways. Among the approaches are (1) conventional test marketing, (2) minimarket tests, and (3) laboratory (or simulated) market tests.

● **Conventional Test Marketing** ● The introduction of the product in one or more test cities that are representative of the market area in which the product is intended to be sold is called *conventional test marketing*. Testing in two or more cities provides an opportunity to measure consumer response to different marketing mixes. For example, the promotion element might consist of advertising in one city and of advertising along with free product samples in another city. A consumer product manufacturer would use its sales force to induce wholesalers and retailers in the test cities to stock the product. Then it could appraise the product's performance by measuring sales in the test stores and measuring the volume of the product each store orders from its wholesaler.

Conventional test marketing is time-consuming, costly, and highly visible to rivals. The time between the test and the evaluation of its results may be long enough to allow rivals to introduce competitive versions. Rivals also sometimes intentionally distort test marketing by lowering the price of their brands in test cities or by greatly increasing spending on promotion. Thus some marketers skip conventional test marketing and others take approaches that shorten and simplify the conventional approach.

● **Minimarket Tests** ● The marketer's use of an outside research firm that has contracts with retailers in specific market areas to accept new products and place them on their shelves for testing purposes is called a *minimarket test*. The product is delivered to the stores by the research firm, which uses information from electronic scanners at checkout counters to track households' purchases during minimarket tests. The panelists are given coded identification cards to use when they shop at supermarkets covered by the firm's scanner network.

Minimarket tests are conducted in smaller geographic areas, take less time, and cost less money than conventional test marketing. Some marketers, however, question whether minimarkets and consumer panelists are truly representative of the markets into which the products will be introduced and of the customers to whom the products will be targeted. Another drawback is that, as in conventional tests, rivals can see the product that is being tested.

● **Laboratory (or Simulated) Market Tests** ● Still another approach to market testing is the *laboratory (or simulated) market test*. Research firms offer laboratory market tests that cost between $35,000 and $75,000 (instead of the typical $1 million or more that a traditional test can cost). These tests, which can be run in eight weeks instead of six months, also are shielded from observation by rivals. Although simulated market tests are available in many forms, they usually involve taking a small sample (for example, five hundred) from the target market and showing the people ads and other promotional material for several products, including the test product. The people are then taken to shop in either a mockup or a real store, where their purchases are recorded electronically. Shopper behavior (especially repeat purchase behavior) is analyzed by computerized models, which are

FIGURE 10–5
· ·

An Overview of the New-Product Development Process ▪

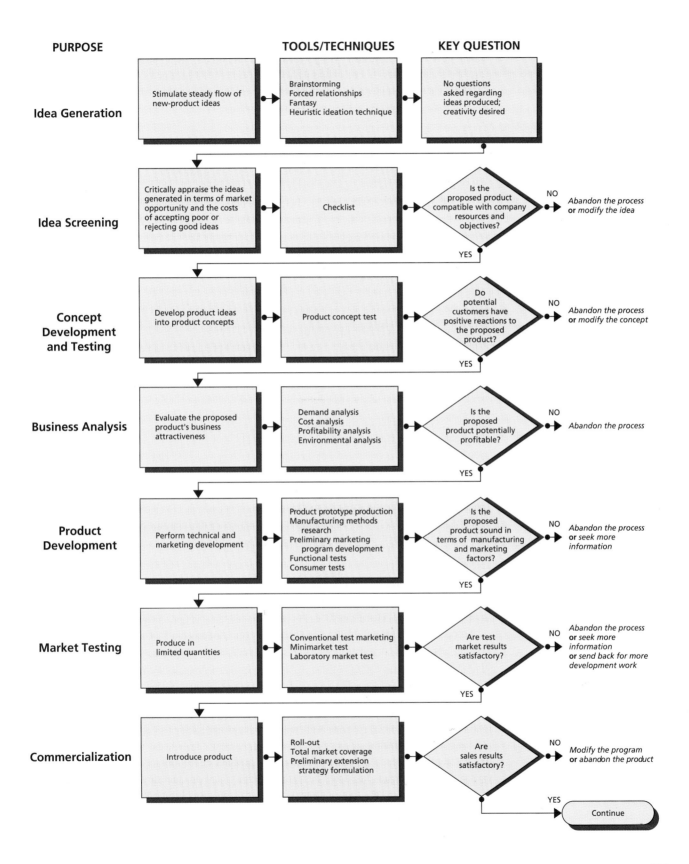

PURPOSE		TOOLS/TECHNIQUES	KEY QUESTION	
Idea Generation	Stimulate steady flow of new-product ideas	Brainstorming Forced relationships Fantasy Heuristic ideation technique	No questions asked regarding ideas produced; creativity desired	
Idea Screening	Critically appraise the ideas generated in terms of market opportunity and the costs of accepting poor or rejecting good ideas	Checklist	Is the proposed product compatible with company resources and objectives?	NO → *Abandon the process or modify the idea* / YES
Concept Development and Testing	Develop product ideas into product concepts	Product concept test	Do potential customers have positive reactions to the proposed product?	NO → *Abandon the process or modify the concept* / YES
Business Analysis	Evaluate the proposed product's business attractiveness	Demand analysis Cost analysis Profitability analysis Environmental analysis	Is the proposed product potentially profitable?	NO → *Abandon the process* / YES
Product Development	Perform technical and marketing development	Product prototype production Manufacturing methods research Preliminary marketing program development Functional tests Consumer tests	Is the proposed product sound in terms of manufacturing and marketing factors?	NO → *Abandon the process or seek more information* / YES
Market Testing	Produce in limited quantities	Conventional test marketing Minimarket test Laboratory market test	Are test market results satisfactory?	NO → *Abandon the process or seek more information or send back for more development work* / YES
Commercialization	Introduce product	Roll-out Total market coverage Preliminary extension strategy formulation	Are sales results satisfactory?	NO → *Modify the program or abandon the product* / YES → Continue

essentially sets of equations that simulate the market. The results of this analysis should reveal how well the product will perform in its intended market and should provide insight into the targeted customers' response to variations in the product's price and promotional support. Critics, however, say that laboratory market tests are not as accurate or reliable as tests that are conducted in real-world markets.

Unfortunately, regardless of the method selected, market testing cannot eliminate the risk in new-product introductions. For example, Campbell Soup successfully test marketed its Souper Combos, a set of microwaveable soups and entrées designed for both home and office lunches. But soon after the product was launched nationally, sales fell off sharply. Campbell managers attributed the difference between test market and national market results to two factors. First, by the time of the national launch two new products (Healthy Choice and Kid's Cuisine) were introduced by a competitor. Second, Campbell had paid an inordinate amount of attention (in terms of advertising and in-store displays) to Souper Combos during the test marketing—a level of attention it could not afford to duplicate in the full national market.[9]

Commercialization

If the market test results are favorable, the marketer prepares to launch the product into the introductory stage of its life cycle. This requires finalizing the product's introductory marketing strategy. During commercialization, the marketer also develops the product's marketing plan over its projected life cycle. Expenditures are greatest in this stage, and interdepartmental cooperation and coordination are required in planning, implementing, and controlling the marketing effort for the new product. Among the activities that take place are acquiring production facilities to produce the product in volume and preparing final budgets. The sales force and intermediaries must be acquainted with the new product and be trained and motivated to help ensure a successful introduction. The ad agency and the marketer must work together in developing the promotional program, and final plans for physical distribution must be made.

DuPont created a tremendous amount of attention with its humorous advertising during the successful launch of its Stainmaster carpets. Company executives have suggested that a high level of coordination with ad agency BBD&O, with the independent carpet mills that produced the product, and with the retail carpet dealers who sold Stainmaster were critical in assuring that product availability was coordinated with the start of advertising and with local promotional activities. By the second year of Stainmaster's life the brand was selling at an annual rate of $1 billion.[10]

To coordinate the hundreds of activities in the commercialization stage many organizations use advanced scheduling techniques, such as the critical path method (CPM), to map out sequentially the necessary activities and the time required for each activity. The result is an elaborate flowchart that coordinates all these activities and identifies the critical path. Any delays on the path will hold up the commercialization of the product.

There is also increasing concern about bringing new products to market quickly and about involving managers from both marketing and the other functional areas throughout the process. *Simultaneous product development* is the term used to describe highly coordinated project team approaches to the new-product development process. A critical aspect of this approach is the need to begin some physical product development activities as early as possible and to share technical problems and developments with marketing personnel as they arise so that necessary modifications can be quickly communicated and coordinated.[11]

...■......

simultaneous product development

Figure 10–5 summarizes the purpose, the tools and techniques, and the key questions during each stage of the new-product development process. In the remainder of this chapter, we focus on the processes of market adoption and diffusion for new products and on the life cycle that follows commercialization.

THE ADOPTION AND DIFFUSION PROCESSES

The basic objective of the commercialization stage of the new-product development process is to gain market acceptance for the new product. As we noted earlier in this chapter, market acceptance will generally be more difficult for products that are more innovative.

Consider, for example, the Telestrator. Pro football fans have seen announcer John Madden use the Telestrator to sketch football plays on what appears to be a TV chalkboard. During the war in Kuwait in 1991 military analysts used it to sketch movements of allied forces in the Middle East for TV audiences. But the Telestrator was patented in 1968 and barely sold at all until Madden began using it in 1982. Since then sales have approached thirty to forty units per year at a price of $8,000 a unit.[12]

Certainly the rate of market acceptance for a breakthrough product will be slower than for product line developments such as the Sensor razor. This is because of differences in the rate of adoption and the rate of diffusion.

The Adoption Process

The series of stages a prospective buyer goes through in deciding to buy and make regular use of a new product is the *adoption process*. The stages are shown in Figure 10–6. Marketing efforts seek to move potential customers rapidly to final adoption. Marketers hope that promotion in the introductory stage of the product life cycle will create awareness of the product and whet the appetites of potential buyers for more information about it so they will evaluate it. (The product life cycle is the subject of the next major section of the chapter.)

Notice that in Figure 10–6 a trial purchase is not made until rather late in the adoption process. If the product is expensive, radically new, or complex, prospects may perceive the risk of a trial purchase to be greater than its benefits. Less expensive and less complex products are often distributed as free samples. The goal is to induce prospects to try them by reducing perceived risk.

adoption process

FIGURE 10–6

Stages in the Adoption Process

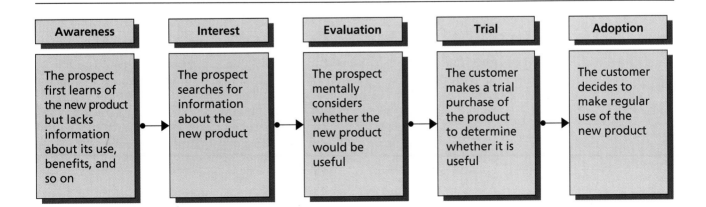

Customers who make a trial purchase make a monetary commitment to the product and then carefully evaluate the "rightness" of the decision. Rivals may attempt to switch them to their brands. There is no assurance customers will remain committed even after adoption. As we saw in chapter 5, they may experience cognitive dissonance, which may lead them to search for additional information to confirm the wisdom of the decision. Providing this information may help the marketer reduce dissonance and raise buyer commitment, or loyalty, to the brand.

• **Adoption Rate** • Five characteristics of the new product affect the rate at which individual buyers adopt it: (1) relative advantage, (2) compatibility, (3) complexity, (4) trialability, and (5) observability.[13]

• *Relative Advantage* • The greater a product's perceived degree of superiority over previous products in terms of price, convenience, ease of use, and so on, the greater its relative advantage and the faster its adoption rate.

• *Compatibility* • A product's compatibility is its consistency with prospects' cultural values and habitual ways of doing things. It includes the perceived risk (personal and social consequences) of using the product. Low-sudsing detergents were accepted slowly because consumers associated plenty of suds with cleaning power. Directions on the labels recommending one-half cup of detergent were contradictory to what consumers expected: a full cup. Sizzlean, a breakfast strip that is leaner than bacon, offers the benefit of leanness, not available with regular bacon, while also being compatible with traditional ways of preparing breakfast.

• *Complexity* • A product's complexity is the relative difficulty consumers have in understanding or using the product. Highly complex products require more time for acceptance. Examples of such products are heat pumps, sophisticated microwave ovens, food processors, VCRs, and home computers.

In-store taste tests can be used to persuade consumers to make a trial purchase.

- *Trialability* • A product's trialability (or divisibility) is the ease with which consumers can make use of the product on a trial basis. A free sample, a low-cost trial sample, a test drive, or a no-charge, two-week, in-home trial could all help a buyer reduce uncertainty about the product's performance.

- *Observability* • A product's observability is the degree to which the benefits or other results of using the product are visible to others. Farmers can observe the yield of a new hybrid corn seed, and the sound quality of compact disc players can be compared to the sound quality of other sound systems. The more observable the benefit, the less risk the buyer encounters and the easier the marketing task.

The rate at which any new product is accepted in the market is partly a function of the rate of adoption. If the adoption rate is high (because of the characteristics just discussed), then the overall rate of market acceptance will be fast. Because the Sensor razor had a clear relative advantage, compatibility with regular shaving habits, a lack of complexity, and observable benefits, the rate of its adoption was very rapid.

But many innovative products do not score as well on these characteristics. Especially if high price is a factor, the relative advantage may be unclear. Moreover, the results may not be easily observable and the product may be complex. In such situations market acceptance will be influenced largely by the diffusion process.

The Diffusion Process

··· ■ ······

diffusion process

The spread of an idea or the penetration of a market by a new product is the *diffusion process*. The process works by a combination of independent adoption and (in situations where the adoption rate is low) word-of-mouth communication and imitation.

In the diffusion process for any product, some buyers are more willing to take the risks associated with new products. Others then rely on the experiences and recommendations of these buyers before buying. Lowering the price of a new product will speed the diffusion process if the product is expensive. The lower price means that nonadopters face less risk and thus have less need for information from adopters.

Figure 10–7 shows the traditional view of the diffusion process, including five categories of adopters and the typical percentage of adopters in each category. The categories are

FIGURE 10–7
·······················

The Product Diffusion Process

Source: Reprinted with permission of The Free Press, a Division of Macmillan, Inc., from *Diffusion of Innovations*, Third Edition, by Everett M. Rogers. Copyright © 1983 by The Free Press. ■

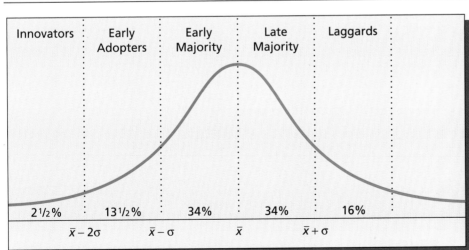

Time of Adoption of Innovations

(1) innovators, (2) early adopters, (3) early majority, (4) late majority, and (5) laggards. A new product that has been adopted by innovators and early adopters still has 84 percent of its potential customers in the nonadopter category. But if innovators and early adopters do not adopt, the product is doomed to failure.

On the surface it would appear that innovators, those who first try new products, would be different in their attitudes and personality traits from laggards, those who adopt products very late. There is, however, no general personality pattern for innovators or laggards. The differences in their behavior can be more easily predicted and explained by using social class, income levels, and status positions in reference groups. These characteristics seem to be related to the degree of risk taking, or lack of it, in buying decisions. A person may be an innovator for one product and a laggard for another.

An innovating organization, therefore, should engage in marketing research to identify the demographic and psychographic characteristics of innovators and early adopters in its particular product area. This information, along with information about consumers' media habits, helps marketers target their initial promotion effort to innovators and early adopters.

THE PRODUCT LIFE CYCLE

**product life cycle
(PLC)**

Because the diffusion process represents the spread of an innovation throughout the marketplace, it portrays the growth in first-time sales of a new product. The *product life cycle (PLC),* which is shown in Figure 10–8, is a concept that depicts a product's sales history over time and includes repeat purchases, not just first-time sales.[14] It was originally derived from the diffusion curve. Essentially, the curve in Figure 10–8 is the cumulative version of the curve in Figure 10–7.

The product life cycle concept suggests that a product goes through different stages of development during and after its diffusion through the marketplace. These stages are

FIGURE 10–8

The Product Life Cycle

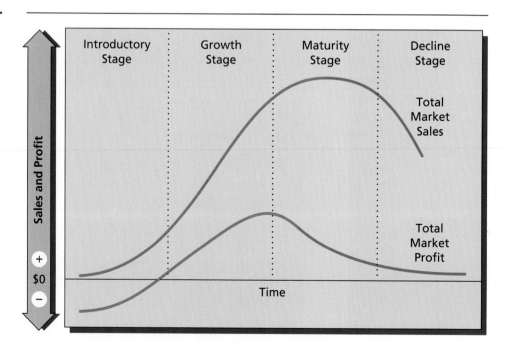

(1) introduction, (2) growth, (3) maturity, and (4) decline. The stages differ in terms of the degree of market knowledge and acceptance of the product and in terms of the competitive situation the product confronts. Because the concept was derived from the diffusion curve, it is most useful when the sales curve depicts the sales of a product category (such as personal computers, color televisions, or microwaveable entrées) rather than a particular brand or supplier. Indeed, most new brands enter a market after the diffusion process for a product category is well under way.

The PLC concept also applies to celebrities, ideas, concepts, practices, places, and social concerns. Some celebrities enjoy long life cycles; others lose the public's interest quickly. Concepts such as the desirability of breastfeeding and of strenuous exercise vary in popularity over time, as do places. Atlantic City legalized casino gambling partly in response to the city's decline as a resort area. Social issues such as quality education, ecology, and consumerism enjoy various degrees of concern and support over time.

Introductory Stage

Also known as the market development stage, the introductory stage of the PLC represents the period during which a product innovation is first commercialized. The first firm to launch a new product category is known as the *pioneer*. Examples are Procter & Gamble with its Pampers disposable diapers, Amana with its microwave ovens, and California Cooler with its wine coolers.

Since the pioneer has no direct competitors, its primary marketing task is to start the diffusion process by stimulating innovators and early adopters to buy and to gain distribution so potential buyers will have access to the new product. Because pioneering can be very costly (recall the cost of launching Sensor) profits are negative during this stage, as Figure 10–8 suggests.

The length of time a product remains in the introductory stage is primarily a function of how long it takes to gain market acceptance. As the diffusion curve demonstrated, until innovators and early adopters have purchased, we cannot expect rapid diffusion through the rest of the market. So the more innovative the product is, the slower its diffusion and the longer the first stage will be. Of course, the more marketing dollars committed to building the adoption rate, the shorter the introductory stage. Because Sensor was a relatively modest innovation and was heavily supported in terms of marketing, its introductory stage lasted only a few months. But VCRs were available for a half dozen years before achieving substantial sales growth, and Telestrator sales languished for fifteen years before John Madden made the device famous.

Growth Stage

If a product is successful in establishing a customer base, the sales growth rate will eventually speed up as the "early majority" of the market begins to buy. This is the growth stage of the product life cycle. Not only do new customers enter the market, but some repeat purchasing from old customers begins. The amount of repeat purchasing during growth will be much higher for nondurables such as microwaveable entrées than for durables such as compact disc players. The market growth attracts new competitors, which imitate (or try to improve on) the pioneer's product. Often this new competition leads to lower prices, which in turn, stimulate more growth. The market growth for VCRs accelerated between 1983 and 1985 in large part because of price reductions. Annual sales rose from about 1.9 million units in 1982 (the start of the growth stage) to 12 million in 1985 (the last year of the growth stage).

As the market evolves, firms often extend their product lines by offering new options or quality levels to reach new market segments. (Recall Gillette's addition of platinum Sensor razors.) Also, the focus of advertising shifts from providing information about the product category to providing information about brands.

Because of the high rate of market growth in this stage of the PLC, most competitors in the market experience rapid sales growth as well. Unless these firms spend prohibitively large sums on promotion, overall industry profitability grows. But as we saw in chapter 3, the leading brands (the "stars") will be much more profitable than the smaller brands.

Maturity Stage

The main clue that a product life cycle is in the maturity stage is that sales growth has leveled off. In the VCR market this occurred in 1986 and 1987, when sales peaked at 14 million units. But the lack of continued growth is not the only market attribute that characterizes maturity. Important buyer and competitive dimensions of maturity are

- Repeat sales become much more extensive than first-time sales.
- Buyers are knowledgeable about the alternatives, so brand preferences become well established.
- Few major technical advances will be forthcoming, so there are few competitive advantages on technical dimensions.

As a consequence, new firms find it difficult to enter the market and existing firms find it difficult to increase their market share. Weaker competitors are often squeezed out of the market at this point, a process called *shake-out*. As growth slows, price competition may heat up, leading to overall declines in market (industry) profits. But the leading firms (the cash cows) will be very profitable because their ratio of sales to advertising and promotional spending will be high.

Most products in the U.S. market are mature products, and they account for far more sales and profits than new products do. Obviously there is a need for mature-product strategy. The rest of this section of the chapter focuses on strategies marketers often use in the hope of extending a mature product's life.

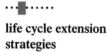

life cycle extension strategies

Because of the risk and high cost of introducing new products, many organizations try to get as much mileage as possible from their established products. To do so they use *life cycle extension strategies*—strategies designed to lengthen the product life cycle. These strategies are used during the early part of the maturity stage. Depending on the circumstances, an extension strategy might involve penetrating new market segments, differentiating the products, or making other changes in marketing strategy. Ideally, such strategies should be planned before a product is launched. There are four basic extension strategies: promoting more frequent usage, developing more varied usage among current users, creating new users by expanding the market, and finding new uses.[15]

More frequent usage can often be stimulated by packaging changes. Aseptic packaging has expanded the usage of many fruit drinks by enabling more people to bring the products to work or school. The market growth for durable goods such as VCRs can be stimulated through the addition of new optional features that make the product easier to use, thereby encouraging faster replacement purchases. Of course, as the Ethics in Marketing box suggests, obsolescence is sometimes planned.

Developing more varied usage means expanding the situations in which the product would be selected. VISA cards were once used primarily for travel and entertainment. Now they are increasingly promoted for use in a variety of other ways, including the payment of some state and local taxes, the purchases of mail-order products, and the purchases at fast-food outlets.

To expand the market, product line development is usually necessary. The Suave ad illustrates the use of product line extensions to attract new skin lotion customers with modest differences in needs.

It may often be possible to develop entirely new uses for the product. Thanks to customer suggestions, Arm & Hammer baking soda is advertised as a refrigerator deodorant, a bath water softener, and a carpet freshener, among other things.

ETHICS IN MARKETING

One of the consequences of technological advancement is that some existing products are rendered obsolete. Compact disc players, for example, are making record players obsolete, just as the electronic calculator ended most uses of the slide rule. In these examples the new products provided major advances in the functional benefits received by consumers.

Three issues associated with planned obsolescence involve ethical concerns: (1) postponed obsolescence, (2) intentionally designed (or planned) obsolescence, and (3) fashion (or style) obsolescence. *Postponed obsolescence* means holding back on product improvements until present inventories run out or demand falls off sharply. *Intentionally designed obsolescence* involves designing a product, or a critical part of it, to wear out within a given period of time. *Fashion obsolescence* is psychological; new-model cars make last year's models obsolete.

A marketer may try to defend postponed obsolescence by saying a product improvement was withheld to provide more time to test it and to research potential customer desire for and willingness to pay for it. Or the marketer may claim that the premature introduction of an improvement would render some inventory worthless and that the inventory losses would have to be offset by higher prices on the improved product.

Marketers are unlikely to accept the term ''intentionally designed obsolescence'' as a fair characterization of any product policies. They often argue that buyers don't want most products to last forever but instead want new, improved automobiles and appliances. Or they argue that the cost of designing long-lasting products would make the price of those products prohibitive.

Fashion obsolescence may result from a marketer's effort to cater to market segments that demand ''newness.'' Defenders contend that such obsolescence helps make products available for the second-hand market and that it may be a natural result of the dynamic competitive and technological environment in which marketers operate.

Opponents of planned obsolescence may argue that marketers waste natural resources in devoting too much effort to developing new products when existing ones are satisfactory. They may also say that marketers are too concerned with creating a never-ending desire for newness. A third argument is that too many products are designed to be short-lived, which creates a solid waste disposal problem as old models are discarded for new ones.

Is planned obsolescence an ethical marketing practice? What other ethical issues are related to it?

Line extensions of a brand can help a firm meet subtle differences in consumer needs.

(Helene Curtis, Inc.)

In some cases extension strategies launch a mature product into a new growth cycle. In other cases the best that can be done is to buy additional time until a new product is ready to replace the mature one.

In the first part of Figure 10–9 the extension strategy recycles the product, starting a new life cycle before the original one runs its course. It is a break-out extension. There may be several recycles, depending on the effectiveness of the extension strategies. In the second part of the figure the extension strategy lengthens the original life cycle by extending the maturity or decline stage. It is a stretch-out extension.

Decline Stage

The decline stage is the final stage in the life cycle. Product forms and brands typically enter into this stage more quickly than do product categories. An example of a declining product form is unfiltered cigarettes. Shifts in consumer tastes, technological progress, and competitive attacks from domestic and foreign rivals are among the reasons products enter the decline stage.

Sales and profits fall off rapidly and competitors become more cost-conscious in the decline stage. But brands with strong acceptance by some customer segments may continue

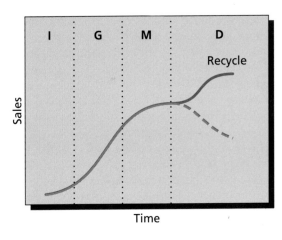

A Break-Out Extension

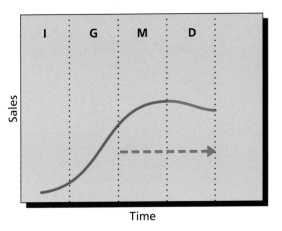

A Stretch-Out Extension

I = Introductory stage   **G** = Growth stage   **M** = Maturity stage   **D** = Decline stage

FIGURE 10–9

Two Types of Extension
Strategies

to produce profits. Thus Spic and Span still is a leading household cleaner even though its powdered form is less popular than liquids and sprays.

Declining (sick) products drain company resources and effort from healthy products. Some firms conduct *product audits,* or product reviews, to identify declining products. Often these products are dropped. Sometimes, however, a careful study of a product may lead to changes in manufacturing or marketing methods that permit the firm to reduce costs and increase profit.

Consider how a declining product's marketing mix may need adjustment. A declining product ordinarily has lost its distinctiveness because of excessive copying by rivals. The appearance of these me-too (parity) products leads to brand switching because there is little to hold buyers' loyalty. Technological development and societal or other environmental developments may also bring on a product's decline. Consider the impact of the introduction of compact disc players on sales of conventional turntables, cassette decks, records, and tapes.

Distribution strategy often focuses on removing the product from unprofitable outlets and concentrating it in outlets that service the few remaining loyal customers. Interestingly, the product probably is considered a specialty product by these buyers, and they will make a concerted effort to locate and buy it.

Promotional support usually is reduced, often practically to zero. The product, however, may continue to be promoted to loyal buyers. Instead of being withdrawn from the market, it may petrify at a low level of sales and remain at that level for many years.

A declining product's price may be increased if there is a group of hard-core loyal buyers. Usually, however, price is subject to extreme downward pressure. In many cases marketers will lower prices to clear out inventories.

Product Deletion

Each candidate for deletion should be evaluated to determine if its life can be extended. If profits have been declining, the causes should be investigated. Perhaps a slight change in manufacturing methods or in the marketing program will permit a reduction in cost and higher profits.

When a product is scheduled for deletion, the timing of its withdrawal and the interim commitment of resources to it become crucial decisions. For the firm, ideal timing would permit the resources that are freed by deleting the product to be used more profitably elsewhere—perhaps in developing a new product to replace it. During this time finished goods, goods in process, and parts and materials inventories would be depleted. For customers, ideal timing means adequate advance warning and, in the case of durable products, available replacement and repair parts. Intermediaries should be notified in advance so they can work off their inventories. Sometimes they are permitted to return products for credit.

Products selected for deletion need not be unprofitable. Environmental factors may be as important in deletion decisions as in new-product development decisions. Tougher Environmental Protection Agency regulations on pesticides led to the abandonment of some pesticides. A product may be deleted because it does not fit the company's mission.

If some loyal customers remain and a new product is not ready to replace the old product, distribution and some promotional support may be provided until the old product is phased out and replaced by the new product. But if a product cannot return a profit on its out-of-pocket costs and a new product is ready for immediate launching, the product should be dropped as soon as possible.

Product Recalls

The Consumer Product Safety Act of 1972 makes quality control a crucial factor in product management. A product that reaches the market but represents ''a substantial product hazard'' must be reported to the Consumer Product Safety Commission within twenty-four hours of the discovery that it is hazardous. The speed and efficiency with which a product is recalled can affect company, product, and brand images. Accountability for quality control and for production should be assigned to different managers. Recall authority often is delegated to yet another person, one who can order a production halt, initiate intermediary and customer notification, and coordinate the actual recall.

A recall involves notification, retrieval of the product from intermediaries and customers (a reverse marketing channel), distribution of replacement units or repair parts along with information so dealers can repair defective units, and communication to keep intermediary support and customer loyalty. Locating owners may be difficult, especially for small products, and elaborate coding systems are needed to keep track of individual units in marketing channels.

Product recalls can be costly. In 1982, Johnson & Johnson spent $100 million to recall 31 million bottles of Tylenol after some capsules were found to have been poisoned with cyanide. All told, the company spent an estimated $300 million to reclaim Tylenol's market position. The 1986 Tylenol scare, which played a big part in Johnson & Johnson's decision to stop offering over-the-counter drugs in capsule form, cost the company an estimated $150 million to recall the capsules and rebuild Tylenol's market share.[16] A similar event occurred in 1991, when some Sudafed capsules were found to have been injected with cyanide.

Product Liability

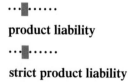

product liability

strict product liability

The issue of product liability often arises in connection with product recalls but is not limited to them. *Product liability* is the concept that businesses are liable for injuries caused by negligence in the design, manufacture, sale, and use of products. Some states have extended the concept to strict product liability. *Strict product liability* is the concept that businesses are liable for injuries caused by their products even if there is no proof of negligence or fault in the design, manufacture, sale, and use of products.

Efforts have been under way for some time to reform product liability law. Various bills have been introduced in Congress to do so. Some of them would limit damage awards in product liability suits.

Although the adoption and diffusion processes and the product life cycle concept apply generally to most products, fashion products present a special case.

FASHION CYCLES

Three terms are important in understanding fashion cycles: *style, fashion,* and *fad*. A *style* is a distinctive way of presenting a product. Bikinis, tanks, maillots, and swimdresses are styles of swimwear. A *fashion* is a style that is currently popular. Thus bikinis are more in fashion during some years than during others. A *fad* is a fashion that is popular for a short time. Over the years there have been many fads in swimwear.

Diffusion theory emphasizes the flow of adoption from innovators to laggards. Thus a designer of women's apparel might seek to induce the "fast track" to adopt a new design and hope it will catch on with early adopters and move on to the other classes of adopters (emulators). But by the time emulators have adopted, the fashion's distinctiveness is eroded and innovators have already begun to accept a new style and make it fashionable.

Fashion's key element is newness, or novelty. As fashions are diffused more rapidly, the fashion cycle becomes shorter and effort focuses on finding new fashions. Firms often use trial-and-error procedures to come up with fashionable products; some will always be losers. Inevitably, this increases the cost of producing and marketing products.

The significance of fashion is not limited to clothing. Consider the fashion element in eyeglasses, telephones, and office furniture.

7-3

SUMMARY OF LEARNING OBJECTIVES

1. Explain the various meanings of *new product*.
The "newness" of a product should be defined from two distinct points of view: newness to the firm and newness to the market. From the firm's point of view, a new product can fall into any of four categories: product modification, product line development, entry into related category, and entry into entirely new category. From the market's point of view, new products include breakthrough innovations, pioneering innovations, adaptive innovations, and imitative new products.

2. Identify organizational arrangements for new-product development.
Four popular approaches to new-product development are (1) the new-product committee, (2) the new-product department, (3) the product (or brand) manager, and (4) the project team.

3. Identify and explain the stages in the new-product development process.
The new-product development process involves seven stages: (1) idea generation, (2) idea screening, (3) concept development and testing, (4) business analysis, (5) product development,

(6) market testing, and (7) commercialization. At each stage management decides whether to proceed, seek more information, or abandon the new-product development process.

4. Explain the elements of the product adoption and diffusion processes.
The adoption process is the stages a prospective buyer goes through in deciding to buy and make regular use of a particular product: (1) awareness, (2) interest, (3) evaluation, (4) trial, and (5) adoption. The diffusion process is the spread of an idea or the penetration of a market by a new product. The diffusion process includes five categories of adopters: innovators, early adopters, early majority, late majority, and laggards.

5. Explain the concept of the product life cycle and discuss the use of the product life cycle concept in product management.
The product life cycle is a concept that depicts a product's sales history and includes repeat purchases, not just first-time sales. There are four stages: (1) introduction, (2) growth, (3) maturity, and (4) decline.

36

The primary task during the introductory stage is to start the diffusion process. During the growth stage firms often extend their product lines and refocus their advertising. Life cycle extension strategies are very important during the maturity stage. During the decline stage, declining products must be identified and evaluated to determine if their lives can be extended.

. . . .

Review Questions

1. What are the types of newness to the firm?

2. What are the types of newness to the market?

3. What are four approaches to organizing for new-product development? Explain each.

4. What is the goal of the idea generation stage of the new-product development process?

5. What are the two main costs associated with idea screening?

6. What is the significance of a go decision in the product development stage of the new-product development process?

7. How do conventional test marketing, minimarket tests, and laboratory (simulated) market tests differ?

8. What are the adoption and diffusion processes?

9. What are the five stages in the adoption process?

10. How is the product life cycle related to the diffusion process?

11. What strategies might extend a mature product's life cycle? Give examples.

12. How does a fad differ from a fashion?

Discussion Questions

1. Royal Crown Companies created the diet soft-drink category in 1962 when it introduced Diet Rite Cola. Coca-Cola Company launched Tab in 1963. What are the relative advantages and disadvantages of being the first entrant in a new-product category?

2. Under what circumstances would a firm be most apt to skip some stages of the new-product development process?

3. "If a manager believes her product is entering the decline stage of the product life cycle, her actions may result in a self-fulfilling prophecy." Explain.

4. How does the product life cycle relate to the process of portfolio analysis discussed in chapter 3?

Application Exercise

Reread the material about the Gillette Sensor razor at the beginning of this chapter and answer the following questions:

1. Would you classify the Sensor as a pioneering innovation or an adaptive innovation? What, in general, are the relative advantages and disadvantages of each of those two types of innovation?

2. If Gillette had used the screening criteria in Table 10–2 to evaluate the Sensor idea, which criteria would have been the most difficult for it to assess? How important are these criteria? Explain. How could Gillette acquire more information about Sensor's expected performance by using those criteria?

3. What marketing activities would help speed the adoption process for Sensor?

4. Explain Sensor's importance to Gillette, taking into account the text discussion of the product life cycle and the Ethics in Marketing discussion of obsolescence.

Key Concepts

The following key terms were introduced in this chapter:

breakthrough innovations
pioneering innovations
adaptive innovations
imitative new products
new-product committee
new-product department
product (or brand) manager

project team
new-product development
   process
product concept test
simultaneous product
   development
adoption process

diffusion process
product life cycle (PLC)
life cycle extension strategies
product liability
strict product liability

CASES

Oasis Laundries

The trip to the laundromat is the low point of the week for many otherwise happy Americans. It's not just that watching your clothes slosh around is so stultifying. It's also that the majority of the 45,000 laundromats in the United States are full of ancient and often dead washers and dryers, are dirty and depressing, and are even sometimes—due to the occasional menacing fellow customer—downright creepy. Small wonder, then, that a billboard for the new Oasis Laundries company asking the question, ''Are you buying underwear to avoid using your laundromat?'' seemed to speak directly to so many.

Cor Bregman, head of Oasis Laundries, hopes to do Fruit-of-the-Loom and Jockey out of some business by removing the dread from the laundromat experience. In San Jose in 1987, Bregman and a partner opened the first Oasis, a bright, clean space where you could wash and dry your clothes and watch sports or music videos on big-screen TVs, play video games, relax with your friends on clean, comfortable couches, or even catch a few rays in the on-site tanning salon. On a more practical level, there were lots of clean surfaces on which to fold your clothes and attendants present to make sure the place stayed tidy and to keep an eye on who wandered in and out.

This first Oasis made washing fun for its customers but didn't make any money for Bregman: there were too many amenities and too few machines. Many potential customers returned to their regular laundries, where at least they could get a machine and get home faster. Bregman learned the crucial lesson that while clothes-washers would rather go to Oasis than to other laundromats, they still didn't want to spend any more time there than necessary. So he rearranged the shop in order to bring the lounge into the folding area and to increase the number of machines. Oasis sprouted.

Four years later there are more than 35 Oasis laundromats—most of them franchises—scattered in West Coast cities from Seattle to Southern California. Each adheres to Bregman's revised formula of plenty of machines and plenty of diversions in a clean, friendly atmosphere. Most now also offer drop-off laundry and dry-cleaning services for those customers who would rather avoid the laundromat completely. Some offer senior citizens' nights and other promotions to try to keep the laundromats busy during off-peak hours.

Although Bregman was apparently the first to dream up the dream laundromat, he's not alone anymore. Copy-cat chains have opened in other cities, including Chicago and Boston. Bregman thinks the competition is good for Oasis because it will raise laundraphobics' standards of acceptable surroundings for performing the dreaded chore, thereby creating more demand for his shops. And he's confident that the pool of potential customers won't dry up: 30 percent of U.S. households don't own washing or drying machines.

Questions

1. The original product design of Oasis was not a success. How might Cor Bregman have avoided this problem?

2. How would you state the product concept of Oasis Laundries?

3. Discuss how the five product characteristics usually affecting the rate of product adoption will help or hinder the adoption of Oasis Laundries.

4. What stage of the product life cycle is the laundromat in? What stage of the product life cycle is Oasis in? What are the implications of this relationship?

EPI Products

In 1987, Solomon Krok bought the U.S., Canadian, New Zealand, and Australian distribution rights to an Israeli-made hand-held gadget that used rotating coils to pull the hairs out of women's legs. He gave the rights to this product, dubbed Epilady, to his daughters. Within a very short time, the Krok sisters, all under age thirty-five, had parlayed Epilady into an entire personal grooming products empire called EPI Products.

The Kroks' fast drive to the top started when they convinced Bloomingdale's, one of New York's most prestigious department stores, to grant Epilady prime display space in its cosmetics section in return for a massive EPI Products advertising campaign boosting both the product and the store. In just five days, customers snatched up 1500 Epiladies, and other department stores stood

in line to sign on. Within five months, Epilady was the top-selling department store item of any kind in the nation. By the end of their first year in business, the Kroks had racked up more than $27 million in sales.

Realizing that they were onto an amazingly good thing, the Kroks decided to extend their brand franchise. They seemed to have a knack for finding inventors of other unusual personal care products who were happy to sell either total or distribution rights to such an obviously successful marketer. During 1988 and 1989, the Kroks launched EpiSauna, a facial sauna; EpiPed, a foot whirlpool and massager; EpiSage, a handheld shower massager; and EpiSmile, a tooth whitener, among other EPI products. All had impressive initial sales spurts in the top-notch department stores where they were exclusively sold.

When the Kroks began to face stiff competition for Epilady in the shape of Smooth & Silky, a similar Remington product that was to be sold in mass market outlets, they came up with a strategy many analysts described as brilliant. They began to package Epilady in a deluxe box that included Epilady accessories. This box was to be sold—at a luxury price—only in department stores so that EPI Products could hold on to both its high profit margins and its prestige image. Once the deluxe Epilady set was established, the Kroks would begin to sell the original Epilady solo in mass market outlets at sharply discounted prices.

As the Kroks continued to expand their range of products, they ran more ads that featured several of the products at once. They also shifted the ads' focus away from selling the products' functions and toward selling the prestige and ingenuity of the "Epi" brand. The strategy seemed to work: the Epilady mass-market launch met expectations and plenty of customers came forward for every other new EPI product. Industry analysts crowed about the $200 million worth of products the Kroks sold in 1989.

But in the spring of 1990, the crowing turned to jeers. Women no longer bought Epiladies in department stores, realizing they could buy the same product for less elsewhere. Subsequent sales of the other EPI products never matched their initial surges. Analysts now said that this wasn't surprising: no other EPI product was as innovative as Epilady or considered by most customers to be as essential. Many analysts also said that EPI had been too new a company to abandon a "function and benefits" advertising strategy in favor of a brand-awareness strategy. By the fall of 1990, EPI Products had filed for bankruptcy, and few analysts expected the company to rise again.

Questions

1. How new a product was Epilady?

2. What causes may have been behind the ultimate failure of EPI Products' brand franchise extension strategy?

3. What stages in the new product development process do the Kroks seem to have omitted in introducing their new products?

4. What did the Kroks do to extend the life cycle of Epilady? How did their strategy backfire?

The Body Shop: The Right Products for Today

"All a moisturizer is is oil and water; every one of them works," says Anita Roddick about the products sold in the Body Shop, her chain of cosmetics stores. "What makes the difference for our company is that we get our ingredients from different sources than do other companies, and we do something different with our profits."

That difference has propelled Roddick from being the indebted owner of a single shop in 1976 to being the fourth-wealthiest woman in Britain today. There are now more than 600 Body Shops scattered across forty countries. And many business analysts see Anita Roddick—once frequently dismissed as a flower-power left-over riding a short-lived fad—as the leading advocate for what may prove a dominant doctrine of 1990s marketing and corporate practice.

• The Birth of the Body Shop •

In 1976, Anita Roddick and her husband Gordon decided that it was now or never for him to fulfill his lifelong ambition of riding a horse from Buenos Aires to New York City. It would take Gordon about a year to complete the journey, they figured, and in the meantime 33-year-old Anita would have to provide for the care and financial support of their two young daughters. Before she met Gordon, Anita had been certified as an English and history teacher and had worked for the United Nations in Geneva. Working with the International Labor Organization, she had also travelled in Polynesia, New Caledonia, Australia, and Africa, meeting with ordinary people and taking note of how they earned their livings and kept their homes running. After they married—and taking a cue from her parents, who ran a café—Anita and Gordon had embarked on a series of relatively successful restaurant and inn-keeping ventures, which provided an adequate income, independence, plenty of contact with other people, and a way to spend time with their children during the day. Anita now needed a business that she could run by herself but that would yield the same combination of benefits. Her solution was the Body Shop.

During her travels in the southern hemisphere, Anita had been fascinated by how village women used locally grown plants and foods rather than factory-made soaps and shampoos to wash and protect their skin and hair. Back in England, she had grown cynical about the promises of everlasting youth doled out by the big cosmetic companies and tired of paying money for lots of packaging and advertising when all she really wanted was the stuff that was inside the bottle inside the box inside the wrapper. So she decided to make her own line of natural hair and skin care products and to sell them from her own shop. She borrowed the equivalent of $6,500, found a tiny shop in a backstreet in Brighton, and concocted about fifteen product formulas using such ingredients as cocoa butter (which she had seen women use as a hair conditioner in Polynesia), citrus juices, nutshells, and pineapple (which she had seen women use in Sri Lanka as a skin cleanser). She packaged them in plain plastic bottles and hand-wrote the stick-on labels. Because she had so few products to sell, she bottled each in five different sizes so her inventory would look more impressive. And because she had so little money to reorder supplies, she offered a bottle refill-discount service, meanwhile touting the ecological benefits of recycling.

The Body Shop name came from an auto-body shop Anita had seen in the United States. That wasn't a good enough explanation for the owners of the next-door undertakers, however, who worried about what their clients' loved ones might think. And so Anita's first lesson in the power of public relations: receiving a formal letter of complaint from the morticians, she called the local newspaper, and told a reporter that the business establishment was harassing a young woman shopkeeper just trying to keep food in the mouths of her children. Their curiosity piqued, readers who probably would never have heard about the Body Shop otherwise—Anita couldn't afford advertising—came by to take a look. Most liked what they saw: Anita sold about $200 worth of her strange-looking products the day after the article appeared. These first customers soon started spreading the word that the Body Shop had tantalizing cosmetics for sale and a cheerful, homey atmosphere totally unlike the sterile supermarket and drugstore aisles and the snooty department-store counters where most beauty products were sold.

• Learning By Doing •

The Body Shop philosophy was forged in this Brighton shop from marketing practices that resulted largely from Anita's initial financial problems and naivete about the cosmetics business. There was no money for advertising, for instance. This meant there was no way Anita could make claims about Body Shop products that oversold their benefits to potential customers before they entered the shop. It also meant that—even if they came on the advice of friends who had already visited the Body Shop—customers usually didn't know much at all about Anita's products. Her response was to explain personally what the ingredients were in any product, why she had developed that formula, and whether it would suit the customer's own particular skin or hair type. Each label also contained a full explanation: ''We thought we had to explain them because they looked so

bizarre. I mean, there were little black things in some of them. We had to say these were not worms.''

As the shop started to fill with customers and Anita could spend less time with each, she began to write and duplicate pamphlets and notecards telling where she got the ideas for her formulas and where the ingredients came from. She soon realized that this cheap in-store effort was worth much more than any expensive advertising campaign: the more substantive information people took in about her products, the more likely they were to buy them. Customers seemed to appreciate the contrast between the Body Shop's down-to-earth, no-nonsense

---

She scoured ancient apothecary manuals for cosmetics recipes to expand her product line.

---

approach and the usual hard-sell, ''these mysterious ingredients will transform your life'' approach of most cosmetics companies, and Body Shop sales quickly began to multiply.

To Anita Roddick's own considerable amazement, the success of the Brighton store was so great that she was able to open a second Body

Shop—this time in Chichester—only six months after the opening of the original. Gordon returned from the Americas to find that his wife had gone far beyond simply providing for their children: she had uncovered a previously unmined, seemingly huge vein of consumer desire for natural yet unusual, unhyped yet intriguing personal care products and she had developed a stunningly effective marketing approach. He now suggested to Anita that, in order to enable rapid growth of the Body Shop and thereby gain a long head-start on any potential competitors, they should franchise the store. In 1977, the first franchised Body Shops opened in England; in 1978, the first Body Shop to open outside the United Kingdom opened in Belgium. Over the next few years, as new Body Shop branches continued to sprout all over Britain, franchises also opened in Sweden, Canada, and Australia. In 1984, the company went public, and its shares increased in value so quickly and so steadily that the Body Shop came to be known by stockbrokers as ''the share that defies gravity.''

• The Body Shop Formula •

As Anita and Gordon Roddick took the Body Shop through the enormous changes involved in transforming a small, local business into an international manufacturing-retail chain, they knew that its continued success relied on their sticking to the basic Body Shop formula. At the core of that formula were the Body Shop hair and skin products themselves.

Anita's original fifteen formulas for shampoos, skin cleansers, and moisturizers had been based on products she had seen village women use during her earlier travels. Now that she had gained experience in what sold and what didn't to customers in industrialized nations she set out to expand her product lines. She scoured ancient English apothecary manuals for soap and other cosmetics recipes. She began travelling again, from equatorial Africa to rural India to the frozen Laplands, seeking out women who would explain their traditional cleansers and cosmetics and farmers and traders who would provide information about the supply availability of various ingredients. Anita's object was to find ingredients that were natural and biodegradable, as well as plant- rather than animal-based. She also made sure that the farming or harvesting of these ingredients wouldn't cause environmental damage. These ingredients were mixed with synthetic ingredients when necessary, but Anita made sure that these too were biodegradable. The results were such classic Body Shop products as Jojoba Oil Conditioning Shampoo, Pineapple Facial Wash, and Cocoa Butter Hand & Body Lotion.

Hunting down and gathering ingredients in this way allowed Anita to develop and adhere to two other central Body Shop policies: *Trade Not Aid* and *Against Animal Testing*. Both the ideas and the ingredients for many Body Shop products originated in the Third World. Buying Third World materials is very profitable for many Western companies because labor costs in such economically depressed areas tends to be both much lower than labor costs in industrialized countries and a tiny fraction of the price people in industrialized countries are able and willing to pay for the fruit of this labor. Anita Roddick's *Trade Not Aid* idea, germinating since her time with the U.N.'s International Labor Organization, was to pay the

same prices for Third World products that she would pay for equivalent First World products—in other words, she tried to pass a fair share of her potential profits back to the people who actually supplied the bulk of each Body Shop product's mass.

Trade Not Aid involved more than simply paying First World prices, however. Body Shop representatives often tried to help communities set up cooperatives or other employee-run corporations that ensured not only a steady flow of ingredients to the Body Shop but also a steady source of employment and income, as well as bargaining power with Body Shop executives, to the communities' people. In Nepal, the Body Shop helped one community set up a project for making various kinds of paper for the stores from banana fibre, recycled waste paper, and water hyacinth. In Brazil, the Body Shop undertook a major ingredient-sourcing project intended to provide the Kayapo people a way to

make a living by remaining in the rain forest and harvesting its fruits, thereby providing an alternative to both community resettlement and slash-and-burn agricultural ventures. In India, the Body Shop sponsored a Boy's Town by commissioning products such as wooden foot massage rollers. The street children served by the Boy's Town were thus able to generate income for the Boy's Town Trust, which paid for their classroom education and for their training in skills—such as farming, woodwork, and printing—that would enable them to earn a living when they were older. And in Easterhouse, Scotland, an area of such deep economic depression that European Community officials had recognized as a First World pocket of Third World living conditions, the Body Shop built and equipped a soap factory, called Soapworks, that currently employs more than 100 local people, many of whom had been out of work for more than 10 years. The Body Shop formed a trust fund to

channel 25 percent of the factory's profits back to the Easterhouse community.

Using natural ingredients allowed the Roddicks to adhere to Anita's *Against Animal Testing* policy, which she introduced with the opening of the first Body Shop. Most cosmetics companies test their products for toxicity and eye and skin irritation on animals. The results of these tests are used to determine whether a product is safe for human use. Anita took the stance that it was cruel to subject animals to these often painful tests when most beauty products are essentially unnecessary. By using such ingredients as honey, cocoa butter, or aloe vera that either are foods or have been applied to people's hair and skin for thousands of years, the Body Shop could be relatively secure in the knowledge that its products would not be toxic or irritating. Still, further tests were carried out, but on human volunteers. And to be sure that the Body Shop wasn't unwittingly using animal-tested products, it required all its ingredient suppliers to provide regular documentation that "no animal testing for cosmetics or toiletry purposes has been carried out on the material for the five years prior to its use in Body Shop products."

Even as the Body Shop grew to become a huge international chain—and came up against more and more big-time competitors—the Roddicks stuck to their minimal-packaging and no-advertising policies, which set them apart even from most other natural-ingredient cosmetic companies. Both policies reenforced the Body Shop's image as a retailer of simple, natural, honest products sold on their own merits rather than on hype.

In fact, the Roddicks' marketing of the Body Shop image is anything but simple or unsophisticated. At the Body Shop central office, a crack team of writers and graphic artists—usually working closely with Anita—produces the pamphlets, posters, T-shirt slogans, and window display material found in each Body Shop. These materials publicize not only Body Shop products, but also the *Trade Not Aid* projects, the *Against Animal Testing* policy, and the many public service projects and political activities—such as Save the Whales and Save the Rainforest campaigns, recycling projects, programs for troubled youth, and a relief drive to Romanian orphanages—to which the Body Shop contributes company money and employee time. (All Body Shop employees must spend at least one hour a week on a service project of their choosing; the Body Shop pays employees for the time they spend volunteering.) The Body Shop also retains two public relations firms which keep the various news media informed about all new Body Shop projects and corporate developments—and about Anita's appearances at demonstrations or other events designed to draw attention to specific social issues. The result: even though the Body Shop has never spent a penny on advertising, it garners about $3.5 million worth of free publicity every year.

The look and feel of every Body Shop is stage-managed by Anita, who helps franchisees develop floorplans, shop color-schemes, and product displays. Franchisees and other employees are carefully selected on the basis of enthusiasm for the Body Shop product lines and corporate policies, interest in the wider world and in getting involved in some kind of service project, and desire to serve customers rather than merely sell products. And every Body Shop franchisee or employee is invited to attend the company's school in London free of charge to learn not accounting or management techniques but the fundamentals of hair and skin anatomy and of the Body Shop's products' ingredients and uses.

Among the results of this total corporate program, virtually all outside commentators agree, is a tremendously motivated Body Shop workforce that believes not only in the value of its products but in the value of the entire Body Shop enterprise. Body Shop customers, too, report that—rather than just buying, say, a bottle of shampoo—they feel they are investing in a larger cause when they buy Anita's products. And it's virtually impossible to find anyone who will argue with the Body Shop's staggering financial success. Fiscal year 1990 sales totalled $141 million and profits $15.3 million—37 percent higher than 1989 profits—even as a horrendous recession dragged down other retailers in the United Kingdom, where the Body Shop still collects 75 percent of its profits.

In fact, most analysts see no reason why the Body Shop shouldn't continue to grow, as it has for the past five years, at a rate between 35 and 50 percent annually. Anita and Gordon Roddick believe that none of their current markets are saturated yet; even in England, where there are currently more than 100 Body Shops, they believe there is room for a total of about 200. Anita has taken her time granting U.S. franchises in order to ensure that the Body Shop image isn't watered down here; there are currently only about fifty U.S. Body Shops, but most analysts believe there may eventually be about 1000.

Some analysts, however, wonder whether Roddick's formula will retain its potency in the cutthroat U.S. market. Some wonder whether the Body Shop will be able to get by without advertising; others whether the Body Shop storefront displays will make as much of a splash in American malls as on European high fashion streets. Then, too, many say that the American marketplace is more likely to sprout formidable competitors than were the Body Shop's first marketing environments. Estée Lauder, for instance, one of the country's biggest cosmetics marketers, has already launched Origins, a line of natural-ingredient, no-animal-testing cosmetics in refillable bottles.

• **Questions** •

1. What product is the Body Shop marketing?

2. In terms of the consumer product classification system discussed in chapter 9, how do you think the Body Shop would classify its products? What are the implications for the company's marketing strategies?

3. Is there any danger that the Body Shop is simply benefiting from a fad? Explain.

4. How important do you think the Body Shop brand is to the company's marketing strategy? What implications has this had or should this have for the growth of the company?

5. *Inc.* magazine has said about the Body Shop: "Its success raises questions . . . about some of the most fundamental aspects of business . . . Are [customers] motivated by forces that traditional marketing efforts ignore, and that traditional test-marketing techniques can't pick up?" Discuss.

Sociocultural and Ethical Variables

Technological Variables

Product

Price **Target Market** Place

Economic Variables

Competitive Variables

Promotion

Political-Legal Variables

Section three focused on the product variable of the marketing mix. Developing customer-oriented product offerings is a crucial task of marketers. Marketers must then distribute the products so that they are available in the quantities target customers desire them at the place and time they want to buy them. The three chapters in this section look at the distribution (or place) element of the marketing mix.

Chapter 11 focuses on marketing channels. It explains what channels are, their functions, and their structure. The chapter also explains the major influences on channel development and the channel planning process. Channel integration and expansion also receive attention, as do the issues of channel cooperation, conflict, and competition. The chapter ends with a discussion of vertical and horizontal marketing systems.

Chapter 12 looks at retailing. It explains what retailing is, shows how retail firms can be classified, and compares in-store and nonstore retailing. Next comes an examination of franchising, followed by an analysis of major retailing decisions and trends. The emergence of new types of retailers is explained by the wheel of retailing hypothesis.

Chapter 13 explores wholesaling and logistics. It explains what wholesaling is, identifies the various types of wholesaling intermediaries, and examines the major wholesaling decisions and trends. The chapter also discusses the nature and importance of logistics.

The comprehensive case for Section 4 traces the birth and growth of Macy's department store. Macy's history reflects practically every retailing trend in the United States for the past 130 years. The case illustrates the impact of environmental change on distribution, relationships among channel members, channel leadership, retailing decisions and trends, and the importance of logistics management in retailing.

11

MARKETING
CHANNELS

After reading this chapter you will be able to

1. explain how marketing channels create utility, improve exchange efficiency, and help match supply and demand.

2. distinguish between the vertical and horizontal dimensions of a marketing channel.

3. identify the major factors that influence channel development.

4. explain what is involved in channel planning.

5. distinguish between channel integration and expansion.

6. explain the nature of channel cooperation, conflict, and competition.

7. differentiate among and give examples of the types of vertical and horizontal marketing systems.

It would take too long and cost too much for Platinum Technology Inc. to grow from a handful of employees into a company with offices worldwide, Andrew "Flip" Filipowski once thought. But by the end of 1990, just four years after he founded Platinum, it had thirty-two offices in eighteen countries on six continents. The secret was a simple, innovative distribution network.

Soon after IBM had introduced DB2, a database management program for its mainframe computers, management information systems departments all over the corporate world were trying to figure out how to install the system, customize it, and teach their people how to use it. Filipowski knew there would be a demand for DB2 training and for software accessories that would make DB2 programs easier to customize and use.

Creating the software and designing the training programs would be a technical challenge, but once Filipowski tackled that, Platinum was still going to have a problem selling them. "We needed distribution," he says. His potential customers included every company that used DB2. They were relatively easy to reach through advertising at trade shows and in computer trade publications. Platinum's larger challenge was to locate technically competent people to run training courses and help users install the add-on software in scores of cities. The company's people would have to work one-on-one with their clients for extended periods. But there were no Platinum people in scores of cities.

Filipowski considered several options. He could open and staff some field offices, starting with key domestic markets. But that would have been costly and time-consuming.

He could go the franchise route, which young companies with limited capital often do to spread themselves out moderately quickly. The licensing and regulatory constraints that apply to franchising, however, didn't appeal to him.

He could try to license his products to IBM, letting its sales engineers be Platinum's sales force. But that didn't appeal either.

Filipowski believed he could achieve broad distribution and acquire brand-name recognition if he could recruit a network of consultants who would take on the Platinum name as well as selling the products. In fact, if he could get the network set up soon, Platinum would look like a large, even global, company far more quickly than it would if he franchised or built field offices from scratch.

But why would consulting firms want to join Platinum's network, and, more important, why would they want to change their names? The firms were local and small—two or three partners competing for large corporate contracts against consultancies with prestigious names. Not only did they have to work harder to get the acceptance automatically afforded a larger firm, but even if they got the contracts, they couldn't charge the same rates as a Big Six accounting firm. "The little guys' margins," says Filipowski, "were constantly being squeezed." So he reasoned, if the small consultancies, too, could look like international firms capable of providing local service, it could only help them. Consequently, his idea was to recruit independent consultants.

By the end of 1990 Platinum's affiliates around the world were employing nearly 2,700 people. Network affiliates pay Platinum $500 to $600 on average per month, which feeds a national advertising fund to which Filipowski's corporate headquarters contributes an equal amount. That fund pays for national and international ads, exposure that no small firm operating on its own could afford.

Platinum corporate assigns one of its telemarketers to each affiliate's territory—which typically covers one telephone area code. The telemarketers pass all sales leads on to the appropriate affiliates. Filipowski's operation also trains and certifies instructors from the affiliated consulting firms, which then teach private DB2 courses to client companies. The corporate office handles all the course administration. In a typical fee arrangement, 15 percent goes to the affiliate that made the sale, 50 percent goes to the firm that does the teaching, and 35 percent goes to Filipowski's Platinum office.[1]

Platinum Technology's choice of a marketing channel reflects a careful analysis of the possibilities for achieving distribution. Filipowski chose an innovative distribution network composed of affiliates. The system has proven effective for Platinum and its affiliated companies. Fortunately, Filipowski quickly recognized the importance of achieving distribution of his goods and services. As he said at the outset, "We needed distribution."

A marketing organization's distribution capability is an important determinant of its success—in some cases the major determinant. In this chapter we look at what marketing channels are and how they are structured. We also look at the major influences on channel development, channel planning, channel integration and expansion, the relationships among channel members, and vertical and horizontal marketing systems.

WHAT ARE MARKETING CHANNELS AND WHY ARE THEY NECESSARY?

A product cannot reach its target market if its distribution is not planned and carried out carefully. In bringing their products to market, producers often entrust some of their selling tasks to intermediaries. The producer, the intermediaries, and the consumer or industrial user constitute the marketing channel for the product. The effectiveness and efficiency of this marketing channel help determine the overall success of the marketing effort.

A *marketing channel* (also called a channel of distribution or a distribution channel) is the series of interdependent marketing institutions that facilitate transfer of title to a product as it moves from producer to ultimate consumer or industrial user. Producers, intermediaries, and final buyers are participants in a channel (channel members).

An *intermediary* (also called a reseller or a middleman) is a person or firm in a marketing channel, such as a wholesaler or retailer, that operates between the producer and the final buyer of a product. Intermediaries specialize in buying and selling but may also perform the other marketing functions that we discussed in chapter 1—transporting, storing, standardizing and grading, financing, risk taking, and supplying market information. If the producer and final buyers are unable to perform all the functions necessary to establish and maintain exchange relationships, intermediaries will provide whatever functions are needed.

All channels have a producer and an ultimate consumer or industrial user. But when a producer sells directly to the final buyer, there are no intermediaries in the channel. The producer or the buyers must perform these functions. In other words, functions can be shifted and shared among the channel members, but functions *cannot* be eliminated.

Figure 11–1 shows some of the title and nontitle flows that might occur in a marketing channel for heavy-duty industrial air compressors. Consider the physical flow, which involves the movement of raw materials and parts from suppliers to the manufacturer's warehouses and manufacturing plants. After the compressors are manufactured, they are warehoused and then shipped to the distributors, which in turn warehouse, sell, and ship them to their customers. Of course, if the manufacturer sold directly to the users, there would be no physical flow to a distributor. The intermediary would not be needed.

Transportation companies might provide the physical flow, banks and other financial institutions might assist in the financing and payment flows, insurance companies might handle the risk flow, marketing research companies might manage the information flow, and advertising agencies might be involved in the promotion flow. These are examples of facilitating intermediaries. *Facilitating intermediaries,* or facilitators, are persons or firms outside the marketing channel that may assist channel members in handling various flows (physical, financial, risk, information, promotion) more effectively and efficiently than the channel members could themselves. Channel members use facilitators when they believe the facilitators can perform the functions more economically and efficiently than they themselves can.

The physical flow in Figure 11–1 also shows a reverse flow from users back to suppliers. This would occur, for example, if a compressor failed to operate and had to be returned to the distributor or manufacturer or perhaps to a supplier who sold a major component part to the manufacturer. The same reverse flow occurs during a product recall and in recycling programs. Recyclable materials can efficiently flow in reverse order from consumers or industrial users back to manufacturers and their suppliers. DuPont's ad discusses the plastic recycling program it operates with Waste Management Inc.

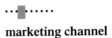

marketing channel

intermediary

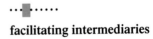

facilitating intermediaries

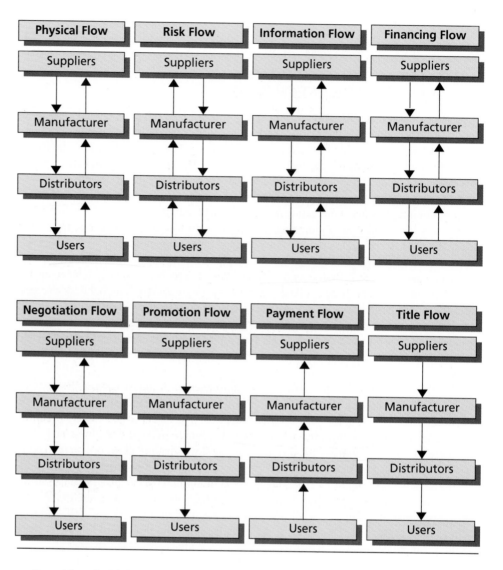

FIGURE 11–1

Examples of Marketing Flows in the Channel for Air Compressors

Reusable soft-drink bottles flow back to the bottler through supermarkets. So do one-way (disposable) containers in states that have deposit laws. Some supermarkets in states without deposit laws are buying one-way aluminum cans from their customers. Manufacturers of aluminum and other packaging materials operate recycling centers, and some breweries operate recycling programs for aluminum cans through their distributors. In all these cases consumers must take the initiative in starting the reverse flow. But curbside recycling programs do not require the consumer to go to a recycling center. The recyclable materials are picked up along garbage collection routes.

Recall that we are using the term *product* throughout this book to mean a tangible good or an intangible service. Thus marketing channels are also necessary for intangible services. For example, in Texas and Louisiana, Southwest Airlines sells standby tickets through automated teller machines in convenience stores. We present an in-depth look at the special considerations in designing marketing channels for services in chapter 21.

The discussions that follow focus on how marketing channels create utility, improve exchange efficiency, and help match supply and demand.

WE'VE GOT TO STOP TREATING OUR GARBAGE LIKE GARBAGE.

The bottle may be empty, yet it's anything but trash. In fact, this empty bottle is actually full of potential. Thanks to recycling.

Over 20% of all plastic soft drink containers are already being recycled into additional consumer and industrial products and the demand for recycled plastic is growing.

At DuPont, we're making sure this growth continues. Together with Waste Management Inc., we've pioneered the country's largest and most comprehensive plastic recycling program. In this, its first year, the operation will recycle more than 80 million pounds of plastic.

With recycling, we believe that plastic will be increasingly appreciated for filling valuable human needs instead of valuable land.

At DuPont, our dedication to quality makes the things that make a difference.

DUPONT
BETTER THINGS FOR BETTER LIVING.

Recycling programs require reverse marketing channels.

(DuPont.)

Creating Utility

We distinguished among form, place, time, and possession utility in chapter 1. Channels bring suppliers and buyers together by creating place, time, and possession utility. They bridge the distance, time, and possession gaps between producers and customers. In the soft-drink industry independent bottlers participate in creating form utility. For example, the Coca-Cola Company supplies the extract to its independent bottlers, which blend, package, and distribute the soft drink. Thus intermediaries also can help create form utility.

Improving Exchange Efficiency

Figure 11–2 shows how the use of an intermediary can improve exchange efficiency by reducing the number of transactions. Without the intermediary, each of the four producers must deal directly with each of the four customers, for a total of sixteen contacts. The presence of an intermediary requires each producer to deal directly with only one firm—the intermediary; the total number of contacts required is only eight.

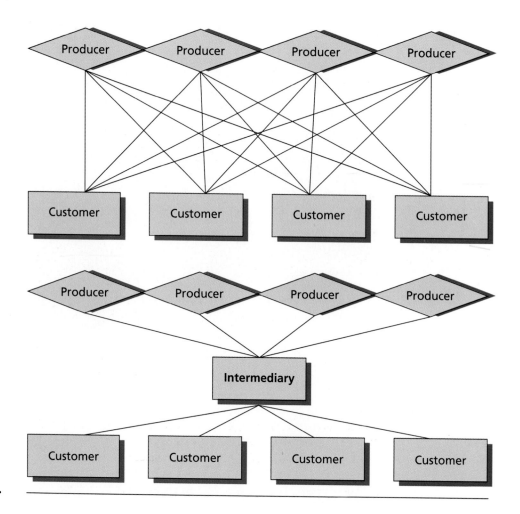

FIGURE 11–2

How an Intermediary Increases
Exchange Efficiency

As mentioned earlier, the marketing functions must be performed in all channels whether a producer distributes directly to final buyers or indirectly through intermediaries. Remember that the functions can be shifted and shared among channel members, but they *cannot* be eliminated. Thus, even though a supermarket ad states, ''We've eliminated the middleman and we're passing the savings on to you,'' no marketing *functions* have been eliminated. The supermarket is bypassing the wholesaler and dealing directly with the producer. The supermarket is thus assuming functions formerly performed by the wholesaler. Distribution costs go down if the supermarket can perform the functions more efficiently than the wholesaler. But the supermarket's inventory costs may go up because it must place larger orders with producers than it would have placed with wholesalers. If inventory costs are more than the savings realized by bypassing the wholesaler, the supermarket's operating costs will also go up. There will be no savings to pass on to customers.

Matching Supply and Demand

Channels concentrate and disperse products in response to effective demand. Therefore they help match supply and demand.

Supermarkets help adjust quantity and assortment discrepancies.

[© Arthur D'Aazien/The Image Bank]

• **Quantity Discrepancy** • The Green Giant Company is not interested in selling two cans of peas directly to a consumer. It wants to sell caseloads and truckloads. The quantity discrepancy between Green Giant and the household buyer is adjusted in marketing channels. Green Giant might sell a truckload of canned peas to a wholesaler, which breaks it down into case lots for sale to supermarkets. The supermarkets break down the cases and stock their shelves with cans of peas. This permits the household buyer to pick two cans from the shelf. (See Figure 11–3.)

Wholesalers and retailers help in adjusting the quantity discrepancy. But when Safeway buys in truckload volume from Green Giant, there is no quantity discrepancy and the wholesaler is not needed. Nor are wholesalers needed when a coal producer mines coal and ships it in trainload quantities directly to an electric company generating station.

FIGURE 11–3

Adjusting a Quantity Discrepancy

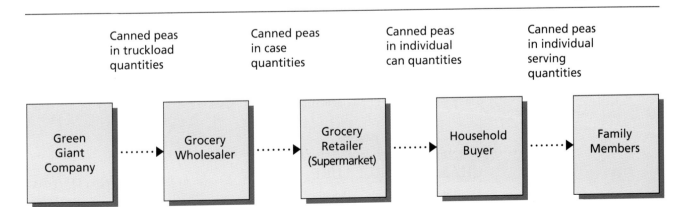

| Canned peas in truckload quantities | Canned peas in case quantities | Canned peas in individual can quantities | Canned peas in individual serving quantities |

Green Giant Company → Grocery Wholesaler → Grocery Retailer (Supermarket) → Household Buyer → Family Members

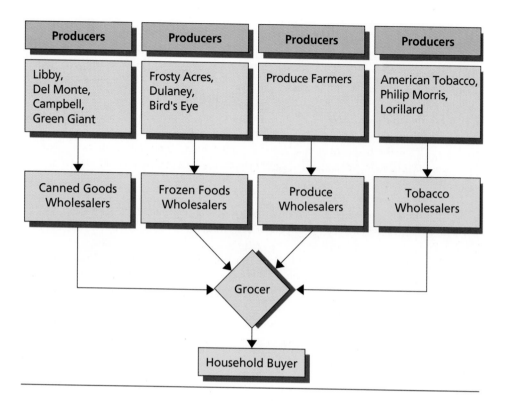

FIGURE 11–4

Adjusting an Assortment
Discrepancy

• **Assortment Discrepancy** • Household buyers want to buy a broad assortment of products when they go grocery shopping. Even giant firms such as General Mills do not produce the full assortment of products a household buyer wants. Thus an assortment discrepancy exists between the household buyer and the producer.

This discrepancy also is adjusted in marketing channels. A supermarket brings together (builds up) the product assortment its customers want by buying products from many producers. It might buy directly from the producer if there is no quantity discrepancy. But this very direct buying and selling can be carried only so far. Because a large supermarket stocks thousands of products made by hundreds of producers, the supermarket operator would have to spend too much time buying and too little time selling. Thus supermarkets buy a large part of their merchandise from wholesalers. Big chains such as Safeway and Kroger, however, buy many of the products they sell directly from producers.

Suppose a supermarket buys canned goods from a canned goods wholesaler, tobacco products from a tobacco wholesaler, meat products from a meat wholesaler, and frozen foods from a frozen foods wholesaler. Each wholesaler buys products from producers whose products fit the wholesaler's line of products. For example, the canned goods wholesaler buys from Green Giant, Libby's, and Del Monte. The supermarket can buy canned peas from one canned goods wholesaler instead of from many canned goods producers and can buy other types of products from other wholesalers. (See Figure 11–4.)

CHANNEL STRUCTURE

Marketing channels have a vertical dimension and a horizontal dimension. The dimensions are interrelated, and together they determine a channel's structure.

The Vertical Dimension

A channel's vertical dimension (length) is determined by the number of types of participants making up the channel. Channel 1 in Figure 11–5 has two types of participants, a producer and a consumer. It is a more direct (shorter) channel than channel 4, which has five types of participants. Channel 4 is a less direct (longer) channel than channel 1.

The number of intermediary levels *between* the producer and final buyers is used to designate a channel's length. Clearly, there are more levels in indirect channels than in direct channels. Channel 1 is a zero-level channel because there are no intermediaries. Channel 4 is a three-level channel because there are three levels of intermediaries: (1) agent or broker, (2) wholesaler, and (3) retailer.

• **Direct Channels** • In the most direct channel there are no intermediaries between the producer and the final buyers. The producer sells directly to the final buyers, not through intermediaries.

Channel 1 in Figure 11–5 illustrates the most direct consumer product channel: producer → consumer. The most direct industrial product channel is channel 5: producer → industrial user. Direct channels are much more common in industrial than in consumer product marketing because industrial buyers often are concentrated geographically, buy in large quantities, buy products with a high unit value, buy complex products that require after-sale service, and insist on dealing directly with producers.

Direct (zero-level) channels are sometimes used for consumer products. Electrolux sells vacuum cleaners door-to-door. Esprit sells some of its clothing through mail-order catalogs and its own retail stores. Most services are sold directly by the producer to the consumer. But intermediaries (agent middlemen) commonly market airline tickets and some types of insurance. Of course, airlines and insurance companies also sell directly to consumers. In fact, a growing number of insurance companies are bypassing independent agents and selling directly to consumers. We will discuss direct selling in chapter 12 and direct marketing in chapter 16.

Producers who sell directly to their final buyers do so for a variety of reasons. They may believe they can do a better job than available intermediaries. Also, they can have greater control over the distribution of their products when they handle the job themselves. Perhaps

FIGURE 11–5

Typical Channels for Consumer and Industrial Products

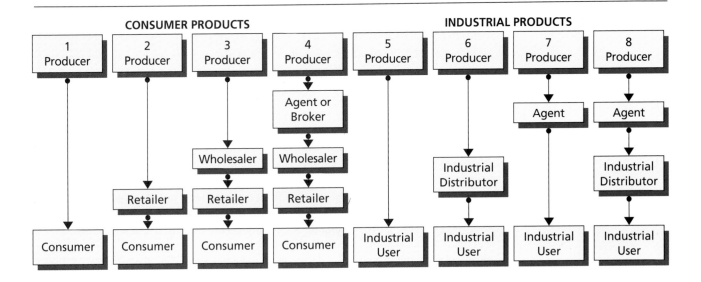

CHAPTER 11   MARKETING CHANNELS   **355**

acceptable intermediaries are unavailable or, if available, are unwilling to handle the producer's product. Producers of products that are heavy or bulky do not want to transport their products to intermediaries when they can send them directly to the final buyer. Producers that have only a few customers, who buy in large quantities, are not likely to use intermediaries. Nor are producers whose products are complex and require after-sale service or training in their use.

Producers who use direct distribution are also able to keep in direct contact with their final buyers. This closeness to the customer makes it easier to keep tabs on buying behavior and customers' changing wants. Thus conducting marketing research and making adjustments to the marketing mix are easier.

• **Indirect Channels** • In an indirect channel the producer entrusts some parts of the distribution task to independent intermediaries. The producer, however, must work closely with the intermediaries to ensure final buyer satisfaction. This is why many manufacturers' ads provide toll-free numbers that prospective buyers can call for the name of their nearest authorized dealer.

In consumer product marketing the producer → retailer → ultimate consumer channel is common for shopping products such as cars, clothing, and home appliances. (See channel 2 in Figure 11–5.) The producer → wholesaler → retailer → ultimate consumer channel is common for convenience products. (See channel 3 in Figure 11–5.) Channels for convenience products tend to be long because consumers want to buy these products with a minimum of effort. Thus producers have to sell through a large number of outlets.

Indirect channels are fairly common for industrial products, except for installations and products manufactured to the buyer's specifications. Generally, however, indirect channels for industrial products are shorter than consumer product channels.

Why are producers willing to give intermediaries some control over the distribution of their products? General Electric has 20,000 consumer product dealers, and Goodyear Tire & Rubber Company has over 6,000 independent dealers. It is doubtful that these manufacturers could assume the financial burden of performing for themselves the distribution activities that the intermediaries perform for them.

Even if a manufacturer has the financial resources to sell directly to its final buyers, it will often choose to use intermediaries. Intermediaries specialize in distribution activities and, as a result, can realize considerable economies of scale. Manufacturers that have a choice between investing additional funds in manufacturing or in distribution typically will invest in manufacturing. The return on funds invested in manufacturing is likely to be greater and faster.

Manufacturers of convenience products such as chewing gum would have a difficult job selling directly to the tens of thousands of retail outlets, including vending machines, that sell chewing gum. Instead they use wholesalers that also carry related products produced by other manufacturers. This spreads the distribution costs among several manufacturers.

The Horizontal Dimension

A channel's horizontal dimension (or channel width) is determined by the number of participants of one type at the same level in the channel. The larger that number, the wider the channel. Chevrolet's channel is much wider at the retail level than Rolls-Royce's because there are many more Chevrolet dealerships than Rolls-Royce dealerships.

Buyers of Rolls-Royce automobiles typically perceive them as specialty products and will make a special effort to locate a Rolls-Royce dealer—even one 200 miles away. Most buyers of Chevrolets probably perceive them to be heterogeneous shopping products and would be unwilling to make such an effort. Thus a greater number of Chevrolet dealers is needed.

INFLUENCES ON CHANNEL DEVELOPMENT

The ideal starting place in developing channel strategy is final buyer wants. This helps the marketer think of channels as market-serving possibilities. Thus the channels shown in Figure 11-5 are only a few of the many types in use. In developing its channel strategy, the firm will estimate the sales it might achieve and the cost of achieving those sales for each channel possibility. In addition, the firm will compare the channel possibilities in terms of their implications for maintaining control over how products are marketed and to whom they are marketed. Finally, some channels require the producer to make a long-term commitment to intermediaries—for example, granting them exclusive rights to distribute the product in specified territories for a stated number of years.

Among the many factors that affect channel development are characteristics of customers, the product, the company, the intermediaries, and the environment. Customer-oriented firms attach great importance to final-buyer wants in developing their distribution strategy. (See Figure 11–6.)

FIGURE 11–6

Factors Influencing Channel Development

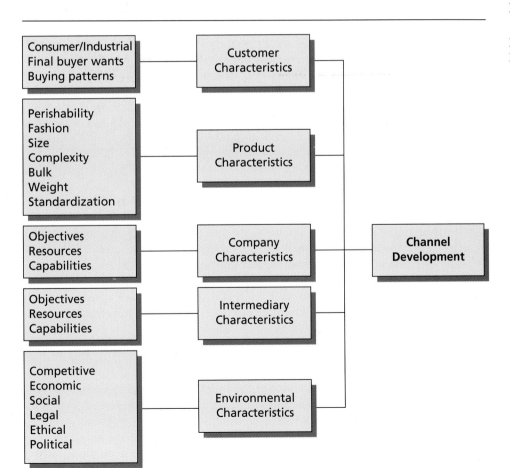

Customer Characteristics

Unlike consumers, industrial users often prefer to deal directly with producers, except when buying small accessory equipment and operating supplies. They also tend to be more concentrated geographically, and there are fewer of them for a typical industrial product. These factors favor shorter channels for industrial products.

Marketing channels for typical consumer products tend to be longer because the number of consumers is greater, they are much more geographically dispersed, they buy in smaller quantities, and changes in their buying patterns are often harder for producers to detect as quickly as they can in the case of industrial products. Intermediaries, who are closer to consumers, can often detect these changes and react to them more rapidly.

Changes in consumers' buying patterns can affect a channel's horizontal and vertical dimensions or lead to the development of entirely new channels. Because of consumer preference for one-stop shopping, supermarkets have become an important outlet for house plants, cut flowers, small appliances, and lawn care products. Faucet producers used to distribute through plumbing supply houses that sold to plumbers, builders, and remodelers. With the growth of do-it-yourself projects, producers are also selling through retail stores.

Product Characteristics

Among the product characteristics are perishability, fashion, size, complexity, value and, standardization. Highly perishable products move through short channels to avoid rehandling and spoilage. Short channels reduce the time a fashion product is in the distribution pipeline from producer to consumer. Low-value, bulky products such as cement and iron ore move through short channels to reduce transportation and rehandling costs. Complex products such as mainframe computers move through short channels because they require specialized training and other after-sale services from producers. High-value products also tend to move through short channels because they usually require the seller to convey product knowledge and, frequently, after-sale services. Highly standardized products, however, tend to move through longer channels than those built to individual customer specification.

Company Characteristics

An organization's objectives, resources, and capabilities also affect channel selection. Kodak has started to sell its products directly to Japanese retailers instead of through a Japanese distributor. Kodak's objective is to persuade dealers to stock more Kodak film and to get consumers, who automatically think of Fuji, to begin thinking of Kodak.[2]

Companies with wide product mixes, such as Colgate-Palmolive, can afford to do more direct selling to large retailers than can smaller firms with narrow product mixes. The smaller firms rely on wholesalers to reach retailers. Colgate-Palmolive's promotion skill also reduces its dependence on intermediaries to push retail sales. Firms lacking this capability must rely more on intermediaries for promotional push.

Intermediary Characteristics

The characteristics of intermediaries, such as their particular resource strengths and capabilities, must also be considered. The Connecting Point Computer Centers ad focuses on this intermediary's resource strengths and capabilities.

Some wholesalers are reluctant to carry inventory and provide credit and delivery to their customers. When suitable intermediaries are absent or unwilling to handle a product,

An ad that focuses on the intermediary's resource strengths and capabilities.

(Mark Bennett, Doug Scott, and Miles Advertising.)

the producer has to go directly to final buyers. If it lacks the resources and capability to do this, distribution may be impossible.

Environmental Characteristics

Environmental factors such as the competitive environment must be considered. A small canned foods producer may have trouble convincing wholesalers to stock a new fruit juice if they are under pressure from present suppliers to keep the new product off the market.

Sociocultural developments have great meaning to channel planners. The big increase in nonstore retailing and direct marketing, which we will discuss in chapters 12 and 16, are due in large part to the fact that women who are in the labor force have little time for shopping. Marketers wishing to sell in some foreign markets find that channels for many consumer products are much longer than in the United States. For example, there is strong resistance in Japan to changing traditional marketing channels. The politically powerful small "papa-mama" retail stores provide excellent customer service, but they are inefficient and keep prices high. Nevertheless, these stores control 56 percent of Japan's retail sales (versus 3 percent for U.S. mom-and-pop stores and 5 percent for European ones).[3]

Political, legal, and ethical factors are important too. Bigness may be looked upon favorably or unfavorably by government regulatory agencies. This could influence the actions of organizations that are contemplating vertical or horizontal integration. Organizational codes of ethics must also be considered when a producer wants to replace an independent distributor with company salespeople.

Economic and technological factors are yet another influence on channel selection. During recessions, for example, intermediaries may be unwilling to stock new products.

CHANNEL PLANNING

Channel planning is important for producers and intermediaries. Wholesalers have to decide on the number and types of retailers through which to distribute. But the closer a channel member is to the ultimate consumer or industrial user, the less need it has to develop a channel from scratch.

If direct distribution (a zero-level channel) is ruled out, a producer must select independent intermediaries. The producer must determine (1) the types of intermediaries to use, (2) the number of each type to use, (3) which specific intermediaries to use, and (4) how to motivate intermediaries.

Determining the Types of Intermediaries

A producer's ultimate objective in selecting intermediaries is to satisfy the final buyer of the product. Thus producers must sell to and through intermediaries. The final buyers' requirements influence the type of retailers selected, and the retailers' requirements influence the type of wholesalers selected. This customer-oriented approach satisfies the producer's final and intermediate customers.

Evian drinking water is distributed through soft-drink bottlers instead of through the usual channels of food and beverage distributors. The big soft-drink bottlers have more clout with supermarkets, which helps Evian get better shelf space and more frequent deliveries.[4]

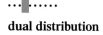

dual distribution

Some producers practice dual distribution. *Dual distribution* is the practice of selling the same brand or product line through two or more competing channels to reach the same target market. For example, Goodyear Tire & Rubber Company sells tires to consumers in the replacement market through 6,300 outlets. The company owns 1,200 of them, and the rest are franchised or independent dealerships.[5]

Dual distribution is a way for producers to reduce the risk that one channel will be inadequate to reach target customers or that channel members will not do a good job of distribution. Dealers often complain, however, that producers use dual distribution to compete directly with their own customers—by undercutting the dealers' prices, for example. Thus the practice can be a source of channel conflict. Although dual distribution in itself is not illegal, producers that are dominant in their industries and that use it to run their independent dealers out of business will likely be charged with violating antitrust laws.

Determining the Number of Intermediaries

The Maytag Company used to distribute its home appliances only through appliance stores but has now added mass merchandisers such as Montgomery Ward and Sears. Apple Computer, on the other hand, became more selective and canceled contracts with some outlets. Apple hoped to sell more computers by limiting availability to only strong dealers capable of sophisticated marketing.[6]

A producer's decisions about the number of intermediaries to use at each channel level determine the channel's width. The intensity of distribution—that is, a product's market exposure—is crucial in channel planning and is a function of the channel's width. The degrees of market exposure are (1) intensive distribution, (2) selective distribution, and (3) exclusive distribution. (See Figure 11–7.)

• **Intensive Distribution** • Producers of convenience products such as cigarettes, chewing gum, and soft drinks want intensive distribution. *Intensive distribution* is a producer's strategy of making a product available to buyers in as many outlets as possible for maximum market exposure. McCormick & Company is the largest producer of spices in the United States. Because more and more consumers are buying spices in discount and variety stores, McCormick expanded distribution to include those types of retailers in addition to supermarkets.[7]

A producer's ability to achieve intensive distribution depends on the willingness of relevant intermediaries to stock the product. Intermediaries are especially reluctant to stock new products produced by small firms with narrow product mixes. Intensive distribution is hard to achieve if the producer cannot afford the promotion effort needed to pull the product through the channel. Trade promotions, such as big discounts, may be required to get intermediaries to push the product.

• **Selective Distribution** • The L'Effleur ad includes a toll-free number that consumers can call to find the location of the nearest store carrying L'Effleur products. The products

intensive distribution

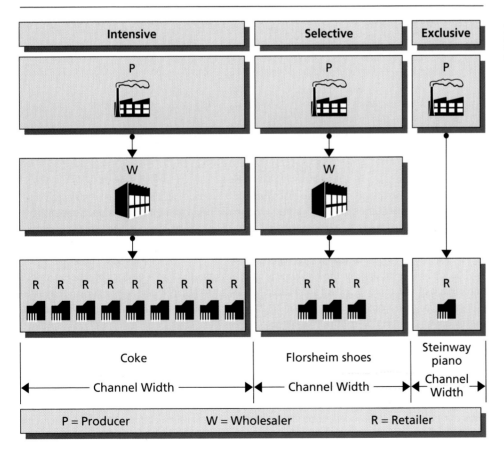

FIGURE 11–7

Intensity of Distribution at the Retail Level in a Specified Geographical Area

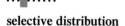

An example of selective distribution.

(Reproduced with permission of Coty Division, Pfizer Inc.)

selective distribution

are selectively distributed. ***Selective distribution*** is a producer's strategy of restricting distribution to intermediaries in a geographic area on the basis of their performance capability. The outlets selected must also be compatible with the product's image. Shopping products, specialty products, and industrial products that require specialized selling effort from intermediaries are often distributed selectively.

The iceberg principle, or the 80/20 principle (see chapter 7), is operating when a small percentage of customers account for a large part of a producer's total sales. A firm may sell 80 percent of its output to 20 percent of its customers; selective distribution is appealing in such a case. Limiting distribution to large accounts cuts selling expenses and, it is hoped, will increase sales to each account. But care is needed to avoid cutting off accounts that have good growth potential.

Selective distribution benefits intermediaries by limiting the number of rival outlets that carry the brand. This often helps build cooperation among channel members. The producer can devote more effort to building a good relationship with the selected intermediaries and does not have to waste money, time, and effort dealing with marginal ones. The producer can also exercise greater control over the product's distribution than would be possible with intensive distribution.

• **Exclusive Distribution** • Products that many consumers consider to be specialty products—Rolex watches, Ferrari cars, and Steinway pianos are examples—are exclusively distributed. *Exclusive distribution* is a producer's strategy of using only one outlet in a geographic area.

...■......
exclusive distribution

Exclusive distribution appeals to producers that want maximum push from intermediaries for their products. They expect dealers that have no competition from other resellers of the brand in their market areas to do a better job of promoting it. Getting these exclusive dealers to carry a complete inventory and to provide service and repair facilities is also easier. The producer's sales force calls on fewer dealer-customers, and fewer accounts are carried. This cuts bad debt losses, reduces working capital needs, and may lower total marketing costs. Producer-dealer cooperation is easier to achieve since both firms work under a contract that spells out their rights and obligations.

Exclusive distribution is also attractive to dealers. The producer's promotion effort benefits the dealer exclusively in its market area. There are no other dealers to underprice an exclusive dealer in its area. Thus inventory may turn over faster. Dealer investment in service and repair facilities creates customer goodwill and greater profit potential.

There are some limitations, however. Convenience products, shopping products, and many types of industrial products do not lend themselves to exclusive distribution. Producers can lose market coverage in an area if the dealer goes out of business or withdraws from the exclusive dealing agreement. Dealers also face the risk that producers will abandon their exclusive distribution policy.

Exclusive distribution is often accompanied by an exclusive dealing contract and a vertical territorial restriction. An *exclusive dealing contract* is an agreement in which the producer does not allow the marketing channel member to sell competitive products. Such a contract can be illegal, especially if the producer is dominant and the intermediary is a small dealer.

...■......
exclusive dealing contract

A *vertical territorial restriction* is an agreement in which a producer grants a marketing channel member the exclusive right to sell its product in a specified geographic area. No other channel member will be granted the right to sell in this area. Exclusive territories are illegal if they restrain trade.

...■......
vertical territorial restriction

Exclusive distribution may also be accompanied by a *tying contract*—an agreement in which the seller requires the buyer to buy some of the seller's other products in order to be able to buy the desired product. This is often called *full-line forcing*. For example, an exclusive dealer may be required to carry a producer's entire line of products in order to become an exclusive distributor of one or more of these products. If the producer prohibits the dealer from carrying competitive products of the nonexclusive items, it is using the tying contract illegally to restrain competition. In general, tying contracts are permitted if they pertain to products that must be used jointly in order to function properly and if they are used by small firms trying to enter a market. In the late 1980s two former licensees of Benetton sued the company, saying it "used its power to impose a tying agreement whereby plaintiffs must buy distinct, unwanted Benetton products in which the defendants have a financial interest."[8]

...■......
tying contract

Tying contracts have been especially popular in franchising agreements. In the past a franchisee legally could be required to buy supplies from the franchisor, even if the franchisee could get products of equal or higher quality at a better price elsewhere. Now a franchisee who can get a better price without sacrificing quality can buy from any supplier.

Determining Which Specific Intermediaries to Use

After the producer has determined the types of intermediaries to use, the channel's *vertical* dimension is set. After the number of intermediaries to use at each level is determined, the channel's *width* is set. Effort then focuses on choosing the specific intermediaries that will become part of the marketing channel. Producers are free to choose their intermediaries as long as there is no intent to establish or maintain a monopoly. They cannot, however, drop an intermediary that refuses to participate in a questionable arrangement, such as a tying contract or an exclusive dealing contract. But in a 1988 case the U.S. Supreme Court ruled that producers can terminate price-cutting dealers as long as there is no agreement with remaining dealers to fix prices. The case involved Sharp Electronics, which had dropped Business Electronics as an authorized dealer after receiving complaints about price discounting from another authorized dealer located in the same city.[9]

Producers seek to attract high-quality intermediaries, which are extensions of the producers' marketing efforts. Selection criteria for intermediaries include their experience, financial stability, management capacity, reputation in the industry, current product mix, sales force size, and ability to provide support to customers.

In some cases there may be only one intermediary serving an area, and the producer will have to either use that one (if the intermediary is willing) or go directly to target customers. Even when several intermediaries are available in an area, the better ones may be unavailable to the producer because they are members of competitors' channels. The producer may have to settle for a less effective and less efficient intermediary or else go direct.

Determining How to Motivate Intermediaries

Producers generally recognize the need to motivate their own sales personnel. Some, however, fail to fully recognize the need to motivate their intermediaries and their intermediaries' sales personnel. Sales to intermediaries are the means to the end of selling to final buyers.

Producers once relied mainly on their sales managers and sales personnel to engage in some nonselling goodwill activities with intermediaries. These efforts are now being supplemented with temporary trade promotions, such as selling to intermediaries at special prices so they can make more profit. Producers often use "push money" to motivate their resellers. Push money is cash payments to resellers and their salespeople to give the producers' products extra selling effort. Increasingly, producers are setting up trade relations departments to handle and coordinate such programs as training for intermediaries and their sales personnel.

CHANNEL INTEGRATION AND EXPANSION

A marketing channel's vertical dimension and horizontal dimension determine the channel's structure. This structure, however, can be altered through integration or internal expansion. Such integration or expansion can be vertical or horizontal.

Vertical Integration and Expansion

Several years ago Coca-Cola formed Coca-Cola Enterprises (CCE) to gain greater control over the packaging and distribution of the company's soft drinks. To form CCE Coca-Cola bought several independent bottlers and combined them.[10] This is an example of vertical integration. *Vertical integration* is the act of combining two or more levels of a marketing channel under one participant's control. One participant buys out another participant's operations.

vertical integration

forward vertical integration

We can distinguish between forward and backward vertical integration. *Forward vertical integration* is the act of acquiring the operations of a firm that is closer to the final buyer in the marketing channel—for example, a manufacturer buying out a wholesaler or a wholesaler buying out a retailer. **Backward vertical integration** is the act of acquiring the operations of a firm that is farther away from the final buyer in the marketing channel—for example, a retailer buying out a wholesaler or a wholesaler buying out a manufacturer.

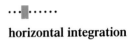

backward vertical integration

Organizations achieve vertical expansion through internal growth instead of through acquiring other organizations. Competitive and other environmental developments and a desire to achieve economies of scale may lead an organization to integrate or expand vertically. The hope of assuring supplies and the desire to improve quality control often are incentives for *backward* vertical integration or expansion, whereas the hope of better control over distribution and the desire for closer contact with final buyers often are incentives for *forward* vertical integration or expansion. The potential drawbacks, however, include getting into a new business about which the firm may know very little and spreading its resources too thinly.

Horizontal Integration and Expansion

Hardee's acquisition of the Roy Rogers hamburger chain is an example of horizontal integration. **Horizontal integration** is the act of acquiring the operations of one or more organizations at the same level in a marketing channel to strengthen one's own position at that level in the channel.

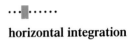

horizontal integration

Instead of acquiring other organizations, organizations can achieve horizontal expansion through internal growth. Thus the firm expands the number of units it operates by opening new ones at a given level in the channel. Hardee's expands horizontally when it opens additional Hardee's restaurants.

An organization might seek to integrate or expand horizontally in the hope of achieving economies in advertising, marketing research, buying, and so on. Such action may also be desirable for achieving a sales volume sufficient to justify vertical integration. The major potential drawback to horizontal integration is that there may be problems in coordinating the operations of a greater number of units.

Legality of Integration and Expansion

The distinction between integration and internal expansion is important in terms of the laws that cover such activity. Vertical and horizontal integration involve one organization acquiring the stock or assets of another and controlling it. The Clayton Act (1914) and the Celler-Kefauver Act (1950) allow the Federal Trade Commission (FTC) to prevent mergers between firms engaged in interstate commerce if the effect "may be to substantially lessen competition or tend to create a monopoly."

For example, several years ago the FTC stopped two proposed horizontal mergers—PepsiCo's proposed acquisition of 7-Up and Coca-Cola's proposed acquisition of Dr Pepper. The FTC contended that if either soft-drink deal had been completed, it would have increased the concentration significantly in a market that was already highly concentrated. If both deals had gone through, the two resulting beverage giants would have controlled about 80 percent of the soft-drink market in the United States.[11]

CHANNEL COOPERATION, CONFLICT, AND COMPETITION

The members of a channel are part of a social system. Each member has certain roles to fulfill and certain functions to perform. Other members expect that member to behave in

An example of a cooperative relationship between channel members.

(Courtesy of Toyota Motor Sales, U.S.A., Inc.)

predictable ways. But channel systems compete with one another; and the members in a given channel may also cooperate, conflict, or compete with one another.

Cooperative Relationships

Cooperative relationships among channel members are necessary for the channel to function as an integrated system of effort for creating and delivering customer satisfactions. The channel will remain a viable structure only if each member recognizes the members' interdependence and perceives some benefit from being on the team. Only then will the members cooperate and coordinate their various roles and functions. The Toyota ad focuses on the cooperative relationship between Toyota and its dealers.

Clearly, each channel member expects to gain something from others in the channel. Harley-Davidson has targeted upscale riders in recent years. In addition to improving the

quality of its motorcycles, the company has sought to dispel the image that Harley riders wear only black. Harley dealers, many of which traditionally conveyed a dark, menacing atmosphere, have cleaned up their stores. The newest "designer store" dealerships sell motorcycle fashion clothing amid neon lights, mirrored dressing rooms, and revolving jewelry cases next to the 20-W-50 motor oil.[12]

Many manufacturers are working more closely with their dealers. Often they come to consider themselves distribution partners. For example, Anheuser-Busch, Exxon, Caterpillar, and Hallmark Cards are tackling family-business issues during sales and management seminars for their dealers. They are doing this because most of their dealerships are family-run.[13]

Conflict Relationships

Channel members are interdependent and should cooperate to achieve overall channel goals. But conflict is inevitable when their individual short-run goals are incompatible and when they disagree on their respective roles and functions. *Channel conflict,* which occurs within a given marketing channel, is the opposing interests that exist among firms at the same level (horizontal conflict) or among firms at different levels (vertical conflict) in the channel.

channel conflict

When Honda started marketing the upscale Acura Legend in the United States, it set up a new division with a dealer network separate from the regular Honda dealerships. The company wanted Honda dealers to specialize in small cars and Acura dealers to specialize in more luxurious cars. But many Honda dealers protested to Honda that the new Acura dealerships would take sales from existing Honda dealerships.[14] This is an example of *vertical conflict*. More recently, similar problems were experienced with Toyota's Lexus and Nissan's Infiniti. The desire of manufacturers for exclusivity conflicts with many dealers' desire to offer a wide selection of brands.

Of course, within a channel vertical and horizontal conflict can exist at the same time. Honda offered the first Acura dealerships to Honda dealers only. But because there were far more Honda dealers who wanted Acura dealerships than there were available dealerships, *horizontal conflict* was likely to arise among Honda dealers over which ones should get the Acura dealerships.

Horizontal conflict is less common than vertical conflict. When horizontal conflict does arise, it is up to the channel leader to solve it. We discuss the channel leader concept later in this chapter. Vertical conflict is not only more common, it is also more complex.

• **Sources of Channel Conflict** • A major source of channel conflict is different perspectives of channel participants' roles. A producer that relies on independent intermediaries for distribution often assumes these wholesalers and retailers are in business to serve that producer's interests. But the intermediaries believe that they are in business to serve their customers and that the producer is merely the supplier.

Another source of conflict involves the use of power by channel members. Some big supermarket chains are trying to force food manufacturers to standardize their prices throughout the United States instead of regionalizing them. The retailers say the change would enable them to streamline their operations and save consumers money. The manufacturers, however, say that abandoning regional pricing would curtail special offers and wind up costing consumers more. The supermarkets have an alternative to buying brand-name products directly from the manufacturers. They can buy from diverters instead.[15] *Diverters* are intermediaries that buy goods from manufacturers at "deal" prices and then resell them to retailers. In many cases diverters are themselves retailers.

Conflict may also arise over the issue of who in the channel is to perform certain functions, such as after-sale service. Other areas of conflict are which products wholesalers will stock and how much promotion they will give each one. Manufacturers with wide product lines want wholesalers to stock and promote all items in a line. Wholesalers want to stock fast sellers but cannot give much push to slow movers because they carry many products of many manufacturers.

Poor communication between manufacturers and intermediaries can also lead to conflict. Intermediaries want to be informed of future model changes, price changes, and so on. The introduction of a new model hair dryer may reduce the value of older models in the intermediary's inventory. Unless the intermediary is informed in advance so the old models can be worked out of inventory or the intermediary is permitted to sell the old units at reduced prices without cutting into the profit margin, conflict may develop.

• **Resolving Channel Conflict** • Conflict is inevitable in a channel with independent intermediaries. The cooperative relationships among channel members, however, must outweigh the conflicting ones or else the members would not participate.

Some degree of conflict may even be beneficial. For example, a manufacturer and a wholesaler may have a conflict over the issue of transportation. For years the manufacturer has shipped in large volumes by rail to the wholesaler. But the wholesaler's customers are placing smaller orders more frequently. The wholesaler's inventory is increasing and a good deal of working capital is tied up in unneeded inventory. This conflict could lead to a new method of transportation that would reduce the wholesaler's inventory and help the manufacturer even out production scheduling. Truck transportation in smaller volumes might be substituted for rail transportation in larger volumes.

If the manufacturer and the wholesaler work out a more efficient method of transportation that benefits both, the same method could be used with the manufacturer's other wholesalers. This type of constructive conflict is called *functional conflict*. It results in new methods that increase channel efficiency and effectiveness. *Dysfunctional conflict* leads channel members to become uncooperative. The goal is to differentiate between the two, reduce dysfunctional conflict, and capitalize on functional conflict. The development of vertical marketing systems is a major step toward resolving dysfunctional conflict. Before we examine these systems, let's look at competition within and between channels.

Competitive Relationships

Channel systems that seek to serve a given market compete with one another. In some cases competing channel systems are basically similar. General Motors and its dealers compete with the other domestic and foreign car manufacturers and their dealers. In this type of *interchannel competition*, each auto manufacturer distributes through its independently owned dealerships.

There is also *intrachannel competition*—competitive relationships within a given channel. An appliance manufacturer that sells through appliance stores will often find the stores competing for sales. This is *intratype competition* because the stores are of the same type. If the manufacturer also sells through discount stores, *intertype competition* would also exist. One type of retailer (appliance store) is competing with another type of retailer (discount store).

Another type of competition is that between authorized and unauthorized channels in the gray market. The **gray market** is unauthorized intermediaries that circumvent authorized marketing channels by buying in low-price markets and reselling in high-price markets at prices that are lower than those charged by authorized channel members. Perfumes, automobiles, tires, cameras, watches, toothpaste, deodorant, and many other consumer goods are often purchased in the gray market.[16]

gray market

A typical case of gray marketing involves a broker who buys goods from distributors overseas, where wholesale prices are low, then diverts them to the United States, where the diverter undersells domestic distributors that have paid a higher wholesale price. Although the practice is not illegal, many manufacturers have fought it in court. The gray market reduces sales for authorized intermediaries and disrupts distribution strategies. In 1988 the U.S. Supreme Court, in the *Kmart Corporation v. Cartier Inc.* case, upheld U.S. Customs Service rules that allow the importation of gray market goods.[17] In effect the Supreme Court ruled that products manufactured under license from the original manufacturer are legal regardless of national origin. The Ethics in Marketing box raises questions about the ethics of gray marketing and of several other distribution issues.

In the discussions that follow we take a closer look at vertical marketing systems and horizontal marketing systems. Both seek to develop greater cooperation among channel members.

VERTICAL MARKETING SYSTEMS

The systems view of channels focuses on the interdependence, or linkage, of channel members. When this linkage is overlooked, the channel consists of a loosely organized group of independent firms (producers, wholesalers, and retailers) in which no one member is able to exert much control over the behavior of other members. No organized systems perspective of a total channel exists.

The traditional view of channels focuses on transactions between buyers and sellers in direct contact. A different channel is created whenever the form of a product changes. For example, where does the channel for steel modular buildings begin and end? Does it begin with a miner of iron ore, a steel producer, a steel fabricator, or the building's manufacturer? The steel producer makes rolled sheet steel from iron ore. The fabricator makes the steel into the shapes and forms its customers want. The manufacturer uses the formed steel to create a modular building its customers want and sells it to a retailer. The retailer in turn sells it to a consumer. Although traditionally the channel for the modular building begins with the modular building manufacturer, we have described four different channels:

iron ore miner → steel producer
steel producer → steel fabricator
steel fabricator → modular building manufacturer
modular building manufacturer → retailer → consumer

The total-system view of channels focuses on a framework for matching natural resources with ultimate consumer demand. This matching process occurs through a single integrated marketing system, not a collection of independent producers and intermediaries. The channel for the modular building starts with the mining of ore and ends with the ultimate consumer. Any institution that increases the efficiency of mining and transforming iron ore into modular buildings and delivering them to consumers is part of the total-channel system.

ETHICS IN
MARKETING

In marketing channels for many types of consumer products, big retail chains now enjoy considerable power over their producer-suppliers. Is it ethical for them to take advantage of this power? For example, what about a large drugstore chain demanding that suppliers deliver emergency and small orders directly to the chain's individual stores in order to reduce the chain's inventory and delivery costs? What about a large supermarket chain that forces suppliers to use their salespeople to provide in-store services, such as setting up point-of-purchase displays? What about fining suppliers for late deliveries?

What about the ethics of dual distribution? What ethical obligations does a company have to its independent dealers that compete with company-owned stores? Suppose a manufacturer that has traditionally sold its products through its own retail stores decides to broaden distribution and sell through a big retail chain. Suppose further that the manufacturer wants to avoid competing with itself. Would it be ethical for the manufacturer to supply the resellers with a slightly outdated model of the product the manufacturer sells in its own stores?

What about the ethics of participating in the gray market? Large consumer products companies such as Procter & Gamble and Colgate-Palmolive license firms overseas to produce products under the U.S. companies' brand names. Is it ethical for these foreign manufacturers or their dealers to divert those products to

This total-channel concept is a key to understanding the tremendous growth in recent years of vertical marketing systems. These systems are set up to maximize intrachannel cooperation and coordination by viewing the channel from the total-system perspective. A *vertical marketing system (VMS)* is a distribution arrangement in which the marketing channel operates as an integrated system with unified objectives instead of as a loosely organized group of independent firms. It is an approach to managing relationships among channel members. Three types of vertical marketing systems are (1) administered, (2) contractual, and (3) corporate. (See Figure 11–8.)

vertical marketing system (VMS)

Administered Vertical Marketing Systems

The main difference between a conventional marketing channel and an administered VMS is that there is a greater degree of effective interorganizational management in an administered channel. An important part of that management is the channel leader. A *channel leader* is the marketing channel member in an administered VMS that exerts power over the other channel members and can influence their decisions and actions. Channel members that are dependent on the leader need to maintain a relationship with the leader in order to accomplish their goals. The channel leader can manage conflict within the channel and exercise a leadership role when other members perceive it to be in their best interests.

The channel leader can be a producer or an intermediary. Producers whose products have good brand images and that spend heavily on consumer advertising, such as General

channel leader

the United States, where they are sold at prices far lower than the prices charged for the American-made versions? Are there any ethical issues associated with the practice of some large retailers of buying from diverters?

Is it ethical for automobile repair shops to buy counterfeit auto replacement parts from counterfeiters in the United States and abroad who stamp the automakers' logos on the parts? The counterfeiters sell these parts to auto dealers, service stations, auto-repair shops, and auto-body shops at lower prices than the purchaser would have to pay for the automakers' own components. Would it make any difference if the replacement parts were manufactured by legitimate independent producers?

Are retailers under any ethical obligation to ensure that the products supplied to them by their suppliers are not fakes or counterfeits? For example, are department stores and specialty shops obligated to ensure that the cashmere clothing they sell is in fact made of genuine cashmere?

Several years ago E & J Gallo Winery, the largest wine maker in the world, voluntarily told its distributors to stop selling fortified wines such as Thunderbird and Night Train to liquor stores in skid-row areas. This action to restrict distribution was intended to reduce the easy availability of the high-alcohol wines to alcoholics in these areas. Can you think of any other products whose distribution perhaps should be restricted in a similar fashion?

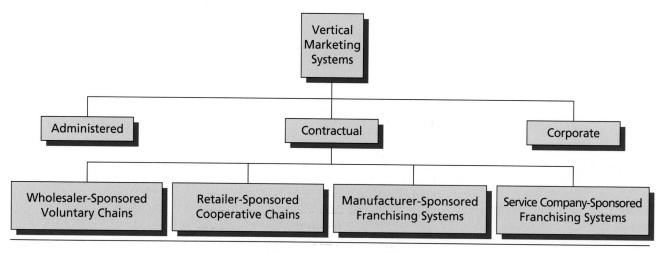

FIGURE 11–8
....

Types of Vertical Marketing
Systems ▮

Electric and Procter & Gamble help create a strong demand that ''pulls'' their products through their marketing channels.

Some producers spend heavily on trade promotions to ''push'' their products through marketing channels. This often gives a firm enough influence to exert a leadership role. White Consolidated Industries, for example, gives push money to appliance dealers and their salespeople to push sales of White's brands. Such producers rely more on the ability of their dealers to push products through channels than on consumer advertising to pull the products through channels. Most producers use a combination of push and pull.

McKesson Corporation is a huge San Francisco–based wholesaler that serves as a channel leader because of its power in the channel. More than half of the 20,000 independent drugstores in the United States are McKesson customers. The company also supplies 27 percent of the chain drugstores and 19 percent of the hospitals in the United States.[18]

Retailers often serve as channel leaders. The ability of giant retailers such as Sears, J. C. Penney, Kmart, and Wal-Mart to move huge volumes of merchandise gives them considerable power in marketing channels. Sears is the only customer for some of its suppliers, thereby giving it a great deal of power over those suppliers. Mergers and the widespread use of scanners at the check-out counter are giving big supermarket chains a growing amount of power. Consider that a hundred supermarket chains now account for about 80 percent of Procter & Gamble's U.S. grocery sales versus 15 percent about twenty years ago.[19]

Contractual Vertical Marketing Systems

The contractual VMS is a further progression toward the total channel concept. In a contractual VMS, independently owned firms in the channel are tied together by formalized contracts that spell out their roles in the channel system. As Figure 11–8 indicates, the four types of contractual systems are (1) wholesaler-sponsored voluntary chains, (2) retailer-sponsored cooperative chains, (3) manufacturer-sponsored franchising systems, and (4) service company–sponsored franchising systems.

Wholesaler-sponsored voluntary chains are started by wholesalers. Super Valu Stores is the largest food wholesaler in the United States. It offers a broad package of services—including accounting, merchandising, site location, store design, and financing—to more than 2,300 independent food retailers that voluntarily enter into buying contracts with it.

The group's combined buying power enables each member to compete effectively with big corporate chains such as Kroger and Safeway.

Retailer-sponsored cooperative chains function in a similar manner except that the retailers set up their own wholesaling operation. They own and buy from it. Each member receives a patronage dividend based on the volume of its purchases.

Manufacturer-sponsored franchising systems exist at the wholesale and retail levels. The Coca-Cola Company franchises wholesalers (bottlers) to buy its concentrate and produce Coke to sell to retailers in their market areas. Midas Muffler Shops are independently owned retail outlets franchised to buy and install Midas products from the manufacturer.

Service company–sponsored franchising systems serve both consumers and industrial buyers. McDonald's serves consumers, and Uniforce supplies temporary workers to business and nonbusiness organizations.

Franchise systems vary in terms of the percentage of units owned by the franchisor. Prior to its acquisition by Hardee's, 60 percent of the Roy Rogers restaurants were owned by the franchisor.[20] Sonic has over 1,000 hamburger outlets, all but 90 of which are owned by franchisees.[21] Mail Boxes Etc. has over 1,300 franchised stores, only 1 of which is owned by the franchisor.[22] In recent years some fast-food franchisors have been buying back franchises from independent franchisees and operating them. The independent franchises that remain are often concentrated in large regional chains or minichains. Finally, some large franchisors operate multiple franchising systems. For example, International Dairy Queen owns Dairy Queen, Orange Julius, and Karmelkorn Shops.

Although the contractual VMS seeks to remove conflict, it still may arise. For example, Fotomat Corporation, an operator of retail photo-developing outlets, was successfully sued by several of its franchisees, which alleged that the company placed new outlets too close to existing franchises.[23] We discuss service company–sponsored franchising systems in greater detail in the next chapter.

Corporate Vertical Marketing Systems

The corporate VMS comes closest to implementing the total-channel concept. A corporate VMS exists when channel participants on two or more levels are owned and operated by one organization. The ultimate corporate VMS occurs when a single firm owns every level in the channel. Oil companies that explore for oil and own producing oil wells, refineries, means of transportation, and retail gas stations are corporate VMSs.

Producers, wholesalers, or retailers can initiate a corporate VMS through forward or backward vertical integration or through internal expansion. Kimball, which was once the biggest piano maker in the United States, now makes most of its sales and profits from office furniture. The company operates its own sawmills and makes the lumber and plywood used in its furniture. It also owns some hardwood forest land, makes plastic accessories for its products, and operates a fleet of delivery trucks.[24] Tandy Corporation designs, manufactures, and retails its products through Radio Shack stores.

HORIZONTAL MARKETING SYSTEMS

A *horizontal marketing system (HMS)* is a distribution arrangement in which two or more organizations at the same level of distribution cooperate to accomplish common goals, each giving up some authority to make independent decisions. The organizations may work

horizontal marketing system (HMS)

together temporarily or permanently. They may even create a separate organization. Sometimes HMs are called joint ventures or strategic alliances.

DuPont and Merck formed a new company called DuPont Merck Pharmaceuticals Company. Merck achieved access to all of DuPont's experimental drugs and its research

GLOBAL
MARKETING

Late in 1990 U.S.-based Coca-Cola and Switzerland-based Nestlé announced their plans to form an alliance to cash in on a potentially hot new growth area in beverages: ready-to-drink coffees and teas. They were looking into the possibility of making and distributing iced or hot beverages under the Nescafe and Nestea brand names. Coca-Cola is the world's largest soft-drink company. Nestlé is the world's largest food company.

By combining Nestlé's well-known trademarks with Coca-Cola's massive global distribution system, the joint venture would be able to bring coffee and tea products to worldwide markets much faster than either company could do alone. Nestlé's expertise is with dry goods such as instant coffee and tea, not ready-to-drink products.

For Coca-Cola the venture would be the latest in an on-again, off-again relationship with coffee. After more than two decades in the business, Coke sold its coffee subsidiary in 1988. The company had been examining the possibility of marketing an iced coffee beverage in the United States for years. But it decided to exploit the "equity already existing" in the Nestlé brands to save time and money developing its own, a spokesperson said. In addition to selling ready-to-drink Nestea in cans, Nestlé in 1990 began test marketing Nescafe Mocha Cooler, a combination of coffee, chocolate, and milk, in the United States. The company now sells an iced coffee beverage in Europe.

But the alliance has risks. Although such joint ventures have immediate benefits, the interests of the two parties, whose coffees and soft drinks are competing beverage products, eventually could clash in certain countries. Image-conscious Coca-Cola also could be exposing itself to some of the negative publicity surrounding a boycott sparked by Nestlé's infant formula marketing practices in the Third World. But since the formula business and the joint venture are "totally separate, we don't think it will have an impact," said a Coca-Cola spokesperson.

The only country excluded from the joint venture plans is Japan, Coca-Cola's most profitable market. There Coke has carved out a major position in the ready-to-drink coffee business with its Georgia Coffee. That product, which it began selling in Japan in 1975, has benefited because it is widely available through Japanese vending machines.

Nestlé has a similar arrangement with General Mills. In 1990 they formed a joint venture to develop a major breakfast cereal business starting in Europe. That venture eventually intends to market cereals in worldwide markets, excluding the United States and Canada.

Source: Adapted from Michael J. McCarthy, ''Coke, Nestlé Get Together over Coffee,'' *Wall Street Journal*, November 30, 1990, pp. B1, B6. Reprinted by permission of the *Wall Street Journal*, © Dow Jones & Company, Inc., 1990. All rights reserved.

operation. Merck provided the new company with foreign marketing rights to some pre-scription medicines plus some cash.[25] The Global Marketing box discusses plans by Coca-Cola and Nestlé to form an alliance.

Another example of an HMS is retailers sharing warehouse facilities and participating in joint advertising campaigns. But it is illegal for them to agree to a horizontal territorial restriction. A *horizontal territorial restriction* is an agreement among retailers not to com-pete with one another in selling products from the same manufacturer.

Downtown merchants' associations are also HMSs. Individual merchants may get together to set up a joint fund to promote downtown shopping. Both beef producers and packers promote the consumption of beef through the activities of their trade association, the Beef Industry Council and Beef Board.

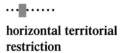

horizontal territorial restriction

SUMMARY OF LEARNING OBJECTIVES

1. Explain how marketing channels create utility, improve exchange efficiency, and help match supply and demand.

Channels bridge the distance, time, and possession gaps between producers and customers, thereby creating place, time, and posses-sion utility. The use of an intermediary can improve exchange effi-ciency by reducing the number of transactions necessary between producers and customers. Channels concentrate and disperse prod-ucts in response to effective demand, thereby helping match supply and demand.

2. Distinguish between the vertical and horizontal dimensions of a marketing channel.

A channel's vertical dimension (length) is determined by the num-ber of types of participants making up the channel. A channel's hor-izontal dimension (width) is determined by the number of participants of one type at the same level in the channel.

3. Identify the major factors that influence channel development.

The major factors are the characteristics of customers, the product, the company, the intermediaries, and the environment.

4. Explain what is involved in channel planning.

If direct distribution is ruled out, a producer must select indepen-dent intermediaries. The producer determines (1) the types of inter-mediaries to use, (2) the number of each type to use, (3) which specific intermediaries to use, and (4) how to motivate intermediaries.

5. Distinguish between channel integration and expansion.

Channel integration can be vertical or horizontal. Vertical integra-tion is the act of combining two or more levels of a marketing chan-nel under one participant's control. One participant buys out another participant's operations. Organizations can achieve vertical

expansion through internal growth instead of through acquiring other organizations. Horizontal integration is the act of acquiring the operations of one or more organizations at the same level in a marketing channel to strengthen one's own position at that level in the channel. Instead of acquiring other organizations, organizations can achieve horizontal expansion through internal growth.

6. Explain the nature of channel cooperation, conflict, and competition.

In a vertical channel, cooperative relationships among members are necessary for the channel to function as an integrated system of effort for creating and delivering customer satisfactions. Channel conflict, which occurs within a given marketing channel, is the opposing interests that exist among firms at the same level (hori-zontal conflict) or among firms at different levels (vertical conflict) in the channel. Channel systems that seek to serve a given market compete with one another. This competition can be interchannel, intrachannel, intratype, or intertype. Another type of competition is that between authorized and unauthorized channels in the gray market.

7. Differentiate among and give examples of the types of ver-tical and horizontal marketing systems.

A vertical marketing system is a distribution arrangement in which the marketing channel operates as an integrated system with unified objectives instead of as a loosely organized group of independent firms. The three types are administered, contractual, and corporate. A horizontal marketing system is a distribution arrangement in which two or more organizations at the same level of distribution cooperate to accomplish common goals, each giving up some authority to make independent decisions.

Review Questions

1. Are intermediaries necessary in a marketing channel? Explain.

2. How do facilitating intermediaries assist in handling the various types of flows through marketing channels?

3. "The more direct the marketing channel, the greater the number of marketing functions that are eliminated." Do you agree or disagree? Explain.

4. How do channels adjust quantity and assortment discrepancies?

5. What is meant by a marketing channel's vertical and horizontal dimensions?

6. What factors influence marketing channel development?

7. What are the relative advantages and disadvantages to a producer that practices dual distribution?

8. Why would a producer settle for less than intensive distribution?

9. What is forward vertical integration in a marketing channel?

10. How does the existence of channel conflict affect the functioning of a marketing channel?

11. What is a vertical marketing system? What are the three major types of vertical marketing systems?

12. What is a horizontal marketing system? Give an example.

Discussion Questions

1. Gucci became a great name in fashion in the late 1950s. By the 1980s the Gucci name had declined. Among the causes were too intensive distribution of Gucci products, licensing of the name to too many producers of too wide a variety of products, and counterfeiting of Gucci products. To restore its good name, Gucci undertook several actions, including paring its product line and taking many of its remaining products out of department stores and restricting their distribution to Gucci-owned or Gucci-franchised stores worldwide. What lessons can other image-conscious firms learn from Gucci's experience?

2. Lance Inc. markets snack foods such as peanut butter sandwiched in cheese crackers and salted peanuts. It does not distribute its products throughout the United States, but it does sell through outlets such as gas stations, mom-and-pop grocery stores, barbershops, beauty salons, and even funeral homes. How would you describe Lance's intensity of distribution?

3. Tandy Corporation designs and builds its products and retails them in its Radio Shack stores. Hitachi produces semiconductors, which go into Hitachi computers, which are used to create robots, which go into Hitachi factories to make more semiconductors. Some oil companies explore for oil and own producing oil wells, refineries, means of transportation, and retail gas stations. What are the advantages and disadvantages of vertical integration?

4. What should a manufacturer whose products end up in the gray market do about the situation?

5. Why is the issue of channel leadership important in an administered vertical marketing system?

Application Exercise

Reread the material on Platinum Technology Inc. at the beginning of this chapter and answer the following questions:

1. What are the relative advantages and disadvantages of each of the distribution options Filipowski considered: (a) opening and staffing field offices, (b) going the franchise route, (c) licensing his products to IBM, and (d) recruiting a network of consultants who would take on the Platinum name as well as selling the products.

2. How would you describe the intensity of distribution for Platinum's offering?

3. How would you describe the relationship between Platinum and its affiliated consulting firms?

The following key terms were introduced in this chapter:

marketing channel
intermediary
facilitating intermediaries
dual distribution
intensive distribution
selective distribution
exclusive distribution
exclusive dealing contract

vertical territorial restriction
tying contract
vertical integration
forward vertical integration
backward vertical integration
horizontal integration
channel conflict
gray market

vertical marketing system
  (VMS)
channel leader
horizontal marketing system
  (HMS)
horizontal territorial
  restriction

CASES

H.O.G. Wild for Harley

DENNIS J. ELBERT, *University of North Dakota*
W. FRED LAWRENCE, *University of North Dakota*

Grim Reapers and Hell's Angels beware: a new breed of bikers is taking on the product you have been associated with for years. Often referred to as Rubbies—Rich Urban Bikers—they are purchasing Harleys the way they used to purchase Perrier, BMW's, and button-down shirts. This interest and escalating sales have helped Harley-Davidson return to the dominant position in the heavyweight (750cc and above) motorcycle category. Dealers can't keep inventory on showroom floors. All this has happened to a product that in the 1970s was displayed with a rug under the motor to catch the oil drips. What caused the turnaround? Why are sales of what many consider a technologically inferior machine growing so fast? Most people attribute the success to what is often referred to in hushed terms as the ''Harley Mystique.''

The story begins in Milwaukee, Wisconsin, in 1903 with a motorcycle called the Silent Grey Fellow. This was the same year Henry Ford introduced the Model A and the Wright Brothers flew at Kitty Hawk. Through the years Harley survived while a multitude of other motorcycle firms like Indian, Excelsior, Ace, and Herring all fell by the wayside. In the late 1960s and early 1970s Japanese bikes such as Honda, Yamaha, Suzuki, and Kawasaki dominated the motorcycle scene. Harley lumbered along. The AMF Corporation nearly demolished the company in the 1970s, when quality and dependability hit an all-time low. In 1981 Harley went private and started to make its move in the heavyweight market.

The center of this resurgence is probably the 883 Sportster. This is the company's entry-level bike and retails for just under $4500. The 883 is a clone of the 1975 XL Sportster with a slightly downsized engine (883cc versus 1000cc). The smaller engine allows a break on insurance yet retains the low-end, torque-producing power and throaty sound unique to Harleys. This bike is not designed for touring but for city cruising. At the low end of the Harley price range it is designed to get customers who ''always wanted a Harley'' to try one. Dealer incentives during the 1988 and 1989 model years, for example, allowed customers to trade in and get full retail value if they traded up to a larger machine within one year of purchase.

The turnaround is largely credited to Chairman Vaughn Beals and President Richard Teerlink. The motorcycles were redesigned to reduce vibration and oil leakage while retaining the traditional styling. Employee involvement and just-in-time inventory systems for parts were initiated. During a five-year period production costs were reduced by almost 50 percent and tariff protection, at Harley's own request, was removed. Styling has proven to be a critical element in the turnaround. Here styling vice president William G. Davidson, grandson of one of the company's founders, provides the key and the ''hi touch'' with the consumer. Known as ''Willie G.'' among the Harley lovers, this stylist has taken a fashion approach to his product. Custom models including the Low Rider, the Wide Glide, and the Fat Boy have resulted from his genius with decals, paint, and styling concepts.

Beyond product innovation, Harley also utilized extensive marketing efforts during the turnaround process. During the mid-1980s a program called SuperRide allowed the company to give almost 100,000 rides to potential consumers. In 1983 the Harley Owner Group (HOG) was formed to enhance contacts with customers. Dealers are heavily involved in HOG and usually sponsor some type of motorcycle event on weekends. Harley owners have been very involved in raising money for the Muscular Dystrophy Association. A company magazine, touring guides, membership cards, and rally event information all are provided through local HOG chapters. All of these activities have helped improve Harley's image.

Harley has targeted the female market also. A separate group called Ladies of Harley has its own newsletter, special activities, and promotional events. The female market was grown because married "biker widows" wanted a way to enjoy the sport with their husbands. Women have a tremendous influence on the purchasing behavior of potential and existing owners. Most male consumers cannot or will not spend between $4500 and $15,000 for a motorcycle without the approval of their girlfriend or wife.

So far Harley has been able to expand and market to the new groups without alienating its existing, and very loyal, clientele. In a sense Harley has a very definite marketing orchestration challenge, to maintain the new growth without hurting relationships with existing customers. The latest Harley moves include strong efforts in designer stores and soft lines. Harley is strongly pushing its line of clothing and motorcycle accessories. Dealers are strongly encouraged to rework their stores in new formats, purchase new display equipment and cabinets, and use new color and decorating schemes.

Some analysts are concerned that Harleys are becoming too much the "in thing." When celebrities and weekend rebels (a Chicago group calls itself the Rolex Rangers) tire of Harleys and move on to the next craze, what will happen to Harley? Harley is counting on the international market to counter any departure of baby boomers. Currently HOG chapters are being aggressively set up in Europe and Japan.

Questions

1. How would you describe Harley's intensity of distribution?

2. How do Harley's marketing activities help motivate its dealers?

3. Is Harley part of a vertical marketing system? If so, which type? Explain.

4. What channel obstacles might Harley expect to find as it attempts to expand into the international market?

Karaoke

DENNIS J. ELBERT, *University of North Dakota*
DONALD G. ANDERSON, *Ouachita Baptist University*

OK, put away your books, notes, and course materials! It's time for a marketing quiz. Open your minds, sharpen your pencils and complete the following statement: Karaoke is _____ .
(a) what you do when you have a sore throat; (b) something frogs do for fun; (c) an appetizer served in a sushi bar; (d) taped music that people can sing along with. The correct answer is: d.

Karaoke, pronounced kar-ah-oh-kay, is a Japanese word meaning "empty orchestra." Japan, especially Tokyo, is famous for karaoke bars where hard working, stressed-out businessmen relax by singing Japanese and English songs to prerecorded background music. Karaoke has started to take hold in American bars and even in some living rooms. Interest in sing-along music fun escalated when Billy Crystal used a karaoke machine in the movie, *When Harry Met Sally*. Electronics distributors are hopeful that Americans will get sufficiently enthused about karaoke in bars and to want home machines. This strategy worked successfully for video games several years ago.

In bars across the country, two or three nights a week are being devoted to karaoke. Themes vary from bar to bar. At "Crooner" in Los Angeles a "dead singer contest" revived Ritchie Valens, Janis Joplin, and Karen Carpenter. Some bars provide performing patrons with a video of their time in the spotlight, for a fee of course. A typical karaoke format has a master of ceremonies who collects cards from patrons who wish to perform: these impromptu acts appear in sequential order. In karaoke, anything can happen: for example, five guys might start singing Helen Reddy's classic hit, *I Am Woman*.

Unit sales of karaoke machines in the United States in 1991 are predicted to be in the range of three-quarters of a million, which is almost three times the 1990 figure. Basic, no-frills machines sell in toy stores for less than $100. More sophisticated models are sold through music stores and karaoke specialty stores in major cities. These home versions are similar to the high-end models used in bars and lounges. For example, Seiko has a Carry-A-Tune cassette player which offers an echo feature. Low price models allow the user to slow down, speed up, or change the key of a song. More expensive machines can also electronically modify the pitch. The idea is that users can train their ear and learn the rhythm in the privacy of their own home.

Karaoke cassettes usually include songs performed by anonymous performers on one side to help the singer recreate the lyrics. After practicing, the singer can switch the cassette to the other side where the lyrics have been eliminated and he can sing along. A well known company which markets sing-along cassettes is New York-based Music Minus One (MMO). It offers a wide variety of cassettes from its catalog, all of which allow buyers to imitate Sinatra, Madonna, Springsteen, or whoever they choose to become.

New technology will assist the karaoke enthusiast who has an extensive collection of traditional recordings. Nikkodo and Citizen are both bringing out portable CD players which will let users digitally mute 70 to 85 percent of the lead vocals from traditional CDs. This will save buyers from having to invest in cassettes or CDs designed only for karaoke machines. Consumers can also purchase laser karaoke machines from companies like Pioneer and Sanyo-Fisher. These combination machines play conventional CDs, CD-videos, and video discs. Super enthusiasts can purchase CD-graphics machines, which enable lyrics to be scrolled on the television screen.

The karaoke craze has encouraged would-be Paula Abdul, Madonna, Beatles, and Elvis impersonators to get on stage. Whether the stage is in a living room or at a local bar, karaoke machines are letting people sing outside the shower and live out their fantasies.

Questions

1. Is there potential for channel conflict among sellers/distributors of karaoke systems? Explain.

2. Which environmental characteristics might affect channel development for Karaoke manufacturers? Explain.

3. What kind of operation would a karaoke manufacturer buy in order to engage in forward vertical integration?

4. Suggest some nontraditional channels manufacturers of karaoke machines or karaoke tapes might choose.

12

coming to **you.**

B A R N E Y S
N E W Y O R K

RETAILING

When Barney Pressman heard that his grandsons wanted to expand the Manhattan discount men's store he started in the early 1920s, he had one piece of advice: "Go north," he said. "I like markets where you can sell overcoats."

His grandsons, Gene and Bob Pressman, who now guide the privately held corporation, chose not to listen. In early 1990 they opened the store's first branches outside the Northeast—one in Costa Mesa, California, the other in Seattle. They plan to open twenty-five to thirty more stores and to make Barneys a nationwide chain. They are also expanding into Japan. Says Gene Pressman, "We're going to be the largest American retailer in Japan."

Once known for its low prices and downscale location on lower Seventh Avenue in Manhattan, Barneys has been transformed. First by Fred Pressman, Barney's son, who expanded into European goods, then by Fred's sons Gene and Bob, who pushed Barneys into high-fashion and mostly high-priced women's wear.

The main Manhattan store, now expanded to 170,000 square feet, sells everything from English hand-painted ceramics to Armani and Chanel. The newer stores sell a much narrower range of merchandise, and the mix differs from store to store. Entirely unlike the New York store, which made its name on tailored men's suits and slacks and is still 65 percent menswear, the stores opening across the country are 70 percent women's merchandise. And no men's suits, only sportswear. So although the stores are called Barneys New York, they will be a disappointment to any customer who comes looking for a New York replica. At 7,000 to 20,000 square feet, the stores are a fraction of the size of the New York store.

The new Costa Mesa store offers $40 Matsuda socks and $85 Yamamoto baseball caps—"fashion forward" stuff seen more in magazines than on real people. In Seattle Barneys is the only store in town carrying Romeo Gigli, an Italian designer whose blouses start at $275 and go up to $480.

The women's boutiques are a joint venture with Japan's Isetan Company Ltd. As part of the Japanese joint venture a 30,000-square-foot Barneys also opened in Tokyo in late 1990.

But the Pressman family itself is also planning to open a wholly owned, 110,000-square-foot store in Beverly Hills in 1993. That store will attempt to match the breadth and depth of men's and women's fashions offered in New York.

Thus Barneys is in a bit of a marketing quandary. In the past the clothing store's advertising generally featured the merchandise, usually draped on high-profile personalities. But with Barneys now a full-scale department store in one location, a men's boutique in another, and (mostly) a women's boutique in several others, the advertising has grown less focused.

As the company's vice president of advertising puts it, ''We found we were trying to be too many things to too many people, so now we're doing generic ads.'' The ads feature single black-and-white photos ranging from tourists gawking at the John F. Kennedy Space Center to a pensive, bespectacled James Dean sitting on a school desk in an empty classroom. The tag lines: ''Select don't settle'' and ''In a class by itself,'' respectively. There is no indication what Barneys is selling to the public. If Barneys bombs in its efforts to go national, it will be because the Pressmans made a common mistake in thinking that the whole world is like Manhattan.[1]

Like many other retailers, Barneys is in the process of being transformed. It started as a discount men's store in Manhattan. The plan is to make it a nationwide chain and to penetrate the Japanese market. There is little doubt that Barneys today is very different from the Barneys of the early 1920s.

In this chapter we look at what retailing is, how retail firms can be classified, the different types of retail stores, and the growth in nonstore retailing. We also examine franchising, the major decisions of retail management, and important trends in retailing.

WHAT IS RETAILING?

retailing

Retailing is the combination of activities involved in selling or renting consumer goods and services directly to ultimate consumers for their personal or household use. In addition to selling, retailing includes such diverse activities as buying, advertising, data processing, and maintaining inventory.

retailer

Retailing does not include sales of industrial products or sales of consumer products to resellers. Furthermore, not all firms that engage in retailing are retailers. A *retailer* is a firm that derives more than half of its sales revenues from sales made directly to ultimate consumers.

Retailing's Role in Marketing Channels

In organizational marketing, producers often sell directly to their final buyers and so are linked to their final buyers in marketing channels. Such direct channels are much less common in consumer product marketing. Ultimate consumers make most of their purchases in retail stores that are independent of the producer. Retailing therefore is the final stage in marketing channels for consumer products. Retailers provide the vital final link between producers and ultimate consumers.

Retailers often have considerable power in marketing channels because a majority of shoppers make most of their buying decisions within the retailing environment (inside the store).[2] In the do-it-yourself market Home Depot, the largest home repair chain in the business, uses its volume buying clout to back up its demand that makers of products such as light fixtures and gas grills rewrite instructions Home Depot deems incomprehensible.[3]

Retailing's Economic and Social Importance

Approximately one out of every seven full-time workers in the United States is employed in retailing. Many thousands of people, including many college students, also hold part-time jobs in retail businesses. Every year thousands of people go into business for themselves by opening retail businesses. Thus retailing has a significant impact on the economy.

The efficiency of retailing activities affects the aggregate demand for goods and services in the United States. The efficiency of individual retailers affects their sales and profits. Thus the quality and efficiency of retailing affects the efficiency of mass distribution.

Value Added by Retailing

Retailing benefits consumers in that retailers perform marketing functions that enable them to make available to consumers a broad variety of products. Retailing helps create place, time, and possession utility. It may add form utility, as when a clothing retailer alters a suit to fit a customer. A retailer's services also help create a product's image.

Retailers add value to product items through (1) the services they offer, such as credit, delivery, and extensive store hours; (2) the image they present, which can enhance the product's image; (3) the personnel they hire, such as salespeople who help identify and solve customer problems; and (4) the store's location, perhaps near other stores to facilitate comparison shopping. The Global Marketing box explains how Sweden-based Ikea creates value for the customer.

Classifying Retail Firms

Regardless of the particular type of retailer (such as a supermarket or a department store), a retail firm can be classified according to (1) form of ownership, (2) operational structure, (3) price and service orientation, (4) merchandise offering, and (5) where the retail sales take place.

• **Form of Ownership** • A retail business, like any other type of business firm, can be owned by a sole proprietor, partners, or a corporation. The majority of retail businesses are sole proprietorships and partnerships. Corporations, however, account for the majority of total retail *sales*.

Consumer cooperatives (co-ops) are customer-owned retail stores. Usually consumer-investors receive interest on their investment, and each has one vote in running the co-op. In most co-ops members and nonmember shoppers pay prices similar to those charged by other retailers in the area, and any profit is returned to the member-owners on the basis of their purchases from the co-op. This helps build customer loyalty. Although important in many other countries, co-ops are less important in the United States. In general they succeed best in areas where traditional retailers are inefficient or have high markups. Most of them are food co-ops, many started by consumers in low-income neighborhoods.

• **Operational Structure** • Regardless of the form of ownership, a retail firm can be operated as (1) an independent retailer, (2) a chain retailer, (3) an association of independents, or (4) a franchise organization. A person or firm that owns and operates one store is an *independent retailer*. Most retail firms are independents, and most independent retailers are sole proprietorships and partnerships.

A *retail chain* is made up of two or more similar, centrally owned stores (chain stores). In some types of retailing, however, a greater number of stores are necessary for classification as a retail chain. For example, in the supermarket business a firm must own and operate eleven stores to be classified as a chain. Most retail chains are corporations.

Wholesaler-sponsored voluntary chains and retailer-sponsored cooperative chains are formed primarily to compete more effectively with corporate chain stores. The member stores, although independently owned, enjoy many of the same advantages enjoyed by cor-

GLOBAL
MARKETING

Foreign-based retailers are doing more and more business in the United States. One example is Sweden-based Ikea, a retailer of furniture and housewares. Ikea has ninety stores in twenty-two countries, including recent openings in Hungary and Poland.

Ikea opened its first store in the United States in 1983. The company laid low until 1991, after it had spread its Scandinavian ideal of retailing to Eastern Europe. Then it launched a bicoastal blitz in the United States. The privately held company expects to have eight of its enormous stores (each is about six times the size of an average supermarket) in the Los Angeles and New York markets by 1993.

The fact that the U.S. furniture market is stagnant does not bother Ikea's chief executive, Anders Moberg. Says he: "It is an interesting time for us to go into expansion. We have a situation in the U.S. similar to what we had in Germany in 1974 and in France in 1982. Furniture was a low-interest category. We have changed that."

Ikea's offer is value, intelligently presented, and it is as persuasive a selling proposition as consumers are ever likely to hear. The response to the store opening in Elizabeth, New Jersey, about 15 miles from Manhattan, bordered on riot. The New Jersey Turnpike was backed up for 9 miles as 26,000 shoppers jammed into the place on opening day. Months later embarrassed Ikea workers were still telling shoppers that the $285 armchairs, $116 oak veneer bookcases, and couches they wanted were out of stock. One clerk was taking reservations to place orders on a particular bookcase, which like most items was selling at 20 to 40 percent below competitive offerings. Managers had underestimated sales by 40 percent.

Ikea idolizes the customer. "It's a very basic concept that stresses cutting out anything that doesn't give the consumer some value," says Moberg. Salespeople, for instance. Shoppers move through a cleverly designed layout that allows them to look, get information, and make purchase decisions without any sales help. A couch, for instance, is displayed both in a real-life setting and in a group of other couches for sale so people can compare.

porate chain stores. Examples of voluntary chains include Independent Grocers Alliance (IGA); Western Auto, Pro, Liberty, and True Value in hardware; and NAPA in auto parts. Notice the toll-free numbers in the True Value ad—one for professional advice about painting and one for the location of the nearest True Value store. Examples of cooperative chains include Associated Grocers, Certified Grocers, and Wakefern (ShopRite).

Manufacturer-sponsored and service company–sponsored franchising systems combine the advantages of independent ownership with those of the chain organization. A *franchise* is a license to do business, granted by a franchisor to a franchisee. The U.S. Department of Commerce forecasts that by the year 2000 franchising will account for half of retail sales.[4] Franchising not only provides the franchisor with capital and rapid expansion, it often provides the franchisee with a workable "blueprint" for retail success. We devote a separate section to franchising later in the chapter.

What consumers really need are information and time to browse, and at Ikea they get plenty of both. The key selling tool is a catalog that includes prices and specifications. On the floor each piece of furniture is graded by a code called *Mobelfakta,* an adaptation of the Swedish testing-board standards that identify materials, construction, and durability on an A, B, C scale.

As for time, take all you want: Ikea staffers will mind the toddlers in a playroom. The company also provides an infant changing room and someone to warm the baby's bottle. There are a restaurant and a snack bar that sell Swedish specialties at low prices, which gives people places to think their decisions through. If they can't make up their minds on big-ticket furniture purchases, and the company doesn't necessarily expect them to, the family can wander through the lower level, called the Marketplace. It is stacked with glassware, linens, rugs, and other household items at deep discounts.

Ikea has the ability to shift a variety of cost burdens onto consumers and get

them to like it. A shopper who selects, for instance, a bookcase, pays for it at a central location and then picks it up from a separate distribution area or selects it from warehouse shelves. The company won't deliver—that's an added cost it doesn't want—but it will arrange delivery with an outside contractor. Once the consumer is home, he or she must assemble the bookcase. Only one tool is needed—an Allen wrench that comes with each purchase.

To keep prices down Ikea designs all its furniture for low-cost manufacture and distribution and contracts out to suppliers in nearly fifty countries, many in Eastern Europe and the Soviet Union. Ikea's next move is to find more suppliers in the United States. Would-be applicants should prepare for high volume and high standards. Says Moberg, "We have very tough demands."

Source: Adapted by permission from Bill Saporito, "Ikea's Got 'Em Lining Up," *Fortune,* March 11, 1991, p. 72. © 1991 Time Inc. All rights reserved.

True Value is a voluntary chain.

(Courtesy of True Value.)

• **Price and Service Orientation** • Figure 12–1 identifies the four price/service positioning options available to retailers.[5] Keep in mind that services (delivery, gift wrapping, knowledgeable salespeople, credit, and so on) are costly for the retailer. Those costs must be built into the *margin*—the amount added onto the price the retailer pays for the goods to arrive at a retail selling price.

Quadrants 1 and 4 in Figure 12–1 are not viable positioning alternatives. Quadrant 1 provides the retailer with poor profit performance. New stores often fall into this trap as they try to provide many services for the customer but are fearful of charging accordingly. Quadrant 4 presents the opposite problem. Here retailers are charging for services that are not being delivered.

Although positioning in quadrants 1 and 4 may work in the short run, it is unlikely to work in the long run. In quadrant 1 the retailers cheat themselves. In quadrant 4 it is the customer who gets cheated.

Quadrant 2 is the service-oriented retail strategy. The retailer offers a wide variety of customer services and charges accordingly. Specialty stores that emphasize one type of product are well suited to this strategy. For example, Tiffany & Company offers expensive,

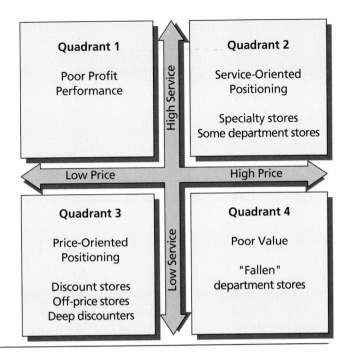

FIGURE 12–1
. . . .

Price/Service Positioning
for Retailers

Source: Adapted by permission from
George H. Lucas, Jr., and Larry
G. Gresham, "How to Position for
Retail Success," *Business,* April–June
1988, p. 5. Georgia State
University.

exquisite jewelry and genteel service. Many department stores once took this approach. Each department was run as a specialty shop. Faced with stiff price competition from retailers in quadrant 3, however, many of these stores elected to centralize their operations, cut prices, and cut services. The frequent result was a slide into quadrant 4.

The low price–low service positioning alternative (quadrant 3) has seen the largest number of innovations in recent years. Here the retailer eliminates all but the most necessary services (parking, lighting, security, and check-out) and charges the lowest possible price for the items. The key for the quadrant 3 retailer is to sell a large number of items, because the profit on each item is quite small. This strategy was first used by *discount retailers.*

As discount stores began to add services and a greater selection of national brands, new entrants emerged in the 1970s, with lower prices and fewer services. These entrants, *off-price retailers,* buy at less than the wholesale prices discounters pay. They also offer fewer services than discounters. Examples of off-price clothing chains include Burlington Coat Factory Warehouse, Marshall's, T. J. Maxx, and Loehmann's. Typically off-price retailers purchase excess merchandise from manufacturers after the normal buying season has ended and display it in shipping boxes to cut costs.

Over time off-price retailers started providing better selection and more services, partly in response to intense competition among department stores, which caused them to cut their prices. In other words, low prices no longer were enough. Thus some off-price clothing chains reorganized their stores to provide separate sections for petites, large sizes, maternity clothes, and so on. T. J. Maxx's "related separates" department, for example, groups a variety of pieces to help customers put outfits together. Some off-price retailers have even opened specialty shops. Off-price lingerie is available at Carole Hochman Lingerie, and off-price handbags and luggage are available at Bag and Baggage.[6]

The improvement in selection and services by off-price retailers left room in quadrant 3 for more new entrants—*deep discounters*. An example is Tuesday Morning, with stores in fifty-two cities. This discounter buys manufacturers' close-out merchandise—whatever is available—at 50 to 80 percent off normal wholesale. Its stores are open just four times a year for seasonal sales. A sale lasts from four to nine weeks.[7]

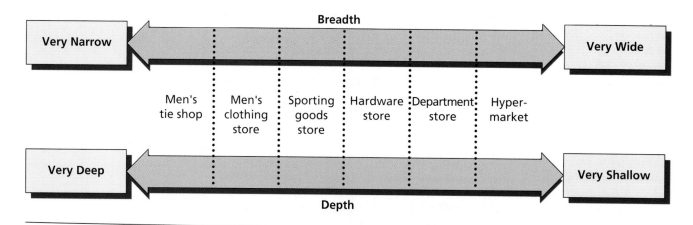

FIGURE 12–2

Merchandise Breadth and Depth

Merchandise Offering
- **Merchandise Offering** • A *merchandise mix* is composed of all the products a retailer makes available to target customers. The two dimensions of a merchandise mix are breadth (narrow to wide) and depth (shallow to deep).

merchandise breadth

merchandise depth

Merchandise breadth is the variety of products that a retailer offers for sale. As Figure 12–2 indicates, a shop that sells only ties offers very narrow merchandise breadth. In general, specialty shops offer very narrow merchandise offerings and department stores and discount stores offer much broader assortments. The ultimate in merchandise breadth is provided by *hypermarkets*. These stores, which are discussed in more detail later in the chapter, offer shoppers everything from food to lumber.

Merchandise depth is the selection a merchandise offering provides. A tie shop does not sell shirts and slacks, but it offers customers a large number of styles, patterns, fabrics, brands, and colors of ties from which to choose. The hypermarket offers great breadth, but the offering is very shallow—for example, one brand of canned corn and one brand (and few models) of TV sets. Because the hypermarket stocks so many different product lines, it does not offer much depth in any given line. (See Figure 12–2.)

nonstore retailing

- **Where the Retail Sales Take Place** • Most retail sales take place in retail stores. *In-store retailing* means that customers go to the retailer's store to shop. During recent years, however, there has been a tremendous growth in nonstore retailing. *Nonstore retailing* is selling to consumers by means other than through stores.

IN-STORE VERSUS NONSTORE RETAILING

In the discussions that follow we contrast in-store and nonstore retailing. Although there are many similarities between the two types of retailing, there are also significant differences.

In-Store Retailing

scrambled merchandising

Scrambled merchandising is the retail practice of carrying product lines that appear to be unrelated. Thus not only do drugstores carry prescription and over-the-counter drugs, but many also carry magazines, toys, hardware, beer, wine, soft drinks, milk, bread, cosmetics, camera film, and housewares. On the one hand they look like convenience stores. On the other hand they look like variety stores.[8] Scrambled merchandising helps retailers generate more sales volume, and it fits consumers' desire for one-stop shopping.

Figure 12–3 divides retail stores into three broad categories: (1) specialty merchandisers, (2) general merchandisers, and (3) mass merchandisers. It has become increasingly difficult to classify retailers solely on the basis of the merchandise they carry because of scrambled merchandising.

Specialty Merchandisers • Stores that offer a narrow product line with a deep assortment within that line are called *specialty merchandisers*. Examples of specialty merchandisers include furniture stores, jewelry stores, toy stores, sporting goods stores, bookstores, health food stores, and apparel stores. As Figure 12–3 shows, single-line stores, limited-line stores, and specialty shops are types of specialty merchandisers. Which type a particular retailer is depends on the degree of narrowness of the product line. For example, an apparel store is a single-line store. A men's apparel store is a limited-line store. A men's tie shop is a specialty shop.

A *specialty shop* is a single-line retail store that carries the narrowest merchandise offering and provides the greatest depth. These shops represent the ultimate in single-line stores. Motherhood is a specialty shop that sells career dresses for pregnant women. Montgomery Ward operates many of its stores in the mall-under-one-roof format. Its retailing focuses on several specialty stores—Electric Avenue, Auto Express, Home Ideas, the Apparel Store, and Gold N' Gems—each run as an autonomous business.[9] Sears too is becoming a

specialty merchandisers

specialty shop

FIGURE 12–3

Retail Stores Classified by Merchandising Approach

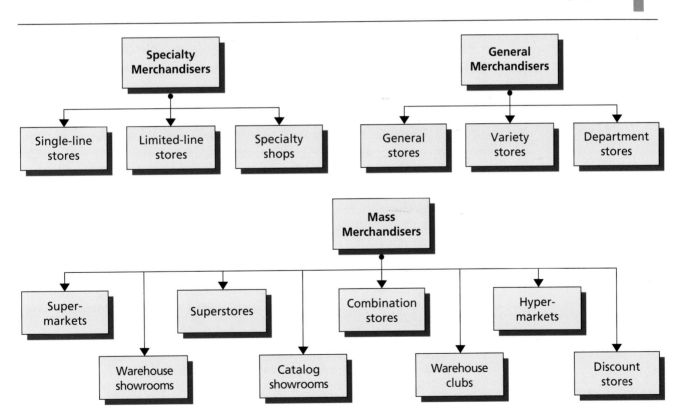

A New Leaf is a specialty merchandiser.

[© Fredrik D. Bodin]

collection of specialty stores.[10] Specialty shops are proliferating as retailers focus more carefully on segmenting markets and tailoring merchandise offerings for specifically targeted markets.

general store

• **General Stores** • The merchandise offering of a general store is much wider and shallower than the offerings of single-line stores. *General stores* are nondepartmentalized stores that sell a wide variety of such staple products as sugar, flour, dried meat, medicines, tobacco, and hardware items. They were very important during the nineteenth century. The few remaining today are mostly in rural areas and small towns, where the limited concentration of people makes it feasible to serve a broad variety of needs rather than specializing in only a few.

variety store

• **Variety Stores** • Once called 5-and-10-cent stores, *variety stores* are retail stores that provide considerable breadth but limited depth in their merchandise offerings, which consist mostly of relatively inexpensive products. F. W. Woolworth started as a chain of variety stores, expanded to include a chain of discount stores (Woolco), closed its Woolco stores, and is focusing increasingly on specialty stores. Today Woolworth operates more than forty types of specialty stores, including Foot Locker, Lady Foot Locker, Kids Foot Locker, Champs (sporting goods), Herald Square (party goods), and Afterthoughts (fashion accessories).

Woolworth management believes specialty outlets will continue to take business from the bigger general merchandise stores. As for the variety stores, Woolworth plans to build few of the traditional general merchandise type and has closed many of them. It is opening Woolworth Express, a stripped-down version that stocks about a quarter of the items sold in the larger stores—the best-selling items. On the other hand, Woolworth's traditional variety stores are very popular in Europe.[11]

• **Department Stores** • Some of the most famous names in retailing belong to department stores: Macy's, Bloomingdale's, Marshall Field's, Foley's, Rich's, Jordan Marsh, Nordstrom, and Dillard. A *department store* is a retail store that carries wide and fairly deep merchandise lines and is departmentalized according to product lines, such as clothing, furniture, appliances, toys, books, sporting goods, and housewares.

A department store's *traditional* strengths lie in its presenting a fashion image and in its offering numerous customer services and a wide variety of product lines in considerable depth in a downtown shopping district. Department stores were the first to promote shopping as an enjoyable social activity. During the past several decades, however, the decline of many downtown shopping districts caused many department stores either to abandon downtown or to scale back their operations in their downtown stores and expand into the suburbs. Greater competition from discount stores, specialty shop chains, and other types of retailers has also hurt department stores.

Some department stores are becoming more similar to the types of retailers that stress low price and few services. They are opening or expanding bargain basements or budget shops in their stores, holding warehouse outlet sales, cutting services such as delivery, reducing the number of employees, and turning more to self-service retailing. Others are entering into other types of retailing.

Other department stores are remodeling existing stores and opening designer departments and boutiques. They are adding restaurants, beauty salons, optical shops, and departments that offer travel advice, insurance, and various types of financial programs. Often these units are operated as *leased departments*. The retailer leases the departments to independent entrepreneurs, who run the departments and pay the department store a percentage of the sales revenues. The lessee's merchandise offering is typically narrow and shallow but profitable because the store generates traffic for the lessee's department.

• **Supermarkets** • Safeway Stores, Kroger, Grand Union, A&P, Alpha Beta Stores, and Winn-Dixie are all supermarkets. A *supermarket* is a large, departmentalized, self-service retail store that sells meat, produce, canned goods, dairy products, frozen foods, and such nonfood items as toys, magazines, records, small kitchen utensils, and toiletries.

Some supermarket chains have opened warehouse and box stores to appeal to consumers who want rock-bottom prices and no-frills service. *Warehouse stores* feature a full line of manufacturer brands, but customers must bring or buy their bags and pack their own groceries. *Box stores* are similar but stock fewer items and emphasize dealer brands. To hold down costs they typically do not stock refrigerated items.

To help offset the price-cutting strategy that can hurt profits (a typical supermarket's after-tax profit is about 1.5 percent of sales), supermarkets are adding fast-turnover, high-margin nonfood items such as prescription drugs, small kitchen appliances, personal care items, and cut flowers. Whereas the gross margin (selling price minus cost) on a can of soup is roughly 19 percent, that on cut flowers runs 50 percent or more.[12] Because people are buying more prepared meals and consuming them at home, many supermarkets are selling prepared take-out foods such as hot pizzas and fried chicken. Today 91 percent of U.S. supermarkets have delicatessens.[13]

Catering to the need for special items and specialized service by two-income households, smaller specialty supermarkets are appearing. Cooking courses, party consulting, wine education, and the acceptance of credit cards are among the attractions. Selection, convenience, and high-level customer service are the key success ingredients for specialty supermarkets. A&P targets high-end buyers with its A&P Food Bazaars and Food Emporiums, budget shoppers with A&P Sav-A-Center and Super Fresh Food Markets, and upscale suburbanites with A&P Futurestores.[14]

department store

supermarket

Supermarkets face strong competition from the nation's roughly 70,000 *convenience stores,* among them 7-Eleven, Lil' General, and Stop N Go. Convenience stores stock a limited number of high-turnover food and nonfood items and charge higher prices than supermarkets. They seek to appeal to people who want maximum shopping convenience (locations close to jobs and homes, late hours, no long lines) and who are willing to pay higher prices than in supermarkets. Increasingly, convenience stores are entering the fast-food business by selling hot lunches, sandwiches, and specialty drinks.

···■·······

superstore

• **Superstores** • A retail store that is larger than a conventional supermarket and provides a more diversified merchandise offering—including services such as banking, dry cleaning, and lunch counters—is a **superstore**. Whereas a typical supermarket has about 23,000 square feet of selling space, a superstore averages around 38,000. In addition to a full line of grocery products, a superstore stocks hardware, garden supplies, health and beauty aids, clothing, gifts, toys, home appliances, video rentals, and so on. For the consumer, superstores go a step beyond traditional supermarkets in offering one-stop shopping convenience. For the retailer, the superstore is a way to do more business in higher-margin nonfood items and to compete more effectively against convenience stores and fast-food outlets for a larger share of the consumer's food budget.

Some supermarket chains—for example, Safeway—are building superstores. For its superstores Safeway is testing Service Village, a kiosk offering shoe repair, key cutting, fax machines, and other services that are important to shoppers at superstores.[15]

A growing number of retail stores are referring to themselves as supermarkets or superstores. For example, some appliance stores call themselves appliance supermarkets and some home repair chains refer to themselves as superstores. In other words, other types of retail stores are adopting "supermarketing" and "superstoring" as methods of doing business.

···■·······

combination store

• **Combination Stores** • A combination food store and drugstore that is larger than a superstore and offers even more diversified merchandise and services is a **combination**

···■·······

HyperMart USA in Arlington, Texas, is an example of a hypermarket. The concept originated in France.

[© Bob Daemmrich]

store. Roughly half of the selling space is devoted to nonfood items. Half of Kroger's approximately 1,300 stores are "combo" stores. Some of them are 60,000 square feet, the size of a football field.[16]

• **Hypermarkets** •   The hypermarket began in France in 1963 as the *hypermarché* and has since spread to other countries, including Spain, Brazil, Argentina, and the United States. A *hypermarket* is a retail store whose operations represent a combination of discount store, supermarket, and warehouse store under one roof. The merchandise offering includes grocery products, prescription drugs, hardware, automobile supplies, major appliances, and furniture. A hypermarket also typically has a cafeteria, a bank, a bakery, and a beauty salon. Some people refer to hypermarkets as "malls without walls."

hypermarket

Although there are more than two thousand hypermarkets in Europe, this retailing concept is still in its infancy in North America. In general U.S. hypermarkets are smaller than in Europe, though still six times larger than an average supermarket. American discount retail organizations are leading the way in the expansion of hypermarkets in the United States. Wal-Mart opened its first 222,000-square-foot Hypermart USA in the Dallas suburb of Garland in December 1987. Kmart, in a joint venture with a supermarket chain, launched the American Fare hypermarket in Atlanta in 1989. European firms such as Carrefour and Euromarche continue to expand their U.S. presence.

Hypermarkets have enormous buying power and frequently deal directly with manufacturers. Although sales have been extremely healthy, profits have been slow to materialize. The key to profitability appears to be finding the appropriate mix of food and nonfood items. Americans prefer more food items and fewer high-profit nonfood items in the merchandise mix.[17] Kmart recently supplanted its hypermarket efforts with experiments in combination stores.[18]

• **Discount Stores** •   Kmart, Wal-Mart, Caldor, Target, and Rose's are discount stores. A *discount store* is a large, self-service, departmentalized volume retailer that sells a wide variety of merchandise at low markup for a high turnover. Examples of the merchandise offered in a typical discount store are appliances, photographic equipment, furniture, jewelry, groceries, and clothing. Competition between discount stores and such normal-margin retailers as department stores is intense; it is also intense among discount stores themselves.

discount store

Single-line stores also engage in discount retailing. Examples include many sporting goods stores, appliance stores, stereo equipment stores, bookstores, and toy stores. Retailers that offer a nearly complete selection of one type of merchandise and that become the giants of their narrow merchandise segments are called specialty discounters, or "category killers." Examples are Crown Books, Tower Records, and Toys "R" Us.[19] Traditional discounters, such as Kmart and Caldor, offer considerable merchandise breadth but shallow depth. Category killers offer narrow breadth but a great deal of depth. They offer greater selection within their product area and steeper price cuts. In recent years some traditional discount stores have purchased several category killers. For example, Kmart recently bought Sports Authority, a sporting goods specialist.[20]

CONVENANT STORES

• **Warehouse Showrooms** •   Levitz Furniture Corporation is a pioneer in the field of warehouse showrooms. A *warehouse showroom* is a discount retailer that sets up a facility in a low-rent area, often next to a major highway intersection or a railroad siding, and focuses on high volume at low prices. The location helps keep operating costs low and facilitates buying in full carloads from manufacturers. The warehouse facility is on one level; therefore operations involve little rehandling of merchandise. Mechanization and automation of operations also help keep costs down.

warehouse showroom

Warehouse showrooms engage in heavy promotion to generate the volume of traffic necessary to justify the huge investment in inventory. Sample items of merchandise are neatly displayed for inspection in the showroom. Salespeople in the showroom write up customers' orders, and shoppers can take the merchandise home with them in cartons or have it delivered for an additional charge.

• **Catalog Showrooms** • Best Products Company, Service Merchandise Company, and W. Bell and Company operate catalog showrooms. A *catalog showroom* is a discount retail facility whose customers preshop—compare quality and prices in the catalog at home before going to the store to shop—through a catalog mailed to them and then select merchandise from samples that are often featured in display cases in the showroom. To keep costs down, shoppers are sometimes required to write up their own orders and present them to clerks. The merchandise is then brought from the storage area to the customers. Typical products sold through this type of retailer include luggage, jewelry, cameras, and small appliances.

Catalog showrooms are able to hold costs down by offering very limited merchandise display areas. Because customers have preshopped before coming to the showroom, few salespeople are needed. Nevertheless, many catalog showrooms have been hurt in recent years by intense competition from traditional discount retailers, such as Kmart, which have matched catalog showrooms' prices for durable goods while offering more services.[21]

• **Warehouse Clubs** • Price Club, Costco Wholesale Club, Pace Membership Warehouse (a division of Kmart), and Sam's Wholesale Club (a division of Wal-Mart) are all warehouse clubs. A *warehouse club* is a wholesale-retail, cash-and-carry, membership-only operation that sells high-turnover manufacturer brands typically from a combination warehouse and store. The annual dues requirement, usually $25 or $30, gives the warehouse clubs a defined customer base.

A club is usually housed in a low-rent combination warehouse-store building that is bigger than two football fields and has a concrete floor and racks on which the merchandise is displayed. Among the items stocked are groceries, liquor, office supplies, hardware, appliances, apparel, and tires. Some warehouse clubs even sell cars and motor homes.[22] Whereas a typical discount store might stock 100,000 items, warehouse clubs carry about 3,500 items and usually just 1 name-brand appliance, athletic shoe, fax machine, and so on. Although the selection is limited, it is becoming more and more upscale. Prices average 8 to 10 percent over cost, about one-third the typical discount store markup.[23]

The first warehouse club, Price Club, was opened in 1976 in San Diego. The huge success of this type of retailing explains why in recent years discount retailers and supermarket chains have expanded into warehouse club retailing. Much of the growth in warehouse club sales has been at their expense.[24]

Nonstore Retailing

The retailers we have discussed are in-store retailers; their customers go to their stores to shop. In *nonstore retailing* customers do not go to a store to buy. Although consumers buy most of their goods and services from stores, nonstore retailing is growing much faster than in-store retailing. Among the reasons are the growing number of women in the labor force who have less time to shop in stores, the growing number of elderly people who tend to shop less in stores, and the presence of unskilled retail store salespeople who cannot provide information to help shoppers make buying decisions.

In chapter 16 we will discuss direct marketing, a major type of retailing that occurs away from a retail store environment. Examples are buying through catalogs and over the phone. In the discussions that follow we look briefly at direct selling and automatic vending.

• **Direct Selling** • Door-to-door selling, route selling, party-plan selling, and custom selling are examples of direct selling. ***Direct selling*** is a method of marketing that is based on direct sales contact between the marketer and the prospective customer.

direct selling

Among the many marketers that engage in *door-to-door selling* are World Book, Kirby, Amway, and Avon. As the president of World Book Educational Products says: "We're not sales clerks waiting for someone to come in and buy something. We go out and sell." Some Kirby vacuum cleaner salespeople make more than $250,000 a year working strictly on commission.[25] Amway's products include detergents, vitamins, and cosmetics. The company has achieved a great deal of success selling door-to-door in Japan. Selling through acquaintances works very well in Japan, a country in which building networks of contacts is very important.[26]

Milk, newspapers, doughnuts, and potato chips are often sold by *route salespeople*. Tupperware and Sarah Coventry use *party-plan selling*. The salesperson recruits hosts or hostesses to sponsor parties in their homes. The party sponsor receives free merchandise at levels based on the orders written at the party. Examples of *custom sellers* include home improvement product companies and clothing companies that tailor suits in their customers' offices.

Door-to-door selling, route selling, party-plan selling, and custom selling are types of *in-home retailing*. They give salespeople an opportunity to demonstrate products in a personal manner that is free of in-store distractions. But in-home retailing is the most expensive form of retailing. For example, commissions paid to the salesperson typically range between 30 and 50 percent of the product's retail selling price.

• **Automatic Vending** • The ultimate in nonpersonal selling is ***automatic vending,*** or automatic merchandising—a type of nonstore retailing in which products are sold directly to buyers from machines. Vending machines make it possible to serve customers where and when it is not practical for stores to serve them, such as in restrooms.

automatic vending

Automatic vending is an especially popular type of retailing in Japan.

[© Chuck Fishman]

Vending machines have long played a major role in retailing convenience products such as cigarettes, beverages, newspapers, and candy bars. Other products include flight insurance, videocassettes, cash, complete meals, paperback books, record albums, computer time, and air for tires at service stations.

Prices of products sold through vending machines are typically higher than they are in stores. In addition to paying for convenience, consumers also pay for the high cost of maintaining the machines. Vandalism and pilferage are major problems. In many cases the firms that own the machines are service companies that lease space in high-traffic areas and install and service the machines. Because of the limited storage capacity of typical machines and because of their scattered locations, restocking them can be costly.

Automatic vending is very important in Japan. For example, roughly 50 percent of the soft-drink retail sales in Japan are made through vending machines, compared with 10 percent in the United States. The importance of automatic vending in Japan is due in part to the fact that the machines are mostly on city sidewalks instead of in offices and factories, as they are in the United States. Machine vandalism in Japan is virtually nonexistent, and a well-placed vending machine can move as much soft drink as a medium-sized convenience store.[27]

FRANCHISING

We discussed four types of contractual vertical marketing systems in chapter 11: (1) wholesaler-sponsored voluntary chains, (2) retailer-sponsored cooperative chains, (3) manufacturer-sponsored franchising systems, and (4) service company–sponsored franchising systems.

Super Valu Stores Inc., a grocery wholesaler, sponsors a voluntary chain. The independent grocers affiliated with Super Valu could also be called franchised stores.

Associated Grocers and Certified Grocers are retailer-sponsored cooperative chains. The retailers that are members of the cooperative chain established their own wholesaling operation.

Manufacturer-sponsored franchising systems exist at the wholesale and retail level. Soft-drink manufacturers franchise wholesalers (bottlers) to buy their concentrate and produce beverages to sell to retailers in their market areas. Automobile manufacturers franchise retailers (auto dealers) to sell their cars to consumers. Such wholesalers and retailers are often referred to as *authorized,* or *franchised,* distributors or dealers.

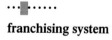

franchising system

In this section our focus is the service company–sponsored franchising system, because it represents the fullest development of the concept of franchising as a system for doing business. A *franchising system* is an arrangement in which a franchisor, which has developed an idea and business procedures that can be duplicated, licenses franchisees to copy the idea and procedures. Examples include Subway Sandwiches, Jazzercise fitness centers, ServiceMaster, Budget Rent A Car, and H&R Block. As mentioned earlier in this chapter, franchised businesses account for one-third of retail sales in the United States. The Department of Commerce forecasts that by the year 2000 franchising will account for half of retail sales.[28] Franchising is a very popular way for people to go into business for themselves.

Among the types of businesses that are involved in franchising are banks, accounting firms, dating services, skin care centers, tub and tile refinishers, tutoring firms, funeral homes, dentistry firms, popcorn stores, cookie bakeries, and suppliers of maid service, lawn care, and solar greenhouses. A recent form of franchise expansion is ''standchising.'' The standchise is a franchised small retail outlet, or kiosk, positioned in high-traffic lanes in malls.[29] A franchising expert at the Department of Commerce says, "Any business that can be taught to someone is being franchised."[30]

According to the International Franchise Association, less than 5 percent of franchised outlets fail or are discontinued each year. On the other hand, 65 percent of independent business start-ups fail within the first five years of operation.[31] Thus, on the average, people who become franchisees with established and reputable franchisors stand a much better chance of succeeding than if they were to go into business strictly on their own.

Franchising specialists expect a significant increase in the number of women and minorities who purchase franchises in the 1990s. According to the president of Chicago-based Women in Franchising, "Franchisors are gradually waking up to the reality that their pool of available franchisees in the 1990s is shifting from white males to minority groups and women."[32]

Three essentials for success as a franchisor are (1) a sound concept, (2) adequate financing, and (3) a good relationship with franchisees. The concept must have recognizable individuality, be practical and easy to replicate, and have staying power. It is also suggested that a would-be franchisor operate one or more prototype outlets to test the concept.[33]

The franchisor gives advice and help to franchisees, including finding a good location, providing blueprints for building the shop or store, and giving financial, marketing, and management assistance. Franchisees own their businesses but must adhere to the franchisor's requirements regarding merchandising and operations to preserve uniformity and control.

Franchisee Benefits

A franchising operation offers franchisees many potential benefits. On a personal level it provides opportunities to retired people, to people who are concerned about job security, and to those who are frustrated with corporate politics and the "rat race."[34] The PIP Printing ad is targeted to these types of prospective franchisees.

A recent study revealed that about 25 percent of franchises are sold to "corporate dropouts." The study also indicated that 42 percent of franchises are purchased by husband-and-wife teams.[35] For a growing number of working mothers who have difficulty getting flexible working hours from their employers, operating a franchise from the home is becoming an attractive option. According to a spokesperson for the International Franchise Association, "You'll find franchise companies beating a path to their door because these women offer past business experience, stability and motivation."[36]

Franchising also offers franchisees other benefits. First, belonging to a recognized franchise organization gives the franchisee quick recognition by potential customers. Second, the franchisor provides management training and assistance to the franchisee and employees. Third, the franchisor either makes or buys ingredients, supplies, and parts in large volume and resells them to franchisees, usually at lower prices than they would pay if each franchisee made or bought them independently. Thus the franchisee enjoys economies in buying. Fourth, franchisors often provide financial assistance to the franchisee. Usually a franchisee puts up a certain percentage of the cost of land, building, equipment, and initial promotion. The franchisor finances the rest and is paid back out of the revenues the franchisee earns. Jiffy Lube International and Uniforce Temporary Personnel are examples of franchisors that directly fund the expansion of their franchisees. For example, when the owner of a temporary services franchise could not get banks to finance her purchase of another temporary agency, her own franchisor, Uniforce, gave her 50 percent of the acquisition price, without any repayment required.[37] Fifth, franchisors usually develop and run

An ad that invites prospective franchisees to call toll-free for franchise information.

(Reprinted with the permission of PIP Printing.)

national promotion campaigns and supply franchisees with various types of promotional aids, such as in-store displays, radio scripts, and publicity releases.

Franchisor Benefits

Franchising also offers a franchisor many potential benefits. First, the franchisor may achieve national and perhaps international expansion much faster than by any other approach. The franchisor's expansion is being financed partly by the franchisees' payment of royalties and fees. Second, a local franchisee pays a lower rate for newspaper advertising than a national franchisor. The franchisor and the franchisee can share the cost of advertising (cooperative advertising), and both benefit. This also helps the franchisor avoid wasted coverage—advertising in areas where there are no franchisees. Third, as the owners of their businesses, franchisees may be motivated to work harder than employees the franchisor might hire. Franchisees are entrepreneurs and owners, not employees. Fourth, whereas the headquarters of a chain-store operation must keep payroll, tax, and other records on all of its units and concern itself with local laws regarding sales taxes, licenses, and permits, these are the responsibility of each franchisee.

In recent years some chains have been selling some of their company-owned outlets to franchisees. This can help improve sales, help raise cash, and streamline operations. After opening seven video outlets in Phoenix, Arizona, the co-founder of Movie Superstore realized that the massive restructurings of recent years had put a lot of experienced executives out of work. He reasoned that these people did not want to return to big corporations, but they did not want to start businesses from scratch either. Thus Movie Superstore sold some stores as freestanding going concerns. The franchisees also will open new outlets of their own—and finance most of that growth themselves.[38]

The Franchising Agreement

A *franchising agreement* is a contract between the franchisor and the franchisee that spells out their respective rights and obligations. Thus McDonald's Corporation (the franchisor) grants the right to make and sell its hamburgers and use its trademarks (a franchise) to independent businesspeople (franchisees) in designated areas. The terms of franchising agreements vary greatly but usually provide that the franchisee will (1) pay a flat fee to the franchisor to buy and operate the franchise; (2) pay the franchisor a royalty (a percentage of the shop's or store's gross income); (3) buy supplies and merchandise from the franchisor or, if buying from other sources, buy products of equal quality; and (4) pay a set amount or a percentage of gross receipts into a fund that the franchisor uses to promote the franchised outlets to consumers.

The franchising agreement also stipulates what the franchisor will do. Typically this includes granting a license to the franchisee to do business in a specified territory and specifying the types of financial and managerial assistance available from the franchisor. The Federal Trade Commission requires franchisors to give prospective franchisees a disclosure document and then ten business days to decide whether to sign a franchising agreement. The franchisor and franchisees have many common interests and objectives. But there is also an element of conflict in that the franchisees want independence and the franchisor wants control. The franchisor must take the initiative in managing the franchisor-franchisee relationship to maximize cooperation and minimize damaging conflict.[39]

MAJOR TYPES OF RETAILING DECISIONS

Among the major types of retailing decisions are those related to (1) target markets, (2) merchandise management, (3) store location, (4) store image, (5) store personnel, (6) store design, and (7) promotion.

Target Market Decisions

Although some retailers still aim at the mass market, a growing number are engaging in marketing research and market segmentation because they are finding it increasingly difficult to satisfy everyone. By carefully defining target markets, retailers can use their resources and capabilities to position themselves more effectively relative to rivals and to achieve a differential advantage. The tremendous growth in the number of specialty shops in recent years is due in large part to their ability to define precisely the type of customer they seek to serve and to put together a merchandise offering that appeals to that target customer. Duty Free International is a chain of stores in North American airport terminals and along the U.S.-Canadian border that targets a captive audience of international travelers. The company also operates a wholesaling business that sells merchandise to cruise ships and international airlines.[40]

Merchandise Management Decisions

The goal of merchandise management is to identify the merchandise that target customers want and to have it available in the right quantities and at the right prices where and when

customers want it. Merchandise management includes (1) merchandise planning, (2) merchandise buying, and (3) merchandise control.

Merchandise planning seeks to put together a merchandise mix that has the breadth and depth needed to satisfy target customers and to achieve the retailer's return on investment goal. Cultural diversity makes merchandise planning more challenging. For example, more and more chains of convenience stores are tailoring their merchandise to their neighborhoods. Supermarkets too are doing a more careful job of targeting. For example, a Safeway store in a Hispanic neighborhood of San Jose, California, has a tortillaria on the premises that makes 500 dozen fresh corn and flour tortillas every day.[41]

Merchandise buying involves making decisions about (1) centralized or decentralized buying, (2) merchandise resources, and (3) negotiations with suppliers. A few years ago, for example, J. C. Penney decentralized much of the buying of fashion merchandise, giving individual store managers a greater role in deciding which items they would carry. Traditionally, Penney's New York buyers had ordered the products, which were then shown to merchandise specialists from Penney's four national regions. These specialists in turn decided which merchandise their regional stores would carry.[42]

The choice of merchandise resources (suppliers) is crucial. Limited Inc. bought Mast Industries in 1978. Mast takes orders for apparel from retailers and then arranges for production through a worldwide network of contract manufacturing units. In addition to helping Limited executives predict fashion trends, Mast helps make possible speedy delivery of "hot" items to Limited stores.[43]

Negotiations with suppliers focus on such issues as who pays the freight costs and what the merchandise return policy will be. The financial difficulties many department store chains have experienced in recent years have complicated the relationship between them and their suppliers. *Factors* are facilitating intermediaries that buy retail receivables from apparel makers at a discount and assume the risk that the bills will not be paid by the apparel makers' customers. Factors have become more choosy about accepting receivables from suppliers that sell to retailers experiencing financial difficulties.[44]

Merchandise control involves maintaining proper levels of merchandise inventories and protecting inventory against shrinkage (employee theft, shoplifting, and other causes of lost merchandise). Merchandise inventory is the average retailer's biggest asset. Dillard Department Stores and Home Depot have computer software that links stores directly to vendors so they can respond quickly to demands for additional inventory. The Limited uses a satellite to speed orders from its Asian factories.[45]

A basic stock list states the minimum number of units of staple merchandise to keep in inventory and the quantity to reorder. The model stock plan is used for fashion merchandise. It is expressed in dollars instead of units because this merchandise changes from season to season. The model stock plan breaks the merchandise down by color, size, and type instead of listing specific units.

Inventory shrinkage occurs when the dollar amount on hand is less than that carried in the inventory records. A physical inventory is needed to detect shrinkage. Shoplifting means taking merchandise without paying for it or paying less than the correct price by switching price tags or altering the price. The fastest-growing larceny crime, shoplifting is a $9 billion-a-year problem for the nation's retailers.[46] Shoplifting controls range from low-tech to high-tech. Cub Foods in Colorado Springs places low-tech life-sized cardboard figures of local police officers next to products such as film and cosmetics. A high-tech control is the "ink tag," a plastic disk containing three glass vials of indelible ink attached to a garment and removable only with a special tool. If the tag is tampered with, the ink spills and ruins the fabric.[47] Table is 12–1 lists several other types of shoplifting controls.

Employee theft causes even more shrinkage than shoplifting. Controls include establishing an ethic of honesty in managing the store, informing employees that the store has a system to detect theft, and prosecuting offenders.

Store Location Decisions

Location is crucial to the success of retail stores. A store's trading area is the area surrounding the store from which the store draws the majority of its customers. The extent of a

TABLE 12–1   Examples of Shoplifting Controls for Retailers

1. Encouraging manufacturers to discontinue making bottle caps that are interchangeable on different sizes of bottles.

2. Using price tags that are impossible to switch, such as the plastic string that goes through an item of clothing and can be removed only by cutting.

3. Designing stores with fewer exits, fewer partitions, and fitting rooms with doors that do not touch the bottom of the floor.

4. Locating easily shoplifted merchandise away from store entrances.

5. Putting signs in stores that remind shoppers that shoplifting is a crime and that management will prosecute shoplifters.

6. Placing mirrors in isolated store areas.

7. Using closed-circuit television to monitor shopper activity.

8. Hiring security guards and plain-clothes store detectives.

9. Training personnel to be alert to shoplifting activity.

10. Establishing in-store policies, such as limiting the number of garments a customer can take to a fitting room.

11. Keeping easily pilfered products locked in specially designed display cases.

12. Avoiding the use of ordinary pens to mark down merchandise prices.

store's trading area depends in part on the merchandise sold. For example, some people are willing to travel further to shop at Neiman-Marcus than to shop at Kmart, largely because of the unique and prestigious merchandise offered at Neiman-Marcus.

Once the trading area is delineated, the retailer must select a specific site within the area. Factors to consider include traffic patterns, accessibility, competitors' locations, site availability and cost, and population shifts within the area. There are two basic types of shopping areas within which retail stores are located—unplanned shopping areas and planned shopping centers.

unplanned shopping area

• **Unplanned Shopping Areas** •   An area in which a group of stores are located close together, but without the benefit of a master plan regulating the types or the number of stores, is an *unplanned shopping area.* As several stores begin to attract customer traffic, others locate nearby.

The *downtown shopping area* is usually in the center of town. Traffic congestion, lack of parking, movement of people to the suburbs, and urban decay have reduced the importance of this area in many cities. Downtown revitalization projects, however, are improving the downtown areas in many cities. The person who oversees the Gap's real estate deals says: "We're already in all the best malls, and since mall growth is slowing, it's time to find other locations. We think downtowns are going to be the place to shop."[48]

Secondary shopping areas develop as people move out from the center of town and form neighborhoods. This attracts retailers to these areas. On-street parking is common, and there is little apparent planning of types of stores. *Strip shopping areas* are made up of several stores clustered in a row, usually on one side of the street. Many are close to large apartment buildings, which provide a large number of people in a small area. Stores that target their offerings to college students often locate in strip shopping areas near college campuses.

planned shopping center

• **Planned Shopping Centers** •   During the 1950s, as many people began moving from the central cities to the suburbs, planned shopping centers appeared. A *planned shopping*

This modern shopping mall in Singapore has a roof-top playground.

center is a location for retailing activity that is planned, built, and managed by a development company, which leases space to tenant retailers. Tenants pay rent for their sites, and in most cases a percentage of their sales receipts goes to the development company. One major advantage of locating in a shopping center is the expansion of the retailer's trading area. The combined pulling power of the mix of stores in a shopping center is greater than that of a freestanding store. Table 12–2 lists several advantages and disadvantages of planned shopping centers.

The *neighborhood shopping center* is the smallest type of shopping center. The main store is usually a supermarket, and it is accompanied by a hardware store, a beauty salon, a laundry, a drugstore, and a barbershop. A *community shopping center* includes, in addition to the types of stores in a neighborhood center, a small department store, several convenience stores, and perhaps several types of apparel stores.

The *regional shopping center* is the largest. First-generation centers are built around suburban branches of one or two downtown department stores. These anchor stores draw a lot of traffic. Numerous specialty shops facilitate comparison shopping between their merchandise and that offered in the anchor department stores. Second-generation centers are supercenters that may have well over a hundred stores, including several major anchor stores and numerous specialty shops. They typically are enclosed, climate-controlled shopping malls that feature fountains, pedestrian rest areas, fashion shows, and other coordinated promotional activities. Theaters, health clubs, day-care facilities, children's playgrounds, restaurants, branch banks and libraries, and professionals such as physicians, dentists, public accountants, and lawyers are often located in these malls. Some malls issue credit cards that have no annual fee.

The largest mall in the United States, the Mall of America, is in the Minneapolis suburb of Bloomington, Minnesota. The 4.5-million-square-foot mall has 4 department stores, 400 specialty shops, and 12,000 parking spaces.[49]

Because of intense competition among malls in most urban areas, mall operators are constantly looking for new retailing concepts with which to differentiate themselves. Over a decade ago the Rouse Company, which operates shopping centers across the United States, started allowing cash-poor entrepreneurs to sell merchandise from mobile carts or stalls in mall locations. This enables the pushcart operator to test the market without having to make a big investment. Those that succeed can then graduate to leased store space.[50]

TABLE 12–2 ▮ Advantages and Disadvantages of Planned Shopping Centers

Advantages	Disadvantages
1. There is free parking for shoppers.	1. Some developers do not provide adequate maintenance and upkeep.
2. Buildings in the center are carefully planned, designed, and constructed.	2. Some developers plan only for the short run, and these centers may be too small soon after they are built.
3. Maintenance services are provided to tenants in the center.	3. Some small retailers, especially new businesses, may be excluded because they may not help in building customer traffic in the center.
4. Individual retailers can cooperate in promoting shopping at the center.	4. Rents usually are high because a large amount of space is taken up by parking areas, which do not produce any sales per square foot.
5. All tenants must abide by the developer's rules, which helps to develop and maintain an overall uniform shopper image of the center.	
6. People in the center are there to shop, not on their way to work, as is common of downtown traffic.	
7. A center with a good image helps to build the store's image.	

Some retailers prefer to locate at a freestanding site. They do not want to locate near other stores because they believe their merchandise offering is sufficiently broad and deep and they do not want to share the traffic they generate.

Store Image Decisions

To a retailer a store's image is the mental picture, or personality, of the store that the retailer tries to project to consumers. To a consumer a store's image is the person's attitude about the store. Image is affected by advertising, services, convenience, store layout, and personnel, as well as by the quality, price, breadth, and depth of merchandise. Consumers tend to shop in stores that fit their images of themselves, and successful retailers project store images that fit the images that target customers have of themselves. The Saks Fifth Avenue ad reinforces this retailer's fashion image.

When the Gap bought Banana Republic in 1983, the stores featured an Indiana Jones safari look. The customers loved it. But several years later nothing much had been done to update the merchandise or the stores, and the image of Banana Republic declined. Thus the jungle motif was toned down and more fashionable, higher-priced goods were added to the clothing mix.[51]

An ad that reinforces this retailer's fashion image.

(Saks Fifth Avenue.)

VERY SAKS FIFTH AVENUE

CASUAL LUXURY GOES OVER THE TOP WITH THIS, THE LATEST MOVE IN CASHMERE. EXCLUSIVELY AT SAKS IN MEN'S SWEATER COLLECTIONS, OUR MULTI-COLOR ARGYLE CREW-NECK FOR SIZES S,M,L,XL, $595 (95-908). TO ORDER BY PHONE, CALL 1-800-345-3454. BY FAX, 1-800-221-3297. TO RECEIVE A COMPLIMENTARY COPY OF OUR LATEST FOLIO CATALOGUE, CALL 1-800-322-7257. WE ACCEPT ALL MAJOR CREDIT CARDS.

Frederick's of Hollywood has remodeled its stores, changed its advertising, and altered its merchandise mix to move its salacious image closer to the mainstream. According to a retail consultant: "They've gone from X-rated to R. They've abandoned their sluttishness." Store mannequins are less brassy, ads now appear in *Vogue* and *Redbook* and not in *Hustler* and *Penthouse,* and explicit books and sex games are no longer stocked.[52]

Store Personnel Decisions

A retailer's sales personnel can help build customer loyalty and store image. Unfortunately, a main complaint in many lines of retailing is the poor job done by salesclerks. The causes include the low esteem often accorded by people to retail sales work and the tendency of many retailers to underinvest in training. More and more retailers, however, are recognizing the role that store personnel play in providing customer service. They are investing in training programs to convert order-taking salesclerks into effective sales associates.

The sales staff at Home Depot, the do-it-yourself home repair chain, is known for giving good advice. The company hires workers with experience in the building trades, and before a new store is opened nearly every new worker receives four weeks of training. The training costs can amount to $400,000 per store.[53]

On the other hand, many retailers are focusing more on self-service. Some stores are even experimenting with electronic salesclerks. To prevent long delays at the check-out line, Pathmark has installed Check Robot, an automatic check-out machine, in some stores. You check yourself out. Eight months after installing Check Robot, Pathmark found 30 percent of its customers using the system. According to a company spokesperson, "They do it themselves so they have the perception that they get out of the store faster."[54]

Store Design Decisions

A store's exterior design and interior design affect its image and profit potential. *Atmospherics* is the term used to refer to a retailer's effort to design a store's physical surroundings to attract target customers.[55] A discount store wants to avoid an atmosphere of exclusiveness, and a prestige dress shop wants exclusivity.

Merchandise display is also important. For example, effective layout in a supermarket helps ensure that shoppers are directed through the produce department, where margins are high, before they reach the departments that sell low-margin products.

Promotion Decisions

Retail promotion includes all communication from retailers to consumers and between salespeople and consumers. Its objectives are to build and enhance the store's image, build customer traffic, and sell specific products. It includes personal and nonpersonal promotion.

Personal promotion is personal selling—face-to-face communication between salespeople and consumers. Department stores, fashionable-clothing stores, and jewelry stores stress it; supermarkets and discount stores stress nonpersonal promotion.

The major type of nonpersonal promotion is advertising. Retailers use such advertising media as TV, radio, newspapers, and billboards. Other promotion methods include displays, special sales, and contests. Retailers also engage in direct marketing, as we will see in chapter 16.

Wal-Mart, Sears, and Home Depot are among the many retailers that have adopted everyday low prices. They no longer have to advertise weekly sales. Home Depot's ad expenses were 3.2 percent of sales in 1985. The company adopted the everyday low price policy in 1987. In 1989 ad expenses were just 1.5 percent of sales.[56]

MAJOR TRENDS IN RETAILING

Retailing is changing. Several of the major trends in retailing are discussed in the sections that follow.

Growth of Mini-Malls

From the 1950s through the 1970s real estate developers built shopping centers in the suburbs, and the downtown areas of most larger cities deteriorated as centers of retail activity. During the 1980s many downtown shopping malls were built. Examples include The Gallery in Philadelphia, Harborplace in Baltimore, and Union Station in St. Louis. These malls differ from the second-generation suburban supercenters discussed earlier. Many combine retail stores with new hotels, condominiums, or office buildings. People who work downtown, conventioneers, and tourists make up a big part of their customer base. In general they target higher-income customers with their prestigious specialty shops, restaurants, and department stores. This also helps attract suburbanites.

In the 1990s more and more mini-malls are being built. For example, the Gap is working with a mall developer to build an anchorless, open-air miniature mall in Wheaton, Illinois. The Gap will set up its clothing store in a small "town square" format, with about fifty other upscale specialty shops taking up some 180,000 square feet. Big regional malls, in contrast, usually have more than a hundred shops and two or three department stores and can occupy millions of square feet.[57] A major attraction of mini-malls is that they are more accessible than regional malls and reduce shopping hassles. The developers of the mini-mall in Wheaton describe it as "automobile and pedestrian friendly."[58]

Strip malls are also gaining increasing favor over the more expensive enclosed malls as retailers seek lower operating costs. Increasingly these strip malls will attract big-name tenants, thereby making the malls more upscale.

In general, strip shopping center developers and mall developers are encountering more difficulty in securing financing for new projects. This is due in part to tougher lending restrictions by financial institutions in light of the difficulties in the savings and loan and banking industries.[59] Financial problems have caused some major anchor department stores to close. This hurts the malls and many of their smaller tenants, which depend on the traffic the anchors generate. One result may be that department store anchors may play a lesser role in malls. We are likely to see more and more anchorless mini-malls.

Growth of Factory Outlet and Discount Malls

Manufacturers opened the first factory outlet stores to sell off surplus inventories, outdated merchandise, and rejects. This gave manufacturers greater control over the distribution of the merchandise than would selling it to off-price retailers. The newer factory outlets are more attractive and carry the same kind of top-quality merchandise they sell through higher-margin retailers. To prevent channel conflict a manufacturer opening an outlet store will locate it away from its traditional retailers and often operate it under a different name. For example, Oshkosh B'Gosh, a manufacturer of children's clothing, uses the name "Genuine Article" in its outlet stores.[60]

Factory outlets are being opened in malls that also contain a large number of discount outlets, many of which are operated by traditional retailers, such as Saks Fifth Avenue and

Neiman-Marcus. Travelers and tourists account for a big proportion of the customers in outlet-and-discount malls. That's one reason a 1.5 million-square-foot outlet mall was recently built in Niagara Falls.[61]

The world's biggest outlet-and-discount mall is Sawgrass Mills, near Fort Lauderdale. The 2.2-million-square-foot mall has 2 miles of storefronts, and the parking lot covers 170 acres. All factory outlets and discount outlets offer goods at 20 to 60 percent off the usual retail price, a requirement that is specified in the stores' leases. Sawgrass Mills is an upscale discount mega-mall.[62]

Factory outlet and discount malls are going increasingly upscale. Many of the malls are located near vacation spots because consumers on holiday are less pressed for time and are in a good mood for spending.[63] It can be expected that factory outlet and discount malls will take more and more business from department stores.

Growth of Nonstore Retailing

As we said earlier, nonstore retailing is growing at a faster rate than in-store retailing, and this growth will probably accelerate. The Direct Selling Education Foundation and the Direct Marketing Association are especially active in promoting this rapidly growing area of retailing. We will discuss direct marketing in chapter 16.

Diversification and Concentration of Offerings

Many retailers are diversifying their offerings. In recent years Sears has earned more from its financial services arm (including Dean Witter, Allstate Insurance, Coldwell Banker Real Estate, and Discover Card) than it has from its retail division.[64] Another approach to diversification is buying or starting specialty shops. Limited Inc. operates The Limited, Limited Express, Lerner Shops, Lane Bryant, Victoria's Secret, Bendel, and Abercrombie & Fitch.

The trend among some large retailers of serving market niches with specialty shops is likely to continue, although competition is becoming more and more intense. Consider the children's clothing market. Among the many "nichers" are Kids "R" Us, Gap Kids, and Limited with its Limited Too children's sections in its specialty stores. Others include Woolworth's Kids Mart and Little Folk Shop chains and Sears's Kids & More departments.[65]

On the other hand, some retailers are succeeding by concentrating their offerings. Although the retail video industry is becoming dominated by big national chains, such as Blockbuster Entertainment, some firms are concentrating on niches. An example is Video Vault in Alexandria, Virginia. Among its many titles is a specialty collection of hard-to-find cult movie classics.[66] A growing number of entrepreneurs are entering retailing with kiosks and carts, usually in malls. Some malls rent carts to merchants for short terms of three days to several months, often before holidays and around back-to-school time. The ability to move or to make a business seasonal attracts some people into the cart and kiosk business.[67]

What appears to be happening is that medium-sized retailers are being pressured from the top by large diversified retailers and from the bottom by small specialty shops. They are finding it more difficult to compete solely on a price or service basis.

Greater Emphasis on Productivity and Professional Management

In 1978 the average revenue per square foot in retail stores was $191.47. In 1990 it was $160.90.[68] Retailers therefore are seeking ways to become more productive. For example,

Safeway's 1989 revenues worked out to $400 per square foot. Management knows that if it can increase sales by just 4 percent, the bottom line will grow 21 percent.[69]

More and more retailers are taking steps to control their costs. Consider that Wal-Mart's operating expenses are about 15 percent of revenues. Sears's run closer to 30 percent.[70] The Cerritos Auto Square is an 80-acre outdoor auto mall near Los Angeles. Customers can walk or drive the half-mile stretch, where eighteen franchises are scattered. According to a spokesperson, the eight dealers who own more than one franchise there are able to lower their operational costs by consolidating some management positions and collectively training personnel. They enjoy economies of scale.[71]

Retailers are also placing more emphasis on professional management—executives who have both merchandising and management skills. Retailers generally have been slower than manufacturers in applying management science techniques because they have not had up-to-the-minute data on sales by department and customer. Modern point-of-sale terminals are remedying this situation.

Greater Impact of Technology on Shopping Behavior

The ways retailers present their merchandise and conduct their transactions are changing. (We will discuss this in greater detail in chapter 16.) The use of cable-TV channels to present merchandise, of videos for catalogs, and of computer linkages to both acquire product information and make purchases will continue to increase. Retailers are gaining increased understanding of their customers from more intensive use of the data they have available from scanners and computerized terminals.

Walgreen Company recently squeezed a prototype mini-store into a narrow shop about a mile and a half from three other Walgreen drugstores. Part of the company's marketing strategy is computer screening of prescription orders by zip code. This analysis indicated that the three drugstores were not getting many customers from the area between them. Walgreen therefore opened the new store with prescriptions as the basic attraction.[72]

Greater Focus on Differentiation

A recent study on shopping found that for many people "the thrill is gone." "Retailers hawk look-alike merchandise in stores that are numbingly similar in appearance."[73] To generate loyalty retailers are increasingly striving for differentiation. Without taking a true leadership role in some aspect of its retail offering, a retailer cannot expect to achieve a loyal following of shoppers.

Another recent study found that "baby boomer families are often debt-stressed, time-stressed, and in search of quiet downtime." Consumers are growing more cautious and less interested in flashy consumption. "Shop-till-you-drop" has become less appealing, and attracting reluctant customers into stores is getting tougher.[74]

One retailing expert advises retailers to pay more attention to demographics: "Every part of the country really is different, with clear differences in how people dress, where people go out to dinner. That dictates different shopping habits." Thus homogenized national chains will find the going tough. Those that cater to regional tastes and cultural diversity will succeed.[75]

While many malls in the United States are having difficulty, Tysons Corner Center, 11 miles west of Washington, D.C., is among the nation's most prosperous. Tysons Corner Center knows its customers' demographics, and it tailors events to its customers. It also offers sales training courses free to its mall tenants. At least three times a year the mall owner dispatches ten undercover shoppers to identify inattentive store managers and testy cashiers. A concierge booth offers copying and fax transmission services, local theater tickets, and travel planning to help set Tysons Corner Center apart from rival malls.[76]

Greater Attention to Environmental Monitoring

Retailers are monitoring the environment more closely and responding to change. According to a retail consulting firm, by the year 2000 the number of U.S. households with an annual income of $15,000 or less (in 1984 dollars) will be about 36 percent of total households, versus 31.2 percent in 1970. Those 40 million families constitute a downscale market that is too large for many retailers to ignore.[77]

For example, before Limited Inc. bought Lerner's in 1985, Lerner's was a collection of poorly lit stores that catered to lower-income working women. Limited renovated the stores to create elegant shops that still offer low prices but make the consumer feel good about herself. The flagship store in Manhattan has a high rotunda and a tuxedo-clad piano player. Nevertheless, a rayon dress costs only $60. The chain plans to expand from 800 stores in 1990 to 1,200 within two years.[78]

Haggling over retail prices traditionally has been much more common in some other countries than in the United States. During the recent recession, however, American consumers became more conscious of prices and more sensitive to price differentials. Many retailers for the first time focused on price in their ads. Some department stores started mailing their charge customers discount coupons, and many fast-food restaurants started value pricing some of their food items. Under pressure, department stores were quick to press their suppliers for price concessions.[79] Among the issues raised in the Ethics in Marketing box is retail pricing practices.

Often it is not easy to interpret the significance of environmental developments. New York's Place des Antiquaires is the city's most glamorous shopping mall. The underground mall opened in November 1987, one month after the stock market crash and one week after Vincent van Gogh's *Irises* was auctioned for $53.9 million. Mall merchants targeted the upper-middle market, where affluent young professionals pay thousands of dollars for less-than-masterpiece works. But the strategy backfired. Although demand from the wealthy continued to inflate prices of masterpieces, the upper-middle market was hurt by the economic slowdown in the Northeast, including extensive layoffs in the financial industry.[80]

THE WHEEL OF RETAILING

Like products, retail institutions have a life cycle. For example, the warehouse club is in the growth stage, the discount store is in the maturity stage, and the variety store is in the decline stage. Furthermore, just as life cycles are getting shorter for products, they are getting shorter for retail institutions.

The *wheel of retailing* is a hypothesis that attempts to explain the emergence of new retailing institutions and their eventual decline and replacement by newer retailing institutions.[81] According to this hypothesis, new retail institutions enter the market as low-margin, low-price, low-status institutions. They locate their bare-bones facilities in low-rent areas and offer few customer services. They do, however, challenge conventional retailers, whose costs and prices have gone up over time. But the innovative retailers' suc-

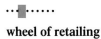

wheel of retailing

ETHICS IN MARKETING

Retailers appear to be bombarding consumers with a never-ending series of sales and markdowns. Is it ethical to put highly inflated fictitious price tags on merchandise, mark down the prices to a realistic level, and then advertise a "sale"? Suppose a chain of consumer electronics stores challenges consumers in its advertising to find a lower price for identical merchandise. Suppose further that the particular items of merchandise featured in the ads are manufactured exclusively for this retail chain. Is that ethical?

Retailers were among the first to focus on environmental concerns in their advertising. Environmental efforts of "green retailers" range from supermarkets selling their own lines of "green" products to department stores proclaiming ivory "out of fashion." It is less costly for retailers to become involved in environmentalism than it is for manufacturers. Retailers, for example, do not have to invest resources in costly product research and development activities. The low cost of entry into green marketing for retailers makes the cause an easy one to hype in their advertising. Is it ethical for them to build ad campaigns around an environmental theme while they still sell products that are known to cause environmental damage? What about charging very high prices for some "green products"? Might that discourage some consumers from buying them?

What about *slotting allowances*—payments that supermarket chains demand up front from manufacturers that want the retailer to make space for a new product? In recent years there has been a big increase in the practice of supermarkets demanding cash and local media advertising from food manufacturers. Among the results of the growing trend are fewer choices for consumers and a barrier to entry for smaller food manufacturers, which cannot afford to buy their way into supermarkets. Some supermarkets also demand *pay-to-stay* fees. These are payments to keep the manufacturer's products on the shelves. Are supermarkets acting ethically when they require manufacturers to make such payments?

Some retail stores and shopping malls have taken steps to discourage teenagers from shopping. Some convenience stores have made it more difficult for teens to "hang out." Actions include removing video games, window ledges, and flat-topped trash cans that teenagers sit on. Some malls have banned teens who are unaccompanied by adults. Others regulate the hours during which teens can shop. What ethical issues are involved in such actions?

Retailers today are dedicating themselves as never before to providing unparalleled customer service. Can management go overboard with demands on retail salespeople? For example, would it be ethical for a department store to require its salespeople to engage in non-selling activities on their own time and without being paid for them? Examples of such activities are writing thank-you letters to customers and sending out postcards informing customers of newly arrived merchandise.

Employee pilferage and shoplifting are major problems for retailers. What ethical issues might arise as retailers attempt to cope with these problems? What about the use of honesty tests for job applicants and surveillance of employees and shoppers?

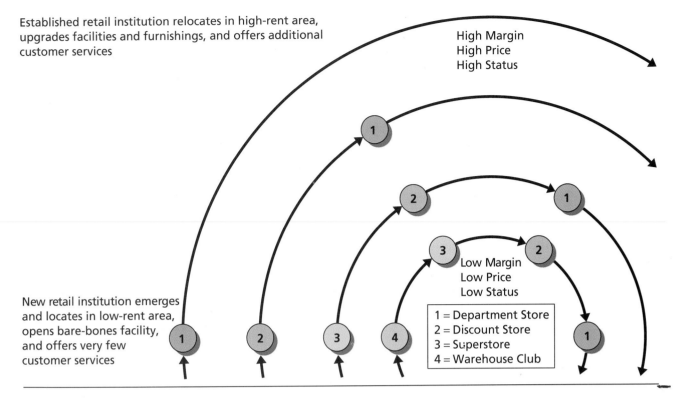

Established retail institution relocates in high-rent area, upgrades facilities and furnishings, and offers additional customer services

High Margin
High Price
High Status

Low Margin
Low Price
Low Status

1 = Department Store
2 = Discount Store
3 = Superstore
4 = Warehouse Club

New retail institution emerges and locates in low-rent area, opens bare-bones facility, and offers very few customer services

FIGURE 12–4
. . . .

The Wheel of Retailing

cess leads the innovators to relocate in higher-rent areas, to upgrade their facilities and furnishings, and to add numerous customer services. Thus they become increasingly similar to the conventional retailers they originally displaced. They too become high-margin, high-price, high-status retailers—vulnerable to newer types of low-margin, low-price, low-status retailers. Thus the wheel turns again.

Figure 12–4 shows the wheel of retailing for the department store, discount store, superstore, and warehouse club. Each emerged as a low-margin, low-price, low-status retail institution. Gradually, however, each moved up the wheel in the direction of becoming a higher-margin, higher-price, higher-status institution. As each successive retail institution emerges, it in effect turns the wheel, moving its predecessor up the wheel.

The wheel of retailing appears to explain the development of such retailing institutions as supermarkets and discount stores. It also seems to explain why supermarkets and discount stores have developed difficulties in competing with warehouse stores and warehouse clubs. The hypothesis, however, does not explain the evolution and growth of suburban shopping centers and downtown malls. They emerged as high-margin, high-price, high-status institutions. The hypothesis does not enable us to predict which specific type of institutions will emerge or when they will appear.

The factory outlet and discount mall emerged as a result of discount stores going increasingly upscale. As we saw earlier however, Sawgrass Mills is an upscale form of the factory outlet and discount mall. What will eventually replace this form of retailing?

To keep out of the wheel of retailing spiral, an innovative retailer should avoid changes that make it more like the conventional retailer it originally displaced. This, however, is difficult to do. For example, it would require the innovative retailer to continue focusing on price competition, and many retailers are reluctant to do so. New retailing forms and institutions will therefore continue to emerge.

SUMMARY OF LEARNING OBJECTIVES

1. Identify several bases for classifying retail firms.

Five bases are (a) form of ownership—sole proprietorship, partnership, corporation, and consumer cooperative; (b) operational structure—independent retailer, chain retailer, association of independents, and franchise organization; (c) price and service orientation—high service–low price, high service–high price, high price–low service, and low price–low service; (d) merchandise offering—merchandise breadth and depth; and (e) where the retail sale takes place—in-store retailing and nonstore retailing.

2. Identify the major types of in-store retailers.

In-store retailers include (a) specialty merchandisers—single-line stores, limited-line stores, and specialty shops; (b) general merchandisers—general stores, variety stores, and department stores; and (c) mass merchandisers—supermarkets, warehouse showrooms, superstores, catalog showrooms, combination stores, warehouse clubs, hypermarkets, and discount stores.

3. Give examples of nonstore retailing.

Examples include direct selling (door-to-door selling, route selling, party-plan selling, and custom selling) and automatic vending.

4. Describe how a franchising system works.

A franchising system is an arrangement in which a franchisor, which has developed an idea and business procedures that can be duplicated, licenses franchisees to copy the idea and procedures. A franchising agreement is a contract between the franchisor and the franchisee that spells out their respective rights and obligations.

5. Identify several major types of retailing decisions.

Among the major types of retailing decisions are those related to target markets, merchandise management, store location, store image, store personnel, store design, and promotion.

6. Identify several major trends in retailing.

Among the major trends are the growth of mini-malls, the growth of factory outlet and discount malls, the growth of nonstore retailing, diversification and concentration of offerings, greater emphasis on productivity and professional management, greater impact of technology on shopping behavior, greater focus on differentiation, and greater attention to environmental monitoring.

7. Explain the wheel of retailing hypothesis.

The wheel of retailing is a hypothesis that attempts to explain the emergence of new retailing institutions and their eventual decline and replacement by newer retailing institutions. According to this hypothesis, new retail institutions enter the market as low-margin, low-price, low-status institutions. Eventually they become increasingly similar to the conventional retailers they originally displaced. That is, they become high-margin, high-price, high-status retailers—vulnerable to newer types of low-margin, low-price, low-status retailers. Thus the wheel turns again.

Review Questions

1. What is retailing's role in marketing channels?

2. How do retailers add value to the merchandise they sell?

3. How does the positioning of a service-oriented retailer differ from that of a price-oriented retailer?

4. What are merchandise breadth and depth? Give examples.

5. What are specialty merchandisers, general merchandisers, and mass merchandisers? Give examples of each.

6. What is scrambled merchandising? Why do so many retailers practice it?

7. What is nonstore retailing?

8. How does a franchising system work?

9. What is involved in merchandise management?

10. How do unplanned shopping areas differ from planned shopping centers?

11. What does the wheel of retailing attempt to do?

Discussion Questions

1. Sears, J. C. Penney, and Kmart have put forth a lot of effort in recent years to develop a trendier image among consumers. Why? How successful do you think each company has been?

2. European retailers are far ahead of American retailers in terms of airport operations. What types of goods and services would lend themselves to successful airport retailing?

3. Are department stores becoming an endangered species of retail stores? Explain.

4. Safeway recently introduced a home delivery service called Shoppers Express. For a $12 fee, customers can order groceries over the phone and have them delivered to their homes.

Neighborhood grocery stores provided home delivery many years ago. Nevertheless, the majority of people in the supermarket business today would probably say that Safeway's home delivery service is innovative. What do you think?

Application Exercise

Reread the material about Barneys at the beginning of this chapter and answer the following questions:

1. Is the Barneys that exists today a specialty merchandiser, a general merchandiser, or a mass merchandiser? Explain.

2. How would you describe Barneys in terms of breadth and depth of merchandise?

3. How would you describe Barneys' image?

4. What is the nature of Barneys' marketing quandary?

5. Do you think Barneys will be successful in its efforts to go national? Explain.

Key Concepts

The following key terms were introduced in this chapter:

retailing
retailer
merchandise breadth
merchandise depth
nonstore retailing
scrambled merchandising
specialty merchandisers
specialty shop
general store

variety store
department store
supermarket
superstore
combination store
hypermarket
discount store
warehouse showroom

catalog showroom
warehouse club
direct selling
automatic vending
franchising system
unplanned shopping area
planned shopping center
wheel of retailing

CASES

Kmart Fights Back

Wal-Mart Stores, the fantastically successful chain of discount stores headquartered in Bentonville, Arkansas, is on top of the world. It is currently rated as the fifth most valuable corporation in the United States, with sales of $32.6 billion in 1990, and the company has just announced its first international expansion, a joint venture with a Mexican retailer.

Running slightly behind Wal-Mart, with sales of $32.1 billion in 1990, is Kmart; behind Kmart comes Sears, formerly number one in the United States, with sales of $32 billion. But Wal-Mart has been growing much faster than either of its rivals, with a 34 percent rate of sales increase since 1980, compared with 8 percent for Kmart. Neither Kmart nor Sears seems ready to give in to the pressure of Wal-Mart's competition, and Kmart in particular has laid plans for a comeback.

Kmart CEO Joseph Antonini concedes that Kmart made some crucial mistakes in the 1970s by moving away from the concept of the giant store. The company decided that smaller stores could better serve smaller markets, and the company opened 1,100 new stores that were as small as 40,000 square feet, instead of the 80,000-square-foot store that had been Kmart's standard. The company also passed up an opportunity to get into the membership warehouse club market, which has yielded big profits for Wal-Mart, choosing instead to diversify into other kinds of chains such as Builders Square, Waldenbooks, and Pay Less Drug Stores. Today, Antonini's plans call for reversing the pattern of shrinking stores. By the end of 1995, the company will have refurbished, expanded, closed, or relocated almost all of its 2,300 North American stores. And Kmart is moving into the warehouse market through acquisition of existing warehouse clubs.

Kmart's old discount stores looked dilapidated, small, and crowded compared to the newer Wal-Mart or Target stores, and prices were often higher. An outdated inventory system meant that items were frequently out of stock. Finally, store personnel were less than friendly and enthusiastic. Kmart's new stores will look like the recently opened prototype in Oak Park, Michigan: brightly lit, with wide aisles, larger racks, big signs, and contemporary graphics. The inventory system has been replaced with computerized point-of-sale registers that are linked by satellite to corporate headquarters, so sales and inventories can be closely tracked. And Antonini communicates directly with all employees several times a month via the satellite system, to explain goals and boost morale.

Will Kmart be able to make a turnaround in a declining or static economy? So far, sales at the new Oak Park store have exceeded the sales plan by 40 percent; the store produces $280 in sales per square foot, versus the Kmart average of $189. By the end of 1991 Antonini expects to have 30 percent of Kmart's stores transformed into the new format, and he plans to have completed the overhaul by 1995. Kmart and its CEO are determined to give Wal-Mart—and Sears—a run for their money.

Questions

1. Which of Kmart's recent problems probably affected the retailer's image? Explain.

2. How would you evaluate Kmart's merchandise control?

3. Does Antonini's expansion into warehouse clubs make sense? Why?

4. Is Kmart trapped in the world of retailing spiral? Explain.

TCBY: Lifecycle Swirl

DONALD G. ANDERSON, *Ouachita Baptist University*
DENNIS J. ELBERT, *University of North Dakota*

TCBY Enterprises is the largest franchiser of frozen yogurt stores in the United States. Headquartered in Little Rock, Arkansas, the company accounts for approximately one-third of industry sales through its more than 1900 stores. The founder and head of TCBY Enterprises is Frank Hickingbotham. Hickingbotham opened his first frozen yogurt store in Little Rock in 1981 under the name, "This Can't Be Yogurt." He soon determined that his operation had potential for franchising.

Within two years Hickingbotham started more than forty stores, most of which were franchised outlets. The company continued its rapid expansion during the next several years. By the end of 1984 TCBY had 102 outlets. In 1986, there were 458 stores in operation and 1582 in 1989. Company sales grew from $1.5 million in 1982 to $132 million in 1989.

During the 1980s TCBY capitalized on the growing demand for frozen yogurt. Although yogurt had been marketed for many years, *frozen* yogurt was a somewhat unique product when the first TCBY store was established. TCBY used such slogans as, "All the pleasure, none of the guilt," to appeal to consumers who saw frozen yogurt as a healthy alternative to other dairy desserts. The company's success in marketing both yogurt and the company enabled TCBY to state in its 1988 annual report that it was the fourth fastest growth company in America.

Starting in 1990, TCBY's fortunes experienced a downturn. Company sales increased slightly to $134 million. However, profits declined from a 1989 high of $28 million to $20 million. Some store sales had begun to fall even while the company was achieving its record increases in sales and profits. Thus, the sales increase was mainly due to the addition of new outlets. In late 1990 an independent analyst estimated that nearly a quarter of TCBY franchisees were failing. In Florida, a TCBY franchisee with thirty-four stores filed for bankruptcy. Franchisees were faced with increased competition from recent entrants into the frozen yogurt industry. Frozen yogurt was now dispensed in such outlets as supermarkets and gas stations. Traditional ice cream competitors—including Dairy Queen and Baskin-Robbins—now offered frozen yogurt as part of their product line. Even fast-food restaurants began to sell frozen yogurt.

Some TCBY franchisees have said that TCBY should be doing more to help them meet the increased competition; they are concerned about the decline in store sales. On the other hand, a company representative has indicated that the present unfavorable situation may be short-lived. Although franchisees may temporarily lose some customers to competition, in the long run competitors' promotional efforts could expand the total number of customers for frozen yogurt.

Nevertheless, to ease short-run problems, TCBY has considered a number of changes and has begun to implement some. The company has begun to follow the lead of fast-food restaurants such as Taco Bell and McDonald's in the adoption of "value pricing." This entails reducing the prices of some menu items. TCBY has offered its franchisees the option of setting lower prices on selected menu items, such as frozen yogurt cones. The company is also adding new products to enable its stores to differentiate their product line from generic yogurt sold elsewhere. For example, TCBY has introduced "Ultra Slim Fast" yogurt desserts for the diet-conscious consumer. In addition, franchisees are now allowed to sell products such as frozen yogurt bars to restaurants and other vendors.

As TCBY faces increased competition in the next decade it must seek to maintain its position as the industry leader and rectify its sales and earnings problem. One solution might be to enable and equip stores to prepare and market food items which would make up an entire meal. Another possible solution would be to emphasize sales to grocery stores and to expand overseas franchising. Whatever action the company elects to take must be taken soon if it is to remain the industry leader.

Questions

1. How would you describe the depth and breath of TCBY's offering?

2. What advantages do you see in opening a TCBY franchise, as opposed to opening your own frozen yogurt store?

3. Do you think that TCBY should have adopted value pricing? Why?

4. To enable its franchisees to compete more effectively, should TCBY Enterprises permit them to broaden their product line to include nonyogurt products? Explain.

13

WHOLESALING AND
LOGISTICS

It was in 1985 that Sheila West realized she had a problem. She was expanding her archery business from retail to wholesale, and to succeed as a distributor, she needed a reliable base of archery dealerships. That was the rub. Archery dealers were notoriously unreliable as retailers. They typically set up shop out of devotion to bow hunting, not commerce. A pastime would become a passion and, finally, a business. All too often those businesses failed.

For her company's sake, West decided she had to help her would-be customers become more reliable. She struck on the idea of a trade show. Now, once a year, West's Archery Center International (ACI) stages the Pow Wow, a trade show with a difference. Unlike other such events it is not designed primarily to push products. Rather, its purpose is to instruct customers in the fundamentals of business. "The bottom line is that an educated dealer will be a better dealer and run a better store and sell more merchandise," says West. "When that happens, it's good for us."

Indeed, it has been very good for ACI. Since 1985 the company has increased its annual sales from $540,000 to $3.8 million, while establishing a customer base of some 800 dealers. The Pow Wow has played an important role in that growth. It has also placed ACI in the thick of a quiet but intriguing trend. In a wide range of industries, companies are developing marketing campaigns built around customer education. Their premise is simple enough: they believe that, to succeed in business, it's not enough to have customers—what you really need are smart customers.

The Wests entered the archery business in 1980 by buying a small pro shop in Monroe, Michigan. By 1984 they had moved into wholesaling and were planning to open a large distribution facility on a 10-acre site outside town. With 5,000 or so archery dealers nationwide, the market was certainly large enough. What concerned Sheila West, the company's CEO, was its volatility. She thought she could minimize the problem with education, but that presented a challenge. These guys were hunters, after all, not bookworms. They were not likely to show up for a weekend of seminars.

A trade show, on the other hand, had drawing power. In the archery business technology is always changing. West figured that dealers would welcome an opportunity to see the latest equipment and get a jump on competitors by being first with the best new gear. If the event generated sales for ACI, so much the better. But she believed the company would benefit most over the long term by making the dealers better businesspeople, and that was her primary goal.

Whether she could pull it off was another matter. One industry expert told her she'd be lucky to draw fifty dealers. The industry's major event, the Shooting and Hunting Outdoor Trade Show, brings in upwards of 30,000 people. But a show thrown by a single distributor? That was unheard of.

It wasn't even clear that West could attract the manufacturers she needed to fill booths with bows, sights, camouflage clothing, and other items of the trade. She called up the biggest names in the business and asked them to come. Much to her surprise, nearly 50 factory reps and company presidents accepted invitations.

As it turned out, the first show in 1986 attracted seventy-five dealers. The 1987 show attracted 110 dealers, and thereafter the Pow Wow continued to grow in size, sophistication, and recognition. By 1989 the trade press was writing it up in glowing terms and heaping accolades on ACI. The 1990 show drew more than 100 manufacturers and 250 dealers, many of whom brought their spouses. The total turnout topped 600.

West attributes the gain to the popularity of the numerous show specials that provide product discounts as high as 8 percent. For small retailers who don't usually make the major industry shows, the specials are an important part of the Pow Wow's appeal. For ACI, the benefits go beyond sales. With all those dealers in one place, the company has an opportunity to garner a wealth of marketing information. Among other things, it uses trade-show purchasing trends to help fine-tune its inventory requirements.

What West finds most gratifying, however, is the growing popularity of the Pow Wow's educational offerings. At the first show, only one-third of the attendees went to the seminars. Now sessions on such topics as tax law, pricing, and marketing routinely pull in 80 to 90 percent of the dealers.[1]

Archery Center International (ACI) is an example of a wholesaling intermediary that is getting closer to its retail customers and its manufacturer-suppliers. The Pow Wow trade show is a key part of ACI's efforts to help its retail customers to become more effective businesspeople. The educational seminars which are held during the trade show enhance ACI's retail customers' business skills. The trade show also benefits ACI and its manufacturer-suppliers.

In this chapter we study what wholesaling is and identify the various types of wholesaling intermediaries. We also look at major wholesaling decisions and trends in the industry. The second major topic in the chapter is logistics, which is concerned primarily with the physical flows through marketing channels. We examine its growing importance in marketing channels and identify its major components—warehousing, inventory control, materials handling, order processing, and transportation.

WHAT IS WHOLESALING?

wholesaling

Wholesaling is the activities of firms that sell to retailers, to other intermediaries, or to other organizational buyers but do not sell (except perhaps in small amounts) to ultimate consumers. The price at which a product is sold does not determine whether the seller is a retailer or a wholesaling intermediary. The classification depends on which type of customer (ultimate consumer or organizational buyer) accounts for more than half of the firm's sales revenues.

Sometimes it is difficult to determine whether a firm should be classified as a wholesaling intermediary or a retailer. Take, for example, 4day Tire Stores, based in Irvine, California. The stores are open Wednesday through Saturday. On Tuesdays store managers work as wholesalers, selling to service stations and other independent tire dealers. The wholesaling business accounts for half of 4day's overall sales. The added volume gives the chain the leverage to negotiate lower prices from tire manufacturers. Thus 4day's prices are about 10 percent lower than local competitors'. According to 4day's chief executive, ''We tell the little [retailing] guy, 'Let us stock the tires for you.' '' This is a good deal for many small retailers. The owner of two small tire stores near Disneyland says, ''It's cheaper for me to buy from 4day than to go to a manufacturer.''[2]

Because wholesale sales receipts do not include a retailer's markup and because many products sold at retail never pass through a wholesaling intermediary, one might expect total retail sales to be greater than total wholesale sales. But in fact total wholesale sales are greater. One reason is that more than half of wholesaling intermediaries' sales are made to customers other than retailers. These sales involve industrial products. Another reason

TABLE 13–1 ▌ Examples of Marketing Functions That Wholesaling Intermediaries Perform for Their Suppliers

1. Selling.	Act as extensions of manufacturers' sales force; Seek out supply sources and reduce manufacturers' need for sales personnel.
2. Stocking.	Reduce manufacturers' need to carry large inventories and make heavy investment in warehousing by dispersing inventories instead of concentrating them at factories.
3. Financing.	Reduce warehousing costs; Reduce manufacturers' commitment of working capital to inventory; Enable manufacturers to conserve working capital by receiving payment for products before they are sold to final buyers; Screen credit applicants, which reduces bad debts.
4. Gathering market information.	Reduce manufacturers' need for marketing research because of closer contact with manufacturers' final buyers.
5. Reducing risk.	Assume risk in credit sales; Assume risk of owning title to products; Assume risk of carrying inventory; Order in advance and help even out production scheduling.

is that a product, as it moves through its marketing channel, may be sold to a sequence of several wholesalers, and each sale constitutes a wholesale sale. The sale of the product at the retail level, however, counts as only one sale.

Table 13–1 shows some of the marketing functions wholesaling intermediaries help their *suppliers* perform—selling, stocking, financing, gathering market information, and reducing risk. Table 13–2 shows some of the marketing functions wholesaling intermediaries help their *customers* perform—buying, stocking, gathering market information, financing, reducing risk, contacting, and concentrating and dispersing.

Although the marketing functions cannot be eliminated, they can be shifted and shared among channel members. When a retailer buys directly from a producer, the retailer and the producer perform activities that could have been performed by a wholesaling intermediary. Thus some firms engage in wholesaling activities although they are not wholesaling intermediaries.

Wholesaling intermediaries perform one or more services for their customers and suppliers. In some channels they perform very few services. This occurs when other channel members assume services or functions. When Campbell Soup Company sells directly to Safeway, it bypasses wholesaling intermediaries. Instead of having the intermediaries provide credit, delivery, and other services, either Campbell or Safeway provides them. Wholesaling intermediaries can be eliminated, but the marketing functions cannot.

In general, intermediaries that do not perform marketing functions efficiently are eliminated and their functions are assumed by other channel members. Look at Figure 13–1. In

TABLE 13–2   Examples of Marketing Functions That Wholesaling Intermediaries Perform for Their Customers

1. Buying.	Forecast customer product requirements; Buy products to meet those requirements; Have sales representatives call on customers.
2. Stocking.	Carry inventory so customers can operate with smaller inventories; Help customers avoid over- and underbuying; Share with customers economies in operating large-scale warehouses.
3. Gathering market information.	Provide information about manufacturers and their products; Detect developing trends in their industries; Keep customers informed of competitive developments.
4. Financing.	Sell on credit; Carry inventory; Reduce customer need to commit fixed capital to construction and operation of large warehouses.
5. Reducing Risk.	Enable customers not to have to tie up as much working capital in inventory; Make it possible for small firms that might be turned down by manufacturers to buy on credit.
6. Contacting.	Own and transfer title to products without customer need to negotiate directly with manufacturers; Enable customers to spend more time on the selling function and less time on the buying function.
7. Concentrating and dispersing.	Bring together the quantity and assortment of products to meet customer requirements and disperse them to adjust for quantity and assortment discrepancies between manufacturers and customers of wholesaling intermediaries: Concentrating—buying in large quantities reduces transportation costs; Dispersing—frequent and speedy delivery reduces inventory investment.

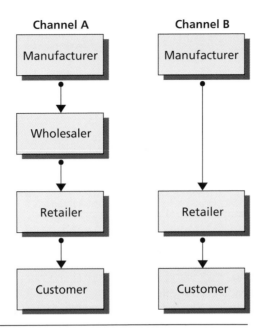

Channel A | Channel B

Manufacturer → Wholesaler → Retailer → Customer

Manufacturer → Retailer → Customer

FIGURE 13–1

Bypassing an Independent
Wholesaling Intermediary

channel B the wholesaling intermediary is bypassed and the manufacturer or retailer must perform the functions that would have been performed by the intermediary.

TYPES OF WHOLESALING INTERMEDIARIES

The Census of Wholesale Trade, which is conducted every five years, identifies five categories of wholesaling intermediaries: (1) merchant wholesalers, (2) manufacturers' sales branches and sales offices, (3) merchandise agents and brokers, (4) petroleum bulk plants and terminals, and (5) assemblers of farm products.

Merchant Wholesalers

Merchant wholesalers account for about 80 percent of all wholesaling establishments and for slightly more than half of total wholesale sales. A *merchant wholesaler* is an independently owned business that owns title to the products it offers for sale to organizational buyers. It is often referred to simply as a *wholesaler*. Merchant wholesalers that specialize in industrial products are often called *industrial distributors*. Those that specialize in consumer products are often called *jobbers*. On the basis of the services, or functions, they perform, merchant wholesalers can be divided into two types: full-service (full-function) wholesalers and limited-service (limited-function) wholesalers. (See Figure 13–2.)

merchant wholesaler

• **Full-Service Wholesalers** • The most important type of merchant wholesaler in terms of number of establishments and dollar sales volume is the full-service wholesaler. A *full-service wholesaler* is a merchant wholesaler that performs most or all of the marketing functions for its suppliers and customers. The categories of full-service wholesalers

full-service wholesaler

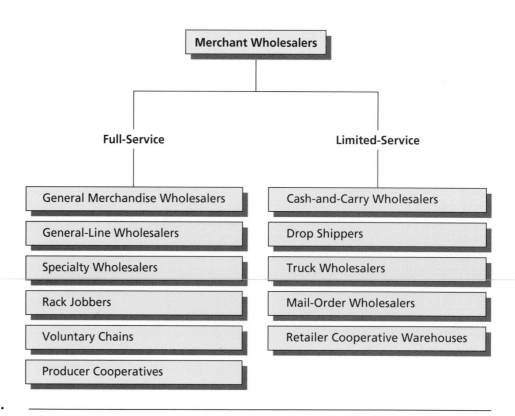

FIGURE 13–2
· ·

Merchant Wholesalers Classified
by Service Offering

are general merchandise wholesalers, general-line wholesalers, specialty wholesalers, rack jobbers, voluntary chains, and producer cooperatives.

• *General Merchandise Wholesalers* • Full-service wholesalers that stock a wide assortment of unrelated product lines, such as drug sundries, hardware, electrical supplies, auto equipment, plumbing supplies, nonperishable foods, detergents, and cosmetics, are general merchandise wholesalers. Their major customers are small grocery and department stores and small nonbusiness organizations. Their importance declined as the general store was largely replaced by retailers that carry more specialized product mixes.

• *General-Line Wholesalers* • The single most important type of wholesaler in terms of dollar sales volume is general-line wholesalers. These full-service wholesalers carry only one or two product lines but stock them in great depth. Examples are drug wholesalers, grocery wholesalers, and hardware wholesalers.

Industrial distributors are often general-line wholesalers. They might carry plumbing supplies, oil-well drilling equipment, or electrical equipment and supplies. Manufacturers often devote much effort to building good manufacturer-distributor relations—or ''partnerships.'' They realize that the use of distributors is often the most economical way to achieve total market coverage. In some cases it may be the only way.

• *Specialty Wholesalers* • Full-service wholesalers that carry one particular part of a line of products are specialty wholesalers. In the foods line, for example, they might stock only health foods, seafood, or produce. Also, because they deal with fewer producers than general merchandise and general-line wholesalers, they can provide more promotional and other types of support for their manufacturer-suppliers.

• *Rack Jobbers* • The full-service wholesalers known as rack jobbers, or service merchandisers, came about when supermarkets began expanding into high-margin nonfood items such as paperback books, health and beauty aids, and hardware. These wholesalers relieve retailers of the need to order, price, display, and keep inventory records on the racked items. The jobbers stock displays (racks or shelves) with their products and regu· larly call on retailers to restock and to take back damaged or slow-moving products. Rack jobbers collect from retailers only after the merchandise is sold. In effect, they rent space from retailers, to whom they pay a commission on the products that are sold.

• *Voluntary Chains* • Wholesaler-sponsored voluntary chains were discussed in chapters 11 and 12. Super Valu Stores, the largest grocery wholesaler in the United States, is an example of this type of full-service wholesaler. The services it provides its 2,300 affiliated retailers help them compete effectively with big corporate chain supermarkets. In fact, an executive at Super Valu prefers to think of the company as a "retail support company" rather than a wholesaler: "Super Valu can find the site, design the store, finance the equipment, set the shelves, train the butchers and clerks, plan the promotion, write the advertising, count the money, and insure the whole works, bologna to bagboy."[3]

Voluntary chains are most common in grocery retailing but also exist in hardware retailing (Ace), variety store retailing (Ben Franklin Stores), and so on. The independent retailers contract with the initiating wholesaler, which combines their purchases and gets quantity discounts. The wholesaler also may handle their advertising, inventory control, and other functions. The members use a common store name and buy from the wholesaler.

• *Producer Cooperatives* • Full-service wholesalers that are especially popular in agriculture are producer cooperatives, which are set up by farmers to help them buy and sell in large quantities. *Supply co-ops* sell fertilizer, chemicals, and petroleum to member farmers. *Marketing co-ops* enable farmers to get better prices for their output than they would if each member sold individually. Also, having a variety of agricultural products produced by member farmers permits the co-op to spread the risk inherent in farming, which would be impossible for a single-crop producer. Thus a tomato producer that has a bad year can still make a profit if other members' products sell well, because the co-op's profits are distributed among all the members. Farmland Industries, Sun-Diamond Growers of California, and Ocean Spray Cranberries are examples of producer cooperatives.

Over the years these co-ops have become more deeply involved in marketing their output. Sun-Diamond, for example, is a 6,000-member co-op. Its brands include Sun-Maid raisins, Diamond walnuts, Sunsweet prunes, and Valley figs. Sun-Diamond promotes these brand names by spending on joint promotions with supermarkets. This enables the co-op to sell to large supermarket chains directly rather than through independent food brokers, thereby gaining greater control over the distribution of its products.[4]

• **Limited-Service Wholesalers** • Figure 13–2 also identifies several types of limited-service wholesalers. A *limited-service wholesaler* is a merchant wholesaler that performs fewer marketing functions for its suppliers and customers than a full-service wholesaler performs. Limited-service wholesalers may offer their customers lower prices for forgoing services. Their appeal depends on whether their customers can perform the services they do not offer. The categories of limited-service wholesalers are cash-and-carry whole-

limited-service wholesaler

salers, drop shippers, truck wholesalers, mail-order wholesalers, and retailer cooperative warehouses.

• *Cash-and-Carry Wholesalers* • Limited-service wholesalers whose customers are willing to give up services such as credit and delivery for lower wholesale prices are cash-and-carry wholesalers. These wholesalers usually stock a limited line of products, mostly staples and fast-turnover items. Their customers tend to buy frequently and in small quantities. Small grocers and small building contractors are examples. Cash-and-carry wholesalers also fill emergency orders for larger buyers. Some full-service wholesalers have separate departments to serve customers that want to buy on a cash-and-carry basis.

• *Drop Shippers* • Limited-service wholesalers known as drop shippers, or desk jobbers, take orders from their customers and give them to producers, which ship directly to the drop shippers' customers. Drop shippers buy in their own name (take title), assume the risk of owning products, arrange for transportation, and may extend credit. Since they do not store, handle, or deliver the products, their operating costs are lower than those of full-service wholesalers.

Drop shippers deal mainly in bulky products. They eliminate the need for costly rehandling of products at the wholesale level. They often are used when there is no quantity discrepancy between the producer and the drop shipper's customer, such as a firm that buys lumber or coal in rail carload quantities. Thus there is no need for intermediate bulk breaking (breaking down larger shipments into smaller shipments).

• *Truck Wholesalers* • Limited-service wholesalers termed truck wholesalers (also wagon, or truck, jobbers) operate rolling warehouses and sell a limited line of products directly from their trucks to their customers. They often specialize in perishable or semi-perishable fast-selling products. They call on their accounts regularly.

Truck wholesalers handle goods such as potato chips, candy, dairy products, and

A truck wholesaler selling Ecuadorean food to small grocers in New York.

[© Chuck Fishman]

WHAT IS LOGISTICS?

As we saw in chapter 11, the total systems view of a marketing channel holds that a channel is a framework for matching natural resources with ultimate consumers' demand. *Logistics* is the activities of moving raw materials from their sources to the production process; moving raw materials, semimanufactured products, and finished products within and among plants and warehouses; moving finished products through warehouses and intermediaries; and moving finished products to final buyers. As suggested in the Nedlloyd ad, logistics is concerned with the physical flow through marketing channels.

Some organizations distinguish between physical supply and physical distribution. In Figure 13–3 *physical supply* is the activities involved in moving raw materials into the plant, the various in-plant movements, and the movement of products to warehouses. *Physical distribution* is the activities involved in moving finished products to intermediaries and on to final buyers.

logistics

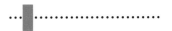

An ad that explains the logistics services this firm provides.

(Nedlloyd Lines [U.S.A.] Corp., a company of the Royal Nedlloyd Group.)

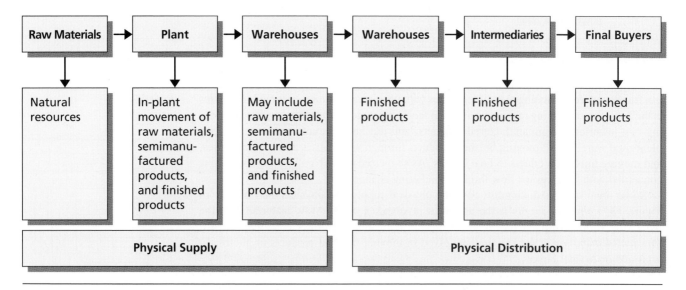

Raw Materials	Plant	Warehouses	Warehouses	Intermediaries	Final Buyers
Natural resources	In-plant movement of raw materials, semimanu-factured products, and finished products	May include raw materials, semimanu-factured products, and finished products	Finished products	Finished products	Finished products

Physical Supply	Physical Distribution

FIGURE 13–3

A Systems View of Logistics

The strategic importance of logistics is increasingly being recognized. For example, surveys indicate that reliable delivery is more critical to most customers than is rapid but inconsistent service. Thus all components of a logistics system—including purchasing, inbound and outbound freight, forecasting, inventory management, order processing, warehousing, materials handling, and customer service—must also be coordinated.

In order for the logistics function to contribute to profits, and not merely add to costs, its role in marketing strategies must be defined, communicated, and understood. For example, involving the firm's chief logistics executive in the development of marketing plans can help ensure that he or she will do a good job of supporting marketing strategies and tactics.[12]

The Objective of Logistics Management

Logistics service means such things as order size limitations, the amount of time that elapses between the placement of an order and its delivery, accurate and complete filling of orders, dependable delivery of undamaged products, and supplier willingness to accommodate special requests such as emergency deliveries.

In setting customer service policies, firms often survey their target customers. A survey may indicate that customers would be satisfied with less service if they were charged less or that they want more service and are willing to pay more for it. A firm can vary its service according to the requirements of different customers.

Logistics managers play a major role in both setting and achieving customer service standards. They provide the cost data that top management needs to set the standards. If top management wants to move from filling 80 percent of customer orders from inventory on hand to filling 90 percent from inventory on hand, logistics managers provide the estimated costs of raising the service level. They know that costs go up at an increasing rate as the level of service goes up.

Once top management has set the customer service standard with input from logistics management, the objective for logistics management is to minimize total logistics cost through efficiency while providing the predetermined level of customer service. Firms set a customer-oriented level of service and then seek to minimize the cost of providing it.

Care, however, is necessary when measuring customer service. For example, Baxter Healthcare Corporation sought to improve delivery of medical products to a major hospital. But it took Baxter three months to figure out what was required, mainly because the two defined on-time delivery differently. The hospital would order a package of six hundred to seven hundred items and then measure the first shipment against the invoice and conclude that, say, only 58 percent of the order was being shipped on time. Baxter, on the other hand, would take the total of two or three shipments and say that the order fill rate was much higher. The two discussed how much of the delivery absolutely had to be on the first truck, and then they agreed on which items would go in which shipment.[13]

The Growing Importance of Logistics

Logistics used to involve little more than traffic management. Production managers scheduled their production runs and told traffic managers to find the cheapest way to get the products to customers. This production-oriented view often resulted in customers receiving less service than they wanted.

Modern marketers, however, recognize that the logistics system must offer target customers what they want. Thus Georgia-Pacific consolidated several distribution branches into larger distribution centers because its customers wanted to be able to buy a full line of the company's products at each center. The consolidations improved customer service and reduced costs.[14]

Marketers focus on logistics because they realize it is the area in which they have the greatest opportunity to increase productivity through automation. On the average, logistics costs eat up more than 21 cents of every U.S. sales dollar.[15] Automation of such activities as order processing, inventory control, and warehousing increases logistics productivity, just as it increases manufacturing productivity.

Another reason for the focus on logistics is that efficient logistics management can have a major impact on overall marketing strategy. For example, a firm that wishes to sell in distant markets may have to meet or beat local marketers' prices. Low-cost, dependable transportation may be a key requirement for entry into those markets.

The Systems View of Logistics Management

The *systems view of logistics management* recognizes the diversity of logistics activities and the need to coordinate them under a logistics manager. This avoids dividing up and assigning logistics activities to different executives, such as traffic to the production manager and inventory control to the finance manager. Some firms create a manager of logistics who reports directly to the marketing manager and is accountable for coordinating all logistics activities. Other firms, however, may want to elevate the executive's status, having the person report directly to the firm's chief executive officer. Thus the marketing manager and the logistics manager are equals.

Logistics provides a good example of how the systems view of management can be applied to achieve an optimum blend of activities. Three key concepts are part of this systems view: (1) the total-cost concept, (2) the cost trade-off concept, and (3) the optimization concept.

• **The Total-Cost Concept** • As indicated earlier in the chapter, the basic objective of logistics management is to minimize total logistics costs given a predetermined level of customer service. The total-cost concept of logistics focuses on the cost of logistics activities taken as a whole instead of separately. Included are the costs of warehousing, transporting, inventorying, and handling products. Less obvious, but nevertheless important, are the costs associated with inventory obsolescence, damaged goods, and customer dissatisfaction caused by such factors as failure to meet promised delivery dates or inaccurate filling of orders.

• **The Cost Trade-off Concept** • Implementing the total-cost concept requires that logistics managers recognize the necessity for cost trade-offs, because the goals of different logistics activities often conflict. Suppose we want to provide next-day delivery to customers and also minimize freight costs. The desired level of service (next-day delivery) conflicts with the transportation goal (cost minimization). Salespeople want quick delivery to customers, whereas the traffic manager wants minimum freight bills. A possible cost trade-off would be second-day delivery to customers for lower transportation costs. If customers accept that service reduction, the trade-off will be profitable and will result in lower total distribution costs.

• **The Optimization Concept** • Underlying the systems view is a desire to optimize overall performance. In optimization, the various logistics activities are balanced in such a way that overall costs are minimized while the predetermined level of customer service is maintained. This is hard to achieve when (1) top management thinks other objectives are more important than logistics objectives; (2) different logistics activities are assigned to different departments, which makes coordinating them difficult; and (3) the firm is reluctant to specify the level of customer service it will provide.

It is hard to coordinate logistics activities when they are assigned to different departments. Inventory management may be assigned to production, and order processing may be assigned to accounting. Furthermore, when management fails to set a specific level of customer service, performance varies according to the department or person performing each activity. The result is suboptimization, in which overall costs are not minimized subject to the customer service constraint. This will likely continue until top management recognizes the role of logistics in helping the firm achieve its objectives and concentrates logistics activities under one executive.

THE LOGISTICS SYSTEM

The focus of the rest of this chapter is on the major subsystems of the logistics system, which are shown in Figure 13–4. Although these subsystems are discussed separately, they are, of course, interdependent.

The Warehousing Subsystem

Logistics activities have one unifying goal—to develop and maintain a steady flow of products. Ideally this flow begins with natural resources and ends with manufactured products in the hands of ultimate consumers.

• **Storage** • Although maintaining a steady flow of products is desirable, there are valid reasons for interrupting the flow. Grain is produced seasonally, but some must be stored for off-season consumption. Swimsuits are consumed seasonally but produced year-round. Storage interrupts the flow from producer to final buyer but makes longer and more efficient production runs possible. Production cost savings may be greater than the storage costs.

Storage provides time utility to products. It helps firms balance supply (production) and

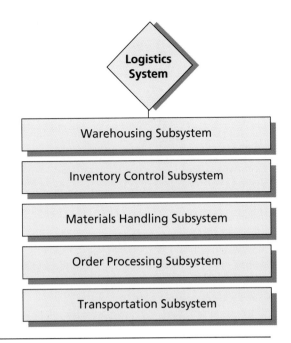

FIGURE 13–4

Major Subsystems of the
Logistics System

demand (consumption). Even when products are consumed as they are produced, firms usually store some output in case actual demand exceeds forecasted demand.

As suggested in the Ballantine's ad, storage may add form utility to products. Storage may include stockpiling in case of strikes by supplier and transportation workers and anticipated materials shortages or price increases. Some firms incur increased storage costs to get bigger quantity discounts on their purchases. This is an example of a trade-off. Again, the systems view of logistics is essential to effective management of logistics trade-offs. Clearly there are advantages to storing products. But there also are costs, such as insurance, taxes, obsolescence, warehouse operations, interest on borrowed funds, and the opportunity cost of funds (that is, the lost opportunities of using the funds elsewhere) invested in stored products.

• **Warehousing** • Warehousing serves as a valve to regulate the flow of products through a marketing channel. Storage is static; the focus is holding. Warehousing is dynamic; the focus is moving (throughput, or the efficient flow of products from producer to consumers). Warehouse planning involves determining the number, location, size, and ownership of warehouses.

The number of warehouses needed, their size, and their locations depend primarily on the desired level of customer service and the distance between supply sources and markets. In general, fewer and smaller warehouses are needed when supply sources and markets are located nearby than when they are separated by great distances. When plant locations are fixed, the warehousing decision involves finding locations between plants and markets for inventories of finished products.

Finished products can be concentrated at the plant or at a centrally located warehouse; dispersed to many warehouses, each of which serves customers in its local area; or dispersed to a few large warehouses and concentrated there for shipment to customers. A centralized inventory requires building and stocking one warehouse. Because all products that the firm markets are in one warehouse, order changes can be handled easily and fewer

······ | ························

Storage adds form utility to this product.

(Ballantine's and Foote, Cone & Belding.)

··■·····

public warehouse

customers will receive only partial shipments. Inventory control is easier with only one warehouse. Warehousing cost per unit of product should be low because the large-scale operation makes it economical to use mechanical and automated equipment to handle products and process orders.

On the other hand, a centralized inventory means slower delivery to customers on the fringes of the distribution area. Total transportation cost is also higher.

Warehousing strategy requires an investment decision. Firms must invest heavily in building and operating private warehouses (branch warehouses). If a firm could invest those funds more profitably elsewhere, it should consider using public warehouses. A *public warehouse* is an independently owned profit-seeking business that offers services such as storage and break-bulk (breaking a big, bulky shipment into smaller lots) and reshipping to firms and individuals. Because the user pays only for space used, public warehousing is a variable cost, as opposed to the largely fixed cost of building and operating private warehouses. No capital investment is required, and warehouse space may be added or deleted as market conditions dictate.

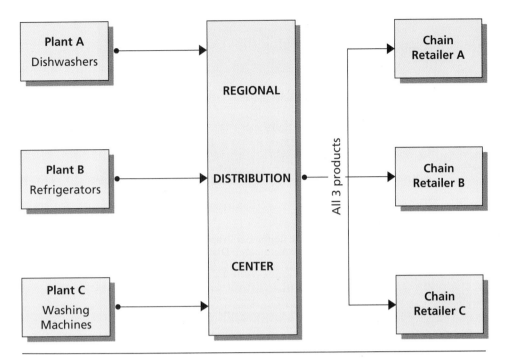

FIGURE 13–5

The Distribution Center Concept

distribution center

• **Distribution Centers** • A compromise between total centralization and total decentralization of inventory is the distribution center. A *distribution center* is a facility that coordinates order taking, order filling, and delivery activities under one roof to accomplish throughput. It is planned around markets to maintain an efficient flow of products from producer to customers. The goal is to move products, not store them. Orders are processed rapidly because modern handling equipment, scientific inventory management, and computer technology make automation practical. This reduces costs, improves customer service, and speeds inventory turnover. In most cases major dealers get overnight deliveries from General Electric distribution centers. As a competing Frigidaire distributor said, this system "had more to do with Frigidaire losing market share than pricing has."[16]

Figure 13–5 shows how a distribution center works. The manufacturer of home appliances has three plants. One produces dishwashers, one produces refrigerators, and one produces washing machines. Each plant ships its product in volume quantities to the distribution center, where order taking, order filling, and delivery activities are coordinated and the products flow to large retail chain buyers in the region.

Many supermarkets, discount, fast-food, convenience, and department store chains also use distribution centers. Fleming Companies, which sponsors a voluntary chain of supermarkets, operates nineteen full-line distribution centers that provide complete inventory needs for its customers. Wal-Mart's distribution centers are mostly within a day's drive of the stores they serve. The Austin Company's ad discusses the U.S. Army's distribution center at New Cumberland, Pennsylvania.

The Inventory Control Subsystem

One reason for manufacturer's L.A. Gear's recent decline in sales and profitability was huge inventories of shoes. Unlike Reebok and Nike, which stock shoes on the basis of

An ad that discusses the U.S. Army's distribution center at New Cumberland, Pennsylvania.

(The Austin Company—Consultants, Designers, Engineers, Constructors.)

future orders, L.A. Gear kept huge inventories on hand to ship as orders came in.[17] The goal of inventory management is to minimize the amount of working capital tied up in ntory while providing the specified level of customer service. The two major inventory control decisions are *when* to order (order timing) and *how much* to order (order quantity). Both decisions are made in light of the company's sales forecast.

• **Order Timing** • A *reorder point* is the inventory level at which the firm will reorder stock to replenish the inventory. This answers the question of when to reorder.

Order lead time and usage rate must be considered in setting the reorder point. *Order lead time* is the number of days that elapse between order placement and order receipt. For a manufacturer this means the number of days between ordering component products and having them available for incorporation into the product. For an intermediary it means the number of days between ordering products for resale and having them available for resale. For a manufacturer the *usage rate* is the rate at which a component product is used in producing the manufacturer's product. For an intermediary it is the average number of units of the product the firm sells each day.

The reorder point is determined by multiplying the order lead time by the usage rate. Thus, if the usage rate is 5 units per day and the order lead time is 15 days, an order would be placed when the inventory fell to 75 units (the reorder point). These 75 units constitute the firm's *basic stock*.

Most firms, however, carry *safety stock* to offset variations in order lead time caused by strikes, transportation problems, supplier out-of-stock situations (stock-outs), and so on. For example, if an order is received in 20 days instead of 15, the firm will experience stock-outs. Likewise, most firms carry *seasonal stock* to offset variations in the usage rate. In our example, if the usage rate increases from 5 to 7 units per day, the firm will experience stock-outs. Most firms therefore include provisions for safety stock and seasonal stock when they set the reorder point. The reorder point is: (order lead time × usage rate) + safety stock and seasonal stock. Because reductions in order lead time or usage rates will cause a firm to be overstocked, inventory managers are careful to balance the costs of overstock against the risks of stock-outs when they set their reorder points.

• **Order Quantity** • The reorder point tells the inventory manager how much inventory to keep on hand and when to reorder to maintain that level of inventory. It does not, however, tell how many units to order when the reorder point is reached. This order quantity decision involves a trade-off between the inventory carrying cost and the order processing cost.

The inventory carrying cost includes the costs of storage, record keeping, insurance, taxes, handling, depreciation, damage, interest, and obsolescence. The inventory carrying cost per unit of product increases as the size of each individual order (the order quantity) increases. This is because each unit of product will remain in inventory longer as the order quantity increases.

The order processing cost is the cost of placing an order—the cost of preparing and processing order forms. Unlike the carrying cost, the order processing cost per unit of product decreases as the order quantity increases because the largely fixed order processing cost is spread over a larger number of units. We will discuss the order processing subsystem from the seller's perspective in greater detail later in the chapter.

The *economic order quantity (EOQ)* is the quantity of goods that should be ordered for inventory each time to minimize total cost (carrying cost and ordering cost). (See Figure 13–6.) But the EOQ is not necessarily the quantity that will be ordered. If the EOQ is 460 units and sellers accept orders only in multiples of 100, the firm probably will order 500 units. If the firm produces the product for itself and its most efficient production run is 490 units, then 490 units probably will be produced.

economic order quantity (EOQ)

• **Inventory Control** • As the Radio Shack ad states, excess inventory hurts profitability. Thus inventory control is necessary. Inventories are controlled by the setting of upper and lower limits. The firm's desired level of customer service determines the upper limit. It sets the percentage of orders that can be filled from inventory on hand. The lower limit depends on how fast inventories can be replenished by more production or by buying from suppliers. When inventory on hand reaches the lower limit (the reorder point), an order is placed to replenish it. Many firms use computers to handle reordering details.

Different factors affect the upper and lower limits for inventories of finished products, goods in process, and raw materials. Finished product inventories are managed with a view to all marketing mix elements. An upcoming ad campaign or a temporary price cut may favor an increase in the upper limit. The greater the number of customers, the less frequent model changes are; and the greater the efficiency of long production runs, the higher the

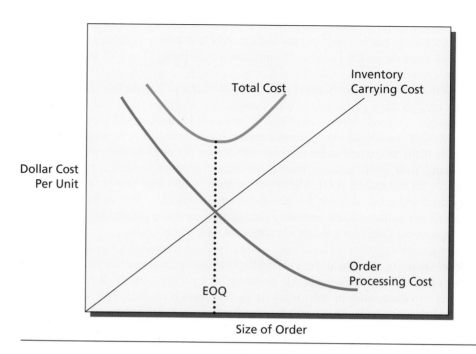

Dollar Cost Per Unit

Total Cost

Inventory Carrying Cost

Order Processing Cost

EOQ

Size of Order

. . . . ■ . . . . . .

just-in-time (JIT) system

upper limit for goods-in-process inventories. The more distant and undependable suppliers are and the greater the risk of product shortages, the higher the upper limit for raw materials inventories.

To evaluate inventory management a firm could compare its inventory turnover rate with the rates of other firms in its industry. But a high turnover rate could be achieved by keeping small inventories and ignoring ordering costs and out-of-stock costs. Some firms set a desired rate of return on inventory investment. Regardless of the evaluation approach, the desired level of customer service should not be sacrificed for cost savings.

The *just-in-time (JIT) system* is an inventory management system that focuses on maintaining a steady and coordinated flow of materials and parts into the manufacturing process and at the same time maintaining a steady flow of products off the assembly line. Materials and parts inventories are kept at the lowest level at which operations can be maintained so as to save on inventory and materials handling costs. Production schedules are fixed weeks in advance, and materials and component parts are delivered as needed by suppliers directly to assembly stations, not accumulated and stored there for future use. Managers can do an efficient job of monitoring the production process because there is little inventory on the shop floor to obscure production operations.

The biggest users of the JIT philosophy are the Japanese. Traditionally, U.S. firms have viewed inventory as insurance—a substitute for planning. It is a hedge against unexpected increases in demand, machine breakdowns, and faulty inputs. Japanese firms take the position that excessive inventory simply masks inefficiency and that a JIT system will uncover problems and force management to correct them. For example, suppose a manufacturer runs out of a critical part because the vendor does not deliver as promised or because the parts that are delivered are defective. The entire assembly line must be shut down at a cost of tens of thousands of dollars per hour.

The non-JIT philosophy would advocate keeping additional inventory of the critical part on hand to avoid incurring the huge shutdown costs. The JIT view would be that these costs

The purpose of an inventory control subsystem is to avoid excess inventory.

(Reprinted by permission of Tandy Corp.)

should be exposed so the underlying problems that created them can be dealt with. This might involve changing vendors or transportation companies.

Levi Strauss's LeviLink is a computer hookup that enables Levi's retailers to order and pay electronically for new inventory. Direct connections with fabric suppliers enable Levi Strauss to constantly fine-tune the amounts and kinds of fabrics it orders. There is no longer a need for it to have big fabric warehouses next to its apparel plants. Furthermore, some of its retailers have done away with their warehouses too. The goal "is to order electronically the manufacture of a pair of jeans when the customer buys one in the store."[18]

The Materials Handling Subsystem

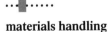

materials handling

Materials handling is the activities of physically moving products into and out of plants, warehouses, and transportation terminals. How products are handled may alter their characteristics or quality. For example, rolls of newsprint must be handled carefully because out-of-round rolls impair the efficiency of high-speed presses. The handling of nuclear wastes and other hazardous cargo is especially critical. Grain in storage elevators can self-ignite and burn, and sugar and grain dust can explode under some conditions.

- **Bulk and Packaged Products** • *Bulk products* are handled in loose rather than packaged form. For example, raw sugar can be handled in hundred-pound sacks or in bulk by the barge load (dry bulk). Liquid chemicals can be handled in barrels or in bulk by rail tank cars (liquid bulk). Bulk materials typically require highly specialized, perhaps custom-built, materials handling equipment—pumping systems, suctioning systems, conveyor belt systems, and shoveling systems, for example. To reduce environmental damage, vapor controls for dangerous chemicals and dust controls for grain, wood chips, and mineral products are now part of bulk transport and storage facilities.

Packaged products come in bottles, boxes, cans, jars, and so on. The package, which both protects and promotes the contents, is usually enclosed in a series of larger packages as the product moves from the producer to the consumer. For example, a supermarket will receive a dozen or so packages of cereal enclosed in a case.

- **Handling Efficiency** • High labor costs and new warehousing tools make the selection of materials handling equipment a crucial decision. The cost trade-off concept applies here also. For example, the use of high-stacking equipment in warehouses increases the usage of space in high-ceilinged warehouses, but it may be costly in terms of the equipment, packaging, and time needed to store and retrieve products. Thus focusing on maximum space utilization may be more desirable for products that are placed in storage for long periods of time and less desirable for distribution centers, where the focus should be on throughput.

Unitization and containerization are important elements of modern materials handling. *Unitization,* or unitizing, is a technique for increasing the efficiency of handling small packages. It usually involves palletization, or combining several small packages and strapping them to a wooden pallet or a heavy cardboard slip-sheet to move them. In shrink palletizing the entire unit is covered with plastic film. The plastic is heated and then cooled so it shrinks and holds the products together for shipment. Unitized pallets move faster and cheaper than individual items handled separately. Damage and pilferage are also reduced.

A British firm and an Australian firm have brought to the United States a more durable pallet made of stronger timber. In addition, a software system tracks pallet movement from food company to retailer and back. Tougher pallets and tighter controls can be expected to reduce damaged goods and the demand for new pallets. A societal benefit should be the saving of trees.[19]

containerization

Containerization is a materials handling system that encloses a shipment of products (perhaps several unitized loads) in a container, seals it, and transports it from shipper to receiver without rehandling the products in the container. Containerization reduces transit time, loading and unloading time, handling costs, damage, and theft.

Baltimore's new Seagirt Marine Terminal houses what may be the world's best container handling cranes as well as a computerized truck plaza. The Terminal's seven 20-story Sumitomo cranes are the largest, fastest, and most fully automated container handling cranes in existence. Their legs could span a six-lane highway with ease. The Seagirt facility provides unprecedented speed, efficiency, and ease in transferring containers from ship to shore and vice versa.[20]

The Order Processing Subsystem

The accuracy, reliability, and speed with which orders are received, handled, and filled are crucial customer service factors. Order processing activities include order receipt, credit approval, invoice preparation, and collection of accounts receivable. These activities also cross departmental lines. Coordination between sales and office personnel is a must. The longer salespeople wait to submit orders to office personnel, the less efficient the system becomes. Once an order is received in the office, it must be invoiced quickly; order picking instructions must be sent to the warehouse, and transportation instructions must be sent to the traffic department. Variability in the timing of these activities causes unreliable delivery and customer complaints. Logistics managers also should be able to give customers up-to-date information about the status of their orders.

Fast and accurate filling of orders reduces the time customers must wait to receive shipments. The more reliable a seller is in meeting delivery dates, the better its customers can manage their inventories. This is often a major factor in a buyer's choice of suppliers. McKesson Corporation, the largest U.S. drug wholesaler, has an automated ordering system, which features a base system linked to hand-held computers at major drugstores. This makes it possible for retailers to reorder inventory with the touch of a button. An added benefit is that the system practically locks the retailer into the products that McKesson distributes.[21]

The Transportation Subsystem

Transportation is needed to move raw materials to production points, semimanufactured products among manufacturing points, and finished products to resellers or final buyers. For many manufacturers, transportation cost is the third largest expense, after labor and materials. The **modes of transportation** are the methods of moving freight: railroads, motor carriers, airlines, pipelines, and water carriers.

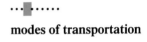

modes of transportation

• **Railroads** • The major inherent advantage of railroads has always been low-cost long-haul (over 300 miles) transportation for heavy and bulky commodities that have a relatively low value in relation to weight. Examples are coal, sand, gravel, steel, iron ore, lumber, and grain. Heavy, bulky commodities still provide railroads with most of their freight revenues, and the railroads are anxious to strengthen their competitive advantage in moving these products. A *unit train* moves one bulk commodity for one shipper from one point to another without stopping in between. A trainload of coal can be transported from a coal mine directly to an electricity generating station. Once the train is unloaded, it returns to the coal mine for another load.

• **Motor Carriers** • The major inherent advantages of trucks are speed and flexibility, especially for small loads over short distances. Small shipments weigh less than 1,000 pounds and account for three-fourths of all truck shipments.[22] Some firms can penetrate new market areas with truck transportation. Retailers and wholesalers can also operate with smaller inventories when speedy transportation is available. Faster transportation reduces the need for products in the distribution pipeline.

• **Airlines** • The volume of air freight has increased greatly in recent years but still accounts for less than 1 percent of total ton-miles shipped in intercity commerce. Air freight is the highest-quality type of transportation available. Speedy service is the major advantage, but air freight also exposes cargo to less potential for damage, pilferage, deterioration, and obsolescence. Fashion merchandise, fragile and highly perishable products, emergency shipments, and expensive and intricate industrial products account for the bulk of air freight.

• **Pipelines** • Pipelines are used mainly to transport natural gas, crude petroleum, and petroleum products from production fields to refineries. Natural gas, of course, is piped

Intermodal transportation facilitates international business.

[© George Hall]

intermodal transportation

from production fields to distribution companies in local market areas and to large industrial users.

Service is very dependable because pipelines are not affected much by weather and labor strikes. They are the least labor-intensive mode, and maintenance expenses are low.

• **Water Carriers** • Ocean vessels include general cargo ships and bulk vessels. *General cargo ships* move a wide variety of cargoes. *Bulk vessels* make large-volume movements of individual bulk commodities, which are loaded and unloaded directly into and from the ships' tanks or holds by on-board or shipside equipment. Towboats and tugboats move barges on inland waterways. The major advantage is low cost for low-value bulk commodities. There is a lot of competition between barges, railroads, and pipelines. Table 13–3 summarizes several cost and quality factors for various modes of transportation.

• **Intermodal Transportation** • Perhaps the most significant development in transportation is the tremendous growth in intermodal transportation. *Intermodal transportation* is the combination of two or more methods of moving freight in order to more fully exploit the major advantages of each.

Piggyback service, or trailer on flat car (TOFC), is a joint rail-truck service in which the railroad provides long-haul movement and trucks provide door-to-door service. Containers also move in piggyback service called container on flat car (COFC).

Other examples of intermodal service in domestic commerce include *birdyback* (truck–air freight–truck) and *fishyback* (truck/rail–ship/barge–truck/rail). Much of this coordinated transportation involves the movement of containerized freight.

• **Supplementary Carriers** • The logistics manager also may use supplementary carriers, mainly for small shipments. Freight forwarders sell the services of railroads, airlines, water carriers, and truckers. They do not own transportation equipment except perhaps

TABLE 13–3 ▎ Cost and Quality of the Different Modes of Transportation

Cost and Quality Factors	Railroads	Motor Carriers	Airlines	Pipelines	Water Carriers (Ocean and Inland)
Transportation cost	Medium	High	Highest	Low	Lowest
Door-to-door transit time	Medium	Fast	Fastest	Slow	Slowest
Dependability in meeting schedules	Medium	Good	Very good	Best	Fair
Scope of products economically transportable	Broad	Medium	Narrow	Narrowest	Broad
Major inherent advantages	Low cost for long hauls of bulk commodities	Speed and door-to-door service	Fastest and highest-quality transport	Low cost and dependability	Low cost for long hauls of bulk commodities
Necessity of intermodal transfer for door-to-door transit	Often*	No	Practically always	Often*	Often*
Ability to reach shippers over widespread areas	Very good	Best	Very good	Very limited	Very limited
Products ideally suited to movement	Low-value bulk commodities	High-value manufactured products	High-value perishable products	Petroleum, natural gas	Low-value bulk commodities

*Except when shipper and receiver are located on rail spurs (for railroads), when they are connected by pipeline (for pipelines), and when they are located on navigable waterways (for water carriers).

pickup and delivery trucks. They pick up less-than-truckload (l.t.l.) or less-than-carload (l.c.l., for rail transportation) shipments at their customers' plants or warehouses, consolidate them into truckload or carload shipments, and arrange for delivery at destination points. Their margin is the difference between the l.t.l. or l.c.l. rates they charge their customer and the truckload (t.l.) or carload (c.l.) rates they pay to the carrier. Many exporters rely on foreign freight forwarders to handle their export documentation problems and to deliver their products to customers in other countries. The Global Marketing box discusses the operations of an international freight forwarder.

The U.S. Postal Service handles a large volume of freight through its parcel post service. UPS is privately owned and offers shippers pickup and delivery service. A large volume of small packages moves via intercity bus lines. Courier express companies such as Federal Express provide overnight delivery of documents and other small packages.

Shippers' cooperatives are somewhat like freight forwarders. The members set up a facility to collect their shipments and hire a local pickup carrier to move the products to a terminal for loading. At the destination terminal the products are picked up and delivered to customers by local pickup carriers. Each shipper's share in the cooperative's transportation bill is based on its shipment's percentage of total weight.

• **Transportation Rates** • The transportation industry has traditionally operated under strict regulations regarding rates and services. The Interstate Commerce Commission (ICC) was created in 1887 to regulate railroads. Later, pipelines, motor carriers, and inland water carriers were brought under ICC regulation. Other regulatory bodies were also created. Among them are the Federal Maritime Commission and the Civil Aeronautics Board.

In the transportation industry all-cargo aircraft operations were the first to be deregulated, in 1977. Subsequently, the trucking and railroad industries were also deregulated.

GLOBAL MARKETING

Harper Group, an international freight forwarder, purchases cargo space from airlines and ocean carriers at wholesale prices and resells the space to its customers at retail prices. About half of Harper's revenues derive from international air freight, with the balance divided between ocean freight forwarding and customs brokerage.

Harper's biggest clients are IBM and 3M, each of which accounts for about 5 percent of total revenues. Another big client is the United Nations. In 1989 Harper arranged the shipment of the UN's peace-keeping mission to Namibia. Eight ships were chartered to transport the cars, trucks, and household goods. Another significant project was arranging the shipment of 4,000 truckloads of equipment for Toyota's first automobile manufacturing plant in the United States in 1988.

Harper began focusing on developing a global business some time ago. According to the firm's chairman, John Robinson, "I foresaw that multinational customers like Chevron, General Motors, and IBM would move a lot of goods internationally, and they would want somebody with uniform ideas." Whereas other freight forwarders were dealing with agents for their international business, Robinson set up a company-owned office wherever business demanded it, eventually buying out any joint venture partners. The Harper Group now has 3,150 employees working out of more than 280 offices, 90 of which are in the United States and the rest in 42 countries around the world. Robinson is now looking to open offices in Eastern Europe and to collaborate with a freight forwarder in Canton, China.

A central precept is Robinson's belief that, unlike others in the industry, Harper should never own its transportation assets. As he puts it, "If it flies, floats, or has wheels, we won't own it." He is quick to criticize such competitors as Federal Express and American President Companies, both of which own large fleets and are trying to make the job of the independent freight forwarder obsolete by internalizing it themselves.

"Ocean carriers or Federal Express have the job of filling their ships or airplanes," says Robinson. "They are very narrow-minded. The advantage of Harper is that we have much more flexibility because we have a much larger universe to choose from. Federal Express wants to have our head. And me the same, I want their head."

Source: Adapted from Spyros Manolatos, "The Power of Positive Imagery," by permission of *Forbes* magazine, April 16, 1990, pp. 105–112. © Forbes Inc., 1990.

Traffic managers therefore are generally finding it easier to negotiate freight rates with carriers. The Ethics in Marketing box earlier in this chapter discusses some of the ethical issues that might arise in such negotiations.

Measuring Logistics Performance

Logistics performance can be measured in terms of efficiency and effectiveness. Efficiency can be measured by comparing actual performance to budgets and cost standards. Standards include per-unit costs such as transportation and order processing. Within those categories, specific measurements can be taken to assess productivity. Examples include ton-per-mile costs and billing lag time (the time between the shipment date and the invoice date).[23]

It is more difficult to measure logistics effectiveness. Benchmarking is one approach. *Benchmarking* is the continuous process of gathering information about the performance of industry leaders and comparing your performance to theirs. Benchmarking is how Xerox operates its logistics business as well as many other operating functions.[24] Another approach is to conduct surveys of customers to ascertain their perceptions of logistics effectiveness in terms of such factors as on-time delivery and responsiveness to emergencies. Ideally the surveys should be conducted by a third party.[25]

SUMMARY OF LEARNING OBJECTIVES

1. Identify the marketing functions wholesaling intermediaries might perform for their suppliers and customers.
Marketing functions for suppliers include selling, stocking, financing, gathering market information, and reducing risk. Marketing functions for customers include buying, stocking, gathering market information, financing, reducing risk, contacting, and concentrating and dispersing.

2. Identify the five categories of wholesaling intermediaries that are recognized by the Census of Wholesale Trade.
The categories are merchant wholesalers, manufacturers' sales branches and sales offices, merchandise agents and brokers, petroleum bulk plants and terminals, and assemblers of farm products.

3. Describe the major types of wholesaling decisions and the major wholesaling trends.
The major types of wholesaling decisions include target markets, personnel, product, promotion, credit and collections, image, warehouse location and design, and inventory control. The major trends in wholesaling include greater participation in multiple competitive environments, greater attention to margin management and quality, greater attention to environmental monitoring, greater effort to bypass wholesaling intermediaries, continued increases in corporate concentration, and greater impact of technology.

4. Explain the basic objective of logistics management.
Once top management has set the customer service standard with input from logistics management, the objective for logistics management is to minimize total logistics cost through efficiency while providing a predetermined level of customer service.

5. Identify the major subsystems of the logistics system.
The major subsystems are the warehousing subsystem, the inventory control subsystem, the materials handling subsystem, the order processing subsystem, and the transportation subsystem.

Review Questions

1. What marketing functions do wholesaling intermediaries perform for their suppliers and customers?

2. What are the various types of full-service wholesalers and limited-service wholesalers?

3. What are the advantages to manufacturers of manufacturer-owned wholesaling establishments?

4. How do merchandise agents and brokers differ from merchant wholesalers?

5. What are the various types of regular representation agents and irregular representation agents and brokers?

6. What are the major types of wholesaling decisions and the major wholesaling trends?

7. What is the basic objective of logistics management?

8. What are the three key concepts that are part of the systems view of logistics management?

9. What are the major subsystems of the logistics system?

10. What is a distribution center?

11. How can unitization and containerization improve materials handling efficiency?

12. What are the relative advantages of each of the five modes of transportation?

Discussion Questions

1. We discussed warehouse clubs in chapter 12. Do you think they compete with cash-and-carry wholesalers? Explain.

2. Do you think manufacturers' sales branches and sales offices will eventually make merchant wholesalers obsolete? Explain.

3. Suppose a manufacturer's current logistics system enables it to deliver on time to 90 percent of its customers. Logistics costs would double if the firm were to raise the service level so that 95 percent of its customers would receive on-time delivery. Should it increase the service level? Explain.

4. How might a major crisis such as the 1991 Persian Gulf War impact some just-in-time inventory management systems?

5. How important to the international competitiveness of the United States is the effectiveness and efficiency of our transportation system?

Application Exercise

Reread the material about West's Archery Center International (ACI) at the beginning of this chapter and answer the following questions:

1. Why do you think the Wests decided to expand from retailing into wholesaling?

2. How would you describe the relationship between ACI and its retailer-customers?

3. Why do you think Sheila West decided to stage the Pow Wow trade show?

4. How does the Pow Wow benefit the Wests and the manufacturers and retailers who attend the show?

Key Concepts

The following key terms were introduced in this chapter:

wholesaling
merchant wholesaler
full-service wholesaler
limited-service wholesaler
manufacturer's sales branch
manufacturer's sales office
merchandise agents and
   brokers

petroleum bulk plant and
   terminal
assembler of farm products
logistics
public warehouse
distribution center
economic order quantity
   (EOQ)

just-in-time (JIT) system
materials handling
containerization
modes of transportation
intermodal transportation

CASES

Speeding Through Europe

LYN S. AMINE, *St. Louis University*

As plans for an integrated market inside the European Community (EC) proceed, changes are being made in European rail infrastructure that will eventually allow businesspeople, vacationers, and merchandise to whiz through Europe on what is commonly referred to as the "TGV." TGV stands for "train à grande vitesse," or high-speed train, and is the name given to the new and highly efficient train service in France. Germany has a similar network, developed as a competitor to the TGV, called the Inter-City Express (ICE). The ICE is heavier than the TGV, its carriages are wider, and its electrical systems are different.

The forerunners of the European high-speed trains were the Japanese "bullet trains," or shinkansen, introduced in 1964 to serve Tokyo and Osaka at a speed of 125 mph. European trains are much faster, reaching speeds of 180 mph. Since 1981 France's TGV has carried 100 million passengers on the Paris—Lyons line at 167 mph during the two-hour trip.

By the turn of the century it should be possible to speed through the EC from the southern extremities of Portugal, Spain, Italy, or Greece through the countries of central Europe northward to Britain and Denmark. Passage through the English Channel Tunnel, or "Chunnel," due to open in 1993, will slow the train's speed to about 100 mph, and progress through the English countryside toward London will be even slower. Improvements in existing rail service in southeast England have been severely hampered by protests against noise pollution from ecologists and homeowners, and by the failure of British Rail to gain government subsidies for construction of new track and purchase of new rolling stock.

The European high-speed train network is still a long way from completion. Some 4,600 miles of new track need to be laid and 12,000 miles require upgrading, at a total estimated cost of $90 billion. Public opposition must be reconciled in some countries, and differences in specifications worked out in others. Yet despite all these setbacks the Community of European Railways, which represents EC state railroad companies, hopes to achieve an 18,000-mile network of lines with 120–180 mph trains by the year 2015.

The French remain pioneers. By the mid-1990s they expect to bring Bordeaux in the west, London in the north, and Rotterdam and Cologne in the northeast within three and a half hours of Paris. In the future, airlines are expected to come under severe pressure to compete for the attention of the business traveller who, by choosing the high-speed train, will be spared the hassle of late-arriving airplanes and gridlocked airports.

Questions

1. Which of the major trends in wholesaling described in the text might be affected by the availability of high-speed trains in Europe? Explain.

2. In what ways can marketers benefit specifically from the availability of (a) high-speed rail service and (b) a trans-European rail network?

3. How is the planned European rail network likely to affect logistical planning in the future?

4. What are the implications of these developments in Europe for U.S.-based firms that wish to sell in these countries?

Cardinal Distribution's Automated Link to Customers

Hospital pharmacies need to have a wide range of drugs and supplies on hand. They also need to be able to order and reorder medicines and supplies quickly, and to receive fast delivery. Wholesalers that supply hospital pharmacies need to be able to distribute materials quickly and to keep an inventory of many different types of products. One wholesaler that has met this challenge is Cardinal Distribution, a pharmaceutical and hospital supplies company that uses a new, automated ordering system to stay competitive.

Cardinal devised its own order-taking and inventory-tracking system, called AccuNet. The system requires only an IBM-compatible PC and a modem at the customer site. Customers enter their orders into the AccuNet system and send them by modem to the nearest Cardinal distribution center. There Cardinal's mini-computers sort the requests, confirm the order on the customer's screen within minutes, and send the materials to the customer within 24 hours.

AccuNet is an important tool for Cardinal's customers. By providing hospitals with a quick and easy ordering process it helps the pharmacy to keep less inventory on hand. Cardinal claims that a hospital can reduce the administrative costs of its pharmacy operations by 80 percent using the system. Said Cardinal Chief Financial Officer David Bearman, "It can manage the hospital pharmacy almost on a just-in-time basis."

Not only does this system benefit the customer, it is also an important marketing tool for Cardinal Distributors, allowing the company to stand among the frontrunners in the wholesale pharmaceutical and hospital supplies business. By carrying inventory for the customer, Cardinal ensures a firm relationship between itself and the AccuNet user. It also improves Cardinal's operations, by allowing orders to be filled more quickly. In fiscal 1990 alone, Cardinal's earnings rose from $8.5 million to $12.8 million.

In addition to providing an easy ordering system, AccuNet allows a hospital pharmacy to keep its own inventory on the system, and even informs pharmacies of less expensive or generic brands of medicine. It can also alert a customer a month before its contract with Cardinal is due to expire.

According to David Bearman, AccuNet has played an important role in winning Cardinal new customers. He asserts, "Systems like AccuNet are essential if you want to win and keep customers."

Questions

1. What marketing functions does Cardinal Distribution perform for its customers?

2. How would you describe the relationship between Cardinal Distribution and its customers?

3. How does AccuNet help Cardinal to provide customer service?

4. Which logistics subsystems does the AccuNet system most closely resemble?

Macy's: A Rollercoaster Retailer?

• Introduction •

In 1858, lots of people had 36-year old Rowland H. Macy of Massachusetts booked as a five-time loser: he had already run four retail businesses into the ground. It certainly didn't seem auspicious that the site he had picked for his first New York retail venture was quite a distance uptown from the city's retail center, and that he insisted on an unusual cash-only sales policy.

But by the end of 1859, Macy's dry goods store had sold about $85,000 worth of merchandise. Due to his previously dormant talents in advertising and promotion—and to his store's low prices—R. H. Macy was finally a success. By the 1870s, "Macy's" was synonymous with the new phenomenon of department store shopping.

Macy's is still a New York landmark, one of those few stores whose name is known around the globe. In addition to the famous Herald Square Macy's—known as "The World's Largest Store"—there are now more than 100 Macy's branches across the United States and even Macy's departments in Japanese stores. Macy's also owns and operates the prestigious I. Magnin and Bullock's department store chains on the West Coast. But many in the financial and retail communities doubt whether Macy's will survive the 1990s, or even the coming five years. Many department stores with names just as venerable as Macy's—including Bonwit Teller, B. Altman, and Bloomingdale's in New York alone—have recently either filed for bankruptcy or been put up for sale. If Macy's does go under, many analysts will see it as a major blow to the department store concept itself, for Macy's history has reflected virtually every trend in consumer goods retailing for the past 130 years.

• A Changing Environment •

R. H. Macy had established a formula that would bring shoppers from all over the city to Macy's: many and various departments staffed with excellent sales help, marvelous promotions, and reasonable prices. Macy's was one-stop shopping in style and, unlike at some of New York's other department stores, you didn't have to be rich to be treated as a valued customer. Macy's continued to grow in strength through the early 20th century as the city grew around it.

But by the 1960s, changes in the typical department store customer's lifestyle and in the general economic environment began to take some of the shine off Macy's formula. First, following World War II, many Macy's shoppers had moved to the suburbs. Many still returned to the city to buy clothes and housewares that they could carry home themselves. But one of the many attractions department stores held for city dwellers was that they arranged quick—and usually free—delivery of big-ticket items such as furniture, rugs, and mattresses. For customers who lived miles and miles from Herald Square, Macy's had either to charge for delivery or to decline the service, depending on how far away the customer lived. Many ex-Macy's loyalists thus found that it now made more sense to buy such items locally, even if Macy's prices were usually lower and its selection usually better. There were still plenty of Macy's customers left in the city. But, publicly owned, Macy's was obliged to grow, and the source of growth was obviously the suburbs. For the first time, Macy's began to open suburban branches.

Meanwhile, the department store business was becoming increasingly competitive both in New York and in the suburbs. On New York's prestige scale, Macy's had always ranked below Bloomingdale's: although there were always plenty of top-of-the-line, very expensive products for sale at Macy's, there were also plenty of bargains. This had always been Macy's strength—whereas Bloomingdale's appealed to fairly conservative, upper-middle-class and upper-class clientele, Macy's had something for everybody. In the 1970s, though, Bloomingdale's started to encroach on Macy's territory. The store went on a marketing blitz, updating the designs of everything from its floor layouts to its newspaper ads to its shopping bags, always emphasizing its new informality by stressing its traditional nickname—Bloomie's. Buyers stocked up on the latest fashions, and, in many departments, musak was dropped in favor of the top 40. Prices still stayed higher on average than at Macy's, but new customers came pouring through the doors. Bloomie's was suddenly *the* trendy place to shop, and Macy's was left looking rather fuddy-duddy by comparison.

Bloomingdale's wasn't Macy's only worry. Like most other suburban department store branches, Macy's branches were usually located in planned shopping centers or in malls, and now some new specialty stores in these centers and malls began to give Macy's a run for its money. There were two main reasons why Macy's and other department stores used to have an advantage over specialty stores. First, department-store credit cards used to be the only ones found in most people's wallets: if you wanted to buy on credit, department stores were just about your only option. But with the coming of the credit card boom of the 1970s, the department stores lost this advantage.

Second, their size, history, and expertise had in the past given the department store chains a huge amount of clout with clothes designers and other vendors, ensuring that they got access to designers' thinking on new trends as well as the best of every season's new products. Single-outlet specialty stores could usu-

ally compete with the department stores only on the basis of price; because they didn't have either the kind of fashion forecasting information or the kind of influence with vendors that the department stores had, they couldn't hope to set fashion trends. Specialty store chains had more of a chance at competing with the department stores, but were still at a serious disadvantage. They, too, had less influence with vendors. And it was difficult for their buyers to keep on top of sales trends: it was almost impossible to collect timely sales information from widely dispersed stores and to cater to tastes that differed from one suburb to another. As a result, like the single-outlet specialists, they tended to play safe—which often meant boring—with their product lines.

Macy's was one-stop shopping in style. . . .

During the 1970s, however, a few independent-minded specialty store managers began to wise up. They began to target more narrow segments of the market, segments that had traditionally been of secondary importance to department store managers—younger men and women, for instance, who didn't find the "Juniors" or "Young Men's" sections of the department stores very exciting, and aspiring gourmet cooks who often couldn't find the specialized equipment they wanted in the housewares sections. They also began to make use of emerging

information technologies to keep closer track of sales trends in their various branches. They began to form special relationships with newer vendors so that some began to carry certain trend-setting products even before the department stores could get hold of them. And they paid more attention to store design and to promotion. In the malls, Macy's suddenly found attractive, competitive stores right outside its doors. It was easy for shoppers to zip in to these stores to compare products and prices against those in the neighboring Macy's.

Stretched by its expansion in the suburbs, challenged at home by Bloomingdale's, and starting to feel the specialty stores bite at its heels, by the mid-1970s Macy's seemed in danger of becoming a dinosaur.

• Minding the Store •

When Edward Finkelstein, a career Macy's employee, took charge of the Herald Square store in the mid-1970s, the landmark had seen better days. Fewer and fewer customers passed through the grand entrance into what had once been one of the most inviting shop floors in the world but which now seemed more like a slightly dingy airport lobby divided up by perfume and hosiery counters. It was clear to Finkelstein that something had to be done and done soon if Macy's was to survive in this newly competitive marketplace. The answer, he believed, was to return to Macy's original formula of one-stop shopping convenience, excellent service, and reasonable prices. And each department, Finkelstein believed, would have to compete head on with the specialty stores.

Finkelstein conferred with buyers, customer service representatives, personnel managers, retail trade analysts, and his top management and set about transforming the store. Whole floors were redesigned to make them more alluring to fashion-conscious shoppers. Promotional material was updated to provide a challenge to Bloomingdale's. And the breadth and depth of departments was expanded so that customers would be more likely to find what they wanted at Macy's. The kitchen department, for instance, became a showcase for the hottest new trends in food and equipment. Shopping mavens in New York soon started saying that if you wanted anything for the kitchen— from your first set of budget-priced plates to a $400, top-of-the-line food processor—Macy's was the place to go. And as the new department designs and product selections were installed in the branches, Macy's repolished reputation spread to the suburbs. For the first time in years, Macy's profits started to increase substantially. In 1980, Ed Finkelstein was appointed Macy's CEO.

• **Dangerous Debts** •

With new money in Macy's corporate coffers, Finkelstein faced a new challenge. Michael Milkin's popularization of the junk bond had unleashed a wave of unfriendly corporate takeovers. "I actually made the decision sometime in 1984 that . . . with the availability of high-yield securities, with various takeovers in the media area and in retailing, that sooner or later, somebody was going to make a thrust at us and take Macy's," says Finkelstein. "So after a great deal of thought, I decided the best thing was for the management to buy the company."

This was no easy decision: a man-

agement buyout of Macy's would involve taking on $3.7 billion in debt. But it meant not only that Macy's was safe from takeovers but also that stockholder pressure to constantly increase short-term profits would vanish. Finkelstein believed private ownership would give him the freedom to run Macy's in the best long-term interests of the company. In 1986, he and about 300 other employees bought Macy's.

The buyout was controversial, but a year later many analysts were calling it a model deal. Finkelstein increased earnings by selling off some weak suburban branches and by continuing to refashion the remaining stores to make them more competitive. In the first years following debt-heavy buyouts, interest payments usually cover the balance sheet in red ink. But Macy's sales were so strong that Finkelstein almost made a net profit in 1987. He soon embarked on a much-applauded plan to start paying off his bonds early, thereby reducing the costs of his debt service.

In 1988, however, a chain of events began that would show that even a model employee buyout wasn't enough to insulate Macy's from the effects of the decade's merger mania. Robert Campeau, a Canadian real estate developer, had acquired the Allied retail company, which included Jordan Marsh, and Stern's department stores as well as the Ann Taylor and Brooks Brothers specialty chains, in late 1986 for $3.5 billion. Following this deal, Campeau was heavily in debt and Allied was losing close to $200 million a year. But the availability of junk bonds meant that this didn't disqualify him from putting together a hostile takeover bid for Federated Department Stores, which included Abraham and Straus, Blooming-

dale's, Bullock's, I. Magnin, Filene's, Burdines, Foley's, Goldsmith's, Lazarus, and Rich's. The Federated board of directors saw Campeau as a threat to their company's long-term welfare and called in Macy's as a "white knight"—a buyer more palatable to the board. Finkelstein and Campeau's battle finally ended with Campeau's winning bid of $6.6 billion. But Macy's wasn't left completely out in the cold: its reward for acting as white knight was that Federated had written an option for it to buy Bullock's and I. Magnin into the final Campeau deal. Finkelstein believed that these prestigious California retailers would boost Macy's earnings and image, so he took the option, adding $1 billion in new Macy's debt.

Macy's interest payments alone now ran to about $600 million a year. Finkelstein had planned for Macy's newly strong sales figures and tightened management practices to outweigh the burden of his debt service. But things didn't turn out quite that way. First, Finkelstein was by no means free of Campeau's shadow. Campeau had virtually no experience in managing retail businesses and this fact, in addition to Allied's horrendous debt burden, led to a quick slide in Allied's earnings starting in the fall of 1989. At the same time, consumer confidence went into its own slide following a series of setbacks in the national economy, and all of the retail industry started to feel the pinch. In a desperate attempt to boost his earnings—and to keep up with his interest payments—Campeau started to slash prices in his stores. Most of his stores were in direct competition with Finkelstein's, and Macy's began to respond with its own discounts in an attempt to hold on to customers. The trade-off was that

Macy's own earnings went into a downward spin and more cents from every sales dollar went for debt service.

The Christmas season usually accounts for about 30 percent of retailers' annual sales. Following an autumn full of doubt about the state of the economy, the 1989 Christmas season was the worst in years, and Macy's and the Allied stores, like most of their competitors, took the blow hard. ''With the Campeau failure and the fact that we had accumulated much more inventory than we would have had our systems been under control, that was a very bad quarter,'' Finkelstein says. ''I think we made a decision that should have been applauded by the financial community. What we said was, 'Let's take our mark-downs, . . . get our inventories clean, . . . get a lot of cash, and . . . be as lean as we can for the next year. And let's not

worry that, on an accounting basis, we will show a bad statistical quarter.' '' All that most people in the financial community saw, however, was that Macy's posted a $39 million loss in the Christmas quarter. Allied filed for bankruptcy in the spring, sparking a new round of price-cutting. Macy's future didn't look very bright.

The paradox for Finkelstein was that his retailing instincts were intact. In the twelve months ending July 1990, a year marked by consumer skittishness, Macy's annual sales had actually increased by 4.2 percent, which compared favorably to many of his competitors. But, due to deep discounting and to his interest costs, his annual losses had more than tripled to $215 million. Cash flow, which Finkelstein had to keep strong in order to stay even with his interest payments, was slowing, too. At the same time, the economy was

sliding deeper into recession. The looming Christmas 1990 season didn't give most retailers much hope.

Meanwhile, its heavy debt burden was seriously hobbling Macy's in its desperate race against the new breed of specialty stores, the best of which, like The Limited and The Gap, had little or no operating debt. By dint of brilliant marketing techniques, these chains were selling their products better than ever. They were now large enough to wield considerable influence with vendors and to start new fashion trends. They had invested in the best new computerized inventory and ordering systems so that they almost always had what customers wanted when they wanted it. And because they had little or no interest obligations, a large percentage of every sales dollar was free to be reinvested in expansion or store refurbishment or to be returned to customers in the form of lower prices. At Macy's, it was now getting hard to find enough pennies in every sales dollar to keep the store clean, let alone enough to invest in what was really needed—such as new stores or department redesigns—to stay competitive. Macy's was also losing out to new vendor-retailers—such as the Ralph Lauren, Burberry, Laura Ashley, and Timberland stores—that now offered the same brand-name prestige products that used to be found only in the department stores. And respected West Coast department stores, such as Nordstrom, were beginning to expand to the East.

Christmas 1990 turned out to be abysmal for Macy's. Sales for the quarter were down more than 10 percent from Christmas 1989 and cash flow was now even slower. Many analysts believed Macy's was staying afloat solely due to the hundreds of millions of dollars invested in the company since 1988 by interests including the Loews Corporation, the Mutual Shares Corporation, the real estate developer Alfred Taubman, and the General Electric Company, which had also agreed to buy Macy's credit subsidiary. In early 1991, these investors and other shareholders invested $150 million more, which Macy's used to buy back junk bonds originally worth about $400 million. (The sharply discounted, $150 million actual purchase price reflected how little confidence the bond markets had in Macy's future.) This would save the company about $40 million in cash interest payments, but interest payments were still expected to monopolize about seven cents of every Macy's sales dollar—a depressing figure when Finkelstein knew that Nordstrom, for instance, had to earmark less than two cents of every sales dollar for interest payments.

Finkelstein and his top managers repeatedly tried to reassure Macy's investors that lower inventories, more efficient operating practices, and sound marketing approaches would carry the store through this rough patch. But in February 1991, yet another department store chain—

this time Carter Hawley Hale Stores of California—declared bankruptcy. Every analyst in the industry knew that Ed Finkelstein was hoping that the recession would be short and shallow. Most thought that, if it wasn't, Macy's wouldn't long outlive Carter Hawley Hale. Plenty thought that even if the recession were short and shallow, Macy's didn't have long to live.

In May of 1991 Finkelstein hosted a black-tie party for major suppliers, with singer Melissa Manchester and the Peter Duchin orchestra. Finkelstein announced to guests that the worst was over, and pledged to build sales to $10.5 billion in 1996, up from $7.3 billion in 1990. But seven days later, April-quarter 1991 results revealed that Macy's had lost $101 million, the worst quarterly showing in three years. Some analysts felt that Finkelstein's optimism was still justified—that the quarter's gross margins were only slightly worse than last year's. But others speculated that Finkelstein could be preparing for a public offering or a sale of part of the company. In either case, a turnaround still appears to be some way off for R. H. Macy & Co.

• Questions •

1. How did the specialty store chains such as The Limited and The Gap gain more power in marketing channels?

2. When Macy's and other department stores began opening suburban branches, they opened some as stand-alone stores and others in malls or planned shopping centers. What are some of the likely advantages and disadvantages of these two suburban location choices for department stores?

3. What are some of the challenges the department stores were likely to face as they expanded into the suburbs?

4. Why do you think some new, trendsetting vendors would choose to sell their products in certain specialty stores rather than in department stores?

5. How important is logistics management to department stores and specialty store chains?

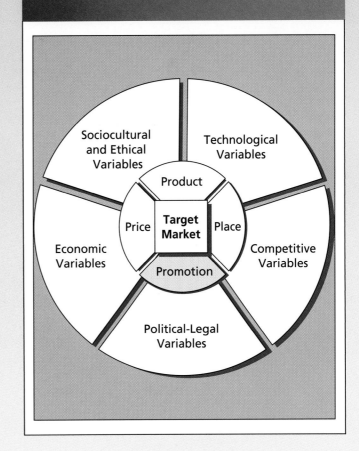

Sections three and four dealt with the product and distribution variables of the marketing mix. The four chapters in this section focus on the promotion element of the marketing mix: communicating with target customers.

Chapter 14 explains promotion in terms of a communication process. It develops the concept of the promotion mix and the objectives of promotion activities. Next comes a look at promotion management and an examination of the criticisms directed at promotion.

Chapter 15 looks at advertising. It examines the nature and types of advertising and the tasks of advertis-

ing management. The chapter also explains what an advertising agency does.

Chapter 16 examines direct marketing, sales promotion, and public relations. It looks at the nature of direct marketing and its advantages to marketers and customers. This is followed by discussion of direct response media, marketing databases, direct marketing management, and the future of direct marketing. The chapter also looks at sales promotion, public relations, and their management.

Chapter 17 looks at the objectives and tasks of personal selling. It focuses on the steps in the personal

selling process and the nature of sales force management. It also examines the functions of professional salespeople and the various types of selling jobs.

The comprehensive case examines the public relations firm Hill & Knowlton's efforts to cope with a crisis brought on by the decision to handle the National Conference of Catholic Bishops account. The firm's task included making plain and persuasive the reasoning behind the Bishops' opposition to abortion. The case illustrates the nature of the communication process and the promotion mix. It also raises ethical issues.

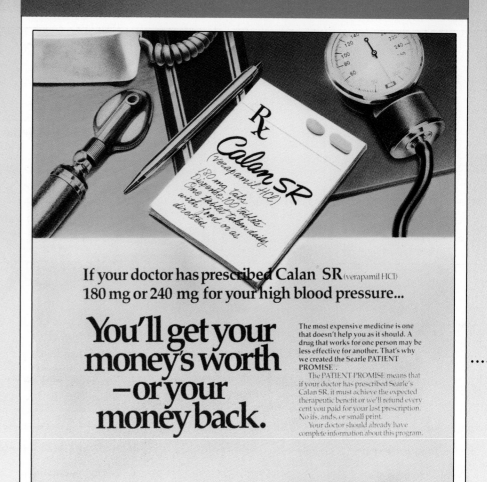

THE PROMOTION
EFFORT

After reading this chapter you will be able to

1. identify and explain the elements in the communication process.

2. explain what a promotion mix is and identify some of the many factors that influence its development.

3. identify several major examples of generalized promotion objectives.

4. identify the major steps in managing the promotion effort.

5. cite examples of criticisms about promotion that often are framed as questions.

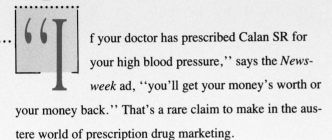

"If your doctor has prescribed Calan SR for your high blood pressure," says the *Newsweek* ad, "you'll get your money's worth or your money back." That's a rare claim to make in the austere world of prescription drug marketing.

Monsanto's Searle unit, however, has made Calan SR a marketing standout and transformed Searle from an anemic money loser to a profitable go-getter. The stakes are high and the competition is intense. Sales of calcium channel blocker drugs like Calan—which relaxes the arteries—are growing rapidly. But similar drugs are offered by Lederle Laboratories, Pfizer, and Knoll, a German company. Yet Searle, by dint of its superior marketing as much as anything else, has a dominant and highly profitable share of the market.

The marketing is narrowly focused on about 120,000 doctors who prescribe the drugs, mostly internists and general practitioners, but also key specialists like kidney and heart doctors. With its *Newsweek* ad, however, Searle goes beyond the doctors to the ultimate consumer. Recent Searle ads touted Searle's Patient Promise program, which pays for any unused portion of a drug that proves to be ineffec-

tive. So far, Searle has paid out only a minimal amount of money, but the campaign attracted a lot of attention.

"Most doctors don't prescribe a chemical compound, they prescribe a brand name," according to one kidney specialist. "Marketing is everything." Searle's chemical compound—verapamil—is considered highly effective against hypertension and puts less strain on the heart than some other treatments. An identical drug, Isoptin SR, made by Knoll, the company that licenses the verapamil formula to Searle, does a fraction of Calan's business. The difference, according to a pharmaceutical analyst, is Searle's strong marketing.

The Food and Drug Administration (FDA) sternly polices drug promotion, so Searle must design its marketing programs within very strict boundaries. The backbone of pharmaceutical marketing remains the sober communication of detailed medical findings about drugs to doctors. But within the confines of FDA rules, Searle plays creatively and effectively. Searle's army of over 700 salespeople, like those of other drug companies, makes frequent calls to physicians in their offices and in hospitals, and commonly gives away prescription pads preprinted with drugs' brand names. To generate data on which to base its marketing efforts, Searle works with physicians to initiate studies on how effective the drug is.

Searle began their Patient in Need program with Calan SR, and gave away $10 million worth of Calan to indigent hypertension sufferers. The effort won Searle considerable goodwill among both doctors and the African-American community, an important market for Calan SR since African-Americans are disproportionately affected by hypertension. After one year Searle expanded this program to include 75 percent of its product line.

Searle also developed Patients in the Know—detailed informational literature for distribution by doctors to their patients, who often forget or ignore what their doctors tell them about prescription drugs. Again, none of this is startling for a consumer product, but it's delicate stuff for a drug-marketer. The Patient Promise program, for instance, was hotly debated within Searle. Some critics contended that a money-back offer might undermine confidence in the drug by suggesting it might not work. And just before Searle ran its *Newsweek* ad, it bought space in medical journals to inform physicians what it was about to do. Why? "Doctors don't like surprises," says a Searle executive.[1]

Marketers refer to efforts to communicate with target audiences as *promotion*. Searle is using various promotional approaches to communicate with physicians and ultimate consumers. These approaches include advertising, personal selling, direct marketing, sales promotion, and public relations—the promotion mix.

In this chapter we examine how the communication process works, what a promotion mix is, what the factors that influence its development are, and what the objectives of promotion activities are. We also look at the management of the promotion effort and some of the criticisms directed at promotion.

THE COMMUNICATION PROCESS

communication

Communication is the process of influencing others' behavior by sharing ideas, information, or feelings with them. The two major participants are the *sender* (source) and the *receiver* (destination or audience). The sender has a meaning and seeks to share it with one or more receivers. The tools senders use to reach their intended receivers are called messages and channels. Thus communication occurs when (1) a sender transmits a message, (2) a receiver receives that message, and (3) the sender and the receiver have a shared meaning. Figure 14–1 shows the basic elements in the communication process.

The Sender

The message sender can be an individual, a business organization, or a nonbusiness organization. How target receivers perceive the sender can have a major impact on communi-

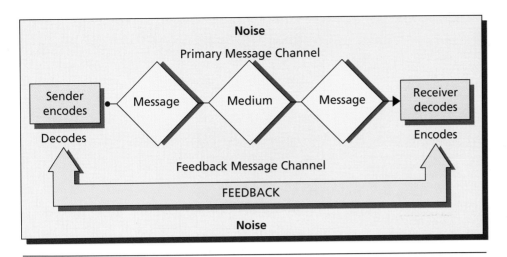

FIGURE 14–1
....

Elements in the Communications
Process ▮

cation effectiveness. In the communication process, ***source credibility*** is target receivers'
perceptions regarding the sender's believability. The more believable the sender is perceived to be, the more likely the message will be perceived as credible. Source credibility
influences how target receivers will evaluate and react to the message. The Rolex ad features a very credible spokesperson, General Chuck Yeager.

···▮······
source credibility

A source's credibility can be attributed to such factors as experience, perceived expertise, trustworthiness, and likability. In the athletic shoe industry Nike uses only athletes as
spokespersons in its ads. Reebok and L. A. Gear use athletes and entertainers. For example, L. A. Gear's products have been promoted by Michael Jackson, Joe Montana, and
Paula Abdul. Prior to serving as a spokesperson for L. A. Gear, Paula Abdul endorsed Reebok shoes.[2] Retired politicians and retired network TV people are also popular as
spokespersons.

Some advertisers are shying away from using a single spokesperson to personify their
brand because of the possibility of a "spokesperson scandal." Several years ago Pepsi
launched a campaign featuring Madonna. The initial ad included the premiere of her new
song, "Like a Prayer." Soon thereafter Madonna's music video of the same song appeared
on TV and sparked a public outcry because of its mingling of Christian imagery and sug-
gestive scenes.[3]

Some advertisers believe real people make ads more believable than do professional
models. Beefeater gin, Breck hair care products, and Jockey hosiery run contests to find
people to appear in their ads.[4]

To communicate effectively the sender must (1) identify the intended receiver's characteristics and the desired change in behavior, (2) formulate the message and place it in a
form the receiver can interpret (encoding), (3) select the channels that can best reach the
receiver and carry the message, and (4) interpret feedback from the receiver (decoding) and
determine the changes that may be needed to improve the communication process.

Encoding

Because meaning cannot be transmitted directly, it must be converted into symbols that can
be transmitted. ***Encoding*** is the process of putting meaning into symbols to be conveyed
as messages in the communication process. These symbols must be chosen carefully, however, because the receiver will assign meaning to them (interpret or decode them) in light
of personal experience and knowledge. Thus the symbols must be tied to some common

···▮······
encoding

To the first man to break the sound barrier, Rolex is essential equipment.

Chuck Yeager first flew when he was 18. Three years later, he was a World War II ace. And at only 24, he became the first man to fly faster than the speed of sound.

The Bell X-1, first to fly faster than the speed of sound.

An uncommon mix of drives and talents contributes to the general's achievements: the grit to press to the outer limits of speed, an insatiable lust for flight, extraordinary eyesight and reflexes, and an instinct for choosing the right equipment. Like the Rolex Oyster that has served him through 4 decades, even on punishing supersonic flights.

Now retired from the military, the general is still a man on the move. He's a consulting test pilot, a lecturer, and a lifelong outdoorsman with a passion for hunting and fishing.

Honors abound for such a man. His many awards include a peacetime Congressional Medal of Honor and the gold medal of the Fédération Aéronautique Internationale.

Today, General Yeager may well be America's most celebrated pilot. His exploits were featured in the Academy Award-winning film

The Right Stuff. And his autobiography, *Yeager,* became a best-seller.

Keeping one of history's greatest test pilots on schedule takes an extraordinarily tough and reliable timepiece. For over 40 years, Rolex has been Chuck Yeager's choice to meet that challenge. And he ought to know.

Gold Medal, Fédération Aéronautique Internationale.

ROLEX

GMT-Master II Oyster Perpetual Chronometer in stainless steel.
Write for brochure. Rolex Watch U.S.A., Inc., Dept. 612, Rolex Building, 665 Fifth Avenue, New York, New York 10022-5383.
GMT-Master II, Oyster Perpetual are trademarks. © 1986 Rolex Watch U.S.A., Inc.

point of reference between the sender and the receiver. The Carefree ad is an example of an effective combination of symbols to convey a message.

To share meaning the sender must choose symbols that the receiver perceives as familiar and will use in referring to the meaning intended by the sender. Benetton's long-running ad campaign stressing harmony among the races encountered difficulty several years ago. The ad that caused problems showed a white hand and a black hand, both denim-clad and handcuffed together at the wrists. Benetton received many complaints from people who believed it depicted an African-American man under arrest. The company was accused of racism.[5]

Language differences often cause problems in encoding messages. This is a problem for marketers in the United States that target ethnic segments in our culturally diverse society. It is also a problem for marketers that target markets overseas. Unilever's Timotei shampoo is a big hit in Europe but failed its market test in the United States. One reason was that Americans had trouble pronouncing the name.

The Message

• • • ▪ • • • • •

message

Sources must first determine what change in receiver behavior they want to achieve and then develop a message to induce that change. A *message* is the combination of symbols

representing objects or experiences that a communicator transmits in order to induce a change in a receiver's behavior. Most symbols, including words, can have more than one meaning, so those selected for messages should be familiar to intended receivers and should be arranged in the simplest structure possible.

As we will see more fully in chapters 15–17, message development is a complex and especially important part of the communication process. It involves determining *what* to say and *how* to say it to produce the change in receiver behavior the sender wants to achieve.

VISA had difficulty airing a TV ad in New Zealand and Australia that promoted VISA's "exclusive" sponsorship of the 1990 Commonwealth Games. The ad was like other VISA ads: "Bring your VISA card . . . they don't take American Express." It was criticized by advertising standards boards in both countries, which said the ad reflected poorly on the games by suggesting that American Express cardholders weren't welcome in Auckland, New Zealand, where the competition was held.[6]

The content of some messages focuses on product benefits, quality, and performance. Ads for natural gas often stress the economy and dependability of the product. Fear, guilt, pride, and moral responsibility are other examples of appeals. The National Parkinson Foundation uses a fear appeal: "Let's get it, before it gets you." Ads for Foster Parents

Three engines are best appreciated eight miles above the Pacific.

More than 1600 miles ahead: Guam. 1600 miles behind: Hawaii. You're in one of many places where the security of a Falcon's third engine is especially meaningful. Where deeper systems redundancy is priceless. Where, in the unlikely event of an engine failure, the assurance of reaching an airport is immeasurably valuable. Assurance that's yours from any point on the globe.

That's why the three-engine Falcon 50 and 900 are the only business jets that meet the most stringent FAA safety standards for extended overwater flight. Yet, surprisingly, both Falcons cost *less* to operate than competing twins.

For detailed information on the many benefits that an extra engine can provide, contact your nearby Falcon Jet Regional Sales Manager or call Falcon Jet at (201) 393-8056.

FalconJet
Teterboro, New Jersey 07608

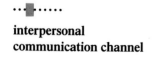

What appeals are used in this ad?

(Falcon Jet Corporation)

Plan often focus on moral responsibility: ''It's the right thing to do.'' As the Falcon Jet ad suggests, some ads use more than one appeal.

Structure (organization) must also be considered in message development. For example, in making their sales presentations, salespeople may be instructed to use the same sales talk (a canned sales presentation) for all prospects or to tailor their presentations to each individual prospect. Structuring also requires decisions about the sequencing of selling propositions. For example, should the product's strongest selling points come at the beginning or the end of the presentation? Generally, if the prospect lacks interest, they should appear early. The elements in print and broadcast ads must also be carefully structured, as we will see in the next chapter.

The Communication Channel

A communication channel is anything that carries a message—a means by which the sender conveys or transmits a message to receivers. Two broad types are interpersonal communication channels and mass communication channels.

An *interpersonal communication channel* is a type of message carrier that provides direct contact between the sender and the receiver. Examples include salesperson-to-prospect communication and word-of-mouth.

interpersonal communication channel

In salesperson-to-prospect communication, salespeople are in direct face-to-face contact with one or more prospective buyers. Such channels are selective; that is, the message can be tailored to the individual receiver. If the prospective buyer has been screened (qualified) in terms of desire for the product and ability to buy it, the channel is even more selective. Communication flows in both directions, and the salesperson receives immediate and direct feedback. This enables the salesperson to largely control the communication process.

In word-of-mouth communication, friends and relatives influence the receiver's behavior. In many cases this channel is more effective than a salesperson-to-prospect channel because salespeople are typically perceived as biased in favor of the source.

A *mass communication channel* is a type of message carrier that provides contact between the sender and a large number of receivers simultaneously. Examples include print media (newspapers and magazines) and broadcast media (radio and television).

mass communication channel

The Receiver

A receiver, a potential customer perhaps, is an active participant in communication who (1) on the basis of knowledge and experience, assigns meanings to (decodes) messages received; and (2) reacts to the decoded meaning by asking questions, making comments, and buying or not buying. The meanings a receiver assigns to a message depend on many factors, including attitudes, values, previous experiences, timing, the receiver's needs, and the interpretation of the message. Growing cultural diversity in the United States is contributing to greater use of specialized ads for different receiver groups.

The sender should understand the wants and characteristics of targeted receivers, whether they are present or potential customers, deciders, gatekeepers, or influencers. The factors that influence consumer and organizational buying behavior are all relevant to developing a true understanding of the target audience. Some of these factors complicate the communication effort. For example, when groups influence purchase decisions, the sender has a more difficult task in determining which people should receive the message and how it should be targeted to them.

Decoding

decoding

Just as the sender must encode the message, the receiver must decode it. *Decoding* is the process by which the receiver attempts to convert symbols conveyed by the sender into a message. Different receivers may decode, or interpret, the message in different ways because of their individual characteristics, biases, and backgrounds. Whenever a receiver does not decode the meaning the sender encoded, the result is noise, which we will discuss shortly.

As we saw in chapter 5, consumers are constantly bombarded by an ever-changing flow of stimuli. Attempts by advertisers to communicate with consumers are part of this flow. In order to cope, consumers are selective in the messages they receive (selective exposure), in how they decode them (selective perception), and in how much of the decoded message is remembered (selective retention). Not all messages are received or decoded as the sender intends. Thus a message by Alcoholics Anonymous on TV may be ignored by nondrinkers while angering some of the alcoholics at whom it is targeted.

Feedback

feedback

After a message has been sent, the sender is interested in securing feedback. *Feedback* is communication from receivers to the sender about the meaning they assigned to the message and how they reacted to it. Feedback generally is more frequent, more direct, and more immediate when the sender uses interpersonal communication channels such as personal selling rather than mass communication channels such as television and radio. Effective salespeople are skilled in receiving feedback from their prospects and can adapt their sales presentations on the spot to fit the individual prospect's requirements. Even when feedback through mass communication channels does exist, it is usually indirect, slow, and hard to obtain. It may require the sender to sample people in the target audience to determine if they recall the message and how many times they saw or heard it.

Companies that offer toll-free telephone numbers and invite customers to call for information about product usage or to express satisfaction or make complaints are actively encouraging customer feedback. So are restaurants, hotels, and hospitals that place questionnaires on tables and in guest and patient rooms. General Electric's Answer Center is an 800-number network. Since GE first installed the 800 number in 1982, calls have gone from 1,000 to 65,000 a week. The 150 Answer Center representatives must have a college degree and sales experience. They are expected to spot trends in consumer complaints and alert the appropriate GE division so it can take prompt action.[7]

Noise

noise

Anything that interferes with the communication process so the receiver gets a message that is different from the one the sender sent or gets no message at all is *noise*. Noise can come from many sources and can affect any or all elements of the communication process.

The vehicle within a given medium (for example, *Time* in the magazine medium) that is chosen for a particular message may create noise if target receivers do not expect that message to be channeled through that vehicle. Commercials for products targeted to people aged sixty-five and over would likely encounter considerable noise on MTV.

Noise can originate in the actions and perceptions of the receiver too. TV viewers who go to the refrigerator or who switch channels during commercials or "zap" them create noise.

As mentioned earlier, a receiver may assign meanings to symbols (decode) that are different from meanings the sender intended, especially when sender and receiver have very different backgrounds. Thus receivers' perceptual processes create noise by screening out or distorting messages.

Noise may even originate in the message itself. For many years Norelco used special Christmas ads—ones with an animated Santa Claus riding snowy hills atop a Norelco shaver. But the ads fostered an image that Norelco was in the toy business—and they did not help in increasing sales.[8] Coca-Cola's "Coke Is It" campaign became meaningless after the company introduced the new Coke. Thus it switched to "Can't Beat the Feeling."[9]

In order to communicate with their target receivers, marketers must develop promotion mixes. The elements in such a mix must be carefully selected and blended to produce an effective promotion program.

THE PROMOTION MIX ELEMENTS

Creating a marketing mix involves a careful blending of the product, place, promotion, and price elements. Each of these elements, not just the promotion element, communicates something to potential customers. For example, packaging is an integral component of the product element in the marketing mix. But because of its promotional role as a ''silent salesperson,'' packaging could also be included among the elements in a promotion mix. What a product costs and where it can be purchased also say something to potential customers. Thus the entire marketing mix must be managed carefully to deliver maximum communication impact.

The promotion mix, one of the four major components of the marketing mix, also requires blending. A **_promotion mix_** is a careful blending of advertising, personal selling, direct marketing, sales promotion, and public relations to accomplish an organization's promotion objectives. (See Figure 14–2.)

Industries and organizations vary with respect to the relative importance they place on the different elements in the marketing mix. The same is true of the promotion mix. For example, firms in the cosmetics industry typically spend a higher percentage of their sales revenues on promotion than do firms in the bulk chemicals business.

Even within a given industry, firms often vary in terms of the percentage of sales revenues they spend on promotion. Dean Foods Company is a major producer of diverse food products. Unlike most other big food companies, Dean keeps a low profile, marketing mostly regional brands and knock-offs of other companies' new-product hits. Dean spends only about 1 percent of sales on advertising—far below the average for the packaged-foods industry.[10]

There is often considerable variation in the way rivals allocate their promotion budgets among the various elements in their promotion mixes. Avon, for example, emphasizes personal selling, whereas Revlon emphasizes advertising.

The elements in the promotion mix must be coordinated and integrated so they reinforce and complement each other in order to create a blend that accomplishes the organization's

promotion mix

FIGURE 14–2

The Promotion Mix
Elements

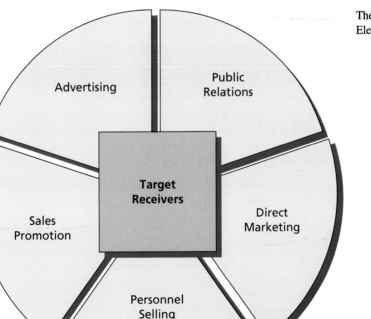

promotion objectives. Some promotion mix elements are better suited than others to accomplishing certain promotion objectives. For example, advertising might be emphasized in creating rapid consumer awareness of a new product, and personal selling might be needed to answer prospective buyers' questions at the point of purchase and to create the conviction to buy.

In chapter 10 we discussed the adoption process—the series of stages a prospective buyer goes through in deciding whether to buy and make regular use of a new product. The stages are awareness, interest, evaluation, trial, and adoption. Promotion can help in moving prospective buyers through this process.

From an overall perspective, promotion seeks to inform, remind, and persuade target receivers about the organization and its products. Different types of advertising are used to accomplish these three objectives. But in order to inform, persuade, or remind target customers, the organization must first get their attention. Advertisers more than ever are struggling to come up with attention-grabbers.

The Sanctuary shelter in San Francisco dramatized the plight of the homeless with a billboard featuring the message "Don't leave the homeless out in the cold." Volunteers standing on a platform and harnessed to the billboard (to prevent accidents) helped draw attention to the message.[11]

If prospective customers are to become adopters (be converted into customers), however, the marketer must develop their interest, arouse their desire, and generate action on their part. The *AIDA process* is the sequence of stages (attention, interest, desire, and action) that a marketer hopes to lead target customers through with its promotion effort. The AIDA process, for example, guides the development of ads and personal sales presentations. The following overview of each promotion mix element provides a foundation for the discussion in the remainder of this chapter.

Advertising

The advertising element is used when sponsors want to communicate with a number of people who cannot be reached economically and effectively through personal means. *Advertising* is any paid form of nonpersonal communication through the mass media about a good, service, or idea by an identified sponsor. The media used include magazines, direct mail, radio, television, billboards, and newspapers. Sponsors may be nonprofit organizations, political candidates, companies, or individuals. Advertising differs from news and publicity in that an identified sponsor pays for placing the message in the media.

Personal Selling

Nonprofit organizations, political candidates, companies, and individuals use personal selling to communicate with their publics. *Personal selling* is a person-to-person process by which the seller learns about the prospective buyer's wants and seeks to satisfy them by making a sale.

In chapter 17 we will look at several types of selling jobs. Although they are all examples of personal selling, there are significant differences among them. For example, personal selling means something entirely different to Kmart than to IBM.

Direct Marketing

As we will see in chapter 16, direct marketing is becoming more and more important in many marketers' promotion mixes. The Direct Marketing Association defines the term as follows: *Direct marketing* is an interactive system of marketing which uses one or more

AIDA process

advertising

personal selling

direct marketing

advertising media to effect a measurable response and/or transaction at any location. If you have ever received a phone call or a brochure in the mail from someone trying to sell you something or if you have ordered merchandise from a catalog, you were the target of a direct marketer. We will discuss other forms of direct marketing in chapter 16.

Sales Promotion

The element of sales promotion is a means of communicating with target receivers in a way that is not feasible by using other elements of the promotion mix. *Sales promotion* is any activity that offers an incentive for a limited period to induce a desired response from target customers, company salespeople, or intermediaries. Sales promotion activities add value to the product because the incentives ordinarily do not accompany the product. For example, consumer contests add value for consumers, and sales contests add value for salespeople.

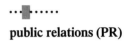
sales promotion

A new kind of vending machine in supermarkets dispenses free samples with the pull of a lever. It also hands out a coupon to be used toward the purchase of a full-size package and offers a thank you from a synthesized voice.[12] The Oakland Athletics use novel promotions to make the ballpark experience more fun for casual fans and families as well as for baseball diehards. Among them are animated dot races on the giant TV screen in center field, free diapers in the restrooms, and high-decibel rock-and-roll interludes (rather than tunes played on an organ).[13]

Public Relations

Modern organizations are concerned about the effects of their actions on people outside their target markets. These people may have little contact with an organization but believe it affects their welfare in some way. Unless the organization understands their concerns and communicates its goals and interests, they may misinterpret, distort, or be openly hostile to the organization's actions. *Public relations (PR)* is communication to build and maintain a favorable image for an organization, maintain the goodwill of its many publics, and explain its goals and purposes.

public relations (PR)

Unlike the other promotion mix elements, public relations is concerned primarily with people outside the target market, although it may include them. Government agencies, communities in which plants are located, consumerists, environmentalists, stockholders, and college professors are some of the groups reached by an organization's PR efforts.

Publicity is a type of communication that comes under the heading of public relations. *Publicity* is news carried in the mass media about an organization and its products, policies, personnel, or actions; it can originate with the media or the marketer and is published or aired at no charge to the organization for media space or time. The U.S. distributor of Nevica skiwear does virtually no advertising. Instead the distributor developed a list of the thirty most prolific photographers whose work appears in major ski magazines. It then began offering these photographers free skiwear and a fee if they got photos with Nevica-clad models into major ski magazines. As a result, Nevica gear shows up regularly in ads for ski products such as boots—as well as in ski resort promotions.[14] This is an example of positive publicity. Animal welfare groups such as People for the Ethical Treatment of Animals and Friends of Animals have helped generate negative publicity for the fur and beef industries. Unfavorable publicity about an organization is ''news'' originated by the media.

publicity

Although publicity does not require any payment to the broadcast media for time or to the print media for space, it is not free communication. The marketer, for example, may have to pay for the cost of preparing news releases.

FACTORS INFLUENCING THE PROMOTION MIX

Most marketers use a combination of elements in their promotion mixes, and each element should reinforce the messages of the others. Among the many factors influencing the choice of elements and the relative emphasis placed on each are (1) product-related factors, (2) customer-related factors, (3) organization-related factors, and (4) situation-related factors. (See Figure 14–3.)

Product-Related Factors

Among the product-related factors that affect the promotion mix are (1) the amount and complexity of product information to be communicated, (2) the product's stage in its life cycle, and (3) the product type and unit price.

• **Amount and Complexity of Product Information** • To get across simple ideas or to make consumers aware of a product whose features are easily observed, emphasis is usually placed on advertising. Advertising also is used for products that are familiar to consumers. The messages are relatively simple and easily understood.

To demonstrate complex ideas, emphasis is placed on personal selling and sales promotions, such as printed brochures, demonstrations, and point-of-purchase displays. Salespeople and product demonstrations convert complex information to a form consumers

FIGURE 14–3

Factors Influencing the
Promotion Mix

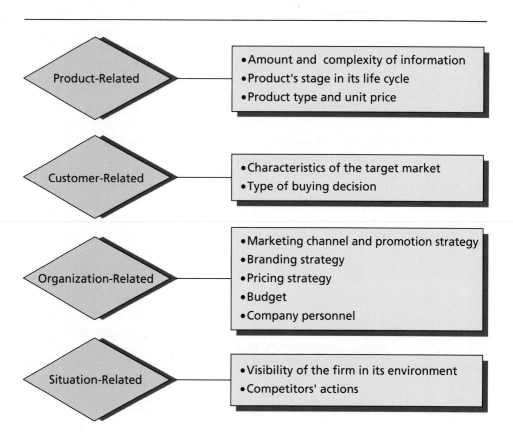

A product's stage in its life cycle influences its promotion mix. Disney's announcement that it would open Disney stores generated a great deal of publicity for the stores during the introduction stage of their life cycle.

[© David Dempster]

can understand. Such personal contact also enables consumers to experience the product and ask questions.

Some organizations use videotapes to sell products that are hard to describe or demonstrate. Datavision Technologies has developed video sales pitches that are the counterpart of personalized form letters. Datavision's technology enables firms to create individualized videotapes to target consumers in various economic brackets or geographical regions.[15]

• **Product's Stage in the Life Cycle** • The objectives and the tools used for the promotion effort differ in each stage of a product's life cycle. During the introduction stage, the basic promotion objective is to inform. This helps create awareness of and interest in the product. Extensive advertising, direct marketing, sales promotions (such as coupons and free samples), and publicity help reach potential customers and induce trial purchases. Personal selling also helps reach intermediaries to ensure adequate distribution.

During the growth stage, as an increasing number of rivals are entering the market, promotion efforts shift to differentiating the brand by showing its advantages relative to rival brands'. Promotion is increasingly persuasive in order to build and maintain brand loyalty—repeat purchases. Because a larger number of people are trying and adopting the product, marketers of each brand in the product category find advertising to be more economical. Personal selling efforts, however, are still needed to increase the intensity of the product's distribution—to recruit additional intermediaries and to maintain established ones.

Because competition tends to be most intense during the maturity stage, promotion efforts and expenditures are at their highest levels. Promotion becomes even more persuasive, and advertising tends to dominate the promotion mix. Product improvements may be introduced to combat or discourage introduction of new brands, especially dealer brands, and to extend the brand's life. These product changes may require new promotion campaigns.

Marketers usually reduce promotion in the decline stage. But they may continue aggressive promotion to a particularly loyal segment of customers. Otherwise, much of the promotion is left to intermediaries, because the manufacturer's profit margin can no longer support the heavy promotion expenditures of earlier stages.

• **Product Type and Unit Price** • The interaction of product type (consumer or industrial) and unit price affects the promotion mix. Heavy emphasis is placed on advertising for relatively inexpensive consumer products. Items with a high unit price receive more personal selling support because consumers want more detailed and personalized information. Personal selling is more important at all price levels for industrial products but receives even greater emphasis at the higher unit price levels. Again, the need for more accurate and tailored information for large purchases probably accounts for this.

Customer-Related Factors

Two customer-related factors influence the promotion mix: characteristics of the target market and type of buying decision.

• **Characteristics of the Target Market** • Advertising is a nonpersonal form of promotion in that there is no direct contact between the advertiser and the promotion target. Personal selling is a personal form of promotion because there is direct contact between the salesperson and the prospect.

Public relations, sales promotion, and direct marketing are more difficult to classify as personal or nonpersonal. An example of a personal type of public relations is a company spokesperson announcing at a local Chamber of Commerce luncheon the company's decision to expand its plant. An example of nonpersonal public relations is publicity. Coupons are an example of nonpersonal sales promotion. Store demonstrations are an example of personal sales promotion. In a store demonstration the manufacturer arranges with retailers a special in-store demonstration of its products and supplies them to the representatives who conduct the demonstrations. Although face-to-face contact does not occur in direct marketing, some forms of direct marketing are more personal than others. For example, a conversation between a telemarketer and a prospect is more personal than is ordering by mail from a catalog.

In general, nonpersonal forms of promotion are emphasized in promotion mixes targeted to ultimate consumers. Personal selling tends to receive more emphasis in promotion mixes targeted to organizational buyers.

Nonpersonal forms of promotion to consumers are especially favored as the size of the target market increases. But as the size increases, the people in the target become more heterogeneous with respect to demographic and lifestyle characteristics. This makes nonpersonal forms of promotion less effective.

Beyond a certain point, therefore, marketers usually engage in market segmentation and product differentiation. Even if the product remains the same, the promotion efforts may be radically different. Regional TV ads for nationally distributed products may be used as well as different ads in various regional magazines. On the other hand, as we will discuss more fully in chapter 22, it may be possible to reach some market segments throughout the world with a global ad campaign. For example, Benetton, Coca-Cola, PepsiCo, Levi

Strauss, Gillette, and Swatch International are among the firms that are now behaving as if there is one generic type of teenager in most parts of the world.[16]

The choice of a promotion mix for products with a relatively small target market depends on whether people in the market are relatively similar. If so, special-interest or local mass media may be used. If not, personal contact through personal selling or telephone sales calls may be used.

• **Type of Buying Decision** • The second customer-related influence on the promotion mix is the type of buying decision involved—programmed or complex. Consumers making programmed decisions are not receptive to information. If they make programmed purchases of the firm's brand, promotion focuses on calling attention to the brand at the point of purchase, reminding them that the brand remains better than others, and combating the introductory campaigns of new brands. If they make programmed purchases of rival brands, promotion might focus on appeals such as "if you're tired of your brand, try ours."

When complex decisions are being made, the promotion mix must be heavily informative and tailored to the consumer's primary concerns. The effects of rivals' promotional campaigns also must be considered. Reassuring the consumer after the decision through individualized communications such as a personal letter may help reduce cognitive dissonance, which we discussed in chapter 5.

Convenience, shopping, specialty, and unsought products require different promotion mixes. But the type of buying decision for a product may change, thereby placing the product in a different category. The introduction of similar rival brands may switch it from a specialty product to a shopping product. For example, nothing on the market was an adequate substitute for Merrill Lynch's Cash Management Account when it was introduced. Subsequently other brokerage firms introduced their versions of this type of account. Shifts in a product's classification require changes in the content, goals, and elements of the promotion mix.

Organization-Related Factors

A promotion mix must take into account these preexisting organization-related factors: (1) marketing channel and promotion strategy, (2) branding strategy, (3) pricing strategy, (4) budget, and (5) company personnel.

• **Marketing Channel and Promotion Strategy** • Probably the single most important factor influencing the development of a promotion mix is the marketer's choice of a strategy to build sales—a push strategy or a pull strategy.

A *push strategy* is a sales-building strategy in which the producer actively promotes its product to intermediaries, which actively promote it to final buyers. Thus a consumer product manufacturer using this strategy would actively promote the product to wholesalers, wholesalers would actively promote it to retailers, and retailers would actively promote it to consumers. Each channel participant directs its promotion effort to the next lower level in the vertical marketing channel. (See Figure 14–4.)

A push strategy typically involves heavy reliance by the producer on the company's sales force (personal selling) and various types of sales promotion directed to company salespeople and to intermediaries and their sales forces. Examples are sales contests for company salespeople, dealer contests for intermediaries, and producer-supplied incentives for dealer salespeople as an extra reward for selling the producer's product. As we saw in chapter 11, producers often use "push money" to motivate their resellers to give the product extra push through the marketing channel.

push strategy

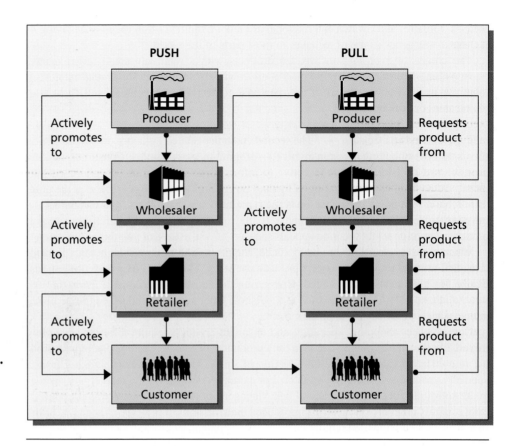

FIGURE 14–4

Push versus Pull Promotion
Strategies for a Consumer
Product

pull strategy

A *pull strategy* is a sales-building strategy in which the producer focuses promotion efforts directly on the final buyer, rather than on intermediaries in the marketing channel, in order to control product presentation to final buyers. Thus, in the case of a consumer product, the objective is to stimulate consumers to ask retailers for the product, retailers to ask wholesalers for the product, and wholesalers to ask the producer for the product. Consumers "pull" the product through the marketing channel. (See Figure 14–4.)

A pull strategy typically involves heavy spending by the producer on advertising and various types of sales promotions directed to final buyers. Examples include coupons and consumer sweepstakes. A pull strategy allows the producer to control how the product is presented to consumers. Pull is more appropriate when the producer wants to create a strong corporate image.

Big food and consumer product producers are emphasizing the push strategy in an effort to win shelf space amid a skyrocketing number of new products. Partly because of sluggish domestic sales, however, Kellogg announced early in 1990 that it was shifting more of its money to consumer advertising and away from trade promotion. Although Kellogg still spends millions on trade promotion, a company spokesperson said, "It's fair to say that there's growing emphasis on the pull side of the business, to get the consumer."[17]

In most cases marketers use various combinations of push and pull. Salespeople for many cosmetics manufacturers, for example, call on department stores, discount stores, drugstores, supermarkets, and so on to implement a push strategy by perhaps setting up product demonstrations in department stores and encouraging other types of retail stores to give their brands more shelf space. The manufacturers also spend heavily on advertising and on consumer sales promotions such as samples to pull their products through their marketing channels.

- **Branding Strategy** • An organization that selects an individual branding strategy commits itself to heavy promotion expenditures to introduce a new brand. An image must be created for each brand in order for the brand to gain acceptance at each level of the marketing channel. Sales promotion, the concentrated efforts of a sales force, direct marketing, and massive advertising are needed to establish the brand.

Family branding requires less promotion effort to introduce a new product. Perhaps only a small amount of advertising to create consumer awareness will be needed because the new product capitalizes on the family brand's image. Consumers may try it because of their satisfaction with other products with the family brand name. Scotch brand adhesives are an example.

- **Pricing Strategy** • Promotion mix decisions often are affected by pricing strategy. Personal selling plays the major role in marketing high-priced products because buyers typically perceive considerable risk in buying such products. Advertising is emphasized in marketing low-priced convenience products. Getting retailers to honor a manufacturer's suggested retail selling price usually requires a major commitment on the manufacturer's part to invest heavily in advertising in order to build strong consumer demand and brand loyalty. For retailers this means fast turnover without the need to resort to price reductions to stimulate sales.

- **Budget** • Organizations choose among promotion elements on the basis of the relative costs of reaching each intended receiver. Maintaining a sales force, for example, is more expensive per person reached than is advertising. Sales promotions and direct marketing may be expensive or inexpensive, depending on the type used. Public relations generally is considered a necessary part of doing business, and its budget often is considered separately from a firm's promotion budget.

Most marketers try to optimize their return on promotion dollars. The mix they settle for is always less than ideal because there usually is a trade-off among the funds available, the number of people in the target market, the quality of the communication needed, and the relative costs of the different promotion elements. Generally, the cost per person reached is higher for personal selling, personal contact public relations, and sales promotions such as samples and demonstrations than for advertising, many types of direct marketing, other sales promotions, and publicity.

- **Company Personnel** • A fifth organization-related factor is the expertise and peculiarities of an organization's personnel. Some organizations lack experience with certain promotion elements and therefore do not use them. Powerful executives often influence or determine an organization's approach to promotion. Michel Roux is the president of Carillon Importers, the firm that markets Absolut vodka in the United States. For many years Roux has been the driving force behind Absolut's eye-catching print campaign, which plays on the name Absolut and the distinctive shape of its bottle. Roux says much of his inspiration for marketing Absolut has come from his long-standing interest in art.[18]

''Celebrity'' chief executives, such as Chrysler's Lee Iacocca, the Body Shop's Anita Roddick, and Microsoft's Bill Gates, can generate considerable publicity for their organizations. The charisma of Steve Jobs helps create favorable publicity for NeXT Inc. Of course, the publicity chief executives generate is not always favorable. Lisa Olson, a sportswriter for the *Boston Herald,* was allegedly harassed by some members of the New

England Patriots. Subsequently, Victor Kiam, owner of the Patriots and chief executive of Remington Corporation, told a joke about the incident that generated a lot of unfavorable publicity.

Situation-Related Factors

The promotion mix may be affected by situation-related factors, which stem from the firm's environment. Wrigley launched a big ad campaign with a smoking theme for its Spearmint gum. The ads recommend the brand as an alternative "when you'd like to smoke but can't." The ads address three places where smokers find it difficult, if not impossible, to smoke—on planes, at the office, and in the homes of nonsmoking friends.[19]

Over the years 3M Company has had several image campaigns, each built around a corporate slogan—for example, "What will they think of next?" "The kind of climate that grows good products," and "One thing leads to another." A recent one is "Innovation working for you." The company says the revision is justified because the marketplace has changed. According to 3M's manager of corporate communication: "People aren't interested any more in how you do things. They want to know what's in it for them."[20]

Among the situation-related factors that affect the promotion mix are the visibility of the firm in its legal, political, and social environment and competitors' actions.

• **Visibility of the Firm** • More people are concerned about the actions of highly visible firms. Some firms are more visible to the public because of their products, their relative position in an industry, or their potential impact on their communities.

Paper and lumber producers are focusing more attention on public relations in order to portray themselves as environmentally sensitive green marketers. Firms that have large market shares also spend relatively more on public relations; their executives are perceived as spokespersons for their industries. Firms whose actions are essential to or potentially harmful to the public welfare—such as chemical, transportation, pharmaceutical, waste management, petroleum, and steel companies and public utilities—also spend heavily on public relations. On the other hand, firms that prefer to maintain a low profile downplay publicity.

Le Moulin de Mougins is a highly visible gourmet restaurant owned by Roger Vergé in the French village of Mougins. In this line of business big ads often signal that the establishment's reputation is declining. Thus Vergé communicates with the public in other ways, such as through his published cookbooks. During Le Moulin de Mougins's two-month winter holiday, Vergé and several associates travel far and wide, appearing as guest stars in hotel kitchens.[21]

• **Competitors' Actions** • Rivals' promotion activities also affect the promotion mix. Organizations often have to match or counter the promotional activities of rivals to maintain or increase their market share. The "cola wars" and "hamburger wars" have been raging for years. The combatants have to respond to one another's coupon offers, event-oriented ad campaigns, and efforts to generate favorable publicity. The auto makers also have to respond to one another's rebate programs and ad campaigns.

When Atlanta was chosen as the site of the 1996 Olympic Summer Games, officials in some rival cities complained because Coca-Cola had strongly supported the hometown bid to the International Olympic Committee (IOC). Pepsi began suggesting to consumers in three cities that lost out—Athens, Rome, and Melbourne—that they should make their feelings known at the check-out counter. For example, a newspaper ad in Melbourne said, "If you don't like the I.O.C.'s choice, make your own."[22]

OBJECTIVES OF PROMOTION ACTIVITIES

As we saw earlier, promotion seeks to inform, remind, and persuade target customers about the organization and its products. Like other marketing objectives, promotion objectives should be stated clearly and specifically and a time frame should be given for their accomplishment. Otherwise, there is no basis for determining when to begin an evaluation of promotional effectiveness or on what bases to evaluate performance.

For example, one promotion objective for a new firm might be "to develop consumer and intermediary awareness of the firm and its products." This is a very general long-run objective. A more specific and useful statement might be "to develop consumer and intermediary awareness of the firm so that at least 50 percent of consumers and intermediaries will know who we are and what we have to offer by the end of our first two years in business." Another objective may be short run: "to achieve a monthly sales volume of $100,000 on product X within the next six months."

The role of each promotion mix element in achieving promotion objectives should also be stated specifically. For example, if a firm is seeking to increase short-run sales, sales promotions such as coupons and cash rebates are more likely to produce results than advertising that seeks to enhance the firm's image. The discussions that follow explain several generalized types of promotion objectives. (See Figure 14–5.)

Creating Awareness

Every year many firms go out of business simply because target customers never hear about them or what they have to offer. Product awareness also plays a major role in distribution strategy. Consumer product wholesalers, for example, are unwilling to stock products that are unknown to consumers and retailers. Big supermarket chains generally refuse to stock a new product unless the manufacturer backs it with a big promotion budget. According to one expert, approximately 90 percent of new products are withdrawn from the market within two to three years. "In most cases, failures were the result of a lack of product recognition."[23]

In a recent survey only 4 percent of U.S. consumers knew that Avia International is a

FIGURE 14–5

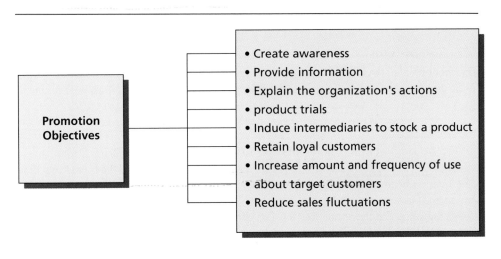

manufacturer of sneakers and sports apparel. Avia's marketing vice president says, "There's a whole segment of people who are not buying our shoes because they don't know who we are." In contrast, Avia's parent, Reebok, and industry leader Nike are known by more than 70 percent of U.S. consumers. Reebok spends more than $70 million and Nike some $100 million annually in product promotions, compared with Avia's $10 million.[24]

Providing Information

Many promotion activities are undertaken to provide information. In the cruise industry, for example, recent promotion efforts have focused on educating people about what a cruise is. The majority of Americans think that cruises are just transportation and that cruising may be boring or too expensive. But the fact is that cruising can be cheaper as a total vacation because the price includes transportation, food, lodging, and entertainment.[25]

Chicken consumption in the United States increased 62 percent between 1977 and 1990, while beef eating fell 26 percent over the same period. Nevertheless, government tests show that lean cooked beef is almost identical in terms of fat, cholesterol, and calories to

The objective of this ad is to provide information.

(Copyright 1990 AT&T.)

skinless roasted chicken. The meat industry clearly has an image problem. Part of this problem may be attributable to the lack of relevant information in the hands of potential consumers.[26]

Consumers and organizational buyers often want specific information about complex products—construction, ingredients, and uses—to help reduce the perceived risk in buying such products. Marketers must provide informative ads about the firm, product warranty, and service facilities. Informative ads, brochures, folders, and store demonstrations also help inform target customers about changes in well-accepted products. The AT&T ad tells the reader how to get AT&T service when the call is being placed from a non AT&T phone.

Explaining the Organization's Actions

As suggested by the American Bankers Association ad, organizations often must explain their actions to people who believe those actions affect them. Failure to do this can lead to misinterpretation, distrust, or open hostility.

The Environmental Protection Agency (EPA) often has to explain what it is doing to clean up toxic waste dumps. American Can Company had to explain that it changed its

An ad that explains why commercial banks may be asking their customers for more information when they make some financial transactions.

(American Bankers Association.)

name to Primerica Corporation because it was transforming itself from a manufacturer to a financial services and retailing concern. The makers of Tylenol and Sudafed had to cope with ''crisis marketing'' and explain to the public what they were doing to cope with the tampering of their products. Perrier voluntarily recalled its bottled water worldwide after traces of benzene, a suspected carcinogen, were found in some bottles. Some people question whether the company explained its actions well enough during the crisis to enable it to recover its position as U.S. market leader in the imported bottled water business.[27]

Inducing Product Trials

Promotion is often used to induce people to try products. The aim is to motivate rather than inform target markets. Getting action rather than awareness often requires different promotional appeals. Some types of direct marketing, coupons, reduced prices, samples, and contests are examples of efforts that can help get people to make trial purchases. McDonald's placed coupons for free McLean burgers in *USA Today* and the *Wall Street Journal* when the new product was introduced.

Inducing Intermediaries to Stock a Product

Wholesalers may have to be persuaded that demand exists or can be stimulated before they will agree to stock a new product. Retailers also want information on the promotion efforts manufacturers and wholesalers will undertake to stimulate consumer demand before they will stock a new product. Thus manufacturers must decide about the relative advantages of push and pull promotion strategies.

Communicating with intermediaries requires information and appeals different from those required in communicating with final buyers, because intermediaries buy for resale. They want to know about cooperative advertising arrangements (in which manufacturers share promotion costs with intermediaries), replacement of stale stock, shelf-space requirements, and profit potential.

Retailers typically carry only two or three brands of photo film. Kodak, with its roughly 80 percent share of the U.S. market, is sure to be one of the brands carried. Fuji has the second largest share of the U.S. market, approximately 11 percent. Other producers of 35 mm film, such as Polaroid and Konica, have to work especially hard to induce retailers to stock their film. Examples of such efforts are intensive advertising campaigns directed to consumers, incentives and promotions offered to retailers, and bonuses for meeting sales targets.[28]

Retaining Loyal Customers

To discourage brand switching and to reduce the chance that a brand name will become a generic name, marketers must communicate with customers who use their brands. This requires marketers to (1) remind customers that the brand is still available; (2) show customers that the brand's benefits are superior to those of rivals; (3) inform customers of changes in the brand that make it better than rivals'; (4) perhaps offer added value (premiums) for using the brand, such as T-shirt giveaways; and (5) remind customers that the brand name is not a generic name for the product category.

Customer loyalty should never be taken for granted. We mentioned Perrier's recall earlier. The recall occurred in February 1990. By mid-July of that year the product was again available throughout most of the United States. But many formerly brand-loyal customers were not buying Perrier. Perrier's marketing research confirmed that the problem was not the benzene, because memory of the incident had all but faded. Instead the contamination crisis exposed the fact that consumers tended to pick Perrier out of inertia and a perceived lack of alternatives, not any true product preference. Perrier faced the difficult task of rebuilding its market share. For example, to win back restaurant business, Perrier created a new fifty-two-member sales force to supplement distributors' efforts.[29]

Increasing Amount and Frequency of Use

A major objective of many promotion efforts is to increase the amount and frequency of use of the product. Airline frequent-flyer programs and hotel/motel frequent-guest programs are examples. So are Coca-Cola's and PepsiCo's ads that urge consumers to drink cola for breakfast.

Learning about Target Customers

Magazine ads sometimes include direct response coupons that help the advertiser determine whether a given magazine reaches the target audience and to identify market segments that might have been overlooked. Some ads include a coupon along with a toll-free telephone number. Follow-up letters and questionnaires to present customers can also help marketers learn more about them. The same is true of warranty registration cards that request information about the purchaser and place of purchase.

demographic

Reducing Sales Fluctuations

Many firms' products have fluctuating demand patterns. When sales are affected by climate, season, and holidays, problems can arise with production scheduling, shipping, inventory management, and financial and personnel requirements.

Promotion

Some resort hotels increase promotion in the off-season to attract people then and reduce promotion during the peak season so as not to stimulate more demand than can be accommodated. Electric utilities promote the use of electricity during periods of relatively low demand. Brewers are working to sell more beer in October, traditionally one of their softest months. In recent years they have developed TV commercials and in-store displays with a Halloween theme.[30]

PROMOTION MANAGEMENT

The overall promotion effort usually includes several individual promotion campaigns. A *promotion campaign* is an interrelated series of promotion activities designed to accomplish a specific objective. Thus some of Procter & Gamble's promotion campaigns focus on extending the lives of mature products and others focus on introducing new products.

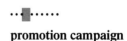
promotion campaign

The goal of promotion management is to ensure that all the individual elements of the promotion mix work together to accomplish the organization's overall promotion objectives. This overall effort may include several or many promotion campaigns. A coordinated effort is needed to (1) set promotion objectives, (2) plan the promotion effort, (3) determine the total promotion budget, (4) allocate the budget among the promotion mix elements, (5) implement the promotion program, and (6) evaluate the promotion program. (See Figure 14–6.)

Setting Promotion Objectives

Promotion objectives should be realistic and specific and should indicate the criteria by which success or failure will be judged, including the time frame for accomplishing them.

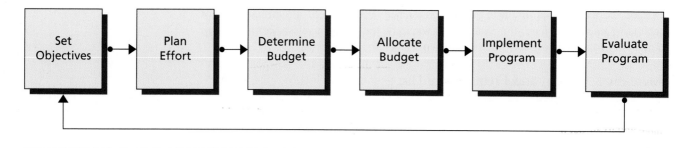

FIGURE 14–6
....

The Tasks of Promotion
Management

Table 14–1 gives some examples of poorly stated and effectively stated promotion objectives.

In 1981 Adolph Coors Company started rolling out its beer a few states at a time from its traditional geographical market west of the Mississippi River. In 1985 the company began preliminary planning for its big move into the New York–New Jersey market. Those two states together account for 10 percent of annual U.S. beer sales. Coors's objective for the promotion campaign in New York–New Jersey was to capture 8 to 10 percent of the market and to maintain and enhance that share after the novelty wore off and the introductory marketing blitz subsided. The campaign was launched in early 1987.[31]

Planning the Promotion Effort

Once objectives are set, the next steps are to (1) determine which promotion elements are most appropriate to reach the target; (2) determine exactly what each element must do and who will be accountable for what; (3) construct a coordinated work sequence for the promotion elements, with a schedule of when each step will be completed; and (4) arrange for feedback.

All elements of the promotion mix were used when Coors entered the New York–New Jersey market. In addition to having to contend with rival brewers in that market, the company's promotion effort had to appeal to a large number of African-Americans, Hispanics,

TABLE 14–1　Comparison of Poorly Stated and Effectively Stated Promotion Objectives

....

Poorly Stated Objectives

1. To create good acceptance of our firm by consumers.
2. To market our product with dignity.
3. To increase the market for our product.

Effectively Stated Objectives

1. To create awareness of our new product in 40 percent of the 16–21 age group this year.
2. To increase market share for our brands by 5 percent in the coming year.
3. To position our product over the next three years as the undisputed leader in the Hispanic market in the United States.

....

and union members—groups with whom Coors had had stormy relations. Prior to Coors's entry into the market, the New York AFL-CIO called on its members to boycott Coors and discouraged taverns and stores from carrying the beer. In an effort to blunt the boycott, Coors contacted local reporters and urged them to include the company's viewpoint in any news stories they wrote. African-Americans and Hispanics ended a Coors boycott in 1984, when the company agreed to recruit more African-American and Hispanic employees and to do business with more minority-owned firms. In order to help build a good-neighbor image and to attract minority customers in the New York area, Coors donated money to the Urban League, sponsored an African-American cowboy rodeo, and lent support to a Puerto Rican theater troupe and program for the homeless.

Determining the Promotion Budget

One of the toughest decisions organizations face is deciding how much to spend on promotion—determining the promotion budget. Typical approaches to setting the promotion budget include (1) taking a percentage of current or forecasted sales, (2) spending all available funds, (3) matching expenditures of a major competitor, (4) calculating return on investment, (5) using an arbitrary amount, and (6) establishing objectives and determining the tasks and their costs.

During the 1970s people who journeyed out West often took Coors beer home with them as a sort of souvenir. But by the time Coors was preparing to enter the New York–New Jersey market, Coors beer was available everywhere except Pennsylvania, Delaware, and Indiana. In other words, Coors beer no longer qualified as a rare and coveted commodity, and the company set a promotion budget of $25 million for the New York–New Jersey market entry.

- **Percentage of Current or Forecasted Sales** • The budget can be figured by taking a percentage of either last year's sales or the forecasted sales for the coming year. A slight variation is to use a fixed amount per unit of product and to multiply it by the forecasted number of units to be sold in the coming year. This approach is rigid and leads to overspending during expanding markets and underspending during declining markets. It also confuses cause and effect. Basing a promotion budget on current sales, for example, means that promotional funds are a function of sales.

- **Spending All Available Funds** • Small firms often use for promotion whatever funds remain after expenses and allowance for a reasonable profit. This method reflects management's desire to maintain liquidity but does not consider promotion a capital investment for which a firm might reasonably borrow money. Also, the budget is not related to the firm's promotion objectives.

- **Matching Expenditures of a Major Competitor** • Matching the expenditures of a major competitor mistakenly assumes that the rival knows what it is doing and that your firm's needs are the same. A variation is to use the average percentage of sales devoted to promotion in the whole industry. This recognizes the activities of rivals but does not tie budgets to promotion objectives or recognize differences in the promotional effectiveness of the different firms.

- **Return on Investment** • The return on investment approach treats promotion as a capital investment. The underlying logic is that since an organization's funds are limited, the allocation of those funds should be based on their projected return on investment. Thus the use of funds for promotion must compete with their use for other purposes, such as building a new plant or buying new equipment. This approach is rarely used because it is difficult to estimate the return on dollars spent on promotion.

- **Arbitrary Amount** • Deciding how much you want to spend and then seeing what you can get for the money is a highly arbitrary method. This approach sometimes leads to overspending for small firms; and owners may receive benefits that are unrelated to the firm's objectives, such as compliments on their appearance in TV commercials.

- **Objective and Task** • Usually the most effective approach to determining the promotion budget is to (1) establish promotion objectives, (2) determine the promotion tasks that will accomplish each objective, and (3) estimate the cost of performing each task. Thus the objective and task approach requires an ability to measure the productivity of each dollar invested in promotion.

Of course, different objectives will require different levels of spending and different promotion mixes. Costs, therefore, will vary accordingly. The budget and the objectives it is supposed to support must be flexible to adjust to changing company and market conditions. The objectives and the mix might have to be adjusted to fit available resources.

Coors knew that when it entered the New York–New Jersey market entrenched brewers would fight hard to defend their market shares. For example, a spokesperson for Miller Brewing Company said, "We'll offer our distributors a whole smorgasbord of sweepstakes, refunds, and other incentives to hold on to Miller customers who are tempted to try Coors." The objective and task approach made sense for Coors.

Allocating the Promotion Budget

Promotion funds must be allocated to different promotion mix elements. Organizations are always trying to increase the productivity of their promotion dollars by, for example, experimenting with substitutions of one element for another. Allocation decisions can be especially complicated when the effective use of one promotion mix element requires the use of another. For example, Coors can easily shift funds between sales promotion and advertising. As we saw earlier, the company sponsored an African-American cowboy rodeo. But to be effective, this sales promotion activity had to be advertised in order to attract people to the event.

In theory, an organization's promotion funds are optimally allocated if the last dollar spent on each element generated the same return. In this way, every available promotion dollar is evaluated in terms of the marginal return available from each promotion mix element. We looked at the major practical factors that influence this allocation decision earlier in this chapter—product-, customer-, organization-, and situation-related factors. Flexibility in allocating funds to different mix elements allows greater use of the elements that prove to be more effective as the program is being implemented.

Implementing and Evaluating the Promotion Program

Once the objectives and budget have been set and funds have been allocated to the different promotion mix elements, *implementation* is necessary. Advertising and sales management become the centers of activity.

Careful monitoring of the promotion program's implementation is a must. For example, the marketing people at Coors knew prior to entering the New York–New Jersey market that sales might grow more slowly in southern New Jersey because consumers there would not see any Coors ads on TV. People in southern New Jersey watch Philadelphia stations, and Coors did not market its beer in Pennsylvania. Consequently, analysis and control of the promotional impact on sales would have to be concentrated in the northern counties.

There is no objective way to determine for sure whether a firm's promotion program is worth the money invested in it. But few firms are willing to risk not communicating with their many publics. Attempts to use such objective techniques as return on investment are themselves subjective because many factors influence sales. In the final analysis, evaluation of the total promotion effort is a subjective judgment based on objective data such as sales data, market share, and subjective feedback from customers and the sales force. We will discuss the evaluation of promotion's effectiveness in greater detail in chapters 15–17.

Several types of feedback, however, signal the need for changes in promotion programs. The programs may (1) stimulate more demand than the firm can meet, (2) confuse intermediaries or final buyers, (3) damage company or brand images, (4) create expectations that cannot be met, or (5) fail to reach their targets. Gillette spent $3 million on TV ads during the 1990 Super Bowl and millions more on newspaper ads and TV spots throughout its launch of Sensor razors. But demand was so strong that Gillette had difficulty supplying its retailers, many of whom became irritated by the shortage. Another effect was to delay the product's launch in some European markets.[32]

CRITICISMS OF PROMOTION

Promotion is criticized more than any other element of the marketing mix. Some attack promotion in general on the ground that it is a waste of money because well-made products will sell themselves. Others focus on specific organizations and their marketing programs. Examples of complaints include those against uninformed, overly aggressive salespeople; misleading, deceptive, tasteless advertisements; invasion of privacy by people trying to sell over the phone; public relations campaigns that seek to cover up major shortcomings in product engineering; underhanded efforts to generate self-serving publicity; and phony sales promotions that seek to make consumers believe they are getting something for nothing.

Ours is a heterogeneous society—a mixture of people with different ethical and social values, abilities, and educational levels. Some types of promotion may be offensive to certain people but helpful to others. However, promotion activities perceived as offensive, deceptive, or otherwise unacceptable by target customers probably will not achieve the promoter's objectives.

The following discussions examine several questions frequently asked about promotion. Keep them in mind as you read the next two chapters.

Does Promotion Misrepresent the Truth?

Puffery is exaggeration in claims made about a product. Practically all marketers use superlatives such as *best* in describing their brands. But the limits on permissible puffery have narrowed over the years. Promotion that misrepresents the truth beyond mere puffery is misleading, deceptive, or fraudulent—and illegal. Thus the Food and Drug Administration (FDA) banned sales of nonprescription antibaldness creams and aphrodisiac products because none has been shown to work. But what about advertisers and the media packaging ads in such a way that they appear to be part of the editorial content of magazines or part of the news on a TV program? What about all the claims about earth-friendly products and the issues raised in the Ethics in Marketing box?

The Federal Trade Commission (FTC) regulates a wide variety of business practices. One of its major responsibilities is to prevent false and deceptive advertising. For example, the FTC has required *corrective advertising* as a remedy for allegedly deceptive advertising. Under the FTC's *ad substantiation doctrine* an advertiser must have a reasonable basis for making an advertising claim. If the FTC believes an advertiser's claims are questionable, it will ask the advertiser to substantiate them.

Each year, the FTC issues complaints against companies it considers to be using questionable advertising or other promotional practices. The FTC can settle cases informally if an advertiser agrees to discontinue the alleged deception. As we saw in chapter 2, the firm may sign a consent order, which is an agreement to "cease and desist" a certain practice. This avoids the need for further action by the FTC. If a firm refuses to stop questionable advertising, the FTC makes a formal complaint and a public hearing is held before an FTC examiner. The examiner reviews the facts and makes a decision, which may be reviewed

ETHICS IN
MARKETING

Advertising executives shook their heads in amazement at North American Volvo's blatant rigging of its "monster truck" commercial. The truth is, though, that some other auto ads aren't exactly what they seem.

In a Volvo ad from 1989 a six-ton truck was lowered onto the roof of a Volvo car, which didn't sag at all under the truck's weight. But the car was propped up with jacks, which were hidden by shadows and thus invisible to viewers.

Nissan touted its antilock brakes in a 1990 spot that shows a side shot of a car screeching to a halt just in front of a standing man. But the man actually is closer to the camera than is the car.

An Oldsmobile ad showed a car being dropped by parachute from the belly of an airborne cargo plane. The Olds 98 hits the ground and is driven away from the scene. But it isn't the same car. The one dropped from the airplane was just the empty shell of a car.

All three companies defend these ads, saying they don't make specific performance claims that are phony. And many ad specialists agree. But these experts add that commercials using trick photography can fall into an ethical gray area.

Volvo's monster truck ad wasn't in a gray area. It depicted a pickup truck with oversized tires driving over the top of a row of cars, crushing the roofs of all except the Volvo. But the Volvo's roof was reinforced with lumber and steel that viewers couldn't see. And the other cars' roof-support pillars were severed or weakened. Volvo has apologized for the ads, and the agency that made them gave up the account.

But Volvo stoutly defends the 1989 ad showing a Volvo holding up a heavy-duty truck. It's a descendant of Volvo commercials from the early 1970s, which showed a Volvo holding up six other Volvos without sagging. In both the earlier and the latest ads, viewers saw the

by the full commission. If a firm believes the FTC has issued an erroneous order, it may bring the case before the appropriate Federal Circuit Court of Appeals and, ultimately, to the U.S. Supreme Court.

Advertisers, ad agencies, and the media have made considerable voluntary progress in eliminating misleading advertising. For example, the National Advertising Review Board (NARB) plays an active role in self-regulation. A consumer who questions the truth or accuracy in a national ad can write to the NARB, and it will ask the advertiser to substantiate the claims made. Where justified, the advertiser will be requested to modify or discontinue any claim for which there is not adequate support.

Does Promotion Lead to Monopoly and Higher Prices?

Some people believe the large promotion budgets of big firms keep smaller firms from competing and thus help create monopolies that can charge very high prices. Although it is clear that many smaller firms have succeeded despite the heavy promotion by giant rivals, it is impossible to determine just how many smaller firms never got started simply because the

Volvos holding up lots of weight, but they didn't see the jacks placed between the cars' tires. The reason: The ads were intended to show the strength of Volvo's roofs and bodies, which weren't reinforced. They weren't meant to claim that Volvo's tires and suspensions can support such loads.

The Nissan commercial, in which a man appears to be standing directly in front of a moving car, wouldn't have looked the same without trick photography. In fact, somebody might have been killed. During filming, the car ran ''through'' the plane of the man a couple of times, forcing reshoots. Still Nissan's national advertising creative manager says the ad is ''an accurate braking demonstration. The car was driving on wet pavement. It didn't skid when the brakes were applied.''

The Oldsmobile air drop commercial didn't discuss the car's performance. Instead, according to a company spokesperson, it touted the Oldsmobile customer satisfaction program; the parachute was meant to represent the security that the program provides.

It isn't just auto ads that fall into gray areas. Food and toy spots are among those that also use special effects to exaggerate their products. Many fast-food companies use coloring and special lighting to make their products look more appealing.

What ethical issues are involved in these situations? Are such commercials common, or are they exceptions?

Source: Adapted from Krystal Miller and Jacqueline Mitchell, ''Car Marketers Test Gray Area of Truth in Advertising,'' *Wall Street Journal*, November 19, 1990, pp. B1, B5. Reprinted by permission of the *Wall Street Journal*, © Dow Jones & Company, Inc., 1990. All rights reserved.

promotion budgets of giant rivals were too big an obstacle to entry. Promotion plans clearly aimed at preventing rivals from entering a market, however, may be construed as a violation of antitrust laws.

A firm may enjoy economies of scale in producing and marketing its product if promotion increases the demand for it. If these economies more than offset the promotion cost, the firm could pass some of the savings on to consumers by lowering prices.

We discussed the role of promotion in nonprice competition earlier in this text. It is interesting that promotion among professionals such as doctors, lawyers, and accountants is encouraged by the FTC as a way of stimulating price competition.

On the other hand, what about the incentives to travel agents offered by some car rental companies, cruise lines, tour operators, and airlines—ranging from free trips to big commissions? Could such offers lead to higher prices for travelers and cause travel agents to be more concerned about winning a prize than providing the best service to their clients?

Does Promotion Brainwash and Stereotype Consumers?

Some critics believe marketers use promotion to create consumer tastes and preferences. Persuasive advertising, they argue, makes consumers mere pawns of mass advertisers. The high failure rate of new products, however, proves that advertisers are not in complete control. Promotion cannot manipulate people against their will. Although much of it seeks to persuade us to do certain things, it cannot brainwash us.

Broadcast programming, editorial content in print media, and advertising often are criticized for stereotyping consumers. Some women complain that many ads depict them as sex objects or in demeaning housewife roles. Men, on the other hand, are seldom depicted doing household chores, when, in fact, many men do them. Lifestyles and sex roles are changing so rapidly in our society that some ads may depict people in outmoded stereotypes.

Maidenform started an ad campaign in early 1991 that drew fire from the National Organization for Women before the ads even appeared on TV. In one ad, for example, a woman's voiceover says, "Somewhere along the line, someone decided to refer to a woman as this," as a chick flashes on the screen. Other images follow: a tomato, a fox, a cat, and a dog. At the end the announcer offers reassurance: "While these images are simple and obvious, women themselves rarely are. Just something we like to keep in mind when designing our lingerie." Maidenform said its intent was to criticize the stereotypes with a touch of humor. Opponents said that bringing out such negative images—even while debunking them—risks offending women simply by reminding them of the prevalence of sexism.[33] As the Global Marketing box suggests, sexual stereotyping can be an even bigger problem for international marketers who are doing business with people from different cultures.

Does Promotion Ignore Good Taste?

Some critics say promotion is guilty of poor taste. Erotic advertising for products ranging from cosmetics to drill presses and fear advertising for deodorants and mouthwashes are often cited. Also cited are ads that insult our intelligence with monotonous and repetitious themes and unbelievable situations. Advertisers are often attacked for damaging the environment with billboards, invading consumers' privacy with junk mail, junk phone calls, and junk fax, and sponsoring broadcast programs that some consumers believe are in very bad taste.

Is it in good taste for lawyers, certified public accountants, dentists, and physicians to advertise? Is it in good taste for a movie star who has gone public with a history of drug abuse to appear in an ad for the chemical dependency unit of a hospital? Is it acceptable for profit-seeking firms to link up with causes and with nonprofit organizations? This *cause-related marketing* started to spread after American Express began its program of contributing one cent to the restoration of the Statue of Liberty for each use of its charge card.

What about an ad for United Way that portrays a reenactment of a rape in a darkened alley? Such ads are said to take their cue from reality-TV programs—for example, "A Current Affair" and "Unsolved Mysteries"—that feature graphic reenactments of crimes.[34] Is it in good taste for public-service ads to be explicit?

There are wide differences of opinion about what constitutes good and bad taste. Taste in advertising is subjective, just as it is in music, dress, and personal behavior. In some cases critics are attacking the product being advertised, and in the process the advertising comes under criticism. For example, some people believe feminine hygiene products and condoms should not be advertised on TV. Although a specific ad for such a product might be tastefully done, the ad is criticized as a result of its association with the product.

GLOBAL MARKETING

Women's groups in the 1970s successfully fought sexist "Fly Me, I'm Diane" advertising campaigns. They now have a fresh target. Asian carriers are pitching pretty, pert flight attendants as their main fare. These ads are popping up frequently as Asian airlines increase U.S. service.

A recent Thai Airlines ad features a graying man wearing a white-collared shirt and dark tie, leaning his head back in his plane seat and smiling contentedly. Behind him a Thai flight attendant leans forward, her head just inches from the man's left ear. The ad reads, in part: "Service that has no end."

"They're trying to sell sex appeal," says the executive vice president at the National Organization for Women and a former Pan Am flight attendant. "It limits women when advertising perpetuates that type of image."

A female executive who travels from the United States to Asia several times a year says: "It's offensive. It's a geisha mentality. They flaunt younger Oriental girls catering to older, white men." U.S. carriers, in contrast, hype fares, routes, and on-time rankings.

The ads of virtually all Asian carriers include a head-shot of female attendants. "We use them because they are the personification of all the exoticness of the cabin service—not because they are sex kittens," says Thai Airlines' U.S. advertising manager. Few show male attendants, though they are 25 to 50 percent of the cabin crews.

Source: Adapted from Asra Q. Nomani, "Tracking Travel: Asian Airline Ads Accused of Sexism," *Wall Street Journal,* October 31, 1990, p. B1. Reprinted by permission of the *Wall Street Journal,* © Dow Jones & Company, Inc., 1990. All rights reserved.

SUMMARY OF LEARNING OBJECTIVES

1. Identify and explain the elements in the communication process.

(1) The sender (source) has a meaning and seeks to share it with one or more receivers. (2) Encoding is the process of putting meaning into symbols to be conveyed as messages. (3) The message is the combination of symbols representing objects or experiences that a communicator transmits in order to induce a change in a receiver's behavior. (4) A communication channel is anything that carries a message—a means by which the sender conveys or transmits a message to receivers. (5) A receiver is an active participant in communication who on the basis of knowledge and experience assigns meanings to (decodes) messages received and reacts to the decoded meaning. (6) Decoding is the process by which the receiver attempts to convert symbols conveyed by the sender into a message. (7) Feedback is communication from receivers to the sender about the meaning they assigned to the message and how they reacted to it. (8) Noise is anything that interferes with the communication process so the receiver gets a message that is different from the one the sender sent or gets no message at all.

2. Explain what a promotion mix is and identify some of the many factors that influence its development.

A promotion mix is a careful blending of advertising, personal selling, direct marketing, sales promotion, and public relations to accomplish an organization's promotion objectives. Among the factors that influence its development are product-related factors, customer-related factors, organization-related factors, and situation-related factors.

3. Identify several major examples of generalized promotion objectives.

Examples include creating awareness, providing information, explaining the organization's actions, inducing product trials, inducing intermediaries to stock a product, retaining loyal customers, increasing amount and frequency of use, learning about target customers, and reducing sales fluctuations.

4. Identify the major steps in managing the promotion effort.

The major steps are (1) setting promotion objectives, (2) planning the promotion effort, (3) determining the total promotion budget, (4) allocating the budget among the promotion mix elements, (5) implementing the promotion program, and (6) evaluating the promotion program.

5. Cite examples of criticisms about promotion that often are framed as questions.

Examples include the following: Does promotion misrepresent the truth? Does promotion lead to monopoly and higher prices? Does promotion brainwash and stereotype consumers? Does promotion ignore good taste?

Review Questions

1. What are the basic elements in the communication process? Explain each.

2. What factors enhance a source's perceived credibility among intended receivers in the communication process?

3. Why is the choice of symbols so important in developing a message?

4. How do interpersonal communication channels differ from mass communication channels?

5. How does noise affect the communication process?

6. What elements make up a promotion mix? Briefly define each element.

7. What types of factors influence the choice of elements in a promotion mix?

8. How do push and pull promotion strategies differ?

9. What are some typical types of promotion objectives?

10. How does the percentage of current or forecasted sales approach to determining the promotion budget differ from the objective and task approach?

11. How does the fact that our society is heterogeneous contribute to criticism of promotion?

Discussion Questions

1. What risks are involved in using celebrities in advertising?

2. The British require that all political commercials on TV run a minimum of three minutes. The belief is that longer ads will ensure that candidates take positions on real issues. Typical political TV ads in the United States last thirty seconds. What are the advantages and disadvantages of the longer political commercials to the candidates and to the electorate?

3. More and more marketers are seeking to have their products featured in movies, home videos, home video games, board games, and even on record albums. Why?

4. During economic slowdowns, most firms cut back on their spending on promotion. Is this wise? Explain.

Application Exercise

Reread the material about Monsanto's Searle unit at the beginning of this chapter and answer the following questions:

1. What are the elements in Searle's promotion mix? Briefly describe the nature of each element.

2. Is Searle using a push strategy, a pull strategy, or both? Explain.

3. Are any ethical issues raised in the way Searle promotes Calan? Explain.

Key Concepts

The following key terms were introduced in this chapter:

communication
source credibility
encoding
message
interpersonal communication
    channel
mass communication channel

decoding
feedback
noise
promotion mix
AIDA process
advertising
personal selling

direct marketing
sales promotion
public relations (PR)
publicity
push strategy
pull strategy
promotion campaign

CASES

Megabucks for Superstars

LYN S. AMINE, *St. Louis University*

Famous faces and voices in television commercials sell products—or do they? Many marketing companies invest heavily in celebrity endorsers in the fervent belief that, at minimum, viewers will pay attention long enough to register the brand name. Attention-getting becomes expensive, though. Many celebrities have lent their faces, names, voices, or personae to advertisers for sometimes exorbitant fees in order to bolster sales in fiercely competitive markets. But the question remains: do consumers actually buy the product, or more specifically the brand, just because a superstar extols its virtues?

In 1988, Video Storyboard Tests, Inc., a New York advertising research agency, conducted over 25,000 tests of viewers' impressions of TV advertising. One third of the respondents could not cite a single commercial, even though the typical viewer sees about 2,000 commercials a month.

Breaking through television advertising clutter is a major problem for many consumer goods companies. When Nike first used sports hero Michael Jordan its ads were a huge success.

Now with Bo Jackson, Paula Abdul, Michael Jackson, and many other famous faces appearing on TV screens, confusion threatens to turn athletic shoes into a commodity, making brands seem interchangeable despite significantly different product features. Similarly, in the cola industry, the proliferation of singing, dancing superstars has created almost total consumer confusion. As one critic states, ''Coke and Pepsi aren't in the product business any more. They're in the image business—in show business.'' In the cola industry, the products are not significantly different, so advertisers have to rely heavily on image as a source of product differentiation.

Some executives believe that the real reason Coke and Pepsi are spending hundreds of millions of dollars on superstars is to try to lure teens to their brand. Soft drinks are about the only food and drink category where teenagers show any brand loyalty. In 1989, the typical teenager spent $61.50 per week, and the annual spending power of the 28 million American teens continues to rise. Keeping up with the shifting tastes of teenagers is no easy task. A famous face that is hot today may fall from favor faster than companies can do their marketing research.

The real challenge in paying out megabucks for superstars is to draw attention from the celebrity toward the product. For celebrity advertising to work there has to be an initial link between the celebrity and the product. If not, then there has to be some potential for creating an emotional appeal. For example, Oldsmobile's television campaign featured well-known celebrities in humorous situations with their not-so-famous children to support the theme: "This is not your father's/(mother's) Oldsmobile." This campaign was not only effective in creating brand recognition and consumer recall, it also succeeded in rejuvenating the rather stuffy and old-fashioned image of the brand name. Sales even increased, a feat not always accomplished by celebrity advertising.

Although more than 25 percent of today's TV ads use celebrities, the ads voted most popular by consumers do not often feature stars. In 1987 only two of the top ten most popular ads included celebrities. Some critics argue that overuse of celebrities is driving advertising costs into an unending, upward spiral as companies vie with one another to "up the ante." Trade characters like the Jolly Green Giant and the pink Ever-Ready Battery bunny seem to fare just as well, if not better, in tests of consumer recall and likeability. Some companies, however, appear to view investment in a superstar as insurance against "zapping" and getting lost in the clutter. If the role of advertising, as some claim, is basically to reinforce current product use and maintain brand-name awareness, then a famous face may give a product a head-start over the competition. In this case, the goal becomes one of merely maintaining the status quo, not increasing market share.

Questions

1. Is it likely that the use of a celebrity in an ad will create noise? Explain.

2. How does the use of celebrities in advertising relate to the AIDA process?

3. Can the use of celebrities help in generating publicity for a company's product? Explain.

4. From memory, which superstars can you link reliably with a specific brand name?

Wave Promotions

It's called "ambush sampling" or "guerilla marketing" and it's the new wave in promotion. This is how it works, as practiced by Wave Promotions, a Washington, D.C., promotions firm:

When Smartfood, maker of gourmet popcorn, wanted to introduce its products to the D.C. area, Wave assembled the SWAT (Smartfood Whacky-Attacky Team) to come to the rescue of bored victims of traffic jams. SWAT members, dressed as bigger-than-life bags of Smartfood, swarmed out of a van and handed real bags of the popcorn through car windows to the stranded motorists. On other days, Wave treated D.C. drivers to the spectacle of human Smartfood billboards prancing around on overpasses. Beachgoers watched as windsurfers appeared in the distance and came careening into shore to distribute Smartfood. Wave's intention was to create an original, off-beat, exciting image for Smartfood. It succeeded: within months of its introduction, Smartfood had wrested 40 percent of the D.C. market from its competitors.

Smartfood executives say Wave's guerilla marketing works because, although it takes longer than traditional advertising to spread product information through a population, its impact lasts longer: those reached by the campaign form a personal memory about the company. And the impact of Wave's Smartfood ambush sampling was felt by more than just the 6,000 or so people a day who actually received Smartfood samples. The ambushes created such a stir that they were covered by local news organizations.

Wave has also worked wonders for other companies. For Bacardi Breezers, a new rum cooler, Wave engineered the Breezer Mobile, a truck filled with samples and "young, sporty, California kind of people," that rolled up at the health clubs, nightclubs, and beaches most favored by young adults and college students. The tactic was cheap and effective—Bacardi sprang from 49th to 6th in distilled spirits sales after hiring Wave—and proved Wave's point that, in promotion, imagination counts more than dollars spent. While the success of Wave's Bacardi strategy spoke for itself, a 1990 Wave survey of departing Daytona Beach spring-breakers found that MTV, Plymouth, and Pepsi, the break's biggest sponsors, ranked near-lowest in sponsor-recognition polls.

According to Wave officials, the only possible drawback of guerilla marketing is that it has the potential to alienate targeted consumers. Creating a scene can cause a scene, and before any ambush, Wave personnel spend a lot of time planning their actions and anticipating possible negative public reactions. Says one Wave executive, ''We want it to be, 'Oh, there's those nuts from Wave,' rather than, 'Let's ban those guys from the city.' ''

Questions

1. What part might the concept of noise play in the Wave ambush sampling strategy?

2. How large a part of the promotion mix do you think guerilla marketing should be?

3. What are the main objectives of Wave's promotion activities?

4. What criticisms could be aimed at Wave's promotion strategies?

15

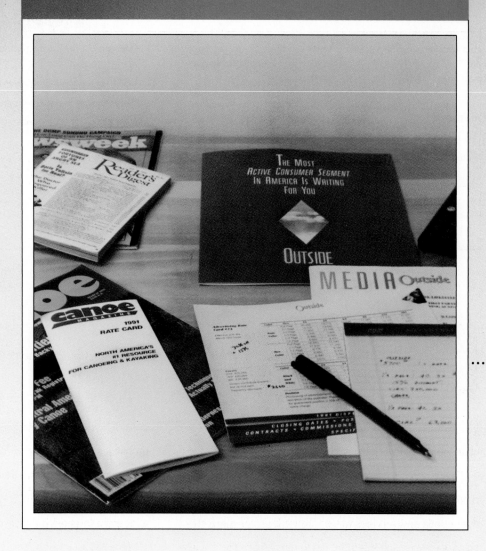

ADVERTISING

After reading this chapter you will be able to

1. identify the three fundamental objectives of advertising.
2. distinguish between product advertising and institutional advertising.
3. distinguish among pioneering, competitive, and reminder product advertising.
4. distinguish among pioneering, competitive, and reminder institutional advertising.
5. identify the major tasks of advertising management.
6. explain the options marketers have for organizing their advertising activities.

In 1978 ABC, NBC, and CBS had a lock on viewers, with 90 percent of the television audience during prime time. By 1989 that had dropped to 64 percent, with independents up to 24 percent and cable channels at 22 percent.

Faced with the decline in network televiewing and with rising prices for TV time and advertising space, people with goods and services to sell are looking for more efficient ways to reach potential customers. Thus the TV networks and mass-circulation magazines are finding they can no longer prosper merely by delivering tons of undifferentiated audiences to advertisers.

"The way mass media work now, advertisers simply 'buy eyeballs,' " as one ad agency media director put it. But in the future advertisers will demand that the media pinpoint not only the ages and incomes of their prospects but also their psychology and buying patterns. Often this won't be done program by program and page by page but in combinations of magazines, TV programs, books, and videotapes. Knowing who it is the advertiser wants to reach with the message, the marketer will demand a media package that promises to deliver the target audience—not just an audience.

Rupert Murdoch's News Corporation is buying and building exactly these sorts of bundled media options on a global scale. Looking ahead to when homes will get a hundred or more cable or satellite channels, Murdoch says there will be "a lot more fragmentation in the audience and a lot more targeted broadcasting."

By 1989 roughly half of U.S. households could choose from among more than thirty TV channels. With so many choices the audience becomes, as Murdoch says, "fragmented." Each fragment offers different viewer profiles and correspondingly different marketing opportunities. Viewing choices will multiply in the 1990s, further undermining network viewing.

Mass-circulation magazines face the same dilemma the TV networks face. They offer a somewhat undifferentiated audience, and that isn't what marketing people generally want. Faced with an avalanche of new competition from special-interest publications—nearly three thousand new titles hit the newsstands in the 1980s—the general-interest, mass-circulation magazine industry is currently suffering through a gruesome downturn.

Most disturbing to advertisers, the defectors from the mass media tend to be richer, better-educated people who can afford specialized material that fits their needs more snugly. This leaves mass television and magazine audiences increasingly made up of a "media underclass" that will only become more impoverished over time.

Take women aged twenty-five to fifty-four, a basic audience sector in TV advertising. On average the poorest 40 percent of the audience sees 77 percent of the prime-time commercials and the richest 40 percent sees only 8 percent. Instead of watching a network show, the more affluent women are probably spending their time reading *Architectural Digest,* the *National Review, Town & Country,* or the *New Republic.* Or, if televiewing, they may be watching Bravo or the Arts & Entertainment Network.[1]

As marketers increasingly practice targeted marketing, they will increasingly seek advertising media that can reach their target audiences. Undifferentiated audiences are becoming less and less attractive to most of today's marketers.

In this chapter we take an in-depth look at one of the elements in the promotion mix, advertising. We begin with a look at the different types of advertising and then focus on advertising management. The chapter ends with a look at how advertising activities are organized.

THE NATURE OF ADVERTISING

Advertising was defined in chapter 14 as any paid form of nonpersonal communication through the mass media about a good, service, or idea by an identified sponsor. As one element in a promotion mix, advertising is used to send messages to target audiences through mass media such as television, radio, outdoor boards, newspapers, and magazines. Marketers hope the recipients, upon being exposed to the advertising, will respond.

How consumers or organizational buyers respond to advertising often depends on the purpose of the ad. Typically, advertising has one or more of three fundamental objectives: (1) to *inform* target audiences, (2) to *persuade* target audiences, or (3) to *remind* target audiences. On the basis of these objectives, advertisers normally set more specific and quantifiable advertising objectives. Advertising objectives should be realistic and specific and should indicate the criteria by which success or failure will be judged, including the time frame for accomplishing them.

Advertising is a pervasive influence in our daily lives. Consider that in 1991 advertisers spent an estimated $136 billion on advertising.[2] Although advertising seeks to inform, persuade, or remind target audiences about marketers and their offerings, it can also irritate and offend people.

In addition to businesses, individuals are big users of advertising, often through the local newspaper classified section. Nonbusiness organizations also know the value of commu-

Atlantic Union College uses out-door advertising to communicate with its target audience. Is the primary purpose of this ad to inform, to persuade, or to remind?

[© David Dempster]

nicating with the marketplace. Examples include political parties, churches, universities, charitable organizations, and governments.

Industries and firms vary in terms of the percentage of their sales revenues they spend on advertising. Firms that make cosmetics spend a greater percentage of their sales revenues on advertising than do many industrial product manufacturers. Charles Revson, the founder of Revlon, said he made his money by selling hope, the kind that comes in a jar. Because firms in the cosmetics business sell hope, they can charge high prices for products that do not cost much to make. But the hope ingredient requires a lot of expensive and effective advertising.[3] Many industrial product manufacturers, however, rely more on personal selling to push their products through marketing channels. For them advertising is not a key sales tool.

There are many ways to categorize advertising. For example, some people consider retail advertising to be a special category. *Retail advertising* is advertising done by department stores, supermarkets, specialty shops, and other retailers. The retail industry typically accounts for half of all newspaper ads.[4] In general, however, advertising can be broken down into two basic types—product advertising and institutional advertising—on the basis of what is advertised.

Product advertising is promotion that focuses on selling specifically identified goods and services. *Institutional advertising* is promotion that focuses on the image of a product category, a company, a nonprofit organization, or an industry association rather than a specific brand. General Motors does a lot of product advertising. An ad for the Buick Road-master is an example of product advertising. GM's "Putting Quality on the Road" image campaign is an example of institutional advertising. Many ads are a combination of product and institutional advertising. An ad for a Buick Roadmaster that discusses GM's overall dedication to building quality cars is an example.

Regardless of the specific type of advertising, however, the underlying objective is still to inform, to persuade, or to remind. (See Table 15–1.) As a product moves through its life

product advertising

institutional advertising

TABLE 15–1 ▪ Examples of Generalized Advertising Objectives

Objective	Product Advertising	Institutional Advertising
To inform (pioneering)	Introduce a new product Announce a price increase Explain a product improvement	Build an organizational image Correct misstatements of fact about the firm in the media Announce a new organizational mission
To persuade (competitive)	Build brand preference Encourage a product trade-in Encourage brand switching	Build customer loyalty to the firm Compare the firm favorably to a rival Encourage intermediaries to become channel members
To remind (reminder)	Keep brand name dominant in product category Recall product's long history Summarize the brand's benefits for customers	Remind voters of the crucial issues in a lengthy campaign Recall a past activity of a trade association that benefited members greatly Summarize past accomplishments of a charitable organization

cycle, advertising's dominant objective tends to shift from informing to persuading to reminding. The discussions that follow look at product and institutional advertising that seeks to inform (pioneering advertising), to persuade (competitive advertising), and to remind (reminder advertising).

Product Advertising

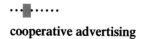

cooperative advertising

Marketers use product advertising to promote the features, benefits, and uses of their goods and services. One type of product advertising is *cooperative advertising*—advertising in which a manufacturer pays part of the retailer's cost of advertising the manufacturer's product in the retailer's local market. It gives retailers an incentive to stock the product and to promote it. Also, retailers often get better prices from local media than national companies are able to get.

• **Pioneering Product Advertising** • Product advertising that seeks to create awareness and understanding and to develop *primary demand* (demand for a new-product category) is *pioneering product advertising*. It seeks to provide information in the early stages of the product adoption process. Ads must create awareness of the new product, teach potential buyers how to use it, and induce channel members to stock it. New-product categories that required this type of advertising include laptop computers, personal facsimile (fax) machines, and zero-coupon bonds. 50's AirPlane

• **Competitive Product Advertising** • Product advertising that tries to stimulate *selective demand* (demand for a specific brand within a product category) is *competitive product advertising.* Once products reach the growth stage of their life cycles, competitive product advertising is used to create a brand image; improve consumer recognition of brand names and trademarks; show why the brand's characteristics, price, or benefits are better than Fighter for SHARe those of competing brands; increase usage of the brand by light users; and attract new users. Competitive product advertising is easy to recognize by its persuasive emphasis. It usually stresses benefits and reasons to buy.

Comparative advertising is advertising in which the marketer compares its brand to rival brands that are identified by brand name. Among the many users of comparative advertising are Coca-Cola, PepsiCo, Subaru, Saab, Chevrolet, Ford, American Express, MasterCard, and Maxwell House.

The Trademark Law Revision Act of 1988 says that anyone who misrepresents "his or her or another person's" goods or services is liable for damages. That wording closed a loophole in the Lanham Act of 1946, which prohibited false claims about one's own product but did not mention "another person's." Some marketers expect the tougher law to lead to less comparative advertising and more brands comparing themselves to "Brand X."

comparative advertising

• **Reminder Product Advertising** • Product advertising that is used when a product has reached the brand preference or insistence stage for a large number of target customers is *reminder product advertising.* It is most commonly used during the maturity stage of the product life cycle.

Reminder advertising also tries to persuade by mentioning brand benefits. It may even be directed at consumers who have *already* purchased in order to help them reduce cognitive dissonance—the fear that they may have chosen the wrong brand. Sometimes reminder advertising introduces new uses for existing products in order to keep sales levels up. For example, Arm & Hammer baking soda, a well-known baking ingredient, was advertised successfully as an odor absorber for the refrigerator and for cat litter boxes.

Institutional Advertising

Used correctly, institutional advertising can create and maintain a corporate or family brand image among target customers and channel members, can supplement public relations activities by building goodwill among noncustomer publics, can counter adverse publicity, and can generate demand for a product category.

Advocacy advertising is a type of institutional advertising in which the advertiser takes a position for or against an issue. Mobil Corporation started running advocacy ads in 1970 and, over the years, has presented its opinions on far-ranging topics—oil taxes, managing the U.S. economy, freedom of the press, and so on. Most companies, however, avoid using controversial ads and, instead, let their trade associations handle advocacy advertising.

advocacy advertising

• **Pioneering Institutional Advertising** • Pioneering institutional advertising helps in building and maintaining the desired image for an organization. When Goodrich got out of the tire business, it used this type of advertising to get across the idea that the firm was no longer in the tire business. When Andersen & Company, a public accounting firm, started Andersen Consulting, it used pioneering institutional advertising to establish a separate identity for the new division. As the Global Marketing box explains, many South Korean firms are using this type of advertising to establish distinctive corporate images in the United States.

• **Competitive Institutional Advertising** • When different product categories compete for the same market segment, competitive institutional advertising is often used. Some of these competitive ads seek to stimulate an immediate buying response, and others point out the advantages of an industry's product. A California Prune Board ad explains, "Six prunes have almost as much fiber as two bowls of bran flakes." The National Dairy Board's ad is an example of competitive institutional advertising.

• **Reminder Institutional Advertising** • Information presented or comparisons made in previous pioneering or competitive campaigns can be summarized in reminder institu-

GLOBAL MARKETING

South Korea's conglomerates have a problem: Most Americans don't know a Sunkyong from a SsangYong or a Samsung. So the largest South Korean companies, including these three sound-alike companies, are spending more on image ads in U.S. business publications. The spending boost marks a growing awareness among South Korean firms that they have to build a distinctive corporate image in the United States, their most important overseas market. Because their number 1 goal is to find overseas business partners, most of the image advertising is aimed at business executives, not consumers. The Koreans want overseas executives to use South Korea as a source of supply, and, even more importantly, to sell advanced technology to South Korean companies so they'll be better able to compete.

Image advertising has become crucial to South Korean companies because the U.S. prices of South Korean–made products are quickly rising to match those of Japanese imports. So South Korean companies must get consumers to trust their brands the way they trust Japanese competitors' names. "It is possible that foreigners might think that Koreans are unreliable," says Lee Sang Chan of the public relations and advertising department at SsangYong, a company that recently began selling a few of is products in the United States under its own name.

Making South Korean companies household names will be an uphill battle. The companies tend to look alike because they make many of the same things. Moreover, they tend to run look-alike ads. A typical South Korean ad will mention that the conglomerate is young, fast-growing, large, and in almost every business from petrochemicals and construction to electronics and finance. And they usually use a bit of nondescript but old-fashioned-looking artwork.

As the companies spend more, they are becoming more sophisticated. Once content to let the in-house staff design the ads, more South Korean conglomerates are seeking outside help.

The best example of the improvement in South Korean ads is that of Daewoo Group. Its first international campaign began in 1983, the first for any South Korean company. In 1990 Daewoo took a giant leap forward. It decided that instead of spending a certain percentage more each year, it would spend as much as it takes to reach 50 percent of its intended audience in major business publications. As a result it increased spending on image ads in the United States 100 percent, to $4.5 million.

Source: Adapted from Damon Darlin, "Advertising: South Koreans Try to Build Image in U.S.," *Wall Street Journal*, June 28, 1990, p. B4. Reprinted by permission of the *Wall Street Journal*, © Dow Jones & Company, Inc., 1990. All rights reserved.

An example of competitive institutional advertising.

(America's Dairy Farmers, National Dairy Board.)

tional advertising. Sunkist Growers, a cooperative of fruit growers, spends millions of dollars each year on advertising to remind consumers of the benefits of California oranges and lemons. The organization began advertising in 1908 and uses reminder institutional advertising to reinforce consumers' positive feelings about California oranges and lemons.

ADVERTISING MANAGEMENT

Like the overall promotion effort, advertising requires management. Advertising management includes (1) defining the target audience, (2) defining advertising objectives, (3) setting the advertising budget, (4) developing the creative strategy, (5) selecting the advertising media, and (6) evaluating advertising effectiveness. (See Figure 15–1.)

Defining the Target Audience

The *target audience* is the people to whom an advertising campaign is directed. Sometimes the target audience and the target market are the same; in other cases they are different. For

target audience

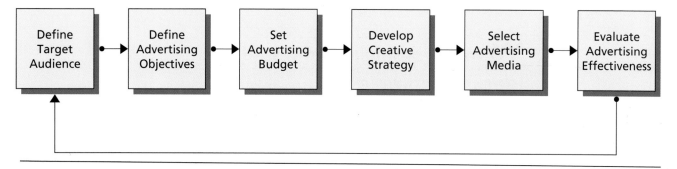

FIGURE 15–1

The Tasks of Advertising
Management

example, the advertising target for Hertz's "America's Wheels" ad campaign was vacationers, although the firm's target market also includes business travelers.[5]

Defining Advertising Objectives

Advertising objectives are derived from a marketer's overall promotion objectives. Typically, advertising objectives are formulated in terms of either sales or communication.
Examples of sales-oriented advertising objectives are "to increase market share by 5 percent," "to increase dollar sales by $3 million," and "to increase sales by 10 percent."

A problem with sales-oriented advertising objectives is that sales usually depend on
many factors, not just advertising. Therefore, many advertisers set objectives in communication terms, in the belief that advertising is mainly a communication tool. Examples of
communication-oriented advertising objectives are "to create awareness for the brand
among 80 percent of the target audience" and "to teach 70 percent of the target audience
the new advertising slogan." Whether a company sets advertising objectives in sales terms
or in communication terms, the objectives should be precise and measurable and a time
frame for their accomplishment should be indicated.

Setting the Advertising Budget

Several approaches to determining the promotion budget were discussed in chapter 14. The
ad budget is a component of the total promotion budget. During economic slowdowns firms
try to stretch their ad budgets. During the recent recession the *Wall Street Journal* included
ads urging advertisers to maintain or increase their advertising spending. Advertisers also
become more cautious during slowdowns and use tried-and-true ads. Some firms engage
in joint advertising. In one H&R Block and Excedrin ad, a well-dressed gentleman sits
behind a desk and offers tax tips. Tip No. 1: "If you receive an audit notice from the IRS
and you lost all your records, what should you use?" He reaches into his desk, pulls out a
bottle of Excedrin, and deadpans, "This, for your headache."[6]

The ad budget must be allocated among markets, brands, and media. Allocation decisions are anything but simple in large multiproduct firms. Many such firms use propor-
tionate budgeting to allocate funds among markets. Thus, if one geographic segment of the
market accounts for 25 percent of total sales, it receives 25 percent of the budget. Such an
approach, however, should not be allowed to become mechanistic. Room is needed for
managerial discretion and flexibility. In allocating advertising funds among brands, some
firms group the brands according to their stage in the product life cycle. Under this system
brands in the introductory stage would receive more funds than those in the maturity stage.

Developing the Creative Strategy

To develop a successful creative strategy, the advertiser (1) decides on a sales message, (2) formulates an execution of the message, (3) creates the ad elements, and (4) provides technical directions for production of the ad. The discussion of message development in chapter 14 is relevant to the development of a creative strategy.

• **Deciding on a Sales Message** • An advertising sales message expresses the basic idea the advertiser wants to communicate. It should motivate recipients to respond by emphasizing *benefits,* not *attributes.* As the saying goes, people don't want quarter-inch drill bits; they want quarter-inch holes.

Good advertising translates the product characteristics into benefits that are meaningful to the target audience. Marketing research and creative intuition are often combined to come up with an effective sales message. In a memorable advertising campaign directed toward business executives, Xerox focused on the benefits, not the attributes, of its office equipment. Magazine ads featured large photographs of wistful-looking children, presumably

Product
Benefit
Drill Holes

TABLE 15–2   Advertising Executions

1. Straight spokespersons:
   Lee Iacocca for Chrysler automobiles
   Orville Redenbacher for popcorn

2. Celebrity testimonials:
   Bo Jackson for Nike shoes
   Bill Cosby for Jell-O gelatin

3. Case histories and slice of life (what actually happened to ordinary people):
   Timex—ordinary people who "experienced something extraordinary. And survived."
   Folgers coffee—"Best Part of Waking Up" (for example, a son on military leave greeting his parents in an emotional homecoming)

4. Showing product uses and recipes:
   Kraft cheeses
   Triscuit crackers

5. Fantasy:
   Calvin Klein's Obsession fragrance
   Guess? jeans

6. Humor:
   Grey Poupon mustard
   Leslie Nielsen Dollar Rent a Car ads

7. Real or animated characters to personify the product:
   The Campbell Kids rap singing in soup jingle
   Kibbles 'n Bits dogs

8. Mood:
   Giorgio Armani perfumes
   Bacardi rum

9. Lifestyle (focus on users rather than product):
   Levi's bluejeans
   Johnnie Walker scotch whiskey

10. Demonstration:
    Porsche automobiles
    Miracle-Gro plant food

waiting for mommy or daddy to come home from work. The headline read, "The real reason for getting my office running smoothly is waiting for me at home." Xerox successfully translated the performance and quality of its office products into an effective sales message.

In the hope of giving its cars a little mystique, Volkswagen's U.S. unit came up with the German word *fahrvergnugen* as the focus of a recent broadcast and print ad campaign. Pronounced "far-fair-nu-ghen," it means "the pleasure of driving." Many VW dealers in the United States, however, were skeptical that buyers would latch on to the term.[7]

• **Formulating an Execution of the Message** • The advertising execution is how the sales message is presented. As Table 15–2 suggests, there are many possible ways to execute the same message. According to creative experts, finding the most effective advertising execution often begins with a "big idea."[8] A big idea is one that dramatizes or demonstrates how the product will benefit the prospective buyer.

• **Creating the Ad Elements** • The big idea will be successful only if it can be translated successfully into a finished ad. The most important guideline is to keep it simple, focusing on one major benefit. In creating the ad elements, advertisers often follow the AIDA model described in chapter 14.

The discussions that follow take a closer look at creating the ad elements for print and broadcast advertising. Many of the ideas discussed here also apply to the creation of ad elements for direct marketing media and out-of-home media.

Figure 15–2 illustrates the application of the AIDA model to print advertising. The *headline* and *illustration* grab attention and interest readers in looking further. Headlines make a promise to readers, give them information, or pose a question to draw people into the ad. Once the ad has the readers' attention, the *copy* talks to them in a believable way about their problems and explains the product's benefits. The copy should include a call to action, stating what the reader should *do,* such as trying the product or calling for more information. All print ads include a *signature,* which identifies the sponsor of the ad. A signature often consists of an organization's slogan or trademark.

Broadcast copywriters, like print copywriters, must grab people's attention and deliver a sales message. In TV and radio the first few seconds of the commercial must engage recipients and motivate them to watch or listen to the entire ad. Once attention is gained, the commercial must communicate product benefits in a meaningful way. Like print ads, broadcast ads typically end by asking the viewers or listeners to do something specific, such as trying the product.

• **Providing Technical Direction** • The mechanical work of producing an ad falls to an art director in print advertising and to a producer/director in broadcast advertising. They take the big idea as the copywriters have executed it and transform it into finished form.

Art directors prepare a *layout,* a rough sketch of a print ad that shows the location of the headline, illustration, copy, and signature. A layout also includes instructions for typesetting and printing the ad.

Radio producers and directors prepare a commercial from a *script,* a sheet of paper that includes the words to be spoken, directions for music or sound effects, and other audio directions. Radio commercials can be either live or produced. A company that wants live commercials will send a script to the radio station, where it will be read on the air by someone at the station, such as a disc jockey. A company that wants to have more control over the precise contents of its ads will produce the script in a studio and send it on tape to the radio station.

1. The Headline

INTRODUCING A NATURAL PHENOMENON

2. The Illustration

3. The Copy

Try new Del Monte Fruit Naturals.® The only way to enjoy the 100% pure taste of fruit cocktail in its own juice, with no sugar added. And no preservatives. Also in three other phenomenal varieties.

4. The Signature

FIGURE 15–2

The Different Parts of a Magazine Ad

Source: Reprinted with permission of Del Monte Corporation.

Television producers and directors also work from a script, but they may use a *storyboard* as well. A storyboard is a series of sketched frames showing actions, spoken words, and technical directions for making the ad.

Selecting the Advertising Media

Advertisers direct their messages to us through a wide variety of media. Media that readily come to mind include newspapers, magazines, radio, and TV. Media that come less readily to mind include *advertising specialties* (free gifts such as calendars, pens, and T-shirts that bear the advertiser's name and perhaps a brief message); *directory advertising* (advertising in the Yellow Pages, college student directories, professional association directories, and so on); and *corporate-sponsored magazines* (magazines owned by the advertiser, such as Delta Air Lines's *Sky* magazine, which is placed aboard Delta flights).

Advertisers seek media vehicles whose audiences match their own target audiences.

[© Gerd Ludwig]

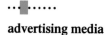

advertising media

audience selectivity

geographic selectivity

Advertising can also reach you at movie theaters, on in-flight movies, on home videos, on grocery carts, on monitors on top of self-serve gas pumps, on monitors mounted over the check-out counter in supermarkets, and so on. Toyota's ad agency even mailed 200,000 eight-minute videotape commercials for its Previa van to prospective buyers.[9]

Advertising media are the communication channels that carry messages from advertisers to their advertising targets, the four basic types of which are print, broadcast, out-of-home, and direct response. Advertisers must select the media through which to send their messages. They also have to decide which particular *vehicles* within each medium to use. For example, if the selected medium is magazines, should the vehicles be *Time, TV Guide,* and so on? These decisions must take into consideration advertising objectives, medium and vehicle characteristics, target audience characteristics, information to be communicated, and funds available for advertising.

Choosing advertising media is known as "matching media to markets." Advertisers seek media vehicles whose audiences match their own target audiences. *Audience selectivity* is an advertising medium's (or vehicle's) relative ability to reach an audience whose members are alike in ways that are important to the advertiser.

Audience selectivity is very important in a culturally diverse market. For example, a marketer that wants to reach Hispanics can turn to an increasing number of Hispanic media. The number of U.S. TV stations carrying Hispanic programming jumped from 46 in 1983 to 102 in 1990. During the same period the number of Spanish-language radio stations went from 371 to 661 and the number of Spanish-language newspapers from 94 to 158.[10]

Geographic selectivity can also be important. *Geographic selectivity* is an advertising medium's (or vehicle's) relative ability to reach people in selected geographic areas. Billboards, for example, enable advertisers to focus on neighborhoods where their target audiences are located.

Most organizations use a *reach* or *frequency* media strategy to guide their selection of media vehicles. **Reach** is the number of people who are exposed to an advertiser's advertising within a certain time period, usually four weeks. Advertisers that focus on reach want as many different targets as possible to see the ad. Reach is usually a goal when the product is new or in the growth stage of the product life cycle.

Frequency is the number of times the target audience is exposed to the advertiser's advertising within some time period, usually four weeks. Advertisers that emphasize frequency want targets to see their ads often. Frequency is an objective when the firm wants to remind prospects to buy. The marketer of a product in the maturity stage of the life cycle typically tries to achieve high frequency.

Prices for media time and space are based on two factors: size of the audience and purchasing power of the audience. A radio station that has a large number of listeners will charge more for time than one that has a small number of listeners. A magazine that is read by corporate executives and professionals will charge more for space than one that is read by college students.

In addition to the total cost of time or space, advertisers also look at *cost efficiency*. They want to avoid waste coverage—that is, paying for a media audience that does not include enough targets. Cost-per-thousand serves as a way to compare various media vehicles to ensure that the most cost-efficient are selected. **Cost-per-thousand (CPM)** is a commonly used tool to determine the cost efficiency of a media vehicle; it is computed by the following formula:

reach

frequency

cost-per-thousand (CPM)

$$CPM = \frac{\text{Cost of the ad} \times 1000}{\text{Number of targets reached}}$$

The cost of the ad should be based on like units in each medium—for example, full pages in magazines or thirty-second spots on radio or TV. The following CPM calculations compare full-page four-color ads targeted to heavy users of yogurt:

Magazine A: $\dfrac{\$72,589 \times 1000}{2,322,000 \text{ readers who heavily use yogurt}} = \$31.26$

Magazine B: $\dfrac{\$45,890 \times 1000}{1,381,000 \text{ readers who heavily use yogurt}} = \$33.23$

Although Magazine A charges a higher price, it is a more efficient media buy, because on a per-thousand basis it is less expensive.

In addition to audience size and prices, other media selection considerations include government regulations and media policies. For example, tobacco companies cannot purchase TV or radio time because of a federal law passed in 1965. Certain media vehicles may have policies regarding the kinds of ads that will be accepted. Some newspapers refuse ads for X-rated movies or alcohol. The Ethics in Marketing box raises several ethical issues about advertising.

The media vehicles used by competitors should be examined. An organization whose ad agency proposes to go head-to-head against competitors will try to select the same media that they use. A firm with a small ad budget, however, may avoid media vehicles dominated by competitors. Instead it may seek vehicles in which its ads can stand out.

The creative content of the advertising may dictate media selection. A product demonstration works best on TV, but a lengthy explanation of a complex product requires newspapers, magazines, or direct mail. A campaign to build recognition of a package or trademark will find out-of-home media effective. Advertising that teaches consumers a slogan or jingle fits radio very well. In selecting advertising media, advertisers should compare the unique characteristics of each medium to the demands of the creative strategy.

• **Print Media** •   Because print media stimulate only one sensory mode directly, they lack the impact of media that stimulate several sensory modes, such as TV. *Print media* are communication channels that sell advertising space to marketers. Newspapers and magazines are print media. More information can be communicated more accurately through print media than through other media, except for some direct response media such as direct mail.

• *Newspapers* •   Advertisers spend more money on newspaper advertising than on advertising in any other medium, probably because newspapers are popular media vehicles with local businesses. Newspapers offer mass coverage of local markets. Ads in a newspaper have high credibility because they appear in a news context. Newspapers have catalog value to consumers—they may be purchased because people want to look at the ads. Newspapers offer an immediacy and flexibility few other media can match. Advertisers may also use newspapers as a means of distributing ads they produce themselves. These *free-standing inserts* are produced on high-quality paper, often use color, and most often come with the Sunday newspaper.

There are some limitations to newspaper advertising. Ad life is short, because readers usually do not keep newspapers around more than one day. This cuts down on the number

ETHICS IN
MARKETING

More and more advertisers are inserting commercial messages into TV programs, videocassettes, movies, and video games—especially those targeted to young people. Product placement in comic books is also becoming more common. In the case of TV, the networks often push for tie-ins between programs and products—for example, showing or mentioning brand names on TV programs in return for increased advertising from the products' manufacturers. What about the ethics of blurring the traditional distinction between advertising and TV programming? More and more pharmaceutical companies are issuing video news releases to TV stations nationwide. The videos are designed to look like segments on a newscast. Does the use of these videos raise ethical issues?

What about the ethics of program-length commercials? These programs generally appear on late-night and weekend TV on cable and independent TV stations and are built around self-help products—products that promise to grow hair, whiten teeth, get rid of cellulite, make you quit smoking, or make you rich. Does it matter that the shows appear to be part of regular TV programming?

What about the use of "supers" in TV commercials—those disclaimers that often are superimposed on the bottom of ads and flash on the screen in tiny type. Are advertisers using the supers to avoid disclosure of information?

How many half-hour TV cartoons amount to little more than program-length commercials for children's games, toys, or rock groups? Is children's TV

of pass-along readers too. Newspaper pages may be cluttered, making it difficult for an ad to stand out from other ads on the page. Newspaper audiences are also declining as young adults turn to TV for news and information. Older people read newspapers more often than young people.

• *Magazines* • On the basis of their readership, magazines can be classified as consumer, business, or farm publications. Consumer magazines range from large-circulation, general-interest magazines such as *Reader's Digest, People,* and *Time* to small-circulation, special-interest magazines such as *Backpacker, Bon Appetit,* and *Video Review*.

Business publications may be general or specific in scope. General business magazines, such as *Business Week* and *Fortune,* cover many broad issues related to trade and commerce. Business magazines that are more specific in scope can be classified as horizontal or vertical. *Marketing News,* which is written for marketing professionals in all types of industries, is a horizontal publication. *Iron Age,* which is written for people who work in the same industry, is a vertical publication.

Farm publications may appeal to broad interests, as does *Farm Journal,* or to specific farm audiences. An example of a farm magazine written for a particular type of farm activity is *Hogs Today*. An example of a farm magazine written for a geographic area is *Alabama Farmer*.

Magazines offer audience selectivity. They are being used more and more as targeting vehicles. For example, general-interest magazines that divide their readerships into discrete

driven too much by commercial considerations?

In print media, magazines in particular, it is often difficult to distinguish between news and ads. Advertorials increasingly look like part of the news being reported in the magazine. Is it ethical to blur the distinction between editorials and advertising?

Several years ago Philip Morris launched an institutional advertising campaign in association with the celebration of the two hundredth anniversary of the Bill of Rights. Was the campaign's intended message that smokers have rights too?

Have the macho themes used to promote smokeless tobacco products made "dipping" a rite of passage for young males? What about targeting mostly white, blue-collar males by sponsoring such events as auto races, tractor pulls, and monster truck shows? What about providing free samples of smokeless tobacco products to professional baseball players?

What about commercial hype in the diet industry? Do "before" and "after" photos mislead consumers about product benefits? Is it ethical for lawyers to run ads in which clients talk about the favorable results lawyers obtained for them in personal injury cases?

Would it be ethical for Hispanic media executives to fight proposed restrictions on alcohol and tobacco advertising if they believe the restrictions will threaten the existence of Hispanic newspapers and magazines?

segments can attract advertisers who want to reach a specialized audience. GM and IBM are exploring new binding technology that would enable them to target ads in *Time* and *Newsweek* to market segments such as affluent retirees. The ads would be inserted only in copies mailed to these people.[11]

Magazines also offer excellent color reproduction and good pass-along readership. Advertisers who emphasize frequency in their media strategies often choose magazines. As ads run month after month, magazine subscribers get greater exposure to them.

Among the limitations of magazine advertising is long lead time. Advertisers must submit their ads for production several weeks before the magazine's issue date. If market conditions change quickly, it may be difficult or impossible to change the ad. Other media allow more flexibility than magazines. As the Roddenbery's ad suggests, clutter also can be a problem.

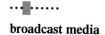

broadcast media

• **Broadcast Media** •   As we have seen, advertisers buy space in print media. They buy time on broadcast media. *Broadcast media* are communication channels that sell advertising time to marketers. Radio and television are broadcast media.

The use of white space can help in dealing with clutter in print media.

(W. B. Roddenbery Company, Inc., Cairo, Georgia; Jones-Kelley & Kilgore Advertising, Atlanta, Georgia.)

Roddenbery's®

Pickles are for smiles.

• *Radio* • Radio stations can be identified by their music (rock, oldies, classical, easy listening, country and western, jazz) or ethnic appeal, such as Spanish-language and African-American. This offers advertisers audience selectivity. Radio also offers geographic selectivity, since most stations are local or regional. However, network radio is available to reach a national target audience.

Radio is a good medium for frequent advertising, since commercial prices and the cost of production are relatively low. Radio is very flexible and is often selected by advertisers that have small budgets and highly specific target audiences. For example, it is an excellent medium for reaching teenagers.

Radio has some disadvantages, however. Prices for radio time are relatively low because radio stations usually lack the large audiences that TV and newspapers possess. In order to reach the majority of adults in a particular city, advertisers may have to purchase time on four or five radio stations, which, of course, drives up the cost of the ad campaign. Radio ads may also suffer from a lack of effectiveness because radio is essentially a background medium. The attention of most listeners is engaged elsewhere; listeners may be driving, reading, working, or talking to other people.

• *Television* • Because virtually everyone watches TV, its main advantage as an advertising medium is mass reach. TV is also a multidimensional medium. Ads can use both sound and motion for the sales message. Another advantage is the cost efficiency brought about by the ability of TV to reach millions of people. Although it is a mass medium, TV offers the advantage of some audience selectivity too. For example, children can be reached on Saturday mornings and young men can be reached during sporting events. Cable TV offers the greatest audience selectivity, with special-interest stations such as the sports-oriented ESPN and the Weather Channel.

Although TV is cost-efficient, one of its major disadvantages as an advertising medium is its high total cost. Many advertisers simply cannot afford TV. In 1990 ''The Simpsons'' commanded $300,000 per thirty-second spot from national advertisers, roughly 40 percent more than ''Monday Night Football'' and only slightly behind ''Cosby.''[12] A thirty-second spot during the 1991 Super Bowl game cost $800,000.[13] TV commercials can also be expensive to produce. And clutter is another problem, especially as more and more advertisers purchase fifteen-second commercials.

• **Out-of-Home Media** • The last advertising media consumers see before they buy may be out-of-home media. *Out-of-home-media* are communication channels that expose the target audience to the sales message when the audience is away from home and closer to the marketplace. Outdoor advertising and transit advertising are examples.

out-of-home media

• *Outdoor Advertising* • The three major types of outdoor advertising are printed posters, painted bulletins, and electric spectaculars. Printed posters and painted bulletins, often called billboards, are owned by outdoor-advertising companies, which rent them to advertisers on a monthly basis. Electric spectaculars are often more permanent and are located in high-traffic locations, such as Times Square in New York City and the Strip in Las Vegas.

Outdoor advertising is a high-frequency medium, since people normally follow the same route each day as they travel to and from work, school, or shopping. Geographic selectivity is another advantage. Advertisers can focus on cities or neighborhoods where targets are located. Like TV, outdoor advertising is cost-efficient (low CPM) because large numbers of people pass boards daily.

A disadvantage of outdoor advertising is the limited attention it receives from drivers and passersby, who may glance at it for less than a second. Therefore, effective outdoor ads must be simple and must contain only a few words.

• *Transit Advertising* • Advertising that appears inside and outside mass transportation vehicles, such as buses and subway cars, is transit advertising. It may also be found at bus stops, train stations, and airports. Transit ads can be geographically selective and, in terms of cost-per-thousand, are one of the least expensive advertising media available. Some advertisers use transit ads to reach target audiences living and working in the inner core of large cities.

Transit advertising is a high-frequency medium. Limitations include the fact that the ads are often subject to vandalism. Also, transit ads are believed by some to have a poor image, probably because of the poor physical appearance and lack of cleanliness of some transit vehicles and facilities.

direct response media

• **Direct Response Media** • The communication channels through which marketers can communicate directly with the target audience are ***direct response media.*** Direct mail advertising is a type of direct response media. With direct mail advertising, the advertising message is delivered by mail. The response can be made by mail or by telephone. We will examine direct response media in greater detail in our discussion of direct marketing in chapter 16. Figure 15–3 shows the share of total advertising volume accounted for by each of the major media in 1990.

• **The Media Plan** • After comparing the various alternatives, the advertiser selects the media that will help most in accomplishing advertising objectives. Media costs account for the largest part of the total advertising budget. In light of the big increases in such costs during recent years, advertisers are paying close attention to media planning. Some have brought media planning and buying in-house, while retaining their ad agencies for creative work. Others have hired media buying services. These firms negotiate prices and buy media time and space on behalf of their clients.

Audience information can be purchased from firms such as Simmons Market Research Bureau and A. C. Nielsen, or obtained free of charge directly from most media vehicles. Audience information is becoming increasingly available through computer databases that advertising agencies and advertisers access by telephone. *Cost information* is available

Transit advertising can be a very cost effective way of reaching particular types of target audiences.

[© Gerd Ludwig]

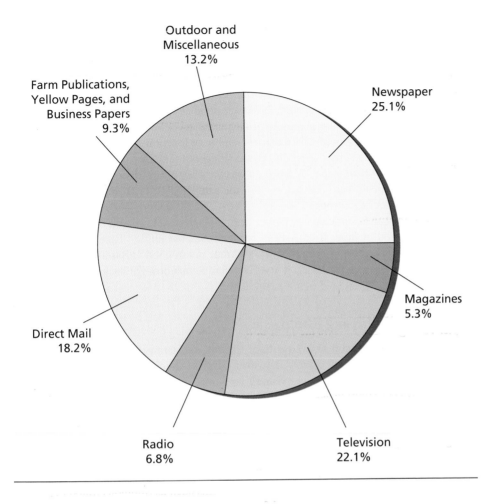

Outdoor and
Miscellaneous
13.2%

Farm Publications,
Yellow Pages, and
Business Papers
9.3%

Newspaper
25.1%

Magazines
5.3%

Direct Mail
18.2%

Radio
6.8%

Television
22.1%

FIGURE 15–3

Share of Total Advertising Volume for Each Medium, 1990.

Source: Reprinted with permission from *Advertising Age,* May 6, 1991. Copyright Crain Communications, Inc. All rights reserved. Data collected by Robert J. Coen, McCann-Erickson.

media plan

from a monthly publication, *Standard Rate and Data Service,* which includes rate cards for all types of media, and directly from media vehicles themselves.

A *media plan* is a written statement of the reach and frequency goals of an advertising campaign and of how these goals will be achieved. It contains the names of media vehicles that will carry the advertising as well as timing information and costs. Computer models are available to help media planners design a plan that achieves reach and frequency goals within a stated budget.

• **Timing** • The timing of ads—when and how often they should appear—is influenced by several factors, including seasonality, competitors' timing, and budget size. Advertising is most effective when it appears just before and during seasonal sales peaks. For example, firms that sell back-to-school supplies typically begin advertising in late July and August.

Advertisers must consider competitors' advertising schedules. The strategy may be to match competitors in similar media at similar times or it may be to avoid them by advertising in different media at different times.

Budget size affects the timing of ads. Small advertisers that cannot afford to advertise continually may save their money until they can buy enough ads over a short period of time to make an impact with the target. After this short period, advertising is stopped. Advertisers hope the impact achieved during the *flights of advertising* will last through periods of no advertising. Advertisers with larger budgets may choose a *pulsing strategy,* in which a basic level of advertising is constantly maintained but there are seasonal periods of heavier advertising.

An ad campaign that has high frequency or that runs for a long period of time may begin to suffer the problem of *advertising wearout.* Consumers tire of the advertising, and its effectiveness declines. Ad campaigns based on popular characters can wear out quickly because the characters are overexposed. Some marketers believe the Mutant Ninja Turtles were overexposed very quickly.[14] Procter & Gamble no longer uses ads based on such characters as Mr. Whipple (Charmin), Mrs. Olson (Folgers), and Rosie the waitress (Bounty). Isuzu's Joe Isuzu ("He's lying") campaign was very popular with consumers. Some marketing experts believe that Isuzu got tired of the campaign before consumers did and that the firm should not have dropped Joe.[15]

On the other hand, some ad campaigns or parts thereof are brought back after they are rested for a period of time. Rice-A-Roni brought back the jingle "Rice-A-Roni, the San Francisco treat"; Campbell brought back "Mmm, mmm good"; Banfi Vintners brought back "Riunite on Ice. That's Nice"; and Hawaiian Punch brought back "Punchy."

Evaluating Advertising Effectiveness

Probably the most difficult task advertisers face is evaluating the effectiveness of their advertising. Evaluation is necessary, however, because it helps advertisers (1) determine whether their advertising is accomplishing its objectives; (2) assess the coordination of advertising with other promotion mix and marketing mix elements; (3) appraise the relative effectiveness of different ads in terms of appeals, ad concepts, layout, and so on; (4) appraise the relative effectiveness of various media and media plans; and (5) improve future advertising efforts. The Cahners Publishing Company ad suggests the importance advertisers attach to evaluating advertising's effectiveness.

Most advertisers would like to link sales results directly to advertising. Thus, in order to measure the sales impact of an entire advertising campaign, some firms try to correlate past sales data to past advertising expenditures by using statistical techniques. Others engage in sophisticated experiments in which they divide their markets into a number of submarkets based on such factors as their relative market shares. Then they vary the level of advertising expenditures in those submarkets in an effort to measure advertising effort response elasticity. *Advertising effort response elasticity* is the relationship between the percentage change in advertising expenditures and the percentage change in sales.

The danger in using sales volume as the criterion for judging advertising effectiveness is that it ignores the roles of other promotion and marketing mix elements. Furthermore, many types of advertising do not seek to produce immediate sales results. For example, it would be difficult to evaluate many types of institutional advertising campaigns on the basis of sales results.

It is a bit simpler, but by no means easy, to link sales results to particular ads. As we will see in chapter 16, in some cases, such as direct response ads on TV and direct mail and mail-order advertising, this linkage can be fairly well established.

One approach to linking advertising and sales is to use split-run tests. Many magazines allow their advertisers to divide their markets so that half the market receives one version of an ad and the other half receives another version. Sales responses for each version are subsequently tabulated and compared as a measure of relative pulling power. Such tests are also possible with cable TV and national newspapers.

Another approach is to conduct a sales test. This involves selecting two market areas that are closely matched by characteristics such as income, educational level, or racial/ethnic makeup and by buying patterns. One receives the ad and the other does not. Sales response in the two areas is then tabulated and any differences are attributed to the ad.

Many advertisers also seek to measure the communication effects of their ads. An ad's communication effectiveness can be tested before (pretest) or after (post-test) it is placed in the media. A *pretest* helps determine whether a proposed ad should be run and, if so, how it might be improved. A *post-test* helps determine whether ads in use should be continued, changed, or dropped.

● **Pretests** ●   Advertisers use techniques such as focus group interviews, consumer juries, semantic differential scales, projective techniques, laboratory techniques, and recall tests to assess proposed ads. *Focus group interviews* (see chapter 4) are often used in the early stages of developing the creative strategy for ads. *Consumer juries* may be used later to evaluate proposed layouts for print media ads by, for example, choosing which ads they prefer among pairs in a series of ads. For ads that are to run on television, jury members might be shown several commercials in a projection room and asked to discuss what they liked and disliked about each one.

Other pretests might use *semantic differential scales* (see chapter 5) and *projective techniques* (see chapter 4) to measure the effects of alternate ads on the way respondents think or feel about the product. Different versions are given to different groups, which rate them on a number of scales that describe the product or how people will think and feel about it.

Laboratory techniques to measure an ad's ability to stimulate action include a variety of psychological measurement devices. Some measure changes in eye pupil size and voice

An ad that discusses a new approach to evaluating advertising's effectiveness.

(Cahners Publishing Company, 1990.)

pitch to indicate the viewer's emotional involvement with the ad. Eye cameras that photograph how people read ads can be especially helpful in making layout decisions.

Recall tests are commonly used to pretest TV commercials. Consumers are recruited ostensibly to view and evaluate TV programming in which test commercials have been placed. Later, typically within twenty-four hours, they are contacted and asked which commercials they recall seeing. Commercials that generate high recall are thought to be more effective.

• **Post-Tests** • As mentioned earlier, post-tests are designed to measure the effectiveness of ads that are running in the media. Examples are readership tests, unaided recall tests, and inquiry tests. These are indirect measurements of an ad's effectiveness.

Readership tests are conducted by research firms such as Starch Readership Service. Starch periodically measures the readership of more than a hundred print media vehicles, including newspapers and magazines. In the case of magazine readership, an interviewer takes readers of a given issue through the magazine and asks them to indicate what they recognize as having seen before. Three different Starch readership scores are prepared for each ad: (1) "noted"—the percentage who say they previously saw the ad, (2) "seen/associated"—the percentage who correctly identify the product with the advertiser, and (3) "read most"—the percentage who say they read more than half the content of the ad.

Unaided recall tests involve interviewing respondents who claim to have read a particular issue of a magazine or to have seen a particular TV program. After proving to the interviewer that they did in fact read that issue or see that program, respondents tell the interviewer what they recall about the ads.

In an *inquiry test* the ad includes an invitation to call or write for additional information or offers a free sample of the product to people who respond to the ad. The number of inquiries received is considered to be a measure of the ad's effectiveness.

ORGANIZING ADVERTISING ACTIVITIES

Marketing organizations have three basic options for organizing their advertising activities. As we will see in greater detail shortly, these activities can be (1) handled by an internal advertising department, (2) handled by an outside advertising agency, or (3) shared between them.

A growing number of large firms are separating their direct marketing activities from their other marketing and advertising functions. Many agencies specialize in direct response and are called direct response agencies. Some major advertising agencies also have created or acquired direct response divisions.

Sales promotion is often a shared responsibility. In many cases advertising managers handle such elements as coupons and consumer contests and sales managers handle trade shows and dealer contests and premiums. Thus advertising managers tend to focus on mass promotion tools and sales managers on more personalized forms of sales promotion. Product, or brand, managers are often accountable for specifying the dates when various sales promotion activities will begin and end. In larger organizations, sales promotion activities are usually handled by specialists either inside the organization or at its advertising agency or sales promotion firm.

Public relations activities in most larger firms are handled out of the public relations department, not the marketing department. These departments may engage in such diverse activities as lobbying legislative groups and coping with damaging rumors. As a result, PR activities, such as generating publicity for new products, are only part of a PR department's responsibilities. Some firms therefore set up publicity units in the marketing department and use advertising agencies or PR firms to help ensure that marketing-related PR activities will not be overlooked.

The discussions that follow take a closer look at how advertising activities are organized. Regardless of organizational approach, the specialized skills needed to create effective advertising are essentially the same—research, creative, managerial, production, and media buying skills.

Advertising Departments

In small manufacturing companies advertising is usually the responsibility of the sales manager, who, with help from one or two others in-house, develops basic ideas for ads. This person also relies on copywriters and other specialists who work for local media to produce, place, and schedule ads. Small retailers rely heavily on local media for assistance, but they can also seek help from the manufacturers whose products they sell.

The larger an organization and the greater its advertising effort, the more likely it will set up an advertising department. An *advertising department* is part of an advertiser's own organization, may include creative and technical personnel, and is headed by a manager, who participates in ad production and media placement and reports to the marketing manager. Advertising department personnel sometimes turn to freelance specialists for assistance.

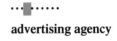

advertising department

Advertising Agencies

An *advertising agency* is a firm that specializes in communication and marketing and that offers these services to clients (advertisers). Ad agencies range in size from large, full-service companies with worldwide operations to one-person firms.

advertising agency

Giant ad agencies such as WPP Group, Saatchi & Saatchi, and Omnicom Group are made up of a number of formerly independent ad agencies, often from different countries. London-based Saatchi & Saatchi's units include formerly independent U.S.-based agencies such as Ted Bates and Backer & Spielvogel. WPP Group's units include J. Walter Thompson, Ogilvy & Mather, Hill & Knowlton, and assorted smaller companies. Such giant agencies were formed largely as a result of pursuing the strategy of *cross-selling*— selling clients one-stop advertising, public relations, and marketing services. More recently, many big ad agencies have abandoned cross-selling.[16] Many clients do not believe that one-stop shopping has provided them with all the benefits that some agencies promised.

At the other end of the spectrum are small agencies in virtually every city of any size in the United States. These agencies consist of one person or a small group of people who create and place advertising for local retailers and others.

• **Agency Organization** • Full-service ad agencies are often organized by function. The *research department* studies the client's target audience and coordinates tests of advertising effectiveness. The *creative department* develops the sales message and execution, which are then turned into actual ads by the *production department*. The *media department* selects media and places ads. The *traffic department* keeps track of an ad campaign while it is being developed and produced and makes sure each department finishes its part in a timely manner. Most agencies have an administrative staff to handle routine business activities such as accounting, payroll, and personnel. Small ad agencies may have no departments and only one or two people to perform all the functions.

• **Agency-Client Interaction** • Personnel in the various departments of an ad agency are assigned to work with one or more clients. The clients themselves are called accounts, and each is assigned to an account executive. An *account executive,* the major link between the advertising agency and the client, is the manager who coordinates all the agency's activities on the client's behalf.

Industry practice is to limit an ad agency to one client in any product category. Thus one agency would not handle advertising for both Toyota and Nissan. Furthermore, multiproduct firms often use several ad agencies. These firms ordinarily have an in-house ad department headed by an advertising manager. This person coordinates the ad campaigns for different products and the sales promotion activities that are tied together with the ad campaigns.

• **Why Use an Ad Agency?** • Many advertisers that have their own ad departments still use ad agencies. They do so for a variety of reasons. Ad agencies (1) are staffed by personnel who have wide advertising experience, (2) maintain closer contact with the media than advertisers do, (3) may introduce more objectivity into the advertiser's decision making because they are outsiders, and (4) may work harder for their clients because they can easily be replaced by rival agencies.

Many firms wanting to become involved in "green marketing" have turned to ad agencies for advice. Saatchi & Saatchi, for example, recently set up a worldwide "Green Team" to help clients track environmentally savvy consumers. In California two new agencies are committed solely to environmentally sensitive goods and services.[17]

• **Agency Compensation** • In a sense, ad agencies are compensated by the media, not the client. If an advertiser contracts with an ad agency for $100,000 worth of magazine space, the agency bills the client for $100,000, deducts a 15 percent commission for itself, and remits $85,000 to the magazine. But only ad agencies that are "recognized" by the media are allowed a commission. So if the advertiser did not use a recognized agency, it would still pay the magazine $100,000 for the space. The advertiser could not keep the $15,000 commission for itself.

The commission system, however, is changing. Large advertisers with in-house ad departments want to receive the same treatment from the media as recognized agencies. Advertisers also complain that the system encourages ad agencies to place ads in high-cost media in order to earn bigger commissions. Some ad agencies are dissatisfied because the straight 15 percent commission does not take into account the fact that some clients require more services than others.

Thus some ad agencies are moving in the direction of charging fees rather than relying on the 15 percent commission. This has stimulated the development of small agencies (boutique agencies) that specialize in the creative part of agency work. It has also stimulated the unbundling of services (pricing various services separately) by full-service agencies.

• **Agency Selection** • In selecting an ad agency a firm must collect information about various agencies and divulge information about itself. The firm may contact prospective ad agencies and ask them several questions, such as what experience they have in the product category, who their current clients are, and who in the agency would be working on the account. The firm will also want to see samples of the agencies' creative work.

The firm must communicate to prospective agencies its own history, overall promotion strategy, specific campaign objectives, product characteristics, campaign budget and tentative division among different media, desired services the agency is to provide, and the role of the firm's in-house ad department in the campaign.

SUMMARY OF LEARNING OBJECTIVES

1. Identify the three fundamental objectives of advertising.
The three objectives are (1) to inform target audiences, (2) to persuade target audiences, and (3) to remind target audiences.

2. Distinguish between product advertising and institutional advertising.
Product advertising is promotion that focuses on selling specifically identified goods and services. Institutional advertising is promotion that focuses on the image of a product category, a company, a nonprofit organization, or an industry association rather than a specific brand.

3. Distinguish among pioneering, competitive, and reminder product advertising.
Pioneering product advertising seeks to create awareness and understanding and to develop primary demand (demand for a new-product category). Competitive product advertising tries to stimulate selective demand (demand for a specific brand within a product category). Reminder product advertising is used when a product has reached the brand preference or insistence stage for a large number of target customers.

4. Distinguish among pioneering, competitive, and reminder institutional advertising.
Pioneering institutional advertising helps in building and maintaining the desired image for an organization. Competitive institutional advertising is often used when different product categories compete for the same market segment. Reminder institutional advertising summarizes information presented or comparisons made in previous pioneering or competitive campaigns.

5. Identify the major tasks of advertising management.
Advertising management includes (1) defining the target audience, (2) defining advertising objectives, (3) setting the advertising budget, (4) developing the creative strategy, (5) selecting the advertising media, and (6) evaluating advertising effectiveness.

6. Explain the options marketers have for organizing their advertising activities.
Marketing organizations have three basic options for organizing their advertising activities. These activities can be handled by an internal advertising department, handled by an outside advertising agency, or shared between them.

Review Questions

1. What are the three fundamental objectives of advertising?

2. What is the basic difference between product advertising and institutional advertising?

3. How do pioneering advertising, competitive advertising, and reminder advertising differ?

4. What are the tasks of advertising management?

5. Do the terms *target audience* and *target market* mean the same thing? Explain.

6. What is meant by *advertising execution*?

7. What are the four basic types of advertising media?

8. What is meant by *audience selectivity*?

9. How do pretests and post-tests of advertising's effectiveness differ?

10. Why would an advertiser use an advertising agency?

Discussion Questions

1. Do advertisers emphasize celebrity commercials too much?

2. In recent years the TV networks appear to be doing more and more multicultural programming? Why?

3. Some marketers feature several of their products in the same ad. Some do it to stretch their advertising budgets. Others do it believing that the company name is a more important selling point than the brand names. Traditionally, however, marketers have been reluctant to feature more than one product in a given ad. Is it wise to feature several products in a single ad? Explain.

4. Recently, Honda and Nissan started advertising some of their cars as having been built in the United States. For example, an ad for the Honda Accord had the following headline: ''The amazing new car from Ohio that goes around corners, up hills, and overseas.'' The ad also pointed out that Honda makes the Accord wagon only in its plant in Ohio, from which some units are exported to Europe and Japan. Why are Honda and Nissan using such ads?

Application Exercise

Reread the material about mass media at the beginning of this chapter and answer the following questions:

1. Is a media package that promises to deliver the target audience more important in the case of product advertising or in the case of institutional advertising? Explain.

2. What is the meaning of the following statement by an ad agency media director? "The way mass media work now, advertisers simply 'buy eyeballs.'"

3. Are mass media in danger of becoming extinct? Explain.

Key Concepts

The following key terms were introduced in this chapter:

product advertising
institutional advertising
cooperative advertising
comparative advertising
advocacy advertising
target audience
advertising media

audience selectivity
geographic selectivity
reach
frequency
cost-per-thousand (CPM)
print media
broadcast media

out-of-home media
direct response media
media plan
advertising department
advertising agency
account executive

·· █ ··

CASES

Beefcake and Babies

LYN S. AMINE, *St. Louis University*

After decades of selling products by depicting women as sex kittens or domestic half-wits, advertisers have switched bimbos. The women's liberation movement of the 1970s and 1980s raised consciousness in the advertising world about negative stereotypes being attached to women. Now, in the 1990s, men are suffering through the creation of new male stereotypes which, in many cases, display reverse sexism. The positive, traditional images of men as providers, protectors, and sports heroes, and the negative images of the sexually dominant male are both being replaced by new images that are not always flattering. Men are commonly portrayed as jerks, boors, kitchen klutzes, or objects of female fantasy. In some instances, they are simply accused of smelling bad. The only concessions made to male integrity are when the man becomes a father. Then intelligence, good looks, and sophistication are permitted—as long as there is a baby or young child in the picture with the man.

Men's Rights, Inc. of Sacramento, an activist organization, has analyzed thousands of print and video ads and commercials and compiled annual lists of the best and worst portrayals of men. The most positive portrayals are seen in ads for Kodak, Omega, and American Express, which use the "beefcake and babies" formula made popular in the movie *Three Men and a Baby*. Other companies (such as Texas Instruments and Pioneer Electronics) have used a more muted version of the father–child relationship,

while one company (Fruit of the Loom) has added the image of "Dad, the sports hero" to the father–son relationship.

The more traditional images of men in advertising have not been completely supplanted. Dewar's "White Label" Scotch whiskey ads show a series of worldly sophisticates listing various pieces of idiosyncratic information about their likes and dislikes. Fujitsu has consistently supported a print ad campaign featuring selected employees; one print ad shows five middle-aged family men who are skilled electronics professionals from Oregon and who are "all proud men with a fierce passion for perfection in their work."

The newer, more controversial images of men as "bimbo objects" are used ironically by Perry Ellis to promote a men's fragrance. The open-shirted model addresses the reader saying "I may model for a living, but I hate being treated like a piece of meat." This both endorses the new stereotype and questions its validity. Dom Deluise is similarly saved from his fate as a kitchen klutz in the Ziploc campaign by his evident interest in good food and his ability to laugh at himself.

In other ad campaigns the men are not allowed to lament their questionable roles or images. The print campaign for Pitney Bowes fax machines pokes fun at incompetent businessmen and adds to this the image of the boorish boss who bellows, "SEALS? I said, bring in more DEALS!!" to his uninspired employee. The warning headline reminds the businessperson that "The Pitney Bowes fax lets you see what you thought you heard."

Men, as consumers, generally tend not to complain. It is not surprising, then, to find many men suffering in silence through this wave of unflattering, new-generation ads featuring men, even though they resent the implications. At this time, there is no research evidence that it sells to any of the newly liberated women who might harbor some of the resentment against men that these ads project. At most, all that can be claimed for these ads is that they get consumers' attention. Whether or not they sell the product is open to debate.

Questions

1. In what ways might the target audience for "beefcake and babies" ads differ from the target audience for ads depicting men as "bimbo objects"?

2. What sales message do you think the Perry Ellis "bimbo" ad conveys? What message is it intended to convey?

3. What changes in sociocultural trends are reflected in reverse sexism ads?

4. Do you think the problem of clutter in advertising media played a part in the appearance of ads depicting men as "bimbo objects"? Explain.

Barq's Root Beer: From Biloxi to the Big Apple

The roots of Barq's Root Beer are found down South, in Biloxi, Mississippi, but Barq's isn't just a regional brand anymore. In 1898 Edward Barq started brewing root beer in tubs in his Louisiana backyard. The family continued the small, regional business in Biloxi, Mississippi, and at one point had 30 percent of the soft drink market in southern Mississippi while doing practically no advertising.

In 1976 two partners, John Koerner and John Oudt, bought the business from the Barq family for $3 million. Through a combination of careful planning and unconventional advertising, the two have expanded Barq's distribution into over 70 percent of the country. The company, now based in New Orleans, is estimated to have a net worth of as much as $50 million.

The partners' strategy included building a network of bottlers across the country. Barq's ensures bottlers' loyalty by providing the traditional advertising allowance with a unique twist: bottlers can use the allowance practically any way they like, including to promote other brands, so long as the promotion includes Barq's. Bottlers can even use the allowance to improve the bottom line in a bad quarter.

The partners realized that they needed to distinguish Barq's from other brands in their advertising. They hired Fred/Alan, the New York agency that created the successful "I want my MTV" advertising spots, to create a unique image for Barq's. In New York Barq's advertising has been characterized by its hip approach: the message on Barq's posters reads, "So try 'em already." The campaign was so successful that Barq's is in a neck-and-neck race with number-one A&W for the top root beer brand in New York, and the Fred/Alan agency has gotten most of Barq's advertising business.

Other advertising, including TV ads that feature Three Stooges-like characters who drink Barq's and proclaim, "That bites," continues the hip theme. Barq's planned to spend $2 million on a summer 1991 ad campaign to be shown on cable and syndicated shows. The company's total advertising expenditure for its root beer and other soda products is about $10 million per year, with a targeted market of young people ages twelve to twenty-four.

Barq's has retained its family identity through Edward (Sonny) Barq IV, great-grandson of the founder, a company employee who meets with bottlers and oversees the mixing of the secret Barq's formula in Biloxi. Every can of Barq's carries Sonny's name and address and asks people to write in; Sonny sends each writer a thank-you and a discount coupon.

The company's strategy has worked: Barq's is now the second-ranked root beer brand in the country, with 8 percent of the $1.8 billion root beer market, ahead of Pepsi's Mug Root Beer, Monarch Co.'s Dad's, and Cadbury, Schweppes' Hires. Number one A&W is still far ahead with 30 percent of the market, but Barq's is running hard. The company had T-shirts printed up that read, "A&Who?"

Questions

1. Should Barq's engage in institutional advertising? Why?

2. How would you evaluate Barq's definition of its target audience?

3. What media do you think Barq's should use to reach its target audience?

4. Why do you think Barq's includes Sonny Barq's name and address on its cans of root beer and encourages drinkers to write?

16

DIRECT MARKETING,
SALES PROMOTION, AND
PUBLIC RELATIONS

OBJECTIVES

After reading this chapter you will be able to

1. explain direct marketing as a marketing channel system and a communication system.

2. explain the role of a marketing database in direct marketing.

3. identify the major tasks involved in direct marketing management.

4. identify the major tasks of sales promotion management.

5. contrast direct contact public relations and publicity.

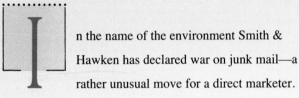

n the name of the environment Smith & Hawken has declared war on junk mail—a rather unusual move for a direct marketer. "Junk mail is anything that comes in the mail box that you don't want," says Paul Hawken, the company's founder. Smith & Hawken is a mail-order company that specializes in garden tools, furniture, and clothing.

According to Hawken, the direct marketing industry is sending an increasing amount of mail to a relatively stable number of potential customers, members, and donors. "This overgrazing of the consumer is excessive, wasteful, and bothersome. It creates pollution, destroys forests, chokes landfills, and squanders energy. The direct marketing industry thrives on waste, and this waste has to stop."

Smith & Hawken decided to do something about the problem with a nine-part junk mail initiative designed to reduce waste and increase environmentally sound practices in the direct marketing industry. As part of its "action agenda," the company uses selective mailings, giving customers a choice of which Smith & Hawken catalogs they will receive.

Customers are encouraged to keep their Smith & Hawken catalogs. In turn the company carries catalog products for longer periods. Remailing, the common practice of repackaging old catalogs to make them seem new, will nearly cease.

Postcards in the catalogs allowed customers to contact the company and have their names removed from the company's mailing list. The firm will help customers learn how to get their names removed from other lists. Catalogs have informed customers about the company's name-rental policy and explain how they can prevent their names from being rented.

The company also hands over $5 gift certificates to customers who send in duplicate address labels from a Smith & Hawken catalog. Catalogs also are being printed with soy-based inks, a practice that if used by all printing companies could save the United States 5 to 6 percent of its oil imports.

Smith & Hawken has set up a sanctuary forest program and has begun using recycled materials for its packaging and catalogs. The company is encouraging the paper industry to produce printing papers higher in recycled content, especially with post-consumer waste, as part of its long-term commitment to using recycled paper.

According to Bonnie Dahan, Smith & Hawken's vice president of communications, the company has always had a strong commitment to environmental concerns. It has a staff environmental director and gives 10 percent of its pretax profits to environmental and horticultural organizations.

The company's motto for the junk mail campaign seems to sum it all up rather nicely: "Plant your beans . . . or get out of the garden." Dahan says it's a fun way of saying, "Stop talking about it and start doing something."

It probably helps that most of Smith & Hawken's customers have a strong interest in the environment. Dahan says the company has received a "real response" from its customers, who often write that they're happier doing business with an environmentally concerned company.

Smith & Hawken may have one of the most comprehensive plans around, but it's not alone. According to the Direct Marketing Association (DMA) in New York, many direct marketers are doing the "green" thing. DMA recently produced a booklet of environmental recommendations for direct marketers. The group also has formed a task force to identify ways in which direct marketers can implement environmentally responsible policies, such as cleaning mailing lists, establishing in-house recycling programs, and using recycled and recyclable paper and packaging.[1]

Smith & Hawken is a direct marketer that is trying to do something about the image the industry has. Many consumers equate direct marketing with such problems as junk mail and junk fax.

In this chapter we look closely at the nature of direct marketing, sales promotion, and public relations. These elements of the promotion mix are perhaps less familiar to and less understood by the average individual than are advertising and personal selling.

WHAT IS DIRECT MARKETING?

As we saw in chapter 14, the Direct Marketing Association defines *direct marketing* as an interactive system of marketing which uses one or more advertising media to effect a measurable response and/or transaction at any location. Let's take a closer look at several key terms in this definition.

Direct marketing is an *interactive system*. The marketer and the prospect engage in two-way, one-on-one communication. For example, even if a direct marketer advertises a product for sale on TV, the prospect must write or call the marketer to order the product. The interactive nature of direct marketing reflects the notion of exchange as the critical focus in marketing.

The *advertising media* used by direct marketers include telephone, television, direct mail, interactive video (such as the touch-screen restaurant guides at downtown hotels), and other means of electronic data exchange. We discuss direct advertising media in greater detail later in the chapter. As we will see, direct marketers often combine media in marketing their products.

Direct marketing programs seek to induce measurable actions, or responses, on the part of the target audience. Examples of such actions include ordering by phone, sending a donation, requesting further information, and scheduling a product demonstration. These actions are *measurable responses*. For example, in a telemarketing operation every call a telephone operator makes to a prospect is trackable. The outcome of every call can be tallied. A response or lack of response can be associated with each individual prospect. The direct marketer can identify not only the specific communication that stimulated the respondent to action but also the action so stimulated, such as a sale or a request for additional information regarding the product warranty.

In direct marketing, communication between the marketer and the prospect can occur at any *location*. The interaction need not take place in a store or purchasing agent's office. It can occur whenever and wherever communication media, such as terminals, phones, or mailboxes, are available. The copy in the Spiegel ad alludes to catalog shopping from a

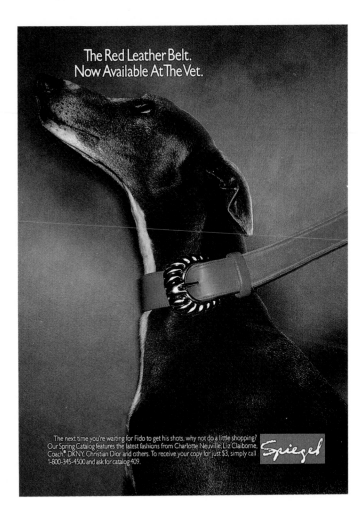

This ad focuses on the convenience of catalog shopping.

(With permission of Spiegel, Inc., Spring 1990 ad campaign.)

veterinarian's office. U.S. Cavalry Inc., a mail-order company specializing in "military and adventure equipment," sent 250,000 copies of its winter 1991 catalog to U.S. soldiers in Saudi Arabia during Operation Desert Shield and Operation Desert Storm.[2]

Direct Marketing's Advantages to Marketers and Customers

As a highly targeted type of marketing, direct marketing offers advantages to both marketers and customers.

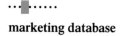

marketing database

• **Advantages to Marketers** • There is little wasted coverage with direct marketing because the marketer can be very selective in targeting prospects. For example, with its own or a rented mailing list, a prestige department store can use direct mail to reach people in certain high-income zip codes instead of using newspaper ads to promote its home furnishings department to the general public. The offer is also shielded from competitors.

When coupled with a marketing database, direct marketing can be an especially highly targeted form of marketing that strengthens relationship marketing, the development of long-term ties with customers. A *marketing database* is a collection of interrelated data about an organization's individual prospects and customers that is intended to satisfy the organization's marketing information requirements. Typically such a database is computerized and contains information about individual prospects and customers that has been collected over a considerable period of time. This information makes possible highly targeted individualized direct marketing efforts.

A marketing database helps the direct marketer get closer to customers on a continuing basis. Customers can be addressed by name; and with customer-specific information in the database, it is possible to go much further in the one-to-one, interactive communication process. For example, a direct marketer might suggest particular articles of clothing in a catalog that would complement items of clothing a particular customer had purchased from an earlier catalog.

Because direct marketing lends itself to accurate measurement of results, it permits marketers to test and to adjust their strategies more often and more rapidly. A telemarketer that is dissatisfied with the rate of response to a telemarketing effort can provide the telemarketing communicators with a new script. Marketing resources therefore can be allocated more effectively and efficiently.

Direct marketing also motivates its targets to respond quickly. An example is "call the toll-free number on your TV screen now to take advantage of this exciting offer."

Direct marketing can increase the efficiency of an organization's marketing effort in many ways. L. L. Bean, for example, can serve many markets with its centralized warehouse in Freeport, Maine. Direct marketing can support the sales force by generating leads (names of people or organizations that might use the marketer's product), qualifying leads, preselling prospects, and handling marginal or small accounts. Craftmatic/Contour Industries runs ads for its beds on local and cable TV. Viewers are urged to call a toll-free number for more information. People who call are sent a brochure, which is followed up by calls from telemarketing salespeople who solicit in-home appointments for Craftmatic salespeople.[3] The American Association of Retired Persons uses direct mail to prospect for new members.

Direct marketing also makes it feasible to serve small niche markets profitably. General Foods sells premium Swedish coffees in a continuity program (shipping coffees at regular intervals) for about $5 per pound. The volume is small compared to the volume of coffee

sold through supermarkets. But General Foods' Gevalia Kaffe is targeted to a special niche and is relatively insulated from the price wars in the traditional coffee category.

Direct marketing provides a means of demonstrating and building demand in order to secure wider subsequent distribution if needed. For example, on the basis of Gevalia's sales, General Foods might consider marketing the product in kiosks in shopping malls to reach new customers.

Direct marketing can help marketers stay in touch and resell—managing customer relationships. Automobile manufacturers can use direct marketing to maintain ongoing contact with their customers. Insurance companies and banks can use direct marketing to help cross-sell their products.

Direct marketing can also help reduce dependence on and vulnerability to channel systems. For example, Mary Kay Cosmetics distributes through independent beauty consultants who supply the names and addresses of their customers. This information is entered into Mary Kay's database, and four times a year the customers receive a direct mail package from the company. Included in each package is the name and phone number of the customer's consultant to make it easy for the customer to call to place orders. This dialogue with customers also can facilitate reassignment of customers whose consultants leave the company.[4]

In organizational marketing many marketers are finding that direct marketing can help reduce costs. A major reason is the escalating cost of face-to-face personal sales calls. Marketers of many industrial products rely on direct marketing to serve customers in the aftermarket. For example, a marketer of office machines might use a sales force to sell the machines and use direct marketing to sell paper and other supplies. Direct marketing can also supplement existing marketing channels and identify sales leads for dealers and distributors. Fund-raising organizations often turn to direct marketing to increase the response rate and reduce the cost of soliciting funds. Direct marketing efforts can also be used to reduce resistance to first-time calls by salespeople.

• **Advantages to Customers** • Direct marketing offers advantages to customers as well. Consumers can use their credit cards to order merchandise advertised on TV by calling a toll-free number and receiving rapid delivery. They can comparison shop from catalogs in the comfort of their homes and order gifts to be delivered directly to the recipients.

Direct marketing gives buyers easy access to merchandise that may be hard to find. The merchandise you want comes to you instead of you having to go from store to store looking for it. Many find this way of buying to be fun, safe, convenient, time saving, money saving, and free of problems such as street crime, fighting traffic, finding a parking place, and coping with uninformed retail salespeople. Direct marketing helps lonely people cope with their loneliness and provides a way for housebound people to shop.

Marketers that sell to small organizational buyers often rely on direct marketing because they cannot justify the cost of selling to these customers through a sales force. Without direct marketing those customers might not be serviced.

Direct Marketing as a Marketing Channel System

Recall from chapter 11 that in a direct distribution channel there are no intermediaries. Direct marketing involves no intermediaries and therefore could be viewed as a direct distribution channel.

Over time the notion of what direct marketing is has changed. At one time *direct marketing* and *direct distribution* meant about the same thing. Thus a company whose salespeople sold directly to final customers was engaged in direct marketing. So was a manufacturer that operated a factory outlet selling directly to final buyers. In chapter 12 we discussed nonstore retailing, which includes direct selling and automatic vending. Direct marketing, of course, does not involve retail stores.

Direct marketing eventually came to be associated mainly with catalog marketing and direct mail marketing. These too are forms of marketing that involve no intermediaries. As technology advanced, direct marketing began to include various forms of telemarketing and electronic media.

Today retailers, wholesalers, manufacturers, charitable organizations, and others engage in direct marketing to deal directly with target customers or donors. Some, such as L. L. Bean, rely almost exclusively on direct marketing. In other cases marketers supplement their traditional channels, such as producer to wholesaler to retailer to final buyer, with direct marketing such as telemarketing. Many retailers that operate large chains of retail stores also engage in direct marketing. Sears and J. C. Penney, for example, operate hundreds of retail stores. Both also engage in catalog and other forms of direct marketing.

Direct Marketing as a Communication System

Direct marketing is a highly focused channel of communication. As we have seen, direct marketers target their communications to very specific individuals.

As a communication system, direct marketing emphasizes measurability, which helps make advertising more accountable. In essence there is a tighter feedback loop for marketing communication. This has had the related benefit of putting the marketing organization in closer contact with customers.

For example, a response device in display ads can enhance the efficiency of media evaluation. Readers might be invited to clip a coded coupon, enter a contest, or send for a free T-shirt. When customers can use toll-free numbers to order merchandise (Lands' End), solve technical problems (GE Answer Center), or locate a dealer (IAMS pet food), sellers are in a position to respond quickly to problems and opportunities.

DIRECT RESPONSE MEDIA

Among the direct response media are phones and mail. In 1983, 36 percent of adult Americans shopped by phone or mail. By 1990 the figure had risen to 55 percent.[5] In the discussions that follow we look at direct marketing media. Keep in mind, however, that these media often are combined in multimedia campaigns. An example is the integration of the telephone with television in direct response TV advertising. Other examples include integration of the telephone with magazines and newspapers in direct response space advertising and telephone ordering from catalogs. Catalog customers can call Spiegel's home fashion consultants toll-free and receive decorating tips.

Telephone

inbound telemarketing

Inbound telemarketing is a system that enables the marketer to receive telephone calls from prospective customers who dial the marketer's number (usually an 800 or 900 number), which is included in the marketer's advertising or catalogs. They also can call the number to register complaints or to request information or service. Inbound telemarketing therefore can help increase the level of customer satisfaction. The data captured can be added to the firm's marketing database. (We will discuss these databases in greater detail shortly.) The AT&T ad describes the company's International 800 Service.

AT&T International 800 Service can help direct marketers do business in other countries.

(© 1990 AT&T.)

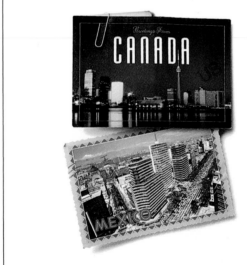

outbound telemarketing

Outbound telemarketing is a system that enables the marketer to initiate contact with prospective customers by telephone. Outbound telemarketing systems are often used to supplement personal selling. Many organizations use automatic dialing systems to deliver prerecorded sales messages. In addition to selling over the phone, the marketer can place calls to customers for a variety of other purposes that affect the level of customer satisfaction. Examples include a telephone call to a customer to verify an order or to service an account. Still other uses include generating and qualifying sales leads. The Global Marketing box discusses the operations of an international telemarketing firm.

For many years marketers ranging from insurance companies to aluminum siding companies have used the telephone to sell their products. Often the people hired to work the phones in "boiler rooms" were minimally trained and the list of consumers or businesses called was not narrowed down to likely prospects. For example, an aluminum siding telemarketing communicator might be given a telephone directory and told to call people whose names begin with *S* and to read them the prepared script. Today many professionals would not consider such use of the telephone to be outbound telemarketing. The modern telemarketer avoids focusing exclusively on generating an immediate response at the expense of losing an opportunity to build, maintain, and enhance a long-term, close relationship. Every contact with a prospect or a customer provides opportunities to gather information that can be entered into the organization's database.

GLOBAL MARKETING

Work begins at 2 A.M. for the overseas operators at Connecticut-based Lester Telemarketing, just as business executives in Bonn, Paris, and Amsterdam start their day. Soon foreign languages fill the crowded room as the operators work the telephones in French, German, Japanese, Chinese, and even Russian. In an age when more and more companies rely on telemarketing to reach potential customers, Lester offers its clients something new: instant access to markets half a world away.

According to Joan Mullen, president of the American Telemarketing Association, a number of U.S. companies have telemarketing operations in Europe, often through a European affiliate. But Lester is unusual in hiring native speakers to make calls overseas from the United States.

Lester handles telemarketing projects for scores of clients, including *Fortune* 500 companies, publishing houses, major cable-TV companies, universities, and charities. The company decided to expand overseas in 1991, as Europe was moving rapidly toward uniting its economic and political forces.

Bob Lester, the company's founder, spent much of his childhood in Italy. His bilingual upbringing shaped his business attitudes. "I guess I was swept up by the shrinking nature of the world," he says. "One day I just realized that everything is becoming international faster and faster and faster. In 10 or 20 years, the company that has marketing abilities in many foreign countries with many foreign languages will have an extraordinary advantage."

Lester's first challenge was to find well-educated bilingual operators fluent in the languages of the dozens of countries he wanted to reach, from Europe and Asia to the Soviet Union. He turned

One fairly recent development in telemarketing is the increasing use of pay-per-call service (900 numbers). Collecting money for the calls is no problem for the marketer because local phone companies handle the billing. The earliest examples were the sex, entertainment, sports, and gab lines. Many marketers of goods and services ranging from jet engines to legal advice are now using 900 numbers. Some have switched from 800 to 900 numbers. Usually callers who pay for 900 calls are more serious prospects than callers who use 800 lines.[6]

Many firms that sell technical services are using 900 numbers to segment their customers by their level of sophistication or their type of inquiry. For example, customers who want warranty information might be directed to an 800 number. Those who want a step-by-step explanation of a computer program might be given a 900 number to call.[7]

Direct Mail, Mail Order, and Catalog Marketing

Direct mail, mail order, and catalog marketing were the earliest forms of direct marketing to emerge. They still are very important in the direct marketing industry.

Direct mail is a type of advertising that uses the mail to deliver the message to the target. The mailing piece can range from a simple postcard announcing a sale to a complex multi-part package that might include an audiotape, a videotape, or a computer diskette. Direct

direct mail

for help to the foreign language departments at nearby Yale University. He also resorted to flipping through the Yellow Pages, calling up Chinese and Japanese restaurants to ask the owners for help.

Another challenge was getting the telephone numbers of the overseas businesses his clients wanted to reach. In the United States, computer lists complete with phone numbers exist for almost everything. Few such lists exist in other countries. So Lester established International Telefind to develop its own lists. Telefind employees spend hours on the phone with other countries' equivalents of directory assistance, trying to put together new lists for clients.

A computer magazine that is mailed out free to 20,000 computer engineers in sixty countries recently hired Lester to conduct market research. The magazine had addresses for those receiving the publication but wanted to know if it was being read both thoroughly and by decision makers. International Telefind first found phone numbers for all those on the magazine's mailing list. Then Lester operators called them in thirty different languages.

Lester also offers a service nobody is using yet: toll-free access to the United States from overseas. An American company can advertise in a Dutch trade magazine, for example, listing a toll-free number direct to Lester's offices. The international projects make good business sense, but Lester also finds them satisfying. "You're sitting in your office," he says, "and you realize that there are people all over the world that have been affected by your work, that are brought closer together because of it."

Source: Adapted by permission of the Associated Press from "Connecticut Telemarketing Company Takes on the World," *Marketing News,* June 10, 1991, pp. 16–17.

mail-order

catalog marketing

mail is especially useful when other distribution channels are absent or when the market is geographically dispersed. Advocates say direct mail is the most efficient way to organize and rally support for public causes.

Mail order is a type of marketing that uses the mail to deliver the product from the marketer directly to the customer regardless of how the order was placed. With mail order, the order can be placed by mail, over the telephone, or by computer terminal.

Catalog marketing is a type of marketing in which the marketer offers its products in a publication, which includes ordering instructions, and the customer orders by mail or phone or at a catalog counter. Retailers and business-to-business marketers (such as mail-order wholesalers) use catalogs, including the videotape catalog (videolog).

Historically the retail catalog was a major seasonal or annual book (such as the Sears and Penney "big books") with hundreds of pages and thousands of items. However, more and more catalog retailers are moving to specialized publications that are carefully targeted to market niches to cater to certain lifestyles or to meet special needs. Next Directory is a hardback catalog that was launched in Great Britain in 1988. In 1990 the producer distributed an Americanized version (American sizing and pricing) of the Next Directory to five thousand select homes across the United States.[8] J. C. Penney's Easy Dressing catalog consists of fashions for arthritic women. Penney also has specialty apparel catalogs for large-sized children, tall women, petites, and big men. Avenues is a fashion catalog targeted to wheelchair users—a group whose buying power is anticipated to increase since passage of the Americans with Disabilities Act in 1990. This act is intended to stop workplace discrimination against the 20 percent of Americans who are disabled.[9] Although the

An ad for one of *Mademoiselle*'s catalog collections.

(Courtesy Mademoiselle, copyright © 1991 by the Condé Nast Publications Inc.)

An example of direct response space advertising with both a response coupon and a toll-free telephone number.

(Franklin Funds Advertising Dept., San Mateo, Calif.)

catalog segment of retailing continues to grow faster than the in-store segment, growth rates are slowing from their highs in the late 1970s and early 1980s.

Direct Response Print Advertising

Direct response ads in newspapers and magazines include instructions for ordering from the marketer. The instructions may come in the form of a response coupon, a mailing address to order by mail, or a telephone number to call to place an order. The ad for Mademoiselle's Catalog Collection appeared in *Mademoiselle*. It invites readers to respond through a coupon. A toll-free number is not included. The Franklin ad appeared in *Fortune*. It invites readers to respond through a coupon or a toll-free number.

Direct Response Broadcast Advertising

Direct response ads often appear on radio and on network and cable television. TV viewers can be reached two ways. One is through home shopping, in which viewers of a particular program or an entire channel, such as QVC or HSN, can place orders for goods and services. The other is through direct response advertising, in which the direct response marketer airs spots featuring goods and services that the viewer can order. The ordering instructions may include an address to write to or a telephone number to call.

P.C. Flowers markets primarily through Prodigy, a videotex service established by IBM and Sears.

[Courtesy of P.C. Flowers]

Electronic Media

Videotex (text on a video screen) is an example of an electronic medium. One form of videotex is a two-way system that enables consumers to order merchandise through their TV sets. The sets are equipped with a device that permits communication with the advertiser's computer banks through cable or telephone lines. Another form involves the use of personal computers equipped with modems, through which consumers can exchange data electronically with videotex services such as Prodigy, Genie, and CompuServe. These services enable consumers to perform such tasks as ordering merchandise from retailers and making airline reservations. In the United States there are roughly 2 million users of videotex—far fewer than many advocates of this technology were predicting in the 1980s. Videotex in the United States exists primarily on the personal computer, with TV and phone applications in an embryonic stage.[10]

An increasing variety of marketers are using order-placing machines to interact with their customers. These machines can be located in shopping malls, stores, airports, and kiosks. For example, Delphi Technology and IBM are putting computerized kiosks that handle film orders in supermarkets and malls. The kiosks are similar to automated teller machines and have a four-minute video menu that tells the customer how to use the machine. The customer can also press a button to get a direct phone link to a customer service representative.[11]

MARKETING DATABASES

Direct marketing is an interactive system of marketing because of the existence of a marketing database, which allows for analysis and identification at the level of individual prospects or customers. Recall that a marketing database is a collection of interrelated data about an organization's individual prospects and customers that is intended to satisfy the organization's marketing information requirements. This information makes it possible for the organization to target highly individualized direct marketing efforts.

The database is a direct marketer's most important asset. The Reader's Digest Association maintains a database of information on 50 million U.S. households, more than half of which have bought products from the Digest within the last two years. The company uses this database to target customers. It recently spent more than $20 million to update its database system.[12]

Users of a marketing database include personnel in new-product development, brand management, customer service, advertising, sales promotion, direct mail, and telemarketing. Our discussion in chapter 4 of the marketing information system (MIS) indicated that communication problems often exist between information users (marketing decision makers) and information suppliers. The same type of communication problem often exists between marketers and marketing database personnel. Ideally, of course, the system should be user friendly, should facilitate marketing objectives such as cross-selling and selling up, and should anticipate customer requirements.

Because the cost of computing and storing data is declining, more and more organizations can afford to build extensive customer databases.[13] Motels, hotels, car rental firms, and airlines are among the heaviest users of marketing databases. They use the information in their systems to enhance their understanding of the consumer behavior patterns of frequent customers. This helps them build lasting relationships with high-priority customers. The more effectively marketers match particular offers to individual customers, the more responsive those targeted will be to the offers.

Anheuser-Busch and Procter & Gamble were among the early users of interactive 900 telephone lines. They found consumers who were willing to pay for a 900 call to enter a sweepstakes, to collect discount coupons by return mail, and so on. The payoff for the marketers is information for their databases.[14]

A direct mail specialist can cross-index lists obtained from credit agencies, political parties, mail-order firms, and other organizations and can merge and compare the data to identify the groups you belong to, the car you drive, the amount you paid for your house, and so on. This, of course, helps direct marketers identify the goods, services, and causes that might interest you. It also helps in determining whether you are a good credit risk.[15]

As part of its promotion of the movie ''Memphis Belle,'' Warner Bros. used direct marketing. Warner, a unit of Time Warner Inc., mailed out 700,000 postcards offering a special $1 discount for each recipient and a guest at evening performances. The names were culled from the lists of households that had purchased Time-Life books or videos on such subjects as World War II and aviation. The head of advertising, publicity, and marketing for Warner said, ''We have to be able to reach the target in a concise manner, or otherwise we'd be spending a lot of money reaching the wrong individuals.''[16]

DIRECT MARKETING MANAGEMENT

In the discussions that follow we look briefly at some management issues in direct marketing. Direct marketing management includes these tasks: (1) defining the direct marketing target, (2) defining direct marketing objectives, (3) setting the direct marketing budget, (4) developing the direct marketing strategy, (5) selecting direct response media, and (6) evaluating direct marketing effectiveness. (See Figure 16–1.)

Defining the Direct Marketing Target

The direct marketing target is the audience at whom a particular direct marketing effort is aimed. In many cases the target is essentially the names of prospects that appear on a list. One type of list is the *house list*—a list of names and addresses of people who have bought the company's products or who have donated to the organization. Another type is the *response list,* which lists the names and addresses of people who have a history of buying by mail and an identifiable product interest, such as advice about personal investments. Still another type is the *compiled list.* The people on this list have an identifiable characteristic, such as being plumbers, but their willingness to buy by mail is not known.

In organizational marketing, marketers often use trade shows to build a list of the prospects who visit their booths. These house lists should be kept as up-to-date and as accurate as possible. In addition to maintaining a house list, direct marketers can swap their lists and rent lists from list brokers. *Direct Mail List Rates and Data* is a bimonthly publication that describes 10,258 rentable mailing lists.[17] Lists are a major source of input for an organization's marketing database. The database should be capable of storing all relevant facts about the people or organizations on the lists. Direct marketers often share their lists, but they do not share their databases.

Direct marketers may target only one or a few segments of a particular list. For example, a marketer might wish to target only the recent purchasers of expensive cars on a list of all recent car buyers in a particular state. Fund-raising direct marketing efforts often are heavily targeted to known heavy contributors. On the other hand, organizational marketers must engage in multiple targeting when multiple buying influence is present. Direct marketing can be especially helpful in bypassing gatekeepers in buying centers.

Defining Direct Marketing Objectives

Generalized direct marketing objectives include securing leads, qualifying leads, securing an immediate purchase, strengthening the brand image, maintaining and enhancing the

FIGURE 16–1

The Tasks of Direct Marketing Management

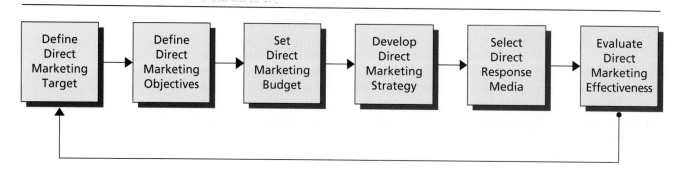

customer relationship (for example, by maintaining contact between personal sales calls), and educating prospective customers about the company and its market offering. Of course, direct marketing objectives should be stated in specific terms.

Setting the Direct Marketing Budget

An important task in setting the overall promotion budget is to determine the desired mix of promotional tools. As marketers learn more about direct marketing and its capabilities, many are allocating more resources to it. For example, many firms are allocating more money to telemarketing and less to personal selling because of the skyrocketing cost of personal sales calls.

Developing the Direct Marketing Strategy

Many decisions are necessary in formulating a direct marketing strategy. For example, consider the fulfillment process—the activities involved in fulfilling a customer's order after it has been received. Many of the topics we covered in the discussion of logistics in chapter 13 are relevant here. Examples include order processing, inventory policy, warehouse policy, and customer service.

What proportion, if any, of the fulfillment activities should be assigned to an *outside fulfillment house*? Should telemarketing activities be handled in-house or by a telemarketing service bureau? An outbound telemarketing service bureau is a firm that places telephone calls on behalf of its clients. An inbound telemarketing service bureau is a firm that takes calls placed to 800 and 900 numbers on behalf of its clients.[18]

Donnelly Marketing, which was recently acquired from Dun & Bradstreet Corporation by an investor management group, is the leading direct mail distributor of cents-off coupons through its Carol Wright co-op program.[19] Should the firm use direct marketing to support sales promotion? In other words, should it hire Donnelly's services?

How sophisticated should the customer database be? Are one-shot messages superior to direct marketing campaigns? How can demoralizing competition between telemarketers and the field sales force be prevented or minimized? These are only a few of the many questions that must be answered during the development of the direct marketing strategy.

Selecting Direct Response Media

The direct marketer must monitor developments in direct marketing media in order to make informed selection decisions. For example, it would be a mistake to assume that contemporary direct response ads on TV are similar to those for vegetable slicing machines and kitchen knives several years ago. In addition to generating sales leads and closing sales, television can play a supporting role in a direct marketing campaign. An ad on TV urging viewers to watch their mailboxes for news about a special offer is an example of the use of TV to support the pulling power of direct mail. It is crucial that the direct marketer stay informed of developments in the technology of direct marketing.

Evaluating Direct Marketing Effectiveness

Because direct marketing activities are measurable, a response (or the lack of one) can be traced to the individual prospect. The specific activity that motivated the prospect to respond can also be identified. Thus the direct marketer knows the activity the prospect responded to and the nature of that response. This information about each prospect is added to the database as input for planning future direct marketing efforts.

THE FUTURE OF DIRECT MARKETING

Direct marketing has grown very rapidly in recent years. Yet it is still in the growth stage of its life cycle.

Many developments in the social and cultural environment bode well for the continued growth of direct marketing. Consumers are valuing their time more and more; and the number of dual-income households, especially time-poor ones with buying power, is growing. These households are attractive targets for direct marketers. The individualization of tastes and lifestyles along with retail service failures are also favorable factors for the direct marketing industry.

The technological outlook is also favorable. Semiconductor costs are decreasing; telecommunication is becoming increasingly sophisticated; and new means of personalization, such as laser printing and custom binding, are being developed. For some time large telemarketing firms have used telecommunications technology that makes it possible to call up the business file of an incoming caller the moment the call is received. Advances in telecommunications are bringing this and other sophisticated technology to smaller businesses.

Economic pressures also affect the industry. High personal selling costs, increasing credit card use worldwide, and the boom in specialized media are positive developments for direct marketing. On the other hand, the pressure of rising U.S. Postal Service and United Parcel Service rates is a definite negative. For example, in 1991 L. L. Bean for the first time started charging customers for shipping. Some experts predict that catalogs in the next few years will be smaller. They also predict that more and more small catalog firms will do joint mailings to qualify for cheaper bulk mailing rates and that catalog companies in general will purge their mailing lists of people who do not order.[20]

What about the political/legal/ethical environment? Concerns are growing about privacy and mail-order and credit card fraud. The growing fiscal problems in many states are causing the states to look for revenue by imposing a sales tax on sales made by out-of-state direct marketers. The Deceptive Mailing Prevention Act of 1990 bans mail solicitations that masquerade as government notices. Junk mail and junk fax also raise many ethical issues. For example, is it ethical for a direct marketer to send unsolicited junk fax to prospects who have to pay for the cost of the paper in their own fax machines? Is it ethical to place junk calls to people with car phones, who are charged for every minute they use a telephone line—whether or not they initiated the call? More than 28 percent of U.S. households had unlisted phone numbers in 1991, up from 21.8 percent in 1984. According to a marketing research firm, the big reason people request unlisted phone numbers is because they don't want calls from telemarketers making sales pitches.[21] The Ethics in Marketing box raises additional ethical issues in direct marketing.

Because of the huge volume of paper used in direct marketing, the environmental movement is a major concern to direct marketers. In a typical recent year about 41 pounds of junk mail were generated for each adult American. This mail accounts for about 3 percent of the total clutter in the nation's landfills. An estimated 44 percent of the junk mail that reaches our mailboxes ends up in trash cans, unopened and unread. Greenpeace USA mails more than 25 million pieces annually.[22]

Direct mail advertisers became worried in the summer of 1990 when more than a million people, an elevenfold increase over the previous summer, signed up with the U.S. Postal Service's preference service, which eliminates many third-class and sales mailings. The Direct Marketing Association blamed the backlash on the 1989 book *50 Simple Things You*

Can Do to Save the Earth. The number 1 recommendation: get rid of unnecessary mail. The book claimed, "if only 100,000 people stopped their junk mail, we could save about 150,000 trees every year."[23] In 1990 the Environmental Defense Fund put out a direct mail fund-raiser (on recycled paper) that offered in exchange for membership a copy of the best-selling book![24]

ETHICS IN MARKETING

Ethical issues abound in the field of direct marketing. Consider telemarketing. What about a 900 number that promises a "guaranteed immediate issue" credit card for a $49.95 call. Callers do not get a credit card but are told to send an additional $30 processing fee to get an "IHS card" allowing them to shop only from the International Home Shopper catalog. Are long-distance telephone companies ethically obligated to monitor programs that run on their networks?

What ethical issues are associated with the development and maintenance of customer databases? Video choices can reveal a lot about a person's tastes and lifestyle. Is it ethical for a video rental store to maintain huge databases of information on the subject matter of the movies its customers rent and to sell the information to direct marketers? A person who rents a mystery movie probably does not know that her name, address, and phone number may be sold to a direct marketer of mystery books. Is it ethical for a merchant to ask customers with credit cards to supply their names and addresses and then sell the information to a mailing list company? What about mailing list companies renting lists to one another? Is it ethical for direct marketers to intrude on consumers' privacy—especially telemarketers who tend to call during the evening meal?

What about the use of direct marketing by charitable organizations? About 90 cents of every dollar spent by some charities goes to sending out more mail, most of it asking for more money. Is it ethical to charge the majority of those direct mail costs to "public education"?

Do some direct marketing efforts prey on uneducated and gullible people? Do they use scare tactics to sell products to the elderly? Do they use questionable appeals to sell products to children and teenagers? Do some telemarketers exploit people who desire instant gratification and cannot resist the urge to "call now"? Are the concerns expressed by some direct marketers, especially mail-order firms, about the environment basically hype? Direct marketers generally resist paying sales taxes in states in which they sell their products. Is that ethical?

Most direct marketers are concerned about some of the questionable practices in the industry. For example, consumers who do not want to receive additional junk mail can write to Mail Preference, Direct Marketing Association, 11 W. 42nd St., P.O. Box 3861, New York, NY 10163-3861, to request that their names not be sold to mailing list companies. This will prevent receipt of new unsolicited mailings, but it will not affect the mailing lists the consumers are currently listed in.

What ethical issues arise in developing sales promotions targeted to college students during spring break?

[© Bob Eighmie]

SALES PROMOTION

As we saw in chapter 14, sales promotion is any activity that offers an incentive for a limited period to induce a desired response from target customers, company salespeople, or intermediaries. Sales promotion activities add value to the product because the incentives ordinarily do not accompany the product. The incentives are designed to induce final customers and intermediaries to buy and to persuade company salespeople, intermediaries, and their sales forces to sell. An additional feature of sales promotion is that it is typically short term. It is designed to get action immediately.

Marketers spend less on advertising than they do on sales promotion. Spending on sales promotion has increased steadily for the past several years as marketers furiously compete in crowded product categories where there is little differentiation among brands. Some marketers have turned to continuous sales promotion as a way of achieving marketing goals in very competitive and often mature markets.

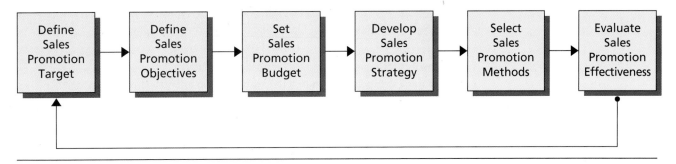

FIGURE 16–2
. . . .

The Tasks of Sales Promotion
Management

There is a controversy as to the relative merits of advertising and sales promotion in marketing a product. Some believe advertising is the best tool for building brand image and brand loyalty over the long term. They think sales promotion teaches consumers that the brand is not worth the full price, and that they deserve a special incentive for buying. In the long run, these critics argue, continuous sales promotion causes the image of the brand as a quality item to decline.

On the other hand, proponents of sales promotion say that it is an integral element in many marketing plans. Pepsi-Cola and Coca-Cola use continuous sales promotion with great success. An expert in the field of sales promotion argues that there are no hard and fast rules for using sales promotion versus advertising. Price, competition, target audience, distribution, trade support, and product features must always be factored into the sales promotion decision.[25] Ideally, advertising and sales promotion should be coordinated to preserve and enhance brand equity.

In the discussions that follow we look at the management of sales promotion. Sales promotion management includes (1) defining the sales promotion target, (2) defining sales promotion objectives, (3) setting the sales promotion budget, (4) developing the sales promotion strategy, (5) selecting sales promotion methods, and (6) evaluating sales promotion effectiveness. (See Figure 16–2.)

Defining the Sales Promotion Target

The sales promotion target is the audience to whom a particular sales promotion is directed. Sales promotion can be directed to consumers, to the company's own salespeople, and to intermediaries and their sales forces.

Defining Sales Promotion Objectives

Sales promotion objectives are derived from the marketer's overall promotion objectives. Table 16–1 lists several examples of generalized sales promotion objectives. Of course, these objectives would be stated more specifically to fit a marketer's specific situation. Notice that sales promotion is used by producers, intermediaries, individuals, and non-profit organizations.

Setting the Sales Promotion Budget

An important task for marketers in setting the overall promotion budget is to determine the desired ratio of sales promotion to advertising. The role each is expected to play in an overall promotion strategy determines its share of the overall promotion budget.

TABLE 16–1 ■ Examples of Generalized Sales Promotion Objectives

1. To encourage trial purchases of new products by consumers.
2. To encourage shoppers in a retail store to drop coins in a container placed there by the local humane society.
3. To encourage intermediaries to increase their order size.
4. To encourage consumers to buy several units of the product at one time.
5. To encourage an intermediary's sales force to give extra selling effort to a mature product.
6. To encourage retailers to devote more shelf space to the product.
7. To encourage wholesalers to cooperate in a manufacturer's effort to generate more feedback from retailers.
8. To encourage voters to vote for a particular candidate.
9. To encourage company sales personnel to increase sales effort for a new product.
10. To acquaint consumers or organizational buyers with product modifications.
11. To identify new consumers or organizational buyers.
12. To develop a mailing list.
13. To attract more attendance at a rock concert.
14. To build customer loyalty.
15. To encourage brand switching by consumers.
16. To encourage off-season purchases by retailers.
17. To gain entry into new retail outlets.

In general, sales promotion is most effective when it is tied to advertising. For example, the initial ad in Diet Pepsi's ''Un-huh!'' campaign featured Ray Charles crooning a new tune: ''You've got the right one baby, un-huh!'' Pepsi quickly followed up by sponsoring a contest in which consumers were invited to submit their home videos of people singing the tune. Pepsi also created a line of ''Un-huh!'' T-shirts and other clothing.[26]

Developing the Sales Promotion Strategy

Numerous decisions are necessary in developing a sales promotion strategy. One concerns the size of the incentive to be offered. For example, a company may have to decide how much a coupon will reduce the retail price of a product. Another decision concerns the means of distributing the incentive. Coupons, for example, can be included in magazine or newspaper ads, can be distributed through the mail, can appear on product packages, and so on.

Criteria for participation in the promotion are often needed. For example, consumer sweepstakes are not open to employees of the sponsoring company or to employees of the company that administers the sweepstakes. Administrative procedures are also necessary to prevent consumers from, say, sending in multiple requests for a refund. Marketers often use outside companies to assist in sales promotion efforts.

The duration of the sales promotion must also be decided. Thus a coupon for a high-frequency-purchase product such as margarine might be valid for a shorter period of time than one for a low-frequency-purchase product such as an oven cleaner. Of course, all sales promotion efforts must be carefully integrated with the other elements in the promotion mix.

Selecting Sales Promotion Methods

A marketer must consider these factors in selecting sales promotion methods: (1) sales promotion objectives, (2) target customer characteristics, (3) product characteristics, (4) marketing channel characteristics, (5) the legal and regulatory environment, (6) the competitive environment, and (7) the economic environment. Consider the following examples.

If the goal is to stimulate intermediaries to increase their sales effort, a contest offering prizes for dealer salespeople makes more sense than a contest for consumers. Target customer characteristics, such as age and education, could influence a manufacturer's decision about the type of consumer contest to sponsor. A product's size, packaging, perishability, weight, volume, bulk, and cost could affect the desirability of mailing free samples.

The choice between point-of-purchase displays or in-store product demonstrations might depend on whether a channel is direct or indirect and on the number and variety of intermediaries. The legal and regulatory environment might be a factor in choosing between a consumer sweepstakes and coupons, since some states outlaw sweepstakes. The competitive environment might discourage a manufacturer from offering push money to dealer sales forces if the manufacturer expects that push money will induce better-financed rivals to offer even more push money. Recession and inflation may increase the attractiveness of using coupons and refund offers to help consumers stretch their buying power.

• **Sales Promotion Targeted to Consumers** • Figure 16–3 identifies specific types of sales promotion targeted to consumers. *Coupons* can be included in printed ads. They also

FIGURE 16–3
....

Examples of Sales Promotion

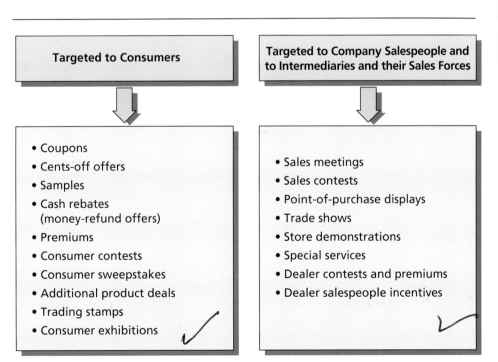

Targeted to Consumers	Targeted to Company Salespeople and to Intermediaries and their Sales Forces
• Coupons • Cents-off offers • Samples • Cash rebates (money-refund offers) • Premiums • Consumer contests • Consumer sweepstakes • Additional product deals • Trading stamps • Consumer exhibitions	• Sales meetings • Sales contests • Point-of-purchase displays • Trade shows • Store demonstrations • Special services • Dealer contests and premiums • Dealer salespeople incentives

can be sent to targets by way of freestanding inserts placed in Sunday newspapers or can be dispensed by machines in retail stores. After research indicated that Hispanics tend not to use coupons, many marketers started targeting Spanish-language coupons to Hispanics living in the United States.[27] In addition to the actual value of the coupon, companies must pay retailers a per-coupon handling fee.

Cents-off offers are printed on, attached to, or included in the product's package and constitute a reduction in the product's retail price. Because attached offers can be removed and used for the current purchase, they probably are more likely to stimulate initial trial purchases than are printed-on or in-package offers.

Sampling involves offering the product free or for sale at a drastically reduced price. *Samples* are often made available in specially designed trial sizes that are smaller than the regular package size.

Cash rebates (refund offers) refund an amount of money to consumers who mail in proofs-of-purchase of a product to the product's manufacturer.

There are several types of *premiums*. One is a continuous offer to redeem some proof-of-purchase for merchandise. This can help build brand loyalty. Another is an item placed in or on the product's package or given to customers by a merchant.

Consumer contests require contestants to compete for prizes by demonstrating a skill, such as writing an essay or baking a cake. In a *consumer sweepstakes* entrants are not required to demonstrate a skill. They fill out and return either an entry form included in a newspaper or magazine ad or a direct mail piece to be included in a drawing for prizes.

Additional product deals give the consumer an extra amount of the product for the regular price—for example, eight free ounces of Scope mouthwash. Some retailers give *trading stamps*. For example, a grocer might give one stamp for each 10 cents of groceries a customer buys. Customers can redeem the stamps at the stamp maker's redemption centers for products or for cash. Marketers sometimes collectively sponsor *consumer exhibitions* of their products; typical examples are boat shows and sporting goods shows.

• **Sales Promotion Targeted to Salespeople and Intermediaries** • Figure 16–3 also identifies specific types of sales promotion targeted to company salespeople and to intermediaries and their sales forces. *Sales meetings* help motivate a sales force by giving them recognition. *Sales contests* offer cash incentives, merchandise, or vacations for company salespeople who reach certain goals in their territories. Contests may be ongoing to encourage salespeople to establish new accounts or temporary to help introduce a new product.

Manufacturers often provide retailers with store signs, display racks, brochures, banners, and other printed materials. These *point-of-purchase displays* direct consumers to the manufacturer's product and help explain it without the aid of a salesclerk. As we saw in chapter 13, many manufacturers exhibit their products at *trade shows* for intermediaries; company representatives can write orders or get leads for salespeople. Manufacturers can also arrange with retailers for a special *store demonstration* of their products.

Manufacturers also offer *special services* for retailers, such as prepricing merchandise at the plant. Another example is the dealer listing in which the manufacturer prepares an ad that promotes a product and lists the names of the retailers that sell it. Manufacturers often sponsor contests for and offer premiums to their salespeople. *Dealer contests and premiums* are very similar to those provided for the company's own salespeople. They usually involve more expensive incentives, however. *Dealer salespeople incentives* often are less expensive forms of promotions to the dealers. Push money is an example. As we saw in chapter 12, *slotting allowances* may be paid to retailers to gain shelf space in stores, particularly supermarkets and drugstores.

Evaluating Sales Promotion Effectiveness

Whenever possible, sales promotion methods should be pretested to gauge their promotional impact. Point-of-purchase displays, for example, should be thoroughly pretested before they are introduced.

The approach most used in evaluating effectiveness involves measuring sales performance before, during, and after the sales promotion effort. Suppose a marketer has easy access to timely market share data. Prior to launching of the sales promotion activities, market share is 10 percent. During the promotion, market share increases to 14 percent. It drops to 11 percent immediately after the activities cease and then increases to 12 percent after several weeks.

Apparently the promotion produced some results during the promotion period. Perhaps the activities attracted new users and increased purchasing by existing customers. The drop-off in sales after the promotion stopped could indicate that consumers who loaded up with the product during the promotion stopped buying and were using what they purchased during the promotion. The fact that market share increased from a prepromotion 10 percent to a sustainable 12 percent several weeks after the promotion ceased suggests that the activities did bring in new customers. If, instead, the share had gone back down to 10 percent, that would mean the promotion simply speeded up sales during the promotion period.

Most marketers do not want to risk spacing sales promotion activities far enough apart to permit this type of evaluation. The major problem with the sales performance approach to evaluation is that it attributes all sales increases to sales promotion activities.

Other approaches to evaluation include consumer panels, consumer surveys, and experiments. Consumer panels can be questioned about their likes and dislikes concerning the sales promotion activities, about whether the activities caused them to switch to the marketer's brand, and, if so, if they intend to continue buying the brand. A field survey could extend the evaluation to a larger number of people and include measuring the percentage of the target audience reached. Experiments might include running two types of sales promotion activities at the same time and comparing results. An example is comparing coupon redemption rates in newspapers and magazines.

PUBLIC RELATIONS

As we saw in chapter 14, public relations (PR) is communication to build and maintain a favorable image for an organization, maintain the goodwill of its many publics, and explain its goals and purposes. Some types of institutional advertising, such as the Domino's Pizza ad, are part of public relations. Such ads attempt mainly to create or enhance a positive image for the organization. The discussions that follow focus on two other approaches to public relations: direct contact and publicity.

Direct Contact Public Relations

Direct contact includes writing letters to customers or others, conducting plant tours, visiting and speaking to schools and civic groups, and sponsoring events. Great West Insurance of Denver, Colorado, wrote its shareholders to encourage them to express their opinions about upcoming federal legislation that would affect their investments. Some firms offer plant tours, but many firms have dropped them in recent years to protect secrets

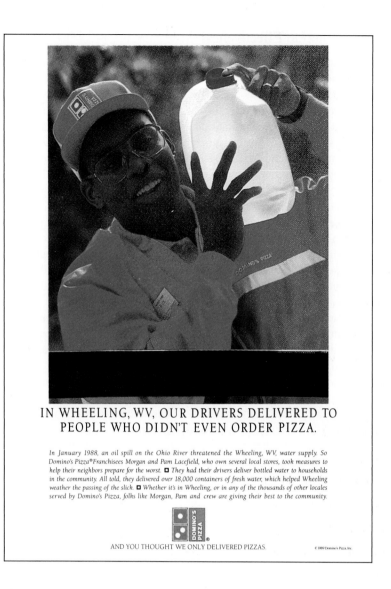

IN WHEELING, WV, OUR DRIVERS DELIVERED TO
PEOPLE WHO DIDN'T EVEN ORDER PIZZA.

In January 1988, an oil spill on the Ohio River threatened the Wheeling, WV, water supply. So Domino's Pizza®Franchisees Morgan and Pam Lacefield, who own several local stores, took measures to help their neighbors prepare for the worst. ❑ They had their drivers deliver bottled water to households in the community. All told, they delivered over 18,000 containers of fresh water, which helped Wheeling weather the passing of the slick. ❑ Whether it's in Wheeling, or in any of the thousands of other locales served by Domino's Pizza, folks like Morgan, Pam and crew are giving their best to the community.

AND YOU THOUGHT WE ONLY DELIVERED PIZZAS.   © 1989 Domino's Pizza, Inc.

An example of public relations.

(Courtesy of Domino's Pizza, Inc.)

and to avoid liability for visitors who might be injured. Coca-Cola, Frederick's of Hollywood, and Tupperware have opened company museums. Public relations representatives of the Phoenix Suns basketball club often visit civic and service clubs in Phoenix to speak about the club and its goals. Chevrolet sponsors Sunrayce, in which student teams design and race solar-powered vehicles.

Publicity

As we also saw in chapter 14, *publicity* is news carried in the mass media about an organization and its products, policies, personnel, or actions; it can originate with the media or the marketer and is published or aired at no charge to the organization for media space or time. Publicity is not completely free, however. Marketers must pay the cost of preparing publicity-generating materials and of developing good working relationships with media editors.

Publicity offers several advantages as a promotion tool. First, it may reach people who ordinarily do not pay attention to advertising, sales promotion, and salespeople. Second, it has greater credibility than advertising because it appears in the context of editorial or program material. Third, it is relatively inexpensive and provides coverage that would cost many advertising dollars.

On the other hand, the marketer has very little control over what media editors do with the publicity materials that marketers prepare. Media people routinely disregard materials they do not consider newsworthy—subject matter that is untimely, uninteresting, or inaccurate. Even if the materials are judged newsworthy, the marketer has no control over how media people edit the content, schedule its appearance in the media, and so on.

• **Generating Publicity** • Sony had little work to do to generate publicity after it signed a partnership deal with Michael Jackson that Sony said was worth a potential $1 billion to him. Ads featuring No Excuses jeans ''spokesmodels'' also tend to generate publicity. The same was true for firms that donated goods and services to U.S. troops during Operation Desert Shield and Operation Desert Storm. Max Factor, for example, said it was ''providing a form of protection'' for the troops by sending more than $800,000 worth of sunscreen.[28]

But events having less news value in the opinion of media editors require more skill on the publicist's part to create a story. Celebrities may have to be present at sponsored events to generate enough interest to merit media attention. Effective publicists have good working relationships with media people (editors, news reporters, and other news personnel) and can prepare materials for them that have a good chance of being used.

• **Publicity Tools** • Great care is needed in preparing materials to help ensure that they will be used by the media. A *news release,* usually one typewritten page, contains information that the organization wants disseminated, along with the name, address, and phone number of the person whom media personnel should contact for more information. *Feature articles* are longer and are prepared for specific publications. Media representatives are invited to *press conferences* to hear about upcoming major events that the marketer hopes will be considered newsworthy and to receive written materials, photographs, and other materials pertaining to the event. *Letters to the editor* are sent to newspapers and magazines, perhaps in response to articles that appeared in those media. Radio and TV stations are given *tapes and films* for broadcasting.

• **Coping with Negative Publicity** • Procter & Gamble has had to cope for many years with negative publicity associated with tales that its moon-and-stars logo is associated with satanism. Perrier also has had to cope with negative publicity associated with the company's worldwide product recall after benzene was found in some bottles of water. Abortion foes helped create negative publicity for firms that funded Planned Parenthood family planning programs, including Dayton Hudson, J. C. Penney, and AT&T.

Marketers try to avoid unfavorable publicity, of course, by using careful quality control procedures, providing use limitation information on product labels, and conducting in-plant safety and training programs. But it is almost impossible to eliminate all potentially damaging events. Thus most firms set up policies for handling news coverage related to such events. It is wise to cooperate with the media in giving speedy and fair coverage to unfavorable events. Impeding regulatory agency and news media access to information will likely start damaging rumors and hurt future efforts to secure favorable publicity from the media.

General Motors stopped producing and selling the limited edition ZR-1 Corvette for three months in 1991 because faulty camshafts caused engines to blow up. None of the cars with the flawed engines left the factory. Finding the problem required tearing apart 250 of the engines. According to a company spokesperson: "It hasn't been a public-relations black eye. It shows we're committed to quality. Ten years ago, a GM manager who said 'That's it; I don't want any of these to go out until we figure out the problem,' probably would have been fired. We've come a long way."[29]

Evaluating Public Relations Effectiveness

Some experts advise spending 10 to 15 percent of the public relations budget on evaluation.[30] The most common approach is to count the number of exposures in the media—for example, how many press releases, feature articles, photographs, and films were published or aired during a given period of time.

Ad agencies and public relations firms clip printed publicity materials from newspapers and magazines and keep track of minutes of broadcast publicity on radio and TV for their clients. They also may convert this space and time to an equivalent amount of advertising cost to give the client some idea of the value of publicity.

Firms that do not use ad agencies or public relations firms can keep track of printed media publicity by hiring a clipping service. It will clip and send relevant printed publicity materials to the client. But there are no similar independent services for broadcast materials.

SUMMARY OF LEARNING OBJECTIVES

1. Explain direct marketing as a marketing channel system and a communication system.
Direct marketing is a marketing channel system. It is a direct distribution channel in which there are no intermediaries and is also a highly focused channel of communication. Marketers can target their communications to very specific individuals with direct marketing.

2. Explain the role of a marketing database in direct marketing.
Direct marketing is an interactive system of marketing. This interactivity is possible because of the existence of a marketing database, which allows for analysis and identification at the level of individual prospects or customers. A marketing database is a collection of interrelated data about an organization's individual prospects and customers that is intended to satisfy the organization's marketing information requirements. The existence of this information makes it possible for the organization to target highly individualized direct marketing efforts.

3. Identify the major tasks involved in direct marketing management.
The major tasks of direct marketing management are (1) defining the direct marketing target, (2) defining direct marketing objectives, (3) setting the direct marketing budget, (4) developing the direct marketing strategy, (5) selecting direct response media, and (6) evaluating direct marketing effectiveness.

4. Identify the major tasks of sales promotion management.
Sales promotion management includes (1) defining the sales promotion target, (2) defining sales promotion objectives, (3) setting the sales promotion budget, (4) developing the sales promotion strategy, (5) selecting sales promotion methods, and (6) evaluating sales promotion effectiveness.

5. Contrast direct contact public relations and publicity.
Direct contact and publicity are two approaches to public relations. Direct contact includes writing letters to customers or others, conducting plant tours, visiting and speaking to schools and civic groups, and sponsoring events. Publicity is news carried in the mass media about an organization and its products, policies, personnel, or actions; it can originate with the media or the marketer and is published or aired at no charge to the organization for media space or time.

····················■·····················

Review Questions

1. What is the significance of the fact that direct marketing is an interactive system of marketing?

2. What are some of the major advantages of direct marketing to marketers?

3. Is direct marketing a highly focused channel of communication? Explain.

4. Why would a marketer install an inbound telemarketing system?

5. Do direct marketers use traditional advertising media such as print and broadcast media? Explain.

6. Is direct marketing a type of databased marketing? Explain.

7. What are the tasks of sales promotion management?

8. In addition to consumers, what other groups can be targeted with sales promotion?

9. How does the direct contact approach to public relations differ from the publicity approach?

Discussion Questions

1. Is direct marketing a highly personalized form of communication? Explain.

2. Is direct marketing more suitable for use by consumer products marketers than by business-to-business marketers?

3. Are some forms of direct marketing too intrusive? In other words, do they invade our privacy? Explain.

4. Does a firm that spends heavily on sales promotion and spends relatively little on advertising harm its brand's image? Explain.

5. Should public relations really be considered part of an organization's promotion mix? Explain.

Application Exercise

Reread the material about Smith & Hawken at the beginning of this chapter and answer the following questions:

1. Do you agree that ''the direct marketing industry thrives on waste''? Explain.

2. Why do you think Smith & Hawken decided to do something about the problem of junk mail?

3. What ethical issues are raised?

4. Why is the Direct Marketing Association interested in ''green'' marketing?

Key Concepts

The following key terms were introduced in this chapter:

marketing database
inbound telemarketing

outbound telemarketing
direct mail

mail-order
catalog marketing

CASES

Lotus's Marketplace Program: An Idea Whose Time Came . . . and Went

One of the biggest challenges for direct marketers is developing an accurate marketing database. Perceiving that need, Lotus Development Corp., a software manufacturer, came up with Marketplace: Household, a program that provides data on some 80 million U.S. households. Lotus intended to market the program to small and mid-sized businesses that wanted to do inexpensive, targeted direct mail marketing.

Marketplace: Household would have provided ''snapshots'' of households by consumer names and by psychographic categories such as ''accumulated wealth'' and ''mobile young families.'' The program would also have provided age and income ranges for the households, although ages and incomes of individuals would not be available. The underlying data were provided by Equifax, Inc., an Atlanta-based credit reporting company.

The great advantage for direct marketers would have been that, instead of the one-time mailing lists that are currently available from companies, the Marketplace: Household program could be used repeatedly. The initial cost was to be $695 for the program itself plus 5,000 names, and $400 for each additional 5,000 names. The user could then manipulate the data to compile the most likely database for his or her products—from targeting potential customers who live on a particular street to targeting all ''inner city singles'' in a particular city.

What happened to Marketplace: Household? The product was announced in the fall of 1990 and scheduled for release in early 1991, but in January of 1991 Lotus announced it was cancelling Marketplace: Household because of the outcry raised by the product's announcement. Consumer groups, individual consumers and journalists, the American Civil Liberties Union, academics, and an organization called Computer Professionals for Social Responsibility raised the alarm, claiming that the program violated consumers' rights to privacy by allowing marketers to command too much information about individual households. The ACLU contended that the development of the program raised legal and ethical issues about data privacy. In the end Lotus cancelled the release, and simultaneously cancelled its Marketplace: Business program for business-to-business marketing.

Debate is still ongoing about the desirability of such a program. Lotus officials and some marketers say that the program would have been a help to small and medium-sized businesses that otherwise could not afford to do direct marketing. Also, say Lotus officials, the program had built-in safeguards for those who might want to use the information for dishonest purposes; phone numbers were not included in the database, and it was to be sold only to ''legitimate businesses,'' whose addresses would be checked against a fraud file. Further, individuals who did not want to be included on the database had the option of contacting Lotus, Equifax, or the Direct Marketing Association's mail preference service in New York. Consumer advocates responded that the program would only increase the rising tide of junk mail and unwanted phone calls.

Several bills are pending before Congress that would limit the use of marketing databases and create a Data Protections Board to set federal policy; this would bring the United States more in line with European countries, which have such regulations.

Questions

1. What are some of the advantages that Marketplace: Household could have offered to businesses interested in direct marketing?

2. How would you feel about being in the Marketplace: Household database? Would you feel comfortable knowing that a business could send you a mailing that accurately targeted your income level and preferences?

3. As a marketer who wants to sell upscale dog biscuits by direct mail, what information would you like to have about consumers? Would you want to use a program such as Marketplace: Household to reach those consumers? Explain.

4. What might be some disadvantages of direct marketing using a database program such as Marketplace: Household?

Quenching Small Businesses's Thirst

THOMAS K. PRITCHETT, *Kennesaw State College*

Coca-Cola USA's research found that there are approximately one million American workplaces, employing less than fifty people, that do not have soft drinks available on site. Apparently there are two reasons why soft drinks are not found in some workplaces. First, low sales volumes are not sufficient to support a standard soda machine. Second, a soft drink machine is too large for the ''break area'' in many workplaces.

Coca-Cola found a way around the size problem by developing a small machine that it calls the BreakMate. The BreakMate is about the size of a microwave oven and dispenses fountain drinks (the kind found in fast-food restaurants) in 6.5 ounce cups.

BreakMate machines can handle up to three different products—for example, Diet Coke, Coke, and Sprite—and can make them available at a cost of about 25 cents per serving.

Before it began promoting the BreakMate to businesses, Coca-Cola established a network of more than 400 office coffee and water vendors to distribute the BreakMate machines and the soft-drink syrup to these small businesses. To promote this service to small businesses Coke mailed a direct mail piece that focused on the convenience of having an in-house soda dispenser to office managers and presidents of small businesses. The promotion also conveyed the fact that the BreakMate is easy to use, easy to maintain, and free.

The first mailing was a four-color self-mailer (a mailing that does not require a separate envelope) held closed with a gold seal. The prospect who unfolded the self-mailer four times found a life-size poster of the BreakMate. In an effort to reinforce size as a key selling point, prospects were encouraged to display the poster next to their coffee machine to see how the real thing would fit into their work environment. They were also provided with an 800 number to call to contact their nearest coffee or bottled water dealer who would distribute BreakMates and syrup.

As businesses reply to Coca-Cola's direct mail campaign, Coke is gathering information to build a database of small businesses. They want to include who the decision maker is, what he or she does, and what motivates the individual.

Coca-Cola Company received thousands of responses to its direct mailpieces. Coca-Cola now has about sixty thousand BreakMate machines pumping more than 1 million gallons of syrups in workplaces. It predicts that BreakMates will be dispensing as many as twenty million gallons by 1999.

Questions

1. What was the measurable response Coca-Cola was seeking with this mailing?

2. By using direct mail as its primary advertising medium to reach prospective customers, what advantage(s) of direct marketing is Coca-Cola using?

3. Why is Coca-Cola gathering information from those who respond to its mailings for a database?

4. Who would consider this mailing to be junk mail?

17

PERSONAL SELLING

After reading this chapter you will be able to

1. identify the basic objectives and basic tasks of personal selling.

2. outline the steps in the personal selling process.

3. identify the major tasks of sales force management.

4. outline the functions of professional salespeople.

5. identify the types of sales calls and sales jobs.

Salespeople seem to be more prone than others to making a mistake when it comes to jobs. To help them choose the right job, prospective salespersons should ask these ten questions before accepting a particular sales job:

1. *Does the sales manager make you feel inferior?* If you feel uncomfortable at the initial interview, imagine how you'll feel once you're on the job.

2. *May I look at your résumé?* What you want to see is the manager's employment track record. If the résumé reveals that the manager has done a lot of jumping around or has stayed a year here and a year there, get out the door as fast as you can!

3. *Where will I get my leads?* If the answer is unclear, you must generate them yourself. Never take a sales job unless there is an effective lead-generation program. It's the company's job to market its goods or services in such a way that people want to do business with you. If that's not happening, you will become a canvasser, not a salesperson.

4. *May I see your office?* A "sales scoreboard" on the wall suggests that this company is not interested in developing customers and wants only to push product. Your only value will be in terms of where you stand in the weekly or monthly ratings. If you're at the top, you're great. If you're at the bottom, you're gone.

5. *May I review your sales literature?* If the promotional materials are customer centered, you can be fairly certain that the company is committed to understanding and fulfilling the needs of the customer. If the brochures focus solely on the wonders of the firm and its position in the field, the company is not customer centered.

6. *When are your slow times?* "May and June are never really very good, and we just write off November and December." Now you know a lot more than just the "slow times" for this company. You also know that everyone has come to accept that sales during one-third of the year are going to be lousy. No one has ever thought of developing a marketing program.

7. *May I go with you on a sales call?* During the call the customer should do 90 percent of the talking and the salesperson 10 percent. If the sales rep does most of the talking, this is probably a product-pushing sales organization.

8. *What gives you an edge in your market?* The more probing you do, the better. You're trying to find out whether the company markets by price. What's the sales manager's philosophy? Is it to offer the lowest price every time? If so, the only way you'll ever keep

a customer is to push to get the price down as low as possible—and then some. The only thing you're good for to the customer is being someone to threaten and intimidate.

9. *What can you teach me?* "Hey, you're good, but you come with us and I'll teach you every trick in the book and then some. I'll make you great. It's all a matter of orchestrating the customer," the manager whispers. "I'll show you how to do it." Without realizing it, the sales manager has let you know he or she believes that clever techniques and tricks are what make sales.

10. *May I visit your marketing department?* If someone takes you down the hall and says, "Turn to your right and it's the second door on your left just beyond the restrooms," you know that the marketing department is the closet where they store sales literature. You've discovered that this company does not understand marketing.[1]

Have you ever considered a career in sales? Or is a career in selling one of the few career options you have absolutely decided against because of negative stereotypes you have about salespeople?

In this chapter we look at the objectives and tasks of personal selling. We focus considerable attention on the personal selling process and on sales force management. We also take note of the increasing professionalism in personal selling.

OBJECTIVES OF PERSONAL SELLING

Few professions have gone through such a radical change as selling has over the last fifty years. The salesperson of the old days has been portrayed in many novels, films, and plays (for example, Willy Loman in *Death of a Salesman*). In these portrayals you learn such "truths" as that salespeople are good talkers who can sell anything to anybody and never take no for an answer, that selling is a game of using trickery and deception to get people to buy things they don't want, and that sales are usually made at golf courses, poker games, and so on. Today's sales professional is not even recognizable under those criteria.

Professional salespeople are primarily good listeners with a sincere desire to determine the exact needs of the customer. They certainly take no for an answer because they don't desire to waste either the prospect's or their own time. They engage in ethical practices, and recognize that sales are made through effective presentations that demonstrate how their good or service meets the prospect's needs.

Professional salespeople also attempt to build long-term relationships and trust with customers by properly servicing the account after the sale. The salesperson and the customer are partners. Managers understand that prospective salespeople can improve their listening, communication, and presentation skills through proper training, dispelling the myth that one has to be born a salesperson.

An organization's salespeople provide the most direct link to its customers. In fact, to many customers the salesperson *is* the organization. In such cases the customer's image of the organization is formulated on the quality of the personal selling effort. Because of their direct contact with the market, salespeople are a valuable source of feedback concerning company products, competitors and their products, and customer requirements. They also play a pivotal role in implementing marketing strategies.

As we saw in chapter 14, personal selling is a person-to-person process by which the seller learns about and seeks to satisfy the prospective buyer's wants by making a sale. This definition clearly illustrates the importance of the marketing concept in selling.

Furthermore, everybody engages in personal selling. College students use it to market themselves to prospective employers. Politicians use it to win votes. College football coaches use it to recruit outstanding players. The Girl Scouts use it to sell cookies. As Figure 17–1 shows, the basic objectives of personal selling are (1) to find prospective customers (prospects), (2) to convert these prospects to customers, and (3) to keep them as satisfied customers.

Finding Prospects

All marketing organizations have to identify and locate prospective customers for their products. Most retail stores try to draw new customers to their stores through advertising; their salespeople ordinarily do not seek out prospects. On the other hand, as we saw in chapter 16, direct marketing can support the sales force by helping salespeople find prospects. For example, many ads in magazines invite prospects to call or write for information. Those who respond are considered prospects by the company's sales force. Still other organizations do little advertising and rely on salespeople to find prospects through a variety of methods.

Converting Prospects to Customers

A marketing organization with a list of prospects but no customers will not be successful unless it can actually convince some of them to buy—that is, convert prospects to buyers. Convincing, or persuading, prospects to buy is a major objective of personal selling.

FIGURE 17–1
••••••••••••••••••••••••••••

The Basic Objectives of
Personal Selling ▮

Salespeople at this trade fair in Leipzig seek to find prospects and convert them to customers.

[© Heimo Aga, Contact Press Images]

For example, Nabisco salespeople convince supermarket managers to order extra stock and to erect an end-of-aisle display that ties in with a major promotional campaign. Without the display, customers might not remember to seek the promoted item or the store might experience a stock-out because of heavier than usual demand.

Maintaining Customer Satisfaction

Some marketing organizations can be successful without repeat sales to the same customer. Unfortunately, a few fly-by-night operators take advantage of this. Even when chances of repeat business with a customer are slim, the salesperson should be concerned about that customer's after-sale satisfaction—if for no other reason than to preclude negative word-of-mouth communication.

To most marketers repeat sales to satisfied customers are more important than first-time sales. It is becoming clear to more and more marketers that they can earn a higher return from repeat sales to existing customers than from spending money to solicit new customers. Repeat sales are also easier to get. These realities help explain the greater focus on building and maintaining long-term relationships with customers and on viewing them as partners. Thus keeping established customers satisfied by providing after-sale service is another objective of personal selling.

GLOBAL MARKETING

The foundation of Japanese selling is respect. Customers are often referred to as *okyaku-sama—sama* referring to God, the emperor, and others deserving honor. Japanese selling relies heavily on support materials and data. Japanese sales reps have slick brochures and carry big notebooks of data, microphotographs, and other material to respond to questions with substantive answers.

U.S. sales reps, on the other hand, often are poorly equipped. They have the slick brochures but nothing more. When asked for the data that prove their product's superiority, they can only skirt the issue and claim it is "guaranteed by design." In the United States the focus is on individual performance. In Japan the sales rep, the engineer, and even the manager are not considered heroes; they are members of a team.

U.S. buyers are responding favorably to "wet" Japanese selling, an approach that may eventually cause them to reject the traditional "dry" U.S. approach. "Wet" in Japanese is flexible, accommodating, caring, and human, as opposed to the logical, inflexible, cut-and-dried approach often encountered in the United States.

Wet selling solidifies relationships with customers, but it's even more effective in landing new accounts. "We haven't had the pleasure of serving you before," says the Japanese sales rep, "so take this product and one of our engineers for a few months and see how you like the performance." The dry U.S. approach is reflected in hard logic, such as; "It's our policy to loan products only when an order of $2 million or more can be expected. Sorry, but you don't qualify."

Wet Japanese-style partnerships, with the truly open-ended obligations they impose on vendors, would drive Americans crazy. But today that may be the

The Global Marketing box contrasts "wet" Japanese selling with the traditional "dry" U.S. approach. Notice that the wet approach is flexible, accommodating, caring, and human. Its focus is providing the ultimate in customer satisfaction.

PERSONAL SELLING TASKS

Many salespeople are accountable for accomplishing all three objectives of personal selling. Thus each Electrolux salesperson finds prospects, converts them to customers, and provides after-sale services, such as making minor repairs, to keep customers satisfied.

On the other hand, some salespeople specialize in accomplishing only one of the objectives of personal selling. For example, a salesperson who works for a wholesaler may only take orders from established customers over the phone. The job is considerably different from that of a salesperson whose primary job is to solicit new customers. Keeping a particular customer satisfied may be so important to a company that it assigns one salesperson to service that account exclusively. The person does not have to find prospects or convert them to customers. There are also new-account development specialists whose sole job is

price of earning a customer. Vendors that work hand-in-glove with their customers to satisfy their special requirements earn solid accounts.

With Japanese vendors service is an integral part of selling, and the standards for service are quite different from those in the United States. It isn't enough to say, "We fixed it." In Japan the salesperson must step in, work with the service and quality control departments, and submit a report to the customer explaining "why the product failed and what we have done so it will never happen again."

For the customer this procedure demonstrates a sincere interest in eliminating problems. Its repetition several times a day every day of the year has also become one of the driving forces that has pushed Japanese product reliability to where it is today.

We may try to convince ourselves that this level of commitment isn't needed in the United States because American expectations are lower. However, the growing incursion of Japanese products into the U.S. market, driven largely by expansion of Japanese manufacturing here, will expose more U.S. engineers to responsive Japanese selling, and customer expectations will rise accordingly.

U.S. managers can view the Japanese challenge as a window on the kind of business that we can expect in the future: responsive salespeople, documented product claims, a team commitment, cooperative "wet" relationships with customers, service that removes the causes of failure, and people who have a fanatical pride in their company and a genuine dedication to doing a good job.

Source: Adapted by permission, from George Leslie, "U.S. Reps Should Learn to Sell 'Japanese Style,' " *Marketing News,* October 29, 1990, p. 6, published by the American Marketing Association.

selling tasks

to identify and locate prospects. They give the information to salespeople, who make the initial contact with prospects.

Selling tasks are activities that incorporate one or more of the three objectives of personal selling and are often classified into three categories (1) order-getting tasks, (2) order-taking tasks, and (3) sales support tasks. As we mentioned before, many salespeople perform all three tasks. On the other hand, some people who perform selling tasks are not called salespeople. Bank tellers, for example, are customer contact personnel who can be trained to solicit new business and to cross-sell the bank's other services. Marketers who recognize the importance of existing customers to their firms' profitability focus on opportunities for cross-selling to these customers.

Order-Getting Tasks

Salespeople who perform order-getting tasks focus primarily on converting prospects to customers and getting present buyers of some of the firm's products to also buy some of its other products. Developing new accounts requires a lot of effort and creativity in finding prospects and converting them to customers. Developing present accounts focuses on building long-term relationships with customers.

Order-Taking Tasks

The focus of order-taking tasks is primarily on building repeat sales of products that customers have previously purchased—making sure that their product requirements continue to be met. Inside order takers, for example, take orders from customers over the counter, over the phone, or by mail. Field order takers call on their customers regularly, check inventory on hand, show customers how much they need to reorder to replenish their normal inventory, and write up the order. Examples are beer, bread, and soft-drink field order takers. These salespeople also deliver the product to the customer.

Sales Support Tasks

Salespeople who perform sales support tasks do not produce sales by themselves but facilitate order getting and order taking. They can help in finding prospects, converting them to customers, and maintaining customer satisfaction after the sale.

Dataflex Corporation is a highly successful personal computer reseller that sells to big companies such as Squibb. Each day fourteen Dataflex people report to three Squibb locations in New Jersey, which together own 13,000 pieces of Dataflex-maintained equipment. This type of service support helps explain why Dataflex's net margins have increased in recent years.[2] Kodak has more than a hundred service representatives who pay regular visits to photographers' labs to help them troubleshoot problems. "If I have a real problem, they'll go over my work with me in the darkroom and sit with me until it's where I want it to be," says an advertising photographer in New York.[3]

The next section focuses on the personal selling process. It explains how salespeople find prospects, convert them to customers, and keep them as customers.

THE PERSONAL SELLING PROCESS

Figure 17–2 shows the steps in the personal selling process: (1) prospecting, (2) preparing the preapproach, (3) approaching the prospect, (4) making the sales presentation,

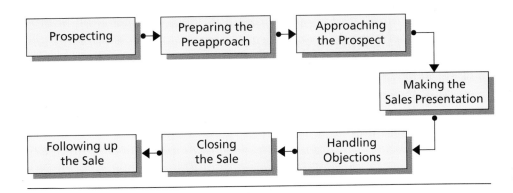

FIGURE 17–2

Steps in the Personal Selling Process

(5) handling objections, (6) closing the sale, and (7) following up the sale. As salespeople go through this process, they seek to create attention, develop interest, arouse desire, and generate action—the AIDA process introduced in chapter 14.

Prospecting

As we saw in chapter 16, sales leads are the names of people or organizations that might use the salesperson's product. *Prospecting* is the process of searching for, identifying, and qualifying potential customers, beginning with getting sales leads. The leads become *qualified prospects* if they (1) can benefit from buying the product, (2) can afford it, and (3) are authorized to make the buying decision. Thus salespeople must generate leads and gather information with which to qualify them. Qualifying is screening out poor leads and ranking qualified prospects in terms of their buying potential. The Dun & Bradstreet ad distinguishes between a sales lead and a qualified prospect.

prospecting

Important internal sources of leads are company records and service, advertising, and credit department personnel. External sources include trade journals, business sections of local newspapers, present customers, trade shows, trade association directories, and mail-in requests for information from prospects who have seen or heard the firm's ads.

As chapter 16 noted, telemarketing helps many organizations generate and qualify leads. *Inbound telemarketing* focuses on generating inquiries by placing a toll-free telephone number in ads and other promotional material. With *outbound telemarketing* the telemarketer initiates the call to a potential prospect. In both cases the prospects can be qualified while they are still on the phone and the names of qualified prospects can be passed on to the sales force. In some cases telemarketing personnel can actually make the sale.

Telemarketing can be used for more than prospecting tasks. For example, it is widely used to set up appointments, maintain contact with present customers, gather information for the firm's marketing information system, and resolve billing, delivery, and installation problems.

Effective salespeople are constantly working to improve their prospecting skills. Life insurance salespeople obtain leads from birth and marriage announcements in newspapers; building materials salespeople get leads from city or county offices that issue building permits; and real estate salespeople get leads by driving through neighborhoods looking for "For Sale by Owner" signs. Salespeople typically seek to qualify leads as soon as possible to avoid wasting their time and that of their prospects. They must be careful, however, to avoid unintentionally screening out otherwise qualified prospects on the basis of style of clothing, level of education, and so on.

This ad focuses on the difference between a sales lead and a qualified prospect.

(Dun & Bradstreet Business Credit Services.)

Preparing the Preapproach

Preapproach preparation is part of the salesperson's homework before contact with the prospect. It involves gathering more specific information about the prospect's background, product needs, personal characteristics, and so on in order to help identify and meet the prospect's needs quickly when the presentation begins.

In in-store retailing, where the prospect goes to the store, there is obviously no opportunity for the salesperson to gather information about the prospect prior to initial contact. Instead, information gathering is part of the approach. The salesperson asks questions designed to provide insight into the prospect's wants and preferences.

The opportunity to gather information is much greater when the salesperson initiates contact, as in some types of nonstore retailing and most types of organizational marketing. The industrial products salesperson, for example, will want to gather information about the prospect's organization—what products it produces, its manufacturing processes, its buying practices, and so on. The salesperson will also want to know the prospect's role in the buying process (influencer, gatekeeper, decider, user, buyer) and the prospect's preferences regarding the type of initial contact—phone call, personal visit, letter.

ScoopLINE is a twenty-four-hour support system for Val-Pak Direct Marketing System's thousand-member internationally dispersed sales force. Salespeople can call the company's toll-free ScoopLINE and receive various types of information prior to making their calls. For example, the Daily Bulletin is a report on hot tips and industry trends relating to industries that Val-Pak services. Sales Call Briefings give salespeople information pertinent to the sales they are trying to make.[4]

Approaching the Prospect

The *approach* is the manner chosen by the salesperson to gain access to the prospect, establish rapport, and get the prospect's attention and interest. Careful preparation of the approach helps the salesperson ensure that a good first impression will be made. Opening statements that attract attention and build interest focus on what the salesperson can do for the prospect. For example:

> Ms. Jones, I'm Bob Johnson from Anniston Energy Corporation. Thank you for the opportunity to discuss with you our energy monitoring systems. One of the systems in particular is ideally suited to your energy-intensive operations. The 10-EX system will cut your electricity costs by a minimum of 15 percent per year. With the cost of electricity being what it is today, the 10-EX can have an especially favorable impact on your company's bottom line. Here are a few examples of what some of our current users are saying about the 10-EX—a product that Anniston guarantees to save you money.

The specific type of approach a salesperson uses depends largely on whether the prospect is a current customer or someone who is being contacted for the first time. The approach to an existing customer may involve little more than setting up an appointment with the prospect over the telephone. In the case of a new lead, the biggest hurdle may be getting past the lead's secretary. One approach is the referral—the salesperson explains to the secretary that an associate of the prospect suggested the call.

Making the Sales Presentation

After capturing the prospect's attention and interest, the salesperson proceeds to the heart of the personal selling process—making the sales presentation and building desire for the product. Miniature models of the product, along with slides, pictures, videotapes, booklets, flip charts, and demonstrations, help communicate the product's message to the prospect.

Salespeople use various sales presentation formats. Among them are (1) stimulus-response selling, (2) formula selling, (3) need satisfaction selling, and (4) problem solution selling.

Stimulus-response selling is a canned sales approach in which the salesperson presents a memorized sales talk, including a number of key words (stimuli) to produce a favorable response by the prospect. Thus in selling to a retailer a salesperson might use words such as *high profit margin* and *high turnover*.

Constructing a stimulus-response sales presentation involves listing all the prospect's possible buying motives. Then the product's features are translated into selling points. The fact that a ball-point pen has a Diamite ball point may have little meaning to a prospect. It must be translated into selling points such as "won't skip" or "won't leak." This is called "benefitizing" the product. After all product features have been benefitized, a sales presentation is written and each salesperson memorizes and uses it on all prospects. If all

approach

stimulus-response selling

buying motives have been identified correctly, those for any one prospect will be covered in the sales presentation.

This approach can generate sales for simple-decision products with a minimum of sales training and therefore is widely used in door-to-door and telephone selling. It can also be a training technique for beginning salespeople, who will stop using it after they develop product knowledge and sales skills.

formula selling

Formula selling is a sales approach in which the salesperson assumes that prospects go through a series of stages and that once the salesperson determines which stage the buyer is currently in, the salesperson can follow a basically canned presentation to move the prospect through the remaining stages and ultimately to buy. The stages are the AIDA ones of *A*ttention, *I*nterest, *D*esire, and *A*ction. Although formula selling is not a totally canned sales approach, it is similar to stimulus-response selling.

Formula selling gives the salesperson an organized way to plan and assess the presentation. The major disadvantage is the mistaken idea that a properly executed formula sales presentation always leads to a sale. This can damage a salesperson's morale. The prospect may want to think it over before deciding, but the salesperson may believe he or she has done something wrong. Another weakness is that the stage of the formula the customer is in determines the salesperson's behavior. In most instances the salesperson's major concern is feedback from the prospect to indicate when to move to the next stage in the formula.

need satisfaction selling

Need satisfaction selling is a sales approach in which the salesperson, operating on the principle that the main reason people buy comes from within, tries to discover the prospect's needs and then demonstrate how the product will satisfy them. This approach forces the salesperson to practice the marketing concept.

The words a salesperson uses to benefitize the product must fit the prospect's frame of reference and situation. In discussing a word processing package with an office manager, the salesperson might emphasize the elimination of several operations by typists, expressed as "increased productivity." With a typist the emphasis might be "makes rearranging sentences and paragraphs a lot easier." The key is to show that the salesperson's offering meets the buyer's needs.

This approach can produce excellent results when the salesperson is sensitive, understands motivation, and knows the product. It emphasizes internal motivation—which benefitizes the product from the prospect's frame of reference. It also relies on customer feedback to determine how the salesperson will handle a given sales presentation.

problem solution selling

Problem solution selling, also called consultative selling, is a sales approach that focuses first on discovering the prospect's needs and then on the salesperson acting as a consultant for the prospect. It is very similar to the need satisfaction approach. The salesperson/consultant's tasks include listing possible solutions to the prospect's problems and then recommending one of them.

Problem solution selling requires time and considerable skill on the part of salespeople. An advantage of this approach is the trust and long-term relationship it builds with the prospect. It is most often used in selling technical goods and services.

Handling Objections

Normally a prospect is going to have some objections to buying a good or service. Salespeople often try to anticipate these objections and incorporate a discussion of them in their presentation. Salespeople also encourage the prospect to voice objections and then try to respond to them.

How a salesperson answers an objection depends on whether it is valid. When a prospect raises an invalid objection, the method used might be *direct denial* ("No, we are not the company that was indicted for price fixing'') or *indirect denial* (''I can see how you might think that, since the name of our company also begins with *Profax;* however, we are not the company that was indicted'').

When a prospect has raised a valid objection, the salesperson can resort to *compensation* (''You're right, but the high price is offset by these features''), *postponement* (''That's a good question, but I would like to explain our delivery times after I've discussed transportation options if that's OK with you''), or *feel-felt-found* (''I can see how you would feel that way; Mr. Jones at UGI felt the same way, but he found after using our service for a month that the return on investment was higher than we had predicted''). The key is to answer truthfully and helpfully so the prospect can make a wise decision.

Closing the Sale

····■·····

close

The *close* is the point in the sales presentation at which the salesperson attempts to secure the order. Some salespeople have great difficulty closing a sale because they do not want the prospect to feel pressured. Or they may not be confident that they made a good case for the prospect's buying the product. Or they simply do not know when to ask for the order and so end up talking themselves out of a sale.

Effective salespeople know how to pick up signals from prospects that indicate they are ready to buy. These include nodding agreement with the salesperson's assertions about the product's superiority, asking questions about financing terms and possible delivery dates, and making comments that translate into ''I'll take it.'' The salesperson often attempts trial closes at one or more places in the presentation. For example, after demonstrating the product the salesperson might ask the prospect about a desired delivery date. If the prospect supplies a desired date, the salesperson knows the sale is made. If the prospect raises objections, closing will be postponed until the prospect's concerns have been addressed.

Closing techniques vary widely, and the salesperson usually tailors the technique to the prospect. The *summary close* involves summarizing the major benefits of the product and then asking for the order. The *balance sheet close* involves the salesperson drawing a T-account and writing down the reasons for purchasing in the left column and the reasons for not purchasing in the right column. A variation of this is the *comparison close,* which involves comparing product features with those of a well-known competitive product, then asking for the order.

The *alternative decision close* presents the prospect with two or more alternatives— ''Would you like a 4-cylinder or a 6-cylinder engine?'' The *standing room only close* focuses on buying now because the product is selling well and may not be available tomorrow. The *extra inducement close* offers something extra at no cost, such as below market interest rate financing, free installation, or no charge for additional options. Successful salespeople avoid using deception or pressure in closing the sale. They recognize the importance of building trust and a long-term relationship.

Following Up the Sale

After closing a sale, an effective salesperson will follow up to make sure the order was delivered on time and the product arrived damage-free and, if necessary, was installed properly. Subsequent checks on product performance also help ensure customer satisfaction and build goodwill, and they may lead to repeat business. Following up is part of the effort to implement the marketing concept at the organization's sales level.

Following up on a sale also helps dispel any cognitive dissonance (post-purchase doubt) after the sale is made. Furthermore, it helps salespeople learn about a customer's future product requirements and contributes to the development of a long-term relationship

An ad that underscores the importance of a good long-term relationship between the customer and the salesperson.

(State Farm Insurance Companies. Home offices: Bloomington, IL.)

between the customer and the salesperson. The State Farm Insurance ad underscores the importance of a good long-term relationship between the customer and the salesperson.

Formats for Salesperson-Prospect Contacts

There are many variations of the format for salesperson-prospect contacts. Instead of one salesperson dealing with one prospect at a time, the salesperson or a team of salespeople (including perhaps one or more sales engineers) may deal with one or more counterparts on a buying team. Team selling is ideally suited for complicated products and for customers that have a complex buying process. General Electric assembled a team of more than fifty people to win a big General Motors contract to supply power equipment at Saturn car plants.[5]

In some cases a team of company salespeople may work with personnel from a third firm to put together an offering for a buying group. Thus Data General Corporation's salespeople may bring together a prospect and a sales representative from an independent software vendor to meet the prospect's unique needs. The nature of the targeted customer's organizational buying unit plays a major role in determining the marketer's contact format.

Negotiation

An increasingly important element in personal selling is negotiation. Factors to be negotiated can include pricing, display allowances, extra services, shelf position, inventory levels, delivery terms, special packaging, end-of-aisle displays, and slotting allowances. For example, it used to be common practice for an S. C. Johnson & Son sales representative to deliver a planned presentation about the company's waxes to a major food retailer such as Kroger and then ask for the order. Today, however, it is just as likely that Kroger's buying team and the Johnson's Wax sales team will agree on a time and place to negotiate an upcoming major promotion. Each side researches and prepares for the negotiation.

The Kroger team will assess the effectiveness of past promotional campaigns by analyzing Kroger's own scanner data, will determine the profit contribution of Johnson wax products and compare it to the competitors', will review recent proposals from other vendors, and so on. During the negotiation session each side attempts to gain concessions from the other by using various strategies and tactics to arrive at a final negotiated purchase. The key is to try to engage in a win-win negotiating session, in which both sides ''win,'' because it builds successful long-term relationships. It takes a great deal of creativity, persistence, planning, and optimism to be successful as a negotiator. As a result, many firms are now sending their salespeople to negotiation courses. Buyers too are attending such courses.

Blending Personal Selling with Other Promotion Mix Elements

Throughout this text we have stressed the necessity of blending the marketing mix elements carefully. We have also seen that the elements in a promotion mix must be blended. Other promotion mix elements are often instrumental in facilitating the steps in the personal selling process. In turn, the personal selling process reinforces other promotion mix elements.

Like the other elements in the promotion mix, the personal selling effort must be managed. Let's look at what is involved in sales force management.

SALES FORCE MANAGEMENT

The sales force plays a crucial role in deciding an organization's fate because the organization's revenues are derived from sales. Thus the sales force must be managed effectively. Figure 17–3 identifies the major tasks of sales force management.

Establishing Sales Force Objectives

As with all marketing objectives, sales force objectives should be stated in precise, measurable terms and should specify a time period for their accomplishment. Typically objectives are first established for the sales force as a whole and then are broken down into objectives for each salesperson. Overall sales force objectives are stated in terms of total dollar or unit volume, market share, or profit. Individual salespeople are then assigned objectives called *quotas*. These may be volume quotas (''You are to sell $400,000 worth of product A''), activity quotas (''You are to make four calls per day and three demonstrations per week''), or financial quotas (''You are to contribute $60,000 to profits'').

Volume for the sake of volume sales objectives are for sales-oriented, not market-oriented, organizations. Thus there is growing emphasis on financial quotas. For example, in multiproduct firms objectives for salespeople may take into account the relative profit

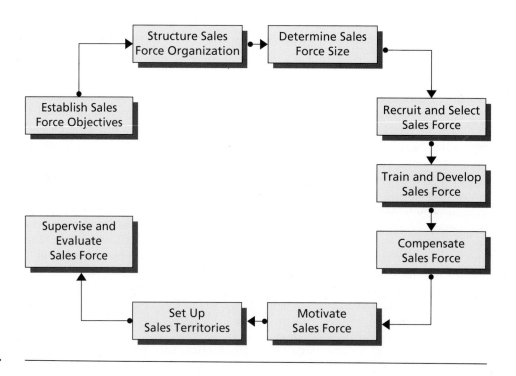

FIGURE 17–3

Tasks of Sales Force
Management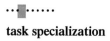

contribution of the firm's various products. Salespeople may then be expected to allocate more time and effort to increasing sales of the products that yield higher profit.

Structuring the Sales Force Organization

How the sales force is structured affects the quality of the firm's communication with its customers. The key is to match the organizational structure with the type of communication the firm needs. A sales force can be organized by (1) geography, (2) product, (3) task, or (4) target market.

Geographic specialization is an approach to structuring the sales force in which each salesperson is assigned a territory and sells all the firm's products to all customers in that territory. It is common among firms that have a small number of closely related, nontechnical products. This type of specialization allows the firm to assess the costs of doing business in each territory and ensures adaptability to changing conditions in each of them. It also helps salespeople develop long-term working relationships with customers.

Product specialization is an approach to structuring the sales force in which some salespeople sell one or a few products to customers in a territory and other salespeople may sell other company products to the same customers. Salespeople thus become very knowledgeable about their products. Overlapping territories, however, are a problem for firms whose products are closely related. Customers may become confused when several salespeople from the same firm call on them. It also is costly to the marketer.

Task specialization is an approach to structuring the sales force in which some salespeople may serve established customers in their territories while a smaller group develops new accounts. Newly established accounts are turned over to the salesperson in whose territory the new accounts are located. The advantage is that the communication skills needed to establish new accounts differ from those needed to maintain existing accounts. Task specialization is usually found in large firms.

geographic specialization

product specialization

task specialization

Target market specialization is an approach to structuring the sales force in which the sales force is divided by target markets and each salesperson calls on only one target group. This approach is often used for complex and technical products whose use varies by target market. It might be used by a computer manufacturer whose products are targeted to different market segments, such as schools, hotels, and hospitals.

target market specialization

Determining Sales Force Size

The optimal size of a firm's sales force depends on how the sales force is structured, its productivity, and numerous other factors. This size changes as the firm's market conditions and marketing objectives change. One approach to approximating the required sales force size is to use the following formula, where SFS = Sales force size, T = Total number of customers, N = Number of calls per account per year, L = Length of time of each sales call, and S = Sales time available per salesperson per year:

$$SFS = \frac{T \times N \times L}{S}$$

The sales time actually available for each salesperson per year takes into account non-selling time—time spent traveling to accounts, waiting to see buyers, and so on. In using this formula, sales managers also consider several other factors. Established accounts and accounts that call in their orders generally require fewer calls per year than new accounts. The sales and profit impact of increasing or reducing the number of calls on accounts should also be evaluated. The formula approach is usually tempered with managerial judgment in light of sales force objectives and company resources.

Recruiting and Selecting the Sales Force

Recruiting is the process of attracting applicants for sales positions. For most firms it should be an ongoing process to ensure an adequate number of recruits from which to select. One method of recruiting is to seek referrals by present employees. Others include word of mouth, newspaper ads, announcements in trade publications, public and private employment agencies, and contacting vocational and technical schools and colleges.

Selection procedures are guided by criteria that either have been validated as predictors of success or are believed to be important. Examples include aptitude tests, interest inventories, role playing, and interviews. Selection criteria and procedures should be validated, and those that are ineffective as predictors of selling success should be dropped.

Most firms use a sequential selection procedure in which unsuitable applicants may be rejected at one of several steps in the selection process. Figure 17–4 shows the sequence used by one firm that recruits nationally on college campuses. This procedure reduces the time and money spent on unsuitable applicants.

Training and Developing the Sales Force

More and more organizations are viewing their salespeople as a strategic resource and investing in training and development of that resource. Training and development is necessary for both new and experienced salespeople and should be an ongoing process.

Among the major trends in sales training during the 1990s are (1) a greater emphasis on listening; (2) knowledge-based selling—knowing more about the product and customers in order to build partnerships; (3) a broad range of interpersonal skills, which are needed by the contact person on the quality management team servicing customers; (4) empowerment

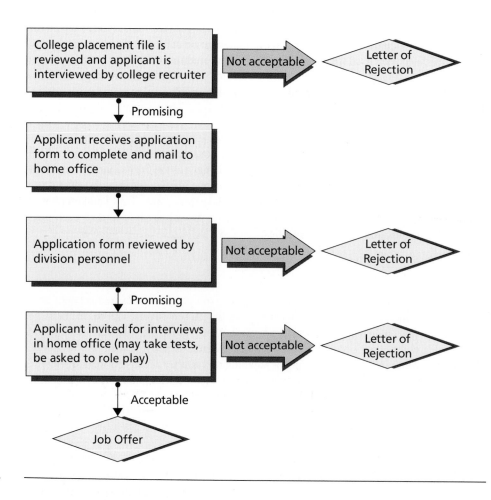

FIGURE 17–4

A Procedure for Selecting
Applicants for Sales
Positions

to change the rules to make a sale; and (5) basic sales techniques for employees who don't sell but who are part of the selling process.[6]

• **Subject Areas Included in Training Programs** • Knowledge areas usually covered in modern sales training programs include the product, the organization's code of ethics, buyer behavior and decision processes, self-assessment and understanding, communication theory and planning problem-solving, and negotiation skills.

Knowledge of product features, construction, applications, and so on is indispensable to a salesperson. Often product knowledge also requires an in-depth understanding of the targeted customer's operations.

Sales training should focus on the ethics of selling. Most firms have codes of ethics that pertain to selling, and they should be communicated to salespeople. The Ethics in Marketing box raises several ethical issues in personal selling.

A good training program also provides basic insight into buyer behavior and relevant buying decision processes. Industrial salespeople, for example, should understand the concept and functioning of a buying center.

Training in self-assessment and understanding helps salespeople recognize and understand their personal strengths and weaknesses. It also helps them cope with rejection and develop self-discipline. This is important because usually there's no boss out in the field looking over the salesperson's shoulder on a daily basis. Understanding learning principles, communication theory, and human relations and interviewing skills helps salespeople digest complex product information, conduct sales interviews, and communicate and establish long-term relationships with customers. As mentioned earlier, the development of listening skills is receiving more attention. In a nationwide survey of corporate buyers, nearly half the buyers said salespeople are ''too talky.'' They wanted salespeople who could really listen.[7] Planning and problem-solving skills help salespeople become effective territorial managers and problem-solving consultants to their customers.

• **Location and Timing of Training** •   Some companies focus primarily on on-the-job training; others stress away-from-the-job training at their company-operated training schools or schools operated by other firms or universities. Most companies use both approaches. In a recent survey, more than 75 percent of sales managers said the type of training their companies offer is essentially on-the-job. The same survey indicated that lack of training was the major cause of dissatisfaction among new salespeople.[8]

ETHICS IN MARKETING

Couples who thought they had a moment alone to discuss a company's offer to buy six year's worth of soap had no idea salespeople were listening in through a concealed speaker. The eavesdropping allegedly took place at Space Tech Industries in Hollywood, Florida, where husbands and wives were invited to receive free prizes after taking part in a marketing survey.

According to the Florida Department of Law Enforcement, which confiscated the hidden microphones and speakers, the couples were intentionally left alone during the sales presentation to facilitate the spying. ''A microphone is left on so all the fears and apprehensions that people have can be dispelled'' by salespeople who listen in on conversations from another room, said one of the special agents assigned to the case.

The Florida attorney general's office has filed a lawsuit charging the company with using unfair and deceptive trade practices and has won a temporary injunction preventing Space Tech from doing business. The suit seeks a court order permanently shutting down Space Tech and fines of $5,000 for each violation.

According to an assistant attorney general, the company mailed cards to families with two working adults, offering free prizes. The cards did not mention Space Tech or soap products. However, when consumers arrived at Space Tech, they eventually were hit with a high-pressure sales pitch for soaps and were escorted to a showroom of ''bonus gifts.'' The gifts were awarded if the couples bought a six-to-eight-year supply of soap. Financing also was offered to the customers.

What ethical issues does this incident raise? Is this an isolated example, or do similar examples occur fairly often?

Source: Adapted by permission of the Associated Press from ''Sales Reps Allegedly Listened in on Customers,'' *Marketing News,* January 21, 1991, p. 17.

Sales training and development is an ongoing process. These experienced salespeople are working to improve their planning and problem-solving skills.

[© Kay Chernush]

The initial training period may range from one or two weeks to several years, depending mainly on the complexity of the product. Sales managers have to consider other factors in the ongoing need to train salespeople. These include the frequency of training efforts, the duration of each training effort, and the scheduling of salespeople for training to avoid diluting coverage of the market.

• **Trainers and Training Techniques** • Trainers are usually experienced salespeople and other personnel at company-operated training schools. However, many firms also use training consultants, university professors, and representatives from professional organizations in the industry.

Training techniques include lectures, role playing, simulation exercises, demonstrations, and cases. Training materials include audio- and videocassettes, films, manuals, programmed learning aids, fax machines, and hand-held and laptop computers. The following box discusses the nature of sales training at Paychex Inc.

Compensating the Sales Force

Salespeople may be compensated in three basic ways: (1) straight commission, (2) straight salary, (3) a combination of salary and incentives, such as commission and bonus, or other benefits.

• **Straight Commission** • Firms with limited resources or in high-ticket industrial sales, such as construction and electronic health care and laboratory equipment, often use straight commissions. Insurance, real estate, and door-to-door consumer product salespeople are also often paid on straight commission. The president of Dataflex Corporation, the personal computer reseller mentioned earlier in this chapter, relies primarily on money as a motivational tool for salespeople. He says, "We want greedy, money-hungry people looking for an opportunity." Salespeople at Dataflex are paid straight commission.[9]

Commissions usually are stated as a flat percentage of sales. But some firms use variable percentages that reflect the different profit margins of various product lines. Straight commission rewards salespeople on the basis of productivity but may not provide the balanced selling effort most firms want. Salespeople tend to concentrate on large accounts, high-commission items, and the immediate sale rather than on long-range development of new accounts, service, and follow-up activities. Turnover also tends to be higher under this system. This limits the resources a firm can invest in training beginning salespeople. Also, the sales manager has less control over personnel because they receive no salary.

SALES TRAINING AT PAYCHEX INC.

Paychex Inc. is a supplier of payroll and other business services. Every new sales person goes through seven weeks of training before ever meeting a prospect. Paychex's vice president of marketing calculates that the firm spends $3,500 per trainee to operate a professionally staffed school at the company's Rochester, New York, headquarters. That amount includes instructors' salaries as well as transportation, housing, and meals for the trainees. It may seem like a lot, but it's a lot less than the roughly $18,600 it costs Paychex to recruit, interview, hire, and train a replacement for a salesperson who gets fired or quits.

The thinking behind the Paychex approach is that every salesperson first has to know and understand the company's products. In Paychex's case, those are payroll and other administrative services provided to a national market of client companies. Consequently, during the first three weeks of the Paychex school, the sixteen or so students that start every month take courses on tax laws and accounting principles and study the services Paychex sells to its clients.

During the three weeks the new hires live in company-owned condominiums, drive company-rented cars, and pay their expenses out of a company-granted stipend. After three weeks they take a comprehensive exam. If they don't pass, they go home to look for another job. Those who pass are sent to work for two weeks at a Paychex operations branch to learn firsthand what the company does. They also accompany branch salespeople on calls, but only to watch and listen.

In the last week it's back to Rochester for more classroom work—now, finally, on selling skills. The courses include sales presentation, visual selling (reading the customer's body language), closing, and time and territory management. Only after graduation does a new salesperson get to solo on an actual sales call.

Paychex's school employs eleven full-time instructors—some former school-teachers and some field personnel. According to Paychex's vice president of marketing, even if a company can't afford a full-blown sales school, whatever time it can spend teaching its salespeople about the company's specific goods or services and procedures can help them get up to speed faster in the field. "Training is an investment that a progressive company can't afford not to make," he says.

Source: Adapted from "Hands On: Sales and Marketing." Reprinted with permission of *Inc.* Magazine, May 1991, pp. 85–86. Copyright © 1991 by Goldhirsh Group, Inc., 38 Commercial Wharf, Boston, MA 02110.

Straight Salary • With the straight salary method the sales manager has greater control over the sales force. This method also creates willingness on the part of salespeople to devote time to the nonselling activities necessary for a balanced selling effort because they are paid on the basis of time. Salespeople are less concerned about an immediate payoff and are more interested in the long-range development of good relationships with target customers. Digital Equipment Corporation pays salespeople straight salary. The company believes this avoids a focus on quotas and puts the focus on customer needs.[10] But straight salary is not as effective as commissions in motivating the sales force to maximum effort.

Combination Plans • The most widely used form of compensation is a combination plan of salary, commission, and other benefits. Although varying widely in details, most plans include a salary that covers living expenses. Commissions usually are figured on a percentage of sales over quota. Other benefits may include a company car, expenses, medical and life insurance, prizes, and bonuses for special achievements. Combination plans relieve the salesperson of anxiety about daily living expenses, offer incentives related directly to productivity, and encourage salespeople to do the nonselling activities that lead to a balanced selling effort.

Motivating the Sales Force

Many outside salespeople are on their own much of the time. Eventually apathy can set in. Salespeople often have no feeling of group identity. Therefore, they need something more than just financial rewards to help motivate them.

As we saw in chapter 16, some types of sales promotions—for example, sales contests and sales meetings in resort areas—can be targeted to a company's sales force. Suppliers of incentive programs market a variety of packaged incentive systems to companies for use in motivating their salespeople.

Improving the sales force's willingness and ability to participate in activities such as sales forecasting often requires special effort on the part of sales managers. An incentive system might motivate salespeople to take forecasting seriously, and such aids as sales recording and reporting systems that minimize the time needed to prepare estimates can help.

Top salespeople often are forced into management, even though many would prefer to remain salespeople. The usual reasons for moving up are to gain promotion and to receive more pay. Some employers, however, are creating career ladders in the field in an effort to keep top-performing salespeople selling. One consultant says, "Employers now recognize the value of keeping experience in the field to build customer relationships." For example, Brooklyn Union Gas Company promoted several of its most experienced salespeople to account managers. They act as the company's representatives to clients, who used to deal with sales reps from several departments.[11]

Setting Up Sales Territories

An important factor in compensating and motivating professional salespeople is setting up sales territories. Some symptoms of the need to redraw territorial lines are poor servicing of existing accounts, a lack of new accounts, low sales for some product lines, high travel expenses, high turnover of sales personnel, and wide, unaccounted-for differences in sales volume among territories. Motivational factors also must be considered. A big complaint of salespeople is that they build sales in a territory and then the sales manager breaks it into

TABLE 17–1   Guidelines for Establishing Sales Territories

1. A salesperson should not have to spend more than two or three nights a week away from home to cover the territory.
2. The number of established customers in a territory should be somewhat less than the salesperson can call on and maintain the call frequency demanded by the product.
3. A territory should provide adequate income for the salesperson and have growth potential.
4. A suitable plan for salespeople to live near the geographical center of their territories should be developed.
5. Travel routes in a territory should be arranged to keep mileage and traveling time to an acceptable minimum.
6. The potential volume of a territory should cover direct expenses of maintaining a salesperson there plus an acceptable profit margin.
7. Territorial lines should be observed by sales personnel—sales in a territory are credited to that territory's salesperson regardless of who makes the sale.

two or three territories. This can undermine morale and reduce a salesperson's compensation. Table 17–1 lists several guidelines for establishing sales territories.

Supervising and Evaluating the Sales Force

A sales manager's main task is to provide a supportive climate and the resources needed to build salesperson effectiveness. Among these resources are training, help in defining problems and generating solutions, technical assistance, and emotional support. Sales managers continually evaluate the performance of their personnel to identify and provide solutions to problems that help maintain a balanced selling effort. Activity reports and open lines of communication help them pull together the information they need in the evaluation process.

The sales manager's goal is to help the salespeople do a better job of selling. Among the indications that a salesperson needs help from the sales manager are increased buying levels followed by small purchases by a customer with a history of regular buying patterns, spending too much time with certain customers, failure to develop new accounts, and loss of long-time regular customers.

Many firms are turning to automation to increase the productivity of their sales departments. Sales managers are using tools such as sales management software packages to free sales reps from manual systems and mountains of paperwork. This enables salespeople to use their time more productively and to increase sales revenues.[12]

PROFESSIONAL SELLING

Of all the types of jobs in marketing—marketing research, product management, public relations, retail store management, sales management, logistics management, and so on— sales jobs are the most numerous. Furthermore, there are more entry-level jobs in sales than in any other type of marketing-related employment.

Professional salespeople realize that sales that do not benefit both customer and salesperson cannot be a basis on which to build a long-term relationship. They attempt to meet customers' needs by gaining product knowledge, upgrading their selling skills, and adhering to strict ethical standards. Professional salespeople are partners with their prospects and customers.

Several years ago the Forum Corporation conducted a study to determine which characteristics distinguish high-performing sales personnel from moderate performers. Among the major findings about high-performers are

1. They have product knowledge, competitive knowledge, and "face-to-face skills" (in selling features and benefits, handling objections, and so on).

2. They are much more than demonstrators and explainers of products. They are clearinghouses of information, advisers, relationship builders, problem solvers, customer advocates, and deal makers.

3. They possess the influence skills needed to work with both internal staff and customers. Because salespeople generally have no subordinates, they must work through others over whom they have little or no direct control. Influencing others to change their priorities and interrupt their schedules is a major part of the job.

4. They recognize that the skills required to service an account are different from those required prior to a sale. For example, they do not abdicate responsibility for installation, implementation, and service to technical support staff. They continue to maintain a client relationship that their customers find valuable.[13]

Functions of Professional Salespeople

Customer-oriented professional salespeople serve their employers and customers by functioning as (1) territorial market managers, (2) educators, (3) communication specialists, (4) human relations experts, and (5) feedback mechanisms.

• **Territorial Market Managers** • Professional salespeople make many of the same types of decisions at a territorial level that marketing managers make at the companywide level.

A daily plan specifies whom to call on that day, what to discuss, and any materials that must be taken to the sales interview. It enables salespeople to evaluate their daily performance. Reviewing these plans over weeks and months can help increase selling effectiveness—for example, by modifying the call mix.

Salespeople must also plan their territorial coverage. Call frequency, geographical location, and customer preferences affect travel time. Salespeople can divide territories into easily covered units by using zones or sections and establishing a call frequency that maintains a working relationship with the prospect.

Territory screening is a continuous process of prospecting and developing new accounts. It requires a personal record-keeping system that should at least include a prospect file and a current customer file. Computerization is enabling salespeople to spend less time on paperwork and more time on customer contact and selling. This increases salespeople's productivity and often enables their companies to increase sales without having to hire additional salespeople.

Laptop computers, fax machines, voice mail, and car phones are among the time-saving equipment that salespeople are using to free them from paperwork. Automation is making pencils and clipboards obsolete for salespeople.[14] Inexpensive software packages enable salespeople to perform such tasks as eliminating duplicate leads, sorting the best prospects by territory, setting up a "tickle file" to prompt sales calls, and even generating demographic information.[15]

Each workday Frito-Lay's 10,000 salespeople plug 10,000 hand-held computers into minicomputers at local sales offices or into modems in their homes. The salespeople can relax while a report of their day's efforts is zapped to Frito-Lay headquarters in Dallas. They don't have to spend many hours each week taking care of routine nonsales tasks.[16] Hewlett-Packard's salespeople have laptop computers backed up by customer-prospecting and relationship-tracking systems at headquarters. The result has been a 33 percent growth in sales, a 31 percent increase in sales force productivity, and a 40 percent drop in the attrition rate of sales personnel.[17]

• **Educators** • Several of the salesperson's tasks come under the education function. Salespeople inform prospects about product features and their meaning. Making highly technical new-product information meaningful to an industrial buyer may require assessing the prospect's level of education, product knowledge, and readiness to learn. Choice of words, use of visual materials, and demonstration techniques are important.

• **Communication Specialists** • Professional salespeople need information-getting skills, information-giving skills, and consultant skills to communicate with their prospects. Information-getting skills are needed to get prospects to talk about their problems so the salesperson can present product information from the prospect's frame of reference. This, of course, also requires information-giving skills. Consultant skills are important because salespeople often act as communication consultants for buyers. For example, retailers

The salesperson-prospect/ customer relationship gives rise to many ethical issues on the part of both the salesperson and the prospect/customer. What are some of those issues?

[© Baron Wolman]

sometimes expect a manufacturer's representative to help them prepare advertising campaigns, the cost of which is shared by the manufacturer and the retailer (cooperative advertising). In a recent survey, seven of eight buyers said most salespeople do not know how to ask the right questions about their company needs. When asked which reason for switching vendors was most familiar to them, 27 percent of buyers cited an out-of-touch sales rep.[18]

• **Human Relations Experts** • Professional salespeople need a high level of human relations skills. Ideally, the salesperson-prospect relationship should be one of warmth, honesty, trust, and confidentiality—a partnership. This is especially important in times of shortages. When a firm cannot produce enough output to meet demand, salespeople must work with customers so they will understand and remain customers. Salespeople play a major role in implementing a demarketing strategy.

• **Feedback Mechanisms** • Salespeople are a vital part of a firm's marketing information system. They hear about problems customers are having with the firm's products and can provide valuable feedback on customer comparisons of rivals' products, prices, and services; on modifications needed in existing products; on effectiveness of mass advertising and other promotional efforts; and on changes needed in marketing channels.

Professional Sales Calls and Interviews

As Table 17–2 shows, professional salespeople make four basic types of sales calls, each based on the purpose of the call: (1) initial contact calls, (2) regular customer calls, (3) follow-up calls, and (4) service calls. Regardless of the type of sales call, listening skills are important.

TABLE 17–2 Types and Purposes of Sales Calls

Type of Call	Purposes of Call
Initial contact call	1. To verify information obtained through prospecting. 2. To gather new information about the prospect to see if the product can be used. 3. To give the prospect information about the firm's products verbally or through printed materials.
Regular customer call	1. To get information about changes in the customer's situation, problems, or attempts at solving problems. 2. To provide information and help the customer consider alternate courses of action and their consequences. 3. To understand the customer's situation from the customer's point of view. 4. To make the sale if it appears to be appropriate for the customer's situation.
Follow-up call	1. To handle any problems the customer is having with the product. 2. To communicate concern for the customer and to build trust in the salesperson and firm. 3. To make auxiliary sales.
Service call	1. To provide requested service on the product. 2. To gather feedback. 3. To gather additional information about the customer's other needs.

Initial contact calls are the first face-to-face contact a salesperson has with a prospect. They may be either cold calls or by appointment. Cold calls help in fully developing a territory. They also build flexibility into a daily plan because they can be omitted if necessary. But they may use up valuable time if the salesperson has to wait to see prospects. Initial contacts by appointment reduce wasted time but at the cost of losing flexibility.

Regular customer calls are calls salespeople make on established customers or prospects who have been called on before. They usually are by appointment and at regular intervals.

Follow-up calls are calls salespeople make about previous sales to help ensure after-sale satisfaction. These calls are often made without an appointment and can help build flexibility into the daily plan.

Service calls are calls salespeople make in response to customer requests for service, to anticipated problems with the product, or to new developments that will affect the performance of products bought for resale. Both follow-up and service calls are important as a feedback mechanism for the salesperson's company.

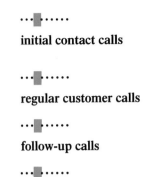

initial contact calls

regular customer calls

follow-up calls

service calls

TYPES OF SELLING JOBS

Salespeople can be classified into four categories based on whom they call on and the characteristics of their work: (1) trade salespeople, (2) missionary salespeople, (3) technical salespeople, and (4) retail salespeople.

Trade Salespeople

The main job of *trade salespeople* is to provide promotional assistance to their established customers. Thus a trade salesperson who works for a canned foods manufacturer might call on supermarket managers to explain the manufacturer's upcoming sales promotion—perhaps a cooperative advertising program or a couponing effort—and attempt to secure an end-of-aisle display. Trade salespeople do relatively little prospecting because their main job is making recurring calls on existing accounts rather than cultivating new customers.

Missionary Salespeople

Salespeople who seek to persuade their organizations' indirect customers to stimulate orders for their organizations' direct customers are *missionary salespeople*. For example, pharmaceutical "detail reps" make regular calls on physicians to persuade them to write prescriptions for the drugs their companies make. Detail reps do not write orders for delivery to physicians. But by explaining (detailing) their products to physicians, these salespeople hope to sell more of their pharmaceutical products through pharmacies. Physicians are the missionary salesperson's indirect customers; pharmacies are the direct customers. Missionary salespeople, however, often call on pharmacists to answer questions and to render assistance.

Missionary salespeople may also be responsible for recruiting new channel members and for working with them and established intermediaries to increase sales of their employers' products. This might involve training the intermediaries' sales and service people to do a better job of selling the missionary salesperson's products and to develop markets for new products in new territories.

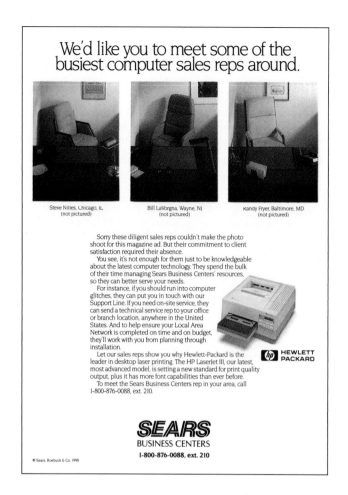

An ad that discusses the role of technical salespeople.

(We wish to thank Sears Business Centers for providing us with a model ad representative of technical salespeople.)

Technical Salespeople

Salespeople who provide technical advice and assistance to their present customers are *technical salespeople*. They require analytical skills and technical expertise to identify and solve problems for their customers, who are the actual users of their products. The Sears Business Centers ad discusses the role of technical service reps.

Retail Salespeople

In-store *retail salespeople* engage mainly in order-taking selling tasks. Some types of non-store retail salespeople, such as door-to-door salespeople, however, devote more effort to order-getting selling tasks.

Perhaps the most important difference between in-store retail selling and other types of selling is that the retail salesperson's customers come to the store. Retail store managers rely on advertising and sales promotion to attract customers—not on the prospecting efforts of their salespeople.

Another important difference has to do with the job itself. Retail salespeople often are part-time employees, their jobs are generally accorded little status by others, and many earn only minimum wage and are little more than clerks who ring up sales, stock shelves, mark prices, and so on. Some retailers, however, are recognizing the importance of training their salespeople and providing appropriate recognition.

SUMMARY OF LEARNING OBJECTIVES

1. Identify the basic objectives and basic tasks of personal selling.

The basic objectives of personal selling are (1) to find prospective customers (prospects), (2) to convert these prospects to customers, and (3) to keep them as satisfied customers. The basic selling tasks are (1) order-getting tasks, (2) order-taking tasks, and (3) sales support tasks.

2. Outline the steps in the personal selling process.

The steps in the personal selling process are (1) prospecting, (2) preparing the preapproach, (3) approaching the prospect, (4) making the sales presentation, (5) handling objections, (6) closing the sale, and (7) following up the sale.

3. Identify the major tasks of sales force management.

The major tasks are: (1) establishing sales force objectives, (2) structuring the sales force organization, (3) determining sales force size, (4) recruiting and selecting the sales force, (5) training and developing the sales force, (6) compensating the sales force, (7) motivating the sales force, (8) setting up sales territories, and (9) supervising and evaluating the sales force.

4. Outline the functions of professional salespeople.

Professional salespeople serve their employers and customers by functioning as (1) territorial market managers, (2) educators, (3) communication specialists, (4) human relations experts, and (5) feedback mechanisms.

5. Identify the types of sales calls and sales jobs.

Salespeople make four basic types of sales calls, each based on the purpose of the call: (1) initial contact calls, (2) regular customer calls, (3) follow-up calls, and (4) service calls. Salespeople can be classified into four categories based on whom they call on and the characteristics of their work: (1) trade salespeople, (2) missionary salespeople, (3) technical salespeople, and (4) retail salespeople.

Review Questions

1. What are the three basic objectives of personal selling?

2. What are the three categories of selling tasks?

3. What are the steps in the personal selling process?

4. How do sales leads differ from qualified prospects?

5. How does stimulus-response selling differ from problem solution selling?

6. What are the major tasks of sales force management?

7. How does the geographic specialization approach to structuring the sales force differ from the task specialization approach?

8. What are the three basic ways of compensating the sales force?

9. In what ways does a professional salesperson function as a territorial market manager?

10. In what major ways do missionary salespeople differ from retail salespeople?

Discussion Questions

1. One way for organizations to generate more business from existing customers is to encourage all personnel who come into contact with customers to engage in cross-selling. If practiced effectively, cross-selling might enable an organization to enhance its revenue without expanding its customer base. How might cross-selling be employed by a bank? What about a hotel?

2. High-technology surveillance and monitoring of employees is common in customer service–oriented industries such as insurance, airline ticketing, and telemarketing. An example is an airline reservation agent being monitored once or more a month by a supervisor to ensure that the agent follows the company's sales procedures. Proponents say monitoring enables employers to supply employees with immediate feedback on their performance. Employees, however, often complain that monitoring amounts to spying. Does surveillance and monitoring of customer service personnel raise ethical issues? Explain.

3. To some organizations, motivating the sales force means hiring a ''rah-rah'' motivational speaker to address the sales force during the annual sales meeting. Do you think this approach is effective in motivating professional salespeople? Explain.

4. Comment on the following statement: ''Anyone can be a successful salesperson.''

Application Exercise

Reread the material at the beginning of this chapter about questions to ask prior to taking a particular sales job and answer the following questions:

1. Do you agree that you should not take a sales job unless there is an effective lead-generation program? Explain.

2. Which sales presentation format do you think the person who prepared the ten questions would advocate? Explain.

3. Do you agree that during a sales call the customer should do 90 percent of the talking and the salesperson 10 percent? Explain.

4. Would you want to sell for a company whose sales manager is like the one described in item 9? Explain.

Key Concepts

The following key terms were introduced in this chapter:

selling tasks
prospecting
approach
stimulus-response selling
formula selling
need satisfaction selling

problem solution selling
close
geographic specialization
product specialization
task specialization

target market specialization
initial contact calls
regular customer calls
follow-up calls
service calls

CASES

Strategic Selling Helps Complex Business-to-Business Sales

A single sale of complex equipment or a database network to an organization can represent millions of dollars and require a team of sales and service representatives. In instances where a single sale is that complex, the selling process often takes months and even years. One company called Private Networks, a division of Scientific Atlanta, offers satellite-based communications networks to *Fortune* 500 corporations; each network can cost from $5 million to $50 million, and the sales cycle can take 12–24 months. The company decided that it had to streamline its procedures in order to reduce the amount of time needed to close a deal.

Enter a new selling tool called Strategic Selling, which was developed by two sales managers, Robert B. Miller and Stephen E. Heiman, who had become frustrated with sales procedures then in use. They decided that there had to be a better way to deal with complex business-to-business sales, and they set out to create a system that could provide a repeatable sales system that could be used throughout an organization. They wrote a book about their methodology in 1985 called *Strategic Selling,* and they subsequently formed a company called Miller-Heiman Inc. to market their system.

The Strategic Selling approach provided Private Networks with ''a set of analytical processes that gave us a handle on the complex sales we were involved in,'' according to Alan Freece, vice president of marketing and sales for Private Networks. The system gives everyone on the sales team access to the same information and allows them to identify weak points or opportunities in the sales process. For example, in a single sale of one of Private Networks's satellite systems, Private Networks may be dealing with end users, a person or persons with the authority to make the purchase, engineers who may be brought in to evaluate the quality of the system, and many others. The Strategic Selling method uses a common language to identify all of these individuals and allows Private Networks to track them all. Then, the sales team can evaluate how the sale is doing and what should be done next. Private Networks creates a Blue Sheet, the system's "road map," which is used by every member of the team, and is used in a monthly management review process.

Private Networks credits Strategic Selling with a $15 million sale to the automotive industry shortly after the system was adopted. The system allowed Private Networks to identify an important person in the buying chain who hadn't previously been identified, which led to closing the sale quickly. "Our competitors never knew what happened," said Freece.

Questions

1. How important are sales support tasks to Private Networks?

2. Which of the two approaches described in the Global Marketing box in this chapter, the Japanese "wet" approach or the the U.S. "dry" approach, would seem to be better suited to Private Networks's type of large sales? Explain.

3. Which sales presentation (stimulus-response, formula, need satisfaction, or problem solution) would seem to be most appropriate for Private Networks in contacting a potential customer? Explain.

4. What benefits does the Blue Sheet provide to the individual member of a sales team like that of Private Networks? To the manager of the sales team?

Chuck Piola Never Underestimates the Power of a Cold Call

Many marketing experts say that the in-person cold call is dead, killed off by the sheer expense of fielding a sales staff. But Chuck Piola, known as the "king of cold calls," doesn't agree. Piola's company, NCO Financial Systems, a collection agency, has grown so fast that it has made *Inc.* magazine's top-500 list for the past three years. That growth is directly attributable to Piola's style—and his cold calls.

Piola and his partner, Michael Barrist, teamed up in 1986 to revive NCO, a collection agency started by Barrist's grandfather in 1926. The client base, which totaled sixty-four when Piola started, has grown to 1,700, and billings have reached $3.5 million a year. Piola now heads a sales staff of six, but he doesn't spend much time sitting around the office; he's out on calls, many of them the dreaded cold call.

Piola routinely walks into office complexes without an appointment, heading right past suspicious security guards to select a floor or a company that he thinks might have business for him. He walks in and chats with the receptionist to find out whom he should see, and asks to see that individual. Often he is turned down, but sometimes he can make an appointment to come back later. Sometimes he finds that he has the wrong person, but he gets some inside information about the right person to see. Piola's rules for cold calling include:

- Everybody you see is a resource. Piola strikes up a conversation with everyone he meets, on the chance of obtaining some useful information.
- Never assume the person you're talking to isn't the decision maker. In other words, treat everyone as if he/she is the decision maker.

- Nothing should bother you. Don't take rejection personally.
- Even in slow times, stay consistent. If three weeks have gone by with no results, your calls in the fourth week should be just as upbeat as when you started. If you don't maintain enthusiasm, prospects will feel it.

Piola also follows the rules for dressing for success: he drives a Mercedes, wears a cashmere topcoat, a conservative suit and impeccable tie, and he always shines his wing tips the night before he makes cold calls. He carries an expensive leather briefcase and wears good cufflinks and an Omega watch. Piola feels that this gives him a psychological edge—he believes that part of the aura of cold calling is feeling good about yourself. He is also combating the perception that collection agencies are sleazy, fly-by-night companies.

Piola's final secret weapon is that he genuinely likes people. "If you walk in the door and are a breath of fresh air for them, you're not an infringement on their time. They'll make room for you."

Questions

1. What are some of the reasons that many marketing experts say cold calling is dead?

2. What personal characteristics would Chuck Piola probably be looking for in the sales representatives that he hires?

3. What do you think Chuck Piola might emphasize in establishing sales objectives for his sales force?

4. Evaluate Chuck Piola's rules for cold calling in terms of what you have learned in the chapter about professional selling.

Hill & Knowlton: Coping with Crises

• Introduction •

In the spring of 1990, Hill & Knowlton, America's largest public relations firm, found itself in the unusual position of having to undertake a crisis-control public relations effort on behalf of its own corporate leadership. The story began when CEO Robert L. Dilenschneider decided that H&K would conduct an anti-abortion campaign for the National Conference of Catholic Bishops. Dilenschneider saw this decision as in the best tradition of public relations: Hill & Knowlton would supply its expertise and contacts in order to help a client persuade the public to accept its interpretation of an issue.

Not everyone else saw it that way, however. Some H&K employees were outraged that Dilenschneider agreed to advance the anti-abortion cause, and many Catholics and others were disgusted that the Church would be spending money on what they saw as essentially a commercial enterprise. Other H&K employees, though, including Dilenschneider, believed that denying the Bishops access to the public relations apparatus would be tantamount to abridging their right to free speech. And many Catholics and

others believed that it was only logical for the Bishops to turn to H&K—abortion-rights advocates had long used PR firms to get their message across to the public.

No matter who was right or wrong in these disputes—and they seemed unlikely ever to be settled—the disputes themselves caused a public relations disaster for both the Bishops and Hill & Knowlton. Every public relations firm wants plenty of media coverage for its accounts. But the flurry of news stories appearing through the spring and summer of 1990 were exactly the kind a PR firm dreads: they focused not on the Bishops' arguments against abortion, but rather on the Bishops' relationship with a public relations firm and on the controversy raging inside Hill & Knowlton itself.

• The Masters of Crisis Control •

By 1990, Hill & Knowlton, a subsidiary of the advertising agency J. Walter Thompson, itself a subsidiary of British advertising giant WPP Group, was a $165 million company that had ongoing relationships with one out of every three *Fortune* 500 companies. Although it had lost its title of world's largest PR firm to Britain's Shandwick agency, H&K was still widely viewed by newspaper editors and other PR firms' executives as the world's most powerful and influential PR outfit. In fact,

since public relations pioneer John W. Hill had founded the firm in 1927, it had served as a laboratory for the development of some of the industry's most advanced techniques and strategies.

Many of those techniques and strategies had been used by Hill & Knowlton in ticklish situations before taking on the Bishops' account. Over the years, the heavy majority of Hill & Knowlton accounts had involved fairly run-of-the-mill publicity activities, including getting media plugs for clients' products, working with newspaper, magazine, and network news reporters and editors to help shape reporting of clients' policies or product development plans, and helping to craft statements and press releases emanating from clients' corporate offices. But the firm had also made a name for itself by specializing in the management of clients' actual or potential public relations disasters.

During the 1950s, for instance, the Tobacco Industry Research Council hired Hill & Knowlton to handle its day-by-day public relations effort. The Council was ostensibly formed to fund impartial research about the health effects of smoking but actually was an advocacy group in charge of counteracting popular press articles beginning to appear in the early 1950s that linked smoking and cancer. Hill & Knowlton worked on this account through the late 1960s, and all concerned in the effort apparently agreed that the firm had played an integral part in successfully defending the industry against lawsuits and regulatory restrictions and in greatly slowing the formation of negative public attitudes about the tobacco companies.

In 1979, when the Three Mile Island nuclear reactor malfunctioned and radioactive gases escaped through the plant's venting system, the electric utility that owned the plant called in H&K to calm the public's nerves and to minimize political damage to the nuclear power generation industry. The firm received generally high marks for its handling of the account, but Robert Dilenschneider believed that the overall campaign was "absolutely not" successful: "There was a 72-hour information gap between the time that the reactor went up and the time the utility decided to do something. And in that 72 hours, the information pipeline was full of fear and demagoguery and misinformation, all of which had to be overcome and even today, has not been overcome."

Almost immediately after a skywalk collapsed in the lobby of the Kansas City Hyatt Hotel in 1981, killing 114 people, Hyatt requested Hill & Knowlton's services. In addition to worrying about potential lawsuits, Hyatt had to be very careful that its handling of this disaster did not give consumers the impression that it was more concerned with protecting its assets than with the safety and well-being of its customers. The combination of H&K's expert handling of Hyatt statements and press releases and Hyatt's own decision to settle all liability claims quickly resulted in relatively little damage to Hyatt's public image.

And when a March 1989 U.S. Food and Drug Administration inspection of grape crates shipped from Chile revealed that two grapes had been tainted by cyanide and resulted in a U.S. quarantine of all Chilean fruit, Chile's government hired Hill & Knowlton to persuade the U.S. government and public that two grapes did not a public health disaster make and that everything possible was being done to ensure

---

Clearly . . . Hill & Knowlton's team knew how to handle crises.

---

future consumer safety. Again, H&K's efforts with reporters and lawmakers were seen to be crucial in the generally successful control of what could have been a runaway crisis. Chilean fruitgrowers were able to breathe a sigh of relief when the FDA lifted its quarantine just four days after it had been imposed, and Hill & Knowlton was able to carve another notch on its corporate belt.

• The Crisis Nobody Expected •

Clearly, then, Robert Dilenschneider and the rest of Hill & Knowlton's team knew how to handle crises. The irony was that the National Conference of Catholic Bishops account was never meant to be a crisis control case—it was meant to be merely a traditional persuasion account, a job in which H&K would marshall all its resources to help a client put

its message before the public as effectively and as often as possible. The Bishops' stand on abortion was already well-known: they believed that abortion—which had been legalized during the first six months of pregnancy by the Supreme Court's 1973 *Roe v. Wade* decision—was the murder of a human being. Hill & Knowlton's job was to make plain and persuasive the reasoning behind the Bishops' position and to counter abortion-rights advocates' arguments that the Bishops were seeking to infringe upon the rights of women and to defy the constitutional separation of church and state.

The Bishops' account became a crisis control case when Rowland Evans and Michael Novak, syndicated columnists who frequently comment on issues involving the Catholic clergy and laity, reported that the Bishops had hired Hill & Knowlton. They had learned about the account from members of the House and Senate who had met earlier with New York's John Cardinal O'Connor. Unfortunately for H&K, Robert Dilenschneider hadn't yet told more than a few top executives at the firm about the account.

The response of many Hill & Knowlton staffers upon reading Evans and Novak's article was pure outrage. Dilenschneider had a good reputation for maintaining open lines of communication with his employees: "Dear Bob" letters—in which individual employees told Dilenschneider exactly what they thought about H&K policies and to which Dilenschneider always wrote personal responses—were famous throughout the PR community. Dilenschneider usually discussed any potentially controversial accounts with key employees throughout the firm before deciding whether to sign an agreement—something he said he did before taking the Bishops' account. But at least a few staffers told reporters that Dilenschneider hadn't followed his usual procedure. This may have led him, they said, to misgauge the amount of controversy the account would stir up within the firm.

Another reason Dilenschneider was taken by surprise may have been that he knew that all H&K employees knew that they could refuse to work on any account they found offensive and that no one would be rewarded or punished for working or not working on accounts involving controversial issues. (This policy is almost universal in the PR community.) Few issues in the United States, however, are as divisive as the abortion issue, and the response Dilenschneider encountered from his employees was more serious than just people declining to work on the Bishops' account. Instead, he found himself the recipient of a petition signed by 136 H&K staffers—including, by one count, nearly a third of the New York staff—stating in part: ''For management to seek out as well as accept an assignment whose ultimate goal is to limit our fundamental rights leaves us with a stinging sense of betrayal. Our rights, it seems, mattered less than the promise of additional revenue.''

The leaking of this petition—as well as of the fact that Dilenschneider's decision to take the account had led, at least in part, to the resignation of two employees and the loss of two major accounts, including Revlon—to the press kept the wrong story in the news, at least from Dilenschneider's and the Bishops' point of view. Employee leaks also made Dilenschneider and other top Hill & Knowlton executives worry whether potential clients would trust their controversial accounts to the

firm in the future. The continuing appearance of opinion pieces and editorials both for and against the Bishops' right to use a PR firm compounded the problem.

And meanwhile, probably as a result of being flustered by all this unexpected brouhaha, Hill & Knowlton and the Bishops kept getting their signals crossed about who should say what and when. Dilenschneider told his employees that the firm wouldn't actually lobby lawmakers to change abortion laws; Church officials told the media that the firm would. Dilenschneider told his employees that the account—at

$3 to $5 million, one of the firm's largest—was already a done deal and there was no backing out; Church officials said no contract had yet been signed. These discrepancies led to more stories in the media. Meanwhile, little attention was being focused upon the Bishops' anti-abortion argument itself.

• An Industry Problem •

Many in the public relations industry saw all of this publicity as detrimental not only to the Bishops' account and to Hill & Knowlton but also to the industry as a whole. Some anti-abortion and abortion-rights advocates agreed on a single point: they believed that it was unseemly for the Bishops to resort to hiring a public relations firm. Their stance was that, given the Bishops' moral authority, learning, and eloquence—their statements frequently had some impact on the formation of opinion and policy even outside the Church—their anti-abortion argument should stand or fall based on its own merits, not on the basis of a PR firm's special relationships with reporters or lawmakers or on its expertise in using the news media. The obvious implication of this argument was that there was something sordid about the use of a public relations firm and that public relations firms' ''persuasion'' techniques were inherently underhanded.

This implication was reinforced as many stories about the Bishops' account focused readers' attention on some of the techniques regularly used by PR firms, including the ''pre-writing'' of editorial pieces and the ''creation'' of media stories by calling press conferences or providing news desks with narrated film footage. Press coverage of the controversy also called attention to the amount of money involved in public relations campaigns: critics of the Bishops said that the $3 to $5 million promised to H&K should be spent on keeping inner-city parish churches and parochial schools open or on serving the homeless. (The Bishops said that the PR campaign would not take money away from other Church causes; money destined specifically for the campaign was being solicited from individual and institutional donors.) Such high-priced accounts were not uncommon in the PR industry and nobody argued that the Catholic Church alone should be responsible for pay-

ing to right the world's ills. But this sudden questioning about how such millions of dollars could otherwise be spent forced the whole PR industry onto the defensive.

The Hill & Knowlton–Catholic Bishops controversy also forced other PR firms to think about their own vulnerability. Although few other issues were as divisive as abortion, the leaders of many other PR firms had begun to notice a new sensitivity among their employees to certain accounts. The Burson-Marsteller firm, for instance, had long ago put into place a no-religious-organizations, no-political-candidates accounts policy to try to avoid the kind of employee factionalization experienced by Hill & Knowlton. But that didn't make Burson-Marsteller immune to controversy: some employees had already expressed resistance to the firm taking on accounts involving liquor or tobacco promotions, certain foreign governments or companies having investments in certain foreign countries, nuclear power generation, or companies involved in controversies over environmental issues. The list of questionable accounts seemed to be growing all the time.

Moreover, crisis control accounts—a minority of most firms' portfolios but usually a significant source of revenue—also seemed to be getting trickier than ever. First, depending on the crisis, many employees didn't want to work on them. And second, and perhaps more worrying, the press had discovered with the Bishops' account what a good source of dramatic, ''behind-the-scenes'' stories the PR firms' handling of such accounts was. Almost any media attention aimed at how crisis control worked tended to undercut the crisis control effort itself.

In the midst of the Bishops' account crisis, *Business Week* ran a postmortem story comparing how Robert Dilenschneider had handled the account with the rules he had set down in his book, *Power & Influence: Mastering the Art of Persuasion*. The writer found Dilenschneider lacking on every count from ''Closely control the timing of announcements,'' to ''Organize all the power centers early on,'' to ''Stay out of the spotlight.'' Dilenschneider himself was quoted in the article as admitting that he had been caught out: ''We knew if we took [the Bishops' account] there was going to be a lot of controversy. But in candor, if the Evans and Novak piece hadn't appeared we would have handled it a lot differently and there would have been nowhere near this amount of controversy.''

Dilenschneider seemed to remember one of his own rules, however—''State your position in terms of the public interest.'' When reporters or others asked why he had grabbed hold of such a hot potato, he consistently replied in more or less the same words: ''We took it, really, because we felt it was a free speech issue. . . . The abortion issue is probably the most divisive issue in American society today. . . . Nobody's listening to one another. People are talking at one another. If we can create a dialogue that somehow helps to resolve the issue, we've done a lot.''

No matter how they felt about either the abortion issue or the free speech issue, however, many in the PR industry believed that the Bishops' account fiasco had seriously bruised the images of both Dilenschneider and Hill & Knowlton.

Many wondered if the firm would be able to recover its lost prestige. They didn't have to wait long to find out. Dilenschneider's next major move concerning the account was seen as masterly: he silenced H&K spokespeople for the Bishops and replaced them with the extremely articulate Helen Alvare, an attorney who was already working for the Bishops.

And then, as the Iraqi army moved into Kuwait during the summer and everyone wondered what the United States' response would be, the Bishops' account story, like many other stories, disappeared from the news. Now, Hill & Knowlton had a different kind of crisis control job on its hands as it accepted the $1 million account of the Citizens for a Free Kuwait, an anti-Iraqi group of Kuwaiti citizens.

Hill & Knowlton wasn't the only American PR firm to take on such an account, but it mounted the largest effort. In September, it arranged a *New York Times* interview with "Major Sam," who claimed to be a Kuwaiti resistance fighter. The firm also set up various press conferences, placed several full-page newspaper advertisements on behalf of Arab-American groups stating support for the multinational action against Iraq, and produced a number of video press conferences, which it sent to national and local TV news desks. The effort went off smoothly, and by December 1990, Hill & Knowlton was once again being praised by PR industry watchers as the masters of the game.

• **Questions** •

1. What other promotion mix elements might have been useful to the National Conference of Catholic Biships in this situation? Explain.

2. Robert Dilenschneider says that refusing the Bishops' account would be tantamount to abridging their right to free speech. Some reporters have suggested that this statement is just another PR technique. What do you think?

3. How might Dilenschneider have avoided his problems with his own employees after taking on the Bishops' account?

4. Why do you think Dilenschneider gives the advice, "Stay out of the spotlight," to other PR practitioners?

5. As more subjects—such as the environment, AIDS, etc.—become "hot-to-handle" topics, do you think the PR firms should stick to their policy of allowing employees to opt out of working on accounts? What are some of the possible implications of your answer?

SECTION

VI

PRICE

. . . .

Sections Three, Four, and Five examined the product, distribution, and promotion elements of the marketing mix. Unless the price element in the marketing mix is equal to, or less than, the value that target customers perceive in the product, the marketing mix will not satisfy them. Price also must return an adequate profit or else a firm cannot survive over the long run. The two chapters in this section examine the price element of the marketing mix.

Chapter 18 explains the roles that price can play in the buyer's decision-making process and the objectives that marketers can achieve through price decisions. It also develops a procedure for setting the list price which is the original base asking price for a product.

Chapter 19 focuses on the marketer's day-to-day administration of prices. In practice, list prices must often be adjusted in individual sales transactions. Examples of such adjustments include discounts, allowances, and price promotions.

The Comprehensive Case at the end of this Section, on Carnival Cruise Lines, focuses on the company's birth and growth and the role pricing plays in its success. It illustrates the concepts of pricing objectives, price and demand analysis, and product line pricing strategies.

18

PRICING
PROCEDURES

OBJECTIVES

After reading this chapter you will be able to

1. explain the two roles of price in buyer decision making.

2. outline a procedure a firm might follow in setting a product's list price.

3. identify the basic objectives marketers can pursue through pricing.

4. understand the relationships among price, total revenue, and elasticity of demand.

5. understand the relationships among cost, volume, and profit.

D uring the 1980s the $60 billion hotel and motel industry witnessed an unparalleled period of expansion and change. One of the most prominent changes was the increasing segmentation of this market. Today the hotel industry is generally considered to consist of three segments: luxury, mid-price, and budget.

The luxury segment includes major big-city and resort hotels where nightly rates exceed $100 and where a variety of amenities and services are provided. Historically, Sheraton Corporation and Hilton have been the largest competitors in this market.

The mid-price segment typically covers a price range of $45 to $60 a night, depending on location. It has long been dominated by Holiday Inn, although Marriott Courtyard and Hampton Inns are increasingly strong competitors.

In the budget segment Motel 6 and Super 8 have dominated the competition. They offer no-frills rooms at rates averaging $35 per night.

The greatest growth has occurred in the budget segment. Moreover, in spite of the growing numbers of budget motel units, data from industry watcher Smith Travel Research show that occupancy rates at budget motels have risen to 70 percent of capacity. By comparison, mid-price segment occupancy rates were expected to fall to 60 percent in the early 1990s.

Not surprisingly, the three segments have different cost structures to go along with the different pricing structures. As the size of rooms and the number of services and amenities rise, so does the cost. The cost differences result in different levels of breakeven occupancy rates—the percentage of rooms that must be occupied each night to fully cover a hotel's cost. For luxury hotels this rate is 67 percent, for mid-price hotels 64 percent, and for budget motels 61 percent.[1]

The variety of prices available from competitors in the hotel and motel industry suggests that product differentiation is widespread in this market. But given the variations in size, location, amenities, and other nonprice aspects of the marketing mix, how do such firms arrive at pricing decisions? In this chapter we will examine a process for developing the *list price*—the base price or initial offering price of a product. This process demonstrates how a firm can integrate the considerations presented in the discussion of the hotel and motel industry: market demand (including differences in demand across segments), cost and its relationship to volume, and pricing objectives and their relationship to competitive strategy.

THE SCOPE AND MEANING OF PRICE

People pay interest on loans, fees to consult with physicians, fares to ride taxis, and premiums to insure their lives and property. All of these are examples of price. In effect, every transaction that occurs involves a price—even if the price is zero.

In order to successfully market any good or service, a seller must establish a price. Indeed, price is often a cornerstone of a firm's marketing strategy. Discounters such as Wal-Mart rely on their low-price image, and many products and brands employ relatively high prices to reinforce an image of superior quality—for example, Gucci, Chivas Regal, and Mercedes.

What ethical questions might arise in pricing upscale cosmetics? Would the approach to pricing differ for cosmetics that are sold through drugstores and discount stores?

[© Sepp Seitz]

Price thus has two roles in buyer decision making: an allocation role and an information role.[2] The *allocation role of price* is the function price performs in helping buyers decide how to derive the greatest expected utility from their buying power. In other words, the existence of price helps buyers decide how to allocate their buying power toward various goods and services. Buyers compare the prices of alternatives and then decide how to spend their money. The Jeep ad provides the buyer with price and product feature information so the buyer can make judgments about the relative desirability of that vehicle.

The *information role of price* is the function price performs in educating consumers about product factors such as quality. It is useful when buyers have a difficult time judging the product factor. For example, higher prices may be taken as indicators of higher quality, especially in cases where the brand or supplier is unfamiliar and where it is difficult to measure the key characteristics or benefits of the product objectively. The soundness of legal advice and the quality of a brand of floppy disks cannot be evaluated in any perfectly objective manner. In most cases buyers will not evaluate cut-rate lawyers or discount floppy disks as being very high in quality.

allocation role of price

information role of price

or buying organic baby food?

Price often helps buyers assess the value of a product.

(Campbell-Mithun-Esty Advertising.)

The Biggest Obstacle You Face In A Jeep Cherokee Shouldn't Be The Price.

The four-door Jeep Cherokee Sport with shift-on-the-fly four-wheel drive and a new 190 horsepower 4.0 litre engine:

$15,946*

There's Only One Jeep.
Advantage: Chrysler

Protects engine and powertrain for 7 years or 70,000 miles and against outerbody rust-through for 7 years or 100,000 miles. See limited warranty at dealer. Deductibles and restrictions apply. *Price includes $500 50th Anniversary discount. $13,343 for two-door two-wheel drive. Price includes $675 50th Anniversary discount. MSRPs exclude title, taxes, dest. charges and options. For further information, or how to buy or lease one, call 1-800-JEEP-EAGLE. Jeep is a registered trademark of Chrysler Corporation. Buckle up for safety.

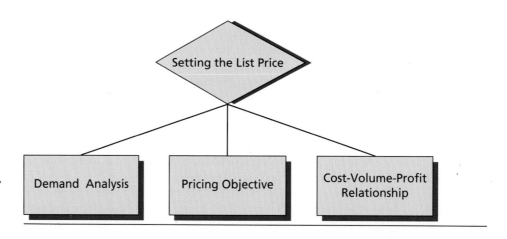

FIGURE 18–1

Key Elements in Setting the
List Price

perceived value pricing

Accordingly, many managers practice perceived value pricing in such cases. ***Perceived value pricing*** is the establishment of prices that are intended to enhance the utility that customers will perceive in the products offered. This type of pricing works best when a high-quality image can be developed through promotion.

Whether the role of price is allocative or informative, however, price influences the demand for a firm's goods or services and is an essential dimension of marketing strategy. Thus any decisions about pricing should be made after evaluating its expected impact on demand and its consistency with the rest of the marketing strategy.

Price can influence the volume demanded as well as the revenue per unit of volume. It therefore has a major potential impact on a firm's (or a product's) profitability. As the volume produced and sold changes, certain costs change as well. Consequently, in price setting, the costs associated with given price and volume expectations must be considered along with any relevant organizational objectives regarding profit expectations.

As Figure 18–1 shows, a logical approach to setting a list, or base, price would include the following elements: (1) pricing objectives, (2) price and demand analysis, and (3) cost-volume-profit relationships.

PRICING OBJECTIVES

Many organizations have established corporate pricing objectives that provide strong direction for pricing decisions. Generally these objectives are designed to reflect the firm's organizational objectives. Although the pricing objectives alone are not sufficient to identify the single best list price, they often help managers narrow the range of possible prices. However, if management determines that the pricing objectives cannot be met for a given product, then that product may be eliminated from the product line.

Although pricing objectives are unique to each organization, we can identify four basic classes of them: (1) profit-oriented, (2) volume-oriented, (3) image-oriented, and (4) stabilization. (See Table 18–1.) The four classes of objectives need not be mutually exclusive. Firms such as Pillsbury and the Kraft division of Philip Morris, which sell super-premium ice creams (Häagen Dazs and Frusen Glädjé, respectively) clearly are pricing these products to reinforce the quality image of the brands. However, the firms would not set premium prices on them unless they anticipated that certain volume and profit goals would also be met.

TABLE 18–1 ▊ Types of Pricing Objectives

. . . .

1. Profit-oriented
   - Profit maximization
   - Target margin
   - Target return on investment
2. Volume-oriented
   - Sales maximization
   - Market share maximization
3. Image-oriented
   - Quality image
   - Value image
4. Stabilization

. . . .

Profit-Oriented Objectives

Classical economic theory assumes that firms always select the price that results in the highest profit—*profit maximization.* If that view were adopted consistently by all companies, then all pricing decisions would be made with this single objective in mind.

profit maximization

Profit maximization is often not a workable objective, however. First, in a competitive market where firms can change their prices, the level of sales that will be achieved at a given price can seldom be predicted with total assurance. Therefore it is usually not possible to know exactly what price will yield profit maximization. Second, where monopolies (such as local electric and telephone services) exist, the government regulates the amount of profit received. Finally, a price that may lead to maximum short-run profits may not be optimal in terms of long-run profits, and vice versa. Thus many firms enter new markets with very low prices to encourage product trial in the hope that, if the products are well accepted, the firms will become profitable in later years.

More typically, firms establish a profit target—a level of profits that is acceptable as a profit goal. There are two types of profit targets: target margin and target return on investment. A *target margin* is a profit target for a product that is stated as a percentage reflecting the ratio of profits to sales. Thus a firm may price its products to achieve a target margin of 20 percent. (As we will see later in the chapter, wholesale and retail intermediaries are especially likely to use target margin pricing.)

target margin

A *target return on investment* is a profit target for a product that is stated as a ratio of profit to the firm's total dollar investment in production facilities and assets supporting the product. For example, a firm may set prices that are expected to yield a 25 percent return on investment.

target return on investment

Volume-Oriented Objectives

In firms that equate sales and market share with profit, the *volume pricing objective*—price setting to meet target sales volumes or market shares—is common. However, higher volume can be expensive if it is achieved through extensive marketing expenditures or through lower price. Therefore, setting price policies that emphasize target sales volume or market share can be risky.

volume pricing objective

Higher volume can help a firm establish a market position quickly or allow more efficient levels of operation. To a large extent airline pricing reflects volume-oriented objectives. Because the difference in the cost of flying a half-empty plane and a plane fully loaded with passengers is very small, there is a great incentive to use price specials to minimize the number of empty seats. The relationships among cost, volume, and profit are discussed in more detail later in the chapter.

Image-Oriented Objectives

Image building may be achieved in part through pricing. Some retailers set high prices to build or maintain a prestige image (Neiman-Marcus, for example), and others (such as Wal-Mart) use low prices to build an image of value. Often, value-oriented retailers reinforce their pricing with guarantees that they have the "lowest price in town."

Whether prices are high or low, the *image pricing objective* is price setting to enhance the consumer's perception of the store's total merchandise mix. Thus Neiman-Marcus enjoys an image of quality and prestige that differentiates it from other department stores. Value-oriented stores, on the other hand, use their overall low-price image to attract bargain-oriented shoppers.

Similarly, manufacturers often use price as a clue to product quality. For example, the Mark Cross ad deliberately focuses on the high price of the company's product line to underscore the prestige of the brand. However, simply raising the price of a product will

image pricing objective

An ad designed to build a product image.

(Photos: Olof Wahlund. Reprinted by permission of Mark Cross, Inc.)

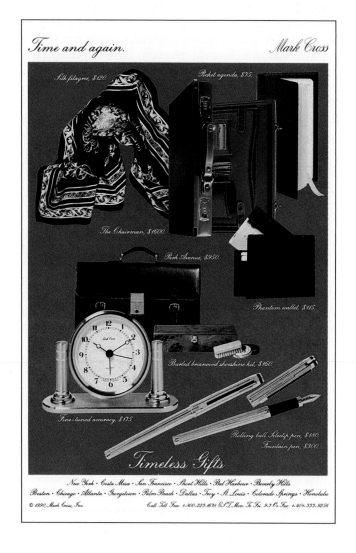

not guarantee that a quality image can be delivered. Revlon's Flex shampoo experienced a decline in market share from 8 percent to 3 percent after the company used a higher price, fancier package, and modified formula to try to establish a quality image for Flex. Consumers apparently were not persuaded that the product had really changed.[3]

Stabilization Objectives

In many industries, if one firm lowers its price, competitors are often obliged to follow suit. This is especially true when buyers are very price-sensitive. In the videotape market, quality is the number 1 purchase criterion, but price is a close second. However, a number of producers are perceived as equal in quality. The result of price cutting in such industries is reduced profits for everyone. Consequently, firms in such industries try to achieve a *price stabilization objective*—setting prices to maintain a stable relationship between the firm's prices and the industry leader's prices. For example, many videotape producers compete on the basis of distribution rather than price, attempting to obtain broader retail availability and to get more prominent retail displays than competitors.

price stabilization objective

Stabilization is not the same as collusion. In the 1970s the objective of the international oil cartel known as OPEC (the Organization of Petroleum Exporting Countries) was price collusion. Price changes were agreed upon and implemented in concert by this group. Such action would constitute illegal price fixing in the United States.

Another form of stabilization can be seen in the pricing of movie theater tickets. Although there are enormous differences in the cost of making movies, a theater owner customarily charges the same price for all films. One explanation offered by those in the industry shows that the informational role of price is partly responsible. Some fear that if they charge less for small-budget pictures, the lower-budget films will be perceived as losers and only the most expensive films will be seen.[4]

Strategic Implications

The various pricing objectives have important implications for a firm's competitive strategy. Thus the chosen objective should be consistent with the way the firm is attempting to position itself relative to the competition.

For example, the selection of a profit objective means that the firm will ignore competitors' prices. This choice may be made because there are no competitors, because the firm is operating at maximum production capacity, or because price is far less important than other attributes to the buyers in the market.

By contrast, the selection of a volume objective might come from the strategy of beating the competition; and the selection of a stabilization objective might come from the strategy of meeting the competition. In both cases management will need to be able to assess competitors' actions.

Finally, when image objectives are dominant, management will usually be avoiding competition by attempting to differentiate the product or to reach a special segment of the market. In all of these cases, however, the firm's ability to achieve the objective will depend in part on the nature of the relationship between price and demand.

PRICE AND DEMAND ANALYSIS

Ultimately, managers must develop some estimate of the level of demand that will result from a given price. In order to understand the demand estimation process, however, it is first necessary to understand some basic concepts relating to price and demand.

Basic Price/Demand Concepts

• **Demand schedules and curves** • A *demand schedule* is a summary of the quantity of a product that is demanded at different prices. A *demand curve* is a graphic portrayal of a demand schedule.

Consider, for example, the data for a hypothetical no-frills motel, the Sleep Inn, shown in Table 18–2. The data portray a typical demand schedule. As Sleep Inn lowers its daily room rates, the number of rooms occupied (quantity demanded) increases. The increase in demand as price is decreased results from two possible sources: (1) people who would otherwise choose competing motels might choose Sleep Inn instead because of the lower price, or (2) people who would otherwise choose not to use any motel (truckers or campers, for example) might use the motel because the price is more reasonable.

Of course, some travelers would not stay at Sleep Inn even at a rate of $10 per night while others might not consider $65 too expensive. Thus firms could define different demand curves for each market segment, and some firms might choose to serve only the segment willing to pay a high price.

• **Price Elasticity of Demand** • The typical demand curve is downward-sloping. Thus, as the price is lowered, the quantity demanded increases. Virtually all demand curves are downward-sloping, even for products that most people believe are not responsive to price. For example, economists have shown that a 10 percent increase in cigarette prices results in a short-term 4 percent decrease in consumption.[5]

Not all downward demand curves have the same degree of slope, however. In effect, demand for some products is much more sensitive to small price changes than is demand for other products.

Because changes in price nearly always have some impact on demand, managers need to be able to classify demand curves according to demand sensitivity to price. The *price elasticity of demand* is the degree of demand sensitivity to price in a given demand curve. In general, if the percentage change in quantity exceeds the percentage change in price, demand is said to be elastic. More specifically, demand is said to be elastic if the effect on total revenue of a change in quantity is greater than the effect on total revenue of a change in price.

As we can see in Table 18–3, Sleep Inn's total revenue (price times quantity) increases as the price is lowered from $32 to $26. However, when the price goes below $26, total revenue begins to drop. The increase in the quantity of rooms occupied reflects the decline in price over the $32 to $26 range, but not below $26. Demand responds readily to price in the $32 to $26 range; it stretches easily, much like a very elastic rubber band. The term

TABLE 18–2 ▎ A Demand Schedule for Sleep Inn: Daily Room Rates and Rooms Occupied

Room Rates	Rooms Occupied
$32	180
30	210
28	240
26	260
24	270
22	275

TABLE 18–3 Total Revenue Schedule for Sleep Inn

Price (P)	Quantity (Q)	Total Revenue (P × Q)
$32	180	$5,760
30	210	6,300
28	240	6,720
26	260	6,760
24	270	6,480
22	275	6,050

price elastic demand describes this situation. A change in price leads to an *opposite* change in direction to total revenue.

If demand is relatively unresponsive to price, it is termed *price inelastic*. In such cases a change in price results in a modest change in the quantity demanded. The price change also leads to a change in total revenue, but the direction of the two changes is the same. In Table 18–3, demand is price inelastic over the range $26 to $22. As the price is reduced, the quantity demanded increases; but the total revenue is also reduced.

Table 18–4 summarizes the relationships involved in price elasticity. As the preceding example indicates, demand can be price elastic over one range of prices and inelastic over another range of prices *for the same product*. For example, the demand for consumer electronics products such as microwave ovens was inelastic at very high prices but became elastic as prices dropped into a range that the majority of households could afford. It is difficult, therefore, to provide meaningful generalizations about the degree of elasticity of a given product.

Moreover, elasticity of demand need not be the same for all brands or suppliers in a product category. To the extent that marketers can convince prospective buyers that their product is unique, demand will more likely be inelastic. In general, however, the greater the number of alternatives of which the customer is aware, the greater the price elasticity of demand.[6]

Demand Estimation

Marketers of consumer products consider the opinions of intermediaries when estimating the final buyer's expected price. They also study the prices of competitors' brands and try

TABLE 18–4 Price Elasticity of Demand

If Change in Price Is:	And Change in Revenue Is:	Then Demand Is:
Down	Up	Elastic
Down	Down	Inelastic
Up	Up	Inelastic
Up	Down	Elastic

to position their brands in relation to them. Some use survey approaches and laboratory experiments to gain insight into potential customers' expected prices, especially for new products. They may also test market the product at different prices in different markets.

As we explained in chapter 6, marketers of complex industrial products, such as installations and accessory equipment, might send representatives into potential buyers' plants to demonstrate and discuss the product concept with engineers. Purchasing agents are a useful source of information for cheaper and less complex industrial products.

After defining the target market's probable price range, the marketer estimates demand at each price within the range. In making these estimates, it is crucial that the marketer answer three questions:

1. What change in sales will occur even if no price changes occur in the market?

2. What price actions are competitors likely to take?

3. What effect will price changes have on other products in our line?

● **Changes in Demand** ● Usually the quantity demanded in a product category will grow even if no price changes occur. The causes include population growth, an increase in the awareness or availability of the product, and increases in income. The growth in demand involves a gradual *upward* shifting of the demand curve, as shown in Figure 18–2.

Of course, demand curves can shift *downward* as well as upward. Poor economic conditions, such as high unemployment or high interest rates, may result in temporary declines in demand for durable goods such as home appliances and cars and in demand for discretionary goods and services such as vacation travel.

From a marketer's viewpoint, demand changes are usually identified in the sales forecasting process. These changes should be factored into the demand estimate but separated from expected changes based on price. The procedure is to first estimate demand at current prices (taking any demand curve shifts into account) to establish a baseline estimate. Then demand estimates at new price levels can be made on the basis of the expected elasticity of demand and of the competitors' actions.

Often changes in demand may be accompanied by changes in elasticity. In the business segment of the personal computer market an economic slowdown (such as the one that began in 1990) will usually result in a downward demand shift because most personal

FIGURE 18–2
· ·

Shifts in the Demand Curve for Sleep Inn

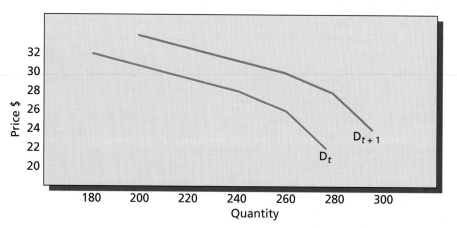

D_{t+1} = Initial demand curve in month *t*.
D_{t+1} = Demand curve in month *t* + 1 (after upward demand shift).

computer purchases can be deferred without seriously affecting operations. Moreover, higher-priced competitors in this market may face another problem. In 1990, with funds for personal computer purchases limited, many Compaq buyers opted for lower-priced alternatives such as Dell in order to be able to buy a larger number of units.[7]

• **Competitors' Price Behavior** • As indicated earlier, price can generate a competitive advantage only if competitors do not match a price cut or if they increase prices by a larger amount. Consequently marketers must attempt to project the pricing behavior of competitors.

In chapter 2 we saw that the nature and extent of price competition depend largely on the type of market structure. Prices tend to be more stable under oligopolies than under monopolistic competition. That is, firms find it difficult to avoid following a competitor's price cut when only a few large competitors exist—especially if the products are undifferentiated.

Although the behavior of competitors is not always predictable, managers can gain insight into probable price behavior from historical behavior. Competitors that have always matched lower prices in the past are likely to do so in the future. As the Global Marketing box suggests, predicting the probable pricing behavior of multinational competitors also involves an understanding of exchange rates and trade barriers.

GLOBAL MARKETING

Firms that operate in multinational settings face an especially dynamic pricing environment. Among their most important challenges are changes in exchange rates and changes in trade barriers.

Because market forces cause the relative value of national currencies to shift over time, a firm may find overseas sales rising or falling in response to changing prices. For example, during the past decade the value of the dollar declined relative to the value of many other currencies, including the German deutsche mark. This meant that the number of dollars required to buy an imported German car would go up unless the German auto maker was willing to reduce the price in deutsche marks. In effect, such currency shifts constitute an important uncontrollable factor affecting pricing strategy.

In one of the most important twentieth century developments in international business, the nations in the European common market—the European Community, or EC—agreed to eliminate all trade barriers among members by 1992. One large market replaces several small and medium-sized ones, and tariffs and other government-supplied protections to industries gradually will disappear.

Some experts have suggested that an increase in price competition can be expected from these changes, because many industries will have more competitors than can readily survive in nonprotected markets. In 1990, for example, the EC countries had twelve national airlines and a half dozen mass-market "domestic" auto makers. Compared to the number of domestic firms in the United States and considering the inroads that American and Japanese competitors are likely to make, this appears to be a surplus of competitors. Moreover, since economies of scale are strong in such industries, price competition could well escalate.

Managers can also try to estimate competitors' relative cost positions. If a firm has invested a large amount of money in automated production facilities or has control over key raw materials, then that firm may have a significant cost advantage and thus may be willing to compete on price.

Consider the case of Dover Publishing. Dover publishes specialized books in areas such as art, science, crafts, and architecture, as well as a number of literature classics. Dover's books sell for at least 30 percent less than comparable books in the retail market, primarily because of cost advantages. In addition to maintaining a smaller staff, Dover sells its books to retailers on a nonreturnable basis. It also pays its authors modest flat fees instead of royalties based on sales.[8]

Clearly, if competitors' reactions do not include any change in the *relative prices* they charge, then no increase in sales should be expected from brand switching. Market share should remain more or less constant. In such cases the only sources of increased volume resulting from a price change are increases in the rate of purchase or in the number of new buyers who decide to purchase something in the product category. For example, if an airline's fare cut is matched by competitors, then demand will be increased only if total airline industry sales increase because of people flying more frequently or more people electing to fly. Generally, such gains will accrue to all firms in proportion to their market share.

• **Product Line Effects** • Most firms offer an array of products, and frequently decisions regarding the list price of one product will influence demand for the other products as well. For example, if a company such as Sears markets several models of refrigerators, then lowering the list price of one model is likely to cause some buyers who would have purchased a more expensive model to trade down. Product line relationships can be complex. However, because most product line pricing issues involve modifications to list prices, they are discussed in more detail in chapter 19.

COST-VOLUME-PROFIT RELATIONSHIPS

Earlier in the chapter we suggested that, in many firms, pricing decisions must be made after due consideration of the firm's profit-oriented objectives. Even if short-run profit maximization is not the primary goal, the firm needs to recognize the profit consequences of pricing decisions. Since prices are expected to influence volume, and volume will influence costs and profits, marketers must consider these relationships when making pricing decisions.

Most marketers take a cost-oriented approach to pricing their products. Because no firm can stay in business over the long run unless the prices it gets for its products cover its costs, marketers put great emphasis on cost data. Cost accounting systems are used to collect these data, which are reported to marketing decision makers. The bottom line on the income statement is preceded by deductions of costs from net sales to arrive at a net profit figure. Thus costs set a floor below which a firm cannot price its products in the long run.

cost-plus pricing

Cost-Plus Pricing

The simplest cost-oriented approach to pricing is *cost-plus pricing*—the approach in which the selling price for each unit of product equals its total cost plus something extra for profit. For example, suppose Sleep Inn wants to price its rooms at 20 percent above the cost of each room. Suppose also that the total cost of staff salaries, utilities, leases, insurance, promotion, and other overhead is $4,000 per day. In addition, suppose that it costs $8 per day per room for laundry, water, and room cleaning. If 200 rooms are occupied on a given day, total costs are $4,000 + ($8 × 200) = $5,600. Adding the 20 percent desired profit, the cost plus profit is $5,600 + (20% × $5,600) = $6,720. Since this cost is based on an assumption of 200 occupied rooms, the daily room rate should be $6,720 ÷ 200 = $33.60.

This approach to pricing is simple but does not explicitly consider that different types of costs behave in different ways. If only 100 rooms are occupied, the total cost will not change very much, since the major portion of it is for salaries, utilities, and leases. In fact, the total cost will now be $4,000 + ($8 × 100) = $4,800. At a price of $33.60 per room, the 100 occupied rooms will generate only $3,360 in revenue, far below the amount required to achieve a profit.

In determining the cost of a product, therefore, it is important to distinguish between two types of costs: fixed costs and variable costs. *Fixed costs (FC)* are costs that remain the same regardless of changes in the volume sold. For example, Sleep Inn's $4,000 fixed cost is the portion of the total cost that is not affected by the number of room occupied. *Variable costs (VC)* are costs that change in relation to volume. For Sleep Inn the variable cost is $8 per room per day.

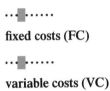

fixed costs (FC)

variable costs (VC)

Total cost (TC) is the sum of fixed and variable costs. To some extent, firms can change the relative size of fixed and variable costs. For example, IBM spent $20 billion on new production facilities during the first half of the 1980s in order to automate a larger share of its production process. Although this effort reduced variable labor costs, it also increased the fixed costs (or overhead) of the plants substantially.[9] Sleep Inn could eliminate some fixed costs by reducing the range of services offered.

In general, the higher the fixed costs relative to the variable costs, the more important volume is to the firm. As volume grows in a high-fixed-cost firm, the business achieves

Homebuilders who use cost-plus pricing should understand the nature of fixed and variable costs.
[© David Dempster]

Organizations with high volumes and economies of scale are better able to compete on price.

(United States Postal Service.)

economies of scale

breakeven analysis

economies of scale—reductions in cost per unit as fixed costs are spread over a larger number of units. The airline industry is an industry in which economies of scale are very significant. The Express Mail ad underscores a low-price strategy that depends on high package volume per airplane flight.

In order to examine these economies of scale and the overall relationship of costs, volume, prices, and profits, marketers often rely on breakeven analysis.

Breakeven Analysis

The method of identifying the level of sales at which total revenue (TR) will equal total cost (TC), given a product's per-unit selling price, is *breakeven analysis*. Suppose Sleep Inn decides to try a room rate of $28. Given the variable cost of $8, we know that $8 of each room charge will be used to cover variable costs. This leaves $20 to be used for fixed costs and any profit. Since fixed costs are $4,000, Sleep Inn will need to have 200 rooms occupied to cover these costs ($4,000 ÷ $20). The breakeven point therefore is 200 rooms.

The formula for the breakeven point in units is

$$\text{Breakeven point} = \frac{\text{Total fixed cost}}{\text{Price} - \text{Variable cost per unit}}$$

By definition the breakeven point is where

$$
\begin{aligned}
\text{TR} &= \text{TC} \\
\text{P} \times \text{Q} &= \text{FC} + \text{VC} \\
\$28 \times \text{Q} &= \$4{,}000 + (\$8 \times \text{Q}) \\
\$28Q - \$8Q &= \$4{,}000 \\
\$20Q &= \$4{,}000 \\
Q &= 200
\end{aligned}
$$

Multiplying the breakeven point in units by the selling price we get $\$28 \times 200 = \$5{,}600$. Thus $5,600 is the amount of total revenue required to break even in this scenario.

Figure 18–3 is a breakeven chart for Sleep Inn. The number of units (rooms occupied) is measured on the horizontal scale. Total cost and total revenue are measured on the vertical scale. The product's selling price is $28; therefore the total revenue line moves up $28 each time it moves to the right by 1 unit. If the firm "sells" all 300 rooms, its total revenue is $8,400.

The fixed cost line is a horizontal line at $4,000 on the vertical scale. Because the total cost line starts from the $4,000 fixed cost level, it also measures variable cost at various quantities. If 200 rooms are occupied, the total cost is $5,600: fixed costs of $4,000 and variable costs of $1,600 (200 × $8).

The total cost and total revenue lines intersect at the level of 200 units. This is the breakeven point. Profit increases rapidly beyond this point because the only cost that must be covered for each unit beyond the breakeven point is variable cost.

Breakeven analysis tells the marketer how many units must be sold in order to break even. It does not, however, determine if that volume of sales can be realized. Furthermore, by using only one total revenue line in Figure 18–3, we are assuming that any number of units can be sold at the selling price of $28 per unit. The assumption is unrealistic, however, because the demand curve for the product would have to be perfectly elastic

FIGURE 18–3

A Breakeven Chart for Sleep Inn

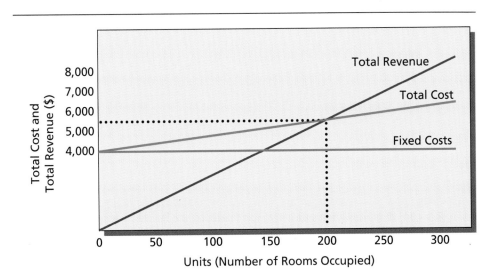

TABLE 18–5   Volume, Cost, and Profit Schedule for Sleep Inn

Price (P)	Quantity (Q)	Total Revenue (TR) (P × Q)	Total Cost (TC) ($4000 + $8Q)	Profit (TR − TC)
$32	180	$5,760	$5,440	$320
30	210	6,300	5,680	620
28	240	6,720	5,920	800
26	260	6,760	6,080	680
24	270	6,480	6,160	320
22	275	6,050	6,200	−150

(horizontal) at that price. This would be highly unusual given that demand curves for most products slope down and to the right.

In situations where the shape of the demand curve is not well known (as is the case for new products) breakeven analyses could be performed for varying prices. Managers could then attempt to determine on the basis of their experience and judgment which combinations of price and breakeven volume levels would be unreasonable. Although Sleep Inn's breakeven point at a price of $28 is 200 units, at a price of $24 it is as follows:

$$\text{Breakeven point} = \frac{\text{Total fixed cost}}{\text{Price} - \text{Variable cost per unit}}$$

$$= \frac{\$4,000}{\$24 - \$8}$$

$$= 250 \text{ rooms}$$

If management believes it is easier to attract 250 occupants at a price of $24 than to attract 200 at a price of $28, it might opt for the lower price.

If we have some estimate of the demand schedule, we will probably be concerned not with breakeven analysis but with the assessment of the cost and profit implications of each price. Table 18–5 provides a volume, cost, and profit schedule for each price under consideration by Sleep Inn. Such a schedule allows management to identify the most profitable list prices, assuming that the demand schedule is accurate. Additionally, with today's personal computers and spreadsheet programs, managers can do what-if analyses to determine the profit consequences of modest errors in demand schedule estimates.

SELECTING THE LIST PRICE

Once the demand, cost, and profit estimates have been made, managers can better understand the potential consequences of various list prices. These estimates will also help managers judge how effective a given list price will be in achieving pricing objectives.

Other considerations are also involved in finalizing the list price decision. In firms that sell through intermediaries, managers must usually determine whether a price change will be accepted by an intermediary. As we will see in the last section of the chapter, price decisions made by intermediaries are affected by the price decisions made by manufacturers.

Managers might also want to have any price changes reviewed by the firm's legal department. The major legal issues associated with price decisions are discussed in chapter 19, along with other aspects of price administration. The Ethics in Marketing box examines some of the ethical questions involved in pricing.

Two special cases of list pricing are new-product pricing and pricing by intermediaries.

NEW-PRODUCT PRICING

One of the most important pricing decisions a firm will ever make is how to price a new product. This is especially critical when the new product is substantially different from

ETHICS IN MARKETING

Many ethical issues arise in the area of pricing, especially when firms use price to underscore an image of high quality or of being the low-priced alternative. Do sellers have any ethical obligations in the area of pricing when they believe buyers rely on price as an indicator of product quality? Is it ethical to set an inordinately high price on a product to convey the impression that the product is higher in quality than it really is?

What ethical issues are involved when retailers advertise ''we won't be undersold'' or ''lowest prices guaranteed''? What do these phrases mean? Does ''lowest prices guaranteed'' mean that the retailer's price is the lowest it has ever charged? That the price is the lowest compared with competitors' prices? Or that the retailer will match any competitor's advertised price? What ethical obligation does the retailer have to divulge the meaning of ''guaranteed lowest prices''?

What about retailers who advertise markdown prices? Is it ethical to use artificially inflated regular prices to create the false impression that the markdowns being offered are very large?

Some industries face additional ethical complexities when making pricing decisions. In the pharmaceutical industry, for example, firms may commit vast sums of money to research and development on a drug, and these sums must be recovered in order for the firm to do more research that will lead to other new products. But often the drugs are sold at prices that many patients cannot afford.

Genentech spent $150 million to develop the drug TPA (tissue plasminogen activator), which helps clear blood clots that cause heart attacks. But the price per dose was $2,200. And Sandoz Pharmaceutical developed a drug to treat schizophrenia. But because of potential side effects, users must be monitored through regular drug tests, which are conducted with a blood-monitoring system controlled by Sandoz. As a consequence the annual cost of treatment was as high as $9,000 per patient when the product was first introduced.

Sources: Information from Joan O'C. Hamilton, ''Genentech: A Textbook Case of Medical Marketing,'' *Business Week,* August 13, 1990, p. 96; Andrew Purvis, ''Way Out of Reach,'' *Time,* October 1, 1990, p. 79.

existing ones in the marketplace. Because direct comparisons are difficult to make in such situations, firms generally have more latitude in setting the price than they will once directly competing versions enter the market. The two pricing strategies for introducing a new product are price skimming and penetration pricing.

Price Skimming

price skimming

The practice of setting an introductory price relatively high in order to attract buyers who are not concerned with price and to recover research and development costs quickly is *price skimming*. In effect, the firm is skimming the top off the market. Early marketers of compact disc players, video games, and personal computers used the skimming strategy.

One practical advantage of skimming is that it is easier to cut a price that is too high in order to be more in line with demand than it is to raise a price. Thus firms that have little knowledge of the demand curve are usually advised to employ skimming and then to gradually reduce prices until a satisfactory level of sales is achieved.

There are, however, a number of other criteria for choosing between price skimming and penetration pricing, as Table 18–6 indicates. Specifically, demand may be inelastic if the new product offers a major improvement in customer satisfaction. Or a firm may not have sufficient capacity to expand production in order to meet a larger volume of demand. Because a high price generates higher revenues per unit, skimming may allow a firm to recover its initial investment before the product becomes technologically obsolete. On the other hand, a high price may attract competitors into the market. Thus skimming is often safer from a competitive point of view when the innovator has a patent or when other barriers to entry (such as extremely high investment requirements) already exist.

Penetration Pricing

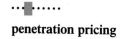

penetration pricing

The practice of setting an introductory price relatively low to gain deep market penetration quickly is *penetration pricing*. In this type of pricing, the expectation is that demand is elastic, often because a number of substitute products offer relatively similar benefits. Even if the new product is innovative, the firm may believe that demand is elastic because the rate of use or consumption might increase if the price is low. For example, people might buy an innovative new sugar substitute more frequently if the price were low.

For innovative new products the market impact of skimming and penetration pricing also seems to depend on the amount of word-of-mouth communication. If such communication is strong, the speed of the diffusion process can be accelerated by lower prices, which (as we discussed in chapter 10) encourage faster trial and adoption. If word-of-

TABLE 18–6   Choosing between Skimming and Penetration Pricing

Criteria	Conditions Favoring	
	Skimming	Penetration
Demand curve	Inelastic	Elastic
Economies of scale or experience curves	Absent	Extensive
Rate of technological change	High	Low
Recovery of investment	Fast	Slow
Barriers to competitive entry	Substantial	None
Production capacity	Limited	Extensive

mouth communication is expected to be weak, price skimming more will likely be the superior choice.[10]

As Table 18–6 shows, managers need to consider other criteria too, the most important of which is economies of scale. If economies of scale allow a firm to drive average costs downward, profitability is enhanced. Additionally, if the firm keeps prices low, the incentive for potential competitors to enter the market will be reduced.

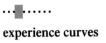

experience curves

Declining costs also can occur because of the existence of experience curves. *Experience curves* are reductions in the per-unit cost of a product that occur over time as the cumulative volume of output (and therefore experience) increases. As the cumulative production volume of a product increases, the per-unit cost of producing it will decline at a predictable rate because of the accumulated experience in producing the product. Managers will develop specialized processes to cut costs, workers will become more productive, plant layout will become more efficient, the work flow will proceed more smoothly, and so on. Depending on the industry and the firm, per-unit production costs might decline 15 to 30 percent every time cumulative production doubles.

If this effect exists, a firm will want to gain the highest market share in its industry as quickly as possible. Thus the penetration pricing strategy should reward the firm with a large market share and declining per-unit production costs as the share grows larger. Because the firm expects per-unit production costs to go down as the share grows larger, the price may be set on the basis of expected future costs rather than on the basis of current costs. This would enable the firm to reduce its price and further discourage potential rivals from entering the market.

From a practical point of view the experience curve theory has little meaning if the output cannot be sold. Concentrating too much on reducing per-unit production costs (a production orientation) may in fact lead the firm to overlook target customer wants—perhaps for a redesigned version of the product—in order to pursue further cost decreases.

PRICING BY INTERMEDIARIES

Cost-plus pricing is the most widely used approach among retailers and wholesalers when setting list prices. Specifically, intermediaries set prices based primarily on the prices they pay to manufacturers. In effect they employ target margin pricing, with the target margin known as the markup.

Markup Calculations

markup

A *markup* is an addition to the cost of a product to reach a selling price. Thus if an electronics store buys a videotape for $4.50 and sells it for $6.00, the markup is $1.50. Retailers and wholesalers hope the markup will cover their operating expenses (salaries, rent, and so on) as well as providing a profit from the sale of the product.

Markups are usually expressed as percentages. For example, the $1.50 markup could be expressed two ways. It could be expressed in relation to cost, as follows:

$$\text{Markup percentage on cost} = \frac{\$ \text{ amount added to cost}}{\$ \text{ cost}}$$

$$= \frac{\$1.50}{\$4.50}$$

$$= 33\tfrac{1}{3}\%$$

It could also be expressed in relation to selling price, as follows:

$$\text{Markup percentage on selling price} = \frac{\$ \text{ amount added to cost}}{\$ \text{ selling price}}$$

$$= \frac{\$1.50}{\$6.00}$$

$$= 25\%$$

Suppose the cost of a videotape is $4.50 and the desired markup percentage on cost is 33⅓ percent. Given this information, we can arrive at the selling price. Since the markup is calculated on the basis of cost, the cost is 100 percent. Thus to determine the selling price we simply fill in the boxes in the following equation. The dollar markup is 33⅓ percent of $4.50, or $1.50; and the selling price is $6.00, or 133⅓ percent of cost.

Selling price	−	Cost	= Markup
Percent [133⅓%]	−	100%	= 33⅓%
Dollars [$6.00]	−	$4.50	= [$1.50]

Now suppose the cost of a videotape is $4.50 and the desired markup percentage on selling price is 25 percent. What price should be set on the item? Since the markup is calculated on the basis of selling price, the selling price is 100 percent. Again the task is to fill in the boxes.

Selling price	−	Cost	= Markup
Percent 100%	−	[75%]	= 25%
Dollars [$6.00]	−	$4.50	= [$1.50]

The dollar markup on a product therefore represents the margin that the intermediary has set as a target. The term *gross margin* is also used to represent the difference between selling price and unit cost.

Calculating Markdown

markdown

Although retailers and wholesalers use cost-plus pricing in setting initial offering prices, if customers do not buy at these prices, the prices will be lowered. Thus intermediaries are also concerned about demand in pricing their products.

A *markdown* is a reduction in the original price set on a product. For example, if our retailer sells some videotapes at $5.70 instead of $6.00, the markdown percentage is figured as follows:

$$\text{Markdown percentage} = \frac{\text{Markdown}}{\text{Net sales price}}$$

$$= \frac{\$.30}{\$5.70}$$

$$= 5.3\%$$

Notice that the markdown percentage is figured on the basis of the new selling price, not the original asking price.

Markdowns are especially important to retailers. Managers of the various departments in a department store are often evaluated in part by the average markdown percentage on the merchandise in their departments. For example, a department manager with a high markdown ratio ($ markdown divided by $ sales) may be buying merchandise that is not what target customers really want.

The markdown calculation shown here reflects the procedure generally used for internal business purposes. From the consumer's point of view the real savings is $.30 ÷ $6.00 = 5 percent. Thus in promoting markdowns, managers should calculate the percentage off on the basis of the original selling price.

Markup Strategies

In selecting a price each intermediary generally relies on an assessment of competitors' prices and on a markup strategy. A *markup strategy* is a policy that governs the size of the markup on the cost of a product.

markup strategy

Some firms, including discount retailers, establish small markups in the expectation that prices will be very competitive and consumers will be price-sensitive. Other firms set higher markups in the belief that price competition will not be as keen. In addition, intermediaries will consider the stock turnover rate when setting wholesale or retail prices.

The *stock turnover rate* is the number of times per year the average inventory (beginning + ending inventory ÷ 2) is sold. The lower the turnover rate, the greater the inventory carrying cost. An inventory that has a turnover rate of 1 ties up five times as much working capital as one that has a turnover rate of 5. A low turnover rate could result from carrying an assortment of products that is not satisfying target customers. In general, products with a seasonal demand pattern, those with a very low repeat purchase frequency, and those that are slow sellers have a relatively low stock turnover rate.

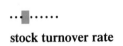

stock turnover rate

When inventory is carried at cost, the formula for determining the stock turnover rate is

$$\text{Stock turnover rate} = \frac{\text{Cost of goods sold}}{\text{Average inventory at cost}}$$

Suppose a retailer maintains a gross margin of 30 percent on net sales of $2,000,000 during a year. The cost of goods sold is therefore $1,400,000.

Net sales	$2,000,000	
− Cost of goods sold	− 1,400,000	(70% of net sales)
Gross margin	$ 600,000	(30% of net sales)

If the inventory (carried at cost) at the beginning of the year is $250,000 and the inventory (carried at cost) at the end of the year is $325,000, the average inventory is ($250,000 + $325,000) ÷ 2 = $287,500. Thus the stock turnover rate is

$$\frac{\$1,400,000}{\$287,500} = 4.87$$

When inventory is carried at the selling price, the formula for determining the stock turnover rate is

$$\text{Stock turnover rate} = \frac{\text{Net sales}}{\text{Average inventory at selling price}}$$

Assume the following for a retail store:

$1,000,000 net sales
   $300,000 beginning inventory carried at selling price
   $200,000 ending inventory carried at selling price

Thus the stock turnover rate is

$$\frac{\$1,000,000}{(\$300,000 + \$200,000) \div 2}$$

$$\frac{\$1,000,000}{\$250,000} = 4.0$$

An understanding of markup strategies is also important to manufacturers that sell through retailers. In establishing a price to charge retailers, manufacturers must allow the retailers to achieve a markup consistent with their needs.

SUMMARY OF LEARNING OBJECTIVES

1. Explain the two roles of price in buyer decision making.
The allocation role of price is the function price performs in helping buyers decide how to derive the greatest expected utility from their buying power. The information role of price is the function price performs in educating consumers about product factors such as quality.

2. Outline a procedure a firm might follow in setting a product's list price.
A logical approach to setting a list price would include the following steps: (1) setting the pricing objective, (2) estimating demand at various prices, and (3) establishing cost-volume-profit relationships.

3. Identify the basic objectives marketers can pursue through pricing.
Pricing objectives can be of four types. Profit-oriented objectives include profit maximization, target margin, and target return on investment. Volume-oriented objectives include sales maximiza-

tion and market share maximization. Image-oriented objectives include quality image and a value image. Stabilization objectives are set when minimal changes in prices are desired.

4. Understand the relationships among price, total revenue, and elasticity of demand.
Price elasticity of demand is the degree to which sales volume changes in response to changes in price. If an increase (decrease) in price results in a decrease (increase) in total revenue (price times quantity) demand is said to be elastic. If an increase (decrease) in price results in an increase (decrease) in total revenue, demand is said to be inelastic.

5. Understand the relationships among cost, volume, and profit.
Prices influence volume, and volume influences costs and total revenue. Although fixed costs are independent of volume, variable costs change in relation to volume. Spreading fixed costs over more volume (a larger number of units) creates economies of scale.

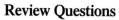

Review Questions

1. What are some examples of purchases in which the information role of price would be emphasized?

2. How does a target return on investment policy differ from a volume-oriented policy?

3. Why would a firm establish an image-oriented objective instead of a profit-oriented objective?

4. How is a firm's total revenue affected when it raises the price of a product that has a highly price elastic demand?

5. Is advertising a fixed or a variable cost? Explain.

6. What are economies of scale? What do they have to do with pricing?

7. How does price skimming differ from penetration pricing?

8. Why do intermediaries usually vary the markup according to the rate of stock turnover?

Discussion Questions

1. Can a person be price-sensitive in buying some products and virtually ignore price in buying other products? Explain.

2. Would the information role of price likely be greatest for buying a watch, an automobile, or a physician's services? Explain.

3. In which of the following industries would you expect the greatest degree of price competition: frozen orange juice, ice cream, or paper plates? Explain.

4. In retailing, budget-oriented stores such as Wal-Mart and swanky stores such as Neiman Marcus are prospering while traditionally middle-level stores such as Sears are having difficulties. Can you offer any reasons for this?

5. A manufacturer of portable radios will incur fixed costs of $10 million to produce a particular model. Variable costs per radio are expected to be $4 each. Calculate breakeven volumes if the radio is sold at $9, at $8, and at $6.

6. Is skimming or penetration used in pricing compact disc players? What would you have recommended?

Application Exercise

Reread the material on hotel and motel pricing at the beginning of the chapter and answer the following questions:

1. What type of pricing objective would you adopt if you were entering this market today? Explain.

2. Why might different competitors adopt different price policies in this market?

3. What factors might cause demand shifts in this industry?

Key Concepts

The following key terms were introduced in this chapter:

list price
allocation role of price
information role of price
perceived value pricing
profit maximization
target margin
target return on investment
volume pricing objective
image pricing objective

price stabilization objective
demand schedule
demand curve
price elasticity of demand
cost-plus pricing
fixed costs (FC)
variable costs (VC)
economies of scale

breakeven analysis
price skimming
penetration pricing
experience curves
markup
markdown
markup strategy
stock turnover rate

CASES

Saturn: Good Deals for New Wheels

LYN S. AMINE, *St. Louis University*

General Motors' new company, Saturn, was named after NASA's Saturn Rocket and is the first new U.S. car line in thirty years. The company's mission is to market automobiles developed and produced in the United States that are world leaders in quality, cost, and customer satisfaction. Specific marketing goals are threefold: (1) to capture current import car owners and import purchase "intenders," many of whom might also consider "buying American"; (2) to compete head-to-head with Japanese compact cars; and (3) to sell 80 percent of Saturn production to import buyers. Saturn is positioned to offer the reliability associated with Japanese small cars and the performance of European touring sedans. Thus, the new Saturn models are designated as *sports sedans*.

The Saturn project was launched in June 1982 and the first test vehicle was ready by September 1984. In 1985 GM Chairman, Roger Smith, announced that GM would invest $5 billion in the all-new Saturn plant to be located in Spring Hill, Tennessee. Six thousand "team members" would be employed, all on salary, and the production goal was to be 500,000 cars a year. In October 1990, Saturn dealerships in the West and Southwest opened their doors for business.

Management and workers operate under a consensus decision-making program which replaces the traditional bureaucratic "us versus them" model prevalent in the U.S. automobile industry. TV and print advertising feature individual workers by name and title who explain what Saturn means to them in terms of their dedication to the creation of a world-class automobile. Saturn dealerships are designed to promote a soft-sell atmosphere which encourages browsing. Saturn salespeople are trained to provide a high level of customer information and service, and car sales are based on a "constant price" concept, replacing traditional adversarial price dickering.

The goal for Saturn was "to perfect simplicity" by offering a good, reliable, well-designed, and exceptionally engineered automobile that would be a significant, price-value contender in the marketplace. Thus, each of the four models—SL, SL1, SL2, and SC—includes many standard equipment features normally found on higher-priced cars. The "popularly equipped" prices for each 1990–91 Saturn model range from a low of $9,215 for the SL to a high of $14,345 for the SC.

GM has chosen to position its new car line not as a luxury line, but as a range of cars for everyone, offering the highest possible value for money. Early on in the seven-year development period, a GM executive stated that Saturn would be priced "somewhere between a Maserati and a Yugo." The question remains whether this new product pricing strategy will effectively accomplish GM's goals of winning over import buyers.

Questions

1. What strategy do you think is being used to position and promote Saturn—skimming or penetration? Why do you think GM chose this strategy?

2. What pricing objective—profit, volume, image, or stabilization—do you think is being pursued by GM?

3. What cues about quality, status, and performance do consumers receive from a new car price that is closer to the price of a Yugo than a Maserati?

4. Do you think Saturn's price/quality message will be sufficient to win over import buyers? Explain.

Quaker State Corporation

JOHN W. GILLETT, *University of North Dakota*
DENNIS J. ELBERT, *University of North Dakota*

Three years ago, five major brands dominated the retail oil market: Pennzoil Products Co., Houston, TX; Quaker State Corp., Oil City, PA; Valvoline Oil Co., Lexington, KY; Havoline (Texas Lubricant Co.), Houston, TX; and Castrol Inc., Wayne, NJ. These five, together with a few private brands, are all retail oriented and bitter rivals. Quaker State and Pennzoil were the top two brands.

What was a highly competitive market then has become even more competitive today as other oil companies have joined the marketplace. In addition, technology—in the form of smaller crankcases, better oils, and new quick-lube operations—has been reducing traditional retail sales, resulting in slower market growth. Without market growth, oil suppliers must steal market share from each other to increase sales. This has resulted in oil companies using extensive advertising, slicing prices, and using many promotions to bring in new or to keep their old customers. Many experts in the oil business believe that price is the major factor in oil sales and any other factors are a distant second.

In 1988, in the face of these circumstances and under the direction of Chief Executive Jack W. Corn, Quaker State adopted a new marketing strategy. Mr. Corn quit the motor oil pricing war, insisting that Quaker State's quality image justified higher prices. The results of this refusal to match rivals' discounting were swift and severe. Quaker State's market share, more than 22 percent five years ago, plunged to about 14 percent, putting it well behind Pennzoil and just ahead of other brands that discount their oil. Quaker State still maintains that a high-end market strategy will prevail; that is, quality motor oil will win out over price.

Quaker State has continued to develop its quick-lube market while sticking with their quality philosophy. Quaker owns Minit-Lube, the number-two quick-lube outlet with shops in more than twenty states. Quaker State has fairly recently acquired McQuik's Oilube Inc., an Indiana chain of quick-lube outlets. They have continued to expand Minit-Lube shops through an agreement with Montgomery Ward & Co. Auto Express stores to install Minit-Lube outlets in selected stores. This will add shops in Michigan, California, Ohio, and Kansas, among others. The move enables Quaker State to expand its Minute-Lube unit without the cost of opening new outlets. It gives the company a presence in high-traffic shopping malls.

On the international front, Quaker State entered the Canadian market through a joint venture with a Canadian quick-lube operator. The new venture, Minit-Lube Ontario Inc., is owned jointly by Canadian quick-lube entrepreneurs Peter and George Walsh of Waterloo, Ontario, and Quaker State. Plans call for rapid expansion in southern Ontario with company-owned and franchise operations with Quaker State partly guaranteeing financing for the outlets which will feature Quaker's motor oil.

Quaker State can control their own quick-lube shops. However, the typical auto parts and supply store wants to carry only four to six brands. The shelf line-up is usually the classic retail brand and a high-end specialty oil. The current trend is to drop, not to add brands. Typically, retailers carry only one or two complete lines. At present, there seems to be no simple solution. The retail oil market remains very competitive.

Questions

1. What pricing objective is Quaker State pursuing?

2. Given Quaker State's reduced market share, demand appears to be elastic. How could we more precisely determine whether demand is elastic?

3. Are there any advantages to retailers from Quaker's pricing strategy?

19

PRICE
ADMINISTRATION

OBJECTIVES

After reading this chapter you will be able to

1. identify the various types of discounts and allowances.

2. give examples of geographic price policies.

3. explain how price promotions can be used for targeted marketing.

4. identify the options available in setting prices for a line of related products.

5. contrast competitive bidding and negotiated contracts.

The $9 billion domestic air express business was largely created by Federal Express. This pioneering company still dominates the market, with a 48 percent share of next-day and second-day delivery of letters and light packages. Among its significant competitors are Airborne (9.2 percent), Emery (6 percent), and the U.S. Postal Service (3.2 percent). Federal Express's main challenger, however, is United Parcel Service (UPS), whose share has climbed to 26 percent.

Although UPS has not fully matched Federal Express's level of service, by 1991 it was guaranteeing next-day delivery by 10:30 A.M. to more locations than was Federal Express. It was also attempting to catch up to Federal Express with regard to on-demand pickup of packages and Saturday deliveries.

At the same time, UPS had come to recognize the significance of price in this industry. Because the company has very little debt and a large ground delivery service that already contacts many businesses, its costs per pickup are quite low. Consequently it was well positioned to initiate a policy of price discounts aimed at drawing away some Federal Express customers.

Specifically, UPS offered 10 to 20 percent reductions in price to many of its larger customers that ship large volumes of packages. Also, although the company made some increases in list price at the end of 1990, industry observers saw this as a way to offset the discount policy for frequent users. Yet to be determined was whether UPS would be similarly aggressive in seeking business that involved competitive bidding. While UPS was initiating its new pricing policies, Federal Express was successfully bidding on $50 million in federal government next-day delivery service.[1]

Price administration is the process of making adjustments to list prices. These adjustments—including discounts and competitive bidding—have become important aspects of air express companies' marketing strategies.

In this chapter we will examine a variety of price administration decisions. Managers involved in pricing must consider not only price promotions for consumers but discounts and allowances and freight charges for intermediaries and organizational buyers. In addition they must consider the impact of price changes on other goods and services they offer. Finally, many firms must also consider price customization for individual buyers and the special circumstances faced by professionals and nonprofit organizations.

DISCOUNTS AND ALLOWANCES

Reductions from list prices that enable marketers to adjust their actual prices without changing their published prices are *discounts and allowances*. Industrial marketers, for example, often revise their discount sheets rather than print new catalogs. The following are examples of discounts and allowances: (1) quantity discounts, (2) trade discounts, (3) cash discounts, (4) brokerage allowances, (5) promotion allowances, and (6) push money allowances.

Quantity Discounts

Marketers offer quantity discounts to encourage customers to remain loyal buyers or to place larger orders. A discount can be based on the dollar value of purchases or on the number of units purchased. The two types of quantity discounts are cumulative and noncumulative.

Have you ever shopped at a going out of business sale? What ethical issues might arise in the pricing of products at such a sale?

[© Freda Leinwand]

- **Cumulative Quantity Discount** • A deduction from list price that applies to the buyer's total purchases made during a specific period of time and intended to encourage customer loyalty is a *cumulative quantity discount*. The buyer's purchases are totaled at the end of the period and the discount received depends on the quantity (dollars or units) bought during that period. The discount percentage usually increases as the quantity purchased increases. This type of discount has a promotional impact because it rewards a customer for being a loyal buyer. It is also called a *patronage dividend*.

···■·····
cumulative quantity discount

Cumulative quantity discounts have been used in industries as diverse as automobiles and computers, with the discount period lasting up to a year or even more. Often the discounts are termed *volume purchasing agreements* and continue for special long-term contractual periods.

Pharmaceutical manufacturers, for example, are increasingly faced with the prospect of selling to large-volume buyers (such as hospitals), which often demand 30 to 40 percent discounts because of their large cumulative volumes. Another large customer, Medicaid, has historically received modest discounts even though it pays the cost of millions of prescriptions. But industry leader Merck recently agreed to a discount formula with Medicaid officials in various states that will cost the company $30 million per year in the short run.[2]

- **Noncumulative Quantity Discount** • A deduction from list price that applies to a single order rather than to the total volume of orders placed during a period of time and that is intended to encourage orders in large quantities is a *noncumulative quantity discount*. The size of this discount generally increases with the size of the order. The purpose is to reward buyers whose purchase patterns help the seller reduce costs. Specifically, as the size of the buyer's order increases, the seller can ship the product in a more efficient way. For example, UPS offers lower rates to companies that are big users because if a courier can pick up one hundred packages on a trip rather than, say, seventy-five, UPS's cost per package will decline. Similarly, it costs a furniture manufacturer less money to ship if each truck is fully loaded with products for a single retailer than if each truck has to deliver to several destinations. Table 19–1 contrasts cumulative and noncumulative discounts.

···■·····
noncumulative quantity discount

TABLE 19–1 ▪ Cumulative and Noncumulative Quantity Discounts

Cumulative	Noncumulative
With a cumulative quantity discount, the buyer's purchases are added up over the year and the discount percentage applies to the total volume of purchases made during the year. A buyer who purchased five hundred cases during the year would be entitled to a 7 percent discount from list price.	A buyer who places a single order for twelve cases gets a 2 percent discount from list price on that particular order. But suppose instead that the buyer places fifty orders for ten cases each over the period of a year. Under a noncumulative quantity discount, the buyer would not receive any quantity discount during the year.

Cases Purchased during Year	Discount Percentage	Cases Purchased on Individual Order	Discount Percentage
1–50	0.0	1–10	0.0
51–125	2.0	11–25	2.0
126–250	4.0	26–40	3.5
Over 250	7.0	Over 40	6.0

Trade Discounts

trade (or functional) discount

A reduction in list price granted to a channel member for performing marketing services is a *trade (or functional) discount*. Suppose the manufacturer of a product that retails for $200 quotes trade discounts of 30 percent and 10 percent. The price to wholesalers is the retail price less discounts of 30 and 10 percent. Each discount percentage is figured on the amount remaining after the preceding percentage has been deducted; this is called a *chain discount*. A chain discount of 30 and 10 percent, therefore, does not mean a total discount of 40 percent. The wholesaler gets the 30 and 10 percent discount and is supposed to keep the 10 percent and pass on the 30 percent to the retailer. For example:

Retailer pays wholesaler:	$200 less 30 percent
	$200 less $60
	$140
Wholesaler pays manufacturer:	$140 less 10 percent
	$140 less $14
	$126

Thus the wholesaler's selling price to the retailer is $140. The manufacturer's selling price to the wholesaler is $126.

Cash Discounts

cash discount

A reduction in list price that rewards customers for paying their bills promptly is a *cash discount*. Terms of 2/10, net 30 mean that the buyer can take a 2 percent discount off the invoice price by paying within 10 days of the invoice date. The buyer gets a 2 percent discount for paying the bill 20 days sooner than it is due. Since there are 18 periods of 20 days in a year during which the buyer could earn the 2 percent, the annual percentage rate for *not* taking the discount would be 36 percent. Many buyers will borrow money to take advantage of cash discounts.

Marketers use cash discounts for promotional reasons, to help cut bad debt losses, and to speed up the collection of accounts receivable. They can extend the credit period by forward dating their invoices. Terms of 2/10, net 30 e.o.m. (end of month), for example, mean that the discount period for an invoice dated March 3 runs until April 10. The invoice is treated as if it were prepared on the first day of the month following the invoice date, April 1, instead of March 3. Terms of 2/10, net r.o.g. (receipt of goods) mean that the discount period does not begin until the buyer receives the goods. Cash discounts are computed after deductions for any trade, seasonal, and quantity discounts from the list prices.

Often cash discount policies are modified to help retail customers during weak economic times. In 1990 women's apparel manufacturer Liz Claiborne increased its cash discount to 10 percent for retailers that pay for their merchandise within 10 days of getting it. The goal was to help retailers' profit margins during a period in which retail sales were weakening. Since the industry standard discount was 8 percent, industry observers expected the move to enhance Liz Claiborne's retailer relationships. Many also expected Liz Claiborne would be the first supplier that troubled retailers would pay, which would result in a smooth cash flow for the firm.[3]

Brokerage Allowances

As we saw in chapter 13, brokers are agent intermediaries that do not own title to the products they sell. They are allowed a discount off list price much like the trade discount offered to wholesalers and retailers. A *brokerage allowance* is a discount granted by sellers to brokers for the services (functions) they perform.

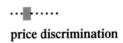

brokerage allowance

Promotion Allowances

Payments made by sellers and reductions from list prices granted by sellers to compensate buyers for performing promotional services are *promotion allowances*. Del Monte, for example, might grant a certain amount of money for each case of its catsup that wholesalers or retailers buy. In turn, wholesalers and retailers would be expected to provide special displays, to feature the product in any local advertising they might do, or to reduce the price to their customers. In practice, many retailers do not always perform the required services, forcing manufacturers to spend time monitoring these programs.

promotion allowances

Trade promotion has grown tremendously in recent years as the battle for shelf space in retail stores, especially in supermarkets, has heated up. Since the mid-1970s the growth in square footage in supermarkets has slowed and scrambled merchandising has led to an increase in the number of nonfood items stocked. The result is stiffer competition for shelf space.

For example, retail food stores usually carry only one line of spices. Thus the major spice company McCormick offers special discounts that range as high as 25 percent off wholesale prices in exchange for one-to-three-year contracts for the shelf space.[4]

Manufacturers whose products have small market shares and that spend little on advertising tend to spend a fair amount on trade promotion. This compensates the retailer for giving additional shelf space to products that lack the pull of consumer demand. It constitutes a push strategy rather than a pull strategy.

Promotion allowances also are used in selling to manufacturers. NutraSweet Company has offered large discounts on its aspartame sweetener to soft-drink manufacturers and other firms that agree to use the red-and-white NutraSweet logo on their products.[5]

Push Money Allowances

As we saw in chapter 11, push money (also called spiffs) is cash or prizes that manufacturers or wholesalers offer their dealers and dealer sales personnel for aggressive selling effort. It can help stimulate the sales of new products, slow-moving products, and high-markup products.

Legality of Discounts and Allowances

Some of the discounts and allowances we have discussed may result in a firm charging different prices to different customers. This can create legal problems, since the Robinson-Patman Act of 1936 outlaws certain types of price discrimination in interstate commerce.

price discrimination

Price discrimination is discrimination that occurs when a manufacturer sells the same product to two intermediaries at different prices or to two industrial buyers at different prices. The type of price discrimination outlawed under the Robinson-Patman Act occurs when a seller knowingly charges different prices to competing resellers or to industrial buyers of "commodities of like grade and quality" when the effect may be to injure competition. The act covers injury to individual customers as well as to competition in general. It also makes it illegal for a buyer to knowingly induce or receive a discriminatorily lower price. This is intended to prevent large buyers from forcing sellers to give them discriminatorily lower prices.

Not all price differentials are illegal, however. Price differentials may be legal when any of the following conditions are met: (1) they do not injure competition, (2) they result from cost differences in selling to different customers, (3) they are used to sell perishable or obsolete products, (4) they are offered in good faith to meet a competitor's equally low price, (5) they are offered to customers that do not compete with one another, or (6) they are offered in conjunction with going-out-of-business sales.

Legal problems ordinarily do not arise with the offering of seasonal and cash discounts or trade-in and damaged goods allowances. Quantity and trade discounts and brokerage, promotion, and push money allowances are more likely to cause problems.

• **Legality of Quantity Discounts** • Marketers should be prepared to justify their discount schedules. Under the Robinson-Patman Act quantity discounts are legal if the resulting price differentials do not exceed the cost differentials in manufacturing, selling, and delivering the product to buyers that are in competition with one another. This cost defense is hard to justify for a cumulative quantity discount; it is easier to defend a noncumulative quantity discount.

• **Legality of Trade Discounts** • The Robinson-Patman Act does not discuss trade discounts specifically. But several court cases seem to uphold the legality of offering separate

GLOBAL MARKETING

Firms exporting overseas generally must modify the discounts they make available to distributors because channel costs and local tax policies can sharply change the final price to the consumer. For example, state and local sales taxes in the United States typically run on the order of 5 to 7 percent, but European value-added taxes (VATs) have historically been in the range of 13 to 19 percent for "standard" goods and as high as 35 to 38 percent for "luxury" goods. Also, gross margins at the retail level tend to be higher outside the United States, reflecting the fact that distribution channels are longer and are composed of smaller-sized firms.

As indicated in chapter 18, the nations in the European Community (EC) agreed to eliminate all trade barriers among its members by 1992. For many years, a major source of revenue for major European airports has been the sale of duty-free products. Indeed, in some cities (for example, Paris) airports have built duty-free malls selling products from Irish

whiskey to Danish furs. Passengers going through the airports can purchase such items without having to pay the home-country VAT—a tax that makes the price of a bottle of Scotch three times more expensive in Copenhagen than at London's Heathrow airport.

Duty-free sales have been a boon both to airports and to manufacturers looking for incremental discount sales volume. However, all this could rapidly change with the elimination of trade barriers among the EC nations. The EC plans to apply a uniform VAT and may eliminate all tax-free markets on the grounds that they are philosophically out of tune with the economic integration of Europe. This would severely limit this particular form of price promotion.

Source: Information from Jean Pierre Jeannet and Hubert D. Hennessey, *International Marketing Management* (Boston: Houghton Mifflin, 1988), pp. 402–404.

discounts to separate classes of buyers as long as the discounts are offered in return for services rendered (marketing functions performed). One discount can be offered to wholesalers and another to retailers. All retailer buyers must be offered the same discount and all wholesaler buyers must be offered the same discount in return for rendering their services.

• **Legality of Brokerage Allowances** • The Robinson-Patman Act makes it illegal for a wholesaler or retailer to receive a brokerage allowance. It also is illegal for manufacturers to pay brokerage fees to a buyer. For example, a large retail chain that performs for itself the services formerly performed by an independent broker cannot legally demand a brokerage allowance from the manufacturer. In practice, however, these allowances sometimes are disguised as promotion allowances to keep large chains as customers.

• **Legality of Promotion and Push Money Allowances** • Sellers are also prohibited from offering various types of promotion allowances and push money unless they offer them to all customers "on proportionately equal terms." For example, a canned goods manufacturer might offer a big supermarket chain an advertising allowance of 5 percent off the cost of its purchase to use in advertising the product. As we saw in chapter 15, this is called cooperative advertising. Under the Robinson-Patman Act, the seller must inform all competing buyers of the allowance and offer them the same percentage.

The seller is also responsible for enforcing any guidelines it establishes regarding performance of the services required for promotion allowances. Moreover, the seller cannot be selective in enforcing these requirements. It cannot threaten to withdraw allowances from some nonperforming intermediaries and allow others to continue to enjoy these allowances.

Discount policies are among the most difficult marketing policies to standardize across national boundaries. Not only are there variations in legal restrictions, but the practicality of various types of discounts can be influenced by tax policies, as the Global Marketing box illustrates.

GEOGRAPHIC PRICE POLICIES

List prices can also be adjusted by the manner in which freight costs are handled. These costs can be paid by the seller, the buyer, or both.

F.o.b. Shipping Point Pricing

When a seller quotes prices f.o.b. (free on board) at the seller's plant or warehouse, the seller pays for loading the freight onto the carrier, at which time title passes to the buyer. *F.o.b. shipping point pricing* is freight cost pricing under which the buyer owns the products while they are in transit, assumes the risks in transporting the products, and pays the entire freight charge.

f.o.b. shipping point pricing

This approach limits a seller's market area because distant buyers will favor nearby suppliers to avoid paying high freight charges. Customer goodwill also suffers when a buyer pays a high freight charge because the seller routed shipments improperly. Quoting prices can be tough for firms that offer a wide product mix to widely scattered customers. Buyers do not know in advance what their delivered prices will be. But the seller receives the same amount of revenue on all sales to customers that buy in the same quantity. This is true regardless of buyers' locations.

Delivered Pricing

Buyers know in advance what their final prices will be when sellers quote *delivered prices*. Three types of delivered pricing are (1) uniform delivered pricing, (2) zone pricing, and (3) basing point pricing.

Under ***uniform delivered pricing or postage-stamp pricing*** all quoted prices include a fixed average freight charge because the seller averages total transportation costs for serving all customers. All buyers pay the same average transportation charge and all are quoted the same delivered price. Thus nearby buyers pay more than the actual cost of shipping to them (phantom freight charges). Distant buyers, on the other hand, pay less than the actual cost of shipping to them because the seller absorbs some of the freight cost. This approach is practical when the freight cost is low in relation to a product's value. It also enables sellers to quote only one price in their national advertising.

Zone pricing is a type of uniform delivered pricing in which buyers in a given zone pay the same delivered price but buyers in different zones pay different delivered prices. A seller who quotes prices that are "slightly higher west of the Mississippi River" is using a two-zone pricing system. Any number of zones could be used, however. Zone pricing is more practical than totally uniform delivered pricing (or one-zone pricing) when the freight cost is large in relation to a product's value. Phantom freight charges and absorption of freight charges by the seller still exist under zone pricing. (See Figure 19–1.)

Basing point pricing is a type of delivered pricing in which prices include freight charges from chosen locations (basing points) regardless of the actual location from which the product will be shipped. It started in the steel industry, which developed in the Pittsburgh area. Each steel producer quoted prices f.o.b. shipping point, which meant distant buyers paid higher prices than local buyers. This stimulated the construction of new mills

uniform delivered pricing (or postage-stamp pricing)

zone pricing

basing point pricing

FIGURE 19–1

Zone Pricing

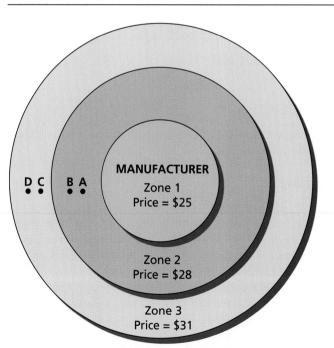

The delivered price for customers A and B in Zone 2 is $28.
The delivered price for customers C and D in Zone 3 is $31.
The delivered price for customers in Zone1, where the manufacturer is located, is $25.

in places such as Chicago and Birmingham, Alabama, that were closer to steel buyers in those areas. Thus Pittsburgh mills could sell in the Chicago area only if they absorbed the freight differences between the Chicago and Pittsburgh mills. Sellers often wanted to broaden their market areas to spread their fixed costs over a wider range of production. But because total industry demand tended to be highly price inelastic, price competition would develop and reduce all rivals' revenues.

Thus steel industry leaders set up a basing point pricing system known as *Pittsburgh-plus*. All mills quoted delivered prices that assumed the steel was being shipped from Pittsburgh. A steel buyer in Jackson, Mississippi, logically would buy from a Birmingham mill even though the delivered price would be identical to that from a Pittsburgh mill. The Pittsburgh mill benefited by being able to sell to more distant customers. The Birmingham mill benefited because it could charge its buyer in Jackson phantom freight from Pittsburgh. This meant extra profit for the Birmingham mill. (See Figure 19–2.)

A single basing point pricing system restricts competition. The steel industry eventually went to a multiple basing point system. Some customers, however, still paid phantom freight because even though the mills they bought from were closer to them, the mills were not basing points. The legality of the basing point system is not entirely clear. Collusion among rivals to set up such a system is illegal; even in the absence of collusion, the system can be illegal. It appears that the presence of phantom freight charges is enough to make the legality questionable.

Freight Absorption Pricing

A firm that wants to penetrate distant markets to maintain or increase market share can practice *freight absorption pricing*—pricing that meets the delivered prices of rivals in distant areas by the seller's absorption of freight costs. This might benefit customers, who

freight absorption pricing

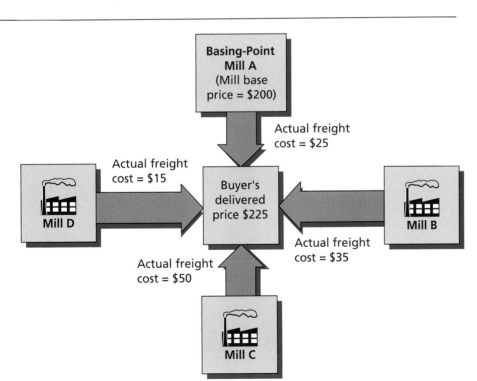

FIGURE 19–2

Basing Point Pricing

would no longer be restricted to buying from local suppliers. The local suppliers might become inefficient if they were insulated from distant rivals.

PRICE PROMOTIONS

In chapter 16 our discussion of sales promotion included a summary of widely used consumer price promotions such as coupons, rebates, and cents-off offers. In effect, these are special discounts off list prices that are used for a limited time to stimulate immediate

**ETHICS IN
MARKETING**

Managers involved in pricing decisions face a variety of ethical questions. Although some pricing practices are clearly illegal (price collusion, for example), frequently the issues are not so clearly drawn.

There is some evidence that airlines may send warning signals about how they will respond to price cuts by competitors. For example, one airline was accused of setting a short-term, very-low-price fare in response to a competitor's reduction to suggest that it planned a price war unless the fare decrease was rescinded. Is such action ethical?

Retailers are not allowed to collude overtly on prices, but they may alert customers, news media, and other interested groups about planned price increases through public speeches or in their advertising. This may allow competitors time to match the price change. On the other hand, retailers may not be so willing to inform customers about impending price *cuts*. Is it ethical for a store to sell a high-priced personal computer or stereo component when the manager knows that the manufacturer is about to sharply reduce prices on that item?

Ethical concerns also arise when price cuts are promoted by retailers. Retailers

that claim to be selling "below cost" are sometimes really receiving a special promotion allowance to offset the special price. Some retailers try to create an illusion of sale prices by setting inflated list prices that are never charged and then advertising the "specials."

Ethical concerns also arise in retailers' dealings with manufacturers. Numerous studies have shown that retailers do not always perform the pricing and promotion activities that manufacturers request in exchange for promotion allowances. Moreover, some manufacturers may offer heavy short-term allowances to get retailers to stock up on a product in an attempt to thwart the introduction of new products by competitors.

Finally, some people believe it is unethical for retailers to attract customers to their stores by advertising very low prices on prestigious brands—prices that manufacturers claim damage their quality image. Others believe ethical issues are involved when shoppers go to full-service retail stores to gather information from sales personnel about such products as stereo equipment and then buy the products from discounters that have no service overhead and can thus sell at much lower prices.

consumer response. They are useful for encouraging the trial of new products and in stimulating inventory movement when sales are sluggish. As the Ethics in Marketing box suggests, however, price promotion policies are often challenged on ethical grounds. Strategically, price promotions are often directed toward and limited to targeted market segments such as types of customers, purchase times, or exchange situations.

• **Customer Type** • Some pure promotions are directed toward specific customer groups that a firm is particularly interested in reaching. When coupons ''good on next purchase'' are included in or on a package of dog food, this usually means the firm is targeting its regular users. Age-based discounts are on the upswing as more firms target the senior citizens' market. A quarter of all the restaurants in the Florida Restaurant Association offer discounts to seniors.[6] The Hertz ad discusses a promotion target at a specific type of business customer.

• **Purchase Time** • Many price promotions are designed to balance sales across peaks and valleys in demand. Termed *off-peak pricing*, this price promotion strategy is widely used by such firms as long distance telephone companies and hotels. Hotels generally target weekends for off-peak pricing discounts. Hilton, for example, ran an $8 million advertising campaign to support its ''Bounceback Weekend'' promotion. Between 1989 and 1991 this

When you're making it on your own, expenses come out of your own pocket. Hertz has your wheels.

Hertz offers special rates and services for independent business people. For more information call 1-800-852-2502.

Hertz
AMERICA'S WHEELS

Hertz rents Fords and other fine cars.

Some price promotions are directed at specific types of customers.

(Copyright Hertz System, Inc., 1990.)

1991 SEDAN DE VILLE–backed by a no-deductible 4-year/50,000-mile bumper-to-bumper warranty† and 24-hour Cadillac Roadside Service.

Special discounts may be made available to customers with different transaction needs, such as different down payment schedules.

(Reprinted with permission of General Motors Corporation.)

promotion enabled Hilton to boost Saturday night from the second worst to the second best night of the week in terms of occupancy rates.[7]

• **Exchange Situations** • Special discounts are often made available to reach customers with special transaction needs. For instance, as the Cadillac ad shows, different automobile promotions, such as financing packages and leases, may target different buyers.

PRODUCT LINE PRICING STRATEGIES

Most firms offer an array of products, and frequently changes in the price of one product will influence demand for complementary or substitute products. A variety of product line pricing strategies may be employed in administering changes from list price. For complementary products, the strategies include leader pricing, mixed bundling, unbundling, and value-added pricing. For substitute products, differential pricing is the basic strategy; but some firms use bait pricing.

Leader Pricing

A retailer's promotion of one product at a sharply reduced price in the expectation that it will attract customers who will then purchase other items is **leader pricing**. The retailer hopes the gain in profits on complementary products will offset the reduced profit on the leader. When the leader is priced below cost, it is known as a *loss leader*.

In selecting effective leaders, sellers should consider products with the following characteristics. The product should be widely used so it will appeal to a wide variety of potential customers. It should be a product that is not easily stocked up on and that is fairly well known so potential buyers will recognize that it is a bargain. There should be a large number of products that complement the leader.

Supermarkets are likely to use milk and hamburger as leaders because of their wide use, perishability, and well-known regular prices. Clothing stores may select sport coats as leaders because they have many complements (slacks, ties, and shirts, for example). McDonald's uses leader pricing when it promotes items such as its hamburger, small shake, and McChicken sandwich, in the hope of selling such high-margin items as french fries and soft drinks.[8]

Mixed Bundling

When a firm is marketing a line of complementary products, it may offer **mixed bundling**—allowing the customer to purchase each of two products separately at their list prices or together at a special price. For example, some banks will offer a VISA or MasterCard credit card at no annual fee to customers who maintain large balances in their savings accounts. Similarly, a washer-dryer combination may be priced below the prices of the two products purchased separately.

The idea behind bundling is to reach a segment of the market that is not effectively reached when the products are sold separately. Some buyers will be more than willing to buy one product but have much less use for the second. Bundling the second product to the first at a slightly reduced price will therefore create some sales that otherwise would not be made.[9]

Unbundling

Another approach is to change the bundle of services that accompanies the basic product. Rather than raise the price of hotel rooms, some hotel chains have started charging registered guests for parking. To help hold the line on costs, some department stores require customers to purchase gift wrapping services. Such steps are often referred to as **unbundling**—pricing by which a firm reduces or eliminates certain elements of its market offering and prices the remaining independent elements separately.

In some cases unbundling is no longer optional. The Federal Trade Commission has adopted and is enforcing the rule that funeral directors must provide an itemized list of services to prospective clients so consumers can select only the specific services they want.[10]

Value-Added Pricing

The seller's addition of a special service or complementary product, at no charge, to the product being priced is **value-added pricing**. Often automobile manufacturers offer special options at no charge. In a novel use of that strategy Pontiac began offering to pay half of any Firebird buyer's insurance deductibles for five years. Owners could then opt for larger deductibles, thereby lowering the high insurance premiums that Pontiac officials believed

leader pricing

mixed bundling

unbundling

value-added pricing

You're tempted by the HP LaserJet IIP's impressive print quality. You're amazed by its low price. Just $1,495.* And now that it comes with a free lower paper cassette, you just can't say no.

With 300 dpi print quality, the affordable HP LaserJet IIP printer does your work justice. It delivers laser-sharp text and graphics at a

quiet four pages per minute.

As far as size goes, the LaserJet IIP fits right in. It's easy to use. And, it's compatible with virtually all popular software.

Beyond this, the LaserJet IIP offers you an extra degree of reliability. The reliability you'd expect from the longtime leader in laser printing.

Your free 250-sheet paper cassette, valued at $195,* is available with purchase of the HP LaserJet IIP printer from October 1 to December 31, 1990. So call **1-800-752-0900,**

Ext. 1908 today for your nearest authorized HP dealer.

Here's one urge you can't afford to resist.

© 1990 Hewlett-Packard Company *Suggested U.S. list price. Dealer prices may vary. PE12042

Value-added pricing is an increasingly popular strategy for marketing complementary products.

(Compliments of Hewlett-Packard Company.)

were hindering Firebird sales.[11] The Hewlett Packard ad provides another example of value-added pricing.

Differential Pricing

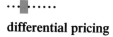

differential pricing

The practice of offering two or more slightly different products (substitutes) at different prices is *differential pricing.* The key to differential pricing is to select the right number of alternatives for meeting the needs of segments with different price-value trade-offs.

For many years differential pricing was greatly simplified by the existence of well-established *price lines* in many industries. Essentially, the various price lines reflected different levels of quality. For example, all lawn mowers might be priced at $79.95, $119.95, or $159.95. With increasing product complexity, however, clearly defined price lines are harder to come by. Setting differentials that are large enough to convey quality differences but small enough to entice customers to trade up is no simple task. In general, the lowest-priced product is more heavily promoted to generate interest and shopping and the highest-priced product is the most profitable.

A major concern in differential pricing is cannibalization, a topic we first addressed in chapter 9. Often low-priced lines are added to meet a competitive threat. But this strategy may backfire if the new line attracts customers from the firm's own higher-priced lines.

Goodyear successfully introduced its All-American Decathlon tires at prices between $27 and $45 depending on size. But profit margins on such tires are only around 8 to 10 percent versus the 25 to 30 percent for premium Goodyear tires, such as the Eagle GT. The risk of cannibalization in this case could be substantial.[12]

Sometimes product differences are limited to differences in package size. In such cases retailers often use *unit pricing*—the practice of breaking down a price in terms of dollars and cents per unit of measure. In supermarkets the price for each product is expressed on the shelf label in terms of dollars and cents per pound, per pint, and so on. This practice enables consumers to do a better job of comparison shopping both within and between product lines.

unit pricing

Bait Pricing

bait pricing

Some retailers use bait pricing with the lowest-priced product in a line of substitutes. *Bait pricing* (also called bait-and-switch pricing) is the practice (often illegal) of advertising a product at a very low price to attract shoppers, only to persuade them to buy a higher-priced item when they respond. For example, a furniture store might advertise a recliner chair at a very low price, but a shopper who comes to inspect the chair will be talked out of buying it by a salesperson who points out its faults and discusses the advantages of buying a higher-priced chair. This bait-and-switch scheme is illegal in interstate commerce. But since it usually is practiced at the retail level in a limited area, the federal law may not apply. Many states, however, also have laws against bait pricing.

CUSTOMIZED PRICING

The needs of a particular customer may be so unique or complex that pricing must be customized to the situation. *Customized pricing* is often used for large customers, for customers

Contractors from many nations typically compete for such huge projects. In such projects, pricing must be customized to the situation.

[© Scott Rutherford]

buying a varied assortment of products, or for products that are custom-designed. It can take three basic forms: price shading, competitive bidding, and negotiated contracts.

Price Shading

The practice in industrial marketing of tailoring the price to the customer's situation is **price shading.** The counterpart in consumer product marketing is the buyer-seller negotiation that often occurs in the purchase of a new car.

As we discussed earlier, such negotiations are prohibited in situations covered by the Robinson-Patman Act. Specifically, price negotiation will most likely be illegal if the customer receiving favored price status is an intermediary in direct competition with other customers. Generally this is not the case in negotiations with final users of the product.

However, several risks are associated with negotiated pricing. Among them is a potential loss of customer goodwill if some buyers learn they paid more than other buyers. Also, salespeople tend to be overly optimistic that price reductions will help them increase sales. Thus their productivity suffers when they devote too much time and effort to price negotiation and not enough to the nonprice elements in their offerings. They may make downward price adjustments (shade prices) routinely, whether or not it helps them close sales. There is also less central control over pricing when salespeople operate under a flexible price policy.

Competitive Bidding

The practice of prospective sellers competing by submitting their prices for goods or services to industrial buyers that are shopping around is **competitive bidding.** The sale could involve a construction project, a physical good, or a service. Competitive bidding requires the seller to have a good accounting system for analyzing costs. Fixed and variable costs must be estimated carefully to avoid the loss that will occur if a bid is accepted and turns out to be too low.

Knowledge of buyer requirements is also necessary. The buyer may present potential sellers with detailed specifications compiled by its purchasing officer, the appropriate department, and technical personnel.

Suppose Apex Plumbing Company wants to bid on a job. Ideally, it wants to know if other firms also will bid and, if so, how many firms, which firms, and what their probable bids will be. Unfortunately, Apex will not likely get this information. In order to achieve its pricing objective, Apex's owner must develop a bid based on the best educated guess about what competitors will do. If the objective is to maximize expected profit, Apex can use a probability approach in its bidding strategy. Suppose Apex's cost estimate for the job is $150,000 and the owner is trying to decide whether to submit a bid of $400,000 or $500,000. Assume that the probability of winning the contract is 60 percent for the lower bid and 45 percent for the higher bid. The formula for expected profit is

Expected profit = P(Bid price − Cost estimate)

where P is the probability of winning the bid. The expected profit on the low bid is $150,000 and the expected profit on the high bid is $157,000. Apex should therefore bid $500,000.

Negotiated Contracts

Some buyers prefer negotiated contracts to competitive bidding. **Negotiated contracts** are an approach to procurement in which the buyer requests bids from several sellers, selects the most attractive (not necessarily the lowest) offering, and then negotiates a contract with the seller—after having had the benefit of consulting with bidders in developing specifications.

Rapidly rising costs pose a problem for marketers that sell products under long-term contracts. A price set in one year may turn out to be too low in the future. Some marketers handle the problem by including in the sales contract an *escalator clause* that ties the price to an industrial index. Another approach is *delayed quotation pricing;* in this approach a final price is set only after the product has been manufactured. This is common in the case of custom-made products that involve long production lead times, such as machine tools.

PROFESSIONAL PRICING

professional pricing

Professionals such as doctors and lawyers often use *professional pricing*—price setting based on the ethical premise that flat fees are more appropriate than fees based on the amount of time spent with individual patients or clients. For example, a routine doctor's office visit might be priced at $40 regardless of how much time the physician spends with the patient.

However, professionals must be careful to avoid restricting price differences through cooperative action—on maximum as well as minimum fees. In the court case *Arizona v. Maricopa County Medical Society* 70 percent of the physicians in the county agreed to a maximum fee schedule and required adherence to the schedule as a condition of membership in the society. However, the Supreme Court stated that even if the objective of the price fixing (containment of medical costs) is beneficial to society, price-fixing agreements made directly by individual providers are illegal.[13]

In recent years some professionals, such as accountants, physicians, lawyers, and dentists, have begun to advertise their fees for specific types of services, including consultation time. This has been encouraged by the Federal Trade Commission. In some cases such advertising has led to price competition among professionals for customers.

The legal industry's standard on contingency fees—in which the lawyer is paid by the client only if a lawsuit is successful—is one-third of the amount awarded. But in many situations—for example, following aviation disasters—lawyers have been known to quote a much lower percentage to prospective plaintiffs.[14]

Whenever the demand for a product is extremely price inelastic, there is the potential for the seller to exploit the buyer. (This is why government agencies regulate rates charged by public utilities.) But a pharmaceutical firm that could charge a very high price for life-extending drugs might instead choose to use ethical pricing. *Ethical pricing* is pricing so as to avoid taking undue advantage of the highly price-inelastic demand for a product.

ethical pricing

PRICING IN NONBUSINESS ORGANIZATIONS

Nonbusiness organizations also make pricing decisions. The U.S. Postal Service, for example, has to set prices for different classes of mail. Similarly, universities set tuition prices, cities set parking meter prices, and state highway authorities set toll road prices. Policymakers appear to believe society is best served by these rates. This, of course, means that any deficits must be made up from other sources of revenue.

Earlier in the chapter we referred to uniform delivered pricing as postage-stamp pricing.

All customers pay the same delivered price regardless of their location. This is the case, for example, with first-class mail. A first-class postage stamp on a letter will take the letter to a receiver across the street or across the nation.

The pricing of some public services can be a means to an end. The cost of car inspections often is set low to encourage car owners to comply with local or state laws designed to keep unsafe cars off the road. High parking fines in congested downtown areas discourage people from taking their cars there. This policy may also help increase the use of mass transit.

SUMMARY OF LEARNING OBJECTIVES

1. Identify the various types of discounts and allowances.
There are quantity discounts, including cumulative quantity discounts and noncumulative quantity discounts; trade, or functional, discounts; cash discounts; brokerage allowances; promotion allowances; and push money allowances.

2. Give examples of geographic price policies.
In f.o.b. shipping point pricing the buyer pays the entire freight cost. In uniform delivered pricing, the quoted price includes a fixed average freight charge. In zone pricing all customers within a particular zone pay the same delivered price but customers in different zones pay different prices. In basing point pricing the prices include freight charges from chosen locations. In freight absorption pricing the seller absorbs the freight costs.

3. Explain how price promotions can be used for targeted marketing.
Customer type price promotions are directed to specific customer groups such as regular users or particular demographic groups. Purchase time price promotions are designed to balance sales across peaks and valleys in demand by offering price cuts at specific times. Exchange situation promotions may be targeted to reach customers with special transaction needs.

4. Identify the options available in setting prices for a line of related products.
Most firms offer an array of complementary or substitute products. For complementary products managers involved in pricing can consider leader pricing, mixed bundling, unbundling, and value-added pricing. Differential pricing is normally used in pricing a line of substitutes, but some firms also use bait pricing.

5. Contrast competitive bidding and negotiated contracts.
In competitive bidding prospective sellers submit prices for goods or services to industrial buyers that are shopping around. Negotiated contracts are an approach to procurement in which the buyer requests bids from several sellers, selects the most attractive offering, and then negotiates a contract with the seller.

Review Questions

1. How do cumulative and noncumulative quantity discounts differ?

2. Assume that the retail price of a product is $100 and the manufacturer quotes trade discounts of 30 percent and 10 percent. What price will the wholesaler pay to the manufacturer? What price will the retailer pay to the wholesaler?

3. Explain the meaning of *3/10, net 30*. Why do some marketers offer cash discounts?

4. What are the relative advantages and disadvantages of f.o.b. shipping point pricing?

5. What are phantom freight charges?

6. Why would a firm practice freight absorption pricing?

7. What are price promotions?

8. What kinds of products make good leaders?

9. Contrast leader pricing and mixed bundling.

10. How is bait pricing related to differential pricing?

11. What is meant by *price shading*?

12. How do competitive bidding and negotiated contracts differ?

Discussion Questions

1. "Promotion allowances stimulate retail price competition by allowing retailers to lower their prices, but quantity discounts ultimately restrict retail price competition because they encourage retailers to buy more of their requirements from one or a few suppliers." Do you agree? Explain.

2. Manufacturers complain that many retailers accept trade promotion allowances but do not provide the expected promotional support in return. If this is true, why would manufacturers continue to offer these discounts?

3. Holiday Inn and other mid-priced motel chains are finding it difficult to keep a full house as the number of competitors increases. What are some kinds of product line pricing strategies that such motel chains might pursue?

4. A catalog marketer offers all-cotton men's chino pants at three prices: $18.50, $34.50, and $51.00. What purpose do the various prices serve?

5. Much of the purchasing by the federal government is done through competitive bidding, but some is done with negotiated contracts. What kinds of goods and services would most likely be purchased through each approach?

6. Is price competition among providers of professional services preferable to professional pricing? Explain.

Application Exercise

Reread the material about UPS at the beginning of this chapter and answer the following questions:

1. From UPS's point of view, what are the relative advantages of offering cumulative versus noncumulative discounts?

2. If UPS decides to use price promotions, what are some likely segments to target?

3. What are some product line pricing options that UPS or its competitors might consider?

4. In pricing to government or large organizations, how feasible is negotiated pricing as opposed to competitive bidding?

Key Concepts

The following key terms were introduced in this chapter:

cumulative quantity discount
noncumulative quantity
    discount
trade (or functional) discount
cash discount
brokerage allowance
promotion allowances
price discrimination
f.o.b. shipping point pricing

uniform delivered pricing (or
    postage-stamp pricing)
zone pricing
basing point pricing
freight absorption pricing
leader pricing
mixed bundling
unbundling
value-added pricing

differential pricing
unit pricing
bait pricing
price shading
competitive bidding
negotiated contracts
professional pricing
ethical pricing

CASES

Mercedes-Benz

Among European luxury automobile makers, only Mercedes-Benz was able to increase its U.S. unit sales during 1990. This sales growth came mostly from cars costing buyers more than $50,000 during a year when a heavy economic recession set in. Mercedes got the message.

During the summer of 1991, the company was to launch a new line of S-class Mercedes. Members of the new S-class line will replace comparable S-class models that Mercedes is retiring from the line, and will carry sticker prices ranging from $60,000 to $90,000, or about 15 to 20 percent more than the retired models. But even as the recession deepened, Mercedes executives pre-

dicted that first-year sales of these cars would amount to about 30,000 units in the United States and 90,000 units globally.

The Mercedes price strategy is based upon past company experiences in the U.S. market. Mercedes suffered setbacks when it introduced the relatively inexpensive—slightly less than $23,000—Model 190 in 1983. At first the car sold well. But soon the U.S. dollar lost strength against the German deutsche mark and Mercedes was forced to raise the 190's U.S. dollar price in order to maintain its profit margins. By 1990 the 190's price had risen to almost $30,000 and Americans were buying only about half as many as they had in 1985. Meanwhile, middle- and top-of-the line Mercedes—whose hefty profit margins allowed Mercedes to swallow the exchange-rate loss—enjoyed unit sales increases. The lesson Mercedes took away: it's not a good idea to raise a price once you've set it.

Another lesson was learned in 1990. That year Mercedes introduced the 300SL—priced at $78,500—and the 500SL—priced at $89,000. These sports cars were priced more than 20 percent higher than the retired SL models they replaced. But huge waiting lines formed for the new cars, and lucky buyers willing to part with their trophies were able to turn around and sell 500SLs for $110,000 almost immediately.

Owners of recent S-line cars who trade up for the 1991 S-line models will get a slightly restyled car body, more room in the back seat, a bit more horsepower, and a few new niceties, including double-glazed windows that reduce both interior noise and windshield condensation. For Mercedes, trading up to the new models will mean hefty profit margins that should more than cushion any future adverse fluctuations in the deutsche mark–dollar relationship.

In early 1991 Mercedes executives were confident that their U.S. unit sales would continue to grow even if the economy slid deeper into recession. If they were wrong, they had a back-up plan: Mercedes sales had been growing even more quickly in Japan than in the United States, and a larger percentage of the cars coming out of Mercedes' German factories would simply be rerouted to Japanese ports.

Questions

1. What market segment is Mercedes trying to target with its pricing policy?

2. If the recession deepens, should Mercedes-Benz consider using price promotions to sell more cars? Explain.

3. Could the introduction of the relatively inexpensive Model 190 in 1983 be considered an example of leader pricing? Explain.

4. Is Mercedes' practice of substantially raising the prices of new model cars that replace comparable old models an example of value-added pricing? Explain.

On the Scent of Success: Oleg Cassini

LYN S. AMINE, *St. Louis University*

In 1978 the famous designer, Oleg Cassini, was introduced to Bernard Mitchell, founder of Jovan Inc., a fragrance producer. Mitchell, a Chicago entrepreneur, started Jovan in 1968 with $100,000 and chose the name Jovan because it sounded like Avon and Revlon and hinted of French origins. Cassini was doing well with a fragrance of his own in Italy but, at the time of his meeting with Mitchell, did not have a perfume line in the United States.

Jovan had typically sold its products through supermarkets and discount stores and was looking for an opportunity to move upmarket into department stores. The meeting proved to be a turning point for both men. Cassini signed an agreement giving Jovan Inc. exclusive rights to the Cassini name in fragrances, cosmetics, toiletries, and beauty aids. It covered ten years and every market in the world except Italy. Cassini was to receive 3.75–4.0 percent of net sales of Jovan's Cassini products. Jovan would benefit by spreading its sales abroad and by being the first company to promote a popularly priced designer fragrance in the United States.

The company hoped to combine mass *and* class. Oleg Cassini was well known in the 1960s as official couturier to the First Lady, Mrs. Jacqueline Kennedy. At the time of the Jovan contract he had thirty-four licensees around the world and received from them annual royalties of $1.2 million.

Sales of the Jovan Cassini line began in June 1979. As the Christmas season began, Cassini was startled to see "tags" on TV commercials indicating local discount stores where the product was on sale. Richard Meyer, CEO of Jovan Inc., had decided to sell the Cassini line through discounters because, as he claimed, he was under pressure to boost profits to satisfy demands of the store owners. In September 1979 Jovan Inc. had been acquired by the British conglomerate, Beecham Group, for $85 million in cash, just three months after the new Cassini product-line launch.

Profit taking continued to be the principal strategy for the Cassini line from 1979 to 1988, when it was finally withdrawn. Advertising support in the first year was just under $2 million. The high level of early sales provided Cassini with almost half a million dollars in royalties, about 40 percent of his total royalty income for that year. By the third year advertising support was down 60 percent to $775,000. It was reduced still further in the following year, 1982–1983, to $560,000. The last TV spot aired in June 1982. In 1983, without Cassini's knowledge, the elegant frosted bottles of the original Cassini fragrance were replaced by clear, stock bottles of a type previously used by another company to sell mouthwash to teenagers. After 1984 advertising support for the Cassini line was completely withdrawn.

The marketing strategy for Jovan's Cassini was a classic example of milking a brand—letting it coast on its own reputation until it finally disappears and using revenues from those sales to support other new products. Jovan Inc., known in the industry as the company of "this year's fragrance," launched Andron and Sculptura on the coattails of Cassini. Then another designer, Diane von Furstenberg, was retained to support a new fragrance, Rouge et Noir. In May 1988 Oleg Cassini sued the company for breach of contract and fraud and was awarded $16 million by a federal jury in New York.

Questions

1. Identify from the case the expectations that Oleg Cassini apparently had regarding price objectives of the new Jovan Cassini line.

2. Recall that first year royalties to Oleg Cassini were $500,000. At a royalty rate of 4 percent, Jovan's total sales that year would have been $12,500,000. (That is, $500,000 ÷ .04.)

Assume that the average price to Jovan dropped from $10 to $8 between 1979 and 1983 and all other variable costs were $2.50 per bottle. What level of sales would be required to cover the cost of advertising in 1979? In 1983?

3. Was any other pricing strategy available to the company to achieve its corporate objectives, other than "milking" the new Cassini brand?

Carnival Cruise Lines: Fun in the Sun

• A Sandy Start •

It's hard to imagine a worse beginning for a new company, but the story goes like this: in the early 1970s, Ted Arison and Meshulam Riklis, Israeli immigrants to the United States from prosperous families, raised $6.5 million to buy the Empress of Canada, a classic cruise liner. They changed its name to the Mardi Gras, and set sail from Miami for the Bahamas with hundreds of travel agents and paying passengers aboard. Thirty minutes later, the Mardi Gras, flagship and only ship of the new Carnival Cruise Lines, ran aground. While their passengers were ferried back to shore in smaller rescue boats, Arison and Riklis counted up their losses.

Although Arison and Riklis were able to repair the Mardi Gras, the story of Carnival's specialty short cruises got around fast. Berths on the Mardi Gras simply didn't sell. By 1975, Carnival Cruise Lines was $5 million in debt and Riklis had enough. He sold his share of the company—and his share of the debts—to Arison for one dollar.

Arison now came up with a new idea. He knew he probably couldn't compete with established cruise companies such as the Cunard, Princess, or Holland America on their own surf. They had fleets of liners, he had one; they had established, classy reputations, he was known for running his ship aground. So instead of competing directly with other cruise lines for vacationers' business, he decided to compete with vacation and entertainment complexes such as Disney World.

"The Mardi Gras was positioned as the flagship of the Golden Fleet," Robert Dickinson, Carnival senior vice president of sales and marketing told *Adweek's Marketing Week*. "But it wasn't golden, and there was no fleet. What we did have was a large ship with three swimming pools. So we created a personality: the Fun Ship."

• The Fun Ship •

Before airplanes, ships were the only way to travel across the oceans. If you were a poor or moderately well-off emigrant, you travelled in the steerage or third-class compartments of ships that had the barest of amenities. But if you were wealthy and needed to travel for business or wanted to winter in a warmer clime or to take a grand tour of another continent, you took ocean liners. These liners were essentially floating first-class hotels that delivered all the services expected of their counterparts on land: luxurious rooms, gourmet dining, bars, dancing, and such activities as lectures, table-tennis, bowling, skeet-shooting, and shuffle-board.

Modern-day cruise ships carried on this old style of travel. The vacationer picked a destination, say a Caribbean island or England. But in accordance with the old style and in contrast to airplane travel, getting there remained half the fun. The dress-up, gourmet dinners, the dancing, the lectures, the skeet-shooting all remained as a way of relaxing away the time it took to reach the port of destination. And prices for such cruises, not surprisingly, reflected this level of luxury.

Carnival's Fun Ship, however, took a completely different tack. "We're not in the cruise business," says Dickinson, "we're in the vacation business." The Mardi Gras, the "Fun Ship," wasn't a way for vacationers to reach a destination: it *was* their destination.

A fairly simple insight led Ted Arison to adopt this new approach. He knew that only a tiny percentage of travellers ever booked a cruise, and that most of these travellers were either quite wealthy or people who had saved for years in order to take such a trip in their retirement. The typical cruise price alone kept many vacationers away. But so did the typical cruise image: sedate, formal, even, in a way, confining—you couldn't get off a liner until it docked, and if you found that the ship's activities or your fellow travellers didn't suit you, you were stuck. On the other hand, Arison knew, a large percentage of people who could afford any kind of vacation at all travelled from everywhere in the nation to such vacation complexes as Disney World and resorts in the Caribbean, Mexico, and Hawaii. Arison's idea was basically to reposition the Fun Ship away from being primarily a means of travel for the well-to-do and toward being a floating resort for the average person.

Rather than taking long cruises to a specific destination, the Mardi Gras set out on four- and seven-day cruises around the Caribbean, making short stopovers in various ports. On the ship, vacationers were treated to an enormous variety of activities ranging from casino gambling, to discos, to endless prix fixe meals and buffets, to swimming and sunbathing, to various contests—including ping-pong and skeet-shooting tournaments and best knobbly-knees and boasting-by-a-grandmother competitions. If they wanted to, they could find a quiet corner of the deck to read in or to sunbathe, a dark corner of the bar for a romantic tête-à-tête. But the emphasis was on providing constant activity for people who wanted to get the most out of their vacation time and money. Every effort was made by the cruise planners and staff to make everything on board comfortable for regular, middle-class Americans of all ages.

Arison also did everything he could to make taking a Carnival vacation easy for first-time cruisers. He put together air–sea packages so that customers could book flights from many cities in the Northeast and Midwest to airports where they were met by ground transportation

taking them straight to the Mardi Gras. Such packages—which were included in the cruise price and could be booked during a single visit to a travel agency—relieved Carnival customers of the hassle of having to figure out flight connections or of having to coordinate the offerings of more than one transportation company. Arison also established good relations with travel agents—often based on promotion programs that brought the agents themselves aboard on free cruises—and set up booking systems that made reserving any of the air–sea packages simple.

Arison's next master stroke was to embark on a huge television advertising campaign on local television stations. His early commercials set the tone for a massive national television campaign launched in 1984 that featured Kathie Lee Gifford singing ''Ain't We Got Fun'' as she engaged in a myriad of Fun Ship activities. These advertisements were instrumental in Arison's plan to dissolve the ''cruises are boring'' image. They were shown frequently

and in all seasons, keeping the Carnival name on people's minds and pounding in the message over and over again that you, too, could afford a Carnival cruise.

• **The Price Is Right** •

And chances were that if you could afford a vacation, you *could* afford a Carnival cruise: Carnival cruises were consistently priced about 20 percent lower than other companies' cruises. A seven-day Carnival air–sea package usually cost about the same as a week's trip to Disney World when round-trip travel, food, and lodging were counted in.

The price of a Carnival cruise was so low because Arison adopted a different pricing method than his competitors, according to his son, Mickey, now CEO of Carnival: ''Our philosophy is that we market the product to be full all the time, so you price it to be full all the time. If you price the product at 100 percent occupancy versus 80 percent [occupancy], right away at the same cost

structure you're pricing 20 percent below your competitors. We've consistently [booked] at 100-plus percent occupancy over the last dozen or so years and because of that, we can confidently price in that fashion.''

One hundred percent occupancy was a vital part of Carnival's overall strategy. It made sure that Carnival's costs were covered so that high service standards were maintained in every facet of its operation. Full occupancy also kept life aboard the Mardi Gras lively and helped to reassure first-time cruisers that they had made the right decision—the same decision hundreds of other people like them had made—about how to spend their vacation. And with hundreds of satisfied cruisers disembarking and returning home full of ''what-I-did-on-my-vacation'' stories every week of the year, word-of-mouth soon began to complement Carnival's aggressive promotion campaign. (It also didn't hurt that *Love Boat,* a long-running prime-time network television show about the adventures of the crew and passengers aboard a cruise liner, helped to popularize the idea that even ordinary middle-class vacationers—albeit fictional ones—could have the time of their lives on a cruise.) Soon, the Arisons had succeeded in convincing tens of thousands of vacationers that it was time to take their first cruise, and to take it on Carnival's Fun Ship.

• Full Speed Ahead •

Profits made on Mardi Gras cruises allowed the Arisons to create an actual Carnival Cruise Lines fleet by buying new liners during the rest of the 1970s and through the 1980s. By

continuing to set prices at a level that insured full occupancy on the entire fleet, Ted and Mickey Arison were able to maintain operating margins and to increase profits every year. In fact, the more profitable Carnival Cruise Lines became, the easier it was for the Arisons to make profits. By expanding the fleet, he introduced economies of scale—achieved in such areas as travel agent promotions, advertising, and the purchase of food and other supplies—that increased the operating margin per passenger. Because the operating margin kept increasing—finally reaching levels as high as 30 percent—Arison was able to hold his price increases to a rate lower than the rate of inflation in the rest of the travel industry. In 1989, prices for a summer cruise on one of Carnival's Fun Ships ranged from $395 to book a lower-deck cabin on a three-day cruise to $2,095 to book a top-deck suite on a seven-day cruise. And these prices included the cost of round-trip air travel from more than 150 cities. Carnival Cruises therefore came to seem more and more of a bargain, which again helped to ensure full occupancy rates even as more ships were added to the fleet. Carnival also used its profits to buy Boeing airliners and hotel chains, both of which were used to cut costs and add value—in terms of both traveller convenience and traveller security in knowing that Carnival was taking care of all the details—to Carnival's cruise packages.

Other factors also contributed to Arison's high operating margins and low prices. Carnival is registered as a corporation in Panama, not the United States, and as a result pays no U.S. corporate income tax. Also, because Carnival isn't an American

corporation, it doesn't have to hire its crews—not the personnel with whom passengers usually come into contact but the people who actually pilot the ships and keep their huge engines running—from the ranks of U.S. maritime unions, which demand comparatively high wages for their members.

• Smooth Sailing Ahead? •

By 1990 Carnival Cruise Lines was the largest cruise company in the world, claiming a $1.4 billion chunk of the $5 billion industry. The company fleet now totalled 15 ships, which transported 953,221 passengers that year. Mickey Arison, now Carnival CEO, stuck to his father's full occupancy formula. Even though 1990 had seen both the advent of a national economic recession and the addition of 15 percent passenger capacity to the Carnival fleet, Carnival occupancy rates for the year remained at their 1989 level of about 106 percent.

Most industry analysts expected Carnival not only to weather the recession, but also to continue to keep up the swift pace of its former growth. Carnival would accomplish this, they said, because it never lost sight of what had made the Fun Ship concept successful in the first place. When Carnival added the $225 million Fantasy cruise ship to its fleet in 1990, for instance, special provisions were made for the care, feeding, and entertainment of children. On a four-day Fantasy cruise, parents paid only $250 for each child sharing a cabin with two adults. For that price, families got not only the expected kiddy pool, video game rooms, cribs, and high chairs, but also a daytime clubroom and evening disco for teen-agers and a children's playroom for younger passengers, a staff of 22 counselors and activity coordinators, dining room and room service menus geared to kids' tastes, and a program of activities—ranging from "pizza pig-outs" to scavenger hunts to Italian lessons—lasting from 10 in the morning until 9:30 at night. Baby sitters were available for $3.50 per hour for parents who wanted some more time to themselves. Such amenities made it even easier and more affordable for middle-class, first-time cruisers to come aboard—they didn't have to worry about their kids back home, and it cost less to bring them along on a Carnival cruise than on most other vacations.

More than 60 percent of Carnival's passengers have never taken a cruise before, and industry analysts estimate that, while 30 million Americans could afford a cruise, only 4 or 5 percent of them have ever taken one. Even though Carnival's competitors have realized that the Arisons are onto a good thing—Norwegian Caribbean rechristened its liners the "Pleasure Ships"; Royal Caribbean equaled Carnival's $15 million national TV advertising budget in 1989; and all cruise lines have started selling air–sea packages—most analysts bet that Carnival has the experience, the reputation, and the resources to guarantee that a huge proportion of inexperienced cruisers will take their first chance on Carnival.

What many analysts are not so sure about is how successful the Arisons will be as they begin to move beyond their tried-and-true business formula. Mickey Arison says that Carnival will always hold on to the affordable Fun Ship concept. But in 1989, Carnival paid $625 million to acquire the Holland America Line. In contrast to Carnival and its imitators, the 116-year-old Holland America had maintained the traditional approach to cruises, including the emphasis on luxurious transport to particular destinations, such as the Alaskan coast (where many passengers went to spot wildlife) and the eastern Caribbean islands. Cruises of the same length were usually priced about a third higher on Holland America than on Carnival. Holland America also served well-to-do vacationers with its Windstar Sail Cruises, three sailing ships offering an even more exclusive vacation experience.

to be headed in the right direction: in its first year under Carnival ownership, Holland America chalked up record profits.

But another Carnival investment—this one on land—seemed a more questionable bet to many analysts. In 1990 Carnival opened its Crystal Palace Resort & Casino in Nassau, the Bahamas. The 150-acre, 1,550-room complex cost Carnival $250 million to develop and is a real change of target audience from the Fun Ships: many of the Crystal Palace's rooms cost more than $180 per night and the Galactica suite—whose staff includes a robot and whose decorations include guest-

---

We . . . price the product to be full all the time.

Carnival's idea was not to convert the Holland America fleet to Fun Ships, according to Mickey Arison: "Holland America is a very upscale line with very first-class service and fine cuisine. We felt as more and more people take Carnival cruises and get hooked on the cruise experience as a way to vacation, then they will want more upscale and more . . . variety in their itineraries . . . and we will have our people trade up to Holland America in the '90s." Until Carnival cruisers do trade up, Arison is counting on the new relationship between the two lines to help both; he has been able to spread advertising and other overhead costs in order to introduce new economies of scale. So far, he seems

selected famous paintings projected on the walls—rents out at $25,000 a night. As with the Holland America purchase, Mickey Arison hopes that many Fun Ship cruisers will eventually become Crystal Palace high rollers. But while all other major divisions of Carnival reported net profits during 1990, the resort lost $10.7 million. Mickey Arison said that although the rest of Carnival seemed to be virtually recession-proof, business at Crystal Palace "continued to deteriorate during the fourth quarter" of 1990 as the recession deepened. Many analysts wondered if the Crystal Palace would prove to be the dragging anchor that would finally slow Carnival Cruise Lines down.

• Questions •

1. What pricing objective does Carnival Cruise Lines have? How is that objective related to Carnival's cost–volume–profit relationship and original new-product pricing strategy?

2. Do you think that the Arisons considered the price elasticity of demand when devising their pricing objectives? Explain.

3. Mickey Arison says that he believes that many Carnival customers will eventually "grow" into more expensive Holland America cruises. Is this an example of leader pricing? Why not?

4. Does mixed bundling play any role in the success of Carnival Cruise Lines? Explain.

IMPLEMENTING, CONTROLLING, AND EXTENDING MARKETING

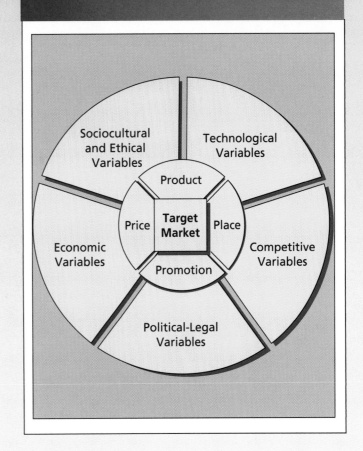

Sections three through six dealt with the various elements of the marketing mix—the key decisions marketing managers make in order to implement the marketing concept. Simply making a decision about one or more aspects of the marketing mix will not assure success. Managers must do whatever they can to assure effective implementation of the marketing strategy and to modify the strategy and marketing mix when necessary.

Chapter 20 focuses on the issues of implementation and control. It examines how the structure of the marketing organization can hinder or facilitate implementation and what managers can do to enhance execution. Additionally, it presents methods for evaluating performance.

Chapter 21 deals with modifications to the marketing mix that are necessary when marketing services. It discusses the special characteristics that distinguish services from goods and examines how service marketers can deal with these characteristics. Additionally, it looks at the special aspects of marketing in nonprofit organizations.

Chapter 22 looks at the increasingly important topic of international marketing. It gives some insight into the ''whys'' of international trade and explains the nature of interna-

tional marketing and multinational companies. It then examines the environment of international marketing and the types of involvement an organization might have in international marketing. The chapter discusses some of the major decisions multinational companies face in conducting marketing efforts.

The Comprehensive Case at the end of this section, on PepsiCo, focuses on the company's penetration of the Soviet Union and Eastern Europe. It illustrates the concepts of implementing and controlling marketing strategies. It also depicts the increasingly international character of a U.S.-based company.

IMPLEMENTING
AND CONTROLLING
MARKETING
STRATEGIES

After reading this chapter you will be able to

1. distinguish product-oriented organization structures from market-oriented organization structures.

2. identify the actions managers can take to help assure effective execution of strategies.

3. present the purpose of sales analysis.

4. describe marketing cost analysis.

5. discuss the importance of quality assessment.

6. explain what is involved in a marketing audit.

There has probably never been a time in American business history during which an announced concern for quality was as pervasive as it is today. Television advertisements trumpeting claims such as "quality is job 1" are widespread, and business magazines are filled with articles on how firms have developed quality enhancement programs. The U.S. Department of Commerce has added to the preeminent role of quality by initiating the annual Malcolm Baldrige Awards, given to businesses for significant achievement in quality.

The purposes of the Baldrige Awards are "to promote quality awareness, to recognize quality achievements of U.S. companies and to publicize successful quality strategies."[1] In 1988 the companies receiving the award were Motorola, Globe Metallurgical, and Westinghouse Electric's Commercial Nuclear Fuel Division. In 1989 the companies were Milliken & Company and Xerox Corporation's Business Products and Systems Divisions. In 1990 they were Federal Express, the Cadillac Division of General Motors, Wallace Inc. (a small Texas distributor of pipes and valves), and the minicomputer division of IBM.

No one would dispute the idea that quality is a desirable performance trait for an organization. However, there are a variety of notions about what constitutes quality. Probably the most traditional and widely accepted view is that quality is a production concept measured by the likelihood of receiving a defect-free product. Indeed, a widely adopted management technique in recent years is *statistical process control,* a technique for monitoring the production of component parts in a way that permits adjustments to the manufacturing process as soon as (or before) defective parts are produced. For example, Motorola's quality image stems largely from improved manufacturing processes designed to achieve a goal of "Six Sigma quality"—statistical jargon for a rate of only 3.4 defects per million products. By 1991 Motorola had achieved an overall performance level of 5.2 Sigma—a seventy-fold increase over 1987—and expected to achieve the Six Sigma goal by 1992.[2]

But defect-free production is being viewed increasingly

as only one dimension of quality. Certainly Motorola's success in the semiconductor industry is not due solely to the Six Sigma program. Dataquest, a marketing research firm specializing in high-technology industries, has twice given Motorola its "Semiconductor Supplier of the Year" award. The award is based on ratings made by semiconductor purchasers in the areas of product quality, on-time delivery, pricing, understanding of the applications, and customer service.

Indeed a multidimensional view of corporate quality performance is emerging. Japanese automotive manufacturers are generally regarded as leading practitioners of production quality. In recent years they have carried the notion of quality beyond simply minimizing defects. The new Japanese concept of quality is *miryokuteki hinshitsu*— developing cars that are fascinating and bewitching to the customer. In the words of a Mitsubishi Motor Sales executive: "We've entered the second phase of quality. Now it's the personality of the product that dictates quality."[3] This philosophy underlies such developments as the new engine mount on the Honda Accord that dissipates engine vibration when the car is idling. In a defect-free industry, will such fine touches be the dominant indicators of quality?

The U.S. Department of Commerce goes further in assessing quality. The criteria for the Baldridge Awards include not only quality assurance, quality results, and customer satisfaction but also management activities designed to maintain and enhance future quality. Thus leadership, information and analysis, planning, and human resource utilization are also evaluated by the Baldridge judges. Why are these managerial factors so important? Because evidence shows that a quality-oriented strategy can be effective only if top management is committed to the program, if the activities of people in the various functional areas are coordinated, and if performance is regularly monitored and analyzed to identify opportunities for improvement.

As Motorola managers will attest, quality is critical to success in today's competitive global marketplace. But the growing importance of quality enhancement programs in organizations represents an aspect of marketing that is not very visible to the casual observer. Specifically, a quality program represents an attempt to enhance the effective *implementation* of a firm's organizational and marketing strategies.

Most of this book has been devoted to showing how marketing strategies are designed. As we discussed in chapter 3, the development of marketing strategies includes the selection of target markets and the design of marketing mixes for each target. In chapters 4 through 8 we presented some of the key marketing tools and concepts for selecting target markets. Chapters 9 through 19 were devoted to examining the elements of the marketing mix. Finally, in chapters 21 and 22 we will discuss some of the unique marketing strategy considerations facing marketers of services and international marketers.

We also showed in chapter 3 that marketing strategy was only part of the marketing

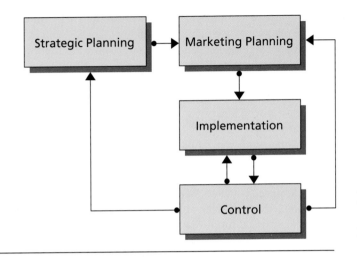

FIGURE 20–1
....

Planning, Implementation, and
Control

planning process. The focus of this chapter is on the remaining two steps in this process: implementation and control. Figure 20–1 shows the relationships among the three steps.

Marketing implementation is the aspects of organizational structure and behavior that determine how a given strategy is carried out; specifically, it is the *actions* of marketing managers, sales and customer service personnel, distributors, and sometimes even non-marketing personnel. The success of any strategy is limited by the effectiveness with which it is implemented. Thus, in achieving customer satisfaction through enhanced quality, marketing managers must often work closely with research and development and manufacturing personnel.

marketing implementation

Marketing control is the monitoring of marketing performance and the identification of problems that have resulted in unsatisfactory levels of performance. Marketing control is necessary because strategies are never perfectly realized. Managers must anticipate that things will never go exactly according to plan, and they must be prepared to modify the strategy or the implementation as necessary in response to unsatisfactory performance. Motorola's manufacturing managers, for example, use statistical process control to adjust manufacturing processes.

marketing control

IMPLEMENTATION

Several years ago one of the nation's most respected management consulting firms, McKinsey & Company, attempted to define the key business practices that seemed to characterize well-run organizations. One of McKinsey's managers, Tom Peters, later summarized the results of the company's work in his popular book *In Search of Excellence*.

Perhaps the most fundamental conclusion of the McKinsey studies was that the most successful companies are not successful because of any superiority in strategic planning. Rather the distinguishing feature is how well strategic plans are implemented.[4] Implementation has two dimensions: organizing and executing.

Organizing

Because of the number and diversity of marketing activities, firms must develop mechanisms to coordinate them. The basic mechanism is the organization structure, which spells out how various positions are related to one another. More specifically, an organization structure should provide an understanding of who will carry out the marketing plans for each product and market and what the reporting relationships among managers and other marketing personnel will be.

Although organization structures are usually developed for entire organizations, our concern is strictly with the organization of the marketing function. That is, we are concerned solely with identifying the basic ways in which the marketing function can be organized to implement marketing plans. There are two basic options for organizing marketing: product-oriented organization and market-oriented organization.

product-oriented organizations

• **Product-Oriented Organizations** • Firms in which each product, product line, or group of related products has its own marketing organization are **product-oriented organizations.** Although there are many variations, Figure 20–2 shows the basic elements of this organizational form.

Note that specific brand or product managers are responsible for overseeing the marketing planning activities of each product. The brands or product groups may be the strategic business units (SBUs) discussed in chapter 3. At the same time, it is unusual for a firm to dedicate a sales force, an advertising manager, or a marketing research department to a single brand. More typically, as is illustrated in Figure 20-2, brand managers will share staff resources and sales forces. That is, a single sales force is responsible for selling all products within a group, and individual advertising managers and marketing research managers work on all brands within a group.

A recent development in the product management system is the introduction of *category managers,* or product group managers, who are responsible for overseeing groups of closely related products. For example, Procter & Gamble reorganized itself into thirty-nine product categories so one manager could coordinate marketing plans and budgets across brands that might compete (such as Puritan and Crisco cooking oils).[5]

Product-oriented organizations are most likely to be firms that have experienced a rapid increase in the number and diversity of the products they carry. In particular, firms that

FIGURE 20–2

A Product-Oriented Organization

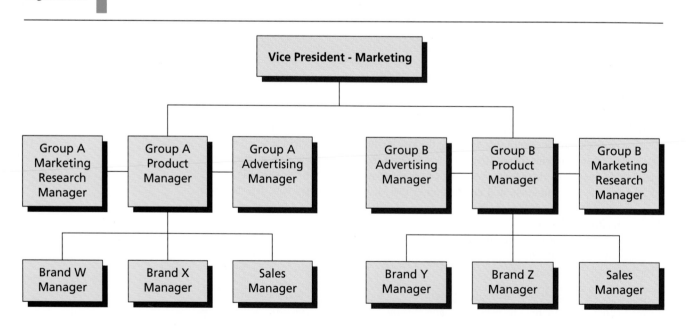

Product managers rely heavily on their interpersonal skills to gain support of their personnel in implementing their marketing strategies.

[© Jeffry W. Myers]

have engaged in diversification strategies are most likely to need this form of organization. Basically, the product-oriented structure provides assurance that someone is paying close attention to the marketing strategy and performance of each brand and product group.

The major difficulty usually associated with product-oriented organizations is that product and brand managers sometimes find it difficult to implement the plans they develop. That is, because brand managers (and sometimes their product group managers) do not have direct supervisory control over the sales force and other marketing units, they must rely on other means (such as their personal negotiating or persuasive skills) to gain the necessary cooperation and support.[6]

market-oriented organizations

• **Market-Oriented Organizations** • In contrast to product-oriented organizations, *market-oriented organizations* are firms structured around market segments. Geographic segments are probably the most common basis for market-oriented structures, but many firms are organized by type of distribution channel. For example, automobile tire manufacturers use separate marketing and sales efforts for selling to original equipment manufacturers (OEMs) such as Ford or Oldsmobile and to the replacement market (through wholesalers or retail distributors). Some firms are also organized by type of customer; for example, some computer manufacturers employ separate sales forces to call on customers with distinct needs, usage patterns, or buying practices. Educational institutions, for instance, need different types of hardware and software and buy in different volumes than do engineering companies.

Figure 20–3 shows one variation of a market-oriented organization. As an industrial company with a relatively limited product line, the firm in Figure 20–3 needs only one advertising department and one marketing research department. Thus the main issue is how to organize the sales force.

This organization is structured first by type of channel. One is a direct channel to OEMs, and the other is a distributor-based channel. The OEM sales force is organized geograph-

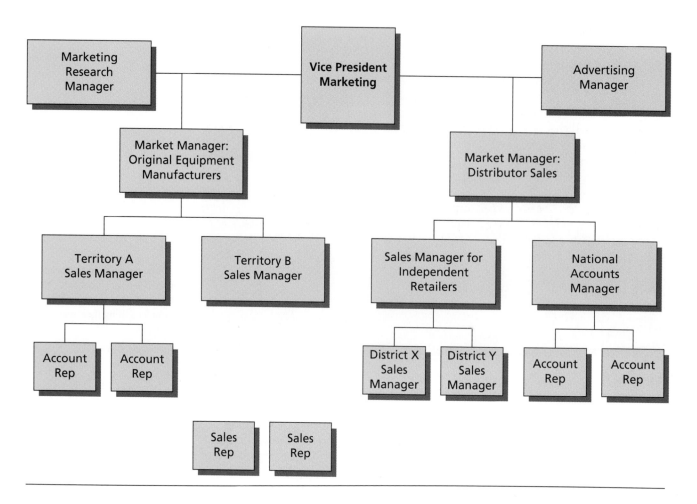

FIGURE 20–3

A Market-Oriented
Organization

ically, and the distributor sales force is organized first by account size (independents versus large national accounts) and then by geography. The decision to use a market-oriented organization structure could reflect either a major shift in the firm's corporate strategy toward market development or a concern with improving execution in existing markets.

• *Corporate Market Development Strategy*   If a firm makes a clear commitment to a corporate growth strategy of market development—taking its existing products into new markets—then a market-oriented structure is needed for success. Without a separate organizational unit marketing the line to new territories, new channels, or new types of customers, a firm risks devoting inadequate attention to the new markets. For example, it is questionable whether IBM would have been successful in selling personal computers through independent retail outlets if a separate sales unit had not been developed for this channel.

• *Improving Execution in Existing Markets* •   Shifting to a more market-oriented structure can enhance the execution of a firm's current corporate strategy in three possible ways. First, efficiency in coverage may be improved if duplication of selling effort can be avoided. Second, if the reorganization enables marketing personnel to be more responsive in meeting local market conditions, performance should be enhanced. Finally, when a small percentage of all customers accounts for a large percentage of sales, a market-oriented structure that emphasizes on these high-volume accounts will enhance efficiency and effectiveness.

Among the firms that have recently shifted to a predominantly market-oriented structure is Hewlett-Packard. In revising the marketing strategy for its computer businesses, the company divided these businesses into two groups. One group handles personal computers, printers, and other products sold through dealers. The second oversees sales of workstations and minicomputers to larger customers. Each group has an entirely separate sales force. As a consequence the company has improved selling efficiency and has become more effective in meeting specific customer needs.[7]

• **Hybrid Organizations** • Most organizations are *hybrid organizations*—firms that combine some features of both the product-oriented and the market-oriented structures. At Minnesota Mining and Manufacturing (3M) the overall organization structure is clearly a hybrid. As Figure 20–4 illustrates, some of the major business sectors and groups (such as tape and medical products) are organized by product while others (commercial markets and consumer markets) are organized by market.

hybrid organizations

GLOBAL MARKETING

The question of how best to organize for multinational business has no single answer. However, for some product categories it is critical that the marketer adapt to the circumstances unique to each nation.

In Europe, for example, Ford has long been a strong competitor in the automobile market. In part this is because Ford has production facilities and sales teams in a number of countries. The European Community's decision to drop trade barriers in 1992 will reduce customers' headaches, permit more standardization of components, and perhaps facilitate centralization of the financing function. But Ford plans to maintain sales offices in each country to tailor marketing and design strategies to meet local tastes.

On the industrial side the fact that many customers are multinational often leads firms to organize along regional lines to assure coordination of marketing policies. For instance, Apple established a separate division, Apple Europe, to

market its products across that continent. Although sales efforts are overseen by individual country managers, most key policies (such as pricing) are managed out of Apple Europe's Paris headquarters.

But even if Europewide or global strategies are important, a decentralized, market-driven organization structure is still effective in implementing strategies. For example, when a large Swedish electrical equipment firm merged with a Swiss counterpart, computer manufacturer Digital Equipment Corporation combined its account teams from those countries to land a large share of the merged company's new business.

Sources Barbara Buell, Jonathan Levine, and Neil Gross, ''Apple: New Team, New Strategy,'' *Business Week,* October 15, 1990, pp. 86–96; ''Ford Is Ready to Roll in the New Europe,'' *Business Week,* December 12, 1988, p. 60; ''SEC: Making the Most of Vanishing Borders,'' *Business Week,* December 12, 1988, p. 60.

MINNESOTA MINING AND MANUFACTURING COMPANY (3M)
Corporate Organization Chart
February 1, 1991

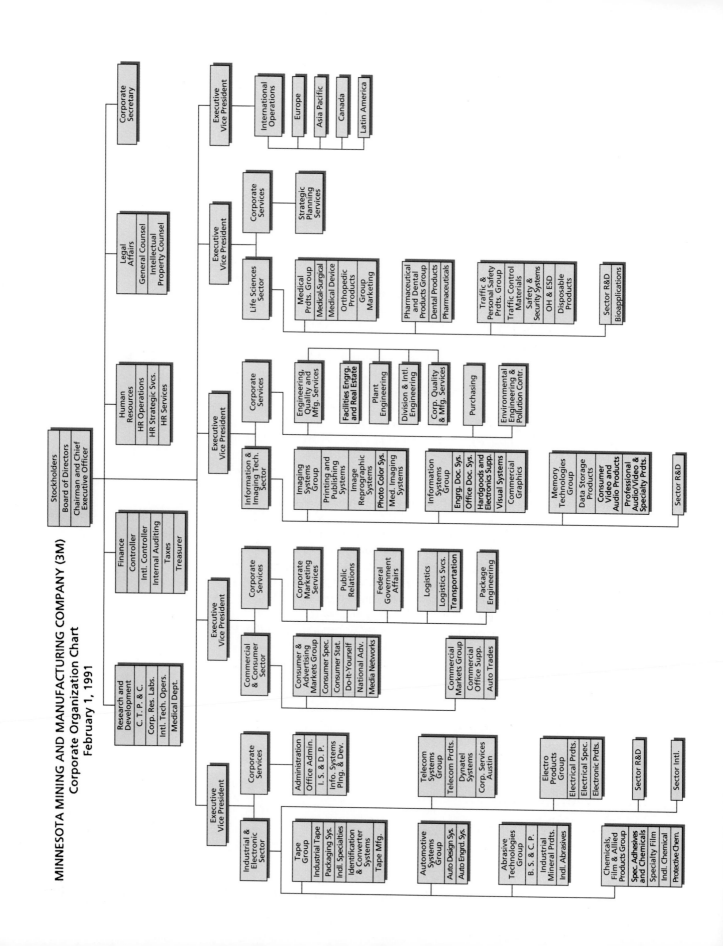

The existence of hybrid organization structures among very successful firms is noteworthy because it reflects the well-known law of organization structure: There is no single best way to organize. Ultimately each firm must develop a structure that fits its corporate growth strategy and that appears to be an effective way to achieve the attention and coordination necessary to implement its marketing strategies. As the Global Marketing box suggests, this guideline also holds true for multinational businesses.

Executing

Coordination can never ensure good execution of a plan. Each of the units being coordinated must execute its assigned tasks in an effective and efficient manner to make the plan work.

Within the marketing function, *execution* is most often a problem for the sales force. When price changes or new sales promotions are contemplated, their execution is relatively straightforward. However, each salesperson is responsible for a complex set of activities. Consequently, there is always some uncertainty about how well a strategy will be executed.

Execution problems may also arise when managers must rely on outside firms (advertising agencies or intermediaries) or on other functional departments within the firm (such as credit or production) to implement a strategy.

Unfortunately, there are no guaranteed routes to effective execution. When the activities of the sales force are critical to the execution of a strategy, it is important to have effective compensation packages and sales training programs, as discussed in chapter 17. More generally, managers can enhance the level of execution to the extent that they are effective in (1) assuring that activities are goal directed, (2) assigning resources to facilitate performance, and (3) building interpersonal relationships and informal networks.

- **Assuring Goal-Directed Actions** • Managers who want to assure that activities will be properly directed toward implementing a strategy must, at a minimum, be sure that those involved in executing the strategy are given clearly stated goals and that motivational packages are designed to support these goals.

Anyone involved in executing a plan should be aware of the firm's priority goals. Often execution depends on recognizing and pursuing goals that are not described in terms of sales volume but that will ultimately lead to increased sales or profit. Thus an advertising agency may pursue a goal of increasing brand awareness and will design (execute) advertisements toward that end. This goal is most likely to be pursued and achieved if it is a clearly established and agreed-upon goal.

Once goals are established, programs should be instituted to reinforce goal-directed behavior. At Fidelity Investments, a mutual fund investment firm, an important new goal is to provide quality telephone responses to customers who are calling with questions or other business related to their investments. Specifically, Fidelity's representatives are expected to be more personable than they used to be and to provide more care in servicing customer needs without sacrificing efficiency. In order to assure that the new quality orientation is successful, the firm has combined telephone etiquette training with a system that

FIGURE 20–4
....

Minnesota Mining and Manufacturing (3M) Corporate Organization Chart

Source: Courtesy of 3M.

eases the pressure for productivity in the hope that workers will pay greater heed to customer needs.[8]

Assuring that activities are goal directed is important, but managers should also be concerned about the ethical content of those activities. The Ethics in Marketing box presents some specific ideas with respect to this issue.

• **Assigning Resources** • When the performance of salespeople or distributors is critical to the successful execution of a strategy, managers should identify ways of facilitating distributor or salesperson performance through the assignment and allocation of resources. These resources can include money, equipment, and even the manager's time.

3M, for instance, prizes innovation and new-product development as primary organizational objectives; 25 percent of sales are expected to come from products developed within the previous five years. To make this goal a reality top management has developed and nurtured a culture that is conducive to innovation by enabling employees to see the resources available to support product development. These resources include technology, time, and special funding. There is extensive technology sharing within the corporation, so researchers in one division can obtain needed technical support from any other division. The company allows technical people to spend up to 15 percent of their time on projects of their own choosing. Finally, new projects for which it is difficult to secure funding within a given group or sector are eligible to compete for $50,000 grants from the 3M Genesis program.[9]

• **Building Relationships and Networks** • In the day-to-day world of the marketing manager, getting things done usually means interacting with individuals who do not report to the marketing manager. As we indicated earlier, product managers often lack authority over the sales force, not to mention individuals in other organizational units. As a result

ETHICS IN MARKETING

What can organizations do to implement marketing strategies ethically? Professor Patrick Murphy has studied this question and has drawn four major conclusions.

First, firms should establish formal codes of ethics that provide specific guidance on often-asked ethical questions. Second, the organization's commitment to ethical standards must be reinforced in a visible way through periodic meetings in which such standards are discussed and through sanctions against those who violate the standards. Third, top management must exert some form of control over the procedures by which extraordinary goals are reached. (Management can't take the attitude "I don't know how you will do it and I don't want to know".) Finally, there should be someone in top management to champion the cause of ethical behavior. Although this person need not be the chief executive officer, it should be someone in a position that requires ethical decision making, not just ethical cheerleading. Who should that person be?

Source: Based on Patrick E. Murphy, "Implementing Business Ethics," *Journal of Business Ethics,* December 1988, p. 914.

the formal organization structure may be inadequate to assure coordination, and a manager may be unable to motivate key individuals. In such cases managers must develop strong interpersonal skills—especially persuasive skills—or be able to develop or find individuals in an informal network who can deal with implementation problems.[10]

Product managers are especially likely to face this type of problem because of the nature of a product-structured organization. Consider, for example, all the interactions likely to be necessary if a product manager at a typical consumer goods company wanted to run a special coupon promotion for one of the company's detergents:

- Funds would be solicited from a group product manager or category manager.
- External agencies (such as advertising agencies and sales promotion specialists) would be contacted and coordinated.
- The sales manager for the detergent sales force would set up a sales campaign to get retailers to increase inventories in preparation for the promotion.
- Production managers might be asked to adjust schedules to produce more detergent prior to the promotion period so higher retail inventories could be achieved.

Some individuals would be better than others at obtaining the support needed to persuade these managers to act in the desired way at the desired time. Such skills come naturally to some, but they can also be developed through training and experience.

CONTROLLING

The management process of controlling involves measuring actual performance, comparing performance to the standards established for a plan, and taking corrective action when necessary. Figure 20–5 shows the major steps in the control process.

The Need for Control

Controlling is an important part of marketing management because a marketing strategy seldom works out exactly as planned. As a result, managers need to be able to spot deviations from the plan as soon as possible in order to adjust the strategy.

FIGURE 20–5

The Control Process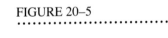

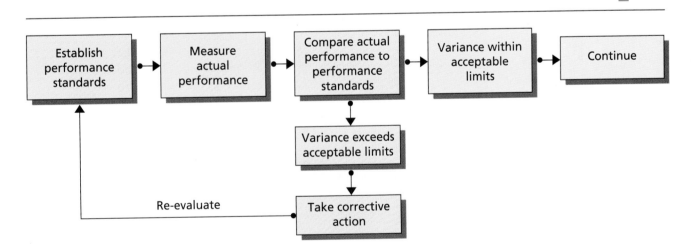

Performance may not achieve the standard that has been set for many reasons: (1) the standard may have been unrealistic, (2) unanticipated environmental changes may have occurred, or (3) implementation may have been ineffective.

- **Unrealistic Standards** • Sometimes managers let their enthusiasm get the best of them. When new products are brought into the marketplace, managers may overestimate the speed with which the market will respond. In many cases these faulty estimates are the result of poor marketing research or of managers' unwillingness to accept research results that do not match their own opinions. In general, the newer the product category, the more difficult it will be to generate realistic sales goals. Although microwave ovens, personal computers, and videocassette recorders are viewed as successful products today, sales in the early years of the life cycles of these products were all considered disappointing.

- **Unanticipated Environmental Changes** • Even the best marketing research cannot enable management to eliminate market risk. A firm may correctly forecast consumer reactions to a price change. However, the sales standards established in a plan that includes the proposed change still may not be realized if competitors make unexpected changes in their prices.

For example, the demise of People Express Airlines came about because the company did not anticipate price changes made by competitive airlines. In order to offset People Express's across-the-board low fares, the major airlines used their computer systems to analyze opportunities for selective discounting. By offering special fares for flying on certain days and with certain advance purchase deadlines to customers in the price-sensitive personal travel market, the major airlines were able to eliminate People Express's advantage.

Similarly, profit standards established in a plan may not be realized if the firms that

Unanticipated environmental changes often require adjustments in marketing strategies. This is why the control process is so important to marketers.

[© Heimo Aga, Contact Press Images]

supply the component parts suddenly decide to increase their prices. The earlier such changes can be identified, the greater the opportunity to adjust the strategy to achieve the original goals.

• **Ineffective Implementation** • When achievable performance standards are not being met and when inadequate performance cannot be traced to environmental factors, then the problem lies with implementation. A number of factors are influential in determining whether a strategy will be effectively implemented. The process of trying to determine the specific cause of poor implementation is difficult for managers. Many managers establish measurable benchmarks that can help isolate implementation problems. For example, managers may set subgoals of making a certain number of sales calls per week or dealing with a certain number of customer complaints. By comparing these benchmarks with weekly or monthly reports on actual sales calls or complaint handling, managers may gain insights into execution problems.

Performance Evaluation Methods

Managers can use several techniques to track and evaluate performance. The most comprehensive techniques are sales analysis, marketing cost analysis, quality assessment, and the marketing audit.

• **Sales Analysis** • The performance evaluation procedure designed to identify the areas in which sales performance problems exist is *sales analysis*. When a company has a complex line of products or serves a variety of distinct sales segments, then the source of the poor performance is seldom obvious without sales analysis.

sales analysis

Consider, for example, the data in Table 20–1 for the hypothetical Cross Roads Running

TABLE 20–1   Sales Analysis of Cross Roads Running Shoe Company

Sales Segment	Sales (in Thousands)		
	Planned	Actual	Actual Minus Planned
Manufacturers' reps			
• Territory A	12.2	10.1	−2.1
• Territory B	5.3	4.3	−1.0
• Territory C	12.5	12.0	−0.5
• Territory D	9.9	5.7	−4.2
• Territory E	8.1	8.1	0
Total	48.0	40.2	−7.8
Direct sales			
• Account M	12.8	14.7	1.9
• Account N	8.2	10.3	2.1
• Account O	7.9	7.6	−0.3
• Account P	5.1	5.2	0.1
Total	34.0	37.8	3.8
All segments total	82.0	78.0	−4.0

Shoe Company. The data show planned and actual sales for a three-month period across different sales segments. In this case the company sells directly to large national retailers using its own sales force and to independent stores and regional sporting goods chains through manufacturers' representatives. Each of the five manufacturers' reps has a distinct geographic territory.

Simply identifying the total gap between planned and actual sales (four thousand pairs) is not helpful in deciding what action to take. But organizing the sales data according to the company's marketing channels, sales territories, and key accounts enables management to readily identify the location, if not the cause, of the problem. Clearly the sales shortfalls in manufacturer rep territories A and D are the major areas of difficulty.

The sales analysis does not tell the company what action to take; it merely clarifies where performance is above or below target. The sales manager for Cross Roads would likely want a further breakdown of sales trends among the specific retailers within the two problem territories to gain more understanding of the source of the sales shortfalls.

With the advent of personal computers a number of software companies have developed sales analysis computer packages that allow managers to sort through various levels of sales analysis quickly and easily. Table 20–2 lists the types of classifications for which sales analyses are most typically conducted.

marketing cost analysis

natural accounts

functional accounts

- **Marketing Cost Analysis** • Although sales analysis helps in evaluating a marketing strategy, it does not indicate anything about the strategy's profitability. A given strategy can be effective in generating sales but inefficient in terms of resource utilization. Marketing costs, like sales figures, should be broken down by product, sales territory, salesperson, customer, or the other types of classifications shown in Table 20–2.

Marketing cost analysis is the process of breaking down and classifying marketing costs to determine which costs are incurred in performing specific marketing activities. This usually requires considerable effort because accounting systems generally assign costs to *natural accounts* —accounts such as rent, salaries, insurance, heat, and supplies that are listed in ledgers and on income statements. *Functional accounts,* on the other hand, are accounts that indicate the purpose or function for which funds have been spent.

Returning to our Cross Roads example, Table 20–3 shows how the natural accounts on an income statement are allocated to the various marketing functions. The only natural account here that is also a functional account is advertising because the account title indicates the marketing function for which the funds were spent.

The right side of Table 20–3 shows how the amounts in the natural accounts are allocated to functional accounts: advertising, shipping, personal selling, and general administration. Thus the amount in the natural account called *salaries* is allocated to these functional accounts to reflect how the money spent on salaries is attributable to advertising, personnel, truck drivers, salespeople, and clerical workers.

TABLE 20–2 | Types of Sales Segment Classifications for Which Sales and Cost Analyses Are Used

- By product
- By model or other product variation
- By package size
- By sales territory
- By salesperson

- By type of channel
- By type of retail outlet
- By type of customer industry
- By size of order

TABLE 20–3
Allocating Natural Accounts to Functional Accounts for Cross Roads Running Shoes (in Thousands of Dollars)

Income Statement				Functional Accounts	
Net sales	$15,000				
Cost of goods sold	11,300				
Gross margin	$ 3,700				

Expenses (Natural Accounts)		Advertising	Shipping	Personal Selling	General Administration
Salaries	$1,120	$ 60	$100	$360	$600
Advertising	1,000	1,000	0	0	0
Rent	200	10	20	10	160
Freight/delivery	300	0	240	20	40
Supplies	80	5	20	20	35
Travel	160	5	0	90	65
Total	$2,860	$1,080	$380	$500	$900
Net profit	$ 840				

Table 20–4 shows how the costs in each of the functional accounts are allocated among the company's sales segments. In making the allocation of functional expenses to products, managers must identify the key factors that determine each cost. For example, personal selling costs might be allocated according to the share of the sales force's time that is devoted to calling on each account, and shipping costs might be allocated from shipping records.

TABLE 20–4
Allocating Functional Expenses to Cross Roads' Sales Segments (in Thousands of Dollars)

Income Statement	Total	Direct Sales to National Accounts	Sales by Reps To Single-Unit Stores	Sales by Reps To Regional Chains
Net sales	$15,000	$7,000	$3,500	$4,500
Cost of goods sold	11,300	4,900	2,800	3,600
Gross margin	$ 3,700	$2,100	$ 700	$ 900
Functional Expenses				
Advertising	$1,080	$ 510	$ 210	$ 360
Shipping	380	120	150	110
Personal selling	500	500	0	0
Total allocated expenses	$1,960	$1,130	$ 360	$ 470
Net contribution	$1,740	$ 970	$ 340	$ 430
Contribution as percent of sales	11.6%	13.9%	9.7%	9.6%
Unallocated general and administrative expense	$ 900			

Whether the allocation is being made to products, to territories, or to some other classification of sales segments, marketing cost analysts generally agree that only the costs that can logically be traced to various sales segments should be allocated. Thus pure overhead costs (such as the salary of the firm's president—a general administrative expense) that cannot be allocated across sales segments except in some arbitrary manner should be excluded.

By examining a marketing cost analysis managers obtain some insights as to where profit performance might be improved. For example, Table 20–4 shows that direct sales to national accounts are the most profitable sales segment even though they carry the full burden of the selling costs. Since manufacturers' reps operate on commission and pay their own expenses, no selling costs are incurred in those segments. However, commissions are deducted from total sales, so lower gross margins are earned (in percentage terms) on sales made by the manufacturers' reps. Additionally, the share of shipping costs allocated to the direct sales segment is proportionately lower, probably because these accounts make larger-sized orders that are more economical to ship.

Customer satisfaction is becoming an increasingly important standard in evaluating marketing performance.

(British Airways/Backer Spielvogel Bates Inc.)

© 1990 British Airways

OUR SERVICE
IS WHY WE'RE
SO FREQUENTLY
CHOSEN.

When it comes to awards, British Airways has won more than its fair share: over 130 top honors in the past five years alone. And every one can be attributed to superior service. Whether it's complimentary cocktails in Economy Class, fine dining on Royal Doulton® china in Club® Class, or the time-saving advantages of Concorde—no airline is more dedicated to the concept of service. British Airways meets the most exacting standards. Because far more important than winning awards, is winning you over.

BRITISH AIRWAYS
The world's favourite airline®

• **Quality Assessment** • Although sales and cost analyses can be combined to track the overall profit performance of marketing strategies, managers also need more precise information on the dimensions of marketing performance that lead to sales and profit results. As chapter 1 noted, the focus on customer satisfaction should be the dominant orientation of a business. And as indicated at the start of this chapter, quality is the route to customer satisfaction. Not surprisingly, then, in many firms the key performance evaluation method is the assessment of quality from the customer's point of view. As the British Airways ad suggests, high ratings for customer satisfaction can be significant additions to a firm's competitive advantage.

Because the concept of quality is a bit elusive, measures of quality that are appropriate for every organization have yet to be developed. However, Harvard professor David Garvin has attempted to define the basic dimensions of quality. His eight dimensions, presented in Table 20–5, are not likely to be of equal significance to each organization. Rather he expects firms to measure their performance on those dimensions that are critical to their strategic success. Garvin also notes that "high quality means pleasing customers, not just protecting them from annoyances." Thus the ultimate goal of quality assessment is to find ways to enhance customer satisfaction.[11]

Although an inspection of Garvin's eight dimensions of quality suggests that some of these dimensions are most influenced by manufacturing or engineering performance, it is ultimately the responsibility of marketing management to see that an appropriate response is forthcoming. In particular, the *customer service function* is most responsible for solving customer problems and for handling complaints or dealing with the firm's inadequacies on the various dimensions.

The paramount role of customer service is undeniable today. A study by Forum Corporation, a Boston consulting firm, suggests that 40 percent of people who stop doing business with a firm do so because of service-related issues.[12] And the Customer Service Institute states that every unhappy customer tells his or her story to ten other people, whereas a customer who experiences good service tells only three people.[13]

Two major issues emerge in charting customer satisfaction and the firm's performance:

TABLE 20–5   The Eight Dimensions of Quality

....

1. Performance—the primary operating characteristics or benefits of a product.
2. Features—additional attributes (including options) that supplement the primary characteristics.
3. Reliability—the probability of a product failing within a specific time period.
4. Conformance—the degree to which the product's characteristics are reasonably consistent with established standards.
5. Durability—the amount of use one gets from a product before it must be replaced.
6. Serviceability—the speed, courtesy, competence, and ease of repair for a product.
7. Aesthetics—how a product looks, feels, sounds, tastes, or smells.
8. Perceived quality—inferences about the other dimensions of quality based on the image and reputation of an organization or its brands.

....

Source: Based on David Garvin, "Competing on the Eight Dimensions of Quality," *Harvard Business Review,* November–December 1987, pp. 101–109.

standards and measures. The prevailing view on standards is revealed in the pledge at catalog retailer L. L. Bean: "All our products are guaranteed to give 100% satisfaction in every way." This standard does not assume zero defects; it does assume that when defects occur, the customer's problem is addressed promptly and effectively. To some marketers the principle of 100 percent satisfaction is "the competitive advantage of the nineties."[14]

With respect to measurement, a number of approaches are possible. Xerox surveys about 40,000 customers every month.[15] American Express has developed a Service Tracking Report, which examines the firm's performance in a hundred separate areas, such as the accuracy of monthly statements and the processing time on new applications.[16] In some cases industrywide surveys are taken and published by independent research firms. J. D. Power & Associates conducts surveys of new automobile buyers for manufacturers and publishes the ratings. The overall satisfaction of 23,000 owners is measured with twenty-three detailed questions, and a summary customer satisfaction index is tabulated. The index reflects both satisfaction with the vehicle itself and satisfaction with the customer service.[17]

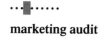

marketing audit

• **The Marketing Audit** • Although quality assessment may provide great insights on the effectiveness of a firm's marketing, from time to time firms should undergo a ***marketing audit***—a comprehensive review of the organization's overall marketing performance and prospects.

The marketing audit is an examination of an organization's environment, objectives, strategies, and activities; it culminates in a plan of action for improving marketing performance. At first glance this may seem much the same as the situational analysis discussed in chapter 3. Actually, it goes far beyond that. A marketing audit not only assesses whether the organization's mission and strategy fit with the environment and the organization's resources, it also yields a detailed assessment of, for example:

- The appropriateness of the target market.
- Needed changes in the product line.
- Degree of fit among prices, costs, and demand.
- Advertising and sales promotion budgeting practices.
- Sales force selection and motivation.
- Organization structure and communications.
- The quality of various research, planning, forecasting, and control systems.

In sum, no area of marketing decision making is off-limits to a marketing audit.

Some managers might argue that such evaluations occur anyway and might question what is so special about a marketing audit. Those who support the concept of an audit, however, point to several of its elements that help answer that question:[18]

1. Marketing audits are *comprehensive*. They cover all of the marketing activities of a firm, not just those for which problems are obvious. This comprehensiveness helps ensure that the sources of problems are identified. For example, if one evaluates only the quality of advertising in attempting to determine why a product is experiencing declining sales, the real cause (say, a decline in quality) might be overlooked.

2. Marketing audits are *systematic*. Because an orderly sequence of steps is followed, the likelihood is great that a plan for corrective action will be identified.

3. Marketing audits are *periodic*. This increases the chances that a potential problem (such as declining sales force morale or declining product quality) will be identified before it becomes serious.

Now what?

Even the best managed companies may find themselves in this seemingly untenable position. With market forces changing so rapidly, the same practices that built a business may now be blocking its path to the future.

Andersen Consulting can show you the way out.

We'll work with you to examine and rethink your basic business practices.

If they're sound, we'll suggest you keep them. If they're getting in your way, we'll help you revise them. And if the new processes can be enhanced by information technology, we'll help you automate them.

In industry after industry, businesses have employed our techniques to get back on track. Because with competition increasing every second, no company can afford to stay cornered for long.

ANDERSEN CONSULTING
ARTHUR ANDERSEN & CO., S.C.

Where we go from here.

© 1990 Andersen Consulting, AA & Co., S.C.

Often firms use consultants to design control systems and perform marketing audits.

(Used by permission of Andersen Consulting.)

4. As the Andersen Consulting ad suggests, the best marketing audits are *independent*. When experienced outside consultants are used, they can devote full time to the audit and can be objective in their assessments. Without objectivity, the whole concept of control is invalidated.

SUMMARY OF LEARNING OBJECTIVES

1. Distinguish product-oriented organization structures from market-oriented organization structures.

In a product-oriented organization structure each product, product line, or group of related products has its own marketing organization. In a market-oriented organization structure the firm is structured around market segments such as geographic territories or types of customers.

2. Identify the actions managers can take to help assure effective execution of strategies.

Managers can help assure effective execution by (1) assuring goal-directed activities, (2) assigning resources to facilitate performance, (3) building interpersonal relationships and informal networks.

3. Present the purpose of sales analysis.

Sales analysis is designed to identify the areas in which sales performance problems exist.

4. Describe marketing cost analysis.

Marketing cost analysis is the process of breaking down and classifying marketing costs to determine which costs are incurred in performing specific marketing activities. The costs are assigned to natural accounts and functional accounts. By examining a marketing cost analysis, managers can obtain insight as to where profit performance might be improved.

5. Discuss the importance of quality assessment.

Quality assessment is important because quality is the route to cus-

tomer satisfaction, which is the dominant orientation of a business. By assessing quality, managers can obtain more precise information on how well the firm is performing on the eight dimensions of quality. This allows management to identify opportunities for enhancing customer satisfaction.

6. Explain what is involved in a marketing audit.

A marketing audit is a comprehensive review of the organization's overall marketing performance and prospects. It examines the firm's environment, objectives, strategies, and activities.

Review Questions

1. What makes a product manager's job difficult?

2. What are the various ways in which an organization structure can be market oriented?

3. What is the relationship between a firm's choice of corporate growth strategy and its type of organization structure?

4. What determines whether actions of marketing personnel are goal directed?

5. What are the major reasons for deviations between planned performance and actual performance?

6. What can a manager learn from doing a sales analysis?

7. What are natural accounts and functional accounts?

8. What is the relationship between customer satisfaction and product quality?

9. What are the characteristics of a good marketing audit?

Discussion Questions

1. For each of the following firms, decide if it would be more effective if the firm were primarily product oriented or primarily market oriented: a publisher of college textbooks, a manufacturer of computers, and a company selling health insurance. Explain.

2. Which type of management activity do you think would be *most* important in assuring effective execution in each of the following situations: getting retail computer stores to carry a new model of personal computer, promoting new pharmaceutical products to physicians through personal sales calls, or coordinating the development of a new product? Explain.

3. An automobile manufacturer brings out a new $25,000 sports car. After six months only 15,000 units have been sold, whereas the planned sales volume for six months was 25,000. What questions should be asked in determining if the original standard was unrealistic?

4. Discuss how a firm's choice of organization structure will influence the type of sales segments used in sales analysis.

5. In developing a marketing cost analysis, managers must find a logical way of allocating functional costs to sales segments.

For each of the following situations, what basis or guide could management use to make the indicated allocations (if you believe there is no reasonable basis for making the allocation, indicate that the cost should not be allocated): the cost of marketing research across products, the cost of media advertising to consumers across marketing channels (for example, discount stores versus supermarkets), and the cost of shipping across customers of different order size classes?

6. Many firms have established "quality management" positions. Should quality managers try to measure the various dimensions of quality by customer surveys or by internal measures (such as calculations of error rates, speed of response to customer inquiries, etc.)? Explain.

7. Which of Garvin's eight dimensions of quality would be most important to each of the following organizations: a manufacturer of construction equipment, a university, a florist? Explain.

Application Exercise

Reread the material about the Baldrige Awards at the beginning of this chapter and answer the following questions:

1. For a firm that is dedicated to quality, such as Motorola, would it be better to be organized along product lines or along market lines?

2. In this chapter we suggest that there are three kinds of actions managers can take in enhancing execution. How might each type of action be designed to enhance quality?

3. If Motorola wanted to design a quality assessment program for its line of cellular telephones, what kinds of measurements should it make?

Key Concepts

The following key terms were introduced in this chapter:

marketing implementation
marketing control
product-oriented
    organizations
market-oriented
    organizations

hybrid organizations
sales analysis
marketing cost analysis

natural accounts
functional accounts
marketing audit

· ·

CASES

What Would Lucky Lindy Think?

DONALD G. ANDERSON, *Ouachita Baptist University*
DENNIS J. ELBERT, *University of North Dakota*

Airlines have been the major commercial carrier of passengers in the United States since the 1950s. Until 1978, The Civil Aeronautics Board (CAB) regulated the rates and services of airlines as well as routes served, mergers, and operating rights. This economic regulation caused critics to charge that the CAB had discouraged price competition while encouraging expensive service competition. Moreover, the CAB was accused of protecting the established carriers from competition by restricting the number of carriers authorized to fly certain routes. By the mid-1970s there was considerable interest in Washington in deregulating the airline industry. The CAB then began to loosen its restrictions. In 1978 Congress passed the Airline Deregulation Act which was signed into law by President Jimmy Carter. The Act provided for the gradual relaxation of economic restrictions on passenger airlines and the abolishment of the CAB in 1985.

As a result of the passage of the Airline Deregulation Act competition changed dramatically in the airline industry. Airlines now had greater freedom to alter fares and routes. The major airlines hastened to build more efficient and extensive route systems around major hub airports. Service competition for passengers was replaced by fare (price) competition. Possibly as a consequence, the number of airline passengers more than doubled in the decade following the start of deregulation. However, wage, interest, and maintenance costs increased even more rapidly. Some airlines, no longer able to compete on a fare basis, became vulnerable to takeovers by stronger airlines. Furthermore, these stronger airlines sought to merge with weaker airlines in order to dominate passenger service at their hub airports.

Airport domination provides an opportunity for the stronger airline to charge higher fares than at more competitive airports. The result has been a number of significant mergers among major airlines. Between 1984 and 1990 the number of airlines accounting for more than 90 percent of domestic passenger miles fell from fifteen to nine. This number is expected to continue to fall as the fight for market share among the major airlines continues. The stronger airlines, such as American, United, and Delta, continue to fortify their position while some of the remaining major airlines seem to be getting weaker. Less competition in the future could bring fare increases, a situation which has occurred at the eight major hubs where one major airline accounts for 75 percent or more of the departures.

Rising fuel costs, labor problems, heavy debt, and the recession of the early 1990s have further exacerbated the competitive challenges faced by airlines. Increasing costs mean that competition on a fare basis will result in operating losses. At the same time, an era of higher fares may discourage travel by price-conscious passengers and magnify the problem of too many empty seats on flights. As a consequence the major airlines are giving increased attention to the international travel market. International fares are generally regulated by bilateral treaties and are therefore less subject to fare wars. Also, most international flights carry a larger complement of business passengers who can better afford high fares. On the other hand, foreign markets are also experiencing competitive conditions similar to those in the United States. Thus, foreign carriers are also aggressively seeking to compete in the global market. The likely result will be increasing competition for passengers by the world's principal airlines during the remainder of the century. Only the strongest are likely to survive.

Questions

1. As marketing manager for one of the major airlines, would your strategic marketing plan be based on price, on service, or on a combination of the two? Describe such a plan.

2. How could an airline's strategic goal be stated in a way that incorporates the concept of quality?

3. Did airlines anticipate the changes that would be created by the passage of the Airline Deregulation Act? What could they have done to monitor such changes?

4. Which of David Garvin's eight dimensions of quality should be of greatest concern to the airlines? Which are of least concern?

Maytag: The Dependability People?

Maytag Corporation's address at its headquarters in Newton, Iowa, is One Dependability Square. The company's reputation is based on quality; the quality of Maytag washers and dryers was established well before quality became a national concern. But lately, Maytag executives have been hearing comments that aren't as favorable as they're used to.

Starting in 1986, in an effort to expand, Maytag made a number of acquisitions. The company believed that, in order to stay competitive, it needed to provide a full line of appliances, both to keep dealers happy and to avoid becoming an acquisition target during the merger frenzy of the 1980s. Maytag purchased Magic Chef, Inc., which manufactures appliance brands Magic Chef, Admiral, and Norge; in 1989, Maytag acquired Chicago Pacific Corporation with its Hoover vacuum cleaner unit. Through these acquisitions Maytag joined the front ranks of appliance manufacturers, alongside Whirlpool, General Electric, and Sweden's Electrolux; sales rose from $684 million in 1985 to an estimated $3.1 billion in 1990. But the purchases have created problems for Maytag's quality image.

Maytag's new appliances, including Magic Chef, Admiral, and Norge, are rated among the lowest in quality by *Consumer Reports*. The new plants didn't do things the "Maytag way"—refrigerators were sent off the line with screws driven in crooked and temperature balances off-kilter. Problems arose when Maytag put its own name on some of these lower-quality brands; customers expected quality from a Maytag appliance and were doubly disappointed if they didn't get it.

The company realized that, in order to maintain the Maytag reputation, it would need to keep the brands separate, and gradually bring the other plants in line with the "Maytag way." Maytag spent $60 million on the Admiral refrigerator plant and made 1,100 engineering changes before turning out a new refrigerator that carried the Maytag name. The Maytag brand sells for about $200 more than the Admiral brand and was in such demand that the company hasn't been able to keep up; Consumer Reports rates Maytag refrigerators far above Admiral and Magic Chef, which are made at the same plant.

Maytag's reputation has been building for most of the twentieth century, since farm equipment maker F. L. Maytag introduced a hand-crank washer in 1907 that became known for its rugged construction. The Maytag company carries on that tradition with quality parts, such as rust-inhibiting coatings for its washers and innovative engineering; Maytag created a new transmission for its washer that has 40 percent fewer parts than the previous model. Many dealers would rather sell a customer a Maytag: they know they're not going to get the appliance back again.

If the Maytag culture is allowed to permeate the new acquisitions, the expansion could bring many benefits, especially to brands such as Hoover that already have some penetration in the European marketplace. But some people, including some Maytag employees and management, are worried that overall quality will suffer. Maytag is building a new plant in Jackson, Tennessee, where its dishwasher production will be centralized. Veteran Maytag workers in Newton feel betrayed, and they are apprehensive that the company plans to rely on its reputation for quality and skimp on actual production. Time will tell whether Maytag will retain its slogan, "the dependability people."

Questions

1. Do you think that Maytag is a product-oriented or a market-oriented organization? Why?

2. Which of the management functions of organizing, executing, or controlling might be most important in the short term in establishing Maytag quality standards for the new brands?

3. David Garvin states that "high quality means pleasing customers, not just protecting them from annoyance." By this standard, is Maytag's reputation for quality deserved?

4. How does Maytag's advertising campaign take advantage of its image for quality?

21

SERVICES AND
NONPROFIT
MARKETING

After reading this chapter you will be able to

1. explain the complexities that result from the special characteristics of services.

2. identify the service marketing strategies available for dealing with service characteristics.

3. explain the purpose of relationship marketing and identify its methods.

4. understand the unique aspects of marketing in nonprofit organizations.

5. contrast the major strategies nonprofits can use in marketing efforts directed toward prospective donors.

Most people's primary contact with the Girl Scouts of America comes through the annual sale of Girl Scout cookies. But the cookie sale is not the real business of the Girl Scouts. This organization is a nonprofit organization that provides an array of educational, recreational, and other personal services for girls.

In the mid-1970s the future of the Girl Scouts was in doubt. It was predominantly a white, middle-class organization in a society that was increasingly diverse. Teenagers were losing interest in scouting. The Boy Scouts were rumored to be thinking about opening their ranks to girls, and an increase in working mothers was reducing the availability of leaders.

The 1976 appointment of Frances Hesselbein as national executive director is widely regarded as a critical turning point in the history of the Girl Scouts. After a period of extensive examination of the organization and its environment, Hesselbein and other leaders concluded that the organizational mission, "helping each girl reach her highest potential," was still valid. However, they also concluded that the organization had not recognized the changing environment and its influence on their "customers" and on what the customers valued. Market studies revealed that more interest needed to be placed on services that emphasized the growing interest girls had in business, science, and the environment, in contrast to the historical emphasis on home-making skills. Today the most popular proficiency badges are in computing and mathematics.

In addition to modifying the services, the Girl Scouts enlisted fashion designers Bill Blass and Halston to redesign uniforms. At the same time a greater importance was attached to getting more troop leaders from the ranks of business and the professions to serve as role models.

To broaden the representation of minorities, separate recruiting drives were designed for African-Americans, Hispanics, and Native Americans. By 1990 minority membership had tripled, to 15 percent. Recognizing the growing number of preschool latch-key kids in the nation, the Scouts abandoned the traditional time of entry (first grade) through the creation of Daisy Scouts for five-year-olds. As the Daisies caught on, Hesselbein developed a collaborative alliance with the federal government's Head Start program. Now graduates of Head Start are immediately accepted into the Daisy Scouts.[1]

Although the Girl Scouts of America is very different from profit-making corporations such as IBM and Procter & Gamble, it faces many of the same challenges that those organizations face. As we can see, the Girl Scouts of America has periodically had to rethink its mission and its organizational strategy. It is also clear that demand for the services it provides is not automatically assured. However, because the Girl Scouts provides services (as opposed to physical goods) and because the organizational goals are nonfinancial, the managers in this organization who are responsible for marketing activities face some challenges that do not confront their IBM or P&G counterparts.

In this chapter our first task is to examine the unique dimensions of and strategies involved in services marketing. Later on we will address the special problems and challenges faced by nonprofit organizations. Although not all services are sold by nonprofit organizations, nearly all nonprofit organizations are involved primarily in the marketing of services.

GROWTH IN SERVICES AND SERVICES MARKETING

As we saw in chapter 2, the U.S. economy has been in transition from a manufacturing orientation to a service orientation. Today roughly half of all consumer expenditures go for the purchase of services rather than goods. Table 21–1 lists some of the major reasons for the growth of the service economy.

Although the sheer growth of the service sector has prompted greater attention to the management of service firms, a number of changes in the sector have led to an increasing emphasis on the marketing function.[2]

- Many service industries (including the airline, banking, and long distance telephone industries) have been deregulated in recent years. AT&T has been forced to compete for long distance customers, and airlines and banks no longer rely on federal agencies to set prices.
- In some areas (such as health care and mail delivery) nonprofit organizations have recognized the need to expand their marketing efforts because of increased competition from for-profit organizations. Consider, for example, the rise of Federal Express, which competes with the U.S. Postal Service.
- Changes in attitudes about acceptable standards of professional conduct have resulted in the increased use of marketing by professionals such as lawyers and physicians.

As the amount of attention given to the marketing of services has increased, it has become apparent that the techniques employed in the marketing of goods must be adapted

TABLE 21–1 Reasons for the Growth in Service Industries

1. Increasing affluence	Greater demand for lawn care, carpet cleaning, and other services that consumers used to provide for themselves
2. More leisure time	Greater demand for travel agencies, travel resorts, adult education courses
3. Higher percentage of women in the labor force	Greater demand for day care nurseries, maid service, away-from-home meals
4. Longer life expectancy	Greater demand for nursing homes and health care services
5. Greater complexity of products	Greater demand for skilled specialists to provide maintenance for such complex products as cars and home computers
6. Increasing complexity of life	Greater demand for marriage counselors, legal advisers, employment services
7. Greater concern about ecology and resource scarcity	Greater demand for purchased or leased services, such as door-to-door bus service and recycling services
8. Increasing technological change	Greater demand for cellular telephone services, complex surgery, home banking

to the marketing of services. That is, although the general processes of marketing strategy and marketing mix development are basically the same, there are some important distinctions between goods marketing and services marketing. These distinctions result from the special characteristics that distinguish services from goods.

Most U.S. service providers that go abroad do so initially to serve U.S. expatriates. Many subsequently make the transition to serving local nationals too.

[© P & G Bowater]

SPECIAL CHARACTERISTICS OF SERVICES

Four special characteristics of services are (1) intangibility, (2) perishability, (3) simultaneous production and consumption, and (4) lack of standardization. Some goods also have some of these characteristics, but *all* services have them. Each of these characteristics has important implications for the design of marketing strategies.

Intangibility

Services are *intangible* in that they cannot be seen, touched, felt, or otherwise sensed. When we purchase a service, we are not purchasing any physical object (although equipment and people may be involved in the delivery of the service). Rather, we are buying processes (such as dry cleaning), experiences (a museum visit), time (car rental), or some other intangible.[3]

Because services are intangible, it is generally difficult for the prospective customer to evaluate a service in advance. The special benefits of a service are not easily displayed or communicated because there are no features that directly demonstrate the existence of a benefit. For example, one can infer the operating economy of an automobile by examining its size and its type of engine. But one cannot inspect the financial counseling offered by an investment broker or banker.

As a consequence, service firms usually spend a good deal of time and effort building a reputation for reliability in providing the key benefits customers desire. The Met Life ad shows how one company is trying to establish such a reputation.

Perishability

Services are *perishable;* they cannot be saved or inventoried. Once an airliner takes off for its destination, the empty seats cannot be reclaimed. Because perishability leads to difficulty in balancing supply and demand, many service providers find it too costly to offer levels of service that will match peak demand. As a consequence, individual service organizations are often criticized for not providing adequate convenience. Bank teller lines are too long, there is standing room only on the bus, and the parking lot is full.

Firms are becoming increasingly aware of the cost of lost sales caused by waiting. One study showed that 27 percent of customers who can't get through to a service firm on the telephone will either buy elsewhere or forget about the whole transaction.[4]

Simultaneous Production and Consumption

For most services, *production and consumption occur simultaneously;* the hair stylist produces as the client consumes. Thus the consumer becomes involved in the production process to some extent, and in many cases the individuals involved in producing the service are the same people who serve as the sales force.

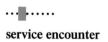

service encounter

The *service encounter* is the moment of interaction between the customer and the firm. The level of customer satisfaction that results from the encounter will depend heavily on the degree to which employees are willing and able to deal with their marketing roles as well as with their production roles.[5] Their attitude toward and their communication with the client or customer are as important in maintaining customer satisfaction as their technical "production" skills. Because many services require personal contact between the seller and the buyer, service firms must also pay special attention to location.

WHO CAN YOU TRUST?

MetLife, of course. From paying claims
promptly to providing expert advice, we'll always
be there when you need us.

GET MET. IT PAYS.
❊ MetLife

PEANUTS Characters © 1950, 1952, 1958, 1960, 1965, 1968 United Feature Syndicate, Inc.   © 1990 Metropolitan Life Insurance Co., N.Y, N.Y.

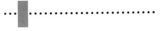

Because services are intangible, customers must rely heavily on a firm's reputation in evaluating the potential benefits they will receive.

(Metropolitan Life Insurance Company.)

Lack of Standardization

Buyers prefer to know what level of quality they are going to receive when they make a purchase. Consistent quality often is a critical basis for customer decisions. However, consistent quality is more difficult to achieve for service providers than for goods providers. For example, no two haircuts or auto repair jobs are exactly alike, because two employees may provide the service in slightly different ways and because the precise needs of the customers receiving the service are slightly different. This is an especially important problem when the essence of the service depends on contact personnel, since the performance of individuals is bound to fluctuate from day to day and from client to client.

Because of the *lack of standardization,* it is difficult to assure consistent quality in the provision of a service. The cost of providing the service may vary from client to client because of differences that often cannot be identified before the fact. For example, two standard physical examinations may vary sharply in terms of time, depending on the problems the physician finds and on the cooperativeness of the patient.

Taken together, the unique characteristics of services result in other, more subtle consequences for service evaluation. Specifically, the intangibility and lack of standardization

TABLE 21–2

How Consumers Rate the Value They Receive from
Goods and Services

What Consumers Like . . .			. . . And Dislike the Most	
Product	% Good		Product	% Poor
Poultry	53.6%		Hospital charges	58.4%
Fruits, vegetables	42.7		Lawyers' fees	49.1
Meat	35.5		Movies at theaters	47.0
Fish	33.9		Credit card charges	45.5
Prescription drugs	33.8		Bank service charges	42.3
Appliances	30.2		Cable TV	41.1
Personal care items	29.6		Health insurance	40.6
Pet food	29.1		Doctors' fees	36.4
Electricity	27.8		U.S. postage	36.3
Shoes	27.6		Used cars	35.6

Source: Reprinted by permission from Sales and Marketing Management magazine, January 13, 1986, p. 34. Copyright 1986.

characteristics make it difficult to evaluate the value received from a service. This problem is even more severe when simultaneous consumption and production mean that there are no retail intermediaries to advise the customer or to screen out low-value services. In addition, it is time-consuming to acquire information about the price and quality of most services, especially as the services become more customized.[6]

As a result, the level of satisfaction with services tends to lag behind the level of satisfaction with goods. In one study consumers were asked to rate a series of goods and services on the basis of the value they received. As Table 21–2 demonstrates, the nine items with the highest percentage of "poor" value ratings were services. Only one of the top ten rated items (electricity) was a service.

Because of the problems posed by these characteristics (as summarized in Table 21–3), services marketers have developed an array of special strategies to enhance the effectiveness of their marketing mixes.

TABLE 21–3   Problems Created by the Unique Characteristics of Services

Characteristic	Problems
Intangibility	Difficult to demonstrate benefits, reputation
Perishability	Inability to build inventory Customer dissatisfaction from waiting
Simultaneous production and consumption	Producers of services are also marketers Potential for locational inconvenience
Lack of standardization	Inconsistent quality

SERVICE MARKETING STRATEGIES

In developing the marketing mix for a service, managers usually make explicit allowance for one or more of the special characteristics of services by attempting to develop a special focus for the marketing mix. This focus is usually developed by selecting one or more of the following service marketing strategies: (1) association, (2) industrialization, (3) demand balancing, and (4) relationship marketing.

Association Strategies

Strategies that emphasize linkages between a service and a brand name, a symbol, or some other observable evidence in order to overcome the handicap of intangibility are *association strategies*.

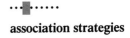

association strategies

• **Corporate Brand Association** • Because service marketers do not as a rule offer branded goods, the brand name is the corporate name. Consequently, the selection of a relevant corporate name is of substantial importance to service marketers. Goods marketers such as Procter & Gamble and Ford may offer an array of different brands that are loosely tied to the corporate name.

For services a relevant and identifiable corporate "brand" helps overcome intangibility by identifying and positioning the company in terms of key benefits. For example, *VISA* is a useful name for a credit card because it implies international access, and *Ticketron* conveys both the nature of the service provided and its electronic delivery.[7]

• **Association with Tangible Objects** • The reputation and benefits of a service organization can also be underscored in communications that associate the organization and its benefits with a tangible object. For example, life insurance companies tend to use advertising and symbolism that links these firms to objects suggesting assurance or protection, such as the Rock of Gibraltar (Prudential) and umbrellas (Travelers). Many organizations also offer tangible objects to symbolize the service being provided and to give the customer something to point to or observe in order to reinforce the service's benefits. Thus colleges award diplomas to make the service of education tangible and banks provide credit cards to make the service of credit tangible.

• **Managing Evidence Associated with the Service** • Services are usually accompanied by some physical objects that are essential or useful to the production or delivery of the service. These physical objects represent tangible cues, or evidence, about the service. They can be managed to provide the customer or client with assurance that the service was or will be performed.

The types of evidence fall into two basic categories: peripheral evidence and essential evidence.[8] *Peripheral evidence* is a tangible item that comes with a service, can be possessed, and represents the service's existence. Examples include theater tickets and savings account passbooks. *Essential evidence* is tangible objects that are associated with the source of production of the service but that cannot be possessed. These objects provide strong proof of the existence of a service. In some cases the most important essential evidence is that which relates to the people providing the service. Such services are said to be people-based. Consequently, uniforms are often provided for unskilled laborers to present

peripheral evidence

essential evidence

a standard or high-quality image. Professional service firms manage evidence through other forms. For example, three-piece suits and prominently displayed diplomas and awards provide evidence of quality for lawyers and accountants. Essential evidence is equipment based when buyers evaluate services on the basis of size, newness, or quality of equipment. A photographer may want clients to be aware of new cameras or processing equipment, and an airline usually tries to keep its aircraft looking new. The American Airlines ad offers essential evidence about the people who provide the safety benefits from air travel.

Regardless of whether the service is people based or equipment based, the *environment* in which a service is offered is also part of the essential evidence. An accountant's office that is painted pink might not inspire total confidence in this service provider.

On the other hand, modest changes in facilities can enhance customer satisfaction. Northwest Airlines embarked on an overhaul of much of its fleet to provide a more comfortable and pleasant environment. On international flights, business class sections were to have only seven-across seating rather than eight-across to allow for wider seats. First-class passengers were to receive new reclining seats. Moreover, the interiors of all aircraft were to receive complete facelifts and more frequent cleaning. The stated goal of the effort was

The qualifications of people performing a service are often used as essential evidence.

(American Airlines, Inc.)

to project an image of concern about the passengers' comfort and thus, over time, to achieve higher levels of customer preference.[9]

Industrialization Strategies

In service industries in which lack of standardization is viewed as a critical problem, service marketers often use an industrialization strategy. An *industrialization strategy* is the application of technology—including tools, machines, or preplanned systems—to reduce reliance on people in performing a service. When this strategy is successful, the consistency of the service or a component of it is improved.

Industrialization can be carried out with either "hard" or "soft" technologies.[10] *Hard technologies* are technologies that involve the substitution of machinery, tools, or facilities to perform tasks that otherwise are performed by people. Automatic car washes, airport X-ray machines, surveillance equipment, and automated bank tellers are examples of industrialization through hard technology. In theory, hard technologies provide services in exactly the same way every time.

Soft technologies by contrast, are technologies that involve the application of organized, preplanned systems (including special equipment and routines) to guide performance. Quality standards are achieved in fast-food restaurants through established routines and the development of specialized roles and tasks. Of course, perfect standardization is not always what the customer wants. Accordingly, many soft technologies have been modified so as to allow the customer to become part of the process. For example, the salad bars at some fast-food restaurants allow the customer to tailor that portion of a meal to suit personal tastes, while overall service standardization is maintained.

Demand-Balancing Strategies

Because inventory can't be built up to meet peaks in demand, such peaks can mean lost sales opportunities. This problem of perishability is compounded by simultaneous production and consumption. When production and consumption cannot be separated, it is even more difficult to meet fluctuating demand. *Demand-balancing strategies* are marketing policies that are designed to reduce demand fluctuations. There are three kinds of demand-balancing strategies: yield management, flexible delivery, and service decoupling.

• **Yield Management** • In chapter 19 we discussed price promotion to build sales during periods of low demand. *Yield management* is the practice of setting prices on services to yield the maximum number of customers at the highest possible prices. Many firms use *off-peak pricing*—encouraging service consumption during off-peak hours by lowering prices. For example, long distance telephone companies offer lower rates on selected days and at selected times when business volume is lower.

However, yield management is more than off-peak pricing because it focuses on the value of the service to the user. With today's computing technology, firms that reserve their services well in advance (such as airlines) can set list prices at rates that may be high but that are acceptable to some market segments (such as business travellers). They then gradually adjust the price of their remaining capacity through discounts to try to draw groups of customers who are willing to buy only at lower prices. Prices continue to decline until the capacity is met.[11]

• **Flexible Delivery** • In the strategy of *flexible delivery* a service marketer attempts to enhance time and space convenience for the customer by changing the method or location

industrialization strategy

hard technologies

soft technologies

demand-balancing strategies

yield management

off-peak pricing

flexible delivery

of service delivery. To the extent that flexibility is achieved, customers will have more non-peak opportunities to acquire or use the service. A good example is the development of automated teller machines (ATMs). These machines allow bank customers to acquire services during nonbank hours (which benefits the customer) while reducing teller lines within the bank during regular hours. Similarly, credit cards enhance the delivery of services because they permit credit to be produced and consumed in a variety of places and times convenient to the customer.

Another method of increasing flexible delivery is through the use of "snakes"—the single lines that feed customers one at a time to a group of bank tellers or airline counters. Studies show that customers prefer snakes to multiple lines because they eliminate the chance of getting stuck in a "slow" line.[12]

Table 21–4 shows various methods of service delivery. Although not all service organizations can employ complex methods, it is important that they determine (1) what level of service delivery they need to be competitive, (2) what level of service delivery they can afford, and (3) whether they can develop innovative delivery mechanisms to gain a competitive advantage.

Obviously, some services can be delivered only in certain ways; pest control services, for example, must come to the customer. However, service marketers should be imaginative in setting and changing delivery policy. Courier services such as Federal Express and Emery enjoy a substantial advantage over the U.S. Postal Service because they pick up from the customer virtually on demand.

·· ·**▪**· ······
decoupling

• **Service Decoupling** • The demand-balancing strategy in which the service is divided into components, some of which can be delivered in different ways, is *decoupling*.[13] Both customer convenience and efficient handling of heavy demand can sometimes be achieved by this strategy. Airlines decouple their service through the use of travel agents and telephone ticketing. Because some elements of the service (providing flight information, taking reservations, and billing) are decoupled, only unusual situations need be handled on a face-to-face basis. Although demand for the basic service (the flights) is unchanged, demand for the peripheral services is more balanced, reducing customer dissatisfaction.

TABLE 21–4 **▮** Methods of Service Delivery

Nature of Interaction between Customer and Service Organization	Availability of Service Outlets	
	Single Site	**Multiple Site**
Customer goes to service organization	Theater Barbershop	Bus service Fast-food chain
Service organization comes to customer	Lawn care service Pest control service Taxi	Mail delivery American Automobile Association emergency repairs
Customer and service organization transact at arm's length (mail or electronic communications)	Credit card company Local TV station	Broadcast network Telephone company

Source: Adapted by permission, from Christopher Lovelock, "Classifying Services to Gain Strategic Marketing Insights," *Journal of Marketing,* Summer 1983, p. 18, published by the American Marketing Association.

Relationship Marketing Strategies

Viewed broadly, *relationship marketing strategies* are marketing strategies designed to enhance the loyalty of customers or to generate more business from existing customers. Because of intangibility and the lack of standardization, it is difficult to differentiate services on the basis of unique attributes or benefits. But services can often be differentiated if a strong ongoing relationship is established with the customer. In recent years, managers in service organizations have given increased attention to relationship marketing strategies. As the Global Marketing box indicates, service firms must often find ways of globalizing their businesses in order to preserve relationships with customers who have global interests.

Figure 21–1 shows how service organizations differ in their customer relationships along two dimensions: whether or not they have some formal "membership" or continuing

relationship marketing strategies

GLOBAL MARKETING

As organizations become more multinational in scope, the service firms they rely on for support must also become multinational. For banks the multinational imperative has been long established. For example, Citicorp has thousands of offices around the world to assist its globalized clients in managing cash, exchanging currencies, and obtaining short-term financing.

Advertising agencies have begun to confront the issue of globalization as well. Large multinationals such as Nestlé, Procter & Gamble, and Sony must adapt their advertising to local languages, symbols, and customs. Often this means that a variety of advertising agencies will be used. Agencies have responded to this need primarily by developing alliances with agencies in other nations to coordinate research and creative strategy.

Possibly the greatest degree of complexity faced by firms doing business in several nations is that arising from legal issues. The advice provided by law firms is not merely a question of technical expertise; reliability and confidentiality

are also important. So even in the case of a minor legal problem, it is desirable to have some sort of relationship with the law firm one will use.

In response to this need, a number of international confederations of law firms have sprung up, some informal and some operating as nonprofit groups with members accepted on an invitation-only basis. One such group is Lex Mundi ("World Law" in Latin), which has members in forty-nine countries. Lex Mundi's eighty-plus law firms are able to provide advice and business contacts in their home areas to clients of associated law firms overseas. By having allied overseas law firms to refer a client to, a local law firm can enhance its credibility with local clients. Additionally, revenues of Lex Mundi members will be enhanced because of the mutual referrals that result.

Source: Information about Lex Mundi from Wayne Green, "Attorneys Form Global Networks," *Wall Street Journal,* July 10, 1990, pp. B1, B6.

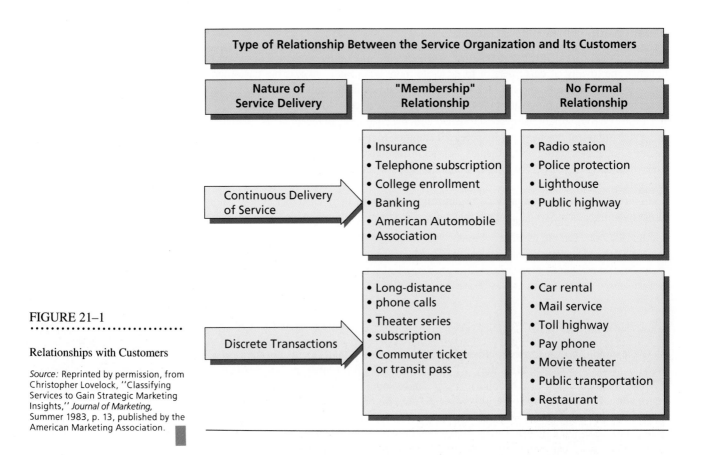

Type of Relationship Between the Service Organization and Its Customers		
Nature of Service Delivery	**"Membership" Relationship**	**No Formal Relationship**
Continuous Delivery of Service	• Insurance • Telephone subscription • College enrollment • Banking • American Automobile • Association	• Radio staion • Police protection • Lighthouse • Public highway
Discrete Transactions	• Long-distance • phone calls • Theater series • subscription • Commuter ticket • or transit pass	• Car rental • Mail service • Toll highway • Pay phone • Movie theater • Public transportation • Restaurant

FIGURE 21–1

Relationships with Customers

Source: Reprinted by permission, from Christopher Lovelock, "Classifying Services to Gain Strategic Marketing Insights," *Journal of Marketing,* Summer 1983, p. 13, published by the American Marketing Association.

account relationship and whether the service is delivered continuously (within a given contract or enrollment period) or purchased at various points in time.

Generally speaking, there are significant advantages to having some sort of membership relationship. A *membership relationship* is a formal exchange relationship in which the customer's identity is known and in which a record of each customer's transactions may be maintained. If a firm is able to develop such a relationship with its customers, it is often able to identify the heaviest users of its services. This enables the firm to target promotional efforts to the largest, most profitable customers. For example, American Express can call up a wealth of information on the spending habits and preferences of its credit card holders. This enables the company to target direct mail promotions of luggage, mutual funds, insurance, and a variety of other goods and services to these customers.[14]

The activities that service marketers can pursue to build relationships fall into three categories: contractual arrangements, systems marketing, and personalizing the service.

membership relationship

• **Contractual Arrangements** • Formal membership relationships usually require some form of contractual arrangement in which the customer has an economic incentive to continue the relationship. Such incentives could be cumulative quantity discounts such as those offered by airline frequent flyer clubs. They could also be initial charges or fees when a customer becomes a member. For example, country clubs have initiation fees and long distance telephone companies have set-up fees. Because these initial investments have to be repeated if a customer switches to a competitor, there is an economic cost to switching.

In 1991 MCI introduced a new version of this strategy with its "Friends and Family" promotion. The program allowed 20 percent discounts to small networks of people who all agreed to use MCI as their long distance carrier. Customers who subsequently left MCI would lose these discounts when making calls to individuals in the group.[15]

• **Systems Marketing** • The relationship marketing strategy of offering a wide array of services to meet a series of related customer needs is *systems marketing.* Although systems marketing is also used by marketers of goods (for example, IBM sells computers and programs), it usually applies to a combination of related services and goods or just services. The essence of systems marketing is the active promotion of a full line of complementary goods and services. For example, most banks view themselves as marketers of a full line of products to meet all of their customers' financial needs (savings, checking, trust services, loans, credit cards, financial counseling, insurance, and so on).[16] The PTT Telecom ad provides an example of a firm emphasizing its system of services.

Usually systems marketers provide the benefit of convenience through one-stop shopping. However, it may also be useful to promote the compatibility advantages of using a single source for multiple services. For example, some banks offer a tailored mix of invest-

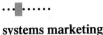

systems marketing

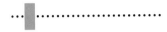

Many firms emphasize their ability to offer systems of related services.

(One of three ads in a worldwide campaign for PTT Telecom Netherlands. Agency: PPGH/JWT Amsterdam.)

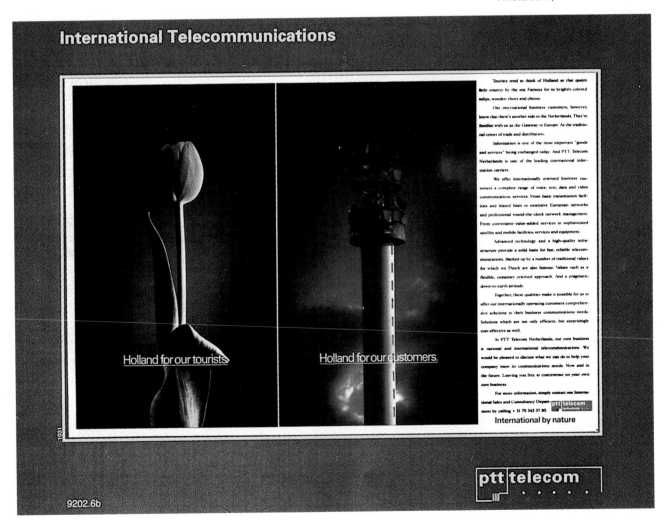

ment alternatives to customers. They argue that by being a complete financial provider, they can best understand and service a customer's total financial needs.

Increasingly, professional services providers have adopted the systems marketing perspective. For example, many law firms specializing in family law have established working relationships with psychiatrists and psychologists because some legal problems (such as divorce) have strong emotional consequences for clients. One Austin, Texas, law firm offers free group therapy sessions in its own law offices.[17]

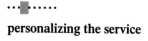

personalizing the service

Germany's largest bank portrays relationships as one of its fundamental principles.

(Courtesy of the Deutsche Bank Group.)

• **Personalizing the Service** • Developing a close business relationship in which the service provider becomes familiar with the needs of individual customers is *personalizing the service*. The most widely accepted example of this strategy is the relationship between hair stylists and their customers—a relationship that combines strong interpersonal ties that complement (and enhance) the knowledge of customers' needs.

Similarly, as the Deutsche Bank Group ad suggests, in many business services, interpersonal contact is critical to successful relationship marketing efforts. Salespeople often perform the role of ''relationship managers'' in complex service businesses. Studies show

Let's talk about relationships

A relationship is more than a history of doing business. It's a link based on mutual understanding and trust. To grow, it must be fostered through tangible effort and attention.

All of us at Deutsche Bank understand what it takes to make a relationship work. This understanding takes shape in all of our policies, practices and plans. Around the world, you'll find us ready to talk business – real business – today and for tomorrow.

Deutsche Bank –
Your Partner in the World

Deutsche Bank Group

Branches, subsidiaries and representative offices in Europe: Amsterdam, Antwerpen, Barcelona and more than 100 branches in Spain. Brussels, Federal Republic of Germany with more than 1300 branches. Geneva, Istanbul, Lisbon, London, Lugano, Luxembourg, Madrid, Manchester, Milan and more than 100 branches in Italy. Moscow, Oporto, Paris, Rotterdam, Strasbourg, Vienna, Zurich.

North and South America: Buenos Aires, Campinas, Caracas, Chicago, Deerfield, Los Angeles, Mexico, Montevideo, New York, Porto Alegre, Santiago de Chile, São Paulo, Toronto, Willemstad. Asia-Pacific: Bangkok, Beijing, Bombay, Colombo, Hong Kong, Jakarta, Karachi, Kuala Lumpur, Lahore, Macao, Manila, Melbourne, Nagoya, New Delhi, Osaka, Pusan, Seoul, Singapore, Surabaya, Sydney, Taipei, Tokyo. Africa and Middle East: Cairo, Johannesburg, Lagos, Manama, Tehran.

Airlines know the names of their frequent flyers. Airlines can also accumulate a lot of other information about these passengers. What ethical issues might arise out of this membership relationship?
[© David E. Dempster]

that the degree of trust and satisfaction that customers experience from their relationship with the sales force is a critical determinant of long-term sales opportunities.[18]

MARKETING IN NONPROFIT ORGANIZATIONS

In the first chapter of this book we showed how marketing is used in nonprofit organizations as well as in businesses. In subsequent chapters we used nonprofit organizations to illustrate some of the basic marketing concepts and techniques.

Because most nonprofit organizations are basically service organizations, the issues and strategies presented earlier in this chapter are pertinent to nonprofit marketers. Additionally, as suggested in the Ethics in Marketing box, numerous ethical issues arise in the marketing of services and nonprofit organizations. In the rest of the chapter we examine special considerations relevant to nonprofit marketing.

Scope of Nonprofit Marketing

As Table 21–5 demonstrates, a wide range of public and private organizations can be labeled as nonprofit. Clearly, not all such organizations have an equal interest in marketing activities. However, marketing concepts are useful to every organization on occasion. For example, state tourist bureaus are public nonprofit organizations that use marketing to compete with one another. The ad that describes the benefits of U.S. savings bonds is another case of marketing by a public nonprofit organization.

Similarly, examples of the use of marketing in private nonprofit organizations include advertising decisions made by political parties, price decisions made by orchestras, and place decisions (such as for home health care programs) made by hospitals. Although all of these organizations may be viewed as service organizations, the focus of their marketing efforts can vary substantially in terms of what is being marketed. Universities are service organizations that market education but that also market a specific *place* (the institution). Social cause organizations are service organizations whose real focus is on marketing specific *social ideas*. Political organizations that support certain candidates for office are service organizations interested in marketing *people*. In many cases a primary role of marketing is to stimulate *membership* in the organization. These complexities reflect the special considerations needed to understand the role of marketing in nonprofit organizations.

ETHICS IN
MARKETING

Because services are intangible, it is often difficult for consumers to evaluate whether a service has been adequately performed. This creates potential opportunities for unethical organizations.

Consider, for example, the high frequency of consumer complaints about auto repair and the apparent ease with which many people are duped into phony investment schemes. Although such problems involve ethical behavior in the operations area as well as in the marketing area, a major concern is how the customer should be protected. Can unethical service be eliminated through consumer education? What kinds of information would be useful in helping consumers evaluate a service business? Is some form of licensing by the government the best answer?

When marketing by nonprofit organizations is considered, several other ethical issues come into play. For example, some people find fault with the marketing of charitable organizations such as United Way, suggesting that marketing activities require scarce resources that should properly be used to conduct charitable work. Others believe that such activities pit one charity against another in terms of fund-raising. How should the

results of such activities be evaluated? Can these objections be addressed?

What about the use of corporate sponsorships to support nonprofit groups? Should such sponsorships be sought if a sponsor stands to gain by association with that organization? For example, should the American Heart Association allow a pharmaceutical firm to pay for commercials that describe risk factors for heart attacks but end with a commercial for the pharmaceutical company's painkiller?

The marketing of political parties and candidates and of social causes is sometimes questioned on the basis that whichever side generates the most funds for use in promoting its point of view stands a better chance of winning. Thus important social and political issues may be decided not on their merits but on their marketing support. Moreover, some groups may not be heard at all because of their small size or lack of wealth. Are these criticisms of nonprofit marketing legitimate? Should the use of marketing be regulated in such cases? Or is the access to and use of marketing expertise a right that all individuals and organizations have?

TABLE 21–5 ▮ Types of Nonprofit Organizations

....

Public Nonprofit Organizations

- Producers of services (postal service, public schools, government tourist bureaus, libraries)
- Funds transfer agencies (Internal Revenue Service, Social Security Administration)
- Intervention-type agencies (courts, Federal Trade Commission)

Private Nonprofit Organizations

- Religious organizations (World Council of Churches, individual churches)
- Social organizations (Junior League, Kiwanis, Boy Scouts, sororities)
- Cultural organizations (orchestras, museums, zoos)
- Educational organizations (private schools and research institutes)
- Trade and professional organizations (trade unions, American Medical Association)
- Political organizations (political parties and lobbying groups)
- Philanthropic organizations (nonprofit hospitals, United Way)
- Social cause organizations (peace groups, Sierra Club, consumer groups)

....

Source: Based on Philip Kotler, *Marketing for Nonprofit Organizations,* 2d ed. (Englewood Cliffs, N.J.: Prentice-Hall, 1982), pp. 13–14.

Many public nonprofit organizations recognize the importance of meeting customer needs.

(U.S. Savings Bonds Division, Department of the Treasury.)

Unique Aspects of Nonprofit Marketing

Managers of nonprofit organizations operate under conditions that are somewhat different than those of for-profit organizations. The most important nonprofit conditions are (1) the dominance of nonfinancial objectives, (2) the existence of multiple constituencies, and (3) the conflict between organizational mission and customer satisfaction.[19]

• **Nonfinancial Objectives** • By definition, nonprofit organizations do not seek to earn profits for the benefit of owners or stockholders. Indeed, many of these organizations (especially public organizations) are not involved in any revenue-generating activities.

One consequence of the dominance of nonfinancial objectives is that some nonfinancial criteria need to be established to evaluate the organization's performance. Thus an orchestra may evaluate its performance by product-oriented criteria (for example, by reviewing the quality of its own performance) or by market-oriented criteria (what the reviews said).

Unfortunately, the criteria used often are solely product oriented. Nonprofits can be so centered around their offering that they think only ignorance or lack of motivation can explain a lack of market interest in it.[20] Increasingly, however, attention is also being paid to customer or client responses and to the development of parallel marketing efforts for enhancing nonfinancial market responses.

For example, a large Catholic hospital chain in the Southwest increased revenues by 15 percent while raising patient care standards. Essentially, management recognized that an increasing amount of health care should be provided *outside* the hospital (in rehabilitation centers and in lab and X-ray networks, for instance). By branching into such services, instead of trying to keep such activities within the old hospitals, the network provided improved health care delivery to the poor while enhancing the hospital's reputation for quality.[21] Similarly, the primary mission of the Girl Scouts is to address the needs of girls growing up in a changing society. To assess how well they achieve that goal, the organization must consider market-oriented measures such as size of membership as well as qualitative judgments of performance.

multiple constituencies

• **Multiple Constituencies** • Although the primary goals of nonprofit organizations are nonfinancial, these organizations still need to acquire resources to perform their functions. Often the resources generated directly from primary operations (such as museum admissions fees and university tuition) are insufficient. In such cases, resources must be sought from other sources. *Multiple constituencies* are the various groups, individuals, and organizations that provide supplemental resources for nonprofit organizations. In the case of the Girl Scouts, outside constituencies include social service agencies such as Head Start, business and professional organizations that provide leaders and that help organize educational and career-related programs, and consumers who purchase Girl Scout cookies.

An important consequence of multiple constituencies is that multiple marketing programs must usually be developed, each targeted to a specific constituency. Moreover, these programs may differ from the programs used to market the basic service. Thus a university engages in separate marketing efforts for potential students, for research-funding government agencies, for foundations, and for alumni.

development-oriented nonprofit marketing

Marketing efforts directed toward prospective donors should be development oriented rather than campaign oriented. *Development-oriented nonprofit marketing* is a marketing approach that emphasizes long-term relationships with targeted donor groups; it is based on the idea of mutually satisfying exchanges. This approach implies the need to understand the benefits donors receive for supporting a nonprofit organization. For instance, university alumni give money for many reasons, including a desire to feel a part of their alma mater.

In a developmental approach the organization finds mechanisms (such as alumni newsletters) for offering this kind of benefit on an ongoing basis.

Campaign-oriented nonprofit marketing is a marketing approach that consists of occasional broad based, money-oriented appeals (for example, annual telethons and media campaigns such as the one portrayed in the Environmental Challenge fund ad). Typically campaign-oriented approaches emphasize only the organization's needs.[22]

Increasingly, nonprofits have begun to cultivate corporate sponsors in their quest to reach their constituencies. For years nonprofits have relied on the media for about $3 billion a year in free public service ads. Now many charities are using paid messages underwritten by corporate partners to more effectively reach their constituencies. Sponsors often receive a direct benefit from such associations. For example, Marion Merrell Dow, manufacturer of Nicorette antismoking gum, has provided several million dollars in support of the American Lung Association's "Non-Dependence Day" for smokers.[23]

campaign-oriented nonprofit marketing

• **Conflict between the Mission and Customer Satisfaction** • The traditional philosophy of the marketing concept does not apply fully to nonprofit organizations. That is, non-

A variety of marketing efforts are used to attract donors for nonprofit social causes.

(This advertisement created as a public service by Lawner Reingold Britton & Partners, Boston, Massachusetts.)

profits cannot always completely satisfy all customer wants and still maintain the philosophical foundations on which their missions rest. Many social cause organizations (such as antidrug groups) exist to stop people from doing things that appeal to them. Similarly, religious and political organizations might choose to pursue programs and policies that alienate some members, and universities might establish requirements that are unpopular but essential to the educational mission.

There are, however, ways of enhancing customer satisfaction without directly affecting the core mission. For example, universities can enhance the quality of housing or recreational opportunities to increase student satisfaction. The Girl Scouts redesigned their uniforms for a more fashionable appearance. This action neither supported nor contradicted the mission of helping girls reach their potential, but it certainly enhanced overall satisfaction. Thus the action indirectly contributed to the nonfinancial objectives of the organization.

SUMMARY OF LEARNING OBJECTIVES

1. Explain the complexities that result from the special characteristics of services.

Services have four special characteristics: (1) intangibility, (2) perishability, (3) simultaneous production and consumption, and (4) lack of standardization. These characteristics lead to several major problems, including difficulties in demonstrating service benefits, supply and demand imbalances, locational inconvenience, and uneven service quality.

2. Identify the service marketing strategies available for dealing with service characteristics.

The four basic service marketing strategies are (1) association, (2) industrialization, (3) demand-balancing, and (4) relationship marketing.

3. Explain the purpose of relationship marketing and identify its methods.

Relationship marketing strategies are strategies designed to enhance the loyalty of customers or to generate more business from existing customers. Three methods of relationship marketing are:

(1) contractual arrangements, (2) systems marketing, and (3) personalizing the service.

4. Understand the unique aspects of marketing in nonprofit organizations.

Marketing in nonprofit organizations is complicated by three key considerations: (1) organizational objectives are primarily nonfinancial, (2) separate marketing efforts may be needed to deal with multiple constituencies, and (3) customer satisfaction and the organizational mission are sometimes in conflict.

5. Contrast the major strategies nonprofits can use in marketing efforts directed toward prospective donors.

Marketing efforts aimed at donors can be either development oriented or campaign oriented. Development-oriented approaches emphasize long-term relationships with targeted donor groups that are based on mutually satisfying exchanges. Campaign-oriented approaches rely on occasional broad-based, money-oriented appeals.

Review Questions

1. What is meant by *intangibility*?

2. What are the implications of simultaneous production and consumption?

3. What major difficulties do consumers face in evaluating the value of a service?

4. Why is a corporate name more important to service businesses than to most goods manufacturers?

5. How do peripheral and essential evidence differ?

6. What is the distinction between hard technologies and soft technologies in an industrialization strategy?

7. What is yield management?

8. What are the purposes of relationship marketing strategies?

9. What do nonprofit organizations market in addition to services?

10. In nonprofit marketing, what is meant by the conflict between organizational mission and customer satisfaction.

Discussion Questions

1. To what extent do the special characteristics of services create a problem for securities brokers such as Merrill Lynch and Prudential-Bache? How should these organizations respond to such problems?

2. Recall a recent service encounter you have experienced and describe the actions of the service personnel that were production oriented and those that were market oriented.

3. Discuss how evidence is typically managed by each of the following types of service organizations: dentists, libraries, and shoe repair shops.

4. Develop a list of services that might be provided either in a highly industrialized manner or in a fairly nonstandardized way. (One example is check cashing—automated tellers versus human tellers.) Discuss the basic advantages and disadvantages associated with each approach.

5. Develop a list of services for which personalizing the service is likely to be an effective way to build relationships. Discuss what the services on your list have in common.

6. What are the various constituencies faced by each of the following: a nonprofit hospital, a public library, the Democratic Party, and the U.S. Park Service?

7. If you were marketing a college baseball team, how would your strategies differ from those used to market a major league baseball team?

Application Exercise

Reread the material about the Girl Scouts of America at the beginning of this chapter and answer the following questions:

1. What strategies could the Girl Scouts use for overcoming the problems associated with intangibility?

2. Is relationship marketing an important strategy for the Girl Scouts? Explain.

3. List some nonfinancial objectives that you think might be appropriate for the Girl Scouts.

4. Can you conceive of situations in which the Girl Scouts' marketing efforts might come into conflict with its primary mission? What boundaries would you set to separate acceptable marketing activities from those that might conflict with or be inconsistent with the mission?

Key Concepts

The following key terms were introduced in this chapter:

service encounter
association strategies
peripheral evidence
essential evidence
industrialization strategy
hard technologies
soft technologies

demand-balancing strategies
yield management
off-peak pricing
flexible delivery
decoupling
relationship marketing
   strategies

membership relationship
systems marketing
personalizing the service
multiple constituencies
development-oriented
   nonprofit marketing
campaign-oriented nonprofit
   marketing

CASES

Pinkerton's

Pinkerton's is the oldest and most famous security firm in the world, its name having become a piece of popular legend when "the Pinkertons"—detectives who were often the only force for law and order in the Wild West—helped track down such outlaws as the Younger brothers, the James brothers, and Butch Cassidy and the Sundance Kid. But by the late 1980s Pinkerton's seemed to be riding off into the sunset. Its owner, American Brands, had unsuccessfully tried to move the firm into new markets, and the company had begun to run up substantial losses.

In 1988, American Brands sold Pinkerton's to Tom Wathen, the owner of California Plant Protection (CPP), a West Coast uniformed-guard firm. If anyone could reverse Pinkerton's fortunes it was Wathen, who knew the security business and knew how to turn a security firm around. He had gained this knowledge the hard way. Only months after joining and then buying the then-tiny CPP in the early 1960s Wathen discovered that CPP was essentially bankrupt.

Before joining CPP Wathen had worked as a security director for the federal government and for several large companies. In those positions, he had usually subcontracted security duties to uniformed-guard firms. Now he had to scramble to turn CPP around the only way he knew how—by running the business so that it would answer his concerns as if he were the customer. He analyzed potential clients' individual problems to show them how they could get better security from CPP for less money. He carefully screened job applicants for reliability and psychological stability and then provided them with continuous training after they were hired. He promoted only guards who had completed a course in security methods and had passed a proctored examination to the position of "certified security officer." And to make his clients' workplaces safer, he allowed less than two percent of his employees to carry guns; the rest were trained to handle security problems without resorting to shooting.

The uniformed-guard business was and is an easy one to enter; most customers are reassured simply by the presence of a uniform and a gun. Competition in this market is fierce, but Wathen soon learned that his marketing approach could get results. By the end of Wathen's first year of ownership CPP was out of debt. By 1984 CPP was big enough to supply about two-thirds of the private-security hours for the 1984 Los Angeles Olympics. By 1987 CPP had offices in 38 states and around $250 million in annual revenues. And by 1988 it was big enough to take over Pinkerton's.

At first Wathen called the new, merged company CPP/Pinkerton. But a few years later he changed it to just plain Pinkerton's. In fact, the Pinkerton name was the most valuable asset Wathen acquired in the Pinkerton purchase, he told *Nation's Business*: "We were buying history. We were buying name recognition."

Now Wathen has done for the once-ailing Pinkerton's what he previously did for the sickly CPP. He has reestablished close relationships with customers in order to service their individual needs. He has reinforced his commitment to training Pinkerton personnel. And he has dropped unprofitable accounts. The result: Pinkerton's 1989 net income, after taxes and interest payments for debt taken on to finance the acquisition, climbed to over $6 million.

Questions

1. How has Tom Wathen tried to overcome the problem of lack of standardization in service marketing?

2. Has Wathen undertaken any association strategies? If so, what types?

3. Is relationship marketing a feasible strategy for Pinkerton's? Why or why not?

McGladrey & Pullen—Who Markets?

JOHN W. GILLETT, *University of North Dakota*
DENNIS J. ELBERT, *University of North Dakota*

McGladrey & Pullen is the nation's tenth largest accounting and consulting firm. It has grown to national stature by helping individuals and businesses succeed for more than 80 years. The firm measures its success by that of its clients.

Those clients run the gamut of commercial and industrial enterprises in the United States today—from manufacturing to wholesaling to retailing. They include financial services businesses such as banks, savings and loan associations, real estate development concerns, and investment and insurance firms; personal services enterprises such as hospitals, nursing homes, individual health care practitioners, government entities, and attorneys; and representatives of specific industries such as agribusiness, construction, communications and publishing, textiles, and mineral extraction.

McGladrey & Pullen currently has over 70 offices located in major metropolitan areas and smaller communities across the nation. The firm also serves their clients through the McGladrey Network. The McGladrey Network is an affiliation of independent accounting firms who share the common bond of a commitment to helping closely held business.

Internationally, McGladrey & Pullen is known as Dunwoody Robson McGladrey & Pullen. This affiliation provides their clients access to financial and management expertise in more than 60 countries around the world.

Currently McGladrey & Pullen has over 2,350 personnel throughout the United States, including 381 partners and nearly 2,000 other highly qualified professionals. In addition, through the McGladrey Network, more than 1,000 other partners and professionals serve clients from an additional 36 offices in 13 states and the District of Columbia.

McGladrey & Pullen's philosophy can be seen in their mission statement. Their mission is to "help their clients grow, prosper and accomplish their objectives." To accomplish this mission they must give their clients more than routine service and assistance. Their standard procedure is to ask themselves, "What would I expect from my CPA firm if I were the client?" The answer to that question forces them to go beyond basic accounting services and provide what the client needs as well as what the client wants.

Like many large accounting firms, McGladrey & Pullen hired a marketing director to establish a marketing culture for their firm. As part of that culture and to ensure that their professionals know what is expected of them, the guidelines shown in Table 1 are shared with all their professionals. The guidelines and anticipated changes in responsibility for marketing activity vary with years of service and experience.

Questions

1. In what ways does McGladrey & Pullen practice relationship marketing?

2. How does McGladrey & Pullen work on its public image?

3. How do the special characteristics of services create a problem for a public accounting firm.

4. Describe several types of marketing activities that a public accounting firm could use. What strategy/objective do these activities have?

TABLE 1   McGladrey & Pullen Marketing Guidelines

Years of Experience	Marketing Activities
1–2	• build technical competence • learn the services and culture of the firm • apprentice with "in-field" client relations • attend firm-sponsored functions
3–4	• strengthen and build technical competence • learn to tell a brief firm history • learn to give a "one minute" commercial about the firm • participate in a civic or professional club • take on Practice Development (PD) assignments, such as attendance at trade fairs; help with proposals . . . • identify new work opportunities and communicate them to the partners • take on a leadership role in a civic or professional club
5–7	• strengthen and expand technical competence and industry concentrations • participate in communications skills and sales training • under the guidance of a partner, write articles, give speeches • apprentice in new sales through going along with a partner or manager on a prospect call • aggressively identify new work opportunities within existing client service • assume greater responsibility for PD committee assignments, such as monitoring, tracking and reporting
7+	• strengthen and deepen technical competence, with focus on industry or service concentrations • develop a personal PD plan • have dollar growth goals • assume responsibility for an element of the office's marketing program; guide others' participation • continue communication skills and sales training • represent the firm at public events and private functions • expand leadership roles in civic and professional organizatons • take the lead in "closing" a new engagement, under the guidance of a partner • "mentor" 1–7 year people

22

INTERNATIONAL
MARKETING

OBJECTIVES

After reading this chapter you will be able to

1. Distinguish among international trade, international marketing, multinational company, and transnational company.

2. Explain why international marketers should engage in environmental monitoring.

3. Identify the various forms of regional trading blocs.

4. Identify various approaches to entering foreign markets.

5. Contrast the globalization and adaptation strategies.

Record numbers of small businesses are turning overseas to bolster their profits. Even the tiniest—and greenest—entrepreneurs are cracking foreign markets. "There's a place in every market for this," says Carewell Industries co-founder Tony Gelbart, pointing to a "Made in the USA" label on one of the hundreds of toothbrushes his eight-person concern exports to fourteen nations.

On the estimated 100,000 U.S. companies that export, roughly 80 percent are small. According to a spokesperson for the National Association of Manufacturers: "It's an awakening. Small companies are finding that there is life beyond the domestic market."

For example, on a hunch about European demand for his leather goods, Earl Thompson, the owner of Torel Inc. of Yoakum, Texas, made his first trip abroad to a leather trade show in Nuremburg, Germany, several years ago. He walked into the auditorium with a cowboy hat, cowboy boots, and a silver belt buckle. "They all called me J.R.," he recalls.

With no interpreter, he pinned a big map and flag of Texas on the wall, then set up his leather display and waited. "I was resorting to international sign language, you know, pointing to the goods," Thompson says. The display drew hundreds. Thompson says he found that German clients want "a little gaudier product than what we sell in the U.S., more of a John Wayne product," such as embossed leather belts with white stitching and big buckles.

He flew back to Germany the following year but this time went to retailers. He teamed up with a U.S. leather distributor based in Germany, and the two drove across the country, visiting nearly fifty retail shops in one week.

On one trip Thompson laid out a line of hand-tooled wallets before a shop owner. "He took one look at them and said, 'They don't have coin purses.' Being from Texas, I said, 'Men use those?' He said 'Yes.'" Now Torel wallets for Germany have coin purses and are deeper to hold German bills.

Quicksilver Enterprises, based in Temecula, California, makes ultralight airplanes in the United States. Flying the 250-pound aluminum-and-fiberglass bird, which looks like a go-cart with wings, has become a cultist hobby among amateur pilots. Recently Broyhill Company, a Dakota City, Nebraska, maker of liquid-spray equipment for tractors, proposed a marriage of products with Quicksilver to make innovative, ultralight crop-dusters. Today many Third World farmers use these "iron butterflies." Priced at $18,000 or less, they're an alternative to standard crop-dusters, which average more than $100,000.

Roughly half of Quicksilver's annual sales are made to foreign buyers. But conducting international business is seldom easy. For example, to get around a steep import tax in Brazil, Quicksilver licensed a local distributor to build and sell the plane there. But six months after Quicksilver engineers taught the concern to build, fly, and fix the plane, the royalties stopped. The Brazilian firm claimed it had "changed the design, and therefore it was a new plane," and they just never paid Quicksilver.[1]

INTERNATIONAL TRADE, MARKETING, AND COMPANIES

It is important to understand the nature and growing importance of international trade, international marketing, and multinational and transnational companies. Each involves activities that cross national boundaries.

International Trade

The movement of goods and services across national borders—the imports and exports of nations—is *international trade*. Although goods have been traded among nations for centuries, services now outrank manufacturing and extractive industries in the United States in terms of their respective rates of growth in international trade. Examples include financial, consulting, advertising, legal, insurance, and data processing services.

International trade is not as big a factor in the U.S. economy as it is in the economies of countries such as the Netherlands, Germany, and the United Kingdom. Exports account for a much higher percentage of their gross national product (GNP) than is the case in the United States. In addition, the U.S. share of total world exports has been declining.

The United States is totally dependent on imports of some products (chromium and coffee are examples) and highly dependent on imports of other products (petroleum is an example). Other imports, such as cars and VCRs, are not critical but are demanded by many Americans.

On the other hand, some U.S. industries, such as the chemical and agricultural industries, depend heavily on exports for sales revenues and profit. Exports of farm products, the biggest export category, are so important that they govern the health of the agricultural industry in the United States. Table 22–1 identifies the ten largest industrial exporters in the United States. As this table and the GM ad suggest, export sales are very important to this company.

TABLE 22–1

The Ten Largest U.S. Industrial Exporters in 1990
(Ranked by Dollar Volume)

Rank	Company	Exports (in Millions of Dollars)	Exports as Percent of Sales
1	Boeing	$16,093.0	58.3
2	General Motors	10,315.9	8.2
3	General Electric	7,128.0	12.2
4	Ford Motor	7,098.0	7.2
5	International Business Machines	6,195.0	9.0
6	Chrysler	5,004.0	16.2
7	E. I. duPont de Nemours	4,352.0	10.9
8	United Technologies	3,606.0	16.6
9	McDonnell Douglas	3,538.0	21.6
10	Caterpillar	3,435.0	29.8

Source: Reprinted by permission from "The *Fortune* Directory of the Biggest U.S. Industrial Exporters," *Fortune,* 1991 Special Issue, Spring–Summer 1991, p. 60 © 1991 Time Inc. All rights reserved.

An ad that focuses on General Motors' involvement in exporting cars from North America.

(Reprinted with permission of General Motors Corporation.)

Americans bought $15 billion worth of products made in China in 1990, up 27 percent from 1989, on top of a 41 percent jump the year before. At $10.4 billion and rising, the U.S. trade deficit with China will soon be second only to the one with Japan.

The only thing that could slow China's export momentum—short of political upheaval in Beijing—would be the loss of its privileged trading status with the United States. Since 1980 China has been one of the few communist countries designated a "most-favored nation" in trading with the United States. Most-favored countries get to trade at normal tariff rates. The unfavored, such as Cuba, face tariffs of 70 percent or more on many products.

The most-favored status has typically been used to encourage liberal emigration policies and human rights protection. Under U.S. trade law the President can grant it to a human rights violator such as China on a year-to-year basis if the President decides that the country is making progress in the right direction.

In late May 1991 President Bush announced he would renew China's status, triggering a sharp response from Senate Democrats, who have been wanting to punish China since the student uprising that culminated in the Tiananmen Square massacre in 1989. There was a similar uproar over renewal of China's privileges in 1990, but it eventually died down. That debate focused mainly on China's dismal human rights record.

What gave the issue greater urgency in 1991 was the swollen trade deficit and the factors enlarging it: China's lax protection of patents and other intellectual property and its severe restrictions on imports. If China were stripped of most-favored status, its exports to the United States would be largely snuffed out by killer tariffs. For example, duties on stuffed toy animals would rise from 6.8 percent to 70 percent, on men's trousers from 17.7 percent to 90 percent. Odyssey International, an American-managed company that produces North Face sleeping bags and a wide range of pricey sportswear brands, says it would move 70 to 80 percent of production out of China.

Wal-Mart, Kmart, Sears, and other mass merchandisers would have to scramble to locate suppliers outside China. The retailers—and American consumers—would almost certainly pay more. A Hong Kong toy manufacturer jokes that Santa Claus would have to shoulder the greatest price increase because the toy industry is so concentrated in southern China that it would take years to move someplace else.

China's export machine is the beneficiary of two formidable advantages: a bountiful supply of people who will cut, sew, twist, and insert for a bowl of rice and as little as $2 a day, and lots of foreign capital and manufacturing expertise, mostly from Hong Kong, Taiwan, and South Korea. When wages and other costs began rising in Taiwan in the late 1980s, entrepreneurs shipped whole shoe-making factories to Fujian province, just across the Formosa Strait. Hong Kong toy makers have been moving their machines over the border into southern China even longer.

Source: Adapted by permission from Ford S. Worthy, "Making It in China," *Fortune,* June 17, 1991, pp. 103–104. © 1991 Time Inc. All rights reserved.

- **Why Do Nations Trade?** • Even if a country can produce everything it needs more efficiently than all other countries, it can still benefit from trade. *Comparative advantage* is the position a country enjoys when it produces the products in which it has the greatest advantage, or the least disadvantage, in relation to other countries. The idea is that each country should specialize in producing products in which it has the greatest comparative advantage and import those in which it has the greatest comparative disadvantage. Mutual trust among all nations would also be necessary because the nations would be highly interdependent.

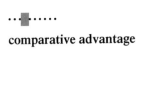

comparative advantage

- **The Balance of Trade** • A country's *balance of trade* is the difference in value between its total exports and total imports. For many decades prior to the 1970s the U.S. balance of trade was *favorable* in almost every year. Exports were greater than imports. But in the 1970s, the 1980s, and thus far the 1990s the United States has had *unfavorable* balances of trade in most years. (The most recent year during which the United States had a favorable balance of trade was 1975.) Imports have been much greater than exports.

balance of trade

The United States' unfavorable balance of trade has a variety of causes, including heavy imports of petroleum, the long-term increasing productivity of many foreign firms and their ability to compete more effectively with U.S. firms (in part because of lower labor costs in many other countries), and the willingness of some foreign marketers to accept reduced profit levels in order to maintain or increase their market share in the United States. Furthermore, some Americans apparently believe that some types of imported products are superior in quality to American-made products. This, as we saw in earlier chapters, has stimulated a major concern about quality on the part of U.S.-based firms. The Global marketing box discusses our trade deficit with China.

Recently the United States has begun to close its trade gap with the rest of the world. For example, in 1990, for the first time in eight years, the United States had a surplus in merchandise trade with twenty-three countries of Western Europe, which receive 29 percent of U.S. exports. American firms sold $4 billion more to Europe than they bought. The recession in the United States played a role, however, as Americans bought fewer imports. The United States' merchandise trade deficit peaked in 1987 at $159 billion. It was $101 billion in 1990.[2] In addition, the United States narrowed its trade gap with Japan from $49.1 billion in 1989 to $41.1 billion in 1990.[3] The challenge for U.S. firms is to continue narrowing the gap between U.S. exports and imports.

International Marketing

International marketing, global marketing, multinational marketing, and *transnational marketing* are some of the terms used to refer to marketing across national boundaries. In unprecedented numbers U.S.-based organizations and organizations headquartered abroad are seeking to participate in the explosive growth in the volume of transborder marketing activity.

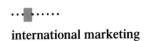

international marketing

Both business and nonbusiness organizations engage in international marketing. *International marketing* is the efforts of individuals and organizations to satisfy human wants by facilitating exchanges across national boundaries. Table 22–1 identified several business organization examples. Nonbusiness organization examples are UNICEF (United Nations International Children's Fund), religious organizations that send missionaries abroad to seek converts, and U.S. universities that recruit international students.

Clearly, the major difference between purely domestic marketing and international marketing is environmental. The basic concepts that underlie the development of marketing strategies are universal. But marketing strategies must be formulated with an understanding

of the uncontrollable environmental variables in each country in which the organization engages in marketing efforts.

Multinational and Transnational Companies

Switzerland-based Nestlé is the world's largest food company. It has more than four hundred plants in sixty countries. Nestlé products are in most every aisle in most every supermarket in most every major country. The company has been described as a kind of corporate United Nations. For example, there are ten nationalities among fourteen market heads in the company's Asia-Pacific territory.[4]

U.S.-based CPC International is the maker of such familiar brands as Mazola corn oil, Skippy peanut butter, and Hellman's mayonnaise. CPC's foreign operations account for 57 percent of its earnings and sales, the highest percentage of any major U.S. food company.[5] One-third of CPC's officers are foreign nationals.[6]

Ireland-based CRH is a building materials producer. It is the product of about sixty mergers and acquisitions. CRH operates in the United Kingdom, mainland Europe, and the United States. The company's chief executive says, ''We're working for the day when CRH will be seen not as an Irish multinational, but a multinational that happens to be located in Ireland.''[7]

U.S.-based Colgate-Palmolive Company derives 64 percent of its sales and 63 percent of its operating profits from foreign operations. It operates in over 160 countries, ranging from Argentina to Zimbabwe. Colgate-Palmolive's CEO says, ''Our real strength is in being truly global.''[8]

Traditionally such companies are called multinational companies—and the greater the number of countries in which they do business, the more international, or multinational, they are. Thus a *multinational company (MNC)* is a firm that is based in one country (the *parent,* or home, country) and produces goods or provides services in one or more foreign countries (*host* countries).

In recent years many internationalists have distinguished between multinational com-

multinational company (MNC)

panies and the evolving transnational companies. A *transnational company* is a firm that views the world as one market, conducts operations in many countries, and makes decisions as if national boundaries did not exist. Thus a transnational manufacturing firm buys supplies, raises capital, conducts research and development, and manufactures its products wherever in the world it can do so most effectively and efficiently. It does not distinguish between its home and host countries; its headquarters can be in any country. It seeks to develop and maintain a single worldwide identity. Its executives are of various nationalities, and they are global managers. Transnational companies also have been called global companies, world companies, stateless companies, and borderless companies.[9]

More and more companies are seeking to become more globally focused. For example, when Procter & Gamble's CEO retired in 1989, he was replaced by Edwin L. Artzt, the vice chairman and president of P&G's international unit. Artzt had turned P&G into a powerful contender in the international market. P&G observers said that he was being rewarded for reviving the company's overseas operations.[10] (We will use *international companies* in the rest of the chapter when there is no need to distinguish between multinational and transnational firms.)

THE ENVIRONMENT OF INTERNATIONAL MARKETING

Organizations that engage in marketing efforts in more than one country must do a thorough job of monitoring environmental variables in targeted domestic and foreign markets (see Figure 22–1). This monitoring effort is relevant to decision making about selecting and entering foreign markets and developing marketing strategies for them.

Even if an organization restricts its operations to its home country, it should at least be

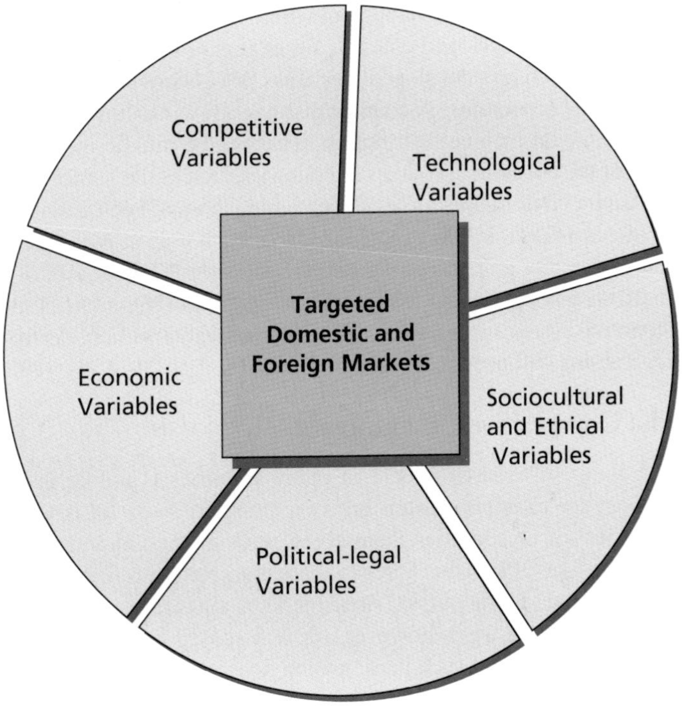

transnational company

FIGURE 22–1

The Focus for Environmental Monitoring in International Marketing

Competitive Variables

Technological Variables

Economic Variables

Targeted Domestic and Foreign Markets

Sociocultural and Ethical Variables

Political-legal Variables

aware of present and potential foreign competitors. Foreign rivals can target entire industries or major sectors of a given industry. If firms in the affected industries are unaware of this, they can lose market share very quickly.

The Economic Environment

Underdeveloped country, Third World nation, less developed country (LDC), emerging nation, newly industrialized country, and *developed nation* are among the many designations used to describe a country's stage of economic development. A country's current and potential levels of economic development determine its capacity for producing and consuming products.

Measures such as gross national product (the sum of the market values of all final goods and services that a nation produces during a year) and disposable personal income (what remains of people's incomes after they have paid their taxes) help in assessing the potential of various countries as markets. But they are often supplemented with other indicators of living standards. Depending on the marketer's offering, these standards might include the number of rooms in the average dwelling, the number of persons per room, and the percentage of dwellings with electricity, piped water, telephones, televisions, and so on. Such indicators also provide insight into the quality of life in a country.

Economic development is a process—a series of stages through which a country progresses as it moves from underdeveloped to developed. As a country becomes more developed economically, it experiences declining employment in agriculture and basic manufacturing industries, increasing urbanization, a rising literacy rate, and high product saturation levels. Rising wage levels stimulate the demand for less labor-intensive methods of production, which in turn creates a market for new types of industrial products. A country's level of economic development also affects marketing mixes. For example, distribution tends to become more self-service, and aggregate advertising expenditures tend to increase greatly as the country becomes more developed.

In addition to different levels of economic development among countries, there often are different levels of development within a country. The economies of one or more major cities in a less developed country, for example, may be highly industrialized, while other areas are much less developed, perhaps "backward" by comparison. Such economies are called *dual economies*. A country that has a few wealthy households and many poor ones has a bimodal income distribution. That is, the middle-income group, the one that buys most of the consumer products in countries such as the United States, is practically absent. Per capita GNP figures are inadequate indicators of such countries' capacity to consume.

sustainable development

Increasingly it is being recognized that economic growth offers the best chance for alleviating poverty and protecting the environment. The concept of sustainable development is also receiving more attention. *Sustainable development* is the process through which economic systems can meet existing human wants without destroying the resources future generations will need to meet their wants.

The Competitive Environment

cartel

The competitive environment in many countries is unlike that in the United States. In Europe, for example, cartels are very popular. A *cartel* is a group of firms in different countries (or of countries themselves, such as the Organization of Petroleum Exporting Countries, or OPEC) that agree to share markets. Thus firms that would otherwise compete agree instead to limit output, share markets, and set prices. Cartels are illegal in the United States. It may be legal, however, for U.S.-based firms to participate in cartel agreements in foreign markets if such participation does not affect the U.S. market.

In some foreign countries international marketers find themselves competing with government-owned enterprises. What are considered to be acceptable business practices also vary among countries. Bribery may be an accepted practice in securing sales in some countries; in other countries rivals may openly engage in industrial espionage in order to keep up with one another's product development efforts.

In a growing number of cases, international competition focuses on countertrading. *Countertrades* are transactions in which purchases are paid for with something other than money and credit as the medium of exchange. In countertrading the terms of sale are as important as the product offering.

••••▪••••••

countertrades

The most elementary type of countertrade is simple *barter*. The buyer and the seller exchange products directly with each other rather than dealing in currency or credit. For example, U.S.-based Coherent Communications Systems took payment in ginger for a sale of $1 million in telephone switching equipment to the government of Colombia. The firm had to hire a commodities broker to tell it how much ginger to demand (2 tons) and to help convert the brown root into U.S. dollars.[11]

In a *counterpurchase* the supplier sells a plant or product for cash but agrees to buy a specified amount of unrelated products from the customer for cash to offset the cost to the buyer. *Buyback* is still another form of countertrade. For example, the supplier might build a plant for the buyer and agree to buy some of the plant's output. In other words, the buyer of the plant pays for it through the sale of part of the plant's output.

The Technological Environment

International companies are affected in many ways by the technological environment. One major way relates to productivity. The cost of producing the same product can vary among countries, depending on the level of technology. A country's level of technological development also affects the attractiveness of doing business and the type of operations possible in the country.

Marketers in developed nations often take for granted the modern transportation systems, communication and data processing facilities, and adequate energy supplies that may be absent in some sections of LDCs. A poor transportation system increases production and logistics costs. Poor communications facilities may rule out advertising on TV and radio and in magazines and may require more costly personal selling. The absence of modern data processing facilities makes it hard to plan, coordinate, and control a foreign subsidiary's operations and to integrate them with the parent firm's operations. Inadequate energy supplies cause production scheduling and inventory management problems.

International firms tend to derive their competitive advantage in foreign markets by introducing something new to those markets—new products, new production methods, new marketing techniques, and so on. In other words, they are engaged in the transfer of technology.

The amount and speed with which technology is transferred from West to East is greatly affected by politics. The Chinese government's crackdown on its student-led people's revolt in 1989 helped slow down the transfer of technology to China. So did the reemergence of more conservative leaders who wanted less contact with the West. On the other hand, the unravelling of the Soviet Union following the failed coup in 1991 aided the transfer of technology to Russia and its aligned republics and to former republics that are now independent.[12]

Technology is also transferred, to a lesser extent, from East to West. For example, a U.S.-based manufacturer of scientific instruments and parts, bought Chinese know-how and equipment to produce a sophisticated helium magnetometer for civilian and military use.[13]

The LDCs have spent a considerable amount of their export earnings to acquire technology with which to speed their economic development. But they are increasingly concerned with the concept of *appropriate technology*. Many LDCs have recognized that the purchase of capital-intensive production equipment may be inappropriate in countries that have many unskilled and unemployed people.

The Sociocultural and Ethical Environment

International companies must understand the cultural environments in their foreign markets because cultural differences affect market behavior. Marketers must adapt their strategies to different cultures in each foreign market and, perhaps, to cultural diversity within a given country. Considerable differences may exist between the domestic and foreign markets with respect to language, aesthetics, religion, cultural values and attitudes, social structures, and customs and taboos (see Figure 22–2).

Of course, it is important for businesspeople from different cultures to understand one another if they are to communicate. But it is a mistake to assume that simply understanding another person's culture will lead to successful negotiations. The executive director of the Japan-America Society of Southern California provides an example: "One of the greatest non-tariff barriers that American businessmen impose on themselves are those 'Doing Business in Japan' seminars. They learn how to bow and pass meishi (business cards) and expect that they now have a secret code on how to do business with the Japanese." He says that by paying so much attention to the formalities, American businesspeople often fail to concentrate on the substance of what they're trying to accomplish in negotiations with prospective Japanese business partners.[14]

• **Language** • There are at least three thousand languages in the world. In the United States people speak and write in the English language. Generally, however, countries are bilingual or multilingual. Canada, for example, is a bilingual country. Quebec province has

FIGURE 22–2

Elements of the Sociocultural Environment

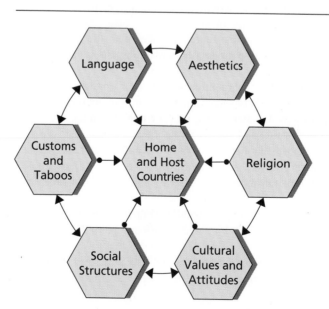

an overwhelmingly French-speaking majority. Other Canadians use English. India is a multilingual country, as are many African nations. In most bilingual and multilingual countries, lingua francas have developed. A *lingua franca* is a language that is used in conducting business and for general communication among people who ordinarily speak their own language but who have this language in common. English, for example, is a lingua franca in many countries, including India, where over two hundred languages and dialects are spoken.

The language problem makes it difficult for marketers to design effective ad campaigns and product labels. In Canada and in some other bilingual and multilingual countries, language differences can lead to deep divisions among the people. Even when people use the same written language, there can be problems with the spoken language. Britons say *boot* for *trunk, bonnet* for *hood* and *petrol* for *gas.*

- **Aesthetics** - A culture's concepts of beauty and good taste, as expressed in its music, dance, folklore, drama, and art, are its *aesthetics*. International marketers must be sensitive to aesthetic preferences in designing products, packages, stores, and advertisements.

For example, the meaning of color can vary among cultures. Purple is associated with death in many Latin American countries. Black is the color of mourning in the United States, white is the color of mourning in Japan, and dark red is the color of mourning along the Ivory Coast. A marketer wishing to sell in these countries should bear this in mind when making advertising and packaging decisions. The same is true when advertisers use music and dancing in their television advertisements.

- **Religion** - Religious beliefs affect our ideas about affluence, materialism, sexual equality, family roles, how and when we shop, and the products we buy. Borrowing from an old European tradition, Adolph Coors started brewing a distinctive-tasting lager called Winterfest to be sold only at Christmastime.[15] PepsiCo markets Shani, a thick currant and blackberry soda that is popular in the Mideast during the Moslem holy month of Ramadan.[16]

Religion is only one aspect of life in most Western societies. It is a total way of life in the Islamic world. The Christmas season is a major sales period in countries with a heritage of Christianity; it is almost impossible to negotiate business contracts during Ramadan.

Hinduism stresses abstinence from beef, and Islam forbids the eating of pork. The women's rights movement has made little headway in the Islamic world, where a woman's place is in the home. A marketer wanting to do business in Northern Ireland must understand the strong hostility between Catholics and Protestants.

• **Cultural Values and Attitudes** • As the Northwest Airlines ad suggests, marketers that want to succeed in foreign markets must understand the cultural values and attitudes of people in those markets. Important dimensions here include values and attitudes related to work, risk taking, change, and wealth.

As we have suggested, many of our cultural values and attitudes spring from religious beliefs. Thus people in the United States and in Western Europe place a much higher value on material well-being and are more likely to buy status symbols than are people in the Islamic countries. But other cultural values relate to other aspects of our lives. The Latin American man, for example, is expected to be very masculine, or "macho." Some cultures consider the elderly to be wisest; other cultures place a much higher value on youth.

An ad that underscores the importance to businesspeople of understanding the cultural environment in the countries in which they do business.

(Reprinted with permission of Northwest Airlines.)

People in the United States are more likely to risk buying a new product than are people in more tradition-bound societies. One of the reasons U.S. firms have had difficulty selling their products in Japan is the fact that the Japanese are so proud of their culture and its achievements that they prefer to buy Japanese-made products.

• **Social Structures** • As we saw in chapter 5 there is a social class structure in the United States, although it is less rigid than that in many other countries. Ad campaigns stressing the idea of upward social mobility are less likely to be effective in those countries.

Multiple-earner families in the United States are creating an affluent segment of consumers. In some cultures, however, it is not acceptable for women to work outside the home; and extended families are common in many of these societies. By pooling their buying power the members of an extended family may be able to purchase goods or services that they otherwise could not afford.

• **Customs and Taboos** • Differences among cultures in customs and taboos can affect buyer behavior and the development of marketing mixes. Salespeople who insist on setting definite times for sales calls will often spend a lot of time waiting for Arab and Latin American prospects, who are less time-bound than people in the United States. Middle Easterners prefer toothpaste that tastes spicy, the Japanese like herbs in their cold medicines, and many Mexicans use laundry detergent to wash dishes. Most of the houses in Thailand are one-story dwellings because the Thais consider it unlucky to have another person's foot over one's head.

• **Ethics** • International companies often face differing expectations about what constitutes good corporate citizenship. They have to think globally but act locally. As the Ethics in Marketing box suggests, issues related to marketing ethics are also much more

Every year, millions of pounds of pesticides that cannot be used in the United States are exported for use oveseas. These pesticides are used on food and beverage crops which the United States regularly imports. The environmental action group, Greenpeace, is lobbying congress to exact stricter laws regarding pesticide exports.

[© L. Cortesi]

complex in international marketing than in purely domestic marketing. What is right in one country may be very wrong in another. For example, people in the United States are straightforward and open in their business dealings, even if such behavior does sometimes hurt others' feelings. They believe such behavior is ethical. But Latin cultures reject this notion. People avoid saying things that would make others feel uncomfortable.

The Political-Legal Environment

Each nation adopts its own internal system of government, policies, and laws and determines how it will deal with other nations. Each nation can also assert its political sovereignty by passing laws to control foreign-owned businesses within its borders. These laws can affect the proportion of ownership the international firm can have in its subsidiary and the subsidiary's objectives, hiring policies, procurement policies, and so on. Governments

ETHICS IN MARKETING

Like purely domestic firms, companies that do business in many countries make marketing decisions that involve ethical issues. In doing so, they often have to decide *whose* ethics apply in a given situation. Is it a case of "When in Rome, do as the Romans do"?

Some governments impose very specific requirements on foreign-based firms as a condition of entry into their markets. A firm either agrees to the conditions or is excluded from the market. What ethical issues can arise here?

More and more firms that do business across national borders are engaging in competitive intelligence—gathering information about their rivals. Some people favor using intelligence specialists in federal agencies to gather information and supply it to U.S. corporations. In addition to the problem of defining what a U.S. corporation is, what ethical issues arise here?

What about selling abroad products that are banned for safety or health reasons in the domestic market? For exam-ple, is it ethical to sell in an LDC a pesticide that is banned in the United States because it is suspected of causing cancer? What about selling in an LDC pharmaceutical products that are past their expiration dates?

Product counterfeiting is an increasingly serious problem for manufacturers of such diverse products as airplane parts, toys, automobile parts, cashmere clothing, and blue jeans. Although many countries have anticounterfeiting laws, the scope of these laws and their enforcement vary tremendously from market to market. What should a manufacturer do about counterfeiters in overseas markets?

As we saw in Chapter 11, the gray market consists of unauthorized intermediaries who circumvent authorized marketing channels by buying in low-price markets and reselling in high-price markets at prices that are lower than those charged by authorized channel members. This gray market is growing rapidly. What ethical issues are involved here? U.S.-based tobacco companies aggres-

that believe in free trade welcome foreign investment and imports. Those that do not believe in it restrict imports and foreign investment and discriminate against foreign-based firms doing business in their countries.

Political stability is a major consideration in a firm's decision to enter and remain in a foreign market. The Tiananmen Square massacre in 1989 brought an end to the euphoria that had existed about political reform in China. But after approximately eighteen months of isolation imposed by other nations, China started making a quiet comeback. Foreign investment started pouring back into the coastal provinces, although the inland provinces continue to languish economically. The coastal provinces are insisting on more economic freedom from Beijing. This too helps create political instability in the eyes of foreign investors.[17] For several years after Gorbachev came to power in the Soviet Union, his reforms made the political system much more unstable. This uncertainty increased the difficulty and political risks of investing in the Soviet Union.[18] Immediately after the failed coup in the Soviet Union, uncertainty increased even more.

sively promote cigarettes in LDCs, very few of which restrict tobacco advertising or require health warnings on packages. In many countries U.S. firms were the first to use mass media cigarette advertising. They also adapt packaging to accommodate very low per capita incomes—for example, by making packages that contain fewer cigarettes than the packages sold elsewhere. Consumption of cigarettes is skyrocketing in the Third World. What ethical issues are involved here?

What about international companies acting as agents of cultural change? In the not too distant past a visit to the neighborhood public bath was a nightly ritual for the Japanese. Now most Japanese have bathtubs and Western-style toilets in their homes. Millions of people have been introduced to and persuaded to use such products as deodorants, toothpaste, and mouthwashes by U.S.-based firms. What about attempts to change cultural values regarding birth control or breast feeding?

The Foreign Corrupt Practices Act of 1977 imposes penalties on U.S. corporations and their officers for offering bribes to win contracts with foreign governments or firms. Few, if any, other nations try to legislate what their firms can and cannot do in their business operations in other countries. Thus managers of U.S.-based firms often complain they cannot compete effectively with foreign-based firms in bidding for contracts in countries where bribery is tolerated. The law was amended in 1988 in an attempt to make the standards for U.S. firms doing international business more workable and to rid the 1977 law of ambiguities. Nevertheless, U.S. firms still are prevented from engaging in activities overseas that rivals consider to be common business practices. What ethical issues might arise here?

International firms assess political risks in the countries in which they are currently doing business or in which they plan to do business. Methods of political risk assessment range from sending a group of executives to the host country to meet with government officials and local businesspeople to using sophisticated quantitative techniques.

The major political risks faced by international firms are confiscation, expropriation, nationalization, and domestication. *Confiscation* means that the host country takes over the firm's property in that country without reimbursing the company. *Expropriation* involves partial payment by the government in a forced sale of the firm's property. The government that confiscates or expropriates plants may turn ownership over to local nationals by selling or giving the plants to them. If, however, the government retains ownership, the plants are said to be *nationalized*. Some people fear that China will nationalize firms in Hong Kong when the British lease on the colony expires in 1997 and it reverts to China. *Domestication* is a variety of efforts by a host country government to pressure international firms to shift ownership or control from themselves to local nationals.

TABLE 22–2   Examples of Government-Created Trade Barriers

Tariff Barriers

Duties or taxes that a government puts on products imported into or exported out of a country. *Revenue tariffs* are set low in order not to reduce imports because their purpose is to raise revenue for the government that imposes them. *Protective tariffs* are set high to keep imported products out of the country. For example, Taiwan imposes a high protective tariff on imported cars.

Nontariff Barriers

Quotas:	Limits on the amount of a product that can enter or leave a country. For example, Japan has a quota on the amount of citrus fruits that can enter Japan.
Embargoes:	Prohibitions on the export or import of certain products into or out of a country. For example, the United States bans the importation of forty-three styles of semiautomatic rifles.
Exchange control:	Government control over access to its country's currency by foreigners—for example, a country controlling how much profit a foreign-based firm in that country can send to its home country.
Tax control:	Use of government's taxing authority in a discriminatory manner to control foreign investments in that country.
Government procurement policies:	Giving preference to domestic suppliers over foreign suppliers in awarding government purchase contracts.
Government regulations and standards:	Government regulations concerning safety and health and other product standards. For example, a West German law derived from a 1516 Bavarian law on beer purity prohibited the sale of beer made from anything but pure water, malt, yeast, and hops. It kept out beers that contain other grains or preservatives. The European Court of Justice, however, overturned the law in 1987.
Customs procedures:	Methods of inspecting and valuing imported products for customs purposes—for example, inspecting each new car imported into a country rather than inspecting a sample of those cars.

Table 22–2 offers several examples of government-created trade barriers. Taiwan's ad discusses what the government has done to eliminate trade barriers. Table 22–3 offers several examples of government-created incentives to trade. Keep in mind, however, that what one country considers an incentive may be considered a barrier by one or more other countries. For example, Japan's Ministry of International Trade and Industry (MITI) helps increase Japanese exports. By subsidizing Japanese industries, however, MITI poses a problem to U.S.-based firms, which receive no government subsidies yet must compete with Japanese firms that do.

In general the U.S. government supports the concept of free trade and helps U.S. firms, both small and large, to export their products. For example, the Bureau of International Commerce in the U.S. Department of Commerce organizes trade missions, operates permanent trade centers in many foreign countries, and sponsors district export expansion councils. The U.S. Department of State provides information and promotion services to U.S. firms interested in business in foreign countries.

On the other hand, there is pressure to limit imports when heavy imports of some products lead to layoffs of U.S. workers. Import competition has been especially intense in recent years in the steel, shoe, TV, clothing, automobile, and semiconductor industries.

Some people in the United States favor "fair trade" over "free trade." They want to

An ad that discusses Taiwan's efforts to open its market to foreign competition.

(Courtesy of Republic of China.)

TABLE 22–3 ▌ Examples of Government-Created Incentives to Trade

Foreign trade zones (United States)	Areas into which products can be imported without being subject to customs duties or quotas. Often the imported materials are manufactured into finished products. If reexported, they are not subject to any tariffs. If they enter domestic commerce, they are subject to regular tariffs.
MITI (Japan)	Ministry of International Trade and Industry—a government agency that subsidizes new industries that have export potential.
Special economic zones (China)	The Shenzhen special economic zone, which borders Hong Kong, permitting foreigners to set up wholly owned manufacturing plants.
International Bank for Reconstruction and Development (World Bank)	Organization to further the economic development of member nations by making loans to them, either directly by using its own funds or indirectly by borrowing from member countries.
International Monetary Fund (IMF)	Organization to eliminate trade barriers and promote financial cooperation among member countries, enabling them to cope with balance of payments problems.
General Agreement on Tariffs and Trade (GATT)	Agreement negotiated by member nations to improve trade relations through reductions and elimination of tariff and nontariff barriers.
International Development Association	Organization affiliated with the World Bank that makes loans to private businesses and to member countries of the World Bank.

limit imports into the United States from countries that limit exports from the United States. The Super 301 provisions of the 1988 U.S. Trade Act requires retaliation if countries do not resolve through negotiation trade practices that are determined by U.S. trade officials to be unfair.

Some people in the United States also advocate *local content laws.* Under a law of this sort, for example, foreign car manufacturers with annual U.S. car sales over a specified amount might be required to use a certain percentage of U.S.-made component parts.

U.S. antitrust law has been amended to allow joint research, production, and other cooperative efforts among firms. The trend toward cooperation among companies, often with government encouragement and university participation, is taking various forms—formal joint ventures, strategic partnering, and global alliances. At least three fundamental forces are driving the trend: (1) the increasing cost, complexity, and risk of developing new technologies; (2) the globalization of markets, leading firms to seek partners who can help them crack foreign markets; and (3) the emergence of powerful foreign competitors, forcing U.S. companies to turn from competing with one another to joining to fend off a common threat.[19]

Family-owned firms in the United States can offer customers continuity that is highly valued in many countries. Unlike big corporations, which are often attacked for focusing too much on short-term results, family-owned firms can take the long-term view that firms in many other countries take. They also have the patience to develop the long-term personal relationships that many foreign-based firms want. ''Evergreen'' contracts are common in many countries. These are contracts that last for generations. Foreign businesspeople who want to know with whom they will be dealing for the next twenty or thirty years often prefer to deal with family-owned foreign firms that have good succession and continuity planning.[20]

REGIONAL TRADING BLOCS

The huge U.S. market provides more market opportunity than any domestic market abroad. This is perhaps the main reason most U.S. firms have hesitated to get involved in international marketing.

In the post–World War II period many other countries have attempted to broaden their "domestic" markets by forming regional trading blocs. A *regional trading bloc* is a group of countries (a cartel) that formally agree to reduce trade barriers among themselves in order to create a larger market.

These blocs can take any of a number of forms—free trade areas, customs unions, common markets, economic unions, and political unions—and each successively more integrated form includes the essential characteristics of the less integrated forms (see Figure 22–3). Thus in a *free trade area*, the least integrated form, there are no tariffs or quotas on products moving among member countries. In a *customs union* there is also a common

regional trading bloc

FIGURE 22–3

Forms of Regional Trading Blocs

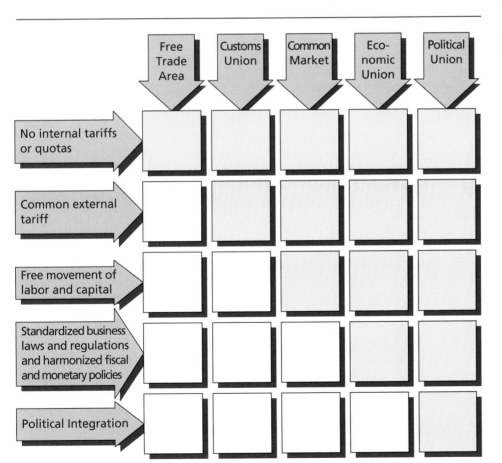

tariff applied to products imported from nonmember countries. In a *common market* there is also free movement of labor and capital among countries. In an *economic union* there are also standardized laws and regulations pertaining to business, and member nations harmonize their fiscal and monetary policies. Finally, in a *political union,* the most integrated form, there is also political integration among member countries. In effect, the members become one nation.

In 1989 the United States and Canada finalized the Canada-U.S. Free Trade Agreement, which closely integrates the two nations' economies. The agreement removes all remaining tariffs on trade between the two countries over the next ten years, thereby creating a free trade area. A U.S.-Mexico free trade agreement is also being pursued. The focus is on creating a unified North American trading bloc including Canada, the United States, and Mexico. Beyond that is President Bush's Enterprise for the Americas, a set of proposals to lower trade and investment barriers between the United States and Latin American countries. The ultimate result could be a thirty-three-nation trading bloc—a hemispheric trading network that would stretch from Point Barrow, Alaska, to Patagonia, Argentina.[21]

The European Community (EC)—the best known of the various regional groupings—includes Belgium, Denmark, France, the United Kingdom, Greece, Ireland, Italy, Luxembourg, the Netherlands, Germany, Spain, and Portugal. Its beginning dates to the 1957 Treaty of Rome. The idea of the treaty was to eventually create a single European market, but it was not until 1968 that all internal tariff barriers were removed. At a 1985 summit meeting, however, EC leaders pledged to create a true single market of goods and services among their nations by the end of 1992.[22] Thus the EC, which currently is essentially a common market, is evolving into an economic union. It is replacing widely varying single-country import restrictions with EC-wide rules.

The EC has enabled former enemies to come together and merge their nationalism into a larger whole.[23] As for the future of the EC, there is considerable debate about "deepening" or "widening" it. *Deepening* means speeding the drive for a single currency, harmonizing disparate legal systems, and otherwise strengthening economic and social bonds. *Widening* means increasing membership to include countries such as Austria, Sweden, Switzerland, and the East European states. Deepening is likely to occur before widening. Eventually, however, the twelve-member EC, a market of 325 million people, is likely to become a free market of 500 million. At that point the EC would be the world's most formidable concentration of economic power.[24]

Some observers believe a "United States of Europe" will emerge, perhaps by the turn of the century. They say that working out the details for implementing treaties dealing with such matters as monetary and political union will require time. With more countries wanting to join, the process may take even longer.[25]

The United States has for decades favored the political and economic integration of the nations of Western Europe. But some people believe the Soviet retreat from Eastern Europe, an apparent end of the Cold War, and the economic and political problems confronting the Soviet Union at home have weakened the geopolitical argument for a united Western Europe.[26]

Other examples of regional trading blocs include the Association of South East Asian Nations (ASEAN), which includes Indonesia, Malaysia, Singapore, the Philippines, and Thailand; and the Andean Common Market (ANCOM), which includes Bolivia, Colombia, Ecuador, Peru, and Venezuela.

The development of such blocs is significant to international marketers, which, instead of viewing global market opportunities in terms of individual nation states, can shift their focus to larger regional groupings that represent greater market potential. Furthermore, these groupings encourage suppliers from nonmember countries to set up plants in one or more member countries. In this way they "get behind the tariff wall" and need not export to members of the bloc. For example, a German firm can export products to France without paying a tariff, but a U.S. exporter would have to pay it. The U.S. firm could avoid the French tariff by setting up manufacturing operations in one or more EC countries.

Marketers inside member countries generally experience greater competition as trade barriers come down. They, along with marketers outside the bloc, also often enjoy greater economies of scale in producing for a larger market. In addition, marketing mixes may achieve greater standardization as laws regulating marketing activities are standardized.

THE FIRM'S APPROACH TO INTERNATIONAL MARKET OPPORTUNITY

Business firms have different perspectives of, or orientations to, the world in terms of what constitutes market opportunity. Firms can be categorized by their orientation as (1) ethnocentric (home country orientation), (2) polycentric (host country orientation), (3) regiocentric (regional orientation), or (4) geocentric (global orientation).[27] These orientations are arranged along a continuum from narrowest to broadest in Figure 22–4.

Two types of *ethnocentric orientation* are domestic only and predominantly domestic. Domestic-only firms limit operations to their domestic markets. They believe too much red tape is involved in international marketing and so make no effort to investigate foreign opportunities. Predominantly domestic firms look to foreign markets to absorb the output they cannot sell at home. They make little or no effort to adapt their products and other marketing mix elements to suit foreign tastes.

Firms with a *polycentric orientation* may set up production and marketing facilities abroad. The underlying belief is that social systems, buying patterns, and legal systems vary so much among nations that it is best to let local people in each country manage the firm's operations there. Marketing mixes in the home and host countries may vary in minor or major ways.

Some firms group host countries by region. Some market segments in Latin America, for example, are alike except that people in the segments live in different countries. Were it not for these political boundaries these people could be treated as one market segment. The *regiocentric orientation* makes this possible, especially for international companies that market to members of a regional trading bloc.

The *geocentric, or global, orientation* is an extension of the regiocentric orientation. The firm pushes national borders aside and looks at the entire world as one big source of market opportunity. But because of significant cultural, social, economic, political, and

FIGURE 22–4

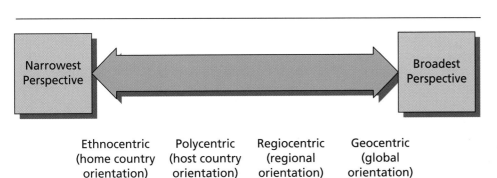

A Continuum of Orientations to International Market Opportunity

legal differences among nations, this orientation may be more useful in functional areas such as production and finance than in some marketing activities because marketing is more culture-bound.

Except for domestic-only firms, a firm can have varying degrees of involvement with international marketing. The next two sections discuss exporting and foreign operations as two vastly different methods of conducting international marketing.

Exporting

Exporting is a low-risk approach to entering foreign markets. Firms export their products for a variety of reasons. Some firms find it less risky and more profitable to diversify by exporting their present products instead of developing new products for domestic consumption. Those firms whose products are in the maturity stage of their life cycle at home may find growth markets elsewhere. For example, many U.S. toy makers turn to export markets for sales of toys that are no longer popular in the United States. Some firms turn to exporting when their domestic markets are in a recession and the economies in export markets are prospering.

Firms whose products have seasonal demand patterns may want to shift their off-season output to foreign markets where the product is in season. Another reason for exporting is less competition in some foreign markets. As the Banca Serfin ad explains, foreign-based firms with subsidiaries in Mexico can import components more cheaply than before. In the discussions that follow we distinguish between unsolicited and solicited exporting.

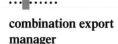

trading company

• **Unsolicited Exporting** • Some firms occasionally receive and fill unsolicited orders from foreign buyers. They are engaging in *unsolicited exporting*. The foreign buyer initiates the contact, and the exporter treats these foreign sales like domestic sales.

A *trading company* is a privately owned business that buys and sells products in many different countries, either in its own name or as an agent for its buyer-seller clients. Such a company can place orders with exporters for their own account or for the account of a client. The best-known trading companies in the world are those based in Japan. They include C. Itoh & Co. Ltd., and Mitsui and Company. These companies offer many services to their clients—importing, exporting, storing and transporting, and getting the products distributed through intermediaries.

In addition to privately controlled trading companies, *state trading companies* handle foreign trade in state-controlled economies. Thus China's state trading companies handle exports and imports between China and foreign countries. In addition to seeking buyers for Chinese products, they also contact foreign firms to supply products needed in China.

combination export manager

• **Solicited Exporting** • Exporters that initiate the contact with buyers, either indirectly or directly, are engaging in *solicited exporting*. Examples of indirect contact are using a combination export manager and engaging in piggyback exporting.

A *combination export manager* is a domestic agent intermediary that serves as the export department for several noncompeting manufacturers. These intermediaries contact foreign customers and negotiate sales for their manufacturer-clients for a commission that ranges between 10 and 20 percent, depending on the services they perform. They are similar to selling agents in domestic marketing.

Piggyback exporting is another type of cooperative exporting. A manufacturer with export facilities and foreign marketing channels (the carrier) handles the foreign wholesaling of one or more other firms' (the riders') noncompetitive but complementary products. This helps the carrier put together a complete product mix and gives the riders fairly

The Beginning Of Mexico's New Foreign Trade Policy.

BANCA SERFIN

Mexico is tearing up its tariffs. And tearing down the barriers to trade.

Which means greater opportunities for you.

Suppose, for example, you seek access to the burgeoning Mexican market. Now your products can compete fairly with local goods. And should you own a subsidiary in Mexico, you can import components more cheaply than before. Thus making your manufactured items more competitive on the world market.

The end of restrictive trade policies is yet another example of how Mexico is now, shall we say, open for business.

Which brings us to Banca Serfin.

We've helped foreign companies do business in our country for more than 125 years. Becoming Mexico's trade finance leader in the process. As well as the bank offering the most comprehensive array of financial services in all Mexico.

If you'd like to learn how Mexico's new foreign trade policy can work to your advantage, talk with Banca Serfin.

And let the gains begin.

Mexico City (525) 512-7768   New York (212) 635-2300   Tokyo (813) 273-5911   London (4471) 408-2151   Toronto (416) 360-8900   Los Angeles (213) 624-6610   Nassau (212) 635-2300   Belize (5012) 78970   Seoul (813) 273-5911

Mexico is eliminating many tariff and nontariff barriers to trade.

(Albert Frank-Guenther Law, Inc., NY, NY, ad agency; art direction: Dominic Algieri; creative director/copy: Jon Saunders; photography: Susumu Sato.)

easy access to foreign markets. The carrier might sell the riders' products on a commission basis or buy them outright and sell them under the carrier's brand.

Direct exporting requires that exporters handle the export tasks themselves by setting up export departments to sell directly to foreign firms. The exporters contact foreign buyers and perform marketing research, physical distribution, and export documentation for themselves.

Direct contact with foreign buyers gives exporters some control over the marketing of their products but requires getting involved in the environment of foreign countries. It may help firms diversify into other export markets or get more involved in multinational operations.

Direct exporters can achieve distribution within foreign markets by dealing with various types of intermediaries in those markets or by setting up foreign sales subsidiaries. These are discussed in Table 22–4. The U.S. and Foreign Commercial Service, an agency of the Commerce Department's International Trade Administration, operates a program designed to match U.S. exporters with foreign agents and distributors at nominal cost.

| | How a Direct Exporter Might Achieve Distribution Within |
| TABLE 22–4 | a Foreign Market |

1. Manufacturers' representatives	Overseas agent intermediaries that sell related but noncompetitive products for a limited number of principals. They often have a continuing relationship with their overseas principals but do not arrange for shipping and seldom take physical possession of the products they sell.
2. Import jobbers	Merchant intermediaries that buy products directly from the exporter and resell to wholesalers, retailers, and industrial users in their countries. A manufacturer might sell to several import jobbers in a given country because they do not have exclusive territorial rights in their countries.
3. Dealers	Merchant intermediaries that work with exporters on a continuing basis because they have exclusive selling rights in their areas. Manufacturer-dealer relationships often are set up as franchisor-franchisee relationships.
4. Wholesalers and retailers	Intermediaries in foreign countries that often engage in direct importing. Large retailers sell to ultimate consumers but also frequently wholesale to smaller retailers the products they import.
5. Foreign sales subsidiaries	The exporter exports its products to its own foreign sales subsidiary. This is a type of direct foreign investment because the firm actually is present in the foreign country.

Other Approaches to Entering Foreign Markets

As Figure 22–5 indicates, there are other ways to enter foreign markets besides exporting. The spirit of nationalism, especially in newly emerging nations, often leads to laws requiring foreign firms to build plants or contract with local firms to produce products in those countries rather than exporting finished products to them. Local production creates jobs, and the government can exercise greater control over the firm's operations.

Industrialized nations also sometimes pressure foreign-based exporters to set up operations in their countries. The U.S. balance of trade deficits of recent years played a big part in stimulating actions to induce foreign-based firms to set up plants in the United States.

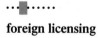

foreign licensing

• **Types of Foreign Operations** • *Foreign licensing* is an agreement in which a licensor gives a licensee in another country the right to use the licensor's patent, trademark, copyright, technology, processes, or products in return for a stated percentage of the licensee's sales revenues or profits resulting from such use. A cross-licensing agreement enables the participating companies to have access to each other's patents in exchange either for license fees or for other technologies.

Franchising, as we saw in chapter 12, is a popular type of licensing arrangement. Many fast-food franchisors have entered foreign markets through licensing. As domestic business slows, more and more fast-food chains are looking overseas for growth.

A recent survey by the International Franchise Association found that about a third of U.S. franchisors have international operations and another third plan to go overseas eventually.[28] Meanwhile foreign-based firms are getting more involved in franchising in the United States. For example, Ito-Yokado, Japan's second-largest supermarket owner, bought 75 percent of Southland Corporation, the parent company of 7-Eleven. The purchase underscores U.S. franchise companies' attractiveness to foreign investors. The

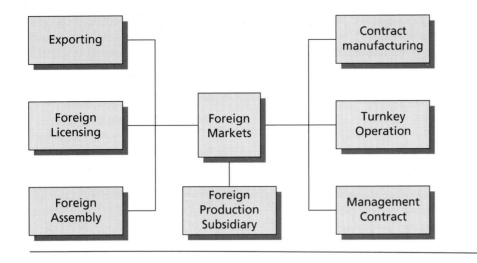

FIGURE 22–5
· ·

Methods of Entering Foreign
Markets ▮

director of marketing and public relations for the International Franchise Association refers to this emerging trend as "the globalization of franchising."[29]

Foreign assembly is an arrangement in which a firm exports component parts to a subsidiary or licensee in a foreign country for local assembly into the finished product. One benefit is that tariffs are lower on unassembled products than on assembled products.

Contract manufacturing is an arrangement in which a firm enters into an agreement with firms in foreign markets to manufacture its product and the firm handles the marketing, usually through its foreign sales subsidiaries. Consumer products manufacturers often take this approach.

A *turnkey operation* is an arrangement in which a supplier designs, builds, and trains the staff of an operating facility for a foreign buyer, which runs the facility. In effect, all the buyer has to do is "turn the key" to make the facility, such as an electricity generating plant, operational.

A *management contract* is a pact in which one firm sells management services to operate a facility owned by another firm. Marriott Corporation receives management fees for operating hotels that are owned by others throughout the world. Management contracts are also often involved in turnkey operations. The contractor-builder agrees to manage the facility until local managers are prepared to take over.

Many firms that do business abroad set up their own production subsidiaries to produce their products in the foreign markets. A *foreign production subsidiary* is a subordinate company established in another country by a parent company for the purpose of production. Mitsubishi Electric America is the U.S. subsidiary of Japan-based Mitsubishi, the parent. Thus Mitsubishi is a direct investor in the United States. *Foreign direct investment* is a commitment of financial resources by an organization for the purpose of owning (totally or partially) and exercising control (total or partial) over an enterprise in a foreign country. Of course, many U.S.-based firms have direct investments abroad.

· **Ownership of Foreign Operations** · An international company must make an investment decision in setting up production or marketing operations in foreign countries. These operations may be owned 100 percent by the company (wholly owned subsidiaries) or only partially owned (joint ventures). Furthermore, the company might buy into or buy outright an existing firm there or build operations from the ground up.

A *wholly owned subsidiary* of an international company is owned outright by the

foreign assembly

contract manufacturing

turnkey operation

management contract

foreign production subsidiary

foreign direct investment

company; there are no local part owners. This gives the company substantial control over its subsidiaries and makes coordinating their operations easier. The host country, however, still has some control because it can require the subsidiary to hire local nationals and can restrict how much profit the subsidiary can send to its foreign owners.

The majority of foreign investments of U.S.-based international companies are wholly owned. But there is a strong trend toward requiring some ownership by local nationals.

joint venture

In international business a *joint venture* is a partnership in which the partners share ownership and control of the venture's operations and property rights. The partners can be (1) two foreign firms doing business in a host country, (2) a foreign firm and a government agency, or (3) a foreign firm and a locally owned firm. Many host countries require joint ventures as a condition of entering their markets.

Numerous joint ventures exist in the auto industry. The most extensive joint venture between Ford and Mazda is the Ford Escort. (Ford owns 25 percent of Mazda.) Mazda engineered the car, Ford designed it, and 80 percent of the car is built in the United States. Most joint ventures between U.S. and Japanese car makers work differently. The U.S. firm has a Japanese firm engineer a car for the U.S. market. The Japanese firm builds and manages a plant in the United States and ships 80 percent of the components from Japan to the plant. The cars are assembled and shipped to dealers with an American nameplate.[30]

More and more firms are trying to get involved in international business rapidly and deeply by forming strategic alliances with rivals, suppliers, and customers. In a growing number of cases the alliances involve partners in different countries. In a typical *strategic alliance* two or three firms make an equity investment in a joint venture or sign an agreement to share marketing, research, or manufacturing. Some refer to it as *strategic partnering*. In 1984 Congress exempted research and development consortiums from U.S. antitrust laws. Sematech is one such consortium. It is an Austin, Texas, nonprofit research group that receives $100 million a year from its fourteen corporate backers and a matching sum from the Department of Defense. Sematech develops the advanced equipment and technology to make semiconductors. Sematech calls its alliance ''precompetitive cooperation.''[31]

INTERNATIONAL MARKETING DECISIONS

globalization

As the Bankers Trust Company ad suggests, ''globalization'' is affecting the way a growing number of organizations conduct their operations. *Globalization* is a worldwide marketing strategy whereby an organization uses the same or very similar marketing mixes in all its markets. Instead of focusing on the differences among people in different countries, this strategy advocates looking first for similarities.

The globalization strategy is based on the belief that mass communication and technology are creating similar patterns of consumption in otherwise diverse cultures. Proponents say that this allows firms to standardize the manufacturing and distribution of products as diverse as Revlon cosmetics and Sony TVs. Opponents argue that the diversity of cultures and of levels of economic development make globalization a risky strategy.

Careful consideration must be given to the relative benefits of globalization (standardization) and adaptation (customization or localization) in each situation. To achieve economies of scale in production and marketing, it is desirable to produce and market highly standardized products. But this must be balanced against the attractiveness of tailoring marketing mixes to the wants of very specific target markets. Marketing research may be

Today, the most hospitable financial climate
may not be close to home.

Yesterday, globalization was a word.

Today, it's a reality.

As the world's markets have become unified, so should
a bank's ability to take advantage of them for you.

Today, Bankers Trust can move effortlessly to wherever
the climate is most favorable to each element of your transaction.

A swap in London, a private placement in New York,
yen from Sydney, dollars from Zurich—we can put the pieces
together swiftly and efficiently.

Long ago, perfecting our ability to take advantage of the
global market became an important part of our merchant
banking strategy. Today, we run a single, integrated book of
worldwide business that encompasses New York, London, Tokyo,
Hong Kong, Sydney and Zurich.

Yesterday, many markets. Today, just one. That dramatic
change is exactly reflected in the way merchant banking goes
about its clients' business.

◪ Bankers Trust Company

Because today isn't yesterday.

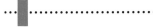

Globalization is affecting the
way a growing number of
organizations conduct their
operations.

(Bankers Trust Company and
Doremus & Company Advertising
Agency.)

needed to determine how much consumers are willing to pay for highly customized market offerings.

In November 1990, 15,000 Procter & Gamble employees attended their annual management meetings. Three days later they returned to their offices worldwide with information about P&G's newest approach to doing business—globalization. This was seventy-five years after P&G entered its first foreign market (Canada) and ten years after the firm dedicated itself to doubling its plants and offices overseas. Henceforth, instead of creating different products for different markets, P&G is to work to create global products. The belief is that with appropriate cultural adjustments most of its brands can appeal to all consumers regardless of where they live.[32]

The Entry Decision

Most firms start out in international marketing with a product orientation—they seek foreign markets for their existing products. Thus they tend to enter countries that are highly similar to the home country in terms of demographics and culture. But the more committed the firm becomes to international marketing, the more market oriented it becomes.

The decision to enter a foreign market should be based on research suggesting that greater market opportunity exists there than in either the firm's home country or other foreign countries. For example, since 1986 H. J. Heinz has been manufacturing in China an instant rice cereal for babies. Heinz has 80 percent ownership in the joint venture with two Chinese partners. Heinz entered China knowing that 22 million babies are born there each year—almost six times the number born every year in the United States. A box of cereal that will last ten days sells for 75 cents. Heinz, of course, knew about China's one-child policy. As an ad executive in China says, ''With the one-child policy, almost all of the disposable income of an urban family will go to the one child.''[33]

U.S. auto makers traditionally have demonstrated little interest in selling cars in the Asian market. But in the few Asian nations where a U.S. auto maker has tried to sell cars, the result has been positive. For example, Ford has well over 25 percent of the market in Taiwan. As Ford's vice president of Asia-Pacific Automotive Operations says: ''To be a major player, you have to be a major player in Asia. If you don't have a presence in Asia, you will have a shrinking world market share.''[34]

Marketing Research Decisions

Population, GNP, and other secondary data about many foreign markets are available from the United Nations. Other international and regional organizations also are available as data sources. The Organization for Economic Cooperation and Development (OECD), for example, publishes reports on business in the industrialized Western nations. Regional trading blocs are another source of information.

Many countries have embassies in the United States that supply information to interested firms. Nongovernment sources include the Chamber of Commerce of the United States and international trade clubs, banks, ad agencies, and shipping companies. After using the available secondary data, the marketer must decide whether to collect primary data. As in domestic marketing, the costs, risks, and expected benefits must be considered. In many LDCs gathering primary data is very costly and risky. High illiteracy rates, poor postal and telephone service, language problems, and a general suspicion of people who ask questions may make telephone, mail, and personal interviews difficult. Because of these and other problems, many firms rely on interviewing other executives who do business in these countries and sending their own executives to the countries for a firsthand look at the markets.

Of course, the marketing research techniques used in the United States can easily be adapted for use in other developed nations. The international company can conduct the research for itself or use research firms there. These firms may be local firms or foreign branches of large U.S. research firms.

Product Decisions

Figure 22–6 identifies three basic product strategies for international marketers: (1) standardization, (2) adaptation, and (3) innovation.

• **Product Standardization** • The strategy of selling the identical product in all countries is *product standardization*. It is the least costly strategy. Economies of scale are possible in producing and marketing the product. Whether a global product strategy will be profitable depends on the product's suitability to its different target markets.

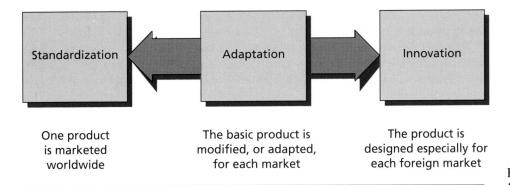

Standardization	Adaptation	Innovation
One product is marketed worldwide	The basic product is modified, or adapted, for each market	The product is designed especially for each foreign market

FIGURE 22–6

A Continuum of Product Strategies for International Markets

Erno Laszlo, a U.S. marketer of skin care products, tried to sell its products identically everywhere. It had been successful in convincing its American clients that they should follow a daily regimen using a series of its products. But it was not successful in selling an identical regimen to fair-skinned Australians, swarthy Italians, and delicate Asian women. In Asia, for example, skin care customs vary widely from region to region.[35] Industrial products probably lend themselves more to globalization than consumer products because cultural differences are less significant in the case of industrial products.

In chapter 2 we defined *regionalization* as a marketing strategy that seeks to cater to regional preferences within a larger market. For example, in the United States CPC International markets a sweeter Skippy peanut butter in southern states and peanut butter with honey on the West Coast.[36] On a broader scale it is likely that there are more opportunities for the profitable marketing of regionalized products than of truly globalized products. Our earlier discussion of the European Community's efforts at unification suggests that highly standardized products will be developed for the member countries of the EC. For years 3M Company's European plants turned out different versions of its products for different countries. Several years ago, however, the company began concentrating production. For example, the 3M plant in Wales makes videotapes and videocassettes for all of Europe. Only the language on the packages is different.[37]

• **Product Adaptation** • The strategy of modifying a product to suit local tastes and uses is *product adaptation*. In contrast to a globalization strategy, it is a *localization strategy*.

Although product adaptation involves greater costs than product standardization, it may also result in greater profit. This strategy is often used when the product performs the same function in different countries but use conditions are different. Boeing's narrow-bodied 737 airplanes are specifically outfitted to protect against damage on Third World runways.[38] In addition to the physical good itself, other product elements that may require modification are (1) packaging, (2) labeling, (3) branding, (4) warranties, and (5) after-sale service.

Consumer products in many countries move through very long marketing channels, and transportation is often crude. This may require stronger packaging materials. Differences in tastes regarding package shapes, colors, and sizes are also important. In the United States people prefer tightly sealed packages for many items, but some foreign consumers insist on opening the package to examine the contents before buying. Nonreturnable plastic soft-drink bottles are banned in Germany.

Labeling decisions are affected by language, laws, literacy rates, and local customs. Multilingual labels and package inserts are necessary in multilingual countries. Pictures can help where illiteracy rates are high. Different systems of weights and measures must also be considered.

Branding decisions can be risky, as Chinese exporters discovered when they tried unsuccessfully to export to the West ''Fang Fang'' lipstick, ''White Elephant'' batteries, and ''Pansy'' underwear for men.[39] Riot police were called out in Bangladesh as Moslem demonstrators protested against a Canadian-based firm whose slippers reputedly bore a logo resembling the Arabic characters for Allah. The government banned the sale of the slippers and seized unsold stocks because many Moslems considered the rubber slippers offensive to Islam.[40]

International firms have three major alternatives when it comes to warranty strategy: (1) offer the same warranty worldwide, (2) offer one warranty for all foreign markets and a separate one for the home market, or (3) customize the warranty for each country. A U.S. auto maker that offers the same warranty worldwide can expect problems in countries with dirt roads for highways.

After-sale service policies are important if the company wants to avoid the reaction of ''you can't get service on those foreign-made products.'' Japanese exporters of machine tools learned quickly that U.S. manufacturers used the machines around the clock to maximize equipment utilization. Breakdowns were a big problem, and the Japanese had to modify their products and strengthen their service policies to fit the tougher use conditions in the United States.

• **Product Innovation** • The product innovation strategy focuses on designing the product especially for each foreign market. In other words, simple product modification is not enough. In Japan, Nestlé markets cereals that taste like seaweed, carrots and zucchini, and coconuts and papaya—tastes the Japanese like.[41]

Distribution Decisions

Intermediaries in most countries tend to be either very large or very small. In Japan many small wholesalers buy and sell from one another many times before products even reach the retail level. Wholesaling in Finland, on the other hand, is dominated by large firms.

Intermediaries in small countries tend not to specialize by product lines as much as intermediaries in the United States. The size of the market limits their ability to specialize. There also is resistance to changing distribution structures and patterns in many countries. This is another factor that makes joint ventures with local nationals attractive to many foreign-based firms.

Marketers also face the standardization/adaptation issue in formulating distribution strategy. For example, franchised American retailers of personal computers discovered that Britons do not buy computers impulsively, as do many Americans, from storefront locations. Entre Computer Centers abandoned the British market several years ago, shutting down its fifteen franchised outlets.[42]

The gray market will become an even bigger issue than it is now as more and more firms seek to market standardized products on a global basis. With numerous licensees producing a standardized toothpaste, for example, it will become almost impossible for the licensor to track the brand. Marketers will have to decide what, if anything, should be done about unauthorized distributors and dealers circumventing their authorized channel arrangements.

Decisions about logistics must also be made carefully. Transportation, warehousing, order processing, and materials handling facilities vary greatly among and within countries and by product type. Mexico's export-based growth is hampered by the decaying infrastructure—roads, bridges, and ports. Recently Mexico decided to allow private investment in infrastructure, a radical change from previous policy.[43] Government regulations concerning logistics activities also vary.

Dreyer's is a premium ice cream. The company recently started exporting the product from California to Japan in a joint venture with a Japanese trading company. Exporting enables the company to avoid the Japanese manufacturing costs incurred by rivals such as Häagen-Dazs and Baskin-Robbins. Dreyer's ships small packages that fit neatly into the tiny freezers in cramped Japanese households.[44]

One especially important facilitating intermediary in international marketing is the *foreign freight forwarder*. Forwarders consolidate small shipments into larger ones and arrange for foreign country transportation. They also handle all the complicated paperwork required by governments for exporting and importing products.

Promotion Decisions

An international firm's promotion strategy also has to consider the relative merits of globalization and adaptation in advertising, personal selling, direct marketing, sales promotion, and publicity.

• **Advertising** • The attitudes of consumers, governments, competitors, intermediaries, and advertising agencies must be considered in advertising decisions. For example, Japanese ad agencies, unlike agencies in the United States, often handle competing accounts; hence comparative ads are considered distasteful in Japan. A government may prohibit advertising altogether, prescribe its content, or determine the types of products that can be advertised.

There also are problems in preparing ads. U.S. ads can be translated into foreign languages, but there will be problems if the translator is not up-to-date on the idioms and dialects of the foreign language. Ads directed to Orientals in Hong Kong must appear in both English and Chinese. If they appear only in Chinese, people may think the product is inferior. Ad themes and appeals also must fit the target audience's culture. Ads featuring the "Marlboro man" were unsuccessful in Hong Kong because it is one of the world's most urbanized areas and the people did not identify with horseback riding in the countryside.[45]

Media selection decisions often require adaptation. The use of print media is greatly limited in countries with high illiteracy rates. Some newspapers will not accept advertising. TV ads in some countries must be contracted one year in advance of their appearance, and it is not unusual for as many as fifty TV commercials to be bunched together for one showing. Circulation figures for magazines and newspapers often are suspect. This makes it harder to select the proper media mix.

The international firm may also have to select an ad agency. It can use an agency in its home country, separate local agencies in each host country, or a large multinational agency with branches in the host countries. U.S.-based ad agencies have been opening foreign branches for many years. The most popular means of entry has been the purchase of existing agencies in foreign countries.

Some ad campaigns that worked well in the United States have been successfully transplanted to Japan. For example, American Express translated its famous "Do you know me?" campaign into Japanese, keeping Jack Nicklaus and his golf clubs.[46] On the other hand, ads depicting women in bikinis would not be acceptable in Islamic countries.

McDonald's, whose operations are often cited as an example of globalization, claims that it is not an advocate of globalization. Consider the company's experience when it expanded into Puerto Rico. Right off it alienated Puerto Ricans with American TV commercials dubbed in Spanish. It also alienated residents with Hispanic ads imported from New York, which research showed looked too Mexican. Finally, a localized campaign was developed featuring ''McNaticos,'' a group of *puertorriquenos* who are fanatical about quality and service. Sales rose 4.4 percent after the campaign's introduction.[47]

- **Personal Selling** • Because of face-to-face contact between the salesperson and the prospect, personal selling is more culture-bound than advertising. Avon discovered some time ago that a standardized door-to-door retailing approach will not always work. For example, most Japanese women are too reserved to make a sales pitch to strangers. Thus the company adapted its approach to personal selling by allowing salespeople to sell to acquaintances.[48]

Most sales of consumer products are made by local nationals, but expensive industrial products often are sold by foreign salespeople. A few examples will show the need to practice cultural empathy in the personal selling effort.

Salespeople in some German-speaking countries should avoid smiling when shaking hands with prospects because the prospects may consider it too affectionate. The French do not say ''thanks'' in response to praise. Using first names is also considered offensive by the French. A salesperson who talks in a loud voice may be perceived as angry by the Chinese. In the Middle East and Latin America people stand much closer together while talking than they do in the United States. One of the worst things an industrial salesperson can ask an Arab businessman is ''How are the wife and children?''

- **Direct Marketing, Sales Promotion, and Public Relations** • As we saw in chapter 16, direct marketing can cross national borders. 7-Eleven Japan Company recently distributed Japanese-language catalogs produced by U.S.-based Shop America. The firm targets the 4 million customers who shop in 7-Eleven's four thousand stores in Japan every day. Shop America sells many items for 30 to 50 percent less than Tokyo stores charge. The catalogs offer products such as compact discs, Canon cameras, Rolex watches, and Remington shavers. Shop America's computer system allows 7-Eleven clerks to send orders straight to the company's home office in New York simply by waving a scanner over bar codes in the catalog. The firm has also arranged for some suppliers to ship directly to Japan.[49]

Promotional programs often include sales promotion and public relations activities. When auto sales declined recently in Europe, European car makers started offering rebates and low-interest financing—promotions that U.S. car makers have used for many years.

Public relations activities are also common. For example, in an attempt to boost exports, the American Soybean Association hired a nutritionist to travel through fifteen Latin American countries with the message that soybeans are a cheap source of protein. In Mexico the nutritionist called on small neighborhood tortilla factories and taught nutrition seminars at schools as part of the effort to persuade Mexicans to enrich the corn product with soy flour.[50]

Pricing Decisions

The globalization versus adaptation decision also arises in connection with pricing. For example, in doing business in China some companies have made the mistake of routinely setting their prices too high in the expectation that people will be anxious to negotiate for reductions. These companies have found instead that the Chinese do considerable research on prices in international markets. A business consultant says this about Chinese businesspeople, ''If you start with sky-high prices, they'll say goodbye.'' Subsequent cuts during negotiations will not help much because the people will think the seller set out to rip them off.[51]

Among the factors that international marketers must take into account in their pricing decisions are tariffs, international shipping costs, export credit terms, and, usually, less control over intermediary margins. As we saw earlier in the chapter, countertrading is also becoming increasingly important in international trade.

International companies conduct business in various currencies—French francs, German marks, U.S. dollars, Italian lira, and so on. In setting their prices and in converting one currency into another, the companies must cope with fluctuating foreign exchange rates. The *exchange rate* between two currencies is the value of one currency in relation to the other. For example, when the German mark goes up in value (appreciates) relative to the U.S. dollar, it can be converted into a greater number of dollars. In other words, fewer marks are needed to buy a dollar. Therefore German-made products become more expensive in the United States and U.S.-made products become cheaper in Germany. Fluctuating exchange rates cause international marketers problems in quoting prices, especially when the prices are to be included in long-term contracts.

• **Export Pricing** • Besides evaluating manufacturing costs, exporters must evaluate demand in each foreign market along with the competitive environment and government regulations. This often results in different prices for domestic and foreign buyers and different prices in different export markets. Table 22–5 lists several reasons exporters may set their f.o.b. factory prices lower on export sales than on domestic sales.

In setting export prices, firms must be careful to avoid dumping. *Dumping* is the shipment of substantial quantities of a product to a foreign country at prices that are below either the home market price of the same product or the full cost (including profit) of producing it. United States firms that complain of foreign dumping must show that the prices of the dumped goods are lower in the United States than in their home markets and that U.S. producers are being directly harmed by the alleged dumping. If the U.S. International Trade Commission finds that dumping has occurred, it can impose a countervailing duty on the dumped products to wipe out the foreign firm's price advantage. The International Trade Commission's Trade Remedy Assistance Office focuses mainly on helping small firms file petitions to the commission to halt unfair trade practices, such as dumping. Examples of dumped products from recent years are foreign-made shoes, semiconductors, forklift trucks, and minivans.

dumping

• **Pricing for Foreign Subsidiaries** • Many U.S.-based international companies are organized into product divisions and an international division. The product divisions sell

TABLE 22–5 Factors Favoring Lower F.o.b. Factory Prices on Exports

1. Lower buying power in the foreign market requires lower selling prices to sell there.
2. Competition in the foreign market is very strong.
3. Add-ons to the f.o.b. price, such as tariffs and shipping costs, are high.
4. Export pricing is based on variable costs and domestic pricing is based on full costs.
5. In the case of consumer products the foreign government sets price ceilings and the export price must be low enough to enable intermediaries to add their margins and still not exceed the prescribed ceiling.

their products to the international division, which in turn, sells the products to the firm's foreign subsidiaries. Typically each of these divisions is operated as a profit center to which costs and revenues are assigned. These intracompany sales (from product divisions to international divisions to foreign subsidiaries) require the setting of *transfer prices*.

Product divisions want to set high transfer prices, but the international division wants to pay low transfer prices. Each wants its operation to show a profit, and this often leads to conflict. This is another case where the systems view is essential.

The international division also has to set transfer prices for foreign subsidiaries. Those in low-tax countries tend to get low transfer prices, and those in high-tax countries tend to get high transfer prices. The company wants subsidiaries in low-tax countries to show more profit than those in high-tax countries. The U.S. Internal Revenue Service, U.S. customs officials, and foreign tax and customs officials can regulate transfer prices when they are being used to avoid taxes or customs duties.

• **Pricing within Foreign Markets** • Once a product enters a foreign country, pricing decisions become domestic pricing decisions in that country. International firms that distribute their products through wholly owned subsidiaries with local sales forces must set prices for final buyers in each host country. Their pricing problems are like those of purely domestic marketers. But companies that distribute through foreign intermediaries in their host countries exercise less control over pricing to final buyers.

SUMMARY OF LEARNING OBJECTIVES

1. Distinguish among international trade, international marketing, multinational company, and transnational company.

International trade is the movement of goods and services across national borders—the imports and exports of nations. International marketing is the efforts of individuals and organizations to satisfy human wants by facilitating exchanges across national boundaries. A multinational company is a firm that is based in one country (the parent, or home, country) and produces goods or provides services in one or more foreign countries (host countries). A transnational company is a firm that views the world as one market, conducts operations in many countries, and makes decisions as if national boundaries did not exist.

2. Explain why international marketers should engage in environmental monitoring.

Environmental monitoring is relevant to decision making about selecting and entering foreign markets and developing marketing strategies for them. The variables that should be monitored are economic, competitive, technological, sociocultural and ethical, and political-legal.

3. Identify the various forms of regional trading blocs.

The various forms are free trade area, customs union, common market, economic union, and political union.

4. Identify various approaches to entering foreign markets.

The various approaches are exporting (unsolicited and solicited), foreign licensing, foreign assembly, contract manufacturing, turn-key operation, management contract, and foreign production subsidiary.

5. Contrast the globalization and adaptation strategies.

Globalization is a worldwide marketing strategy whereby an organization uses the same or very similar marketing mixes in all its markets. Opponents favor the adaptation strategy. They argue that the diversity of cultures and of levels of economic development make globalization a risky strategy. Whereas globalization is a standardization strategy, adaptation is a customization or localization strategy.

Review Questions

1. What is the major difference between purely domestic marketing and international marketing?

2. Is a multinational company the same thing as a transnational company? Explain.

3. What is the significance to international marketers of a country's level of economic development?

4. What are the major elements of the sociocultural environment that are important to marketers?

5. What are the major risks that firms face when doing business in a foreign country?

6. What forms can a regional trading block take? Explain each.

7. What methods might a marketer use to enter foreign markets? Explain each.

8. What does globalization mean?

9. Why would a firm engage in dumping?

10. What is a transfer price?

Discussion Questions

1. What does the concept of social responsibility mean to a transnational company?

2. Why do governments create trade barriers?

3. Are regional trading blocs good for consumers? Explain.

4. Which strategy is more in tune with the marketing concept—globalization or adaptation? Explain.

Application Exercise

Reread the material about small businesses going into international marketing at the beginning of this chapter and answer the following questions:

1. Why do you think more small firms are getting involved in international marketing?

2. Would you describe Earl Thompson, the owner of Torel Inc., as an advocate of globalization (standardization) or adaptation (customization or localization)? Explain.

3. What lesson does Quicksilver Enterprises' experience in Brazil offer?

Key Concepts

The following key terms were introduced in this chapter:

comparative advantage
balance of trade
international marketing
multinational company (MNC)
transnational company
sustainable development
cartel

countertrades
regional trading bloc
trading company
combination export manager
foreign licensing
foreign assembly
contract manufacturing

turnkey operation
management contract
foreign production subsidiary
foreign direct investment
joint venture
globalization
dumping

CASES

Bonjour, Mickey!

LYN S. AMINE, *St. Louis University*

Mickey Mouse is going to Paris. In 1992, Walt Disney Company's new Euro Disneyland is scheduled to open at an estimated cost of $2.6 billion. Located about twenty miles east of Paris in an area called Marne-la-Vallee, Mickey's new home in Europe was chosen from among some 200 competing sites in France and Spain. Why was Paris chosen as the site of preference, despite its dreary winters that are predictably cold, rainy, and even snowy? It was chosen because of its prime location in the center of Europe's heartland. There are estimated to be 17 million people living within a two-hour drive of the new site, 68 million within a four-hour drive, and 310 million within a two-hour flight.

This compares very favorably with Mickey's venture into

Japan, where 35 million people live within 90 minutes' travel of the Tokyo park. Winter weather in Tokyo can be as unfavorable as in Paris but this has not deterred visitors. What they see is pure Americana. All signs are in English, most of the food is American-style, and the attractions are cloned from the American parks. The only changes made were to rename Main Street USA as the World Bazaar and Frontierland as Westernland. The Tiki Room birds, the country bears, and the pirates of the Caribbean also now speak Japanese. Judging by attendance figures, it would seem that the Japanese are just wacky over Mickey.

The question remains whether Europeans will take to the Disney world of characters with the same enthusiasm. Monsier Jack Lang, the French Minister for Culture, expressed fierce hostility in 1989 to American film and TV imports and any other artefacts of American cultural "imperialism." Paris theatre director Ariane Mnouchkine has called Euro Disneyland a "cultural Chernobyl," and French journalist Gilles Smadja denounced the government's commitment to spend $350 million on park-related infrastructure in his 1988 book entitled *Mickey: The Sting*. When Disney Chairman Michael D. Eisner visited Paris, French Communist party members threw eggs at him. Farmers in the area around the new site have complained angrily about the government's intervention to sell their land to Disney Company at preferential prices. Finally, Michael Colombe, mayor of a nearby town, has criticized the company and its American way of doing things as an icon of foreign arrogance.

Introducing "the American way" of doing things may not be easy. Cast members at Euro Disneyland will number some twelve thousand, half of whom will be French. In addition to specific job training, employees will attend the standard day-and-a-half course in Disney culture at Disney University. Recognizing differences in cultural habits and expectations, Disney has relaxed its personal grooming code slightly. Women employees may wear redder nail polish than in the United States, but the taboo for men on facial hair still holds. "We want the clean-shaven, neat-and-tidy look," says the director of the Paris branch of Disney University.

Euro Disneyland is not the only theme-park in Europe. Great Britain has a number of large parks dotted around the countryside, ranging in themes from medieval castles to adventure parks to safari parks and zoos. Also planned for the Paris area are two new film parks, Universal Studios (1994) and Disney MGM Studios (1996), and a Marine World (1993). Britain may see two more parks, Battersea in London and Wonderworld in the north. Spain will be the new home for Busch Gardens in Barcelona (1992), Magic Mountain in Marbella, and Andalusialand in Seville. 1992 will be the year of the Barcelona Summer Olympics and the 500-year anniversary of Christopher Columbus' discovery of the New World.

Questions

1. What economic environment do you think Disney looks for in deciding where to locate its theme parks?

2. Why might Europeans be less enthusiastic about Disney characters and themes than the Japanese? What could Disney have done to lessen the "culture shock" for Europeans?

3. How might Walt Disney Company adapt the new Euro Disneyland to meet the tastes and preferences of European visitors? Do you think any adaptation is necessary?

4. How might the imminent establishment of the European Community affect Euro Disneyland?

Moscow-McDonald's

LYN S. AMINE, *St. Louis University*

After fourteen years of intensive negotiations, McDonald's Corporation finally opened its first restaurant in Moscow on January 31, 1990. McDonalds Restaurants of Canada and the Food Service Administration of the Moscow City Council signed an agreement to form a joint venture called "Moscow-McDonald's." Initially, twenty McDonald's restaurants will be built, along with a food processing and distribution center in Moscow. The location of the first store is in the heart of Moscow, near Gorky Street and just several blocks away from the Kremlin. The restaurant seats some 900 customers. There are 700 indoor and 200 outdoor patio seats, making it the largest McDonald's in the world. It is expected to be the highest-volume McDonald's store in the world, with daily visits of 10,000–15,000 customers.

Since the Iron Curtain was lifted, trading with the Soviet Union has become an intriguing opportunity for many American companies. At least three considerations led McDonald's to decide on expansion into the U.S.S.R. First, the U.S. domestic fast-food market is saturated and over-built with franchises. Market share growth strategies have given way to market share protection tactics. Second, baby boomer families who once crowded fast-food stores are staying home or are frequenting convenience stores for fill-in food purchases. Third, many understand the necessity and advantage of being the first to offer well-known, brand-name goods and services. Over 200 million eager new customers are not easily ignored. McDonald's is the first fast-food company in the Soviet market. Worldwide, McDonald's operates some 11,300 restaurants of which 8,700 are based in the United States. The remainder are located in fifty other countries.

An important challenge for Moscow-McDonald's is to maintain the corporate values expressed by the motto "QSCV" (Quality, Service, Cleanliness, and Value). Intensive training will be used to transfer these distinctive corporate values not only to management and employees, but also to suppliers and even customers. Four Soviet managers have graduated from the Canadian Institute of Hamburgerology. Trainee employees learn everything from how to wash windows to the proper way to assemble a Big Mac. One of the most important cultural changes that training of employees has to accomplish concerns customer relations. Learning to smile, look people in the eye, be courteous, and say "priyatnovo appetita" (or "enjoy your meal"), has been a radical departure from traditional business conduct among local employees.

Vegetable farmers need training in how to harvest and pack produce without bruising. Cattle farmers were instructed to slaughter their cattle one month earlier than usual to raise leaner beef. Customers also require some educational assistance in eating finger food, as their first reaction was to disassemble a Big Mac and eat it layer by layer. Littering inside the store was also a problem.

On opening day, students and office workers marveled at what was by Moscow's standards a short forty-five minute waiting line. A "Big Mak," "Kartotel-fries," and a "milk-koktel" cost about 5.5 rubles, twice the cost of a meal in a state-owned cafeteria.

The first day, over 30,000 Soviets were served. Many were seen slipping plastic forks and styrofoam plates into their coats to take home as souvenirs. Elizaveta Pavlenko, a 74-year-old pensioner, wearing her best fur coat and emerald earrings, was present on opening day. "It's like a holiday," she said. "The food was wonderful." But the thing that struck her most was the service. "Somebody even showed me to my seat and carried my tray. Now that has never happened before!"

Questions

1. Which environmental variables have had a significant impact on the operation of the new Moscow-McDonald's?

2. Would you characterize the orientation of McDonald's as ethnocentric, polycentric, regiocentric, or geocentric? Explain.

3. Which marketing mix variable do you think will be critical to the future success of McDonald's in the U.S.S.R.? Explain.

4. Is it important for Moscow-McDonald's to operate in *exactly* the same way as in Western markets? Explain.

PepsiCo: Swapping Pepsi for Chickens and Tomato Paste

• **"Be Sociable—Have a Pepsi"** •

"Coca-Cola had gone into Europe with the troops [in World War II], and I wasn't going to let them get Eastern Europe, too," says Donald Kendall, chairman of the Executive Committee of PepsiCo. From 1957 to 1971, Kendall was president of Pepsi-Cola International. During that time, he increased the number of countries in which Pepsi sold its soft drinks from about 60 to more than 120 and tripled International's sales. But what he will probably always be remembered for in the business community—and probably in Washington, D.C., and Moscow, too—is making Pepsi the first foreign consumer product to be sold legally in the U.S.S.R.

Although the Soviet leadership didn't finally accept Kendall's overtures until 1972, the picture most people associate with Pepsi's piercing of the Iron Curtain is of Soviet Premier Nikita Khrushchev drinking Pepsis at the 1959 American National Exhibition in Moscow. As the clear leader in the cola wars, Pepsi's arch-rival Coca-Cola had been invited to take part in the exhibition—an opportunity for U.S. companies to show off their best goods to the Soviets and the international news media. But the Cold

War was in one of its frostier periods, and Coke executives thought handing out sodas in Moscow could hurt sales at home.

Donald Kendall thought otherwise: "I was bound and determined that they [Coke] weren't going to get Eastern Europe and I always felt that eventually it was going to open. So I wanted to go to the Soviet Union even though I had very little support even in our own company. We went and, because of the criticism back home, I told . . . then-Vice President Richard Nixon [the top U.S. official at the Exhibition] that we had to get Khrushchev by our kiosk and give him a Pepsi."

Nixon complied, and Kendall handed the infamously ebullient Premier two Pepsis—one, he said, bottled in New York and the other bottled in the Soviet Union for the exhibit. Khrushchev tasted both and declared that, of course, the one made in the U.S.S.R. was better. He ordered another and asked Nixon to join him. As the two continued to banter, cameras clicked away. The next day, pictures of Khrushchev and his Pepsi appeared in newspapers all around the globe. It was one of the PR coups of the century, and it gave Kendall a good leg-up in his dealings with the Soviets.

• **The Great Opportunity** •

When Pepsis were finally sold in Moscow, lines formed every day at

Kendall's kiosks. Soviet citizens—accustomed to a limited choice of consumer goods, many of them frequently unavailable and of unreliable quality—seemed to have an insatiable thirst for the dependable cola with the Western cachet. In the years that followed Pepsi's entrance, a few other Western companies began to make headway in the Soviet marketplace, usually encountering strong consumer demand. And American and Western European tourists knew that they could always sell their Levi's, Nikes, and other brand-name belongings on the Soviet and Eastern European black markets, often for more than twice what they had paid for them at home.

Many Western marketers took note of the Soviets' and Eastern Europeans' apparent pent-up desire for Western goods: to them, the falling of the Berlin Wall in late 1989 symbolized not just the possibility of a new social and political order within the Soviet's former sphere of influence but also the opening of a huge new marketplace. Perhaps, in fact, the most attractive new marketplace in the world: Eastern Europe was already industrialized and its people well-educated and culturally similar in many ways to West Europeans, whose consumption habits were already familiar. Moreover, unlike the emerging Asian and African markets, where Western marketers often had to wait for consumers to amass enough money to be able to afford Western goods, Eastern Europeans were known to have a high personal-savings rate—the result of having industrial jobs but not much to spend their money on.

While Eastern Europe was opening up, Western Europe was preparing for 1992, when trade barriers between European Community countries were set to fall. At the very least, East Germany, now reunified with West Germany, would be part of the European Community. Many hoped that it wouldn't be long before Poland, Hungary, Czechoslovakia, and other ex-Soviet satellites would join in, making the free-trade zone the largest in the world. "Europhoria" took hold as Western marketers rubbed their hands together in anticipation of large returns on relatively little investment in market extension activities. In mid-1990, the Opinion Research Corporation reported that 35 percent of the largest 1,500 U.S. companies had plans in the coming year to market their products in Eastern Europe.

People remembered the picture of Khrushchev and his Pepsi. What many had forgotten was the lesson of Donald Kendall's patience in working over many years with the Soviets to ensure PepsiCo's long-term presence in their market. It was a lesson that many would have to relearn as Europhoria gave way to Eurorealism during late 1990 and early 1991.

• **The Great Disappointment** •

In the first flush of joy following the overthrow of Eastern Europe's Communist governments, many had underestimated the difficulty the new democracies would have in moving toward Western-style capitalism and consumption. Although their populations were generally eager for Western or Western-style goods, the Eastern European countries faced

many impediments to a quick integration with the rest of Europe's economy. First, many of their factories were shockingly antiquated and ill-equipped to produce precision-manufactured goods or even low-tech goods of consistent quality. The contrast between West Germany's precision-engineered Mercedes-Benz and East Germany's belching, testy Trabant was all too symbolic of the contrast between the physical plants, management, and operations of Western and Eastern European factories.

As antiquated as they were, most of the East's factories had been able to run steadily because they were subsidized either by their own governments or by the Soviet Union in order to maintain full employment in the factories' neighborhoods. Many existed only because the Soviets had placed standing orders for products that actually were not really needed or could be bought cheaper elsewhere. Now, as both their town governments and Moscow took drastic measures to move quickly toward market economies, subsidies and guaranteed orders were cut off. Unable to compete, many factories closed, thereby throwing tens of thousands of people out of work. The relatively large savings many Eastern European workers had accumulated dwindled as their pay was cut or stopped altogether and as prices of staples rose to reflect true costs of production rather than old rates of government subsidy. At a national level, there was a dire lack of hard currency reserves needed to pay for capital investments or production materials. It would take millions, and perhaps billions, of dollars to rehabilitate or replace these factories so that they could answer real market demands.

Meanwhile, Westerners were beginning to realize the vast extent of industrial pollution that had been allowed to occur in the East. Millions more dollars would be needed

Soviet premier Nikita Khruschev (left) had his first taste of Pepsi Cola at the American Exhibition in Moscow in 1959.

[© UPI/Bettman]

to make these factories, their neighborhoods, and even the products that came out of them safe for human use.

Because the East's distribution networks had often grown in response to plans dictated by central government officials rather than to customer demands, whole new channels would have to be developed to answer both producer and consumer needs. And the infrastructure necessary to move goods, people, and information around efficiently— roads, rail lines, airports, and telecommunications networks—was in primitive form even within most of Eastern Europe's largest cities. Although Western European and U.S. lawmakers pledged aid grants and loans to help remedy some of these problems, it soon became clear that a deepening recession in the West meant that such help would fall far short of what the new Eastern European governments had hoped for.

The political realities of doing business in Eastern Europe were also complicated. It soon became clear that, although they were adamant about breaking free of Soviet control, many Eastern Europeans were not entirely convinced of the benefits of swinging all the way over to a U.S.-style free-market economy. Many were wary of the prospects of cyclical unemployment and inflation associated with free markets and disgusted by reports of homelessness and limited access to medical care in the U.S. They wanted the benefits of a demand-responsive economy but also to maintain many of their social welfare systems. It soon became clear that it would take as much as a decade or more for their governments to settle on what basic rights or restrictions would be given to businesses as both marketers and

employers. For Western marketers, this meant continuing uncertainty about what kind of political environment they would be operating in.

It was now patently obvious that many early predictions of Eastern economic growth had been overly optimistic. As the disturbing reality of Eastern Europe's condition sank in, many Western marketers abandoned their plans for doing business there.

- **One Way to Deal With Reality** •

When Donald Kendall was asked by *Directors & Boards* magazine to comment on the fact that many Eastern European technologies, facilities, and employee skills were not competitive in a world market, he replied, "Of course they are not. If they were, why would we go over there? They wouldn't need us." Kendall's comments on the Soviet Union also applied to his approach to the rest of Eastern Europe: "There is no place with greater opportunity. If you wait until you have stability and convertible currency, the opportunity is going to be gone. . . . Where there is opportunity there is always risk."

As PepsiCo had begun to move into the Eastern European market, it had the advantage of Kendall's experience in crafting deals in the U.S.S.R. that would be unthinkable

in the West. In the Soviet Union, Kendall had faced the same problems Eastern Europe now faced: a lack of hard currency, an undeveloped infrastructure, antiquated factories, unsuitable distribution channels, workers unused to modern technology or management procedures, and a general lack of understanding or willingness to adhere to general free-market principles. Rather than wait for the Soviet Union to convert to capitalism or to reform its economy within a socialist framework, he tackled individual problems standing in the way of a successful PepsiCo marketing strategy.

For instance, Soviet officials had no interest in the idea of PepsiCo

---

"Where there is opportunity there is always risk."

---

simply exporting its products to the U.S.S.R.: this would send Soviet citizens' money out of the country in exchange for nothing but a nondurable consumer good. And in any case, money coming out of the Soviet Union would be of no use to PepsiCo: because the ruble was nonconvertible, PepsiCo wouldn't be able to buy anything with such money or even to bank it. So Kendall and the Soviets instead agreed that PepsiCo would build a bottling plant in the Soviet Union.

In most other countries where PepsiCo operated, an entity in that country—whether a private concern or the government—would finance the bottling plant in what amounted to a franchise agreement with PepsiCo. To convince the Soviets to go along with the deal, however, Kendall had to agree to finance the first Soviet Pepsi plants. In order to make an adequate return on this investment, he wrote an override—an extra commission paid to PepsiCo on sales of Pepsi concentrate to the Soviets running the plants—into the agreement. Still, this extra commission, as well as the standard profit from Pepsi-Cola sales, was useless to PepsiCo in rubles. So Kendall arranged a barter agreement whereby PepsiCo would accept Stolichnaya vodka instead of cash. By selling the Stolichnaya in the United States and Europe, PepsiCo finally had its hard currency, as well as the prestige of being the first Western consumer products company to crack the Soviet market. Meanwhile, the Soviets got not only Pepsi-Cola to drink but also thousands of new jobs and millions of dollars worth of technology transfer as Soviet managers, engineers, and workers learned how to control the operation of the modern PepsiCo bottling plants. It was a workable deal, but it took Kendall from 1959 until 1972 to complete it.

Following PepsiCo's success in the U.S.S.R., Soviet officials allowed Kendall to pursue similar enterprises in their Eastern European satellites. In return for setting up Pepsi-Cola bottling plants and selling his soft drinks in Romania, Hungary, and Bulgaria, he accepted Romanian, Hungarian, and Bulgarian wine, which he sold in the U.S. through PepsiCo's Monsieur Henri wine division, created for just this purpose. In Bulgaria, where certain industries were in advanced stages of development, PepsiCo accepted bottling equipment, which it used to set up Pepsi bottling plants in China. In Hungary, PepsiCo accepted chickens, which it took out of the country and used in its Kentucky Fried Chicken division restaurants, and tomato paste, which it used in its Pizza Hut division restaurants. In Poland, PepsiCo accepted tables and chairs, which were installed in its U.S. Pizza Hut restaurants, as well as brewer's yeast and assorted other products, which it turned around and sold in the United States and Western Europe.

Back in the U.S.S.R., PepsiCo's business was so successful that by 1991, there were 26 Soviet Pepsi plants and PepsiCo was planning to build 28 more. After the first few plants were built, the Soviets themselves had financed the rest. This meant that PepsiCo had to take less vodka per plant out of the country. But still, Soviet sales of Pepsi had grown so steadily that they had outstripped Western demand for Stolichnaya vodka. When PepsiCo negotiated for the 28 new plants—which would increase Soviet production of Pepsi from 960 million bottles in 1989 to almost 2 billion bottles in 2000—it agreed to increase its take of Stolichnaya from 24 million bottles in 1989 to nearly 50 million bottles in 2000. But the Soviets also agreed to transfer the title of 10 new Soviet-built oil tanker ships to PepsiCo. PepsiCo wasn't in the oil business, but it would either sell or lease the ships in order to get back its investment in hard currency. "You have to have people who have the ability to go into a country and find things that you might be able to sell in the West," Kendall told *Directors & Boards*. "We've been very successful at it, and the result is that we have a very strong market position."

At the same time, PepsiCo executives also negotiated with Soviet officials to loosen up their rules on the kinds of containers Pepsi could be sold in. In the past, PepsiCo had been willing to follow a Soviet mandate that it use only 11.5 ounce glass bottles made in Soviet factories. These bottles were heavy, expensive, and had to be returned to the factory for refilling. The underdeveloped state of the Soviet road and rail systems and shortage of trucks alone curtailed Pepsi's distribution abilities, but these bottles helped to guarantee that Pepsi was rarely found more than 20 km from a Pepsi plant. Now, Soviet officials agreed to let Pepsi produce 8-ounce containers in the new plants and to introduce Western-style aluminum cans and plastic bottles. Nearly 20 years after first launching its products in the Soviet market, Pepsi finally had a chance to develop some kind of efficient nationwide distribution system.

• Constant Challenge •

It was likely that such long time lags between the design of PepsiCo business plans and their implementation would persist for some years in the U.S.S.R. But Kendall and other PepsiCo executives hoped that Eastern Europe's economic and political reform would translate into faster action in Poland, Czechoslovakia, Hungary, and their neighbors for future PepsiCo deals. Still, the fundamental problems of Eastern Europe's lack of hard currency reserves, undeveloped distribution networks, pollution, and underdeveloped skills remained. And in some ways, reform would actually make it harder for PepsiCo and other Western companies to make deals in the new democracies: they now had to contend with many different authorities, many of them competing with each other over turf, rather than the old central authorities, whose word was law.

And, now that Eastern Europe had opened up, PepsiCo faced a tough challenge that was both new and old: the arrival on long-time PepsiCo territory of traditional enemy Coca-Cola. Although Pepsi was the market leader in Poland, Czechoslovakia, Hungary, Bulgaria, and Romania, it trailed far behind Coke in the rest of Europe. As of early 1991, Coca-Cola owned more than half of the European soft-drink market, while Pepsi could claim little more than a tenth. In western Germany, Coke had taken 70 percent of the market, compared to Pepsi's 10 percent share; in eastern Germany, Coke had 70 percent and Pepsi 30 percent. Coca-Cola planned to use its overwhelming market position and new bottling plants in eastern Germany to try to capture the rest of Eastern Europe from Pepsi. Ironically, Pepsi was expected to have a struggle on its hands not in spite of but *because* of its long-time presence in the East: Pepsi had been around so long it almost seemed like a home-grown product; for East Europeans, the thrill came from drinking the formerly unobtainable Coke.

• Questions •

1. It took more than a decade for PepsiCo to execute its plan to enter the Soviet market. Discuss some possible ways in which PepsiCo managers may have (1) assured goal-directed actions, (2) assigned resources, and (3) built interpersonal relationships and informal networks.

2. What unanticipated environmental changes are more likely to affect marketers doing business in the Soviet Union and Eastern Europe than Western marketers who confine themselves to domestic markets? What are the implications for marketers?

3. How successful do you think PepsiCo's countertrade strategy has been?

4. Many Western marketers initially assumed that Eastern European consumers would be essentially equivalent to Western European consumers once they were allowed access to a free market. How may Eastern Europeans differ from their Western cousins?

GLOSSARY

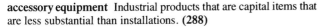

accessory equipment Industrial products that are capital items that are less substantial than installations. **(288)**

account executive The major link between the advertising agency and the client; the person who coordinates all the agency's activities on the client's behalf. **(520)**

adaptive innovations Innovations that involve enhancements to established product forms that will compete with existing brands or suppliers but that may have some special distinctive feature. **(312)**

adoption process The series of stages a prospective buyer goes through in deciding to buy and make regular use of a new product. **(335)**

advertising Any paid form of nonpersonal communication through the mass media about a good, service, or idea by an identified sponsor. **(470)**

advertising agency A firm that specializes in communication and marketing and that offers these services to clients (advertisers). **(519)**

advertising department Part of an advertiser's own organization; may include creative and technical personnel, and is headed by a manager, who participates in ad production and media placement and reports to the marketing manager. **(519)**

advertising media The communication channels that carry messages from advertisers to their targets, the four basic types of which are print, broadcast, out-of-home, and direct response. **(508)**

advocacy advertising Type of institutional advertising in which the advertiser takes a position for or against an issue. **(501)**

AIDA process The sequence of stages (attention, interest, desire, and action) that a marketer hopes to lead target customers through with its promotion effort. **(470)**

allocation role of price The function price performs in helping buyers decide how to derive the greatest expected utility from their buying power. **(593)**

approach The manner chosen by the salesperson to gain access to the prospect, establish rapport, and get the prospect's attention and interest. **(563)**

assembler of farm products A merchant wholesaler that buys in small quantities from many producers and sells in large quantities to fewer customers. **(427)**

association strategies Strategies that emphasize linkages between a service and a brand name, a symbol, or some other observable evidence in order to overcome the handicap of intangibility. **(675)**

attitudes Enduring feelings, evaluations, and response tendencies directed toward an object or idea. **(156)**

audience selectivity An advertising medium's (or vehicle's) relative ability to reach an audience whose members are alike in ways that are important to the advertiser. **(508)**

automatic vending (also called automatic merchandising) The ultimate in nonpersonal selling; a type of nonstore retailing in which products are sold directly to buyers from machines. **(395)**

backward vertical integration The act of acquiring the operations of a firm that is farther away from the final buyer in the marketing channel—for example, a retailer buying out a wholesaler or a wholesaler buying out a manufacturer. **(365)**

bait pricing (also called bait-and-switch pricing) The practice (often illegal) of advertising a product at a very low price to attract shoppers, only to persuade them to buy a higher-priced item when they respond. **(631)**

balance of trade The difference in value between a country's total exports and total imports. **(697)**

basing point pricing A type of delivered pricing in which prices include freight charges from chosen locations (basing points) regardless of the actual location from which the product will be shipped. **(624)**

benefit segmentation The division of a mass market on the basis of the benefits that people seek from the product. **(236)**

blanket ordering A procurement method in which the buyer and supplier enter into a long-term contract under which the supplier offers speedy and reliable delivery or a reduced price for repeat purchases of supplies and the buyer must use that supplier for the duration of the agreement. **(184)**

brand A name, term, design, symbol, or any other feature that identifies one seller's good or service as distinct from those of other sellers. **(291)**

brand equity The added value that a brand name brings to a product beyond the product's functional value. **(295)**

brand franchise extension The application of an old brand to a new product line. **(295)**

brand loyalty The degree to which a buying unit, such as a household, concentrates its purchases over time on a particular brand within a product category. **(236)**

brand mark (also called a logo) That part of a brand name that cannot be spoken and is most commonly a symbol, picture, design, distinctive lettering, color, or a combination of these. **(291)**

brand name That part of a brand that can be spoken—letters, numbers, or words. **(291)**

breakdown approach The approach to estimating sales potential that assumes that a product's sales potential varies with the country's general level of business activity. **(262)**

breakeven analysis The method of identifying the level of sales at which total revenue (TR) will equal total cost (TC), given a product's per-unit selling price. **(604)**

breakthrough innovations Innovations that involve major changes in technology that lead to the creation of new product categories. (312)

broadcast media Communication channels that sell advertising time to marketers. (512)

brokerage allowance A discount granted by sellers to brokers for the services (functions) they perform. (621)

build-up approach The approach to estimating sales potential that begins with an estimate of the number of units of the product category a typical buyer in a typical sales territory will buy, then multiplies that number by the number of potential buyers in that territory, and does the same for all the other territories. (262)

business cycle The sequence of changes (swings) that occur in an economy's overall level of business and economic activity. (37)

business services Intangible industrial products that are expense items and that do not become part of the finished product they are used to make. (289)

buyclasses The three types of industrial buying situations: (1) new task, (2) modified rebuy, and (3) straight rebuy. (188)

buyer's market An environment in which supply is greater than demand. (15)

buying center The set of people who determine both what will be purchased to fill an organization's needs and from whom the products will be purchased. (193)

buyphases The problem-solving steps used by industrial buyers primarily in new task buying: (1) recognizing a need; (2) specifying the need; (3) searching for potential suppliers; (4) inviting, acquiring, and analyzing vendor proposals; (5) selecting the vendor and placing the order; and (6) following up. (190)

campaign-oriented nonprofit marketing A marketing approach that consists of occasional broad based, money-oriented appeals (such as annual telethons) emphasing the organization's needs. (687)

cannibalization Situation that exists when an organization's new product achieves its sales mainly by taking away customers of its established products. (291)

cartel A group of firms in different countries (or of countries themselves, such as the Organization of Petroleum Exporting Countries, or OPEC) that agree to share markets. (700)

cash discount A reduction in list price that rewards customers for paying their bills promptly. (620)

catalog marketing A type of marketing in which the marketer offers its products in a publication, which includes ordering instructions, and the customer orders by mail or phone or at a catalog counter. (534)

catalog showroom A discount retail facility whose customers pre-shop—compare quality and prices in the catalog at home before going to the store to shop—through a catalog mailed to them and then select merchandise from samples which are often featured in display cases in the showroom. (394)

cause-related marketing The process of formulating and implementing marketing activities that are characterized by an offer from the firm to contribute a specified amount to a designated cause when customers engage in revenue-producing exchanges that satisfy organizational and individual objectives. (26)

channel conflict The opposing interests that exist among firms at the same level in a marketing channel (horizontal conflict) or among firms at different levels (vertical conflict) in the channel. (367)

channel leader The marketing channel member in an administered vertical marketing system that exerts power over the other channel members and can influence their decisions and actions. (371)

close The point in the sales presentation at which the salesperson attempts to secure the order. (565)

cognitive dissonance A state of psychological tension or post-purchase doubt that a consumer experiences after making a difficult purchasing choice. (146)

combination export manager A domestic agent intermediary that serves as the export department for several noncompeting manufacturers. (714)

combination store A combination food store and drugstore that is larger than a superstore and offers even more diversified merchandise and services. (392)

communication The process of influencing others' behavior by sharing ideas, information, or feelings with them. (462)

comparative advantage The position a country enjoys when it produces the products in which it has the greatest advantage, or the least disadvantage, in relation to other countries. (697)

comparative advertising Advertising in which the marketer compares its brand to rival brands that are identified by brand name. (501)

competition Rivalry among marketers that seek to satisfy markets. (42)

competitive bidding The practice of prospective sellers competing by submitting their prices for goods or services to industrial buyers that are shopping around. (632)

complementary products Products for which the purchase of one increases the likelihood that the second will be purchased. (290)

complex decisions Decisions that consumers make through extensive problem solving, rather than through routine behavior. (144)

component materials Industrial products that include semi-manufactured and semiprocessed materials that require further processing before becoming part of the finished product. (288)

component parts Industrial products that either are ready for direct assembly into the finished product or require only a minor amount of further processing. (288)

concentration strategy The marketing strategy of focusing marketing effort on one segment of a larger market and developing one marketing mix for that segment. (216)

consent order An agreement by a firm to "cease and desist" a practice that is presumed to be in violation of regulatory rules. (67)

consolidation strategies Methods for achieving organizational objectives that conflict with growth objectives. (83)

consumer behavior The subset of human behavior that is concerned with the decisions and acts of individuals in purchasing and using products. (143)

consumerism A movement to strengthen the power of consumers in relation to the power of producers and sellers. **(15)**

consumer products Goods and services that are bought to satisfy personal and household wants. **(282)**

containerization A materials handling system that encloses a shipment of products (perhaps several unitized loads) in a container, seals it, and transports it from shipper to receiver without rehandling the products in the container. **(444)**

contract manufacturing An arrangement in which a firm enters into an agreement with firms in foreign markets to manufacture its product and the firm handles the marketing, usually through its foreign sales subsidiaries. **(717)**

convenience products Low-priced items or services that consumers buy frequently with a minimum of shopping effort. **(283)**

cooperative advertising Advertising in which a manufacturer pays part of the retailer's cost of advertising the manufacturer's product in the retailer's local market. **(500)**

copyright The granting to creators of dramatic, musical, and other intellectual properties or their heirs exclusive rights to their published or unpublished works for as long as the creator lives, plus fifty years. **(292)**

corporate purchasing agreements Statements of intention by the buyer to buy and the seller to sell a given quantity of a product at a specified price during the next year. **(195)**

cost-per-thousand (CPM) A commonly used tool to determine the cost efficiency of a media vehicle; it is computed by the following formula **(508)**:

$$CPM = \frac{\text{cost of the ad} \times 1000}{\text{number of targets reached}}$$

cost-plus pricing The simplest cost-oriented approach to pricing in which the selling price for each unit of product equals its total cost plus something extra for profit. **(602)**

countertrades Transactions in which purchases are paid for with something other than money and credit as the medium of exchange. **(701)**

cultural values Values that result from assigning worth to objects or behaviors on the basis of need satisfaction; objects and behaviors that are highly valued are transmitted to succeeding generations. **(167)**

culture The sum total of knowledge, beliefs, values, customs, and artifacts that we use to adapt to our environment and that we hand down to succeeding generations. **(166)**

cumulative quantity discount A deduction from list price that applies to the buyer's total purchases made during a specific period of time and intended to encourage customer loyalty. **(619)**

dealer brand (also called distributor, private, store, house, or middleman brand) A brand that is owned by an intermediary such as a wholesaler or retailer. **(297)**

decoding The process by which the receiver attempts to convert symbols conveyed by the sender into a message. **(467)**

decoupling The demand-balancing strategy in which the service is divided into components, some of which can be delivered in different ways. **(678)**

deflation Falling prices. **(40)**

degree of brand familiarity The level of awareness of a product by any given person. **(293)**

Delphi method The sales forecasting method that involves surveying (often by mail) a panel of experts from inside and outside the organization—sometimes from across the nation or throughout the world—to obtain their anonymous estimates and explanations, then having them repeat the process, after they are shown a summary of results, for as many times as necessary until a consensus emerges. **(264)**

demand-balancing strategies Marketing policies that are designed to reduce demand fluctuations. **(677)**

demand curve A graphic portrayal of a demand schedule. **(598)**

demand schedule A summary of the quantity of a product that is demanded at different prices. **(598)**

demarketing A strategy a marketer undertakes in an attempt to reduce demand for its goods or services. **(26)**

demographic segmentation The division of a mass market on the basis of statistical data such as age, sex, and buying power. **(224)**

department store A retail store that carries wide and fairly deep merchandise lines and is departmentalized according to product lines, such as clothing, furniture, appliances, toys, books, sporting goods, and housewares. **(391)**

depth interviewing A marketing research technique that uses open-ended questions to permit respondents to talk to and interact with the interviewer. **(128)**

derived demand A situation in which the demand for one product results from the existing demand for another product. **(179)**

determinant attributes The features of a product that decide the buyer's choice of a particular brand. **(250)**

development-oriented nonprofit marketing A marketing approach that emphasizes long-term relationships with targeted donor groups; it is based on the idea of mutually satisfying exchanges. **(686)**

differential advantage The benefit enjoyed when a marketer offers a unique product that customers will buy from it rather than from its rivals. **(45)**

differential pricing The practice of offering two or more slightly different products (substitutes) at different prices. **(630)**

diffusion process The spread of an idea or the penetration of the market by a new product. **(327)**

direct interviewing A marketing research technique that uses direct questions designed to elicit specific responses. **(128)**

direct mail A type of advertising that uses the mail to deliver the message to the target. **(533)**

direct marketing An interactive system of marketing which uses one or more advertising media to effect a measurable response and/or transaction at any location. **(470)**

direct response media The communication channels through which marketers can communicate directly with the target audience. **(514)**

direct selling A method of marketing that is based on direct sales contact between the marketer and the prospective customer. **(395)**

discount store A large, self-service, departmentalized volume retailer that sells a wide variety of merchandise at low markup for a high turnover. (393)

disinflation A sustained reduction in the inflation rate, caused by prices rising at a declining rate. (40)

distinctive competencies The key resources that provide a foundation for future growth and enable the organization to achieve a distinct competitive advantage. (79)

distribution center A facility that coordinates order taking, order filling, and delivery activities under one roof to accomplish throughput. (439)

dual distribution The practice of selling the same brand or product line through two or more competing channels to reach the same target market. (360)

dumping The shipment of substantial quantities of a product to a foreign country at prices that are be- low either the home market price of the same product or the full cost (including profit) of producing it. (725)

economic order quantity (EOQ) The quantity of goods that should be ordered for inventory each time to minimize total cost (carrying cost and ordering cost). (441)

economies of scale The decline in cost per unit as fixed costs are spread over a larger number of units. (603)

encoding The process of putting meaning into symbols to be conveyed as messages in the communication process. (463)

environmental monitoring The process by which a marketing organization identifies, analyzes, and forecasts the impact of relevant environmental forces on it. (68)

essential evidence Tangible objects that are associated with the source of production of the service but that cannot be possessed. (675)

ethical pricing Pricing so as to avoid taking undue advantage of the highly price-inelastic demand for a product. (633)

exchange A process by which two or more individuals or organizations give and receive something of value. (7)

exclusive dealing contract An agreement in which the producer does not allow the marketing channel member to sell competitive products. (363)

exclusive distribution An extreme form of selective distribution in which the producer uses only one outlet in a geographic area. (363)

experience curves Reductions in the per-unit cost of a product that occur over time as the cumulative volume of output (and therefore experience) increases. (609)

experimental research The gathering of primary data by manipulating an independent variable (such as advertising or price) to observe the effect of the change on a dependent variable (such as sales). (121)

expert survey The sales forecasting method that involves the participation of people outside the organization who have special knowledge and experience in the market under consideration—for example, economists, consultants, and retired executives. (264)

facilitating intermediaries (also called facilitators) Persons or firms outside the marketing channel that may assist channel members in handling various flows (physical, financial, risk, information, promotion) more effectively and efficiently than the channel members could themselves. (349)

family brand (also called blanket brand) A brand that is applied to an entire product mix or to all products in a particular line. (295)

family life cycle The series of life stages people pass through—including childhood, marriage, childbirth, childrearing, and eventual dissolution of marriage through the death of a spouse or by divorce. (159)

feedback Communication from receivers to the sender about the meaning they assigned to the message and how they reacted to it. (467)

fixed costs (FC) Costs that remain the same regardless of changes in the volume sold. (603)

flexible delivery A service marketer's strategy for enhancing time and space convenience for the customer by changing the method or location of service delivery. (677)

f.o.b. shipping point pricing Freight cost pricing under which the buyer owns the products while they are in transit, assumes the risks in transporting the products, and pays the entire freight charge. (623)

focus group interview A form of survey research in which a moderator (a highly trained interviewer) meets with eight to twelve participants and leads them through a discussion on a given topic to develop hypotheses about an existing or potential product or marketing problem that might lead to more specific marketing research projects. (124)

follow-up calls Calls salespeople make about previous sales to help ensure after-sale satisfaction. (579)

foreign assembly An arrangement in which a firm exports component parts to a subsidiary or licensee in a foreign country for local assembly into the finished product. (717)

foreign direct investment A commitment of financial resources by an organization for the purpose of owning (totally or partially) and exercising control (total or partial) over an enterprise in a foreign country. (717)

foreign licensing An agreement in which a licensor gives a licensee in another country the right to use the licensor's patent, trademark, copyright, technology, processes, or products in return for a stated percentage of the licensee's sales revenues or profits resulting from such use. (716)

foreign production subsidiary A subordinate company established in another country by a parent company for the purpose of production. (717)

formula selling The sales approach in which the salesperson assumes that prospects go through a series of stages and that once the salesperson determines which stage the buyer is currently in, the salesperson can follow a basically canned presentation to move the prospect through the remaining stages and ultimately to buy. (564)

forward vertical integration The act of acquiring the operations of a firm that is closer to the final buyer in the marketing channel—for example, a manufacturer buying out a wholesaler or a wholesaler buying out a retailer. (364)

franchising system An arrangement in which a franchisor, which has developed an idea and business procedures that can be duplicated, licenses franchisees to copy the idea and procedures. (396)

freight absorption pricing Pricing that meets the delivered prices of rivals in distant areas by the seller's absorption of freight costs. (625)

frequency The number of times the target audience is exposed to the advertiser's advertising within some time period, usually four weeks. (509)

full-service wholesaler A merchant wholesaler that performs most or all of the marketing functions for its suppliers and customers. (421)

functional accounts Accounts that indicate the purpose or function for which funds have been spent. (658)

general stores Nondepartmentalized stores that sell a wide variety of such staple products as sugar, flour, dried meat, medicines, tobacco, and hardware items. (390)

geodemographic segmentation The division of a mass market that clusters potential customers into neighborhood lifestyle categories that enable the marketer to determine what "type" of people live in a particular area and to identify areas with the greatest demand for a particular good or service. (233)

geographic segmentation The division of a mass market into units such as nations, regions, states, cities, and neighborhoods. (222)

geographic selectivity An advertising medium's (or vehicle's) relative ability to reach people in selected geographic areas. (508)

geographic specialization An approach to structuring the sales force in which each salesperson is assigned a territory and sells all the firm's products to all customers in that territory. (568)

globalization A worldwide marketing strategy whereby an organization uses the same or very similar marketing mixes in all its markets. (718)

gray market Unauthorized intermediaries that circumvent authorized marketing channels by buying in low-price markets and reselling in high-price markets at prices that are lower than those charged by authorized channel members. (369)

green marketing The development and implementation of marketing programs designed to enhance an organization's environmental image. (25)

growth-share matrix A portfolio analysis technique by which strategic business units (SBUs) are categorized according to the rate of growth of the market in which each SBU competes and the SBU's market share relative to the share held by the market leader. (87)

growth strategies The methods by which an organization can expand: (1) market penetration, (2) product development, (3) market development, and (4) diversification. (81)

hard technologies Technologies used in creating a service that involve the substitution of machinery, tools, or facilities to perform tasks that otherwise are performed by people. (677)

hierarchy of needs Abraham Maslow's ranking of human needs, starting with the most basic physiological needs and ranging in decreasing dominance, through safety, love and belonging, esteem, and self-actualization needs. (153)

horizontal integration The act of acquiring the operations of one or more organizations at the same level in a marketing channel to strengthen one's own position at that level in the channel. (365)

horizontal marketing system (HMS) A distribution arrangement in which two or more organizations at the same level of distribution cooperate to accomplish common goals, each giving up some authority to make independent decisions. (373)

horizontal territorial restriction An agreement among retailers not to compete with one another in selling products from the same manufacturer. (375)

hybrid organizations Firms that combine some features of both the product-oriented and the market-oriented approaches to organizing marketing. (651)

hypermarket A retail store whose operations represent a combination of discount store, supermarket, and warehouse store under one roof. (393)

image pricing objective Price setting to enhance the consumer's perception of the store's total merchandise mix. (596)

imitative new products Products that copy an existing product and whose companies try to compete by underpricing the competition or perhaps by providing superior reliability and quality. (312)

inbound telemarketing A system that enables the marketer to receive telephone calls from prospective customers who dial the marketer's (usually an 800 or 900 number) number which is included in the marketer's advertising or catalogs. (531)

industrialization strategy The application of technology—including tools, machines, or preplanned systems—to reduce reliance on people in performing a service. (677)

industrial products Goods and services that are bought to use in producing other consumer or industrial products or in conducting an organization's operations. (283)

inflation A decline in buying power caused by price levels rising more rapidly than incomes. (39)

information role of price The function price performs in educating consumers about product factors such as quality. (593)

initial contact calls The first face-to-face contact a salesperson has with a prospect. (579)

installations Industrial products that are capital items, including land and major equipment. (288)

institutional advertising Promotion that focuses on the image of a product category, a company, a nonprofit organization, or an industry association rather than a specific brand. (499)

intensive distribution A producer's strategy of making a product available to buyers in as many outlets as possible for maximum market exposure. (361)

intermediary (also called a reseller or middleman) A person or firm in a marketing channel, such as a wholesaler or retailer, that operates between the producer and the final buyer of a product. (349)

intermodal transportation The combination of two or more methods of moving freight in order to more fully exploit the major advantages of each. **(446)**

international marketing The efforts of individuals and organizations to satisfy human wants by facilitating exchanges across national boundaries. **(697)**

interpersonal communication channel A type of message carrier that provides direct contact between the sender and the receiver. **(466)**

joint venture A partnership in which the partners share ownership and control of the venture's operations and property rights. **(718)**

jury of executive opinion The sales forecasting method that involves combining and averaging the sales projections of executives in different departments to arrive at a sales forecast. **(263)**

just-in-time (JIT) system An inventory management system that focuses on maintaining a steady and coordinated flow of materials and parts into the manufacturing process and at the same time maintaining a steady flow of products off the assembly-line. **(442)**

label The printed material that appears on a product package. **(302)**

leader pricing A retailer's promotion of one product at a sharply reduced price in the expectation that it will attract customers who will then purchase other items. **(629)**

learning The process through which a relatively permanent change in behavior results from the consequences of past behavior. **(150)**

leasing A renting arrangement in which a lessor grants use of a product to a lessee for a period of time in return for stated regular payments. **(184)**

life cycle extension strategies Strategies designed to lengthen the product life cycle. **(330)**

lifestyles The consistent patterns that people follow in their lives, including how they spend their time and money, and are identified through people's activities, interests, and opinions of themselves and the world around them. **(158)**

limited-service wholesaler A merchant wholesaler that performs fewer marketing functions for its suppliers and customers than a full-service wholesaler performs. **(423)**

list price (also called base price) The initial offering price of a product. **(592)**

logistics The activities of moving raw materials from their sources to the production process; moving raw materials, semimanufactured products, and finished products within and among plants and warehouses; moving finished products through warehouses and intermediaries; and moving finished products to final buyers. **(433)**

mail order A type of marketing that uses the mail to deliver the product from the marketer directly to the customer regardless of how the order was placed. **(534)**

make-or-buy decision The choice an industrial buyer makes between manufacturing its own goods (or performing services) and buying the goods (or hiring the services) from vendors. **(186)**

management contract A pact in which one firm sells management services to operate a facility owned by another firm. **(717)**

manufacturer brand (also called national brand) A brand that is owned by a manufacturer. **(297)**

manufacturer's sales branch A manufacturer-owned wholesaling establishment that carries inventory, is separated physically from the manufacturing plant, and makes deliveries to customers. **(425)**

manufacturer's sales office A manufacturer-owned wholesaling establishment that serves as a regional office for the sales force and does not carry inventory or make deliveries. **(425)**

markdown A reduction in the original price set on a product. **(610)**

market A set of individuals or organizations that desire a product and are willing and able to buy it. **(212)**

market attractiveness–business strength matrix A portfolio analysis technique that rates strategic business units (SBUs) on a series of market attractiveness criteria and on a series of criteria reflecting the company's strengths and competencies. **(88)**

market density The number of people per square mile in an area who are potential customers for a given marketer's offering. **(223)**

marketer An individual or organization that performs marketing functions to facilitate exchanges for the purpose of satisfying human wants. **(10)**

market forecast An estimate of the expected sales of a specific product in a specific market (or market segment) over a specific time period for all sellers in the industry, given an expected level of industry effort and an expected set of environmental conditions. **(259)**

marketing The process of planning and executing the conception, pricing, promotion, and distribution of ideas, goods, and services to create exchanges that satisfy individual and organizational objectives. **(7)**

marketing audit A comprehensive review of the organization's overall marketing performance and prospects. **(662)**

marketing channel (also called a channel of distribution or a distribution channel) The series of interdependent marketing institutions that facilitate transfer of title to a product as it moves from producer to ultimate consumer or industrial user. **(349)**

marketing concept A philosophy of management that advocates that a business organization (1) exists to satisfy targeted customers' wants, (2) approaches decision making from a systems view of management, and (3) seeks to earn a satisfactory return on the owners' investment in the firm. **(17)**

marketing control The monitoring of marketing performance and the identification of problems that have resulted in unsatisfactory levels of performance. **(647)**

marketing cost analysis The process of breaking down and classifying marketing costs to determine which costs are incurred in performing specific marketing activities. **(658)**

marketing database A collection of interrelated data about an organization's individual prospects and customers that is intended to satisfy the organization's marketing information requirements. **(528)**

marketing effort response elasticity The relationship between the percentage change in expenditures on marketing effort and the percentage change in sales. **(262)**

marketing ethics Judgments about what is morally right and wrong for marketing organizations and their employees in their role as marketers. **(23)**

marketing functions The activities that create utility and facilitate the exchange process by bridging the distance, time, and possession gaps that usually separate the participants in an exchange. **(8)**

marketing implementation The aspects of organizational structure and behavior that determine how a given strategy is carried out; specifically, it is the actions of marketing managers, sales and customer service personnel, distributors, and sometimes even non-marketing personnel. **(647)**

marketing information system (MIS) A structured, interacting complex of persons, machines, and procedures designed to generate an orderly flow of pertinent information collected from intra- and extra-firm sources, for use as the bases for decision making in specific responsibility areas of marketing management. **(110)**

marketing management The process of planning, implementing, and controlling marketing activities and decisions in order to facilitate exchanges. **(76)**

marketing mix The combination of the four controllable variables—product, place, promotion, and price (the four Ps)—that an organization creates to satisfy its target market. **(29)**

marketing objective The specific level of performance desired from a product or product line. **(91)**

marketing plan A program that specifies a marketing strategy and lays out the details needed to implement it. **(95)**

marketing planning The ongoing process of (1) establishing clearly specified marketing objectives, (2) selecting marketing strategies, and (3) developing a detailed plan of action to make the strategies work. **(90)**

marketing research The process of identifying and defining a marketing problem or opportunity, specifying and collecting the data required to address these issues, analyzing the results, and communicating information to decision makers. **(113)**

marketing strategy A broad plan of action for using an organization's resources to meet its marketing objectives. **(28)**

market niche An area of unfulfilled need in a market. **(45)**

market offering Anything of value that is presented by a marketer to potential customers. **(11)**

market-oriented organizations Firms structured around market segments. **(649)**

market potential The maximum possible sales of a specific product in a specific market (or market segment) over a specific time period for all sellers in the industry, given that all sellers are putting forth their maximum marketing effort under an assumed set of environmental conditions. **(259)**

market segmentation A process of identifying smaller markets (groups of people or organizations) that exist within a larger market. **(215)**

market segment profile A description of the characteristics and wants of people or organizations in a market segment. **(248)**

market test The sales forecasting method that involves distributing the product in one or more markets to predict potential customer response by measuring actual sales and generalizing test experiences to the entire market. **(264)**

markup An addition to the cost of a product to reach a selling price. **(609)**

markup strategy A policy that governs the size of the markup on cost of a product. **(611)**

mass communication channel A type of message carrier that provides contact between the sender and a large number of receivers simultaneously. **(467)**

mass-market strategy A strategy that defines the market as all potential buyers of brands in a product category and offers them one marketing mix. **(213)**

materials handling The activities of physically moving products into and out of plants, warehouses, and transportation terminals. **(443)**

media plan A written statement of the reach and frequency goals of an advertising campaign and of how these goals will be achieved. **(515)**

membership relationship A formal exchange relationship in which the customer's identity is known and in which a record of each customer's transactions may be maintained. **(680)**

merchandise agents and brokers Functional intermediaries that for a commission bring buyers and sellers together, perhaps physically handling products but not owning title to them. **(425)**

merchandise breadth The variety of products that a retailer offers for sale. **(388)**

merchandise depth The selection a merchandise offering provides. **(388)**

merchant wholesaler An independently owned business that owns title to the products it offers for sale to organizational buyers. **(421)**

message The combination of symbols representing objects or experiences that a communicator transmits in order to induce a change in a receiver's behavior. **(464)**

mixed bundling The practice of allowing the customer to purchase each of two complementary products separately at their list prices or together at a special price. **(629)**

modes of transportation The methods of moving freight: railroads, motor carriers, airlines, pipelines, and water carriers. **(445)**

monopolistic competition A market structure in which there are many sellers and many buyers, but the offerings of each seller are somewhat different. **(42)**

monopoly A market structure in which one firm produces a product that has no close substitute. **(43)**

motivation The driving force that causes a person to take action to satisfy specific needs. **(152)**

motivational research A type of marketing research that attempts to develop deeper insight into the whys of consumer behavior by analyzing the motives behind it. **(130)**

multinational company (MNC) A firm that is based in one country (the parent, or home, country) and produces goods or provides services in one or more foreign countries (host countries). **(698)**

multiple buying influence A situation in which several persons participate in an industrial buyer's buying decision. **(194)**

multiple constituencies The various groups, individuals, and organizations that provide supplemental resources for nonprofit organizations. **(686)**

multiple sourcing The establishment of a buying relationship with two or more vendors rather than with only one. **(199)**

multisegment strategy A marketing strategy of developing two or more marketing mixes for two or more market segments. **(217)**

natural accounts Accounts such as rent, salaries, insurance, heat, and supplies that are listed in ledgers and on income statements. **(658)**

need satisfaction selling The sales approach in which the salesperson, operating on the principle that the main reason people buy comes from within, tries to discover the prospect's needs and then demonstrate how the product will satisfy them. **(564)**

negotiated contracts An approach to procurement in which the buyer requests bids from several sellers, selects the most attractive (not necessarily the lowest) offering, and then negotiates a contract with the seller—after having had the benefit of consulting with bidders in developing specifications. **(632)**

new-product committee An approach to organizing for new product development in which managers from different functional areas (production, marketing, finance, and R&D) review and act on new-product ideas generated elsewhere in the organization. **(313)**

new-product department An approach to organizing for new product development in which a separate, formally structured unit handles all phases of the new-product development process. **(313)**

new-product development process The sequence of stages a product must pass through prior to arriving at the introductory stage of the product life cycle: idea generation, idea screening, concept development and testing, business analysis, product development, market testing, and commercialization. **(315)**

noise Anything that interferes with the communication process so the receiver gets a message that is different from the one the sender sent or gets no message at all. **(468)**

noncumulative quantity discount A deduction from list price that applies to a single order rather than to the total volume of orders placed during a period of time and that is intended to encourage orders in large quantities. **(619)**

nonprice competition A market situation in which rivals minimize the importance of price as a competitive tool. **(45)**

nonprobability (or nonrandom) sample A selection in which not every item in a population has a known chance of being included because researcher judgment enters into the selection. **(131)**

nonstore retailing Selling to consumers by means other than through stores, such as by mail or telephone. **(388)**

observational research The gathering of primary data through direct or indirect monitoring and recording of behavior. **(120)**

off-peak pricing A strategy to encourage service consumption during off-peak hours by lowering prices during those hours. **(677)**

oligopoly A market structure in which a few large firms account for the bulk of the industry's sales. **(43)**

organizational buyers Entitles such as businesses, governments, and nonprofit organizations that purchase products (1) for use in making other products, (2) to resell, or (3) to carry on the organization's operations. **(13)**

organizational marketing The branch of marketing that is concerned with providing products to all buyers except ultimate consumers. **(177)**

organizational mission The organization's fundamental purpose. **(80)**

original equipment manufacturer (OEM) A firm that buys industrial products from a supplier and incorporates them into the product it produces and markets. **(179)**

outbound telemarketing A system that enables the marketer to initiate contact with prospective customers by telephone. **(532)**

out-of-home media Communication channels that expose the target audience to the sales message when the audience is away from home and closer to the market place. **(513)**

packaging The design and production of the container or wrapper for a product. **(299)**

patent Protection of an invention (a product), a chemical formula, or a new way of doing something (a process) from imitation for a period of seventeen years. **(292)**

penetration pricing The practice of setting an introductory price relatively low to gain deep market penetration quickly. **(608)**

perceived value pricing The establishment of prices that are intended to enhance the utility that customers will perceive in the products offered. **(594)**

perception The process through which an individual selects relevant stimuli (information) from the environment, organizes them, and assigns meaning to them. **(154)**

peripheral evidence A tangible item that comes with a service, can be possessed, and represents the service's existence. **(675)**

personality A collection of relatively permanent tendencies to behave in consistent ways in certain situations. **(158)**

personalizing the service Developing a close business relationship in which the service provider becomes familiar with the needs of individual customers. **(682)**

personal selling A person-to-person process by which the seller learns about the prospective buyer's wants and seeks to satisfy them by making a sale. **(470)**

petroleum bulk plant and terminal A wholesaling intermediary that resells petroleum products such as gasoline and fuel oils to petroleum retailers, other wholesaling intermediaries, and industrial users. **(426)**

pioneering innovations Improvements in form or function that are so significant as to make existing products in the category obsolete or to create entirely new benefits and usage options for a product category. (312)

planned shopping center A location for retailing activity that is planned, built, and managed by a development company, which leases space to tenant retailers. (402)

portfolio analysis The process that top management uses to compare and contrast the situation assessments of strategic business units (SBUs) and to gauge the future contributions that can be anticipated from each SBU. (87)

price discrimination Occurs when a manufacturer sells the same product to two intermediaries at different prices or to two industrial buyers at different prices. (621)

price elasticity of demand The degree of demand sensitivity to price in a given demand curve. (598)

price shading The practice in industrial marketing of tailoring the price to the customer's situation. (632)

price skimming The practice of setting an introductory price relatively high in order to attract buyers who are not concerned with price and to recover research and development costs quickly. (608)

price stabilization objective Setting prices to maintain a stable relationship between the firm's prices and the industry leader's prices. (597)

primary data Data that are collected through original research for a specific purpose. (118)

print media Communication channels that sell advertising space to marketers. (510)

probability (or random) sample A selection in which each item in a population has a known chance of being included through strict statistical procedures. (131)

problem solution selling (also called consultative selling) A sales presentation format that focuses first on discovering the prospect's needs and then on the salesperson acting as a consultant for the prospect. (564)

product A bundle of perceived tangible and intangible attributes that has the potential to satisfy present and potential customer wants and is received in exchange for money or other consideration. (278)

product advertising Promotion that focuses on selling specifically identified goods and services. (499)

product concept test An instrument used in the new-product development process to determine potential customers' feelings about new products. (317)

product differentiation A marketing strategy that seeks to create a difference in people's minds between a marketer's brand and rival brands that are serving the same mass market. (213)

product liability The concept that businesses are liable for injuries caused by negligence in the design, manufacture, sale, and use of products. (334)

product life cycle (PLC) A concept that depicts a product's sales history over time and includes repeat purchases, not just first-time sales. (328)

product line A group of products that are related because of customer, marketing, or production considerations. (290)

product line extension The use of an old brand on a new product within an existing product line. (295)

product (or brand) manager A person who is assigned a product, or product line, that has been approved for development and is responsible for determining its objectives and marketing strategies. (313)

product mix An organization's entire offering of product items. (290)

product-oriented organizations Firms in which each product, product line, or group of related products has its own marketing organization. (648)

product positioning The effort aimed at creating and maintaining in the minds of target customers the intended image for the product relative to the image of competitive offerings so target customers will perceive the product as possessing the attributes they want. (250)

product quality The totality of features and characteristics of a product (good) or service that bear on its ability to satisfy stated or implied needs. (281)

product-related segmentation The division of a mass market on the basis of characteristics of the consumer's relationship to the product. (234)

product specialization An approach to structuring the sales force in which some salespeople sell one or a few products to customers in a territory and other salespeople may sell other company products to the same customers. (568)

professional pricing Price setting based on the ethical premise that flat fees are more appropriate than fees based on the amount of time spent with individual patients or clients. (633)

profit maximization Classical economic theory that assumes that firms always select the price that results in the highest profit. (595)

programmed decisions Routine decisions that result from the learning process consumers engage in when making complex decisions. (148)

projective interviewing A marketing research technique that seeks to get respondents to reveal subconscious feelings and opinions. (129)

project team An approach to organizing for new-product development in which specialists from various functional areas who share an interest in a particular new product are given extensive authority in developing a new-product idea. (314)

promotion allowances Payments made by sellers and reductions from list prices granted by sellers to compensate buyers for performing promotional services. (621)

promotion campaign An interrelated series of promotion activities designed to accomplish a specific objective. (483)

promotion mix A careful blending of advertising, personal selling, direct marketing, sales promotion, and public relations to accomplish an organization's promotion objectives. (469)

prospecting The process of searching for, identifying, and qualifying potential customers, beginning with getting sales leads. (561)

psychographic segmentation The division of a mass market on the basis of social class, personality characteristics, or lifestyles. (230)

publicity News carried in the mass media about an organization and its products, policies, personnel, or actions; it can originate with the media or the marketer and is published or aired at no charge to the organization for media space or time. (471)

public relations (PR) Communication to build and maintain a favorable image for an organization, maintain the goodwill of its many publics, and explain its goals and purposes. (471)

public warehouse An independently owned profit-seeking business that offers services such as storage and break-bulk (breaking a big, bulky shipment into smaller lots) and reshipping to firms and individuals. (438)

pull strategy A sales-building strategy in which the producer focuses promotion efforts directly on the final buyer, rather than on intermediaries in the marketing channels, in order to control product presentation to final buyers. (476)

pure competition A market structure in which there are many small buyers and sellers, a homogeneous product, easy entry into and exit from the industry, perfect information in the hands of buyers and sellers, and identical conditions under which all buyers buy and all sellers sell. (42)

push strategy A sales-building strategy in which the producer actively promotes its product to intermediaries which actively promote it to final buyers. (475)

quality function deployment The process of providing a formal way of linking information on customers' preferences for attributes to engineering specifications to ensure that marketing and research and development are collaborating effectively in achieving quality. (281)

range of acceptable behavior (also called a range of group norms) The limits of a group's values, beliefs, and behaviors, to which members must conform more or less according to their status. (163)

raw materials Industrial products that have undergone only enough processing to permit convenient and economical handling, transportation, and storage. (287)

reach The number of people who are exposed to an advertiser's advertising within a certain time period, usually four weeks. (509)

reciprocity An arrangement under which a customer buys from a vendor if the vendor buys from the customer. (199)

reference group Any group that positively or negatively influences a person's attitudes or behavior. (162)

regionalization A marketing strategy that seeks to cater to regional preferences within a larger market. (55)

regional trading bloc A group of countries (a cartel) that formally agree to reduce trade barriers among themselves in order to create a larger market. (711)

regression analysis A statistical technique for developing a mathematical formula that defines a relationship between changes in past sales (the dependent variable) and one or more independent predictor variables (such as gross national product, per capita income, or industry advertising expenditures). (265)

regular customer calls Calls salespeople make on established customers or prospects who have been called on before. (579)

relationship marketing strategies Marketing strategies designed to enhance the loyalty of customers or to generate more business from existing customers. (679)

reliability A measurement instrument's ability to produce essentially identical results after repeated use. (128)

research design The grand plan for conducting a marketing research investigation; it specifies the data that are needed and the procedures for collecting, processing, and analyzing the data. (116)

retailer A firm that derives more than half of its sales revenues from sales made directly to ultimate consumers. (382)

retailing The combination of activities involved in selling or renting consumer goods and services directly to ultimate consumers for their personal or household use. (382)

sales analysis The performance evaluation procedure designed to identify the areas in which sales performance problems exist. (657)

sales forecast An estimate of the number of units or the dollar sales volume a firm expects to reach for a specific product in a specific market (or market segment) over a specific time period, given an intended level and type of marketing effort by the firm and an expected set of environmental conditions. (260)

sales force composite The sales forecasting method that involves asking salespeople to forecast attainable sales volume in their territories for a given time period and combining those projections to produce a total sales forecast. (263)

sales potential The upper limit of sales that a firm could possibly reach for a specific product in a specific market (or market segment) over a specific time period, given a maximum level of marketing effort and an assumed set of environmental conditions. (260)

sales promotion Any activity that offers an incentive for a limited period to induce a desired response from target customers, company salespeople, or intermediaries. (471)

sample A set of units, or items, selected from a population. (130)

scrambled merchandising The retail practice of carrying product lines that appear to be unrelated. (388)

secondary data Data that were previously collected by people either inside or outside the organization to meet their needs. (118)

segmentation variable Some characteristic of people in the overall (mass) market that aids in dividing it. (219)

selective distribution A producer's strategy of restricting distribution to intermediaries in a geographic area on the basis of their performance capability. (362)

self-concept (also called self-image) The image or perception of oneself. (158)

seller's market An environment in which demand is greater than supply. (15)

selling tasks Activities that incorporate one or more of the three objectives of personal selling and are often classified into three categories (1) order-getting tasks, (2) order-taking tasks, and (3) sales support tasks. (560)

semantic differential scales Methods for measuring the meanings consumers attach to products, brand names, or organizations, whereby the consumers rate the subject on a seven-point scale between pairs of antonyms (opposites). (156)

service calls Calls salespeople make in response to customer requests for service, to anticipated problems with the product, or to new developments that will affect the performance of products bought for resale. (579)

service encounter The moment of interaction between the customer and the firm. (672)

shopping products Goods or services that consumers will purchase only after making price and quality comparisons. (284)

simple trend analysis The sales forecasting technique that assumes future sales will be determined by the same variables that caused past sales and that the relationships among the variables will remain the same. (265)

simultaneous product development Highly coordinated project team approaches to the new-product development process. (324)

situation assessment An analysis of the organization's environment and of the organization itself. (78)

social classes The relatively stable and homogeneous divisions in society into which individuals, families, or groups that share similar values, lifestyles, interests, and behaviors can be placed. (164)

social marketing The design, implementation, and control of programs seeking to increase the acceptability of a social idea, cause, or practice in target groups. (11)

social responsibility The concept that businesses are part of the larger society in which they exist and are accountable to society for their performance. (22)

societal marketing concept A philosophy that requires marketers to accept their social responsibility. (24)

soft technologies Technologies used in creating a service that involve the application of organized, preplanned systems (including special equipment and routines) to guide performance. (677)

source credibility In the communication process, target receivers' perceptions regarding the sender's believability. (463)

specialty merchandisers Stores that offer a narrow product line with a deep assortment within that line. (389)

specialty products Goods or services for which the buyer has a strong conviction as to brands, styles, or type. (285)

specialty shop A single-line retail store that carries the narrowest merchandise offering and provides the greatest depth. (389)

Standard Industrial Classification (SIC) system A system developed by the U.S. Bureau of the Census that breaks down organizational markets into eleven major industries, with further divisions into subindustries and products. (177)

stimulus–response selling A canned sales approach in which the salesperson presents a memorized sales talk, including a number of key words (stimuli) to produce a favorable response by the prospect. (563)

stock turnover rate The number of times per year the average inventory (beginning and ending inventory ÷ 2) is sold. (611)

strategic business units (SBUs) Businesses that are operated as separate profit centers within a large organization. (87)

strategic planning The process by which top management establishes the long-term direction of an organization. (77)

strict product liability The concept that businesses are liable for injuries caused by their products even if there is no proof of negligence or fault in the design, manufacture, sale, and use of products. (334)

subculture A group that shares values and behavior patterns that differ in important ways from those of the dominant culture. (169)

substitute method The technique for forecasting sales of a new product that involves analyzing the sales of the older product it will replace and projecting sales of the new product on the basis of that analysis. (265)

substitute products Products that satisfy the same basic needs but differ slightly in terms of specific characteristics. (290)

supermarket A large, departmentalized, self-service retail store that sells meat, produce, canned goods, dairy products, frozen foods, and such nonfood items as toys, magazines, records, small kitchen utensils, and toiletries. (391)

superstore A retail store that is larger than a conventional supermarket and provides a more diversified merchandise offering—including services such as banking, dry cleaning, and lunch counters. (392)

supplies Industrial products that are expense items and include maintenance supplies, repair supplies, and operating supplies. (288)

survey of buyer intentions The sales forecasting method that requires asking potential buyers if they intend to buy a certain product during a specific time period and, if so, how many units and from whom they will buy them. (264)

survey research The gathering of primary data from respondents by mail, telephone, or in person. (123)

sustainable development The process through which economic systems can meet existing human wants without destroying the resources future generations will need to meet their wants. (700)

systems marketing The relationship marketing strategy of offering a wide array of services to meet a series of related customer needs. (681)

systems selling The marketing of a total product offering that will provide a total solution to a customer's problem. (197)

target audience The people to whom an advertising campaign is directed. (503)

target margin A profit target for a product that is stated as a percentage reflecting the ratio of profits to sales. (595)

target market A well-defined set of present and potential customers that an organization attempts to satisfy. (29)

target market specialization An approach to structuring the sales force in which the sales force is divided by target markets and each salesperson calls on only one target group. (569)

target return on investment A profit target for a product that is stated as a ratio of profit to the firm's total dollar investment in production facilities and assets supporting the product. **(595)**

task specialization An approach to structuring the sales force in which some salespeople may serve established customers in their territories while a smaller group develops new accounts. **(568)**

technology The knowledge to do new or old tasks in a better way. **(47)**

trade (or functional) discount A reduction in list price granted to a channel member for performing marketing services. **(620)**

trademark A legal term meaning the same as brand. **(292)**

trade practice rules Purely advisory rules that are developed by regulatory agencies in conjunction with industry representatives to guide firms in avoiding future violations of the law. **(67)**

trade regulation rules Binding rules that are published by regulatory agencies and are used to bring cases against alleged violators. **(67)**

trading company A privately owned business that buys and sells products in many different countries, either in its own name or as an agent for its buyer-seller clients. **(714)**

transnational company A firm that views the world as one market, conducts operations in many countries, and makes decisions as if national boundaries did not exist. **(699)**

turnkey operation An arrangement in which a supplier designs, builds, and trains the staff of an operating facility for a foreign buyer, which runs the facility. **(717)**

tying contract An agreement in which the seller requires the buyer to buy some of the seller's other products in order to be able to buy the desired product. **(363)**

ultimate consumers People who acquire products for their personal or household use. **(13)**

unbundling Pricing by which a firm reduces or eliminates certain elements of its market offering and prices the remaining independent elements separately. **(629)**

uniform delivered pricing (also called postage stamp pricing) All quoted prices include a fixed average freight charge because the seller averages total transportation costs for serving all customers. **(624)**

unit pricing The practice of breaking down a price in terms of dollars and cents per unit of measure. **(631)**

unplanned shopping area An area in which a group of stores can be located close together, but without the benefit of a master plan regulating the types or the number of stores. **(402)**

unsought products Goods or services that potential buyers do not know exist or do not want to think about buying. **(285)**

user account A manufacturer that buys industrial products that facilitate the manufacturer's production process but are not incorporated into the product the manufacturer markets. **(179)**

utility The satisfaction, value, or usefulness a user receives from a good or service in relation to the user's wants. **(5)**

validity A measurement instrument's ability to measure what it is supposed to measure. **(128)**

value added by manufacturing The worth added to a product as a result of processing or manufacturing operations that caused a change in the product's form utility. **(178)**

value added by marketing The worth added to a product by resellers that equals the resellers' sales revenues minus their costs of goods sold and their cost of purchased services. **(188)**

value-added pricing The seller's addition of a special service or complementary product, at no charge, to the product being priced. **(629)**

value analysis The review of existing product specifications to eliminate inessential cost factors and to develop greater capability for the present cost for products purchased or manufactured in house. **(195)**

variable costs (VC) Costs that change in relation to volume. **(603)**

variety stores Retail stores that provide considerable breadth but limited depth in the merchandise offerings, which consist mostly of relatively inexpensive products. **(390)**

vendor analysis The evaluation of the performance capability of potential suppliers through the rating of their past performance in technical, financial, managerial, and other areas. **(196)**

vertical integration The act of combining two or more levels of a marketing channel under one participant's control. **(364)**

vertical marketing system (VMS) A distribution arrangement in which the marketing channel operates as an integrated system with unified objectives instead of as a loosely organized group of independent firms. **(371)**

vertical territorial restriction An agreement in which a producer grants a marketing channel member the exclusive right to sell its product in a specified geographic area. **(363)**

volume pricing objective Price setting to meet target sales volumes or market shares. **(595)**

voluntary compliance A practice by which a firm agrees to do what a regulatory agency advises without the need for a hearing. **(67)**

warehouse club A wholesale-retail, cash-and-carry, membership-only operation that sells high-turnover manufacturer brands typically from a combination warehouse and store. **(394)**

warehouse showroom A discount retailer that sets up a facility in a low-rent area, often next to a major highway intersection or a railroad siding, and focuses on high volume at low prices. **(393)**

wheel of retailing A hypothesis that attempts to explain the emergence of new retailing institutions and their eventual decline and replacement by newer retailing institutions. **(409)**

wholesaling The activities of firms that sell to retailers, to other intermediaries, or to other organizational buyers but do not sell (except perhaps in small amounts) to ultimate consumers. **(419)**

yield management The practice of setting prices on services to yield the maximum number of customers at the highest possible prices. **(677)**

zone pricing A type of uniform delivered pricing in which buyers in a given zone pay the same delivered price but buyers in different zones pay different delivered prices. **(624)**

NOTES AND CREDITS

Chapter 1

1. Adapted from Joshua Levine, ed., "Marketing: How'm I Doin'?" by permission of *Forbes* magazine, December 24, 1990, pp. 106–109. © Forbes Inc., 1990.
2. John Harris, "Good Eggs," *Forbes*, January 7, 1991, pp. 58–60.
3. Lisa Miller Mesdag, "The Appliance Boom Begins," *Fortune*, July 25, 1983, p. 57.
4. "Business Notes," *Time*, December 3, 1990, p. 87.
5. "Ministering to High-Flying Spirits," *Insight*, December 3, 1990, pp. 56–58.
6. "In Business This Week," *Business Week*, May 7, 1990, p. 44.
7. Suzanne Alexander, "Hungry Fast-Food Companies Invade College Eateries as Nutritionists Groan," *Wall Street Journal*, November 27, 1990, pp. B1, B5.
8. Michael J. McCarthy, "Pepsi Spilling into Burgers, Drive-Up Units," *Wall Street Journal*, December 20, 1990, pp. B1, B6; Gene G. Marcial, "Really Fast Drive-Up Fast Food," *Business Week*, May 28, 1990, p. 98.
9. "AMA Board Approves New Marketing Definition," *Marketing News*, March 1, 1985, p. 1.
10. Susan Chace, "Xerox Plans to Sell Most of Its Retail Stores to New Concern Headed by Texas Group," *Wall Street Journal*, October 25, 1983, p. 58.
11. Pamela J. Podger, "Managing," *Wall Street Journal*, December 27, 1990, p. B1.
12. Cindy LaFavre Yorks, "McChurch," *USA Weekend*, April 13–15, 1990, pp. 4–7; Thomas A. Steward, "Turning Around the Lord's Business," *Fortune*, September 25, 1989, pp. 116–128; Peter F. Drucker, "The Non-Profits' Quiet Revolution," *Wall Street Journal*, September 8, 1988, p. 26.
13. Karen Schwartz, "Nonprofits' Bottom-Line: They Mix Lofty Goals and Gutsy Survival Strategies," *Marketing News*, February 13, 1989, pp. 1–2.
14. Philip Kotler and Gerald Zaltman, "Social Marketing: An Approach to Planned Social Change," *Journal of Marketing*, July 1971, p. 5.
15. Charles Siler, "Blocking, Tackling, and Fumbling," *Forbes*, May 29, 1989, p. 92.
16. Timothy D. Schellhardt, "Managing," *Wall Street Journal*, March 22, 1990, p. B1.
17. James Cook, "We're Still Harnessing Power," *Forbes*, May 29, 1989, p. 100.
18. Gilbert Fuchsberg, "Gurus of Quality Are Gaining Clout," *Wall Street Journal*, November 27, 1990, pp. B1, B5.
19. Douglas Danforth, "The Quality Imperative," *Quality Progress*, February 20, 1987, pp. 17–19.
20. Stephen Kindel, "World Washer," *Financial World*, March 20, 1990, pp. 42–46.
21. "Top Mazda Execs Pay for Recall," *USA Today*, December 27, 1990, p. 2B.
22. "Xerox Guarantees 'Total Satisfaction,' " *Marketing News*, October 15, 1990, p. 2.
23. Joan C. Szabo, "Service = Survival," *Nation's Business*, March 1989, pp. 16–24.
24. Patricia Sellers, "How to Handle Customers' Gripes," *Fortune*, October 24, 1988, p. 87.
25. Amanda Bennett, "Making the Grade with the Customer," *Wall Street Journal*, November 12, 1990, pp. B1, B8.
26. Bennett, "Making the Grade with the Customer."
27. Lynn G. Coleman, "Those Were the Days: Satisfaction Was King This Year; Focus Shifted to Service, Employees," *Marketing News*, December 10, 1990, p. 2.
28. Brian Dumaine, "P&G Rewrites the Marketing Rules," *Fortune*, November 6, 1989, pp. 34–48.
29. AT&T Crashes the Credit-Card Party," *Business Week*, April 9, 1990, p. 23.
30. "Business Briefing," *Insight, November 12, 1990, p. 41.*
31. "Business Notes," *Time*, April 30, 1990, p. 77.
32. "The Greening of Corporate America," *Business Week*, April 23, 1990, pp. 96–103.
33. JoAnn S. Lublin, "Advertising: 'Green' Marketing Gets Tougher as States Crack Down on Claims," *Wall Street Journal*, December 24, 1990, p. A11.
34. P. Rajan Varadarajan and Anil Menon, "Cause-Related Marketing: A Coalignment of Marketing Strategy and Corporate Philanthropy," *Journal of Marketing*, July 1988, p. 60.
35. JoAnn S. Lublin, "Creating a 'Green' Ad Campaign Risks Making Consumers See Red," *Wall Street Journal*, December 5, 1990, p. B6.
36. "Utilities Are Making More by Selling Less," *Business Week*, January 9, 1989, p. 90.
37. Sandra Barbier, "P.R. Man: Charities in Trouble," *New Orleans Times-Picayune*, February 19, 1989, p. A36.
38. Barbier, "P.R. Man."
39. Brian Dumaine, "Creating a New Company Culture," *Fortune, January 15, 1990, pp. 127–131.*
40. Jagannath Dubashi, "Old Elephant, New Tricks," *Financial World*, November 27, 1990, pp. 24–25.
41. Robert Johnson, "As More Men Choose Flashy Foreign Suits, a U.S. Maker Squirms," *Wall Street Journal*, August 27, 1990, pp. A1, A2.
42. "The Executive Suite Goes Traveling," *Time*, March 30, 1987, p. 55.
43. "The Right Stuff," *Time*, October 29, 1990, pp. 74–84.

Chapter 2

1. Adapted from Michael J. McCarthy, "History Offers Hope to Some Marketers," *Wall Street Journal*, November 9, 1990, pp. B1, B5. Reprinted by permission of the *Wall Street Journal*, © Dow Jones & Company, Inc., 1990. All rights reserved.
2. Maureen F. Allyn, "The Great American Spending Spree Is Winding Down at Last," *Fortune*, October 24, 1988, p. 41.
3. Elys McLean-Ibrahim, "USA Snapshots," *USA Today*, February 5, 1991, p. 1B.
4. Denise Kalette, "Pawnbrokers See No Signs of Recovery Yet," *USA Today*, July 9, 1991, p. 1B.
5. Alecia Swasy, "Firms Change Pitch as Economy Falters," *Wall Street Journal*, November 9, 1990, pp. B2, B3.
6. Henry F. Myers, "Some Service Jobs May Get Less Stable," *Wall Street Journal*, February 25, 1991, p. A1.
7. Urban C. Lehner and Alan Murray, "Will the U.S. Find the Resolve to Meet Japanese Challenge?" *Wall Street Journal*, July 2, 1990, pp. A1, A4.
8. Arlene Visoda, "Catalog Firms Blame Economy for Late Orders," *USA Today*, December 6, 1990, p. 1D.
9. William Mathewson, "World Wire," *Wall Street Journal*, July 27, 1990, p. A8.

10. Alecia Swasy, "Diaper Failure Shows How Poor Plans, Unexpected Woes Can Kill New Products," *Wall Street Journal*, October 9, 1990, pp. B1, B4.

11. Susan Moffat, "Can Nintendo Keep Winning?" *Fortune*, November 5, 1990, pp. 131–136.

12. This section is based on John Case, "The New Economy: Competitive Advantage," Reprinted with permission of *Inc.* Magazine, April 1989, pp. 33–34. Copyright © 1989 by Goldhirsh Group, Inc., 38 Commercial Wharf, Boston, MA 02110.

13. Jeremy Main, "A Golden Age for Entrepreneurs," *Fortune*, February 12, 1990, pp. 120–125.

14. John Harris, "Your Taste Buds Won't Know, Your Pocketbook Will," *Forbes*, September 3, 1990, pp. 88–90.

15. Michael J. McCarthy, "After Frantic Growth, Blockbuster Faces Host of Video-Rental Rivals," *Wall Street Journal*, March 22, 1991, pp. A1, A6.

16. "These RVs Are Doing Wheelies off Dealers' Lots," *Business Week*, May 21, 1990, p. 104.

17. Ronald Alsop, "Arm & Hammer Baking Soda Going in Toothpaste as Well as Refrigerator," *Wall Street Journal*, June 24, 1988, p. 18.

18. Alyssa A. Lappen, "You Just Work Your Heart Out," *Forbes*, March 5, 1990, pp. 74–77.

19. "Let's Make a Deal," *Time*, December 23, 1985, pp. 42–45.

20. Randall Smith, "The Corporate Raider of the '90s: Big Business," *Wall Street Journal*, December 4, 1990, pp. C1, C9.

21. Christopher Elias, "Glaxo Is Swallowing Market for Prescription Drugs in U.S.," *Insight*, November 12, 1990, pp. 35–37.

22. Gregory A. Patterson, "Big Three Car Firms Say Joint Research Is Fastest Route to Electric-Auto Success," *Wall Street Journal*, January 21, 1991, p. B6.

23. Paul Wiseman, "USA Losing Its Edge in Technology," *USA Today*, March 21, 1991, p. 1B.

24. "Will Uncle Sam Be Dragged Kicking and Screaming into the Lab?" *Business Week*, July 15, 1991, pp. 128–129.

25. Sana Siwolop, "Technology," *Financial World*, November 14, 1989, pp. 38–41.

26. Amy Dockser Marcus, "Medical, Social Changes May Spur Courts to Reformulate Definition of Parenthood," *Wall Street Journal*, September 18, 1990, pp. B1, B8.

27. Michele Manges, "Do-It-Yourself," *Wall Street Journal Reports: Technology*, November 13, 1989, p. R13.

28. "The Search for Superdrugs," *Business Week*, May 13, 1991, pp. 92–96.

29. "Mail Smart," *Forbes*, December 12, 1988, pp. 246–248.

30. Cyndee Miller, "Electronic Monitor Sets Up Frequent-Diner Data Base," *Marketing News*, July 8, 1991, p. 14.

31. Kevin Goldman, "More Radio Stations Play Oldies Songs to Lure Listeners Coveted by Advertisers," *Wall Street Journal*, April 24, 1990, p. B1.

32. Carlee Scott, "As Baby Boomers Age, Fewer Couples Untie the Knot," *Wall Street Journal*, November 7, 1990, pp. B1, B10.

33. David Shribman, "Mobility of U.S. Society Turns Small Cities into Giants," *Wall Street Journal*, February 8, 1991, pp. B1, B4.

34. Julie Connelly, "How Dual-Income Couples Cope," *Fortune*, September 24, 1990, pp. 129–136.

35. Christopher Knowlton, "Consumers: A Tougher Sell," *Fortune*, September 26, 1988, p. 70.

36. Julie Stacey, "USA Snapshots," *USA Today*, March 22, 1991, p. 1A.

37. Web Bryant, "USA Snapshots," *USA Today*, March 27, 1991, p. 1A.

38. William Dunn, "Minorities Gain in Census," *USA Today*, March 11, 1991, p. 1A.

39. "Beyond the Melting Pot," *Time*, April 9, 1990, pp. 28–31.

40. William Dunn, "Rapid Growth Builds Minorities' Power 'Potential,' " *USA Today*, March 11, 1991, p. 5A.

41. "Beyond the Melting Pot."

42. "Suddenly, Asian-Americans Are a Marketer's Dream," *Business Week*, June 17, 1991, pp. 54–55.

43. Mark Robichaux, "Interfaith Cards for Holiday Irk Jewish Leaders," *Wall Street Journal*, December 10, 1990, pp. B1, B2.

44. Marj Charlier, "Youthful Sobriety Tests Liquor Firms," *Wall Street Journal*, June 14, 1990, pp. B1, B7.

45. Meg Cox, "Music Industry Composes Counterpoint as Demands to Censor Lyrics Increase," *Wall Street Journal*, October 19, 1990, pp. B1, B9.

46. "Beyond the Melting Pot."

47. Alix M. Freedman, "National Firms Find That Selling to Local Tastes Is Costly, Complex," *Wall Street Journal*, February 9, 1987, p. 17.

48. Kathleen Deveny, "For Marketers, No Peave Is Too Petty," *Wall Street Journal*, November 14, 1990, pp. B1, B6.

49. Mary Ellin Barrett, "Peddling the Planet," *USA Weekend*, December 14–16, 1990, pp. 4–5.

50. Anne B. Fisher, "What Consumers Want in the 1990s," *Fortune*, January 29, 1990, pp. 108–112.

51. Priscilla Painton, "Greening from the Roots Up," *Time*, April 23, 1990, pp. 76–86.

52. Robert Tomsho, " 'Recycled' Often Doesn't Mean 'Reused' in the Paper Industry," *Wall Street Journal*, November 23, 1990, pp. B1, B3.

53. "Developments to Watch," *Business Week*, April 16, 1990, p. 93.

54. Doug Carroll and Desirée French, "Think Green on the Road," *USA Today*, January 8, 1991, p. 8B.

55. Ellen Neuborne, "Plastic Out, 'Green' L'eggs the Plan," *USA Today*, July 10, 1991, p. 1B; J. Taylor Buckley, "The Incredible, Inedible, L'eggs," *USA Today*, July 12, 1991, p. 11A.

56. Walter Shapiro, "Is Washington in Japan's Pockets?" *Time*, October 1, 1990, pp. 106–107.

57. "Grapevine," *Time*, August 27, 1990, p. 13.

58. Gary S. Becker, "Your Tax Dollars Are at Work—on the Wrong Jobs," *Business Week*, November 26, 1990, p. 18.

59. Alecia Swasy, "P&G Drops Plans to Market Maalox for Rhone-Poulenc," *Wall Street Journal*, August 24, 1990, p. B4.

60. Ron Winslow, "Sandoz Unit Faces States' Antitrust Suit over Marketing of Schizophrenia Drug," *Wall Street Journal*, December 19, 1990, p. B3.

61. Bradford A. McKee, "Planning for the Disabled," *Nation's Business*, November 1990, pp. 24–26.

62. Gerald F. Seib, "Shifting Policies: To a Surprising Extent, Bush Quietly Discards Many Reagan Stands," *Wall Street Journal*, April 20, 1989, pp. A1, A6.

63. "When 'Friends' Become Moles," *Time*, May 28, 1990, p. 50.

64. "Hunkering Down," *Time*, July 23, 1990, pp. 55–57.

65. "The Battle of the 'Burbs: Redrawing the Political Map," *Business Week*, November 26, 1990, pp. 80–86.

Case 1 source: Bradford McKee, "From the Ground Up," *Nation's Business*, January 1991, pp. 39–40. *Case 2 sources:* Jim Williams, 'The Coming Waterloo," *Investment Vision*, November–December 1990, pp. 67–68; Keith R. Yocum, "Ionics: Atop the Clean Water Wave," *Boston Sunday Globe*, March 10, 1991; "The Globe 100," *Boston Globe*, June 11, 1991, p. 71.

Chapter 3

1. Julie Liesse Erickson, "Quaker Boosts Budget, Adds Products," *Advertising Age*, November 19, 1990, p. 2; "Quaker to Focus on Core Brands," *Adweek Eastern Edition*, November 19, 1990, p. 45; Bill Saporito, "How Quaker Oats Got Rolled," *Fortune*, October 8, 1990, pp. 129–138; Julie Liesse Erickson, "Gatorade Gusher Set," *Advertising Age*, April 17, 1990, p. 10; Quaker Oats Company, *1990 Annual Report*.

2. Lois Therrien, "Kraft Is Looking for Fat Growth from Fat-Free Foods," *Business Week*, March 26, 1990, pp. 100–101.

3. Seth Lubove, "Unfinished Business," *Forbes*, December 10, 1990, pp. 170–172.

4. Theodore Levitt, "Marketing Myopia" (reprinted with retrospective commentary), *Harvard Business Review,* September–October 1975, p. 26. Originally published in 1960.

5. Joseph Weber, "From Soup to Nuts and Back to Soup," *Business Week,* November 5, 1990, pp. 114–116; "Campbell Chief Cooks Up Winning Menu," *Wall Street Journal,* February 15, 1991, pp. B1, B5; "Campbell Sells Two Subsidiaries," *Focus,* December 19, 1990, p. 10; "US Food Industry: Campbell Soup," *Strategic Intelligence Systems Research Study,* October 1990, pp. 9–10; "Campbell Announces Major Restructuring and North American Divestitures," *Frozen Food Digest,* October 1990, p. 118.

6. Michael Porter, "From Competitive Advantage to Corporate Strategy," *Harvard Business Review,* May–June 1987, pp. 43–59.

7. The discussion of Gatorade's marketing strategy was developed from "Soda Rivals Are Muscling In on the Success of Gatorade," *New York Times* (National Edition), September 26, 1990, pp. B1, B4; "Business Bulletin: Gator Raidings," *Wall Street Journal* (Eastern Edition), August 2, 1990, p. A1; "Gatorade Introduces Bag-in-Box Program," *Vending Times,* August 1990, p. 3; "Gatorade Quenches Thirst for High School Marketing," *Adweek* (Midwest Edition), September 24, 1990, p. 3; "New Quaker Sports Drink in Test Market," *Crain's Chicago Business,* June 10, 1990, p. 45; "Quaker's 'Cola War,'" *Advertising Age,* May 28, 1990, pp. 3, 62.

Chapter 4

1. Adapted from Martin Mayer, "Scanning the Future," by permission of *Forbes* magazine, October 15, 1990, pp. 114–117. © Forbes Inc., 1990.

2. Richard H. Brien and James E. Stafford, "Marketing Information Systems: A New Dimension for Marketing Research," *Journal of Marketing,* July 1968, p. 21.

3. "New Marketing Research Definition Approved," *Marketing News,* January 2, 1987, pp. 1, 14.

4. "Search for Tomorrow at Pitney Bowes," *Business Week,* March 5, 1990, pp. 50–51.

5. "Has Waterford Set Loose a Bull in Its Shop?" *Business Week,* November 5, 1990, p. 58.

6. "When J. D. Power Talks, Carmakers Listen," *Business Week,* September 26, 1988, p. 134.

7. Amanda Bennett, "Making the Grade with the Customer," *Wall Street Journal,* November 12, 1990, pp. B1, B8.

8. Bennett, "Making the Grade with the Customer."

9. Fern Schumer, "The New Magicians of Market Research," *Fortune,* July 15, 1983, p. 72.

10. Ronald Alsop, "Advertisers Put Consumers on the Couch," *Wall Street Journal,* May 13, 1988, p. 17.

11. "Doesn't Everyone Want to Smell like Cher?" *Forbes,* April 2, 1990, pp. 142–144.

12. "Brokers Filling Businesses' Information Gaps," *Marketing News,* October 11, 1985, p. 3.

13. "Merchandising Ploys Effective? Scanners Know," *Marketing News,* January 4, 1985, p. 17.

14. Alan R. Andreasen, "Cost-Conscious Marketing Research," *Harvard Business Review,* July–August 1983, pp. 74–79.

Chapter 5

1. Adapted from Kathleen Deveny, "Reality of the '90s Hits Yuppie Brands," *Wall Street Journal,* December 20, 1990, pp. B1, B4; and Alix M. Freedman, "With Yuppies Fading, Absolut May Too," *Wall Street Journal,* December 17, 1990, pp. B1, B5. Reprinted by permission of the *Wall Street Journal,* © Down Jones & Company, Inc., 1990. All rights reserved.

2. Richard Gibson, "Super-Cheap and Mid-Priced Eateries Bite Fast-Food Chains from Both Sides," *Wall Street Journal,* June 22, 1990, pp. B1, B5.

3. Brent Bowers, "Pampering Motorists Proves Profitable," *Wall Street Journal,* September 13, 1990, pp. B1, B2.

4. John R. Emshwiller, "Rollover Worry Plagues Utility Vehicles," *Wall Street Journal,* May 23, 1988, p. 19; Robert Daniels, "Suzuki Samurai Is Called Unsafe, Recall Is Urged," *Wall Street Journal,* June 3, 1988, p. 19; Bradley A. Stertz, "Different Data Lies behind Samurai Dispute," *Wall Street Journal,* September 12, 1988, p. 15.

5. "New Lemons from the Auto Lot," *Business Week,* December 3, 1990, p. 148.

6. Peter Newcomb, "Hey, Dude, Let's Consume," *Forbes,* June 11, 1990, pp. 126–131.

7. Ronald Alsop, "Marketing," *Wall Street Journal,* December 27, 1988, p. B1.

8. JoAnn S. Lublin, "Spread of 'Kids Clubs' Is Slowing amid Criticism of the Promotions," *Wall Street Journal,* January 31, 1991, p. B4.

9. Ronald Alsop, "Pepsi Revamps Caffeine-Free Brands of Cola," *Wall Street Journal,* March 2, 1988, p. 28.

10. Stephen MacDonald, "Form = Function," *Wall Street Journal,* January 22, 1988, p. 17.

11. Richard Gibson, "'Shelf-Stable' Foods Seek to Freshen Sales," *Wall Street Journal,* November 2, 1990, pp. B1, B5.

12. "The Van Market Gets Set to Go into Overdrive," *Business Week,* October 17, 1983, p. 101.

13. Yumiko Ono, "Japan Eats Up 'U.S.' Food Never Tasted in America," *Wall Street Journal,* April 4, 1990, pp. B1, B6.

14. Alsop, "Pepsi Revamps Caffeine-Free Brands of Cola."

15. Mason Haire, "Projective Techniques in Market Research," *Journal of Marketing,* April 1950, pp. 649–656; Frederick E. Webster, Jr., and Frederick Von Pechmann, "A Replication of the 'Shopping List' Study," *Journal of Marketing,* April 1970, pp. 61–63.

16. Rick Christie, "Cruise Operators Hope Marketing Push Will Put the Wind Back in Their Sails," *Wall Street Journal,* April 3, 1990, pp. B1, B9.

17. Mindy Fetterman, "For New Items, Timing the Trend Is Everything," *USA Today,* December 24, 1990, p. B1.

18. "The Dangers of Foul Fowl," *Time,* November 26, 1990, p. 78.

19. "People Patterns," *Wall Street Journal,* August 3, 1990, p. B1.

20. "Proceeding with Caution," *Time,* July 16, 1990, pp. 56–62.

21. "Proceeding with Caution."

22. Eugene Carlson, "'Graying' Market May Not Be So Golden," *Wall Street Journal,* December 27, 1989, p. B1.

23. Pauline Yoshihashi, "Gambling Mecca in Nevada Caters to Older Low-Rollers," *Wall Street Journal,* December 1, 1988, pp. B1, B5.

24. "Grandparents Are Filling Empty Nests, Study Finds," *New Orleans Times Picayune,* May 11, 1989, p. A4.

25. Alan L. Otten, "Extended Families: As People Live Longer, Houses Become Home to Several Generations," *Wall Street Journal,* January 27, 1989, pp. A1, A8.

26. Robert E. Allen, "It Pays to Invest in Tomorrow's Work Force," *Wall Street Journal,* November 6, 1989, p. A12.

27. Suzanne H. McCall, "Meet the Workwife," *Journal of Marketing,* July 1977, pp. 55–65.

28. Ellen Graham, "Children's Hour: As Kids Gain Power of Purse, Marketing Takes Aim at Them," *Wall Street Journal,* January 19, 1988, pp. 1, 8.

29. "The Mommy Track," *Business Week,* March 20, 1989, p. 127.

30. Graham, "Children's Hour."

31. Alix M. Freedman, "The Microwave Cooks Up a New Way of Life," *Wall Street Journal,* September 19, 1989, p. B1.

32. Alecia Swasy, "Marketing," *Wall Street Journal,* February 2, 1990, p. B1.

33. "Pampers in the Men's Room." *Fortune,* January 2, 1989, pp. 12–13.

34. "Proceeding with Caution."

35. Kathleen Deveny, "Marketing," *Wall Street Journal,* September 20, 1990, p. B1.

36. "Proceeding with Caution."

37. Kathleen Deveney, "Aiming High, Marketers Shoot for the Hip," *Wall Street Journal*, January 10, 1990, pp. B1, B2.

38. "Saudi Men Aghast at Female GIs," *New Orleans Times- Picayune*, August 17, 1990, p. A2.

39. William Rademaekers, "The Oh So Good Life," *Time*, July 9, 1990, pp. 80–82.

40. Maitlon T. Russell, "Naive Assumptions Cause Unpleasant Surprises When Targeting Ethnic Youth," *Marketing News*, February 19, 1990, pp. 14, 16.

41. "The New Ellis Island," *Time*, June 13, 1983, pp. 19–20.

Chapter 6

1. Adapted from Marc Beauchamp, "No More Weekend Stands," by permission of *Forbes* magazine, September 17, 1990, pp. 191–192. © Forbes Inc., 1990.

2. "ServiceMaster: Gearing Up for a New World," *Financial World*, November 27, 1990, p. 16.

3. Julie Amparano Lopez, "Cellular Phone Concerns Step Up Effort to Get Ordinary Consumers on the Line," *Wall Street Journal*, September 24, 1990, p. B1.

4. Desirée French, "Continental Flying New Colors to Lure Business," *USA Today*, February 13, 1991, p. 2B.

5. "How Well Can Goodyear Take the Bumps Ahead?" *Business Week*, October 15, 1990, pp. 31–32.

6. Brenda L. Rinholm, "Consumer Information May Be Key for Business Marketers," *Marketing News*, March 13, 1989, pp. 13, 34.

7. "USA Snapshots," *USA Today*, February 13, 1991, p. 1B.

8. Jack Willoughby, "Eggshells Everywhere," *Forbes*, May 29, 1989, pp. 254–262.

9. "This Will Melt in Your Mouth, Not in the Sands," *USA Today*, December 12, 1990, p. 4A; "Business Notes," *Time*, December 24, 1990, p. 60.

10. "OEM-Supplier Accords Yield Productivity Improvements," *Marketing News*, October 25, 1985, p. 20.

11. Jacob M. Schlesinger, "GE Wins Contract over Pratt & Whitney to Design Engine for Japan Fighter Jet," *Wall Street Journal*, December 21, 1990, p. A5.

12. John H. Taylor, "Fasten Seat Belts, Please," *Forbes*, April 2, 1990, pp. 84–88.

13. Alexandra Biesada, "Different Drummer," *Financial World*, March 20, 1990, pp. 40–41.

14. Anthony Baldo, "Heavy Metal," *Financial World*, August 21, 1990, pp. 38–44.

15. Janet Guyon, "GE Will Sell Its Chip Line to Harris Corporation," *Wall Street Journal*, August 16, 1988, p. 4.

16. Patrick J. Robinson, Charles W. Faris, and Yoram Wind, *Industrial Buying and Creative Marketing* (Boston: Allyn & Bacon, 1967), p. 14.

17. Joseph B. White, "GM Hopes Plastic Drubs Vans of Steel," *Wall Street Journal*, August 24, 1989, p. B1.

18. Rick Wartzman and Peter Pae, "Alcan Aluminum Sees Opportunities in Car, Airplane Parts for U.S. Market," *Wall Street Journal, December 30, 1988, p. A8*.

19. "Tin Foil Lizzies: Here Come Aluminum Cars," *Business Week*, January 29, 1990, p. 41.

20. Robinson, Faris, and Wind, *Industrial Buying and Creative Marketing*, p. 14.

21. "Developments to Watch," *Business Week*, September 24, 1990, p. 137.

22. Jagannath Dubashi, "Image . . . Is Everything," *Financial World*, October 16, 1990, pp. 55–56.

23. Frederick E. Webster, Jr., and Yoram Wind, "A General Model for Understanding Organizational Buying Behavior," *Journal of Marketing*, April 1972, pp. 17–18.

24. Michele Manges, "Companies Cut Special Air-Fare Deals," *Wall Street Journal*, November 21, 1988, p. B1.

25. Norm Alster, "Thank You, Saddam," *Forbes*, October 15, 1990, pp. 81–85.

26. Dorin P. Levin, "Westinghouse Seeks More Acquisitions to Expand Its Automation Product Lines," *Wall Street Journal*, April 28, 1983, p. 14.

27. "Benetton Strips Back Down to Sportswear," *Business Week*, March 5, 1990, p. 42.

28. Gregory A. Patterson, "Chrysler to Acquire Dollar Rent A Car, Eyeing Broader Market in Rental Sector," *Wall Street Journal*, June 27, 1990, p. A4.

29. John C. Franke, "Marketing to the Government: Contracts There for Those Who Know Where to Look," *Marketing News*, October 9, 1989, pp. 1, 7; John C. Franke, "Military Makes Its Own Purchasing Rules," *Marketing News*, October 9, 1989, pp. 1, 7.

30. "The Top 25 Contractors," *Fortune*, February 25, 1991, pp. 68–69.

31. "Major Defense Department Acquisition System Overhaul Underway," *Impact* (National Association of Purchasing Management Newsletter), March 1990, pp. 1, 2.

32. Jane Easter Bahls, "A Demanding Customer," *Nation's Business*, March 1990, pp. 29–30.

33. Alster, "Thank You, Saddam."

34. "It's Fat and Snazzy—And Worth Billions to Boeing," *Business Week*, October 29, 1990, p. 32.

35. "What's in a Name? A Lot, Says Tandy," *Business Week*, February 27, 1989, p. 109.

Chapter 7

1. Adapted from Alix M. Freedman, "Habit Forming: Fast-Food Chains Play Central Role in Diet of the Inner City Poor," *Wall Street Journal*, December 19, 1990, pp. A1, A10. Reprinted by permission of the *Wall Street Journal*, © Dow Jones & Company, Inc., 1990. All rights reserved.

2. Marj Charlier, "Kimberly-Clark Enlivens Market for Toilet Paper," *Wall Street Journal*, July 23, 1990, pp. B1, B6.

3. Clare Ansberry, "New Kodak and Fuji Films Target Advanced Amateurs," *Wall Street Journal*, March 17, 1989, p. B1.

4. Pauline Yoshihashi, "Players Club Sees a Good Bet in Niche Left by Casinos," *Wall Street Journal*, May 10, 1990, p. B2.

5. Edward Giltenan, "Root Beer Gloat," *Forbes*, December 11, 1989, pp. 156–160.

6. William P. Barrett, "A Wal-Mart for the Movies," *Forbes*, August 22, 1988, pp. 60–61.

7. "Sara Lee: No Fads, No Buyouts, Just Old-Fashioned Growth," *Business Week*, November 14, 1988, pp. 110–112.

8. "News/Trends," *Fortune*, October 24, 1988, pp. 8–9.

9. Melinda Grenier Guiles, "Quiet Ride Ends for Luxury-Car Makers as a Crowded Market Befuddlers Buyers," *Wall Street Journal*, March 22, 1990, pp. B1, B6.

10. "Bad Risks Are This Car Insurer's Best Friends," *Business Week*, November 12, 1990, p. 122.

11. "Alcohol Consumption Found to Be Highest among Southerners," *Wall Street Journal*, August 11, 1988, p. 5.

12. Michael J. McCarthy, "Marketers Zero In on Their Customers," *Wall Street Journal*, March 18, 1991, pp. B1, B5.

13. Kathleen Deveney, "Marketing in the '90s: Segments of One," *Wall Street Journal*, March 22, 1991, p. B4.

14. "People Patterns," *Wall Street Journal*, January 4, 1990, p. B1.

15. Gregory Witcher, "Japanese Auto Makers Target Midwest," *Wall Street Journal*, December 19, 1988, p. B1.

16. Eugene Carlson, "U.S. Population Trends Defy Neat Classification by Experts," *Wall Street Journal*, October 18, 1983, p. 31.

17. "Gerber to Sell Good for Toddlers to Keep Its 'Aging' Customers," *Wall Street Journal*, February 21, 1990, p. B6.

18. Richard Gibson, "Super-Cheap and Mid-Priced Eateries Bite Fast-Food Chains from Both Sides," *Wall Street Journal*, June 22, 1990, pp. B1, B5.

19. "P&G's New Diapers Geared to Stages of Child's Growth," *Wall Street Journal*, September 19, 1990, p. B6.

20. 'Growing Pains at 40," *Time*, May 19, 1986, p. 23.

21. Gwen Hall, "Boomers Hit 40; Marketing Reacts," *Hattiesburg American*, September 24, 1990, p. 6A.

22. Louis Richman, "The New Middle Class: How It Lives," *Fortune*, August 13, 1990, pp. 104–113.

23. Rick Christie, "Marketers Err by Treating Elderly as Uniform Group," *Wall Street Journal*, October 31, 1988, p. B1.

24. Barbara Carton, "Rich, Gray, and Forever Young," *Boston Globe*, January 17, 1989, pp. 41, 46.

25. William Power, "Wall Street Hopes to Strike Gold by Mining the Silver-Haired," *Wall Street Journal*, July 3, 1990, p. C1.

26. Christie, "Marketers Err by Treating Elderly as Uniform Group."

27. "The Health Industry Finally Asks: What Do Women Want?" *Business Week*, August 25, 1986, p. 81.

28. Kathleen Deveny, "Slim-Fast Maker Beefs Up Ads to Rebuff Rivals in Swelling Diet-Powder Market," *Wall Street Journal*, October 18, 1990, pp. B1, B6.

29. "People Patterns," *Wall Street Journal*, January 24, 1989, p. B1.

30. "The Simmons B-School: Striving to Be the Equalizer," *Business Week*, May 21, 1990, pp. 98–100.

31. Peter Waldman, "Tobacco Firms Try Soft, Feminine Sell," *Wall Street Journal*, December 19, 1989, p. B1.

32. Robert Guenther, "First Women's Bank Asks to Defeminize Distinctive Name," *Wall Street Journal*, November 3, 1988, p. B6.

33. Hank Gilman, "Retailers That Target Low-Income Shoppers Are Growing Rapidly," *Wall Street Journal*, June 24, 1985, pp. 1, 8.

34. Edmund Faltermayer, "Who Are the Rich?" *Fortune*, December 17, 1990, pp. 95–106.

35. "People Patterns," *Wall Street Journal*, September 7, 1988, p. 21.

36. William Power, "How Not to Break a Leg; 'Arts Medicine' Helps Performers Stay Healthy on the Job," *Wall Street Journal*, June 5, 1986, p. 29.

37. David Ward, "Leasing the Good Life," *Nation's Business*, January 1990, p. 16.

38. Ronald Alsop, "Marketing," *Wall Street Journal*, October 14, 1988, p. B1.

39. Suzanne Alexander, "Marketers Find College Crowd a Tough Test," *Wall Street Journal*, April 16, 1990, pp. B1, B4.

40. William Dunn, "Asians Build New Lives as Immigrants," *USA Today*, November 26, 1990, pp. A1, A2.

41. Andrea Stone, "Asian Growth: 105% in 10 Years," *USA Today*, February 27, 1991, p. 11A.

42. "People Patterns," *Wall Street Journal*, July 12, 1990, p. B1.

43. Nicandro F. Juarez, "Researcher Debunks Myths Propagated by Self-Appointed 'Spanish Market Gurus,' " *Marketing News*, July 6, 1984, p. 4.

44. Dunn, "Asians Build New Lives as Immigrants."

45. "People Patterns," *Wall Street Journal*, October 20, 1988.

46. Alan L. Otten, "People Patterns," *Wall Street Journal*, September 11, 1990, p. B1.

47. Tatiana Pouschine, "We Will Remove the Cobwebs," *Forbes*, August 22, 1988, pp. 56–60.

48. Gilman, "Retailers That Target Low-Income Shoppers Are Growing Rapidly."

49. Frederick E. Rowe, Jr., "Don't Bet Your Life," *Forbes*, October 15, 1990, p. 233.

50. Elizabeth Snead, "Unwrapping Your Christmas Presence," *USA Today*, December 3, 1990, p. 4D.

51. "Multiple Personalities Emerge in Travel Study," *New Orleans Times-Picayune*, May 17, 1990, p. E1.

52. The examples of geodemographic segmentation are adapted by permission from Lynn G. Coleman, "Marketers Advised to 'Go Regional,' " *Marketing News*, May 8, 1989, pp. 1, 8, published by the American Marketing Association.

53. Marj Charlier, "Coors to Kick Off Ads for the New Beer on NFL Broadcasts," *Wall Street Journal*, September 5, 1989, p. B4.

54. "Will Price Wars Hobble Fed Ex?" *Financial World, December 11, 1990, p. 15.*

55. Gregory A. Patterson, "Chrysler to Acquire Rent A Car, Eyeing Broader Market in Rental Sector," *Wall Street Journal*, June 27, 1990, p. A4.

56. Clare Ansberry, "Marketing," *Wall Street Journal*, March 24, 1988, p. 29.

57. "Warner-Lambert Tests Gum with No Sugar, No Stick," *Wall Street Journal*, August 17, 1990, p. A12.

58. Ronald Henkoff, "This Cat Is Acting like a Tiger," *Fortune*, December 19, 1988, pp. 69–76.

59. Henkoff, "This Cat Is Acting like a Tiger."

60. Henkoff, "This Cat Is Acting like a Tiger."

Chapter 8

1. Adapted from Dana Milbank, "Microbreweries Find Space at the Bar," *Wall Street Journal*, October 16, 1990, pp. B1, B2. Reprinted by permission of the *Wall Street Journal*, © Dow Jones Company, Inc., 1990. All rights reserved.

2. Paul B. Brown, "Marketing: Matters of Import," *Inc.*, October, 1988, pp. 115–118.

3. Yumiko Ono, "Marketing," *Wall Street Journal*, March 26, 1991, p. B1.

4. Marj Charlier, "Brew Pubs Pour into Restaurant Market, Creating Their Own Beers and Ambiance," *Wall Street Journal*, February 22, 1990, pp. B1, B6.

5. Marj Charlier, "New Kinds of Beer to Tap a Flat Market," *Wall Street Journal*, April 20, 1989, p. B1.

Chapter 9

1. Information from Joshua Levine, "But in the Office, No," *Forbes*, October 16, 1989, pp. 272–273; Dan Koeppel, "Dole Wants the Whole Produce Aisle," *Adweek's Marketing Week* October 22, 1990, pp. 20–26.

2. ANSI/ASQC, "Quality Systems Terminology, American National Standard, A3-1987," in *Marketing and Quality* (Milwaukee: American Society for Quality Control, 1989), p. 2.

3. John R. Hauser and Don Clausing, "The House of Quality," *Harvard Business Review*, May–June 1988, pp. 63–73.

4. Stephen MacDonald, "Form + Function," *Wall Street Journal*, October 12, 1988, p. B1.

5. Committee on Definitions, American Marketing Association, *Marketing Definitions: A Glossary of Marketing Terms* (Chicago: American Marketing Association, 1960).

6. "Development to Watch," *Business Week*, October 10, 1988, p. 137.

7. The classification of consumer products into convenience, shopping, and specialty products was proposed by Melvin T. Copeland in "Relation of Consumer's Buying Habits to Marketing Methods," *Harvard Business Review*, April 1923, pp. 282–289. The category of unsought products was proposed by E. Jerome McCarthy in *Basic Marketing: A Managerial Approach* (Homewood, Ill.: Richard D. Irwin, 1960).

8. Subrata Chakravarty, "Philip Morris Is Still Hungry," *Forbes*, April 2, 1990, pp. 96–102.

9. "Cigarette Sales Up—Maybe for the Last Time," *Business Week*, December 17, 1979, p. 54.

10. Peter D. Bennett, *Dictionary of Marketing Terms* (Chicago: American Marketing Association, 1988), pp. 18–19.

11. Bennett, *Dictionary of Marketing Terms*.

12. Ronald Alsop, "It's Slim Pickings in Product Name Game," *Wall Street Journal*, November 29, 1988, p. B1.

13. Peter Farquhar, "Managing Brand Equity," *Marketing Research*, September 1989, pp. 24–32.

14. Marj Charlier, "IBP Inc. Struggles to Regain Beef Industry's Leadership," *Wall Street Journal,* May 3, 1988, p. 6.
15. Farquhar, "Managing Brand Equity."
16. Guy McWilliams, "The Big Brouhaha over the Little Juice Box," *Business Week,* September 17, 1990, p. 36.
17. David Stipp, "Lab Notes," *Wall Street Journal,* July 18, 1988, p. 19.
18. Marj Charlier, "Beer Drinkers in Texas, California Don't Swallow Change in Coors Label," *Wall Street Journal,* December 29, 1988, p. B4.

Chapter 10

1. Stephen Kindel, "Leading Edge," *Financial World,* January 8, 1991, pp. 48–49; "A Cut Above," *USA Today,* December 24, 1990, p. 38; Lawrence Ingrassia, "Schick Razor to Try for Edge against Gillette," *Wall Street Journal,* October 8, 1990, p. B1; "Sensor: A One-Year Success for Gillette," *Business Wire,* January 23, 1991.
2. Gene Bylinsky, "Turning R&D into Real Products," *Fortune,* July 2, 1990, pp. 72–78.
3. Richard Koenig, "P&G Creates New Posts in Latest Step to Alter How Firm Manages Its Brands," *Wall Street Journal,* October 12, 1987, p. 30; "The Marketing Revolution at Procter & Gamble," *Business Week,* July 25, 1988, pp. 72–76.
4. Russell Mitchell, "Masters of Innovation," *Business Week,* April 10, 1989, pp. 58–63.
5. Sue Shellenberger, "McDonald's Low-Fat Burger to Go National," *Wall Street Journal,* March 14, 1991, p. B1.
6. C. Merle Crawford, *New Products Management,* 3d ed. (Homewood, Ill.: Richard D. Irwin, 1991), pp. 74–75.
7. John Bussey and Douglas Sease, "Speeding Up: Manufacturers Strive to Slice Time Needed to Develop Products," *Wall Street Journal,* February 23, 1988, pp. 1, 13.
8. John Bussey, "Next Stop Saturn," *Marketing Insights,* Fall 1990, pp. 70–75.
9. David Kiley, "Conditions That Change," *Adweek's Marketing Week,* November 5, 1990, p. 25.
10. Craig Mellow, "Successful Products of the Eighties," *Across the Board,* November 1988, pp. 40–43.
11. A good discussion of this simultaneous product development is in Hirotaka Takeuchi and Ikujiro Nonaka, "The New Product Development Game," *Harvard Business Review,* January–February 1986, pp. 137–145.
12. James Warren, "Electronic Chalkboard Puts Maker on Map," *Chicago Tribune,* February 28, 1991, sec. 3, pp. 1–2.
13. Everett Rogers, *Diffusion of Innovations,* 3d ed. (New York: Free Press, 1983), pp. 15–16.
14. The best reference on the nature and uses of the product life cycle is Theodore Levitt, "Exploit the Product Life Cycle," *Harvard Business Review,* November–December 1965, pp. 81–94.
15. Levitt, "Exploit the Product LIfe Cycle," p. 89.
16. "In Business This Week," *Business Week,* March 21, 1983, p. 36; Spencer Davidson, "A Replay of the Tylenol Scare," *Time,* February 24, 1986, p. 22; Stephen Koepp, "A Hard Decision to Swallow," *Time,* March 3, 1986, p. 59.

Chapter 11

1. Adapted from Tom Richman, "Recruiting Affiliates." Reprinted with permission of *Inc.* Magazine, December 1990, pp. 157–158. Copyright © by Inc. Publishing Corp., 38 Commercial Wharf, Boston, MA 02110.
2. Clare Ansberry, "Kodak's New Research Lab in Japan Is Latest Weapon Aimed at Fuji Photo," *Wall Street Journal,* October 17, 1988, p. B6.

3. Damon Darlin, "Shelf Control: 'Papa-Mama' Stores in Japan Wield Power to Hold Back Imports," *Wall Street Journal,* November 14, 1988, pp. A1, A5.
4. Steve Weiner, "Debt Focuses the Mind," *Forbes,* January 7, 1991, pp. 40–41.
6. Michael W. Miller, "Apple to Reduce Its 2,600 U.S. Outlets by 600 Stores in Bid to Help Marketing," *Wall Street Journal,* April 7, 1986, p. 4.
7. Reed Abelson, 'Spicy Days at McCormick," *Fortune,* January 15, 1990, p. 97.
8. Teri Agins, "Benetton Is Sued by 2 Ex-Licensees of Oregon Stores," *Wall Street Journal,* September 27, 1988, p. 45.
9. Craig A. Kelley, "Recent Court Decisions Illustrate Dynamic Nature of Distribution," *Marketing Educator,* Fall 1988, p. 4.
10. "Bottling Is Hardly a Classic for Coke," *Business Week,* December 11, 1989, pp. 130–135.
11. Craig C. Carter, "Yes, Antitrust Can Still Say No," *Fortune,* September 1, 1986, pp. 63–64.
12. Robert L. Rose, "Vrooming Back: After Nearly Stalling, Harley-Davidson Finds New Crowd of Riders," *Wall Street Journal,* August 31, 1990, pp. A1, A6.
13. Mark Robichaux, "Family Business Isn't All in the Family," *Wall Street Journal,* November 8, 1989, p. B1.
14. "The Selling of Acura—A Honda That's Not a Honda," *Business Week,* March 17, 1986, p. 93.
15. Alecia Swasy and Gregory Stricharchunk, "Grocery Chains Pressure Suppliers for Uniform Prices," *Wall Street Journal,* October 21, 1988, p. B1; "Squeezin the Charmin," *Fortune,* January 16, 1989, pp. 11–12.
16. "There's Nothing Black-and-White about the Gray Market," *Business Week,* November 7, 1988, pp. 172–180.
17. Craig A. Kelley, "Recent Court Decisions Illustrate Dynamic Nature of Distribution," Marketing Educator, Fall 1988, p. 4; Dan Koeppel, "Brands Dressed in Gray," *Adweek's Marketing Week,* March 20, 1989, pp. 20–24.
18. "McKesson's Hard-Sell Success," Business Week, June 30, 1986, p. 58.
19. Brian Dumaine, "P&G Rewrites the Marketing Rules," *Fortune,* November 6, 1989, pp. 34–48.
20. Rick Christie, "Hardee's Helps Itself to New Markets with Roy Rogers," *Wall Street Journal,* January 31, 1990, pp. B1, B4.
21. Seth Lubove, "People Talk Thin but Eat Fat," *Forbes,* April 2, 1990, pp. 56–58.
22. Julie Schlax, "Rain, Sleet, Snow, and Franchising," *Forbes,* November 26, 1990, pp. 224–225.
23. "Fotomat Agrees to Pay $10 Million to Settle Franchise Holder Suits," *Wall Street Journal,* May 3, 1983, p. 8.
24. Julianne Slovak, "Companies to Watch," Fortune, March 12, 1990, p. 90.
25. Michael Waldholz, "Merck & DuPont Ally to Form Drug Joint Venture," *Wall Street Journal,* July 26, 1990, pp. B1, B3.

Chapter 12

1. Adapted from Lisa Gubernick, "So Where Are the Overcoats?" by permission of *Forbes* magazine June 11, 1990, pp. 178–179. © Forbes Inc., 1990.
2. Kevin Higgins, "In-Store Merchandising Is Attracting More Marketing Dollars with Last Word in Sales," *Marketing News,* August 19, 1983, p. 1.
3. Michael J. McCarthy, "Home Depot's Do-It-Yourself Powerhouse," *Wall Street Journal,* July 17, 1990, pp. B1, B8.
4. "Franchises Are the Best Way to Make a Million Dollars, Trade Group Representative Maintains," *Marketing News,* May 27, 1983, p. 14.
5. This section borrows heavily from George H. Lucas, Jr., and Larry G. Gresham, "How to Position for Retail Success," *Business,* April–June 1988, pp. 3–13.

6. Debra Wise, "Shopping Smart," *Glamour,* September 1990, p. 272.

7. "The Price Is Always Right," *Time,* December 17, 1990, pp. 66–68.

8. Rick Reiff, "Convenience with a Difference," *Forbes,* June 11, 1990, pp. 184–186.

9. Paul Klebnikov, "A Little Brother's Big Score," *Forbes,* November 26, 1990, pp. 148–152.

10. Ellen Neuborne, "CEO Pitching New Vision for Retailer," *USA Today,* April 10, 1991, p. 10B.

11. Alexandra Biesada, "Dumping on the Dime Store," Financial World, October 30, 1990, pp. 62–63; Francine Schwadel, "Woolworth Is Bargaining on Return to East Germany," Wall Street Journal, June 20, 1990, pp. B1, B4.

12. Bill Saporito, "Kroger, the New King of Supermarketing," *Fortune,* February 7, 1986, p. 59.

13. "Nielsen Reports Retail Trends; Edge Goes to One-Stop Shopping," *Marketing News,* April 1, 1991, p. 7.

14. "What Put Pathmark in Such a Pickle?" *Business Week,* February 26, 1990, pp. 68–71.

15. "How Two Big Grocers Are Bringing Home the Bacon," *Business Week,* April 24, 1989, pp. 141–143.

16. "What Put Pathmark in Such a Pickle?"

17. "Hypermart Arrives in Arlington," *Dallas Times Herald,* August 14, 1988, pp. E1–E10; "The Return of the Amazing Colossal Store," *Business Week,* August 22, 1988, pp. 59–61; "News Briefs," *Adweek's Marketing Week,* January 23, 1989, p. 6; John Huey, "Wal-Mart: Will It Take Over the World?" *Fortune,* January 30, 1989, pp. 52–64.

18. Bill Vlasic, "Kmart Turning Kmall," *Hattiesburg American,* August 13, 1990, p. 6A.

19. Steve Weiner, "With Big Selection and Low Prices, 'Category Killer' Stores Are a Hit," *Wall Street Journal,* June 17, 1986, p. 23.

20. Joseph Pereira, "Discount Department Stores Struggle against Rivals That Strike Aisle by Aisle," *Wall Street Journal,* June 19, 1990, pp. B1, B4.

21. Paul M. Barrett, "Best Products Rejects Offer of $522 Million," *Wall Street Journal,* September 27, 1988, p. 21; Mary Lu Carnevale, "Best Products Buy-Out Is Set after Review," *Wall Street Journal* October 11, 1988, p. A14.

22. "Corn Flakes, Aisle 1. Cadillacs, Aisle 12," *Business Week,* April 29, 1991, pp. 68–70.

23. Gary Strauss, "Warehouse Clubs Heat Up Retail Climate," *USA Today,* December 7, 1990, pp. 1B, 1C.

24. Strauss, "Warehouse Clubs Heat Up Retail Climate."

25. Gregory Stricharchuk, "Making Money the Old-Fashioned Way: Door to Door," *Wall Street Journal,* February 19, 1991, p. B2.

26. Yumiko Ono, "Amway Translates with Ease into Japanese," *Wall Street Journal,* September 21, 1990, pp. B1, B4.

27. Andrew Tanzer, "War of the Robots," *Forbes,* January 7, 1991, pp. 293–296.

28. Faye Rice, "How to Succeed at Cloning a Small Business," *Fortune,* October 28, 1985, p. 60.

29. Stanley A. Brown, " 'Standchising' Is New Wave in Franchise Expansion," *Marketing News,* April 1, 1991, p. 10.

30. Rice, "How to Succeed at Cloning a Small Business."

31. "Franchising across the Nation," *USA Today,* February 14, 1991, p. 4B.

32. Meg Whittemore, "Franchising," *Nation's Business,* December 1990, p. 58; Jeffrey A. Tannenbaum, "Franchisee Pool Is Drying Up for Some Firms," *Wall Street Journal,* November 14, 1989, pp. B1, B2.

33. Rice, "How to Succeed at Cloning a Small Business."

34. "Franchising across the Nation."

35. "Franchising Facts from the Franchise Front," *Business Week,* May 6, 1991, p. 70.

36. Suzanne Alexander, "More Working Mothers Opt for Flex of Operating a Franchise from Home," *Wall Street Journal,* January 31, 1991, pp. B1, B2.

37. Udayan Gupta, "Franchisers Chip in; Few Use Method to Fund Research," *Wall Street Journal,* September 17, 1990, p. B2.

38. Michael Selz, "More Concerns Are Franchising Existing Outlets," *Wall Street Journal,* December 17, 1990, pp. B1, B2.

39. Hal Kreiger, Laura Leli, Larry Rouse, and Don Townsend, "Franchising Creates Conflicts and Is No Guarantee of Success," *Marketing News,* February 19, 1990, p. 6.

40. "It's Taking Off with Jet-Lagged Shoppers," *Business Week,* May 21, 1990, p. 108.

41. Gretchen Morgenson, "The Buyout That Saved Safeway," *Forbes,* November 12, 1990, pp. 88–92.

42. Hank Gilman, "J. C. Penney Decentralizes Its Purchasing," *Wall Street Journal,* May 8, 1986, p. 6.

43. Jolie Solomon, "Limited Is a Clothing Retailer on the Move," *Wall Street Journal,* October 31, 1985, p. 6.

44. Jeffrey A. Trachtenberg, "Macy's Smaller Suppliers Forced into Riskier Position," *Wall Street Journal,* November 2, 1990, p. B2.

45. "Retailing: Who Will Survive?" *Business Week,* November 26, 1990, pp. 134–144.

46. Francine Schwadel, "Chicago Retailers' 'Sting' Aims to Put Shoplifting Professionals Out of Business," *Wall Street Journal,* June 5, 1990, p. B1.

47. "The Price Is Always Right," *Time,* December 17, 1990, pp. 66–68.

48. Susan Caminiti, "How the Gap Keeps ahead of the Pack," *Fortune,* February 12, 1990, pp. 129–131.

49. Jeffrey A. Trachtenberg, "Big Spenders: Largest of All Malls in the U.S. Is a Gamble in Bloomington, Minnesota," *Wall Street Journal,* October 30, 1990, pp. A1, A8.

50. Eugene Carlson, "New Retailers Face Struggle Getting in Malls," *Wall Street Journal,* July 24, 1990, pp. B1, B2.

51. Caminiti, "How the Gap Keeps ahead of the Pack."

52. "Frederick's of Hollywood Trades Its X Rating for an R," *Business Week,* December 11, 1989, p. 64.

53. "Will Home Depot Be 'The Wal-Mart of the '90s'?" *Business Week,* March 19, 1990, pp. 124–126.

54. Ellen Neuborne, "Retailers Bolster Customer Service," *USA Today,* April 18, 1991, p. 4B.

55. Philip Kotler, "Atmospherics as a Marketing Took," *Journal of Retailing,* Winter 1973–1974, pp. 48–64.

56. "Will Home Depot Be 'The Wal-Mart of the '90s'?"

57. "Retailing: Who Will Survive?"

58. Francine Schwadel, "Going Without: Gap Drops Anchors in Its Plan to Develop Upscale Malls," *Wall Street Journal,* October 25, 1990, pp. B1, B6.

59. Mitchell Pacelle, "Mall Developers Face Severe Credit Pinch," *Wall Street Journal,* November 13, 1990, p. A2.

60. Peter Weaver, "It's Your Money," *Nation's Business,* March 1991, p. 65.

61. Gretchen Morgenson, "Cheapie Gucci," *Forbes,* May 27, 1991, pp. 43–44.

62. "The Price Is Always Right."

63. Morgenson, "Cheapie Gucci,"

64. "At Sears, the more Things Change . . . ," *Business Week,* November 12, 1990, pp. 66–68.

65. Francine Schwadel, "Spiegel, Crayola Plan Kids' Clothes Line," *Wall Street Journal,* July 2, 1990, pp. B1, B2.

66. Eugene Carlson, "Video Stores Try Sharper Focus in Market Glut," *Wall Street Journal,* July 2, 1990, pp. B1, B2.

67. Dan Moreau, "How to Start a *Really* Small Business," *Changing Times,* May 1991, pp. 57–59.

68. Marty Baumann, "USA Snapshots," *USA Today,* December 4, 1990, p. B1.

69. Gretchen Morgenson, "The Buyout That Saved Safeway," *Forbes,* November 12, 1990, pp. 88–92.

70. Ellen Neuborne, "Wal-Mart Wins with Folksy Approach," *USA Today,* December 12, 1990, pp. 1B, 2B.

71. Susan Dillingham, "Auto Dealers under One Umbrella," *Insight,* June 26, 1989, p. 40.

72. Rick Reiff, "Convenience with a Difference," *Forbes,* June 11, 1990, pp. 184–186.

73. Francine Schwadel, "Shoppers' Blues: The Thrill Is Gone," *Wall Street Journal,* October 13, 1989, pp. B1, B5.

74. "Retailing: Who Will Survive?"

75. "Retailing: Who Will Survive?"

76. "Lessons from Tysons Corner," *Forbes,* April 30, 1990, pp. 186–188.

77. "Looking Downscale—Without Looking Down," *Business Week,* October 8, 1990, pp. 62—67.

78. "Looking Downscale—Without Looking Down."

79. Jeffrey A. Trachtenberg, "A Buyer's Market Has Shoppers Demanding and Getting Discounts," *Wall Street Journal,* February 8, 1991, pp. A1, A8.

80. Alexandra Peers, "Art Mall Tries to Be More than a Still Life," *Wall Street Journal,* March 28, 1990, p. B1.

81. Malcolm P. McNair and Eleanor G. May, "The Next Revolution of the Retailing Wheel," *Harvard Business Review,* September–October 1978, pp. 81–89.

Chapter 13

1. Adapted from Jay Finegan, "Reach Out and Teach Someone." Reprinted with permission, *Inc.* Magazine, October 1990, pp. 112–114. Copyright © 1990 by Goldhirsh Group, Inc., 38 Commercial Wharf, Boston, MA 02110.

2. Ellen Paris, "Welcome, Ladies," *Forbes,* September 3, 1990, p. 96.

3. Bill Saporito, "Super Valu Does Two Things Well," *Fortune,* April 18, 1983, p. 116.

4. "What Makes Sun-Diamond Grow," Business Week, August 9, 1982, p. 83.

5. Allen Konopacki, "CEOs Attend Trade Shows to Grab 'Power Buyers,' " *Marketing News,* October 15, 1990, pp. 5, 18.

6. "Automotive Aftermarket Is Confronted with Turbulent Times," *Marketing News,* February 18, 1983, p. 24.

7. "Wholesalers: The Practice of Making Perfect," *Business Week,* January 14, 1991, p. 86.

8. "Wholesalers: The Practice of Making Perfect."

9. "Mom and Pop Move Out of Wholesaling," *Business Week,* January 9, 1989, p. 91.

10. Steven P. Galante, "Distributors Switch Strategies to Survive Coming Shakeout," *Wall Street Journal,* July 20, 1987, p. 21.

11. "Mom and Pop Move Out of Wholesaling."

12. Howard S. Gochberg, "Don't Underrate Logistics Services as a Strategic Asset," *Marketing News,* November 21, 1988, p. 9.

13. Amanda Bennett, "Making the Grade with the Customer," *Wall Street Journal,* November 12, 1990, p. B1.

14. Georgia-Pacific, *Annual Report,* 1982, p. 8.

15. Roy D. Shapiro, "Get Leverage from Logistics," *Harvard Business Review,* May–June 1984, p. 124.

16. "The Fast-Spinning Machine That Blew a Gasket," *Business Week,* September 10, 1990, pp. 50–52.

17. "L.A. Gear Is Tripping over Its Shoelaces," *Business Week,* August 20, 1990, p. 39.

18. Brenton R. Schlender, "How Levi Strauss Did an LBO Right," *Fortune,* May 7, 1990, pp. 105–107.

19. "Pallets That Save Money—And Trees," *Time,* July 30, 1990, p. 70.

20. Glenn Emery, "Containers, Cranes, and Computers," *Insight,* December 3, 1990, pp. 40–41.

21. Kevin G. Salwen, "McKesson's Prospects Attract Some Investors, Who Cite Firm's Focus on Distribution Unit," *Wall Street Journal,* March 23, 1988, p. 49.

22. Bill Paul, "Trucks's Rates on Small Loads Stir Big Fight," *Wall Street Journal,* July 28, 1983, p. 23.

23. Howard Gochberg, "There's More than One Way to Measure Logistics Performance," *Marketing News,* January 7, 1991, p. 39.

24. Gene Tyndall, "How You Apply Benchmarking Makes All the Difference," *Marketing News,* November 12, 1990, pp. 18–19.

25. Gochberg, "There's More Than One Way to Measure Logistics Performance."

Chapter 14

1. Adapted from Joshua Levine, "Marketing: Selling Hard without Hype," by permission of *Forbes* magazine December 10, 1990, pp. 202–204. © Forbes Inc., 1990.

2. JoAnne Lipman, "Oversupply of Celebrity Hawkers Could Trip Up Sneaker Makers," *Wall Street Journal,* May 23, 1990, p. B6.

3. "The cola Superpowers' Outrageous New Arsenals," *Business Week,* March 20, 1989, pp. 162–166.

4. Ronald Alsop, "Marketing," Wall Street Journal, November 9, 1988, p. B1.

5. "Business Nots," *Time,* December 4, 1989, p. 69.

6. Thomas R. King, "Visa under Fire for Ad Sniping at Arch-Rival American Express," *Wall Street Journal,* December 22, 1989, p. B4.

7. Faye Rice, "How to Deal with Tougher Customers," *Fortune,* December 3, 1990, pp. 38–52.

8. Thomas R. King, "Norelco Fires Santa from Ads; Sales Gain," *Wall Street Journal,* December 29, 1989, p. B4.

9. "The Cola Superpowers' Outrageous New Arsenals."

10. Tananarive Due, "Dean Foods Thrives on Regional, Off-Brand Products," *Wall Street Journal,* September 17, 1987, p. 6; Charles Siler, "Ripe for the Picking," *Forbes,* April 3, 1989, pp. 110–112.

11. Ronald Alsop, "Marketing," *Wall Street Journal,* November 30, 1988, p. B1.

12. "Business Notes," *Time,* July 16, 1990, p. 51.

13. Brenton R. Schlender, "Take Me out to the Gold Mine," *Fortune,* August 13, 1990, pp. 93–100.

14. Rita Koselka, "Pockets Mean Profits," *Forbes,* October 29, 1990, pp. 50–52.

15. "Developments to Watch," *Business Week,* October 8, 1990, p. 83.

16. Andrew Feinberg, "The First Global Generation," *Adweek's Marketing Week,* February 6, 1989, pp. 18–27.

17. Richard Gibson, "Kellogg Shifts Strategy to Pull Consumers In," *Wall Street Journal,* January 22, 1990, pp. B1, B2.

18. Evan McGlinn, "Absolut Marketing," *Forbes,* December 11, 1989, pp. 282–286.

19. Stuart Elliott, "Something to Chew On," *USA Today,* December 27, 1990, p. 1B.

20. Richard Gibson, "Image Campaign by 3M Focuses on Innovation," *Wall Street Journal,* September 7, 1989, p. B8.

21. "Marketing: Three-Star Brands," *Forbes,* November 26, 1990, pp. 251–254.

22. "An Olympic Cola Contest," *Time,* October 15, 1990, p. 27.

23. Joseph Pereira, "Name of the Game: Brand Awareness," *Wall Street Journal,* February 14, 1991, pp. B1, B4.

24. Pereira, "Name of the Game."

25. Vincent Randazzo, "Cruise Lines Urges to Educate Public," *New Orleans Times-Picayune,* September 4, 1988, p. E3.

26. Steve Weiner, "Beef Is a Four-Letter Word," *Forbes,* February 19, 1990, pp. 124–128.

27. Alix M. Freedman, "Perrier Finds Mystique Hard to Restore," *Wall Street Journal,* December 12, 1990, p. B1, B2.

28. Peter Pae, "For Makers of Photo Film, Holidays Are War Days," *Wall Street Journal,* December 13, 1989, pp. B1, B6.

29. Freedman, "Perrier Finds Mystique Hard to Restore."

30. Thomas R. King, "Marketing," *Wall Street Journal,* October 5, 1989, p. B1.

31. Facts about Adolph Coors Company in this section are from Ronald Alsop, "Ready for a Fight, Coors Beef Barrels into New York Region," *Wall Street Journal,* February 12, 1987, p. 25.

32. "It's One Sharp Ad Campaign, but Where's the Blade?" *Business Week,* March 5, 1990, p. 30.

33. Thomas R. King, "Maidenform Draws Fire over Ads Focusing on Sexual Stereotypes," *Wall Street Journal,* December 10, 1990, p. B5.

34. Thomas R. King, "More Public-Service Commercials Take Blunter-Is-Better Approach," *Wall Street Journal,* June 5, 1989, pp. B1, B4.

Chapter 15

1. Adapted from Joshua Levine, "Marketing: The Last Gasp of Mass Media?" by permission of *Forbes* magazine September 17, 1990, pp. 176–182. © Forbes Inc., 1990.

2. Thomas R. King, "Advertising: Spending on Ads Expected to Rise Only 4.6% in '91," *Wall Street Journal,* December 11, 1990, pp. B1, B6.

3. Gretchen Morgenson, "How Different Can a $17 Lipstick Be from a $3 Version?" *Forbes,* September 18, 1989, pp. 128–134.

4. JoAnne Lipman, "Advertising: Newspaper Ad Climate Worsening," *Wall Street Journal,* April 6, 1990, pp. B1, B8.

5. Thomas R. King, "Hertz Rolls Out New Ads to Attract Vacation Travelers," *Wall Street Journal,* March 5, 1990, p. B6.

6. JoAnne Lipman, "Advertising: H&R Block, Excedrin Discover Joint Promotions Can Be Painless," *Wall Street Journal,* February 28, 1991, p. B5.

7. Bradley A. Stertz, "Advertising: Volkswagen Tries for a Little Mystique," *Wall Street Journal,* February 7, 1990, p. B5.

8. Don E. Schultz and Stanley I Tannenbaum, *Essentials of Advertising Strategy,* 2d ed. (Chicago: NTC Business Books, 1988), p. 80.

9. Philip Glouchevitch, "Cruel and Unusual Punishment," *Forbes,* October 15, 1990, p. 182.

10. "Small-Business Update," *Nation's Business,* September 1990, p. 9.

11. "Magazine Publishers Put on Their Thinking Caps," *Business Week,* July 23, 1990, pp. 76–77.

12. "The Fourth Network," *Business Week,* September 17, 1990, pp. 114–121.

13. "USA Snapshots," *USA Today,* January 25, 1991, p. 1B.

14. JoAnne Lipman, "Advertising: Mutant Ninja Turtles May Be Overexposed," *Wall Street Journal,* August 1, 1990, p. B6.

15. Thomas R. King, "Advertising: Isuzu to End Its Popular Liar Campaign," *Wall Street Journal,* August 2, 1990, p. B4; "Business Notes," *Time,* June 18, 1990, p. 67.

16. JoAnne Lipman, "Advertising: WPP to Cut Back 'Cross-Selling' Plans," *Wall Street Journal,* January 7, 1991, p. B5.

17. JoAnn S. Lublin, "Advertising: Agencies Join Rush to Give 'Green' Advice," *Wall Street Journal,* January 25, 1991, p. B6.

Chapter 16

1. Adapted by permission, from Cyndee Miller, "Direct Mailer Leads Fight against Too Much Junk," *Marketing News,* December 10, 1990, pp. 6–7, published by the American Marketing Association.

2. Michael W. Miller, "Catalog Firms Chase GI Dollars in Desert," *Wall Street Journal,* January 25, 1991, pp. B1, B2.

3. Fleming Meeks, "Upselling," *Forbes,* January 8, 1990, pp. 70–72.

4. *Direct Marketing Newsletter,* No. 80.

5. Suzy Parker, "USA Snapshots," *USA Today,* December 19, 1990, p. D1.

6. "900 Numbers Are Being Born Again," *Business Week,* September 17, 1990, pp. 144–149.

7. "It's Not Just for Sleaze Anymore: Serious Marketers Want Consumers to Dial 1-900," *Marketing News,* October 15, 1990, pp. 1, 2.

8. Cyndee Miller, "Slick Brit Book Makes U.S. Foray," *Marketing News,* April 1, 1991, p. 6.

9. Kevin Helliker, "Fashion Catalogs Focus on Consumers' Special Physical Needs," *Wall Street Journal,* November 29, 1990, p. B1.

10. Michael J. Major, "Videotex Never Really Left, but It's Not All Here," *Marketing News,* November 12, 1990, pp. 2, 22.

11. "Business Briefing," *Insight,* December 3, 1990, p. 39.

12. "The Man Who Rewrote Reader's Digest," *Business Week,* June 4, 1990, pp. 148–149.

13. David Churbuck, "Smart Mail," Forbes, February 22, 1990, pp. 107–108.

14. "900 Numbers Are Being Born Again."

15. "Read This!!!!!!!!" *Time,* November 26, 1990, pp. 62–68.

16. Laura Landro, "Warner Tries Target Marketing to Sell Film Lacking Typical Box-Office Appeal," *Wall Street Journal,* October 3, 1990, pp. B1, B10.

17. "Read This!!!!!!!!"

18. Michael Barrier, "An Omaha Telemarketer Rings Up Sales," *Nation's Business,* December 1990, pp. 14–16

19. Cyndee Miller, "Investor Group Buys Donnelley Marketing," *Marketing News,* April 1, 1991, pp. 1, 21.

20. Ellen Neuborne, "Catalogers: Adapting to Soaring Costs," *USA Today,* February 19, 1991, p. 2B.

21. John Schneidawind, "Unlisted Numbers vs. Dialing for Dollars," *USA Today,* June 11, 1991, p. 1B.

22. "Read This!!!!!!!!"

23. "Grapevine," *Time,* September 24, 1990, p. 29.

24. "Read This!!!!!!!!"

25 William A. Robinson, "Continuous Sales (Price) Promotion Destroys Brands—No," *Marketing News,* January 16, 1989, p. 4.

26. Stuart Elliott, "Pepsi Capitalizing on Success of 'Un-huh!' " *USA Today,* February 19, 1991, p. 2B.

27. JoAnne Lipman, "Marketers Turn to Promotions to Attract Hispanic Consumers," *Wall Street Journal,* September 21, 1989, p. B6.

28. Richard Gibson, "Marketing," *Wall Street Journal,* December 26, 1990, p. B1.

29. James R. Healey, "Bad Engine Parts Stall ZR-1 Output," *USA Today,* May 13, 1991, p. 4B.

30. Hugh M. Ryan, "Public Relations Is More than Publicity," *Marketing News,* March 13, 1989, pp. 8–9.

Chapter 17

1. Adapted by permission, from John R. Graham, "If You Don't Get the Right Answers, Don't Take the Job," *Marketing News,* March 19, 1990, pp. 8, 26, published by the American Marketing Association.

2. Matthew Schifrin, "The Magician, the Dry Cleaner, and the Secretary," *Forbes,* December 10, 1990, pp. 152–156.

3. Joan E. Rigdon, "Kodak Zooms in on Pro Photographers," *Wall Street Journal,* February 27, 1991, pp. B1, B5.

4. Cyndee Miller, "Company Expanding Voice Mail Applications," *Marketing News,* December 10, 1990, p. 21.

5. Timothy D. Schellhardt, "Managing," *Wall Street Journal,* December 17, 1990, p. B1.

6. Michael J. Major, "Sales Training Emphasizes Service and Quality," *Marketing News,* March 5, 1990, pp. 5, 8.

7. Timothy D. Schellhardt, "Managing," *Wall Street Journal,* March 22, 1990, p. B1.

8. Marlene L. Rossman, "Marketers Must Realize That Selling Is a Real Job," *Marketing News,* March 5, 1990, p. 5.

9. Schifrin, "The Magician, the Dry Cleaner, and the Secretary."

10. Sharyn Hunt and Ernest F. Cooke, "It's Basic but Necessary: Listen to the Customer," *Marketing News,* March 5, 1990, pp. 22–23.

11. Schellhardt, "Managing," March 22, 1990.

12. Sam Licciardi, "Paper-Pushing Sales Reps Are Less Productive," *Marketing News,* November 12, 1990, p. 15.

13. "Survey Identifies Traits of High-Performing Sales Reps," *Marketing News,* September 16, 1983, sec. 1, p. 14.

14. Gilbert Fuchsberg, ''Hand-Held Computers Help Field Staff Cut Paper Work and Harvest More Data,'' *Wall Street Journal,* January 30, 1990, pp. B1, B8.
15. Richard Gibson, ''Marketing,'' *Wall Street Journal,* December 26, 1990, p. B1.
16. ''Frito-Lay Shortens Its Business Cycle,'' Fortune, January 15, 1990, p. 11.
17. Shawn Clark, ''Sales Force Automation Pays Off,'' *Marketing News,* August 6, 1990, p. 9.
18. Schellhardt, ''Managing,'' March 22, 1990.

Chapter 18

1. Information from Jeffrey Trachtenberg, ''When Cheap Gets Chic,'' *Forbes,* June 13, 1988, pp. 108–109; Brian Bremmer, Chuck Hawkins, and Russell Mitchell, ''America's Innkeepers Brace for the '90s,'' *Business Week,* August 13, 1990, pp. 106–107.
2. Gary Erickson and Johny Johansson, ''The Role of Price in Multi-Attribute Product Evaluations,'' *Journal of Consumer Research,* September 1985, pp. 195–199.
3. Gretchen Morgenson, ''The Perils of Perelman,'' *Forbes,* December 10, 1990, pp. 218–222.
4. Peter Newcomb, ''Adam Smith Goes to the Movies,'' *Forbes,* November 12, 1990, pp. 42–44.
5. ''Economic Trends,'' *Business Week,* June 18, 1990, p. 20.
6. Thomas Nagle, ''Economic Foundations for Pricing,'' *Journal of Business,* January 1984, pp. 3–26.
7. Mark Ivey, Barbara Buell, Jonathan Levine, and Neil Gross, ''Doing unto Compaq as It Did unto IBM,'' *Business Week,* November 19, 1990, pp. 130–137.
8. Fleming Meeks, ''Mom-and-Pop Publishing,'' *Forbes,* September 17, 1990, pp. 170–174.
9. ''America's Computer Heavyweight Slugs It Out in Europe,'' *Business Week,* May 26, 1986, p. 122.
10. Dan Horsky, ''A Diffusion Model Incorporating Product Benefits, Price, Income, and Information,'' *Marketing Science,* Fall 1990, p. 362.

Chapter 19

1. Information from Daniel Pearl, ''UPS Takes on Air-Express Competition,'' *Wall Street Journal,* December 20, 1990, p. A4; Debra Goldman, ''UPS Sells Efficiency, not Price,'' *Adweek Eastern Edition,* November 12, 1990, p. 8.
2. Anthony Baldo, ''Merck Plays Hardball,'' *Financial Week,* June 26, 1990, pp. 22–23.
3. Teri Agins, ''Liz Claiborne to Lift Standard Discount to Stores to 10% on Women's Apparel,''*Wall Street Journal,* July 30, 1990, p. B4; Laura Zinn, ''Liz Claiborne's Sizable Rag Trade-Off,'' *Business Week,* August 13, 1990, pp. 38–40.
4. Dana Wechsler Linden, ''Hot Stuff,'' *Forbes,* November 26, 1990, pp. 164–165.
5. Nancy Ryan, ''Nutra Sweet Faces Stiff Import Duty in Europe,'' *Chicago Tribune,* November 30, 1990, sec. 3, p. 1.
6. ''Niche Marketing Replacing Discounts Based on Age,'' *Marketing News,* October 15, 1990, p. 9.
7. Laurie Petersen, ''Hilton Pushes Its Getaway Weekends,'' *Adweek's Marketing Week,* March 11, 1991, p. 11.
8. Richard Gibson, ''Discount Menu Is Coming to McDonald's as Chain Tries to Win Back Customers,'' *Wall Street Journal,* November 30, 1990, p. B1.
9. Joseph Guiltinan, ''The Price Bundling of Services,'' *Journal of Marketing,* April 1987, pp. 74–85.

10. Ann Hagedorn, ''FTC Tightens Scouting of Funeral Homes,'' *Wall Street Journal,* November 30, 1990, p. B1.
11. James R. Healey, ''Pontiac Tries Easing the Pain of Insurance for Firebird Buyers,'' *USA Today,* November 27, 1990, p. 8B.
12. Gregory Stricharchuk, ''Tire Makers Are Traveling Bumpy Road as Car Sales Fall, Foreign Firms Expand,'' *Wall Street Journal,* September 19, 1990, p. B1.
13. Ray O. Werner, ''Marketing and the Supreme Court in Transition,'' *Journal of Marketing,* Summer 1985, pp. 97–105.
14. Leslie Spencer, ''Are Contingency Fees Legal?'' *Forbes,* February 19, 1990, p. 130.

Chapter 20

1. U.S. Department of Commerce, Malcolm Baldrige Award 1990 Fact Sheet.
2. Lois Therrien, ''The Rival Japan Respects,'' *Business Week,* November 13, 1989, pp. 108–118; ''Motorola Wins 'Dataquest's Semiconductor Producer of the Year' Award,'' *Business Wire,* February 13, 1990; J. B. Miles, ''Motorola: The Six Sigma Challenge,'' *Information Week,* January 7, 1991, p. 39.
3. David Woodruff, Karen Lowry Miller, Larry Armstrong, and Thane Peterson, ''A New Era for Auto Quality,'' *Business Week,* October 22, 1990, p. 84.
4. ''Putting Excellence into Management,'' *Business Week,* July 21, 1980, pp. 196–205.
5. Brian Dumaine, ''P&G Rewrites the Marketing Rules,'' *Fortune,* November 6, 1989, pp. 42–43.
6. Alladi Venkatesh and David L. Wilemon, ''Interpersonal Influence in Product Management,'' *Journal of Marketing,* October 1976, pp. 33–40.
7. Barbara Buell, Robert Hof, and Gary McWilliams, ''Hewlett-Packard Rethinks Itself,'' *Business Week,* April 1, 1991, pp. 76–79.
8. Gilbert Fuchsberg, ''Gurus of Quality Are Gaining Clout,'' *Wall Street Journal,* November 27, 1990, p. B1.
9. Thomas Osborn, ''How 3M Manages for Innovation,'' *Marketing Communications,* November–December 1988, pp. 17–22.
10. Thomas Bonoma, *The Marketing Edge* (New York: Free Press, 1985), pp. 35–48.
11. David Garvin, ''Competing on the Eight Dimensions of Quality,'' *Harvard Business Review,* November–December 1987, p. 104.
12. Amanda Bennett, ''Many Consumers Expect Better Service—And Say They Are Willing to Pay for It,'' *Wall Street Journal,* November 12, 1990, p. B1.
13. Barry Farber and Joyce Wycoff, ''Customer Service: Evolution and Revolution,'' *Sales and Marketing Management,* May 1991, p. 47.
14. Farber and Wycoff, ''Customer Service,'' pp. 44, 46.
15. Farber and Wycoff, ''Customer Service,'' p. 48.
16. Aaron Bernstein, ''Quality is Becoming Job One in the Office, Too,'' *Business Week,* April 29, 1991, pp. 52–54.
17. Larry Armstrong, ''Who's the Most Pampered Motorist of All?'' *Business Week,* June 10, 1991, pp. 90–92.
18. Philip Kotler, *Marketing Management,* 5th ed. (Englewood cliffs, N.J.: Prentice-Hall, 1984), p. 765.

Chapter 21

1. Information from Peter Drucker, ''What Business Can Learn from Nonprofits,'' *Harvard Business Review,* July–August 1989, p. 90; Patricia O'Toole, ''Thrifty, Kind, and Smart as Hell,'' *Lear's,* October 1990, pp. 26–30; John A. Byrne, ''Profiting from the Nonprofits,'' *Business Week,* March 26, 1990, pp. 66–74.
2. Christopher Lovelock, *Services Marketing* (Englewood Cliffs, N.J.: Prentice-Hall, 1984), p. 1.

3. G. Lynn Shostack, "Breaking Free from Product Marketing," *Journal of Marketing,* April 1977, pp. 73–80.

4. Amanda Bennett, "Their Business Is on the Line," *Wall Street Journal,* December 7, 1990, p. B1.

5. Mary Jo Bitner, Bernard H. Booms, and Mary Stanfield Tetreault, "The Service Encounter: Diagnosing Favorable and Unfavorable Incidents," *Journal of Marketing,* January 1990, p. 71.

6. Robert Krughoff, "Service Evaluation," in *Marketing of Services,* ed. James Donnelly and William George (Chicago: American Marketing Association, 1981), pp. 242–244.

7. Leonard Berry, Edwin Lefkowith, and Terry Clark, "In Services, What's in a Name?" *Harvard Business Review,* September–October 1988, pp. 1–3.

8. G. Lynn Shostack, "How to Design a Service," in Donnelly and George, *Marketing of Services,* pp. 221–229.

9. Judith Valente, "Northwest to Invest in Service," *Wall Street Journal,* January 31, 1990, p. B1.

10. Theodore Levitt, "The Industrialization of Service," *Harvard Business Review,* October 1976, pp. 63–74.

11. Esther Dyson, "What the Traffic Will Bear," *Forbes,* May 29, 1989, p. 282.

12. Bennett, "Their Business Is on the Line."

13. John E. G. Bateson, *Managing Services Marketing* (Hinsdale, Ill.: Dryden Press, 1989), pp. 143–147.

14. "How AMEX Is Revamping Its Big, Beautiful Money Machine," *Business Week,* June 13, 1988, pp. 90–92.

15. Jon Berry, "MCI Reaches out for Leads," *Adweek's Marketing Week,* March 25, 1991, p. 4.

16. James H. Donnelly, Leonard L. Berry, and Thomas W. Thompson, *Marketing Financial Services* (Homewood, Ill.: Dow Jones–Irwin, 1985), pp. 112–113.

17. Wayne E. Green, "Divorce and Therapy under the Same Roof," *Wall Street Journal,* August 2, 1990, p. B1.

18. Lawrence A. Crosby, Kenneth R. Evans, and Deborah Cowles, "Relationship Quality in Services Selling: An Interpersonal Influence Perspective," *Journal of Marketing,* July 1990, pp. 68–81.

19. This section is based on Christopher Lovelock and Charles Weinberg, *Marketing for Public and Non-Profit Managers* (New York: Wiley, 1984), pp. 32–36.

20. Alan R. Andreasen, "Non-Profits: Check Your Attention to Customers," *Harvard Business Review,* May–June 1982, pp. 105–110.

21. Peter Drucker, "What Business Can Learn from Nonprofits," *Harvard Business Review,* July–August 1989, pp. 89–90.

22. Charles W. Lamb, Jr., "Non-Profits Need Development Orientation to Survive," *Fund Raising Management,* August 1983, pp. 26–30.

23. Joann S. Lublin, "More Charities Reach out for Corporate Sponsorship," *Wall Street Journal,* October 1, 1990, p. B1.

Chapter 22

1. Adapted from Mark Robichaux, "Three Small Businesses Profit by Taking on the World," *Wall Street Journal,* November 8, 1990, p. B2. Reprinted by permission of the *Wall Street Journal,* © Dow Jones & Company, Inc., 1990. All rights reserved.

2. "Why Europe Is in Dollar Shock," *Business Week,* March 4, 1991, pp. 36–37; "At Last, Good News," *Business Week,* June 3, 1991, pp. 24–25.

3. Marty Baumann, "USA Snapshots," *USA Today,* March 4, 1991, p. 1B.

4. John Marcom, Jr., "Feed the World," *Forbes,* October 1, 1990, pp. 110–118.

5. "How CPC Is Getting Fat on Muffins and Mayonnaise," *Business Week,* April 16, 1990, pp. 46–47.

6. "The Stateless Corporation," *Business Week,* May 14, 1990, pp. 98–106.

7. Richard Phalon, "Growth by Accretion," *Forbes,* December 24, 1990, p. 104.

8. "Can Colgate Import Its Success from Overseas?" *Business Week,* May 7, 1990, pp. 114–116.

9. "The Stateless Corporation"; Jeremy Main, "How to Go Global—and Why," *Fortune,* August 28, 1989, pp. 70–76.

10. "P&G's Worldly New Boss Wants a More Worldly Company," *Business Week,* October 30, 1989, pp. 40–41; Michael K. Ozanian, "P&G's Pinch Hitter," *Financial World,* July 10, 1990, pp. 26–29; Alecia Swasy, "P&G, in Surprise, Appoints Artzt Chairman and Chief," *Wall Street Journal,* October 11, 1989, pp. B1, B4.

11. Louis Kraar, "How to Sell Cashless Buyers," *Fortune,* November 7, 1988, p. 150.

12. Ford S. Worthy, "What's Next for Business in China," *Fortune,* July 17, 1989, pp. 110–112.

13. Adi Ignatius, "China to Export Top Technology to a U.S. Firm," *Wall Street Journal,* July 7, 1988, p. 16.

14. "Global Connections: The U.S.-Japan Macro-Economy," *Time,* June 25, 1990, Special Advertising Section.

15. "Coors, Cap 'N Crunch Get Holiday Spirit," *Wall Street Journal,* December 3, 1987, p. 31.

16. Joanne Lipman, "Ad Fad: Marketers Turn Sour on Global Sales Pitch Harvard Guru Makes," *Wall Street Journal,* May 12, 1988, p. 12.

17. "A Quiet Comeback: How China Broke Out of Isolation," *Business Week,* December 24, 1990, pp. 34–35.

18. "Big Deals Run into Big Trouble in the Soviet Union," *Business Week,* March 19, 1990, pp. 58–59.

19. Christopher J. Chipello, "More Competitors Turn to Cooperation," *Wall Street Journal,* June 23, 1989, p. B1.

20. Sharon Nelton, "Family Firms' Global Reach," *Nation's Business,* February 1990, p. 51.

21. "Mexico: A New Economic Area," *Business Week,* November 12, 1990, pp. 102–113; "Turning the Hemisphere into a Free Trade Bloc," *Business Week,* December 24, 1990, p. 37.

22. "Toward Real Community?" *Time,* April 18, 1988, p. 54.

23. "A Bouquet, Please, for the European Community," *Business Week,* March 5, 1990, p. 16.

24. Allan T. Demaree, "The New Germany's Glowing Future," *Fortune,* December 3, 1990, pp. 146–154.

25. " 'United State of Europe'? Don't Hold Your Breath," *Business Week,* June 17, 1991, p. 50.

26. Peter Brimelow, "The Dark Side of 1992," *Forbes,* January 22, 1990, pp. 85–89.

27. Yoram Wind, Susan P. Douglas, and Howard V. Perlmutter, "Guidelines for Developing International Marketing Strategies," *Journal of Marketing,* April 1973, pp. 14–23.

28. Francis C. Brown III, "Small Business," *Wall Street Journal,* April 25, 1988, p. 23.

29. Meg Whittemore, "Changes Ahead for Franchising," *Nation's Business,* June 1990, pp. 49–54.

30. Robert Wrubel, "If You Can't Beat 'Em . . . .," *Financial World,* April 3, 1990, pp. 30–34.

31. Jeremy Main, "Making Global Alliances Work," *Fortune,* December 17, 1990, pp. 121–126.

32. Patricia Gallagher, "P&G Takes New Look at Its Effort Worldwide," *Hattiesburg (Mississippi) American,* January 19, 1991, p. 8A.

33. Patricia Gallagher, "Feeding China's 'Little Emperors,' " *Forbes,* August 6, 1990, pp. 84–85.

34. Damon Darlin, "U.S. Auto Firms Push Their Efforts to Sell Cars in Asian Markets," *Wall Street Journal,* March 21, 1991, pp. A1, A5.

35. Lipman, "Ad Fad," p. 8.

36. Richard S. Teitelbaum, "CPC's Global Spread," *Fortune,* October 22, 1990, p. 106.

37. Richard I. Kirkland, Jr., "Outsider's Guide to Europe in 1992," *Fortune,* October 24, 1988, p. 122.

38. Kenneth Labich, "America's International Winners," *Fortune,* April 14, 1986, p. 44.

39. "Chinese Commit Faux Pas, Too, in Export Marketing," *Marketing News,* October 14, 1983, p. 13.

40. "Moslems Protest Symbol on Slippers," *Chicago Tribune,* June 25, 1989, sec. 1, p. 5.

41. John Marcom, Jr., "Feed the World," *Forbes,* October 1, 1990, pp. 110–118.

42. Joann S. Lublin, "For U.S. Franchisers, a Common Tongue Isn't a Guarantee of Success in the U.K.," *Wall Street Journal,* August 16, 1988, p. 18.

43. Matt Moffett, "Mexico Boosts Role of Private Investment," *Wall Street Journal,* July 12, 1990, p. A7.

44. "Cone-Ichiwa," *Forbes,* July 9, 1990, p. 107.

45. David A. Ricks, *Big Business Blunders* (Homewood, Ill.: Dow Jones–Irwin, 1983), p. 52.

46. Carla Rapoport, "You Can Make Money in Japan," *Fortune,* February 12, 1990, pp. 85–92.

47. Lipman, "Ad Fad," p. 8.

48. Labich, "America's International Winners."

49. "Can This Catalog Company Crack the Japanese Marketing Maze?" *Business Week,* March 19, 1990, p. 60.

50. "How a Nutritionist Teaches Mexicans to Use Soybeans to Fortify Tortillas," *Wall Street Journal,* May 20, 1983, p. 10.

51. Vigor Fung, "As Chinese Markets Open, Foreign Businessmen Learn the Special Tricks of Making a Deal There," *Wall Street Journal,* August 1, 1985, p. 22.

CASES

Chapter 1
Glen Ellen Wine-Success Through Marketing
Adapted by permission of *Forbes* magazine, February 19, 1990. © Forbes Inc., 1990.

The Greening of Lucky Charms
Reprinted by permission of *The Wall Street Journal,* © 1991 Dow Jones & Company, Inc. All Rights Reserved Worldwide.

Chapter 2
Environmental Clean-Up Makes (Dollars and) Sense
Reprinted by permission, *Nation's Business,* January 1991. Copyright 1991, U.S. Chamber of Commerce.

Chapter 3
Does P&G Want Out of the Food Market?
Reprinted by permission of *The Wall Street Journal,* © 1991 Dow Jones & Company, Inc. All Rights Reserved Worldwide.

Chapter 4
Caller I.D.
Reprinted with the permission of *Marketing News,* September 3, 1990. Published by the American Marketing Association.

What Is Welch's
Reprinted with the permission of *Marketing News,* September 11, 1989. Published by the American Marketing Association.

Chapter 5
Environmentally Mean or Truly "Green"?
Reprinted with the permission of *Marketing News,* December 24, 1990. Published by the American Marketing Association.

Chapter 6
Ball Corp. "Can" Do
Anthony Baldo, "Heavy Metal," *Financial World,* August 21, 1990, pp. 38–44.

Raytheon: From Vacuum Tubes to SCUD-Busting
Adapted by permission of *Forbes* magazine, October 15, 1990. © Forbes Inc., 1990.

Chapter 7
A&W Goes Beyond Root Beer
Adapted by permission of *Forbes* magazine, December 11, 1989. © Forbes Inc., 1989.

A New Generation of American Dolls
Lora Sharpe, "Dolls in All the Colors of a Child's Dream," *The Boston Globe,* February 22, 1991. Reprinted with the permission of the author.

Chapter 8
Enterprise Rent-A-Car
Adapted by permission of *Forbes* magazine, October 15, 1990. © Forbes Inc., 1990.

Chapter 10
Oasis Laundries
Reprinted with the permission of *Marketing News,* February 19, 1990. Published by the American Marketing Association.

Chapter 12
Kmart Fights Back
Subrata N. Chakravarty, "A Tale of Two Companies," *Forbes,* May 27, 1991, pp. 86–96, and Ellen Neuborne, "WalMart: Mexico offers rich retail market," *USA Today,* July 12, 1991, p. 1B.

Chapter 13
Cardinal Distribution's Automated Link to Customers
Dubashi, Jagannath, "The Tie that Binds." *Financial World,* April 30, 1991. p. 66.

Chapter 14
Ware Promotions
Reprinted with the permission of *Marketing News,* August 20, 1990. Published by the American Marketing Association.

Chapter 15
Barq's Root Beer: From Biloxi to the Big Apple
Adapted by permission of *Forbes* magazine, June 24, 1991. © Forbes Inc., 1991.

Chapter 16
Quenching Small Businesses's Thirst
Gloria Savina, "Work Goes Better with Coke," *Direct Marketing,* March 1989, pp. 74–76.

Chapter 17
Strategic Selling Helps Complex Business-to-Business Sales
Reprinted with the permission of *Marketing News,* March 4, 1991. Published by the American Marketing Association.

Chuck Piola Never Underestimates the Power of Cold Call
Reprinted with permission, *Inc.* Magazine, June, 1991. Copyright © 1991 by Goldhirsh Group, Inc. 38 Commercial Wharf, Boston, MA 02110.

Chapter 19
Mercedes-Benz
Adapted by permission of *Forbes* magazine, February 18, 1991. © Forbes Inc., 1991.

Chapter 20
Maytag: The Dependability People?
Reprinted by permission of *The Wall Street Journal,* © 1991 Dow Jones & Company, Inc. All Rights Reserved Worldwide.

Comprehensive Cases
The Comprehensive Cases are based on the following materials.
SECTION 1: Green Marketing   Laura Bird, "Arm & Hammer Stakes Its Name on the Environment," *Adweek's Marketing Week,* November 19,

1990, p. 4; "Friendly to Whom?" *Economist,* April 7, 1990, p. 83; Shelly Garcia, "Green Marketers Facing Questions," *Adweek Eastern Edition,* December 17, 1990, p. 40B; John Holusha, "Coming Clean on Products: Ecological Claims Faulted," *New York Times,* March 12, 1991, p. D1; John Holusha, "The Packaging Industry's New Fancy—Composting Garbage," *New York Times,* February 24, 1991, p. F4; David Kiley, "Earth Island, Bumble Bee Wage Ad War over Dolphins," *Adweek's Marketing Week,* December 10, 1990, p. 5; Jim Kirk, "Green Packaging a War of Words," *Adweek Western Advertising News,* August 27, 1990, p. 42; Cathy Madison, "AGs to Feds: Set the Rules for Environmental Claims," *Adweek Eastern Edition,* November 12, 1990, p. 14; Susan Reed, "When America Thinks Green, Eco-preneurs Alan Newman and Jeffrey Hollender Think Greenbacks," *People,* November 12, 1990, p. 155; "Souper Combo Gets 86'd," *Garbage,* January–February 1991, p. 23; "When Green Is Profitable," *Economist,* September 2, 1989, p. S16.

SECTION 2: Essence "ABC-CCC Sells Four TV's for $485 Million," *Broadcasting,* July 29, 1985, p. 30; "Black Women Enjoy Vogue, but Essence Is a Magazine for Them," *Wall Street Journal,* December 11, 1986, p. 1; "Direct Marketing: Essence, Hanover House Unveil Catalog for Blacks," *Advertising Age,* August 30, 1984, p. 8; Rebecca Fannin, "Reach vs. Environment," *Marketing & Media Decisions,* June 1989, p. 42; "Increasing Affluence in U.S. Ethnic Market," *European Cosmetic Markets,* November 1989, p. 13; Edward Lewis, "In Celebration of Our Twentieth Anniversary," *Essence,* May 1990, p. 20; Liane McAllister, "Black Americans: Acquisitive and Loyal," *Gifts and Decorative Accessories,* August 1983, p. 112; John Masterson, "Essence Signs on 9,157 Product Experts," *Folio,* November 1, 1990, p. 46; Fred Pfaff and Rebecca Fannin, "Media with a Mission," *Marketing & Media Decisions,* March 1986, p. 44; "Pinnacle," Cable News Network, June 16, 1990.

SECTION 3: The Body Shop John Barnes, "A 'Natural' Formula for Success," *U.S. News & World Report,* December 12, 1988, p. 70; Body Shop promotion materials; Bo Burlingham, "This Woman Has Changed Business Forever," *Inc.,* June 1990, p. 34; Anne Furguson, "Soapworks' Good Works," *Management Today,* May 1989, p. 94; George Gendron, "Nice Work, if You Can Get It," *Inc.,* June 1990, p. 11; "Jungle Law," *Sunday Times* (London), September 23, 1990; Dana Longstreet, "Saving Faces," *American Health,* July–August 1990, p. 54; "Makeup Maverick: What Makes Anita Roddick Run?" *Mirabella,* August 1990; Jeannie Ralston, "Cosmetics with a Conscience," *American Way,* March 15, 1991, pp. 84–89; Connie Wallace, "Lessons in Marketing—From a Maverick," *Working Woman,* October 1990, pp. 81–84.

SECTION 4: Macy's Ellen Benoit, "The Hustlers of Herald Square," *Financial World,* October 18, 1988, p. 26; Cable News Network, "Pinnacle," July 21, 1990; Susan Caminiti, "The New Champs of Retailing," *Fortune,* September 24, 1990; "Enter a Different World," *Economist,* February 23, 1991, p. 52; Macy's, "Macy's New York 125th Anniversary," brochure, 1983; Caroline E. Mayer, "Macy's Counters Campeau with New Federated Bid," *Washington Post,* March 15, 1988, p. C1; Eva Pomice, "Macy's Hopes for Santa Claus," *U.S. News & World Report,* December 3, 1990, p. 60; Mark Pots, "Campeau Puts Bloomingdale's on the Bloc," *Washington Post,* September 9, 1989, p. A1; Christopher Power, "Macy's Buyout Loses a Lot of Its Luster," *Business Week,* March 19, 1990, p. 40; Walter J. Salmon and Karen A. Cmar, "Private Labels Are Back in Fashion," *Harvard Business Review,* May–June 1987, p. 99; Laura Zinn, "Macy's: Bad News, Brave Talk," *Business Week,* June 10, 1991, pp. 38–39.

SECTION 5: Hill & Knowlton Dan Balz, "Bishops Retain PR Firm to Assist Abortion Fight," *Washington Post,* April 6, 1990, p. A10; Jon Berry and Dan Koeppel, "PR Firms Fight Sound-Byte War," *Adweek's Marketing Week,* September 10, 1990, p. 4; Cable News Network, "Pinnacle," June 30, 1990; Dan Koeppel, "Abortion Fight Makes H&K a House Divided," *Adweek's Marketing Week,* April 23, 1990, p. 7; Dan Koeppel, "Dilenschneider's Twist of Faith," *Adweek,* April 23, 1990, p. 26; Dan Koeppel, "Rising and Falling," *Adweek's Marketing Week,* December 17, 1990, p. 23; Mark Landler, "When a PR Firm Could Use a PR firm," *Business Week,* May 14, 1990, p. 44; Richard W. Pollay, "Propaganda, Puffing, and the Public Interest," *Public Relations Review,* Fall 1990, p. 39; Adam Shell, "Controversies over Social Issues Causing Firms to Re-Examine Policies," *Public Relations Journal,* June 1990, p. 9.

SECTION 6: Carnival Cruise Lines Ernest Blum, "Carnival Reports Record Year, despite Recession," *Travel Weekly,* January 28, 1991, p. 15; Cable News Network, "Pinnacle," July 14, 1990; Mike Clary, "Carnival's Victory at Sea," *Adweek's Marketing Week,* July 17, 1989, p. 18; Antonio N. Fins, "Carnival Tries Sailing Upstream," *Business Week,* September 25, 1989, p. 82; Gay Nagle Myers, "Carnival's New Fantasy Caters to Kids," *Travel Weekly,* September 6, 1990, p. C19; Eva Pomice, "Cruising to a Fortune Touting 'Love Boats' for the Masses," *U.S. News & World Report,* August 1, 1988, p. 43; Clemens P. Work, "Carnival Shows Cruise Lines How to Hit High Seas," *U.S. News & World Report,* August 29, 1988, p. 87.

SECTION 7: PepsiCo, the Soviet Union, and Eastern Europe Celestine Bohlen, "The Pains Are Sharp in Hungary," *New York Times,* May 6, 1991, p. D3; "Eastern Europe Figures in a Third of Marketing Plans," *Business America,* July 16, 1990, p. 29; Stephen Engelberg, "Eastern Europe's Hardships Grow as Trade with Soviets Dries Up," *New York Times,* May 6, 1991, pp. A1, D3; Steven Greenhouse, "Europe's Economy Is Found to Stall," *New York Times,* April 16, 1991, pp. A1, D6; Michael Harrison, "Back to Barter," *Macleans,* April 23, 1990, p. 32; Jim Impoco, "The New Global Game: Let's Make a Deal," *U.S. News & World Report,* April 23, 1990, p. 53; John Marcom, Jr., "Cola Attack," *Forbes,* November 26, 1990, p. 48; Ferdinand Protzman, "Coke's Splash in Eastern Germany," *New York Times,* May 3, 1991, pp. D1, D6; Miriam Widman, "Pepsi Working to Double Market Share in Germany," *Journal of Commerce,* May 3, 1991, p. 5A.

Chapter Opener and Comprehensive Case photo credits:

Chapter 1, p. 2, Courtesy of Mannington, Inc.; Chapter 2, p. 34, David E. Dempster; Chapter 3, p. 74, Henderson Cartledge Studio; Comprehensive Case 1, p. 100, David E. Dempster; Chapter 4, p. 106, Charles Gupton/Stock Boston; Chapter 5, p. 140, Courtesy of Carillon Importers; Chapter 6, p. 174, Courtesy of Boling Commercial Airplane Group; Chapter 7, p. 210, Peter Menzel/Stock Boston; Chapter 8, p. 244, David E. Dempster; Comprehensive Case 2, p. 270, Courtesy of Essence Magazine; Chapter 9, p. 276, David E. Dempster; Chapter 10, p. 308, David E. Dempster; Comprehensive Case 3, p. 341, Jacques Chenet/Woodfin Camp and Associates; Chapter 11, p. 346, John Sundlof; Chapter 12, p. 380, Courtesy of Barneys New York; Chapter 13, p. 416, Courtesy of Archery Center International/Business Image Group; Comprehensive Case 4, p. 456, Rafael Macia/Photo Researchers, Inc.; Chapter 14, p. 460, Courtesy of Searle Corporation; Chapter 15, p. 496, David E. Dempster; Chapter 16, p. 524, Henderson Cartledge Studio/with assistance of Smith & Hawkins; Chapter 17, p. 554, John Curtis/Offshoot; Comprehensive Case 5, p. 586, Courtesy of Hill & Knowlton/Kuwait American Foundation; Chapter 18, p. 590, David E. Dempster/Offshoot; Chapter 19, p. 616, David E. Dempster; Comprehensive Case 6, p. 639, Courtesy of Carnival Cruise Lines; Chapter 20, p. 644, Courtesy of Cadillac Automotive Corporation; Chapter 21, p. 668, J. Berndt/Stock Boston; Chapter 22, p. 692, Courtesy of Quicksilver Corporation; Comprehensive Case 7, p. 731, The Bettmann Archive.

COMPANY AND BRAND NAME INDEX

A. C. Nielsen, 108, 121, 514
A. Schulman, 46
A&P, 391
A&W, 216, 241–242, 523
ABC, 497
Abercrombie & Fitch, 407
Abraham and Straus, 455
Absolut, 141–142, 477
AccuNet, 451–452
Ace, 423
Action for Children's Television, 64
Acura Legend, 367–368
Admiral, 666
Affinity, 227
AFL-CIO, 485
Afterthoughts, 390
Airborne, 617
Airflow, 15
Alabama Farmer, 511
Alcan Aluminum, 189
Alcoholics Anonymous, 467
Alex, 215
All, 100
All-American Decathlon, 631
All Brand Importers, 247
Allied, 455, 456
Allstate, 295, 407
Alpha Beta Stores, 391
Amana, 12–13, 208, 299, 329
American Airlines, 42, 176, 203, 665, 676
American Association for Public Opinion Research, 126
American Association of Retired People, 528
American Bankers Association, 481
American Brands, 689–690
American Can, 481–482
American Cancer Society, 224, 285
American Civil Liberties Union, 552
American Dental Association, 212
American Enviro Products, 102
American Express, 228, 465, 501, 522, 662, 680, 723
American Heart Association, 684
American Homebrewers' Association, 262
American Lung Association, 687
American Management Association, 20
American Marketing Association, 25, 55–57, 113, 126
American Medical Association, 12
American National Can, 208
American President Companies, 448
American Psychological Association, 126
American Society for Quality Control, 281
American Soybean Association, 724
American Telemarketing Association, 532
AMF, 377
Amstel Light, 258

Amway, 395
Andersen & Company, 501
Andersen Consulting, 45, 46, 501, 663
Andron, 636
Anheuser-Busch, 52, 79, 172, 187, 207, 208, 246, 256–258, 260, 295–296, 367, 537
Ann Taylor, 455
Antique & Contemporary Leasing, 229
Apex Plumbing (hypothetical), 632
Apparel Mart, 427
Apparel Store, 389
Apple Computer, 98, 268, 312, 315, 360, 651
Archer-Daniels-Midland, 101
Archery Center International, 417–418, 427
Architectural Digest, 498
Arm & Hammer, 46, 101, 331, 501
Armani, 381
Arts & Entertainment Network, 498
Asahi Breweries, 260
ASPCA, 107
Associated Grocers, 385
AT&T, 22, 47, 52, 150, 151, 172, 480, 481, 531, 549, 670
Atlanta, 223
Atlantic Union College, 499
Aunt Jemima, 75
Austin Company, 439, 440
Auto Consumers, 145
Auto Critic, 6
Auto Express, 389
Avia International, 479–480
Avis Rent-A-Car, 200, 267
Avon, 395, 469, 636, 724

B. Altman, 453
Bacardi, 494
Backer & Spielvogel, 519
Backpacker, 511
Badger, 208
Bag and Baggage, 387
Ball, 207–208
Ballantine's, 437, 438
Banana Republic, 404
Banca Serfin, 62, 63, 714, 715
Band-Aid, 293
Banfi Vintners, 516
Bankers Trust, 718, 719
Barneys, 381–382
Barq's Root Beer, 523
BASF, 46
Baskin-Robbins, 414, 723
Baxter Healthcare, 435
Bayer, 236, 280, 281
BBD&O, 272, 273, 324
Beck's, 246
Beech Aircraft, 208, 288, 289

Beecham Group, 636
Beefeater, 463
Beer Institute, 26, 27
Bell, W., and Company, 394
Bell Atlantic, 138
Bell System, 22
Ben Franklin Stores, 423
Bendel, 407
Benetton, 199, 363, 464, 474
Best Products, 394
Betty Crocker, 296
Beverage Industry, 262
Bic, 265, 306
Blockbuster Entertainment, 407
Blockbuster Video, 45
Bloomingdale's, 337, 391, 453
BMW, 141
Body Shop, The, 339–343, 477
Boeing, 175, 203, 721
Bold, 26
Bon, The, 455
Bon Appetit, 511
Bonwit Teller, 453
Borden, 300
Boston Consulting Group, 87
Bounty, 516
Boy Scouts, 669
Brand Central, 233, 299
Bravo, 498
BreakMate, 552–553
Breck, 463
Breyer's, 78, 290
Brice Enviro Ventures, 71–72
Briggs & Stratton, 180
Brik Pak, 300
Brim, 290
British Airways, 18, 660, 661
Brooklyn Union Gas, 574
Brooks Brothers, 141, 455
Broyhill, 694
Buckler, 258
Budget Rent A Car, 200, 396
Budweiser, 296
Buick, 281, 499
Builders Square, 413
Bullock's, 453, 455
Bumble Bee, 100, 102
Bunnies, 102
Burberry, 456
Burdines, 455
Burger King, 150, 154, 172, 211
Burlington Coat Factory Warehouse, 387
Burrell Advertising, 212
Burson-Marsteller, 587
Busch, 296
Business Electronics, 364

Electric Avenue, 389
Electrolux, 355, 559, 666
Emery, 617, 678
Enterprise Rent-A-Car, 267
Entre Computer Centers, 722
Environmental Challenge Fund, 687
Environmental Defense Fund, 541
EPI Products, 337–338
Equifax, 133, 134, 552
Equitable, 52
Erno Laszlo, 721
ESPN, 513
Esquire, 64
Essence, 269–278
Essence Communications, 269–278
Essence Direct Mail Marketing, 272
Estée Lauder, 343
Etienne Aigner, 284, 285
Eureka, 299
Euro Disneyland, 727–728
Euromarche, 393
Eve Ultra Light, 228
Eveready Battery, 154, 494
Evian, 360
Excalibur, The, 232
Excedrin, 504
Express Mail, 604
Exxon, 367

Falcon Jet, 466
Familia de Hoy, La, 172
Fanuc, 197
Farm Journal, 511
Farmland Industries, 423
Federal Express, 11, 64, 236, 293, 315, 448,
    617, 645, 670, 678
Federated Department Stores, 455
FemIron, 297
Ferrari, 189, 363
Fidelity Investments, 18, 653–654
Filene's, 455
Filofax, 141
First Response, 229
First Women's Bank (First New Bank for
    Business), 228
Fisher Nuts, 98
Fisher-Price, 76, 78
Fleetwood, 45
Fleming Companies, 439
Flex, 597
Florida Restaurant Association, 627
Foley's, 391, 455
Folgers, 98, 516
Foot Locker, 390
Ford, 15, 43, 47, 54, 147, 148, 189, 196,
    200, 213, 271, 319, 320, 501, 649, 651,
    675, 718, 720
Fortune, 511
40 + Bran Flakes, 226
Forum, 576, 661
Foster Parents Plan, 465–466
Fotomat, 373
4day Tire Stores, 419
Fox Broadcasting, 150
Franklin Funds, 535
Fred/Allan, 523
Frederick's of Hollywood, 405, 548

Friends of Animals, 471
Frigidaire, 439
Frito-Lay, 221, 577
Fruit Classics, 217
Fruit Loops, 45
Fruit of the Loom, 522
Frusen Glädjé, 290, 291, 594
Fuji, 100, 216, 358, 482
Fujitsu, 522

Gainesburgers, 75, 76
Gallery, The, 406
Gallo Winery, 371
Gap, 141, 402, 404, 406, 407, 456
Gatorade, 75, 87, 91–95
GE Capital, 11
Genentech, 315, 607
General Cinema, 216
General Dynamics, 202, 208
General Electric, 6, 10–11, 18, 68, 182, 183,
    187, 196, 202, 299, 356, 371–372, 425,
    439, 456–457, 468, 530, 566, 666
General Foods, 101, 108, 161, 242, 528–529
General Mills, 33, 45, 296, 318, 354, 374
General Motors, 16, 29, 43, 47, 54, 60, 61,
    85, 189, 197, 200, 271, 296–297, 321,
    369, 448, 499, 512, 550, 566, 613–614,
    628, 645, 694, 695
Genie, 536
Genuine Article, 406
Georgia Coffee, 374
Georgia-Pacific, 435
Gerber, 217, 225
Gerstman-Meyers, 172
Gevalia Kaffe, 529
Ghirardelli, 75
Gillette, 100, 205, 309–311, 330, 475, 487
Gilmore Research Group, 233
Girl Scouts, 11, 557, 669, 686, 688
Glass Plus, 297
Glaxo Holdings, 47
Glaxo Pharmaceutical, 318
Gleem, 295
Glen Ellen winery, 32–33
Globe Metallurgical, 645
Gold Label, 84
Gold N' Gems, 389
Golden Grahams, 318
Goldsmith's, 455
Goldstar, 215, 299
Good Sense, 100
Goodrich, B. F., 501
Goodyear, 176–177, 356, 360, 631
Grand Metropolitan, 47
Grand Union, 391
Great West Insurance, 547
Green, 100, 101
Green Giant, 353, 354, 494
Greenpeace USA, 540
Greyhound, 42
Grid Systems, 205
Grumman, 208
Gucci, 141, 592

H&R Block, 396, 504
Häagen-Dazs, 141, 594, 723
Hallmark Cards, 367

Hampton Inns, 591
Hanes, 217, 294
Hanover House, 272
Harborplace, 406
Hardee's, 365, 373
Hardware Age, 205
Harley-Davidson, 295, 366–367, 377–378
Harper Group, 448
Harpoon Ale, 245
Hartmarx, 28
Havoline, 614
Hawaiian Punch, 516
Healthy Choice, 324
Hefty, 102
Heineken, 258
Heinz, 101, 295, 720
Hellman's, 698
Herald Square, 390
Hercules, 300
Hershey, 183, 295, 297
Hertz, 200, 235, 267, 271, 504, 627
Hewlett-Packard, 310, 577, 630, 651
Hickey-Freeman, 28
Hill & Knowlton, 519, 584–588
Hilton, 591, 627–628
Hires, 523
Hitachi, 283
Hoechst, 46
Hoffmann-LaRoche, 47, 292
Hogs Today, 511
Holiday Inn, 591
Holland America, 638, 641
Home Depot, 383, 401, 405–406
Home Ideas, 389
Honda, 147–148, 158, 217, 367–368, 377, 646
Honey Nut Cheerios, 318
Honeycomb Hideout Club, 150–151
Hoover, 299, 666
HSN, 535
Hustler, 405
Hyatt Hotel, 585
Hypermart USA, 393

I. Magnin, 453, 455
IAMS, 530
IBM, 11, 28, 98, 150, 185, 196, 202, 204,
    271, 312, 315, 347, 348, 448, 470, 536,
    645, 650, 681
Ichiban Shibori, 260
Ideal Cement, 297
Ikea, 383–385, 698
Impact, 220
In-N-Out Burger, 236–237
Inc., 583
Independent Grocers Alliance, 385
Infiniti, 368
Information Resources Inc. (IRI), 107, 127
InstAward, 50
Institute for Brewing Studies, 246
Inter-City Express, 451
International Bank for Reconstruction and
    Development, 710
International Bottled Water Association, 72
International Dairy Queen, 373
International Development Association, 710
International Franchise Association, 397,
    716–717

SUBJECT INDEX

Contractual vertical marketing systems, 372–373
Controllable variables, 29–31
Controlling, 95–96, 400–401, 645–647, 655–663, 665–667
Convenience products, 283–284, 286
Convenience sampling, 132
Convenience stores, 392
Conventional test marketing, 322
Cooperative advertising, 500, 623
Cooperative chains, retailer-sponsored, 372, 373, 384–385, 396, 425
Cooperative channel relationships, 366–367
Cooperative warehouses, 425
Cooperatives, 383, 423
Copyrights, 292
Corporate culture, 27
Corporate debt, 40
Corporate market development strategies, 650
Corporate purchasing agreements, 195
Corporate-sponsored magazines, 507
Corporate vertical marketing systems, 373
Corrective advertising, 488
Cosmetics business, 339–343
Cost analysis, 319, 658–660
Cost-per-thousand (CPM), 509
Cost-plus pricing, 602–604, 609
Cost trade-off concept, 436
Costs
   in advertising, 509, 514–515
   controlling, 408
   in logistics management, 435–436
   in pricing, 602–606, 609–612
   in purchasing decisions, 199
   and technology, 49–50
   types of
      fixed, variable, and total, 603–606
      marketing effort, 252–253
Countercyclical businesses, 38
Counterfeiting of products, 706
Counterpurchases, 701
Countertrades, 701, 725
Coupons, 236, 544–546, 627
Creative strategies, 505–507
Credibility, source, 463, 493–494
Credit, 6–7, 39, 429–430
Credit cards, 454, 629
Critical path method (CPM), 324
Cross-licensing agreements, 716
Cross-selling strategy, 519
Cross-tabulation of data, 133
Cultural myths, 168
Cultural values, 52–55, 167–169, 704–705
Culture(s). *See also* Sociocultural environment
   and consumer behavior, 166–170, 172–173
   corporate, 27
   in international marketing, 702–706, 724
   and marketing mix, 51–52
Cumulative quantity discounts, 619
Custom manufacturing, 203
Custom selling, 395
Customer loyalty, 487–488
Customer orientation, 17–22, 202–203, 247–249
Customer relations field, 60
Customer retention strategies, 22

Customer satisfaction, 3–4, 18–22, 281, 558–559, 661–662, 674, 687–688
Customer service function, 661
Customers
   characteristics of, 358
   geographic concentration of, 182
   in promotion mix, 474–475
   from prospects, 557–558
   of service marketers, 679–683
   types of, 627, 649
Customization strategy, 721
Customized pricing, 631–633
Customs (of cultures), 705
Customs procedures, 708
Customs unions, 711–712

Data
   analyzing, 133
   collecting, 107–108, 120–124, 127–130, 132–133
   editing and coding, 133
   versus information, 108–109
   need for, 117–118
   processing, 133
   in research design, 117–132
   selling, 107–108
   sources of, 118–120
   tabulating, 133
   types of
      external, 109, 112, 118–120
      internal, 109, 112, 119
      primary, 118–132, 238, 720
      secondary, 118–120, 237–238, 247, 249, 720
      special-purpose, 112–113
   validity and reliability of, 128
Databases, marketing, 528, 531, 532, 537, 541, 552
Dealer brands, 297–299
Dealer contests and premiums, 546
Dealer salespeople incentives, 546
Dealers in international marketing, 716
Debt, types of, 40–41
Deceptive advertising, 15, 488–489, 501, 631
Deceptive Mailing Prevention Act, 540
Deceptive sales practices, 15
Deciders in industrial markets, 194
Decoding in communication, 467
Decoupling of services, 678
Deep discounters, 387
Defect-free production, 645–646
Deflation, 40
Degree of brand familiarity, 293–295
Delayed quotation pricing, 633
Delivered pricing, 624–625
Delphi method, 264
Demand
   in direct marketing, 529
   elasticity of, 182–183, 598–601, 608
   estimation of, 599–602
   and supply, 15, 352–354
   types of
      derived, 179–183
      price elastic, 182–183, 599
      price inelastic, 182–183, 599
      primary, 182–183, 500
      selective, 182–183, 500

Demand analysis, 319, 597–602
Demand-balancing strategies, 677–678
Demand curves, 598, 600, 605–606
Demand measurement, 252, 258, 260–261
Demand schedules, 598
Demarketing, 26–27, 41
Demographic segmentation, 220, 221, 224–230, 248–251. *See also* Age segmentation; Ethnic groups; Race in segmentation; Sex in segmentation
Demographics in retailing, 408
Demography, defined, 224
Department stores, 387, 391, 411, 453–457
Dependability, 198
Depressions, 37, 65. *See also* Recessions
Depth
   of merchandise, 388
   of product lines, 290, 291, 429, 430
Depth interviewing, 128–130
Deregulation, 44, 67, 99, 432, 448–449, 665–666
Derived demand, 179–183
Descriptive analysis, 133
Descriptive research, 116
Desk jobbers, 424
Destination in communication, 462, 467
Detail reps, 579
Determinant attributes, 250
Development-oriented marketing, 686–687
Differential advantage, 45
Differential pricing, 630–631
Differentiated oligopoly, 43, 44
Differentiation in retailing, 408–409
Diffusion process, 327–328
Direct contact public relations, 547–548
Direct denial, 564–565
Direct distribution (marketing) channels, 355–356, 530
Direct experience, 150, 156–157
Direct exporting, 715–716
Direct interviewing, 128
Direct investment, foreign, 717
Direct mail, 514–516, 533–534, 553
Direct marketing, 469–471, 524–541, 552–553
   advantages of, 528–530
   by catalog, 525–526, 534–535, 540
   as communication system, 530
   databases in, 528, 531, 532, 537, 541, 552
   effectiveness of, 539
   ethics in, 540, 541
   future of, 540–541
   individualized, 221–222
   in international marketing, 724
   in marketing channels, 529, 530
   objectives of, 538–539
   in personal selling, 557
   retailers in, 405
Direct marketing budgets, 539
Direct marketing channels, 355–356, 530
Direct marketing management, 538–539
Direct marketing strategies, 539
Direct marketing targets, 538
Direct response media, 514–516, 531–537, 539
Direct selling, 395
Directly similar offerings, 42

defined, 419
ethics in, 432
trends in, 430–432
Wholesaling intermediaries, 417–432
Wholly owned subsidiaries, 717–718
Wide-Area Telecommunications Service
    (WATS) lines, 124

Women. *See also* Sex in segmentation;
    Sexism in advertising
  marketing to, 268–273, 498
  stereotyping, 490, 491
Word association tests, 129–130
Word-of-mouth, 157, 467

Yield management, 677
Yuppies, 160, 162

Zero-level marketing channels, 355–356
Zone pricing, 624